# www.wadsworth.com

*www.wadsworth.com* is the World Wide Web site for Wadsworth and is your direct source to dozens of online resources.

At *www.wadsworth.com* you can find out about supplements, demonstration software, and student resources. You can also send email to many of our authors and preview new publications and exciting new technologies.

**www.wadsworth.com**
Changing the way the world learns®

# Intervention and Reflection

## Basic Issues in Medical Ethics

Seventh Edition

Ronald Munson
University of Missouri–St. Louis

THOMSON
WADSWORTH

Australia • Canada • Mexico • Singapore • Spain
United Kingdom • United States

Publisher: Holly J. Allen
Philosophy Editor: Steve Wainwright
Assistant Editors: Lee McCracken, Anna Lustig
Editorial Assistant: Melanie Cheng
Technology Project Manager: Susan DeVanna
Marketing Manager: Worth Hawes
Marketing Assistant: Kristi Bostock
Advertising Project Manager: Bryan Vann
Composition Buyer: Ben Schroeter

Print/Media Buyer: Doreen Suruki
Permissions Editor: Elizabeth Zuber
Production Service: The Cooper Company
Text Designer: Harry Voigt
Copy Editor: Ben Kolstad
Cover Designer: Ross Carron
Compositor: Pre-Press Company, Inc.
Printer: RR Donnelley

For more information about our products,
contact us at:
**Thomson Learning Academic
Resource Center
1-800-423-0563**
For permission to use material from this
text, contact us by:
**Phone:** 1-800-730-2214
**Fax:** 1-800-730-2215
**Web:** http://www.thomsonrights.com

**Wadsworth/Thomson Learning
10 Davis Drive
Belmont, CA 94002-3098
USA**

**Asia**
Thomson Learning
5 Shenton Way #01-01
UIC Building
Singapore 068808

**Australia/New Zealand**
Thomson Learning
102 Dodds Street
Southbank, Victoria 3006
Australia

**Canada**
Nelson
1120 Birchmount Road
Toronto, Ontario M1K 5G4
Canada

**Europe/Middle East/Africa**
Thomson Learning
High Holborn House
50/51 Bedford Row
London WC1R 4LR
United Kingdom

**Latin America**
Thomson Learning
Seneca, 53
Colonia Polanco
11560 Mexico D.F.
Mexico

**Spain/Portugal**
Paraninfo
Calle/Magallanes, 25
28015 Madrid, Spain

**Library of Congress Control Number:
2003101802**

Student Edition ISBN 0-534-56507-7

*To Miriam*
"Giver of bright rings"

**Ronald Munson** is Professor of the Philosophy of Science and Medicine at the University of Missouri–St. Louis. He received his Ph.D. from Columbia University and was a Postdoctoral Fellow in Biology at Harvard University. He has been a Visiting Professor at University of California, San Diego, Johns Hopkins School of Medicine, and Harvard Medical School.

A nationally acclaimed bioethicist, Munson is a medical ethicist for the National Eye Institute and a consultant for the National Cancer Institute. He is also a member of the Washington University School of Medicine Human Studies Committee.

His other books include *Raising the Dead: Organ Transplants, Ethics, and Society* (named one of the "Best Science and Medicine Books of 2002" by the National Library Association), *Reasoning in Medicine* (with Daniel Albert and Michael Resnik), *Elements of Reasoning* and *Basics of Reasoning* (both with David Conway), and *Outcome Uncertain: Cases and Contexts in Bioethics*. He is also author of the novels *Nothing Human*, *Fan Mail*, and *Night Vision*.

# Brief Contents

# Contents

# Preface

In shaping the seventh edition of this book, I have tried to capture both the intellectual excitement and the great seriousness that surround bioethics. I've done my best, in particular, to convey these aspects to those new to the field.

By emphasizing cases and presenting relevant medical, scientific, and social information, I've attempted to introduce readers to the basic issues and make them active participants in the enterprise of deliberation and problem solving.

I believe that everyone, whatever the level of knowledge or intellectual sophistication, will find this a useful and engaging book.

## The Topics and Readings

The topics I've selected are all fundamental ones in bioethics. They reflect the range and variety of the problems we now confront and involve ethical and social issues that have excited the most immediate concern. But more than this, the problems raised are ones so profoundly serious that they lead people to turn hopefully to philosophical consideration in search of satisfactory resolutions.

The Readings present current thinking about the topics and show that such consideration can be worthwhile. All are readable and nontechnical, and many reveal bioethics at its best. Although philosophers are strongly represented, the authors also include jurists, scientists, clinical researchers, social critics, and practicing physicians. The moral problems of medicine always have scientific, social, legal, and economic aspects, and to deal with them sensibly and thoroughly, we need the knowledge and perceptions of people from a variety of disciplines.

I have also opted for diversity in another way, by trying to see to it that opposing viewpoints are presented for major topics.

Part of the intellectual excitement of bioethics is generated by the searing controversies surrounding its issues, and to ignore these conflicts would be misleading. Even worse, it would deny readers the opportunity of dealing directly with proposals and arguments incompatible with their own views. Hence, I've felt an obligation to raise issues that some would prefer to ignore and to present proposals to resolve them that others reject as wrong or even immoral. I hold, along with most reasonable people, that we must face our problems and consider seriously all proposed solutions. Otherwise, rational inquiry evaporates and power and prejudice take its place.

## Chapter Structure

Each chapter for the first four Parts of this book is like a sandwich with several layers. Each opens with a Classic Case Presentation, followed by the chapter Briefing Session, then a combination of Social Contexts and Case Presentations. The variety and number of these vary by chapter. The Readings appear next, and after them six or more Decision Scenarios.

In the Case Presentations, I sketch out the most important cases in bioethics in narrative accounts. These are ones that have faced us with crucial issues and shaped our thinking about what we believe is morally legitimate in various areas of clinical practice and medical and biological research.

Some of the people at the focus of the cases are familiar. Nearly everyone has heard of Jesse

Gelsinger, Karen Quinlan, Jack Kevorkian, Louise Brown, and Dax Cowart. Their names have been in the headlines and on the evening news many times—some as recently as last week, others three decades ago.

I call the opening Case Presentations "Classic" because the cases have been at the center of discussion. They raised issues that prompted us to reflect. The image of the young Karen Quinlan slipping into a coma that lasted until her death ten years later, for example, has made us all think hard about when life support ought to be discontinued and whether active euthanasia is ever morally acceptable. Other Classic Cases have forced us to face similar problems. (I should say, however, that some Case Presentations might have been called "classic" with justification equal to those that were. In this respect, my designation may be considered arbitrary.)

Not all Case Presentations center on individuals. Some focus on defining episodes in the history of clinical research or social practice. These include, for example, the Tuskegee Syphilis Study and the hardly less controversial Willowbrook Hospital Experiment. The central concern of such cases is usually with the way groups of individuals were treated by researchers and by society. Or it may be the way a particular therapy has developed and raised issues.

The most important aspect of Case Presentations, in my view, is that they remind us that in dealing with bioethical questions we are not engaged in some purely intellectual abstract game. Real lives are often at stake.

In the Briefing Session section of each chapter, I discuss some of the specific moral problems that occur in actual medical and biological practice, research, and policymaking. I present, in addition, whatever factual information is needed to understand how such problems arise. Finally, I suggest the ways moral theories or principles might be used to resolve some of the problems. Because virtue, care, and feminist ethics don't involve principles, I haven't tried to invoke these theories. My suggestions, in any event, are offered only as starting points in the search for satisfactory answers.

The Social Context sections of each chapter provide information relevant to understanding the current social, political, or biomedical situation in which issues are being debated. They differ from Case Presentations in offering a broader and deeper view of problems like the mammography debate, testing of AIDS drugs in Africa, and the Human Genome Project. If we hope to raise the level of public discussion of an issue and genuinely inform the life of our society, it is essential to consider the relevant scientific and medical facts, as well as the social situation.

The ongoing debate over embryonic stem cells is a good illustration. No one can make a reasoned decision about whether we should allow (or even encourage) embryonic stem-cell research without knowing what embryonic stem cells are and without a sense of the therapeutic possibilities they may offer. The debate is not taking place in a vacuum, however. Policies and laws have been proposed and criticized, and anyone wanting to participate in the debate needs some information about the current situation.

Social Contexts sections, to be blunt but accurate, offer a deep-background briefing to help with the understanding of the issues that are their focus.

The Readings make up the next layer of a chapter sandwich. They provide the variety of basic arguments and viewpoints relevant to the problems addressed by the chapter. While each selection stands alone, I have tried to represent opposing positions in a fair and evenhanded fashion. The multiplicity of topics addressed in the book means, however, that I couldn't always represent the various varieties and strengths of a general point of view. The arguments are offered to prompt inquiry, not make it unnecessary.

The Decision Scenarios constitute the final component of each chapter. These are brief, dramatic presentations of situations in which moral questions are crucial or in which ethical or social-policy decisions have to be made. The scenarios are followed by questions asking the reader to decide what the problems are and how they might be dealt with by a particular moral theory or by principles argued for in the Readings. Thus, the Decision Scenarios are really exercises in bioethics that can direct and structure class discussion.

Because virtue, care, and feminist ethics don't involve principles, I have generally omitted questions invoking these theories. An instructor can easily pursue such questions, however, by engaging in a dialogue with students and making the case described in the scenarios more detailed and concrete.

## Foundations of Bioethics

For some readers, the most important feature of this book may be *Part V: Foundations of Bioethics*. In the first section, I sketch the basics of five major ethical theories and indicate how they might be used to answer particular moral questions in medicine and research. In the second section, I present and illustrate several major moral principles. The principles are ones endorsed (or at least expressed in practice) by virtually all ethical theories. Even so, I don't try to demonstrate how the principles follow from or are consistent with particular theories. In the third section, I present the fundamental ideas of three ethical theories usually framed as not involving principles—virtue ethics, care ethics, and feminist ethics.

The main purpose in these sections is to give those without a background in ethics the information they need to frame and evaluate moral arguments about the issues in bioethics. The three parts of the Foundations section are complementary, but they are also self-contained and may be read separately. The aim of each (and of all three together) is to help prepare readers for independent inquiry into bioethics.

## Independent Components

What I've said about the parts of the Foundations sections being independent also holds for the components of the chapters—the Case Presentations, Briefing Sessions, Social Contexts, Readings, and Decision Scenarios. I have written and arranged everything to stand alone. This makes it possible for a reader to turn to any chapter and pick and choose among the materials presented.

Reading the Briefing Session of a chapter may deepen the understanding of the issues involved in (say) paying for health care, but one might choose to read only the Case Presentation discussing the Canadian system. Or, instead, one might consider only the proposals and arguments presented in the Readings.

Similarly, one might want to focus only on gene therapy by reading the appropriate Case Presentation and Readings and ignore the issues connected with the various other modes of genetic control. The components of the book can be skipped or combined in a variety of ways, depending on one's interests.

This is a useful feature for those using the book as a text. Some instructors, for example, may want to start with *Part V: Foundations of Bioethics* and lay out moral principles or theories, while others may prefer to refer to that section only in the course of discussing some particular topic. Still others may choose to ignore it completely, providing students with whatever information they need in lectures or discussions. This book offers so much flexibility that it is compatible with almost any path an instructor chooses.

## Tables of Contents

This is a big book and includes a wide variety of topics and materials. To make it easier to navigate, in addition to the main Table of Contents, I have included a Contents section at the beginning of each chapter. In addition to listing the Case Presentations and Social Contexts, the section also spells out the major subheadings of the Briefing Sessions. The Contents pages are designed to reveal all the topics covered in the chapter at a glance and prevent readers from getting lost in the thicket of cases and discussions.

## Notes and References

Following the Foundations section, *Notes and References* lists sources for materials used in the Cases, Briefing Sessions, Social Contexts, and Decision Scenarios.

## General Resources in Bioethics

Following the Notes is a brief guide to general resources in bioethics. This includes addresses of some of the more important online databases and Web sites. Sites such as the National Library of Medicine, the National Institutes of Health, and the Centers for Disease Control provide access to Medline, making it possible to carry out extensive research on almost any bioethical, clinical, or biomedical topic. Addresses for other medically related Web sites are easily located by any search engine.

Those interested in diseases like diabetes or breast cancer or therapies such as stem-cell rescue or heart transplant can readily acquire a great deal of up-to-the-minute information by consulting relevant Web sites. Everyone knows by now, of course, that Web sites often evaporate like dew in the sun and that the information supplied by some should not be taken on trust.

Also included in this section is a list of prominent bioethics journals, as well as a list of others that publish articles on bioethics frequently. The section also contains a list of printed bibliographies, some quite specialized, that offer a way of getting access to older publications relevant to bioethics. Most printed bibliographies are no longer updated.

## Additional Resources

The Additional Resources section can be found on the book's Web site. Its bibliographies mirror the topics of each chapter and provide a guide to articles and books. The references are both extensive and recent (although influential older works are also included). Hence, anyone wanting to do additional reading on a topic should have no difficulty locating appropriate works quickly.

## InfoTrac College Edition

Accompanying this book when acquired new is a card permitting access to InfoTrac College Edition. This is a searchable, online database of full-text articles and images drawn from more than 600 periodicals. The database is updated daily, and the articles are kept in it for four years. InfoTrac College Edition is particularly useful for following the course of shifting debates on such topics as embryonic stem cells, abortion, physician-assisted suicide, and health-care costs.

The database offers completely up-to-date information, which means that when new topics emerge (as happened with stem cells) or new information becomes relevant to an ongoing discussion (as happens often with plans for financing health care) the reader can easily go beyond the materials in this book.

## Web Site for This Book

Wadsworth Publishing Company, the publisher of this book, maintains the Wadsworth Philosophy Shoppe site at http://philosophy.wadsworth.com. This book has a Web page at that site, and materials such as supplements to the bibliographies, addresses of additional bioethics Web sites, and any needed corrections will be posted.

## Content Changes in the Seventh Edition

Alterations of importance have been made throughout the book in response to the impact that changes in social circumstances, court decisions, scientific understanding, government regulations, and clinical practice have on moral issues in medicine. Here is a sample of issues freshly discussed:

- The debate over embryonic stem cells, prompted by the conflict between their promise in treating spinal cord injuries and diseases like diabetes, and the need to destroy human embryos to obtain them.

- New controversies about cloning, particularly the possibility of cloning humans.

- Changes in federal privacy regulations.

- New data on AIDS in Africa.

- New steps toward an AIDS vaccine.

- The health gap between African Americans and Whites.

- Updates on the mammogram debate.

- New controversies over gene therapy.

- Postmenopausal motherhood.

- Transplantation of lung segments.

- Updates on health-care costs and new proposals to extend coverage to the uninsured.

- New abortion policies and updates on RU-486.

- New studies relevant to decisions about low-birthweight infants.

- Update on assisted suicide in Oregon.

The Briefing Sessions have been revised in dozens of ways to take into account changes in policies, statistics, and relevant scientific or medical information, or simply to make the text clearer. (For various reasons, by the way, sometimes even the most recent statistics may be several years old. A large-scale study, for example, may have been so expensive and time-consuming it hasn't been repeated.)

The new Case Presentations and Social Contexts include the Jesse Gelsinger case, the debate over embryonic stem cells, proposals to extend the health-care system, health care for Indians, Hispanics, and African Americans, and the search for an AIDS vaccine.

The number of Decision Scenarios has been reduced, as a means of streamlining the book. Yet each chapter still has six or more, and about a dozen Decision Scenarios are new to this edition. Certainly there are enough for class discussion and as sources for paper topics.

The Readings in this edition maintain the scope of those in the last. *Twenty* readings are completely new. Included are selections by (without attempting to be exhaustive) P. Alward, Marcia Angell, Mark T. Brown, Lonnie R. Bristow (for the American Medical Association), Allen Buchanan, Annette Dula, Charles Erin, Michael Gross, Arlene J. Klotzko, John Lachs, Kishore D. Phadke, Pontifical Academy for Life, President's Commission on Bioethics, Bernard Rabinowitz, James Q. Wilson, and Aaron Spital.

The new Readings are particularly good at addressing clearly such complicated issues as late-term abortion, government-financed health care, African-American bioethics, testing AIDS drugs in Africa, physician-assisted suicide, and acquiring human embryonic stem cells. The arguments on all sides of these issues are worth careful consideration by reasonable people.

## Envoi

I have tried to be helpful without being too intrusive. Anyone who teaches bioethics wants enough flexibility to arrange a course in the way she or he sees fit. I have attempted to offer that flexibility, while at the same time supplying readers with the kind of information and support they need.

This book, with its Case Presentations, Briefing Sessions, Social Context sections, Decision Scenarios, and Foundations of Bioethics section, is more ambitious than any similar work. I've been pleased by responses from my colleagues to the earlier editions. Even their criticisms were tempered by a sympathetic understanding of the difficulty of producing a book of this scope that attempts to do so many things.

Thanks to the help of many people who took the trouble to write to me, I was able to correct errors in this edition that I missed in the last. (I am particularly indebted to Karen Lucas for pointing out many mistakes.) I am under no illusion that the book has achieved perfection, and I would still appreciate comments or suggestions from those who use the book and discover ways it needs to be corrected or can be improved. Communications may be e-mailed to me or sent to my university address (Department of Philosophy, University of Missouri–St. Louis, St. Louis, MO 63121).

I owe so many intellectual debts I must declare bankruptcy, and this means that those who invested their help in this project have to settle for an acknowledgment that is less than they are rightly owed. My greatest debt is to those authors who allowed their work to be printed here. I hope they will find no grounds for objecting to the way I have dealt with them. I am also grateful to the following reviewers for their criticisms and recommendations: Jacqueline Colby, University of Colorado; Mary Ann Cutler, University of Colorado, Colorado Springs; Nicholas Hunt-Bull, University of North Carolina, Greensboro; Elysa Koppelman, Oakland University; David Morgan, University of Northern Iowa; Steve Scarlet, SUNY Binghamton; Dave Yount, Mesa Community College.

Steve Wainwright, Wadsworth's Philosophy Editor, has remained, like his predecessors, a strong fan of this book. I'm also grateful to Jerry Holloway and Cecile Joyner, whose expertise and industry were crucial to the production of this book. Benjamin Kolstad's quick eye and sharp intelligence kept me from making many errors, large and small.

Miriam Munson's name deserves to appear on the title page as an indication of how grateful I am to her for her hard work and keen judgment. The book is better because of her. I thank Rebecca Munson for reminding me that there is more to life than the making of books.

I have not always listened to those who have taken the trouble to warn and advise me, and this is reason enough for me to claim the errors here as my own.

*Ronald Munson*

Ronald Munson
University of Missouri–St. Louis, 2003
munson@umsl.edu

# Intervention and Reflection

## Basic Issues in Medical Ethics

### Seventh Edition

# Part I

# Rights

## Chapter 1

# Research Ethics and Informed Consent

## Chapter Contents

## Classic Case Presentation

### *Jesse Gelsinger: The First Gene-Therapy Death*

When Jesse Gelsinger was three months short of his third birthday, he was watching cartoons on TV when he fell asleep. Except it was a sleep from which his parents were unable to arouse him. Panicked, they rushed him to a local hospital.

When Jesse was examined, he responded to stimuli but didn't awaken. The physicians classified him as being in a level-one coma. Laboratory tests showed he had a high level of ammonia in his blood, but it was only after several days and additional blood assays that Jesse's physicians arrived at a diagnosis of ornithine transcarbamylase deficiency—OTC.

OTC is a rare genetic disorder in which the enzyme ornithine transcarbamylase, one of the five involved in the urea cycle, is either missing or in short supply. The enzymes in the cycle break down the ammonia that is a by-product of protein metabolism.

A deficiency of OTC means the body cannot get rid of the ammonia, and it gradually accumulates in the blood. When the ammonia reaches a crucial level, it causes coma, brain damage, and eventually death. The disease results from a mutation on the X chromosome; thus females are carriers of the gene, which they pass on to their sons. The disorder occurs in 1 of every 40,000 births. Infants with the mutation usually become comatose and die within seventy-two hours of birth. Half die within a month of birth, and half of those who remain die before age five.

Although OTC is a genetic disease, no one else in Jesse's immediate family or ancestry had ever been diagnosed with the disease. His disease was probably the result of a spontaneous mutation. He was a genetic mosaic, which meant his body contained a mixture of normal and mutated cells. For this reason, Jesse had a comparatively mild form of OTC. His body produced enough of the enzyme that he could remain in stable health, if he stuck to a low-protein diet and took his medications. These included substances, like sodium benzoate, that chemically bind to ammonia and make it easier for the body to excrete it.

At age ten, after an episode of consuming too much protein, Jesse once again fell into a coma and was hospitalized. But five days later, he was back home with no apparent neurological damage. During his teens, Jesse's condition was monitored by semiannual visits to a metabolic clinic in his hometown of Tucson, Arizona.

In 1998 Jesse, now seventeen, and his father, Paul Gelsinger, heard from Dr. Randy Heidenreich, a doctor at the clinic, about a clinical trial at the University of Pennsylvania. Researchers at the Institute for Human Gene Therapy, Heidenreich told the Gelsingers, were trying to use gene therapy to supply the gene for OTC. Their success would not be a cure for the disease, but it would be a treatment that might be able to bring babies out of comas and prevent their having brain damage.

The Gelsingers were interested, but Jesse was still a year short of being old enough to participate. In April 1999, during another visit to the clinic, they again talked to Dr. Heidenreich about the trial, and Paul mentioned that the family would be taking a trip to New Jersey in June. They would be able to make a side trip to Philadelphia and talk to the investigators.

Dr. Heidenreich contacted an investigator at the Institute and mentioned the Gelsingers' interest in the research, and Paul received a letter from him in April. Jesse would be interviewed and tested at the university hospital on June 22 to determine whether he met the criteria for becoming a research participant.

A bioethicist at the university, Arthur Caplan, had advised the researchers that it would be morally wrong to use infants born with OTC as participants in the gene-therapy trial. Because they could not be expected to live, Caplan reasoned, their parents would be desperate to find a way to save their child's life. Hence, driven by desperation, their consent would not be free. The appropriate participants would be women who were carriers of the gene or men in stable health with only a mild form of the disease. Jesse would celebrate his eighteenth birthday the day the family flew to the East Coast, and his age would then make him eligible to become a participant.

On June 22, 1999, Jesse and Paul Gelsinger met with Dr. Steven Raper for forty-five minutes to review the consent forms and discuss the procedure for which Jesse might volunteer, if he qualified. Dr. Raper, a surgeon, would be the one performing the gene-therapy procedure.

According to Paul Gelsinger's recollections, Raper explained that Jesse would be sedated and two catheters inserted: one in the artery leading to his liver, the second in the vein leaving it. A weakened strain of adenovirus (the virus causing colds), genetically modified to include the OTC gene, would be injected into the hepatic artery. Blood would then be taken from the vein to monitor whether the viral particles were being taken up by the liver cells.

To reduce the risk of a blood clot's breaking loose from the infusion site, Jesse would have to remain in bed for eight hours after the procedure. Most likely, he would soon develop flu-like symptoms lasting for a few days. He might develop hepatitis, an inflammation of the liver. The consent form mentioned that if hepatitis progressed, Jesse might need a liver transplant. The consent form also mentioned that death was a possible outcome.

Paul Gelsinger saw this as such a remote possibility that he was more concerned about the needle biopsy of the liver to be performed a week after the procedure. The risk of death from the biopsy was given as 1 in 10,000. Paul urged Jesse to read the consent document carefully and to make sure he understood it. Paul thought the odds looked very good.

Dr. Raper explained that Jesse couldn't expect to derive any personal medical benefit from participating in the clinical trial. Even if the genes became incorporated into his cells and produced OTC, the effect would only be transitory. His immune system would attack the viral particles and destroy them within a month to six weeks.

Jesse, at the end of the information session, agreed to undergo tests to determine how well the OTC he produced got rid of ammonia in his blood—a measure of OTC efficiency. Samples of his blood were taken; then he drank a small amount of radioactively tagged ammonia. Later, samples of his blood and urine were taken to see how much of the ingested ammonia had been eliminated. The results showed his body's efficiency was only 6 percent of a normal performance.

A month later, the Gelsingers received a letter from Dr. Mark Bratshaw, the pediatrician at the Institute who proposed the clinical trial. Bratshaw confirmed the 6 percent efficiency figure from additional test results and expressed his wish to have Jesse take part in the study. A week later, Bratshaw called Jesse and talked to him. Jesse had already expressed to his father a wish to participate, but he told Bratshaw to talk to his father.

Bratshaw told Paul about the results of their animal studies. The treatment had worked well in mice, preventing the death of those given a lethal injection of ammonia. Also, the most recent patient treated had shown a 50 percent increase in her ability to excrete ammonia. Paul Gelsinger later recalled saying, "Wow! This really works. So, with Jesse at 6 percent efficiency, you may be able to show exactly how well this works."

Bratshaw said their real hope was to find a treatment for newborns lacking any OTC efficiency and with little chance of survival. Also, another twenty-five liver disorders could potentially be treated with the same gene-therapy technique. The promise, then, was that hundreds of thousands, if not millions, of lives might be saved. Bratshaw and Paul never talked about the dangers to Jesse of becoming a subject in the clinical trial.

Paul discussed participation with Jesse. They both agreed that it was the right thing to do. Jesse would be helping babies stay alive and, perhaps in the long run, he might even be helping himself.

## Approval

The clinical trial was supported by a National Institutes of Health grant awarded to Dr. James Wilson, the head of the Institute, and Mark Bratshaw. Their protocol had been reviewed by the federal Recombinant-DNA Advisory Committee (RAC) and the FDA. The animal studies Bratshaw had mentioned to Paul included twenty studies on mice to show the efficacy of the proposed technique. Wilson and his group had also conducted studies on monkeys and baboons to demonstrate the safety of the procedure.

Three of the treated monkeys had died of severe liver inflammation and a blood-clotting disorder when they had been given a stronger strain of adenovirus at a dose twenty times that proposed in the human trial. Both of the scientists assigned by the RAC to review the proposal thought the trial was too dangerous to include stable, asymptomatic volunteers. But Wilson and Bratshaw, using Caplan's argument, convinced the panel that using subjects capable of giving consent was morally preferable to using OTC newborns.

The initial protocol called for the modified viruses to be injected into the right lobe of the liver. The thinking was that if the treatment caused damage, the right lobe could be removed and the left lobe spared. But the RAC objected to injecting the viruses into the liver and the investigators agreed to change the protocol. The decision was later reversed by the FDA, on the grounds that wherever the viruses were injected, they would end up in the liver. The RAC was in the process of being reorganized and, in effect, taken out of the approval loop for proposals; it never received notice of the change. The investigators continued to operate under the modified protocol.

## Protocol

The study was a Phase I Clinical Trial. According to its protocol, eighteen patients were to receive an infusion of the genetically modified adenovirus. The aim of the study was to determine "the maximum tolerated dose." The investigators wanted to determine the point at which the transferred gene would be producing OTC in the maximum amount compatible with side effects that could be tolerated.

The eighteen patients were divided into six groups of three. Each successive group was to receive a slightly higher dose than the preceding one. The idea behind this common procedure is to protect the safety of the study participants. By increasing doses slightly, the hope is to spot the potential for serious side effects in time to avoid causing harm to the participants.

## Preparation

On Thursday, September 9, Jesse Gelsinger, carrying one suitcase of clothes and another of videos, caught a plane for Philadelphia. He checked into the hospital alone. His father, a self-employed handyman, stayed in Tucson to work. Paul planned to arrive on the 18th to be present for what he considered the most dangerous part of the trial—the liver biopsy.

"You're my hero," Paul told Jesse. He looked him in the eye, then gave him a big hug.

The level of ammonia in Jesse's blood was tested on Friday and Sunday. Sunday night he called his father, worried. His ammonia level was high, and his doctors had put him on IV medication to lower it. Paul reassured his son, reminding him that the doctors at the Institute knew more about OTC than anybody else in the world.

## Tragedy

On the morning of Monday, September 13, Gelsinger became the eighteenth patient treated. He was transported from his room to the hospital's interventional radiology suite, where a catheter was snaked through an artery in his groin to the hepatic artery. A second catheter was placed in the vein exiting the liver.

Dr. Raper then slowly injected thirty milliliters of the genetically altered virus into Jesse's hepatic artery. This was the highest dose given to any participant. Patient 17, however, had received the same size dose from a different lot of the virus and had done well. The procedure was completed around noon, and Jesse was returned to his room.

That evening Gelsinger, as expected, began to develop flu-like symptoms. He was feeling ill and feverish when he talked to his father and his stepmother, Mickie, that evening. "I love you, Dad," Jesse told his father. They all said what turned out to be their last goodbyes.

During the night, Jesse's fever soared to 104.5 degrees. A nurse called Dr. Raper at home, and, when he arrived at the hospital around 6:15 that morning, the whites of Jesse's eyes had a yellowish tinge. This was a sign of jaundice, not something the doctors had encountered with the other trial participants. Laboratory findings revealed that Jesse's bilirubin, the product of red blood cell destruction, was four times the normal level.

Raper called Dr. Bratshaw, who was in Washington, to tell him their patient had taken a serious turn. Bratshaw said he would catch the train and arrive in Philadelphia in two hours. Raper also called Paul Gelsinger to explain the situation.

The jaundice was worrying to Jesse's physicians. Either his liver was not functioning adequately or his blood was not clotting properly and his red blood cells were breaking down faster than his liver could process them. Such a breakdown was life threatening for someone with OTC, because the destroyed cells released protein the body would have to metabolize. Jesse was showing the same problem as the monkeys that had been given the stronger strain of the virus.

Tuesday afternoon Paul received a call from Dr. Bratshaw. Jesse's blood-ammonia level had soared to 250 micromoles per deciliter, with 35 being a normal measure. He had slipped into a coma and was on dialysis to try to clear the ammonia from his blood. Paul said he would catch a plane and be at the hospital the next morning.

By the time Paul arrived at eight o'clock on Wednesday and met Bratshaw and Raper, Jesse had additional problems. Dialysis had brought his ammonia level down to 70 from its peak of 393, but he was definitely having a blood-clotting problem. Also, although placed on a ventilator, he continued to breathe for himself, causing hyperventilation. This increased the pH of his blood, which increased the level of ammonia circulating to his brain. Paul gave his permission for the doctors to give Jesse medications that would paralyze his breathing muscles and allow the machine to take over completely.

By Wednesday afternoon, Jesse's breathing was under control. His blood pH had fallen back to normal, and the clotting disorder was improving. Bratshaw returned to Washington. Paul began to relax, and at 5:30 he went out to dinner with his brother and his wife. But he returned to the hospital to find Jesse had been moved to a different intensive care ward, and as he watched the monitors, he saw the oxygen content of Jesse's blood was dropping. A nurse asked him to wait outside.

At 10:30 that evening, a doctor told Paul that Jesse's lungs were failing. Even by putting him on pure oxygen, they were unable to get an adequate amount of oxygen into his blood. The doctors had also talked with a liver transplant team and learned that Jesse was not a good candidate for a transplant.

Raper, very worried, discussed Jesse's problems with Bratshaw and Wilson, and the three of them decided to put Jesse on extracorporeal membrane oxygenation—ECMO. The machine would remove carbon dioxide from Jesse's blood and supply it with the needed oxygen. The procedure was far from standard, however. Only half of the 1000 people placed on ECMO had lived, but Paul was informed that Jesse had only a 10 percent chance of surviving without ECMO.

"If we could just buy his lungs a day or two," Raper later told a reporter, "maybe he would go ahead and heal up."

Jesse was not hooked up to the ECMO unit until five o'clock Thursday morning. Bratshaw attempted to return from Washington, but he was trapped in an Amtrak train outside Baltimore. Hurricane Floyd was headed toward the East Coast; Jesse's stepmother arrived from Tucson just before the airport closed.

The ECMO appeared to be working. But Paul was told that Jesse's lungs were so severely damaged that, if he survived, it would take a long time for him to recover.

When Paul finally saw his son at mid-morning, Jesse was still comatose and bloated beyond recognition. Only the tattoo on his right calf and a scar on his elbow assured Paul that the person in the bed was Jesse.

That evening, unable to sleep, Paul walked the half-mile from his hotel to the hospital to check on Jesse. His son was no better, and Paul noticed that the urine-collecting bag attached to Jesse's bed contained blood. He realized that this meant Jesse's kidneys were shutting down. "He was sliding into multiple-organ-system failure," Raper later recalled.

The next morning, Friday, September 17, Raper and Bratshaw met with Paul and Mickie to give them the bad news that Paul had already predicted. Jesse had suffered irreversible brain damage, and the doctors wanted Paul's permission to turn off the ventilator. At Paul's request, he and Mickie were left alone for a few minutes. He then told the doctors he wanted to bring in his family and have a brief service for Jesse.

Paul and Mickie, seven of Paul's fifteen siblings and their spouses, and about ten staff members crowded into Jesse's room. Paul leaned over Jesse, then turned and told the crowd, "Jesse was a hero." The chaplain said a prayer; then Paul gave a signal. Someone flipped one switch to turn off the ventilator, and flipped a second to turn off the ECMO unit.

Dr. Raper watched the heart monitor. When the line went flat, he put his stethoscope against Jesse's chest. At 2:30 P.M. Raper officially pronounced him dead. "Goodbye, Jesse," he said. "We'll figure this out."

## Gathering Storm

Dr. James Wilson, the head of the Institute, immediately reported Jesse's death to the FDA. Paul Gelsinger, sad as he was, didn't blame Jesse's physicians for what had happened. Indeed, he supported them in the face of an initial round of criticism. "These guys didn't do anything wrong," he told reporters.

Then journalists began to bring to light information that raised questions about whether Jesse and his father had been adequately informed about the risks of the trial that claimed Jesse's life. Also, it raised questions about a conflict of interest that might have led researchers to minimize the risks. The FDA initiated an investigation, and the University of Pennsylvania conducted an internal inquiry.

Paul Gelsinger decided to attend the December 1999 RAC that discussed his son's death. He learned for the first time at that meeting, according to his account, that gene therapy had never been shown to work in humans. He had been misled, not necessarily deliberately, by the researcher's accounts of success in animals. As Paul listened to criticisms of the clinical trial, his faith in the researchers waned and was replaced by anger and a feeling of betrayal.

Other information fed his anger. When a month earlier he had asked James Wilson, "What is your financial position in this?" Wilson's reply, as Paul recalled, was that he was an unpaid consultant to the biotech company Genovo that was partially funding the Institute. Then later Paul learned that both Wilson and the University of Pennsylvania were major stockholders in Genovo and that Wilson had sold his 30 percent share of the company for $13.5 million.

Wilson and the university, as Paul saw it, had good reason to recruit volunteers for the clinical trial and produce positive results. Thus, they might not have been as careful in warning the Gelsingers about the risks of the study as they should have been. Also, the bioethicist approving the trial was someone who held an appointment in the department headed by Wilson. This, in effect, made Wilson his superior and thus automatically raised a question about the independence of his judgment.

A year and a day after Jesse's death, the Gelsinger family filed a wrongful-death lawsuit against the people conducting the clinical trial and the University of Pennsylvania. The university settled the suit out of court. The terms of the settlement were not disclosed.

## FDA Findings

An investigation by the FDA resulted in a report to Wilson and the University of Pennsylvania pointing to two flaws in the way the clinical trial was conducted. First, the investigators failed to follow their protocol and failed to report liver toxicity in four patients treated prior to Gelsinger. Second, the investigators failed to acknowledge the death of two rhesus monkeys injected with a high level of a similar vector.

Wilson's response was that he had sent the FDA the liver–toxicity information prior to the final approval of the protocol, although his report had been late. Further, the two monkeys that died were part of another study that used a different, stronger virus. In effect, then, Wilson was claiming that he and his colleagues had done nothing wrong and the FDA criticisms were unjustified.

Critics point out, apart from the question of how legitimate the criticisms were, that the FDA itself does not have enough power to oversee clinical trials properly. Most important, it is prohibited by law from distributing some so-called "adverse-event" reports. Difficulties encountered by patients in the fifty or so gene-therapy trials are often not made public, or even shared with investigators conducting similar trials, because drug-company sponsors regard information about adverse events as proprietary. This, critics say, puts participants in the position of having to take risks that they know nothing about. The law seems to favor protecting the investments of the pharmaceutical industry more than the protection of human subjects.

## Outcome

What caused the death of Jesse Gelsinger? Even after the autopsy, the answer isn't clear. The most suggestive finding was that Jesse had abnormal cells in his bone marrow. This may have been a pre-existing condition, and it may account for why his immune system reacted in such an unpredicted way to the viral injection. He apparently died from an immunological response.

The FDA, after Jesse's death, shut down all gene-therapy operations temporarily for review. The University of Pennsylvania, after its internal review, restricted the role of the Institute for Human Gene Therapy to conducting basic biological research. Unable to carry out clinical trials, the Institute was de facto put out of business. A year or so later, it ceased to exist.

Because of Jesse's death, the Office for the Protection of Human Research Subjects committed itself to a major effort to educate researchers in the requirements for protecting participants in clinical trials and to stress the importance of Institutional Review Boards in seeing to the safety of participants. Even so, adverse-event reporting is still prohibited by law, when it can be deemed to constitute proprietary information. Critics continue to see this as incompatible with the idea behind informed consent.

## BRIEFING SESSION

In 1947, an international tribunal meeting in Nuremberg convicted fifteen German physicians of "war crimes and crimes against humanity." The physicians were charged with taking part in "medical experiments without the subjects' consent." But the language of the charge fails to indicate the cruel and barbaric nature of the experiments. Here are just some of them:

- At the Ravensbrueck concentration camp, experiments were conducted to test the therapeutic powers of the drug sulfanilamide. Cuts were deliberately made on the bodies of people; then the wounds were infected with bacteria. The infection was worsened by forcing wood shavings and ground glass into the cuts. Then sulfanilamide and other drugs were tested for their effectiveness in combatting the infection.

- At the Dachau concentration camp, healthy inmates were injected with extracts from the mucous glands of mosquitos to produce malaria. Various drugs were then used to determine their relative effectiveness.

- At Buchenwald, numerous healthy people were deliberately infected with the spotted-fever virus merely for the purpose of keeping the virus alive. Over 90 percent of those infected died as a result.

- Also at Buchenwald, various kinds of poisons were secretly administered to a number of inmates to test their efficacy. Either the inmates died or they were killed at once so that autopsies could be performed. Some experimental subjects were shot with poisoned bullets.

- At Dachau, to help the German Air Force, investigations were made into the limits of human endurance and existence at high altitudes. People were placed in sealed chambers, then subjected to very high and very low atmospheric pressures. As the indictment puts it, "Many victims died as a result of these experiments and others suffered grave injury, torture, and ill-treatment."

Seven of the physicians convicted were hanged, and the other eight received long prison terms. From the trial there emerged the Nuremberg Code, a statement of the principles that should be followed in conducting medical research with human subjects.

Despite the moral horrors that were revealed at Nuremberg, few people doubt the need for medical research involving human subjects. The extent to which contemporary medicine has become effective in the treatment of disease and illness is due almost entirely to the fact that it has become scientific medicine. This means that contemporary medicine must conduct inquiries in which data are gathered to test hypotheses and general theories related to disease processes and their treatment. Investigations involving nonhuman organisms are essential, but the ultimate tests of the effectiveness of medical treatments and their side effects must involve human beings as research subjects. Human physiology and psychology are sufficiently different to make animal studies alone inadequate.

The German physicians tried at Nuremberg were charged with conducting experiments without the consent of their subjects. The notion that consent must be given before a person becomes a research subject is still considered the basic requirement that must be met for an experiment to be morally legitimate. Moreover, it is not merely consent—saying yes—but informed consent that is demanded. The basic idea is simply that a person decides to participate in research after he or she has been provided with background information relevant to making the decision.

This same notion of informed consent is also considered a requirement that must be satisfied before a person can legitimately be subjected to medical treatment. Thus, people are asked to agree to submit themselves to such ordinary medical procedures as blood transfusion or to more extraordinary ones such as surgical operations or radiation therapy.

The underlying idea of informed consent in both research and treatment is that people have a right to control what is done to their bodies. The notion of informed consent is thus a recognition of an individual's autonomy—of the right to make decisions governing one's own life. This right is recognized both in practice and in the laws of our society. (Quite often, malpractice suits turn on the issue of whether a patient's informed consent was valid.)

In the abstract, informed consent seems a clear and straightforward notion. After all, we all have an intuitive grasp of what it is to make a decision after we have been supplied with information. Yet in practice informed consent has proved to be a slippery and troublesome concept. We will identify here only a few of the moral and practical difficulties that make the concept controversial and hard to apply.

Our focus will be on informed consent in the context of research involving human subjects. But most of the issues that arise here also arise in connection with giving and securing informed consent for the application of medical therapies. (They also arise in special forms in abortion and euthanasia.) In effect, then, we will be considering the entire topic.

Before discussing informed consent, it will be useful to have an idea of what takes place in a typical clinical trial. Perhaps the most common type of research involves testing new drugs, so let's begin by considering a sketch of what this involves.

## Drug Testing

Traditions of medical research and regulations of the U.S. Food and Drug Administration more or less guarantee that the development of new drugs follows a set procedure. The procedure consists of two major parts: preclinical and clinical testing. When it is thought likely that a chemical substance might be useful, animal experiments are conducted to determine how toxic it is. These tests are also used to estimate the drug's therapeutic index (the ratio of a dose producing toxic effects to a dose producing desired effects). The effects of the substance on particular organs and tissues, as well as on the whole animal, are studied. Efforts are made to determine the drug's potential side effects and hazards. (Does it produce liver or kidney damage? Is it carcinogenic? Does it cause heart arrythmias?)

Clinical testing of the substance occurs in three phases. In Phase I, healthy human volunteers are used to determine whether the drug produces any toxic effects. If the outcome of giving them the drug is acceptable, in Phase II the drug is administered to a limited number of patients who might be expected to benefit from it. If the drug produces desirable results, and has no serious side effects, then Phase III studies are initiated.

The drug is administered to a larger number of patients by a larger number of clinical investigators. Such multicenter trials usually take place at teaching hospitals or in large public institutions. Usually they are sponsored by the drug's manufacturer. Successful results achieved in this phase ordinarily lead to the licensing of the drug for general use.

In the clinical part of testing, careful procedures are followed to attempt to exclude bias in the results. Investigators want their tests to be successful and patients want to get well, and either or both of these factors may influence test results. Investigators may perceive a patient as "improved" just because they want or expect him to be. What is more, medications may produce a "placebo effect." That is, when patients are given inactive substances (placebos), they nevertheless may show improvement.

To rule out these kinds of influences, a common procedure followed in drug testing is the "double-blind" (or "double-masked") test design. In the classic version of this design, a certain number of patients are given the drug being tested, and the remainder of the test group are given placebos. Neither the investigators nor the patients are allowed to know who is receiving the drug and who is not—both are kept "blind." Sometimes a test group is divided so that part receives placebos all of the time, part only some of the time, and part receives genuine medication all of the time.

Often placebos are no more than just sugar pills. Yet, frequently, substances are prepared to produce side effects like those of the drug being tested. If, for example, the drug causes drowsiness, a placebo will be used that produces drowsiness. In this way, investigators will not be able to learn which patients are being given placebos on the basis of irrelevant observations.

In recent decades, placebo trials have been replaced, for the most part, with trials in which an established drug used to treat a condition is compared to a new drug. The old drug represents the "standard of care," and the question is whether the new drug is more effective.

The double-blind test design is employed in many kinds of clinical investigations, not just in drug testing. Thus, the testing of new vaccines and even surgeries often follows the same form. A major variation is the "single-blind" design, in which those who must evaluate the results of some treatment are kept in ignorance of which patients have received it.

## The "Informed" Part of Informed Consent

Consent, at first sight, is no more than agreement. A person consents when he or she says "yes" when asked to become a research subject. But legitimate or valid consent cannot be merely saying yes. If people are to be treated as autonomous agents, they must have the opportunity to decide whether they wish to become participants in research.

Deciding, whatever else it may be, is a process in which we reason about an issue at hand. We consider such matters as the risks of our participation, its possible advantages to ourselves and others, the risks and advantages of other alternatives that are offered to us, and our own values. In short, valid consent requires that we deliberate before we decide.

But genuine deliberation requires both information and understanding. These two requirements are the source of difficulties and controversies. After all, medical research and treatment are highly technical enterprises. They are based on complicated scientific theories that are expressed in a special vocabulary and involve unfamiliar concepts.

For this reason, some physicians and investigators have argued that it is virtually useless to provide patients with relevant scientific information about research and treatment. Patients without the proper scientific background, they argue, simply don't know what to make of the information. Not only do patients find it puzzling, but they find it frightening. Thus, some have suggested, informed consent is at worst a pointless charade and at best a polite fiction. The patient's interest is best served by allowing a physician to make the decision.

This obviously paternalistic point of view (see Chapter 2) implies, in effect, that all patients are incompetent to decide their best interest and that physicians must assume the responsibility of acting for them.

An obvious objection to this view is its assumption that, because patients lack a medical background, they cannot be given information in a form they can understand that is at least adequate to allow them to decide how they are to be treated. Thus, proponents of this view confuse difficulty of communication with impossibility of communication. While it is true that it is often hard to explain technical medical matters to a layperson, this hardly makes it legitimate to conclude that people should turn over their right to determine what is done to them to physicians. Rather, it imposes on physicians and researchers the obligation to find a way to explain medical matters to their patients.

The information provided to patients must be usable. That is, patients must understand enough about the proposed research and treatment to deliberate and reach a decision. From the standpoint of the researcher, the problem here is to determine when the patient has an adequate understanding to make informed consent valid. Patients, being people, do not like to appear stupid and say they don't understand an explanation. Also, they may believe they understand an explanation when, as a matter of fact, they don't.

Until recently, little effort was made to deal with the problem of determining when a patient understands the information provided and is competent to assess it. In the last few years, researchers have investigated situations in which individuals have been asked to consent to become research subjects. Drawing upon these data, some writers have attempted to formulate criteria for assessing competency for giving informed consent. The problem is not one that even now admits of an ideal solution, but, with additional empirical investigation and philosophical analysis, the situation may improve even more.

## The "Consent" Part of Informed Consent

We have talked so far as though the issue of gaining the legitimate agreement of someone to be a research subject or patient involved only providing information to an ordinary person in ordinary circumstances and then allowing the person to decide. But the matter is more complicated than this, because often either the person or the circumstances possess special features. These features can call into question the very possibility of valid consent.

It's generally agreed that, in order to be valid, consent must be voluntary. The person must of his or her "own free will" agree to become a research subject. This means that the person must be capable of acting voluntarily. That is, the person must be competent.

This is an obvious and sensible requirement accepted by all. But the difficulty lies in specifying just what it means to be competent. One answer is that a person is competent if he or she is capable of acting rationally. Because we have some idea of what it is to act rationally, this is a movement in the direction of an answer.

The problem with it, however, is that people sometimes decide to act for the sake of moral (or religious) principles in ways that may not seem reasonable. For example, someone may volunteer to be a subject in a potentially hazardous experiment because she believes the experiment holds out the promise of helping countless others. In terms of self-interest alone, such an action would not be reasonable.

### Vulnerable Populations

Even in the best of circumstances, it is not always easy to determine who is competent to consent and who is not. Yet researchers and ethicists must also face the issue of how children, the mentally retarded, prisoners, and those suffering from psychiatric illnesses are to be considered with respect to consent. Should no one in any of these vulnerable populations be considered capable of giving consent? If so, then is it ever legitimate to secure the consent from some third party—from a parent or guardian—in some cases?

One possibility is simply to rule out all research that involves such people as subjects. But this has the undesirable consequence of severely hampering efforts to gain the knowledge that might be of use either to the people themselves or to others with similar medical problems. Later we will consider some of the special problems that arise with children and other vulnerable groups as research subjects.

The circumstances in which research is done can also call into question the voluntariness of consent. This is particularly so with prisons, nursing homes, and mental hospitals. These are all what the sociologist Erving Goffman called "total institutions," for within them all aspects of a person's life are connected with the social structure. People have a definite place in the structure and particular social roles. Moreover, there are social forces at work that both pressure and encourage an inmate to do what is expected of him or her.

We will discuss later in this chapter some of the special problems that arise in research with prisoners. Here we need only point out that gaining voluntary consent from inmates in institutions may not be possible, even in principle. If it is possible, it's necessary to specify the kinds of safeguards that must be followed to free them from the pressures resulting from the very fact that they are inmates. Those who suffer from psychiatric illnesses may be considered just as capable intellectually of giving consent, but here too safeguards to protect them from the pressures of the institution need to be specified.

In recent years, researchers have expanded the testing of new drugs and drug regimens into developing countries. The citizens of these countries are typically less well educated and less scientifically sophisticated than their counterparts in industrialized nations. They may also be more likely to trust that what they are asked to do by some medical authority will be in their best in-

terest. Hence, securing informed consent from them that is valid presents particular difficulties.

It's important to keep in mind that ordinary patients in hospitals may also be subject to pressures that call into question the voluntariness of the consent that they give. Patients are psychologically predisposed to act in ways that please physicians. Not only do physicians possess a social role that makes them figures of authority, but an ill person feels very dependent on those who may possess the power to make her well. Thus, she will be inclined to go along with any suggestion or recommendation made by a physician.

The ordinary patient, like the inmate in an institution, needs protection from the social and psychological pressures that are exerted by circumstances. Otherwise, the voluntariness of consent will be compromised, and the patient cannot act as a free and autonomous agent.

## Medical Research and Medical Therapy

Medical therapy aims at relieving the suffering of people and restoring them to health. It attempts to cure diseases, correct disorders, and bring about normal bodily functioning. Its focus is on the individual patient, and his or her welfare is its primary concern.

Medical research, by contrast, is a scientific enterprise. Its aim is to acquire a better understanding of the biochemical and physiological processes involved in human functioning. It is concerned with the effectiveness of therapies in ending disease processes and restoring functioning. But this concern is not for the patient as an individual. Rather it's directed toward establishing theories. The hope, of course, is that this theoretical understanding can be used as a basis for treating individuals. But helping a particular patient get well is not a goal of medical research.

The related but distinct aims of medical research and medical therapy are a source of conflict in human experimentation. It's not unusual for a physician to be acting both as a researcher and as a therapist. This means that although she must be concerned with the welfare of her patient, her aims must also include acquiring data that are important to her research project. It is possible, then, that she may quite unconsciously encourage her patients to volunteer to be research subjects, provide them with inadequate information on which to base their decisions, or minimize the risks they are likely to be subject to.

The patient, for his part, may be reluctant to question his physician to acquire more information or to help him understand his role and risks in research. Also, as mentioned previously, the patient may feel pressured into volunteering for research, just because he wants to do what his physician expects of him.

Medical research is a large-scale operation in this country and affects a great many people. It has been estimated that 400,000–800,000 people a year are patients in research programs investigating the effectiveness of drugs and other therapies. Since 1980, the number of clinical studies has increased more than 30 percent, from about 3500 to 5000. Informed consent is more than an abstract moral issue.

The aims of therapy and the aims of research may also cause moral difficulties for the physician that go beyond the question of consent. This is particularly so in certain kinds of research. Let's look at some of the ethical issues more specifically.

## Financial Conflict of Interest

Paul Gelsinger's eighteen-year-old son Jesse died in a clinical trial of gene therapy. Although devastated by his loss, Paul was initially prepared to support the work of James Wilson, the project's principal investigator at the University of Pennsylvania. Then he learned that Wilson and the university were major stockholders in Genovo, the biotech company sponsoring the research, and that Wilson had sold his 30 percent share of the company for $13.5 million. Gelsinger not only stopped defending Wilson, he sued him and

the university. (See the Classic Case Presentation for more details.)

Private industry now supports academic research to the tune of about $1.5 *billion* a year. One study showed that 2.8 percent of researchers in the biomedical sciences received at least some funding from private sponsors. Such sponsors are mainly pharmaceutical, medical-device, and biotech companies that expect to profit from patents based on the research.

It is not unusual, as was the case with James Wilson, for an investigator to have a financial stake in the research. The stake may be slight or, when the investigator is a major shareholder in the company sponsoring the research, it may be significant. In a study of researchers at the University of California, San Francisco published in 2000, 7.6 percent of faculty investigators reported personal financial ties with the sponsors of their research. Some were paid to be speakers (at fees ranging from $250 to $20,000 a year), while 32 percent of them held positions on the company's advisory committee or board of directors.

An investigator who stands to earn a considerable sum of money from the success of the clinical trial he is conducting has a clear conflict of interest. He may (even quite unconsciously) minimize the risks of participating when seeking the consent of a volunteer. Or he may be inclined to delay reporting adverse events associated with the trial to a regulatory agency or institutional review board (IRB) to avoid having the agency or IRB halt the study. He may also be prone to overestimating the value of the treatment or device being tested.

Federal agencies and the IRBs of most institutions now require investigators to reveal whether they have a financial stake in the outcome of the research. Yet having such a stake does not automatically disqualify an investigator from conducting the research, and IRBs work to accommodate the interest of the investigator.

Institutions where research is funded privately, rather than by federal grants, may not require an investigator to inform potential research participants that the investigator has a financial interest in the research. Further, even when investigators are required to reveal a potential conflict of interest, if they fail to do so, the consequences may consist only of a notice of violation or a scolding letter.

Because more and more investigators are acquiring a financial stake in the results of their research, we need to develop national guidelines for dealing with conflicts of interest. It may not be a good idea to forbid researchers to profit financially from the success of their research, but such potential conflicts of interest do raise questions we must address.

## Placebos and Research

As we saw earlier in the description of a typical drug experiment, placebos are often considered essential to determine the true effectiveness of the drug being tested. In practice, this means that during all or some of the time they are being "treated," patients who are also subjects in a research program will not be receiving genuine medication. They are not, then, receiving the best available treatment for their specific condition.

This is one of the risks that a patient needs to know about before consenting to become a research subject. After all, most people become patients in order to be cured, if possible, of their ailments, not to further science or anything of the kind. The physician-as-therapist will continue to provide medical care to a patient, for under double-blind conditions the physician does not know who is being given placebos and who is not. But the physician-as-researcher will know that a certain number of people will be receiving medication that cannot be expected to help their condition. Thus, the aims of the physician who is also a researcher come into conflict.

This conflict is particularly severe in cases in which it is reasonable to believe (on the basis of animal experimentation, in vitro research, and so on) that an effective disease preventative exists, yet, to satisfy scientific rigor, tests of its effectiveness involve the giving of placebos.

This was the case with the development of a polio vaccine by Thomas Weller, John F. Enders, and Frederick C. Robbins in 1960. The initial phase of the clinical testing involved injecting 30,000 children with a substance known to be useless in the prevention of polio—a placebo injection. It was realized, statistically, that some of those children would get the disease and die from it.

Since Weller, Enders, and Robbins believed they had an effective vaccine, they can hardly be regarded as acting in the best interest of these children. As physicians they were not acting to protect the interest and well-being of the children. They did, of course, succeed in proving the safety and effectiveness of the polio vaccine. The moral question is whether they were justified in failing to provide 30,000 children with a vaccine they believed to be effective, even though it had not been tested on a wide scale with humans. That is, did they correctly resolve the conflict between their roles as researchers and their roles as physicians?

Placebos also present physician-researchers with another conflict. As we noticed in the earlier discussion, placebos are not always just "sugar pills." They often contain active ingredients that produce in patients effects that resemble those caused by the medication being tested—nervousness, vomiting, loss of appetite, and so on. This means that a patient receiving a placebo is sometimes not only failing to receive any medication for his illness, but also receiving a medication that may do him some harm. Thus, the physician committed to care for the patient and to relieve his suffering is at odds with the researcher who may be harming the patient. Do the aims of scientific research and its potential benefits to others justify treating patients in this fashion? Here is another moral question that the physician must face in particular and we must face in general.

We should not leave the topic of the use of placebos without the reminder of what was mentioned earlier—that it is possible to make use of an experimental design in research that does not require giving placebos to a control group. An investigator can compare the results of two treatment forms: a standard treatment whose effectiveness is known and a new treatment with a possible but not proven effectiveness. This is not as scientifically satisfactory as the other approach because the researcher must do without a control group that has received no genuine treatment. But it does provide a way out of the dilemma of both providing medical care and conducting research.

This way of proceeding has associated with it another moral issue. If a clinical trial of a drug is scheduled to last for a long period of time (perhaps years) but accumulating statistical results indicate the drug is more effective in the treatment or prevention of a disease than the established one it is being compared with, should the trial be stopped so that all the patients in the study can gain the benefits of the test drug? Or does the informed consent of the participants warrant continuing the trial until the therapeutic value of the test drug is fully established?

The view generally accepted now is that if the evidence strongly indicates that a treatment being tested is more effective than the standard one, researchers have an obligation to discontinue the trial and offer the new treatment to those who were not receiving it.

## Therapeutic and Nontherapeutic Research

We have mentioned the conflict that faces the physician who is also an investigator. But the patient who has to decide whether or not to consent to become a research subject is faced with a similar conflict.

Some research holds out the possibility of a direct and immediate advantage to those patients who agree to become subjects. For example, a new drug may, on the basis of limited trials, promise to be more effective in treating an illness than those drugs in standard use.

Or a new surgical procedure may turn out to give better results than one that would ordinarily

be used. By agreeing to participate in research involving such a drug or procedure, a patient may then have a chance of gaining something more beneficial than he or she would gain otherwise.

Yet the majority of medical research projects do not offer any direct therapeutic advantages to patients who consent to be subjects. The research may eventually benefit many patients, but seldom does it bring more than usual therapeutic benefits to research participants. Ordinarily, the most that participants can expect to gain are the advantages of having the attention of physicians who are experts on their illness and receiving close observation and supervision from researchers.

These are matters that ought to be presented to the patient as information relevant to the decision the patient must make. The patient must then decide whether he or she is willing to become a participant, even if there are no special therapeutic advantages to be gained. It is in making this decision that one's moral beliefs can play a role. Some people volunteer to become research subjects without hope of reward because they believe that their action may eventually be of help to others.

Let us now examine some problems of medical research when special groups are its focus. We will also consider some of the related issues of fetal research.

## Research Involving Children

One of the most controversial areas of all medical research has been that involving children as subjects. The Willowbrook project discussed in the Case Presentation later in the chapter is just one among many investigations that have drawn severe criticism and, quite often, court action.

**Why Study Children at All?** The obvious question is: Why should children ever be made research subjects? Children clearly lack the physical, psychological, and intellectual maturity of adults. It does not seem that they are as capable as adults of giving informed consent because they can hardly be expected to grasp the nature of research and the possible risks to themselves.

Furthermore, because children have not yet developed their capacities, it seems wrong to subject them to risks that might alter, for the worse, the course of their lives. They are in a position of relative dependency, relying upon adults to provide the conditions for their existence and development. It seems almost a betrayal of trust to allow children to be subjected to treatment that is of potential harm to them.

Such considerations help explain why we typically regard research involving children with deep suspicion. It is easy to imagine children being exploited and their lives blighted by callous researchers. Some writers have been sufficiently concerned by the possibility of dangers and abuses that they have advocated an end to all research with children as subjects.

But there is another side to the coin. Biologically, children are not just small adults. Their bodies are developing, growing systems. Not only are there anatomical differences; there are also differences in metabolism and biochemistry. For example, some drugs are absorbed and metabolized more quickly in children than in adults, whereas other drugs continue to be active for a longer time. Often some drugs produce different effects when administered to children.

Also, precisely because the bodies of children are still developing, their nutritional needs are different. Findings based on adult subjects cannot simply be extrapolated to children, any more than results based on animal studies can be extrapolated to human beings.

Further, children are prone to certain kinds of diseases (measles or mumps, for example) that are either less common in adults or occur in different forms. It is important to know the kinds of therapies that are most successful in the treatment of children afflicted with them.

Children also have problems that are not seen in adults, because children with them do not survive unless the problems are treated effectively. Various heart anomalies, for example, must be corrected to keep children alive. Thus, the development of new surgical techniques must necessarily involve children.

Finally, even familiar surgical procedures cannot be employed in a straightforward way with children. Their developing organ systems are sufficiently different that special pediatric techniques must often be devised.

For many medical purposes, children must be thought of almost as if they were wholly different organisms. Their special biological features set them apart and mark them as subjects requiring special study. To gain the kind of knowledge and understanding required for effective medical treatment of children, it is often impossible to limit research solely to adults.

**Excluding Children.** Failing to conduct research on children raises its own set of ethical issues. If children are excluded from investigations, then the development of pediatric medicine will be severely hindered. In general, this would mean that children would receive medical therapies that are less effective than might be possible. Also, since it is known that children differ significantly from adults in drug reactions, it seems wrong to subject children to the risks of drugs and drug dosages that have been tested only on adults.

Research involving children can also be necessary to avoid causing long-term harm to numerous people. The use of pure oxygen in the environments of prematurely born babies in the early 1940s resulted in hundreds of cases of blindness and impaired vision. It was not until a controlled study was done that retinal damage was traced to the effects of the oxygen. Had the research not been allowed, the chances are very good that the practice would have continued and thousands more infants would have been blinded.

**Ethical Issues.** Yet, even if we agree that not all research involving children should be forbidden, we still have to face up to the issues that such research generates. Without attempting to be complete, we can mention the following three issues as among the more prominent.

**Who Is a Child?**  Who is to be considered a child? For infants and children in elementary school, this question is not a difficult one. But what about people in their teens? Then the line becomes hard to draw. Indeed, perhaps it is not possible to draw a line at all without being arbitrary.

The concern behind the question is with the acquisition of autonomy, of self-direction and responsibility. It is obvious on the basis of ordinary experience that people develop at different rates, and some people at sixteen are more capable of taking charge of their own lives than others are at twenty. Some teenagers are more capable of understanding the nature and hazards of a research project than are many people who are much older.

This suggests that many people who are legally children may be quite capable of giving their informed consent. Of course, many others probably are not, so that decisions about capability would have to rest on an assessment of the individual. Where medical procedures that have a purely therapeutic aim are concerned, an individual who is capable of deciding whether it is in his or her best interest should probably be the one to decide. The issue may be somewhat different when the aim is not therapy. In such cases, a better policy might be to set a lower limit on the age at which consent can be given, and those below that limit should not be permitted to consent to participate in research. The problem is, of course, what should that limit be?

**Parental Consent.**  Can anyone else consent on behalf of a child? Parents or guardians have a duty to act for the sake of the welfare of a child under their care. In effect, they have a duty to substitute their judgment for that of the child. We generally agree to this because most often we consider the judgment of an adult more mature and informed than a child's. And because the responsibility for care rests with the adult, we customarily recognize that the adult has a right to decide. It is almost as though the adult's autonomy is being shared with the child—almost as though the child were an extension of the adult.

Society and its courts have recognized limits on the power of adults to decide for children. When it seems that the adult is acting in an irresponsible or unreasonable manner, then society steps in to act as a protector of the child's right to be cared for. Thus, courts have ordered that lifesaving procedures or blood transfusions be performed on children even when their parents or guardians have decided against it. The criterion used in such judgments is "the best interest of the child."

What sort of limits should govern a parent's or guardian's decision to allow a child to become a research subject? Is it reasonable to believe that, if a parent would allow herself to be the subject of research, then it is also right for her to consent to her child's becoming a subject? Or should something more be required before consent for a child's participation can be considered legitimate?

**Therapeutic Benefits.**  Should children be allowed to be subjects of research that does not offer them a chance of direct therapeutic benefits? Perhaps the "something more" that parents or guardians ought to require before consenting on behalf of a child is the genuine possibility that the research will bring the child direct benefits. This would be in accordance with a parent's duty to seek the welfare of the child. It is also a way of recognizing that the parent's autonomy is not identical with that of the child: one may have the right to take a risk oneself without having the right to impose the risk on someone else.

This seems like a reasonable limitation, and it has been advocated by some writers. Yet there are difficulties with the position. Some research virtually free from risk (coordination tests, for example) might be stopped because of its lack of a "direct therapeutic value."

More important, however, much research promising immense long-term benefits would have to be halted. Research frequently involves the withholding of accepted therapies without any guarantee that what is used in their place will be as effective. Sometimes the withholding of accepted treatment is beneficial. Thus, as it turned out, in the research on the incidence of blindness in premature infants in the 1940s, premature infants who were not kept in a pure oxygen environment were better off than those who received ordinary treatment.

But no one could know this in advance, and such research as this is, at best, ambiguous as to the promise of direct therapy. Sheer ignorance imposes restrictions. Yet if the experiment had not been done, the standard treatment would have continued with its ordinary course of (statistically) disastrous results. Here, at least, there was the possibility of better results from the experimental treatment.

But in research that involves the substitution of placebos for medications or vaccines known to be effective, it is known in advance that some children will not receive medical care considered to be the best. A child who is a subject in such research is then put in a situation in which he or she is subjected to a definite hazard. The limitation on consent that we are considering would rule out such research. But the consequence of doing this would be to restrict the development of new and potentially more effective medications and treatment techniques. That is, future generations of children would be deprived of at least some possible medical advances.

These, then, are some of the issues that we have to face in arriving at a view of the role of children in research. Perhaps the greatest threat to children, however, has to do with social organization. Children, like prisoners, are often grouped together in institutions (schools, orphanages, detention centers, and so on) and are attractive targets for clinical investigators because they inhabit a limited and relatively controlled environment, can be made to follow orders, and do not ask too many questions that have to be answered. It is a misimpression to see researchers in such situations as "victimizing" children, but at the same time careful controls are needed to see that research involving children is legitimate and carried out in a morally satisfactory way.

**Guidelines.** In response to some of these difficulties, the Department of Health and Human Services has issued guidelines specifically designed to protect children as research subjects. First, for children to become participants, permission must be obtained from parents or guardians, and children must give their "assent." Second, an Institutional Review Board is assigned the responsibility of considering the "ages, maturity, and psychological states" of the children and determining whether they are capable of assenting. (A failure to object cannot be construed as assent.)

Third, children who are wards of the state or of an institution can become participants only if the research relates to their status as wards or takes place in circumstances in which the majority of subjects are not wards. Each child must also be supplied with an "advocate" to represent her or his interest.

## Research Involving Prisoners

Prisoners are in some respects social outcasts. They have been found guilty of breaking the laws of society and, as a consequence, are removed from it. Stigmatized and isolated, prisoners in the relatively recent past were sometimes thought of as less than human. It seemed only reasonable that such depraved and corrupt creatures should be used as the subjects of experiments that might bring benefits to the members of the society that they wronged. Indeed, it seemed not only reasonable, but fitting.

Accordingly, in the early part of the twentieth century, tropical medicine expert Richard P. Strong obtained permission from the Governor of the Philippines to inoculate a number of condemned criminals with plague bacillus. The prisoners were not asked for their consent, but they were rewarded by being provided with cigarettes and cigars.

Episodes of this sort were relatively common during the late nineteenth and early twentieth centuries. But as theories about the nature of crime and criminals changed, it became standard practice to use only volunteers and to secure the consent of the prisoners themselves.

In the 1940s, for example, the University of Chicago infected over 400 prisoners with malaria in an attempt to discover new drugs to treat and prevent the disease. A committee set up by the Governor of Illinois recommended that potential volunteers be informed of the risks, be permitted to refuse without fear of such reprisals as withdrawal of privileges, and be protected from unnecessary suffering. The committee suggested also that volunteering to be a subject in a medical experiment is a form of good conduct that should be taken into account in deciding whether a prisoner should be paroled or have his sentence reduced.

**Consent and Coercion.**  But the committee also called attention to a problem of great moral significance. They pointed out that, if a prisoner's motive for volunteering is the wish to contribute to human welfare, then a reduction in his sentence would be a reward. But if his motive is to obtain a reduction in sentence, then the possibility of obtaining one is really a form of duress. In this case, the prisoner cannot be regarded as making a free decision. The issue of duress or "undue influence," as it is called in law, is central to the question of deciding whether, and under what conditions, valid informed consent can be obtained for research involving prisoners. Some ethicists have argued that, to avoid undue influence, prisoners should never be promised any substantial advantages for volunteering to be research subjects. If they volunteer, they should do so for primarily moral or humane reasons.

Others have claimed that becoming research subjects offers prisoners personal advantages that they should not be denied. For example, participation in a research project frees them from the boredom of prison life, gives them an opportunity to increase their feelings of self-worth, and allows them to exercise their autonomy as moral agents. It has been argued, in fact, that prisoners have a right to participate in research if the opportunity is offered to them and they wish to do so. To forbid the use of prisoners

as research subjects is thus to deny to them, without adequate grounds, a right that all human beings possess. As a denial of their basic autonomy, of their right to take risks and control their own bodies, not allowing them to be subjects might constitute a form of cruel and unusual punishment.

By contrast, it can also be argued that prisoners do not deserve to be allowed to exercise such autonomy. Because they have been sentenced for crimes, they should be deprived of the right to volunteer to be research subjects: that right belongs to free citizens. Being deprived of the right to act autonomously is part of their punishment. This is basically the position taken by the House of Delegates of the American Medical Association. The Delegates passed a resolution in 1952 expressing disapproval of the use as research subjects of people convicted of "murder, rape, arson, kidnapping, treason, and other heinous crimes."

A more worrisome consideration is the question of whether prisoners can be sufficiently free of undue influence or duress to make their consent legitimate. As we mentioned earlier, prisons are total institutions, and the institutional framework itself puts pressures on people to do what is desired or expected of them.

There need not be, then, promises of rewards (such as reduced sentences) or overt threats (such as withdrawal of ordinary privileges) for coercion to be present. That people may volunteer to relieve boredom is itself an indication that they may be acting under duress. That "good conduct" is a factor in deciding whether to grant parole may function as another source of pressure.

The problem presented by prisoners is fundamentally the same as that presented by inmates in other institutions, such as nursing homes and mental hospitals. In these cases, once it has been determined that potential subjects are mentally competent to give consent, then it must also be decided whether the institutional arrangements allow the consent to be "free and voluntary."

## Research Involving the Poor

In the eighteenth century, Princess Caroline of England requested the use of six "charity children" as subjects in the smallpox vaccination experiments she was directing. Then, and well into the twentieth century, charity cases, like prisoners, were regarded by some medical researchers as prime research subjects.

A horrible example of medical research involving the poor is the Tuskegee Syphilis Study that was conducted under the auspices of the U.S. Department of Public Health (USPH). From 1932 to 1970, a number of black males suffering from the later stages of syphilis were examined at regular intervals to determine the course their disease was taking. The men in the study were poor and uneducated and believed that they were receiving proper medical care from the state and local public health clinics.

As a matter of fact, they were given either no treatment or inadequate treatment, and at least forty of them died as a result of factors connected with their disease. Their consent was never obtained, and the nature of the study, its risks, and the alternatives open to them were never explained.

It was known when the study began that those with untreated syphilis have a higher death rate than those whose condition is treated, and although the study was started before the advent of penicillin (which is highly effective against syphilis), other drugs were available but were not used in ways to produce the best results. When penicillin became generally available, it still was not used.

The Tuskegee Study clearly violated the Nuremberg Code, but it was not stopped even after the War Crimes trials. It was reviewed in 1969 by a USPH ad hoc committee, and it was decided that the study should be phased out in 1970. The reasons for ending the experiment were not moral ones. Rather, it was believed nothing much of scientific value was to be gained by continuing the work. In 1973, a United States Public Health Department Ad Hoc Advisory Panel, which had been established as a result of public and congressional pressure to review the Tuskegee Study, presented its final report. It condemned the study both on moral grounds and because of its lack of worth and rigor. (See the Classic Case Presentation: "Bad Blood, Bad Faith" in Chapter 4 for more details.)

No one today argues that disadvantaged people ought to be made subjects of research simply as a result of their social or economic status. The "back wards" in hospitals whose poor patients once served as a source of research subjects have mostly disappeared as a result of such programs as Medicare and Medicaid. Each person is now entitled to his or her own physician and is not under the general care of the state or of a private charity.

Yet many research projects continue to be based in large public or municipal hospitals. And such hospitals have a higher percentage of disadvantaged people as patients than do private institutions. For this reason, such people are still more likely to become research subjects than are the educated and wealthy. If society continues to accept this state of affairs, special precautions must be taken to see to it that those who volunteer to become research subjects are genuinely informed and free in their decisions.

## Research Involving the Terminally Ill

People who have been diagnosed with a terminal illness characteristically experience overwhelming feelings of despair. Within a few days or weeks, some are able to acknowledge and accept the situation, but others are driven to desperation by the imminent prospect of their death.

When they learn that conventional therapies offer little hope of prolonging their lives, they vow to fight their disease by other means. They look for hope in a situation that seems hopeless, and with the encouragement of family and friends, they seek new therapies.

Some turn to quack medicine or suspect remedies, but others seek out clinical trials of new drugs for their diseases. They seek acceptance into trials from the hospitals and medical centers where they are being conducted.

Critics of the policy of accepting terminally ill patients into clinical trials base their objections on the vulnerability of patients. Most often, critics charge, such patients are not sufficiently aware of what they are getting into, nor are they aware of how little personal payoff they may reasonably expect to receive from an experimental therapy.

To be enrolled in a drug trial, patients must satisfy the study's research protocol. They must meet diagnostic criteria for having a particular disease or their disease must be at a certain stage in its natural history. Or perhaps the patients must not have received certain treatments, such as radiation, or must not have been taking a particular drug for several weeks. Perhaps the patients must not have signs of liver damage or kidney disease. Some of the criteria may require that patients be tested. The testing may involve only drawing blood for analysis, but it may also require submitting to painful and potentially harmful surgical procedures to biopsy tissue.

A patient who qualifies for admission to a study may still have a difficult time ahead. If the study is at an institution that is hundreds, even thousands, of miles away, the patient must either move nearer or travel to the institution regularly. In either case, much expense and inconvenience may be involved.

Critics also charge that patients may have unreasonable expectations about the effectiveness of experimental therapies. Patients may believe, for example, that a drug has at least some record of success, but in fact the therapeutic benefits of the drug may be uncertain at best. Indeed, in the initial stage of drug testing with human subjects, Phase I trials, the aim is not to determine the therapeutic effectiveness of the drug, but to determine such matters as its toxicity, rate of metabolism, or most effective mode of administration.

The chance that a drug under investigation will actually prolong the life of a patient in the final stages of a terminal illness is small. One study reviewed the results of forty-two preliminary reports on drugs used to treat colon cancer and thirty-three on drugs used to treat nonsmall-cell lung cancer, but only one drug was found to have therapeutic effects.

Furthermore, critics charge, patients may not realize the extent to which an experimental drug may turn out to cause unpleasant, painful, or harmful side effects. Patients may suffer nausea, vomiting, chills, fevers, neurological damage, or lowered immunological functioning.

Such effects may not even be known to the investigators, and so they cannot inform patients about them at the time consent is sought. The last weeks or months of terminally ill patients may thus be spent more painfully than if they had simply waited for death, and in fact, patients may even shorten their lives by becoming subjects in a study.

As a sort of final disappointment, critics point out, the study that a dying patient was counting on to give her a last chance at lengthening her life might drop her as a subject. The aim of a clinical trial of a new drug, for example, is to discover such medically important characteristics of the drug as its side effects, what constitutes an effective dosage, and whether the drug has therapeutic benefits. Patients in the study are sources of data, and if a patient who is receiving no therapeutic benefit from a drug turns out to be of no value to the study, she may be dropped from it. Dying patients may be hit particularly hard by such a rejection.

In the view of critics, the desperation of terminally ill patients makes them too vulnerable to be able to give meaningful consent to participate in experimental trials. Even if they are fairly informed that a drug trial will offer them only a remote possibility of prolonging their lives, they are under such pressure from their illness that, in a sense, they are not free to consent. Patients and their families may be so frightened and emotionally distraught that they hear only what they want to hear about an experimental therapy. They may be unable to grasp that the therapy probably will not benefit them and may even harm them.

Opponents of enrolling terminally ill patients in clinical investigations charge that the patients are often treated as though they are only a research resource, a pool from which subjects can be selected for whatever testing needs to be done. That people are dying does not mean that it is justifiable to exploit them, and the only way to avoid this is to exclude them as eligible candidates for research subjects.

While no one advocates the exploitation of terminally ill people, most observers believe it is morally legitimate to include them in clinical trials. The patients themselves may have something to gain. The very act of trying a new drug might make some patients feel better, even if it is only a placebo effect. Also, patients and their families can feel that they are genuinely doing everything possible to improve the patient's health. Moreover, the drug might be of some therapeutic benefit to the patient, even if the chance of its prolonging the patient's life is remote.

Furthermore, defenders of the policy hold, allowing dying patients to participate in research is to recognize their status as autonomous persons, while to exclude them as candidates for research subjects is to deny them that status.

Finally, defenders claim, in connection with their status as moral agents, dying patients deserve to be given a chance to do something for others. In fact, when dying patients are recruited or seek to enroll in a study, instead of stressing the possible therapeutic benefit they might secure, the experimenter should emphasize the contribution that patients' participation might make to helping others in the future.

To put this last point in perspective, consider the responses of twenty-seven cancer patients enrolled in a Phase I clinical trial who were interviewed by Mark Siegler and his colleagues at the University of Chicago. Eighty-five percent of the patients said they had agreed to participate because they hoped for therapeutic benefits, 11 percent enrolled at the suggestion of their physicians, and 4 percent did so at the urging of their families. No one reported enrolling out of a desire to help others.

## Research Involving Fetuses

In 1975 legal charges were brought against several physicians in Boston. They had injected antibiotics into living fetuses that were scheduled to be aborted. The aim of the research was to determine by autopsy, after the death of the fetuses, how much of the drug got into the fetal tissues.

Such information is considered to be of prime importance because it increases our knowledge of how to provide medical treatment for a fetus still developing in its mother's womb. It also helps to determine ways in which drugs taken by a pregnant woman may affect a fetus and so points the way toward improved prenatal care.

Other kinds of research involving the fetus also promise to provide important knowledge. Effective vaccines for preventing viral diseases, techniques for treating children with defective immune-system reactions, and hormonal measurements that indicate the status of the developing fetus are just some of the potential advances that are partially dependent on fetal research.

But a number of moral questions arise in connection with such research. Even assuming that a pregnant woman consents to allow the fetus she is carrying to be injected with drugs prior to abortion, is such research ethical? Does the fact that the fetus is going to be aborted alter in any way the moral situation? For example, prior to abortion should the fetus be treated with the same respect and concern for its well-being as a fetus that is not scheduled for abortion?

After the fetus is aborted, if it is viable—if it can live separated from the mother—then we seem to be under an obligation to protect its life. But what if a prenatal experiment threatens its viability? The expectation in abortion is that the fetus will not be viable, but this is not in fact always the case. Does this mean that it is wrong to do anything before abortion to threaten the life of the fetus or reduce its chance for life, even though we do not expect it to live?

These are difficult questions to answer without first settling the question of whether the fetus is to be considered a person. (See the discussion of this issue in the Briefing Session in Chapter 9.) If the fetus is a person, then it is entitled to the same moral considerations that we extend to other persons. If we decide to take its life, if abortion is considered to be at least sometimes legitimate, then we must be prepared to offer justification. Similarly, if we are to perform experiments on a fetus, even one expected to die, then we must also be prepared to offer justification. Whether the importance of the research is adequate justification is a matter that currently remains to be settled.

If the fetus is not a person, then the question of fetal experimentation becomes less important morally. Since, however, the fetus may be regarded as a potential person, we may still believe it is necessary to treat it with consideration and respect. The burden of justification may be somewhat less weighty, but it may still be there.

Let us assume that the fetus is aborted and is apparently not viable. Typically, before such a fetus dies, its heart beats and its lungs function. Is it morally permissible to conduct research on the fetus before its death? The knowledge that can be gained, particularly of lung functions, can be used to help save the lives of premature infants, and the fetus is virtually certain of dying, whether or not it is made a subject of research.

After the death of a fetus that is either deliberately or spontaneously aborted, are there any moral restraints on what is done with the remains? It is possible to culture fetal tissues and use them for research purposes.

These tissues might, in fact, be commercially grown and distributed by biological supply companies in the way that a variety of animal tissues are now dealt with. Exactly when a fetus can be considered to be dead so that its tissues and organs are available for experimentation, even assuming that one approves of their use in this manner, is itself an unsettled question.

Scientists have long been concerned about federal guidelines and state laws regulating fetal research. Most investigators feel that they are forced to operate under such rigid restrictions that research is slowed and, in some instances,

even prohibited. Everyone agrees, however, that fetal research involves important moral and social issues. (See Chapter 9 for more detail.)

Fetal research has to be considered a part of human research. Not only are some fetuses born alive even when deliberately aborted, but all possess certain human characteristics and potentialities. But who should give approval to what is done with the fetus? Who should be responsible for consent?

To some it seems peculiar to say that a woman who has decided to have an abortion is also the one who should consent to research involving the aborted fetus. It can be argued that in deciding to have an abortion she has renounced all interest and responsibility with respect to the fetus. Yet, if the fetus does live, we would consider her, at least in part, legally and morally responsible for seeing to its continued well-being.

But if the woman (or the parents) is the one who must give consent for fetal experimentation, are there limits to what she can consent to on behalf of the fetus?

With this question we are back where we began. It is obvious that fetal research raises both moral and social issues. We need to decide, then, what is right as a matter of personal conduct and what is right as a matter of social policy. At the moment, issues in each of these areas remain highly controversial.

## Research Involving Animals

The seventeenth-century philosopher René Descartes doubted whether animals experience pain. They may act as if they are in pain, but perhaps they are only complicated pieces of clockwork designed to act that way. Humans feel pain, but then, unlike animals, humans have a "soul" that gives them the capacity to reason, be self-conscious, and experience emotions. The bodies of humans are pieces of machinery, but the mental states that occur within the bodies are not.

If the view of animals represented by Descartes and others in the mechanistic tradition he initiated is correct, we need have no moral concern about the use of animals in research. Animals of whatever species have the status of any other piece of delicate and often expensive lab equipment. They may be used in any way for any purpose.

Here are some of the ways in which animals are or have been used in biomedical research:

- A standard test for determining the toxicity of drugs or chemicals is the "lethal dose-50" (LD-50) test. This is the amount of a substance that, when administered to a group of experimental animals, will kill 50 percent of them.

- The Draize test, once widely used in the cosmetics industry, involves dripping a chemical substance into the lidless eyes of rabbits to determine its potential to cause eye damage.

- The effects of cigarette smoking were investigated by a series of experiments using beagles with tubes inserted into holes cut into their tracheas so that, when breathing, they were forced to inhale cigarette smoke. The dogs were then "sacrificed" and autopsied to look for significant changes in cells and tissues.

- Surgical procedures are both developed and acquired by using animals as experimental subjects. Surgical residents spend much time in "dog labs" learning to perform standard surgical procedures on live dogs. Limbs may be deliberately broken and organs damaged or destroyed to test the usefulness of surgical repair techniques.

- A traditional medical-school demonstration consisted in exsanguinating (bleeding to death) a dog to illustrate the circulation of the blood. High school and college biology courses sometimes require that students destroy the brains of frogs with long needles (pithing) and then dissect the frogs to learn about physiological processes.

- Chimpanzees and other primates have served as experimental subjects for the study of the induction and treatment of infectious diseases. Perfectly healthy chimps and monkeys have been inoculated with viruses resembling the AIDS virus; then the course of the resulting diseases is studied.

A list of the ways in which animals are used would include virtually all basic biomedical research. The discovery of an "animal model" of a disease typically signals a significant advancement in research. It means that the disease can be studied in ways it cannot be in humans. The assumption is that animals can be subjected to experimental conditions and treatments that humans cannot be subjected to without violating basic moral principles.

Is the assumption that we have no moral obligation toward animals warranted? Certainly the crude "animal machine" view of Descartes has been rejected, and no one is prepared to argue that no nonhuman animal can experience pain.

Exactly which animals have the capacity for suffering is a matter of dispute. Mammals undoubtedly do, and vertebrates in general seem to experience pain, but what about insects, worms, lobsters, and clams? Is the identification of endorphins, naturally occurring substances associated with pain relief in humans, adequate grounds for saying that an organism that produces endorphins must experience pain?

Once it is acknowledged that at least some animals can suffer, most philosophers agree that we have some moral responsibility with respect to them. At the least, some (like W. D. Ross) say that, since we have a prima facie duty not to cause unnecessary suffering, we should not inflict needless pain on animals.

This does not necessarily mean that biomedical research should discontinue the use of animals. Strictly construed, it means only that the animals should be treated in a humane way. For example, surgical techniques should be practiced only on dogs that have been anesthetized. Understood in this way, the principle raises no objection to humanely conducted animal research, even if its purpose is relatively trivial.

Philosophers like Kant and most of those in the natural law tradition would deny that we have any duties to animals at all. The only proper objects of duty are rational agents; unless we are prepared to argue that animals are rational, we have to refuse them the status of moral persons. We might treat animals humanely because we are magnanimous, but they are not in a position to lay claims against us. Animals have no rights.

Some contemporary philosophers (Tom Regan, in particular) have argued that, although animals are not rational agents, they have preferences. This gives them an autonomy that makes them "moral patients." Like humans, animals possess the right to respectful treatment, and this entails that they not be treated only as a means to some other end. They are ends in themselves, and this intrinsic worth makes it wrong to use them as subjects in research, even when alternatives to animal research are not available.

Contrary to Regan, a number of philosophers have taken a utilitarian approach to the issue of animal experimentation. Some (like Peter Singer) have argued that, although animals cannot be said to have rights, they have interests. If we recognize that the interests of humans are deserving of equal consideration, then so too are the interests of nonhuman animals. Hence, we can recognize that animals have inherent worth without assigning them rights, but this does not mean that we must treat them exactly as we treat humans.

Most people, whether utilitarians or not, argue that at least some forms of animal experimentation can be justified by the benefits produced. After all, they point out, the understanding of biological processes we have acquired since the time of Aristotle has been heavily dependent on animal experimentation. This understanding has given us insights into the causes and processes of diseases, and, most important, it has put us in a position to invent and test new therapies and modes of prevention.

Without animal experimentation, the identification of the role played by insulin, the development of the polio vaccine, and the perfection of hundreds of major surgical techniques surely would not have been possible. The list could be extended to include virtually every accomplishment of medicine and surgery. Countless millions of human lives have been saved by using the knowledge and understanding gained from animal studies.

Animals, too, have benefited from the theoretical and practical knowledge of research. An understanding of nutritional needs has led to healthier domestic animals, and an understanding of environmental needs has produced a movement to protect and preserve many kinds of wild animals. At the conceptual and scientific levels, veterinary medicine is not really distinct from human medicine. The same sorts of surgical procedures, medicines, and vaccines that benefit the human population also benefit many other species.

However, even from a broadly utilitarian perspective, accepting the general principle that the results justify the practice does not mean that every experiment with animals is warranted. Some experiments might be trivial, unnecessary, or poorly designed. Others might hold no promise of yielding the kind or amount of knowledge sufficient to justify causing the animal subjects to suffer pain and death.

Furthermore, the utilitarian approach supports (as does a rights view like Regan's) looking for an alternative to animal experimentation. If good results can be obtained, for example, by conducting experiments with cell cultures (in vitro), rather than with whole organisms (in vivo), then in vitro experiments are to be preferred. However, if alternatives to animal testing are not available and if the benefits secured promise to outweigh the cost, animal testing may be morally legitimate.

The utilitarian justification faces what some writers see as a major difficulty. It is one posed by the fact that animals like chimpanzees and even dogs and pigs can be shown to possess mental abilities superior to those of humans suffering from severe brain damage and retardation. If experiments on mammals are justifiable by appealing to the benefits, then why aren't experiments on humans with serious mental impairments equally justified? Indeed, shouldn't we experiment on a human in a chronic vegetative state, rather than on a healthy and alert dog?

The use made of animals in biomedical research is a significant issue, but it is no more than one aspect of the general philosophical question about the status of animals. Do animals have rights? If so, what grounds can be offered for them? Do animals have a right to coexist with humans? Do animals have a right to be free? Is it wrong to eat animals or use products made from their remains? These questions and many others like them are now being given the most careful scrutiny they have received since the nineteenth century. How they are answered will do much to shape the character both of medical research and of our society.

## Women and Medical Research

Critics have charged that medical research has traditionally failed to include women as experimental subjects, even when women might also stand to benefit from the results. Most strikingly, a study showing the effectiveness of small doses of aspirin in reducing the risk of heart attack included 2201 subjects—all male. The relevance of the study to women is in doubt, for, although more men than women die of heart disease, after women reach menopause the difference in mortality rates between genders becomes much smaller.

Until recently, studies of the therapeutic effectiveness of drugs characteristically included only males. Although the effects of many drugs are the same for women as for men, this is not always true. Hormonal differences may alter drug reactions, so conclusions based on the reactions of men may be misleading when applied to women.

In the view of critics, the traditionally male-dominated research establishment has been responsible for perpetuating an unacceptable state of affairs. To change the situation so that both women and men are included in studies adds to

their costs. By introducing gender as a variable, a study must include more subjects in order to get the degree of statistical reliability that could be achieved with fewer subjects of the same gender. However, such studies have the additional value of yielding results known to be applicable to women.

That this issue is a matter of social fairness is obvious, but its connection with informed consent is less direct. As we mentioned in connection with prisoners, not allowing someone to consent may be viewed as treating that person as having less worth than someone who is allowed to consent. From this perspective, then, women have traditionally been denied the opportunity to be full persons in the moral sense. They have not been able to exercise their autonomy in ways permitted to men. Of course, they have also not been permitted to gain benefits that might be associated with the research projects from which they have been excluded. (For more details on women and medical research, see Chapter 4, *Race, Gender, and Medicine.*)

## Summary

There are other areas of medical experimentation that present special forms of moral problems. We have not discussed, for example, research involving military personnel or college and university students. Moreover, we mentioned only a few of the special difficulties presented by the mentally retarded, psychiatric patients, and old people confined to institutions.

We have, however, raised such a multiplicity of questions about consent and human research that it is perhaps worthwhile to attempt to restate some of the basic issues in a general form.

*Basic Issues*
Three issues are particularly noteworthy:

1.   Who is competent to consent? (Are children? Are mental patients? If a person is not competent, who—if anyone—should have the power to consent for him or her?) Given that animals have no power to con-

sent, is research involving them legitimate?

2. When is consent voluntary? (Is any institutionalized person in a position to offer free consent? How can even hospitalized patients be made free of pressures to consent?)

3. When are information and understanding adequate for genuine decision making? (Can complicated medical information ever be adequately explained to laypeople? Should we attempt to devise tests for understanding?)

*Standards*

Although we have concentrated on the matter of consent in research, there are other morally relevant matters connected with research that we have not discussed. These often relate to research standards. Among them are the following:

1. Is the research of sufficient scientific and medical worth to justify the human risk involved? Research that involves trivial aims or that is unnecessary (when, for example, it merely serves to confirm what is already well established) cannot be used to justify causing any threat to human well-being.

2. Can the knowledge sought be obtained without human clinical research? Can it be obtained without animal experimentation?

3. Have animal (and other) studies been done to minimize as far as is possible the risk to human subjects? A great deal can be learned about the effects of drugs, for example, by using "animal models," and the knowledge gained can be used to minimize the hazards in human trials. (Ethical issues involving animals in research may also be called into question.)

4. Does the design of the research meet accepted scientific standards? Sloppy research that is scientifically worthless means that people have been subjected to risks for no legitimate purpose and that animals have been harmed or sacrificed needlessly.

5. Do the investigators have the proper medical or scientific background to conduct the research effectively?

6. Is the research designed to minimize the risks and suffering of the participants? As we noted earlier, it is sometimes possible to test new drugs without using placebos. Thus, people in need of medication are not forced to be without treatment for their condition.

7. Have the aims and the design of the research and the qualifications of the investigators been reviewed by a group or committee competent to judge them? Such "peer review" is intended to assure that only research that is worthwhile and that meets accepted scientific standards is conducted. And although such review groups can fail to do their job properly, as they apparently did in the Tuskegee Syphilis Study, they are still necessary instruments of control.

Most writers on experimentation would agree that these are among the questions that must be answered satisfactorily before research involving human subjects is morally acceptable. Obviously, however, a patient who is asked to give his or her consent is in no position to judge whether the research project meets the standards implied by these questions. For this reason, it is important that there be social policies and practices governing research. Everyone should be confident that a research project is, in general, a legitimate one before having to decide whether to volunteer to become a participant.

Special problems are involved in seeing to it that these questions are properly answered. It is enough for our purposes, however, merely to notice that the character of the research and the manner in which it is to be performed are factors that are relevant to determining the moral legitimacy of experimentation involving human subjects.

# Ethical Theories: Medical Research and Informed Consent

We have raised too many issues in too many areas of experimentation to discuss how each of several ethical theories might apply to them all. We must limit ourselves to considering a few suggestions about the general issues of human experimentation and informed consent.

## Utilitarianism

Utilitarianism's principle of utility tells us, in effect, to choose those actions that will produce the greatest amount of benefit. Utilitarianism must approve human research in general, since there are cases in which the sacrifices of a few bring great benefits to many. We might, for example, design our social policies to make it worthwhile for people to volunteer for experiments with the view that, if people are paid to take risks and are compensated for their suffering or for any damage done to them during the course of a research project, then the society as a whole might benefit.

The principle of utility also tells us to design experiments to minimize suffering and the chance of harm. Also, it forbids us to do research of an unnecessary or trivial kind—research that is not worth its cost in either human or economic resources.

As to the matter of informed consent, utilitarianism does not seem to require it. If more social good is to be gained by making people research subjects without securing their agreement, then this is morally legitimate. It is not, of course, necessarily the best procedure to follow. A system of rewards to induce volunteers might be more likely to lead to an increase in general happiness. Furthermore, the principle of utility suggests that the best research subjects would be "less valuable" members of the society, such as the mentally retarded, the habitual criminal, or the dying. This, again, is not a necessary consequence of utilitarianism, although it is a possible one. If the recognition of rights and dignity would produce a better society in general, then a utilitarian would also say that they must be taken into account in experimentation with human beings.

For utilitarianism, that individual is competent to give consent who can balance benefits and risks and decide what course of action is best for him or her. Thus, if informed consent is taken to be a requirement supported by the principle of utility, those who are mentally ill or retarded or senile have to be excluded from the class of potential experimental subjects. Furthermore, investigators must provide enough relevant information to allow competent people to make a meaningful decision about what is likely to serve their own interests the most.

## Kant

For Kant, an individual capable of giving consent is one who is rational and autonomous. Kant's principles would thus also rule out as research subjects people who are not able to understand experimental procedures, aims, risks, and benefits. People may volunteer for clinical trials if they expect them to be of therapeutic benefit to themselves, or they may act out of duty and volunteer, thus discharging their imperfect obligation to advance knowledge or to improve human life.

Yet, for Kant, there are limits to the risks that one should take. We have a duty to preserve our lives, so no one should agree to become a subject in an experiment in which the likelihood of death is great. Additionally, no one should subject himself to research in which there is considerable risk that his capacity for rational thought and autonomy will be destroyed. Indeed, Kant's principles appear to require us to regard as morally illegitimate those experiments that seriously threaten the lives or rationality of their subjects. Not only should we not subject ourselves to them, but we should not subject others to them.

Kant's principles also rule out as potential research participants those who are not in a position to act voluntarily, that is, those who cannot exercise their autonomy. This makes it important to determine, from a Kantian point of view, whether children and institutionalized people (including prisoners) can be regarded as free agents capable of moral choice. Also, as in the case of abortion, the status of the fetus must be determined. If the fetus is not a person, then fetal experimentation presents no particular moral problems. But if the fetus is a person, then we must accord it a moral status and act for its sake and not for the sake of knowledge or for others.

Kant's view of people as autonomous rational beings requires that informed consent be obtained for both medical treatment and research. We cannot be forced to accept treatment for "our own good," nor can we be turned into research subjects for "the good of others." We must always be treated as ends and never as means only. To be treated in this way requires that others never deliberately deceive us, no matter how good their intentions. In short, we have a right to be told what we are getting into so that we can decide whether we want to go through with it or not.

## Ross

Ross's theory imposes on researchers prima facie duties to patients that are similar to Kant's requirements. The nature of people as autonomous moral agents requires that their informed consent be obtained. Researchers ought not to deceive their subjects, and protocols should be designed in ways in which suffering and the risk of injury or death are minimized.

These are all prima facie duties, of course, and it is possible to imagine situations in which other duties might take precedence over them. In general, however, Ross, like Kant, tells us that human research cannot be based on what is useful; it must be based on what is right. Ross's principles, like Kant's, do not tell us, however, how we are to deal with such special problems as research involving children or prisoners.

## Natural Law

The principle of double effect and the principle of totality, which are based on the natural law

theory of morality, have specific applications to experimentation. (See Part V: *Foundations of Bioethics.*) Because we hold our bodies in trust, we are responsible for assessing the degree of risk to which we might be put if we agree to become research subjects. Thus, others have an obligation to supply us with the information that we need in order to make our decision. If we decide to give our consent, it must be given freely and not be the consequence of deception or coercion.

If available evidence shows that a sick person may gain benefits from participating in a research project, then the research is justified. But if the evidence shows that the benefits may be slight or if the chance of serious injury or death is relatively great, then the research is not justified.

In general, the likelihood of a person's benefiting from becoming a participant must exceed the danger of the person's suffering greater losses. The four requirements that govern the application of the principle of double effect determine what is and what is not an allowable experiment. (See Part V: *Foundations of Bioethics* for a discussion of these requirements.)

People can volunteer for experiments from which they expect no direct benefits. The good they seek in doing so is not their own good but the good of others. But there are limits to what they can subject themselves to. A dying patient, for example, cannot be made the subject of a useless or trivial experiment. The probable value of the knowledge to be gained must balance the risk and suffering the patient is subjected to, and there must be no likelihood that the experiment will seriously injure or kill the patient.

These same restrictions also apply to experiments involving healthy people. The principle of totality forbids a healthy person to submit to an experiment that involves the probability of serious injury, impaired health, mutilation, or death.

The status of the fetus is clear in the Roman Catholic version of the natural law theory: the fetus is a person. As such, the fetus is entitled to the same dignity and respect we accord to other persons. Experiments that involve doing it injury or lessening its chances of life are morally prohibited. But not all fetal research is ruled out. That which may be of therapeutic benefit or which does not directly threaten the fetus's well-being is allowable. Furthermore, research involving fetal tissue or remains is permissible, if it is done for a serious and valuable purpose.

## Rawls

From Rawls's point of view, the difficulty with utilitarianism with respect to human experimentation is that the principle of utility would permit the exploitation of some groups (the dying, prisoners, the retarded) for the sake of others. By contrast, Rawls's principles of justice would forbid all research that involves violating a liberty to which a person is entitled by virtue of being a member of society.

As a result, all experiments that make use of coercion or deception are ruled out. And since a person has a right to decide what risks she is willing to subject herself to, voluntary informed consent is required of all subjects. Society might, as in utilitarianism, decide to reward those who volunteer to become research subjects. As long as this is a possibility open to all, it is not objectionable.

It would never be right, according to Rawls, to take advantage of those in the society who are least well off to benefit those who are better off. Inequalities must be arranged so that they bring benefits (ideally) to everyone or, at least, to those who are most disadvantaged. Research involving direct therapeutic benefits is clearly acceptable (assuming informed consent), but research that takes advantage of the sick, the poor, the retarded, or the institutionalized and does not benefit them is unacceptable. The status of the fetus—whether or not it is a person in the moral sense—is an issue that has to be resolved before we know how to apply Rawls's principles to fetal research.

We have been able to provide only the briefest sketch of some of the ways in which our moral theories might apply to the issues in human experimentation. The remarks are not meant to be anything more than suggestive. A satisfactory moral theory of human experimentation requires working out the application of principles to problems in detail, as well as resolving such issues as the status of children and fetuses and the capability of institutionalized people to act freely.

In the Case Presentations and Social Contexts that follow, the issues we have discussed can be recognized as pressing problems requiring decisions about particular situations and general policies.

## Case Presentation

### Baby Fae

On October 14, 1984, a baby was born in a community hospital in southern California with a malformation known as hypoplastic left-heart syndrome. In such a condition, the mitral valve or aorta on the left side of the heart is underdeveloped, and essentially only the right side of the heart functions properly. Some 300 to 2000 infants a year are born with this defect, and most die from it within a few weeks.

The infant, who became known to the public as Baby Fae, was taken to the Loma Linda University Hospital Center. There, on October 26, a surgical team headed by Dr. Leonard Bailey performed a heart transplant; Baby Fae became the first human infant to receive a baboon heart. She died twenty days later.

Baby Fae was not the first human to receive a so-called xenograft, or cross-species transplant. In early 1964, a sixty-eight-year-old deaf man, Boyd Rush, was transplanted with a chimpanzee heart at the University of Mississippi Medical Center. The heart failed after only an hour, and the patient died. Before Baby Fae, three other cross-species transplants had also ended in a quick death.

### Moral Questions

In the case of Baby Fae, questions about the moral correctness and scientific legitimacy of the transplant were raised immediately. Hospital officials revealed that no effort had been made to find a human donor before implanting the baboon heart, and this led some critics to wonder if research interests were not being given priority over the welfare of the patient. Others questioned whether the parents were adequately informed about alternative corrective surgery, the Norwood procedure, available from surgeons in Boston and Philadelphia.

Other observers wondered whether the nature of the surgery and its limited value had been properly explained to the parents. Also, some critics raised objections to sacrificing a healthy young animal as part of an experiment not likely to bring any lasting benefit to Baby Fae.

Scientific critics charged that not enough is known about crossing the species barrier to warrant the use of transplant organs at this time. The previous record of failures, with no major advances in understanding, did not make the prospect of another such transplant reasonable. Furthermore, critics said, chimpanzees and gorillas are genetically more similar to humans than baboons, so the choice of a baboon heart was not a wise one. The only advantage of baboons is that they are easier to breed in captivity. Also, other critics claimed Dr. Bailey was merely engaged in "wishful thinking" in believing that Baby Fae's immune system would not produce a severe rejection response because of its immaturity.

## Postmortem

An autopsy on Baby Fae showed that her death was caused by the incompatibility of her blood with that of the baboon heart. Baby Fae's blood was type O, the baboon's type AB. This resulted in the formation of blood clots and the destruction of kidney function. The heart showed mild signs of rejection.

In an address before a medical conference after Baby Fae's death, Dr. Bailey commented on some of the criticisms. He is reported to have said that it was "an oversight on our part not to search for a human donor from the start." Dr. Bailey also told the conference that he and his team believed that the difference in blood types between Baby Fae and the baboon would be less important than other factors and that the immunosuppressive drugs used to prevent rejection would also solve the problem of blood incompatibility. "We came to regret those assumptions," Dr. Bailey said. The failure to match blood types was "a tactical error that came back to haunt us."

On other occasions Dr. Bailey reiterated his view that, because infant donors are extremely scarce, animal-to-human transplants offer a realistic hope for the future. Before the Baby Fae operation, Dr. Bailey had transplanted organs in more than 150 animals. None of his results were in published papers, however, and he performed all his work on local grants. He indicated that he would use the information obtained from Baby Fae to conduct additional animal experiments before attempting another such transplant.

## NIH Report

In March of 1985 the National Institutes of Health released a report of a committee that made a site visit to Loma Linda to review the Baby Fae matter. The committee found that the informed-consent process was generally satisfactory, in that "the parents were given an appropriate and thorough explanation of the alternatives available, the risks and benefits of the procedure and the experimental nature of the transplant." Moreover, consent was obtained in an "atmosphere which allowed the parents an opportunity to carefully consider, without coercion or undue influence, whether to give permission for the transplant."

The committee also pointed out certain flaws in the consent document. First, it "did not include the possibility of searching for a human heart or performing a human heart transplant." Second, the expected benefits of the procedure "appeared to be overstated," because the consent document "stated that 'long-term survival' is an expected possibility with no further explanation." Finally, the document did not explain "whether compensation and medical treatment were available if injury occurred."

The committee did not question the legitimacy of the cross-species transplant. Moreover, it made no mention of the Norwood procedure, except to say that it had been explained to the mother at the community hospital at the birth of the infant. (The consent document described the procedure as a generally unsuccessful "temporizing operation.")

Although the committee was generally critical of Loma Linda's Institutional Review Board in "evaluating the entire informed-consent process," it reached the conclusion that "the parents of Baby Fae understood the alternatives available as well as the risks and reasonably expected benefits of the transplant."

Officials at Loma Linda University Medical Center promised that before performing another such transplant they would first seek a human infant heart donor.

# SOCIAL CONTEXT: CLINICAL TRIALS, HIV, AND PREGNANCY: A THIRD-WORLD TUSKEGEE?

In 1995 the National Institutes of Health and the Centers for Disease Control and Prevention initiated clinical trials with the aim of finding a cheap and effective way of preventing HIV-positive pregnant women in developing countries from transmitting the virus to their newborn babies. The studies involved 12,211 women in five African countries, Thailand, and the Dominican Republic.

## Regimen 076

The results of clinical trials conducted in the United States and reported in 1994 showed that if pregnant women testing positive for HIV followed a treatment regimen using the drug zidovudine (ZDV, previously called AZT), the risk of the virus being transmitted to their children was reduced by almost two-thirds. The chance of untreated HIV-positive women passing on the virus is about 25 percent, but when the women are treated with ZDV, the transmission drops to around 8 percent. By employing a ZDV treatment regimen, the United States has reduced the number of HIV-positive babies to about 500 per year.

The treatment requires women to take ZDV during the last twelve weeks of their pregnancy, then receive an intravenous dose of it during delivery. The newborns are then given the drug for the first six weeks of their lives. Because the federal study establishing the effectiveness of this treatment was assigned the number 076, the treatment is referred to as the 076 regimen.

## A Thousand HIV-Positive Babies a Day

The CDC estimates that in the world as a whole about one thousand HIV-positive babies are born every day. Most of them are born in countries too poor to pay for the treatment needed to lower this number substantially. The 076 regimen costs about $1000, putting it out of the reach of all but the richest individuals or nations.

Aside from the expense of the drug, other factors stand in the way of using the 076 regimen in underdeveloped countries. Most of them lack the hospitals and equipment needed to administer ZDV intravenously during delivery. Also, most mothers in third-world countries breast-feed their babies, and while generally the practice is beneficial to the infant, the HIV virus can be transmitted through breast milk. Yet feeding infants prepared formula not only goes against custom, it costs more than most women—and their countries—can afford.

Against this backdrop, representatives of the World Health Organization, the United Nations, the National Institutes of Health and the Centers for Disease Control and Prevention met in Geneva in 1994 to design clinical trials to determine whether any short-term regimen using oral doses of ZDV could be effective in reducing the maternal-fetal transmission (vertical transmission) of the HIV virus. A short-term course of oral medication would be both cheaper and easier to administer and thus would make treatments possible in poor countries with limited medical resources.

## How Should Effectiveness Be Judged?

But what comparison group should be used to judge the effectiveness of the experimental regimens? One possibility would be to compare them to 076. This was rejected by the planners, however, because administering 076 to those who might benefit from it in the countries involved was not a realistic prospect. The test regimens needed to be compared to something that was realistic.

Another possibility was to use as a comparison the standard of medical care in the countries where the trials would be conducted. The care received by HIV-positive pregnant women could be measured against the outcome of the clinical trials. But the difficulty with this approach was that the standard of care in the countries where the trials would be conducted didn't exist. Essentially, HIV-positive pregnant women received no care at all. Thus, the Geneva group decided that results of the clinical trials involving different doses of zidovudine could best be judged by comparing them with the results obtained by administering a substance known to possess no therapeutic value—that is, with a placebo.

Tests involving placebos in the United States have become rare when a potentially lethal or disabling disease is involved. The principle is generally accepted that people deserve to receive treatments that represent the standard of medical care for their problem. Experimental treatments must show promise of being superior in at least some respects to the standard of care or there is no justification for employing them. Thus, the results of a test of an experimental treatment are compared with the results of the standard treatment.

The Geneva group, however, took the standard of care for preventing vertical HIV transmission to be that for the countries in which the test would be conducted, not the standard of care in North America or Western Europe. Because women in those countries would receive no treatment, the planners reasoned that women receiving placebos would be no worse off than otherwise. Indeed, because even those in the placebo group would be provided with free general health care, they would gain benefits they wouldn't ordinarily receive.

## Use of Placebos Challenged

The decision to give placebos to about half the women in the ZDV study was controversial from the beginning. Marc Lallemant, an NIH–sponsored investigator working in Thailand, refused to administer them to his patients. (Some Thai women, treated by CDC investigators, did receive placebos.) CDC researchers in Ivory Coast wrote to the agency's headquarters to report that their African collaborators didn't

feel comfortable giving patients placebos. Critics estimated that because of the deliberate withholding of a known and effective treatment, more than a thousand babies would become HIV-positive who might have escaped infection.

"We have turned our backs on these mothers and their babies," said a representative of Public Citizen, a rights organization. The group also wrote to then-Secretary of Health and Human Services, Donna Shalala, and demanded that the clinical trial be redesigned to eliminate placebos. Instead, the group argued, a short course of ZDV should be compared with the 076 regimen, despite the higher cost this would entail. Because ZDV is known to be effective against HIV and in reducing vertical transmission of the virus, all women in the trial would at least be receiving doses of a drug appropriate as a treatment for their disease.

The head of the CDC's AIDS program, Helene Gayle, defended the clinical trial as it was designed. "This was done with a lot of discussion from the international community, following international codes of ethics," she said. "Part of doing ethical trials is that you are answering questions that are relevant for those countries."

Physicians and officials in some of the countries objected to ethical questions being raised about the trials. Viewing the objections as a form of condescension, they saw them as suggesting Africans were unable to decide what was in their best interest. "One has the impression that foreigners think that once white people arrive here they can impose what they want and we just accept it in ignorance," said Dr. Toussaint Sibailly of Ivory Coast. "If that was once the case, those days are long past."

"We already know what the alternative is to what we are doing," said Dr. Rene Ekpini in Abidjan. "The alternative is giving everyone here the placebo treatment, because that is what pregnant women with the disease are getting here—nothing."

This view was supported by AIDS researchers Joseph Saba and Arthur Ammann. They suggested that yielding to critics and giving every pregnant woman some level of treatment with an effective drug would require extending the studies several more years. But with over 1000 children a day becoming HIV infected, they suggested such a delay was unacceptable. "Americans should not impose their standard of care on developing countries," they claimed.

## Another Tuskegee?

In contrast to the defenders of the trial, Marcia Angell, the Executive Editor of the *New England Journal of Medicine,* denounced the study in an editorial in the journal, comparing it to the Tuskegee syphilis experiments. "Some of the same arguments that were made in favor of the Tuskegee study are emerging in a new form in the [ZDV] studies in the third world," she said. (See in Chapter 4 the Classic Case Presentation: "Bad Blood, Bad Faith.")

Investigators in the Tuskegee syphilis study never told the participants they were experimental subjects who might receive no relevant treatment for their disease. Indeed, participants with syphilis were never given a specific diagnosis of their disease. In this respect, at least, the ZDV clinical trials can be distinguished from the Tuskegee study. The design of the trials required that participants be informed of their diagnosis and consent to treatment. Investigators were also required to inform potential participants that they might be receiving a placebo, rather than an effective drug.

Even given the requirement of informed consent, some observers have questioned whether ordinary people in underdeveloped countries were capable of giving legitimate consent to becoming participants. Most of the people in the countries in which the trials took place are generally uneducated and technically unsophisticated. It is not clear whether they could be considered capable of understanding the medical and scientific information provided to them. But if they were not, their consent could not be considered genuine.

## Is Informed Consent Genuine?

When some patients agreed to become participants in the clinical trials, they appeared to have had little or no grasp of what they were consenting to and what the potential risks might be. After interviewing study participants in Abidjan, Ivory Coast, reporter Howard W. French concluded that "despite repeated explanations by project case workers, the understanding of these mostly poor and scantily educated subjects does not match the complexity of the ethical and scientific issues involved."

One educated woman, a thirty-one-year-old mother with a law degree, who spoke with French said she hadn't received an explanation making it clear to her that ZDV was already known to be effective in controlling the transmission of HIV from mother to infant. How would she feel if she learned she had been in the placebo group? "I would say it was an injustice for sure," she told French.

This attitude was in contrast with that of another woman in the study. "People are trying to help us," she said. "And if a bunch of people have to die first, I am ready to risk my life too, so that other women and their babies survive. If I got the placebo, that will hurt for sure. But there is no evil involved."

## An End to Placebos

On February 18, 1998, the Centers for Disease Control and Prevention announced that placebos would no longer be used in the clinical trials. The use was not discontinued for moral reasons, but because data showed that the use of about $80 worth of ZDV administered in the last four weeks of pregnancy could reduce transmission of the HIV virus by about 50 percent.

The decision was based on a study of 393 women in Thailand, some of whom received placebos. "We are very pleased," Philip Nieburg said. "The controversy was unfortunate, but we feel the placebo-controlled trial that we did was very necessary."

Sidney Wolfe, Director the Public Citizen's Health Research Group, claimed the trial was unnecessary, because data supporting the outcome were already known from the trials of the 076 regimen. "This is inexcusable, sloppy research," he charged. "They have wasted a large number of lives and a huge amount of money."

## Equivocal Results

More recent findings make it unclear how effective a drug regimen can be in reducing maternal-fetal transmission of the HIV virus. A study conducted by the United Nations involved giving AZT and 3TC (lamivudine) to the mother for four weeks before expected delivery and during labor, then giving both mother and infant the drugs for an additional week.

The study showed that after eighteen months, the rate at which the infants acquired the virus through breast-feeding cancelled the preventive effects of the drug regimen. If this is the case, preventing the transmission of the virus at birth is probably not worth the investment of cost and effort.

Yet a second study by the National Institute of Allergy and Infectious Disease offers more hope. Researchers gave a single dose of the drug nevirapine to women during labor, then a dose to the newborn. After six to eight weeks, infants and mothers receiving the treatment were 42 percent less likely to be infected with HIV than those treated with AZT. This figure held for eighteen months, but mothers continued to infect their infants through breast-feeding.

In Africa breast-feeding may last for two years or longer. Hence, whether drugs are effective or not in preventing the transmission of HIV at birth, ways must be found to make breast-feeding safer.

Was it worth a widespread clinical trial using a placebo control to acquire data relevant to formulating public health and political policies about controlling the transmission of AIDS to infants in Africa? The question is still being debated.

# SOCIAL CONTEXT: THE COLD-WAR RADIATION EXPERIMENTS

Amelia Jackson was a cook at Pogue's department store in Cincinnati, in 1966, when she was diagnosed with colon cancer. In October, she was treated with 100 rads of full-body radiation—the equivalent of 7500 chest X rays. Until the treatment, Ms. Jackson was strong and still working, but after the treatment, she bled and vomited for days and was never again able to care for herself.

Ms. Jackson was treated as part of a program operated by the University of Cincinnati and supported in part by funds from the Pentagon. She was one of several cancer patients in a research program in which people were subjected to radiation in massive doses to determine its biological effects.

The aim of the study, according to researchers, was to develop more effective cancer treatments. However, the military was interested in determining how much radiation military personnel could be subjected to before becoming disoriented and unable to function effectively.

## A Patchwork of Radiation Experiments

The Cincinnati project was only one of a patchwork of human experiments involving radiation that were carried out with funding from a variety of military and civilian agencies of the U.S. government over a period of at least thirty years. The experiments took place at government laboratories and university hospitals and research centers. Some experiments involved exposing patients to high-energy beams of radiation, while others involved injecting them with such dangerous radioactive substances as plutonium.

The experiments started toward the end of World War II. They were prompted by both scientific curiosity and the practical and military need to know more about the damaging effects of radiation on people. The advent of the Cold War between the United States and the Soviet Union and the real possibility that the political conflict would lead to nuclear war gave a sense of urgency to the research. Little was known about the harmful effects of radiation, and researchers believed their experiments would not only contribute to understanding, but would provide the basis for more effective medical therapies.

In the late 1940s, Vanderbilt University exposed about 800 pregnant women to radiation to determine its effects on fetal development. A follow-up study of the children born to the women showed a higher-than-average rate of cancer.

At the Oak Ridge National Laboratory in Tennessee, patients with leukemia and other forms of cancer were exposed to extremely high levels of radiation from isotopes of cesium and cobalt. Almost two hundred patients, including a six-year-old boy, were subjected to such treatment, until the experiment was ended in 1974 by the Atomic Energy Commission, on the grounds of lack of patient benefit.

From 1963 to 1971, experiments were conducted at Oregon State Prison in which the testicles of sixty-seven inmates were exposed to X rays to determine the effects of radiation on sperm production. Prisoners signed consent statements that mentioned some of the risks of the radiation. However, the possibility that the radiation might cause cancer was not mentioned. A similar experiment was conducted on sixty-four inmates at Washington State Prison.

At Columbia University and Montefiore Hospital in New York, during the late 1950s, twelve terminally ill cancer patients were injected with concentrations of radioactive calcium and strontium-85 to measure the rate at which the substances are absorbed by various types of tissues.

At a state residential school in Fernald, Massachusetts, from 1946 to 1956, nineteen mentally retarded teenaged boys were fed radioactive iron and calcium in their breakfast oatmeal. The aim of the research was to provide information about nutrition and metabolism. In the consent form mailed to parents of the boys, no mention was made of radiation.

## The Experiments Become Public

The radiation experiments became public only in 1993 when reporters for the *Albuquerque Tribune* tracked down five of the eighteen patients who had been subjects in an experiment conducted from 1945 to 1957, in which patients were injected with plutonium. The work was done at the University of Rochester, Oak Ridge Laboratory, the University of Chicago, and the University of California, San Francisco Hospital. Apparently, some of the patients did not receive information about their treatment and were injected with radioactive materials without first giving consent.

Relying on the Freedom of Information Act, Eileen Welsome, a reporter for the newspaper, attempted to get documents from the Department of Energy concerning the radiation research, including ones containing the names of subjects. However, she was able to secure little information, and Tara O'Toole, the Assistant Secretary of Energy for Environment, Safety, and Health at the time, expressed reservations about releasing documents containing the names of research subjects. "Does the public's right to know include releasing names?" O'Toole asked. "It is not clear to me that it is part of the ethical obligation of the Government."

## Did Participants Give Their Informed Consent?

Secretary of Energy Hazel R. O'Leary soon committed her department to a full investigation of the radiation experiments. A major focus of the inquiry was on whether patients were fully informed about the risks of the treatments they received and whether they gave meaningful consent to them.

In a number of cases, the government discovered, the experimental subjects were not informed of the risks they faced and did not consent to participate in the research. Patients were sometimes misled about the character of the treatments and in some cases even the signatures on consent forms were forged. Ms. Jackson's granddaughter claims that although her grandmother was illiterate, she could sign her name, and the signature on the form used by the University of Cincinnati was not hers. The same claim is made by other relatives of subjects in the study.

In one known instance, a researcher found the radiation experiments to be morally suspect and warned his colleagues against pursuing them. C. E. Newton at the Hanford nuclear weapons plant wrote in an internal memorandum about the work done with prisoners at Washington State Prison: "The experiments do not appear to have been in compliance with the criminal codes of the state of Washington, and there is some question as to whether they were conducted in compliance with Federal laws."

Similarly, in a 1950 memorandum, Joseph G. Hamilton, a radiation biologist, warned his supervisors that the experiments "might have a little of the Buchenwald touch." Hamilton warned that the Atomic Energy Commission would be "subject to considerable criticism."

Some observers claim that work carried out twenty or thirty years ago cannot be judged by the same ethical standards as we would use today. Robert Loeb, speaking for Strong Memorial Hospital, where some of the studies were carried out, put the point this way: "In the 1940s, what was typical in research involving human subjects was for physicians to tell the patients that they would be involved in a study and not always give full details. That is not the standard today. Many of these studies would be impossible to conduct today."

By contrast, Dr. David S. Egilman, who has investigated instances of research with human subjects conducted by the military and the Atomic Energy Commission, claims there is adequate evidence to conclude the researchers and their supporting agencies knew they were conducting immoral experiments. "They called the work, in effect, Nazi-like," he says. "The argument we hear is that these experiments were ethical at the time they were done. It's simply not true."

The initial question about the use of human subjects in radiation experiments conducted under the auspices of what is now the Department of Energy was expanded to include those conducted by several federal agencies. It seems as if at least 1000 people were exposed to varying levels of radiation in a variety of experiments conducted over a number of years at various locations. Some observers believe the actual figures are much higher.

The President's Advisory Committee on Human Radiation Experiments reviewed records from the Energy Department, Defense Department, Central Intelligence Agency, NASA, and federal health agencies to attempt to locate research projects involving radiation and identify the people who were their experimental subjects. After eighteen months of investigation, the committee reported in 1995 that many of the government-sponsored experiments had been illegal and that their survivors ought to be compensated.

## Compensation

In November 1996 the federal government agreed to pay $4.8 million as compensation for injecting twelve people with plutonium or uranium. At the time of the settlement, only one of the twelve was still alive, and the $400,000 award was paid to the families of the other participants. In 1998 the Quaker Oats Company and M.I.T. agreed to pay $1.85 million to the more than one hundred men who, as boys, had been fed the radioactive oatmeal at the Fernald School and other study sites.

A large number of claims from other experiments involving radiation and consent were filed against the Federal government, universities, and hospitals. Advocates for those whose rights may have been violated charge the government with failing to make an effort to find the names of the people who were participants in the various radiation experiments. This would be a difficult and time-consuming process, because often names and addresses were not made a part of the experimental records.

⭐ IMO → given times of Cold-War & all, these exp's must have served a military-like purpose & ∴ w/held all background behind experiments

The National Archives has placed all the hundreds of thousands of pages of records acquired by the Presidential Commission in files available to the public, and instead of the government notifying people that they may have a legal claim for compensation, individuals must come forward on their own initiative.

## New Regulations

In 1997 President Clinton endorsed a stringent set of policies governing all human research receiving federal support. Under the new rules, explicit informed consent is required, the sponsor of the experiment must be identified to the subject, the subject must be told whether the experiment is classified, and permanent records of the experiment and the subjects must be kept. Further, an external review must be conducted before the experiment can proceed. The hope was that the new rules would put an end to secret experiments in which human subjects are subjected to radioactive, chemical, or other dangerous substances without their knowledge or consent.

With respect to the radiation experiments, Representative David Mann of Ohio summed up the views of most citizens: "I believe we have no choice but to conclude that the radiation experiments were simply wrong and that the Government owes a huge apology to the victims, their families, and the nation."

## Case Presentation

### The Willowbrook Hepatitis Experiments

The Willowbrook State School in Staten Island, New York, is an institution devoted to housing and caring for mentally retarded children. In 1956 a research group led by Saul Krugman and Joan P. Giles of the New York University School of Medicine initiated a long-range study of viral hepatitis at Willowbrook. The children confined there were made experimental subjects of the study.

Hepatitis, a disease affecting the liver, is now known to be caused by one of two (possibly more) viruses. Although the viruses are distinct, the results they produce are the same. The liver becomes inflamed and increases in size as the invading viruses replicate themselves. Also, part of the tissue of the liver may be destroyed and the liver's normal functions impaired. Often the flow of bile through the ducts is blocked, and bilirubin (the major pigment in bile) is forced into the blood and urine. This produces the symptom of yellowish or jaundiced skin.

The disease is generally relatively mild, although permanent liver damage can be produced. The symptoms are ordinarily flu-like—mild fever, tiredness, inability to keep food down. The viruses causing the disease are transmitted orally through contact with the feces and bodily secretions of infected people.

Krugman and Giles were interested in determining the natural history of viral hepatitis—the mode of infection and the course of the disease over time. They also wanted to test the effectiveness of gamma globulin as an agent for inoculating against hepatitis. (Gamma globulin is a protein complex extracted from the blood serum that contains antigens, substances that trigger the production of specific antibodies to counter infectious agents.)

## Endemic Hepatitis

Krugman and Giles considered Willowbrook to be a good choice for investigation because viral hepatitis occurred more or less constantly in the institution. In the jargon of medicine, the disease was endemic. That this was so was recognized in 1949, and it continued to be so as the number of children in the school increased to over 5000 in 1960. Krugman and Giles claimed that "under the chronic circumstances of multiple and repeated exposure . . . most newly admitted children became infected within the first six to twelve months of residence in the institution."

Over a fourteen-year period, Krugman and Giles collected over 25,000 serum specimens from more than 700 patients. Samples were taken before exposure, during the incubation period of the virus, and for periods after the infection. In an effort to get the kind of precise data they considered most useful, Krugman and Giles decided to deliberately infect some of the incoming children with the strain of the hepatitis virus prevalent at Willowbrook.

## Justifying Deliberate Infection

They justified their decision in the following way: It was inevitable that susceptible children would become infected in the institution. Hepatitis was especially mild in the three- to ten-year age group at Willowbrook. These studies would be carried out in a special unit with optimum isolation facilities to protect the children from other infectious diseases such as shigellosis (dysentery caused by a bacillus), and parasitic and respiratory infections which are prevalent in the institution.

Most important, Krugman and Giles claimed that being an experimental subject was in the best medical interest of the child, for not only would the child receive special care, but infection with the milder form of hepatitis would provide protection against the more virulent and damaging forms. As they say: "It should be emphasized that the artificial induction of hepatitis implies a 'therapeutic' effect because of the immunity which is conferred."

## Consent

Krugman and Giles obtained what they considered to be adequate consent from the parents of the children used as subjects. Where they were unable to obtain consent, they did not include the child in the experiment. In the earlier phases of the study, parents were provided with relevant information either by letter or orally, and written consent was secured from them. In the later phases, a group procedure was used:

> First, a psychiatric social worker discusses the project with the parents during a preliminary interview. Those who are interested are invited to attend a group session at the institution to discuss the project in greater detail. These sessions are conducted by the staff responsible for the program, including the physician, supervising nurses, staff attendants, and psychiatric social workers. . . . Parents in groups of six to eight are given a tour of the facilities. The purposes, potential benefits, and potential hazards of the program are discussed with them, and they are encouraged to ask questions. Thus, all parents can hear the response to questions posed by the more articulate members of the group. After leaving this briefing session parents have an opportunity to talk with their private physicians who may call the unit for more information. Approximately two weeks after each visit, the psychiatric social worker contacts the parents for their decision. If the decision is in the affirmative, the consent is signed but parents are informed that signed consent may be withdrawn any time before the beginning of the pro-

gram. It has been clear that the group method has enabled us to obtain more thorough informed consent. Children who are wards of the state or children without parents have never been included in our studies.

Krugman and Giles point out that their studies were reviewed and approved by the New York State Department of Mental Hygiene, the New York State Department of Mental Health, the Armed Forces Epidemiological Board, and the human-experimentation committees of the New York University School of Medicine and the Willowbrook School. They also stress that, although they were under no obligation to do so, they chose to meet the World Medical Association's Draft Code on Human Experimentation.

## Ethical Concerns

The value of the research conducted by Krugman and Giles has been recognized as significant in furthering a scientific understanding of viral hepatitis and methods for treating it. Yet serious moral doubts have been raised about the nature and conduct of the experiments. In particular, many have questioned the use of retarded children as experimental subjects, some claiming children should never be experimental subjects in investigations that are not directly therapeutic. Others have raised questions about the ways in which consent was obtained from the parents of the children, suggesting that parents were implicitly blackmailed into giving their consent

## Case Presentation

### *Echoes of Willowbrook or Tuskegee? Experimenting with Children*

In April 1998 the National Bioethics Advisory Committee was asked to investigate three experiments conducted from 1993 to 1996 at the New York State Psychiatric Institute.

The subjects of the experiment were almost 100 boys ranging in age from six to eleven. All were from New York City, and many were Black or Hispanic. The boys were chosen as subjects because their older brothers had been legally charged with some form of delinquency.

Researchers identified the potential subjects by combing through court records and by interviewing the mothers of the boys charged with crimes. The ones chosen for the experiment were considered by the researchers to be boys who had experienced "adverse rearing practices." The mothers of the boys selected were asked to take their children to the Psychiatric Institute to take part in the experiment. Mothers bringing in their boys were given a $125 cash payment.

The research subjects were given a small intravenously administered dose of the drug fenfluramine, and their blood was then assayed for a change in the level of neurotransmitters. The aim of the experiment was to test the hypothesis that violent behavior can be predicted by the use of neurochemical markers. The boys were given only a single dose of the drug.

In two of the three studies conducted at the Psychiatric Institute, the sixty-six boys who served as subjects were between seven and eleven and had been diagnosed as having Attention Deficit Hyperactivity Disorder. They were taken off their medication for a period of time before the fenfluramine was administered.

Fenfluramine has now been withdrawn from medical practice by the Federal Drug Administration. In combination with another drug ("fen-phen"), it was used to treat obesity, until it was discovered that in some people it caused damage to the heart valves. Experts on the use of fenfluramine consider it unlikely that the boys in the experiments suffered any harm from the drug. They were given only a single small dose, whereas those with heart damage used the drug in larger doses over a period of months.

Even so, critics of the experiments charge that the boys were exposed to a substantial risk in experiments in which they had no chance of receiving any benefit. The experiments were for the sake of science, not for their own sake. Further, the drug is not free of such side effects as nausea, headache, dizziness, anxiety, and irritability. The children, then, suffered to some extent without gaining any advantage.

While the critics have not mentioned the role played by the boys' mothers, we might ask whether they can be said to have acted in the best interest of their children. Some of the women may have been induced by the $125 payment to ignore their child's interest. Thus the payment itself raises the question of whether the consent of the mothers to their children's participation was legitimate. If their income was low, the prospect of receiving money may have tainted the quality of their consent.

"What value does the President's apology for Tuskegee have when there are no safeguards to prevent such abuses now?" asked Vera Sharay, director of Citizens for Responsible Care in Psychiatry and Research. "These racist and morally offensive studies put minority children at the risk of harm in order to prove they are generally predisposed to violence in the future," she charged. "It demonstrates that psychiatric research is out of control."

A spokesperson for Mount Sinai Hospital, which participated in the studies, refused to reveal how many of the subjects were black or Hispanic. He commented only that the subjects chosen reflected "the ethnically diverse population of the catchment area."

Dr. John Oldham, director of the New York Psychiatric Institute, said during an interview that such studies are crucial to acquiring an understanding of the biological basis of behavior. "Is there a correlation between certain biological markers and conduct disorders or antisocial behaviors?" he asked. "This study was an effort to look at this with a relatively simple method using fenfluramine."

## Case Presentation

### The Use of Morally Tainted Sources: The Pernkopf Anatomy

In November 1996 Howard A. Israel and William E. Seidelman wrote a letter to *JAMA*, the Journal of the American Medical Association, asking that the University of Vienna attempt to determine the source of the cadavers used as subjects of the illustrations in the multi-volume book known as the *Pernkopf Anatomy*. Rumors surrounding the book's author and artists had long suggested that some of the cadavers employed in the dissections might have been victims of the Nazis.

Eduard Pernkopf, the book's author, was a member of the Nazi party, and, although never charged with war crimes, he spent three years in an Allied prison camp. He returned afterward to his academic position at the University of Vienna and worked on his atlas of anatomy until he died in 1955. The four main artists illustrating the anatomy were also Nazi party members, and one of them sometimes incorporated into his signature a swastika and the lightning bolts of the SS. These have been airbrushed out in contemporary printings of the book.

Pernkopf began his work in 1933, well before the beginning of the war, but he died in 1955, and the book was completed by others and published in 1960. While the American edition has dropped Pernkopf's text, it uses the original illustrations, which some anatomists consider to be masterpieces of medical paintings. The atlas is admired for its accuracy and is widely used by anatomists and others in medical schools.

After investigating the charge that cadavers from concentration camps or the bodies of Nazi opponents from the district prison were used as subjects, the anatomist David P. Williams concluded that either was possible but couldn't be proved one way or the other. Because of this doubt about the source of the cadavers, uncertainty about the moral legitimacy of using the atlas continues to be debated.

Anatomist E. W. April expressed the opinion of one faction. The atlas is "a phenomenal book," he told reporter Nicholas Wade, "very complete and thorough and authoritative, and you can't detract from that regardless of the fact that [Pernkopf] might not have been a good person or belonged to the wrong party."

The opposite view is expressed by Howard Israel, the coauthor of the letter to *JAMA*. "I have looked at a lot of anatomy textbooks, and these [volumes] are terrific in terms of the quality of pictures," he told Wade. "But that doesn't mean it's right to use them."

What if the source of the cadavers was known? What if they turned out to be the bodies of victims of the Holocaust? Would it be wrong to use an anatomy text based on the dissection of the victims? This is one aspect of the general question of whether it is morally acceptable to use scientific data or any other sort of information that has been obtained in an immoral way. In the view of some, we have a moral duty to avoid tainted data, because to use it is in an indirect way to benefit from the wrongdoing that produced it. Others, however, believe that using the data is a way of rescuing something worthwhile from something that was wrong. As such, it is a way of honoring those who suffered a terrible injustice by making sure their sacrifice is not wasted.

<hr>

## READINGS

# Section 1: Consent and Experimentation

## Phase I Cancer Trials: A Collusion of Misunderstanding

Matthew Miller

Matthew Miller points out that although Phase I cancer trials are designed to test only a drug's toxicity, the great majority of participants enroll in the hope of benefit. Despite protocols pointing out the low probability of getting a therapeutic effect, most patients' consent is not genuinely informed because physicians and patients focus on the fact that a positive outcome is not impossible. Miller claims that modifying the doses of drugs might add a therapeutic element to trials, but that physicians need to take responsibility for finding ways to promote disclosure and so obtain genuine informed consent.

. . . To be considered for Phase I cancer trials patients must have exhausted all known therapeutic options and have a life expectancy of at least three to four months. Typically, patients are referred by their primary

Matthew Miller, "Phase I Cancer Trials: A Collusion of Misunderstanding," *Hastings Center Report* 30, no. 4 (2000): 34–42. Reprinted with permission of The Hastings Center.

oncologist to a major cancer program where a physician-investigator from the cancer center performs a physical examination, takes a medical history, and then invites eligible patients to enroll. For the duration of enrollment, a physician-investigator at the cancer center usually assumes substantial responsibility for monitoring and caring for each patient.

Phase I dose-toxicity information is usually gathered by administering increasing doses of a new drug (or less often, of novel combinations of known agents) to successive cohorts of three to six patients. The trial ends once serious but reversible toxic effects are produced in a fixed proportion of patients, often one-third of the patients in the highest-dose cohort.[1] . . .

Given that the remission rate [during the studies] is less than 1 percent and that the rate of death due to drug toxicity is comparable, few would claim any aggregate survival advantage for participants. In fact, consent documents state that Phase I cancer trials are primarily toxicity studies and that response is neither intended nor expected. Yet patients enrolled in these trials overwhelmingly cite hope of physical benefit (rarely altruism) as their primary motivation for enrolling.[2]

That patients generally fail to understand the nature of Phase I trials surprises few who work with terminally ill patients. In fact, in one study 94 percent of Phase I investigators and 85 percent of IRB chairs believe that patients enroll in these trials for physical benefit, not for altruistic reasons.[3] What is somewhat more surprising is the finding that physicians involved in these trials tend to overestimate both the likelihood of severe and fatal toxicity and the likelihood of anticancer effect.[4] Although the presumption that the patient's interests come first is challenged in several venues of human investigation (such as in the design of placebo-controlled trials), Phase I trials embody peculiarly contrasting tensions at opposing ends of the dosing spectrum. At one end, Phase I trials are intended to ensure that at least one patient suffers severe (but reversible) toxicity; at the other end, they subject 60 to 80 percent of patients to doses that clinical models suggest will not prove therapeutic.[5] . . .

## Enrolling Patients

At some point during our initial encounter, most patients would turn to me and says something to the effect that having a small chance of responding to an untested agent is better than having no chance. . . .

At this point the conversation veered in one of two radically different directions: toward a hopeful and almost always short-lived intermission from despair, or toward a final and often desperate reckoning with the likelihood of a looming death. The direction our conversation took and, it turned out, the likelihood patients would enroll, largely depended on whether and the extent to which we discussed the way

the protocol opposed customary medical practice. Yet since terminally ill patients rarely if ever initiate such a discussion, no discussion was easier or more tempting to avoid.

Despite the extensive experience my patients had with previous physicians and medical institutions, they seldom approached our initial meeting with any understanding that the drug on which their hopes were pinned would be administered at levels that depended on contingencies unrelated to maximizing the likelihood of response. Perhaps this should not be surprising, since most of my patients' prior medical experience involved (and would thus reinforce assumptions about) customary patient care. Even those patients who had previously participated in Phase II and III studies had been given drugs at doses expected to have the greatest possible anticancer effect. . . .

Patients came to see me ready to wage battle. Many feared being seen as quitters. Speaking of their previous experience with cancer, patients and their families often spoke in martial terms and transferred these battle metaphors to the conversation we were having about Phase I trials. Whatever the psychological advantage bestowed by this language, it also affected the way patients viewed their options. Speaking of continuing to fight their cancer, for example, helped patients conceive of Phase I trials as a forum in which they could continue to battle against their disease, as if the trial were merely a continuation of the medical care that had applied to their struggles thus far. Consequently, this figure of speech buoyed spirits as it dissipated the boundaries between the research they were being asked to consider and the therapy that they had previously received. For many, however, this same language also reinforced their predisposition to see not enrolling as a capitulation, and in this way it coerced enrollment.

In time I came to understand what others had long observed: that the words I used, the setting in which the invitation took place, and the intimate act of taking a medical history and performing a physical examination all reinforced a tendency among sick persons to distort those elements of experimental investigation that threatened to undermine hope of clinical benefit.[6] Even factually accurate information abetted this confusion, depending on how it was given. If one tells a patient, for example, that on the one hand the probability of remission is slight, but that on the other hand one never knows when a miracle drug will come along, equal rhetorical weight is given both to clinical success and failure. This rhetorical parity creates a valuation more in keeping with therapeutic than with nontherapeutic experimentation, promoting Phase I trials as conventional patient care that is simply received under unusual and less optimistic conditions.

It took far longer for me to appreciate that these same words, accouterments, and surrounds performed a similar function for me, preserving the illusion that what I was engaged in was an extension of usual clinical practice. This in turn made it easier for me to assume that my patient's interests were not in conflict with those of protocol, nor with my own interests for career advancement. . . .

## Consent and Empirical Literature

In 1955 a prominent team of ethicists and oncologists at the University of Chicago published one of the first empirical studies to explore the motivations and perceptions of cancer patients to enroll in Phase I trials.[7] Thirty consecutive cancer patients enrolled in Phase I trials were surveyed. Althought 93 percent of patients said that they understood most of the information given them, only 33 percent were able to state that the purpose of the trial in which they were subjects was to determine toxicities, tolerability, or the safest dose of the administered agents. Fewer than one-third said that the option of no treatment was discussed. Eighty-five percent decided to participate for reasons of possible therepeutic benefit, 11 percent because of advice or trust in a physician, and 4 percent because of family pressure. No one identified altruism as the primary motivation for participating. Interestingly, patients who were unable to state the purpose of Phase I trials were more likely to believe that they would derive benefit from the study. These findings are consistent with others demonstrating that patients seldom understand that the purpose of Phase I studies is not to treat a tumor or reduce human suffering but only to estimate toxicity.[8]

Though patients engaged in human experimentation always remain a means to an end, this is not what is most troubling about making a person an experimental subject. The wrong, as Hans Jonas has written, is rather that of making a person into a passive thing to be acted upon in the service of ends that they do not themselves find compelling enough to pursue without the expectation of personal reciprocity.[9] Since Phase I trials are not therapeutic enterprises, the quixotic goal of clinical benefit, however much everybody involved hopes for it, is not an end

that can justify these trials. In nontherapeutic trials patients are means to the ends of research and their participation can only be considered free and dignified "by such authentic identification with the cause that it is the subject's as well as the researcher's cause—whereby his role in its service is not just permitted but willed" (p. 236). By definition, those patients in the University of Chicago trial who could not state the scientific goals of the Phase I trial in which they were already enrolled failed to satisfy this criterion. In my experience, only one patient among several dozen willed his service. A medical journalist by training, this gentleman well understood what was being asked of him and wanted to give something back to science since science had provided him with both livelihood and fascination for over fifty years and expected nothing in return for this gift—no anticancer miracle, as he told me. Ironically, he was too ill to participate and died two days after our first visit.

Pointing to the evidence of poor patient comprehension, some of my colleagues assert that desperately ill patients cannot make truly informed decisions about participating in clinical trials. Some investigators have demonstrated, however, that patients can be taught to recognize that research sometimes conflicts with the goals of ordinary treatment.[10] Indeed, it has been forcibly argued that it is irresponsible to reach any conclusive judgments about what patients can and cannot understand when we know so little about how a patient's capacity to understand can be constrained by illness, fear, being kept ignorant, or being considered incompetent.[11] In my own experience, patients could recognize that the requirements of Phase I trials were those of science, not of medicine, but only if and when we discussed how a particular protocol undermined fundamental assumptions they held about the doctor-patient relationship.

Customary incentives aimed at ensuring that researchers take specific steps (such as obtaining a signature on the consent form) often take the form of sanctions for failure to take those steps. The punitive approach predictably does get people to comply with those requirements that can easily be monitored,[12] but does not encourage them to achieve better patient comprehension. This results in an inefficient expenditure of time and effort by physicians and monitoring bodies. A better way is to change the rules of the game so that the incentives acting on patients and physicians are more in accord. For example, if Phase I trials adopted innovative approaches that aimed at maximizing the chance each patient has at a favorable clinical response, physician's conflicts—psychic, professional, and ethical—could be reduced, though not eliminated, and a more open dialogue with patients could be facilitated.

Improving patient understanding is of course not the only goal. Consent that is informed, understanding, and voluntary is a necessary and non-negotiable but minimum and not sufficient criterion for human experimentation.[13] The Nuremberg Code specifies a range of other requirements that must be met prior to seeking consent, requirements that cannot be waived by the subject. These include that the information sought is for the good of society and that the research design sets out to acquire this information in the least onerous way possible; that unnecessary suffering and injury are avoided and that death or disabling injury are not anticipated; that risks never exceed benefits and that the experiment will be stopped if it becomes likely that injury, disability, or death will result. Each of these requirements is, to some extent, called into question by Phase I trials. Nevertheless, the closer patients come to understanding the nature of these possible violations in present-day trials, the better their awareness can stimulate creative attempts to safeguard their authority and to make "identification" with the research goals the principle of recruitment in general. . . .

## Why Has Tradition Prevailed?

The persistence of a tradition, especially one that is inimical to the long-range goals of those involved in it, usually requires that it serve some deeply felt, if dimly understood, immediate, and overmastering need. . . .

One of the deeply embedded functions of Phase I trials may be as an instrument of affect management, as a magic card that referring physicians, physician-investigators, and patients can play together to avoid the difficult and uncomfortable discussions that loom when therapeutic options have been exhausted.[14] Referring physicians can rationalize putting off these difficult matters because the physician-investigator is offering one last hope. Physician-investigators, in a compromised state to speak about the lack of therapeutic options because they have not had the chance to earn the trust of a new recruit, can focus instead on the possibility of benefit to both society and patients. And patients, perhaps in the most compromised position of all to raise questions about their fears and about possible conflicts of interest, can acquiesce in this avoidance and misunderstanding as a way of preserving a desperate hope. . . .

## Compassion *and* Objectivity

. . . What can be done? I make a four-fold plea: First, incorporate innovative dosing strategies, but avoid being seduced into believing that these technical changes adequately address the more durable, residual problems embedded in these trials such as whether and under what conditions we may justifiably trade on patients' hopes. Second, acknowledge that we know too little about what patients can and cannot comprehend to allow our assumptions about patients' incapacities to limit disclosure or to keep us from thinking creatively about improving the consenting process. Third, recognize that full disclosure and voluntary, comprehending consent are necessary but not sufficient criteria for human experimentation and that, in the words of Hans Jonas, progress is an optional goal, not an unconditional commitment. And last, continue to study empirically how the deeply felt but dimly recognized needs of patients, physicians, and society at large interact to obscure conflicts of interest and impoverish the capacity for self-reflection.

### *References*

1. E. Frei, "Clinical Trials of Antitumor Agents: Experimental Design and Timeline Considerations," *Scientific American, the Cancer Journal* 3 (1997):127–36; B. Storer, "Design and Analysis of Phase I Clinical Trials," *Biometrics* 45 (1989): 925–37; N. L. Geller, "Design of Phase I and II Clinical Trials in Cancer: A Statistician's View," *Cancer Investigations* 2 (1984): 483–91.

2. C. K. Daugherty et al., "Pushing the Envelope: Informed Consent in Phase I Trials," *Annals of Oncology* 6 (1995): 321–23; M. Schaeffer et al., "The Impact of Disease Severity on the Informed Consent Process in Clinical Research," *American Journal of Medicine* 100 (1996): 261–68.

3. E. Kodish et al., "Ethical Issues in Phase I Oncology Research: A Comparison of Investigators and Institutional Review Board Chairpersons," *Journal of Clinical Oncology* 10 (1992): 1810–16.

4. See ref. 2, Daugherty et al., "Pushing the Envelope."

5. See ref. 1, Frei, "Clinical Trials of Antitumor Agents," p. 128.

6. J. Katz, *The Silent World of Doctor and Patient* (New York: N.Y.: The Free Press, 1984); N. M. King, "Experimental Treatment: Oxymoron or Aspiration," *Hastings Center Report* 25, no. 4 (1995): 6–15; P. S. Appelbaum et al., "False Hopes and Best Data: Consent to Research and the Therapeutic Misconception," *Hastings Center Report* 17, no. 2 (1987): 20–24.

7. See ref. 2, Daugherty et al., "Pushing the Envelope."

8. See ref. 2, Daugherty et al., "Pushing the Envelope."; C. K. Daugherty et al., "Study of Cohort-Specific Consent and Patient Control in Phase I Cancer Trials," *Journal of Clinical Oncology* 16 (1998): 2305–12; W. E. Berdel et al., "Influence of Phase I Early Clinical Trials on the Quality of Life of Cancer Patients: A Pilot Study," *Anticancer Research* 8 (1988): 313–21; M. Tomamichell et al., "Informed Consent for Phase I Studies: Evaluation of the Information Provided to Patients," *Annals of Oncology* 6 (1995): 363–369.

9. H. Jonas, "Philosophical Reflections on Human Experimentation," *Daedalus* (1969): 219–45.

10.  See ref. 2, Schaeffer et al., "The Impact of Disease Severity"; ref. 6, Appelbaum et al., "The Therapeutic Misconception," and Appelbaum et al., "False Hopes and Best Data"; also P. S. Appelbaum and T. Grisso, "Assessing Patients Capacities to Consent to Treatment," *NEJM* 319 (1988): 1635–38 [erratum appears in *NJEM* 320 (1989): 748].

11.  J. Katz, "Informed Consent—Must It Remain a Fairy Tale," *Journal of Contemporary Health Law Policy* 10 (1994): 69–91.

12.  D. M. Berwick, "Continuous Improvement as an Ideal in Health Care," *NEJM* 320 (1989): 53–56.

13.  See ref. 9, Jonas, "Philosophical Reflections."

14.  See ref. 6, Katz, *The Silent World of Doctor and Patient.*

# Philosophical Reflections on Experimenting with Human Subjects

## Hans Jonas

Hans Jonas argues that, if we justify experiments by considering them a right of society, then we are exposing individuals to dangers for the general good. This, for Jonas, is inherently wrong, and no individual should be forced to surrender himself or herself to a social goal.

Any risk that is taken must be voluntary, but obtaining informed consent, Jonas claims, is not sufficient to justify the experimental use of human beings. Two other conditions must be met: First, subjects must be recruited from those who are most knowledgeable about the circumstances of research and who are intellectually most capable of grasping its purposes and procedures; second, the experiment must be undertaken for an adequate cause. Jonas cautions us that the progress that may come from research is not necessarily worth our efforts or approval, and he reminds us that there are moral values that we ought not to lose in the pursuit of science.

Experimenting with human subjects is going on in many fields of scientific and technological progress. It is designed to replace the overall instruction by natural, occasional experience with the selective information from artificial, systematic experiment which physical science has found so effective in dealing with inanimate nature. Of the new experimentation with man, medical is surely the most legitimate; psychological, the most dubious; biological (still to come), the most dangerous. I have chosen here to deal with the first only, where the case *for* it is strongest and the task of adjudicating conflicting claims hardest. . . .

Reprinted by permission of *Daedalus,* Journal of the American Academy of Arts and Sciences, Spring 1969, Boston, Mass. This essay is included, on pp. 105–131, in a 1980 reedition of Jonas's *Philosophical Essays: From Current Creed to Technological Man,* published by the University of Chicago Press.

## The Peculiarity of Human Experimentation

Experimentation was originally sanctioned by natural science. There it is performed on inanimate objects, and this raises no moral problems. But as soon as animate, feeling beings became the subjects of experiment, as they do in the life sciences and especially in medical research, this innocence of the search for knowledge is lost and questions of conscience arise. The depth to which moral and religious sensibilities can become aroused over these questions is shown by the vivisection issue. Human experimentation must sharpen the issue as it involves ultimate questions of personal dignity and sacrosanctity. One profound difference between the human experiment and the physical (besides that between animate and inanimate, feeling and unfeeling nature) is this: The physical experiment employs small-scale, artificially devised substitutes for that about which knowledge is to be obtained, and the experimenter extrapolates from these models and simulated conditions to nature at large. Something deputizes for the "real thing"—balls rolling down an inclined plane for sun and planets, electric discharges from a condenser for real lightning, and so on. For the most part, no such substitution is possible in the biological sphere. We must operate on the original itself, the real thing in the fullest sense, and perhaps affect it irreversibly. No simulacrum can take its place. Especially in the human sphere, experimentation loses entirely the advantage of the clear division between vicarious model and true object. Up to a point, animals may fulfill the proxy role of the classical physical experiment. But in the end man himself must furnish knowledge about himself, and the comfortable separation of noncommittal experiment and definitive action vanishes. An experiment in education affects the lives of its subjects, perhaps a whole generation of schoolchildren. Human experimentation for whatever purpose is always *also* a responsible, nonexperimental, definitive dealing with the subject himself. And not even the noblest purpose abrogates the obligations this involves.

This is the root of the problem with which we are faced: Can both that purpose and this obligation be satisfied? If not, what would be a just compromise? Which side should give way to the other? The question is inherently philosophical as it concerns not merely pragmatic difficulties and their arbitration, but a genuine conflict of values involving principles of a high order. May I put conflict in these terms. On principle, it is felt, human beings *ought* not to be dealt with in that way (the "guinea pig" protest); on the other hand, such dealings are increasingly urged on us by considerations, in turn appealing to principle, that claim to override those objections. Such a claim must be carefully assessed, especially when it is swept along by a mighty tide. Putting the matter thus, we have already made one important assumption rooted in our "Western" cultural tradition: The prohibitive rule is, to that way of thinking, the primary and axiomatic one; the permissive counter-rule, as qualifying the first, is secondary and stands in need of justification. We must justify the infringement of a primary inviolability, which needs no justification itself; and the justification of its infringement must be by values and needs of a dignity commensurate with those to be sacrificed.

## Health as a Public Good

The cause invoked [for medical experimentation] is health and, in its more critical aspect, life itself—clearly superlative goods that the physician serves directly by curing and the researcher indirectly by the knowledge gained through his experiments. There is no question about the good served or about the evil fought—disease and premature death. But a good to whom and an evil to whom? Here the issue tends to become somewhat clouded. In the attempt to give experimentation the proper dignity (on the problematic view that a value becomes greater by being "social" instead of merely individual), the health in question or the disease in question is somehow predicated on the social whole, as if it were society that, in the persons of its members enjoyed the one and suffered the other. For the purposes of our problem, public interest can then be pitted against private interest, the common good against the individual good. Indeed, I have found health called a national resource, which of course it is, but surely not in the first place.

In trying to resolve some of the complexities and ambiguities lurking in these conceptualizations, I have pondered a particular statement, made in the form of a question, which I found in the *Proceedings* of the earlier *Daedalus* conference: "Can society afford to discard the tissues and organs of the hopelessly unconscious patient when they could be used to restore the otherwise hopelessly ill, but still salvageable individual?" And somewhat later: "A strong case can be made that society can ill afford to discard the tissues and organs of the hopelessly unconscious patient; they are greatly needed for study and experimental trial to help those who can be salvaged."[1] I hasten to add that any suspicion of callousness that the "commodity" language of these statements may suggest is immediately dispelled by the name of the speaker, Dr. Henry K. Beecher, for whose humanity and moral sensibility there can be nothing but admiration. But the use, in all innocence, of this language gives food for thought. Let me, for a moment, take the question literally. "Discarding" implies proprietary rights—nobody can discard what does not belong to him in the first place. Does society then own my body? "Salvaging" implies the same and, moreover, a use-value to the owner. Is the life-extension of certain individuals then a public interest—that is, of the loss or gain involved. And "society" itself— what is it? When does a need, an aim, an obligation become social? Let us reflect on some of these terms.

## What Society Can Afford

"Can Society afford . . . ?" Afford what? To let people die intact, thereby withholding something from other people who desperately need it, who in consequence will have to die too? These other, unfortunate people indeed cannot afford not to have a kidney, heart, or other organ of the dying patient, on which they depend for an extension of their lease on life; but does that give them a right to it? And does it oblige society to procure it for them? What is it that *society* can or cannot afford—leaving aside for the moment the question of what it has a *right* to? It surely can afford to lose members through death; more than that, it is built on the balance of death and birth decreed by the order of life. This is too general, of course, for our question, but perhaps it is well to remember. The specific question seems to be whether society can afford to let some people die whose death might be deferred by particular means if these were authorized by society. Again, if it is merely a question of what society can or cannot afford, rather than of what it ought or ought not to do, the answer must be: Of course, it can. If cancer, heart disease, and other organic, noncontagious ills, especially those tending to strike the old more than the young, continue to exact their toll at the normal rate of incidence (including the toll of private anguish and misery), society can go on flourishing in every way.

Here, by contrast, are some examples of what, in sober truth, society cannot afford. It cannot afford to let an epidemic rage unchecked; a persistent excess of deaths over births, but neither—we must add—too great an excess of births over deaths; too low an average life expectancy even if demographically balanced by fertility, but neither too great a longevity with the necessitated correlative dearth of youth in the social body; a debilitating state of general health; and things of this kind. These are plain cases where the whole condition of society is critically affected, and the public interest can make its imperative claims. The Black Death of the Middle Ages was a *public* calamity of the acute kind; the life-sapping ravages of endemic malaria or sleeping sickness in certain areas are a public calamity of the chronic kind. Such situations a society as a whole can truly not "afford," and they may call for extraordinary remedies, including, perhaps, the invasion of private sacrosanctities.

This is not entirely a matter of numbers and numerical ratios. Society, in a subtler sense, cannot "afford" a single miscarriage of justice, a single inequity in the dispensation of its laws, the violation of the rights of even the tiniest minority, because these undermine the moral basis on which society's existence rests. Nor can it, for a similar reason, afford the ab-

sence or atrophy in its midst of compassion and of the effort to alleviate suffering—be it widespread or rare—one form of which is the effort to conquer disease of any kind, whether "socially" significant (by reasons of number) or not. And in short, society cannot afford the absence among its members of *virtue*, with its readiness for sacrifice beyond defined duty. Since its presence—that is to say, that of personal idealism—is a matter of grace and not of decree, we have the paradox that society depends for its existence on intangibles of nothing less than a religious order, for which it can hope, but which it cannot enforce. All the more must it protect this most precious capital from abuse.

For what objectives connected with the medico-biological sphere should this reserve be drawn upon—for example, in the form of accepting, soliciting, perhaps even imposing the submission of human subjects to experimentation? We postulate that this must be not just a worthy cause, as any promotion of the health of anybody doubtlessly is, but a cause qualifying for transcendent social sanction. Here one thinks first of those cases critically affecting the whole condition, present and future, of the community we have illustrated. Something equivalent to what in the political sphere is called "clear and present danger" may be invoked and a state of emergency proclaimed, thereby suspending certain otherwise inviolable prohibitions and taboos. We may observe that averting a disaster always carries greater weight than promoting a good. Extraordinary danger excuses extraordinary means. This covers human experimentation, which we would like to count, as far as possible, among the extraordinary rather than the ordinary means of serving the common good under public auspices. Naturally, since foresight and responsibility for the future are of the essence of institutional society, averting disaster extends into long-term prevention, although the lesser urgency will warrant less sweeping licenses.

## Society and the Cause of Progress

Much weaker is the case where it is a matter not of saving but of improving society. Much of medical research falls into this category. As stated before, a permanent death rate from heart failure or cancer does not threaten society. So long as certain statistical ratios are maintained, the incidence of disease and of disease-induced mortality is not (in the strict sense) a "social" misfortune. I hasten to add that it is not therefore less of a human misfortune, and the call for relief issuing with silent eloquence from each victim and all potential victims is of no lesser dignity. But it is misleading to equate the fundamentally human response to it with what is owed to society: it is owed by man to man—and it is thereby owed by society to the individuals as soon as the adequate ministering to these concerns outgrows (as it progressively does) the scope of private spontaneity and is made a public mandate. It is thus that society assumes responsibility for medical care, research, old age, and innumerable other things not originally of the public realm (in the original "social contract"), and they become duties toward "society" (rather than directly toward one's fellow man) by the fact that they are socially operated.

Indeed, we expect from organized society no longer mere protection against harm and the securing of the conditions of our preservation, but active and constant improvement in all the domains of life: the waging of the battle against nature, the enhancement of the human estate—in short, the promotion of progress. This is an expansive goal, one far surpassing the disaster norm of our previous reflections. It lacks the urgency of the latter, but has the nobility of the free, forward thrust. It surely is worth sacrifices. It is not at all a question of what society can afford, but of what it is committed to, beyond all necessity, by our mandate. Its trusteeship has become an established, ongoing, institutionalized business of the body politic. As eager beneficiaries of its gains, we now owe to "society," as its chief agent, our individual contributions toward its *continued pursuit*. I emphasize "continued pursuit." Maintaining the existing level requires no more than the orthodox means of taxation and enforcement of professional standards that raise no problems. The more optional goal of pushing forward is also more exacting. We have this syndrome: Progress is by our choosing an acknowledged interest of society, in which we have a stake in various degrees; science is a necessary instrument of progress; research is a necessary instrument of science; and in medical science experimentation on human subjects is a necessary instrument of research. Therefore, human experimentation has come to be a societal interest.

The destination of research is essentially melioristic. It does not serve the preservation of the existing good from which I profit myself and to which I am obligated. Unless the present state is intolerable, the melioristic goal is in a sense gratuitous, and this not only from the vantage point of the present. Our descendants have a right to be left an unplundered planet; they do not have a right to new miracle cures. We have

sinned against them, if by our doing we have destroyed their inheritance—which we are doing at full blast; we have not sinned against them if by the time they come around arthritis has not yet been conquered (unless by sheer neglect). And generally, in the matter of progress, as humanity had no claim on a Newton, a Michelangelo, or a St. Francis to appear, and no right to the blessings of their unscheduled deeds, so progress, with all our methodical labor for it, cannot be budgeted in advance and its fruits received as a due. Its coming-about at all and its turning out for good (of which we can never be sure) must rather be regarded as something akin to grace.

## The Melioristic Goal, Medical Research, and Individual Duty

Nowhere is the melioristic goal more inherent than in medicine. To the physician, it is not gratuitous. He is committed to curing and thus to improving the power to cure. Gratuitous we called it (outside disaster conditions) as a *social* goal, but noble at the same time. Both the nobility and the gratuitousness must influence the manner in which self-sacrifice for it is elicited, and even its free offer accepted. Freedom is certainly the first condition to be observed here. The surrender of one's body to medical experimentation is entirely outside the enforceable "social contract."

Or can it be construed to fall within its terms—namely, as repayment for benefits from past experimentation that I have enjoyed myself? But I am indebted for these benefits not to society, but to the past "martyrs" to whom society is indebted itself, and society has no right to call in my personal debt by way of adding new to its own. Moreover, gratitude is not an enforceable social obligation; it anyway does not mean that I must emulate the deed. Most of all, if it was wrong to exact such sacrifice in the first place, it does not become right to exact it again with the plea of the profit it has brought me. If, however, it was not exacted, but entirely free, as it ought to have been, then it should remain so, and its precedence must not be used as a social pressure on others for doing the same under the sign of duty. . . .

## The "Conscription" of Consent

The mere issuing of the appeal, the calling for volunteers, with the moral and social pressures it inevitably generates, amounts even under the most meticulous rules of consent to a sort of *conscripting*. And some soliciting is necessarily involved. . . . And this is why "consent," surely a nonnegotiable minimum requirement, is not the full answer to the problem. Granting then that soliciting and therefore some degree of conscripting are part of the situation, who may conscript and who may be conscripted? Or less harshly expressed: Who should issue appeals and to whom?

The naturally qualified issuer of the appeal is the research scientist himself, collectively the main carrier of the impulse and the only one with the technical competence to judge. But his being very much an interested party (with vested interests, indeed, not purely in the public good, but in the scientific enterprise as such, in "his" project, and even in his career) makes him also suspect. The ineradicable dialectic of this situation—a delicate incompatibility problem—calls for particular controls by the research community and by public authority that we need not discuss. They can mitigate, but not eliminate the problem. We have to live with the ambiguity, the treacherous impurity of everything human.

### Self-Recruitment of the Community

To whom should the appeal be addressed? The natural issuer of the call is also the first natural addressee: the physician-researcher himself and the scientific confraternity at large. With such a coincidence—indeed, the noble tradition with which the whole business of human experimentation started—almost all of the associated legal, ethical, and metaphysical problems vanish. If it is full, autonomous identification of the subject with the purpose that is required for the dignifying of his serving as a subject—here it is; if strongest motivation—here it is; if fullest understanding—here it is; if freest decision—here it is; if greatest integration with the person's total, chosen pursuit—here it is. With the fact of self-solicitation the issue of consent in all its insoluble equivocality is bypassed per se. Not even the condition that the particular purpose be truly important and the project reasonably promising, which must hold in any solicitation of others, need be satisfied here. By himself, the scientist is free to obey his obsession, to play his hunch, to wager on chance, to follow the lure of ambition. It is all part of the "divine madness" that somehow animates the ceaseless pressing against frontiers. For the rest of society, which

has a deep-seated disposition to look with reverence and awe upon the guardians of the mysteries of life, the profession assumes with this proof of its devotion the role of a self-chosen, consecrated fraternity, not unlike the monastic orders of the past, and this would come nearest to the actual, religious origins of the art of healing. . . .

### "Identification" as the Principle of Recruitment in General

If the properties we adduced as the particular qualifications of the members of the scientific fraternity itself are taken as general criteria of selection, then one should look for additional subjects where a maximum of identification, understanding, and spontaneity can be expected—that is, among the most highly motivated, the most highly educated, and the least "captive" members of the community. From this naturally scarce resource, a descending order of permissibility leads to greater abundance and ease of supply, whose use should become proportionately more hesitant as the exculpating criteria are relaxed. An inversion of normal "market" behavior is demanded here—namely, to accept the lowest quotation last (and excused only by the greatest pressure of need); to pay the highest price first.

The ruling principle in our considerations is that the "wrong" of reification can only be made "right" by such authentic identification with the cause that it is the subject's as well as the researcher's cause—whereby his role in its service is not just permitted by him, but *willed.* That sovereign will of his which embraces the end as his own restores his personhood to the otherwise depersonalizing context. To be valid it must be autonomous and informed. The latter condition can, outside the research community, only be fulfilled by degrees; but the higher the degree of understanding regarding the purpose and the technique, the more valid becomes the endorsement of the will. A margin of mere trust inevitably remains. Ultimately, the appeal for volunteers should seek this free and generous endorsement, the appropriation of the research purpose into the person's own scheme of ends. Thus, the appeal is in truth addressed to the one, mysterious, and sacred source of any such generosity of the will—"devotion," whose forms and objects of commitment are various and may invest different motivations in different individuals. The following, for instance, may be responsive to the "call" we are discussing: compassion with human suffering, zeal for humanity, reverence for the Golden Rule, enthusiasm for progress, homage to the cause of knowledge, even longing for sacrificial justification (do not call that "masochism," please). On all these, I say, it is defensible and right to draw when the research objective is worthy enough; and it is a prime duty of the research community (especially in view of what we called the "margin of trust") to see that this sacred source is never abused for frivolous ends. For a less than adequate cause, not even the freest, unsolicited offer should be accepted.

## The Rule of the "Descending Order" and Its Counterutility Sense

We have laid down what must seem to be a forbidding rule to the number-hungry research industry. Having faith in the transcendent potential of man, I do not fear that the "source" will ever fail a society that does not destroy it—and only such a one is worthy of the blessings of progress. But "elitistic" the rule is (as is the enterprise of progress itself), and elites are by nature small. The combined attribute of motivation and information, plus the absence of external pressures, tends to be socially so circumscribed that strict adherence to the rule might numerically starve the research process. This is why I spoke of a descending order of permissibility, which is itself permissive, but where the realization that it is a *descending* order is not without pragmatic import. Departing from the august norm, the appeal must needs shift from idealism to docility, from high-mindedness to compliance, from judgment to trust. Consent spreads over the whole spectrum. I will not go into the casuistics of this penumbral area. I merely indicate the principle of the order of preference: The poorer in knowledge, motivation, and freedom of decision (and that, alas, means the more readily available in terms of numbers and possible manipulation), the more sparingly and indeed reluctantly should the reservoir be used, and the more compelling must therefore become the countervailing justification.

Let us note that this is the opposite of a social utility standard, the reverse of the order by "availability and expendability": The most valuable and scarcest, the least expendable elements of the social organism, are to be the first candidates for risk and sacrifice. It is the standard of *noblesse oblige,* and with all its coun-

terutility and seeming "wastefulness," we feel a rightness about it and perhaps even a higher "utility," for the soul of the community lives by this spirit.[2] It is also the opposite of what the day-to-day interests of research clamor for, and for the scientific community to honor it will mean that it will have to fight a strong temptation to go by routine to the readiest sources of supply—the suggestible, the ignorant, the dependent, the "captive" in various senses.[3] I do not believe that heightened resistance here must cripple research, which cannot be permitted; but it may indeed slow it down by the smaller numbers fed into experimentation in consequence. This price—a possibly slower rate of progress—may have to be paid for the preservation of the most precious capital of higher communal life.

## Experimentation on Patients

So far we have been speaking on the tacit assumption that the subjects of experimentation are recruited from among the healthy. To the question "Who is conscriptable?" the spontaneous answer is: Least and last of all the sick—the most available of all as they are under treatment and observation anyway. That the afflicted should not be called upon to bear additional burden and risk, that they are society's special trust and the physician's trust in particular—these are elementary responses of our moral sense. Yet the very destination of medical research, the conquest of disease, requires at the crucial stage trial and verification on precisely the sufferers from the disease, and their total exemption would defeat the purpose itself. In acknowledging this inescapable necessity, we enter the most sensitive area of the whole complex, the one most keenly felt and most searchingly discussed by the practitioners themselves. No wonder, it touches the heart of the doctor–patient relation, putting its most solemn obligations to the test. There is nothing new in what I have to say about the ethics of the doctor-patient relation, but for the purpose of confronting it with the issue of experimentation some of the oldest verities must be recalled.

## The Fundamental Privilege of the Sick

In the course of treatment, the physician is obligated to the patient and to no one else. He is not the agent of society, nor of the interests of medical science, nor of the patient's family, nor of his co-sufferers, nor of future sufferers from the same disease. The patient alone counts when he is under the physician's care. By the simple law of bilateral contract (analogous, for example, to the relation of lawyer to client and its "conflict of interest" rule), the physician is bound not to let any other interest interfere with that of the patient in being cured. But manifestly more sublime norms than contractual ones are involved. We may speak of a sacred trust; strictly by its terms, the doctor is, as it were, alone with his patient and God.

There is one normal exception to this—that is, to the doctor's not being the agent of society vis-à-vis the patient, but the trustee of his interests alone: the quarantining of the contagious sick. This is plainly not for the patient's interest, but for that of others threatened by him. (In vaccination, we have a combination of both: protection of the individual and others.) But preventing the patient from causing harm to others is not the same as exploiting him for the advantage of others. And there is, of course, the abnormal exception of collective catastrophe, the analogue to a state of war. The physician who desperately battles a raging epidemic is under a unique dispensation that suspends in a nonspecifiable way some of the structures of normal practice, including possibly those against experimental liberties with his patients. No rules can be devised for the waiving of rules in extremities. And as with the famous shipwreck examples of ethical theory, the less said about it the better. But what is allowable there and may later be passed over in forgiving silence cannot serve as a precedent. We are concerned with non-extreme, non-emergency conditions where the voice of principle can be heard and claims can be adjudicated free from duress. We have conceded that there are such claims, and that if there is to be medical advance at all, not even the superlative privilege of the suffering and the sick can be kept wholly intact from the intrusion of its needs. About this least palatable, most disquieting part of our subject, I have to offer only groping, inconclusive remarks.

### The Principle of "Identification" Applied to Patients

On the whole, the same principles would seem to hold here as are found to hold with "normal subjects": motivation, identification, understanding on the part of the subject. But it is clear that these conditions are

peculiarly difficult to satisfy with regard to a patient. His physical state, psychic preoccupation, dependent relation to the doctor, the submissive attitude induced by treatment—everything connected with his condition and situation makes the sick person inherently less of a sovereign person than the healthy one. Spontaneity of self-offering was almost to be ruled out; consent is marred by lower resistance or captive circumstance, and so on. In fact, all the factors that make the patient, as a category, particularly accessible and welcome for experimentation at the same time compromise the quality of the responding affirmation that must morally redeem the making use of them. This, in addition to the primacy of the physician's duty, puts a heightened onus on the physician-researcher to limit his undue power to the most important and defensible research objectives and, of course, to keep persuasion at a minimum.

Still, with all the disabilities noted, there is scope among patients for observing the rule of the "descending order of permissibility" that we have laid down for normal subjects, in vexing inversion of the utility order of quantitative abundance and qualitative "expendability." By the principle of this order, those patients who most identify with and are cognizant of the cause of research—members of the medical profession (who after all are sometimes patients themselves)—come first; the highly motivated and educated, also least dependent, among the lay patients come next; and so on down the line. An added consideration here is seriousness of condition, which again operates in inverse proportion. Here the profession must fight the tempting sophistry that the hopeless case is expendable (because in prospect already expended) and therefore especially usable; and generally the attitude that the poorer the chances of the patient, the more justifiable his recruitment for experimentation (other than for his own benefit). The opposite is true.

### Nondisclosure as a Borderline Case

Then there is the case where ignorance of the subject, sometimes even of the experimenter, is of the essence of the experiment (the "double-blind"-control group–placebo syndrome). It is said to be a necessary element of the scientific process. Whatever may be said about its ethics in regard to normal subjects, especially volunteers, it is an outright betrayal of trust in regard to the patient who believes that he is receiving treatment. Only supreme importance of the objective can exonerate it, without making it less of a transgression. The patient is definitely wronged even when not harmed. And ethics apart, the practice of such deception holds the danger of undermining the faith in the *bona fides* of treatment, the beneficial intent of the physician—the very basis of the doctor–patient relationship. In every respect it follows that concealed experiment on patients—that is, experiment under the guise of treatment—should be the rarest exception, at best, if it cannot be wholly avoided.

This has still the merit of a borderline problem. The same is not true of the other case of necessary ignorance of the subject—that of the unconscious patient. Drafting him for nontherapeutic experiments is simply and unqualifiedly impermissible; progress or not, he must never be used, on the inflexible principle that utter helplessness demands utter protection.

When preparing this paper, I filled pages with a casuistics of this harrowing field, but then scrapped most of it, realizing my dilettante status. The shadings are endless, and only the physician-researcher can discern them properly as the cases arise. Into his lap the decision is thrown. The philosophical rule, once it has admitted into itself the idea of a sliding scale, cannot really specify its own application. It can only impress on the practitioner a general maxim or attitude for the exercise of his judgment and conscience in the concrete occasions of his work. In our case, I am afraid, it means making life more difficult for him.

It will also be noted that, somewhat at variance with the emphasis in the literature, I have not dwelt on the element of "risk" and very little on that of "consent." Discussion of the first is beyond the layman's competence; the emphasis on the second has been lessened because of its equivocal character. It is a truism to say that one should strive to minimize the risk and to maximize the consent. The more demanding concept of "identification," which I have used, includes "consent" in its maximal or authentic form, and the assumption of risk is its privilege.

## No Experiments on Patients Unrelated to Their Own Disease

Although my ponderings have, on the whole, yielded points of view rather than definite prescriptions, premises rather than conclusions, they have led me to a few unequivocal yeses and nos. The first is the emphatic rule that patients should be experimented upon, if at all, *only* with reference to *their disease.* Never should there be added to the gratuitousness of the experiment as such the gratuitousness of service to an unrelated cause. This follows simply from what we have found to be the only excuse for infracting the special exemption of the sick at all—namely, that the scientific war on disease cannot accomplish its goal without drawing the sufferers from disease into the investigative process. If under this excuse they become subjects of experiment, they do so *because*, and only because, of *their* disease.

This is the fundamental and self-sufficient consideration. That the patient cannot possibly benefit from the unrelated experiment therapeutically, while he might from experiment related to his condition, is also true, but lies beyond the problem area of pure experiment. I am in any case discussing nontherapeutic experimentation only, where *ex hypothesi* the patient does not benefit. Experiment as part of therapy—that is, directed toward helping the subject himself—is a different matter altogether and raises its own problems but hardly philosophical ones. As long as a doctor can say, even if only in his own thought: "There is no known cure for your condition (or: You have responded to none); but there is promise in a new treatment still under investigation, not quite tested yet as to effectiveness and safety; you will be taking a chance, but all things considered, I judge it in your best interest to let me try it on you"—as long as he can speak thus, he speaks as the patient's physician and may err, but does not transform the patient into a subject of experimentation. Introduction of an untried therapy into the treatment where the tried ones have failed is not "experimentation on the patient."

Generally, and almost needless to say, with all the rules of the book, there is something "experimental" (because tentative) about every individual treatment, beginning with the diagnosis itself; and he would be a poor doctor who would not learn from every case for the benefit of future cases, and a poor member of the profession who would not make any new insights gained from his treatments available to the profession at large. Thus, knowledge may be advanced in the treatment of any patient, and the interest of the medical art and all sufferers from the same affliction as well as the patient himself may be served if something happens to be learned from his case. But his gain to knowledge and future therapy is incidental to the *bona fide* service to the present patient. He has the right to expect that the doctor does nothing to him just in order to learn.

In that case, the doctor's imaginary speech would run, for instance, like this: "There is nothing more I can do for you. But you can do something for me. Speaking no longer as your physician but on behalf of medical science, we could learn a great deal about future cases of this kind if you would permit me to perform certain experiments on you. It is understood that you yourself would not benefit from any knowledge we might gain; but future patients would." This statement would express the purely experimental situation, assumedly here with the subject's concurrence and with all cards on the table. In Alexander Bicker's words: "It is a different situation when the doctor is no longer trying to make [the patient] well, but is trying to find out how to make others well in the future."[4]

But even in the second case, that of the nontherapeutic experiment where the patient does not benefit, at least the patient's own disease is enlisted in the cause of fighting that disease, even if only in others. It is yet another thing to say or think: "Since you are here—in the hospital with its facilities—anyway, under our care and observation anyway, away from your job (or, perhaps, doomed) anyway, we wish to profit from your being available for some other research of great interest we are presently engaged in." From the standpoint of merely medical ethics, which has only to consider risk, consent, and the worth of the objective, there may be no cardinal difference between this case and the last one. I hope that the medical reader will not think I am making too fine a point when I say that from the standpoint of the subject and his dignity there is a cardinal difference that crosses the line between the permissible and the impermissible, and this by the same principle of "Identification" I have been invoking all along. Whatever the rights and wrongs of any experimentation on any patient—in the one case, at least that residue of identification is left him that it is his own affliction by which he can contribute to the conquest of that affliction, his own kind of suffering which he helps to alleviate in others; and so in a sense it is his own cause. It is totally indefensi-

ble to rob the unfortunate of this intimacy with the purpose and make his misfortune a convenience for the furtherance of alien concerns.

## Conclusion

. . . I wish only to say in conclusion that if some of the practical implications of my reasonings are felt to work out toward a slower rate of progress, this should not cause too great dismay. Let us not forget that progress is an optional goal, not an unconditional commitment, and that its tempo in particular, compulsive as it may become, has nothing sacred about it. Let us also remember that a slower progress in the conquest of disease would not threaten society, grievous as it is to those who have to deplore that their particular disease be not yet conquered, but that society would indeed be threatened by the erosion of those moral values whose loss, possibly caused by too ruthless a pursuit of scientific progress, would make its most dazzling triumphs not worth having. Let us finally remember that it cannot be the aim of progress to abolish the lot of mortality. Of some ill or other, each of us will die. Our mortal condition is upon us with its harshness but also its wisdom—because without it there would not be the eternally renewed promise of the freshness, immediacy, and eagerness of youth; nor would there be for any of us the incentive to number our days and make them count. With all our striving to wrest from our mortality what we can, we should bear its burden with patience and dignity.

### Notes

1. *Proceedings of the Conference on the Ethical Aspects of Experimentation on Human Subjects,* November 3–4, 1967 (Boston, Mass.; hereafter called *Proceedings*), pp. 50–51.

2. Socially, everyone is expendable relatively—that is, in different degrees; religiously, no one is expendable absolutely: The "image of God" is in all. If it can be enhanced, then it is not by anyone being expended, but by someone expending himself.

3. This refers to captives of circumstance, not of justice. Prison inmates are, with respect to our problem, in a special class. If we hold to some idea of guilt, and to the supposition that our judicial system is not entirely at fault, they may be held to stand in a special debt to society, and their offer to serve—from whatever motive—may be accepted with a minimum of qualms as a means of reparation.

4. *Proceedings,* p. 33.

# The Willowbrook Letters: Criticism and Defense

Stephen Goldby, Saul Krugman, M. H. Pappworth, and
Geoffrey Edsall

"The Willowbrook Letters," by Stephen Goldby, Saul Krugman, M. H. Pappworth,
and Geoffrey Edsall, concern the moral legitimacy of the study of viral hepatitis
that was conducted at the Willowbrook School by Krugman and his associates.
(See the Case Presentation for more detail.) Goldby charges that the study was
"quite unjustifiable" because it was morally wrong to infect children when no
benefit to them could result. Krugman defends himself by claiming that his results
demonstrated a "therapeutic effect" for the children involved, as well as for others. He presents four reasons for holding that the infecting of the children was
justified.

Pappworth claims that Krugman's defense is presented only after the fact,
whereas an experiment is ethical or not in its inception. Moreover, he asserts,
consent was obtained through the use of coercion. Parents who wished to put
their children in the institution were told there was room only in the "hepatitis
unit."

In the final letter, Edsall defends the Krugman study. The experiments, he asserts, involved no greater risk to the children involved than they would have run
in any case. What is more, the results obtained were of general benefit.

SIR.—You have referred to the work of Krugman and
his colleagues at the Willowbrook State School in
three editorials. In the first article the work was cited
as a notable study of hepatitis and a model for this
type of investigation. No comment was made on the
rightness of attempting to infect mentally retarded
children with hepatitis for experimental purposes, in
an institution where the disease was already endemic.

The second editorial again did not remark on the
ethics of the study, but the third sounded a note of
doubt as to the justification for extending these experiments. The reason given was that some children might
have been made more susceptible to serious hepatitis
as the result of the administration of previously heated
icterogenic material.

I believe that not only this last experiment, but
the whole of Krugman's study, is quite unjustifiable,
whatever the aims, and however academically or therapeutically important are the results. I am amazed that
the work was published and that it has been actively

Reprinted by permission of the authors and publisher from
*The Lancet*, April 10, May 8, June 5, and July 10, 1971.

supported editorially by the *Journal of the American
Medical Association* and by Ingelfinger in the 1967–68
*Year Book of Medicine.* To my knowledge only the
*British Journal of Hospital Medicine* has clearly stated
the ethical position on these experiments and shown
that it was indefensible to give potentially dangerous
infected material to children, particularly those who
were mentally retarded, with or without parental consent, when no benefit to the child could conceivably
result.

Krugman and Giles have continued to publish
the results of their study, and in a recent paper go to
some length to describe their method of obtaining
parental consent and list a number of influential medical boards and committees that have approved the
study. They point out again that, in their opinion, their
work conforms to the World Medical Association Draft
Code of Ethics on Human Experimentation. They also
say that hepatitis is still highly endemic in the school.

This attempted defense is irrelevant to the central
issue. Is it right to perform an experiment on a normal
or mentally retarded child when no benefit can result
to that individual? I think that the answer is no, and
that the question of parental consent is irrelevant. In

my view the studies of Krugman serve only to show that there is a serious loophole in the Draft Code, which under General Principles and Definitions puts the onus of consent for experimentation on children on the parent or guardian. It is this section that is quoted by Krugman. I would class his work as "experiments conducted solely for the acquisition of knowledge," under which heading the code states that "persons retained in mental hospital or hospitals for mental defectives should not be used for human experiment." Krugman may believe that his experiments were for the benefit of his patients, meaning the individual patients used in the study. If this is his belief he has a difficult case to defend. The duty of a pediatrician in a situation such as exists at Willowbrook State School is to attempt to improve that situation, not to turn it to his advantage for experimental purposes, however lofty the aims.

Every new reference to the work of Krugman and Giles adds to its apparent ethical respectability, and in my view such references should stop, or at least be heavily qualified. The editorial attitude of *The Lancet* to the work should be reviewed and openly stated. The issue is too important to be ignored.

If Krugman and Giles are keen to continue their experiments I suggest that they invite the parents of the children involved to participate. I wonder what the response would be.

*Stephen Goldby*

Sir.—Dr. Stephen Goldby's critical comments about our Willowbrook studies and our motives for conducting them were published without extending us the courtesy of replying in the same issue of *The Lancet.* Your acceptance of his criticisms without benefit of our response implies a blackout of all comment related to our studies. This decision is unfortunate because our recent studies on active and passive immunization for the prevention of viral hepatitis, type B, have clearly demonstrated a "therapeutic effect" for the children involved. These studies have provided us with the first indication and hope that it may be possible to control hepatitis in this institution. If this aim can be achieved, it will benefit not only the children, but also their families and the employees who care for them in the school. It is unnecessary to point out the additional benefit to the worldwide populations which have been plagued by an insoluble hepatitis problem for many generations.

Dr. Joan Giles and I have been actively engaged in studies aimed to solve two infectious-disease prob-

lems in the Willowbrook State School—measles and viral hepatitis. These studies were investigated in this institution because they represented major health problems for the 5000 or more mentally retarded children who were residents. Uninformed critics have assumed or implied that we came to Willowbrook to "conduct experiments on mentally retarded children."

The results of our Willowbrook studies with the experimental live attenuated measles vaccine developed by Enders and his colleagues are well documented in the medical literature. As early as 1960 we demonstrated the protective effect of this vaccine during the course of an epidemic. Prior to licensure of the vaccine in 1963 epidemics occurred at two-year intervals in this institution. During the 1960 epidemic there were more than 600 cases of measles and 60 deaths. In the wake of our ongoing measles vaccine programme, measles has been eradicated as a disease in the Willowbrook State School. We have not had a single case of measles since 1963. In this regard the children at the Willowbrook State School have been more fortunate than unimmunized children in Oxford, England, other areas in Great Britain, as well as certain groups of children in the United States and other parts of the world.

The background of our hepatitis studies at Willowbrook has been described in detail in various publications. Viral hepatitis is so prevalent that newly admitted susceptible children become infected within 6 to 12 months after entry in the institution. These children are a source of infection for the personnel who care for them and for their families if they visit with them. We were convinced that the solution of the hepatitis problem in this institution was dependent on the acquisition of new knowledge leading to the development of an effective immunizing agent. The achievements with smallpox, diphtheria, poliomyelitis, and more recently measles represent dramatic illustrations of this approach.

It is well known that viral hepatitis in children is milder and more benign than the same disease in adults. Experience has revealed that hepatitis in institutionalized, mentally retarded children is also mild, in contrast with measles, which is a more severe disease when it occurs in institutional epidemics involving the mentally retarded. Our proposal to expose a small number of newly admitted children to the Willowbrook strains of hepatitis virus was justified in our opinion for the following reasons: (1) they were bound to be exposed to the same strains under the natural conditions existing in the institution; (2) they would be admitted to a special, well-equipped, and well-staffed unit where they would be isolated from exposure to other infectious diseases which were prevalent in the institution—namely, shigellosis, parasitic infections, and respiratory infections—thus, their exposure in the hepatitis unit would be associated with less risk than the type of institutional exposure where multiple infections could occur; (3) they were likely to have a subclinical infection followed by immunity to the particular hepatitis virus; and (4) only children with parents who gave informed consent would be included.

The statement by Dr. Goldby accusing us of conducting experiments exclusively for the acquisition of knowledge with no benefit for the children cannot be supported by the true facts.

*Saul Krugman*

SIR.—The experiments at Willowbrook raise two important issues: What constitutes valid consent, and do ends justify means? English law definitely forbids experimentation on children, even if both parents consent, unless done specifically in the interests of each individual child. Perhaps in the U.S.A. the law is not so clear-cut. According to Beecher, the parents of the children at Willowbrook were informed that, because of overcrowding, the institution was to be closed; but only a week or two later they were told that there would be vacancies in the "hepatitis unit" for children whose parents allowed them to form part of the hepatitis research study. Such consent, ethically if not legally, is invalid because of its element of coercion, some parents being desperately anxious to institutionalize their mentally defective children. Moreover, obtaining consent after talking to parents in groups, as described by Krugman, is extremely unsatisfactory because even a single enthusiast can sway the diffident who do not wish to appear churlish in front of their fellow citizens.

Do ends justify the means? Krugman maintains that any newly admitted children would inevitably have contracted infective hepatitis, which was rife in the hospital. But this ignores the statement by the head of the State Department of Mental Hygiene that, during the major part of the 15 years these experiments have been conducted, a gamma-globulin inoculation programme had already resulted in over an 80 percent reduction of that disease in that hospital. Krugman and Pasamanick claim that subsequent therapeutic effects justify these experiments. This attitude

is frequently adopted by experimenters and enthusiastic medical writers who wish us to forget completely how results are obtained but instead enjoy any benefits that may accrue. Immunization was not the purpose of these Willowbrook experiments but merely a by-product that incidentally proved beneficial to the victims. Any experiment is ethical or not at its inception, and does not become so because it achieved some measure of success in extending the frontiers of medicine. I particularly object strongly to the views of Willey, ". . . risk being assumed by the subjects of the experimentation balanced against the potential benefit to the subjects *and* [Willey's italics] to society in general." I believe that experimental physicians never have the right to select martyrs for society. Every human being has the right to be treated with decency, and that right must always supersede every consideration of what may benefit mankind, what may advance medical science, what may contribute to public welfare. No doctor is ever justified in placing society or science first and his obligation to patients second. Any claim to act for the good of society should be regarded with distaste because it may be merely a highflown expression to cloak outrageous acts.

*M. H. Pappworth*

SIR.—I am astonished at the unquestioning way in which *The Lancet* has accepted the intemperate position taken by Dr. Stephen Goldby concerning the experimental studies of Krugman and Giles on hepatitis at the Willowbrook State School. These investigators have repeatedly explained for over a decade that natural hepatitis infection occurs sooner or later in virtually 100% of the patients admitted to Willowbrook, and that it is better for the patient to have a known, timed, controlled infection than an untimed, uncontrolled one. Moreover, the wisdom and human justification of these studies have been repeatedly and carefully examined and verified by a number of very distinguished, able individuals who are respected leaders in the making of such decisions.

The real issue is: Is it not proper and ethical to carry out experiments in children, which would apparently incur no greater risk than the children were likely to run by nature, in which the children generally receive better medical care when artificially infected than if they had been naturally infected, and in which the parents as well as the physician feel that a significant contribution to the future well-being of similar children is likely to result from the studies? It is true, to be sure, that the W.M.A. code says, "Children in institutions and not under the care of relatives should not be the subjects of human experiments." But this unqualified *obiter dictum* may represent merely the well-known inability of committees to think a problem through. However, it has been thought through by Sir Austin Bradford Hill, who has pointed out the unfortunate effects for these very children that would have resulted, were such a code to have been applied over the years.

*Geoffrey Edsall*

## Judgment on Willowbrook

Paul Ramsey

Paul Ramsey reviews the justifications offered for the Willowbrook experiments presented by Krugman. Ramsey observes that there is nothing about hepatitis that requires that research be conducted on children, that no justification except the needs of the experiment is given for withholding gamma globulin from the subjects, and that nothing is said about attempting to control the low-grade epidemic by other means. Furthermore, Ramsey questions the morality of consent secured from the parents of the children. His basic recommendation is that the use of captive populations of children ought to be made legally impossible.

In 1958 and 1959 the *New England Journal of Medicine* reported a series of experiments performed upon patients and new admittees to the Willowbrook State School, a home for retarded children in Staten Island, New York.[1] These experiments were described as "an attempt to control the high prevalence of infectious hepatitis in an institution for mentally defective patients." The experiments were said to be justified because, under conditions of an existing uncontrolled outbreak of hepatitis in the institution, "knowledge obtained from a series of suitable studies could well lead to its control." In actuality, the experiments were designed to duplicate and confirm the efficacy of gamma globulin in immunization against hepatitis, to develop and improve or improve upon that inoculum, and to learn more about infectious hepatitis in general.

The experiments were justified—doubtless, after a great deal of soul searching—for the following reasons: there was a smoldering epidemic throughout the

institution and "it was apparent that most of the patients at Willowbrook were naturally exposed to hepatitis virus"; infectious hepatitis is a much milder disease in children; the strain at Willowbrook was especially mild; only the strain or strains of the virus already disseminated at Willowbrook were used; and only those small and incompetent patients whose parents gave consent were used.

The patient population at Willowbrook was 4478, growing at a rate of one patient a day over a three-year span, or from 10 to 15 new admissions per week. In the first trial the existing population was divided into two groups: one group served as uninoculated controls, and the other group was inoculated with 0.01 ml. of gamma globulin per pound of body weight. Then for a second trial new admittees and those left uninoculated before were again divided: one group served as uninoculated controls and the other was inoculated with 0.06 ml. of gamma globulin per pound of body weight. This proved that Stokes et al. had correctly demonstrated that the larger amount would give significant immunity for up to seven or eight months.[2]

Serious ethical questions may be raised about the trials so far described. No mention is made of any attempt to enlist the adult personnel of the institution,

Reprinted by permission of Yale University Press from *The Patient as Person* by Paul Ramsey. Copyright © 1970 by Yale University. Editor's Note: The footnotes in this article have been renumbered.

numbering nearly 1,000 including nearly 600 attendants on ward duty, and new additions to the staff, in these studies whose excusing reason was that almost everyone was "naturally" exposed to the Willowbrook virus. Nothing requires that major research into the natural history of hepatitis be first undertaken in children. Experiments have been carried out in the military and with prisoners as subjects. There have been fatalities from the experiments; but surely in all these cases the consent of the volunteers was as valid or better than the proxy consent of these children's "representatives." There would have been no question of the understanding consent that might have been given by the adult personnel at Willowbrook, if significant benefits were expected from studying that virus.

Second, nothing is said that would warrant withholding an inoculation of some degree of known efficacy from part of the population, or for withholding in the first trial less than the full amount of gamma globulin that had served to immunize in previous tests, except the need to test, confirm, and improve the inoculum. That, of course, was a desirable goal; but it does not seem possible to warrant withholding gamma globulin for the reason that is often said to justify controlled trials, namely, that one procedure is *as likely* to succeed as the other.

Third, nothing is said about attempts to control or defeat the low-grade epidemic at Willowbrook by more ordinary, if more costly and less experimental, procedures. Nor is anything said about admitting no more patients until this goal had been accomplished. This was not a massive urban hospital whose teeming population would have to be turned out into the streets, with resulting dangers to themselves and to public health, in order to sanitize the place. Instead, between 200 and 250 patients were housed in each of 18 buildings over approximately 400 acres in a semi-rural setting of fields, woods, and well-kept, spacious lawns. Clearly it would have been possible to secure other accommodation for new admissions away from the infection, while eradicating the infection at Willowbrook building by building. This might have cost money, and it would certainly have required astute detective work to discover the source of the infection. The doctors determined that the new patients likely were not carrying the infection upon admission, and that it did not arise from the procedures and routine inoculations given them at the time of admission. Why not go further in the search for the source of the epidemic? If this had been an orphanage for normal children or a floor of private patients, instead of a school

for mentally defective children, one wonders whether the doctors would so readily have accepted the hepatitis as a "natural" occurrence and even as an opportunity for study.

The next step was to attempt to induce "passive–active immunity" by feeding the virus to patients already protected by gamma globulin. In this attempt to improve the inoculum, permission was obtained from the parents of children from 5 to 10 years of age newly admitted to Willowbrook, who were then isolated from contact with the rest of the institution. All were inoculated with gamma globulin and then divided into two groups: one served as controls while the other group of new patients were fed the Willowbrook virus, obtained from feces, in doses having 50 percent infectivity, i.e., in concentrations estimated to produce hepatitis with jaundice in half the subjects tested. Then twice the 50 percent infectivity was tried. This proved, among other things, that hepatitis has an "alimentary-tract phase" in which it can be transmitted from one person to another while still "inapparent" in the first person. This, doubtless, is exceedingly important information in learning how to control epidemics of infectious hepatitis. The second of the two articles mentioned above describes studies of the incubation period of the virus and of whether pooled serum remained infectious when aged and frozen. Still the small, mentally defective patients who were deliberately fed infectious hepatitis are described as having suffered mildly in most cases: "The liver became enlarged in the majority, occasionally a week or two before the onset of jaundice. Vomiting and anorexia usually lasted only a few days. Most of the children gained weight during the course of hepatitis."

That mild description of what happened to the children who were fed hepatitis (and who continued to be introduced into the unaltered environment of Willowbrook) is itself alarming, since it is now definitely known that cirrhosis of the liver results from infectious hepatitis more frequently than from excessive consumption of alcohol! Now, or in 1958 and 1959, no one knows what may be other serious consequences of contracting infectious hepatitis. Understanding human volunteers were then and are now needed in the study of this disease, although a South American monkey has now successfully been given a form of hepatitis, and can henceforth serve as our ally in its conquest. But not children who cannot consent knowingly. If Peace Corps workers are regularly given gamma globulin before going abroad as a guard against their contracting hepatitis, and are inoculated at intervals thereafter, it seems that this is the least we should do for mentally defective children before they "go abroad" to Willowbrook or other institutions set up for their care.

Discussions pro and con of the Willowbrook experiments that have come to my attention serve only to reinforce the ethical objections that can be raised against what was done simply from a careful analysis of the original articles reporting the research design and findings. In an address at the 1968 Ross Conference on Pediatric Research, Dr. Saul Krugman raised the question, Should vaccine trials be carried out in adult volunteers before subjecting children to similar tests?[3] He answered this question in the negative. The reason adduced was simply that "a vaccine trial may be a more hazardous procedure for adults than for children." Medical researchers, of course, are required to minimize the hazards, but not by moving from consenting to unconsenting subjects. This apology clearly shows that adults and children have become interchangeable in face of the overriding importance of obtaining the research goal. This means that the special moral claims of children for care and protection are forgotten, and especially the claims of children who are most weak and vulnerable. (Krugman's reference to the measles vaccine trials is not to the point.)

The *Medical Tribune* explains that the 16-bed isolation unit set up at Willowbrook served "to protect the study subjects from Willowbrook's other endemic diseases—such as shigellosis, measles, rubella and respiratory and parasitic infections—while exposing them to hepatitis."[4] This presumably compensated for the infection they were given. It is not convincingly shown that the children could by no means, however costly, have been protected from the epidemic of hepatitis. The statement that Willowbrook "had endemic infectious hepatitis and a sufficiently open population so that the disease could never be quieted by exhausting the supply of susceptibles" is at best enigmatic.

Oddly, physicians defending the propriety of the Willowbrook hepatitis project soon began talking like poorly instructed "natural lawyers"! Dr. Louis Lasagna and Dr. Geoffrey Edsall, for example, find these experiments unobjectionable—both, for the reason stated by Edsall: "the children would apparently incur no greater risk than they were likely to run by nature." In any case, Edsall's example of parents consenting with a son 17 years of age for him to go to war, and society's agreements with minors that they can drive cars and hurt themselves were entirely beside the point. Dr. David D. Rutstein adheres to a stricter standard in regard to research on infectious hepatitis: "It is not ethical to use human subjects for the growth of a virus for any purpose."[5]

The latter sweeping verdict may depend on knowledge of the effects of viruses on chromosomal difficulties, mongolism, etc., that was not available to the Willowbrook group when their researches were begun thirteen years ago. If so, this is a telling point against appeal to "no discernible risks" as the sole standard applicable to the use of children in medical experimentation. That would lend support to the proposition that we always know that there are unknown and undiscerned risks in the case of an invasion of the fortress of the body—which then can be consented to by an adult in behalf of a child only if it is in the child's behalf medically.

When asked what she told the parents of the subject children at Willowbrook, Dr. Joan Giles replied, "I explain that there is no vaccine against infectious hepatitis. . . . I also tell them that we can modify the disease with gamma globulin but we can't provide lasting immunity without letting them get the disease."[6] Obviously vaccines giving "lasting immunity" are not the only kinds of vaccine to be used in caring for patients.

Doubtless the studies at Willowbrook resulted in improvement in the vaccine, to the benefit of present and future patients. In September 1966, "a routine program of GG [gamma globulin] administration to every new patient at Willowbrook" was begun. This cut the incidence of icteric hepatitis 80 to 85 percent. Then follows a significant statement in the *Medical Tribune* article: "A similar reduction in the icteric form of the disease has been accomplished among the employees, who began getting routine GG earlier in the study."[7] Not only did the research team (so far as these reports show) fail to consider and adopt the alternative that new admittees to the staff be asked to become volunteers for an investigation that might improve the vaccine against the strain of infectious hepatitis to which they as well as the children were exposed. Instead, the staff was routinely protected earlier than the inmates were! And, as we have seen, there was evidence from the beginning that gamma globulin provided at least some protection. A "modification" of the disease was still an inoculum, even if this provided no lasting immunization and had to be repeated. It is axiomatic to medical ethics that a known remedy or protection—even if not perfect or even if the best exact administration of it has not been proved—should not be withheld from individual patients. It seems to a layman that from the beginning various trials at immunization of all new admittees might have been made, and controlled observation made of their different degrees of effectiveness against "nature" at Willowbrook. This would doubtless have been a longer way round, namely, the "anecdotal" method of investigative treatment that comes off second best in comparison with controlled trials. Yet this seems to be the alternative dictated by our received medical ethics, and the only one expressive of minimal care of the primary patients themselves.

Finally, except for one episode, the obtaining of parental consent (on the premise that this is ethically valid) seems to have been very well handled. Wards of the state were not used, though by law the administrator at Willowbrook could have signed consent for them. Only new admittees whose parents were available were entered by proxy consent into the project. Explanation was made to groups of these parents, and they were given time to think about it and consult with their own family physicians. Then late in 1964 Willowbrook was closed to all new admissions because of overcrowding. What then happened can most impartially be described in the words of an article defending the Willowbrook project on medical and ethical grounds:

> Parents who applied for their children to get in were sent a form letter over Dr. Hammond's signature saying that there was no space for new admissions and that their name was being put on a waiting list.
>
> But the hepatitis program, occupying its own space in the institution, continued to admit new patients as each new study group began. "Where do you find new admissions except by canvassing the people who have applied for admission?" Dr. Hammond asked.
>
> So a new batch of form letters went out, saying that there were a few vacancies in the hepatitis research unit if the parents cared to consider volunteering their child for that. In some instances the second form letter apparently was received as closely as a week after the first letter arrived.[8]

Granting—as I do not—the validity of parental consent to research upon children not in their behalf medically, what sort of consent was that? Surely, the duress upon these parents with children so defective as to require institutionalization was far greater than the duress on prisoners given tobacco or paid or promised parole for their cooperation! I grant that the timing of these events was inadvertent. Since, however, ethics is a matter of criticizing institutions and not only of exculpating or making culprits of individ-

ual men, the inadvertence does not matter. This is the strongest possible argument for saying that even if parents have the right to consent to submit the children who are directly and continuously in their care to nonbeneficial medical experimentation, this should not be the rule of practice governing institutions set up for their care.

Such use of captive populations of children for purely experimental purposes ought to be made legally impossible. My view is that this should be stopped by legal acknowledgement of the moral invalidity of parental or legal proxy consent for the child to procedures having no relation to a child's own diagnosis or treatment. If this is not done, canons of loyalty require that the rule of practice (by law, or otherwise) be that children in institutions and not directly under the care of parents or relatives should *never* be used in medical investigations having present pain or discomfort and unknown present and future risks to them, and promising future possible benefits only for others.

### Notes

1.  Robert Ward, Saul Krugman, Joan P. Giles, A. Milton Jacobs, and Oscar Bodansky, "Infectious Hepatitis: Studies of Its Natural History and Prevention," *New England Journal of Medicine* 258, no. 9 (February 27, 1958): 407–16; Saul Krugman, Robert Ward, Joan P. Giles, Oscar Bodansky, and A. Milton Jacobs, "Infectious Hepatitis: Detection of the Virus during the Incubation Period and in Clinically Inapparent Infection," *New England Journal of Medicine* 261, no. 15 (October 8, 1959): 729–34. The following account and unannotated quotations are taken from these articles.

2.  J. Stokes, Jr., et al., "Infectious Hepatitis: Length of Protection by Immune Serum Globulin (Gamma Globulin) during Epidemics," *Journal of the American Medical Association* 147 (1951): 714–19. Since the half-life of gamma globulin is three weeks, no one knows exactly why it immunizes for so long a period. The "highly significant protection against hepatitis obtained by the use of gamma globulin," however, had been confirmed as early as 1945 (see Edward B. Grossman, Sloan G. Stewart, and Joseph Stokes, "Post-Transfusion Hepatitis in Battle Casualties," *Journal of the American Medical Association* 129, no. 15 [December 8, 1945]: 991–94). The inoculation *withheld* in the Willowbrook experiments had, therefore, proved valuable.

3.  Saul Krugman, "Reflections on Pediatric Clinical Investigations," in *Problems of Drug Evaluation in Infants and Children,* Report of the Fifty-eighth Ross Conference on Pediatric Research, Dorado Beach, Puerto Rico, May 5–7, 1968 (Columbus: Ross Laboratories), pp. 41–42.

4.  "Studies with Children Backed on Medical, Ethical Grounds," *Medical Tribune and Medical News* 8, no. 19 (February 20, 1967): 1, 23.

5.  *Daedalus,* Spring 1969, pp. 471–72, 529. See also pp. 458, 470–72. Since it is the proper business of an ethicist to uphold the proposition that only retrogression in civility can result from bad moral reasoning and the use of inept examples, however innocent, it is fair to point out the startling comparison between Edsall's "argument" and the statement of Dr. Karl Brandt, plenipotentiary in charge of all medical activities in the Nazi Reich: "Do you think that one can obtain any worthwhile, funda-

mental results without a definite toll of lives? The same goes for technological development. You cannot build a great bridge, a gigantic building—you cannot establish a speed record without deaths!" (quoted by Leo Alexander, "War Crimes: Their Social-Psychological Aspects," *American Journal of Psychiatry* 105, no. 3 [September 1948]: 172). Casualties to progress, or injuries ac-

cepted in setting speed limits, are morally quite different from death or maiming or even only risks, or unknown risks, directly and deliberately imposed upon an unconsenting human being.

6.   *Medical Tribune,* February 20, 1967, p. 23.

7.   *Medical Tribune,* February 20, 1967, p. 23.

8.   *Medical Tribune,* February 20, 1967, p. 23.

# Principles of the Nuremberg Code

1.   The voluntary consent of the human subject is absolutely essential.

   This means that the person involved should have legal capacity to give consent; should be so situated as to be able to exercise free power of choice, without the intervention of any element of force, fraud, deceit, duress, over-reaching, or other ulterior form of constraint or coercion; and should have sufficient knowledge and comprehension of the elements of the subject matter involved as to enable him to make an understanding and enlightened decision. This latter element requires that before the acceptance of an affirmative decision by the experimental subject there should be made known to him the nature, duration, and purpose of the experiment; the method and means by which it is to be conducted; all inconveniences and hazards reasonably to be expected; and the effects upon his health or person which may possibly come from his participation in the experiment.

   The duty and responsibility for ascertaining the quality of the consent rests upon each individual who initiates, directs or engages in the experiment. It is a personal duty and responsibility which may not be delegated to another with impunity.

2.   The experiment should be such as to yield fruitful results for the good of society, unprocurable by other methods or means of study, and not random and unnecessary in nature.

3.   The experiment should be so designed and based on the results of animal experimentation and a knowledge of the natural history of the disease or

other problem under study that the anticipated results will justify the performance of the experiment.

4.   The experiment should be so conducted as to avoid all unnecessary physical and mental suffering and injury.

5.   No experiment should be conducted where there is an *a priori* reason to believe that death or disabling injury will occur; except, perhaps, in those experiments where the experimental physicians also serve as subjects.

6.   The degree of risk to be taken should never exceed that determined by the humanitarian importance of the problem to be solved by the experiment.

7.   Proper preparations should be made and adequate facilities provided to protect the experimental subject against even remote possibilities of injury, disability, or death.

8.   The experiment should be conducted only by scientifically qualified persons. The highest degree of skill and care should be required through all stages of the experiment of those who conduct or engage in the experiment.

9.   During the course of the experiment the human subject should be at liberty to bring the experiment to an end if he has reached the physical or mental state where continuation of the experiment seems to him to be impossible.

10.   During the course of the experiment the scientist in charge must be prepared to terminate the experiment at any stage, if he has probable cause to believe, in the exercise of the good faith, superior skill and careful judgment required of him that a continuation of the experiment is likely to result in injury, disability, or death to the experimental subject.

From "Permissible Medical Experiments," *Trials of War Criminals Before the Nuremberg Military Tribunals Under Control Council Law No. 10: Nuremberg, October 1946–April 1949* (Washington: Government Printing Office, n.d., vol. 2), 181–182.

# Section 2: The Ethics of Randomized Clinical Trials

## Of Mice but Not Men: Problems of the Randomized Clinical Trial

### Samuel Hellman and Deborah S. Hellman

Samuel and Deborah Hellman show how randomized clinical trials (RCTs) in medicine may create an ethical dilemma for the physician who is also acting as a scientist. A physician is committed to seeing to the interest of an individual patient, while a scientist may have to sacrifice the interest of present patients to benefit future ones, thus undermining the physician–patient relationship.

The Hellmans reject a utilitarian justification for sacrificing the interest of the individual for the benefit of future patients. They argue that the physician–patient relationship implies that patients have a right to receive a physician's best judgment and care and that physicians have a duty to provide them. The methods typically used in an RCT may require a physician to violate this duty by remaining ignorant of whether a patient is receiving the best therapy available or by continuing to use a therapy after it is believed to be of less worth than an alternative.

The Hellmans conclude by sketching ways in which the problems of observer bias and patient selection, currently solved by using RCTs, may be overcome without violating the rights inherent in the physician–patient relationship.

As medicine has become increasingly scientific and less accepting of unsupported opinion or proof by anecdote, the randomized controlled clinical trial has become the standard technique for changing diagnostic or therapeutic methods. The use of this technique creates an ethical dilemma.[1,2] Researchers participating in such studies are required to modify their ethical commitments to individual patients and do serious damage to the concept of the physician as a practicing, empathetic professional who is primarily concerned with each patient as an individual. Researchers using a randomized clinical trial can be described as physician-scientists, a term that expresses the tension between the two roles. The physician, by entering into a relationship with an individual patient, assumes certain obligations, including the commitment always to act in the patient's best interests. As Leon Kass has rightly maintained, "the physician must produce unswervingly the virtues of loyalty and fidelity to his patient."[3] Though the ethical requirements of this relationship

From the *New England Journal of Medicine,* Vol. 324, no. 22 (1991), pp. 1585–1589.

have been modified by legal obligations to report wounds of a suspicious nature and certain infectious diseases, these obligations in no way conflict with the central ethical obligation to act in the best interests of the patient medically. Instead, certain nonmedical interests of the patient are preempted by other social concerns.

The role of the scientist is quite different. The clinical scientist is concerned with answering questions—i.e., determining the validity of formally constructed hypotheses. Such scientific information, it is presumed, will benefit humanity in general. The clinical scientist's role has been well described by Dr. Anthony Fauci, director of the National Institute of Allergy and Infectious Diseases, who states the goals of the randomized clinical trial in these words: "It's not to deliver therapy. It's to answer a scientific question so that the drug can be available for everybody once you've established safety and efficacy."[4] The demands of such a study can conflict in a number of ways with the physician's duty to minister to patients. The study may create a false dichotomy in the physician's opinions: according to the premise of the randomized clinical trial, the physician may only know or not know whether a proposed course of treatment represents an improvement; no middle position is permitted. What the physician thinks, suspects, believes, or has a hunch about is assigned to the "not knowing" category, because knowing is defined on the basis of an arbitrary but accepted statistical test performed in a randomized clinical trial. Thus, little credence is given to information gained beforehand in other ways or to information accrued during the trial but without the required statistical degree of assurance that a difference is not due to chance. The randomized clinical trial also prevents the treatment technique from being modified on the basis of the growing knowledge of the physicians during their participation in the trial. Moreover, it limits access to the data as they are collected until specific milestones are achieved. This prevents physicians from profiting not only from their individual experience, but also from the collective experience of the other participants.

The randomized clinical trial requires doctors to act simultaneously as physicians and as scientists. This puts them in a difficult and sometimes untenable ethical position. The conflicting moral demands arising from the use of the randomized clinical trial reflect the classic conflict between rights-based moral theories and utilitarian ones. The first of these, which depend on the moral theory of Immanuel Kant (and seen more recently in neo-Kantian philosophers, such as John Rawls[5]), asserts that human beings, by virtue of their unique capacity for rational thought, are bearers of dignity. As such, they ought not to be treated merely as means to an end; rather, they must always be treated as ends in themselves. Utilitarianism, by contrast, defines what is right as the greatest good for the greatest number—that is, as social utility. This view, articulated by Jeremy Bentham and John Stuart Mill, requires that pleasures (understood broadly, to include such pleasures as health and well-being) and pains be added together. The morally correct act is the act that produces the most pleasure and the least pain overall.

A classic objection to the utilitarian position is that according to that theory, the distribution of pleasures and pains is of no moral consequence. This element of the theory severely restricts physicians from being utilitarians, or at least from following the theory's dictates. Physicians must care very deeply about the distribution of pain and pleasure, for they have entered into a relationship with one or a number of individual patients. They cannot be indifferent to whether it is these patients or others that suffer for the general benefit of society. Even though society might gain from the suffering of a few, and even though the doctor might believe that such a benefit is worth a given patient's suffering (i.e., that utilitarianism is right in the particular case), the ethical obligation created by the covenant between doctor and patient requires the doctor to see the interests of the individual patient as primary and compelling. In essence, the doctor–patient relationship requires doctors to see their patients as bearers of rights who cannot be merely used for the greater good of humanity.

As Fauci has suggested,[4] the randomized clinical trial routinely asks physicians to sacrifice the interests of their particular patients for the sake of the study and that of the information that it will make available for the benefit of society. This practice is ethically problematic. Consider first the initial formulation of a trial. In particular, consider the case of a disease for which there is no satisfactory therapy—for example, advanced cancer or the acquired immunodeficiency syndrome (AIDS). A new agent that promises more effectiveness is the subject of the study. The control group must be given either an unsatisfactory treatment or a placebo. Even though the therapeutic value of the new agent is unproved, if physicians think that it has promise, are they acting in the best interests of their patients in allowing them to be randomly assigned to the control group? Is persisting in such an assignment consistent with the specific commitments taken on in the doctor–patient relationship? As a result of interactions with patients with AIDS and their advocates, Merigan[6] recently suggested modifications in the design of clinical trials that attempt to deal with the unsatisfactory treatment given to the control group. The view of such activists has been expressed by Rebecca Pringle Smith of Community Research Initiative in New York. "Even if you have a supply of compliant martyrs, trials must have some ethical validity."[4]

If the physician has no opinion about whether the new treatment is acceptable, then random assignment is ethically acceptable, but such lack of enthusiasm for the new treatment does not augur well for either the patient or the study. Alternatively, the treatment may show promise of beneficial results but also present a risk of undesirable complications. When the physician believes that the severity and likelihood of harm and good are evenly balanced, randomization may be ethically acceptable. If the physician has no preference for either treatment (is in a state of equipoise[7, 8]), then randomization is acceptable. If, however, he or she believes that the new treatment may be either more or less successful or more or less toxic, the use of randomization is not consistent with fidelity to the patient.

The argument usually used to justify randomization is that it provides, in essence, a critique of the usefulness of the physician's beliefs and opinions, those that have not yet been validated by a randomized clinical trial. As the argument goes, these not-yet-validated beliefs are as likely to be wrong as right. Although physicians are ethically required to provide their patients with the best available treatment, there simply is no best treatment yet known.

The reply to this argument takes two forms. First, and most important, even if this view of the reliability of a physician's opinions is accurate, the ethical constraints of an individual doctor's relationship with a particular patient require the doctor to provide individual care. Although physicians must take pains to make clear the speculative nature of their views, they cannot withhold these views from the patient. The patient asks from the doctor both knowledge and judgment. The relationship established between them rightfully allows patients to ask for the judgment of their particular physicians, not merely that of the medical profession in general. Second, it may not be true, in fact, that the not-yet-validated beliefs of physicians are as likely to be wrong as right. The greater certainty obtained with a randomized clinical trial is beneficial, but that does not mean that a lesser degree of certainty is without value. Physicians can acquire knowledge through methods other than the randomized clinical trial. Such knowledge, acquired over time and less formally than is required in a randomized clinical trial, may be of great value to a patient.

Even if it is ethically acceptable to begin a study, one often forms an opinion during its course—especially in studies that are impossible to conduct in a truly double-blinded fashion—that makes it ethically problematic to continue. The inability to remain blinded usually occurs in studies of cancer or AIDS, for example, because the therapy is associated by nature with serious side effects. Trials attempt to restrict the physician's access to the data in order to prevent such unblinding. Such restrictions should make physicians eschew the trial, since their ability to act in the patient's best interests will be limited. Even supporters of randomized clinical trials, such as Merigan, agree that interim findings should be presented to patients to ensure that no one receives what seems an inferior treatment.[6] Once physicians have formed a view about the new treatment, can they continue randomization? If random assignment is stopped, the study may be lost and the participation of the previous patients wasted. However, if physicians continue the randomization when they have a definite opinion about the efficacy of the experimental drug, they are not acting in accordance with the requirements of the doctor–patient relationship. Furthermore, as their opinion becomes more firm, stopping the randomization may not be enough. Physicians may be ethically required to treat the patients formerly placed in the control group with the therapy that now seems probably effective. To do so would be faithful to the obligations created by the doctor–patient relationship, but it would destroy the study.

To resolve this dilemma, one might suggest that the patient has abrogated the rights implicit in a doctor–patient relationship by signing an informed-consent form. We argue that such rights cannot be waived or abrogated. They are inalienable. The right to be treated as an individual deserving the physician's best judgment and care, rather than to be used as a means to determine the best treatment for others, is inherent in every person. This right, based on the concept of dignity, cannot be waived. What of altruism, then? Is it not the patient's right to make a sacrifice for the general good? This question must be considered from both positions—that of the patient and that of the physician. Although patients may decide to waive this right, it is not consistent with the role of a physician to ask that they do so. In asking, the doctor acts as a scientist instead. The physician's role here is to propose what he or she believes is best medically for the specific patient, not to suggest participation in a study from which the patient cannot gain. Because the opportunity to help future patients is of potential value to a patient, some would say physicians should not deny it. Although this point has merit, it offers so many opportunities for abuse that we are extremely uncomfortable about accepting it. The responsibilities of physicians are much clearer; they are to minister to the current patient.

Moreover, even if patients could waive this right, it is questionable whether those with terminal illness would be truly able to give voluntary informed consent. Such patients are extremely dependent on both their physicians and the health care system. Aware of this dependence, physicians must not ask for consent, for in such cases the very asking breaches the doctor–patient relationship. Anxious to please their physicians, patients may have difficulty refusing to participate in the trial the physicians describe. The patients may perceive their refusal as damaging to the relationship, whether or not it is so. Such perceptions of coercion affect the decision. Informed-consent forms are difficult to understand, especially for patients under the stress of serious illness for which there is no satisfactory treatment. The forms are usually lengthy, somewhat legalistic, complicated, and confusing, and they hardly bespeak the compassion expected of the medical profession. It is important to remember that those who have studied the doctor–patient relationship have emphasized its empathetic nature.

> [The] relationship between doctor and patient partakes of a peculiar intimacy. It presupposes on the part of the physician not only knowledge of his fellow men but sympathy. . . . This aspect of the practice of medicine has been designated as the art; yet I wonder whether it should not, most properly, be called the essence.[9]

How is such a view of the relationship consonant with random assignment and informed consent? The Physician's Oath of the World Medical Association affirms the primacy of the deontologic view of patients' rights: "Concern for the interests of the subject must always prevail over the interests of science and society."[10]

Furthermore, a single study is often not considered sufficient. Before a new form of therapy is generally accepted, confirmatory trials must be conducted. How can one conduct such trials ethically unless one is convinced that the first trial was in error? The ethical problems we have discussed are only exacerbated when a completed randomized clinical trial indicates that a given treatment is preferable. Even if the physician believes the initial trial was in error, the physician must indicate to the patient the full results of that trial.

The most common reply to the ethical arguments has been that the alternative is to return to the physician's intuition, to anecdotes, or to both as the basis of medical opinion. We all accept the dangers of such a practice. The argument states that we must therefore accept randomized, controlled clinical trials regardless of their ethical problems because of the great social benefit they make possible, and we salve our conscience with the knowledge that informed consent has been given. This returns us to the conflict between patients' rights and social utility. Some would argue that this tension can be resolved by placing a relative value on each. If the patient's right that is being compromised is not a fundamental right and the social gain is very great, then the study might be justified. When the

right is fundamental, however, no amount of social gain, or almost none, will justify its sacrifice. Consider, for example, the experiments on humans done by physicians under the Nazi regime. All would agree that these are unacceptable regardless of the value of the scientific information gained. Some people go so far as to say that no use should be made of the results of those experiments because of the clearly unethical manner in which the data were collected. This extreme example may not seem relevant, but we believe that in its hyperbole it clarifies the fallacy of a utilitarian approach to the physician's relationship with the patient. To consider the utilitarian gain is consistent neither with the physician's role nor with the patient's rights.

It is fallacious to suggest that only the randomized clinical trial can provide valid information or that all information acquired by this technique is valid. Such experimental methods are intended to reduce error and bias and therefore reduce the uncertainty of the result. Uncertainty cannot be eliminated, however. The scientific method is based on increasing probabilities and increasingly refined approximations of truth.[11] Although the randomized clinical trial contributes to these ends, it is neither unique nor perfect. Other techniques may also be useful.[12]

Randomized trials often place physicians in the ethically intolerable position of choosing between the good of the patient and that of society. We urge that such situations be avoided and that other techniques of acquiring clinical information be adopted. For example, concerning trials of treatments for AIDS, Byar et al.[13] have said that "some traditional approaches to the clinical-trials process may be unnecessarily rigid and unsuitable for this disease." In this case, AIDS is not what is so different; rather, the difference is in the presence of AIDS activists, articulate spokespersons for the ethical problems created by the application of the randomized clinical trial to terminal illnesses. Such arguments are equally applicable to advanced cancer and other serious illnesses. Byar et al. agree that there are even circumstances in which uncontrolled clinical trials may be justified: when there is no effective treatment to use as a control, when the prognosis is uniformly poor, and when there is a reasonable expectation of benefit without excessive toxicity. These conditions are usually found in clinical trials of advanced cancer.

The purpose of the randomized clinical trial is to avoid the problems of observer bias and patient selection. It seems to us that techniques might be developed to deal with these issues in other ways.

Randomized clinical trials deal with them in a cumbersome and heavy-handed manner, by requiring large numbers of patients in the hope that random assignment will balance the heterogeneous distribution of patients into the different groups. By observing known characteristics of patients, such as age and sex, and distributing them equally between groups, it is thought that unknown factors important in determining outcomes will also be distributed equally. Surely, other techniques can be developed to deal with both observer bias and patient selection. Prospective studies without randomization, but with the evaluation of patients by uninvolved third parties, should remove observer bias. Similar methods have been suggested by Royall.[12] Prospective matched-pair analysis, in which patients are treated in a manner consistent with their physician's views, ought to help ensure equivalence between the groups and thus mitigate the effect of patient selection, at least with regard to known covariates. With regard to unknown covariates, the security would rest, as in randomized trials, in the enrollment of large numbers of patients and in confirmatory studies. This method would not pose ethical difficulties, since patients would receive the treatment recommended by their physician. They would be included in the study by independent observers matching patients with respect to known characteristics, a process that would not affect patient care and that could be performed independently any number of times.

This brief discussion of alternatives to randomized clinical trials is sketchy and incomplete. We wish only to point out that there may be satisfactory alternatives, not to describe and evaluate them completely. Even if randomized clinical trials were much better than any alternative, however, the ethical dilemmas they present may put their use at variance with the primary obligations of the physician. In this regard, Angell cautions, "If this commitment to the patient is attenuated, even for so good a cause as benefits to future patients, the implicit assumptions of the doctor–patient relationship are violated."[14] The risk of such attenuation by the randomized trial is great. The AIDS activists have brought this dramatically to the attention of the academic medical community. Techniques appropriate to the laboratory may not be applicable to humans. We must develop and use alternative methods for acquiring clinical knowledge.

### Notes

1. Hellman S. Randomized clinical trials and the doctor–patient relationship: an ethical dilemma. *Cancer Clin Trials* 1979: 2: 189–93.

2. *Idem.* A doctor's dilemma: the doctor–patient relationship in clinical investigation. In: Proceedings of the Fourth National Conference on Human Values and Cancer. New York, March 15–17, 1984. New York: American Cancer Society, 1984: 144–6.

3. Kass LR. *Toward a more natural science: biology and human affairs.* New York: Free Press, 1985: 196.

4. Palca J. AIDS drug trials enter new age. *Science* 1989: 246: 19–21.

5. Rawls J. *A theory of justice.* Cambridge, Mass.: Belknap Press of Harvard University Press, 1971: 183–92, 446–52.

6. Merigan TC. You *can* teach an old dog new tricks—how AIDS trials are pioneering new strategies. *N Engl J Med* 1990: 323: 1341–3.

7. Freedman B. Equipoise and the ethics of clinical research. *N Engl J Med* 1987: 317: 141–5.

8. Singer PA, Lantos JD, Whitington PF, Broelsch CE, Siegler M. Equipoise and the ethics of segmental liver transplantation. *Clin Res* 1988: 36: 539–45.

9. Longcope WT. Methods and medicine. *Bull Johns Hopkins Hosp* 1932: 50: 4–20.

10. Report on medical ethics. *World Med Assoc Bull* 1949: 1: 109, 111.

11. Popper K. The problem of induction. In: Miller D, ed. *Popper selections.* Princeton, N.J.: Princeton University Press, 1985: 101–17.

12. Royall RM. Ethics and statistics in randomized clinical trials. *Stat Sci* 1991: 6(1): 52–62.

13. Byar DP, Schoenfeld DA, Green SB, et al. Design considerations for AIDS trials. *N Engl J Med* 1990: 323: 1343–8.

14. Angell M. Patients' preferences in randomized clinical trials. *N Engl J Med* 1984: 310: 1385–7.

# Clinical Trials: Are They Ethical?

## Eugene Passamani

Eugene Passamani argues that randomized clinical trials (RCTs) are the most reliable means of evaluating new therapies. Without RCTs, chance and bias may affect our conclusions.

Passamani rejects the argument that the physician–patient relationship demands that physicians recommend the "best" therapy for patients, no matter how poor the data on which the recommendation is based. He acknowledges that

RCTs pose ethical problems for physician-researchers but believes the difficulties can be overcome by employing three procedural safeguards.

First, all participants must give their informed consent. They must be told about the goals of the research and its potential benefits and risks. Moreover, they must be informed about alternatives to their participation, and they must be permitted to withdraw from the trial at any time they choose.

Second, for an RCT to be legitimate, a state of clinical *equipoise* must exist. Competent physicians must be genuinely uncertain about which of the alternative therapies in the trial is superior and content to allow their patients to be treated with any of them.

Finally, the clinical trial must be designed as a critical test of the therapeutic alternatives.

Properly carried out, Passamani holds, RCTs protect physicians and patients from therapies that are ineffective or toxic.

[A type I error consists in deciding that therapy A is better than therapy B, when, in fact, both are of equal worth (i.e., a true null hypothesis is rejected). A type II error consists in deciding that the treatments are equally good, when A is actually better than B (i.e., a false null hypothesis is accepted).—ED.]

Biomedical research leads to better understanding of biology and ultimately to improved health. Physicians have for millenniums attempted to understand disease, to use this knowledge to cure or palliate, and to relieve attendant suffering. Improving strategies for prevention and treatment remains an ethical imperative for medicine. Until very recently, progress depended largely on a process of carefully observing groups of patients given a new and promising therapy; outcome was then compared with that previously observed in groups undergoing a standard treatment. Outcome in a series of case patients as compared with that in nonrandomized controls can be used to assess the treatment of disorders in which therapeutic effects are dramatic and the pathophysiologic features are relatively uncomplicated, such as vitamin deficiency or some infectious diseases. Observational methods are not very useful, however, in the detection of small treatment effects in disorders in which there is substantial variability in expected outcome and imperfect knowledge of complicated pathophysiologic features (many vascular disorders and most cancers, for example). The effect of a treatment cannot easily be extracted from variations in disease severity and the effects of concomitant treatments. Clinical trials have thus become a preferred means of evaluating an ever increasing flow of innovative diagnostic and therapeu-

tic maneuvers. The randomized, double-blind clinical trial is a powerful technique because of the efficiency and credibility associated with treatment comparisons involving randomized concurrent controls.

The modern era of randomized trials began in the early 1950s with the evaluation of streptomycin in patients with tuberculosis.[1] Since that time trial techniques and methods have continuously been refined.[2] In addition, the ethical aspects of these experiments in patients have been actively discussed.[3-7]

In what follows I argue that randomized trials are in fact the most scientifically sound and ethically correct means of evaluating new therapies. There is potential conflict between the roles of physician and physician-scientist, and for this reason society has created mechanisms to ensure that the interests of individual patients are served should they elect to participate in a clinical trial.[6]

### Clinical Research

The history of medicine is richly endowed with therapies that were widely used and then shown to be ineffective or frankly toxic. Relatively recent examples of such therapeutic maneuvers include gastric freezing for peptic ulcer disease, radiation therapy for acne, MER-29 (triparanol) for cholesterol reduction, and thalidomide for sedation in pregnant women. The 19th century was even more gruesome, with purging and bloodletting. The reasons for this march of folly

From the *New England Journal of Medicine,* Vol. 324, no. 22 (1991), pp. 1589–1591. Reprinted by permission.

are many and include, perhaps most importantly, the lack of complete understanding of human biology and pathophysiology, the use of observational methods coupled with the failure to appreciate substantial variability between patients in their response to illness and to therapy, and the shared desire of physicians and their patients for cure or palliation.

Chance or bias can result in the selection of patients for innovative treatment who are either the least diseased or the most severely affected. Depending on the case mix, a treatment that has no effect can appear to be effective or toxic when historical controls are used. With the improvement in diagnostic accuracy and the understanding of disease that has occurred with the passage of time, today's patients are identified earlier in the natural history of their disease. Recently selected case series therefore often have patients who are less ill and an outcome that is considerably better than that of past case series, even without changes in treatment.

Randomization tends to produce treatment and control groups that are evenly balanced in both known and unrecognized prognostic factors, which permits a more accurate estimate of treatment effect in groups of patients assigned to experimental and standard therapies. A number of independent randomized trials with congruent results are powerful evidence indeed.

A physician's daily practice includes an array of preventive, diagnostic, and therapeutic maneuvers, some of which have been established by a plausible biologic mechanism and substantial evidence from randomized clinical trials (e.g., the use of beta-blockers, thrombolytic therapy, and aspirin in patients with myocardial infarction).[8] It is unlikely that our distant descendants in medicine will discover that we late-20th-century physicians were wrong in these matters. However, new therapeutic maneuvers that have not undergone rigorous assessment may well turn out to be ineffective or toxic. Every therapy adopted by common consent on the basis of observational studies and plausible mechanism, but without the benefit of randomized studies, may be categorized by future physicians as useless or worse. Physicians are aware of the fragility of the evidence supporting many common therapies, and this is why properly performed randomized clinical trials have profound effects on medical practice. The scientific importance of randomized, controlled trials is in safeguarding current and future patients from our therapeutic passions. Most physicians recognize this fact.

Like any human activity, experimentation involving patients can be performed in an unethical and even criminal fashion. Nazi war crimes led to substantial efforts to curb abuse, beginning with the Nuremberg Code and the Helsinki Declaration and culminating in the promulgation of clearly articulated regulations in the United States and elsewhere.[4-6] There are abuses more subtle than those of the Gestapo and the SS. Involving patients in experiments that are poorly conceived and poorly executed is unethical. Patients who participate in such research may incur risk without the hope of contributing to a body of knowledge that will benefit them or others in the future. The regulations governing human experimentation are very important, as is continuing discussion and debate to improve the scientific and ethical aspects of this effort.

Several general features must be part of properly designed trials. The first is informed consent, which involves explicitly informing a potential participant of the goals of the research, its potential benefits and risks, the alternatives to participating, and the right to withdraw from the trial at any time. Whether informed consent is required in all trials has been debated.[9] I believe that patients must always be aware that they are part of an experiment. Second, a state of clinical equipoise must exist. Clinical equipoise means that on the basis of the available data, a community of competent physicians would be content to have their patients pursue any of the treatment strategies being tested in a randomized trial, since none of them have been clearly established as preferable.[7] The chief purpose of a data-monitoring committee is to stop the trial if the accumulating data destroy the state of clinical equipoise—that is, indicate efficacy or suggest toxicity. Finally, the trial must be designed as a critical test of the therapeutic alternatives being assessed. The question must be clearly articulated, with carefully defined measures of outcome; with realistic estimates of sample size, including probable event rates in the control group and a postulated and plausible reduction in the event rates in the treatment group; with Type I and II errors specified; and with subgroup hypotheses clearly stated if appropriate. The trial must have a good chance of settling an open question.[2]

## Ethical Dimensions of Properly Constituted Trials

Experimentation in the clinic by means of randomized, controlled clinical trials has been periodically attacked as violating the covenant between doctor and patient.[10–12] Critics have charged that physicians engaged in clinical trials sacrifice the interests of the patient they ask to participate to the good of all similarly affected patients in the future. The argument is that physicians have a personal obligation to use their best judgment and recommend the "best" therapy, no matter how tentative or inconclusive the data on which that judgment is based. Physicians must play their hunches. According to this argument, randomized clinical trials may be useful in seeking the truth, but carefully designed, legitimate trials are unethical and perhaps even criminal because they prevent individual physicians from playing their hunches about individual patients. Therefore, it is argued, physicians should not participate in such trials.

It is surely unethical for physicians to engage knowingly in an activity that will result in inferior therapy for their patients. It is also important that the community of physicians be clear in distinguishing between established therapies and those that are promising but unproved. It is this gulf between proved therapies and possibly effective therapies (all the rest) that defines the ethical and unethical uses of randomized clinical trials. Proved therapies involve a consensus of the competent medical community that the data in hand justify using a treatment in a given disorder. It is this consensus that defines an ethical boundary. The physician–investigator who asks a patient to participate in a randomized, controlled trial represents this competent medical community in asserting that the community is unpersuaded by existing data that an innovative treatment is superior to standard therapy. Arguments that a physician who believes that such a treatment *might be* useful commits an unethical act by randomizing patients are simply wrong. Given the history of promising but discarded therapies, hunches about potential effectiveness are not the ideal currency of the patient–doctor interchange.

Lest readers conclude that modern hunches are more accurate than older ones, I have selected an example from the current cardiovascular literature that reveals the problems inherent in relying on hunches to the exclusion of carefully done experiments.

## The Cardiac Arrhythmia Suppression Trial

Sudden death occurs in approximately 300,000 persons in the United States each year and is thus a problem worthy of our best efforts. In the vast majority of cases the mechanism is ventricular fibrillation superimposed on a scarred or ischemic myocardium. It had been observed that the ventricular extrasystoles seen on the ambulatory electrocardiographic recordings of survivors of myocardial infarction were independently and reproducibly associated with an increased incidence of subsequent mortality.[13, 14] It had been established that a variety of antiarrhythmic drugs can suppress ventricular extrasystoles. Accordingly, physicians had the hunch that suppressing ventricular extrasystoles in the survivors of myocardial infarction would reduce the incidence of ventricular fibrillation and sudden death.

The Cardiac Arrhythmia Suppression Trial (CAST) investigators decided to test this hypothesis in a randomized, controlled trial. They sought survivors of myocardial infarction who had frequent extrasystoles on electrocardiographic recordings. The trial design included a run-in period during which one of three active drugs was administered and its effect on extrasystoles noted. Those in whom arrhythmias were suppressed were randomly assigned to active drug or placebo. The trial had to be stopped prematurely because of an unacceptable incidence of sudden death in the treatment group.[15] During an average follow-up of 10 months, 56 of 730 patients (7.7 percent) assigned to active drug and 22 of 725 patient (3.0 percent) assigned to placebo died. Clinical equipoise was destroyed by this striking effect. It is quite unlikely that observational (nonrandomized) methods would have detected this presumably toxic effect.

The CAST trial was a major advance in the treatment of patients with coronary disease and ventricular arrhythmia. It clearly revealed that the hunches of many physicians were incorrect. The trial's results are applicable not only to future patients with coronary disease and ventricular arrhythmia but also to the patients who participated in the study. By randomizing, investigators ensured that half the participants received the better therapy—in this case placebo—and, contrary to intuition, most of them ultimately received the better therapy after the trial ended prematurely and drugs were withdrawn.

To summarize, randomized clinical trials are an important element in the spectrum of biomedical research. Not all questions can or should be addressed by this technique; feasibility, cost, and the relative importance of the issues to be addressed are weighed by investigators before they elect to proceed. Properly carried out, with informed consent, clinical equipoise, and a design adequate to answer the question posed, randomized clinical trials protect physicians and their patients from therapies that are ineffective or toxic. Physicians and their patients must be clear about the vast gulf separating promising and proved therapies. The only reliable way to make this distinction in the face of incomplete information about pathophysiology and treatment mechanism is to experiment, and this will increasingly involve randomized trials. The alternative—a retreat to older methods—is unacceptable.

Physicians regularly apply therapies tested in groups of patients to an individual patient. The likelihood of success in an individual patient depends on the degree of certainty evident in the group and the scientific strength of the methods used. We owe patients involved in the assessment of new therapies the best that science and ethics can deliver. Today, for most unproved treatments, that is a properly performed randomized clinical trial.

### Notes

1. Streptomycin in Tuberculosis Trials Committee, Medical Research Council. Streptomycin treatment of pulmonary tuberculosis: a Medical Research Council investigation. *BMJ* 1948: 2: 769–82.

2. Friedman LM, Furberg CD, DeMets DL. *Fundamentals of clinical trials.* Boston: John Wright/PSG, 1981.

3. Beecher HK. Ethics and clinical research. *N Engl J Med* 1966: 274: 1354–60.

4. Appendix II (The Nuremberg Code). In: Beauchamp TL, Childress JF. *Principles of biomedical ethics.* New York: Oxford University Press, 1979: 287–9.

5. Appendix II (The World Medical Association Declaration of Helsinki). In: Beauchamp TL, Childress JF. *Principles of biomedical ethics.* New York: Oxford University Press, 1979: 289–93.

6. The National Commission for the Protection of Human Subjects of Biomedical and Behavioral Research. The Belmont report: ethical principles and guidelines for the protection of human subjects of research. Washington, D.C.: Government Printing Office, 1978. (DHEW publication no. (05) 78-0012.)

7. Freedman B. Equipoise and the ethics of clinical research. *N Engl J Med* 1987: 317: 141–5.

8. Yusuf S, Wittes J, Friedman L. Overview of results of randomized clinical trials in heart disease. I. Treatments following myocardial infarction. *JAMA* 1988: 260: 2088–93.

9. Brahams D. Randomized trials and informed consent. *Lancet* 1988: 1033–4.

10. Burkhardt R, Kienle G. Controlled clinical trials and medical ethics. *Lancet* 1978: 2: 1356–9.

11. Marquis D. Leaving therapy to chance. *Hastings Cent Rep* 1983: 13(4): 40–7.

12. Gifford F. The conflict between randomized clinical trials and the therapeutic obligation. *J Med Philos* 1986: 1: 347–66.

13. Ruberman W, Weinblatt E, Goldberg JD, Frank CW, Shapiro S. Ventricular premature beats and mortality after myocardial infarction. *N Engl J Med* 1977: 297: 750–7.

14. Lown B. Sudden cardiac death: the major challenge confronting contemporary cardiology. *Am J Cardiol* 1979: 43: 313–28.

15. The Cardiac Arrhythmia Suppression Trial (CAST) investigators. Preliminary report: effect of encainide and flecainide on mortality in a randomized trial of arrhythmia suppression after myocardial infarction. *N Engl J Med* 1989: 321: 406–12.

# The Continuing Unethical Conduct of Underpowered Clinical Trials

## Scott D. Halpern, Jason T. Karlawish, and Jesse A. Berlin

Scott Halpern, Jason Karlawish, and Jesse Berlin critically assess two recent arguments aiming to justify enrolling research subjects in clinical trials too small to produce statistically meaningful results. They argue that these "underpowered" trials are ethical in only two circumstances: either (1) the disease being treated is rare and the investigators have explicit plans to combine their results with similar trials, or (2) the trial's aim is to determine if a drug or device shows enough promise of effectiveness to warrant additional study.

More than 20 years have passed since investigators first described the ethical problems of conducting randomized controlled trials (RECs) with insufficient statistical power. Because such studies may not

*JAMA,* Vol 288, no. 3 (2002), pp. 358–362. References omitted. Reprinted by permission of the American Medical Association.

adequately test the underlying hypotheses, they have been considered "scientifically useless" and therefore unethical in their exposure of participants to the risks and burdens of human research. Despite this long-standing challenge, many clinical investigators continue to conduct underpowered studies and fail to calculate or report appropriate (a priori) power analyses. Not only do these scientific and ethical errors persist in the general medical literature, but 3 recent reports also highlight the alarming prevalence of these problems in more specialized fields.

Patients and healthy volunteers thus continue to participate in research that may be of limited clinical value. Furthermore, authors recently have offered 2 related arguments to support the validity and value of underpowered clinical trials. First, meta-analysis may "save" small studies by providing a means to combine the results with those of other similar studies to enable estimates of an intervention's efficacy. Second, although small studies may not provide a good basis for testing hypotheses, they may provide valuable estimates of treatment effects using confidence intervals. Based on these arguments, authors have suggested that institutional review boards (IRBs) drop the documentation of statistical power as a criterion for study approval.

If meta-analysis and estimating treatment effects provided investigators and IRBs with a means to justify underpowered research, challenges to the ethics of underpowered studies would have to cease. In this article, we examine these arguments in light of the distinctive moral issues associated with the conduct of underpowered trials, the disclosures that are owed to potential participants in underpowered trials so they may make autonomous enrollment decisions, and the circumstances in which the prospects for future meta-analyses may justify individually underpowered trials.

We conclude that underpowered trials can be ethical in only 2 situations. First, small trials of interventions for rare diseases may be justified if investigators document explicit plans for including their results with those of similar trials in a prospective meta-analysis. Second, early-phase trials in the development of drugs, devices, or other interventions need not be powered to make randomized treatment comparisons provided they are adequately powered for other defined purposes and designed to guide the conduct of subsequent, comparative trials. In both cases, investigators must inform prospective participants that their participation may only indirectly contribute to future health care benefits.

## Statistical Power and the Planning of Clinical Trials

Investigators use power analysis to determine the probability that a given study will reject the null hypothesis when it is, in fact, false. In other words, power

analysis determines the chance of detecting a true-positive result. By tradition, researchers consider a study to be adequately powered if it has at least an 80% chance of detecting a clinically significant effect when one exists. This exact value is arbitrary; higher power will always be preferable and should be set with consideration of the importance of limiting both false-negative conclusions (ie, type II errors ) and false-positive conclusions (ie, type I errors).

To calculate a study's power to detect a given effect, investigators use a set of other variables, including the number of individuals to be enrolled, the expected variability of their outcomes, and the chosen probability of making a type I error. Reformulating these variables allows one to calculate the numbers of study participants needed to detect a clinically important effect size with acceptable power. Although consensus among reasonable clinicians will generally enable determinations of how small an effect would be clinically important to detect, disagreement about this value may occasionally emerge. In such cases, we advocate a 3-tiered, hierarchical approach for investigators to use in determining the effect size to be entered into sample size calculations.

First, when empirical definitions of clinically meaningful effects exist, such as in the percentage reduction of reported pain necessary to define analgesic efficacy, these values ought to be used. Second, if there is neither clinical consensus nor empirical evidence to guide definitions of clinically important effects, but data from earlier trials or observational studies reliably indicate an intervention's plausible effect, this value may be used. Finally, if none of the foregoing criteria are met, then previously published definitions of moderate effect sizes, such as those described by Cohen, should be used. Trials that cannot reliably detect effect sizes defined used this hierarchical approach may be defined as underpowered.

## Arguments for Allowing Underpowered Trials

There are several practical barriers to conducting large RCTs, particularly for rare diseases. Because the results of smaller, underpowered trials may later be combined in meta-analyses, authors have argued that prohibiting underpowered trials would "thwart many independent investigations . . . [which] may seriously diminish the stock of the world's knowledge." There are both practical and ethical problems with this argument.

The first practical problem stems from an overly optimistic view of the usefulness of the information that underpowered trials may provide. Acknowledging that hypothesis tests are inordinately likely to produce false-negative results when inadequately powered, proponents argue that quantifying the range of plausible effect sizes will still be possible by examining confidence intervals. However, studies containing too few subjects to detect a positive effect (if one exists) via hypothesis testing will also yield unacceptably wide confidence intervals around the point estimate of this effect. Because such confidence intervals will often contain both the null and clinically important effect sizes, the approach provides ambiguous conclusions.

One might argue that if no trials were conducted, the confidence intervals around the (unknown) effect would remain infinitely wide. Thus, any well-designed trial, no matter how small, would at least reduce this uncertainty. However, the marginal value of narrowing confidence intervals to widths still compatible with both positive and negative results generally is insufficient to justify exposing individuals to the common risks and burdens of research. Although these risks and burdens may often be outweighed by the benefits of trial participation, these beneficial effects are not uniform, and their potential is insufficient to justify human research.

The second practical problem with meta-analysis is that even if investigators conducted multiple underpowered trials, difficulties in synthesizing the results may prevent the calculation of valid treatment effects. Under ideal conditions, meta-analyses offer potential advantages over a single RCT in gauging a treatment effect. Meta-analyses may enhance generalizability by incorporating more heterogeneous populations and may overcome the risk that any single RCT, even a very large one, could be weakened by bias.

For meta-analyses to be useful, however, comparable research methods must have been used among the primary trials, and these trials must be selected for inclusion in an unbiased fashion. The infrequency with which these ideal conditions are met may help explain why 2 independent meta-analyses of the same literature sometimes arrive at different conclusions. As Bailar notes, "Such disagreement argues powerfully against any notion that meta-analysis offers an assured way to distill the 'truth' from a collection of research papers."

Finally, because underpowered trials are more likely to produce negative results and consequently may not be published (the so-called publication bias),

underpowered trials may be less accessible for inclusion in meta-analyses. This may fatally bias the approach. Thus, the ideal conditions for combining evidence may be particularly unlikely when the component trials are underpowered; therefore, even the most rigorously conducted meta-analyses will be unable to augment such trials' abilities to further medical knowledge. Only if widely accessible registries of RCTs are expanded to include privately sponsored trials could the potential for publication bias in retrospective meta-analyses be eliminated.

## Sample Size and Informed Consent

In addition to the practical problems mentioned herein, underpowered studies will also be ethically deficient if investigators do not convey these studies' limited value to prospective participants. Failure to communicate a study's value (or lack thereof) limits the quality of the information on which individuals must base their enrollment decisions. Individuals commonly participate in research to fulfill altruistic motives, such as desires to advance medical science and thereby help others. Therefore, to respect prospective participants' autonomy, investigators must inform them of the limited capacities of small trials to produce public benefit.

Investigators occasionally deprive participants of such information for 3 reasons. First, investigators may simply fail to conduct an a priori power analysis. Such investigators are acting negligently. In addition to risking the enrollment of too few participants to answer the research question, investigators who fail to conduct or improperly conduct a power analysis may enroll too many individuals. This outcome is also troubling because it exposes too many individuals to the risks of research and overconsumes limited societal resources.

Second, investigators might conduct an appropriate power calculation but fail to recruit sufficient numbers of participants in a timely fashion. Such cases may arise, for example, when prospective participants' clinicians have reservations about enrolling their patients or when patients themselves are dissuaded by some feature of the trial, such as the existence of a placebo group. Investigators should attempt to identify potential recruitment problems beforehand and modify their approaches accordingly.

Perhaps most concerning is the third scenario, in which investigators conduct an appropriate power analysis, find they will be unlikely to recruit an adequate number of participants, and choose to proceed without conveying this information to participants in the informed consent process. This knowing failure of information disclosure entails deception. In addition to abrogating participants' rights, if such deception were publicized, it could undermine people's trust in science, further curtailing future enrollment.

Investigators may fear that disclosing information regarding power will itself reduce enrollment. Because study participants so often seek to fulfill altruistic motives, it seems logical that they would rather participate in adequately powered trials. Nonetheless, this potential barrier to efficient recruitment does not justify enrolling individuals without full disclosure.

## Rare Diseases

For research on diseases with low prevalence or incidence, the numbers of afflicted (or newly afflicted) individuals at any one time may make it impossible to conduct even a multicenter RCT that could reliably distinguish between interventions. It has been argued that in such cases some evidence is better than none. This view ignores the fact that only when the effect sizes are extremely large—indeed, larger than anticipated—will small trials be able serendipitously to document them. In all other cases, false-negative conclusions may be drawn and post hoc power analyses will be unable to elucidate the error. Although investigators commonly relax inferential standards to avoid this result, doing so increases the risk of drawing false-positive conclusions.

Instead, if investigators explicitly plan to make the results of a small trial available for inclusion in a prospective meta-analysis, excessive risks of both types of false conclusions may be averted. Prospectively designed meta-analyses are less susceptible to the problems with traditional, retrospective meta-analyses because the methods of the component studies may be synchronized in advance. This avoids the possibility that component studies may not be combinable if, for example, one study investigated a high-dose intervention among men and another study investigated a lower dose of the intervention among women. Because dose and sex would be inextricably confounded between these studies, retrospective meta-analysis would be of little use.

Therefore, only prospectively designed meta-analyses can justify the risks to participants in individually underpowered trials because they provide sufficient assurance that a study's results will eventually contribute to valuable or important knowledge.

Although a multicenter trial could similarly contribute to generalizable knowledge and may provide more internally valid results, it requires that investigators have access to a sufficient number of patients during the trial's conduct. This may not be possible for very rare diseases, making prospective meta-analyses of single-center and multicenter trials necessary to obtain adequate power. Furthermore, prospectively designed meta-analyses retain the innovation possible in conducting several smaller studies, while providing the organizational framework to ensure that their results can be synthesized.

## Early-Phase Studies of Experimental Interventions

Just as prospective meta-analyses may ensure the value of small single studies for rare diseases, plans for large, comparative trials of experimental interventions can justify the conduct of small studies in earlier phases of drug or device development. Thus, several smaller phase 1/2 trials may be justified as long as each is adequately powered for another aim, such as reliably determining whether a new therapy shows at least some promise of benefit, and is explicitly aimed at guiding a definitive phase 3 trial that will be adequately powered to make a reliable treatment comparison. Investigators conducting these studies must tell participants that their participation will not directly provide information of immediate clinical value, but rather will guide future studies that may do so.

## Conclusion

Despite long-standing critiques of the conduct of underpowered clinical trials, the practice not only remains widespread, but also has garnered increasing support. We have provided 2 main arguments for why these trends cannot be ethically reconciled. First, failing to conduct a priori power analyses fails to respect participants' decision-making autonomy by limiting the information disclosed during the informed consent process. Second, proceeding with underpowered trials, in the absence of explicit plans for definitive studies in the future, shifts the risk-benefit calculus that helps justify research in an unfavorable direction. Participants in such trials experience personal risks and benefits commensurate with those in adequately powered trials, but are denied the same opportunity to contribute to the improved care of future patients.

Therefore, IRB members should carefully monitor the statements made in the consent forms regarding the potential benefits of participation to ensure that these statements accurately reflect the strength of the underlying study design.

Low statistical power is merely one manifestation of a much larger problem: that many clinical investigators are not properly trained in research methods. The consequences are not only that investigators fail to properly assess the required sample size. Poor training may also explain why investigators may improperly assess the state of knowledge before initiating new studies, fail to appreciate how new trials ought to be conducted to advance this knowledge, choose inappropriate end points, and poorly report the results of their work.

We have focused our discussion on power because it remains one prominent problem, both scientifically and ethically, for which a workable solution is possible. We recommend that investigators always conduct a

priori power calculations and relay the results to potential study participants. This should not be an overwhelming task. Simplified statements regarding both the inherent uncertainty in all research and whether the relative level of uncertainty in the proposed study conforms to standards of clinical investigation should be understandable by potential participants.

After conveying information in this way, the research must still meet one of the following conditions: either enough patients will be enrolled to obtain at least 80% power to detect a clinically important effect or, if this is not possible, the researchers will be able to document a clear and practical plan to integrate the results of their trial with those of future trials. Absent one of these 2 circumstances, ethics review boards, research funding agencies, and medical journal editors should maintain strict requirements for adequate research methods, including appropriate statistical power, for any clinical trial to be approved, funded, or published, respectively.

## READINGS

## Section 3: Relativism and Retrospective Judgments

## Judging the Past: The Case of the Human Radiation Experiments

### Allen Buchanan

Allen Buchanan uses the case of the human radiation experiments to argue that we can and ought to judge the morality of actions in the past. He rejects the view that we can make judgments only within the context of a particular culture's beliefs (cultural ethical relativism). Also, while acknowledging that individuals may sometimes not be blameworthy because of what they have learned from their culture ("culturally induced ignorance"), he finds no such grounds for excusing those who conducted the radiation experiments.

Buchanan examines the possibility that the evolving notion of what informed consent requires might excuse the experimenters, but he points out that the subjects of the experiments gave no consent at all. Finally, he tries to show that the experiments violated the Hippocratic principle of "Do no harm," because they caused harm without the possibility of therapeutic benefit.

Buchanan concludes by stressing the importance of retrospective moral judgments in deterring future wrongdoing by holding accountable individuals in governments, agencies, and professions who seek institutional anonymity.

"It was a different world then." "They weren't as sensitive to these issues as we are nowadays." "You can't judge people of that time by our standards." Such remarks are common. They express a reluctance to make moral judgments about the past—even a conviction that such judgments are invalid. There seems to be a special reluctance to make moral judgments about particular individuals in the past. Even if we are willing to say that what they did was wrong, or that the institutions within which they operated were unjust or corrupt, we may be reluctant to blame them as individuals for doing what they did.

Exactly what is supposed to be wrong or dubious about making retrospective moral judgments is not usually made explicit. If something is wrong about applying current moral standards to past actions, institutions, or persons, we need an account of what that something is. For we do in fact make some retrospective moral judgments with complete confidence. For example, few of us would say that slavery is wrong now but was not wrong a hundred and fifty years ago (unless we mean it was not *legally* wrong). We believe it was wrong a hundred and fifty years ago, even though it was widely practiced and many people did not see that it was wrong, or at least refused to admit that it was. How can our willingness to make some retrospective moral judgments with confidence be reconciled with the belief that there is something problematic about retrospective moral judgments as such?

This is not just a puzzle for moral theorists. It is an urgent practical question. What position we take on retrospective moral judgment has fundamental implications for what should be done *now*. If we cannot judge that rights were violated in the past, then we cannot accept arguments for compensation grounded on the assumption that rights were violated.

Something else is at stake: the very possibility of moral progress. If we cannot apply the same moral yardstick to the past and the present, then we cannot say either that there has been or that there has not been moral progress.

### The Task of the Advisory Committee on Human Radiation Experimentation

The investigation of radiation experiments conducted on human beings under the auspices of several agen-

Allen Buchanan, "Judging the Past: The Case of the Human Radiation Experiments," *Hastings Center Report,* Vol. 26, no. 3 (1996): 25–30.

cies of the federal government between 1944 and 1974 provides a concrete focus for the problem of retrospective moral judgment. The Advisory Committee on Human Radiation Experiments, which was created by President Clinton and which recently published its final report, was asked to evaluate the ethics of these experiments and make recommendations for how to avoid abuses in the future. The committee was also charged with a prior task to determine what ethics criteria should be used to evaluate the experiments.[1] To answer this question, the committee had to take a stand on the problem of retrospective moral judgment.

Even if it had not been implicated in the committee's formal mandate, the problem of retrospective moral judgment could not have been avoided easily. Although the first revelations of the human radiation experiments evoked confident condemnation in some quarters, some members of the general public and of the press expressed the belief that there would be something inappropriate about blaming those responsible for the experiments. The proper task, rather, was to learn from past mistakes and try to ensure that they did not occur again. This view, I shall argue, mistakenly assumes either that we cannot make valid retrospective moral judgments or that making them is not relevant to the task of minimizing the possibility of future abuses.

Contrary to appearances, there is no distinct problem about the validity of *retrospective* moral judgments as such. The mere passage of time could not possibly affect the validity of moral judgments. The fact that it has now been fifty years since Hitler tried to destroy the Jews and to enslave the greater part of mankind in no way diminishes the wrongness of his actions. Nor does it reduce his culpability. The validity of these moral judgments will not be affected by the passing of another fifty years, nor a hundred, nor a thousand. So if there is some reason to refrain from making retrospective moral judgments, it must be something other than the mere passage of time.

### Cultural Ethical Relativism

Remarks such as "It was a different world then" and "We can't judge the past by contemporary standards" are revealing. The assumption must be that the validity of moral judgments depends upon their cultural context, and that cultural contexts change over time. In other words, skepticism about retrospective moral judgments is simply a special case of the more general position known as cultural ethical relativism. According to this position, the validity of all moral judgments is culturally relative. This position implies that moral judgments about the past are invalid *if* they are applied across cultural boundaries.

According to cultural ethical relativism, moral judgments applied across cultural boundaries are invalid because moral judgments can be justified only by reference to shared values, and shared values are found only within a particular culture. We cannot validly apply ethical standards that can be justified only by reference to the shared values of our culture to actions, agents, or institutions in other cultures that do not share those values, whether they are contemporaneous with ours or existed in the past.

Strictly speaking, this position denies that there are any human rights. Human rights, by definition, are rights we have simply by virtue of our humanity, regardless of differences in our cultures, and regardless of when or where we live. The fundamental idea behind human rights is that because of the kind of beings they are, humans are entitled to be treated in certain ways (and not treated in certain ways). Thus, statements about human rights are justified by appeal to the morally relevant features of human beings, all human beings, as such. The implication is that cultural differences among human beings do not and cannot vitiate this justification because it appeals to features that all human beings have in all cultures.

According to the very concept of human rights, the validity of statements about human rights does *not* depend upon the fact (if it is a fact) that all cultures happen to share certain values by reference to which such statements can be justified. Even if it should turn out that there exists a culture whose values cannot be appealed to to justify the statement that there is a human right not to be tortured, for example, it does not follow that there is no such human right. Whether there is a human right not to be tortured depends only on whether the statement "The right not to be tortured is a human right" can be justified by reference to the morally relevant features of human beings as such, not upon whether all cultures happen to include values that can be invoked in such a justification.

In denying that there are any human rights, cultural ethical relativism not only invalidates *retrospective* moral judgments about actions or institutions occurring in different cultural contexts, it also implies that some of the most basic moral judgments we make about *our own contemporaries* are unjustified. We are barred from saying not only that agents in the past,

such as Hitler, violated human rights, but also that human rights violations are occurring in the world at the present time. At most we can say that there are actions which most (or perhaps even all) cultures happen to recognize as violations of rights. If those who engage in the actions in question belong to a culture that does not recognize those actions as violations of rights, we cannot even say they are violating anyone's rights, much less that human rights are being violated. At most we can say that according to our culture they are violating rights. Thus, for example, whether we can say that Bosnian Serbs who killed unarmed Muslim prisoners are guilty of violating rights will depend upon whether the cultural values of the killers justify the statement that they violated the rights of those they killed. Even if we conclude that they do, we cannot say that human rights were violated. At most we can say that the Bosnian Serbs did something that happens to be wrong in all cultures, because all cultures happen to have values that justify saying that what they did is wrong. If a culture comes to embrace genocide, then those within it who commit genocide cannot coherently be judged to have committed a wrong, according to cultural ethical relativism. And if genocide is wrong only because it is regarded as such by certain cultures, we cannot say that it is wrong simply by virtue of what human beings as such are entitled to. So we cannot say that there is a human right against genocide.

Presumably, most of us do not believe that we must first determine whether the cultural values of the Bosnian Serbs condemn the killing of prisoners to know that the rights of those who were killed were violated. And presumably, most of us who condemn the killings believe that those who were killed were wronged simply as human beings—that they were treated in ways that human beings as such ought not to be treated. For those of us who believe these things, cultural ethical relativism must be rejected.

Assuming that we do reject this position we cannot then appeal to it to explain why "we cannot judge the past by present standards." Instead, we must consider whether there are other ways in which differences between the present cultural milieu and the milieu in which past actions occurred can invalidate or qualify moral judgments we make about the past. Before exploring these, however, another limitation of cultural ethical relativism is worth emphasizing. Even if we were to accept such relativism it still would not follow that it is "wrong to judge the past by present standards." That would follow only if the past objects of our moral judgment existed in a culture that did not include among its values those values by reference to which we make the moral judgments in question. And notice also how implausible it would be to assume that there are no basic values that are shared across otherwise quite different cultures.

This simple point has great significance for how we ought to evaluate some of the actions that occurred during the human radiation experiments. When we attempt to evaluate these actions we are not making judgments about an alien culture. It is our culture, American culture, of fifty to twenty years ago. In some cases, those who authorized or conducted the experiments violated very general moral principles that were widely accepted at the time and that we continue to endorse today. Among these are prohibitions against deceit, against harming innocent persons without their consent, against treating persons as mere means, and against exploiting the vulnerable. We regard such principles as so fundamental that we assume, with reason, that they are applicable in any cultural setting in which morality itself has meaning.

To take only one example, all of these very general principles were violated during the course of an experiment conducted under the auspices of the U.S. government at the Fernald School in the late 1940s and early 1950s. With the complicity of the school's highest administrator, physicians tricked the parents of retarded children at the school into giving permission for their children to participate in a "science club." In fact "science club" was a cover for an experiment in which the children were fed radioisotopes mixed with oatmeal at special "science club breakfasts" (pp. 344–47). Whether the ingestion of the isotopes posed a significant physical risk is perhaps disputable. What is beyond dispute is that these children and their parents were treated as mere means for others' ends, that they were exploited, and that they were chosen for exploitation because their powerlessness made them vulnerable. As one witness before the committee bitterly observed: "They didn't conduct experiments like this at Choate or Andover."

It would be nonsense to suggest that American culture has changed so much in the past few decades that it is inappropriate to apply these very general moral principles to the case of the experiments at the Fernald School. Changes there have certainly been, but the prohibitions against exploiting the vulnerable, against using persons as mere means, and against manipulating people in deceptive and demeaning ways are hardly new moral insights.

Of course, some might agree that these fundamental principles were accepted in the American culture of a few decades ago, but point to a difference in the cultural context that might be thought to invalidate our condemnation of the Fernald experiments. These and most of the other human radiation experiments occurred in the depths of the Cold War. Even if American culture of that time included these general moral principles, perhaps at the time they were thought to be overridden by the requirement of national security. Indeed, this period was called the Cold War to emphasize the urgency of the situation. And in desperate situations, otherwise compelling moral restraints may be relaxed.

One of the most significant findings of the committee is that the so-called "national security exception" was not in fact invoked to justify any of the morally dubious actions undertaken in any of the human radiation experiments, including those at the Fernald School (p. 793). None of the hundreds of memoranda, transcripts of meetings, and official policy statements reviewed by the committee even imply that the justification for infringing otherwise valid moral principles was that national security considerations overrode them. Extensive and often candid discussions of ethical issues did take place at the highest levels of policymaking, but the national security exception was not invoked. Instead, it was the need to avoid legal liability and public outrage that the participants invoked to justify their deceptions and manipulations.

Furthermore, even if the national security exception had been invoked, it is doubtful that doing so would have provided a valid excuse. The reason for using retarded children at a state school, and for duping them and their parents, was to capitalize on their powerlessness—to avoid the risk of resistance had the truth about the experiment been told and to minimize the risk of exposure that would have existed had better off children been used. The committee found no evidence to support the hypothesis that government officials first sought to conduct the experiments without deception and without singling out a vulnerable group, but then found that the only way to serve vital national security interests was to deceive and exploit the vulnerable. So even if American culture during the period of the radiation experiments included a heightened concern about national security there is little reason to conclude that this cultural difference removes blame for what was done.

## Culturally Induced Ignorance

There is another way in which a different cultural context in the past might be thought to invalidate retrospective moral judgments. Recognizing it does not commit one to cultural ethical relativism (and hence to the denial that there are human rights). Nor does it require us to swallow the implausible thesis that a few decades can lead to the abandonment of the most basic of general moral principles. Culturally induced ignorance—if it is nonculpable ignorance—can invalidate the moral judgments we make about the behavior of persons in another cultural setting. This ignorance exists when enculturated beliefs and concepts prevent individuals from discerning what they ought to do and is nonculpable when individuals cannot be blamed for not escaping the effects of such ignorance. Where individuals are prevented from discerning what they ought to do because of such nonculpable ignorance, it would be wrong to blame them for the actions they perform as a result of it.

There are two distinct ways in which a person's ability to discern what he ought to do can be impaired by his enculturated beliefs and concepts. First, morally relevant *factual* information simply may not be available in the culture. Second, the individual, like other members of the culture, may be *morally* ignorant. Due to his deeply enculturated beliefs and conceptual framework, he may be unable to discern what he ought to do because he is unable to make certain moral distinctions or even to recognize certain individuals as beings with rights, as members of the moral community.

To illustrate how culturally induced factual ignorance can undercut an otherwise valid retrospective moral judgment, consider the following case. Suppose we agree that persons should not be subjected to extremely risky medical experiments without a reasonable prospect of significant benefit to themselves. Suppose also that a scientist working in the 1940s subscribed to this tenet of the ethics of experimentation, but believed that the experiment for which he was recruiting subjects involved only minimal risk. Finally, suppose that his belief about the level of risk, though quite false, was supported by the best scientific evidence of his day, which he had conscientiously studied. Under such conditions we might well conclude that even if the patients' rights were violated, the scientist was not blameworthy. It is not hard to imagine errors of scientific fact that could have led to wrongful actions in the human radiation experiments. If we, from the vantage point of superior data, believe that certain experiments were too risky, we might conclude that they never should have been performed. Yet if we believe that the best-informed scientific opinion of the day erroneously regarded certain experiments as being of minimal risk, we might also conclude that the scientists conducting them were not culpable. Given what they knew—and all they could have known at the time—they acted responsibly. They were ignorant of morally relevant facts, but their ignorance was nonculpable.

In at least four groups of experiments, however, the advisory committee's research uncovered no basis for arguing that factual error, culturally induced or otherwise, mitigates blame for wrongdoing. As we have already seen, the moral fault in the case of the Fernald School experiments had nothing to do with estimates of risk. Even if it is true that the amounts of radioisotopes given to the children in their "science club breakfasts" posed no significant risk of physical injury, they were treated wrongly nonetheless. The same was true in the plutonium injection experiments conducted at the University of Rochester and at the University of California between 1947 and 1950 and the total body irradiation experiments conducted at the University of Cincinnati Medical Center, which continued for over a decade until 1972 (pp. 243–46, pp. 390–97).

In the experiments at Rochester and California, sick individuals were subjected to radioactive substances without being informed of the nature of the procedure and without being told that the procedure was expected to yield no therapeutic benefit for them. In the case of the total body irradiation experiments, the researchers were aware that the doses being administered were extremely risky and even collected data that they concluded showed that the "treatment" carried a one in four risk of death from suppression of bone marrow production; yet the experiments continued (pp. 385–90). Similarly, although a government study had shown that American uranium workers were subject to dangerous levels of radon, the miners were not informed of the results of the study (pp. 565–75).

In none of these four groups of experiments can it be argued that factual errors that were widespread or uncorrectable at the time invalidated judgments of wrongdoing. So if the different cultural context of these human radiation experiments is to provide a reason why we should not make moral judgments about them, it is not because those who authorized and conducted the experiments were prevented from knowing what they ought and ought not to have done due to factual ignorance that was pervasive in their culture.

Earlier, a distinction was made between culturally induced factual ignorance and culturally induced moral ignorance, and it was noted that both can vitiate judgments of moral blame. Moral ignorance may be a less familiar notion than that of factual ignorance, but it is equally debilitating and in some cases may be harder to correct.

History provides all too many examples in which the dominant culture of a society recognized that it is wrong to exploit persons or to kill persons wantonly or for trivial reasons, but failed to recognize that certain classes of individuals are persons, and hence that they possess the rights that persons possess. At least some of those thoroughly embued with the ideology of slavery in the antebellum may have been morally blind in precisely this way, and their culture may have induced this dreadful and debilitating condition. Because they did not recognize blacks as persons, they did not see slavery as a violation of the rights of persons.

As with culturally induced factual ignorance, it is important to distinguish between culpable and nonculpable enculturated moral ignorance. Whether a person's moral ignorance is something for which he is culpable depends chiefly upon whether he had access to corrective beliefs and whether he availed himself of them. In other words, the fact that false beliefs are prevalent in a culture does not mean that they are not remediable. And if they are remediable, we may be blamed for maintaining them. *Culpable* moral ignorance cannot exculpate one of the wrongs that result from it.

Is there reason to believe that whatever wrongs were done in the course of the radiation experiments were the result of nonculpable, culturally induced moral ignorance? It is not possible here to answer this question with regard to all of the thousands of actions that are grouped together under the heading "the human radiation experiments." Nevertheless, a strong prima facie case can be made that the excuse of nonculpable culturally induced moral ignorance is not plausible in some of the most morally troubling experiments.

Consider again the four groups of experiments described above. In the case of the uranium miners, the excuse of cultural moral blindness would be farfetched. Nothing in the cultural milieu of the United States in the 1940s and 1950s encouraged the belief that individuals who happened to be miners had no

rights or were expendable. (Some of the miners were Native Americans, and strong prejudices existed against this group, but many were not.) Moreover, the desperate attempts of the government to suppress disclosure of the study results indicate an awareness of the public outrage that would have followed revelation that the government knew the miners' lives were threatened but did nothing to prevent them from dying.

Nor is there any reason to believe that culturally induced moral ignorance undercuts the judgments by which we condemn the actions at the Fernald School. It is one thing to say that the retarded have often been discriminated against, perhaps more so in the past than at present. It is another to suggest that cultural biases toward them were so extreme—and so incorrigible—that individuals who violated the most basic moral principles in their treatment of these children are blameless. Moreover, had there been strong cultural agreement that it was permissible to use retarded persons as mere means, there would have been no need to practice such an elaborate deception.

The plutonium and total body irradiation experiments require a more complicated analysis because they were performed in a medical context in which more specialized ethical principles were operative.

## The Evolving Requirement of Consent

Perhaps the most plausible argument for not blaming physicians involved in radiation experiments that we now regard as wrongful is one based on the very plausible premise that the current standard of informed consent was not generally accepted at the time. Here it is important to distinguish between two modes of moral progress: compliance with the same standards may increase over time, or better standards may emerge over time. The fact that moral standards evolve (rather than being replaced instantaneously by entirely different standards) complicates retrospective moral judgment. The evolution of the requirement of informed consent is an excellent example of this complication. It is also directly relevant to our case study, the moral evaluation of the human radiation experiments.

We now recognize that medical treatment requires the *informed* consent of the patient (if the patient has decisional capacity). For a considerable period prior to the general acceptance of this principle, there was widespread acceptance of the principle that the consent of the patient is necessary. The replacement of the requirement of bare consent with the requirement of informed consent can certainly be viewed as moral progress.

Furthermore, the notion of informed consent itself has undergone a process of refinement and development—through common law rulings, through analyses and explanations of these rulings in the legal literature, through philosophical treatments of the key concepts of autonomy and decisional capacity, and through guidelines advanced in reports by government and professional bodies. As a rough generalization, it can be said that the current dominant understanding of informed consent is more complex and more demanding than either the much earlier requirement of consent or the first interpretations of what constitutes informed consent. If this is the case, then, a question arises: Is it appropriate to judge the actions of physicians in the past by the current standard of informed consent?

There is one reason not to do so. The principle of informed consent is both a principle of the professional ethics of physicians and a legal standard. As such it is an institutional product, or rather the product of the interactions of two institutions, medicine and law. For this reason, the principle of informed consent cannot be lumped together with the very general, commonsense moral prohibitions against deception, against treating persons as mere means, and against exploiting the vulnerable. It would, therefore, be wrong to hold individual physicians to the current, rather refined standard, if the institutions of law and medicine that existed when they acted had not yet developed such a standard.

Having said this, one must hasten to add that in none of the four groups of experiments discussed above was there even bare consent. So at least for these experiments, the fact that there has been progress in the development of the standard of consent is irrelevant.

## The Hippocratic Tenet

Since the time of Hippocrates, it has been a fundamental ethical tenet of the medical profession (at least in the West) that the physician is not to harm his or her patient. Because it is universally acknowledged that even the best medical treatment sometimes involves incidental harms, the "First do no harm" admonition of the Hippocratic corpus is generally and quite reasonably understood to mean that the physician may harm the patient only for therapeutic reasons, that is, only when a significant net benefit to the patient is expected.

Thus, any experiments that physicians subjected their patients to that could be expected to cause harm without compensating therapeutic benefits violated this fundamental tenet of medical ethics. This is precisely what occurred, repeatedly over a ten-year period, in the case of the total body irradiation experiments at the University of Cincinnati Medical Center. Quite apart from whether these experiments also violated the requirement of informed consent, and independently of whether they violated the Nuremburg code (which was accepted by the American Medical Association in 1946), the physicians who conducted them are blameworthy.

## Why We Should Make Retrospective Moral Judgments

I have argued that there is a moral basis for making judgments of individual and professional culpability regarding some of the human radiation experiments. Even if my argument succeeds, another question remains: Granted that such judgments are valid, ought we to make them? Some might argue that there is nothing to gain from issuing judgments of culpability, that energies should be focused instead on the future—on realistic efforts to ensure that these sorts of wrongs will not occur again.

It would be a grave mistake, however, to assume that the choice is *either* to make judgments of culpability *or* to focus on future prevention, as if the two were unconnected. Effective preventive action must include serious efforts to make government officials and biomedical researchers today and in the future accountable for complying with sound ethical principles and procedures for the protection of human subjects. Holding people accountable—and deterring wrongdoing by putting people on notice that they will be held accountable—means specifying what their obligations are and making it clear that they will be judged culpable if they fail to honor those obligations.

Efforts to deter future wrongdoing are likely to be more effective, other things being equal, if individuals know that they personally will be held accountable. If this is not made clear, then individuals operating within complex institutions and organizations may console themselves with the thought that even if "the government" or "the agency" or "the profession" is found blameworthy, no serious consequence will be visited upon them as individuals. Refraining from making judgments of individual culpability about past abuses of human subjects can only feed this dangerous tendency to seek shelter behind the institutional or professional veil.

Perhaps even more importantly, it will be very hard if not impossible to explain and to justify effective proposals for institutional or professional reform without making clear references to particular instances of culpable action performed by identifiable individuals. Unless this is done, the specifics of reform proposals may appear unmotivated or of dubious relevance.

For these reasons, we *should* make judgments of individual culpability about wrongdoings in the past, if we have sufficient empirical evidence to do so responsibly. What I have argued in this essay is that there is in general no conceptual bar to making judgments of individual culpability about agents in the past. Whether there is sufficient empirical evidence will depend upon the particulars of the case. The herculean research effort mounted by the Advisory Committee on Human Radiation Experimentation supplies a wealth of such evidence.

### Acknowledgments

The present essay is based on a background paper the author prepared when working as staff on the advisory committee. The enclosed views are those of the author and do not represent the views of the committee. The findings, recommendations, and analysis of the advisory committee are expressed in the *Final Report.*

### Note

1.   *Final Report: Advisory Committee on Human Radiation Experiments* (Washington, D.C.: Government Printing Office, 1995). Also available from Oxford University Press.

---

### READINGS

## Section 4: Animal Experimentation

## Animal Experimentation

Peter Singer

Peter Singer argues that the vast majority of animal experiments cannot be justified. They exact an extraordinary cost in animal suffering, while producing little or no knowledge—and that can usually be obtained in other ways.

Singer provides multiple examples of painful, pointless experiments leading to the death of animal subjects. He argues that our willingness to tolerate such experiments can be explained only by our "speciesism"—the notion that the interests of nonhuman animals need not be considered. Speciesism, Singer holds, is analogous to racism and is just as indefensible.

Singer argues that the fundamental issue in determining how we may treat animals is whether they suffer and that the pains of animals and humans deserve equal consideration. Many animals are more intelligent than severely retarded or infant humans, so that if lack of intelligence would justify painful animal experiments, it would also justify the same experiments on retarded and infant humans. Because it is immoral to subject humans to such experiments, we have good reason to believe it is also wrong to subject animals to them.

Singer holds that researchers should be required to demonstrate that the benefits of their research will outweigh the suffering of the animals involved. He recommends that ethics committees, with members representing the welfare of animals, be established to oversee experiments.

There has been opposition to experimenting on animals for a long time. This opposition has made little headway because experimenters, backed by commercial firms that profit by supplying laboratory animals and equipment, have been able to convince legislators and the public that opposition comes from uninformed fanatics who consider the interests of animals more important than the interests of human beings. But to be opposed to what is going on now it is not necessary to insist that all animal experiments stop immediately. All we need to say is that experiments serving no direct and urgent purpose should stop immediately, and in the remaining fields of research, we should, whenever possible, seek to replace experiments that involve animals with alternative methods that do not. . . .

. . . Professor [Harry] Harlow, who worked at the Primate Research Center in Madison, Wisconsin, was for many years editor of a leading psychology journal, and until his death a few years ago was held in high esteem by his colleagues in psychological research. His work has been cited approvingly in many basic textbooks of psychology, read by millions of students taking introductory psychology courses over the last twenty years. The line of research he began has been continued after his death by his associates and former students.

In a 1965 paper, Harlow describes his work as follows:

> For the past ten years we have studied the effects of partial social isolation by raising monkeys from birth onwards in bare wire cages. . . . These monkeys suffer total maternal deprivation. . . . More recently we have initiated a series of studies on the effects of total social isolation by rearing monkeys from a few hours after birth until 3, 6, or 12 months of age in [a] stainless steel chamber. During the prescribed sentence in this apparatus the monkey has no contact with any animal, human or sub-human.

These studies, Harlow continues, found that

> sufficiently severe and enduring early isolation reduces these animals to a social–emotional level in which the primary social responsiveness is fear.

In another article Harlow and his former student and associate Stephen Suomi described how they were trying to induce psychopathology in infant mon-

From *Animal Liberation*, 2d ed., by Peter Singer (Random House/New York Review of Books, New York, 1990), pp. 31–33, 40, 45–46, 48, 61–63, 65, 90–92. (Notes and references omitted.)

keys by a technique that appeared not to be working. They were then visited by John Bowlby, a British psychiatrist. According to Harlow's account, Bowlby listened to the story of their troubles and then toured the Wisconsin laboratory. After he had seen the monkeys individually housed in bare wire cages he asked, "Why are you trying to produce psychopathology in monkeys? You already have more psychopathological monkeys in the laboratory than have ever been seen on the face of the earth."

Bowlby, incidentally, was a leading researcher on the consequences of maternal deprivation, but his research was conducted with children, primarily war orphans, refugees, and institutionalized children. As far back as 1951, before Harlow even began his research on nonhuman primates, Bowlby concluded:

> The evidence has been reviewed. It is submitted that evidence is now such that it leaves no room for doubt regarding the general proposition that the prolonged deprivation of the young child of maternal care may have grave and far-reaching effects on his character and so on the whole of his future life.

This did not deter Harlow and his colleagues from devising and carrying out their monkey experiments.

In the same article in which they tell of Bowlby's visit, Harlow and Suomi describe how they had the "fascinating idea" of inducing depression by "allowing baby monkeys to attach to cloth surrogate mothers who could become monsters":

> The first of these monsters was a cloth monkey mother who, upon schedule or demand, would eject high-pressure compressed air. It would blow the animal's skin practically off its body. What did the baby monkey do? It simply clung tighter and tighter to the mother, because a frightened infant clings to its mother at all costs. We did not achieve any psychopathology.
>
> However, we did not give up. We built another surrogate monster mother that would rock so violently that the baby's head and teeth would rattle. All the baby did was cling tighter and tighter to the surrogate. The third monster we built had an embedded wire frame within its body which would spring forward and eject the infant from its ventral surface. The infant would subsequently pick itself off the floor, wait for the frame to return into the cloth body, and then cling again to the surrogate. Finally, we built our porcupine mother. On command, this mother would eject sharp brass spikes over all of the ventral surface of its body. Although the infants were distressed by these pointed rebuffs, they simply waited until the spikes receded and then returned and clung to the mother.

These results, the experimenters remark, were not so surprising, since the only recourse of an injured child is to cling to its mother. . . .

Harlow is now dead, but his students and admirers have spread across the United States and continue to perform experiments in a similar vein. . . .

Since Harlow began his maternal deprivation experiments some thirty years ago, over 250 such experiments have been conducted in the United States. These experiments subjected over seven thousand animals to procedures that induced distress, despair, anxiety, general psychological devastation, and death. . . .

An equally sad tale of futility is that of experiments designed to produce what is known as "learned helplessness"—supposedly a model of depression in human beings. In 1953 R. Solomon, L. Kamin, and L. Wynne, experimenters at Harvard University, placed forty dogs in a device called a "shuttlebox," which consists of a box divided into two compartments, separated by a barrier. Initially the barrier was set at the height of the dog's back. Hundreds of intense electric shocks were delivered to the dogs' feet through a grid floor. At first the dogs could escape the shock if they learned to jump the barrier into the other compartment. In an attempt to "discourage" one dog from jumping, the experimenters forced the dog to jump one hundred times onto a grid floor in the other compartment that also delivered a shock to the dog's feet. They said that as the dog jumped he gave a "sharp anticipatory yip which turned into a yelp when he landed on the electrified grid." They then blocked the passage between the compartments with a piece of plate glass and tested the dog again. The dog "jumped forward and smashed his head against the glass." The dogs began by showing symptoms such as defecation, urination, yelping and shrieking, trembling, attacking the apparatus, and so on; but after ten or twelve days of trials dogs who were prevented from escaping shock ceased to resist. The experimenters reported themselves "impressed" by this, and concluded that a combination of the plate glass barrier and foot shock was "very effective" in eliminating jumping by dogs.

This study showed that it was possible to induce a state of hopelessness and despair by repeated administration of severe inescapable shock. Such "learned helplessness" studies were further refined in the 1960s. One prominent experimenter was Martin Seligman of the University of Pennsylvania. He electrically shocked dogs through a steel grid with such intensity and persistence that the dogs stopped trying to escape and "learned" to be helpless. In one study,

written with colleagues Steven Maier and James Geer, Seligman describes his work as follows:

> When a normal, naive dog receives escape/avoidance training in a shuttlebox, the following behavior typically occurs: at the onset of electric shock the dog runs frantically about, defecating, urinating, and howling until it scrambles over the barrier and so escapes from shock. On the next trial the dog, running and howling, crosses the barrier more quickly, and so on, until efficient avoidance emerges.

Seligman altered this pattern by strapping dogs in harnesses and giving them shocks from which they had no means of escape. When the dogs were then placed in the original shuttlebox situation from which escape was possible, he found that

> such a dog reacts initially to shock in the shuttlebox in the same manner as the naive dog. However in dramatic contrast to the naive dog it soon stops running and remains silent until shock terminates. The dog does not cross the barrier and escape from shock. Rather it seems to "give up" and passively "accept" the shock. On succeeding trials the dog continues to fail to make escape movements and thus takes 50 seconds of severe, pulsating shock on each trial. . . . A dog previously exposed to inescapable shock . . . may take unlimited shock without escaping or avoiding at all. . . .

Electric shock has also been used to produce aggressive behavior in animals. In one study at the University of Iowa, Richard Viken and John Knutson divided 160 rats into groups and "trained" them in a stainless steel cage with an electrified floor. Pairs of rats were given electric shocks until they learned to fight by striking out at the other rat while facing each other in an upright position or by biting. It took an average of thirty training trials before the rats learned to do this immediately on the first shock. The researchers then placed the shock-trained rats in the cage of untrained rats and recorded their behavior. After one day, all the rats were killed, shaved, and examined for wounds. The experimenters concluded that their "results were not useful in understanding the offensive or defensive nature of the shock-induced response. . . ."

. . . When experiments can be brought under the heading "medical" we are inclined to think that any suffering they involve must be justifiable because the research is contributing to the alleviation of suffering. But . . . the testing of therapeutic drugs is less likely to be motivated by the desire for maximum good to all than by the desire for maximum profit. The broad label "medical research" can also be used to cover research that is motivated by a general intellectual curiosity.

Such curiosity may be acceptable as part of a basic search for knowledge when it involves no suffering, but should not be tolerated if it causes pain. Very often, too, basic medical research has been going on for decades and much of it, in the long run, turns out to have been quite pointless. As an illustration, consider the following series of experiments stretching back nearly a century, on the effects of heat on animals:

In 1880 H. C. Wood placed a number of animals in boxes with glass lids and placed the boxes on a brick pavement on a hot day. He used rabbits, pigeons, and cats. His observations on a rabbit are typical. At a temperature of 109.5 degrees Fahrenheit the rabbit jumps and "kicks hind legs with great fury." The rabbit then has a convulsive attack. At 112 degrees Fahrenheit the animal lies on its side slobbering. At 120 degrees Fahrenheit it is gasping and squealing weakly. Soon after it dies.

In 1881 a report appeared in *The Lancet* on dogs and rabbits whose temperatures had been raised to 113 degrees Fahrenheit. It was found that death could be prevented by cool air currents, and the results were said to indicate "the importance of keeping down the temperature in those cases in which it exhibits a tendency to rise to [an] extreme height."

In 1927 W. W. Hall and E. G. Wakefield of the U.S. Naval Medical School placed ten dogs in a hot humid chamber to produce experimental heatstroke. The animals first showed restlessness, breathing difficulties, swelling and congestion of the eyes, and thirst. Some had convulsions. Some died early in the experiment. Those who did not had severe diarrhea and died after removal from the chamber.

In 1954 at Yale University School of Medicine, M. Lennox, W. Sibley, and H. Zimmerman placed thirty-two kittens in a "radiant-heating" chamber. The kittens were "subjected to a total of 49 heating periods. . . . Struggling was common, particularly as the temperature rose." Convulsions occurred on nine occasions: "Repeated convulsions were the rule." As many as thirty convulsions occurred in rapid sequence. Five kittens died during convulsions, and six without convulsions. The other kittens were killed by the experimenters for autopsies. The experimenters reported: "The findings in artificially induced fever in kittens conform to the clinical and EEG findings in human beings and previous clinical findings in kittens. . . ."

In 1969 S. Michaelson, a veterinarian at the University of Rochester, exposed dogs and rabbits to heat-producing microwaves until their temperatures reached the critical level of 107 degrees Fahrenheit or greater. He observed that dogs start panting shortly after microwave exposure begins. Most "display increased activity varying from restlessness to extreme agitation." Near the point of death, weakness and prostration occur. In the case of rabbits "within 5 minutes, desperate attempts are made to escape the cage," and the rabbits die within forty minutes. Michaelson concluded that an increase in heat from microwaves produces damage "indistinguishable from fever in general. . . ."

In 1984 experimenters working for the Federal Aviation Administration, stating that "animals occasionally die from heat stress encountered during shipping in the nation's transportation systems," subjected ten beagles to experimental heat. The dogs were isolated in chambers, fitted with muzzles, and exposed to 95 degrees Fahrenheit combined with high humidity. They were given no food or water, and were kept in these conditions for twenty-four hours. The behavior of the dogs was observed; it included "deliberate agitated activity such as pawing at the crate walls, continuous circling, tossing of the head to shed the muzzle, rubbing the muzzle back and forth on the floor of the crate, and aggressive acts on the sensor guards." Some of the dogs died in the chambers. When the survivors were removed, some vomited blood, and all were weak and exhausted. The experimenters refer to "subsequent experiments on more than 100 beagles. . . ."

Here we have cited a series of experiments going back into the nineteenth century—and I have had space sufficient to include only a fraction of the published literature. The experiments obviously caused great suffering; and the major finding seems to be the advice that heatstroke victims should be cooled. . . . Similar series of experiments are to be found in many other fields of medicine. In the New York City offices of United Action for Animals there are filing cabinets full of photocopies of experiments reported in the journals. Each thick file contains reports on numerous experiments, often fifty or more, and the labels on the files tell their own story: "Acceleration," "Aggression," "Asphyxiation," "Blinding," "Burning," "Centrifuge," "Compression," "Concussion," "Crowding," "Crushing," "Decompression," "Drug Tests," "Experimental Neurosis," "Freezing," "Heating," "Hemorrhage," "Hindleg Beating," "Immobilization," "Isolation," "Multiple Injuries," "Prey Killing," "Protein Deprivation," "Punishment," "Radiation," "Starvation," "Shock," "Spinal Cord Injuries," "Stress," "Thirst," and many more. While some of the experiments may have led to advances in medical knowledge, the value of this knowledge is often questionable, and in some cases the knowledge might have been gained in other ways. Many of the experiments appear to be trivial or misconceived, and some of them were not even designed to yield important benefits. . . .

When are experiments on animals justifiable? Upon learning of the nature of many of the experiments carried out, some people react by saying that all experiments on animals should be prohibited immediately. But if we make our demands as absolute as this, the experimenters have a ready reply: Would we be prepared to let thousands of humans die if they could be saved by a single experiment on a single animal?

This question is, of course, purely hypothetical. There has never been and never could be a single experiment that saved thousands of lives. The way to reply to this hypothetical question is to pose another. Would the experimenters be prepared to carry out their experiment on a human orphan under six months old if that were the only way to save thousands of lives?

If the experimenters would not be prepared to use a human infant then their readiness to use nonhuman animals reveals an unjustifiable form of discrimination on the basis of species, since adult apes, monkeys, dogs, cats, rats, and other animals are more aware of what is happening to them, more self-directing, and, so far as we can tell, at least as sensitive to pain as a human infant. (I have specified that the human infant be an orphan, to avoid the complications of the feelings of parents. Specifying the case in this way is, if anything, overgenerous to those defending the use of nonhuman animals in experiments, since mammals intended for experimental use are usually separated from their mothers at an early age, when the separation causes distress for both mother and young.)

So far as we know, human infants possess no morally relevant characteristic to a higher degree than adult nonhuman animals, unless we are to count the infants' potential as a characteristic that makes it wrong to experiment on them. Whether this characteristic should count is controversial—if we count it, we shall have to condemn abortion along with experiments on infants, since the potential of the infant and the fetus is the same. To avoid the complexities of this issue, however, we can alter our original question a little and assume that the infant is one with irreversible brain damage so severe as to rule out any mental development beyond the level of a six-month-old infant. There are, unfortunately, many such human beings,

locked away in special wards throughout the country, some of them long since abandoned by their parents and other relatives, and, sadly, sometimes unloved by anyone else. Despite their mental deficiencies, the anatomy and physiology of these infants are in nearly all respects identical with those of normal humans. If, therefore, we were to force-feed them with large quantities of floor polish or drip concentrated solutions of cosmetics into their eyes, we would have a much more reliable indication of the safety of these products for humans than we now get by attempting to extrapolate the results of tests on a variety of other species. The LD50 tests, the Draize eye tests, the radiation experiments, the heatstroke experiments, and many others could have told us more about human reactions to the experimental situation if they had been carried out on severely brain-damaged humans instead of dogs or rabbits.

So whenever experimenters claim that their experiments are important enough to justify the use of animals, we should ask them whether they would be prepared to use a brain-damaged human being at a similar mental level to the animals they are planning to use. I cannot imagine that anyone would seriously propose carrying out the experiments described in this chapter on brain-damaged human beings. Occasionally it has become known that medical experiments have been performed on human beings without their consent; one case did concern institutionalized intellectually disabled children, who were given hepatitis. When such harmful experiments on human beings become known, they usually lead to an outcry against the experimenters, and rightly so. They are, very often, a further example of the arrogance of the research worker who justifies everything on the grounds of increasing knowledge. But if the experimenter claims that the experiment is important enough to justify inflicting suffering on animals, why is it not important enough to justify inflicting suffering on humans at the same mental level? What difference is there between the two? Only that one is a member of our species and the other is not? But to appeal to that difference is to reveal a bias no more defensible than racism or any other form of arbitrary discrimination.

The analogy between speciesism and racism applies in practice as well as in theory in the area of experimentation. Blatant speciesism leads to painful experiments on other species, defended on the grounds of their contribution to knowledge and possible usefulness for our species. Blatant racism has led to painful experiments on other races, defended on the grounds of their contribution to knowledge and possible usefulness for the experimenting race. Under the Nazi regime in Germany, nearly two hundred doctors, some of them eminent in the world of medicine, took part in experiments on Jews and Russian and Polish prisoners. Thousands of other physicians knew of these experiments, some of which were the subject of lectures at medical academies. Yet the records show that the doctors sat through verbal reports by doctors on how horrible injuries were inflicted on these "lesser races," and then proceeded to discuss the medical lessons to be learned from them, without anyone making even a mild protest about the nature of the experiments. The parallels between this attitude and that of experimenters today toward animals are striking. Then, as now, subjects were frozen, heated, and put in decompression chambers. Then, as now, these events were written up in dispassionate scientific jargon. The following paragraph is taken from a report by a Nazi scientist of an experiment on a human being, placed in a decompression chamber:

> After five minutes spasms appeared; between the sixth and tenth minute respiration increased in frequency, the TP [test person] losing consciousness. From the eleventh to the thirtieth minute respiration slowed down to three inhalations per minute, only to cease entirely at the end of that period. . . . About half an hour after breathing ceased, an autopsy was begun.

Decompression chamber experimentation did not stop with the defeat of the Nazis. It shifted to nonhuman animals. At the University of Newcastle on Tyne, in England, for instance, scientists used pigs. The pigs were subjected to up to eighty-one periods of decompression over a period of nine months. All suffered attacks of decompression sickness, and some died from these attacks. The example illustrates only too well what the great Jewish writer Isaac Bashevis Singer has written: "In their behavior towards creatures, all men [are] Nazis. . . ."

We have still not answered the question of when an experiment might be justifiable. It will not do to say "Never!" Putting morality in such black-and-white terms is appealing, because it eliminates the need to think about particular cases; but in extreme circumstances, such absolutist answers always break down. Torturing a human being is almost always wrong, but it is not absolutely wrong. If torture were the only way in which we could discover the location of a nuclear bomb hidden in a New York City basement and timed to go off within the hour, then torture would be justifiable. Similarly, if a single experiment could cure a dis-

ease like leukemia, that experiment would be justifiable. But in actual life the benefits are always more remote, and more often than not they are nonexistent. So how do we decide when an experiment is justifiable?

We have seen that experimenters reveal a bias in favor of their own species whenever they carry out experiments on nonhumans for purposes that they would not think justified them in using human beings, even brain-damaged ones. This principle gives us a guide toward an answer to our question. Since a speciesist bias, like a racist bias, is unjustifiable, an experiment cannot be justified unless the experiment is so important that the use of a brain-damaged human would also be justifiable.

This is not an absolutist principle. I do not believe that it could never be justifiable to experiment on a brain-damaged human. If it really were possible to save several lives by an experiment that would take just one life, and there were no other way those lives could be saved, it would be right to do the experiment. But this would be an extremely rare case. Certainly none of the experiments described in this chapter could pass this test. Admittedly, as with any dividing line, there would be a gray area where it was difficult to decide if an experiment could be justified. But we need not get distracted by such considerations now. As this chapter has shown, we are in the midst of an emergency in which appalling suffering is being inflicted on millions of animals for purposes that on any impartial view are obviously inadequate to justify the suffering. When we have ceased to carry out all those experiments, then there will be time enough to discuss what to do about the remaining ones which are claimed to be essential to save lives or prevent greater suffering. . . .

. . . In the United States, where experimenters can do virtually as they please with animals, one way of making progress might be to ask those who use this argument to defend the need for animal experiments whether they would be prepared to accept the verdict of an ethics committee that, like those in many other countries, includes animal welfare representatives and is entitled to weigh the costs to the animals against the possible benefits of the research. If the answer is no, the defense of animal experimentation by reference to the need to cure major diseases has been proved to be simply a deceitful distraction that serves to mislead the public about what the experimenters want: permission to do whatever they like with animals. For otherwise why would the experimenter not be prepared to leave the decision on carrying out the experiment to an ethics committee, which would surely be as keen to see major diseases ended as the rest of the community? If the answer is yes, the experimenter should be asked to sign a statement asking for the creation of such an ethics committee.

Suppose that we were able to go beyond minimal reforms of the sort that already exist in the more enlightened nations. Suppose we could reach a point at which the interests of animals really were given equal consideration with the similar interests of human beings. That would mean the end of the vast industry of animal experimentation as we know it today. Around the world, cages would empty and laboratories would close down. It should not be thought, though, that medical research would grind to a halt or that a flood of untested products would come onto the market. So far as new products are concerned it is true, as I have already said, that we would have to make do with fewer of them, using ingredients already known to be safe. That does not seem to be any great loss. But for testing really essential products, as well as for other kinds of research, alternative methods not requiring animals can and would be found. . . .

The defenders of animal experimentation are fond of telling us that animal experimentation has greatly increased our life expectancy. In the midst of the debate over reform of the British law on animal experimentation, for example, the Association of the British Pharmaceutical Industry ran a full-page advertisement in the *Guardian* under the headline "They say life begins at forty. Not so long ago, that's about when it ended." The advertisement went on to say that it is now considered to be a tragedy if a man dies in his forties, whereas in the nineteenth century it was commonplace to attend the funeral of a man in his forties, for the average life expectancy was only forty-two. The advertisement stated that "it is thanks largely to the breakthroughs that have been made through research which requires animals that most of us are able to live into our seventies."

Such claims are simply false. In fact, this particular advertisement was so blatantly misleading that a specialist in community medicine, Dr. David St. George, wrote to *The Lancet* saying "the advertisement is good teaching material, since it illustrates two major errors in the interpretation of statistics." He also referred to Thomas McKeown's influential book *The Role of Medicine,* published in 1976, which set off a debate about the relative contributions of social and environmental changes, as compared with medical interven-

tion, in improvements in mortality since the mid-nineteenth century; and he added:

> This debate has been resolved, and it is now widely accepted that medical interventions had only a marginal effect on population mortality and mainly at a very late stage, after death rates had already fallen strikingly.

J. B. and S. M. McKinley reached a similar conclusion in a study of the decline of ten major infectious diseases in the United States. They showed that in every case except poliomyelitis the death rate had already fallen dramatically (presumably because of improved sanitation and diet) before any new form of medical treatment was introduced. Concentrating on the 40 percent fall in crude mortality in the United States between 1910 and 1984, they estimated "conservatively" that

> perhaps 3.5 percent of the fall in the overall death rate can be explained through medical interventions for the major infectious diseases. Indeed, given that it is precisely for these diseases that medicine claims most success in lowering mortality, 3.5 percent probably represents a reasonable upper-limit estimate of the total contribution of medical measures to the decline in infectious disease mortality in the United States.

Remember that this 3.5 percent is a figure for all medical intervention. The contribution of animal experimentation itself can be, at most, only a fraction of this tiny contribution to the decline in mortality. . . .

Finally, it is important to realize that the major health problems of the world largely continue to exist, not because we do not know how to prevent disease and keep people healthy, but because no one is putting enough effort and money into doing what we already know how to do. The diseases that ravage Asia, Africa, Latin America, and the pockets of poverty in the industrialized West are diseases that, by and large, we know how to cure. They have been eliminated in communities that have adequate nutrition, sanitation, and health care. It has been estimated that 250,000 children die each week around the world, and that one quarter of these deaths are by dehydration caused by diarrhea. A simple treatment, already known and needing no animal experimentation, could prevent the deaths of these children. Those who are genuinely concerned about improving health care would probably make a more effective contribution to human health if they left the laboratories and saw to it that our existing stock of medical knowledge reached those who need it most.

# The Case for the Use of Animals in Biomedical Research

## Carl Cohen

Carl Cohen rejects arguments by those who favor severely curbing or eliminating animal experimentation, then defends the position that we have a strong duty to conduct such experiments to alleviate human suffering and extend human lives.

Animals have no rights, Cohen claims. To have a right is to have a moral claim against others. This means having the capacity to recognize conflicts between one's self-interest and what is right and being able to restrain one's self-interest when appropriate. Animals lack these capacities. Hence, they are not the sort of beings who *can* possess rights, and lacking rights, their interests may be sacrificed for the welfare of others.

Cohen rejects Peter Singer's argument that the pleasures and pains of animals deserve consideration equal to those of humans in calculating the overall benefits of animal experiments, because holding otherwise is "speciesism." Singer's analogy with racism and sexism does not hold, Cohen claims, because animals lack autonomy and membership in the moral community. Indeed, speciesism is "essential to right conduct," because those who fail to make the relevant distinctions between humans and nonhumans will fail to recognize their moral duties.

In his conclusion, Cohen claims that a proper analysis of animal experimentation shows that, contrary to Singer, instead of having a duty to decrease the use of animal experimentation, we have a duty to increase it.

Using animals as research subjects in medical investigations is widely condemned on two grounds: first, because it wrongly violates the *rights* of animals,[1] and second, because it wrongly imposes on sentient creatures much avoidable *suffering.*[2] Neither of these arguments is sound. The first relies on a mistaken understanding of rights; the second relies on a mistaken calculation of consequences. Both deserve definitive dismissal.

## Why Animals Have No Rights

A right, properly understood, is a claim, or potential claim, that one party may exercise against another. The target against whom such a claim may be registered can be a single person, a group, a community, or (perhaps) all humankind. The content of rights claims also varies greatly: repayment of loans, nondiscrimination by employers, noninterference by the state, and so on.

From the *New England Journal of Medicine,* Vol. 315, no. 14 (1986), pp. 865–870.

To comprehend any genuine right fully, therefore, we must know *who* holds the right, *against whom* it is held, and *to what* it is a right.

Alternative sources of rights add complexity. Some rights are grounded in constitution and law (e.g., the right of an accused to trial by jury); some rights are moral but give no legal claims (e.g., my right to your keeping the promise you gave me); and some rights (e.g., against theft or assault) are rooted both in morals and in law.

The differing targets, contents, and sources of rights, and their inevitable conflict, together weave a tangled web. Notwithstanding all such complications, this much is clear about rights in general: they are in every case claims, or potential claims, within a community of moral agents. Rights arise, and can be intelligibly defended, only among beings who actually do, or can, make moral claims against one another. Whatever else rights may be, therefore, they are necessarily human; their possessors are persons, human beings.

The attributes of human beings from which this moral capability arises have been described variously by philosophers, both ancient and modern: the inner consciousness of a free will (Saint Augustine[3]); the grasp, by human reason, of the binding character of moral law (Saint Thomas[4]); the self-conscious participation of human beings in an objective ethical order (Hegel[5]); human membership in an organic moral community (Bradley[6]); the development of the human self through the consciousness of other moral selves (Mead[7]); and the underivative, intuitive cognition of the rightness of an action (Prichard[8]). Most influential has been Immanuel Kant's emphasis on the universal human possession of a uniquely moral will and the autonomy its use entails.[9] Humans confront choices that are purely moral; humans—but certainly not dogs or mice—lay down moral laws, for others and for themselves. Human beings are self-legislative, morally *auto-nomous*.

Animals (that is, nonhuman animals, the ordinary sense of that word) lack this capacity for free moral judgment. They are not beings of a kind capable of exercising or responding to moral claims. Animals therefore have no rights, and they can have none. This is the core of the argument about the alleged rights of animals. The holders of rights must have the capacity to comprehend rules of duty, governing all including themselves. In applying such rules, the holders of rights must recognize possible conflicts between what is in their own interest and what is just. Only in a community of beings capable of self-restricting moral judgments can the concept of a right be correctly invoked.

Humans have such moral capacities. They are in this sense self-legislative, are members of communities governed by moral rules, and do possess rights. Animals do not have such moral capacities. They are not morally self-legislative, cannot possibly be members of a truly moral community, and therefore cannot possess rights. In conducting research on animal subjects, therefore, we do not violate their rights, because they have none to violate.

To animate life, even in its simplest forms, we give a certain natural reverence. But the possession of rights presupposes a moral status not attained by the vast majority of living things. We must not infer, therefore, that a live being has, simply in being alive, a "right" to its life. The assertion that all animals, only because they are alive and have interests, also possess the "right to life"[10] is an abuse of that phrase, and wholly without warrant.

It does not follow from this, however, that we are morally free to do anything we please to animals. Cer-

tainly not. In our dealings with animals, as in our dealings with other human beings, we have obligations that do not arise from claims against us based on rights. Rights entail obligations, but many of the things one ought to do are in no way tied to another's entitlement. Rights and obligations are not reciprocals of one another, and it is a serious mistake to suppose that they are.

Illustrations are helpful. Obligations may arise from internal commitments made: physicians have obligations to their patients not grounded merely in their patients' rights. Teachers have such obligations to their students, shepherds to their dogs, and cowboys to their horses. Obligations may arise from differences of status: adults owe special care when playing with young children, and children owe special care when playing with young pets. Obligations may arise from special relationships: the payment of my son's college tuition is something to which he may have no right, although it may be my obligation to bear the burden if I reasonably can; my dog has no right to daily exercise and veterinary care, but I do have the obligation to provide these things for her. Obligations may arise from particular acts or circumstances: one may be obliged to another for a special kindness done, or obliged to put an animal out of its misery in view of its condition—although neither the human benefactor nor the dying animal may have had a claim of right.

Plainly, the grounds of our obligations to humans and to animals are manifold and cannot be formulated simply. Some hold that there is a general obligation to do no gratuitous harm to sentient creatures (the principle of nonmaleficence); some hold that there is a general obligation to do good to sentient creatures when that is reasonably within one's power (the principle of beneficence). In our dealings with animals, few will deny that we are at least obliged to act humanely—that is, to treat them with the decency and concern that we owe, as sensitive human beings, to other sentient creatures. To treat animals humanely, however, is not to treat them as humans or as the holders of rights.

A common objection, which deserves a response, may be paraphrased as follows:

> If having rights requires being able to make moral claims, to grasp and apply moral laws, then many humans—the brain-damaged, the comatose, the senile—who plainly lack those capacities must be without rights. But that is absurd. This proves [the critic concludes] that rights do not depend on the presence of moral capacities.[1, 10]

This objection fails; it mistakenly treats an essential feature of humanity as though it were a screen for sorting humans. The capacity for moral judgment that distinguishes humans from animals is not a test to be administered to human beings one by one. Persons who are unable, because of some disability, to perform the full moral functions natural to human beings are certainly not for that reason ejected from the moral community. The issue is one of kind. Humans are of such a kind that they may be the subject of experiments only with their voluntary consent. The choices they make freely must be respected. Animals are of such a kind that it is impossible for them, in principle, to give or withhold voluntary consent or to make a moral choice. What humans retain when disabled, animals have never had.

A second objection, also often made, may be paraphrased as follows:

Capacities will not succeed in distinguishing humans from the other animals. Animals also reason; animals also communicate with one another; animals also care passionately for their young; animals also exhibit desires and preferences.[11, 12] Features of moral relevance —rationality, interdependence, and love—are not exhibited uniquely by human beings. Therefore [this critic concludes] there can be no solid moral distinction between humans and other animals.[10]

This criticism misses the central point. It is not the ability to communicate or to reason, or dependence on one another, or care for the young, or the exhibition of preference, or any such behavior that marks the critical divide. Analogies between human families and those of monkeys, or between human communities and those of wolves, and the like, are entirely beside the point. Patterns of conduct are not at issue. Animals do indeed exhibit remarkable behavior at times. Conditioning, fear, instinct, and intelligence all contribute to species survival. Membership in a community of moral agents nevertheless remains impossible for them. Actors subject to moral judgment must be capable of grasping the generality of an ethical premise in a practical syllogism. Humans act immorally often enough, but only they—never wolves or monkeys—can discern, by applying some moral rule to the facts of a case, that a given act ought or ought not to be performed. The moral restraints imposed by humans on themselves are thus highly abstract and are often in conflict with the self-interest of the agent. Communal behavior among animals, even when most intelligent and most endearing, does not approach autonomous morality in this fundamental sense.

Genuinely moral acts have an internal as well as an external dimension. Thus, in law, an act can be criminal only when the guilty deed, the actus reus, is done with a guilty mind, mens rea. No animal can ever commit a crime; bringing animals to criminal trial is the mark of primitive ignorance. The claims of moral right are similarly inapplicable to them. Does a lion have a right to eat a baby zebra? Does a baby zebra have a right not to be eaten? Such questions, mistakenly invoking the concept of right where it does not belong, do not make good sense. Those who condemn biomedical research because it violates "animal rights" commit the same blunder.

## In Defense of "Speciesism"

Abandoning reliance on animal rights, some critics resort instead to animal sentience—their feelings of pain and distress. We ought to desist from the imposition of pain insofar as we can. Since all or nearly all experimentation on animals does impose pain and could be readily forgone, say these critics, it should be stopped. The ends sought may be worthy, but those ends do not justify imposing agonies on humans, and by animals the agonies are felt no less. The laboratory use of animals (these critics conclude) must therefore be ended—or at least very sharply curtailed.

Argument of this variety is essentially utilitarian, often expressly so[13]; it is based on the calculation of the net product, in pains and pleasures, resulting from experiments on animals. Jeremy Bentham, comparing horses and dogs with other sentient creatures, is thus commonly quoted: "The question is not, Can they reason? nor Can they talk? but, Can they suffer?"[14]

Animals certainly can suffer and surely ought not to be made to suffer needlessly. But in inferring, from these uncontroversial premises, that biomedical research causing animals distress is largely (or wholly) wrong, the critic commits two serious errors.

The first error is the assumption, often explicitly defended, that all sentient animals have equal moral standing. Between a dog and a human being, according to this view, there is no moral difference; hence the pains suffered by dogs must be weighed no differently from the pains suffered by humans. To deny such equality, according to this critic, is to give unjust preference to one species over another; it is "speciesism." The most influential statement of this moral equality of species was made by Peter Singer:

The racist violates the principle of equality by giving greater weight to the interests of members of his own race when there is a clash between their interests and the interests of those of another race. The sexist violates the principle of equality by favoring the interests of his own sex. Similarly the speciesist allows the interests of his own species to override the greater interests of members of other species. The pattern is identical in each case.[2]

This argument is worse than unsound; it is atrocious. It draws an offensive moral conclusion from a deliberately devised verbal parallelism that is utterly specious. Racism has no rational ground whatever. Differing degrees of respect or concern for humans for no other reason than that they are members of different races is an injustice totally without foundation in the nature of the races themselves. Racists, even if acting on the basis of mistaken factual beliefs, do grave moral wrong precisely because there is no morally relevant distinction among the races. The supposition of such differences has led to outright horror. The same is true of the sexes, neither sex being entitled by right to greater respect or concern than the other. No dispute here.

Between species of animate life, however— between (for example) humans on the one hand and cats or rats on the other—the morally relevant differences are enormous, and almost universally appreciated. Humans engage in moral reflection; humans are morally autonomous; humans are members of moral communities, recognizing just claims against their own interest. Human beings do have rights; theirs is a moral status very different from that of cats or rats.

I am a speciesist. Speciesism is not merely plausible; it is essential for right conduct, because those who will not make the morally relevant distinctions among species are almost certain, in consequence, to misapprehend their true obligations. The analogy between speciesism and racism is insidious. Every sensitive moral judgment requires that the differing natures of the beings to whom obligations are owed be considered. If all forms of animate life—or vertebrate animal life?—must be treated equally, and if therefore in evaluating a research program the pains of a rodent count equally with the pains of a human, we are forced to conclude (1) that neither humans nor rodents possess rights, or (2) that rodents possess all the rights that humans possess. Both alternatives are absurd. Yet one or the other must be swallowed if the moral equality of all species is to be defended.

Humans owe to other humans a degree of moral regard that cannot be owed to animals. Some humans take on the obligation to support and heal others, both humans and animals, as a principal duty in their lives; the fulfillment of that duty may require the sacrifice of many animals. If biomedical investigators abandon the effective pursuit of their professional objectives because they are convinced that they may not do to animals what the service of humans requires, they will fail, objectively, to do their duty. Refusing to recognize the moral differences among species is a sure path to calamity. (The largest animal rights group in the country is People for the Ethical Treatment of Animals; its codirector, Ingrid Newkirk, calls research using animal subjects, "fascism" and "supremacism." "Animal liberationists do not separate out the *human* animal," she says, "so there is no rational basis for saying that a human being has special rights. A rat is a pig is a dog is a boy. They're all mammals."[15])

Those who claim to base their objection to the use of animals in biomedical research on their reckoning of the net pleasures and pains produced make a second error, equally grave. Even if it were true—as it is surely not—that the pains of all animate beings must be counted equally, a cogent utilitarian calculation requires that we weigh all the consequences of the use, and of the nonuse, of animals in laboratory research. Critics relying (however mistakenly) on animal rights may claim to ignore the beneficial results of such research, rights being trump cards to which interest and advantage must give way. But an argument that is explicitly framed in terms of interest and benefit for all over the long run must attend also to the disadvantageous consequences of not using animals in research, and to all the achievements attained and attainable only through their use. The sum of the benefits of their use is utterly beyond quantification. The elimination of horrible disease, the increase of longevity, the avoidance of great pain, the saving of lives, and the improvement of the quality of lives (for humans and for animals) achieved through research using animals is so incalculably great that the argument of these critics, systematically pursued, establishes not their conclusion but its reverse: to refrain from using animals in biomedical research is, on utilitarian grounds, morally wrong.

When balancing the pleasures and pains resulting from the use of animals in research, we must not fail to place on the scales the terrible pains that would have resulted, would be suffered now, and would long continue had animals not been used. Every disease eliminated, every vaccine developed, every method of pain relief devised, every surgical procedure invented, every prosthetic device implanted—indeed, virtually every modern medical therapy is due, in part or in whole, to experimentation using animals. Nor may we ignore, in the balancing process, the predictable gains in human (and animal) well-being that are probably achievable in the future but that will not be achieved if the decision is made now to desist from such research or to curtail it.

Medical investigators are seldom insensitive to the distress their work may cause animal subjects. Opponents of research using animals are frequently insensitive to the cruelty of the results of the restrictions they would impose.[2] Untold numbers of human beings—real persons, although not now identifiable—would suffer grievously as the consequence of this well-meaning but shortsighted tenderness. If the morally relevant differences between humans and animals are borne in mind, and if all relevant considerations are weighed, the calculation of long-term consequences must give overwhelming support for biomedical research using animals.

## Concluding Remarks

### Substitution

The humane treatment of animals requires that we desist from experimenting on them if we can accomplish the same result using alternative methods—in vitro experimentation, computer simulation, or others. Critics of some experiments using animals rightly make this point.

It would be a serious error to suppose, however, that alternative techniques could soon be used in most research now using live animal subjects. No other methods now on the horizon—or perhaps ever to be available—can fully replace the testing of a drug, a procedure, or a vaccine, in live organisms. The flood of new medical possibilities being opened by the successes of recombinant DNA technology will turn to a trickle if testing on live animals is forbidden. When initial trials entail great risks, there may be no forward movement whatever without the use of live animal subjects. In seeking knowledge that may prove critical in later clinical applications, the unavailability of animals for inquiry may spell complete stymie. In the United States, federal regulations require the testing of new drugs and other products on animals, for efficacy

and safety, before human beings are exposed to them.[16, 17] We would not want it otherwise.

Every advance in medicine—every new drug, new operation, new therapy of any kind—must sooner or later be tried on a living being for the first time. That trial, controlled or uncontrolled, will be an experiment. The subject of that experiment, if it is not an animal, will be a human being. Prohibiting the use of live animals in biomedical research, therefore, or sharply restricting it, must result either in the blockage of much valuable research or in the replacement of animal subjects with human subjects. These are the consequences—unacceptable to most reasonable persons—of not using animals in research.

### Reduction

Should we not at least reduce the use of animals in biomedical research? No, we should increase it, to avoid when feasible the use of humans as experimental subjects. Medical investigations putting human subjects at some risk are numerous and greatly varied. The risks run in such experiments are usually unavoidable, and (thanks to earlier experiments on animals) most such risks are minimal or moderate. But some experimental risks are substantial.

When an experimental protocol that entails substantial risk to humans comes before an institutional review board, what response is appropriate? The investigation, we may suppose, is promising and deserves support, so long as its human subjects are protected against unnecessary dangers. May not the investigators be fairly asked, Have you done all that you can to eliminate risk to humans by the extensive testing of that drug, that procedure, or that device on animals? To achieve maximal safety for humans we are right to require thorough experimentation on animal subjects before humans are involved.

Opportunities to increase human safety in this way are commonly missed; trials in which risks may be shifted from humans to animals are often not devised, sometimes not even considered. Why? For the investigator, the use of animals as subjects is often more expensive, in money and time, than the use of human subjects. Access to suitable human subjects is often quick and convenient, whereas access to appropriate animal subjects may be awkward, costly, and burdened with red tape. Physician-investigators have often had more experience working with human beings and know precisely where the needed pool of subjects is to be found and how they may be enlisted.

Animals, and the procedures for their use, are often less familiar to these investigators. Moreover, the use of animals in place of humans is now more likely to be the target of zealous protests from without. The upshot is that humans are sometimes subjected to risks that animals could have borne, and should have borne, in their place. To maximize the protection of human subjects, I conclude, the wide and imaginative use of live animal subjects should be encouraged rather than discouraged. This enlargement in the use of animals is our obligation.

### Consistency

Finally, inconsistency between the profession and the practice of many who oppose research using animals deserves comment. This frankly *ad hominem* observation aims chiefly to show that a coherent position rejecting the use of animals in medical research imposes costs so high as to be intolerable even to the critics themselves.

One cannot coherently object to the killing of animals in biomedical investigations while continuing to eat them. Anesthetics and thoughtful animal husbandry render the level of actual animal distress in the laboratory generally lower than that in the abattoir. So long as death and discomfort do not substantially differ in the two contexts, the consistent objector must not only refrain from all eating of animals but also protest as vehemently against others eating them as against others experimenting on them. No less vigorously must the critic object to the wearing of animal hides in coats and shoes, to employment in any industrial enterprise that uses animal parts, and to any commercial development that will cause death or distress to animals.

Killing animals to meet human needs for food, clothing, and shelter is judged entirely reasonable by most persons. The ubiquity of these uses and the virtual universality of moral support for them confront the opponent of research using animals with an inescapable difficulty. How can the many common uses of animals be judged morally worthy, while their use in scientific investigation is judged unworthy?

The number of animals used in research is but the tiniest fraction of the total used to satisfy assorted human appetites. That these appetites, often base and satisfiable in other ways, morally justify the far larger consumption of animals, whereas the quest for improved human health and understanding cannot justify the far smaller, is wholly implausible. Aside from the numbers of animals involved, the distinction in terms of worthiness of use, drawn with regard to any single animal, is not defensible. A given sheep is surely not more justifiably used to put lamb chops on the supermarket counter than to serve in testing a new contraceptive or a new prosthetic device. The needless killing of animals is wrong; if the common killing of them for our food or convenience is right, the less common but more humane uses of animals in the service of medical science are certainly not less right.

Scrupulous vegetarianism, in matters of food, clothing, shelter, commerce, and recreation, and in all other spheres, is the only fully coherent position the critic may adopt. At great human cost, the lives of fish and crustaceans must also be protected, with equal vigor, if speciesism has been forsworn. A very few consistent critics adopt this position. It is the *reductio ad absurdum* of the rejection of moral distinctions between animals and human beings.

Opposition to the use of animals in research is based on arguments of two different kinds—those relying on the alleged rights of animals and those relying on the consequences for animals. I have argued that arguments of both kinds must fail. We surely do have obligations to animals, but they have, and can have, no rights against us on which research can infringe. In calculating the consequences of animal research, we must weigh all the long-term benefits of the results achieved—to animals and to humans—and in that calculation we must not assume the moral equality of all animate species.

### Notes

1.  Regan T. *The case for animal rights.* Berkeley, Calif.: University of California Press, 1983.
2.  Singer P. *Animal liberation.* New York: Avon Books, 1977.
3.  St. Augustine. *Confessions. Book Seven.* 397 A.D. New York: Pocketbooks, 1957: 104–26.
4.  St. Thomas Aquinas. *Summa theologica.* 1273 A.D. *Philosophic texts.* New York: Oxford University Press, 1960: 353–66.
5.  Hegel GWF. *Philosophy of right.* 1821. London: Oxford University Press, 1952: 105–10.
6.  Bradley FH. Why should I be moral? 1876. In: Melden AI, ed. *Ethical theories.* New York: Prentice-Hall, 1950: 345–59.
7.  Mead GH. The genesis of the self and social control. 1925. In: Reck AJ, ed. *Selected writings.* Indianapolis: Bobbs-Merrill, 1964: 264–93.
8.  Prichard HA. Does moral philosophy rest on a mistake? 1912. In: Cellars W, Hospers J, eds. *Readings in ethical theory.* New York: Appleton-Century-Crofts, 1952: 149–63.
9.  Kant I. *Fundamental principles of the metaphysic of morals.* 1785. New York: Liberal Arts Press, 1949.

10. Rollin BE. *Animal rights and human morality*. New York: Prometheus Books, 1981.

11. Hoff C. Immoral and moral uses of animals. *N Engl J Med* 1980: 302: 115–8.

12. Jamieson D. "Killing persons and other beings. In: Miller HB, Williams WH, eds. *Ethics and animals*. Clifton, N.J.: Humana Press, 1983: 135–46.

13. Singer P. Ten years of animal liberation. *New York Review of Books*. 1985: 31: 46–52.

14. Bentham J. *Introduction to the principles of morals and legislation*. London: Athlone Press, 1970.

15. McCabe K. Who will live, who will die? *Washingtonian Magazine*. August 1986: 115.

16. U.S. Code of Federal Regulations. Title 21, Sect. 505(i). Food, drug, and cosmetic regulations.

17. U.S. Code of Federal Regulations. Title 16, Sect. 1500.40–2. Consumer product regulations.

## Decision Scenario 1

On April 6, 1998, researchers at the National Cancer Institute announced that the clinical trials of the drug tamoxifen had produced enough statistical data to show that there was a clear difference in the incidence of breast cancer among women taking the drug, compared with women who were not. Because half of the 13,388 women in the study were receiving a placebo instead of an active drug, the study was stopped before its originally planned date so that all of them could receive the drug's benefits. The trial had lasted six years and was intended to determine whether tamoxifen had a protective effect against breast cancer. "We all felt that question had been answered," said Leslie Ford of the National Cancer Institute.

British researchers were unhappy with the American decision and called the cancellation of the clinical trial premature. "The Americans have unblinded the trial, which means it will be unbalanced, and they will not be able to answer many questions," said Trevor Powles, the head of the pilot study with tamoxifen.

"Our emphasis is to try to get long-term data from the trial," said Tony Howell of Christie's Hospital, co-chair of the seven-nation British study. "Unfortunately the Americans will not be able to do that now."

1. Assuming the data show women who take the drug are less likely to get breast cancer, would it be morally wrong to continue the study? What position might Hellman and Hellman take on this issue? Would Jonas agree with the American decision?

2. Suppose Tony Howell is right and that canceling the trial makes it impossible to answer a number of important questions. Would it be wrong to continue the trial? Those who are receiving a placebo are not being given something that will cause them harm. Also, because they gave their consent, they knew they might be receiving placebo, so why isn't it all right to continue the trial? Might this be the line of reasoning taken by Passamani?

## Decision Scenario 2

"Mrs, Wilkins," Dr. Blake said, "I want to ask you to participate in what we call a Phase I trial of a new drug called Novamed. The aim of such a trial, it's my duty to tell you, isn't to treat your disease, but to help us determine how toxic Novamed is. What we learn may help us figure out how to help other people."

"You mean Novamed won't help me?" Mrs. Wilkins asked.

"I can't say that it won't," Dr. Blake said. "Quite frankly, we just don't know. That possibility is always there, but that's not why you should agree to participate. If you do agree, that is."

"I've been told my disease is terminal," Mrs.

Wilkins said. "I'm in the last stage of life right now. So it looks to me like I don't have anything to lose and, potentially, I've got something to gain. It's a gamble, and I'm ready to take it."

"So long as you know Novamed isn't likely to help you," Dr. Blake said. "I'll get the consent forms, and you can ask me any other questions that occur to you."

1. According to Miller, should Mrs. Wilkins' consent to participate in a Phase I trial be regarded as informed?

2. Would Jonas regard Mrs. Wilkins as an appropriate candidate to participate in a Phase I clinical trial?

3. How does Miller suggest that investigators go about getting people to consent legitimately to Phase I trials?

---

## Decision Scenario 3

In 1988 the Environmental Protection Agency decided to exclude from a study it had commissioned the use of all Nazi data on the effects of phosgene gas. Those favoring the exclusion held that data obtained by unethical means should never be used. Opponents of this view held that making use of such data is a way of honoring and remembering those who were sacrificed to obtain it.

1. On what grounds, according to Buchanan, can we say that the data obtained by the Nazis were unethical? According to their principles, they were doing nothing wrong.

2. Suppose the data had never been published but were available as research notes. Would this make any difference to the question of whether the data ought to be used?

---

## Decision Scenario 4

"You realize," Dr. Thorne said, "that you may not be in the group that receives medication. You may be in the placebo group for at least part of the time."

"Right," Ms. Ross said. "You're just going to give me some medicine."

"And do you understand the aims of the research?"

"You want to help me get better," Ms. Ross suggested hesitantly.

"We hope you get better, of course. But that's not what we're trying to accomplish here. We're trying to find out if this medication will help other people in your condition if we can treat them earlier than we were able to treat you."

"You want to help people," Ms. Ross said.

"That's right. But you do understand that we may not be helping you in this experiment?"

"But you're going to try?"

"Not exactly. I mean, we aren't going to try to harm you. But we aren't necessarily going to be giving you the preferred treatment for your complaint either. Do you know the difference between research and therapy?"

"Research is when you're trying to find something out. You're searching around."

"That's right. And we're asking you to be part of a research effort. As I told you, there are some risks. Besides the possibility of not getting treatment that you need, the drug may produce limited hepatic portal damage. We're not sure how much."

"I think I understand," Ms. Ross said.

"I'm sure you do," said Dr. Thorne. "I understand that you are freely volunteering to participate in this research."

"Yes, sir. Mrs. Woolerd, she told me if I volunteered I'd get a letter put in my file and I could get early release."

"Mrs. Woolerd told you the review board would take your volunteering into account when they considered whether you should be put on work-release."

"Yes, sir. And I'm awfully anxious to get out of here. I've got two children staying with my aunt, and I need to get out of this place as quick as I can."

"I understand. We can't promise you release, of course. But your participation will look good on your record. Now I have some papers here I want you to sign."

1. Discuss some of the difficulties involved in explaining research procedures to nonexperts and determining whether they are aware of the nature and risks of their participation.

2. What reasons are there for believing that Ms. Ross does not understand what she is volunteering for?

3. Also, discuss the problems involved in securing free and voluntary consent from a person involuntarily confined to an institution (a prisoner, for example).

4. Would the concept of equipoise in this case be the same for Hellman and Hellman and Passamani?

5. Is experimentation in this case justified on Passamani's criteria? On what grounds might Hellman and Hellman object to a clinical trial of this kind?

6. Why does Miller find it necessary for researchers to find a way to obtain genuine consent from patients in Phase I cancer trials?

## Decision Scenario 5

"The Human Subjects Committee has reviewed your protocol for using MK-47 to treat patients with Napier's syndrome," Dr. Helen Laski announced to Dr. Tom Kline. "We can't approve it, because it would be unethical to enroll only six patients, as you propose. Such a clinical trial would involve so few patients as to have no statistical significance."

1. Suppose Napier's syndrome (a fictitious disease) is relatively common. Explain why Halpern and his co-authors would support the decision of the Human Subjects Committee.

2. Suppose MK-47 is a drug that anecdotal evidence suggests may be appropriate for treating Napier's syndrome. Would this be grounds for Halpern et al. to approve the protocol?

3. Suppose Napier's syndrome is a rare disease. What sort of evidence would they require Dr. Kline to present to the committee to persuade them to approve his protocol?

## Decision Scenario 6

The first human heart was transplanted in 1967 in South Africa by Dr. Christiaan Barnard. However, this was not the first heart transplant on a human being. In January 1964, Dr. James Hardy of the University of Mississippi transplanted a chimpanzee heart into Boyd Rush.

Boyd Rush was a deaf-mute who was brought to the University of Mississippi Medical Center unconscious and on the verge of dying. A stepsister, the only relative who could be located, signed a consent form permitting, if necessary, "the insertion of a suitable heart transplant." The form made no reference to the sort of heart that might be employed. Mr. Rush lived for two hours after the transplant.

Dr. Hardy justified the use of the chimpanzee heart on the ground that it was impossible to obtain a human heart. Also, he was encouraged to think the transplant might be successful because of the limited success obtained by Dr. Keith Reentsma in transplanting chimpanzee kidneys into a man dying of glomerulonephritis. The kidney recipient lived for two months.

Dr. Leonard Bailey, the surgeon who transplanted the baboon heart into the child known as Baby Fae, expressed his view of Dr. Hardy in an interview: "He's an idol of mine because he followed through and did what he should have done . . . he took a gamble to try to save a human life."

1. Evaluate the quality of the consent that was secured for transplant surgery in this case.

2. Suppose Mr. Rush's stepsister did know that it was possible that a chimpanzee heart might be used. Should anyone be permitted to give consent to such a transplant on behalf of someone else?

3. If the only way to save Mr. Rush's life was to transplant a chimpanzee heart, was the surgery justified?

4. Suppose the transplant could have been expected to postpone Mr. Rush's death for only a relatively short time. Would Singer regard the sacrifice of a baboon as justified? Would Cohen?

5. Evaluate the criticism that Dr. Hardy was doing no more than performing a medical experiment in which Mr. Rush was the unknowing and unconsenting subject.

---

## Decision Scenario 7

Cardiologist William O'Neill decided he would have to go to Germany to do a clinical test on a device to clean out clogged arteries. Several years previously, researchers at the Centers for Disease Control planned to test the effectiveness of giving vitamin supplements to pregnant women to prevent spina bifida in their children. The National Institute for Child Health and Development objected to the plan to withhold vitamins from the control group. The researchers found Chinese collaborators who arranged for the clinical studies to be done.

Some clinical researchers believe cases like these are widespread and increasing. More and more often, researchers and drug companies are choosing to test medical devices, therapies, and drugs in foreign countries.

Two reasons are mentioned as responsible for the increase. First, the FDA and other federal agencies require so many levels of approval and so much paperwork that efforts to mount clinical trials are discouraged. Second, overzealous advocates of patients' rights have both complicated the approval process and made it difficult to recruit test subjects. Speaking of informed-consent forms to test a new

clot-dissolving drug used during a heart attack, one British researcher said: "The American documents were three pages of legalistic junk. That's not the sort of thing you want to push under someone's nose as he's having a heart attack, terrified with chest pain, on morphine. You want to tell him about the trial, but you want to be humane."

Furthermore, critics of testing have made people so suspicious of medical research that they refuse to participate when asked. By contrast, patients in other countries are more trusting and give their consent more readily.

The situation has been encouraged by an FDA decision to accept data from some foreign trials. The aim of the policy change was to make effective drugs more quickly available in the United States, but a consequence has been to encourage researchers to avoid problems at home by going abroad.

1. Do we have an obligation to make sure that clinical trials in other countries involve the free and informed consent of participants? How might a Kantian answer this question? Do we have a prima facie duty to protect research subjects everywhere?

2. Suppose that in a scientifically well-designed trial a drug to prevent strokes was found to be highly effective, but we learn that the trial was conducted in a third-world country and that the patients in the study were not aware of their status as experimental subjects. Should we refuse to use the drug until the same studies were repeated with subjects who were informed and consenting participants?

3. Suppose the drug was first tested in the United States with consenting subjects and found effec-

tive. Because it is too expensive to use in a third-world country, researchers decide to initiate a clinical trial that will test a cheaper drug against a placebo in Namibia and Zaire. Is it legitimate to use a placebo in such a situation? Could there be a better alternative?

4. Might a utilitarian find the reasons mentioned for shifting testing to foreign countries relevant grounds for weakening current laws designed to protect research subjects?

---

## Decision Scenario 8

During the two years he had worked for the Bioplus Foundation, Dennis Quade had been in many labs. Before he could renew the funding of a grant, he was required to make an on-site inspection of the facilities and review the work of the investigators. Now he was sitting in a small, chilly conference room about to watch a videotape of a phase of the work done at Carolyn Sing's lab.

Sing herself was sitting at the table with him, and she leaned forward and pushed the play button. "The experimental subjects we used are baboons," she told him. "We think they possess facial and cranial structures sufficiently similar to humans to make them the best animal models." Dennis nodded, then watched the monitor in complete silence. He was appalled by what he saw. An adult animal, apparently limp from anesthesia, was strapped to a stainless-steel table. Its head was fitted into a viselike device, and several clamps tightened to hold it immobile. The upper-left side of the baboon's head had been shaved and the area painted with a faintly purple antiseptic solution. A dark circle had been drawn in the center of the painted area.

The white-coated arms of an assistant appeared in the tight focus of the picture. The assistant was holding a device that looked like an oversized electric drill. A long, transparent plastic sleeve stuck out from the chuck-end of the device, and through it Dennis could see a round, stainless-steel plate. A calibrated dial was visible on the side of the device, but Dennis couldn't read the marks.

"That's an impact hammer," Dr. Sing said. "We thought at first we were going to be able to use one off the shelf, but we had to modify one. That's an item we didn't anticipate in our initial budget."

The assistant centered the plastic tube over the spot marked on the baboon's head and pulled the trigger of the impact hammer. The motion of the steel plate was too swift for Dennis to see, but he saw the results. The animal's body jerked in spasm, and a froth of blood, brain tissue, and bone fragments welled up from the purple spot.

Dennis Quade turned away from the monitor, unable to stand the images any longer.

"Through induced head trauma studies, we have been able to learn an enormous amount," Carolyn Sing said. "Not only do we know more about what happens to brain tissue during the first few minutes after trauma, but we've used that knowledge to develop some new management techniques that may save literally tens of thousands of people from permanent brain damage."

Dennis Quade nodded.

1. Would Peter Singer oppose such experiments? Suppose it is true that brain damage from head trauma may be reduced or eliminated in thousands of people. Would this make a difference to Singer?

2. If you knew that the information gained from the study described would prevent your child from suffering from brain damage, should this count in your decision about whether such an experiment is justifiable?

3. Is there any reason to suppose that a human life (of any sort) is worth more than an animal life (of any sort)? On what moral grounds, if any, might one object to using patients in a chronic vegetative state as experimental subjects in the study?

4. Would Cohen find the experiment described morally justified? What features does the experiment have that might lead him to approve it? What importance does he attach to animal suffering in an experimental context?

# Chapter 2

# Physicians, Patients, and Others:
# Autonomy, Truth Telling, and Confidentiality

## Chapter Contents

## Classic Case Presentation

### *Donald (Dax) Cowart Rejects Treatment—and Is Ignored*

The man stretched out on the steel platform of the sling with his knees drawn up is thin to the point of emaciation. His face and numerous patches of bare, raw flesh are slathered with layers of thick white salve. A pad covers one eye, and the eyelid of the other is sewn shut. Bandages wrapped around his legs and torso give him the look of a mummy in a low-budget horror movie.

In obvious pain, he writhes on the platform. With rock music playing in the background, white-uniformed attendants in gauze masks raise the sling and lower him into a steel tank of clear liquid.

The real horror began for Donald Cowart in July of 1973. The previous May he had left active duty in the Air Force after three years of service, including a tour of duty in Vietnam, to take a slot in the Air Force Reserve. He returned to his family home in east Texas to wait for an opening as a commercial airline pilot. He was twenty-five years old, a college graduate, unmarried, and in excellent health and top physical condition. A high school athlete who had played football and basketball and run track, he had stayed athletic. He played golf, surfed when he could, and rodeoed. As a pilot for a large airline, he'd be busy, but not too busy to continue the active life he was used to. But in 1973

the airlines weren't looking for new pilots, and while Don waited for them to start hiring again, he decided to join his father as a real estate broker. The two had always been close, so working together was a pleasure for both of them.

And then everything changed forever.

One hot Wednesday afternoon in July, Don and his father drove out to the country to take a look at a piece of land Don thought might be a good buy. They parked the car in a shady, cool spot at a low place in the road beside a bridge. They took a walking tour of the land, but when they returned to the car, it wouldn't start.

Mr. Cowart got out, raised the hood, and tinkered with the carburetor. Don, in the driver's seat, turned the key repeatedly, grinding the engine around so much he got afraid he would run down the battery. Then, after three or four minutes of trying, a blue flame suddenly shot from the carburetor, and a tremendous explosion rocked the car, throwing Don sideways onto the passenger seat. A huge ball of live fire enveloped the car.

Don managed to get the door open, then, still surrounded by fire, he ran three steps toward the woods, the only place that wasn't on fire. But seeing that the undergrowth was so thick that he was likely to get trapped in it and burn to death, he turned away and ran straight down the road. He hurtled through three thick walls of fire, and when he cleared the last one, he threw himself to the ground and rolled to smother the flames.

Getting to his feet, he ran again, shouting for help. He noticed his vision was blurred, as if he were looking at everything from under water, and he realized his eyes had been seared by the fire. *This can't be happening,* he thought as he ran. But the pain assured him that it was. He heard a voice shouting, "I'm coming!" and only then did he stop running and lie down beside the road.

He thought at the time that the car's gas tank had exploded, and only after he had been in a hospital for several days did he learn that the blast and fire were caused by a leak in a propane gas transmission line. Seeping from the line, the gas had collected in the hollow by the bridge, saturating the air to such an extent that the car wouldn't start because the engine couldn't get enough oxygen. The spark from the starter had ignited the gas.

When the farmer who had heard Don's shouts arrived, he said, "Oh, my God." Then Don knew for the first time that he was burned more badly than he had thought. After the farmer came back from looking for Mr. Cowart, Don asked him to get him a gun. "Why?" the man asked.

"Can't you see I'm a dead man," Don told him. "I'm going to die anyway."

"I can't do that," the farmer said gently.

When the first ambulance arrived, Don sent it to pick up his father. When the second came, he didn't want to go to the hospital. "All I wanted to do was die and to die as quickly as possible," he recalled nine years later. Despite his protest, the attendants put him in the ambulance. He asked them to pick him up by his belt, because his burns were so excruciating he couldn't bear to be touched.

Don and his father were taken to a small nearby hospital, but because of the extent of their injuries, they were soon transported to the burn unit of Parkland Hospital in Dallas, 140 miles away. "I'm sorry, Donny boy," his father told him as they were placed in the ambulance. Mr. Cowart died on the way to Parkland. Don continued to insist that he be allowed to die.

Charles Baxter, Don's attending physician, estimated that Don had extremely deep burns over about 65 percent of his body. His face, upper arms, torso, and legs had suffered severe third-degree burns, and both ears were virtually destroyed. His eyes were so damaged that his left eye had to be surgically removed, and he eventually lost the vision in his right eye. His

fingers were burned off down to the second joint, making it impossible for him to pick up anything. The pain was tremendous, and even though he was given substantial doses of narcotics, it remained unbearable for more than a year.

Don's mother had heard about an accidental explosion on the radio, but she learned her husband and son were involved only when the police called her out of an evening church service to tell her. After rushing to Dallas to be with Don, she was approached by his physicians to sign consent forms for surgery and treatment. Knowing nothing about burn therapies, she took the advice offered to her by the physicians. She knew of Don's protest against being treated, but she expected his wish to be allowed to die to pass as soon as he began to recover.

Rex Houston, the family's attorney and close friend, filed a lawsuit with the owners of the propane transmission line for damages resulting from the explosion. He was concerned with going to trial as soon as possible. Don was unmarried and had nobody depending on him, so if he died before the case was heard, the lawsuit would be likely to produce little money. But with Don as a living plaintiff and a young man who had lost the use of both hands and both eyes, the suit had the potential to be of tremendous value. "I had to have a living plaintiff," Houston said years later. Dr. Baxter later said he had discussed the legal and moral aspects of Don's treatment with Mr. Houston.

Don continued to want to die. He asked a nurse with whom he had developed a rapport to give him a drug that would kill him or at least to help him do something to take his own life. As sympathetic as she was, she was forced to refuse his request. Don also asked a family friend to get a gun for him, but then, even while he was asking, he observed that getting him a gun would be pointless, because he had no fingers to pull the trigger.

Dr. Baxter's initial response to Don's request to die was dismissive: "Oh, you don't want to do that," he would say. For a while, though, Don convinced Dr. Baxter he was serious and not simply reacting out of the immediate pain and shock. But eventually Dr. Baxter decided Don talked about wanting to die only to manipulate the people around him and gain control over his environment. Don later rejected this interpretation.

Mrs. Cowart considered her son's medical condition too serious to allow him to make decisions about accepting or rejecting treatment. "Everything was discussed with her in detail," Dr. Baxter recalled. "She was most cooperative and most helpful. We approached the problem of his desire to die very openly." Also, Dr. Baxter remembered, "Even the possibility that it could be allowed was discussed with her. She was never in favor of it, because basically she thought he did not have this desire."

When his burns had healed enough that he was out of danger, Don was moved to the Texas Institute of Rehabilitation in Houston. He agreed to give the program a try, but after about three weeks, he began to refuse treatment again. He had learned that rehabilitation would take years of pain and suffering. The doctors at the Institute honored his request that he not be treated, and in a few days, the burns on his legs became infected again, and the grafted skin peeled away. He came near death.

Dr. Robert Meier, a rehabilitation specialist responsible for Don's care, called a meeting with Don's mother and attorney. They decided that because Don's burns had become infected again due to his refusal to have his dressings changed, he should be hospitalized in an acute care center again.

Don was transferred to the University of Texas Medical Branch at Galveston in April of 1974. Once there, he again refused treatment. Psychiatrist Robert B. White was called in by the surgeons in charge of Don's case, because they thought Don's refusal might be the result of clinical depression or some form of mental illness. If he were found incompetent, a legal guardian could be appointed to give permission for the additional surgery he needed. After examining Don and with the concurrence of a second psychiatrist, Dr. White concluded that Don was fully competent and not suffering from any kind of mental illness. He was, moreover, intelligent, self-aware, and highly articulate.

To control the many infected areas on his body, Don had to be submerged daily in a tank of highly chlorinated water to destroy the microorganisms breeding on the surface of his wounds. The experience was excruciatingly painful, and despite Don's protests and refusals, the "tankings" were carried out anyway. He refused to give his permission for surgery on his hands, which had become more clawlike due to scarring and contracture. Eventually, he consented, with his surgeon's assurance that he would give Don enough drugs to control the pain.

Don wanted to leave the hospital so he could go home and die. But he couldn't leave without help, and neither his physicians nor his mother would agree to help. His mother wanted him taken care of, and moving him home to die of massive infection was more than she could accept. Don accused her of being responsible for prolonging his hopeless condition.

Surgeon Duane Larson was puzzled by Don's ongoing insistence that he wanted to die. Don wasn't on the verge of death and would surely recover some degree of normalcy. He would find new ways to enjoy life. "In essence he was asking people to participate in his death," Dr. Larson recalled.

One alternative Dr. Larson mentioned to Don was for him to be treated until he was well enough to leave the hospital, then he could kill himself, if he still wanted to. Another alternative was to get Don to see that new things could be done to lessen his pain and make him more comfortable. But Dr. Larson also thought Don might be brought to see that some of his outbursts were merely angry "little boy feelings" anyone would experience after going through such a terrible ordeal.

The tankings were by far the worst treatments. "It was like pouring alcohol on an open wound," Don remembered. Being lifted out of the tank was even worse, because the room was freezing, and every nerve in the damaged parts of his body produced agony. "All I could do was scream at the top of my lungs until I would finally pass out with exhaustion. The tankings took place seven days a week—week after week after week."

"Don't ask us to let you die," Dr. Meier had told Don at the rehabilitation center, "because in a sense what that means is we're killing you. If you want to die, then let me fix your hands, operate on them and open them up so at least you can do something with them, and if you want to commit suicide then, you can. But don't ask us to stand here and literally kill you."

"The argument that not treating a patient is the same as killing borders on the ridiculous," Don said years later. "If letting the patient die is characterized as playing God, then treating the patient to save his life has to be as well. In the final analysis, I was nothing but a hostage to the current state of medical technology." Just a few years earlier, he would have died, but the management of burns had advanced sufficiently to keep him alive. He was, he said, "forced to receive treatment," because he was "too weak to resist and unable to walk out on my own." Ironically, as Don later saw the situation, what was happening to him was taking place when the country was emphasizing the importance of individual liberties and freedom of choice by the individual.

Don was treated for ten months. He lost all ten fingers, was blind and terribly scarred and disfigured. He had to have help with everything and was unable to take care of even his most basic bodily needs. His pain was still constant, and he couldn't walk.

Discharged from the hospital, he took up residence in his mother's house. At first he was relieved to be out of the hospital, but in a few weeks he fell into a deep depression. Frustration built up as he experienced his loss of independence, grew bored, and worried about what he was going to do with the rest of his life. Marriage seemed at best a remote possibility.

Because of his disfigurement, he thought about never going out in public, but eventually he began to go to stores and restaurants, protected by his blindness from the stares and reactions of others. Money from the court settlement gave him the financial independence to do what he wanted and was able to do.

Starting law school, he lived with a married couple and learned to do some things for himself. But in the spring of that year, beset by a sleep disturbance and upset by the breakdown of a personal relationship, he tried to kill himself with an overdose of sleeping pills and tranquilizers. He was found in time for him to be taken to the hospital and have his stomach pumped. Despite what Dr. Larson and others had told him while his burns were being treated, he wasn't going to be allowed to kill himself. Don was rehospitalized for depression and insomnia for about a month and eventually returned to law school.

After graduating, Don—who was called Dax—set up a practice in Corpus Christi. He married Karen, someone he had known in high school, in 1983.

His mother is sure she made the right decision in signing the consent forms for treatment, particularly now that her son's life is filled with the satisfactions of marriage and a job he likes. She wishes she had asked the doctors to give him more pain medication, though. They hadn't told her it was possible.

Dax doesn't blame his mother for her decisions. He blames his doctors for putting her in the position of having to make them. *He* should have been the one asked. "The individual freedom of a competent adult should never be restricted," he says, "except when it conflicts with the freedom of some other individual." For him the individual should be able to decide what minimum quality of life is acceptable to him or her. This is not a decision that should be made by physicians or anyone else on behalf of another person.

Now that Donald Cowart is living a satisfactory life, is he glad his physicians and his mother continued his treatment against his wishes? "I'm enjoying life now, and I'm glad to be alive," Cowart says. "But I still think it was wrong to force me to undergo what I had to, to be alive."

Nor would the assurance of pulling through be enough to make him change his mind. "If the same thing were to occur tomorrow, knowing I could reach this same point, I still would not want to undergo the pain and agony that I had to undergo to be alive now. I should want that choice to lie entirely with myself and not others."

## BRIEFING SESSION

Consider the following cases:

1. A state decides to require that all behavioral therapists (that is, all who make use of psychological conditioning techniques to alter behavior patterns) be either licensed psychologists or psychiatrists.

2. A member of the Jehovah's Witnesses religion, which is opposed to the transfusion of blood and blood products, refuses to consent to a needed appendectomy. But when his appendix ruptures and he lapses into unconsciousness, the surgical resident operates and saves his life.

3. A physician decides not to tell the parents of an infant who died shortly after birth that the cause of death was an unpredictable birth defect, because he does not wish to influence their desire to have a child.

4. A janitor employed in an elementary school consults a psychiatrist retained by the school board and tells her that he has on two occasions molested young children; the psychiatrist decides that it is her duty to inform the school board.

5. A six-year-old develops a high fever accompanied by violent vomiting and convulsions while at school. The child is

rushed to a nearby hospital. The attending physician makes a diagnosis of meningitis and telephones the parents for permission to initiate treatment. Both parents are Christian Scientists, and they insist that no medical treatment be given to her. The physician initiates treatment anyway, and the parents later sue the physician and the hospital.

6.    A thirty-year-old woman who is twenty-four weeks pregnant is involved in an automobile accident that leaves her with a spinal cord injury. Her physician tells her that she would have had a greater chance of recovery had she not been pregnant. She then requests an abortion. The hospital disagrees with her decision and gets a court order forbidding the abortion.

There is perhaps no single moral issue that is present in all these cases. Rather, there is a complex of related issues. Each case involves acting on the behalf of someone else—another individual, the public at large, or a special group. And each action comes into conflict with the autonomy, wishes, or expectations of some person or persons. Even though the issues are related, it is most fruitful to discuss them under separate headings. We will begin with a brief account of autonomy, then turn to a discussion of paternalism and imposed restrictions on autonomy.

## Autonomy

We are said to act autonomously when our actions are the outcome of our deliberations and choices. To be autonomous is to be self-determining. Hence, autonomy is violated when we are coerced to act by actual force or by explicit and implicit threats or when we act under misapprehension or under the influence of factors that impair our judgment.

We associate autonomy with the status we ascribe to rational agents as persons in the moral sense. Moral theories are committed to the idea that persons are by their nature uniquely qualified to decide what is in their own best interest.

This is because they are ends in themselves, not means to some other end. As such, persons have inherent worth, rather than instrumental worth. Others have a duty to recognize this worth and to avoid treating persons as though they were only instruments to be employed to achieve a goal chosen by someone else. To treat someone as if she lacks autonomy is thus to treat her as less than a person.

All the cases previously listed may be viewed as involving violations of the autonomy of the individuals concerned. Consider: (1) laws requiring a license to provide therapy restrict the actions of individuals who do not qualify for a license; (2) the Jehovah's Witness is given blood he does not want; (3) information crucial to decision making is withheld from the parents of the child with the genetic disease, so their future decision cannot be a properly informed one; (4) by breaking confidentiality, the psychiatrist is usurping the prerogative of the janitor to keep secret information that may harm him; (5) by treating the girl with meningitis, the physician is violating the generally recognized right of parents to make decisions concerning their child's welfare; (6) by refusing the woman's request for an abortion, the hospital and the court are forcing her to remain pregnant against her will.

The high value we place on autonomy is based on the realization that without it we can make very little of our lives. In its absence, we become the creatures of others, and our lives assume the forms they choose for us. Without being able to act in ways to shape our own destiny by pursuing our aims and making our own decisions, we are not realizing the potential we have as rational agents. Autonomy permits us the opportunity to make ourselves; even if we are dissatisfied with the result, we have the satisfaction of knowing that the mistakes were our own. We at least acted as rational agents.

One of the traditional problems of social organization is to structure society in such a way that the autonomy of individuals will be preserved and promoted. However, autonomy is not an absolute or unconditional value, but just one among others. For example, few would wish to live in a society in which you could do what you wanted only if you had enough physical power to get your way. Because one person's exercise of autonomy is likely to come into conflict with another's, we are willing to accept some restrictions to preserve as much of our own freedom as possible. We value our own safety, the opportunity to carry out our plans in peace, the lives of other rational beings, and perhaps even their welfare.

Because autonomy is so basic to us, we usually view it as not requiring any justification. However, this predisposition in favor of autonomy means that to violate someone's autonomy, to set aside that person's wishes and render impotent her power of action, requires that we offer a strong justification. Various principles have been proposed to justify conditions under which we are warranted in restricting autonomy.

The most relevant principle in discussing the relationships among physicians, patients, and society is that of paternalism. The connection of paternalism with the physician–patient relationship and with truth telling and confidentiality in the medical and social context will be discussed in the following section. (For a fuller account of autonomy, as well as the principles invoked to justify restricting its exercise, see the *Foundations of Bioethics* in Part V of this book. The harm principle is of particular relevance to the topics presented here.)

## Paternalism

Exactly what paternalism is, is itself a matter of dispute. Roughly speaking, we can say that paternalism consists in acting in a way that is believed to protect or advance the interest of a person, even if acting in this way goes against the person's own immediate desires, or limits the person's freedom of choice. Oversimplifying, paternalism is the view that "Father knows best." (The word "parentalism" is now sometimes preferred to "paternalism," because of the latter's gender association. See Part V for the distinction between the weak and strong versions of the principle of paternalism.) Thus, the first three

cases presented on page 104 are instances of paternalistic behavior.

It is useful to distinguish what we can call "state paternalism" from "personal paternalism." State paternalism, as the name suggests, is the control exerted by a legislature, agency, or other governmental body over particular kinds of practices or procedures. Such control is typically exercised through laws, licensing requirements, technical specifications, and operational guidelines and regulations. (The first case listed is an example of state paternalism.)

By contrast, personal paternalism consists in an individual's deciding, on the basis of his own principles or values, that he knows what is best for another person. The individual then acts in a way that deprives the other person of genuine and effective choice. (Cases two and three are examples of this.) Paternalism is personal when it is not a matter of public or semipublic policy but is a result of private, moral decision making.

The line between public and private paternalism is often blurred. For example, suppose a physician on the staff of a hospital believes a pregnant patient should have surgery to improve the chances for the normal development of the fetus. The physician presents his view to the hospital's attorney, and, agreeing with him, the attorney goes to court to request a court order for the surgery. The judge is persuaded and issues the order. Although the order is based on arguments that certain laws are applicable in the case, the order itself is neither a personal decision nor a matter of public policy. The order reflects the judgment of a physician who has succeeded in getting others to agree.

Despite the sometimes blurred distinction between state and personal paternalism, the distinction is useful. Most important, it permits us to separate issues associated with decisions about public policies affecting classes of individuals (for example, people needing medication) from issues associated with decisions by particular people affecting specific individuals (for example, a Dr. Latvia explaining treatment options to a Mr. Zonda).

## State Paternalism in Medical and Health Care

At first sight, state paternalism seems wholly unobjectionable in the medical context. We are all certain to feel more confident in consulting a physician when we know that she or he has had to meet the standards for education, competence, and character set by a state licensing board and medical society. We feel relatively sure that we aren't putting ourselves in the hands of an incompetent quack.

Indeed, that we can feel such assurance can be regarded as one of the marks of the social advancement of medicine. As late as the early twentieth century in the United States, the standards for physicians were low, and licensing laws were either nonexistent or poorly enforced. It was possible to qualify as a physician with as little as four months' formal schooling and a two-year apprenticeship.

Rigorous standards and strictly enforced laws have undoubtedly done much to improve medical care in this country. At the very least, they have made it less dangerous to consult a physician. At the same time, however, they have also placed close restrictions on individual freedom of choice. In the nineteenth century, a person could choose among a wide variety of medical viewpoints. That is no longer so today.

We now recognize that some medical viewpoints are simply wrong and, if implemented, may endanger a patient. At the least, people treated by those who espouse such views run the risk of not getting the best kind of medical care available. Unlike people in the nineteenth century, we are confident that we know (within limits) what kinds of medical therapies are effective and what kinds are useless or harmful. The scientific character of contemporary medicine gives us this assurance.

Secure in these beliefs, our society generally endorses paternalism by the state in the regulation of medical practice. We believe it is important to protect sick people from quacks and charlatans, from those who raise false hopes and take advantage of human suffering. We generally accept, then, that the range of choice of health therapy ought to be limited to what we consider to be legitimate and scientific.

This point of view is not one that everyone is pleased to endorse. In particular, those seeking treatment for cancer have sometimes wanted to try drugs rumored to be effective but not approved by the Food and Drug Administration. Such drugs cannot be legally prescribed in the United States, and those wishing to gain access to them must travel to foreign clinics, often at considerable discomfort and expense. Some have claimed that FDA regulations make it impossible for them to choose the therapy they wish and that this is an unwarranted restriction of their rights. It should be enough, they claim, for the government to issue a warning if it thinks one is called for. But after that, people should be free to act as they choose.

The debate about unapproved therapies raises a more general question: To what extent is it legitimate for a government to restrict the actions and choices of its citizens for their own good? It is perhaps not possible to give a wholly satisfactory general answer to this question. People don't object that they are not permitted to drink polluted water from the city water supply or that they are not able to buy candy bars contaminated with insect parts. Yet some do object if they have to drink water that contains fluorides or if they cannot buy candy bars that contain saccharine. But all such limitations result from governmental attempts to protect the health of citizens. Seeing to the well-being of its citizens certainly must be recognized as one of the legitimate aims of a government. And this aim may easily include seeing to their physical health. State paternalism with respect to health seems, in general, to be justifiable. Yet the laws and regulations through which the paternal concern is expressed are certain to come into conflict with the exercise of individual liberties. Perhaps the only way in which such conflicts can be resolved is on an issue-by-issue basis. Later, we will discuss some of the limitations that moral theories place on state paternalism.

State paternalism in medical and health-care matters may be more pervasive than it seems at first sight. Laws regulating medical practice, the licensing of physicians and medical personnel, regulations governing the licensing and testing of drugs, and guidelines that must be followed in scientific research are some of the more obvious expressions of paternalism. Less obvious is the fact that government research funds can be expended only in prescribed ways and that only certain approved forms of medical care and therapy will be paid for under government-sponsored health programs. For example, it was a political and social triumph for chiropractors and Christian Science readers when some of their services were included under Medicare coverage. Thus, government money, as well as laws and regulations, can be used in paternalistic ways.

## Personal Paternalism in Medical and Health Care

That patients occupy a dependent role with respect to their physicians seems to be true historically, sociologically, and psychologically. The patient is sick, the physician is well. The patient is in need of the knowledge and skills of the physician, but the physician does not need those of the patient. The patient seeks out the physician to ask for help, but the physician does not seek out the patient. The patient is a single individual, while the physician represents the institution of medicine with its hospitals, nurses, technicians, consultants, and so on. In his dependence on the physician, the patient willingly surrenders some of his autonomy. Explicitly or implicitly, he agrees to allow the physician to make certain decisions for him that he would ordinarily make for himself.

The physician tells him what to eat and drink and what to avoid, what medicine he should take and when to take it, how much exercise he should get and what kind it should be. The patient consents to run at least part of his life by "doctor's orders" in the hope that he will regain his health or at least improve his condition.

The physician acquires a great amount of power in this relationship. But she also acquires a great responsibility. It has been recognized at least since the time of Hippocrates that the physician has an obligation to act in the best interest of the patient. The patient is willing to transfer part of his autonomy because he is confident that the physician will act in this way. If this analysis of the present form of the physician–patient relationship is roughly correct, two questions are appropriate.

First, should the relationship be one in which the patient is so dependent on the paternalism of the physician? Perhaps it would be better if patients did not think of themselves as transferring any of their autonomy to physicians. Physicians might better be thought of as people offering advice, rather than as ones issuing orders. Thus, patients, free to accept or reject advice, would retain fully their power to govern their own lives. If this is a desirable goal, it is clear that the present nature of the physician–patient relationship needs to be drastically altered.

The problem with this point of view is that the patient is ordinarily not in a position to judge the advice that is offered. The reason for consulting a physician in the first place is to gain the advantage of her knowledge and judgment. Moreover, courses of medical therapy are often complicated ones involving many interdependent steps. A patient could not expect the best treatment if he insisted on accepting some of the steps and rejecting others. As a practical matter, a patient who expects good medical care must rather much put himself in the hands of his physician.

For this reason, the second question is perhaps based on a more realistic assessment of the nature of medical care: How much autonomy must be given up by the patient? The power of the physician over the patient cannot be absolute. The patient cannot become the slave or creature of the physician—this is not what a patient consents to when he agrees to place himself under the care of a physician. What, then, are the limits of the paternalism that can be legitimately exercised by the physician?

# Informed Consent and Medical Treatment

Traditionally, many physicians believed they could do almost anything to a patient so long as it was in the patient's best interest. Indeed, many thought they could act even against the patient's wishes, because they considered themselves to know the patient's interest better than the patient himself and thought that eventually the patient would thank them for taking charge and making hard decisions about treatment. (See the Dax Cowart Classic Case Presentation which begins this chapter for what has become the standard example of this way of thinking.)

While some physicians may still wish to press treatments on patients for the patients' own good, patients need not choose to do as they are advised. Some people refuse to take needed medications, change their diets, quit smoking, exercise more, or undergo surgical procedures that promise to improve the quality of their lives, if not lengthen them. Valuing autonomy, we now realize, requires recognizing that people do not always do what is good for them in a medical way, and accepting this outcome as a consequence of the exercise of autonomy.

People may even choose to reject treatment necessary to save their lives. Over the past two decades, the courts have recognized repeatedly and explicitly that the right to refuse or discontinue medical treatment has a basis in the Constitution and in common law. To receive medical treatment, people must first give their consent, and if they wish to reject it, even after it has been started, they are legally and morally entitled to do so.

## Free and Informed Consent

Both ethicists and the courts have understood *consent* (in the context of agreeing to treatment) to mean that several specific conditions must be fulfilled. For consent to be morally and legally meaningful, individuals must be: (1) competent to understand what they are told about their condition and capable of exercising judgment;

(2) provided with relevant information about their illness and the proposed treatment for it in an understandable form; (3) free to make a decision about their treatment without coercion. (For a fuller discussion of consent in the context of becoming an experimental subject, see the Briefing Session in the previous chapter.)

Most public and legal attention to the topic of refusing to consent to therapy has focused on cases in which terminally ill patients wished to have ventilators disconnected or in which the guardians of patients in chronic vegetative states wanted their nutrition and hydration to be discontinued. The issues have concerned the rights of patients themselves, and in this respect the questions were more or less straightforward.

The matter of refusing treatment becomes more complicated when the interest of someone other than or in addition to the patient is involved. Two sorts of cases, in particular, present difficulties: cases in which parents' beliefs cause them to deny their children necessary medical attention and cases in which a pregnant woman's behavior results in damage to her fetus.

## Parents and Children

First is the situation in which parents, acting on the basis of their beliefs, refuse to authorize needed medical treatment for their child. The duty of the physician is to provide the child the best medical care possible. The duty of the parent is to protect and promote the welfare of the child. Ordinarily, in the medical context, these two duties are convergent with respect to the line of action they lead to. The parents ask the physician to "do what is best" for their child, and the physician discusses the options and risks with the parents and secures their consent on behalf of the child. (See the discussion of informed consent in the previous chapter for details.)

However, this convergence of duties leading to agreement about action is dependent on physicians and parents sharing some fundamental beliefs about the nature of disease and the efficacy of medical therapy in controlling it. When these beliefs are not shared, then the outcome is a divergence of opinion about what should be done in the best interest of the child. The actions favored by the physician will be incompatible with the actions favored by the parents.

As in the Case Presentation about Robyn Twitchell in this chapter and example 5 on page 104, some parents are adherents of religions like Christian Science that teach that disease has no reality but is a manifestation of incorrect or disordered thinking. People with such beliefs think that the appropriate response to illness is to seek spiritual healing, rather than to employ medical modalities.

What about the children of those with such beliefs? Their parents can legitimately claim that by refusing to seek or accept medical treatment for their children they are doing what they consider best. It is a recognized principle that parents should decide the best interest of their children, except in very special circumstances. We don't think, for example, that a psychotic or clinically depressed parent should be allowed to decide about a child's welfare. Should Christian Scientists and others with similar beliefs be put in the category of incompetent parents and forced to act against their beliefs and seek medical care for their children?

A strong case can be made for answering yes. If mentally competent adults wish to avoid or reject medical treatment for themselves, the principle of autonomy supports a public policy permitting this. However, when the interest of someone who lacks the abilities to deliberate and decide for himself is concerned, it is reasonable to favor a policy that will protect that person from harm. This is particularly so when matters as basic as the person's health and safety are at stake.

Hence, to warrant restricting the generally recognized right of parents to see to the welfare of their children, we can appeal to the harm principle. We might say that, if a parent's action or failure to take action tends to result in harm to a child, then we are justified in restricting his or her freedom to make decisions on behalf of the child. We could then look to someone else—a

court or an appointed guardian—to represent the child's best interest.

In general, we consider a legitimate function of the state to be the protection of its citizens. When parents fail to take reasonable steps to secure the welfare of their children, then doing so becomes a matter of interest to the state.

## Pregnancy and Autonomy

The second kind of case is one that involves an actual or potential conflict between the actions of a pregnant woman and the interest of the fetus she is carrying. (This kind of case is illustrated in example 6 on page 105 and discussed in the Social Context: "Autonomy and Pregnancy" later in the chapter.)

An obvious way of dealing with an alleged conflict between what a pregnant woman wants or does and the interest of her fetus is to deny that conflict is possible. If one holds that the fetus, at every developmental stage, is a part of the woman's body and that she is free to do with her body as she pleases, then there can be no conflict. The woman is simply deciding for herself, and it would be an unjustifiable violation of her autonomy to regulate her actions in ways that the actions of men or nonpregnant women are not regulated.

However, a number of difficulties are associated with this position. The most significant one is that as a fetus continues to develop, it becomes increasingly implausible to hold that it is no different from any other "part" of a woman's body. The problem of when the fetus is a person in the moral sense is one that plagues the abortion dispute (see Chapter 9), and it is no less relevant to this issue.

Furthermore, even if one is not prepared to say that the fetus can claim any serious consideration to life, particularly at the very early stages of pregnancy, it seems prima facie wrong to act as if the fetus (barring miscarriage or abortion) is not going to develop into a child.

Suppose a woman knows that she is pregnant and knows that continuing to drink alcohol even moderately is likely to cause the child who will be born to suffer from birth defects. Most people would consider it wrong for her to disregard the consequences of her actions. Once she has decided against (or failed to secure) an abortion, then it seems she must accept the responsibility that goes with carrying a child to term. On even a moderate view, this would imply avoiding behavior she knows will be likely to cause birth defects.

However, another aspect of the question of whether a pregnant woman has any responsibility to protect the welfare of the fetus is to what extent, if any, we are justified in regulating the woman's actions. Should a pregnant woman retain her autonomy intact? Or is it legitimate for us to require her, by virtue of being pregnant, to follow a set of rules or laws not applicable to other people?

Once again, the status of the fetus as a person makes such a question hard to answer. Should we regard cases of "fetal neglect" or "fetal abuse" as no different from cases of child neglect or abuse? If the answer is yes, then the pregnant woman does not differ from the parent of a minor child. In the same way the state might order a Christian Science parent to seek medical help for a sick child, we might consider ourselves justified in insisting that a pregnant woman get prenatal care and avoid drugs and alcohol. Just as parents are subject to laws and rules that other people are not, so then are pregnant women.

Assuming this answer is accepted, then the question becomes one of how far we should go in prescribing behavior for a pregnant woman. Should we require a basic minimum, or should we establish an obtainable ideal? Even the basic questions surrounding the issue of pregnancy and responsibility remain unanswered by our society. We have yet to develop a social policy to reduce the incidence of fetal alcohol syndrome and drug-damaged babies while also protecting the autonomy of pregnant women.

## Truth Telling in Medicine

The question of the limits of paternalism arises most forcefully when physicians deceive patients.

When, if ever, is it justifiable for a physician to deceive her or his patient?

The paternalistic answer is that deception by the physician is justified when it is in the best interest of the patient. Suppose, for example, that a transplant surgeon detects signs of tissue rejection in a patient who has just received a donor kidney. The surgeon is virtually certain that within a week the kidney will have to be surgically removed and the patient transferred to dialysis equipment again. Although in no immediate clinical danger, the patient is suffering from postoperative depression. It is altogether possible that, if the patient is told at this time that the transplant appears to be a failure, his depression will become more severe. This, in turn, might lead to a worsening of the patient's physical condition, perhaps even to a life-threatening extent.

Eventually the patient will have to be told of the need for another operation. But by the time that need arises, his psychological condition may have improved. Is the surgeon justified in avoiding giving a direct and honest answer to the patient when he asks about his condition? In the surgeon's assessment of the situation, the answer is likely to do the patient harm. His duty as a physician, then, seems to require that he deceive the patient, either by lying to him (an act of commission) or by allowing him to believe (an act of omission) that his condition is satisfactory and the transplant was successful.

Yet doesn't the patient have a right to know the truth from his physician? After all, it is his life that is being threatened. Should he not be told how things stand with him so that he will be in a position to make decisions that affect his own future? Is the surgeon not exceeding the bounds of the powers granted to him by the patient? The patient surely had no intention of completely turning over his autonomy to the surgeon.

The issue is one of "truth telling." Does the physician always owe it to the patient to tell the truth? Some writers make a distinction between lying to the patient and merely being nonresponsive or evasive. But is this really a morally relevant distinction? In either case, the truth is being kept from the patient. Both are instances of medical paternalism.

## Placebos

The use of placebos (from the Latin *placebo,* meaning "I shall please") in medical therapy is another issue that raises questions about the legitimate limits of paternalism in medicine. The "placebo effect" is a well-documented psychological phenomenon: even patients who are seriously ill will sometimes show improvement when they are given any kind of medication (a sugar pill, for example) or treatment. This can happen even when the medication or treatment is irrelevant to their condition.

The placebo effect can be exploited by physicians for the (apparent) good of their patients. Many patients cannot accept a physician's well-considered judgments. When they come to a physician with a complaint and are told that there is nothing organically wrong with them, that no treatment or medication is called for, they continue to ail. They may then lose confidence in their physician or be less inclined to seek medical advice for more serious complaints.

One way to avoid these consequences is for the physician to prescribe a placebo for the patient. Since the patient (we can assume) suffers from no organic disease condition, he is not in need of any genuine medication. And because of the placebo effect, he may actually find himself relieved of the symptoms that caused him to seek medical help. Moreover, the patient feels satisfied that he has been treated, and his confidence in his physician and in medicine in general remains intact.

Since the placebo effect is not likely to be produced if the patient knows he is being given an ineffective medication, the physician cannot be candid about the "treatment" prescribed. She must either be silent, say something indefinite like "I think this might help your condition," or lie. Since the placebo effect is more likely to be achieved if the medication is touted as being amazingly effective against complaints like those

of the patient, there is a reason for the physician to lie outright. Because the patient may stand to gain a considerable amount of good from placebo therapy, the physician may think of herself as acting in the best interest of her patient.

Despite its apparent advantages, placebo therapy may be open to two ethical criticisms. First, we can ask whether giving placebos is really in the best interest of a patient. It encourages many patients in their belief that drugs can solve their problems. Patients with vague and general complaints may need some kind of psychological counseling, and giving them placebos merely discourages them from coming to grips with their genuine problems. Also, not all placebos are harmless (see the discussion in the Briefing Session to Chapter 1). Some contain active chemicals that produce side-effects (something likely to enhance the placebo effect) so the physician who prescribes placebos may be subjecting her patient to some degree of risk.

Second, by deceiving her patient, the physician is depriving him of the chance to make genuine decisions about his own life. Because the person is not genuinely sick, it does not seem legitimate to regard him as having deputized his physician to act in his behalf or as having transferred any of his power or autonomy to the physician. In Kant's terms, the physician is not acknowledging the patient's status as an autonomous rational agent. She is not according him the dignity that he possesses simply by virtue of being human. (A utilitarian who wished to claim that telling the truth to patients is a policy that will produce the best overall benefits could offer essentially the same criticism.)

Some of the traditional ethical problems about using placebos as a form of treatment rests, in part, on the assumption that placebos can be an effective form of therapy. At least one recent study analyzing investigations employing placebos as part of the experimental design casts doubt on the so-called placebo effect. Yet, even assuming the result is correct, we still must deal with the issue of whether it is ever morally legitimate to mislead a patient by giving her an inactive substance in the guise of an effective medication.

## Dignity and Consent

Deception is not the only issue raised by the general question of the legitimacy of medical paternalism. Another of some importance is difficult to state precisely, but it has to do with the attitude and behavior of physicians toward their patients. Patients often feel that physicians deal with them in a way that is literally paternalistic—that physicians treat them like children.

The physician, like the magician or shaman, is often seen as a figure of power and mystery, one who controls the forces of nature and, by doing so, relieves suffering and restores health. Some physicians like this role and act in accordance with it. They resent having their authority questioned and fail to treat their patients with dignity and respect.

For example, many physicians call their patients by their first names, while expecting patients to refer to them as "Dr. X." In our society, women in particular have been most critical of such condescending attitudes displayed by physicians.

More serious is the fact that many physicians do not make a genuine effort to educate patients about the state of their health, the significance of laboratory findings, or the reasons why medication or other therapy is being prescribed. Patients are not only expected to follow orders, but they are expected to do so without questioning them. Patients are, in effect, denied an opportunity to refuse treatment and consent is taken for granted.

The amount of time that it takes to help a patient understand his medical condition and the reason for the prescribed therapy is, particularly in this era of managed care, one reason why physicians do not attempt to provide such information. A busy physician in an office practice might see thirty or forty patients a day, and it is difficult to give each of them the necessary amount of attention. Also, patients without a medical background obviously can find it hard to understand medical explanations—particularly in the ways in which they are often given.

The result, for whatever reasons, is a situation in which physicians make decisions about patients without allowing patients to know the basis for them. Explanations are not given, physicians sometimes say, because patients "wouldn't understand" or "might draw the wrong conclusions about their illness" or "might worry needlessly." Patients are thus not only not provided information, they are discouraged from asking questions or revealing their doubts.

The moral questions here concern the responsibility of the physician. Is it ultimately useful for patients that physicians should play the role of a distant and mysterious figure of power? Do patients have a right to ask that physicians treat them with the same dignity as physicians treat one another? Should a physician attempt to educate her patients about their illnesses? Or is a physician's only real responsibility to provide patients with needed medical treatment?

Furthermore, is it always obvious that the physician knows what will count as the all-around best treatment for a patient? Patients, being human, have values of their own, and they may well not rank their best chance for effective medical treatment above all else. A woman with breast cancer, for example, may wish to avoid having a breast surgically removed (mastectomy) and so prefer another mode of treatment, even though her physician may consider it less effective. Can her physician legitimately withhold from her knowledge of alternative modes of treatment and so allow her no choice? Can he make the decision about treatment himself on the grounds that it is a purely medical matter, one about which the patient has no expert knowledge?

If patients have a right to decide about their treatment, physicians have an obligation to provide them with an account of their options and with the information they need to make a reasonable choice. Thus, treating patients with dignity requires recognizing their status as autonomous agents and securing their free and informed consent.

# Confidentiality (Privacy)

"Whatever I see or hear, professionally or privately, which ought not be divulged, I will keep secret and tell no one," runs one of the pledges in the Hippocratic Oath.

The tradition of medical practice in the West has taken this injunction very seriously. That it has done so is not entirely due to the high moral character of physicians, for the pledge to secrecy also serves an important practical function. Physicians need to have information of an intimate and highly personal sort to make diagnoses and prescribe therapies. If physicians were known to reveal such personal information, then patients would be reluctant to cooperate, and the practice of medicine would be adversely affected.

Furthermore, because psychological factors play a role in medical therapy, the chances of success in medical treatment are improved when patients can place trust and confidence in their physicians. This aspect of the physician–patient relationship actually forms a part of medical therapy. This is particularly so for the "talking cures" characteristic of some forms of psychiatry and psychotherapy.

## Breaching Confidentiality

A number of states recognize the need for "privileged communication" between physician and patient and have laws to protect physicians from being compelled to testify about their patients in court. Yet physicians are also members of a society, and the society must attempt to protect the general interest. This sometimes places the physician in the middle of a conflict between the interest of the individual and the interest of society.

For example, physicians are often required by law to act in ways that force them to reveal certain information about their patients. The clearest instance of this is the legal obligation to report to health departments the names of those patients who are carriers of such communicable diseases as syphilis and tuberculosis. This permits health authorities to warn those with whom the carriers have come into contact and to guard against the spread of the diseases. Thus, the interest of society is given precedence over physician–patient confidentiality.

Confidentiality may also be breached in cases when the interest of the patient is at stake. Thus, a woman seeking medical attention for trauma resulting from abuse by a husband or boyfriend may have no choice about whether the police are notified. State laws may give the physician no choice about whether to report a suspected case of assault.

Similarly, physicians usually have no discretion about whether to report cases of suspected child abuse. While the parents of the child may deny responsibility for the child's injuries, if the physician suspects the parents of abuse, she must make a report notifying police of her suspicions.

Few people question society's right to demand that physicians violate a patient's confidence when protecting the health of great numbers of people is at stake. More open to question are laws that require physicians to report gunshot wounds or other injuries that might be connected with criminal actions. (In some states, before abortion became legal, physicians were required to report cases of attempted abortion.) Furthermore, physicians as citizens have a legal duty to report any information they may have about crime unless they are protected by a privileged-communication law.

Thus, the physician can be placed in a position of conflict. If he acts to protect the patient's confidences, then he runs the risk of acting illegally. If he acts in accordance with the law, then he must violate the confidence of his patients. What needs to be decided from a moral point of view is to what extent the laws that place a physician in such a situation are justified.

The physician who is not in private practice but is employed by a government agency or a business organization also encounters similar conflicts. Her obligations run in two directions: to her patients and to her employer.

Should a physician who works for a government agency, for example, tell her superiors that an employee has confided in her that he is a drug addict? If she does not, the employee may be subject to blackmail or bribery. If she does, then she must violate the patient's confidence.

Or what if a psychiatrist retained by a company decides one of its employees is so psychologically disturbed that she cannot function effectively in her job? Should the psychiatrist inform the employer, even if it means going against the wishes of the patient? (Consider also the fourth case cited at the beginning of the Briefing Session.)

## Duty to Warn?

Even more serious problems arise in psychiatry. Suppose that a patient expresses to his psychiatrist feelings of great anger against someone and even announces that he intends to go out and kill that person. What should the psychiatrist do? Should he report the threat to the police? Does he have an obligation to warn the person being threatened?

This is the fundamental issue dealt with by the California Supreme Court in the *Tarasoff* case. The court ruled that therapists at the student health service of the University of California, Berkeley were negligent in their duty to warn Tatiana Tarasoff that Prosenjit Poddar, one of their patients, had threatened her life. The therapists reported the threat orally to the police, but they did not warn Tarasoff. Two months later, after her return from a trip to Brazil, she was murdered by Poddar.

Poddar was tried and convicted of second-degree murder. The conviction was overturned on appeal, on the grounds that the jury had not been properly instructed. The state decided against a second trial, and Poddar was released on condition that he return to India.

The parents of Tatiana Tarasoff sued the university for damages and eventually won a favorable judgment in the California Supreme Court. The court ruled that not only were the therapists justified in breaking the confidentiality of a patient, they had a duty to warn her that her life was in danger. Since this ruling, many psychia-

trists and other therapists have argued that the court went too far in its demands.

## Managed Care

A worrying trend, with the rise of managed care, is the availability of intimate information about patients that the patients provided to their physicians on the assumption that it would remain confidential. For patients to have their medical bills paid, their physicians may have to reveal to the insurer information concerning such matters as a patient's sexual history and practices, drug use, and troubling psychological problems. Most observers now believe that the assumption that what one tells one's physician will remain private no longer holds. The result is that patients are becoming less willing to tell their physicians anything that might cause them harm if it were known to their spouse, employer, or insurance company.

The basic question about confidentiality concerns the extent to which we are willing to go to protect it. It is doubtful that anyone would want to assert that confidentiality should be absolutely guaranteed. But, if not, then under what conditions is it better to violate it than to preserve it?

## Federal Privacy Regulations

On April 14, 2003 the first comprehensive federal rules governing medical privacy went into effect. The rules represent a weaker version of those framed by the outgoing Clinton administration in 1999.

The original proposals required that physicians, hospitals, and health-care providers in general obtain the written consent of patients before disclosing or using the patient's medical information for treatment, referrals, or paying insurance claims. When the proposed rules were made public, they were praised by privacy advocates as protecting for the first time the medical privacy of individuals. However, insurers, hospitals, and some medical organizations condemned the proposals as unrealistic and un-workable.

Critics claimed that a physician wouldn't even be able to question a patient about her symptoms without first securing her written consent and that pharmacies wouldn't be able to fill a called-in prescription. The health-care industry said the rules would impose on it an unrealistically heavy burden of paperwork and that this, in turn, would cause the cost of medical care to soar.

The Bush administration, after initially endorsing the proposed rules, took these criticisms to heart and dropped the written-consent requirement. The rules now require only that health-care providers notify patients of their legally acknowledged rights with respect to privacy and make a "good-faith effort" to obtain from patients a written acknowledgment that they have been notified.

The rights acknowledged by the rules include a number of important ones:

- Patients have a right to examine their medical records, secure copies, and correct errors.

- Medical information from a patient's records cannot be disclosed to an employer without the patient's explicit authorization.

- Researchers may use medical records for epidemiological studies, but they must remove all uniquely identifying information such as names, addresses, and social security numbers.

- Pharmacists are forbidden to use data about a patient for marketing purposes (for example, selling prescription information to a pharmaceutical company that may try to get patients to ask their doctors to switch them from drugs produced by a rival company).

- The rules guarantee that parents will have "appropriate access" to the medical records of their minor children, including information about abortion, psychotherapy, and drug use.

Defenders of the rules as originally proposed claim that without the written-consent requirement, the new rules are inadequate to protect patients from the breaches of privacy made possible by computers and the electronic storage of information. Even so, it is too soon to say how effective the rules will be in curbing violations of medical confidentiality and assuring patients that information that they wish to keep private will be protected.

## Ethical Theories: Autonomy, Truth Telling, Confidentiality

What we have called state paternalism and personal paternalism are compatible with utilitarian ethical theory. But whether they are justifiable is a matter of controversy. According to the principle of utility, if governmental laws, policies, practices, or regulations serve the general interest, then they are justified. It can be argued that they are justified even if they restrict the individual's freedom of choice or action, because for utilitarianism autonomy has no absolute value. Personal paternalism is justified in a similar way. If a physician believes that she can protect her patient from unnecessary suffering or relieve his pain by keeping him in ignorance, by lying to him, by giving him placebos, or by otherwise deceiving him, these actions are morally legitimate.

However, John Stuart Mill did not take this view of paternalism. Mill argued that freedom of choice (autonomy) is of such importance that it can be justifiably restricted only when it can be shown that unregulated choice would cause harm to other people. Mill claimed that compelling people to act in certain ways "for their own good" is never legitimate. This position, Mill argued, is one that is justified by the principle of utility. Ordinarily, then, people have the freedom to decide what is going to be done to them, so free and informed consent is a prerequisite for medical treatment. Clearly, utilitarianism does not offer a straightforward answer to the question of the legitimacy of paternalism.

What we have said about paternalism applies also to confidentiality. Generally speaking, if violating confidentiality seems necessary to produce a state of affairs in which happiness is increased, then the violation is justified. This might be the case when, for example, someone's life is in danger or someone is being tried for a serious crime and the testimony of a physician is needed to help establish her innocence. Yet it also might be argued from the point of view of rule utilitarianism that confidentiality is such a basic ingredient in the physician–patient relationship that, in the long run, more good will be produced if confidentiality is never violated.

The Kantian view of paternalism, truth telling, and confidentiality is more clear-cut. Every person is a rational and autonomous agent. As such he or she is entitled to make decisions that affect his or her own life. This means that a person is entitled to receive information relevant to making such decisions and is entitled to the truth, no matter how painful it might be. Thus, for treatment to be justified, the informed consent of the individual is required.

The use of placebos or any other kind of deception in medicine is morally illegitimate in a Kantian view, because this would involve denying a person the respect and dignity to which he or she is entitled. The categorical imperative also rules out lying, for the maxim involved in such an action produces a contradiction. (There are special difficulties in applying the categorical imperative that are discussed in the *Foundations of Bioethics*. When these are taken into account, Kant's view is perhaps not quite so straightforward and definite as it first appears.)

It can be argued that Kant's principles also establish that confidentiality should be regarded as absolute. When a person becomes a patient, she does so with the expectation that what she tells her physician will be kept confidential. Thus, in the physician–patient relationship there is an implicit promise. The physician implicitly promises that he will not reveal any information about his patient, either what he has been told or what he has learned for himself. If this analysis is correct, then the physician is under an obligation to preserve confidentiality, because keeping promises is an absolute duty. Here, as in the case of lying, there are difficulties connected with the way a maxim is stated. (See *Foundations of Bioethics* for a discussion.)

Ross's principles recognize that everyone has a moral right to be treated as an autonomous agent who is entitled to make decisions affecting his own life. Thus, free and informed consent to medical treatment is required. Also, everyone is entitled to know the truth and to be educated in helpful ways. Similarly, if confidentiality is a form of promise keeping, everyone is entitled to expect that it will be maintained. Thus, paternalism, lying, and violation of confidence are prima facie morally objectionable.

But of course it is possible to imagine circumstances in which they would be justified. The right course of action that a physician must follow is one that can be determined only on the basis of the physician's knowledge of the patient, the patient's problem, and the general situation. Thus, Ross's principles rule out paternalism, deception, and violations of confidence as general policies, but they do not make them morally illegitimate in an absolute way.

Rawls's theory of social and political morality is compatible with state paternalism of a restricted kind. No laws, practices, or policies can legitimately violate the rights of individuals. At the same time, however, a society, viewing arrangements from the original position, might decide to institute a set of practices that would promote what they agreed to be their interests. If, for example, health is agreed to be an interest, then they might be willing to grant to the state the power to regulate a large range of matters connected with the promotion of health. Establishing standards for physicians would be an example of such regulation.

But they might also go so far as to give the state power to decide (on the advice of experts) what medical treatments are legitimate, what drugs are safe and effective to use, what substances should be controlled or prohibited, and so on. So long as the principles of justice are not violated and so long as the society can be regarded as imposing these regulations on itself for the promotion of its own good, then such paternalistic practices are unobjectionable.

With respect to personal paternalism, consent, deception, and confidentiality, Rawls's general theory offers no specific answers. But since Rawls endorses Ross's account of prima facie duties (while rejecting Ross's intuitionism), it seems reasonable to believe that Rawls's view on these matters would be the same as Ross's.

The natural law doctrine of Roman Catholicism suggests that paternalism in both its forms is legitimate. When the state is organized to bring about such "natural goods" as health, then laws and practices that promote those goods are morally right. Individuals do have a worth in themselves and should be free to direct and organize their own lives. Thus, they generally should be informed and should make their own medical decisions. Yet at the same time, individuals may be ignorant of sufficient relevant information, lack the intellectual capacities to determine what is really in their best interest, or be moved by momentary passions and circumstances. For these reasons, the state may act so that people are protected from their own shortcomings, and yet their genuine desires, their "natural ends," are satisfied.

Thus, natural law doctrine concludes that because each individual has an inherent worth, she is entitled to be told the truth in medical situations (and others) and not deceived. But it reasons too that because a physician has superior knowledge, he may often perceive the interest of the patient better than the patient herself. Accordingly, natural law doctrine indicates that, although the physician should avoid lying, he is still under an obligation to act for the best interest of his patient. This may mean allowing the patient to believe something that is not so (as in placebo therapy) or withholding information from the patient. In order for this to be morally legitimate, however, the physician's motive must always be that of advancing the welfare of the patient.

In the matter of confidentiality, the natural law doctrine recognizes that the relationship between physician and patient is one of trust, and a physician has a duty not to betray the confidences of her patients. But the relationship is not sacrosanct and the duty is not absolute. When the physician finds herself in a situation in which a greater wrong will be done if she does not reveal a confidence entrusted to her by a patient, then she has a duty to reveal the confidence. If, for example, the physician possesses knowledge that would save someone from death or unmerited suffering, then it is her duty to make this knowledge available, even if by doing so she violates a patient's trust.

We have only sketched an outline of the possible ways in which ethical theories might deal with the issues involved in paternalism, consent to treatment, truth telling, and confidentiality. Some of the views presented are open to challenge, and none has been worked out in a completely useful way. That is one of the tasks that remains to be performed.

Autonomy, paternalism, truth telling, and confidentiality are bound together in a complicated web of moral issues. We have not identified all the strands of the web, nor have we traced out their connections with one another. We have, however, mentioned enough difficulties to reveal the seriousness of the issues.

As the following cases and contexts illustrate, some of the issues are social ones and require that we decide about the moral legitimacy of certain kinds of laws, practices, and policies. Others are matters of personal morality, ones that concern our obligations to society and to other people. Our ethical theories, we can hope, will provide us with the means of arriving at workable and justifiable resolutions of the issues. But before this point is reached, much intellectual effort and ingenuity will have to be invested.

## Case Presentation

### *Medical ID Cards and Privacy*

When Tod Whitman, a Denver police officer, saw Carol Kanfield collapse on the sidewalk outside a coffee shop, he rushed over to her and checked to see whether she required CPR. Seeing that she didn't, he called the EMS and gave the operator the medical ID number from the card he found in her purse.

By the time the ambulance arrived, the EMTs and Denver General knew she was a twenty-four-year-old insulin dependent diabetic who was allergic both to penicillin and to animal-derived insulin. The information had been retrieved by using Carol's medical ID number from the National Medical Database and displayed on the EMS and hospital computers. The technicians were able to stabilize Carol and bring her out of her coma by using insulin produced by genetically altered bacteria. Without the information from the database, it would have taken much longer to diagnose Carol's problem, and even then, had she been given bovine insulin, an allergic reaction might have killed her. The case of Carol Kanfield is imaginary, but in the near future, cases like it may become common. In 1996, Congress mandated that every American be assigned a "unique health identifier" or medical identification number, which can be used to create a national computer database containing the lifetime medical records of every citizen. This was passed as a part of the Health Insurance Portability Act, which is supposed to allow people to keep their insurance when they change jobs.

Such a database would benefit everyone considerably. Individuals would have their medical records available for inspection by any physician or hospital whenever they need treatment. This might be of crucial importance in an emergency, but even for a scheduled examination it would be helpful. Patients would no longer have to make an effort to get their records sent to a new physician, and physicians would no longer have to examine patients without having the details of their known medical history. Patients with a complex of disorders or a rare disease might also benefit, if their physicians were able to find out how other patients with the same problem responded to specific treatments.

Insurance companies would benefit, because patients could no longer hide the parts of their medical history that might make them a bad risk or show a preexisting condition. Also, billing would be streamlined. This would reduce the administrative cost of medical care and thus lower the overall cost of care. Scientists would benefit, because they would be able to analyze genetic factors in disease and look for geographical or seasonal patterns. They would also be able to compare the effectiveness of various treatments for the same disease.

Critics of assigning a medical ID number to each person and establishing a medical-records databank point to several serious potential abuses. Connected databases of health records, financial and credit histories, and criminal records would make it possible for government agencies and knowledgeable individuals to pry into almost every aspect of a person's life.

Those gaining access to the records could make decisions about such matters as employment, admission to college, approving home loans or life or health insurance policies without the applicant knowing what information is being used. Someone who is HIV positive, for example, might be turned down for a sales job, because the employer doesn't want to risk hiring a person with an infectious disease. Laws protecting against discrimination would be weakened.

People are already reluctant to tell their physicians intimate details of their lives, even though some of the information may be important to diagnosing their problem or providing them with the right treatment. If they knew that everything they revealed could end up in a database accessible to a large number of people, they would probably reveal even less about themselves than now. This would undercut the quality of medical care.

While at least thirty-five states have passed laws to protect patient privacy and insurance companies are legally required to develop procedures to protect the privacy of their policy holders, no uniform and generally accepted standards currently protect the information in databases or regulate access to it. In part this is because no national consensus on patient privacy appears to exist. Critics of a medical ID system fear that, given the nature of political compromises, any federal privacy standards Congress passes to regulate it will be weaker than most current state standards.

Do people care about their medical privacy? A 1993 Lou Harris poll showed that only 18 percent of those surveyed thought it was all right for medical records to be used in research without a person's consent. Some 60 percent thought it was unacceptable for pharmacists to supply medical data about their customers to marketing companies, and 96 percent wanted legal penalties for the unauthorized disclosure of medical information.

Privacy is clearly valued, but equally clearly, having people's medical records easily available in a national database can benefit them, even to the extent of saving their lives. Further, the database can benefit society by lowering health-care costs and by allowing us to discover more about the causes of disease and the most effective ways to treat them. Perhaps the basic question is whether we can gain the benefits of a national medical identification system without having to surrender the benefits of privacy.

## SOCIAL CONTEXT: AUTONOMY AND PREGNANCY

Pamela Rae Monson was a twenty-seven-year-old mother of two living in San Diego, California. When she became pregnant again, toward the end of her term, she began to experience vaginal bleeding. The cause was diagnosed as placenta previa, and her physician advised her to stay off her feet as much as possible and to get immediate medical treatment if she began to bleed again. She was also told not to engage in sexual intercourse and not to use amphetamines.

Monson disregarded virtually all of these instructions. On November 23 she began to bleed, but instead of seeking medical treatment, she stayed home, took illegally obtained amphetamines, and had sex with her husband. Later that day, she began to have contractions, and several hours after they began, she finally went to a hospital. She gave birth that evening to a boy with massive brain damage. He lived for six weeks.

The San Diego police wanted Monson prosecuted for homicide, but the district attorney charged her with a misdemeanor under a child-support statute. Under the California law, a parent must provide "medical attendance" to a child who requires it. However, the judge threw out the case, on the grounds that an appeals court had already ruled that a conceived but unborn child is not to be considered a person within the intended scope of the child-abuse law.

### Other Cases

The 1985 Monson case was the first of its kind, and despite its legal outcome, it had considerable national influence. In particular, the case suggested to prosecutors in various states that they might use the law to punish pregnant women for acting in ways that cause harm to the fetuses they are carrying.

After Monson, at least 200 women in at least thirty states were charged with threatening the safety of their unborn children by engaging in behavior that put them at risk. Most often, the behavior involved the pregnant woman's use of alcohol or illegal drugs. For example:

- In Laramie, Wyoming, in February 1990, Diane Pfannensteil, twenty-nine years old, was charged with felony child abuse because she drank alcohol while pregnant. A blood test had earlier determined that Pfannensteil was legally intoxicated, and a judge had ordered her to remain alcohol free to protect the fetus. The charge against her was dismissed by a judge who ruled that, according to the law, "the child already has to have suffered," and it might be years before it could be determined whether Pfannensteil's child was damaged.

- In May 1990, a New York State appeals court ruled that the presence of cocaine in the blood of a newborn infant and admission of drug use by the mother were grounds enough to hold a child-neglect hearing to consider what action should be taken in the best interest of the child.

- On August 7, 1992, twenty-four-day-old Hanna Gillispie of Corona, California, was found dead in the apartment of her mother, Alicia. The coroner determined that the child had died from ingesting methamphetamine obtained from her mother's milk. Her mother was said to be a habitual user of illegal drugs. In October, Ms. Gillispie pleaded guilty to three counts of child endangerment and was sentenced to six years in prison. Her other two children, ages two and five, were placed in foster homes. The public defender explained the guilty plea by saying that it avoided the possibility of Ms. Gillispie's being charged with second-degree murder.

## Why Prosecute?

Civil liberties groups have been highly critical of the prosecutorial approach toward pregnant women taken by some cities and states. Even prosecutors admit that the cases they bring are on novel legal grounds, but they claim that something must be done to protect developing fetuses and newborns. "We're really not interested in arresting women and sending them to jail," the solicitor of Charleston said. "We're just interested in getting them to stop using drugs before they do something horrible to their babies."

This also seems to be the motivation of physicians who cooperate in the prosecution of pregnant women who use drugs. However, the actions physicians take in the interest of protecting the developing child may conflict with their traditional commitment to preserving the confidentiality of their patients.

Is it morally permissible for a physician to inform the police that a pregnant patient tested positive for illegal drugs? Should there be laws requiring physicians to make such reports? The preservation of confidentiality is not a value that overrides all others. For example, we justify requiring physicians to report communicable diseases and gunshot wounds on the grounds that the social good this produces (controlling dis-

eases and crime) outweighs infringing on an individual's privacy.

The obvious drawback to such a reporting requirement is that drug-using pregnant women might not seek medical care to avoid the risk of being prosecuted for a crime. Hence, a law intended to benefit the developing child might work in the opposite way in some cases. Indeed, if physicians made it a practice of reporting pregnant women for drug use even though not required to do so, these women might be expected to avoid getting prenatal care.

## Cases Reversed

The great majority of the legal cases of "pregnancy abuse" were appealed and lower court decisions reversed. Indeed, court decisions tended to recognize that pregnant women are not guilty of child abuse, even though their actions might result in harm to the developing fetus:

- The Connecticut Supreme Court ruled in 1992 that a pregnant woman who injected cocaine into a vein as she was about to go into labor was not guilty of abusing her child, even though when the child was born he was traumatized, pale, and suffering from oxygen deprivation. The court decided that state laws give no legal rights to the unborn and that, until the child was born, the mother could not be considered to have engaged in abusive "parental conduct" toward a "child."

- In July 1992, the Florida Supreme Court overturned the 1989 conviction of Jennifer Johnson for "delivering" drugs to her children through the umbilical cord during the first few moments after their birth. Johnson was tested after the births of two of her children in 1987 and 1989 and found positive for cocaine each time.

In the nineteen cases prosecuted in Florida, Johnson was the only defendant convicted. The court reasoned that she could have avoided delivering the drugs only by severing the umbilical cord, which might have killed her children. Further, the court held, the legislature's concept of "delivering" drugs was not intended to cover such cases. In fact, an attempt to pass legislation punishing pregnant women for actions endangering their fetuses had failed.

## South Carolina—Charge Upheld by State Supreme Court

Matters played out in a different way in South Carolina. On June 6, 1995, Talitha Renee Garrick called paramedics complaining of abdominal pains and cramps. She admitted to having smoked crack cocaine an hour or two earlier. Physicians at the hospital to which she was taken found that her placenta had detached and her fetus had suffocated. On autopsy metabolic products of cocaine were detected, indicating that the fetus had been alive. In 1996 Garrick was charged with murder by child abuse and faced a maximum of five years in prison.

In 1997, on appeal, the state Supreme Court allowed her to plead guilty to involuntary manslaughter and handed down a sentence of three years probation and two hundred hours of community service, to take the form of speaking to expectant mothers about the dangers of drugs. South Carolina was the only appellate court to uphold charges against a woman for actions resulting in the death of her fetus.

## Racial Bias

At least one study shows a racial bias in the prosecution of pregnant women addicted to illegal drugs. In Florida, all drug use during pregnancy must be reported to health departments and pregnant women using illegal drugs prosecuted. A study of urine collected during a one-month period in public health clinics and obstetricians' offices showed a 15 percent incidence of drug use by both blacks and whites. Blacks were ten times more likely to be prosecuted than whites, however, and poor women more likely than middle-class women.

Although the incidence of illegal drug use is about the same for black and white women, the frequency of cocaine use is much higher among black women. White women use marijuana more frequently, and although it is associated with fetal harm, the harm is much less than that caused by cocaine.

## Drug Damage

Everyone agrees the problem of infants damaged or put at risk by drug use is enormous. By some estimates, as many as 375,000 newborns each year may be affected by drug abuse by pregnant women. Alcohol is estimated to cause harm in 2 or 3 of every 1000 fetuses.

Cocaine or crack cocaine used by women during pregnancy poses severe risks to newborns. Because the drug triggers spasms in the fetus's blood vessels, oxygen and nutrients can be severely restricted for long periods. Prenatal strokes and seizures may occur, and malformations of the kidneys, genitals, intestines, and spinal cord may develop. "Crack babies" are twice as likely to be premature and 50 percent more likely to need intensive care. Although intensive therapy may reverse effects of the drug to a greater extent than was once thought, "crack babies" still suffer from a high incidence of irreversible brain damage.

Pregnant women who consume alcohol put their developing fetuses at risk for the same kind of damage. Fetal alcohol syndrome includes growth retardation before and after birth, facial malformations, such abnormal organ development as heart and urinary tract defects and underdeveloped genitals, and various degrees of brain damage. Alcohol use is believed to be one of the leading causes of retardation. Furthermore, the damage done by alcohol seems permanent, so that even excellent postnatal nutrition and compassionate care cannot alter the growth retardation or the brain damage.

Some studies suggest that even three or four drinks a week can cause fetal damage. Further, more women are consuming alcohol during pregnancy than ever before. A 1997 Centers for

Disease Control survey found that 3.5 percent of 1313 pregnant women surveyed admitted to having seven or more drinks a week or to binging on five or more drinks at least once during the previous month. This was an increase from 1 percent of 1053 pregnant women surveyed in 1991.

The sample indicates 140,000 women admitted to frequent drinking in 1995, compared to 32,000 in 1991. The study also showed 16.3 percent of pregnant women in 1995 had at least one drink in the preceding month, compared with 12.4 percent in 1991.

## Fetal Interest?

Cases against pregnant women were usually based on the notion that the fetus has legally recognizable interests apart from the woman, while acknowledging that the pregnant woman has a legally recognizable right to seek an abortion. The basic idea is that if a woman decides not to have an abortion, then she acquires a duty to protect the fetus.

This position faces a number of problems. First, the legal basis is at best murky. Most courts do not consider a fetus a child, so child-abuse laws do not apply in any obvious way. Similarly, the notion of "delivering" drugs by maternal–fetal circulation is an apparently significant departure from the notion of "delivering" that lies behind antidrug legislation.

Second, what counts as "fetal abuse" is unclear and elastic. Should a pregnant woman who has two drinks be seen as endangering the fetus? Since there is no safe level of alcohol consumption, the answer might be yes. But what about making sure she eats a diet proper to nourishing the developing fetus? Should the woman be charged with a crime if she fails to provide whatever the medical profession believes to be proper prenatal care? Should she be prosecuted even though she cannot afford to provide the right care?

Third, what about the interests of the pregnant woman herself? Does becoming pregnant and not having an abortion commit her to sub-ordinating her own welfare to that of the fetus? Does she have an obligation to avoid using drugs and alcohol, even though no one else—woman or man—may have such an obligation? Does she have an obligation to avoid engaging in any activities likely to cause a miscarriage?

In general, does the pregnant woman have a duty to live in such a way that whenever there is a conflict of interest between what she wishes to do and what others consider the best interest of the fetus, the conflict must be resolved in favor of the fetus?

The prospect of a continuing number of children damaged by preventable causes is appalling. No one believes that the legal punishment of pregnant women is a satisfactory solution. It is more an act of frustration and desperation. But what solution is satisfactory?

## United States Supreme Court Decision

In a six-to-three decision in March 2001, the United States Supreme Court overturned a Court of Appeals Decision in a South Carolina case. A public hospital in Charleston had an arrangement with the police department that led to the arrest of pregnant women whose urine tested positive for cocaine. Under the program, the women were offered the chance to enter a treatment program or go to trial on drug charges. The aim was to protect the unborn child from the effects of cocaine use.

Before Charleston altered, then eliminated, its program, thirty women were arrested after drug screening. Nearly all charges were dropped after the women agreed to participate in a drug rehabilitation program. Crystal Ferguson was one of the women tested by the hospital.

The Supreme Court ruled in *Ferguson v. Charleston* that it is unconstitutional to order pregnant women tested for drugs without a warrant on the grounds of the "special needs" of getting the women into a treatment program. A "special needs" exception to the Fourth Amendment guarantee against unlawful searches and seizures has been recognized by the court to hold in circumstances in which drug testing was needed to protect health and safety (e.g., testing railroad workers), but the Court rejected the notion that the Charleston program satisfied this criterion.

"While the ultimate goal of the [Charleston] program may well have been to get the women into substance abuse treatment and off drugs," Justice John Paul Stevens wrote in the majority opinion, the immediate objective of the searches [i.e., drug test] was to generate evidence *for law enforcement purposes* in order to reach that goal." Because law enforcement "always serves some broader social purpose or objective," a reference to such a purpose does not justify a constitutional exception.

The "stark and unique" fact of the Charleston case, Justice Stevens said, is that the relationship between the hospital and the police was such that it was designed to collect evidence against patients to be turned over to the police for potential use in a criminal prosecution.

The Supreme Court decision effectively blocks programs that involve the involuntary screening of pregnant women for drug use. Thus, unless women agree to be tested or ask for help with drug rehabilitation, states have little power to intervene for the purpose of protecting the developing fetus.

Whether the state should have such power continues to be a matter of debate. Further, the questions we raised earlier about whether and to what extent a pregnant woman has responsibility for the developing child remain unanswered.

## Case Presentation

### The Death of Robyn Twitchell and Christian Science

Two-year-old Robyn Twitchell ate very little for dinner on April 3. Then, shortly after eating, he began to cry. The crying was soon replaced by vomiting and screaming.

Robyn lived in Boston, the city where the Christian Science religion was founded, and both his parents, David and Ginger Twitchell, were devout Christian Scientists. The tenets of the religion hold that disease has no physical being or reality but, rather, is the absence of being. Because God is complete being, disease is an indication of the absence of God, of being away from God. Healing must be mental and spiritual, for it consists in bringing someone back to God, of breaking down the fears, misperceptions, and disordered thinking that stand in the way of having the proper relationship with God. When someone is ill, the person may need help getting to the root cause of the estrangement from God. The role of a Christian Science practitioner is to employ teaching, discussion, and prayer to assist someone suffering from an illness to discover its spiritual source.

Acting on the basis of their beliefs, the Twitchells called in Nancy Calkins, a Christian Science practitioner, to help Robyn. She prayed for Robyn and sang hymns, and, although she visited him three times during the next five days, he showed no signs of getting better. A Christian Scientist nurse was brought in to help feed and bathe Robyn, and on her chart she described him as "listless at times, rejecting all food, and moaning in pain" and "vomiting." On April 8, 1986, Robyn began to have spasms, and his eyes rolled up into his head. He finally lost consciousness, and that evening he died.

Robyn was found to have died of a bowel obstruction that could have been treated by medicine and surgery. Medical experts were sure that he wouldn't have died had his parents sought medical attention for him.

### Manslaughter Charges

David and Ginger Twitchell were charged with involuntary manslaughter. In a trial lasting two months, the prosecution and defense both claimed rights had been violated. The Twitchells' attorneys appealed, in particular, to the First Amendment guarantee of the free exercise of religion and claimed that the state was attempting to deny it to them.

Prosecutors responded by pointing out that courts have repeatedly held that not all religious practices are protected. Laws against polygamy and laws requiring vaccinations or blood transfusions for minors, for example, have all been held to be constitutional.

The prosecutors also claimed that Robyn's rights had been violated by his parents' failure to seek care for him as required by law. They also cited the 1923 Supreme Court ruling in *Prince v. Massachusetts* that held that "Parents may be free to become martyrs of themselves, but it does not follow they are free to make martyrs of their children."

## Guilty

The jury found the Twitchells guilty of the charge, and the judge sentenced them to ten years' probation. John Kiernan, the prosecutor, had not recommended a jail sentence. "The intent of our recommendation was to protect the other Twitchell children." Judge Sandra Hamlin instructed the Twitchells that they must seek medical care for their three children, if they showed signs of needing it, and they must take the children to a physician for regular checkups.

"This has been a prosecution against our faith," David Twitchell said. Although, speaking of Robyn, at one point he also said most sadly, "If medicine could have saved him, I wish I had turned to it."

The prosecutor called the decision "a victory for children." However, Stephen Lyons, one of the defense attorneys, said it was wrong to "substitute the imperfect and flawed judgment of medicine for the judgment of a parent." A spokesman for the Christian Science church said it was not possible to combine spiritual and medical healing as the ruling required. "They're trying to prosecute out of existence this method of treatment," he said.

During the last several years a number of children have died because religious beliefs kept their parents from getting them necessary medical care. Christian Science parents have been convicted of involuntary manslaughter, felony child abuse, or child endangerment in California, Arizona, and Florida.

The Twitchell case was one of several initially successful prosecutions. The case directly challenged the First Church of Christ Scientist (the proper name of the church) in the city where it was founded and has its headquarters, and the church recognized the challenge and helped in providing leading attorneys to defend the case. "The message has been sent," John Kiernan said after the Twitchells were sentenced. "Every parent of whatever religious belief or persuasion is obligated to include medical care in taking care of his child."

## Appeal

The Twitchells' attorneys immediately announced they would appeal the decision on the grounds that the ruling rested on the judge's misinterpretation of a Massachusetts child-neglect law, which explicitly exempts those who believe in spiritual healing. Because of this, legal authorities considered it possible the Twitchell decision would be overturned on appeal.

A spiritual-healing exemption is found in similar laws in forty-four states. Such exclusions make it difficult to successfully prosecute Christian Scientists or others on the grounds of child neglect. The American Academy of Pediatrics is one of several groups that have campaigned to eliminate the exceptions from child-protection laws, but so far only South Dakota has actually changed its laws.

Despite legal exemptions, parents belonging to religious groups like the Church of the First Born, Faith Assembly, and True Followers of Christ have been convicted and imprisoned for failing to provide their children with medical care. However, so far no Christian Scientist has gone to jail. When a Christian Scientist has been convicted, the sentence has been suspended or has involved probation or community service and the promise to seek medical care for their children in the future.

Critics claim Christian Scientists have been treated more leniently than members of more fundamentalist groups, because a high proportion of church members are middle to upper-middle class and occupy influential positions in business, government, and the law. They also suggest that the legal exceptions for spiritual healing in child-protection laws are there because of the influence of the Christian Science church and its members.

Some legal observers initially believed that the Twitchell case would spur wider and more intense efforts to eliminate the spiritual-healing exception, and groups representing the rights of children consider such a change to be long overdue.

However, the Twitchell conviction was overturned on appeal in 1993, and it did not turn out to have the impact on the law many hoped it would. Except in exceptional cases, the religious beliefs of parents continue to take precedence over the medical welfare of their children.

# Section 1: Consent to Medical Treatment

## Paternalism

### Gerald Dworkin

Gerald Dworkin attempts to show that, even if we place an absolute value on individual choice, a variety of paternalistic policies can still be justified. In consenting to a system of representative government, we understand that it may act to safeguard our interests in certain ways. But, Dworkin asks, what are the "kinds of conditions which make it plausible to suppose that rational men could reach agreement to limit their liberty even when other men's interests are not affected?"

Dworkin suggests that such conditions are satisfied in cases in which there is a "good" such as health involved—one that everybody needs to pursue other goods. Rational people would agree that attaining such a good should be promoted by the government even when individuals don't recognize it as a good at a particular time. There is a sense, Dworkin argues, in which we are not really imposing such a good on people. What we are really saying is that, if everyone knew the facts and assessed them properly, this is what they would choose. Also, we are sometimes influenced by immediate alternatives that look more attractive, or we are careless or depressed and so do not act for what we acknowledge as a good. Thus, we might approve of laws such as ones against cigarette smoking because we know we should not smoke cigarettes.

It is plausible, Dworkin suggests, that rational people would grant to a legislature the right to impose such restrictions on their conduct. But the government has to demonstrate the exact nature of the harmful effects to be avoided. Also, if there is an alternative way of accomplishing the end without restricting liberty, then the society should adopt it.

Neither one person, nor any number of persons, is warranted in saying to another human creature of ripe years, that he shall not do with his life for his own benefit what he chooses to do with it. *Mill*

I do not want to go along with a volunteer basis. I think a fellow should be compelled to become better and not let him use his discretion whether he wants to get smarter, more healthy or more honest. *General Hershey*

I take as my starting point the "one very simple principle" proclaimed by Mill in *On Liberty* . . . "That principle is, that the sole end for which mankind are warranted, individually or collectively, in interfering with the liberty of action of any of their number, is

self-protection. That the only purpose for which power can be rightfully exercised over any member of a civilized community, against his will, is to prevent harm to others. He cannot rightfully be compelled to do or forbear because it will be better for him to do so, because it will make him happier, because, in the opinion of others, to do so would be wise, or even right."[1]

This principle is neither "one" nor "very simple." It is at least two principles; one asserting that self-protection or the prevention of harm to others is sometimes a sufficient warrant and the other claiming that the individual's own good is *never* a sufficient warrant for the exercise of compulsion either by the society as a whole or by its individual members. I assume that no one with the possible exception of extreme pacifists or anarchists questions the correctness of the first half

Reprinted from *The Monist*, LaSalle, IL, Vol. 56, No. 1, with the permission of the author and the publisher. (Notes renumbered.)

of the principle. This essay is an examination of the negative claim embodied in Mill's principle— the objection to paternalistic interferences with a man's liberty.

# I

By paternalism I shall understand roughly the interference with a person's liberty of action justified by reasons referring exclusively to the welfare, good, happiness, needs, interests or values of the person being coerced. One is always well-advised to illustrate one's definitions by examples but it is not easy to find "pure" examples of paternalistic interferences. For almost any piece of legislation is justified by several different kinds of reasons and even if historically a piece of legislation can be shown to have been introduced for purely paternalistic motives, it may be that advocates of the legislation with an anti-paternalistic outlook can find sufficient reasons justifying the legislation without appealing to the reasons which were originally adduced to support it. Thus, for example, it may be that the original legislation requiring motorcyclists to wear safety helmets was introduced for purely paternalistic reasons. But the Rhode Island Supreme Court recently upheld such legislation on the grounds that it was "not persuaded that the legislature is powerless to prohibit individuals from pursuing a course of conduct which could conceivably result in their becoming public charges," thus clearly introducing reasons of a quite different kind. Now I regard this decision as being based on reasoning of a very dubious nature but it illustrates the kind of problem one has in finding examples. The following is a list of the kinds of interferences I have in mind as being paternalistic.

# II

1. Laws requiring motorcyclists to wear safety helmets when operating their machines.
2. Laws forbidding persons from swimming at a public beach when lifeguards are not on duty.
3. Laws making suicide a criminal offense.
4. Laws making it illegal for women and children to work at certain types of jobs.
5. Laws regulating certain kinds of sexual conduct, e.g. homosexuality among consenting adults in private.
6. Laws regulating the use of certain drugs which

may have harmful consequences to the user but do not lead to anti-social conduct.
7. Laws requiring a license to engage in certain professions with those not receiving a license subject to fine or jail sentence if they do engage in the practice.
8. Laws compelling people to spend a specified fraction of their income on the purchase of retirement annuities. (Social Security)
9. Laws forbidding various forms of gambling (often justified on the grounds that the poor are more likely to throw away their money on such activities than the rich who can afford to).
10. Laws regulating the maximum rates of interest for loans.
11. Laws against duelling.

In addition to laws which attach criminal or civil penalties to certain kinds of action there are laws, rules, regulations, decrees, which make it either difficult or impossible for people to carry out their plans and which are also justified on paternalistic grounds. Examples of this are:

1. Laws regulating the types of contracts which will be upheld as valid by the courts, e.g. (an example of Mill's to which I shall return) no man may make a valid contract for perpetual involuntary servitude.
2. Not allowing as a defense to a charge of murder or assault the consent of the victim.
3. Requiring members of certain religious sects to have compulsory blood transfusions. This is made possible by not allowing the patient to have recourse to civil suits for assault and battery and by means of injunctions.
4. Civil commitment procedures when these are specifically justified on the basis of preventing the person being committed from harming himself. (The D.C. Hospitalization of the Mentally Ill Act provides for involuntary hospitalization of a person who "is mentally ill, and because of that illness, is likely to injure *himself* or others if allowed to remain at liberty." The term injure in this context applies to unintentional as well as intentional injuries.)
5. Putting fluorides in the community water supply.

All of my examples are of existing restrictions on the liberty of individuals. Obviously one can think of interferences which have not yet been imposed. Thus one might ban the sale of cigarettes, or require that people wear safety-belts in automobiles (as opposed to merely having them installed) enforcing this by not allowing motorists to sue for injuries even when caused by other drivers if the motorist was not wearing a seat-belt at the time of the accident. . . .

## III

Bearing these examples in mind let me return to a characterization of paternalism. I said earlier that I meant by the term, roughly, interference with a person's liberty for his own good. But as some of the examples show the class of persons whose good is invoiced is not always identical with the class of persons whose freedom is restricted. Thus in the case of professional licensing it is the practitioner who is directly interfered with and it is the would-be patient whose interests are presumably being served. Not allowing the consent of the victim to be a defense to certain types of crime primarily affects the would-be aggressor but it is the interests of the willing victim that we are trying to protect. Sometimes a person may fall into both classes as would be the case if we banned the manufacture and sale of cigarettes and a given manufacturer happened to be a smoker as well.

Thus we may first divide paternalistic interferences into "pure" and "impure" cases. In "pure" paternalism the class of persons whose freedom is restricted is identical with the class of persons whose benefit is intended to be promoted by such restrictions. Examples: the making of suicide a crime, requiring passengers in automobiles to wear seat-belts, requiring a Christian Scientist to receive a blood transfusion. In the case of "impure" paternalism in trying to protect the welfare of a class of persons we find that the only way to do so will involve restricting the freedom of other persons besides those who are benefitted. Now it might be thought that there are no cases of "impure" paternalism since any such case could always be justified on non-paternalistic grounds, i.e. in terms of preventing harm to others. Thus we might ban cigarette manufacturers from continuing to manufacture their product on the grounds that we are preventing them from causing illness to others in the same way that we prevent other manufacturers from releasing pollutants into the atmosphere, thereby causing danger to the members of the community. The difference is, however, that in the former but not the latter case the harm is of such a nature that it could be

avoided by those individuals affected if they so chose. The incurring of the harm requires, so to speak, the active co-operation of the victim. It would be mistaken theoretically and hypocritical in practice to assert that our interference in such cases is just like our interference in standard cases of protecting others from harm. At the very least someone interfered with in this way can reply that no one is complaining about his activities. It may be that impure paternalism requires arguments or reasons of a stronger kind in order to be justified since there are persons who are losing a portion of their liberty and they do not even have the solace of having it be done "in their own interest." Of course in some sense, if paternalistic justifications are ever correct then we are protecting others, we are preventing some from injuring others, but it is important to see the differences between this and the standard case.

Paternalism then will always involve limitations on the liberty of some individuals in their own interest but it may also extend to interferences with the liberty of parties whose interests are not in question.

## IV

Finally, by way of some more preliminary analysis, I want to distinguish paternalistic interferences with liberty from a related type with which it is often confused. Consider, for example, legislation which forbids employees to work more than, say, 40 hours per week. It is sometimes argued that such legislation is paternalistic for if employees desired such a restriction on their hours of work they could agree among themselves to impose it voluntarily. But because they do not the society imposes its own conception of their best interests upon them by the use of coercion. Hence this is paternalism.

Now it may be that some legislation of this nature is, in fact, paternalistically motivated. I am not denying that. All I want to point out is that there is another possible way of justifying such measures which is not paternalistic in nature. It is not paternalistic because as Mill puts it in a similar context such measures are "required not to overrule the judgment of individuals respecting their own interest, but to give effect to that judgment they being unable to give effect to it except by concert, which concert again cannot be effectual unless it receives validity and sanction from the law."[2]

The line of reasoning here is a familiar one first found in Hobbes and developed with great sophistication by contemporary economists in the last decade or so. There are restrictions which are in the interests of a class of persons taken collectively but are such that the immediate interest of each individual is furthered by his violating the rule when others adhere to it. In such cases the individuals involved may need the use of compulsion to give effect to their collective judgment of their own interest by guaranteeing each individual compliance by the others. In these cases compulsion is not used to achieve some benefit which is not recognized to be a benefit by those concerned, but rather because it is the only feasible means of achieving some benefit which *is* recognized as such by all concerned. This way of viewing matters provides us with another characterization of paternalism in general. Paternalism might be thought of as the use of coercion to achieve a good which is not recognized as such by those persons for whom the good is intended. Again while this formulation captures the heart of the matter—it is surely what Mill is objecting to in *Our Liberty*—the matter is not always quite like that. For example when we force motorcyclists to wear helmets we are trying to promote a good — the protection of the person from injury—which is surely recognized by most of the individuals concerned. It is not that a cyclist doesn't value his bodily integrity; rather, as a supporter of such legislation would put it, he either places, perhaps irrationally, another value or good (freedom from wearing a helmet) above that of physical well-being or, perhaps, while recognizing the danger in the abstract, he either does not fully appreciate it or he underestimates the likelihood of its occurring. But now we are approaching the question of possible justifications of paternalistic measures and the rest of this essay will be devoted to that question.

## V

I shall begin for dialectical purposes by discussing Mill's objections to paternalism and then go on to discuss more positive proposals.

An initial feature that strikes one is the absolute nature of Mill's prohibitions against paternalism. It is so unlike the carefully qualified admonitions of Mill and his fellow Utilitarians on other moral issues. He speaks of self-protection as the *sole* end warranting coercion, of the individual's own goals as *never* being a sufficient warrant . . . The structure of Mill's argument is as follows:

1. Since restraint is an evil the burden of proof is on those who propose such restraint.

2. Since the conduct which is being considered is purely self-regarding, the normal appeal to the protection of the interests of others is not available.

3. Therefore we have to consider whether reasons involving reference to the individual's own good, happiness, welfare, or interests are sufficient to overcome the burden of justification.

4. We either cannot advance the interests of the individual by compulsion, or the attempt to do so involves evil which outweighs the good done.

5. Hence the promotion of the individual's own interests does not provide a sufficient warrant for the use of compulsion.

Clearly the operative premise here is 4 and it is bolstered by claims about the status of the individual as judge and appraiser of his welfare, interests, needs, etc.

> With respect to his own feelings and circumstances, the most ordinary man or woman has means of knowledge immeasurably surpassing those that can be possessed by any one else.[3]
> He is the man most interested in his own well-being: the interest which any other person, except in cases of strong personal attachment, can have in it, is trifling, compared to that which he himself has.[4]

These claims are used to support the following generalizations concerning the utility of compulsion for paternalistic purposes.

> The interferences of society to overrule his judgment and purposes in what only regards himself must be grounded in general presumptions; which may be altogether wrong, and even if right, are as likely as not to be misapplied to individual cases.[5]
> But the strongest of all the arguments against the interference of the public with purely personal conduct is that when it does interfere, the odds are that it interferes wrongly and in the wrong place.[6]
> All errors which the individual is likely to commit against advice and warning are far outweighed by the evil of allowing others to constrain him to what they deem his good.[7]

Performing the utilitarian calculation by balancing the advantages and disadvantages we find that:

> Mankind are greater gainers by suffering each other to live as seems good to themselves, than by compelling each other to live as seems good to the rest.[8]

From which follows the operative premise 4.

. . . [T]his is clearly the main channel of Mill's thought and it is one which has been subjected to vigorous attack from the moment it appeared—most often by fellow Utilitarians. The link that they have usually seized on is, as Fitzjames Stephen put it, the absence of proof that the "mass of adults are so well acquainted with their own interests and so much disposed to pursue them that no compulsion or restraint put upon them by any others for the purpose of promoting their interest can really promote them."[9] . . .

Now it is interesting to note that Mill himself was aware of some of the limitations on the doctrine that the individual is the best judge of his own interests. In his discussion of government intervention in general (even where the intervention does not interfere with liberty but provides alternative institutions to those of the market) after making claims which are parallel to those just discussed, e.g.

> People understand their own business and their own interests better, and care for them more, than the government does, or can be expected to do.[10]

He goes on to an intelligent discussion of the "very large and conspicuous exceptions" to the maxim that:

> Most persons take a juster and more intelligent view of their own interest, and of the means of promoting it than can either be prescribed to them by a general enactment of the legislature, or pointed out in the particular case by a public functionary.[11]

Thus there are things

> of which the utility does not consist in ministering to inclinations, nor in serving the daily uses of life, and the want of which is least felt where the need is greatest. This is peculiarly true of those things which are chiefly useful as tending to raise the character of human beings. The uncultivated cannot be competent judges of cultivation. Those who most need to be made wiser and better, usually desire it least, and, if they desired it, would be incapable of finding the way to it by their own lights.
> . . . A second exception to the doctrine that individuals are the best judges of their own interest, is when an individual attempts to decide irrevocably now what will be best for his interest at some future and distant time. The presumption in favor of individual judgment is only legitimate, where the judgment is grounded on actual, and especially on present, personal experience; not where it is formed antecedently to experience, and not suffered to be reversed even after experience has condemned it.[12]

The upshot of these exceptions is that Mill does not declare that there should never be government interference with the economy but rather that

> . . . in every instance, the burden of making out a strong case should be thrown not on those who resist but on those who recommend government interference. Letting alone, in short, should be the general practice: every departure from it, unless required by some great good, is a certain evil.[13]

In short, we get a presumption not an absolute prohibition. The question is why doesn't the argument against paternalism go the same way?

I suggest that the answer lies in seeing that in addition to a purely utilitarian argument Mill uses another as well . . . A consistent Utilitarian can only argue against paternalism on the grounds that it (as a matter of fact) does not maximize the good. It is always a contingent question that may be refuted by the evidence. But there is also a non-contingent argument which runs through *On Liberty*. When Mill states that "there is a part of the life of every person who has come to years of discretion, within which the individuality of that person ought to rein uncontrolled either by any other person or by the public collectively" he is saying something about what it means to be a person, an autonomous agent. It is because coercing a person for his own good denies this status as an independent entity that Mill objects to it so strongly and in such absolute terms. To be able to choose is a good that is independent of the wisdom of what is chosen. A man's "mode" of laying out his existence is the best, not because it is the best in itself, but because it is his own mode.[14]

> It is the privilege and proper condition of a human being, arrived at the maturity of his faculties, to use and interpret experience in his own way.[15]

As further evidence of this line of reasoning in Mill consider the one exception to his prohibition against paternalism.

> In this and most civilised countries, for example, an engagement by which a person should sell himself, or allow himself to be sold, as a slave, would be null and void; neither enforced by law nor by opinion. The ground for thus limiting his power of voluntarily disposing of his own lot in life, is apparent, and is very clearly seen in this extreme case. The reason for not interfering, unless for the sake of others, with a person's voluntary acts, is consideration for his liberty. His

voluntary choice is evidence that what he so chooses is desirable, or at least endurable, to him, and his good is on the whole best provided for by allowing him to take his own means of pursuing it. But by selling himself for a slave, he abdicates his liberty; he foregoes any future use of it beyond that single act.

He therefore defeats, in his own case, the very purpose which is the justification of allowing him to dispose of himself. He is no longer free; but is thenceforth in a position which has no longer the presumption in its favour, that would be afforded by his voluntarily remaining in it. The principle of freedom cannot require that he should be free not to be free. It is not freedom to be allowed to alienate his freedom.[16]

Now leaving aside the fudging on the meaning of freedom in the last line it is clear that part of this argument is incorrect. While it is true that *future* choices of the slave are not reasons for thinking that what he chooses then is desirable for him, what is at issue is limiting his immediate choice; and since this choice is made freely, the individual may be correct in thinking that his interests are best provided for by entering such a contract. But the main consideration for not allowing such a contract is the need to preserve the liberty of the person to make future choices. This gives us a principle—a very narrow one, by which to justify some paternalistic interferences. Paternalism is justified only to preserve a wider range of freedom for the individual in question. How far this principle could be extended, whether it can justify all the cases in which we are inclined upon reflection to think paternalistic measures justified remains to be discussed. What I have tried to show so far is that there are two strains of argument in Mill—one a straight-forward Utilitarian mode of reasoning and one which relies not on the goods which free choice leads to but on the absolute value of the choice itself. The first cannot establish any absolute prohibition but at most a presumption and indeed a fairly weak one given some fairly plausible assumptions about human psychology; the second while a stronger line of argument seems to me to allow on its own grounds a wider range of paternalism than might be suspected. I turn now to a consideration of these matters.

## VI

We might begin looking for principles governing the acceptable use of paternalistic power in cases where it is generally agreed that it is legitimate. Even Mill intends his principles to be applicable only to mature individuals, not those in what he calls "non-age." What is it that justifies us in interfering with children? The fact that they lack some of the emotional and cognitive capacities required in order to make fully rational decisions. It is an empirical question to just what extent children have an adequate conception of their own present and future interests but there is not much doubt that there are many deficiencies. For example it is very difficult for a child to defer gratification for any considerable period of time. Given these deficiencies and given the very real and permanent dangers that may befall the child it becomes not only permissible but even a duty of the parent to restrict the child's freedom in various ways. There is however an important moral limitation on the exercise of such parental power which is provided by the notion of the child eventually coming to see the correctness of his parent's interventions. Parental paternalism may be thought of as a wager by the parent on the child's subsequent recognition of the wisdom of the restrictions. There is an emphasis on what could be called future-oriented consent—on what the child will come to welcome, rather than on what he does welcome.

The essence of this idea has been incorporated by idealist philosophers into various types of "real-will" theory as applied to fully adult persons. Extensions of paternalism are argued for by claiming that in various respects, chronologically mature individuals share the same deficiencies in knowledge, capacity to think rationally, and the ability to carry out decisions that children possess. Hence in interfering with such people we are in effect doing what they would do if they were fully rational. Hence we are not really opposing their will, hence we are not really interfering with their freedom. The dangers of this move has been sufficiently exposed by Berlin in his "Two Concepts of Liberty." I see no gain in theoretical clarity nor in practical advantage in trying to pass over the real nature of the interferences with liberty that we impose on others. Still the basic notion of consent is important and seems to me the only acceptable way of trying to delimit an area of justified paternalism.

Let me start by considering a case where the consent is not hypothetical in nature. Under certain conditions it is rational for an individual to agree that others should force him to act in ways in which, at the time of action, the individual may not see as desirable.

If, for example, a man knows that he is subject to breaking his resolves when temptation is present, he may ask a friend to refuse to entertain his requests at some later stage.

A classical example is given in the Odyssey when Odysseus commands his men to tie him to the mast and refuse all future orders to be set free because he knows the power of the Sirens to enchant men with their songs. Here we are on relatively sound ground in later refusing Odysseus' request to be set free. He may even claim to have changed his mind but since it is just such changes that he wishes to guard against we are entitled to ignore them.

A process analogous to this may take place on a social rather than individual basis. An electorate may mandate its representatives to pass legislation which when it comes time to "pay the price"" may be unpalatable. I may believe that a tax increase is necessary to halt inflation though I may resent the lower pay check each month. However in both this case and that of Odysseus the measure to be enforced is specifically requested by the party involved and at some point in time there is genuine consent and agreement on the part of those persons whose liberty is infringed. Such is not the case for the paternalistic measures we have been speaking about. What must be involved here is not consent to specific measures but rather consent to a system of government, run by elected representatives, with an understanding that they may act to safeguard our interests in certain limited ways.

I suggest that since we are all aware of our irrational propensities, deficiencies in cognitive and emotional capacities and avoidable and unavoidable ignorance it is rational and prudent for us to in effect take out "social insurance policies." We may argue for and against proposed paternalistic measures in terms of what fully rational individuals would accept as forms of protection. Now, clearly since the initial agreement is not about specific measures we are dealing with a more-or-less blank check and therefore there have to be carefully defined limits. What I am looking for are certain kinds of conditions which make it plausible to suppose that rational men could reach agreement to limit their liberty even when other men's interests are not affected.

Of course as in any kind of agreement schema there are great difficulties in deciding what rational individuals would or would not accept. Particularly in sensitive areas of personal liberty, there is always a danger of the dispute over agreement and rationality being a disguised version of evaluative and normative disagreement.

Let me suggest types of situations in which it seems plausible to suppose that fully rational individuals would agree to having paternalistic restrictions imposed upon them. It is reasonable to suppose that there are "goods" such as health which any person would want to have in order to pursue his own good—no matter how that good is conceived. This is an argument that is used in connection with compulsory education for children but it seems to me that it can be extended to other goods which have this character. Then one could agree that the attainment of such goods should be promoted even when not recognized to be such, at the moment, by the individuals concerned.

An immediate difficulty that arises stems from the fact that men are always faced with competing goods and that there may be reasons why even a value such as health—or indeed life—may be overridden by competing values. Thus the problem with the Christian Scientist and blood transfusions. It may be more important for him to reject "impure substances" than to go on living. The difficult problem that must be faced is whether one can give sense to the notion of a person irrationally attaching weights to competing values.

Consider a person who knows the statistical data on the probability of being injured when not wearing seat-belts in an automobile and knows the types and gravity of the various injuries. He also insists that the inconvenience attached to fastening the belt every time he gets in and out of the car outweighs for him the possible risks to himself. I am inclined in this case to think that such a weighing is irrational. Given his life plans which we are assuming are those of the average person, his interests and commitments already undertaken, I think it is safe to predict that we can find inconsistencies in his calculations at some point. I am assuming that this is not a man who for some conscious or unconscious reasons is trying to injure himself nor is he a man who just likes to "live dangerously." I am assuming that he is like us in all the relevant respects but just puts an enormously high negative value on inconvenience—one which does not seem comprehensible or reasonable.

It is always possible, of course to assimilate this person to creatures like myself. I, also, neglect to fasten my seat-belt and I concede such behavior is not rational but not because I weigh the inconvenience differently from those who fasten the belts. It is just that having made (roughly) the same calculation as everybody else I ignore it in my actions. [Note: a much better case of weakness of the will than those usually given in ethics texts.] A plausible explanation for this deplorable habit is that although I know in some intellectual sense what the probabilities and risks are I do not fully appreciate them in an emotionally genuine manner.

We have two distinct types of situation in which a man acts in a non-rational fashion. In one case he attaches incorrect weights to some of his values; in the other he neglects to act in accordance with his actual preferences and desires. Clearly there is a stronger and more persuasive argument for paternalism in the latter situation. Here we are really not—by assumption—imposing a good on another person. But why may we not extend our interference to what we might call evaluative delusions? After all in the case of cognitive delusions we are prepared, often, to act against the expressed will of the person involved. If a man believes that when he jumps out the window he will float upwards—Robert Nozick's example—would not we detain him, forcibly if necessary? The reply will be that this man doesn't wish to be injured and if we could convince him that he is mistaken as to the consequences of his action he would not wish to perform the action. But part of what is involved in claiming that a man who doesn't fasten his seat-belts is attaching an irrational weight to the inconvenience of fastening them is that if he were to be involved in an accident and severely injured he would look back and admit that the inconvenience wasn't as bad as all that. So there is a sense in which if I could convince him of the consequences of his action he also would not wish to continue his present course of action. Now the notion of consequences being used here is covering a lot of ground. In one case it's being used to indicate what will or can happen as a result of a course of action and in the other it's making a prediction about the future evaluation of the consequences—in the first sense—of a course of action. And whatever the difference between facts and values—whether it be hard and fast or soft and slow—we are genuinely more reluctant to consent to interferences where evaluative differences are the issue. Let me now consider another factor which comes into play in some of these situations which may make an important difference in our willingness to consent to paternalistic restrictions.

Some of the decisions we make are of such a character that they produce changes which are in one or another way irreversible. Situations are created in which it is difficult or impossible to return to anything like the initial stage at which the decision was made. In particular some of these changes will make it impossible to continue to make reasoned choices in the future. I am thinking specifically of decisions which involve taking drugs that are physically or psychologically addictive and those which are destructive of one's mental and physical capacities.

I suggest we think of the imposition of paternalistic interferences in situations of this kind as being a kind of insurance policy which we take out against making decisions which are far-reaching, potentially dangerous and irreversible. . . .

A second class of cases concerns decisions which are made under extreme psychological and sociological pressures. I am not thinking here of the making of the decision as being something one is pressured into—e.g. a good reason for making duelling illegal is that unless this is done many people might have to manifest their courage and integrity in ways in which they would rather not do so—but rather of decisions such as that to commit suicide which are usually made at a point where the individual is not thinking clearly and calmly about the nature of his decision. In addition, of course, this comes under the previous heading of all-too-irrevocable decision. Now there are practical steps which a society could take if it wanted to decrease the possibility of suicide—for example not paying social security benefits to the survivors or as religious institutions do, not allowing such persons to be buried with the same status as natural deaths. I think we may count these as interferences with the liberty of persons to attempt suicide and the question is whether they are justifiable.

Using my argument schema the question is whether rational individuals would consent to such limitations. I see no reason for them to consent to an absolute prohibition but I do think it is reasonable for them to agree to some kind of enforced waiting period. Since we are all aware of the possibility of temporary states, such as great fear or depression, that are inimical to the making of well-informed and rational decisions, it would be prudent for all of us if there were some kind of institutional arrangement whereby we were restrained from making a decision which is (all too) irreversible. What this would be like in practice is difficult to envisage and it may be that if no practical arrangements were feasible then we would have to conclude that there should be no restriction at all on this kind of action. But we might have a "cooling off" period, in much the same way that we now require couples who file for divorce to go through a waiting period. Or, more far-fetched, we might imagine a Suicide Board composed of a psychologist and another member picked by the applicant. The Board would be required to meet and talk with the person proposing to take his life, though its approval would not be required.

A third class of decisions—these classes are not supposed to be disjoint—involves dangers which are either not sufficiently understood or appreciated correctly by the persons involved. Let me illustrate, using the example of cigarette smoking, a number of possible cases.

1.  A man may not know the facts—e.g. smoking between 1 and 2 packs a day shortens life expectancy 6.2 years, the costs and pain of the illness caused by smoking, etc.

2.  A man may know the facts, wish to stop smoking, but not have the requisite willpower.

3.  A man may know the facts but not have them play the correct role in his calculation because, say, he discounts the danger psychologically because it is remote in time and/or inflates the attractiveness of other consequences of his decision which he regards as beneficial.

In case 1 what is called for is education, the posting of warnings, etc. In case 2 there is no theoretical problem. We are not imposing a good on someone who rejects it. We are simply using coercion to enable people to carry out their own goals. (Note: There obviously is a difficulty in that only a subclass of the individuals affected wish to be prevented from doing what they are doing.) In case 3 there is a sense in which we are imposing a good on someone since given his current appraisal of the facts he doesn't wish to be restricted. But in another sense we are not imposing a good since what is being claimed—and what must be shown or at least argued for—is that an accurate accounting on his part would lead him to reject his current course of action. Now we all know that such cases exist, that we are prone to disregard dangers that are only possibilities, that immediate pleasures are often magnified and distorted.

If in addition the dangers are severe and far-reaching we could agree to allowing the state a certain degree of power to intervene in such situations. The difficulty is in specifying in advance, even vaguely, the class of cases in which intervention will be legitimate.

A related difficulty is that of drawing a line so that it is not the case that all ultra-hazardous activities are ruled out, e.g. mountain-climbing, bullfighting, sports-car racing, etc. There are some risks—even very great ones—which a person is entitled to take with his life.

A good deal depends on the nature of the deprivation—e.g. does it prevent the person from engaging in the activity completely or merely limit his participation—and how important to the nature of the activity is the absence of restriction when this is weighed against the role that the activity plays in the life of the person. In the case of automobile seat-belts, for example, the restriction is trivial in nature, interferes not at all with the use or enjoyment of the activity, and does, I am assuming, considerably reduce a high risk of serious injury. Whereas, for example, making mountain climbing illegal prevents completely a person engaging in an activity which may play an important role in his life and his conception of the person he is.

In general the easiest cases to handle are those which can be argued about in the terms which Mill thought to be so important—a concern not just for the happiness or welfare, in some broad sense, of the individual but rather a concern for the autonomy and freedom of the person. I suggest that we would be most likely to consent to paternalism in those instances in which it preserves and enhances for the individual his ability to rationally consider and carry out his own decisions.

I have suggested in this essay a number of types of situations in which it seems plausible that rational men would agree to granting the legislative powers of a society the right to impose restrictions on what Mill calls "self-regarding" conduct. However, rational men knowing something about the resources of ignorance, ill-will and stupidity available to the lawmakers of a society—a good case in point is the history of drug legislation in the United States—will be concerned to limit such intervention to minimum. I suggest in closing two principles designed to achieve this end.

In all cases of paternalistic legislation there must be a heavy and clear burden of proof placed on the authorities to demonstrate the exact nature of the harmful effects (or beneficial consequences) to be avoided (or achieved) and the probability of their occurrence. The burden of proof here is twofold—what lawyers distinguish as the burden of going forward and the burden of persuasion. That the authorities have the burden of going forward means that it is up to them to raise the question and bring forward evidence of the evils to be avoided. Unlike the case of new drugs where the manufacturer must produce some evidence that the drug has been tested and found not harmful, no citizen has to show with respect to self-regarding conduct that it is not harmful or promotes his best interests. In addition the nature and cogency of the evidence for the harmfulness of the course of action must be set at a high level. To paraphrase a formulation of the burden of proof for criminal proceedings—better 10 men ruin themselves than one man be unjustly deprived of liberty.

Finally I suggest a principle of the least restrictive alternative. If there is an alternative way of accomplishing the desired end without restricting liberty then although it may involve great expense, inconvenience, etc. the society must adopt it.

### Notes

1. J. S. Mill, *Utilitarianism* and *On Liberty* (Fontana Library Edition, ed. by Mary Warnock, London, 1962), p. 135. All further quotes from Mill are from this edition unless otherwise noted.
2. J. S. Mill, *Principles of Political Economy* (New York: P. F. Collier and Sons, 1900), p. 442.
3. Mill, *Utilitarianism* and *On Liberty*, p. 214.
4. *Ibid.,* p. 206.
5. *Ibid.,* p. 207.
6. *Ibid.,* p. 214.
7. *Ibid.,* p. 207.
8. *Ibid.,* p. 138.
9. J. F. Stephen, *Liberty, Equality, Fraternity* (New York: Henry Holt & Co., n.d.), p. 24.
10. *Ibid.,* p. 33.
11. Mill, *Principles*, II, 458.
12. *Ibid.,* II, 459.
13. *Ibid.,* II, 451.
14. Mill, *Utilitarianism* and *On Liberty*, p. 197.
15. *Ibid.,* p. 186.
16. *Ibid.,* pp. 235–236.

## Confronting Death: Who Chooses, Who Controls? A Dialogue

### Dax Cowart and Robert Burt

Dax Cowart and Robert Burt agree that the principle of autonomy gives competent patients the right to refuse or discontinue medical treatment. Burt suggests, however, that the physician should stop treatment only after a time during which the physician explores the patient's reasons for refusing it and perhaps even argues with him to get him to set aside any preconceptions that may be influencing his decision.

Cowart does not reject Burt's general views, but he is inclined to see the need for physicians to accept patients' decisions relatively quickly. Mentioning his own experiences, Cowart stresses that severe pain permits little delay and that patients should not be forced to endure what they do not wish to endure. That they may later be glad to be alive does not justify violating their autonomy and forcing treatment on them. For Cowart, respecting autonomy means recognizing that a patient is free to make wrong choices, as well as right ones.

**Background Note:** For background, see *Classic Case Presentation: Donald (Dax) Cowart Rejects Treatment—And Is Ignored.*

From "Confronting Death: Who Chooses, Who Controls? A Dialogue Between Dax Cowart and Robert Burt," *Hastings Center Report,* Vol. 28, No. 1 (1998), pp. 14–17. Reprinted by permission of the publisher.

**Robert Burt:** Let me start at a place where I think we agree. Before 1974, the dominant attitude of physicians toward patients was by and large intensely disrespectful of patients' autonomy. The basic posture was paternalistic. Physicians knew what was best for patients, and the patient's job was just to go along. Dax himself has been a critically important actor and symbol in identifying the wrongdoing in that attitude, and raising into high social visibility the proposition that autonomy is a vitally important value; patients are the central actors here and physicians must attend to them in a respectful and careful way. On that point we agree.

The place at which I get troubled or confused is what exactly follows if we embrace this important norm of autonomy. Start with a simple version of two alternatives, perhaps extreme alternatives, to try and sharpen what the issues are. One version of autonomy says: well, it's the physician's job, like it's anybody's job who needs to respect autonomy, to say to a patient, "What do you want?"; the patient says "I want A, B, C," or "I don't want A, B, and C," and then it's just the physician's job to implement that. That is a possible interpretation of the law and way of proceeding.

I find that interpretation of the law, however, to be quite unsatisfactory. It is not only permissible, but important—I would even say essential—that a somewhat different step be taken by a physician (or anyone dealing with a patient). "What do you want?" Dax says, "I don't want treatment." At that point I think it is not only permissible but imperative that whoever hears that respond not with "OK, great, let's go ahead," but instead with, "Well, why exactly do you want that? Why have you come to that conclusion? I want to explore that with you." Now imagine the next step. Dax says, "None of your business." I think it is then both permissible and essential for the doctor to say, "No, no, it is my business, and not because I'm a doctor but because I am another human being who is necessarily involved in your life. We define one another in important kinds of ways, and while, of course, I can't define you, we have to negotiate together what our shared meanings are about, what it is that you want me to do or not to do." It is correct not only for me to say, "Why do you want to do that?" but also permissible for me to argue with you if I disagree, and to argue strenuously with you on a variety of grounds.

Now come the end of the day, yes, it's your life, it's not my life. But the question is, When have we reached the end of the day? When may we terminate this conversation so that I believe that the choice that you're making is as considerate a choice as I think it is morally obligatory for you to make? I know that this can become a kind of trick, and it shouldn't be that; this is only the first step in a conversation.

Why do I think it's not just important but imperative that anybody hearing such a request on Dax's part explore it with him and even quarrel with him? I think we define one another for one another. We are not isolated creatures, popped into this world, who chart ourselves only by what's in our head. We are intensely social creatures. Dax himself has become more than just an individual, he has become a symbol and independent force that shapes our way of thinking about ourselves when we imagine ourselves to be patients. We are mutually shaped by our expectation in lots of ways.

There is one way I want to particularize that in Dax's case. All of us, as members of a society, have attitudes toward people with disabilities. Those of us who are able-bodied or, as they say correctly among disability advocates, those of us who are temporarily able-bodied, often spend an enormous amount of energy denying the fact that our able-bodied status is, in fact, temporary. It is for many, many of us an unattractive, if not to say frightening, possibility to think of ourselves as significantly disabled. Many people in this society, for lots of different reasons, have stereotypical views of disabled people and what their possibilities are. You correct me if I misstep here, Dax, but just on the face of the matter, it seems to me that until your accident you were a member of the able-bodied community, and a very able-bodied member at that, for whom your physical prowess was a matter of great importance and pride to you. Suddenly and deeply beyond your control, in a way that can happen frighteningly to any of us, you found yourself pushed over this divide between the able-bodied and the not-able-bodied. But you inevitably brought with you attitudes that were shaped at a time when you were comfortably, happily, proudly a member of the able-bodied community.

Now it seems to me that having been pushed over that divide in physical terms, there still was a question, at least, about your attitudinal concerns, your attitudinal shift.

Let me read one passage from this initial conversation that Dax had with Dr. White.[1] Dr. White said to Dax, "From the very beginning, according to what you've told me, and what's been written in your hospital record, you had very strong feelings that you didn't want the doctors to go on with your treatment, that you wanted them to leave you alone and not attempt to sustain your life. How do you feel about that at this point?" Dax said in response, "At this point I feel much the same way. If I felt that I could be rehabilitated to where I could walk and do other things normally, I might have a different feeling about it. I don't know. But being blind itself is one big factor that influences my thinking on the matter. I know that there's no way that I want to go on as a blind and a cripple."

Now human communication is a chancy and somewhat crude thing. I only have your words. Dr. White only had Dax's words. Reading those words and putting myself imaginatively in the shoes of your physician, or your lawyer asked to represent you, I have a whole series of questions. How realistic was your perception at that point, just a few months after your accident? How realistic was it of the full range of capacities that could be held out to you, even if you were permanently blind, and even if you were permanently unable to walk (which it turns out, of course, you were not)? How much contact had you had with people with significant disabilities of these sorts? How much were you devaluing your own capacity, thinking that in fact you would be able to do nothing more than your mother's observation in the subsequent videotape interview. She said that you said at one point, "You know, all I'm going to be able do is to sit on a street corner and sell pencils." Well, of course we see today that you are very active and don't sell pencils. But this is a very common fear of able-bodied people who have had no substantial contact with people with disabilities.

So I would ask myself first of all, how realistic is someone like Dax's sense of the real possibilities open for him? But then second of all, how can I as a helper, someone who wants to be useful and helpful to him, communicate in a way that is fully understandable and believable what the real range of options are to him, disabled, that he, formerly able-bodied and now still able-bodied in his image of himself, is not able to see. What do you do? There are many possibilities. You bring people to talk, you discuss, you challenge. All this takes time. It's not something that you can just say to Dax, "Well, how realistic are you? Let's have a brief discussion." In the kind of immensely difficult, immensely traumatic situation in which he found himself, in the midst of his treatment and with the physical pain that he was feeling, and with the psychological pain of his losses including the loss of his father in the same accident, this is not a conversation that can take place in ten minutes or one day. Over how much time and with what kind of constraints?

**Dax Cowart:** Now I know how it feels to be killed with kindness. It makes it more difficult to take the opposing position, but being the good lawyer that I am I will do my best (audience laughter).

The right to control your own body is a right you're born with, not something that you have to ask anyone else for, not the government, not your treating physician, not your next-of-kin. No one has the right to amputate your arms or your legs without your consent. No one has the right to remove your internal organs without your consent. No one has the right to force other kinds of medical treatment upon you without your consent. There is no legitimate law, there is no legitimate authority, there is no legitimate power anywhere on the face of this earth that can take the right away from a mentally competent human being and give it to a state, to a federal government, or to any other person.

A number of quotations constitute a brief overview of what others have said throughout history and also give insight into my own feelings. In *A Connecticut Yankee in King Arthur's Court,* the leading character and one of his companions come across a whole family which has almost died of smallpox. The mother appears to be the only one still alive. Later on they discover she has a fifteen-year-old daughter up in a sleeping loft who is in a near-comatose state and almost dead. So they rushed the young girl down and began administering aid to her. I'll pick up the quotation there. "I snatched my liquor flask from my knapsack, but the woman forbade me and said: 'No, she does not suffer; it is better so. It might bring her back to life. None that be so good and kind as ye are would do her that cruel hurt. Thou go on thy way, and be merciful friends that will not hinder.'"

I was asking my own physicians to be merciful friends who go on their way and do not hinder. But they would not listen. In the first part of this century, Justice Louis Brandeis wrote in one of his Supreme Court opinions: "The makers of our Constitution sought to protect Americans, and their beliefs, their thoughts, their emotions, and their sensations. They conferred as against the government the right to be left alone, the most comprehensive of rights and the right most valued by civilized man."

Warren Burger, who later became chief justice, referred to Justice Brandeis: "Nothing suggests that Justice Brandeis thought an individual possessed these rights only as to sensible beliefs, valid thoughts, reasonable emotions or well-founded sensations. I suggest that he intended to include a great many foolish, unreasonable and even absurd ideas that do not conform, such as refusing medical treatment even at great risk."

Justice Burger did not want to encourage foolish, unreasonable, or absurd conduct, but he did recognize the importance that the individual has in making his or her own decision. He understood that what some of us might think of as foolish, unreasonable, or absurd can also be something that is very precious and dear to someone else.

The English poet John Keats, almost 200 years ago, wrote simply, "Until we are sick, we understand not." That is so true—until we are the ones who are feeling the pain, until we are the ones who are on the sick bed, we cannot fully appreciate what the other person is going through. And even having been there myself, today I cannot fully appreciate what someone who has been badly burned is going through on the burn ward. Our mind mercifully blocks out much of that pain.

When I was in the second grade, a popular joke concerned a mother who severely reprimanded her young son for coming home late from school. He said, "Mom, now that I'm a Boy Scout, I stopped to do my good deed for the day and helped this little old granny lady cross the street." She said, "Young man, it sure doesn't take an hour to help one little old granny lady cross the street." He said, "Well, it sure did this one, 'cause she didn't want to go." I was like that little old granny lady; I didn't want to go. And even today there are many patients who are being forced to endure things that they do not wish to endure, while being taken places that they don't even want to go.

John Stuart Mill, the English philosopher, in his essay *On Liberty,* came down on the side of the right to self-determination by dividing acts into those that are self-regarding and those that are other-regarding in nature. Mill concluded that when the act is self-regarding in nature, the individual should be left to make his or her own decisions. That is precisely my view. In a medical context, I am saying that before a physician is allowed to pick up a saw and saw off a patient's fingers or pick up a scalpel and cut out a patient's eyes, we must make sure that the physician has first obtained that patient's informed consent. I always like to stick the word "voluntary" in there—informed and voluntary consent—because consent that is obtained through coercion or by telling half-truths or withholding the full measure of risk and benefit is not truly consent. Medical providers need to understand that patients do not lose their constitutional rights simply because they find themselves behind a hospital wall. They have the same constitutional rights that the rest of us have, that we expect and enjoy outside hospital walls.

Fortunately today we have many protections that we did not have when I was in the hospital in 1973 and 1974. We have legally enforceable advance directives such as durable power of attorney and other health care proxies. Studies, though, have shown that even when these advance directives are part of the patient's hospital records, over half the time they are ignored by the patient's physician.

When I was in the hospital there were many reasons I wanted to refuse treatment, but one was overriding—the pain. The pain was so excruciating, it was so far beyond any pain that I ever knew was possible, that I simply could not endure it. I was very naive. I had always thought in that day and age, 1973, that a doctor would not let his or her patient undergo that kind of pain; they would be given whatever was needed to control it. Then I found out that was not true. I found out later that much more could have been done for my pain.

There were other important issues, too. One, though it was a distant second, was what Dr. Burt mentioned, my quality of life. I just did not feel that living my life blind, disfigured, with my fingers amputated and at that time not even able to walk, would be worthwhile. With that quality of life it did not seem that I would ever want to live. I have freely admitted for many years now that I was wrong about that.

I want to clarify this, though. Freedom, true freedom, not only gives us the right to make the correct choices; it also has to give us the right sometimes to make the wrong choices. In my case, however, it was a moot point whether I was wrong as far as my quality of life went, because that was a secondary issue. The immediate issue, the urgent issue, was that my pain was not being taken care of. That was why I wanted to die.

Today I'm happy; in fact I even feel that I'm happier than most people. I'm more active physically than I thought I ever would be. I've taken karate for a couple of years, I've climbed a 50-foot utility pole with the assistance of a belay line on the ropes course. I do other mental things, like write poetry and practice law. That is not to say, though, that the doctors were right. To say that would reflect a mentality that says, all's well that ends well, or the ends justify the means— whatever means necessary to achieve the results are okay to use. That totally ignores the pain that I had to go through. I check myself on this very often, several times a year, since I do speak so much. I ask if the same thing were to happen today under identical circumstance, would I still want the freedom? Knowing what I know now, would I still want the freedom to refuse treatment and die? And the answer is always yes, a resounding yes. If I think about having to go through that kind of pain again, I know that it's not something I would want. Another individual may well make a different decision. That's the beauty of freedom; that's his or her choice to do so. . . .

## Acknowledgments

Quotation from "Dax's Case" used with permission of Choice in Dying, 1035 30th Street, N.W., Washington, D.C. 20007.

### Note

1. From the transcript made of the initial videotape and published as an appendix to Robert Burt, *Taking Care of Strangers: The Rule of Law in Doctor–Patient Relations* (New York: The Free Press, 1979), pp. 174–80.

# Transparency: Informed Consent in Primary Care

## Howard Brody

Howard Brody argues that the current standard for informed consent needs to be replaced by one that not only promotes patient autonomy but also enables the physician to determine when informed consent has been given. The usual "reasonable patient" standard leaves physicians uncertain about whether they have provided enough information to constitute informed consent because it is almost always possible to fail to mention a risk that may affect some patient.

Brody favors a "transparency standard," under which physicians explain the thinking behind their selection of treatment and then encourage patients to ask questions. Informed consent is achieved if a patient agrees to a treatment after the thinking has been made transparent. Rather than having to list every possible risk a "reasonable patient" might wish to know to make a decision, physicians would be legally responsible only for explaining their own reasoning.

While the patient's right to give informed consent to medical treatment is now well-established both in U.S. law and in biomedical ethics, evidence continues to suggest that the concept has been poorly integrated into American medical practice, and that in many instances the needs and desires of patients are not being well met by current policies.[1] It appears that the theory and the practice of informed consent are out of joint in some crucial ways. This is particularly true for primary care settings, a context typically ignored by medical ethics literature, but where the majority of doctor–patient encounters occur. Indeed, some have suggested that the concept of informed consent is virtually foreign to primary care medicine where benign paternalism appropriately reigns and where respect for patient autonomy is almost completely absent.[2]

It is worth asking whether current legal standards for informed consent tend to resolve the problem or to exacerbate it. I will maintain that accepted legal standards, at least in the form commonly employed by courts, send physicians the wrong message about what is expected of them. An alternative standard that would send physicians the correct message, a conversation standard, is probably unworkable legally. As an alternative, I will propose a transparency standard as a compromise that gives physicians a doable task and allows courts to review appropriately. I must begin, however, by briefly identifying some assumptions crucial to the development of this position even though space precludes complete argumentation and documentation.

### Crucial Assumptions

Informed consent is a meaningful ethical concept only to the extent that it can be realized and promoted within the ongoing practice of good medicine. This need not imply diminished respect for patient autonomy, for there are excellent reasons to regard respect for patient autonomy as a central feature of good

From *Hastings Center Report,* Vol. 19, No. 5 (September–October 1989), pp. 5–9. Reprinted with permission.

medical care. Informed consent, properly understood, must be considered an essential ingredient of good patient care, and a physician who lacks the skills to inform patients appropriately and obtain proper consent should be viewed as lacking essential medical skills necessary for practice. It is not enough to see informed consent as a nonmedical, legalistic exercise designed to promote patient autonomy, one that interrupts the process of medical care.

However, available empirical evidence strongly suggests that this is precisely how physicians currently view informed consent practices. Informed consent is still seen as bureaucratic legalism rather than as part of patient care. Physicians often deny the existence of realistic treatment alternatives, thereby attenuating the perceived need to inform the patient of meaningful options. While patients may be informed, efforts are seldom made to assess accurately the patient's actual need or desire for information, or what the patient then proceeds to do with the information provided. Physicians typically underestimate patients' desire to be informed and overestimate their desire to be involved in decisionmaking. Physicians may also view informed consent as an empty charade, since they are confident in their abilities to manipulate consent by how they discuss or divulge information.[3]

A third assumption is that there are important differences between the practice of primary care medicine and the tertiary care settings that have been most frequently discussed in the literature on informed consent. The models of informed consent discussed below typically take as the paradigm case something like surgery for breast cancer or the performance of an invasive and risky radiologic procedure. It is assumed that the risks to the patient are significant, and the values placed on alternative forms of treatment are quite weighty. Moreover, it is assumed that the specialist physician performing the procedure probably does a fairly limited number of procedures and thus could be expected to know exhaustively the precise risks, benefits, and alternatives for each.

Primary care medicine, however, fails to fit this model. The primary care physician, instead of performing five or six complicated and risky procedures frequently, may engage in several hundred treatment modalities during an average week of practice. In many cases, risks to the patient are negligible and conflicts over patient values and the goals of treatment or nontreatment are of little consequence. Moreover, in contrast to the tertiary care patient, the typical ambulatory patient is much better able to exercise freedom of choice and somewhat less likely to be intimidated by either the severity of the disease or the expertise of the physician; the opportunities for changing one's mind once treatment has begun are also much greater. Indeed, in primary care, it is much more likely for the full process of informed consent to treatment (such as the beginning and the dose adjustment of an antihypertensive medication) to occur over several office visits rather than at one single point in time.

It might be argued that for all these reasons, the stakes are so low in primary care that it is fully appropriate for informed consent to be interpreted only with regard to the specialized or tertiary care setting. I believe that this is quite incorrect for three reasons. First, good primary care medicine ought to embrace respect for patient autonomy, and if patient autonomy is operationalized in informed consent, properly understood, then it ought to be part and parcel of good primary care. Second, the claim that the primary care physician cannot be expected to obtain the patient's informed consent seems to undermine the idea that informed consent could or ought to be part of the daily practice of medicine. Third, primary care encounters are statistically more common than the highly specialized encounters previously used as models for the concept of informed consent.[4]

## Accepted Legal Standards

Most of the literature on legal approaches to informed consent addresses the tension between the community practice standard and the reasonable patient standard, with the latter seen as the more satisfactory, emerging legal standard.[5] However, neither standard sends the proper message to the physician about what is expected of her to promote patient autonomy effectively and to serve the informational needs of patients in daily practice.

The community practice standard sends the wrong message because it leaves the door open too wide for physician paternalism. The physician is instructed to behave as other physicians in that specialty behave, regardless of how well or how poorly that behavior serves patients' needs. Certainly, behaving the way other physicians behave is a task we might expect physicians to readily accomplish; unfortunately, the standard fails to inform them of the end toward which the task is aimed.

The reasonable patient standard does a much better job of indicating the centrality of respect for patient autonomy and the desired outcome of the informed consent process, which is revealing the information that a reasonable person would need to make an informed and rational decision. This standard is particularly valuable when modified to include the specific informational and decisional needs of a particular patient.

If certain things were true about the relationship between medicine and law in today's society, the reasonable patient standard would provide acceptable guidance to physicians. One feature would be that physicians esteem the law as a positive force in guiding their practice, rather than as a threat to their well-being that must be handled defensively. Another element would be a prospective consideration by the law of what the physician could reasonably have been expected to do in practice, rather than a retrospective review armed with the foreknowledge that some significant patient harm has already occurred.

Unfortunately, given the present legal climate, the physician is much more likely to get a mixed or an undesirable message from the reasonable patient standard. The message the physician hears from the reasonable patient standard is that one must exhaustively lay out all possible risks as well as benefits and alternatives of the proposed procedure. If one remembers to discuss fifty possible risks, and the patient in a particular case suffers the fifty-first, the physician might subsequently be found liable for incomplete disclosure. Since lawsuits are triggered when patients suffer harm, disclosure of risk becomes relatively more important than disclosure of benefits. Moreover, disclosure of information becomes much more critical than effective patient participation in decisionmaking. Physicians consider it more important to document what they said to the patient than to document how the patient used or thought about that information subsequently.

In specialty practice, many of these concerns can be nicely met by detailed written or videotaped consent documents, which can provide the depth of information required while still putting the benefits and alternatives in proper context. This is workable when one engages in a limited number of procedures and can have a complete document or videotape for each.[6] However, this approach is not feasible for primary care, when the number of procedures may be much more numerous and the time available with each patient may be considerably less. Moreover, it is simply not realistic to expect even the best educated of primary care physicians to rattle off at a moment's notice a detailed list of significant risks attached to any

of the many drugs and therapeutic modalities they recommend.

This sets informed consent apart from all other aspects of medical practice in a way that I believe is widely perceived by nonpaternalistic primary care physicians, but which is almost never commented upon in the medical ethics literature. To the physician obtaining informed consent, *you never know when you are finished.* When a primary care physician is told to treat a patient for strep throat or to counsel a person suffering a normal grief reaction from the recent death of a relative, the physician has a good sense of what it means to complete the task at hand. When a physician is told to obtain the patient's informed consent for a medical intervention, the impression is quite different. A list of as many possible risks as can be thought of may still omit some significant ones. A list of all the risks that actually have occurred may still not have dealt with the patient's need to know risks in relation to benefits and alternatives. A description of all benefits, risks, and alternatives may not establish whether the patient has understood the information. If the patient says he understands, the physician has to wonder whether he really understands or whether he is simply saying this to be accommodating. As the law currently *appears* to operate (in the perception of the defensively minded physician), there never comes a point at which you can be certain that you have adequately completed your legal as well as your ethical task.

The point is not simply that physicians are paranoid about the law; more fundamentally, physicians are getting a message that informed consent is very different from any other task they are asked to perform in medicine. If physicians conclude that informed consent is therefore not properly part of medicine at all, but is rather a legalistic and bureaucratic hurdle they must overcome at their own peril, blame cannot be attributed to paternalistic attitudes or lack of respect for patient autonomy.

### The Conversation Model

A metaphor employed by Jay Katz, informed consent as conversation, provides an approach to respect for patient autonomy that can be readily integrated within primary care practice.[7] Just as the specific needs of an individual patient for information, or the meaning that patient will attach to the information as it is presented, cannot be known in advance, one cannot always tell in advance how a conversation is going to turn out. One must follow the process along and take one's cues from the unfolding conversation itself. Despite the absence of any formal rules for carrying out or completing a conversation on a specific subject, most people have a good intuitive grasp of what it means for a conversation to be finished, what it means to change the subject in the middle of a conversation, and what it means to later reopen a conversation one had thought was completed when something new has just arisen. Thus, the metaphor suggests that informed consent consists not in a formal process carried out strictly by protocol but in a conversation designed to encourage patient participation in all medical decisions to the extent that the patient wishes to be included. The idea of informed consent as physician–patient conversation could, when properly developed, be a useful analytic tool for ethical issues in informed consent, and could also be a powerful educational tool for highlighting the skills and attitudes that a physician needs to successfully integrate this process within patient care.

If primary care physicians understand informed consent as this sort of conversation process, the idea that exact rules cannot be given for its successful management could cease to be a mystery. Physicians would instead be guided to rely on their own intuitions and communication skills, with careful attention to information received from the patient, to determine when an adequate job had been done in the informed consent process. Moreover, physicians would be encouraged to see informed consent as a genuinely mutual and participatory process, instead of being reduced to the one-way disclosure of information. In effect, informed consent could be demystified, and located within the context of the everyday relationships between physician and patient, albeit with a renewed emphasis on patient participation.[8]

Unfortunately, the conversation metaphor does not lend itself to ready translation into a legal standard for determining whether or not the physician has satisfied her basic responsibilities to the patient. There seems to be an inherently subjective element to conversation that makes it ill-suited as a legal standard for review of controversial cases. A conversation in which one participates is by its nature a very different thing from the same conversation described to an outsider. It is hard to imagine how a jury could be instructed to determine in retrospect whether or not a particular conversation was adequate for its purposes. However, without the possibility for legal review, the message that patient autonomy is an important value and that patients have important rights within primary care would seem to be severely undermined. The question then is whether some of the important strengths of the conversation model can be retained in another model that does allow better guidance.

## The Transparency Standard

I propose the transparency standard as a means to operationalize the best features of the conversation model in medical practice. According to this standard, adequate informed consent is obtained when a reasonably informed patient is allowed to participate in the medical decision to the extent that patient wishes. In turn, "reasonably informed" consists of two features: (1) the physician discloses the basis on which the proposed treatment, or alternative possible treatments, have been chosen; and (2) the patient is allowed to ask questions suggested by the disclosure of the physician's reasoning, and those questions are answered to the patient's satisfaction.

According to the transparency model, the key to reasonable disclosure is not adherence to existing standards of other practitioners, nor is it adherence to a list of risks that a hypothetical reasonable patient would want to know. Instead, disclosure is adequate when the physician's basic thinking has been rendered transparent to the patient. If the physician arrives at a recommended therapeutic or diagnostic intervention only after carefully examining a list of risks and benefits, then rendering the physician's thinking transparent requires that those risks and benefits be detailed for the patient. If the physician's thinking has not followed that route but has reached its conclusion by other considerations, then what needs to be disclosed to the patient is accordingly different. Essentially, the transparency standard requires the physician to engage in the typical patient-management thought process, only to *do it out loud in language understandable to the patient.*[9]

To see how this might work in practice, consider the following as possible general decision-making strategies that might be used by a primary physician:

1. The intervention, in addition to being presumably low-risk, is also routine and automatic. The physician, faced with a case like that presented by the patient, almost always chooses this treatment.

2. The decision is not routine but seems to offer clear benefit with minimal risk.

3. The proposed procedure offers substantial chances for benefit, but also very substantial risks.

4. The proposed intervention offers substantial risks and extremely questionable benefits. Unfortunately, possible alternative courses of action also have high risk and uncertain benefit.

The exact risks entailed by treatment loom much larger in the physician's own thinking in cases 3 and 4 than in cases 1 and 2. The transparency standard would require that physicians at least mention the various risks to patients in scenarios 3 and 4, but would not necessarily require physicians exhaustively to describe risks, unless the patient asked, in scenarios 1 and 2.

The transparency standard seems to offer some considerable advantages for informing physicians what can legitimately be expected of them in the promotion of patient autonomy while carrying out the activities of primary care medicine. We would hope that the well-trained primary care physician generally thinks before acting. On that assumption, the physician can be told exactly when she is finished obtaining informed consent—first, she has to share her thinking with the patient; secondly, she has to encourage and answer questions; and third, she has to discover how participatory he wishes to be and facilitate that level of participation. This seems a much more reasonable task within primary care than an exhaustive listing of often irrelevant risk factors.

There are also considerable advantages for the patient in this approach. The patient retains the right to ask for an exhaustive recital of risks and alternatives. However, the vast majority of patients, in a primary care setting particularly, would wish to supplement a standardized recital of risks and benefits of treatment with some questions like, "Yes, doctor, but what does this really mean for me? What meaning am I supposed to attach to the information that you've just given?" For example, in scenarios 1 and 2, the precise and specific risk probabilities and possibilities are very small considerations in the thinking of the physician, and reciting an exhaustive list of risks would seriously misstate just what the physician was thinking. If the physician did detail a laundry list of risk factors, the patient might very well ask, "Well, doctor, just what should I think about what you have just told me?" and the thoughtful and concerned physician might well reply, "There's certainly a small possibility that one of these bad things will happen to you; but I

think the chance is extremely remote and in my own practice I have never seen anything like that occur." The patient is very likely to give much more weight to that statement, putting the risks in perspective, than he is to the listing of risks. And that emphasis corresponds with an understanding of how the physician herself has reached the decision.

The transparency standard should further facilitate and encourage useful questions from patients. If a patient is given a routine list of risks and benefits and then is asked "Do you have any questions?" the response may well be perfunctory and automatic. If the patient is told precisely the grounds on which the physician has made her recommendation, and then asked the same question, the response is much more likely to be individualized and meaningful.

There certainly would be problems in applying the transparency standard in the courtroom, but these do not appear to be materially more difficult than those encountered in applying other standards; moreover, this standard could call attention to more important features in the ethical relationship between physician and patient. Consider the fairly typical case, in which a patient suffers harm from the occurrence of a rare but predictable complication of a procedure, and then claims that he would not have consented had he known about that risk. Under the present "enlightened" court standards, the jury would examine whether a reasonable patient would have needed to know about that risk factor prior to making a decision on the proposed intervention. Under the transparency standard, the question would instead be whether the physician thought about that risk factor as a relevant consideration prior to recommending the course of action to the patient. If the physician did seriously consider that risk factor, but failed to reveal that to the patient, he was in effect making up the patient's mind in advance about what risks were worth accepting. In that situation, the physician could easily be held liable. If, on the other hand, that risk was considered too insignificant to play a role in determining which intervention ought to be performed, the physician may still have rendered his thinking completely transparent to the patient even though that specific risk factor was not mentioned. In this circumstance, the physician would be held to have done an adequate job of disclosing information.[10] A question would still exist as to whether a competent physician ought to have known about that risk factor and ought to have considered it more carefully prior to doing the procedure. But that question raises the issue of negligence, which is where such considerations properly belong, and removes the problem from the context of informed consent. Obviously, the standard of informed consent is misapplied if it is intended by itself to prevent the practice of negligent medicine.

## Transparency in Medical Practice

Will adopting a legal standard like transparency change medical practice for the better? Ultimately only empirical research will answer this question. We know almost nothing about the sorts of conversations primary care physicians now have with their patients, or what would happen if these physicians routinely tried harder to share their basic thinking about therapeutic choices. In this setting it is possible to argue that the transparency standard will have deleterious effects. Perhaps the physician's basic thinking will fail to include risk issues that patients, from their perspective, would regard as substantial. Perhaps how physicians think about therapeutic choice will prove to be too idiosyncratic and variable to serve as any sort of standard. Perhaps disclosing basic thinking processes will impede rather than promote optimal patient participation in decisions.

But the transparency standard must be judged not only against ideal medical practice, but also against the present-day standard and the message it sends to practitioners. I have argued that that message is, "You can protect yourself legally only by guessing all bad outcomes that might occur and warning each patient explicitly that he might suffer any of them." The transparency standard is an attempt to send the message, "You can protect yourself legally by conversing with your patients in a way that promotes their participation in medical decisions, and more specifically by making sure that they see the basic reasoning you used to arrive at the recommended treatment." It seems at least plausible to me that the attempt is worth making.

The reasonable person standard may still be the best way to view informed consent in highly specialized settings where a relatively small number of discrete and potentially risky procedures are the daily order of business. In primary settings, the best ethical advice we can give physicians is to view informed consent as an ongoing process of conversation designed to maximize patient participation after adequately revealing the key facts. Because the conversation metaphor does not by itself suggest measures for later judicial review, a transparency standard, or something like it, may be a reasonable way to operationalize that concept in primary care practice. Some positive side-effects of this might be more focus on good diagnostic and therapeutic decisionmaking on the physician's part, since it will be understood that the patient will be made aware of what the physician's reasoning process has been like, and better documentation of management decisions in the patient record. If these occur, then it will be clearer that the standard of informed consent has promoted rather than impeded high quality patient care.

### References

1. Charles W. Lidz *et al.*, "Barriers to Informed Consent," *Annals of Internal Medicine* 99:4 (1983), 539–43.

2. Tom L. Beauchamp and Laurence McCullough, *Medical Ethics: The Moral Responsibilities of Physicians* (Englewood Cliffs, NJ: Prentice-Hall, 1984).

3. For a concise overview of empirical data about contemporary informed consent practices see Ruth R. Faden and Tom L. Beauchamp, *A History and Theory of Informed Consent* (New York: Oxford University Press, 1986), 98–99 and associated footnotes.

4. For efforts to address ethical aspects of primary care practice, see Ronald J. Christie and Barry Hoffmaster, *Ethical Issues in Family Medicine* (New York: Oxford University Press, 1986); and Harmon L. Smith and Larry R. Churchill, *Professional Ethics and Primary Care Medicine* (Durham, NC: Duke University Press, 1986).

5. Faden and Beauchamp, *A History and Theory of Informed Consent*, 23–49 and 114–50. I have also greatly benefitted from an unpublished paper by Margaret Wallace.

6. For a specialty opinion to the contrary, see W. H. Coles *et al.*, "Teaching Informed Consent," in *Further Developments in Assessing Clinical Competence*, Ian R. Hart and Ronald M. Harden, eds. (Montreal: Can-Heal Publications, 1987), 241–70. This paper is interesting in applying to specialty care a model very much like the one I propose for primary care.

7. Jay Katz, *The Silent World of Doctor and Patient* (New York: Free Press, 1984).

8. Howard Brody, *Stories of Sickness* (New Haven: Yale University Press, 1987), 171–181.

9. For an interesting study of physicians' practices on this point, see William C. Wu and Robert A. Pearlman, "Consent in Medical Decisionmaking: The Role of Communication," *Journal of General Internal Medicine* 3:1 (1988), 9–14.

10. A court case that might point the way toward this line of reasoning is *Precourt v. Frederick*, 395 Mass. 689 (1985). See William J. Curran, "Informed Consent in Malpractice Cases: A Turn Toward Reality," *New England Journal of Medicine* 314:7 (1986), 429–31.

# Section 2: Autonomy and Pregnancy

## Punishing Mothers

### Alexander Morgan Capron

Alexander Capron argues that behavior endangering fetuses should not be prosecuted but should be prevented to the extent possible by education and persuasion. He attempts to show that how we judge a woman who puts her fetus at risk varies with the circumstances. The mother of the McCaughey septuplets endangered them by her use of fertility drugs, then received sympathy and support. By contrast, Cornelia Whitner endangered her fetus similarly by using crack cocaine, but she was sentenced to prison.

Capron argues that Whitner's conviction violates the autonomy of pregnant women and poses new threats to their health and to their fetuses. While prosecution will be most likely for drinking alcohol, the endangerment statute could extend to any failure to heed medical advice. This might include deciding to attempt a pregnancy after using fertility drugs, if the woman is informed of the high risks entailed by multiple pregnancies.

Capron urges the medical profession to do more to help prospective parents act in ways that will give children a better start in life.

What should society do when a woman, in producing children, exposes them to avoidable risks? That recurring question—which plunges one quickly and deeply into the murky waters of child protection, women's rights, and the far reaches of medical science—has been back on the front pages recently. Two very different stories illustrate how context affects our answer.

## Multiple Births

This fall the international media cast the bright, warm glow of an approving spotlight on Carlisle, Iowa, the home of Kenny and Bobbi McCaughey, who gave birth to four boys and three girls on 20 November. The babies, who were born two months premature and ranged from 2.5 to 3.4 pounds, seem to be doing well, making them the first surviving septuplets in the

From *Hastings Center Report* (January–February 1998), pp. 31–33. Reprinted by permission.

world. With the use of fertility drugs and in vitro fertilization, multiple births are becoming more frequent; for example, fifty-seven quintuplets were born in the United States in 1995. A few months before the McCaugheys' babies, septuplets were born in Saudi Arabia but six died, and in May 1985 an American woman carrying seven fetuses gave birth to six (the seventh was stillborn) but lost three within nineteen days.

Most media coverage was supportive of the McCaugheys, as were friends and neighbors in their small town, the governor of Iowa, and numerous business enterprises, which promised a new house (to replace the two bedroom home the couple had shared with their two-year-old daughter Mikayla), an extra-large van, and life-time supplies of such items as disposable diapers. While parents who had experienced the heavy demands of multiple births warned of everything from sleepless nights to bankruptcy, the general sentiment was summed up by the septuplets' maternal grandfather Robert Hepworth, who termed their births "a miracle."

Still, a few objections were voiced by physicians as well as ethicists. Fertility specialists in Britain, where artificial reproduction (but not the use of fertility drugs) is closely regulated, raised "serious questions about whether such a multiple pregnancy should have been allowed to happen," viewing it less as a triumph of medicine than as a "medical disaster."[1]

Though most critics did not go so far as to argue that the McCaugheys should not have used fertility drugs unless they were willing to undergo "selective reduction" early in the pregnancy (in which the number of fetuses would have been reduced from seven to at most two or three), Gregory Pence did suggest they had made an unethical choice. Rather than claiming it was "God's will," the McCaugheys should take responsibility for the choice they made. "They took bad odds and hoped that all seven would be healthy, and in so doing, they took the risk of having seven disabled or dead babies."[2]

More frequently, the criticism focused instead on the physicians involved. Through ultrasound scans and other means of monitoring, fertility specialists can tell when their interventions will lead to the release of a dangerously high number of eggs, so the woman can avoid conceiving that month or can undergo egg harvesting and in vitro fertilization, with only a few of the resulting embryos being transferred to the uterus and the rest frozen for later use if needed. Peter Brinsden, medical director at Bourn Hall in Cambridge where Louise Brown, the first test-tube baby, was born in 1978, chided physicians who do not use their medical powers responsibly. "The aim of fertility treatment should be to give couples one or two children at most."

Besides the stress that multiple births place on parents (and on their marriage) after the children are born, the general experience with such pregnancies is that they are very dangerous for mother and fetuses alike. Overstimulation of the ovaries can lead in rare cases to heart failure, and carrying many fetuses is associated with potentially fatal blood clots and miscarriages.

Even when such fetuses survive their crowded uterine environment, they will almost certainly be born many weeks early and very small, conditions that give rise to a litany of medical and developmental risks, such as chronic lung disease, mental retardation, and blindness. If, like the McCaughey babies, they succeed in weathering the risks of pregnancy, prematurity, and low birth weight, and emerge relatively intact from weeks of vigorous and very expensive care in a neonatal intensive care unit (NICU), such children still face an elevated risk of child abuse.

## Addicted Babies

Direct charges of child neglect lay at the heart of another recent motherhood story, as recounted in a decision handed down by the Supreme Court of South Carolina less than a month before the McCaughey septuplets' birth.[3] The spotlight of public attention that shone on Cornelia Whitner after she gave birth in Pickens County several years ago was certainly less intense but also much less warm than that which greeted the birth of the McCaughey septuplets in Des Moines.

Ms. Whitner's baby was born with cocaine metabolites in his system, and she admitted using crack cocaine during the third trimester of her pregnancy. Charged with criminal child neglect under S.C. Code §20-7-50, Ms. Whitner pled guilty and was sentenced to eight years in prison.

Rather than appealing her conviction, Ms. Whitner filed a petition for Post Conviction Relief, arguing that §20-7-50 covered children but not fetuses. Thus, she claimed, she had received ineffective assistance of her trial counsel, who failed to advise her that the statute might not apply to prenatal drug abuse, and the trial court lacked jurisdiction to accept a guilty plea to a nonexistent offense. After her petition was granted on both grounds, the state appealed to the Supreme Court of South Carolina.

The South Carolina Children's Code provides that "Any person having the legal custody of any child . . . who shall, without lawful excuse, refuse or neglect to provide . . . the proper care and attention for such child . . . so that the life, health or comfort of such child . . . is endangered or is likely to be endangered, shall be guilty of a misdemeanor." Another provision of the code defines "child" as "a person under the age of eighteen."

Is a fetus a "person" for the purposes of the children's code? Looking to the language of the statute (in light of comparable language in other contexts) as well as to the policy behind the law, the state supreme court answered "yes." It thus reached a different conclusion from other courts in similar prosecutions over the past dozen years around the country.

As the abuse of illegal drugs—particularly but not exclusively crack cocaine—swelled in the late 1980s to epidemic levels, physicians became concerned about the growing number of babies who had been exposed to these drugs prenatally. Though early medical reports—magnified through the lens of the popular media into a picture of NICUs filled with the Charles Mansons of the future—probably overstated the physical and behavioral consequences of prenatal drug exposure, studies have by now established that many babies whose mothers used cocaine and other drugs during pregnancy will have been harmed, in ways that are not always remediable.

Thus, it is hardly surprising that public officials took steps to deter maternal drug abuse and to punish women whose use of drugs exposed their children to harm before birth. Prosecutions took two forms. In some cases, women were charged under statutes forbidding delivery or distribution of illicit substances, in other cases, under statutes that punish child endangerment. Yet in decision after decision in the early 1990s, state courts rejected these prosecutions and held the statutes inapplicable to pregnant women's drug use insofar as the harm alleged occurred before a child's birth.

### The *Whitner* Decision

The South Carolina Supreme Court reached a different conclusion in the *Whitner* case. Since the case involved only a child endangerment provision, the court did not need to deal with the issue of how "delivery" of a drug would be established under a statute forbidding drug distribution. And the court found "no question" that "Whitner endangered the life, health, and comfort of her child" when she ingested crack cocaine in the third trimester of the pregnancy.

Nor did the court have much difficulty in interpreting its statute to include a fetus within the meaning of "child" because, unlike most of the other states that had rejected prosecutions for prenatal drug abuse, South Carolina had substantial case law construing "person" to include a viable fetus.

The earlier cases dealt with two situations. Going back to 1960, South Carolina's courts have allowed wrongful death actions arising from injuries sustained prenatally by a viable fetus, whether born alive or (after a 1964 decision) stillborn. The second context first arose in a homicide prosecution of a man who stabbed his nine-months-pregnant wife in the neck, arms, and abdomen. Despite an attempted caesarean delivery, the child died while still in utero, and the defendant was convicted of voluntary manslaughter.[4] Proclaiming a desire to be consistent with its holdings in the civil cases, the state supreme court upheld the conviction and recognized the crime of feticide, at least as to fetuses who were capable of surviving outside the womb.

In light of these earlier holdings, the *Whitner* court felt there was no "rational basis for finding a viable fetus is not a 'person' in the . . . context" of the child endangerment statute. In this ruling, it departed from the conclusion reached by a Massachusetts court that refused to recognize criminal liability of a pregnant woman for transmitting cocaine to her viable fetus, even though that state, like South Carolina, allows wrongful death actions for viable fetuses injured in utero and homicide prosecutions of third parties who kill viable fetuses. While the Massachusetts court had read its precedents as limited to cases in which the "mother's or parents' interest in the potentiality of life, not the state's interest, are sought to be vindicated,"[5] the South Carolina court held that the state may protect the interests of a viable fetus even from its mother.

### Maternal Liability

Since South Carolina is not unusual in vindicating the interests of children for prenatal injuries in torts cases, adoption of the *Whitner* court's reasoning by other courts would have profound implications for state regulation of the behavior of expectant mothers.

First, the implication of the decision—though nowhere directly addressed—is that it is acceptable for the state to monitor the status of pregnant women and of their babies, such as by doing tests for illicit drugs without consent. If toxicology screening requires informed consent, then women who know that such tests will label them child abusers will refuse permission.

Conversely, if such screening is seen as acceptable without consent, under some general public health doctrine, then pregnant addicts may avoid routine prenatal care so as not to be arrested and incarcerated, and they may even seek to deliver their children outside usual medical settings—all to the detriment of their health and that of their child-to-be. Further, some pregnant addicts might seek late-term abortions, rather than deliver a baby with telltale signs of drug usage.[6]

It is also hard to believe that the court's holding in *Whitner* will stay confined to viable fetuses. While the courts may feel constrained to limit feticide prosecutions to cases where the victim is viable, civil damages are awarded for injuries that occur not just before viability but even before conception and are then manifested after birth. A similar reading of the child endangerment statute can be expected, especially in light of the medical evidence that the developing fetus is probably at greater risk of injury from maternal drug abuse in the first few months of gestation than in the final months.

While the *Whitner* court repeatedly emphasized that it was only addressing the situation before it—a pregnant woman's abuse of an illegal substance—there is nothing in the child protection law that limits the range of acts for which prosecution is possible. The focus of §20-7-50 is on preventing action or inaction that endangers a child's "life, health or comfort." While the statute excepts acts done with "lawful excuse," it is not clear that anything short of necessity would provide such an excuse—certainly not the mere comfort or convenience of an expectant mother.

The conduct that would therefore be most likely to lead to prosecution would be maternal drinking, since the link between fetal harm and prenatal exposure to alcohol is, if anything, even better documented than the link to prenatal exposure to illegal drugs. Alcoholic beverages carry warnings of this risk, and obstetricians routinely warn their patients to refrain from drinking even before their pregnancies are confirmed. Failure to follow such advice, or medical advice either to take or to refrain from taking prescription drugs or following other medical regimes, could thus lay the basis for a child endangerment prosecution if shown to have led to serious harm to a child.

Indeed, in the words of the South Carolina court, there does not appear to be "any rational basis" for

limiting the wrongful acts that could form the basis for a prosecution, whether the conduct occurred pre-viability or was otherwise legal for a woman who was not pregnant. And, to return to the Iowa septuplets, application of the *Whitner* doctrine would appear to expose to prosecution any woman who decided to initiate a pregnancy following fertility treatment if she was informed about the great risks of multiple births.

Of course, future Bobbi McCaugheys are unlikely to give much thought to such matters, and for good reason, as society regards the decision to proceed with a multiple pregnancy very differently from the abuse of illegal drugs. Yet both are situations in which children are exposed to the risk of death or severe handicaps, and both are situations in which the medical profession needs to do much more to help women (and their partners) to adjust their behavior in ways that offer their children a better start in life.

### References

1. Chris Mihill and Sarah Boseley, "Multiple Births: When the Shine Wears Off a Miracle." *The Guardian* (London), 21 November 1997, p. 17.

2. Gregory Pence, "McCaughey Septuplets: God's Will or Human Choice?" *Birmingham Sunday News*, 30 November 1997, p. C1.

3. Whitner v. State, 1997 W.L. 680091 (S.C.), filed 15 July 1997 and amended and refiled on grant of rehearing 27 October 1997.

4. State v. Horne, 282 S.C. 444, 319 S.E.2d 703 (1984).

5. Commonwealth v. Pellegrini, No. 87970 (Mass. Super. Ct., 15 October 1990), slip op. at 11.

6. The *Whitner* court rejected the argument that the pressure to take this step amounted to a penalty on the decision to carry a pregnancy to term in violation of the woman's right of privacy recognized in Cleveland Board of Education v. LaFleur, 414 U.S. 632 (1974).

## Pregnancy and Prenatal Harm to Offspring

### John A. Robertson and Joseph D. Schulman

John Robertson and Joseph Schulman argue that individuals can be held morally and legally responsible for the harm they cause their children before birth. In the case of pregnant women, the responsibilities and the ways they are enforced must be determined by balancing a child's welfare against the woman's interest in preserving her liberty and bodily integrity.

The most desirable social policy is to inform pregnant women of risks to their unborn child and make needed services (such as drug rehabilitation) available to them. However, if these voluntary measures fail, coercive measures by the state to protect the child's interest may be justified. These may include holding a woman liable to civil and criminal penalties after the birth of a child, prenatal seizure of a woman to prevent her from acting in ways harmful to her developing child, and the forcible treatment of a pregnant woman who has refused therapy medically necessary to protect the interest of the child.

None of this infringes on the right to an abortion, the authors assert, because the duties of a pregnant woman to her unborn child are conditional upon the live birth of the child. We have no duty to see that fetuses are born alive. However, we do have a duty to see that if they are, they show no effects of needless harm as a result of the actions of the pregnant woman or anyone else.

The growing ability to prevent the birth of handicapped infants has raised new issues about the scope of reproductive freedom. For example, recent research in obstetrics and fetal medicine has shown many ways in which behavior during pregnancy can harm babies who would otherwise be born healthy. Most women at risk welcome this knowledge. They avoid risky behavior and accept medical treatments or surgery that will ensure a healthy birth. If a healthy birth is not possible, they may avoid conception or terminate the pregnancy.

Yet not all women benefit from existing knowledge of prenatal risks. Some may not know of the dangers that certain behaviors pose or of the treatment available for congenital conditions. Others may lack access to the prenatal screening and treatment that would prevent handicaps. Sometimes, however, women ignore the knowledge and engage in conduct that causes their children to be born handicapped.

The need for public policies to prevent avoidable prenatal injuries has arisen in several different contexts: prenatal medical or surgical treatment and caesarean section; prenatal abuse of alcohol, heroin and cocaine; exclusion from workplaces posing prenatal hazards to offspring; and prenatal transmission of herpes and syphilis. As more instances of prenatal harm become known, pressure to change the behavior of pregnant women will increase.

Public efforts to modify the behavior of pregnant women are controversial on several grounds. The idea that women could with impunity cause or fail to prevent handicapped births is, of course, troubling. Yet there is no consensus about the seriousness of the problem and the appropriateness of particular remedies. In addition, feminists and others are suspicious of public control of women's bodies during pregnancy for the sake of the unborn child. They view it as a significant intrusion on personal liberty with the potential to accord fetuses a legal status that could diminish the right to have an abortion. . . .

## Obligations to the Unborn Child

Questions of prenatal obligations to offspring are ethically complex because of the prenatal timing of the harmful conduct and the unborn child's location in the mother's uterus when the harmful conduct occurs. Meeting obligations to the unborn child may require placing limits on the mother's conduct that would not arise if she were not pregnant. Thus the mother's interest in autonomy and bodily integrity must be balanced against her baby's welfare.

Yet it is not unreasonable to regard her as having a moral duty to the baby she is choosing to deliver. All persons have obligations to refrain from harming children after birth. Similarly, they have obligations to refrain from harming children by prenatal actions. There is no reason why the mother who has chosen to go to term should not also have a duty to prevent harm when she may reasonably do so. The timing of the conduct does not affect the duty to avoid causing harm.

Nevertheless, the interests of actual offspring to be free of prenatally caused harm rather than the right of the fetus to complete gestation is at issue. But the offspring's right is contingent on live birth and the mother's decision to continue a pregnancy. Protecting offspring against prenatally caused harm does not diminish the woman's right to terminate pregnancy.

In [a] PKU case, failure to [follow] the [appropriate] diet will not prevent the fetus from being born. Rather it will cause a child that could have been born healthy to be born with severe damage. The ethical obligation to future offspring may arise before birth, but it is a duty conditional on the planned and likely possibility of live birth. It is not a duty owed to fetuses to assure that they are born alive.

Thus the tendency of physicians to speak of the fetus as a "patient" should be clarified. The fetus going to term is a "patient" by virtue of the expectation that

From John A. Robertson and Joseph D. Schulman, "Pregnancy and Prenatal Harm to Offspring: The Case of Mothers with PKU," *Hastings Center Report* (August 1987), pp. 23–32. (Notes and references omitted.)

it will be born alive, and not because physicians have an independent duty to bring all fetuses to term regardless of the mother's wishes.

Prenatal duties owed the planned offspring may arise before viability. The mother's plans, and not the state of fetal development, are determinative. A woman who is undecided or ambivalent about a first-trimester pregnancy may still be morally obligated to act as if she will carry the fetus to term if first-trimester conduct poses serious risk to a baby that is born. Although she is free to terminate the pregnancy later, she is not free to injure offspring prenatally just because she is uncertain about whether to continue the pregnancy.

Ethical analysis must balance the mother's interest in freedom and bodily integrity against the offspring's interest in being born healthy. This balance will vary with the burdens of altering the mother's conduct and the risk of prenatally caused harm to offspring. Depending on the balance of risk, benefits, and burdens, prenatal conduct may be discretionary, advisable, prudent, or even obligatory. . . .

## Policy Options: Voluntary Compliance or Compulsion?

Several policy options are available to influence the behavior of women and others during pregnancy, ranging from voluntary compliance to coercive sanctions and seizures.

Relying on voluntary compliance is the most desirable policy, since it raises fewer civil liberties and privacy issues and is more likely to be effective. Most women will welcome such knowledge and act accordingly. If they have not been able to avoid the damaging conduct, many will choose abortion rather than bring the damaged fetus to term. The main need here is to assure that women are adequately informed and have access to treatments that can avoid the harm to offspring.

But women who will not or cannot comply with proper conduct will end up injuring a child who could be born healthy. Should the state go beyond informing and penalize irresponsible maternal behavior during pregnancy by imposing civil or criminal sanctions when actual damage to offspring has occurred? Should it prevent the harm to offspring by incarceration or forced treatment of the pregnant woman? . . .

## Coercive Measures: The Noncompliant Mother

Yet some women, even though they are informed of prenatal risks and given access to needed services, may still refuse or be unable to comply with the measures needed to avert harm to their offspring. Given the harm that their behavior will cause offspring and the reasonableness of expecting them to act differently, some persons have proposed that coercive measures, including postbirth sanctions and even prebirth seizures, be employed when education and counseling fail.

However, policies that seek to coerce noncompliant women into adopting the desired behavior are controversial on several grounds. Some of the controversy arises from a failure to distinguish the question of a fetus's right to be born alive from the very different question of the right of offspring who will be born, to be born free of avoidable harm.

However, even when this crucial distinction is made, many people find the notion of sanctions or seizures for conduct during pregnancy to be highly distasteful and an arguably unjustified limitation on personal liberty. They fear that coercive measures would be used without proper justification to restrain a wide range of personal choices by pregnant women. They also foresee a slide down a slippery slope to a state in which every conceivable protective measure is required of pregnant women, including mandatory pregnancy registration and monitoring of the pregnant woman's conduct, leading to seizures and forced treatment if the code of proper prenatal conduct is violated. They view such policies as expressions of hostility toward women and reinforcement of the stereotype of women as vessels of reproduction.

In assessing these claims a distinction must be made between state sanctions applied after the birth of a child severely damaged by culpable prenatal conduct and prebirth seizures that aim to prevent the damage before it occurs. The analysis will show that although coercive sanctions should not be foreclosed as a matter of principle, their role is narrow and should be carefully circumscribed. Only rarely will prebirth seizures ever be justified.

## Sanctions After Birth: Civil and Criminal Liability

The law has long recognized that actions or omissions during pregnancy can be as harmful to children as actions or omissions after the child is born. Since the sixteenth century, prenatal actions that cause a child to die after live birth have been prosecuted as homicide. Similarly, under the civil law, damages have been awarded for injuries that occur during pregnancy or before conception when a child is born damaged, who could have been born healthy. Recent developments allowing family members to sue each other now permit such suits by children against parents if the latter have culpably caused the children avoidable injury. Since these duties arise only if the woman chooses to continue a pregnancy that she is legally free to end, penalizing culpable maternal behavior that unreasonably damages offspring does not conflict with *Roe v. Wade*.

In theory a child who is severely retarded as a result of culpable prenatal conduct could sue the mother. However, suits by damaged offspring against mothers will rarely be brought. Thus the threat of civil suit is not likely to deter harmful prenatal conduct.

The state might pursue criminal prosecution for culpable prenatal conduct that causes severe damage to offspring. Although only a few prosecutions for prenatal child abuse have been reported and the applicability of current child abuse and neglect laws to prenatal conduct is uncertain, this avenue may be increasingly pursued as the number of prenatally caused injuries increases.

A highly publicized example of such a prosecution occurred in San Diego when Pamela Stewart, a pregnant woman with placenta previa (a condition in which the placenta blocks part of the cervix, leading to a risk of hemorrhage and oxygen deprivation for the fetus) allegedly ignored her doctor's advice to stop using amphetamines, avoid sex, and go to the hospital when she began bleeding. On the day her child was born she allegedly took amphetamines, had sex with her husband, and delayed going to the hospital for "many hours" after she began bleeding. Her baby was born alive with severe brain damage and died within six weeks in a neonatal intensive care unit.

The district attorney filed misdemeanor charges against the mother under a California statute that penalizes a "parent of a minor child who willfully omits, without lawful excuse, to furnish necessary . . . medical attendance or other remedial care for his or her child. The statute included a provision that "a child conceived but not yet born . . . [is] an existing person" within the meaning of the statute. The father, whose knowledge of the risks to the offspring was less clear, was not prosecuted.

The Stewart case was eventually dismissed on the ground that the statute had not been intended to apply to prenatal acts and omissions. A similar result might occur in other states, since most child abuse and neglect statutes do not explicitly mention prenatal action. However, many state child abuse laws could also reasonably be interpreted to protect born children from prenatal injury, just as homicide statutes have been interpreted. In any event, ambiguities in current statutes could be clarified by legislation specifically directed to prenatal conduct where a live birth is reasonably foreseeable.

Since the state clearly has the constitutional authority to punish mothers (and fathers) for culpable prenatal conduct, the major policy question is whether such statutes are desirable, and whether prosecutions under them should ever be brought for culpably caused prenatal harm. Let us examine this question in the context of a noncompliant PKU woman who gives birth to a severely damaged child as a result of her failure to resume the diet after she has been appropriately notified and counseled of the need to do so.

The argument in favor of prosecution in such cases is that serious child abuse should be punished whether it occurs before or after birth. The mother has substantially harmed another person by avoidable conduct that falls below reasonable community standards, after notice and counseling. The offspring was seriously and willfully harmed. If brain damage caused after birth is punished, then brain damage caused prenatally should also be punished when avoidance of the prenatal harm does not unreasonably risk the mother's life or health. A statute penalizing culpable prenatal conduct is thus desirable "to announce to society that these actions are not to be done and to secure that fewer of them are done."

Yet one would hope that prosecutors would be very careful in their use of such statutes. Uncertainties about the effects of prenatal conduct and the pregnant woman's culpability, and the danger that prosecution will be sought in less clear-cut cases caution against the use of criminal sanctions except in the most egregious cases of harm and culpability. . . .

. . . Each situation must be considered individually, with the certainty and substantiality of the harm to offspring weighed against the burden on the mother of avoiding the harm. Some situations may appear both to be morally obligatory and also rise to levels of egregiousness that justify prosecution. Heavy use of alcohol and cocaine and refusal of minimally intrusive medical treatments could constitute such unreasonable risky behavior that prosecution for prenatal child abuse is justified in particular cases, if maternal culpability is found.

On the other hand, many behaviors that might appear harmful would not justify prosecution as prenatal child abuse. For example, moderate use of alcohol and nicotine do not appear to present a severe enough threat in terms of certainty and substantiality of harm to justify prosecution, even though a prudent person might refrain. If further research establishes a greater certainty of more substantial harm from these drugs, the calculus would change. Similarly, prosecution would rarely be appropriate for conduct that occurs prior to viability because of the difficulty in establishing maternal culpability.

Prosecution for refusing fetal surgery or medical treatment also depends on the burdens and benefits involved. Prenatal treatment would not be morally or legally obligatory where the treatment is experimental, has low efficacy, or imposes unreasonable physical burdens or risks to the woman's life or health. Few kinds of fetal surgery currently have clear enough benefits to be legally mandatory. Yet the risks of future forms of fetal surgery could become so minimal and the benefits to offspring so clear that reasonable persons would consider them to be morally mandatory; refusal would then fit the requirement for criminal prosecution.

The refusal of cesarean section is more difficult to assess because the more certain benefits in particular cases for the baby may be outweighed by the physical burdens required of the mother. However, one could argue that willful refusal of cesarean section is so irresponsible as to justify prenatal child abuse charges when the child is born with extensive brain damage that the cesarean section would have prevented. But a clear medical need that reasonable persons would not refuse would have to be established.

By now it should be clear that a slide down a slippery slope toward extensive, loosely justified limits on maternal conduct during pregnancy—a fear animating much of the controversy over this issue—is by no means inevitable. Egregious cases of culpable prenatal conduct causing substantial harm and suitable for prosecution can be distinguished from less egregious cases, just as is done with allegations of postnatal child abuse. Fears that obstetricians will become "pregnancy policemen" are no more valid than fears that pediatricians will become "childrearing policemen" under statutes requiring the reporting of postnatal child abuse. Meaningful lines can be drawn here just as they are drawn in myriad other legal situations.

The parallel with postnatal duties is instructive. We cannot ask parents to do more prenatally for their children than we can after birth. Since we do not prosecute for merely imprudent or inadvisable postnatal parental conduct, we should not punish for similar prenatal conduct. Persuasion and voluntary compliance are then the preferred techniques.

Because the pregnant woman may be liable for failing to take medications or to consent to surgery, prosecution for prenatal misconduct may appear to hold the mother to a higher standard before birth than after. But the unborn child's location inside the mother, rather than a more rigorous standard of parental conduct, explains the difference. If the risk to the child were great and the bodily intrusion to the parents minimal, the state might constitutionally hold parents accountable for failing to accept postnatal treatment necessary for their child's well-being.

Finally, it is important to note that legal sanctions to deter harmful prenatal conduct should be used against all persons who culpably injure offspring prenatally, and not solely against pregnant women. For example, harmful conduct by fathers should not be ignored. A father's smoking during his wife's pregnancy should also be subject to sanctions if substantial harm to offspring from passive ingestion of his smoke can be demonstrated. Mr. Stewart should also have been prosecuted if he had culpably engaged in prenatal conduct harmful to the child. Refusing to prosecute culpable fathers for harmful conduct will cast doubt on the legitimacy of prosecuting mothers.

## Prebirth Seizures

The most extreme and controversial policy option is incarceration or forced treatment of pregnant women who are unlikely or unwilling to avoid the behavior that is damaging to offspring. From the perspective of the child at risk, this approach is preferable to punishing after the damage occurs, since it prevents the damage altogether.

Direct intervention on the mother, however, is the most troubling option because it involves bodily seizures of varying duration and risk without the woman's consent. The right to be free of seizure and forced bodily intrusions, except for very compelling justification, is a very basic right. It is debatable whether forced treatment in maternal PKU and other situations is compelling and whether such extreme remedies are available under existing law. Few cases would meet the high standards necessary to justify a direct seizure for the benefit of unborn offspring.

In principle, seizures and forced treatment are within state power if a compelling need that outweighs the burdens of the seizure can be shown. While direct bodily seizures are rare in the law, they are not unknown. They occur in civil commitment, prison sentences, capital punishment, the draft, forced treatment of adults for the sake of minor children, and blood tests and surgery to recover evidence of crime. Their validity depends on a sufficient state interest to justify the intrusion on protected personal interests in bodily integrity, liberty, and privacy.

While this standard is purposely high and difficult to meet, there may be rare situations in which prenatal protection of offspring satisfies it because the benefits to offspring clearly outweigh the burdens of the intrusion.

However, prenatal seizures for the benefit of offspring would have to be specifically authorized by statute and accord the woman procedural due process, including judicial review of the need for the seizure. No state has enacted statutes specifically for that purpose, though a few courts have interpreted statutes that protect minor children from neglect as granting the power to order a cesarean section against the mother's wishes. A Baltimore court in 1984 ordered a pregnant drug abuser committed for the last two months of pregnancy. Civil commitment of mentally ill mothers to protect their offspring has also occurred.

What situations would justify seizure or forced treatment of the pregnant woman? The strongest case is when the intrusion or seizure is minimal in length and the harm to be prevented is certain and substantial. Even then, considerable doubt and controversy remain about whether the power should be used. The case for seizure weakens rapidly as the length, risk, and burdens of the seizure increase, and the benefit to the offspring diminishes. . . .

Forcing medical treatment on pregnant women would be justified only in very exceptional cases. The forced treatment could maintain the mother for the sake of her offspring or be administered directly to the fetus. The strongest case for forced treatment is a one-time intervention of minimal risk to the mother, administering a drug, blood, or surgery to avert severe handicap in her offspring. A one-time surgical procedure without high risk and with great benefit, such as Rh transfusion or even an established fetal surgery, could meet these standards in particular cases. . . .

Ordering a cesarean section over the mother's refusal is the most difficult case, since it forces an unwilling person to undergo general anesthesia, abdominal surgery, and the risk of infection and other complications. Yet the benefits to the offspring also appear substantial—avoidance of anoxia and severe brain damage. Several court orders have been granted for cesarean delivery and one has been upheld by the Georgia Supreme Court. Their appropriateness is hotly debated, both because of the degree of intrusion and the likelihood of error in estimating the need. It is widely thought that physicians overuse cesarean section because of malpractice fears and the higher fees it generates. In several cases where physicians have sought to force a cesarean section on an unwilling woman, their predictions proved erroneous. In addition, there is seldom sufficient time for adequate due process and judicial review. . . .

No physician should be required to seek a mandatory cesarean section. Informing the mother of the risks and reporting damaging refusals to child welfare authorities satisfy the physician's duty. The benefit to the few children who would avoid injury seems to be outweighed by the errors likely to occur under forced treatment policies. Sanctions after birth, however, may be imposed for culpable refusals that caused serious damage to offspring.

This discussion of prebirth seizures appears to single out pregnant women for a forced bodily burden that is not placed on fathers or on parents after birth occurs. Yet the situations are very different. The unborn child is inside the mother and at risk because of her voluntary actions or omissions. There are few situations in which fathers during pregnancy or parents after birth create risks to offspring that bodily intrusions on them could avert. Yet the principle that would in exceptional cases allow prebirth seizures of pregnant women would allow postbirth seizures of both parents and prebirth seizures of fathers if the same balance of burdens and benefits arose and specific statutory authorization existed, reflecting the community's conception of parental duties.

For example, the balance of burdens and benefits might justify physical intrusions on a parent for blood and possibly for bone marrow if no other source could save the child's life or prevent substantial harm. A forced kidney donation is more difficult, because the intrusion is greater and dialysis is an alternative. But lesser intrusions could be imposed in rare cases of sufficient cause if statutes specifically authorized such intrusions. Arguably, such a redefinition of parental duties is within the state's authority. . . .

In sum, prebirth seizures may fall within state power in a narrow class of compelling cases, yet rarely if ever should be sought. The likelihood of error in predicting benefit, the difficulty in assuring due process, and the burden of forced treatment and incarceration make such an extreme remedy, except in a few exceptional cases, a dubious avenue to reduction of handicapped births. Given the risks of such an intrusive policy, postbirth sanctions are preferable when coercive measures are deemed justified. . . .

## A Tragic Choice

Developments in obstetrics, genetics, fetal medicine, and infectious diseases will continue to provide knowledge and technologies that will enable many handicapped births to be prevented. While most women will welcome this knowledge and gladly act on it, others will not. The ethical, legal, and policy aspects of this situation require a careful balancing of the offspring's welfare and the pregnant woman's interest in liberty and bodily integrity. Each situation has to be examined in light of the burdens and benefits of the prenatal conduct.

. . . The most desirable approach is education, counseling, and assuring access to treatment. Yet ethical and legal traditions do not exclude consideration of punitive measures in very special circumstances. When voluntary measures fail, the interests of children require us to address questions of culpability regarding prenatal conduct that harms offspring.

---

R E A D I N G S

# Section 3: Truth Telling

## On Telling Patients the Truth

Mack Lipkin

Mack Lipkin provides a defense of the paternalistic practice of withholding information from patients. Lipkin claims it is usually a practical impossibility to tell patients "the whole truth." They usually simply do not possess enough information about how their bodies work to understand the nature of their disease, and their understanding of the terms used by a physician is likely to be quite different from the meaning intended. Besides, some patients do not wish to be told the truth about their illness. Whether it is a matter of telling the truth or of deceiving patients by giving them placebos, the crucial question, according to Lipkin, is "whether the deception was intended to benefit the patient or the doctor."

Should a doctor always tell his patients the truth? In recent years there has been an extraordinary increase in public discussion of the ethical problems involved in this question. But little has been heard from physicians themselves. I believe that gaps in understanding the complex interactions between doctors and patients have led many laymen astray in this debate.

It is easy to make an attractive case for always telling patients the truth. But as L. J. Henderson, the

Reprinted by permission from *Newsweek,* 4 June 1979, p. 13.

great Harvard physiologist-philosopher of decades ago, commented:

> To speak of telling the truth, the whole truth and nothing but the truth to a patient is absurd. Like absurdity in mathematics, it is absurd simply because it is impossible. . . . The notion that the truth, the whole truth, and nothing but the truth can be conveyed to the patient is a good specimen of that class of fallacies called by Whitehead "the fallacy of misplaced concreteness." It results from neglecting factors that cannot be excluded from the concrete situation and that

are of an order of magnitude and relevancy that make it imperative to consider them. Of course, another fallacy is also often involved, the belief that diagnosis and prognosis are more certain than they are. But that is another question.

Words, especially medical terms, inevitably carry different implications for different people. When these words are said in the presence of anxiety-laden illness, there is a strong tendency to hear selectively and with emphases not intended by the doctor. Thus, what the doctor means to convey is obscured.

Indeed, thoughtful physicians know that transmittal of accurate information to patients is often impossible. Patients rarely know how the body functions in health and disease, but instead have inaccurate ideas of what is going on; this hampers the attempts to "tell the truth."

Take cancer, for example. Patients seldom know that while some cancers are rapidly fatal, others never amount to much; some have a cure rate of 99 percent, others less than 1 percent; a cancer may grow rapidly for months and then stop growing for years; may remain localized for years or spread all over the body almost from the beginning; some can be arrested for long periods of time, others not. Thus, one patient thinks of cancer as curable, the next thinks it means certain death.

How many patients understand that "heart trouble" may refer to literally hundreds of different abnormalities ranging in severity from the trivial to the instantly fatal? How many know that the term "arthritis" may refer to dozens of different types of joint involvement? "Arthritis" may raise a vision of the appalling disease that made Aunt Eulalee a helpless invalid until her death years later; the next patient remembers Grandpa grumbling about the damned arthritis as he got up from his chair. Unfortunately but understandably, most people's ideas about the implications of medical terms are based on what they have heard about a few cases.

The news of serious illness drives some patients to irrational and destructive behavior; others handle it sensibly. A distinguished philosopher forestalled my telling him about his cancer by saying, "I want to know the truth. The only thing I couldn't take and wouldn't want to know about is cancer." For two years he had watched his mother die slowly of a painful form of cancer. Several of my physician patients have indicated they would not want to know if they had a fatal illness.

Most patients should be told "the truth" to the extent that they can comprehend it. Indeed, most doctors, like most other people, are uncomfortable with lies. Good physicians, aware that some may be badly damaged by being told more than they want or need to know, can usually ascertain the patient's preference and needs.

Discussions about lying often center about the use of placebos. In medical usage, a "placebo" is a treatment that has no specific physical or chemical action on the condition being treated, but is given to affect symptoms by a psychologic mechanism, rather than a purely physical one. Ethicists believe that placebos necessarily involve a partial or complete deception by the doctor, since the patient is allowed to believe that the treatment has a specific effect. They seem unaware that placebos, far from being inert (except in the rigid pharmacological sense), are among the most powerful agents known to medicine.

Placebos are a form of suggestion, which is a direct or indirect presentation of an idea, followed by an uncritical, i.e., not thought-out, acceptance. Those who have studied suggestion or looked at medical history know its almost unbelievable potency; it is involved to a greater or lesser extent in the treatment of every conscious patient. It can induce or remove almost any kind of feeling or thought. It can strengthen the weak or paralyze the strong; transform sleeping, feeding, or sexual patterns; remove or induce a vast array of symptoms; mimic or abolish the effect of very powerful drugs. It can alter the function of most organs. It can cause illness or a great sense of well-being. It can kill. In fact, doctors often add a measure of suggestion when they prescribe even potent medications for those who also need psychologic support. Like all potent agents, its proper use requires judgment based on experience and skill.

Communication between physician and the apprehensive and often confused patient is delicate and uncertain. Honesty should be evaluated not only in terms of a slavish devotion to language often misinterpreted by the patient, but also in terms of intent. *The crucial question is whether the deception was intended to benefit the patient or the doctor.*

Physicians, like most people, hope to see good results and are disappointed when patients do poorly. Their reputations and their livelihood depend on doing effective work; purely selfish reasons would dictate they do their best for their patients. Most important, all good physicians have a deep sense of responsibility toward those who have entrusted their welfare to them.

As I have explained, it is usually a practical impossibility to tell patients "the whole truth." Moreover, often enough, the ethics of the situation, the true moral responsibility, may demand that the naked facts not be revealed. The now popular complaint that doctors are too authoritarian is misguided more often than not. Some patients who insist on exercising their right to know may be doing themselves a disservice.

Judgment is often difficult and uncertain. Simplistic assertions about telling the truth may not be helpful to patients or physicians in times of trouble.

## Respect for Patients, Physicians, and the Truth

### Susan Cullen and Margaret Klein

Susan Cullen and Margaret Klein argue that a respect for persons makes it wrong for physicians to deceive patients. Lying to patients outright or withholding crucial information about their medical condition violates their autonomy and prevents them from making informed choices about their lives. Telling the truth, they claim, should be the "default position" for physicians.

In reviewing three "critical questions," the authors hold, first, that a patient's wish not to be informed should be respected, except when a serious harm to others may result. Second, they claim, only a confusion between the "whole truth" and "wholly true" makes it plausible to believe it is impossible for physicians to tell patients "the truth." Finally, they maintain a physician may legitimately deceive a patient only in rare cases in which the deception is brief and the end sought is of great importance (for example, saving the patient's life) and is likely to be achieved. Deceiving a patient "for his own good" shows disrespect for the person and thus is, in general, an unacceptable way for physicians to try to help patients.

A long tradition in medicine holds that because medicine aims to promote the health of patients, it is permissible for a physician to deceive a patient if the deception would contribute to that end. "The crucial question," as one writer observes, "is whether the deception is intended to benefit the patient."[1]

Thus, according to this view, if Dr. Allison tells Mr. Barton he is making a good recovery from a kidney transplant, when in fact the transplanted kidney is not functioning well and his recovery is slower than expected, Dr. Allison's action is justified on the grounds that she is trying to keep up her patient's spirits and encouraging him to fight to regain his health. A sick person isn't made better by gloomy assessments.

This deception-to-benefit-the-patient (DBP) view has a prima facie appeal. At the least it is motivated by the physician's effort to do something to help the patient. Were a physician to tell a healthy patient he had a vitamin deficiency so she could sell him vitamin supplements or recommend unneeded surgery so she could collect a fee for performing it, we would condemn such actions outright. The physician is practicing deception in such cases to benefit herself, not the patient.

We all realize that a physician wouldn't be justified in engaging in just any form of action to benefit her patients. We reject as morally grotesque, for example, the notion that a surgeon should remove the vital organs from a healthy person and use them to save the lives of four others. Having the aim of benefiting a patient does not license using any means whatsoever. Rather, the physician must use means that are morally acceptable. While deceiving a patient for his own good is very different from killing an innocent person to provide the patient a benefit, we will argue that such deception is nonetheless wrong. In all but the rarest cases, deceiving a patient "for his own good" is an unacceptable way for a physician to try to help her patient.

## Respect for Persons

While the DBP view seems unobjectionable at first sight, it is wrong for the same reason it is wrong for a physician to tell a healthy patient he needs vitamins so she can benefit from selling them to him. Such behavior is wrong (in both cases), because it doesn't treat a human being with respect.

Humans are, at the very least, rational beings. We have the capacity to guide our actions on the basis of deliberation, rather than being moved only by instinct or psychological conditioning. Our ability to reason makes all of us worth more than a tree, a dog, or maybe anything else in the natural world.[2]

If we are each special because of our ability to make choices, then others should not destroy this ability or interfere with our exercise of it. All of us have an equal right to choose how to lead our lives, and others have a responsibility to respect that right. (Working out arrangements allowing each person maximum freedom while also guaranteeing the freedom of others is a major task of social and political philosophy.) Treating humans with respect means recognizing their autonomy by allowing them the freedom to make choices about their lives. By contrast, to disrespect people means taking away their freedom to live as they choose.

## Disrespect and the Physician's Good

If Dr. Mires, a gynecological surgeon, tells Ms. Sligh she needs a hysterectomy, when in fact the medical indications are insufficient to justify the surgery and he is recommending it only for the money he will receive for the operation, Dr. Mires is treating Ms. Sligh with disrespect. By lying to Ms. Sligh, Dr. Mires is damaging her autonomy. She is put in the position of having to make a decision on the basis of the false information Dr. Mires provides to her. Hence, the option of deciding to do what is most likely to contribute to protecting and promoting her health is closed off to her. She can only *believe* she is making that decision, for Dr.

Mires has forced her to deliberate on the basis of a false assumption.

When knowledge is power, ignorance is slavery. When Dr. Mires deliberately misinforms Ms. Sligh, he cripples her ability to carry out any plans she might have. It doesn't matter if she decides she doesn't want to have a hysterectomy and so avoids the risks, pain, and expense of surgery. Not only has she been made to worry needlessly and perhaps agonize over her decision, Dr. Mires' deception has put her in a false position with respect to making decisions about her life. Unknown to her, he has restricted her freedom to make meaningful choices. He has discounted her ability to reason and make decisions, and in this way, he has treated her with disrespect.

## Disrespect and the Patient's Good

The most serious cases in which physicians have traditionally considered themselves justified (and perhaps even obligated) to deceive a patient are ones in which the patient is dying and the disease can no longer be treated effectively.[3] In the past, the question was most often one of whether to tell a patient he had cancer. Now that cancer treatments have become more effective, the question has usually become one of whether to tell a patient a treatment is not likely to be effective in extending his life. The central issue remains the same, because the physician must still decide whether to deceive the patient.

Consider the following case. Susan Cruz, a thirty-four-year-old single mother of a six-year-old boy, suffered for more than two months from excruciating headaches that were often accompanied by vomiting and dizziness. Yet it wasn't until after she lost control of the left side of her body and collapsed in the bathroom in what she thought of as a fit that she went to see her HMO doctor. He immediately referred her to Dr. Charles Lambert, a neurologist, who, after a detailed examination, ordered an MRI of her brain. Susan had two seizures in the hospital, right after the scan. She was admitted, and the MRI was followed by a brain biopsy performed by Dr. Clare Williams, a neurosurgeon.

The results of the tests showed Susan had an aggressive form of malignant brain cancer affecting the glial cells. The cancer was so extensive Dr. Williams advised Dr. Lambert that not only was a surgical cure out of the question, surgery to reduce the amount of cancerous tissue would not be worth the risk of additional brain damage. Radiation treatments might shrink some of the tumor, but Susan's disease was so far advanced they would have little effect on the outcome.

After reviewing all the information in Susan's case, Dr. Lambert concluded it was not likely that whatever was done would extend Susan's life to an appreciable extent. Most likely, she would be dead within a few weeks, a month or two at the most. But should he tell her this? Wouldn't it be better to allow her to spend her last days free of the dread and anxiety that knowledge of the imminence of her death was sure to cause her? She and her son, Bryan, could share sometime together free from the worst kind of worry. She could do nothing to prevent her death, so shouldn't he leave her feeling hopeful about the future? After all, he couldn't *know* she would die in a few weeks.

"You have a disease of the supporting cells in the brain," Dr. Lambert told Susan. "That's the reason for the headaches, dizziness, vomiting, muscular weakness, and seizures."

"Is there a treatment?" Susan asked. "Will I have to have brain surgery?"

"Not for your stage of the disease," Dr. Lambert said. To avoid explaining why, he quickly added, "Radiation therapy is the best treatment we can offer, because X-rays will help kill off the abnormal tissue putting pressure on your brain."

"Will that make the headaches and all the rest go away?"

"It will help," Dr. Lambert said. "But we have medications that will help also. I can give you steroids to reduce the brain swelling and an anticonvulsant to control your seizures. I can also treat the headaches with effective drugs."

"When do my treatments start?"

"I'll prescribe some drugs today and set you up with the therapeutic radiologists," Dr. Lambert said. "I imagine they can start your treatments in a day or so."

"Great," Susan said. "I've got to get well so I can take care of Bryan. He's staying with my mom, and she's got a heart problem. A six-year-old boy can be a real handful."

Susan followed the treatment plan outlined by Dr. Lambert. She took the drugs prescribed and, with the help of her friend Mandy, showed up at the hospital for her radiation treatments for four weeks. She missed the fifth treatment, because she began having uncontrollable seizures and was taken to the hospital. She died the day after her admission.

Dr. Lambert never told Susan she had brain cancer, nor that the reason surgery wasn't appropriate was that the disease was so far advanced it would be useless. He didn't tell her that, by his estimation, she had only a few weeks of life remaining. Dr. Lambert didn't lie to Susan, but he deceived her. What he told her about her medical condition was vague and limited. He didn't share with her information he possessed that was relevant to her condition. He chose his words so that she would believe she had a disease that might be either cured or controlled by the treatments he prescribed.

While Susan did not (we may suppose) press Dr. Lambert for more information than he provided or ask him questions about her illness, this does not mean Dr. Lambert was not engaged in deception.[4] Susan (like many people) may not have known enough about medicine or her own body to ask the right sort of questions, may have been so intimidated by doctors not to dare to ask questions, or may have been psychologically incapable of asking questions about her illness, preferring to leave everything in the hands of her physician. Dr. Lambert, at the least, should have found out from Susan how much she wanted to know. A willful ignorance is, after all, quite different from an enforced ignorance.

It was also disingenuous for Dr. Lambert to reason that because he cannot be *certain* Susan will die of her disease within a few weeks, he should withhold information from her. Uncertainty of that kind is an ineliminable part of medical practice, and Dr. Lambert has every reason to believe Susan has a relatively short time to live. Judges instructing juries in death penalty cases often distinguish between real doubt and philosophical doubt in explaining the meaning of "reasonable doubt." Dr. Lambert has no real doubt about Susan's fate, and she is entitled to his best medical judgment.

Dr. Lambert's deception of Susan Cruz, like Dr. Mires' deception of Ms. Sligh, is morally wrong. Dr. Lambert deceives Susan with the aim of doing something good for her, while Dr. Mires deceives Ms. Sligh with the aim of doing something good for himself. We might thus say that the deception practiced by Dr. Mires is morally worse than that practiced by Dr. Lambert. Even so, Dr. Lambert's deception of Susan Cruz is still wrong, because it treats her disrespectfully.

By failing to provide Susan with crucial information, Dr. Lambert violates Susan's right to shape what is left of her own life. He deceives her into believing that, with the treatments he prescribes, she can go back to living a normal life and might eventually become healthy again. Because this is not so, Susan is thus denied the opportunity to decide how to spend the final weeks of her life.

She is unable to do what she might prefer to do, if she knew she had a fatal disease and a relatively short time left to live. She might reestablish a connection with her ex-husband, complete the novel she was writing, or visit New York. Most important, she might arrange for someone to take care of her six-year-old son. Prevented by Dr. Lambert's deception from knowing she may soon die, Susan is barred from pursuing what she values most in the time she has remaining.

Respect for persons bars the deception of patients. When the deception is for the physician's benefit, the wrong is obvious. Yet even when the deception is intended to benefit the patient, the physician's good intention doesn't alter the fact that the deception violates the patient's autonomy.

## Three Critical Questions

Three questions about physicians' telling the truth to their patients arise with sufficient frequency as to warrant their being addressed explicitly.

1. *What if a patient doesn't want to know about his disease or the state of his health?* Some writers have argued that many patients don't want to know what's wrong with them.[5] Although they may say they do, some don't mean it. Part of the physician's job is to assess how much information and what sort a patient can handle, then provide him with an appropriate amount and kind. Thus, a physician may decide that a man in his mid-thirties doesn't want to know he is showing the first symptoms of (say) Huntington's disease. Although the disease is invariably fatal and essentially untreatable, it is slow acting, and the patient may have another ten or fifteen years of more-or-less normal life before the worst symptoms of the disease manifest themselves. The physician may decide to spare the patient the anguish of living with the knowledge that he is eventually going to develop a fatal and particularly nasty disease. The patient, she judges, really wants her to protect him from the years of agony and uncertainty.

But with no more than her own assessment to guide her, in making judgments about what a patient wants to know, the physician is taking too much on herself. Huntington's disease is a genetic disorder that occurs when a parent passes on the HD gene to a child. Someone with one parent who has HD may al-ready know he has a fifty-fifty chance of developing the disorder. He may want to know whether the problems he is experiencing are symptoms of the disease. If they are, he may choose to live his life in a way very different than he might if the problems are not symptoms. He might decide, for example, not to have a child and to avoid the risk of passing on the gene for the disease. Or if he and his partner decide to have a child, they might opt for artificial insemination and embryo screening to eliminate embryos carrying the HD gene. The physician is generally in no position to decide what information needs to be withheld from a patient. Full disclosure should be the default position for physicians.

### The Patient Is Explicit

If a patient clearly and explicitly expresses the wish not to know the truth about his medical condition physicians should generally respect this desire. No disrespect is involved in not telling the truth (not providing information) to someone who decides he does not want to know it. The ignorance he imposes on himself may be necessary for him to go on with his life in the way he wishes.

Thus, someone may know himself well enough to realize that if he were diagnosed with inoperable cancer, he wouldn't be able to think about anything else, and the remainder of his life would be a misery of anxiety and fear. His physician should respect such a wish to remain ignorant, for it is as much an expression of autonomy as is the wish to be informed.

When a patient expresses the desire not to be informed about his medical condition, this does not justify his physician's *deceiving* him about his condition. The physician is warranted in withholding the truth from a patient who has asked to be kept ignorant, but the physician is not warranted in telling the patient nothing is wrong with him when there is or falsely assuring him he doesn't have metastatic prostate cancer.

### Overriding Considerations?

Cases in which patients do not wish to know about their medical condition may not be as rare as they once were. Some patients don't want to know if they are infected with HIV, for example, and request that they not be informed of test results that might show they are HIV-positive.

Such cases raise the question of whether the respect for persons that grounds the physician's obligation to allow a patient to make his own decisions requires the physician always to be bound by a patient's explicit wish not to be informed about his medical condition. We think not.

Where HIV or some other contagious disease is involved, the patient has a need to know, not necessarily for his own sake, but for the sake of others. Those who do not want to know they are HIV-positive lack information crucial to decisions concerning their own behavior with respect to others. The physician has an obligation to a particular patient, but she also has an obligation to prevent harm to others who may come into contact with that patient. Failing to tell a patient he is HIV-positive, even if he has requested not to know, makes her complicitous in the spread of the disease. She is not responsible for her patient's actions, but she is responsible for making sure he has information relevant to decisions affecting others. Violating his autonomy to the extent needed to inform him is justified by the possibility that it may save the lives of others. (If she discovered an airline pilot suffered from a seizure disorder, it would be morally wrong for her not to make sure the airline was informed.)

A question similar to that about infectious diseases arises about the "vertical transmission" of genetic diseases. Suppose a thirty-four-year-old man whose mother died of Huntington's doesn't want to be tested to find out whether he is carrying the gene (and so will develop the disease). He is bothered by some movement problems and episodes of mental confusion. He wants his physician to treat him for these but not tell him whether they are symptoms of the onset of Huntington's. The man is about to be married, and he has told his physician he and his wife intend to have children.

After examination and testing, the physician believes the patient's problems are symptoms of HD and are likely to get progressively worse. Moreover, the physician knows that offspring of the man have a fifty percent chance of inheriting the gene that causes the disease. Should the physician go against the patient's explicit request and inform him it is likely he has HD?

Once again, violating a patient's autonomy to the extent of telling him something he does not want to hear seems warranted. If the patient knows he may have HD, he might decide either not to have children or to employ embryo screening to avoid having a child that inherits the HD gene. In the absence of this knowledge, he may be more likely to have a child who will inherit the gene and eventually develop a painful, lingering, and fatal disease. Decreasing the likelihood of bringing a child into the world who will eventually develop such a disease justifies the physician's going against her patient's wishes. (Before reaching this stage, the physician might talk to the patient and attempt to get him to change his mind by telling him what might be at stake and making sure he understands his reproductive options.)

In summary, we hold that while a physician has a prima facie obligation to withhold the truth about a patient's condition from the patient at the patient's request, in some circumstances the physician may have a duty to ignore the request and provide the patient with information he doesn't want to hear.

### Patients Who Don't Say

What about patients like Susan Cruz who express neither a desire to be fully informed nor a wish to be kept ignorant? Physicians are justified in presuming that patients want to know about the state of their health, diseases they may have, and the appropriate treatments for them. This presumption is no less than the recognition that patients are persons, that they are rational agents who may be assumed to want to make informed decisions about matters affecting their lives. Setting aside this prior presumption requires that a patient explicitly inform a physician that he or she wishes to remain in ignorance. Informing patients about their medical condition is, again, the default position for physicians.

Further, if a physician has doubts about whether a patient wants to be informed about her medical condition (as we discussed earlier in connection with Susan Cruz), he should make an effort to determine at the beginning of the relationship whether the patient wants to know about the nature and seriousness of her disease. "Don't ask, don't tell" is by no means an appropriate model for physician–patient communication, and because the physician holds the stronger position in the relationship, it is up to him to find out about how much his patient wants to know.

Studies indicate that a significant majority of patients do want to know about the state of their health. In most studies, over eighty percent of patients surveyed reported that they would want to be informed if they were diagnosed with cancer or some other serious disease.[6] Thus, telling a patient the truth can be regarded as the default position for the physician on grounds that are empirical as well as moral.

2. *What if a physician is unable to tell a patient the truth?* Physicians cannot tell patients what they don't know themselves. Nothing is wrong with a physician's

admitting that little is known about the patient's disease or that the patient's symptoms don't point to a clear diagnosis. Patients are aware that physicians aren't omniscient, and a physician who confesses to ignorance or puzzlement may be showing respect for the patient. A physician must recognize his own limitations, as distinct from the limitations of the state of medicine, and be prepared to refer a patient to someone more able to address the patient's problem.

Actual ignorance and the consequent impossibility of telling a patient the truth is not the issue that physicians and patients typically focus on in the conflict over truth-telling. The issue is usually about whether physicians, when they know the truth, are able to tell it to their patients.

A complaint often expressed by physicians about the need to get a patient's informed consent before carrying out a surgical procedure is that patients are unable to understand their explanations. The notion underlying this complaint is that, even when physicians try, it is impossible to inform patients about their medical condition.

This notion lies at the base of the argument that physicians, even when they do their best, cannot tell their patients the truth. Patients (the argument goes) lack the technical background and experience of physicians, so even intelligent and educated patients are not able to understand the medical terms and concepts physicians must use to describe a patient's condition. Physicians, if they are to communicate at all with the patient, must then switch to using terms and concepts that neither adequately nor accurately convey to the patient what is wrong with him. Thus, it is impossible for physicians to tell patients the truth.

Critics have pointed out that this argument that physicians are not able even in principle to tell patients "the truth" rests on a confusion between "whole truth" and "wholly true." Physicians, we can agree, cannot tell patients the "whole truth," meaning that no patient is going to be able to understand all the known details of a disease process as it affects him. Medicine is an information-rich enterprise, and even physicians are quickly out of their depth in areas beyond their expertise. How many of us really understand the pancreas?

Even so, the explanation of a complicated situation in ways a layperson can understand is not a challenge unique to physicians. The same problem is faced by lawyers, electricians, automobile mechanics, and computer help-line workers. In none of these fields, including medicine, is it necessary to provide the layperson with a complete explanation (the "complete truth") of a situation. All a patient requires is an understanding adequate to appreciate the nature and seriousness of his illness and the potential benefits and risks of the available therapies. A diabetic need not know the stages of oxidative phosphorylation to grasp the importance of insulin and role of diet in maintaining her health.

The argument also does not support the claim endorsed by some writers that, because a physician cannot tell their patients "the truth" (the "whole truth"), it's all right to tell them what is not "wholly true"—that is, to deceive them. Such deception may involve using vague language to explain a patient's medical condition. Thus, Dr. Lambert tells Susan Cruz, "You have a disease of the supporting cells in the brain," when he should have explained to her that she had a particular kind of brain cancer, one that was aggressive and that had advanced to an inoperable stage. The view that the impossibility of telling a patient "the whole truth" makes it all right to tell the patient something not wholly true is analogous to saying, "Because I can't pay you the money I owe you, it's okay for me to rob you." Not being able to tell "the truth" is not a license to deceive.

Respect for persons requires that physicians tell their patients the relevant facts about their medical condition in a comprehensible way. It doesn't require trying to tell patients all the facts. Telling the truth is no more an impossibility for physicians than it is for automobile mechanics.

3. *Don't physicians sometimes have a duty to lie to their patients?* Some writers have argued that respect for persons and their autonomy sometimes permits physicians to deliberately deceive their patients. Granting that a sick patient desires to regain his health, then if that desire can most likely be attained by his physician's deceiving him, the physician is justified in carrying out the deception.[7] Deceiving the patient in such a case assists him in securing his goal, so a respect for the patient's goal makes the deception permissible. The physician violates the patient's autonomy a little while the patient is sick so that he will regain his health.

This is not a view that can be dismissed as obviously flawed, but it is one we ought to be cautious about adopting without qualification.

First, it is easy to overestimate the extent to which lying to a patient will be useful in helping him regain his health. We certainly don't have any data that show the relative advantage of deceiving patients about their illnesses. The old notion that if a patient with a serious illness is protected from anxiety and worry about his condition, he will heal faster is no more than speculation. As such, it will not justify our infringing someone's autonomy for the sake of what is at best a hypothetical gain.

Second, it is easy to underestimate the benefits of informing patients about the character of disease and the aim of the treatment. Most treatments for serious diseases require the full cooperation of the patient. A woman diagnosed with metastatic breast cancer must go through a rigorous course of therapy, ranging from surgery through chemotherapy and radiation treatments. If she knows that her cancer has spread from the breast to other places in her body and knows her chances of survival, she is more likely to adhere to the treatment plan mapped out by her oncologist. Deceiving the patient about her medical problem is probably, in most cases, more likely to work against her goal of preserving her life and regaining her health. Thus, deception may not only violate her autonomy, it may contribute to the loss of her life.

Let us suppose, however, that in some cases we can know with reasonable certainty that if we deceive someone about her illness this will contribute to her recovery. Is it acceptable to use deception and violate autonomy in the short run, if the deception can be expected to promote autonomy in the longer run?

Recalling an example mentioned earlier should make us wary of answering this question in the affirmative. It would be wrong, we said, to kill one healthy person to obtain organs to save the lives of four people. Such examples suggest it is wrong to interfere with autonomy (that of the healthy person) for the sake of promoting autonomy (that of the four sick ones).

Yet we generally agree it is acceptable for the federal government to tax people with a certain income, then use part of the money to help feed starving foreigners. This suggests it is *not* wrong to interfere with autonomy (that of taxpayers) to promote autonomy (that of the starving). Are our responses in these two cases inconsistent, or is there a difference between the cases? We suggest there is a difference.

In both cases, the gain in autonomy is great (lives saved), but in the tax case, the infringement of autonomy needed to achieve a great gain is minor. Taxing us

as citizens takes away some of our resources and thus counts as an infringement of our autonomy. Yet we still retain a substantial degree of control over the important parts of our lives.

The contrast between these two cases suggests the following principle: It does not show a disrespect for persons to violate their autonomy, if the violation is minor and the potential gain is both probable and significant. Thus, for example, if a physician is confident she can save a patient's life by deceiving him for a short while, it is not wrong for her to deceive him. Suppose Ms. Cohen has an irrational fear of taking antibiotics, yet if she is not treated for a bacterial lung infection, she will almost certainly die. Her physician, in such circumstances, would be justified in telling her something like, "The pills I'm giving you will help your body fight the infection."

Such cases are sure to be rare, however. In most cases, either the stakes will not be high enough (someone's life) to justify deception or deception will not be likely to help. Most often, the physician's only legitimate course is to respect her patient's status as an autonomous agent. This means not trying to deceive him and helping him make decisions by providing him with information relevant to his disease and the treatment options open to him.

## Conclusion

We have argued that a principle of respect for persons requires that physicians not engage in deceiving patients. It is clearly wrong for physicians to tell patients they need surgery that they don't need. Such a lie is wrong, we have contended, because it prevents patients from making informed choices about their lives. This is also true of deception intended to benefit a patient. In all but the rarest cases, deceiving a patient "for his own good" is an unacceptable way for physicians to try to help their patients.

### Notes

1.  Mark Lipkin, *Newsweek* (June 4, 1979), p. 13. See also Joseph Ellin, "Lying and Deception: The Solution to a Dilemma in Medical Ethics," *Westminster Institute Review* (May 1981), pp. 3–6, and Joseph Collins, "Should Doctors Tell the Truth?" in Samuel Gorovitz *et al.*, eds., *Moral Problems in Medicine,* 2nd ed. (New York: Prentice-Hall, 1983), pp. 199–201.

2.  Immanuel Kant was the first to articulate this idea. See his *Groundwork of the Metaphysic of Morals,* tr. H. Paton (New York: Harper Torchbooks, 1964), esp. p. 96.

3.  Lipkin, *loc. cit.*

4.  Sissela Bok, *Lying: Moral Choice in Public and Private Life* (New York: Pantheon Books, 1978), p. 229.

5.  Lipkin, *loc. cit.* See also Lawrence Henderson, "Physician and Patient as a Social System," *New England Journal of Medicine* (1955), p. 212.

6.  Bok, p. 227.

7.  Jane Zembaty, "A Limited Defense of Paternalism in Medicine," *Proceedings of the 13th Conference on Value Inquiry: The Life Sciences and Human Values* (Geneseo, NY: State University of New York, 1979), pp. 145–158. See also Terence Ackerman, "Why Doctors Should Intervene," *Hastings Center Report* (August 1982), pp. 14–17.

## READINGS

# Section 4: Confidentiality

## Confidentiality in Medicine—A Decrepit Concept

### Mark Siegler

Mark Siegler calls attention to the impossibility of preserving the confidentiality traditionally associated with the physician–patient relationship. In the modern hospital, a great many people have legitimate access to a patient's chart and so to all medical, social, and financial information the patient has provided. Yet the loss of confidentiality is a threat to good medical care. Confidentiality protects a patient at a time of vulnerability and promotes the trust that is necessary for effective diagnosis and treatment. Siegler concludes by suggesting some possible solutions for preserving confidentiality while meeting the needs of others to know certain things about the patient.

Medical confidentiality, as it has traditionally been understood by patients and doctors, no longer exists. This ancient medical principle, which has been included in every physician's oath and code of ethics since Hippocratic times, has become old, worn-out, and useless; it is a decrepit concept. Efforts to preserve it appear doomed to failure and often give rise to more problems than solutions. Psychiatrists have tacitly acknowledged the impossibility of ensuring the confidentiality of medical records by choosing to establish a separate, more secret record. The following case illustrates how the confidentiality principle is compromised systematically in the course of routine medical care.

Supported by a grant (OSS-8018097) from the National Science Foundation and by the National Endowment for the Humanities. The views expressed are those of the author and do not necessarily reflect those of the National Science Foundation or the National Endowment for the Humanities. Reprinted by permission from the *New England Journal of Medicine,* Vol. 307, No. 24 (9 Dec. 1982), pp. 518–521. Copyright 1982 by the Massachusetts Medical Society.

A patient of mine with mild chronic obstructive pulmonary disease was transferred from the surgical intensive-care unit to a surgical nursing floor two days after an elective cholecystectomy. On the day of transfer, the patient saw a respiratory therapist writing in his medical chart (the therapist was recording the results of an arterial blood gas analysis) and became concerned about the confidentiality of his hospital records. The patient threatened to leave the hospital prematurely unless I could guarantee that the confidentiality of his hospital record would be respected.

The patient's complaint prompted me to enumerate the number of persons who had both access to his hospital record and a reason to examine it. I was amazed to learn that at least 25 and possibly as many as 100 health professionals and administrative personnel at our university hospital had access to the patient's record and that all of them had a legitimate need, indeed a professional responsibility, to open and use that chart. These persons included 6 attending physicians (the primary physician, the surgeon, the pulmonary consultant, and others); 12 house officers (medical, surgical, intensive-care unit, and "covering" house staff); 20 nursing personnel (on three shifts); 6 respiratory therapists; 3 nutritionists; 2 clinical pharmacists; 15 students (from medicine, nursing, respiratory therapy, and clinical pharmacy); 4 unit secretaries; 4 hospital financial officers; and 4 chart reviewers (utilization review, quality assurance review, tissue review, and insurance auditor). It is of interest that this patient's problem was straightforward, and he therefore did not require many other technical and support services that the modern hospital provides. For example, he did not need multiple consultants and fellows, such specialized procedures as dialysis, or social workers, chaplains, physical therapists, occupational therapists, and the like.

Upon completing my survey I reported to the patient that I estimated that at least 75 health professionals and hospital personnel had access to his medical record. I suggested to the patient that these people were all involved in providing or supporting his health-care services. They were, I assured him, working for him. Despite my reassurances the patient was obviously distressed and retorted, "I always believed that medical confidentiality was part of a doctor's code of ethics. Perhaps you should tell me just what you people mean by 'confidentiality'!"

## Two Aspects of Medical Confidentiality

### Confidentiality and Third-Party Interests

Previous discussions of medical confidentiality usually have focused on the tension between a physician's responsibility to keep information divulged by patients secret and a physician's legal and moral duty, on occasion, to reveal such confidences to third parties, such as families, employers, public health authorities, or police authorities. In all these instances, the central question relates to the stringency of the physician's obligation to maintain patient confidentiality when the health, well-being, and safety of identifiable others or of society in general would be threatened by a failure to reveal information about the patient. The tension in such cases is between the good of the patient and the good of others.

### Confidentiality and the Patient's Interest

As the example above illustrates, further challenges to confidentiality arise because the patient's personal interest in maintaining confidentiality comes into conflict with his personal interest in receiving the best possible health care. Modern high-technology health care is available principally in hospitals (often, teaching hospitals), requires many trained and specialized workers (a "health-care team"), and is very costly. The existence of such teams means that information that previously had been held in confidence by an individual physician will now necessarily be disseminated to many members of the team. Furthermore, since health-care teams are expensive and few patients can afford to pay such costs directly, it becomes essential to grant access to the patient's medical record to persons who are responsible for obtaining third-party payment. These persons include chart reviewers, financial officers, insurance auditors, and quality-of-care assessors. Finally, as medicine expands from a narrow, disease-based model to a model that encompasses psychological, social, and economic problems, not only will the size of the health-care team and medical costs increase, but more sensitive information (such as one's personal habits and financial condition) will now be included in the medical record and will no longer be confidential.

The point I wish to establish is that hospital medicine, the rise of health-care teams, the existence of third-party insurance programs, and the expanding limits of medicine all appear to be responses to the wishes of people for better and more comprehensive medical care. But each of these developments necessarily modifies our traditional understanding of medical confidentiality.

## The Role of Confidentiality in Medicine

Confidentiality serves a dual purpose in medicine. In the first place, it acknowledges respect for the patient's sense of individuality and privacy. The patient's most personal physical and psychological secrets are kept confidential in order to decrease a sense of shame and vulnerability. Secondly, confidentiality is important in improving the patient's health care—a basic goal of medicine. The promise of confidentiality permits people to trust (i.e., have confidence) that information revealed to a physician in the course of a medical encounter will not be disseminated further. In this way patients are encouraged to communicate honestly and forthrightly with their doctors. This bond of trust between patient and doctor is vitally important both in the diagnostic process (which relies on an accurate history) and subsequently in the treatment phase, which often depends as much on the patient's trust in the physician as it does on medications and surgery. These two important functions of confidentiality are as important now as they were in the past. They will not be supplanted entirely either by improvements in medical technology or by recent changes in relations between some patients and doctors toward a rights-based, consumerist model.

## Possible Solutions to the Confidentiality Problem

First of all, in all nonbureaucratic, noninstitutional medical encounters—that is, in the millions of doctor–patient encounters that take place in physicians' offices, where more privacy can be preserved—meticulous care should be taken to guarantee that patients' medical and personal information will be kept confidential.

Secondly, in such settings as hospitals or large-scale group practices, where many persons have opportunities to examine the medical record, we should aim to provide access only to those who have "a need to know." This could be accomplished through such administrative changes as dividing the entire record into several sections—for example, a medical and financial section—and permitting only health professionals access to the medical information.

The approach favored by many psychiatrists—that of keeping a psychiatric record separate from the general medical record—is an understandable strategy but one that is not entirely satisfactory and that should not be generalized. The keeping of separate psychiatric records implies that psychiatry and medicine are different undertakings and thus drives deeper the wedge between them and between physical and psychological illness. Furthermore, it is often vitally important for internists or surgeons to know that a patient is being seen by a psychiatrist or is taking a particular medication. When separate records are kept, this information may not be available. Finally, if generalized, the practice of keeping a separate psychiatric record could lead to the unacceptable consequence of having a separate record for each type of medical problem.

Patients should be informed about what is meant by "medical confidentiality." We should establish the distinction between information about the patient that generally will be kept confidential regardless of the interest of third parties and information that will be exchanged among members of the health-care team in

order to provide care for the patient. Patients should be made aware of the large number of persons in the modern hospital who require access to the medical record in order to serve the patient's medical and financial interests.

Finally, at some point most patients should have an opportunity to review their medical record and to make informed choices about whether their entire record is to be available to everyone or whether certain portions of the record are privileged and should be accessible only to their principal physician or to others designated explicitly by the patient. This approach would rely on traditional informed-consent procedural standards and might permit the patient to balance the personal value of medical confidentiality against the personal value of high-technology, team health care. There is no reason that the same procedure should not be used with psychiatric records instead of the arbitrary system now employed, in which everything related to psychiatry is kept secret.

## Afterthought: Confidentiality and Indiscretion

There is one additional aspect of confidentiality that is rarely included in discussions of the subject. I am referring here to the wanton, often inadvertent, but avoidable exchanges of confidential information that occur frequently in hospital rooms, elevators, cafeterias, doctors' offices, and at cocktail parties. Of course, as more people have access to medical information about the patient the potential for this irresponsible abuse of confidentiality increases geometrically.

Such mundane breaches of confidentiality are probably of greater concern to most patients than the broader issue of whether their medical records may be entered into a computerized data bank or whether a respiratory therapist is reviewing the results of an arterial blood gas determination. Somehow, privacy is violated and a sense of shame is heightened when intimate secrets are revealed to people one knows or is close to—friends, neighbors, acquaintances, or hospital roommates—rather than when they are disclosed to an anonymous bureaucrat sitting at a computer terminal in a distant city or to a health professional who is acting in an official capacity.

I suspect that the principles of medical confidentiality, particularly those reflected in most medical codes of ethics, were designed principally to prevent just this sort of embarrassing personal indiscretion rather than to maintain (for social, political, or economic reasons) the absolute secrecy of doctor–patient communications. In this regard, it is worth noting that Percival's Code of Medical Ethics (1803) includes the following admonition: "Patients should be interrogated concerning their complaint in a tone of voice which cannot be overheard" [Leake, C. D., ed., *Percival's Medical Ethics*. Baltimore: Williams and Wilkins, 1927]. We in the medical profession frequently neglect these simple courtesies.

## Conclusion

The principle of medical confidentiality described in medical codes of ethics and still believed in by patients no longer exists. In this respect, it is a decrepit concept. Rather than perpetuate the myth of confidentiality and invest energy vainly to preserve it, the public and the profession would be better served if they devoted their attention to determining which aspects of the original principle of confidentiality are worth retaining. Efforts could then be directed to salvaging those.

## Decision in the *Tarasoff* Case

### Supreme Court of California

This ruling of the California Supreme Court has been of particular concern to psychiatrists and psychotherapists. The court ruled that therapists at the student health center of the University of California, Berkeley, were negligent in their duty to warn Tatiana Tarasoff that Prosenjit Poddar, one of their patients, had threatened her life. Although the therapists reported the threat to the police, Tarasoff herself was not warned, and she was murdered by Poddar.

The ruling and dissenting opinions in this case address the issue of balancing the state's interest in protecting its citizens from injury against the interest of patients and therapists in preserving confidentiality. Does a therapist have a duty to warn at all? Should a patient be informed that not everything he tells his therapist will be held in confidence? Is a therapist obliged to seek a court order committing a patient involuntarily to an institution, if the patient poses a threat the therapist deems to be seriously motivated?

In the majority opinion, Justice Matthew Tobriner argues that a therapist whose patient poses a serious danger to someone has a legal obligation to use "reasonable care" to protect the intended victim. This may involve warning the person, but if it is reasonable to believe that a warning is not enough, then the therapist has a duty to seek to have the patient involuntarily institutionalized.

In the dissenting opinion, Justice William Clark argues that the law should not interfere with the confidentiality between therapist and patient for three reasons: (1) Without the guarantee of confidentiality, those needing treatment may not seek it; (2) violence may increase, because those needing treatment were deterred from getting it; and (3) therapists, to protect their interest, will seek more involuntary commitments, thus violating the rights of their patients and undermining the trust needed for effective treatment.

Poddar was convicted of second-degree murder. The conviction was overturned on appeal, on the grounds that the jury had not been properly instructed. The state decided against a second trial, and Poddar was released on the condition that he return to India. Although Poddar escaped punishment for his actions, the issues of confidentiality raised by the case have yet to be satisfactorily resolved.

## Justice Matthew O. Tobriner, Majority Opinion

On October 27, 1969, Prosenjit Poddar killed Tatiana Tarasoff. Plaintiffs, Tatiana's parents, allege that two months earlier Poddar confided his intention to kill Tatiana to Dr. Lawrence Moore, a psychologist employed by the Cowell Memorial Hospital at the University of California at Berkeley. They allege that on Moore's request, the campus police briefly detained Poddar, but released him when he appeared rational. They further claim that Dr. Harvey Powelson, Moore's superior, then directed that no further action be taken to detain Poddar. No one warned plaintiffs of Tatiana's peril. . . .

We shall explain that defendant therapists cannot escape liability merely because Tatiana herself was not their patient. When a therapist determines, or pursuant to the standards of his profession should determine, that his patient presents a serious danger of violence to another, he incurs an obligation to use reasonable care to protect the intended victim against such danger. The discharge of this duty may require the therapist to take one or more of various steps, depending upon the nature of the case. Thus it may call for him to warn the intended victim or others likely to apprise the victim of the danger, to notify the police, or to take whatever other steps are reasonably necessary under the circumstances. . . .

### 1. Plaintiffs' Complaints.

. . . Plaintiffs' first cause of action, entitled "Failure to Detain a Dangerous Patient," alleges that on August 20, 1969, Poddar was a voluntary outpatient receiving therapy at Cowell Memorial Hospital. Poddar informed Moore, his therapist, that he was going to kill an unnamed girl, readily identifiable as Tatiana, when she returned home from spending the summer in Brazil. Moore, with the concurrence of Dr. Gold, who had initially examined Poddar, and Dr. Yandell, assistant to the director of the department of psychiatry, decided that Poddar should be committed for observation in a mental hospital. Moore orally notified Officers Atkinson and Teel of the campus police that he would request commitment. He then sent a letter to Police Chief William Beall requesting the assistance of the police department in securing Poddar's confinement.

California Supreme Court, *Tarasoff* v. *Regents of the University of California*, 131 *California Reporter* 14 (July 1, 1976). (Notes omitted.)

Officers Atkinson, Brownrigg, and Halleran took Poddar into custody, but, satisfied that Poddar was rational, released him on his promise to stay away from Tatiana. Powelson, director of the department of psychiatry at Cowell Memorial Hospital, then asked the police to return Moore's letter, directed that all copies of the letter and notes that Moore had taken as therapist be destroyed, and "ordered no action to place Prosenjit Poddar in 72-hour treatment and evaluation facility."

Plaintiffs' second cause of action, entitled "Failure to Warn On a Dangerous Patient," incorporates the allegations of the first cause of action, but adds the assertion that defendants negligently permitted Poddar to be released from police custody without "notifying the parents of Tatiana Tarasoff that their daughter was in grave danger from Prosenjit Poddar." Poddar persuaded Tatiana's brother to share an apartment with him near Tatiana's residence; shortly after her return from Brazil, Poddar went to her residence and killed her. . . .

### 2. Plaintiffs Can State a Cause of Action Against Defendant Therapists for Negligent Failure to Protect Tatiana.

The second cause of action can be amended to allege that Tatiana's death proximately resulted from defendants' negligent failure to warn Tatiana or others likely to apprise her of her danger. Plaintiffs contend that as amended, such allegations of negligence and proximate causation, with resulting damages, establish a cause of action. Defendants, however, contend that in the circumstances of the present case they owed no duty of care to Tatiana or her parents and that, in the absence of such duty, they were free to act in careless disregard of Tatiana's life and safety.

. . . In analyzing this issue, we bear in mind that legal duties are not discoverable facts of nature, but merely conclusory expressions that, in cases of a particular type, liability should be imposed for damage done. As stated in *Dillon* v. *Legg* (1968): . . . "The assertion that liability must . . . be denied because defendant bears no 'duty' to plaintiff 'begs the essential question—whether the plaintiff's interests are entitled to legal protection against the defendant's conduct. . . . [Duty] is not sacrosanct in itself, but only an expression of the sum total of those considerations of policy which lead the law to say that the particular plaintiff is entitled to protection.'" . . .

In the landmark case of *Rowland* v. *Christian* (1968), . . . Justice Peters recognized that liability should be imposed "for an injury occasioned to another by his want of ordinary care or skill" as expressed in section 1714 of the Civil Code. Thus, Justice Peters, quoting from *Heaven* v. *Pender* (1883) . . . stated: "'whenever one person is by circumstances placed in such a position with regard to another . . . that if he did not use ordinary care and skill in his own conduct . . . he would cause danger of injury to the person or property of the other, a duty arises to use ordinary care and skill to avoid such danger.'"

. . . We depart from "this fundamental principle" only upon the "balancing of a number of considerations"; major ones "are the foreseeability of harm to the plaintiff, the degree of certainty that the plaintiff suffered injury, the closeness of the connection between the defendant's conduct and the injury suffered, the moral blame attached to the defendant's conduct, the policy of preventing future harm, the extent of the burden to the defendant and consequences to the community of imposing a duty to exercise care with resulting liability for breach, and the availability, cost and prevalence of insurance for the risk involved."

The most important of these considerations in establishing duty is foreseeability. As a general principle, a "defendant owes a duty of care to all persons who are foreseeably endangered by his conduct, with respect to all risks which make the conduct unreasonably dangerous." As we shall explain, however, when the avoidance of foreseeable harm requires a defendant to control the conduct of another person, or to warn of such conduct, the common law has traditionally imposed liability only if the defendant bears some special relationship to the dangerous person or to the potential victim. Since the relationship between a therapist and his patient satisfies this requirement, we need not here decide whether foreseeability alone is sufficient to create a duty to exercise reasonable care to protect a potential victim of another's conduct. . . .

. . . Although plaintiffs' pleadings assert no special relation between Tatiana and defendant therapists, they establish as between Poddar and defendant therapists the special relation that arises between a patient and his doctor or psychotherapist. Such a relationship may support affirmative duties for the benefit of third persons. Thus, for example, a hospital must exercise reasonable care to control the behavior of a patient which may endanger other persons. A doctor must also warn a patient if the patient's condition or medication renders certain conduct, such as driving a car, dangerous to others.

. . . Although the California decisions that recognize this duty have involved cases in which the defendant stood in a special relationship *both* to the victim and to the person whose conduct created the danger, we do not think that the duty should logically be constricted to such situations. Decisions of other jurisdictions hold that the single relationship of a doctor to his patient is sufficient to support the duty to exercise reasonable care to protect others against dangers emanating from the patient's illness. The courts hold that a doctor is liable to persons infected by his patient if he negligently fails to diagnose a contagious disease, . . . or, having diagnosed the illness, fails to warn members of the patient's family.

Since it involved a dangerous mental patient, the decision in *Merchants Nat. Bank Trust Co. of Fargo* v. *United States* . . . comes closer to the issue. The Veterans Administration arranged for the patient to work on a local farm, but did not inform the farmer of the man's background. The farmer consequently permitted the patient to come and go freely during nonworking hours; the patient borrowed a car, drove to his wife's residence and killed her. Notwithstanding the lack of any "special relationship" between the Veterans Administration and the wife, the court found the Veterans Administration liable for the wrongful death of the wife.

In their summary of the relevant rulings Fleming and Maximov conclude that the "case law should dispel any notion that to impose on the therapists a duty to take precautions for the safety of persons threatened by a patient, where due care so requires, is in any way opposed to contemporary ground rules on the duty relationship. On the contrary, there now seems to be sufficient authority to support the conclusion that by entering into a doctor–patient relationship the therapist becomes sufficiently involved to assume some responsibility for the safety, not only of the patient himself, but also of any third person whom the doctor knows to be threatened by the patient." . . .

Defendants contend, however, that imposition of a duty to exercise reasonable care to protect third persons is unworkable because therapists cannot accurately predict whether or not a patient will resort to violence. In support of this argument amicus representing the American Psychiatric Association and other professional societies cites numerous articles which indicate that therapists, in the present state of the art, are unable reliably to predict violent acts; their forecasts, amicus claims, tend consistently to overpredict violence, and indeed are more often wrong than right. . . .

. . . We recognize the difficulty that a therapist encounters in attempting to forecast whether a patient presents a serious danger of violence. Obviously we do not require that the therapist, in making that determination, render a perfect performance; the therapist need only exercise "that reasonable degree of skill, knowledge, and care ordinarily possessed and exercised by members of [that professional specialty] under similar circumstances." Within the broad range of reasonable practice and treatment in which professional opinion and judgment may differ, the therapist is free to exercise his or her own best judgment without liability; proof, aided by hindsight, that he or she judged wrongly is insufficient to establish negligence.

In the instant case, however, the pleadings do not raise any question as to failure of defendant therapists to predict that Poddar presented a serious danger of violence. On the contrary, the present complaints allege that defendant therapists did in fact predict that Poddar would kill, but were negligent in failing to warn.

. . . Amicus contends, however, that even when a therapist does in fact predict that a patient poses a serious danger of violence to others, the therapist should be absolved of any responsibility for failing to act to protect the potential victim. In our view, however, once a therapist does in fact determine, or under applicable professional standards reasonably should have determined, that a patient poses a serious danger of violence to others, he bears a duty to exercise reasonable care to protect the foreseeable victim of that danger. While the discharge of this duty of due care will necessarily vary with the facts of each case, in each instance the adequacy of the therapist's conduct must be measured against the traditional negligence standard of the rendition of reasonable care under the circumstances. . . . As explained in Fleming and Maximov, *The Patient or His Victim: The Therapist's Dilemma* (1974): " . . . the ultimate question of resolving the tension between the conflicting interests of patient and potential victim is one of social policy, not professional expertise. . . . In sum, the therapist owes a legal duty not only to his patient, but also to his patient's would-

be victim and is subject in both respects to scrutiny by judge and jury." . . .

The risk that unnecessary warnings may be given is a reasonable price to pay for the lives of possible victims that may be saved. We would hesitate to hold that the therapist who is aware that his patient expects to attempt to assassinate the President of the United States would not be obligated to warn the authorities because the therapist cannot predict with accuracy that his patient will commit the crime.

Defendants further argue that free and open communication is essential to psychotherapy; . . . that "Unless a patient . . . is assured that . . . information [revealed by him] can and will be held in utmost confidence, he will be reluctant to make the full disclosure upon which diagnosis and treatment . . . depends." . . . The giving of a warning, defendants contend, constitutes a breach of trust which entails the revelation of confidential communications.

. . . We recognize the public interest in supporting effective treatment of mental illness and in protecting the rights of patients to privacy, . . . and the consequent public importance of safeguarding the confidential character of psychotherapeutic communication. Against this interest, however, we must weigh the public interest in safety from violent assault. . . .

. . . We realize that the open and confidential character of psychotherapeutic dialogue encourages patients to express threats of violence, few of which are ever executed. Certainly a therapist should not be encouraged routinely to reveal such threats; such disclosures could seriously disrupt the patient's relationship with his therapist and with the persons threatened. To the contrary, the therapist's obligations to his patient require that he not disclose a confidence unless such disclosure is necessary to avert danger to others, and even then that he do so discreetly, and in a fashion that would preserve the privacy of his patient to the fullest extent compatible with the prevention of the threatened danger.

The revelation of a communication under the above circumstances is not a breach of trust or a violation of professional ethics; as stated in the Principles of Medical Ethics of the American Medical Association (1957), section 9: "A physician may not reveal the confidence entrusted to him in the course of medical attendance . . . *unless he is required to do so by law or unless it becomes necessary in order to protect the welfare of the individual or of the community.*" (Emphasis added.) We conclude that the public policy favoring protection of the confidential character of patient–psychotherapist communications must yield to the extent to which disclosure is essential to avert danger to others. The protective privilege ends where the public peril begins. . . .

For the foregoing reasons, we find that plaintiffs' complaints can be amended to state a cause of action against defendants Moore, Powelson, Gold, and Yandell and against the Regents as their employer, for breach of a duty to exercise reasonable care to protect Tatiana.

## Justice William P. Clark, Dissenting Opinion

Until today's majority opinion, both legal and medical authorities have agreed that confidentiality is essential to effectively treat the mentally ill, and that imposing a duty on doctors to disclose patient threats to potential victims would greatly impair treatment. Further, recognizing that effective treatment and society's safety are necessarily intertwined, the Legislature has already decided effective and confidential treatment is preferred over imposition of a duty to warn.

The issue whether effective treatment for the mentally ill should be sacrificed to a system of warnings is, in my opinion, properly one for the Legislature, and we are bound by its judgment. Moreover, even in the absence of clear legislative direction, we must reach the same conclusion because imposing the majority's new duty is certain to result in a net increase in violence. . . .

Overwhelming policy considerations weigh against imposing a duty on psychotherapists to warn a potential victim against harm. While offering virtually no benefit to society, such a duty will frustrate psychiatric treatment, invade fundamental patient rights and increase violence. . . .

Assurance of confidentiality is important for three reasons.

### Deterrence from Treatment

First, without substantial assurance of confidentiality, those requiring treatment will be deterred from seeking assistance. It remains an unfortunate fact in our society that people seeking psychiatric guidance tend to become stigmatized. Apprehension of such stigma—apparently increased by the propensity of people considering treatment to see themselves in the worst possible light—creates a well-recognized reluctance to seek aid. This reluctance is alleviated by the psychiatrist's assurance of confidentiality.

### Full Disclosure

Second, the guarantee of confidentiality is essential in eliciting the full disclosure necessary for effective treatment. The psychiatric patient approaches treatment with conscious and unconscious inhibitions against revealing his innermost thoughts. "Every person, however well-motivated, has to overcome resistance to therapeutic exploration. These resistances seek support from every possible source and the possibility of disclosure would easily be employed in the service of resistance." . . . Until a patient can trust his psychiatrist not to violate their confidential relationship, "the unconscious psychological control mechanism of repression will prevent the recall of past experiences." . . .

### Successful Treatment

Third, even if the patient fully discloses his thoughts, assurance that the confidential relationship will not be breached is necessary to maintain his trust in his psychiatrist—the very means by which treatment is effected. "[T]he essence of much psychotherapy is the contribution of trust in the external world and ultimately in the self, modelled upon the trusting relationship established during therapy." . . . Patients will be helped only if they can form a trusting relationship with the psychiatrist. . . . All authorities appear to agree that if the trust relationship cannot be developed because of collusive communication between the psychiatrist and others, treatment will be frustrated.

Given the importance of confidentiality to the practice of psychiatry, it becomes clear the duty to warn imposed by the majority will cripple the use and effectiveness of psychiatry. Many people, potentially violent—yet susceptible to treatment—will be deterred from seeking it; those seeking it will be inhibited from making revelations necessary to effective treatment; and, forcing the psychiatrist to violate the patient's trust will destroy the interpersonal relationship by which treatment is effected.

## Violence and Civil Commitment

By imposing a duty to warn, the majority contributes to the danger to society of violence by the mentally ill and greatly increases the risk of civil commitment—the total deprivation of liberty—of those who should not be confined. The impairment of treatment and risk of improper commitment resulting from the new duty to warn will not be limited to a few patients but will extend to a large number of the mentally ill. Although under existing psychiatric procedures only a relatively few receiving treatment will ever present a risk of violence, the number making threats is huge, and it is the latter group—not just the former—whose treatment will be impaired and whose risk of commitment will be increased.

Both the legal and psychiatric communities recognize that the process of determining potential violence in a patient is far from exact, being fraught with complexity and uncertainty. In fact precision has not even been attained in predicting who of those having already committed violent acts will again become violent, a task recognized to be of much simpler proportions. . . .

This predictive uncertainty means that the number of disclosures will necessarily be large. As noted above, psychiatric patients are encouraged to discuss all thoughts of violence, and they often express such thoughts. However, unlike this court, the psychiatrist does not enjoy the benefit of overwhelming hindsight in seeing which few, if any, of his patients will ultimately become violent. Now, confronted by the majority's new duty, the psychiatrist must instantaneously calculate potential violence from each patient on each visit. The difficulties researchers have encountered in accurately predicting violence will be heightened for the practicing psychiatrist dealing for brief periods in his office with heretofore nonviolent patients. And, given the decision not to warn or commit must always be made at the psychiatrist's civil peril, one can expect most doubts will be resolved in favor of the psychiatrist protecting himself.

Neither alternative open to the psychiatrist seeking to protect himself is in the public interest. The warning itself is an impairment of the psychiatrist's ability to treat, depriving many patients of adequate treatment. It is to be expected that after disclosing their threats, a significant number of patients, who would not become violent if treated according to existing practices, will engage in violent conduct as a result of unsuccessful treatment. In short, the majority's duty to warn will not only impair treatment of many who would never become violent but worse, will result in a net increase in violence.

The second alternative open to the psychiatrist is to commit his patient rather than to warn. Even in the absence of threat of civil liability, the doubts of psychiatrists as to the seriousness of patient threats have led psychiatrists to overcommit to mental institutions. This overcommitment has been authoritatively documented in both legal and psychiatric studies. This practice is so prevalent that it has been estimated that "as many as twenty harmless persons are incarcerated for every one who will commit a violent act." . . .

Given the incentive to commit created by the majority's duty, this already serious situation will be worsened, contrary to Chief Justice Wright's admonition "that liberty is no less precious because forfeited in a civil proceeding than when taken as a consequence of a criminal conviction."

---

## Decision Scenario 1

"I don't want to be treated," Alice Nuvo said. "According to the statistics you gave me, even with the best treatment I've got no more than a five percent chance of surviving for another year."

"Pancreatic cancer is a bad customer," Dr. Cervando Lupe said. "I wish the numbers were better."

"So why should I suffer the pain and nausea of chemotherapy and then radiation if I'm going to die anyway?" Alice snorted in contempt. "It's absurd. I'd rather spend the remaining time with my husband and two daughters, then die in peace, instead of puking up my guts in some hospital."

"We can use drugs to control the nausea from the chemotherapy," Dr. Lupe said. "And we don't know that the statistics apply to you. They apply to a whole group of people, and I never tell a patient that *she* has a five percent chance."

"Just give me something to control the pain and let me go home," Alice said. "I don't want to talk about it anymore."

1. According to Burt, should Dr. Lupe argue with Alice and try to persuade her to undergo treatment?

2. In Cowart's view, if Dr. Lupe thinks Alice is making the wrong decision, how far should he go to try to persuade her to accept the treatment?

3. What method does Brody recommend for getting patients to give their informed consent to treatment?

4. Can a proponent of care ethics ever justify forcing treatment on someone who refuses it?

---

### Decision Scenario 2

Angela Carter was diagnosed as having bone cancer when she was thirteen years old. Over the following years, she received a variety of treatments and underwent surgery several times. In one operation, her leg was amputated. By the time she was twenty-seven, the cancer had been in remission for three years, and she became pregnant. Twenty-five weeks into the pregnancy, she went for a routine checkup, and her physician discovered a large tumor in a lung. She was told she might have only days to live. She was admitted to George Washington Hospital, and five days later her condition worsened.

Despite the objections of Angela, her family, and even her physician, the hospital decided to attempt to save the developing child. The hospital went to court, and at a hearing staff physicians stated that, despite the fact that the fetus was only twenty-six weeks old, there was a 50 to 60 percent chance that it would survive if a cesarean section was performed. Furthermore, they estimated that there was a less than 20 percent chance that the child would be disabled. The physicians also testified that the surgery would increase the chances of Angela Carter's death.

The hospital obtained a court order, which was immediately appealed. Because the case demanded a quick resolution, the three judges on the appeals court consulted by telephone. The whole process, hearing and appeal, took less than six hours. During this time, the hospital had ordered Angela prepared for surgery.

The appeals court let the lower-court ruling stand, and Angela underwent the court-ordered surgery. The child, a girl, lived for only two hours. Angela lived for two days. The surgery was listed as a contributing cause to her death.

1. Does Capron offer any grounds for objecting to the court-ordered surgery?

2. Is there any reason to view this case as different from ones involving drug abuse by a pregnant woman? That is, are the issues the same in both kinds of cases?

3. Suppose Angela Carter had been further along in her pregnancy so that the chance of her child's survival was virtually certain and that she refused to have a cesarean birth. Would Robertson and Schulman's views imply that it would be right to force her to have a cesarean delivery against her will?

4. Robertson and Schulman claim that while a woman has a right to seek an abortion, if she decides to carry the fetus to term it has a right to have her promote its best interest. Is this position consistent?

## Decision Scenario 3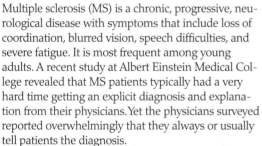

For five years, the hospital of the Medical University of South Carolina followed a controversial policy with respect to pregnant women. Pregnant women admitted to the hospital were asked to sign a consent form agreeing to drug testing, if their physicians decided they needed it. Those who tested positive for cocaine were turned in to local police and were arrested, unless they agreed to take part in a drug rehabilitation program. Forty-two women were turned in. Some agreed to drug treatment, while others were charged with distributing drugs to minors—their fetuses. (These charges were later dropped.)

Critics of the policy claimed that it focused on poor, black women, who form a large proportion of the hospital's patient population. Furthermore, the policy violated the confidentiality of the physician–patient relationship and the woman's right to privacy.

In September 1994, responding to pressure from the federal government, the hospital agreed to change its policy. Had the hospital not complied with federal demands, it stood to lose $18 million of federal research money.

1. What would Capron see as the gravest dangers of a policy like the hospital's? What sort would he be likely to approve?

2. Under what conditions, according to the position on pregnancy and prenatal harm taken by Robertson and Schulman, would the hospital's policy be justified?

3. Is there a policy that the hospital might pursue that would prevent prenatal harm, while also avoiding violating the autonomy of the pregnant woman and preserving the confidentiality of the physician–patient relationship?

## Decision Scenario 4

Multiple sclerosis (MS) is a chronic, progressive, neurological disease with symptoms that include loss of coordination, blurred vision, speech difficulties, and severe fatigue. It is most frequent among young adults. A recent study at Albert Einstein Medical College revealed that MS patients typically had a very hard time getting an explicit diagnosis and explanation from their physicians. Yet the physicians surveyed reported overwhelmingly that they always or usually tell patients the diagnosis.

The researchers learned that a variety of factors account for this discrepancy. Physicians find many reasons for delay—the patient may be under twenty years old, emotionally unstable, or apparently incapable of understanding the diagnosis. Also, the patient may not ask specifically; a relative may ask that the patient not be told; the patient may be medically unsophisticated

or in the midst of an emotional crisis. Most important, there is no cure or wholly effective therapy for MS, and emotional stress seems to aggravate its symptoms. Thus, telling a patient that she or he has a progressive, incurable disease may do no good and may do harm.

Instead of being told they have MS, patients are frequently told that they have "a chronic virus infection," "neuritis," and "inflammation of the nervous system." This sometimes leads patients to consult several physicians and to undergo expensive and unnecessary diagnostic tests in the attempt to get a diagnosis.

1. Are the physicians who claim they believe in telling MS patients the diagnosis but then don't do so necessarily being hypocritical?

2. What sorts of arguments or considerations might Lipkin offer in their defense?

3. In what sort of cases would it be justifiable to withhold a diagnosis from a patient?

4. If there is a chance that knowing the diagnosis will make the symptoms of an MS patient worse and if there is no wholly effective therapy for MS, why is it not the duty of a physician to withhold the diagnosis? After all, "Do no harm" is perhaps the most important of the Hippocratic maxims.

---

## Decision Scenario 5

In 1998 CVS, a national chain of drug stores, accepted payment from pharmaceutical manufacturers to sort through the prescriptions in their database and provide the names of patients taking drugs associated with particular medical problems. After CVS gave the lists to the manufacturers, the manufacturers turned them over to a direct marketing company. The marketing company then sent letters to patients promoting drugs from the manufacturers, designed to treat their specific medical problems.

The program was ended abruptly when the *Washington Post* published an article about it. CVS insisted it had violated no patient's confidentiality and was surprised by the criticisms it received.

1. The CVS program was following the dictates of good marketing strategy by putting specific information in the hands of those for whom it was most relevant. Moreover, patients received information that might be of value to them. On what grounds, then, might one object to the CVS program?

2. If patients supply information about their health problems voluntarily (for example, by answering a questionnaire on a health-information website), does this mean they are giving tacit consent for the information to be used in any way the recipient wishes?

---

## Decision Scenario 6

Jane Montrose told herself that it was just one of the things you had to do if you wanted to get promoted. Talking to eleven department heads might be anxiety provoking, but so far they had all been quite nice. If she were going to be working as an assistant vice president, she would have to deal with all of them frequently. It made sense for them to have an opportunity to say whether they would feel comfortable working with her.

"How are you doing with your psychiatrist?" Art Davis asked.

Jane felt her stomach clutch. She had assumed only her closest friends knew about her therapy. "Fine," she said. "I've been able to work through a lot of problems."

She didn't want to talk to Davis about her feelings of depression and lack of self-worth that had been troubling her for the last few years. None of it was any of his business.

"Will you be able to handle new responsibilities?"

"Yes. I've always done well at every job I've had."

"I know you have," Davis said. "But when we see that an employee has been going to a psychiatrist . . . well, that raises a red flag. It makes us wonder if that person is really to be trusted with a lot of responsibility. I'm sure you understand."

"I don't see what my personal problems have to do with my work, assuming they don't get in the way of my doing it. And they never have."

Davis smiled at her in a way that made her angry. It was the kind of tolerant but superior smile adults usually reserve for children who are talking about things they don't understand.

"How do you know about my seeing a psychiatrist?" Jane asked. "I thought my medical records were all confidential."

"They are, so far as I know. But you did put in an insurance claim for payment, and I have to sign off on all the claims. When I did that, I saw you were getting psychiatric help."

1. Managed care has made information about medical treatment available to more employers than ever before. Is this a necessary result of an employer's need to know the source of costs or is there a way of also protecting employees' privacy?

2. Employees of the New York state government have the right to send medical claims for psychiatric or psychological services directly to the insurance company. Should this be made a legal right for all employees in all states?

3. The federal Privacy Protection Act permits federal law-enforcement agencies to secure search warrants and gain access to all private records, except those of the media. Should the act be restricted to exclude medical and mental health records?

---

### Decision Scenario 7

"Sometimes I think that what I really want to do is to kill people and drink their blood."

Dr. Allen Wolfe looked at the young man in the chair across from him. The face was round and soft and innocent looking, like that of a large baby. But the body had the powerful shoulders of a college wrestler. There was no doubt that Hal Crane had the strength to carry out his fantasies.

"Any people in particular?" Dr. Wolfe asked.

"Women. Girls about my age. Maybe their early twenties."

"But no one you're personally acquainted with."

"That's right. Just girls I see walking down the street or getting off a bus. I have a tremendous urge to stick a knife into their stomachs and feel the blood come out on my hands."

"But you've never done anything like that?"

Crane shook his head. "No, but I'm afraid I might."

Dr. Wolfe considered Crane a paranoid schizophrenic with compulsive tendencies, someone who might possibly act out his fantasies. He was a potentially dangerous person.

"Would you be willing to take my advice and put yourself in a hospital under my care for a while?"

"I don't want to do that," Crane said. "I don't want to be locked up like an animal."

"But you don't really want to hurt other people, do you?"

"I guess not," Crane said. "I haven't done anything yet."

"But you might," Dr. Wolfe said. "I'm afraid you might let yourself go and kill someone."

Crane smiled. "That's just the chance the world will have to take, isn't it?"

1. Suppose that you are Dr. Wolfe. To take the legal steps necessary to have Crane committed against his will requires that you violate his confidentiality. What justification might a utilitarian offer for doing this?

2. Might a Kantian oppose commitment on the grounds that it would violate Crane's dignity as a person?

3. As a physician, how would you justify acting to protect others while going against the wishes of your patient?

4. Should a physician be required by law to act to protect the welfare of others?

5. How does this case compare to the *Tarasoff* case? What might Justice Tobriner require of Dr. Wolfe in this situation? How does Justice Clark think such situations should be handled?

### Decision Scenario 8

In October 1993, fifteen-year-old Benito Agrela stopped taking FK506, a toxic drug that suppresses the immune response. Agrela was taking the drug to prevent the rejection of his second liver transplant.

In June, the Florida Department of Health learned that he was no longer taking his medicine and forcibly removed him from his parents' home. Agrela was confined to the transplant floor of a Miami hospital for four days, but he refused to give blood or to cooperate in any examination other than a basic physical. Agrela had been born with an enlarged liver, and at the age of eight he had his first transplant. After a few years, the donor organ failed, and a second transplant was necessary. However, Agrela did not have an easy time with the result. The drug's side effects left him feeling weak and constantly ill, and finally he decided that he did not want to continue to take the medication. He wanted only to die in peace.

Judge Arthur Birken of Broward County Circuit Court ruled that Agrela could stop taking his medication and return to his family's home to live out the remainder of his life. Judge Birken reached his decision after a long visit with Agrela and listening to four hours of testimony from his physicians.

"I should have the right to make my own decisions," Agrela said as he left the hospital after the judge's ruling. "I know the consequences, I know the problems."

Benito Agrela died shortly before 5 A.M. on Saturday, August 21. "He went in a very good way," his sister said. "He didn't complain of any pain."

1. Benito Agrela was only fifteen years old. Should a minor ever be allowed to decide whether to reject a lifesaving therapy?

2. What criteria might be helpful in deciding whether a minor is capable of giving informed consent?

Chapter **3**

# HIV/AIDS

## Chapter Contents

## Classic Case Presentation

### *The Way It Was: Tod Thompson, Dallas, 1993–1994*

Tod Thompson opened his sock drawer and took out a round, white-enameled snuff box. A green dragon breathing a jagged tongue of fire was painted on the lid. Alan Lauder had given him the box almost five years earlier as a memento of their trip to Cancun.

Tod had never bought cocaine, but when somebody gave him a little he kept it in the dragon box. Those days now seemed as obscure and fragmentary as scenes from a movie watched in childhood. After Alan got sick, Tod never felt happy enough to risk doing drugs of any kind.

After Alan died, he even stopped drinking. He had actually stopped a few months before that. Alan had been too sick even to eat, and Tod had no wish to drink alone. Now he drank only water and fruit juice, not even wine.

Tod opened the hinged lid of the snuff box and looked at the blunt purple and gray capsules of Seconal inside. He dumped them into the palm of his hand and counted them, pushing each to one side with a fingertip.

Eight. Six was supposed to be enough, but with eight he felt much better. How ghastly it would be to wake up in a hospital feeling very sick and knowing you had failed. If you were going to do it, you should be sure you could pull it off. And he was sure he was going to do it. He had watched Alan, and nothing would make him want to go through that.

Tod put the snuff box under his socks in the back corner and closed the drawer. He looked up at the mirror hanging above the dresser, and the reflection still shocked him. He couldn't believe how he had changed.

He still looked young, but in the way photographs of children in concentration camps made them look simultaneously young and old. His gray eyes were abnormally large as they stared out of deep sockets, and his cheeks were drawn into dark hollows beneath sharp cheekbones. His blond hair was fine and wispy, barely hiding the pale skin of his scalp. His body was shrunken, and his thin shoulders hunched inward like the folded wings of a bat.

He pulled back his shirt collar, exposing an edge of one of the bluish patches that ran across his chest and back and covered his arms and legs—Kaposi's

sarcoma. The patches had been late in coming. Maybe the ZDV had slowed down the process. The drug had appeared too late to do much for Alan.

Alan had introduced him to a world he never suspected existed. A world of glittering parties, long weekends on yachts, trips to Mexico, San Francisco, and New York. Above all, abundant and virtually unrestrained sex. Tod found himself the object of much attention, and he liked it.

Hardly two months after Alan died, Tod got sick. First the night sweats started. He would wake up at three or four in the morning so drenched with sweat he would be freezing and burning up simultaneously. Then the mild but persistent fever had started, and diarrhea had come along with it.

He had put off seeing his doctor for almost a month. He hadn't taken the blood test, because he was sure he would test positive, and then he wouldn't be able to deny that something so horrible was going to happen to him. When the symptoms finally started, it was almost a relief in a twisted way. Now he knew the worst and didn't have to fear it anymore.

He finally went to his doctor—to Alan's doctor—when he developed shingles on his legs. The rash was too painful to ignore. By then he had already lost a lot of weight. The diarrhea and the fever seemed to keep him tired. That and the lack of sleep. He was exhausted, but he felt too anxious to sleep. He would wake in the early morning hours while it was still dark and lie in bed and wonder what was going to happen to him.

He always asked for the early shift at the bookstore where he worked. Because he couldn't sleep, it was a relief to get up and have a place to go to. Also, few customers came in during the morning hours. Keeping up a normal front was very hard. He started the day by stocking the shelves, and usually he did as much as necessary before getting too exhausted. He was working only half-days now, but even so he was tired all the time.

When he first got the diagnosis, he resolved to fight the disease and not give in. He wanted to try everything that people told him to try. He spent six weeks eating a macrobiotic diet, but it seemed to make his diarrhea worse. He tried smuggled doses of Compound Q, but he could tell no difference in what was happening to him. Eventually he simply took ZDV.

It was the only drug he took for half a year. Then, when the first bruiselike Kaposi patch appeared on his leg, his doctor put him on alpha-interferon. When he developed a cough and a fever and was found to have pneumonocystis pneumonia, he was given pentamidine spray. And now he was also trying one drug after another to try to control the diarrhea that had become chronic.

He knew he was lucky to be an employee of the bookstore. He was covered by the Blue Cross group policy, and so far it had paid for everything except 20 percent of his medical bills and medicines. He had tried to get a supplemental policy before Alan died, but he couldn't find a company willing to accept him without a blood test. So far he had been able to pay his part of the bills, but it wouldn't be long before he became so weak he would have to quit his job.

He couldn't ask his parents to help him. They knew the kind of life he had been living, and they didn't approve of it. But that's not why he couldn't turn to them. It was because they themselves had nothing, and he would become another burden for them. Besides, to be honest, he was afraid of their reaction to him. He couldn't stand the idea that they would treat him like a leper, not wanting to touch him or come near him. In sparing them, he was also sparing himself.

When he could no longer work, he knew what would happen, because he had seen it happen to other people. First they moved to a cheaper apartment, if they could find someone willing to rent to them. Then they sold their car. After that, they began to sell whatever furniture, stereo, or video equipment they had. Finally, they were forced to turn to Medicaid and the state welfare agencies for everything—medical care, medicine, rent money, telephone, and even the food they didn't want to eat. Most people grew poorer faster than they grew sicker, and that guaranteed their dying in complete poverty.

He heard the sharp ding of the kitchen timer. His frozen pasta dinner was ready. He'd have to get it out of the oven before it burned. He picked up his cane from the bed and started to walk away. Then he turned around and pulled open the drawer. He picked up the snuff box and shook it. The capsules inside rattled reassuringly.

He put the box back inside and closed the drawer.

On a warm April day in 1994, Tod was sitting in a chair by the window when a call came from Dr. Katz at Southwest Medical Center. For the first time since he had been diagnosed with HIV, his viral load had dropped. One of the experimental drugs he had been taking along with the ZDV was a protease inhibitor, and Dr. Katz proposed adding another drug to the ones he was taking.

"You've responded so well, I think you can look forward to seeing some of your symptoms regressing," Dr. Katz said. "I can't promise you'll be cured, but I believe you can count on seeing your life return to something like normal." He paused. "I'd say you're one of the lucky ones."

Tod felt a tightness in his throat that made it impossible to speak, and tears stung the corners of his eyes. He'd keep the snuff box, but it was time to throw away the contents.

---

## Briefing Session

Only a few years ago, the disease known as Acquired Immunodeficiency Syndrome, or AIDS, was routinely described as the worst plague to strike the world since the Black Death devastated Europe and much of Asia in the fourteenth century. Now that treatment with a combination of new drugs can keep HIV infection from progressing to full-blown AIDS and can extend the life of those with the disease, some of the fear and dread associated with AIDS have lessened.

Yet the majority of the pressing moral and social issues associated with the disease have not gone away. We are still faced with questions about such matters as deciding what proportion of medical research funding should be allocated for AIDS, restricting individual freedom to protect society, balancing the need to protect confidentiality against the need to inform, and allocating the new and effective AIDS drugs. Further, while the burden of AIDS has lessened for the United States and other industrialized countries, it has increased for the rest of the world. The infectious and fatal character of AIDS continues to give its issues an immediacy and urgency with few parallels in the history of medicine.

### Combination Therapy: AIDS on the Run

Like a snarling werewolf in a horror movie, AIDS has devastated the lives of hundreds of thousands of people unlucky enough to encounter the virus. The disease doomed friends and family, destroyed sons and daughters, fathers and mothers, and condemned children to short, unhappy lives.

Causing heartbreak and sorrow, the virus has also generated unreasoning fear and sweaty terror. *Am I infected?* people asked themselves. *I have a fever—could it be AIDS?* The disease abolished all hope, because becoming infected with HIV (the human immunodeficiency virus) was the equivalent of receiving a death sentence.

The virus is still a threat, the AIDS monster still stalks the streets, but in 1994–1995 for the first time in the sixteen years since the disease made its appearance, the number of cases of AIDS started to go down. In 1997, for the first time since 1990, AIDS was no longer among the top ten causes of death in the United States. The trend has continued. New drugs and combinations of drugs have been so effective that AIDS has become a chronic disease most people can treat and live with, instead of an invariably fatal one.

Cocktails of the new protease inhibitors plus one or more other antivirals—combination drug therapy or HAART (highly active antiviral therapy)—have worked treatment wonders. The new drugs may make it possible for someone to be infected with HIV and stay alive without symptoms for decades, living long enough to die of something besides AIDS. Those infected with HIV can now contemplate a future that includes them. Instead of studying about death and dying, they can think about living.

A silver bullet to slay the werewolf hasn't been found, but the new combination drug therapy at least provides protection. It thus offers hope where once there was only despair.

## Decline in Death Rate

The effects of combination drug therapy are most obvious in the decline in the number of deaths due to AIDS that resulted when HAART was first introduced. In a study sponsored by the Centers for Disease Control and Prevention and involving 1255 patients at nine medical centers,

researchers found the AIDS death rate declined an astounding 75 percent from January 1994 to June 1997.

The sharpest decline began in early 1996 when people who were HIV positive began to take drug combinations that included a protease inhibitor. Between the first and second quarter of the year, AIDS-related deaths dropped almost 50 percent, and by the end of the next six months, they fell another 50 percent.

In the first quarter of 1994, the AIDS death rate was 35.2 per 100 person-years; in the first quarter of 1995, it was 31.2. The rate began to drop when physicians started using the antiviral drugs ZDV (also called AZT) and 3TC in combination and began aggressively treating the adventitious infections that the compromised immune systems of AIDS patients couldn't fight off.

Then in 1996 protease-inhibiting drugs came into widespread use, and the death rates plunged. In the first quarter of the year they dropped from 29.4 (per 100 person-years) to 15.4, and by the end of the first quarter of 1997, they had dropped again to 8.8. The results of the CDC study showed that HIV infections could be treated successfully and that the great majority of premature deaths caused by AIDS could be prevented.

## Infection Rates

The rate at which people are becoming infected with HIV has remained relatively constant, although the rate at which they develop AIDS has dropped significantly. The CDC reported that from 1994 to 2000 the number of people newly diagnosed with an HIV infection was a relatively steady 40,000 a year.

Data indicate that more than 900,000 people in the United States are HIV positive. Despite a high level of AIDS awareness, the number has increased by 50,000 since 1998. Gay men account for 43 percent of all new infections. Heterosexual sexual contact is responsible for 27 percent and IV drug use for 23 percent. Nearly half of those infected through heterosexual sex were black women.

Although African Americans make up only 12 percent of the population, they constitute 55 percent of new HIV infections. Data from 2000 (the most recent available) indicate that 43 percent of HIV-infected people who develop AIDS are Black, 34 percent are White, and 21 percent are Hispanic. (Hispanics make up 13 percent of the population.)

Combination drug therapy has reduced the number of people dying from AIDS, but to bring the epidemic under control, the number of people who become infected with the virus must be reduced. The CDC has committed itself to spending $3.8 million a year to support a variety of programs that aim to cut the HIV infection rate from 40,000 a year to 20,000 by 2006.

## Protease Inhibitors and Combination Drug Therapy

About 200,000 people in the United States are now taking a protease-inhibiting drug. The number almost doubled from 1996 to 1997, and by now almost everyone who has been diagnosed as HIV positive either is being treated or has been treated by one of the drugs. The protease inhibitor is usually administered in combination with one or more other antiretrovirals.

The first drug to treat HIV infection, Zidovudine (AZT or ZDV), was introduced in 1986. A failed cancer drug, ZDV turned out to be highly effective against reverse transcriptase, an enzyme essential in the early phases of HIV replication. Researchers quickly developed a number of other drugs to interrupt reverse transcriptase. The family is called nucleoside analogs and includes widely used drugs like ddC and 3TC.

Because of HIV's rapid mutation rate, new strains soon emerged that could survive attacks by the available nucleoside analogs. Researchers eventually developed a second class of drugs known as non-nucleoside reverse-transcriptase inhibitors. While drugs in this class also work on the earlier part of the HIV replication cycle, they employ a different mechanism to inhibit reverse transcriptase. Thus, they can be successful in treating HIV, even after ZDV-type drugs have failed.

Protease inhibitors belong to a third family of drugs that prevent HIV from making copies of itself. They work by blocking a necessary enzyme—protease. Protease cuts a long protein chain into fragments that ordinarily form the functioning virus. Thus, protease inhibitors forestall the increase of viral particles, and so protect uninfected cells from infection.

Protease inhibitors work at a later stage of HIV replication than nucleoside analogs and non-nucleoside reverse-transcriptase inhibitors. Thus, it is possible to combine the three types of drugs in ways that attack replication at different stages of the cyle. Viral particles not prevented from replicating by drugs of the first two types may be stopped by protease inhibitors. This is the basic idea of HAART.

None of the drugs do anything to treat cells that are already infected. But if the viral particles can be kept from multiplying, this will prevent the infection of additional cells. The infected cells will then eventually die off, and the symptoms caused by the virus will retreat.

## Limits of the Therapy

As effective as protease inhibitors in combination with other drugs have shown themselves to be in preventing the development of AIDS in people infected with HIV, HAART has definite limitations. It is by no means a cure for AIDS, and it is not effective nor tolerable for everyone who is HIV positive.

### Best with New Infections

Some evidence indicates that protease inhibitors work best in recently infected people whose immune systems have not yet been severely damaged by the AIDS virus. Those who have been infected for ten or fifteen years and have devastated immune systems may not get any long-term benefits from adding a protease-inhibiting drug to the antiviral drugs.

Thus, what offers a new hope for some HIV-positive people may be only another source of frustration and sorrow for those who have become long-term survivors. They still haven't hung on long enough for the long-anticipated "cure" for AIDS.

## Drug Resistance

The mechanisms of HIV infection are still not adequately understood, and the precise manner in which the virus becomes drug resistant is unknown. But protease-inhibiting drugs, like the standard antiviral drugs, can lose their effectiveness due to drug resistance.

From a therapeutic standpoint, the strategy is to change drugs as soon as patients stop responding to the ones they are taking. Even so, it is possible for someone to stop responding to all available drugs. Almost thirty protease inhibitors are now available, and pharmaceutical companies are working rapidly to produce new ones. Drugs from the three types are used in as many as 250 combinations. For some HIV-infected people, there is a race between the virus' development of drug resistance and the companies' development of new drugs, and their lives are at stake.

There is a race, too, for those who are newly infected and don't respond to the standard therapies, because they are infected by a mutant strain. A 2001 study showed that drug-resistant strains of HIV have increased to 14 percent among newly diagnosed HIV cases. This is up from 5.8 percent during the years 1999–2000, which was significantly higher than .04 percent for the period 1995–1998.

In 2002, however, researchers announced encouraging results in treating people infected with drug-resistant strains of HIV. Two series of clinical trials of the drug T-20 or enfuvirtide showed that it could lower the HIV load to the recommended level in a statistically significant number of people.

T-20 belongs to a new class of drugs called *fusion inhibitors.* These are drugs that interfere with the proteins on the surface of viral cells and keep them from locking onto (fusing with) healthy cells. Protease inhibitors keep infected cells from dividing and producing more HIV particles, but fusion inhibitors keep cells from being infected in the first place. Those infected with resistant strains of HIV must be treated with the standard combination therapy, as well as with T-20.

## Virus Remains

Viral load, rather than a count of T-cells or CD4 cells, is now considered to be the best prediction of the outcome of someone who is HIV positive. A follow-up study of infected people who gave blood samples in 1984–1985 showed that at the end of a decade only 17 of 45 men with a viral load averaging less than 5300 RNA strands (per cubic milliliter of blood) had died of AIDS. Out of 45 with a viral load average of above 37,000 RNA strands, 34 had died. In short, the lower the viral load, the more likely an infected person is to survive.

While combination drug therapy can reduce the viral load so low that the presence of HIV particles cannot be detected by a blood test, the drugs never completely eliminate the virus from the body. Despite initial hopes, several studies have shown that copies of the virus remain hidden in the memory T-cells of the immune system.

The memory cells may remain in a resting phase for years (perhaps decades), waiting to make copies of themselves or the viruses infecting them. It is this mechanism that makes vaccinations against polio and measles possible—the immune system remembers the viruses and can produce antibodies against them whenever it needs to. Combination drug therapy works only against actively reproducing viral particles. Thus, it is ineffective against the HIV particles hidden in the memory cells. Ironically, the same adaptation that protects us against some infectious diseases also preserves the agents that cause others.

The discovery of HIV in the memory cells explains why HIV-infected people eventually develop a new viral load after no particles could be detected in their blood. The discovery also means that those who are HIV positive must continue to take their drugs, even when they no longer have a detectable viral load and their CD-4 (or T-cell) count is in the normal range.

On the positive side, however, knowing that copies of the virus are stored in the memory T-cells gives researchers a new target. If a drug or combination of drugs could be found to eliminate the sequestered copies of the virus, as well as the viral particles in the blood, this would constitute a cure for HIV infection.

## Costs

A typical combination-therapy cocktail for HIV infections includes the drugs ZDV, 3TC, and a protease inhibitor like Crixivan. The cost of treating someone with this combination, not counting other drugs, is $10,000–$15,000 a year. In addition, monitoring the effectiveness of the treatment costs another $5000 to $6000 for laboratory work and physician's office visits. Thus, when the expense of other drugs is added, it costs about $25,000–$30,000 a year to treat someone who is HIV positive.

Only about 20 percent of the roughly 1 million people who are HIV positive have insurance adequate to cover most of the expense of HIV treatment. All fifty states have established joint state and federal AIDS Drug Assistance programs (ADAPS), but a patchwork of regulations that differ from state to state make it difficult for many in need of treatment to find the money to pay for it.

While the $20,000 a year treatment costs are high, the costs for treating full-blown AIDS can be $100,000 a year or more. As usual in medicine, just in terms of dollars, preventing a problem from becoming worse costs less than neglecting it, then dealing with the consequences.

## Side-Effects

The immediate side-effects of the combination therapy can be worse than the earlier effects of AIDS itself. Uncontrollable diarrhea, severe stomach cramps, nausea, dizziness, disorientation, skin sensitivity, and a feverish feeling are among the more common reactions to the drugs. Some people find the side-effects so devastating that they can't take the drugs, even though they are potentially life saving. "I early reached the point where death was the preferable alternative," one person with AIDS told a reporter.

The drugs may also cause life-threatening harm. In some susceptible people, they may damage the liver. Those affected develop jaundice as their liver becomes unable to function effectively in breaking down red blood cells. Continuing to take the drugs may lead to liver failure and death.

By mechanisms that are not understood, the drugs may also affect fat metabolism and blood sugar levels. Some taking the drugs experience a potentially dangerous rise in the level of blood cholesterol and even grow a fatty hump between their shoulder blades. A recent study has revealed a rare bone disorder called avascular necrosis, in which bone dies because its blood supply is cut off, in 4 percent of the HIV patients studied. It is unclear whether this is a result of protease inhibitors or other drugs taken by HIV patients.

Some in whom the drugs produce an increase in the level of sugar in their blood may develop diabetes, indicating some sort of failure in the metabolic process. If they are not taken off the drugs or treated for diabetes, they may suffer damage to their eyes, kidneys, and other organ systems caused by diabetes.

The side-effects of combination drug therapy are not ones that need to be tolerated for only a short time while the individual recovers from the infection. Because the drugs do not eliminate all HIV particles from the body, those who are infected must continue to take the drugs for the rest of their lives. If the reactions are too severe or too toxic, this may prove to be impossible.

A question not yet answered is what the long-term effects of combination drug therapy for HIV will be. While the risks are unknown at present, most people who are HIV positive are willing to bet that combination drug therapy will save their lives. They have a better chance of surviving it than they do surviving AIDS.

## Difficult Regimen

When combination therapy was first initiated, some of the drugs had to be taken five or six times a day, some with food, and others on an empty stomach. Some had to be taken every six hours and kept refrigerated, requirements making it difficult to travel very far from home or even stay overnight in most hotels. Responding to these problems, drug companies have made following the necessary regimens easier. They have developed tablets that include a combination of three drugs and have reduced both the number of tablets and the number of times they must be taken. More sophisticated treatment regimens have also been developed. A patient with few complications and a low viral load typically has to take fewer drugs than someone at an advanced stage of HIV infection.

Even with such advances, an HIV-infected patient typically must still follow a demanding drug regimen. While the number of tablets involved in the triple therapy may be fewer, most patients must also take drugs to prevent side-effects from the anti-retrovirals or to treat secondary infections resulting from a damaged immune system.

Missing a dose of some of the drugs can have serious consequences for some patients. It presents a window of opportunity to mutant strains of the virus, allowing them to replicate and spread to new cells. As a result, the drugs in that particular combination may cease being effective against the new drug-resistant strains. Physicians must then try new combinations of drugs and hope they are effective for the patient. Patients who continue to miss doses for different combinations of drugs may find themselves in the unhappy position of being infected with a strain of the virus that is resistant to all drugs currently available. Further, such patients pose a threat, for if they should spread the drug-resistant strain, a rekindling of the AIDS epidemic is possible.

The ideal drug against HIV is one that is taken orally and is easily tolerated, has no serious side-effects, does not interact dangerously with other drugs, is effective against the AIDS virus in all tissues and cell types, and is inexpensive. No drug promising even most of these characteristics is expected to be available soon. Until then, adherence to the regimen of combination therapy offers the most hope of keeping the virus under control in the individual and the nation.

## False Security

About 1 million Americans are infected with HIV, and some 350,000 of them have gone on to develop AIDS. Each year, about 40,000 more become infected with the virus. The rate of HIV infection has remained more or less constant, even though the death rate from AIDS has dropped.

Many public-health researchers think the failure of the infection rate to decline is due, in part, to a false sense of security produced by combination therapy. Supporting this is a 1999 study of 416 gay men that found that the more optimistic they were about new drug treatments, the more likely they were to practice unsafe sex.

Too many people appear to believe that HIV infection is no longer worth worrying about—that someone infected need take only a few pills to bring it under control. But, of course, the infection remains life-threatening, and its treatment, even when it succeeds in bringing the infection under control, is difficult, fraught with severe side-effects, and expensive.

Even more worrying, a 2002 CDC study showed that almost half of those who are HIV positive have never been given a diagnosis or treated for the infection. In the category of "men who have sex with men," black males ages 16–29, 91 percent didn't even know they were HIV positive. In the 16–22 range, 75 percent of Hispanics and 74 percent of Whites were ignorant of their HIV status.

The FDA took a step toward promoting a more realistic view of HIV infection in 2001. In a letter to drug companies, the FDA insisted that advertising eliminate images that are "not generally representative" of patients with HIV. Particularly, the ads should not show "robust individuals engaged in strenuous physical activities" like mountain climbing.

Such ads do not provide an accurate picture of people living with AIDS. While their aim may be to encourage people with AIDS to have a positive attitude, an unintended consequence may be that they encourage the false belief that the disease is no more debilitating than a bout with the flu. This may then translate into rationalizations for avoiding practices known to reduce the risk of HIV infection.

## Origin of the AIDS Virus

In 1999 Beatrice Hahn of the University of Alabama at Birmingham announced that she and her collaborators had established a close connection between a simian virus and HIV-I, the virus that causes AIDS. The simian virus, known as SIV.cpz (simian immunodeficiency virus.chimpanzee) has such a close resemblance to HIV-I that differences can easily be accounted for by changes that have taken place as the virus has crossed to the human species.

Hahn and her coworkers recovered the simian virus from the frozen remains of a chimpanzee named Marilyn that had been brought to the United States from Africa in 1959. Marilyn was used as a breeder for research animals, and in 1985 she was the only member of the breeding colony to test positive for the virus. She died that same year, although an autopsy showed no evidence she had an immunodeficiency disease.

Hahn's group found that the virus recovered from Marilyn and two other viruses from another two infected chimpanzees could be arranged in a phylogenetic tree that demonstrated the closeness of their relationship. A fourth virus from another chimp was very different, and it was this virus that had led some researchers to doubt the connection between chimpanzee viruses and HIV-I. Additional tests by Hahn's group showed that all known strains of HIV-I are closely related to strains of SIV.cpz. These strains infect only a subspecies of chimpanzees known as *Pan troglodytes troglodytes.*

The natural habitat of *troglodytes* includes the areas of central and western Africa where HIV-I was first identified. Hahn and her collaborators speculate that the simian virus was transmitted to humans by means of an exposure to chimpanzee blood as a result of the slaughtering of chimpanzees for meat. The opening of roads into what were once isolated tribal areas then promoted the spread of the virus to human population centers.

The oldest documented case of infection with the AIDS virus is that of a Bantu man from what is now Kinshasa in the Democratic Republic of Congo. Molecular analysis of the 1959 blood sample and comparisons with other examples of the virus suggest AIDS probably occurred in people in the late 1940s or early 1950s. It may have been accidentally spread in local populations by the use of needles in smallpox and polio vaccination programs.

As a result of easier access to transportation, from Africa the disease spread to the Caribbean, was acquired by American homosexuals in Haiti, then began to spread in the United States, probably from New York, then to San Francisco. Recent evidence indicates that the disease appeared several times as early as the late 1950s and 1960s in Britain, the United States, and elsewhere but failed to establish itself within the local population. That did not happen until the 1980s. (The retrospective diagnosis of a British sailor who died, perhaps of AIDS, in 1959 has not been confirmed.)

Discovering the origin of the AIDS virus will make it possible to study the virus in new ways. Chimpanzees, despite infection with SIV.cpz, apparently do not develop AIDS or AIDS-like diseases. An understanding of the mechanisms preventing this from happening might allow the development of an AIDS vaccine or new and more effective drugs to treat the disease.

## Spread of the Disease

The World Health Organization reported in 1997 that an improved method of gathering statistics showed that earlier estimates of the spread of HIV should be doubled, and figures released in 2000–2002 reveal a world burdened by infection. The most recent estimates indicate that 36.1 million adults and children in the world are infected with HIV. The infections are split almost evenly between males and females.

Cases in Western Europe number 600,000, with 30,000 new cases every year. Eastern Europe and central Asia report more than 375,000–475,000. The number has increased to fifteen times the number three years previously (1999). Ukraine alone in 2002 had an estimated 300,000–400,000 cases, making it the first country in Europe with 1 percent of the adult population infected.

South and Southeast Asia now have more than 6.4 million cases; Latin America has 1.3 million and the Caribbean half a million. North American cases now number some 920,000, with 45,000 new cases per year. The Middle East and North Africa have 400,000 cases, with an estimated 80,000 new cases within the last year. Australia and New Zealand have dropped to around 15,000 infections, with only 500 new cases a year.

Two-thirds of the people now thought to be infected with HIV live in the countries of sub-Saharan Africa. The most accurate figure now available puts the figure at an astounding 25.3 million. South Africa, with 4.5 million cases, has the highest number of any single country. (Countries with the highest number of infected people also include Ivory Coast, Kenya, Tanzania, Uganda, and Zimbabwe.) In 2000, however, for the first time the number of new infections in the region stabilized.

### Children

The U.N. estimates that 600,000 children under age 15 become infected with HIV each year. In addition, 1200 children a day die of AIDS. About 10 percent of all new infections are in children under the age of 15. More than half are in people 15 to 24.

### Deaths

As many as 21.8 million people have died of AIDS since the beginning of the epidemic in the late 1970s. By U.N. estimates, 9.7 million of the deaths have been among people in sub-Saharan Africa. South Asia and Southeast Asia account for 740,000 deaths, Latin America 470,000, Western Europe 190,000, and Caribbean countries 110,000. Deaths in North America are estimated to have been 420,000. Deaths in China, with an estimated 500,000–700,000 cases, are expected to increase at a rapid rate over the next few years, both because of the size of the population and the slow response of the government in providing needed treatments.

### The Future

The spread of the disease is a worldwide phenomenon. As the numbers show, the African continent has been hit particularly hard as AIDS has spread from the cities to the countryside. African nations face a bad situation that is likely to worsen, but other countries are also experiencing an increase in infection.

Infection rates in India have tripled since 1992 and risen tenfold in Thailand. Within ten to fifteen years, as many as 37 million people could be infected in India. In China the number of people infected is increasing at a rate of almost 30 percent a year. Sexually transmitted diseases are on the rise there, and HIV infection may follow. Health officials fear that the virus will break out in an unprepared population before steps can be taken to combat its spread. New outbreaks have already occurred in Eastern Europe, Russia, Vietnam, and Cambodia.

U.N. experts believe China, India, and Thailand are likely to follow the pattern set by Africa. Poverty and cultural attitudes will allow outbreaks of HIV to spread in the population until the incidence rate becomes massive.

The North American and Western European countries have been able to use new drugs to prevent HIV infection from developing into AIDS. Yet even wealthy and technologically advanced countries have been able to do very little to reduce the rate of HIV transmission. The underdeveloped countries in Africa and Asia are unable to afford the huge cost of treating HIV with combination drug therapy. The only way they can have a hope of controlling the epidemic is through preventive measures, but those measures often come into conflict with such cultural practices as a refusal to use condoms. Also, cultural disapproval of homosexuality and IV drug use makes it difficult for public health officials to speak openly about prevention strategies. In the view of some observers, only a vaccine will make it possible to bring AIDS under control in impoverished nations.

What everyone in public health accepts is that HIV/AIDS is a worldwide catastrophe. The developed nations, out of self-interest, if not out of altruism, will eventually have to invest billions to bring the pandemic under control. But as the Social Contexts and Cases in this chapter illustrate, the ethical issues in our own country have not disappeared either.

## Case Presentation

### Will Teresa Blair Take Her Medicine?

Teresa Blair (as we will call her) is twenty years old, and for two years she had been infected with HIV—the human immunodeficiency virus.

Dr. Martha McIntosh, Teresa's physician at the Gilman Street Clinic, has explained Teresa's disease to her and warned her that without treatment she will develop the life-threatening symptoms of AIDS. It is unclear to Dr. McIntosh whether Teresa grasps the seriousness of her condition. Teresa appears to understand the explanation, but she doesn't seem able to keep in mind the need to take her medicine and have her regularly scheduled checkups.

But Teresa doesn't seem able to keep much of anything in mind. "I'm the kind of person who likes

to stay on the go and have fun," she says. "I do what I want when I want. I don't sit around and study about what's happening to me or what I'm going to be doing next week. Or even tomorrow, really."

Teresa doesn't have a regular job. She lives with various aunts and cousins, moving frequently, and she picks up work as a cleaner or busperson when she needs some cash. She dropped off the welfare roll, rather than show up five days a week for the required eleven to two shift of picking up trash in the city parks. "It was demeaning," she said. "Besides, it interfered with my social life." Because she has no income or insurance, her medical expenses are paid for under Medicaid.

### No Protease Inhibitor

Although Dr. McIntosh has prescribed ZDV (AZT) to treat Teresa's HIV infection, after a lot of thought she decided not to prescribe a protease inhibitor. The most effective treatment for Teresa would be a combination therapy of a protease inhibitor and one or more antiviral agents, but Dr. McIntosh doesn't think Teresa's life is sufficiently organized for her to adhere to such a demanding drug regimen. This judgment is based on what she knows about Teresa. Teresa has missed six of her last ten appointments and takes the ZDV only when she happens to think about it.

Like many physicians who treat a large number of HIV-positive patients, Dr. McIntosh is reluctant to prescribe a protease inhibitor for patients who are likely to be careless about taking it. Physicians who withhold the combination therapy say they do so out of a concern for the patient and for the public.

To bring an HIV infection under control requires that a patient adhere religiously to the doses, times, and restrictions of the prescribed drugs. Even when only three drugs are involved—a protease inhibitor and two antivirals—the drug-taking regimen can be bewilderingly complex. Some drugs must be taken three times a day, some twice, others once. Some must be taken without food or water, others after eating. When other drugs to prevent or treat the infections commonly found in people with a compromised immune system are added, the number of pills, tablets, and capsules taken daily may increase to fifty or sixty or even more.

An HIV-positive person who starts with a combination drug therapy but misses scheduled doses gives the virus a chance to mutate and rebound. The patient may then stop responding to the drugs, and some other combination will have to be tried. Eventually, if the patient continues to be careless about taking the drugs as prescribed, the virus might stop responding to all available drugs.

What worries some physicians and scientists even more is that some of the new mutated strains of HIV might spread from the individual to the population. If that happened, the recently acquired ability to beat back, if not eliminate, the virus could be lost. Once again, HIV would sweep through vulnerable groups, unchecked by any of the drugs in our arsenal.

## A Duty to Withhold?

Some physicians believe they have a duty to withhold combination therapy from patients who are a poor risk for adherence. This view is highly controversial, however, and some critics of the practice hold that all who might benefit from combination therapy are entitled to at least a chance to show whether they can take the drugs as prescribed. In their view, excluding people who are homeless, drug addicts, or live chaotic lives without a trial run of the medication most effective for their problem is unfair.

A number of social workers and physicians claim that their experience shows that no matter how unplanned their lives, some HIV-infected people find the resources to keep to the demanding regimen of combination therapy. This is particularly so when they realize that their lives are at stake and that the therapy is effective. Also, when those who have not been feeling well for a long time experience the difference the drugs can make, they become more motivated to follow the schedule.

The other side of this, however, is that some HIV-positive people, like Teresa, don't feel sick. Indeed, the combination therapy, with its diarrhea, stomach cramps and worse, may well make them feel much worse than they ordinarily do. When this is coupled with a free-spirited, disorganized approach to life, the chance someone will take the drugs as prescribed becomes slim.

Teresa has people she can stay with, but not everyone is even that fortunate. Being homeless presents immense difficulties for anyone who must take drugs according to a schedule. Some people don't even have a watch. Moreover, some of the drugs must be refrigerated, an impossibility for a homeless person.

In the view of some, prescribing combination therapy for people who have no means of complying

with it is, at best, foolish. At worst, it's against the best interest of the individual and potentially dangerous to anyone who might become infected with the human immunodeficiency virus.

Dr. McIntosh hasn't written off Teresa. If Teresa takes her ZDV, the virus will be kept in check for an indeterminate time, and perhaps before it stops working, Teresa's life will become less chaotic. Maybe she will get a steady job, enroll in a training program, or at least settle down enough to focus on her future. Or perhaps as the virus continues to damage her immune system, she will start developing more symptoms and lose the feeling that she's not sick.

If the time comes when Teresa takes seriously the need to treat her disease, Dr. McIntosh is prepared to prescribe combination therapy for her. The main danger for Teresa, though, is that the time will never come. Or it will come too late for combination therapy to be effective.

---

# SOCIAL CONTEXT: WHAT ABOUT A VACCINE?

When the AIDS virus was identified, people hoped that a vaccine for it would be developed immediately. AIDS would then become a member of the family of diseases like smallpox and rabies that can be effectively prevented by vaccination. Unfortunately, HIV has turned out to be a virus that mutates rapidly and exists in many variant forms. Some researchers have expressed skepticism about the possibility of developing a vaccine that will provide protection against all forms of the disease.

Even so, researchers have invested considerable effort in the last decade, and more than sixty trials involving thirty candidate vaccines are currently under way. Various vaccines have been shown to protect chimpanzees from HIV infection, but the same vaccines have not been effective for humans. Some vaccines have turned out to increase the number of circulating antibodies against the HIV virus, producing so-called humoral immunity. Humoral immunity is often enough to protect against an infectious agent, but this does not seem to be the case with the HIV virus. Even in the presence of antibodies, it continues to infect cells.

Thus many experts think it is necessary to find a vaccine that will also activate the body's system of cellular immunity. Cells infected with HIV display a characteristic protein marker on their surface. Thus, if researchers can find a way of provoking the body to produce killer T-cells that can recognize this marker, they will destroy the infected cells.

The search for an effective vaccine has so far proved elusive, but even partial success would have its rewards. The usual measure of effectiveness of a vaccine is that it produces immunity in 90 percent of the cases in which it is administered. Yet with 15,000 people (worldwide) becoming infected every day, even a vaccine that produces immunity only 50 percent of the time would save millions of lives. Indeed, according to some calculations, a vaccine available now that is 60 percent effective would prevent twice as many infections as one that is 90 percent effective but will not be available until five years from now.

The cost of treating AIDS and its rapid spread in poor countries in Africa, in particular, make finding a vaccine to prevent or reduce HIV infection a matter of global concern.

---

# SOCIAL CONTEXT: AIDS IN AFRICA: WHAT SHOULD BE DONE?

---

Only a few times has the world been faced with a pandemic, the ravaging of an infectious disease on a global scale. It happened most notably with the spread of the Black Death (the bubonic plague) in the fourteenth century. During the long period of its initial outbreak, it killed from 20 to 30 percent of the world's population. Only the remotest regions of the planet were safe from it.

HIV/AIDS is now a global phenomenon. While the developed countries of the West have reduced its ravages, the disease is out of control in many of the countries of sub-Saharan Africa. Those with a high incidence of infection include South Africa, Ivory Coast, Tanzania, Zimbabwe, and Kenya.

Home to only one-tenth of the world's population, the region accounted for 72 percent of new HIV infections in 2000. Seventy percent of all people infected with HIV (including those with AIDS) live in the region, and 80 percent of HIV deaths occur there.

The number infected with HIV is more than 40 million, and the figure is going up by about 4 million a year. The United Nations estimates that in the most affected countries more than one-third of the children now 15 years old are destined to die of AIDS. By 2010 the life expectancy is calculated to be thirty for those living in sub-Saharan Africa. Already 13 million children have been orphaned by AIDS, most of them in that region. This number is expected to rise to 20 million by 2010.

## A Broader Problem

In the United States and other developed countries, infection with HIV is a straightforward medical problem with a limited scope. Those infected are started on a drug regimen, then examined and tested regularly. They are given instructions about safe sex and referred to social programs for help with diet and living problems. Also, a variety of public health programs (TV and radio ads, school talks, counseling sessions for parents, etc.) spread the word about preventive measures and the options open to those who believe they may be HIV infected.

The situation is radically different in undeveloped countries. People may lack a general trust in medicine and may not even share the general scientific worldview needed for understanding diseases and their treatment. They may be unable to read and have no access to testing; they may not believe they could be infected, and, if they are, they cannot afford to buy the drugs most effective in treating HIV/AIDS.

People cannot, in general, do what is best for their health, for they lack the education and the resources. HIV infection is just one among many other disease conditions they may not understand or see themselves as able to do much about.

Dealing with HIV in third-world countries is not simply a matter of addressing a medical problem. It involves educational, social, and economic factors in an essential way. Some factors, particularly the economic one, are so serious that some observers doubt the problems of HIV in Africa can be solved at all. The most the world might be able to do is to slow the spread of infection and work to develop a vaccine to prevent it.

The U.N. estimates that by 2005 it will take $2 billion a year to reduce the spread of HIV to the level achieved by countries like Uganda and Senegal. This will involve putting into place modest programs like distributing condoms, counseling prostitutes, educating students about risks, treating sexually-transmitted diseases (which increase the likelihood of HIV infections), and testing for HIV. Even this would be only for people with access to a medical system able to treat diseases like tuberculosis that accompany HIV infection and to administer drugs to prevent maternal–infant transmission of HIV.

The money for drugs will go for relatively cheap antibiotics to treat people with compromised immune systems. Some will buy antiretroviral drugs, but these will go only to a fraction of those infected with HIV. The reason for this is not so much the costs (see page 191), but that their administration must be carefully monitored. Undeveloped countries lack the physicians, nurses, clinics, and hospitals to make this possible on a wide scale.

By 2005 the U.N. plans to see about 40 percent of Africans dying of AIDS receiving some form of care and 10 percent of those who are HIV positive receiving treatment with antiretroviral drugs. The U.N. calculations assume that the cost of the anti-retrovirals will be $1400 a year per patient, compared to about ten times that amount for an American patient.

No one believes it is possible for Africans (or Asians) to receive the sort of care given in the developed world. To provide it would cost hundreds of billions of dollars, because an entire health-care infrastructure would have to be built to provide what by Western standards would be adequate treatment.

## Drugs

The Pharmaceutical Manufactures Association of South Africa, representing some thirty-nine major international drug companies, filed a suit against the South African government in 1999. The suit alleged that a law that would allow the country to import brand-name drugs from wherever they could be most cheaply obtained would violate the patent rights of the drug companies. The government, for its part, argued that the country was facing a crisis of HIV infection that it could not afford to buy medicines for and that it was unfair for the companies to sell the same drug in South Africa that could be bought from another country for only a fraction of the price.

The lawsuit was only another skirmish in a battle between the international drug companies and those working to make cheap drugs available to those needing them. Human rights groups had been pressuring the companies for several years to lower the prices of their patent drugs for all poor countries. The companies initially resisted, arguing that doing so would both weaken their patent claims and make them lose money on the drugs they had spent millions developing. Then in a sudden shift led by Merck, the companies offered to negotiate deep discounts for African countries. The cost of treating someone with AIDS for a year with combination therapy (see the Briefing Session in this chapter) would then drop from $10,000 to $350.

But critics quickly pointed out that cutting the price of combination therapy would not be enough to assure adequate treatment. The tendency of HIV-infected people to develop adventitious infections, because of their impaired immune systems, means that treating them requires antibiotics, antifungals, and a range of other medications. The companies would have to offer discounts on all the drugs necessary, if those needing treatment were to benefit.

Deciding they were losing the public relations battle and tarnishing their reputations, in April 2001, the pharmaceutical companies dropped the lawsuit. South Africa was thus free to import drugs from wherever they could buy them most cheaply. This included brand-name drugs manufactured by the pharmaceutical companies. Left unresolved was whether the drugs could come from manufacturers of generic versions in countries like India that were not signatories of the international patent agreements.

Some countries have broken the agreements. In May 2002, Zimbabwe declared its HIV epidemic a national emergency. This permits it to ignore drug patents and import generic versions of whatever drugs it needs. With a quarter of its population HIV positive and torn by civil strife, the country's health establishment saw no other acceptable option.

China, in September 2002, raised its estimate of HIV-infected people to 1 million and announced that if the Western patent holders didn't lower their prices, the country would manufacture the full range of AIDS drugs for domestic use. China has sophisticated drug-manufacturing facilities and already makes some of the drugs under licensing agreements.

By contrast, fifteen Caribbean nations met with pharmaceutical manufacturers and arranged to buy AIDS drugs at steep discounts. The group of nations, after Africa, have the second-highest rate of HIV infection in the world, with 500,000 people affected.

Whatever the source of drugs and however cheap they are, they would still be expensive for countries like South Africa. When the costs of distributing and administering the drugs in complicated treatment regimens and testing and monitoring patients is taken into account, the price of the drugs is seen as only one component of an expensive process.

## Money

In an unprecedented meeting in June 2001, the United Nations General Assembly met to discuss the problem of HIV/AIDS in the developing world. The meeting was contentious, but in the end the delegates approved a "Declaration of Commitment" that calls on governments to show leadership in dealing with the AIDS epidemic. "Prevention must be the mainstay of our response," the document declares. The Assembly then laid out a timetable for bringing the disease under control, which includes helping countries develop their own national strategies.

The cost of the program the Declaration set at $7–$10 billion, with countries with an increasing number of cases of HIV/AIDS being given priority in spending. The Declaration urges developed countries to strive to meet the target of contributing about 10 percent of their GNP to the program. The resolution also calls on lender nations to cancel the debts owed by poor countries, on the understanding that the countries will take measurable steps to eradicate poverty and improve health care for people with HIV/AIDS and other infections.

The U.N. Declaration underscored the position taken by Secretary-General Kofi Annan at an AIDS conference in Nigeria in April 2001. Annan announced the establishment of a Global Fund to Fight AIDS that would begin operation in 2002.

The Fund, Annan said, would need from $7 billion to $10 billion a year to deal with HIV/AIDS alone. (This is seven to ten times the $1 billion spent in 2000 in developing countries.) He recommended that the money go to prevent the spread of the disease by reducing mother–infant transmission, educating people about risks, and buying drugs to treat the disease.

The money is supposed to go initially to the African countries most devastated by AIDS, and leaders from 43 African states have committed themselves to increase spending on health in their countries and on HIV/AIDS in particular.

The World Bank, International Monetary Fund, and Group of Seven (the world's most industrialized nations) endorsed the idea of a global fund. Initially it was to be operated by the United Nations, but dissatisfaction with the management of other U.N. programs raised questions about whether the money contributed to the fund would be properly used. The fund was established with independent management.

The money for the fund has been slow in coming. The United States contributed $200 million in 2001 and committed itself to $480 million in 2002. Critics called the amounts paltry and urged the United States, the country that produces 26 percent of the world's wealth, to make a stronger effort. The country should be offering at least $1 billion a year. This, critics point out, would be only 10 percent of the amount needed to slow the progress of the epidemic.

## HIV in Competition

The focus on treating HIV/AIDS, despite its humanitarian appeal, worries some experts on public health. Their major fear is that scarce funds will not be put to the most effective use for saving lives.

Each year some 54 million people die of various causes worldwide. Most (31 percent) of them die of heart disease, but 25 percent die from an infectious disease. Ninety percent of these deaths are caused by six diseases: measles, malaria, tuberculosis, diarrhoeal diseases, acute respiratory infections, and AIDS.

People in developed countries often respond sympathetically when they think about people with AIDS, because they may know of someone who died of the disease. While the other diseases are not unknown in the developed world, relatively few people die of them. This is not the case in the undeveloped world, where the combined deaths from the other five infectious diseases greatly outnumber deaths from AIDS.

Talk of responding to AIDS in Africa by spending large amounts of money makes some public health officials worry that this may divert resources from other diseases and problems that, if not more pressing than HIV/AIDS, are more likely to be solvable.

If resources are shifted away from (for example) childhood vaccination programs, a great number of preventable deaths will occur. Providing retrovirals to treat an HIV-positive African

may cost $1100–$1400, but childhood immunizations for diseases like measles, mumps, diphtheria, whooping cough, and polio cost no more than a few cents per child. Immunization programs save as many as 3 million lives a year in Africa alone. Also, millions of lives could be saved (and many millions more significantly improved) in remote areas if people were guaranteed a supply of safe drinking water.

The basic way of dealing with epidemics before HIV was to focus on preventing the spread of the disease. We do not, even now, have a cure for polio, influenza, or smallpox. We have developed therapies for supporting patients to help their bodies cope with the disease, but historically, we have invested most resources in preventing the diseases. (The eradication of smallpox is a major triumph of public health.)

Only with the arrival of AIDS and the rise of AIDS activism did the biomedical establishment began to focus on finding a cure for the disease. While one has yet to emerge, treatments for the disease have grown more effective over the decades. Yet they are so expensive and require such a large and sophisticated system of medical care, some public health experts question whether the treatment model is the best way to approach dealing with AIDS in Africa.

The most realistic approach may be the classical one of focusing on reducing the spread of the infection. The U.N. resolution recognizes that prevention is the "mainstay" of dealing with the disease. Public education must be a key ingredient in any effective prevention plan, but the real hope for the future lies in the development of a vaccine to prevent infection. Even a vaccine falling short of the 90 percent protection typically required would be a major step forward. If a vaccine were effective only 50 percent of the time, in Africa alone it could cut the number of new cases of infection from about 4 million to 2 million.

Emphasizing the prevention strategy means recognizing that millions of people in Africa and other undeveloped regions will die without receiving medical treatment that developed nations consider standard. No strategy has to be all-or-none, however, and strong financial support from the developed nations can do much to relieve the suffering of millions of people with HIV/AIDS, even if not enough money is available to prolong their lives.

What is most pressing is that decisive steps be taken immediately to prevent the spread of HIV and end the most devastating epidemic to sweep across the world in 600 years.

## Section 1: Responsibility and Confidentiality

### The Irresponsibility That Spreads AIDS

Alan J. Mayer

Alan Mayer criticizes the AIDS community for not encouraging those infected with HIV to make this fact known to potential sex partners. According to Mayer, AIDS advocates and even the CDC emphasize people's rights without emphasizing equally their responsibility. By focusing on "safe sex," they shift responsibility from those who are infected to those who aren't.

AIDS organizations should encourage and teach those who are HIV positive to do what is right.

Two and a half years ago I tested positive for H.I.V. Since then I have discovered a support system that steadfastly refuses to encourage responsible behavior and a society whose silence insures the continued spread of this disease.

The recent case of Nushawn Williams, who is believed to have infected numerous people in New York State, could have been used to clearly illustrate this point. Instead, by focusing on Mr. Williams's criminal record and moral character, the news media strengthened the dangerous myth that most people are somehow safe from harm. We were allowed to view this horror from a distance, comforted in the belief that we would never meet a Nushawn Williams or that if we did, we would recognize him immediately.

Most H.I.V.-positive people I have encountered, regardless of their social standing, do not voluntarily disclose their status to potential partners. Indeed, even people in long-term, committed relationships lie about their status. These are the realities of H.I.V. transmission today.

The people I am talking about are nothing like Nushawn Williams. They did not grow up in ghettos or belong to street gangs. They come from stable homes in safe neighborhoods. They went to your high school and college and graduate school.

They remain silent not because they are evil, but because it is difficult to tell the truth, and because their friends and community support them in their silence. Their doctors, their psychiatrists, even the AIDS organizations they call for help offer comfort and sympathy but don't encourage them to tell the truth.

Certainly, it is difficult to disclose one's status to a partner, but it is necessary, and it does get easier. It is a skill that can and must be learned. But the H.I.V. community has adopted its own "don't ask, don't tell" policy.

We are 15 years into the AIDS epidemic, and I have been asked my status by prospective partners only twice. Since testing positive, I have made a point of disclosing my status to any potential partner; each one told me that I was the first person to do so. Each believed that if he practiced safe sex, there would be no need to know. I practiced safe sex. There is no such thing as safe sex.

Leading advocacy groups perpetuate the culture of irresponsibility. The Gay Men's Health Crisis will not recommend or encourage full disclosure. When I called the group's hot line earlier this year, I was advised to "experiment"—informing some partners of my H.I.V. status while remaining silent with others. In this way I could decide which was more comfortable for me.

The Centers for Disease Control and Prevention will only "suggest that you might want to consider informing your partner," a hot-line counselor told me last week. Counselors at the San Francisco AIDS Foundation said it was their job to dispense information, not moral or ethical recommendations, and, again, that I must do what makes me feel comfortable.

We are not talking about comfortable here. We are talking about life and death.

The emphasis on the individual's rights without an equally strong emphasis on the individual's responsibility is wrong and is a direct cause of the spread of this disease.

By hiding behind the cover of "safe sex," AIDS groups have shifted responsibility off the shoulders of those infected with the virus—this despite the fact that, in their own words, there is no such thing as safe sex, only levels of risk that one must choose. In making that choice, a partner's H.I.V. status is *the* critical piece of information.

Groups like Gay Men's Health Crisis claim they cannot dictate behavior. Granted. But that is all the more reason that AIDS organizations have a responsibility to encourage, to teach and to train people who are H.I.V. positive to do what is right.

For years the AIDS community has rallied around the battle cry "Silence = Death." What it has failed to realize is that silence comes in many forms and that all are lethal.

# The Great Hijack

## Bernard Rabinowitz

Bernard Rabinowitz argues that laws in the United States granting individuals the right to refuse HIV tests and to keep their HIV status confidential run counter to measures medicine has traditionally used to combat infectious diseases. The spread of HIV to the developing world is prompting some to claim the same rights for all HIV-infected people. But to deal effectively with the AIDS epidemic, physicians must be able to test and label those with HIV and have access to records revealing patients' HIV status. The medical system must be recaptured from the hijackers.

It is over 40 years since I qualified as a doctor and 35 since I was awarded the fellowship of the Royal College of Surgeons of England. As a student I read with enthusiasm about the revolution wrought by Pasteur, Jenner, and Lister. Later I was stirred as polio was defeated, diphtheria became a rarity, and smallpox vanished. We were taught and in turn passed on to our students the principles so decisively developed by these great men.

Any epidemic imposes obligations on the doctor. We must diagnose, isolate, localise, and treat. An overriding concern is the protection of the uninfected. That

is the modern and proved way to limit and end an outbreak of an infectious disease. Indeed, it is a catechism for even our junior students.

In the early 1980s some hundred or more people who were immunocompromised came to light in the homosexual community in the United States. A diagnostic test was developed and an infecting agent was identified. Then modern medicine was made to run for cover. A positive test labelled the carrier as a homosexual. That community, generally erudite, articulate, and eloquent, was prominent in the arts, the media, and often in public life. The fear of possible labelling was real and immediate. It hit interested parties in the administration, which handed down speedy and even

*British Medical Journal,* 313 (7060) (September 28, 1996), p. 826. Reprinted with permission from the BMJ Publishing Group.

panicky legislation mandating secrecy and confidentiality and prohibiting testing without consent.

The medical profession remained obediently silent as this disease emerged as a lethal, spreadable infection. We, the doctors, were told that the standard approaches to an infectious disease would land us in court. Our professional bodies raced, with politically correct zeal, to endorse the criminalising of normal diagnostic protocols. With heavy ethical breathing we had endorsed the first legally protected epidemic in medical history.

Some of the jargon then and now bears looking at as we balance on the wobbly ethical platform. The sanctity of confidentiality is a prime example. We have never respected confidentiality at the expense of the common good. The profession has never permitted the rights of an individual to compromise the community. Would any doctor who sees a patient known to have epilepsy driving a school bus keep quiet? Would a person with angina be allowed to pilot an airliner? Doctors employed by insurance and building societies have never felt constrained to protect the secrecy of the person with tuberculosis or hypertension who is now refused a mortgage loan. Yet with AIDS the rights to secrecy of a tiny minority were deemed ethically more important than the rights of the huge uninfected majority.

The medical voices raised in protest at our feeble acquiescence were blasted with the labels of callous, unethical, and not compassionate. Our profession forgot its heritage and its duty. It abandoned its science and its obligation to apply it. As the years passed, young people died in their hundreds, then thousands, and soon, as heterosexual contacts spread, the figures will be millions. Secrecy and confidentiality have served the epidemic well.

What might we have achieved had we identified, labelled, and campaigned? The epidemic would not have been stopped, but millions of people who now have HIV would not have contracted the virus. Homosexuals and carriers identified as such would have had to live with whatever exposure ensued. The HIV infected developing world is, like the developed West, battling with the ethical nonsense formed in the United States 15 years ago. Earnest doctors, people who know better, are shackled by fear of prosecution if they identify a person with HIV. Yet ethical debates have never arisen on cholera, tuberculosis, or lassa fever. We even indulge the indefensible practice of anonymous testing without consent to gain statistics. Those identified as positive are not informed.

Medical law endorses the patient's right to refuse a test for HIV—a test that could be vital in an emergency or other cases. The law demands that the surgeon should proceed or risk prosecution. Can you envisage a scenario where a patient presents for, say, a hip replacement, or a partial gastrectomy and tells the surgeon that he or she cannot take an x ray examination of the chest or do renal functions but must do the operation anyway?

In years to come the profession may well label these past years as the great hijack. As doctors we can still save millions. We must be free to test, diagnose, and label. Families, lovers, and contacts must not be denied information. Obligatory tests for HIV, as in other countries for other diseases, should precede marriage and pregnancy. All patients; blood, organ, and sperm donors; school-children; medical students; surgeons; boxers; rugby players; and anyone in an occupation where blood can be shed should be freely tested as and when indicated with no specific consent required. The person with AIDS will become an accepted feature of society. The hijackers have facilitated a worldwide disaster; I would urge that we speedily do what we can to minimise it.

---

# Controlling HIV/AIDS Forever: Guidelines for Using Protease Inhibitors

## Daniel Saturn

Daniel Saturn argues for the introduction of guidelines to govern the use of protease-inhibiting drugs. He points out that antibiotics, the original "miracle drugs," have lost much of their power, because careless use has led to the emergence of drug-resistant strains of bacteria.

While protease-inhibiting drugs are highly successful in controlling HIV infection and preventing the development of AIDS, Saturn warns that these new "miracle drugs" may also lose their power if they are prescribed for people who don't take them properly. Variant strains of HIV that are drug resistant may emerge, and we will have another AIDS crisis. To keep this from happening, Saturn offers a set of four guidelines to govern the use of the drugs.

Anyone who becomes a patient in a hospital nowadays risks becoming infected with potentially lethal drug-resistant bacteria. Even though scores of antibiotics have been developed since the advent of penicillin, the vast majority of them have become useless against some types of bacteria. Indeed, until recently vancomycin was the only one that could be counted on to treat the strains of bacteria that had defeated other antibiotics, and even it has failed in a few new cases. In hardly more than fifty years, we have slipped from the golden age of miracle drugs into a darker time of uncertainty and even defeat.

How this came about is well known. Antibiotics were (and are) so widely and indiscriminately used that they exerted a selection pressure on bacteria. While most bacteria were destroyed, the variants that were resistant to the drugs reproduced themselves. Over time, more and more drug-resistant variants spread in a niche left empty by variants that weren't resistant. Natural selection did its job, and we are now faced with the result of not having antibiotics we can rely on.

## Protease Inhibitors as Miracle Drugs

Before the group of drugs known as protease inhibitors was developed, people infected with HIV could count on nothing much but an early death. The drug AZT that earlier had been touted as effective turned out not to keep those who took it alive any longer than those who didn't. But the protease inhibitors are different—they work. In combination with AZT and other drugs, they work very well indeed. After such combination therapy was introduced, the death rate for people with AIDS dropped 75 percent.

Combination therapy is not a cure for AIDS any more than insulin is a cure for diabetes or aspirin is a cure for arthritis, but it's a death preventer. Combination therapy is letting people grow old and maybe even die of something besides an HIV-associated

disease. AIDS in our society may become as rare as leprosy. If this isn't a good enough reason to bestow the title "miracle drugs" on protease inhibitors, it'll do until a cure for AIDS or a vaccine to prevent it comes along.

Besides being miracle drugs, protease inhibitors resemble antibiotics in another way. It's necessary to take them as prescribed for them to be effective. More accurately, it's necessary for the HIV-infected person to follow the drug regimen of combination therapy as planned by his or her doctor. This may mean taking from fifteen to fifty (or more) pills each day in a pattern as complicated as a quadrille. Some drugs are taken two at a time, some one at a time. Some are swallowed on an empty stomach, some are taken with food. Some are taken four times a day, while others are taken twice a week.

Being a "good patient" and taking your drugs the way you're told offers a wonderful reward. It can drive down the viral load so far that it can't be detected by an ordinary blood test, and particles of the virus can be discovered only by highly technical laboratory methods.

## Rejecting the Miracle

With so much to gain, you might think anybody infected with HIV would be eager to sign up for combination therapy and to stick to it with all the fervor of religious people acting out their rituals. But such is not the case. Physicians already report that they are having trouble getting some of their HIV patients to stick to the drug-taking pattern they must follow to control the AIDS virus. Exactly how many people can't be counted on to take their drugs is unknown.

It's tempting to think that such people must be out of their minds. At last, after almost two harrowing decades of disability and death, a group of drugs is finally available to keep HIV under control and prevent the development of AIDS, and some people ignore them. What's going on here?

What the public generally doesn't realize is that someone can be infected with HIV for years and not develop AIDS or show any signs of being sick. Because many people are willing to take drugs only when the drugs make them feel better, if being HIV infected doesn't make them feel sick, then they won't take the drugs prescribed for them. Or at least they won't take them *as* prescribed but will only take them in a hit-or-miss, lackadaisical way.

Following the plan for combination therapy isn't a picnic either. Some people infected with HIV (like some people with cancer, diabetes, or whatever) find it hard to get dressed in the morning and to get enough to eat during the day. They don't have the social and personal wherewithal to stick to a complicated schedule for taking drugs or doing much of anything else. If they were hospitalized, they might take their drugs. But left to their own devices, they won't.

The pattern for drug taking in combination therapy is complicated, but what's more the drugs themselves are often unpleasant. Instead of making you feel better, they make you feel sick. They cause nausea, headaches, dizziness, and fatigue. They can cause deposits of fat to build up around the neck and shoulders, giving you a physically altered appearance. Not much of a recommendation for somebody who is infected with HIV but doesn't have any symptoms. "Take drugs that will make me feel worse and look worse? You've got to be kidding."

## A Threat to All

So why not just say, "Let the people infected with HIV take the combination therapy if they want to, and if they don't that's their problem. It's a free country, after all, and everybody has the right to accept or reject treatment. They can give combination therapy a try and see if they can tolerate the drugs and keep to their drug-taking schedule. If they can't, they're the losers. We may feel sorry for them or think they're foolish, but no harm is done."

The problem with this point of view is that harm is done. It's done to everyone who is infected with HIV and to everyone who might become infected—which is to say, all of us. Protease inhibitors, like antibiotics, are miracle drugs, but they're also like antibiotics in another respect. The human immunodeficiency virus, the virus that causes AIDS, is an active organism that mutates rapidly. As a result, it exists in millions of slightly different variants. It's this fact about the virus that makes many researchers despair of being able to develop a vaccine to prevent it from infecting us. What works for one group of variants won't work for an-

other, and what might work for a period of time might not work for a later time because the virus will have changed.

This is a situation exactly analogous to the one in which we first began to use antibiotics. The microorganisms are mutating and changing. Some of them may be resistant to the drug, but others may not be. If the patient stops taking the drug, the variants that are harder to kill will begin to multiply. They will then spread, and eventually the population of infectious organisms will become dominated by those that are hard to kill.

This is what led us to the crisis with antibiotics, and if protease inhibitors are used in the same laissez-faire fashion that we've used antibiotics, we will sooner or later end up in a similar fix. We can now control HIV, but it's highly likely that the indiscriminate use of protease inhibitors will wrest that control from us. Drug-resistant strains of the virus will spread through the population, and the AIDS crisis will revisit us again.

## Guidelines

How can we keep this nightmare scenario from playing in the future? By exerting tight control over the use of the protease inhibitors. This might be done by adhering to the following general guidelines:

1. *Allow physicians to prescribe protease inhibitors only to patients who can reasonably be expected to comply with the rules for taking them.*

To assist physicians, a protocol for assessing patients in terms of their likelihood of adhering to medication directions should be drawn up by a group including HIV/AIDS experts, public health workers, advocates for people with HIV/AIDS, medical social workers, and psychiatrists. The process of selection cannot be made automatic, but it can be routinized in a useful fashion.

In most medical therapies, patients are given (as they ought to be) the benefit of the doubt. While some may abuse the narcotic drug prescribed for them, the condition they complain of warrants prescribing such a drug. If they do not take it or if they take it but don't need it, less harm is done than if they needed it but didn't get it.

The situation must be different from those who are HIV infected because the stakes are different. Their failure to take protease inhibitors in the manner prescribed may lead to the development of resistant HIV strains and so put other people at risk. Thus, the physician (perhaps with help of information provided by social workers and psychologists) needs to be convinced that a patient infected with HIV who is a candidate for protease inhibitors will comply with the proper regimen. The physician should err on the side of caution and deny to the patient the traditional benefit of the doubt.

2. *Establish an appeals procedure open to all who are denied access to protease-inhibiting drugs.*

Because of the danger of the abuse of the power to deny a patient access to a drug that might bring benefit, the decision of a physician to withhold a prescription of protease-inhibiting drugs from a patient should be subject to an appeals process.

It is crucial to keep physicians from acting in arbitrary and discriminatory ways, and an appeal mechanism will have the effect of blocking this possibility. While such vulnerable populations as homeless people and addicts are likely to be the ones most often denied access to protease inhibitors, physicians, hospitals, and clinics need to make a special effort to familiarize them with the availability of the appeals procedure.

Such a procedure might be hospital based or community based. It should include a physician experienced in treating HIV, a representative of people with HIV/AIDS, a social worker or psychologist, a community representative, an attorney, and a medical ethicist.

3. *Develop a set of criteria to determine the safety of various treatment approaches and periods.*

Scientific experts on HIV and AIDS should offer formal opinions on the safety of such practices as taking a protease inhibitor in erratic ways over a period of time. A realistic appreciation of the dangers of noncompliance is needed to settle questions about the risks involved in prescribing protease inhibitors to patients of doubtful reliability.

4. *Require physicians or public health workers to monitor patients taking protease inhibitors to determine that they are taking them as prescribed.*

While monitoring each day's dose of protease inhibitors is not a realistic financial possibility, it is possible to arrange for spot checks and general monitoring of patients considered at risk for failing to comply with their medication regimen. Such a public health function would be expensive, but in the long run it would both be cheaper and would save more lives than a resurgence of AIDS initiated by the spread of a deadly new variant of the virus.

Protease-inhibiting drugs offer us the chance to eliminate AIDS (for the most part) by turning HIV infection into a chronic disorder than can be treated. The ghastly deaths of tens of thousands in the past need not be repeated in the future. But to keep such a tragedy from playing out again, we must be prepared to use our knowledge of biology to restrict the promiscuous use of protease inhibitors. We must not abuse them the way we have abused antibiotics.

## READINGS

# Section 2: HIV Testing

## Insurers Are Right on AIDS Testing

### Bob Hunter and Jay Angoff

Bob Hunter and Jay Angoff assert that the principle of an individual's sharing the risk with *similar* individuals warrants testing, because otherwise the cost of insurance is unfair to those who do not carry the AIDS virus. They admit that other considerations might override this principle, but they do not regard any of the four factors they examine as sufficient. In their view, national health insurance offers the best solution of paying for the care of AIDS patients.

The insurance industry has filed suit to block a regulation proposed by the New York Insurance Department that would prohibit insurance companies from testing applicants for health insurance for exposure to the AIDS virus. The insurance industry has a valid point.

Insurance companies are supposed to charge insurance buyers a price that reflects the risk presented by an individual buyer or by a group of similarly situated buyers.

In seeking to test insurance applicants for exposure to the AIDS virus, life and health insurers are trying to abide by this principle. For example, out of 1,000 34-year-old males who test positive for the presence of the AIDS antibody, which indicates infection by the virus, at least 200 will die of AIDS within seven years, according to the National Centers for Disease Control.

By contrast, actuarial tables tell us that of 1,000 34-year-old males in standard health, 7.5 will die within seven years. Those who test positive, therefore, are 26.6 times more likely to die within seven years than 34-year-old males in standard health. To ignore the risk factor responsible for this 2,666 percent risk differential is bad insurance policy.

However, other factors must be considered in assessing whether a particular restriction on AIDS testing might nevertheless be good social policy. They include the following:

■   *The magnitude of the impact of a particular restriction on the insurance industry.*

People who apply for insurance as individuals are tested to determine the likelihood of their developing various diseases, such as diabetes and heart disease, but those who buy insurance as a group are not.

Because group insurance accounts for 90 percent of all health insurance, but less than 50 percent of all life insurance, prohibiting AIDS testing for health insurance would have a relatively minor impact on the health insurance business, while prohibiting testing for life insurance would have a more substantial effect.

■   *The effect of permitting testing on those at risk for AIDS.*

The gay community argues that insurers cannot possibly guarantee confidentiality and that a breach of it to someone who tests positive can be devastating. A proposed Massachusetts regulation, however, if enforced, would seem to offer true confidentiality: It sets up a "need to know" standard for disclosing the results of an AIDS test even to other individuals in an insurance company.

■   *The effect of prohibiting testing on those not at risk for AIDS.*

If testing for AIDS is prohibited, people in standard health and people at risk for other diseases will subsidize those at risk for AIDS. Whether lawmakers are willing to accept such a subsidy would seem to depend on its cost for each policy holder, which insurers could easily calculate. So far, however, they have failed to do so.

■   *The alternatives to permitting testing.*

If insurers are prohibited from testing, they will use less accurate, and more offensive, methods of determining who is at risk for AIDS. For example, they may seek to charge higher rates to all unmarried males living in zip code areas with a large proportion of gay men.

States may prohibit insurers from either testing for AIDS or using sexual preference or any surrogate for sexual preference as a risk factor, as the District of Columbia has done. But they cannot force insurers to write insurance under those conditions. The heavy-handed but not entirely unjustified response of several insurers to the District's AIDS law has been to stop doing business there.

The best solution to providing health insurance for those at risk for AIDS is national health insurance. By spreading the cost of AIDS as widely as possible throughout society, the burden on any individual will be minimal.

Unless such a system is enacted, any "solution" will be a compromise. The compromise reached by the New York Insurance Department may be reasonable. But we should recognize that insurers that want to test for infection by the AIDS virus—and to decline to insure those testing positive—have sound insurance principles on their side.

# An Insidious Test for AIDS

## William C. Gifford III

William Gifford explains why he refused to consent to be tested for the AIDS virus as part of an insurance application. Anyone testing positive would be "uninsurable," and the results might become known to prospective employers, the federal government, or others. Also, those who are seropositive must then rely on public clinics rather than private physicians. Most important, in Gifford's view, "the test not only amounts to a subsidy of the insurance industry, it could also create a vast class of young people who are uninsurable." At the same time as it wants to avoid insuring those who might have AIDS, the industry campaigns against national health insurance.

One morning not long ago a young woman came to my apartment to take blood and urine samples, as required by the company to which I had applied for an individual health insurance policy. She opened her briefcase and began arranging needles, vials and bandages on the kitchen table.

Then she asked me to sign a form. In very fine print, it said that my blood and urine would be tested for the presence of HIV, the virus that causes AIDS, and for cocaine and other drugs. The results would determine my eligibility for insurance.

For a straight, white, young middle class male like me, AIDS remains a remote possibility. And I don't use drugs. Though my sense of civil liberties was a bit ruffled, my first instinct was to sign and get the test over with.

But as I reread the statement, its implications became clear. If the test showed I carry HIV, then I would be denied insurance—and not just by one company. A call to the company's agent revealed I would be "uninsurable."

In addition, this information would be recorded in a medical information bank. I asked who else would see my test results. Prospective employers? The Federal Government? What if the confidentiality rules changed, and drug users or HIV carriers were reported?

The company agent was annoyed that I would bother to ask these questions. Such a climate of hysteria surrounds both AIDS and drugs, however, that I

needed to know how this sensitive information would be used.

I couldn't sign the form. The unlikely scenario played in my head: What if I did test positive? With HIV, and thus without insurance, I would have to pay all my health care expenses—even the podiatrist's bills. That would mean going to public clinics rather than a private physician. If and when I developed the disease, I would become dependent on Medicare and would qualify for some treatments like AZT, but not others. I would get by, a burden to the taxpayers rather than the private sector.

The AIDS test not only amounts to a subsidy of the insurance industry, it could create a vast class of young people who are uninsurable.

According to a recent news article, teenagers are becoming infected at very high rates. Unlike the situation in the adult population, the article pointed out, among teenagers the disease is spread equally between males and females. That means the Government will soon be picking up the medical expenses of many more young people with AIDS who are ineligible for private insurance, thereby absorbing much of the risk and the losses that would ordinarily belong to the insurance companies.

Typically, insurance works by spreading the health care costs of very sick people around the general insured population. The insurance company gambles that its premiums will be greater than its outlays, and takes steps, like raising premiums to improve the odds.

Excluding carriers of HIV keeps down premiums for most people, the company agent informed me. But this is an illusory savings. First, according to an article in *The New England Journal of Medicine* the actual cost of treating a person with AIDS has turned out to be much lower than the initial estimates cited by insurance companies. Second, we all end up paying for AIDS care through taxes.

These companies and their political spokesmen squeal in agony at the mention of national health insurance. Nevertheless, insurance companies that require an AIDS test seem to be quite willing to let the Government pick up the tab for people with HIV.

They can get away with it because AIDS remains largely a disease of homosexuals, drug users, blacks and Hispanics. But as AIDS slowly seeps into the straight, white majority, discrimination against HIV carriers will no longer be acceptable.

It shouldn't be acceptable now, when between one million and 1.5 million Americans are estimated to carry the AIDS virus. If insurance companies are going to campaign against national health care, they should be held to their argument. The private sector must accept full responsibility for the nation's health, or step aside.

# Section 3: AIDS Trials in Africa

## Human Rights and Maternal–Fetal HIV Transmission Prevention Trials in Africa

George J. Annas and Michael A. Grodin

George Annas and Michael Grodin argue that unless a therapy that is being tested in an "impoverished" country will actually be made available to those needing it in that country, research subjects are being exploited to benefit developed countries. The mere possibility that the therapy will be feasible for use in the impoverished country is not enough to justify the testing. Nor is the fact that scientists from that country are involved; nor is the existence of a professional consensus favoring the testing. Even when the testing is justified, research subjects must not be drawn from the most vulnerable groups and informed consent of participants is required.

### Introduction

Since the adoption of the Universal Declaration of Human Rights by the United National General Assembly in 1948, the countries of the world have agreed that all humans have dignity and rights. In 1998, the 50th anniversary of the Universal Declaration of Human Rights, the Declaration's aspirations have yet to be realized, and poverty, racism, and sexism continue to conspire to frustrate the worldwide human rights movement. The human rights and public health issues of maternal–fetal human immunodeficiency virus (HIV) transmission prevention trials in Africa, Asia, and the Caribbean are not unique to acquired immunodeficiency syndrome (AIDS) or to those countries.

From *American Journal of Public Health,* 88    4 (April 1998), pp. 560–563. With permission from The American Public Health Association.

Open discussion of these issues provides an opportunity to move the real human rights agenda forward. This is why Global Lawyers and Physicians (GLP), a transnational organization dedicated to promoting and protecting the health-related provisions of the Universal Declaration of Human Rights, joined with Ralph Nader's Public Citizen organization to challenge the conduct of a series of AIDS clinical trials in these developing countries.[1]

### The Clinical Trials

In 1994, the first effective intervention to reduce the perinatal transmission of HIV was developed in the United States in AIDS Clinical Trials Group (ACTG) Study 076. In that trial, use of zidovudine administered orally to HIV-positive pregnant women as early as the second trimester of pregnancy, intravenously during labor, and orally to their newborns for 6 weeks reduced the incidence of HIV infection by two thirds (from about 25% to about 8%).[2] Six months after stopping the study, the US Public Health Service recommended the ACTG 076 regimen as the standard of care in the United States. In June 1994, the World Health Organization (WHO) convened a meeting in Geneva at which it was concluded (in an unpublished report) that the 076 regime was not feasible in the developing world. At least 16 randomized clinical trials (15 using placebos as controls) were subsequently approved for conduct in developing countries, primarily in Africa. These trials involve more than 17,000 pregnant women. Nine of the studies, most of them comparing shorter courses of zidovudine, Vitamin A, or HIV immunoglobulin with placebo, are funded by the Centers for Disease Control and Prevention (CDC) or the National Institutes of Health (NIH).

Most of the public discussion about these trials has centered on the use of the placebos.[1] The question of placebo use is a central one in determining how a study should be conducted. But we believe the more important issue these trials raise is the question of whether they should be done at all. Specifically, when is medical research ethically justified in developing countries that do not have adequate health services (or on US populations that have no access to basic health care)? This question is especially pertinent since February 1998 when, on the basis of a Thailand study that demonstrated that a short course of zidovudine reduced HIV transmission by 50%, CDC, NIH, and the United Nations Program on AIDS (UNAIDS) officials announced that they would recommend that the use of placebo be halted in all mother-to-fetus transmission studies.

## Research on Impoverished Populations

The central issue involved in doing research with impoverished populations is exploitation. Harold Varmus, speaking for NIH, and David Satcher, speaking for CDC, both seem to realize this. They wrote in the *New England Journal of Medicine* last year that "trials that make use of impoverished populations to test drugs for use solely in developed countries violate our most basic understanding of ethical behavior."[3] However, instead of trying to demonstrate how the study interventions, such as a shorter course of zidovudine (AZT), could actually be delivered to the populations

of the countries in the studies, they assert that the studies can be justified because they will provide information that the host country can use to "make a sound judgment about the appropriateness and financial feasibility of providing the intervention.[3] However, what these countries require is not good intentions, but a real plan to deliver the intervention, should it be proven beneficial.

Unless the interventions being tested will actually be made available to the impoverished populations that are being used as research subjects, developed countries are simply exploiting them in order to quickly use the knowledge gained from the clinical trials for the developed countries' own benefit. If the research reveals regimens of equal efficacy at less cost, these regimens will surely be implemented in the developed world. If the research reveals the regimens to be less efficacious, these results will be added to the scientific literature, and the developed world will not conduct those studies. Ethics and basic human rights principles require not a thin promise, but a real plan as to how the intervention will actually be delivered. Actual delivery is also, of course, required to support even the utilitarian justification for the trials, which is to find a simple, inexpensive, and feasible intervention in as short a time frame as possible because so many people are dying of AIDS. No justification is supportable unless the intervention is actually made widely available to the relevant populations.

Neither NIH nor CDC (nor the host countries) has a plan that would make the interventions they are studying available in Africa, where more than two thirds of the people in the world reside who are infected with HIV. As an example, Varmus and Satcher point out that the wholesale cost of zidovudine in the 076 protocol is estimated to be in excess of $800 per mother and infant and that this amount is far greater than what most developing countries can pay for standard care. The CDC estimates the cost of the "short course" zidovudine regimens being investigated to be roughly $50 per person. The cost of merely screening for HIV disease, a precondition for any course of therapy, is approximately $10, and all pregnant women must be screened to find the cases to treat. These costs must be compared with the total per capita health care expenditures of the countries where this research is being conducted. Given this fact, African countries involved in the clinical trials (or some other funder) must make realistic assurances that if a research regimen proves effective in reducing mother-to-fetus transmission of HIV, resources will be made available so that the HIV-positive pregnant women in their countries will receive this regimen.

However, the mere assertion that the intervention will be feasible for use in the developing countries is simply not good enough, given our experience and knowledge of what happens in Africa now. For example, we already know that effectively treating sexually transmitted diseases such as syphilis, gonorrhea, and chancroid with the simple and effective treatments that are now available can drastically lower the incidence of HIV infection. Yet, these inexpensive and effective treatments are not delivered to poor Africans. For example, a recent study showed that improving the treatment of sexually transmitted diseases in rural Tanzania could reduce HIV infections by 40%.[4] Nonetheless, this relatively inexpensive and effective intervention is not delivered. Vaccines against devastating diseases have also been developed with sub-Saharan African populations as test subjects.[5]

## Cultural Relativism or Universal Human Rights?

In their article in the *New England Journal of Medicine,* Varmus and Satcher sought to bolster their ethical position by quoting the chair of the AIDS Research Committee of the Uganda Cancer Institute, who wrote a letter to Dr. Varmus:

> These are Ugandan studies conducted by Ugandan investigators on Ugandans. . . . It is not NIH conducting the studies in Uganda, but Ugandans conducting their study on their people for the good of their people.[3]

Two points are especially striking about Varmus' and Satcher's using this justification. First, their justification is simply not accurate. If NIH and CDC were not involved in these studies, these agencies would not have to justify them; indeed, the studies would not have been undertaken. These US agencies *are* involved—these trials are not just Ugandans doing research on other Ugandans. Second, and more importantly, the use of this quotation implies support for an outdated and dangerous view of cultural relativism.

Even if it were true that the studies in question were done by Ugandans on Ugandans, this would not mean that the United States or the international community could conclude that they should not be criticized. (This rationale did not inhibit criticism of apartheid in South Africa, genocide in Rwanda, or torture and murder in the Congo.) Human Rights Watch, referring to repression in Central Africa, said in its December 1997 review of the year on the issue of human rights that the slogan "African solutions to African problems" is now used as a "thin cover" for abusing citizens.[6] That observation can be applicable to experimentation on citizens as well.

The other major justification both NIH and CDC use for the trials is the consensus reached at the June 1994 meeting of researchers at WHO. Of the many analogies that have been drawn between the HIV transmission prevention trials and the US Public Health Service's Tuskegee syphilis study, perhaps most striking is their reliance on professional consensus instead of ethical principle to justify research on poor, black populations. As historian James Jones wrote in his book *Bad Blood,* which was written about the Tuskegee experiment: "The consensus was that the experiment was worth doing, and in a profession whose members did not have a well-developed system of normative ethics, consensus formed the functional equivalent of moral sanction."[7]

Neither researcher consensus nor host country agreement is ethically sufficient justification for choosing a research population. As the National Research Council's committee on Human Genome Diversity properly put it, in the context of international research on human subjects, "[s]ensitivity to the specific practices and beliefs of a community cannot be used as a justification for violating universal human rights."[8] Justice and equity questions are also important to the ability of individual research subjects to give informed consent.

## Informed Consent

Research subjects should not be drawn from populations who are especially vulnerable (e.g., the poor, children, or mentally impaired persons) unless the population is the only group in which the research can be conducted and the group itself will derive benefits from the research. Even when these conditions are met, informed consent must also be obtained. In most settings in Africa, voluntary, informed consent will be problematic and difficult, and it may even preclude ethical research. This is because, in the absence of health care, virtually any offer of medical assistance (even in the guise of research) will be accepted as "better than nothing" and research will almost inevitably be confused with treatment, making informed consent difficult.

Interviews with women subjects of the placebo-controlled trial in the Ivory Coast support this conclusion. For example, one subject, Cecile Guede, a 23-year-old HIV-infected mother participating in a US-financed trial, told the *New York Times,* "They gave me a bunch of pills to take, and told me how to take them. Some were for malaria, some were for fevers, and some were supposed to be for the virus. I knew that there were different kinds, but I figured that if one of them didn't work against AIDS, then one of the others would."[9] The *Times* reporter who wrote the front-page story, Howard W. French, said, "For Ms Guede, the reason to enroll in the study last year was clear: it offered her and her infant free health care and a hope to shield her baby from deadly infection. . . . [T]he prospect of help as she brought her baby into the world made taking part in the experiment all but irresistible."[9]

Persons can make a gift of themselves by volunteering for research. However, it is extremely unlikely that poor African women would knowingly volunteer to participate in research that offered no benefit to their communities (because the intervention would not be made available) and that would only serve to enrich the multinational drug companies and the developed world.[8] Thus, a good ethical working rule is that researchers should presume that valid consent cannot be obtained from impoverished populations in the absence of a realistic plan to deliver the intervention to the population. Informed consent, by itself, can protect many subjects of research in developed countries, but its protective power is much more compromised in impoverished populations who are being offered what looks like medical care that is otherwise unavailable to them.

## The International Community and the AIDS Pandemic

If the goal of the clinical trials is to reduce the spread of HIV infection in developing countries, what strategy should public health adopt to achieve this end? It is not obvious that the answer is to conduct clinical trials of short-term zidovudine treatment. In the developed world, for example, HIV-infected women are advised not to breast-feed their infants because 8% to 18% of them will be infected with HIV from breast milk.[10] However, in much of the developing world, including in most African countries, WHO continues to recommend breast-feeding because the lack of clean water

still makes formula-feeding more dangerous. As long as this recommendation stays in effect, and is followed, even universal use of the ACTG 076 regimen, which would lower the overall newborn infection rate by about 16%, would only likely serve to reduce the incidence of HIV infection in infants by about the same amount that it is increased by breast-feeding (8% to 18%). A more effective public health intervention to improve the health of women and their children may be to put more efforts into providing clean water and sanitation. This will help not only to deal with HIV, but also to alleviate many other problems, including diarrheal diseases.

President Jacques Chirac of France was on target in his December 1997 speech to the 10th International Conference on Sexually Transmitted Disease and AIDS in Africa, which was held in the Ivory Coast. President Chirac proposed creating an international "therapy support fund" that is primarily funded by European countries (the former colonial powers in Africa).[11] Although he put emphasis on the new drugs available for AIDS treatments, it would be more useful to consider the public health priorities of the countries themselves, for example, prevention, especially in areas such as sanitation, water supply, nutrition, education, and the delivery of simple and effective vaccines and medical treatments for sexually transmitted diseases.

## Conclusion

Actual delivery of health care requires more than just paying lip service to the principles of the Universal Declaration of Human Rights; it requires a real commitment to human rights and a willingness on the part of the developed countries to take economic, social, and cultural rights as seriously as political and civil rights.

### References

1. Lurie, P, Wolfe SM. Unethical trials of interventions to reduce prenatal transmission of human immunodeficiency virus in developing countries. *N Engl J Med.* 1997;337:853–856.

2. Connor EM, Sperling RS, Gelber R, et al. Reduction of maternal-infant transmission of human immunodeficiency virus type 1 with zidovudine treatment. *N Engl J Med.* 1994;331:1173–1180.

3. Varmus H., Satcher D. Ethical complexities of conducting research in developing countries. *N Engl J Med.* 1997;337:1003–1005.

4. Grosskurth H, Mosha F, Todd J, Mwijarubi E, et al. Impact of improved treatment of sexually transmitted diseases on HIV infection in rural Tanzania: randomized controlled trial. *Lancet.* 1995;346:530–536.

5. Robbins JB, Towne DW, Gotschlich EC, Schneerson R. 'Love's labours lost': failure to implement mass vaccination against

group A meningococcal meningitis in sub-Saharan Africa. *Lancet.* 1997;350:880–882.

6. Clines FX. Rights group assails US on land mines and ties with China. *New York Times.* December 5, 1997:A13.

7. Jones JH. *Bad Blood: The Tuskegee Syphilis Experiment.* New York, NY: Free Press, 1981.

8. Committee on Human Genome Diversity. Evaluating Human Genetic Diversity. Washington, DC: National Academy Press; 1997:65.

9. French HW. AIDS research in Africa: juggling risks and hopes. *New York Times.* October 9, 1997:A1.

10. Van de Perre P. Postnatal transmission of human immunodeficiency virus type 1: the breast-feeding dilemma. *Am J Ob Gyn.* 1995;173:483–487.

11. Bunce M. Chirac seeks worldwide relief for AIDS in Africa. *Boston Globe.* December 8, 1997:A2.

# We're Trying to Help Our Sickest People, Not Exploit Them

Danstan Bagenda and Philippa Musoke-Mudido

Danstan Bagenda and Philippa Musoke-Mudido respond to critics of the clinical trials in Africa involving comparing the effectiveness of new therapies with placebos in preventing the transmission of HIV from mothers to their infants. The authors argue that such factors as cost, nutrition, social practices, culture, and environmental circumstances make it inappropriate to compare testing in developed countries with testing in Africa.

Also, women enrolled in the trials received intensive education and individual counseling, were given a consent form written in their local language and explaining their potential risks and chances of getting a placebo. Only after their questions and concerns were addressed by counselors were they asked to sign. The authors express skepticism about those who claim to speak on behalf of Africa, yet have never worked with its people.

Every day, like the beat of a drum heard throughout Africa, 1,000 more infants here are infected with HIV, the virus that causes AIDS. At Old Mulago Hospital, we are trying to educate people about AIDS, as well as study new therapies to prevent the disease's rampant spread. Recently, some of these studies have been attacked, with comparisons made to the notorious Tuskegee experiment in which black men in the United States were denied treatment for syphilis. Tuskegee? Is this really what is happening here in our mother-child clinic?

Our country lies in the heart of Africa, along the Great Rift Valley and Lake Victoria. It is one of those hardest hit by the AIDS epidemic. A few years ago, visitors here in the capital were greeted by the macabre sight of empty coffins for sale—piled in pyramids from adult to baby size—along the main road.

These grim reminders have since been removed by city authorities, but the AIDS epidemic is omnipresent. In this city of 1 million, about one out of every six adults is infected with HIV. Hospitals and clinics like ours, which provide free medical care and therefore serve the poorest communities, are stretched beyond their resources.

At the Mulago Hospital, where more than 20,000 women deliver each year, we are trying to find effective therapies to stop transmission of HIV from pregnant women to their babies. About one in five babies becomes infected with HIV during pregnancy and delivery. If he mother breast-feeds her baby, there is an additional 15- to 25-percent chance that the baby will later become infected. There is no available treatment for the disease in Uganda. After careful consideration among researchers from developing and developed countries, the World Health Organization (WHO) recommended in 1994 that the best way to find safe and effective treatment for sufferers in countries in the developing world is to conduct studies in which new treatments, better tailored to the local population, are compared with placebos (inactive pills).

Women who enroll in our studies undergo intensive education and individual counseling. They are given a comprehensive consent form, written in the local language, which they are encouraged to take home and discuss with their families. It describes the potential risks of participating in the study and their chances of receiving a placebo. Only when they and their counselors are satisfied that all questions have been answered are they asked to sign the form. Our careful attention to these measures has consistently met the standards of national and international ethical review committees.

Results from a clinical trial in the United States and France, known as the ACTG 076 protocol, showed as long ago as 1994 that if a mother takes zidovudine (AZT) daily from the middle of her pregnancy until delivery, receives intravenous AZT during delivery, gives her infant oral AZT for the first six weeks of life and does not breast-feed, the transmission of HIV from mother to child can be reduced by two-thirds. The ACTG 076 protocol immediately became the recommended therapy in the United States. But it is not possible to simply transplant this protocol to Uganda for three main reasons: At a cost of between $800 and $1,000 per person, it is far too expensive; it requires treatment to begin in the middle of a pregnancy; and it means mothers must abstain from breast-feeding.

Some critics in the United States have asserted that we should compare new therapies with the ACTG 076 protocol rather than with a placebo. But in Uganda, the government health expenditure is $3 per person per year, and the average citizen makes less than $1 per day. We think it is unethical to impose expensive treatment protocols that could never be used here. The situations are not parallel. In America, for instance, antibiotics are often over-prescribed; but here in Uganda we have difficulty even obtaining many needed antibiotics—to treat common complaints like ear infections. It is also naive to assume that what works for Americans will work for the rest of the world. Differences in nutrition, economics, societal norms and culture, and the frequency of tropical diseases make such extrapolations dangerously ethnocentric and wrong.

Many pregnant women here never show up for prenatal care and, of those who do, 70 percent make their first visit after the 30th week of pregnancy—too late for the U.S. treatment protocol. Should we make a study available only to the minority of women who come early for care and tell the others, sorry, you came too late? We need to find treatments that will reach the most women possible—ones that can be given late in pregnancy or during labor.

There is also a huge gap between the United States and Uganda in breast-feeding practices. Should we apply the ACTG 076 protocol and tell women in the clinic not to breast-feed and instead give their babies infant formula? Access to clean water is a formidable challenge here, and we still remember the shocking epidemics of infant diarrhea and mortality in the early 1970s, when multinational companies shamelessly marketed formula in Africa. Despite the known risks of transmitting HIV through breast milk, the Ugandan Ministry of Health, UNICEF and WHO still encourage African women to breast-feed as the nutritional benefits outweigh the risks of HIV transmission.

There are other factors we need to take into account. Every day, we treat both mothers and infants for malaria and iron deficiency. Both diseases contribute to anemia, which is also a major side effect of AZT. We are worried that AZT will exacerbate anemia in women and infants here. If we are to find out whether the new treatments are safe, the best way is to compare them with a placebo. How could we evaluate the safety of a new treatment if we compared it with the treatment used in America—one that has its own side effects? Could we really tell Ugandans that we had evaluated a new therapy for side effects using the best possible methods?

The AIDS epidemic has touched all our lives. Each of the 90 staff members in the mother-child health clinic has lost a family member, a loved one or a close friend. There is no dividing line between patients with HIV and those of us who care for them. A few years ago, we all chipped in money when a staff member needed to pay for the burial of a loved one, but recently we realized that we were all giving and receiving the same.

The ethical issues in our studies are complicated, but they have been given careful thought by the local community, ethicists, physicians and activists. Those who can speak with credibility for AIDS patients in Africa are those who live among and know the people here or have some basic cross-cultural sensitivity. We are suspicious of those who claim to speak for our people, yet have never worked with them. Callous accusations may help sell newspapers and journals, but they demean the people here and the horrible tragedy that we live daily.

In the next several months, we expect to see results from our study and others like it in Ivory Coast, South Africa, Tanzania and Thailand. We hope they will help bring appropriate and safe therapies to the people of the developing world. That hope is the driving force that brings us back to our work in the clinic after each of the all-too frequent burials.

## Decision Scenario 1

Prisoners are infected with HIV at a rate that is six times higher than that for the general population. But the budget for treating those who are infected has become woefully inadequate.

When an antiviral like AZT (ZDV) was the only effective medication, the cost of treatment was about $2000 a year per prisoner, but with the coming of combination drug therapy, the cost has soared above $16,000. As a result, in many prisons in this country, the most effective treatment is simply not available to inmates.

Apart from the issue of funds to pay for combination therapy, the demands therapy makes on people are hard to satisfy within a prison. The need to take a number of drugs according to a rigid schedule is hard for the administrators of a prison to accommodate.

The proper treatment of HIV infection in prisons is of obvious value to infected prisoners, but it is also of importance from the public health point of view. Along with HIV, prisons are a reservoir of infectious diseases like tuberculosis, hepatitis, and syphilis. Eliminating them in prisons keeps released prisoners from spreading them in the society.

1. If prisoners are unable to adhere to the drug schedule, would a view like Saturn's imply that they shouldn't be treated?

2. Is it morally justifiable to imprison people for crimes, then not provide them with the most effective therapy for HIV? If it is not, then are prisoners also entitled to heart and liver transplants? On the outside, only those who have the means to pay for transplants receive them.

3. Can a case be made on utilitarian grounds that it is in the self-interest of society to provide care for infectious diseases in prison?

4. Medicaid has a program that, in conjunction with state programs, helps pay for combination drug therapy, but because of the demand and a shortage of state funds, many people who might benefit from the treatment cannot pay for it. Would it be unfair to provide free therapy to criminals, while many law-abiding citizens are unable to obtain it?

## Decision Scenario 2

Nushawn Williams was a drug dealer in the upstate New York county of Chautaqua. The number of people infected with HIV in the county is relatively low, but Williams became responsible for a significant outbreak.

In September 1996, while in the Chautaqua County jail on a charge of car theft, Williams learned he was HIV positive. Later it was established by public health officials that Williams was responsible for transmitting the virus to thirteen women and teenaged girls in Chautaqua and New York City. Further, two of the women he infected gave birth to babies who are also infected with HIV, and another of the women passed on the virus to a man she had sex with. Officials estimate that at least ten of the women were infected by Williams after he had been informed that he was infected with the AIDS virus.

After the Williams case was made public, some in the New York state legislature proposed establishing a registry of HIV-positive people and requiring that the names of each person diagnosed be reported. This would make it possible for public health authorities to monitor the behavior of HIV-infected people and intervene if, like Williams, one begins spread the virus.

Another legislative proposal prompted by the Williams case was to make it a felony for an HIV-positive person to fail to warn a sexual partner of that fact.

1. Laws already permit public health officials to register those infected with tuberculosis. Why should HIV be treated any differently? What evidence does Rabinowitz offer to support treating HIV/AIDS as just another infectious disease?

2. What are the drawbacks of establishing an HIV registry with a mandatory reporting requirement?

3. Does Mayer's position offer an alternative to the view that failing to warn a sexual partner that one is HIV positive should be made a crime punishable by imprisonment?

4. If a failure to warn is not made a crime, are there other ways to discourage HIV-infected individuals from putting other people at risk from HIV infection?

## Decision Scenario 3

"I believe it is wrong to have to submit to a blood test to get health insurance," John Tshe said. "If I test positive for HIV, which I'm virtually certain I will not do, then nobody will give me any insurance."

"That's the way it should be," Aerial Stipps said. "No insurance company should have to accept people who have an existing disease. Otherwise, you could just not pay any premiums until you got sick, and then an insurance company would be forced to accept your application and pay your bills."

"But not everyone who tests positive for HIV has AIDS," Tshe said.

"That may be true at the moment, but, let's face it, people who carry the virus are at risk for developing the disease."

"All right, but I thought insurance companies were supposed to spread the risk around."

1. Why does Gifford believe a blood test for the HIV virus should not be part of an insurance application?

2. Why do Hunter and Angoff believe it is a mistake not to allow insurance companies to test for the AIDS virus?

3. Explain the conflict between Tshe and Stipps on the matter of having an insurance company take the financial risk of paying the medical costs of someone with the AIDS virus.

4. How do Hunter and Angoff answer the charge of Gifford and Tshe that, by its very nature, insurance is supposed to spread the risk of financial loss?

## Decision Scenario 4

"You don't understand," L'aga said. "In my culture, men do what they want with women, and women are glad of it. That's why no Ta'gee man would use a condom."

"I understand what you're saying," Dr. Clare Malloy said. "But just because your culture treats women that way is not justification for putting someone at risk for infection with the AIDS virus."

1. On what grounds does Mayer support the position taken by Dr. Malloy?

2. Explain, if possible, why it isn't "cultural imperialism" for Western medicine to impose on the Ta'gee standards of sexual behavior that violate their traditional practices.

3. On what grounds might a proponent of feminist ethics object to the attitude toward women expressed by L'aga?

---

### Decision Scenario 5

"But I know Ben Therman is positive," Dr. Tad Knowles said. "He's been in therapy with me for almost five years. He tells me about his viral load and about how hard it is to take all those drugs." He shook his head. "He got the virus from the needle when he was a user, but he's been clean for a couple of years."

"He didn't tell Margo any of that," Dr. Sissa Toms said. "She's been my patient for a couple of years, and he's the first man she's had sex with in that time. I asked her if she'd checked out Ben, and she said, no, she'd been too embarrassed to ask. Besides, he was so wonderful, she was sure he would have told her."

"Oh, brother," Dr. Knowles said. "She needs to know, so she can take care of herself. What are we going to do about this?"

1. Apparent in this case is a conflict between two duties—the duty to warn and the duty to maintain patient confidentiality. How does Rabinowitz propose resolving this conflict?

2. If Dr. Knowles and Dr. Toms are in the same practice and Toms learns something that's important for Margo to know, can Toms give her the information without violating Ben's confidentiality? After all, Ben isn't her patient.

3. Explain why Rabinowitz thinks the U.S. medical system has been "hijacked" by AIDS activists.

---

### Decision Scenario 6

"I can't believe you don't tell the people you have sex with that you're infected with HIV," Angelo Mateo said.

"I thought about it," Juan Jiminez said. "I even called up the Gay Guidance Committee, and the counselor there said I should tell only if I could handle it. You know, only if it didn't make me feel ashamed or embarrassed or nothing like that."

"Yeah, but what about the other guy?" Angelo said. "You're making him take a risk without knowing it."

"I'm not *making* him," Juan said. "He's taking a risk because he wants to. He can protect himself."

"Not perfectly," Angelo said. "There can be slipups, and he could get infected."

1. On what grounds would Mayer disapprove of Juan's failure to warn a potential sexual partner?

2. Assess Juan's claim that by choosing to have sex the other person is taking a voluntary risk.

3. Why does Mayer believe agencies and counselors have been more concerned with protecting those infected with HIV than with protecting others?

## Decision Scenario 7

"It's a moral outrage to conduct a placebo-controlled clinical trial of the AIDS drug Exhiv in countries like Congo," Sally Andrews said. "We know Exhiv at the standard dose is effective against HIV, so to enroll people who may get a placebo is denying them treatment for their disease."

"Worse than that," Bob Brenner said, "it's deceiving people into thinking they're getting treated when they aren't. The investigators should be comparing Exhiv with ZDV or some other effective drug. The Congo study is no different from the Tuskegee experiments."

Charlene Stein shook her head. "You can't compare what's standard in the U.S. with practices in third-world countries. Almost no one in Congo who is HIV positive gets any sort of treatment, so the Congo study offers participants at least a fifty-fifty chance of being treated. Also, even those who receive placebos get regular medical exams and are treated for other infections they might develop. They also receive regular food supplements from the clinic, just like those getting the active drug."

"And don't forget something else," Charles LaPorte said. "Every volunteer has gone through a long and informative consent procedure. They all know they might get a placebo."

"You shouldn't discount the importance of the Congo study either," Stein said. "If Exhiv acts the ways the investigators think it will, we will be able to provide poor countries with a cheap drug to treat tens of millions of HIV-positive people that will otherwise go untreated."

"But you're sacrificing individuals to benefit others," Andrews objected. "Don't you see how wrong that is?"

1. Explain how the arguments presented by Bagenda and Musoke-Mudido might be used to support the Stein-LaPorte position.

2. On what grounds might Annas and Grodin regard the Congo study as "exploitation"?

3. Is it possible for Annas and Grodin to support the Stein-LaPorte point of view? What requirements must be satisfied, according to Annas and Grodin, to justify testing a drug in an "impoverished" country?

4. How might a utilitarian respond to Andrew's final objection? Granted Kant's notion that individuals possess inherent worth, would this objection be decisive?

Chapter 4

# Race, Gender, and Medicine

## Chapter Contents

## Classic Case Presentation

### Bad Blood, Bad Faith: The Tuskegee Syphilis Study

The way the United States Public Health Service conducted the Tuskegee Study of Untreated Syphilis in the Negro Male probably did more than any other single event to promote suspicion and distrust of physicians, treatment, and the entire medical establishment in the African-American community.

Ironically, the Tuskegee Study was the outgrowth of a program of deliberate efforts to improve the health of poor African Americans in the rural South. It is a story of good intentions paving the road to hell.

Medicine at the beginning of the twentieth century was in the process of becoming scientific, and thanks to the work of bacteriologists like Pasteur, Koch, and Ehrlich in the preceding century, it was able to diagnose and treat a wide range of infectious diseases. Perhaps more important, it had acquired a good understanding of the ways in which such diseases spread, and public health medicine had been founded to put the new knowledge into practice. The prevention of disease on a grand scale became a major goal of public health, and because preventing disease often meant treating those capable of spreading it, joint public programs of treatment and prevention became common.

Since its occurrence in Europe in the fifteenth century, syphilis had been viewed much the way AIDS was when it made its first appearance in the United States during the early 1980s. Syphilis was spread primarily by sexual contact, and so could be passed on to sexual partners. Women could infect their children, and the children could be born dead or blind and diseased. Its association with sex, particularly illicit sex, turned it into a shameful disease for many and made its diagno-

sis and treatment difficult. In the Victorian age mental hospitals housed many people suffering from the "insanity" marking the final stage of the disease, and this underscored the idea that syphilis was a disease affecting only people with loose moral conduct.

The causative agent of syphilis, a small corkscrew shaped bacterium, was isolated in 1905, and a year later August Wassermann introduced a diagnostic blood test for the disease. In 1911 Paul Ehrlich (who coined the phrase "magic bullet") tested over six hundred chemical compounds before identifying one, salvarsan (number 606), that seemed effective in the treatment of syphilis. The hope of public health officials in developed countries was that, armed with the Wassermann test and salvarsan, they could soon eradicate syphilis.

### Macon County, Alabama

Salversan did not turn out to be the miracle drug public health officials had hoped for, but even so researchers soon discovered that injections of arsenic derivatives over a period of about eighteen months would halt the disease and render it noninfectious. This kept alive the dream of eliminating syphilis, and it was in pursuit of that dream that in 1930 in Macon County, Alabama, the United States Public Health Service, building on experience recently acquired in Mississippi, initiated a program to diagnose and treat 10,000 African Americans for syphilis.

Sampling showed that 35 percent of the black population was infected with syphilis, however, and the Public Health Service soon realized it had underestimated the costs of eradicating the disease in even one county. By 1931, in the midst of the Depression, the money for the program ran out, with only some 1400 people receiving even partial treatment. Additional money from the federal government or the

Julius Rosenwald Fund, a Chicago charitable foundation that had supported the project, could not be expected.

Taliaferro Clark of the Public Health Service (PHS) was determined to salvage something from the Macon Project. He decided that if there was no money for the extensive treatments, the Service could at little cost do a six-month study of the natural history of untreated syphilis. Did the disease behave the same in Blacks as in Whites or did genetic differences make Blacks more susceptible? Or were Blacks, once infected, more resistant than Whites to the effects of the disease?

The PHS accepted Clark's proposal and, in doing so, tacitly endorsed a research program that involved deceiving a group of people about the nature of their illness and deliberately withholding potentially effective treatments from them, while giving them the impression that they were being appropriately treated. That the people were all rural, impoverished, and poorly-educated black males makes it hard to avoid the conclusion that the PHS regarded the subjects as hardly more than experimental animals.

Representatives of the PHS approached the Tuskegee Institute with its research proposal, and in 1932 Tuskegee agreed to participate in the observational study. The institute would be paid for its participation, and its interns and nurses would have the opportunity to work for the government, a major incentive during the worst of the depression in the rural South.

With the help of Tuskegee and black churches and community leaders, men were recruited for the study. They were promised free medical examinations, blood tests, and medicines. In rural Alabama, where few people, black or white, could afford to consult a physician even when sick, such an offer by an agency of the federal government seemed a golden opportunity.

## No Diagnosis, No Treatment

What the subjects weren't told was that they wouldn't be given a more specific diagnosis than "bad blood" and would be treated only with placebos. The Public Health doctors sometimes claimed that "bad blood" was the term used by rural Blacks to mean syphilis. But the term was really a catch-all category that could

include anything from iron deficiency and sickle cell disease to leukemia and syphilis. It was used to explain why people felt sluggish, tired easily, or had a low energy level.

In its primary stage syphilis causes a genital, anal, or mouth ulcer. Known as a chancre, this is a pus-filled sore teeming with bacterial spirochetes that heals within a month or two. Six to twelve weeks after infection, the disease enters its secondary stage. It is marked by skin rashes that may last for months, swollen lymph nodes, headaches, bone pain, fever, loss of appetite, and fatigue. Sores that are highly infectious may develop on the skin. The secondary stage lasts for about a year, then the disease becomes latent. During this inactive stage, which may last for many years or even a lifetime, the person seems wholly normal.

About 30 percent of the time, however, people with untreated syphilis progress to the tertiary stage. One marked effect is the destruction of the tissues making up the bones, palate, nasal septum, tongue, skin, or almost any organ in the body. The infection of the heart may lead to the destruction of the valves or the aorta, causing aneurysms that can rupture and cause immediate death. The infection of the brain can lead to general paralysis and to progressive brain damage, which produces the "insanity" noted in the nineteenth century.

Study participants diagnosed with "bad blood" were given, at different times, vials of liquids, round pills, and capsules. But the drugs were nothing more than placebos, vitamins at best, and contained no ingredient active against syphilis. A sham diagnosis was matched by a sham treatment.

Unfortunately, despite the medical counterfeiting, the disease was real enough to maim and kill. At the end of the six-month study period, the data showed that untreated syphilis in Blacks was just as deadly as in Whites. This was seen as an important and exciting finding, because it contradicted the widely-held opinion that Blacks tolerated syphilis better and were less harmed by it.

## Study Extended

Raymond A. Vonderlehr, a Public Health Service officer, obtained permission to extend the study to collect more data. An African-American nurse, Eunice Rivers, was added to the staff. She was assigned to recruit men to the study who were free of the disease and so could serve as a control group. The study came to involve six hundred black men—399 diagnosed with syphilis and 201 free of the disease.

Nurse Rivers also had the job of keeping up with the study participants and making sure they showed up for their annual examinations and tests administered by the PHS physicians. She was given a government car, and it was a sign of pride in the black community of Macon County to be driven by Miss Rivers to the school where the exams were conducted. Because the study offered participants $50 for burial expenses if they agreed to an autopsy at their death, they spoke of themselves as belonging to Nurse Rivers's Burial Society.

Reports from the Tuskegee Study were published in peer-reviewed medical journals like the *Journal of the American Medical Association,* and from time to time Public Health Service officers presented the study results to Congress. No one raised any questions about the ethics of the study or asked whether the men participating in it had been informed that they had syphilis and weren't being treated for it.

In 1938 the passage of the National Venereal Disease Control Act required the PHS to provide treatment for people suffering from syphilis or other venereal diseases, even if they couldn't afford to pay for it. Yet participants in the study were considered experimental subjects and not subject to the requirements of the law. Participants who sought treatment from venereal disease clinics were turned away.

At the outbreak of the Second World War, local draft boards were persuaded to exempt at least fifty participants from military service so their symptoms wouldn't be diagnosed and treated by military physicians. When penicillin, which is highly effective against the syphilis spirochete, became available in the mid-1940s, the PHS withheld it from the study participants. Even as participants became blind or insane, the study went on without any treatments being offered.

In 1947 Nazi physicians and scientists who had taken part in vicious, senseless, and often deadly human experiments were tried for war crimes at Nuremberg. One of the outcomes of the trial was the formulation of the Nuremberg Code to govern the participation of subjects in experimentation. (See the Briefing Session in Chapter 1.) The key element of the Code is the requirement that subjects give their free and informed consent before becoming participants. Although this requirement was consistently violated by the Tuskegee Study, even after the Nuremberg Code was enunciated, officials at the PHS failed to grasp its relevance to the research they were conducting.

## Beginning of the End

In 1964 Irwin J. Schatz, a Detroit physician responding to an article, wrote to PHS researcher Anne Q. Yobs that he was "utterly astounded by the fact that physicians allow patients with a potentially fatal disease to remain untreated when effective therapy is available," but Schatz received no reply. Two years later Peter Buxtun, a social worker hired by the PHS as a venereal disease investigator, heard rumors about the Tuskegee Study, and after reading the research publications based on it, sent a letter to the director of the Division of Venereal Disease, William J. Brown, to express his serious moral concerns about the experiment.

Buxtun received no response, but eventually, he was invited to a meeting at the headquarters of the Centers for Disease Control, and there he was verbally attacked by John Cutler, a health officer knowledgeable about the study. "He was infuriated," Buxtun said. He "thought of me as some sort of lunatic who needed immediate chastisement." Cutler explained to Buxtun the importance the experiment would have in helping physicians treat black patients with syphilis.

Buxtun left the PHS voluntarily to go to law school, but he didn't forget about Tuskegee. In 1968 he wrote another letter to Brown. Pulling few punches, he pointed out that the racial makeup of the study supported "the thinking of Negro militants that Negroes have long been used for 'medical experiments' and 'teaching cases' in the emergency wards of county hospitals." He said they could hardly be regarded as volunteers and observed that whatever justification could have been offered for the experiment in 1932 was no longer relevant. He expressed the hope that the subjects in the study would be given appropriate treatments.

This time Buxtun's letter produced action—but not much. In 1969 the Centers for Disease Control convened a panel to review the Tuskegee Study. With only one dissenting member, it concluded that the study should go on, because it had gone on so long already that treating the subjects with penicillin might cause them more harm than leaving them untreated would. (More than half of the patients treated for syphilis with penicillin suffer a severe reaction in response to the sudden killing of so many spirochetes.)

In short, treatment might cause the participants more harm than doing nothing would.

Early in July 1972 Peter Buxtun turned over the materials he had accumulated on the Tuskegee Study to Associated Press reporter Jean Heller, and on July 25, after interviewing officials in the PHS, Heller broke the story nationally.

Public anger was swift in coming. The experiment was denounced by the Assistant Secretary of Health, Education, and Welfare, who launched an investigation into why study participants never received treatment for their disease. Congressional hearings were conducted, government research agencies reviewed their recruiting practices, and human subject committees were established to oversee all research involving people.

Most important, the Tuskegee Study came to an immediate halt. It lasted for forty years, and twenty-eight of its participants had died by the time it ended. Since 1972, the federal government has paid out $10 million in out-of-court settlements to the subjects, their families, or heirs. Eight of the participants were still alive in 1998, but their number is dwindling.

On May 16, 1997, President Bill Clinton formally apologized to the survivors of the Tuskegee Study. "What is done cannot be undone, but we can end the silence," he said in a White House ceremony. "We can stop turning our heads away. We can look at you in the eye and finally say on behalf of the American people: 'What the United States did was shameful, and I am sorry.' "

# BRIEFING SESSION

Ethical and social issues connected with the health of minorities, particularly African Americans, and women have received little attention until recent decades.

Traditional Western medicine centered the great majority of its efforts on understanding and treating the disorders of the white male. The white male was implicitly taken as the standard patient and research subject. Perhaps this is not surprising, considering that the white male was also the standard physician and researcher.

Society has changed. It has become more diverse, and people of color and women in increasing numbers have become scientists and health-care professionals. Even so, the past has left both thumbprints and bruises on the present. Social inequalities, including those connected with inequalities of income, are still with us, as are entrenched differences in the ways women and people belonging to ethnic minorities are dealt with, despite changed public policies. Clashes of cultures continue to occur, particularly as an increasing number of immigrants from a variety of non-European countries become residents and citizens.

All these factors have consequences for the health of individuals belonging to groups that to various degrees have been marginalized or neglected. As a result, decisions we make about health-care policy and the treatment of individuals must take into consideration both economic and cultural differences and the ways women and minorities have been dealt with in the past.

African Americans can lay a strong claim to special attention in any discussion of social issues connected with health care. To a considerable extent, the black population continues to suffer from the effects of social prejudice, including an endemic distrust of physicians and hospitals rooted in historical and personal experience. Further, not only do African Americans constitute the largest minority in the United States, they have the highest death rate of any group, minority or not. Thus, we need to be particularly concerned about the impact of social practices and policies on the black community.

African Americans are not the only minorities with health problems, of course. American Indians have a higher level of diabetes, and Hispanic Americans suffer more from fatal and disabling strokes. Puerto Rican–American children are more prone to asthma, and tuberculosis among Asian Americans is some fifteen times higher than among Whites and twice as high as among Blacks. Each ethnic group has its own health problems, and while in some instances the problems can be connected with prejudice, negative attitudes, or flawed social policies, in other cases they may be the result of language difficulties or differences in cultural beliefs and patterns.

# African Americans and Health Care

The cost of hospitalization and treatment, the cost of insurance, and the rise of HMOs and other managed care schemes lead some observers to worry that the United States is moving in the direction of a two-tier health-care system—one for the rich and the other for everybody else. Yet in the view of many critics, the United States already has a two-tier system, only the marker for separation isn't money alone. It's also race.

The gap between the health of African Americans and that of the general population is evident in the overall mortality, infant mortality, and most major chronic and fatal diseases. While heart attacks, strokes, and cancer have declined overall, Blacks are still more likely to suffer them sooner than Whites.

The situation is tellingly reflected in a comment by Donald Berwick, a member of the President's Commission on Health Care Quality. "Tell me someone's race," says Dr. Berwick. "Tell me their income. And tell me whether they smoke. The answers to those three questions will tell me more about their longevity and health status than any other questions I could possibly ask. There's no genetic blood test that would have anything like that for predictive value."

The numbers comparing black Americans with the entire population support the view that when it comes to health, race matters very much.

## Programs Haven't Eliminated the Difference

Medicare and Medicaid, along with a variety of new social programs introduced in the 1990s, were expected to close the yawning gap between the health of Blacks and Whites, but the results have been mixed.

Research by the National Institute for Aging shows that black people enjoy eight fewer years of relatively good health than do white people or Hispanic Americans. The Institute also found that while only one-fifth of Whites from 51 to 61 described their health as fair to poor, one-third of Blacks applied the description to themselves.

Far from having diminished, the incidence of asthma, obesity, maternal mortality, and fetal alcohol syndrome in the black population has actually increased. Further, cases of all types of cancer have dropped or stayed the same for men and women of all races—except for black men. Since the early 1960s, deaths from cancer among black males have increased some 62 percent, compared with 19 percent for all American males. The incidence of prostate cancer is 30 percent higher for black men. This means they have the highest rate of cancer of any group in the nation.

In addition, while 81 percent of white men survive for at least five years after diagnosis, the figure for black men is 66 percent. (This is partly explained by the later diagnosis of the disease in

## Death Rates by Ethnicity*

|  | White | Black | Hispanic | American Indian/ Alaska Native | Asian/Pacific Islander |
|---|---|---|---|---|---|
| Total Deaths | 452.7 | 710.7 | 342.8 | 458.1 | 264.6 |
| Heart Disease | 123.6 | 188.0 | 84.2 | 97.1 | 67.4 |
| Stroke | 23.3 | 42.5 | 19.0 | 19.6 | 22.7 |
| Lung Cancer | 38.3 | 46.0 | 13.6 | 25.1 | 17.2 |
| Breast Cancer | 18.7 | 26.1 | 12.1 | 10.3 | 9.8 |
| Suicide | 11.8 | 6.1 | 6.0 | 13.4 | 5.9 |
| Homicide | 3.2 | 26.1 | 9.9 | 9.9 | 3.7 |

*Per 100,000; figures are for 1998.
*Source:* Centers for Disease Control

Blacks; because the cancer is at a later stage, its treatment is less successful.)

From 1980 to 1994 (the most recent comprehensive figures), the number of cases of diabetes increased 33 percent among Blacks—three times the increase among Whites. Infectious diseases like tuberculosis have increased among Blacks in a similar proportion.

African Americans are more likely than Whites to die of heart disease. Yet a study published in 2001 showed that black people who have a heart attack are less likely than Whites to undergo diagnostic cardiac catheterization, regardless of the race of their physicians. A review of the hospital records from various regions of the country of 40,000 Medicare patients (35,675 Whites, 4039 Blacks) who had experienced a heart attack showed that doctors referred white patients for catheterization 40 percent more often than Blacks, no matter what the physician's race.

## Deaths from Heart Disease in Men*

| African American | 398.9 |
| White | 324.7 |
| American Indian/Alaska Native | 211.7 |
| Hispanic | 212.7 |
| Asian/Pacific Islander | 196.7 |

*Per 100,000; figures are for 1999.
*Source:* Centers for Disease Control

This may happen because Whites have access to better medical care, or black patients may be more reluctant to agree to the procedure than white patients. Another possibility is that doctors may be more aggressive in treating white patients. Whatever the explanation, the findings support the general view that Blacks receive less care and less sophisticated care than Whites.

For most American women, advances in the diagnosis and treatment of breast cancer have been, to some extent, a success story. Between 1990 and 1995 the death rate from breast cancer fell 10 percent, going from 23.1 per 100,000 women to 21. But the success story didn't extend to black women. The death rate for them didn't increase, but it did remain steady at 27.5 per 100,000 women. Black women are also more than twice as likely as white women to die of breast cancer, primarily because their disease more often reaches an advanced stage before it is diagnosed and treatment is initiated.

In a 1994 study involving 1100 women (roughly half black and half white) who had just received a diagnosis of breast cancer, researchers found black women were 2.2 times more likely to die than white women. Forty percent of the higher death rate was attributed to the cancer's being more advanced when it was detected. One of the authors of the study, J. W. Eley, was satisfied with the way medicine treats breast cancer in black women, but not with the lateness of the diagnosis: "So we have to concentrate on access to mammography and physical breast exams and educating women to understanding the risk of breast cancer."

Late diagnosis wasn't the only factor involved in the higher rate of breast cancer deaths among black women, according to the researchers. In their view, 15 percent of the death rate was the result of the cancer's being more aggressive in black women. "That's not to say the difference is due to genetics," said Eley. Differences in diet or unknown environmental factors might account for the more aggressive tumors.

A hopeful sign is that since 1992 black women have been having mammograms at the same rate as white women. The decline in breast cancer deaths among Blacks should begin to approach that of Whites.

### Why the Gap?

The failure of social programs to close the health gap is a matter of considerable puzzlement to public health experts. Blacks have generally improved their status in American society over the last few decades. They have increased the level of their education, found better jobs, raised their incomes, and moved into better housing. While prejudice and discrimination have not ended, many black people have become highly successful, and even more have entered the mainstream of American life.

Despite such major changes, the health of African Americans has not improved. The gap between them and the rest of society has remained the same or even widened during the decades when so much else was getting better.

Evidence suggests African Americans as a population have a genetic predisposition to develop diseases like sickle-cell anemia and perhaps prostate cancer; they may also have a predisposition to obesity and to the hazards that accompany it, such as high blood pressure. Yet even if all such predispositions were known to have a genetic basis (and most are still matters of scientific controversy or speculation), they would still not account for the large discrepancies between Blacks and others for diseases like cancer (all forms) and for the significant differences in life spans or in the number of well years of life. Others factors have to be involved.

Blacks generally receive less health care than Whites, and often it is received later in an illness when it is not as likely to be effective. Also, sometimes the care delivered is not as good as that delivered to Whites. Some evidence indicates that when white patients and black, both with insurance, are hospitalized for a heart attack, white patients receive more advanced care more often than black patients.

A greater proportion of African Americans are poor and so are more likely to lack insurance or means to pay for medical care. This may keep more Blacks out of doctor's offices or hospitals. Yet it can't be the whole explanation of the gap between the health of Blacks and the rest of the population. Hispanic Americans are also poor and are even less likely to have health insurance. Yet data from the Centers for Disease Control indicate that they stay healthy longer than all other groups.

Also, even when Blacks have adequate insurance, they don't always make use of it. A study carried out by Roshan Bastani, an expert on cancer and minorities, found that when white women were diagnosed with a breast abnormality, almost 99 percent of them returned to their physicians for follow-up treatment. However, when the same diagnosis was made in a group of minority women, who were predominantly Black or Hispanic, only 75 percent returned for additional care. "Part of this has to do with attitude," according to Bastani. "Like, 'It may go away' or 'I don't have sick leave, so if I go in for this, I'm going to lose a day's pay.'"

Prejudice may also play a role in determining not only the quality of health care provided, but in directly affecting health. A 1996 study of hypertension found that hypertension may be connected with the way black people respond to racial discrimination. When working class Blacks experienced two or more cases of discrimination (such as in looking for a job), they had higher normal blood pressure than working class Whites or black professionals. Black professionals, by contrast, who were aware of experiencing cases of racial discrimination and challenged them, were at a lower risk of developing higher blood pressure. However, as the investigators acknowledged, the study, while suggestive, did not give a full account of why Blacks are more likely to be hypertensive than other groups.

A study published in 2002 by the Institute of Medicine found that members of minorities are less likely than Whites to be treated appropriately for heart disease (including coronary-artery-bypass surgery), receive kidney transplants or dialysis, be tested and treated appropriately for cancer, and receive combination therapy for HIV infection. Such findings lead some researchers to suspect that subtle or unconscious racism may be a factor affecting the health care of black people.

## The Tuskegee Effect

The medical establishment—physicians, nurses, therapists, clinics, and hospitals—is viewed with suspicion and distrust by millions of poor people in the United States. Distrust is especially high among black people, but it extends to white, Hispanic, and Indian people as well.

While public programs like Medicaid and Medicare now offer mostly equal care to all people, this was not the case in the past. Those unable to pay physicians avoided consulting them until their illness or that of a family member was so serious that desperation forced them to act. If they were hospitalized, it was most likely in a charity ward. They were dependent on the benevolence of their physicians and, given the paternalistic attitude prevalent in medicine until recent years, constrained to do what they were told without asking for information or explanations. Further, the doctrine of informed consent had not yet achieved general acceptance in a form offering much protection to a patient's autonomy and well-being. Hence, the poor often received second-rate medical care and, without being told anything in useful detail, could become the subjects of medical or surgical experimentation.

The emblem of the way in which the trust of black patients was taken advantage of and betrayed by the biomedical establishment is the Tuskegee Study. (See the Classic Case Presentation: "Bad Blood, Bad Faith.") But while Tuskegee illustrates the most flagrant abuse of medical authority, it was preceded by a more general pattern of abuse.

The distrust of physicians and hospitals was present before Tuskegee, which only confirmed and reinforced the fears and doubts of people in the black community. But all poor people knew you couldn't trust doctors and hospitals to look out for your interest. Thus, while we may talk of a "Tuskegee effect" to suggest why Blacks are suspicious of medicine, the phrase isn't historically accurate. (Vanessa Gamble has documented the distrust as preceding Tuskegee by decades.)

Also, even now those who have never heard of the Tuskegee study are distrustful. The distrust has been passed along to them as part of the lore of what's involved in coping with being poor. Probably at least years and perhaps decades must pass before the medical establishment can overcome the faults of its own past and earn the trust of all people, whatever their income or race.

## AIDS

HIV/AIDS is a major health problem among African Americans. In 1999 the death rate per 100,000 of population for black males from AIDS was about 61; for black females it was 27. (The comparable figures for Whites were 10 and 2.) In 2001 the number of black males with AIDS was 107 per 100,000, and the number of black females was 47. For Whites the figures are 14 and 2.

Protease-inhibiting drugs are effective in reducing levels of virus in people who are HIV positive, and when the drugs are used in combination with others, life-threatening or debilitating infections can often be brought under control. Yet the distrust of the medical establishment by African Americans hampers the efforts of the medical community to deliver the appropriate care to many who are HIV positive or have developed AIDS.

People delay seeking care until they are suffering from consequences of the disease that are harder to bring under control, and some begin treatment only to drop out because they don't trust those involved in their care to be acting in their best interest. Some are afraid they are being used as subjects in life-threatening experiments which they are told nothing about.

With respect to HIV, the distrust of the medical establishment extends further and deeper than doubt about receiving good care. A significant number of people in the black community believe that AIDS is a genocidal plot against them. A study by the University of North Carolina at Chapel Hill discovered that about 33 percent of 1054 churchgoers in five cities believed that HIV/AIDS was created by Whites as a form of genocide, and another 30 percent said they weren't sure. Other studies have produced similar results.

A variant of the story is that although a cure for AIDS exists, it is not being used, because the disease affects many more black people than white. As soon as enough Blacks die off, "the doctors" will start using the cure.

## Clinical Trials

African Americans participate in clinical trials of new drugs at a rate significantly below their number in the population. Some fear they are being used as "guinea pigs" by physicians who will "poison" them with experimental drugs. The result is unfortunate both for individuals and for the group. Without a representative number of black participants, it is impossible to acquire the data needed to determine whether Blacks respond to drugs and drug regimens in the same way as the population in general. Not until ten years after the introduction of ACE inhibitor beta blockers and converting enzyme inhibitors were researchers able to compile enough data to realize that these groups of drugs are less effective in the treatment of hypertension among Blacks than in Whites.

By not participating in clinical trials, African Americans can also miss the chance to benefit from experimental drugs. Until recently, promising drugs like taxol for breast cancer and anti-retroviral drugs for HIV infection could be obtained by patients only through programs of experimental investigation. While receiving experimental drugs can be a mixed blessing for patients, everyone should at least have the opportunity to decide whether to participate in a drug trial on the basis of relevant considerations. For many African Americans, distrust does not permit them to get so far as to make an informed choice about participation.

African Americans are underrepresented in drug trials for reasons other than their own suspicion. A 1996 survey of some 500 physicians in central Tennessee found that black urban physicians were more likely to refer black and white AIDS patients to clinical trials than were white or rural physicians. In interviews, the nonreferring physicians explained that they didn't think the drug testing system was set up to deal with AIDS patients who were African American, women, or IV-drug abusers.

Factors such as the costs of transportation and the difficulty of scheduling office visits also play a role in keeping African Americans from enrolling in clinical trials. Further, one study has shown that black women, in particular, tend to consider clinical trials unethical. They feel that researchers don't care about them and that by participating in research they would deprive themselves of the best treatment available.

The traditional underrepresentation of black people in clinical trials is likely to change eventually under the influence of a new federal policy. Since 1993 the National Institutes of Health has required that all NIH-supported biomedical research include minorities and women, unless there are clear and compelling reasons to justify their exclusion.

Implementing the mandate, however, is likely to require special recruitment efforts. Patients need to be educated about clinical trials and their importance, more African-American health-care personnel need to be involved, and attempts need to be made to involve community groups. Most of all a strong and continuing effort must be made to earn and deserve the trust of the black community.

## Children's Health

Surveys show that twice as many African-American children as white children under the age of fifteen are in fair or poor health. To a considerable extent, this is the result of poverty. In 2000 the poverty rate for black children was 31 percent, while the rate for white children was 12 percent. Lack of money can translate into poor diet, unsafe housing, and inadequate health care.

Even a small sampling of relevant statistics shows the impact of poverty:

- In 2000, 21 percent of poor respondents reported fair or poor health, compared with 6.3 percent of non-poor respondents.

- A study of women who plan and prepare their family's main meal found that

African-American women were less likely than white women to know the relationship between diet and health.

- In 2000, only 71 percent of children living in poverty received the standard course of immunization, while 78 percent of those living at or above the poverty line were immunized.

- In 1999, the infant mortality rate for African Americans was twice the rate of the general population.

- In 1999–2000, 19 percent of black children under 18 made no health care visits to an office or clinic.

Disproportionate numbers of African-American babies are born with low birth weight (under 5.5 pounds). These infants are more likely to die or suffer from such severe long-term disabilities as brain damage and blindness.

For many years, the mortality rates have been twice as high for African Americans as for Whites, and in 1999 the rate for Blacks was more than twice that of Whites. The infant mortality gap between Blacks and Whites can be explained in part by such factors as a greater frequency of drug use among black women and a lower level of nutrition, but even when these factors are taken into account, a gap still remains. Why it does has become something of a medical mystery.

The health of African-American children is likely to be improved by a 1997 federal program. Under the program, $20 billion will be available to states over a period of five years for health care for children in families not eligible for Medicaid. Each state must develop eligibility requirements and provide matching funds. States are also required to pay for such health services as immunizations, X rays, laboratory tests, outpatient care, and hospital stays.

## Organ Transplants

African Americans are at a higher risk for hypertension and kidney disease than the general population, and this increases the chances that they will eventually suffer from kidney failure and need a transplant. Blacks make up 12 percent of the population, but they constitute 30 percent of end-stage kidney disease patients needing dialysis. They also constitute 30 percent of those on the waiting list for a kidney transplant.

About 20 percent of African Americans needing a kidney transplant are likely to do better with a kidney donated by someone of their own race. Kidneys are matched with patients not only by blood type, but by protein antigens, and the closer the match, the more likely the transplanted kidney will "take." Kidney donation by Blacks is significantly lower than donation by Whites, but from a rate of 8 per million in 1980, it rose to 20 per million in 1996.

Why don't African Americans donate organs as often as others? Some people don't donate for personal religious reasons (no organized religion in the United States objects to organ donation), but many are simply inadequately informed about how donated organs are distributed and don't trust the fairness of the system.

"There's a belief that only rich Whites, especially those who are famous, become organ recipients," said Jackie Lynch, a recruiter of minorities for the Regional Organ Bank of Illinois. "They don't see a black role, other than as those who are dying and donating the organs." (Ironically, because of their relatively low rate of donation, it is Blacks who receive a disproportionate number of organs.) Lynch said that black families sometimes ask his non-black colleagues to leave the room so they can ask him about the fairness of the organ distribution system. The rise in organ donation among African Americans suggests it will continue to increase to at least the level of other ethnic groups. For this to happen, however, more public education about donation and the fairness of the system is needed. Black people will have to come to trust that the organs they donate will be used to save or extend the lives of people who may belong to any ethnic or racial group.

## Closing the Gap

Discrimination, genetics, cultural patterns, education, and personal history are among the numerous factors that play a role in producing the relatively poor health of African Americans in the United States. But there are signs that improvements are taking place. In 1993 the overall death rate for Blacks was 785 per 100,000; for Whites it was 465. In 1995 (the latest available figures), the rate for Blacks had dropped to 571. This is still considerably higher than the 365 rate for Whites, but the size of the decline is greater.

Also, the Centers for Disease Control, in a 2002 survey of seventeen "health indicators," reported that death rates from lung, breast, colorectal, and prostate cancer fell for all groups during the 1990s. The decline was not as much for Blacks as for the general population, but the trend was in the right direction.

New federal and state programs to assist children living in poverty and provide prenatal care for expectant mothers should eventually be reflected in improved health statistics. New federal requirements that African Americans be included in clinical trials have been accompanied by discussions in the research community of ways to recruit Blacks by providing them with information and transportation expenses and making it easier for them to become part of a study. Organ donations by African Americans have increased over the years, and as more black people come to have confidence in the integrity and fairness of the distribution system, donations should continue to rise.

Perhaps the most important change likely to lead to improvements in the health of African Americans is the development of trust in the black community for the medical establishment. The Tuskegee effect is likely to linger for years, and to overcome it the medical establishment must make a special effort to earn and deserve the trust of black patients. Treating patients with respect, taking seriously their reservations about diagnostic tests or proposed treatments, and tak-ing the time to educate them about their medical condition and the therapy for it are important in securing the trust of any group of patients. If African Americans are more distrustful, it's because they have more reason to be.

# American Indians and Alaska Natives and Health Care

With respect to health care, the native peoples of the United States have a relationship with the federal government shared by no other minority group. As a result of the historical evolution of a hodgepodge of treaties and laws, the United States is obligated to build hospitals and provide physicians and medical supplies to see to the health needs of the native people. Finding ways to discharge this obligation eventually led to the creation of the Indian Health Service.

## Indian Health Service

More than 2 million Indians and Alaska natives live in the United States, and the Indian Health Service (IHS) serves about 1.5 million of them. It operates 76 clinics and 42 hospitals and contracts with a number of tribes to administer their own heath care in 64 clinics and 8 hospitals located on Indian reservations and in 172 village clinics in Alaska. The IHS also runs a small urban Indian Health Program with clinics and referral centers that is intended to provide health resources to those who live off reservations.

The IHS budget is around $2 billion, and while this may seem like a lot of money, given the size of the population that must be served, the per capita expenditure is less than half the average for other U.S. citizens. For each Native American, the spending on health care is $1500, while for someone in the general population it is $3100.

Severe budget constraints have put the IHS in the business of rationing care, and not even all necessary health services can be provided to their patient population. Only about fifteen of the 500 IHS health facilities can supply patients with the basic health benefits outlined in the American Health Security Act.

Also, the distribution of resources is skewed and inequitable, with some geographical regions or locations within regions allocated resources to provide a wider range of care than others. The discrepancies are often the result of such factors as historical commitments, population density, and relative isolation. Indians who live in areas without hospitals or clinics within a reasonable distance are often de facto denied the care supplied to others.

Health is generally connected to a large extent with income, and the income of Indians on reservations is substantially below that of the U.S. average. Median household income in the United States is $30,000, while that of Indians is below $20,000. About half the population of Indians and Alaskan Natives live on reservations, and 46 percent of them are unemployed. Of those who have jobs, only 28 percent earn as much as $7000 a year. Most Indians who receive health care are almost completely dependent on its being provided by the Indian Health Service. Because the IHS lacks the budget to provide a level of heath care comparable to that provided to private citizens or military veterans, Indians and Alaskan Natives have no guarantee of receiving what for others is the basic minimum of care.

## Causes of Death

Many of the causes of death among Indians, as among other populations, are related to lifestyle. Although heart disease and cancer are among the leading killers of Indians, the rates are lower for Indians than for the general population. But alcoholism and alcohol abuse are associated with five of the top ten causes of death. This includes accidents and violence connected with excessive drinking.

## Leading Causes of Death

| | American Indian or Alaska Native* | U.S.* |
|---|---|---|
| Heart disease | 171.4 | 267.8 |
| Cancer | 126.4 | 202.7 |
| Accident | 61.1 | 35.9 |
| Diabetes | 50.2 | 25.2 |
| Stroke | 39.7 | 61.8 |
| Liver disease | 28.2 | 9.7 |

*Per 100,000 population.
*Source:* U.S. Department of Health and Human Services, *Health, United States, 2002* (Washington, D.C.: Government Printing Office)

The two leading causes of death for those 15–44 are accidents and liver disease. Research shows that Indian women die from liver disease at 3 times the rate of black women and 6 times the rate for white women. Women account for half of all deaths of Indians from cirrhosis. The rate of alcohol-related mortality for Indians in the age group 35–44 is 5 times the overall U.S. rate, and for those 45–54, it is 8 times the U.S. rate.

While it has been suggested for decades that Indians are genetically predisposed to become alcoholics, the best evidence at present indicates that historical, cultural, and social factors, not genes, are responsible for the high incidence of alcoholism in Indian populations.

Diabetes, like liver disease, is connected with alcohol consumption, and diabetes is a major health problem in Indian communities. Three times as many Indian men and women die from diabetic complications as do in the general U.S. population. Type II or "adult onset" diabetes is responsible for the high rate of amputations among Indian women. Critics claim that IHS policies restrict the foot care diabetics need for the treatment of ulcers and tissue breakdown and that, as a result, a disproportionate number of diabetics lose legs that could be saved with proper medical care. Sadly, 70 percent of the amputees will have a second leg amputated within five years of the first.

Diabetes among Indians may be connected with both predisposing genetic factors and diet. Some evidence suggests that when Indians eat their traditional foods and avoid the high carbohydrate–high fat diet that has become typical in the United States, obesity goes down and the incidence of diabetes declines.

Although the rate for cancer is lower than for the U.S. population as a whole, in Indians it is diagnosed later on the average. This means that the death rate for the disease is greater. Certainly screening and prevention services are woefully inadequate. Some of the clinics have historically treated mammography not as a screening technique, but as a diagnostic test to be used only when a women is discovered to have a lump in her breast. The severe budget limitation of the IHS has seriously restricted the use of procedures that are not immediately life-saving.

## Summary

The American Indian and Native Alaskan people are caught in a situation in which they have little control over their health care. The federal government is responsible for seeing to their welfare, but generally the government has done a poor job. Facilities and funding remain inadequate.

The health status of Native Americans does show some signs of improving, however. The population is growing at the rate of 2.7 percent per year, and the median age is 22.6, compared to the general population age of 30. This partly reflects the fact that from 1955 to 2002 the infant mortality rate fell 85 percent. During this same period, life expectancy for both males (69.1 years) and females (77.5 years) has increased 19 percent. Also, the mortality rate for tuberculosis, once a major killer, has declined 96 percent, and maternal mortality has dropped 91 percent.

The need for increasing the level and quality of care is pressing, and only a strong and continuing political and financial commitment can eventually raise the health of the Indian population to the level of that of the general population. Evidence also suggests that prevention and treatment programs that build on Indian cultures and make use of traditional ways are more likely to succeed than ones imported from the majority culture.

## Asian and Pacific Islanders and Health Care

The hospital staff was worried about Mrs. Tai Li. After giving birth to a healthy baby boy, the thirty-two-year-old woman wouldn't accept the cold water that was offered to her. Her refusal continued for the next five days, with the nurses trying to give her juice and even soft drinks. She was on the verge of becoming seriously dehydrated, and her physicians were on the verge of giving her fluid intravenously, so a translator was called in to explain the situation to her.

As soon as the translator arrived, the situation became clear. Mrs. Li was refusing to drink, because all the beverages that had been offered to her were cold. In Chinese culture, it is thought to bring bad luck to the child for the mother to consume anything cold immediately after childbirth. She willingly accepted the cups of tea that were then offered to her.

By the year 2010 the Asian American–Pacific Islander (AAPI) population will have increased by more than 100 percent, making it the fastest growing minority group. In 1980 the number of people of Asian origin in the United States was roughly 3.5 million. By the time of the 1990 census, it had more than doubled to 7.2 million, and it has continued to increase. About 62 percent of Asian Americans are foreign born, and more than 75 percent speak a language other than English at home.

Present day Asian Americans and Pacific Islanders are not a homogenous group. Rather, the category is made up of as many as forty-eight distinct ethnic populations. Those of Chinese, Japanese, Filipino, Vietnamese, or Hawaiian ancestry, for example, all qualify as members of the group, but all have different cultural backgrounds. They differ in beliefs, diets, lifestyles, and general attitude toward life, and all these factors may play a role in determining their health or the way that they seek health care. Capturing much of importance that is true of the group in a generalization is virtually impossible.

## Health Profile

Partly because the Asian-American population has increased so rapidly, it has not been studied by epidemiologists and medical sociologists as much as other minority groups. Even so, it is possible to make out some of the significant features of its health profile by looking at death rates for major diseases. (At the moment, state agencies reporting health data usually do not distinguish among the various groups.)

Asian-American females die of cancer at a rate of about 74 per 100,000 and males as a rate of 89; comparable figures for Whites are 201 and 224. Lung cancer kills Asian-American females at a rate of 13.5 per 100,000 and males at 22.8. Breast cancer for Asian-American women is comparatively low at a rate of 10.4 per 100,000, compared to a population figure of 29.5.

Death by stroke, at a rate of 28.8 per 100,000 for Asian-American women, is less than half that for white women, and a rate of 28.6 for Asian-American men is somewhat over half that for white men. The rate of death by heart disease for Asian-American women is 70 per 100,000 and much lower than the 286.6 per 100,000 rate for white females. The rate for Asian-American males, 99 per 100,000, is closer to that for white males, 264, but still much lower. Hypertension is less common among Asian Americans, but it is also less successfully controlled.

Deaths from chronic lower respiratory disease among Asian Americans, at 7.2 per 100,000

for women and 14 for men, is near the low end of the population spread. The death rate from AIDS is also low, negligible for Asian-American females and 1.5 per 100,000 for males.

Hepatitis B is endemic in the Asian-American community. The infection occurs in the U.S. population at a rate of only 0.2 percent, but for those claiming origin from China, Korea, Philippines, Southeast Asia, or the Pacific Islands, the rate of infection ranges from 5 to 15 percent.

About 11 percent of those infected are pregnant women, and 54 percent of all infants that carry hepatitis B in the United States are born to these women. Most of the women are foreign born and have received late or no prenatal care and have not been tested for the virus. The good news, though, is that from 1987 to 1995, the number of cases among AAPI children declined, even though it remains two to three times higher than for other children.

The tuberculosis incidence for AAPIs is about five times higher than the rate for the general population. What is more, the rate is increasing for them, while it is decreasing for others. From 1988 to 1995, it went from 36 to 46 per 100,000.

The population of Asian-American women is not receiving proper screening for cancer. While only 5 percent of white women report they have never had a Pap smear to test for cervical cancer, 45 percent of Chinese-American women and 51 percent of Vietnamese-American women say they have never had one.

The situation is comparable for mammograms. Seventy-one percent of white women have had mammograms within the last two years, but only 53 percent of Asian-American women and almost no Native Hawaiians or Pacific Islanders.

On the positive side, life expectancy for Asian Americans and Pacific Islanders is more than 80 years, about five years higher than that of the general population. Japanese have the highest life expectancy at 82.1 years, while native Hawaiians have the shortest at 68.3 years.

## Summary

As much as or more than those belonging to any minority population, the majority of Asian American–Pacific Islanders face formidable barriers to acquiring appropriate medical care. The rate of poverty and unemployment is high, making it difficult for them to obtain private insurance or purchase health care. But perhaps more important, because so many are foreign born and have come to the United States relatively recently, they speak little or no English. Even those who might qualify for Medicaid or Medicare programs may be unable to take advantage of them. Either they don't know about the programs or, if they do, they aren't able to cope with the demands of the social and medical systems to gain access.

Moreover, as a non-Western population with many new immigrants, AAPIs are more likely to come into conflict with the medical establishment. Their entrenched cultural beliefs and practices include ones about the causes of diseases and the proper way to prevent or deal with them. Effective treatments by Western medicine may be delayed or replaced by less effective or even harmful folk treatments. The need for medical care may not be recognized or may be delayed, and the importance of taking prescribed drugs, adhering to a treatment regimen, or taking advantage of life-saving surgery may not be appreciated or even accepted.

# Hispanic Americans/Latinos and Health Care

Like the "Asian American" category, the "Hispanic American" or "Latino" category is made up of people from more than twenty countries. It includes those who identify themselves as having their origins in Mexico, Puerto Rico, Cuba, Central or South America, Spain, and some locations in the Caribbean. While all the subgroups may share a Spanish or Latino heritage, they differ significantly from one another. Data on Hispanics are usually not collected in terms of such refined categories; most data are about Mexican Americans.

In 2002, 32.8 million Hispanic Americans were living in the United States. They constitute roughly 12 percent of the total population, and approximately one in eight people is of Hispanic background. In terms of origin, 66 percent were Mexican, 19 percent Puerto Rican, 15 percent from Central or South America or the Caribbean, while 6 percent were classified as "Other Hispanics." By the year 2010, demographers estimate that Hispanics will become the largest minority group in the United States and constitute about 15 percent of the population.

Hispanic individuals are the youngest of any minority group. In 2000, 35.7 percent were under 18, compared with 23.5 percent for non-Hispanic Whites. A smaller proportion of Hispanics fell in to the 18 to 64 category—the group most often in need of medical care.

About a quarter of the Hispanic population lives in poverty, however, and Hispanic families are more likely to be living in poverty than non-Hispanic Whites. Similarly, with the exception of those of Cuban origin, Hispanics make up the lowest proportion of people with at least a high school diploma. Both income and education have an effect on the medical care people receive, with high-income, high-education groups receiving the best care.

### Health Profile

The Hispanic population is perhaps the healthiest of minority groups. AIDS and lung disease kill a disproportionate number of Hispanic males. Even so, compared with the population as a whole, Hispanics are doing well.

## Leading Causes of Death*

|  | Males | Females | Population |
|---|---|---|---|
| AIDS | 11.5 | 2.2 | 5.4 |
| Lung disease | 45.5 | 9.8 | 8.4 |
| Lung cancer | 15.1 | 7.5 | 55.8 |
| Breast cancer | — | 9.9 | 29.5 |
| Cancer (all) | 67.7 | 61.4 | 201.6 |
| Stroke | 17.8 | 19.9 | 61.4 |
| Heart disease | 86.0 | 79.0 | 265.9 |
| All causes | 515 | 274.4 | 77.0 |

*Per 100,000; figures are for 1999.
*Source:* U.S. Department of Health and Human Services, *Health, United States, 2002* (Washington, D.C.: Government Printing Office)

### Recent Changes

Several recent changes reveal that in some respects the health of Hispanic Americans has taken a turn for the worse compared with the rest of the population. A 2002 study revealed that the incidence of invasive cervical cancer is about twice that for Hispanic women as for others (16.9 vs. 8.9 per 100,000). Another survey, also published in 2002, showed that the incidence of syphilis was three times that of Whites, and that tuberculosis was six times as high. Most striking, the survey showed that homicide was six times as high for Hispanics as for Whites. This makes it a significant public-health problem for Hispanics, as it is for African Americans.

Diabetes is another reason for concern. While the prevalence of the diseases in the U.S. population increased from 28 to 30 cases per thousand in less than a decade, for Mexican Americans the increase went from 54 to 66. Also, the number of pregnancies among Hispanic females between 15 and 19 has increased from 143 per thousand to 180. However, the number of pregnant Hispanic women receiving care in the first trimester of pregnancy increased to 74 percent in 1999.

Some other changes have also been positive. The most recent data show that 86.4 percent of Hispanic-American women who are 50 or older have received a breast examination and a mammogram. Data gathered in 2002 showed that the death rate from breast cancer in Hispanic women had declined by 13 percent. (It fell 18 percent for Whites, but only 4 percent for Blacks.) Further, the proportion of Hispanic-American women receiving a Pap test has increaseed from about 75 percent ten years ago to over 91 percent today.

While these figures are encouraging, the proportion of Hispanic Americans without health-care coverage increased from 31.5 in 1999 to 35.4 in 2002, a much higher rate than for any group except American Indians. This is a trend going in the wrong direction.

## Women and Health Care

Researcher Charles H. Hennekens showed in a 1982 study, the Physician's Health Survey, that small, regular doses of aspirin could reduce the likelihood of a first heart attack by as much as 30 percent. This was an important finding from the standpoint of preventive medicine, and it served as the basis for physicians to recommend that those at risk of heart disease take aspirin in low doses prophylactically.

But did the study's finding also apply to women?

Critics immediately pointed out that the 22,071 subjects in Hennekens' study were all men. What grounds were there to be sure that the same measure that prevented a heart attack in men would also prevent one in women? Why weren't women included in the study?

Cardiovascular disease kills about as many women as men.

Hennekens replied to his critics that the study participants had all been physicians, and at the time the study was initiated, only about 10 percent of physicians in the country were women. The population was simply not large enough to supply him with subjects. Also, twice as many women as men would have been needed in the study to get the same statistically significant result, because while one in five men has a heart attack by age sixty, only one in seventeen women does.

"We didn't want to neglect women," Hennekens said later, "but we couldn't study them in that population."

Whatever the merits of Hennekens' explanation, the gender-exclusive character of the study led many advocates for women to look at other scientific studies. When they did, many decided women weren't being adequately represented as subjects in medical research. Important studies, such as the Multiple Risk Factor Intervention Trial (MR FIT) involved 15,000 men and no women. Drug trials were just as exclusive. The great majority of tests to determine the safety and effectiveness of new drugs included no women. They were routinely excluded on the basis of concerns about the effects of the drugs on actual or future pregnancies. Pregnant women were excluded because new drugs of unknown effects might harm the fetus and cause birth impairments.

Also, because some women might be pregnant without knowing it or become pregnant while taking the experimental drug, most researchers considered it safer and easier simply to exclude women of childbearing age. Some drugs, they said, might also affect a woman's potential for becoming pregnant. Further, researchers argued, the variation in hormone levels associated with menstruation made it difficult to separate the effects of a drug from the effects of biochemical changes.

A result of this systematic exclusion of women, as advocates pointed out, is that most drugs and treatment regimens have been developed (until recently) using data from studies conducted exclusively with men as subjects. For the most part, it has simply been taken for granted that the best drugs and most effective treatments for men are also the best and most effective for women. Yet without studies that include women or ones that focus on the way women respond to treatment, there is no way of knowing to what extent a particular drug (or a certain dose of a drug) or treatment may benefit women. Man cannot be the measure of all things medical.

## Include Women, Study Women

Beginning in the late 1980s, advocates for women, armed with facts about the exclusionary practices of scientific research, began pressing researchers, first of all, to include more women in their studies. It was unacceptable to exclude women from all studies on the slim grounds that a woman's capacity to become pregnant might sometimes lead to harm. Most often, pregnancy was at best a speculative consideration, and women deserved to have confidence that conclusions about their medical treatments were based on data acquired from studies including women. What could be more relevant to predicting the response of women to a drug than a study of the drug that included women as subjects?

Second, advocates demanded that more attention be paid to the variations in responses between men and women. They pointed out that even when women were included in a study, investigators typically failed to make an effort to determine how the gender of the research subjects affected the study's results.

For example, although asthma deaths increase in women during the time before menstruation occurs, researchers have not attempted to determine whether the hormonal changes taking place during menstruation affect the bronchi or interact with asthma medications. Differences in men and women that are connected with differences in responses are often ignored and simply buried in statistical measurements that count men and women as the same.

Third, advocates for women also claimed that health problems specific to women have received relatively little attention from researchers. Perhaps because researchers are predominantly male, they have traditionally focused on problems or diseases affecting mostly men. Thus, data are scarce on the effects of hormone replacement therapy on heart disease, of a low-fat diet on breast cancer, or of alcohol consumption on ovarian cancer.

Fourth, advocates demanded that women receive medical care equal to that of men. One study found that women with kidney disease sufficiently severe to require dialysis were 30 percent less likely to receive a kidney transplant than were men. A second study found there was a 25 percent difference. Moreover, men in every age category were more likely to receive a transplant than were women in the same category.

Similar disparities were found in diagnostic testing. All smokers, regardless of gender, have the same risk of lung cancer, yet a study found that men were twice as likely as women to be tested for the disease. Also, a 1987 study found that men with symptoms of heart disease were much more likely to receive a diagnostic cardiac catheterization than women.

Interpreting diagnostic results showed the same sort of bias as did the tests themselves. When abnormal results were found in thallium scans of the heart, women were more than twice as likely to have their symptoms attributed to psychiatric or noncardiac causes than were men.

### Additional Support

In 1985 the Task Force on Women's Health Issues of the United States Public Health Service concluded that because of the lack of research data on women, it was difficult to assess women's health needs. This conclusion was taken by advocates to endorse the view that gender bias had deprived us of the information needed to recognize and deal with the health needs of women. Women, it appeared clear, were being shortchanged.

The American Medical Association's Council on Ethical and Judicial Affairs 1990 Report "Gender Disparities in Clinical Decision-Making" offered additional support to the contention that women were not being treated fairly by the American health care system. The Council reviewed forty-eight studies published in a variety of medical journals between 1970 and 1990. The basic question was whether gender improperly affected the amount and kind of medical care patients received. (The findings on diagnostic testing and kidney transplants have already been mentioned.)

The Council's conclusion was that there were definitely "non-biological or nonclinical factors which affect clinical decision making." Although the Council did not have the data to identify the exact nature of the nonclinical factors, it pointed to their existence as a cause for concern.

The Council recommended that "physicians examine their practices and attitudes for the influence of social or cultural biases which could be inadvertently affecting the delivery of medical care" and eliminate them. Furthermore, "more research in women's health issues and women's health problems should be pursued." The Council ended by encouraging the promotion of more female physicians to positions of leadership in teaching, research, and the practice of medicine.

### Positive Changes

Partly in response to political pressure from the women's movement but also as a result of the recognition that women had a good case and hadn't been dealt with fairly in medical research and practice, several significant changes were made in the treatment of women by the biomedical research establishment.

In 1990 the National Institutes of Health established the Office of Research on Women's Health. It was given the responsibility of determining what research of benefit to women needed to be done and of making sure women were included in future federally-funded research projects intended to benefit both genders.

It is currently sponsoring research into heart disease and cancer among women.

Researcher Charles Hennekens, who had conducted the study showing the benefit of aspirin therapy in preventing heart attacks in men, proposed a study to establish the effects of aspirin in preventing heart attacks in women. Scientists who reviewed the proposal for the federal granting agency to which it was submitted, the National Heart, Lung, and Blood Institute, rejected the proposal twice. They held that the preliminary data did not support a case for repeating Hennekens' original study with women. The proposal was rejected a third time on a 5-to-4 vote on technical grounds, although the reviewing panel said that determining the benefits and risks of aspirin therapy in a healthy population of women was of "the highest priority."

The director of the Institute, Claude J. Lenfant, decided to set aside the recommendation of the grant reviewing panel and approve the $10 million needed to fund the study. In addition to intense Congressional interest in the project, he cited the potential health significance of the study. He mentioned several differences between men and women with respect to heart disease:

- Women develop heart disease about ten years later than men and tend to be twenty years older than men when they have a first heart attack.

- Women learn they have heart disease when they experience the chest pain of angina, men when they have a heart attack.

- A first heart attack is more often fatal in women, and the death rate during the following year is greater.

- Women have more painless heart attacks.

- Women suffer more complications from clot-dissolving drugs used to treat heart attacks.

Hennekens' study was designed to include 45,000 women nurses. The sample size was designed to be large enough to assess whether the findings apply to Whites, Blacks, Hispanics, and other minorities.

The funding for programs affecting women's health significantly increased during the 1990s. This is particularly true for breast cancer, a disease of particular concern to women. In 1990 the federal funding for breast cancer research was $90 billion, and in 1997 it rose to a phenomenal $600 billion. The increase in research funding for studying health issues affecting women has been accompanied by an increase in the number of professional journals devoted to women's health. At least eight new titles have appeared since 1990.

The increase in research findings concerning women is also reflected in the increase in the number of publications. From 1986 to 1991, Medline, the database for medical research, listed 159 articles with the key words "women's health." For the period 1992 to 1996, the number had increased to 1426. More recent numbers suggest a continuing upward trend.

## Backlash or Balance?

In the view of some critics, the success of advocates for women in shifting the focus of research and funding onto women's health issues has produced a bias against men's health, with a disproportionate amount of resources being spent on women.

First, the claim that diseases affecting women have been studied less than those affecting men has been used by advocates as a basis for demanding that women's diseases receive more attention. The factual basis for this claim has been denied by some, however. Curtis L. Meinert, an epidemiologist at Johns Hopkins University, asserts that when research published in the period 1980 to 1993 is surveyed, the number of projects focusing only on men is virtually matched by ones focusing only on women.

Second, critics charge, the politics of health care have been manipulated to favor women, even when the scientific evidence does not support the demands made by advocates. The principal example of this was a policy change concerning the use of mammography in breast-cancer screening. Because of pressure from Congress, particularly from the women members, the National Cancer Institute reversed its original position. A panel of experts convened by the NCI considered the question of whether women in their forties with no family history of breast cancer should have regular mammograms. The panel found that the evidence did not establish that mammograms saved lives in women in their forties and recommended that the test not be made a part of every woman's medical exam. Although the NCI initially endorsed the recommendation, the director reversed this position in response to public and political pressure. Bills were then immediately introduced in Congress to require that insurers pay for the procedure for women under fifty.

(Critics point out that the director of the Heart Institute acted similarly in setting aside the recommendations of the grant reviewing panel and funding Hennekens' study of the effect of aspirin on heart attacks in women.)

Congress has also devoted considerable attention to whether insurers should be required to pay for longer hospital stays for women recovering from mastectomies. Yet Congress has completely ignored the same question about prostate surgery, although prostate cancer kills almost as many people every year as breast cancer.

Third, research money is spent on women disproportionately. In 1996, 16 percent of National Institutes of Health funds were directed to the study of diseases exclusive to women, while only 5.7 percent went to studies of diseases exclusive to men. The majority of funds, 78.3 percent, went to diseases affecting both genders. Past funding was similar. In 1987, the figures were 13.5 percent for women's diseases, 6.5 percent for men's, and 80 percent for both. Furthermore, the National Cancer Institute spends more on cancers affecting women (breast and ovarian) than on prostate cancer.

Defenders of this pattern of research spending claim that, even though it appears to favor women, the appearance is deceiving. The spending is disproportionate because our ignorance is

disproportionate. We simply lack an understanding of the diseases affecting women. A larger amount of research money goes for research on women because that is where our scientific understanding is most incomplete.

So far as breast cancer is concerned, it should be given special consideration—more consideration than prostate cancer. Breast cancer kills women at an earlier age than prostate cancer. Thus, the money spent on preventing it or treating it buys more years of life than does money spent on prostate cancer.

Nevertheless, some critics reject the whole idea that American medicine has not served women well. If anything, they charge, women receive better health care than men. "There's no question that women seek out medical attention more," says A. G. Kadar. "Whether they are less healthy is another issue . . . especially since there are diseases that keep you from feeling your best but don't shorten your life expectancy." Kadar suggests that a better measure is life expectancy. Given that women live about 5.5 years longer than men, this may be taken as showing that women are healthier than men.

While no one can doubt the influence of politics on health-care research and policy, the historical record supports the claim of advocates that women have received scant attention as research subjects. It may be true that women's response to drugs and treatments do not, for the most part, differ significantly from those of men. But the point some critics miss is that we have little scientific evidence for embracing this view. Past practices have kept us so ignorant of how women may respond that we have scant grounds for generalization.

Things may not be significantly changing either. A 2000 report from the General Accounting Office suggests that the 1993 law requiring that women be included in federally supported clinical trials in numbers sufficient to determine whether men and women respond differently to drugs, surgical procedures, and treatments is being followed only in the letter.

While scientists generally include women in the study group, they don't always analyze the data to look for differences in gender-specific responses to treatments. Also, sometimes the number of women included is not large enough for a reliable statistical analysis of the data to indicate whether a therapy leads to different outcomes for women and men.

Debates over research related to women's health are likely to continue. Eventually, as more is learned about how diseases affect women and how women respond to treatment, funding may reach something like parity. What is more important is that the health needs of women have now been explicitly recognized, because this makes it unlikely that women will ever be completely left out of scientific studies. Women, as well as men, will then be in a position to benefit from new knowledge and understanding.

## Conclusion

In a society committed to fairness, no one questions in principle that we must be sure that disadvantaged groups receive a just allocation of the society's health-care resources. A number of significant steps have been taken to see to it that research into issues affecting women's health is given the same emphasis as that affecting the health of men. Eventually, the institutional structures that have been put into place, such as the Office of Research on Women's Health, are likely to bring about and sustain gender equity in medical research. Attitudes toward women as patients may be slower to change.

The society has been more effective in correcting the imbalance of resources with respect to gender than it has with respect to minority status. Evidence suggests that the health of African Americans and American Indians and Native Alaskans, in particular, is considerably more at risk than that of the general population. The gap between both minority groups and others is so wide that special and continuing efforts need to be made to close it.

A larger budget for the Indian Health Service would solve part of the problem of providing the basic care not currently supplied, and per-

haps a way could be devised to extend the care to Indians living in isolated areas.

But Indians are in need of more preventive care. Disease screening, such as mammograms and PSA testing, needs to be made available to a larger proportion of the population. Further, problems like unemployment and alcoholism that are connected with high death rates need a social and political solution. Public health programs can educate people about the importance of good health habits and make a strong contribution to disease prevention, but it cannot give people jobs.

Many of the factors responsible for the gap between the health of African Americans and that of the general population are unknown. Yet many of them are known and can be modified in a positive direction by political, social, and individual effort. Programs designed to promote preventive screening among Blacks have shown themselves to be effective. Programs to encourage Blacks to participate in clinical trials, to consult physicians when a health concern arises (instead of waiting until it becomes unbearable), and to become organ donors could make use of the same principles. All such programs need to take into account the distrust of the medical establishment in the black community (the Tuskegee effect), as well as restrictions imposed by income and transportation and child-care needs.

Part of the public health message to Indians and Blacks also needs to stress the importance of personal responsibility in health. Louis Sullivan, President George Bush's Secretary of Health and Human Services, stressed that "the top ten causes of premature death in our nation are significantly influenced by personal behavior and life-style choices." He advised African Americans to give up smoking, reduce drinking, and lose weight. Taking such steps, he claimed, could eliminate 45 percent of deaths from heart disease, 23 percent of deaths from cancer, and more than 50 percent of the disabling consequences of diabetes.

The death rates for cancer for African Americans were once lower than for Whites, but as more Blacks took up smoking, the rates surpassed that of Whites. Heart disease rose along with cancer. But it might be due in part to the traditional African-American diet that is high in both salt and fat. Also, almost half of black women are seriously overweight, as are almost a third of black men. This is a risk factor for heart disease and also for diabetes and hypertension. Because African Americans are particularly prone to these diseases, a change in personal behavior might lead to significant changes in health statistics.

If we want to improve the health of minority groups in our society, a crucial step is to bridge the gap between the dominant culture and minority cultures. This is particularly true for Hispanics, who may have to cope with a language difficulty, and with Asian Americans, who may have to cope both with a language difficulty and a radically different cultural understanding of disease and its treatment.

Interpreters for non-English speakers are crucial for providing even adequate health care for many minority individuals. Increasing the number of minorities in the health-care profession is another obvious way to help bring minorities into the health-care system. So, too, is opening clinics in urban areas where immigrant populations are concentrated. All these steps have been taken by some major medical centers and several health maintenance organizations.

From the national perspective, perhaps the most important project was Healthy People 2000: National Health Promotion and Disease Prevention. The effort was a collaboration between private organizations, public agencies, and health professionals led by the U.S. Public Health Service. The project attempted to reduce preventable death and disability, enhance the quality of life, and reduce disparities in health status among Americans.

Listing 300 objectives to be achieved, the project enjoined all participants to work in a professional and personal capacity to achieve whatever targets (increasing immunizations among the Hmong, reducing amputations among the Plains Indians, encouraging African Americans

to quit smoking) were most appropriate for their situation.

Project 2000 was successful in moving in the direction of achieving its goals. Yet for the majority of minority people, a Project 2025 or maybe even a Project 2050 will be needed before the disparities in health care can be expected to disappear.

## Case Presentation

### Lee Lor: Caught in a Culture Conflict

The Hmong are a Southeast Asian mountain people who were American allies during the Vietnam war. At the end of the war, to protect them from reprisals, whole families of Hmong were airlifted to the United States. Most of the Hmong settled in California, and more than 35,000 now live in or near Fresno.

The Hmong (pronounced *mung*) brought their culture with them and have not abandoned it in favor of the general Western or American culture in which they now live. This is unproblematic so far as matters like dress, food preferences, and modes of worship are concerned. But some Hmong practices have brought them into conflict with the law. Over the years, the Fresno police have been required to deal with complaints about the Hmong slaughtering pigs and other animals in their apartments. The police have also raided the patches of ground where the Hmong were growing opium poppies and mounted an education campaign to discourage Hmong men from pursuing their traditional practice of abducting teenage girls to marry.

Hmong beliefs about illness, its causes, and its treatment have led to even more conflicts with sometimes tragic results. Adhering to their traditional beliefs, the Hmong don't accept the view of the world put forward by Western science. They are animists who view the everyday world as a place shared with spirits, and the interactions between spirits and humans help to shape the course of human life. Spirits can be angered or seek revenge for insults or wrongs, and often the vengeful actions of the spirits are manifested as diseases. Propitiating the spirits may involve praying, performing healing rituals, burning incense, and carrying out animal sacrifices.

The cultures of the Hmong and of the West come into sharp conflict where the treatment of sick children is concerned. Hmong parents of a child with club feet avoided getting the child treated, because they thought the child's feet were deformed to atone for the wrongdoing of an ancestor. To try to correct the problem might result in another family member's becoming sick.

Other Hmong parents have refused surgery, because they believe it maims the body and makes it impossible for the child to be reincarnated. But one case of conflict between Hmong cultural beliefs and the Western notion of the legal and moral responsibility to provide children with appropriate medical care was the focus of considerable attention.

## Lee Lor

Lee Lor, a fifteen-year-old girl, was admitted to Valley Children's Hospital in late September of 1994 with a complaint of severe stomach pains. Her physicians diagnosed acute appendicitis and operated immediately. During the surgery, however, they discovered that Lee Lor had a cancerous tumor growing in her abdomen. In removing the tumor, the surgeon took out an ovary and part of one of her fallopian tubes. Her family later claimed they were not told about the cancer or the surgery for it until three days later. A hospital spokesman said the Lees were told, but he suggested they may not have understood because of problems with the translation.

Failing to get permission from Lee's family to initiate chemotherapy, the hospital notified the Fresno County Department of Social Services of the situation. The agency obtained a court order requiring Lee to submit to chemotherapy. The police, facing a barrage of stones hurled by a group of Hmong, removed Lee from her home strapped to a stretcher. Her father was so upset that a police officer had to wrestle a knife out of his hand to keep him from killing himself. A guard was posted outside Lee's room in the hospital.

To protest Lee's forced treatment, several hundred Hmong marched through the city twice. At a town meeting, they accused the county and the hospital of racism.

Lee was given chemotherapy for a week, then allowed to return home. On the day of her discharge, a court hearing was initiated to determine whether she should be placed in a foster home until the completion of her course of chemotherapy. Her physicians estimated that with treatment she had an 80 percent chance of survival, but without it her chances dropped to 10 percent.

Lee made her own decision about treatment by running away from home on October 28. Her parents saw her as she slept on a couch with her eight siblings, but the next morning she was gone. She left with little or no money but with a supply of herbal medicines. Her parents notified the police, but they also called in the family shaman. She reported that she had a vision of Lee out in the open and well.

Some two months later, Lee returned home. She had spent the time wandering around the state and was apparently no worse for the wear. While she was gone, the Department of Social Services had dropped its efforts to get a court order to continue Lee's chemotherapy. In one sense, Lee and her parents and the Hmong community had won their battle against Western medicine.

## Lingering Questions

While the parents of Lee Lor were devoted to their daughter, they could not free themselves of their culturally acquired beliefs and adopt in their place the scientific ones of Western medicine.

They did what they believed best for their child. Yet the fact remains that the beliefs of Western medicine are more effective in dealing with cancer than are ones based on the Hmong's animistic view of the world. Granted this is so, does a respect for the beliefs of others require us to refrain from interfering when a sick child is given a treatment we consider ineffective?

Or, by contrast, does our knowledge of what is more likely to be effective require us to intervene to make sure the child receives the treatment most likely to benefit her—even if this means acting against the wishes of her parents?

These questions are not prompted just by "alien" cultures like that of the Hmong. It's necessary only to think of Jehovah's Witnesses or Christian Scientists (see the Case Presentation: "The Death of Robyn Twitchell" in Chapter 2) to realize that where the best treatment for a child's illness is at issue, the beliefs of parents can come into conflict with the beliefs of scientific medicine.

Our society is strongly committed to individual autonomy and to recognizing the responsibility of parents in caring for their children. Hence, we are ambivalent about abnegating parental responsibility. When the beliefs of an entire culture are concerned, we become even more ambivalent, not wishing to be guilty of cultural arrogance.

But the question that must be addressed above all is—What is in the best interest of the child? Allowing a competent adult to refuse medical care or choose a treatment with little or no chance of success is quite different from allowing an adult to make a similar choice for a child. Children are not in a position to have any say in the matter and must look to society to see that their interest is protected.

# SOCIAL CONTEXT: THE MAMMOGRAPHY DEBATE

Susan Arcadan, as we will call her, was forty-one years old and enjoying life to the fullest.

She had a nice apartment, a wide circle of friends, and best of all, she had recently been promoted to head a new products group at the online computer company where she worked.

Not bad for a college history major who had known next to nothing about computers when she was hired as a sales representative six years earlier. Now she was riding herd over bright, talented, amusing people and loving it.

Susan took care of her health too. She ate lots of fruits and vegetables, avoided fats, biked or jogged every day, and when the weather permitted, worked in the garden she had carved out of the wasteland behind her building. She had regular physical exams, and when she turned thirty-nine, she started getting mammograms, even though no one in her family had ever been diagnosed with breast cancer. She was the sort of person who took pride in being cautious.

Despite her exercise and careful diet, a couple of weeks after her promotion Susan began to gain weight. At first she thought it was only because she was over forty and cut back on her calories, but when she noticed a dimpling in the skin of her left breast, she decided she should see her doctor. Her methods of weight control weren't working.

After only the briefest exam, Dr. Long found a lump in her left breast. "You need a biopsy im-

mediately," he told Susan. "I'll arrange for you to see a surgeon." The dimpling in the skin, she learned, was a sign of breast cancer past its earliest stage.

Susan was numb with shock. She had gotten her yearly mammogram eight months earlier, and it had shown nothing abnormal. She had done everything, and it had turned out to be useless.

## Statistical Pictures

Susan was one of the roughly 200,000 women in the United States diagnosed with breast cancer every year. In about 140,000 of these women, the cancer has not spread beyond the breast, but in 60,000 of them the cancer is not a new diagnosis but a recurrence of the disease. Eventually, around 56,000 women in the group of 200,000 will die of the disease, and by this estimate, during the last ten years, breast cancer killed more than half a million women.

Studies show that women fear breast cancer more than any other disease. Fearing the disease is quite reasonable, because it is one of the major causes of death in women. It is far from being the leading cause, however, and many women believe they are at greater risk for the disease than they are. An unfortunate aspect of this is that they may fail to take steps that might prevent some of the diseases more likely to kill them.

Heart disease, which causes death in women at a rate of 278.8 per 100,000, is a far greater threat to their lives. The same is true of lung cancer, which has a death rate of 45.0, and stroke, with a death rate of 73.8. By contrast with these diseases, breast cancer has a death rate of 29.5 per 100,000—high, but about one-fifth that of heart disease.

While little is known about how to prevent breast cancer, much is known about reducing the risk for heart disease, lung cancer, and stroke. This is why women's health experts worry that too restricted a focus on breast cancer may fail to promote the overall health of women.

A woman's lifetime risk of dying of breast cancer is one in nine, while her risk of dying of heart disease is one in two. Her risk of dying of diabetes is one in three and of stroke one in five.

But even the one in nine figure, high as it is, needs to be kept in perspective. What the figure taken alone does not show is that the risk of breast cancer increases with age. Relatively few women die of the disease in their twenties, thirties, or even early- to mid-forties, but when they reach their fifties, the incidence begins to rise. It then soars for women in their sixties and beyond. The lifetime risk is one in nine, but the longer a woman lives, the greater her risk becomes. The following chart illustrates this.

## Breast Cancer Deaths by Age*

| | |
|---|---|
| 25–34 | 2.3 |
| 35–44 | 12.1 |
| 45–54 | 33.5 |
| 55–64 | 59.9 |
| 65–74 | 89.9 |
| 75–84 | 131.3 |
| 85– | 202.6 |

*Per 100,000; figures are for 1999.
*Source:* U.S. Department of Health and Human Services, *Health, United States, 2002* (Washington, D.C.: Government Printing Office)

At thirty-eight Susan Arcadan was statistically unlikely to develop breast cancer. With good health habits and no family history of the disease, she was only one of the unlucky so-called sporadic cases that have no explanation. (For a discussion of known breast cancer genes, see Chapter 5.) Susan was also unlucky in another way. Although she had gotten a mammogram eight months before she was diagnosed with breast cancer, the X-ray image had appeared to be completely normal.

## Mammograms

In 1987 the National Cancer Institute recommended that women start having breast-cancer screening mammograms at age forty and get one every year or two. The American Cancer Society endorsed the recommendation and continued an intensive advertising campaign stressing the importance of early detection in cancer treatment, and the message that "Mammograms Save Lives" was widely disseminated.

No one questioned the diagnostic usefulness of mammograms, and the number of cases of cancer detected in women over fifty made their importance in examining this group unquestionable. However, even while the general value of mammograms was being promoted, a long-simmering scientific debate over the value of using them for women in their forties continued over the next six years.

Then, in 1993, the National Cancer Institute changed its original recommendation and announced that "experts do not agree on the value of routine screening mammography for women ages 40 to 49." The American Cancer Society and a dozen or more cancer advocacy groups continued to adhere to the original guidelines.

Hoping to resolve the long dispute, in 1997 the Director of the National Cancer Institute, Richard Klausner, convened a panel of thirteen medical experts and public representatives and asked them to address a number of specific questions. They were to consider, for example, "Do mammograms prevent women in their forties from dying of breast cancer?" and "What are the disadvantages of mammograms for women in their forties?" Klausner hoped the panel would function as a consensus conference and establish guidelines for the use of mammograms that could be adopted by both clinicians and public groups.

The panel, headed by Leon Gordis, an epidemiologist from Johns Hopkins, met for six weeks, considered hundreds of scientific papers, and listened to presentations from thirty-five authorities on breast cancer. The scientific findings presented to the committee were not always clear-cut and didn't support an obvious conclusion.

Studies done in Sweden and Scotland indicated women in their forties getting mammograms were less likely to die of breast cancer, but another study conducted in Canada found no such effect. All researchers agreed that even if there was a positive effect, it was so slight that huge numbers of women would have to be screened to save even a few.

Suzanne W. Fletcher pointed out that if the most optimistic estimate of the value of mammograms was correct, for every 1000 women having a yearly mammogram, in a ten-year period only one or two would be saved from death by breast cancer. Ordinarily, eight women could be expected to die of the disease in that time, so mammograms would not save the lives of six or seven of them.

Lazlo Tabar, a principal investigator in the Swedish study, claimed mammograms had "a tremendous potential" to reduce breast-cancer deaths in women in their forties by as much as 16 percent, but Ingvar Andersson, also a Swedish researcher, disagreed. According to his figures, a yearly screening of 10,000 women for ten years would save 15 women from dying of breast cancer. However, the test would produce 1250 false positives—results indicating women have tumors when they don't. Further testing would be required in each case. Biopsies would be performed fifty-six times, and they would lead to ten cases of surgery for noncancerous lumps. Further, at least one woman every ten years would die of cancer caused by radiation exposure from mammograms.

A 1998 study showed that a woman who has a yearly mammogram for ten years has a 50 percent chance of having at least one false positive. She has a 19 percent chance of undergoing an unnecessary biopsy. For the 32 million American women between ages forty and seventy-nine, this could mean 16 million false positives in ten years and over 5 million biopsies. The worry, anxiety, and general difficulties are incalculable.

## Recommendation

On January 23, 1997, the panel made public the results of its deliberations. "At the present time," it said in a public statement, "the available data do not warrant a single recommendation for mammography for all women in their 40s. Each woman should decide for herself whether to undergo mammography."

At best, the panel concluded, mammography might prolong, but not necessarily save, the lives of 10 women of every 10,000 getting a yearly mammogram. While mammograms can reduce the breast-cancer death rate for women fifty and above by as much as 30 percent, the panel found no evidence for any such reduction for women in their forties. Some studies found no effect in the death rate at all, and some found only a slight effect.

As a statistician on the panel put the point, 98.5 percent of women in their forties who have yearly mammograms get no benefit at all. The other 1.5 percent have their lives extended 200 days, but how the days are distributed—all to one person or some to all ten—cannot be known.

Also, mammograms would involve much worry, additional testing, and surgery with its hazards and potential complications. During the ten-year period from forty to fifty, with the women getting yearly mammograms, 30 percent of the supposed abnormalities detected will be false positives. All these women will have to have additional tests, and some will need surgery to be sure cancer is not present. Forty percent of the tumors detected in women in their forties turn out to be intraductal carcinoma in situ, which may or may not turn into invasive lethal tumors. Forty percent of the women with tumors of this type have mastectomies, while the others have lumpectomies, sometimes with radiation and sometimes without. Many women must suffer worry, expense, pain, surgical mutilation, and the risks of surgery and radiation to benefit only a few.

Further, for every 10,000 women getting an annual mammogram, 3 or so might develop breast cancer as a result of the exposure to radiation. Also, because mammograms miss about 25 percent of invasive tumors in women in their forties, having mammograms might give women a false sense of security. The breast tissue in women fifty or older is less dense, and tumors are missed only about 10 percent of the time.

## Responses

The Director of the National Cancer Institute said he was shocked by the panel's recommendation. He himself was persuaded of the importance of the Swedish study indicating the value of mammograms in reducing deaths in women in their forties and thought the panel hadn't given it the weight it deserved.

The American Cancer Society said it was "disappointed" in the report. Some radiologists were outraged. "I do feel this is tantamount to a death sentence for women in their forties," one said. Another said the panel's report was "fraudulent" and should not be released to the public. The former Director of the National Institutes of Health, Bernardine Healy, said she was shocked by the panel's conclusion. "I am very disturbed that a group of so-called experts challenged the notion of early detection," she said. "What they are saying is that ignorance is bliss."

Women who had recovered after a diagnosis of breast cancer were among the sharpest critics of the report. In an op-ed piece in the *New York Times* titled "Luckily, I Had a Mammogram," Kathlyn Conway told how, thanks to a mammogram, she had been diagnosed with breast cancer at the age of forty-three. What is more, while waiting to get a second opinion on a biopsy, she talked to several women in the waiting room, and none was over fifty. "Yes, my evidence is anecdotal," she wrote. "But it is evidence I can't ignore." Conway and others pointed out that the insurance industry would use the panel's report to deny coverage for mammograms for women under fifty.

Politicians were quick to respond to the panel's report. Leon Gordis, the head of the panel, was called to testify before Congress on the panel's report. The Senate voted 98 to 0 in favor of a nonbinding resolution endorsing the value of mammograms for women in their forties.

Some thought the panel's conclusion about the value of mammograms was reasonable but were dissatisfied with its recommendation. It was supposed to be an expert panel, but it said to women, you've got to decide for yourself. But how could women be expected to decide for themselves, if a group of experts couldn't decide?

While most of the responses to the panel's report were ones of angry disbelief, some praised the panel for its courage and candor. Some breast-cancer activists pointed out that the idea of early detection of breast cancer had been oversold and most people were unaware of how often mammograms failed to reveal the presence of a tumor in women in their forties.

Also, despite the repeated message, early detection doesn't always save lives. Some cancers aren't deadly even if they aren't found, while others are still deadly even if they are. This was not a message the public wanted to hear about breast cancer. Instead, they wanted to hear the old, simplistic message that a mammogram would lead to early detection, which would save your life.

Others suggested that many radiologists, hospitals, breast centers, and equipment manufacturers had too much of a professional and financial stake in promoting mammograms to be happy with the panel's report. Mammography has become a big business and a profit center for institutions providing the service, so those with something to lose by reducing the number of mammograms might be expected to object.

## A Reversal

In April 1997, Klausner called a press conference and announced that the NCI was retracting the panel's recommendation. Instead, the NCI recommended that women between forty and forty-nine should have a mammogram every one to two years. Women with a family history of breast cancer would talk to their doctors and perhaps have the procedure sooner and more often.

President Bill Clinton immediately praised the new NCI policy and announced that future federal health-care programs would pay for mammograms. He encouraged private insurers to follow the federal example.

Critics charged that the NCI was giving in to public opinion and heavy lobbying by members of Congress and women's advocacy groups. What should have been settled by scientific evidence was being resolved on political grounds. NCI officials claimed they had never planned for the panel's recommendation to be the final word on mammograms. "More evidence from clinical trials led us, about a year ago, to begin a process of reevaluating our recommendations," Klausner said.

A study appearing in late 2002 gave support to the view that early detection may do little to save lives. Aggressive tumors that did not respond well to treatment, even when detected early, were found to have a "genetic signature" (the action of some seventy genes) that was different from that of tumors that responded well, even when large and detected late. The study also raises the question of whether a tumor with a less-aggressive signature should be treated with the whole range of surgery, chemotherapy, and radiation that is now standard for all breast cancer.

Without a doubt, the change in the NCI position reflected the opinion of most women. Of those surveyed in a *New York Times*/CBS poll, 44 percent said they thought mammograms should start at age forty, and 40 percent thought they should begin even earlier.

## Debate Continues

In October 2001, *Lancet,* a leading British medical journal, published an article in which the authors claimed that a review of past studies showed that mammography had only a marginal benefit in saving lives. Moreover, the studies contained statistical flaws so significant as to make it doubtful it had any value at all in preventing breast-cancer deaths.

A couple of months later, in January 2002, a group of experts called the P.D.Q. Screening and Editorial Board, which is responsible for reviewing the information for the National Cancer Society database, expressed similar doubt. The P.D.Q. said that its review of seven large studies of mammography revealed that they had such serious statistical flaws as to cast doubt on the reliability of their conclusions.

While the debate continues, such health organizations as the American Cancer Society recommend that women continue to have regular mammograms for breast-cancer screening.

## Treatment

Susan Arcadan was among the 25 percent of women in their forties whose breast cancer went undetected by mammography. After a biopsy, her disease was staged.

The clinical staging of breast cancer is the best predictor of the patient's chances of recovery. The stage of the cancer is determined by three variables: tumor size, number of lymph nodes involved, and whether the cancer has metastasized (spread) to other parts of the body. Using a classification scheme worked out by the American Joint Committee on Cancer, a patient's breast cancer is assigned a stage ranging from Stage I (carcinoma in situ) to Stage IV (an invasive tumor that has spread beyond the lymph nodes to distant sites).

Cells that are well differentiated are likely to grow slowly, while cells that are undifferentiated are more abnormal and faster growing. The presence of estrogen or progesterone receptors on the cancer cells are also indicators of how malignant a tumor is. The more receptors on the cells, the less malignant the tumor.

(The 2002 study mentioned earlier suggested a tumor's "genetic signature" is a better predictor of its aggressiveness than its clinical stage.)

Susan Arcadan's cancer was classified as a Type III that was negative for estrogen receptors. It had spread to seven lymph nodes but couldn't be detected at other sites. The cancer was aggressive, and Susan had a mastectomy, with the removal of affected lymph nodes. The surgery was followed by a course of chemotherapy, then radiation treatments.

A year after her breast cancer was diagnosed, Susan showed no sign of the disease. She was in remission. Perhaps the cancer was gone forever, perhaps not. The question of whether to have mammograms during her forties was moot for her.

# SOCIAL CONTEXT: THE PROSTATE CANCER EPIDEMIC

The prostate is a walnut-sized gland unique to men.

It contributes secretions that go to make up the seminal fluid discharged in ejaculation. It surrounds the upper part of the urethra and is located directly under the bladder and in front of the rectum.

The prostate reaches its normal size around age twenty, but it starts to grow again in most men around fifty. Called benign prostatic hyperplasia, the condition may require surgery, if the prostate begins to compress the urethra and makes urination difficult or even impossible. While prostate cancer can also make the prostate increase in size, benign prostatic hyperplasia doesn't lead to cancer.

## Prostate Cancer

The American Cancer Society estimates that about 182,000 men will be diagnosed with prostate cancer in the United States this year. This exceeds the 142,000 new cases of breast cancer, and excluding skin cancer, prostate cancer accounts for almost a quarter of all cancers.

The number of deaths predicted from prostate cancer for the year is roughly 37,000; the number predicted for breast cancer is 44,000. The lifetime odds for a man being diagnosed with prostate cancer is 1 in 6, compared to the 1 in 8 risk of breast cancer in women. If it can be said there is an epidemic of breast cancer, then there is also an epidemic of prostate cancer.

Like breast cancer, the risk of prostate cancer increases with age. It most often develops in men in their sixties and seventies. As life expectancy has increased and men have escaped death from accidents, heart disease, and strokes, more are likely to develop prostate cancer and die from it. About 20 percent of American men will develop prostate cancer in their fifties, and the risk rises with age. Although deaths from breast and prostate cancer are similar, women with breast cancer tend to die at an earlier age. Thus, more years of life are lost to breast cancer than to prostate cancer.

The increase in diagnosed cases of prostate cancer is also due to a better diagnostic test. The traditional test was limited to a digital rectal examination (DRE), in which the physician uses a finger inserted into the rectum to palpate the prostate. If it felt abnormal, the next step was to have a biopsy.

The PSA (for prostate specific antigen) test was pioneered in the late 1980s and has now become a standard test for men of fifty or older. The test measures the blood level of a protein produced by prostate cells. Measured in nanograms of PSA per milliliter of blood, measurements usually rise gradually with age, because after fifty, the number of cells in the prostate increase. A sharp increase in the PSA measurement can indicate the presence of cancer, because it involves the rapid increase of cells.

The normal range for PSA is from 0 to 4 (some researchers put the upper limit at 3 or even 2.5), and a measurement of 4 or above is a cause for further diagnostic inquiry. This now involves an examination of the prostate by ultrasound and, most likely, a needle biopsy of all quadrants of the prostate.

A PSA level below 4 is an indicator that prostate cancer is not likely to be present, but it doesn't rule it out. The probability of cancer increases as the measurement rises to between 2 and 22. When the PSA is within the 4–10 range, the chance of prostate cancer is about 25 percent. When the measurement is over 10, cancer is very likely.

The PSA tests became relatively common in the late 1980s, and a study of Medicare recipients by the National Cancer Institute found that by 1994 half of American men over sixty-five had had at least one. The incidence of prostate cancer per 100,000 men was 190.4 in 1990, but it dropped to 139.1 in 1997. This may not reflect a genuine decrease, but only more precise diagnoses.

Since 1991, the death rate from prostate cancer has dropped 16 percent among white men. In black men, who have a higher incidence of prostate cancer, the death rate has dropped 11 percent since 1993.

No one can be sure to what extent this decrease can be attributed to early detection. A clinical trial was initiated in 1973 to follow 75,000 men with the aim of determining whether early diagnosis prolongs lives, but the trial will not be finished for years. Even those who were initially skeptics have come to regard the PSA test as a valuable tool, but whether their confidence can be given a scientific basis can only be determined when more data are available.

## Treatments

Treatments for prostate cancer are all hard on the patient, offer no certainty of success, and have results that can substantially affect the patient's quality of life.

**Prostatectomy.** The prostate is surgically removed through an incision in the abdomen or behind the scrotum. This is major surgery, with a hospital stay of several days and a recovery time of months. If the cancer has not spread beyond the prostate, the surgery can be curative.

Because sphincter muscles may be cut or damaged, about 8 percent of patients are incontinent, and 20 to 50 percent will have only partial bladder control. Until recently impotence was virtually inevitable, but the development of a nerve-sparing surgical technique has reduced its incidence.

**Radiation Therapy.** Treatment can be performed on an outpatient basis, eliminating the need for a hospital stay and for coping with the trauma of surgery. But while radiation can shrink the tumor, it does not always kill all the cancer cells. After ten years, 75 to 80 percent of those treated show signs of recurrence. Impotence occurs in as many as half the patients.

**Radioactive Seeds.** Instead of using an external source of radiation, dozens of tiny pellets of radioactive palladium or iodine are implanted in the prostate. The damage to healthy tissue produced by a beam of radiation going into the body is reduced, but incontinence is common for several weeks and is permanent in about 5 percent of those treated. Men under seventy have a 15 percent ratio of impotence, with a higher rate for older men. Short-term studies suggest the method has a lower rate of tumor recurrence, but the cure rate is not established.

**Cryotherapy.** The destruction of prostate tissue by liquid nitrogen circulating through a transurethral probe may be most useful after a tumor returns. The tissue destruction usually includes nerves, producing impotence in 60 percent of the men treated, but incontinence is usually not a problem. An important limitation of the procedure is that cancer cells may escape destruction and grow again and spread.

**Hormone Therapy.** Testosterone stimulates the growth of prostate cancer cells, so treatment with another hormone that shuts it down may stop the cells from multiplying and even shrink the tumor. The treatment produces a loss of sex drive and is limited in its effects. Within a year or two, the cancer cells will start to multiply again.

Whatever treatment is chosen, about 35 percent of the men diagnosed with prostate cancer eventually will have a recurrence of cancer. At this point, options are limited and their outcomes not encouraging.

## A Dilemma

The availability of the PSA test, coupled with the lack of a benign and effective way of treating prostate cancer, often presents a dilemma to men and their physicians. The average prostate cancer takes a decade to produce symptoms. Someone advanced in years may choose "watchful waiting," instead of treatment. He will have regular PSA tests, DREs, and occasional biopsies to monitor the cancer. If it shows signs of becoming more aggressive, treatment can be instituted. The aim is for an elderly man to die *with* the cancer, not *from* it.

But what about men who might reasonably be expected to live for more than ten years? Should they choose watchful waiting? The answer is controversial. "Men with prostate cancer should have two goals," according to researcher William Catalona. "One should be to live longer if they can, and the second should be to avoid dying of prostate cancer. A quick heart attack is far preferable." Catalona advocates widespread PSA testing and aggressive intervention.

Unfortunately, PSA readings are insufficient to distinguish between aggressive and slow-growing tumors. A high reading may incline men, with the encouragement of their physicians, to choose treatments that are not needed and are themselves harmful. Thus, widespread PSA testing may lead to an increase in the number of cases treated unnecessarily.

"How many people is it okay to treat without benefit, and even with harm, in order to save one life?" asks urologist Gerald Chodak. Chodak presents his patients with relevant information about the PSA test, then allows them to make the decision as to whether to have it. He tells his patients, "If you want to see if you have cancer, then take the test. If you want to minimize your risk of undue harm, then don't take the test."

Part of the doubt about how men diagnosed with prostate cancer should be treated may be resolved eventually by the results of the Prostate Cancer Intervention Versus Observation Trial. PIVOT will monitor 2000 prostate cancer patients for fifteen years to determine if prostatectomies save enough lives to make surgery preferable to watchful waiting.

The causes of prostate cancer are unknown. Evidence suggests that diet plays a role. The disease is relatively rare in Japan, but incidence among second- and third-generation Japanese Americans is much higher. The incidence in Japan has also increased as many have switched to a more Western diet.

African Americans have a 37 percent higher risk of getting prostate cancer than Whites and are two to three times more likely to die of the disease. Why this is so is not known. Genetic factors may be at work, but perhaps not.

Unanswered questions about prostate cancer are more numerous than answered ones: Is there a gene or genes that predispose men to prostate cancer? How can the disease be prevented? How can its incidence be reduced? Does early detection save lives? What is the best of the available treatments? What treatment might be better than the ones we have? "Our knowledge of prostate cancer is woefully limited," says the head of the American Cancer Society.

## Funding

If it were possible to find a cellular marker to distinguish between aggressive and slow-growing prostate tumors when they are detected early, this would help resolve the question of who should be treated and who kept under surveillance. But that knowledge is currently lacking. While a gene may have been identified for prostate cancer that runs in some families, none is known that predisposes men in general to the disease.

Only recently has prostate cancer received much attention from researchers. Prostate cancer activists point out that the lack of research attention is almost certainly due to a lack of funding. In their view, prostate cancer has been unjustly ignored, considering the number of people it kills.

The number of deaths from prostate cancer each year is comparable to the number of deaths from AIDS and breast cancer, yet the funding for prostate cancer is much lower than for either of the other two diseases. The federal government spends about $1.3 billion a year on AIDS research and about $313 million on breast cancer research. Yet it spends only $59 million on prostate cancer research.

Until quite recently, men didn't talk openly about prostate cancer. Having the disease was almost shameful, and most men suffered and died in silence. They didn't speak out and demand

more research, and there was no prostate cancer lobby or political action group. As a result of silence, activists say, research into prostate cancer is only now moving ahead.

Like other kinds of research, it would move faster if only more research money were available. The drugs, chemotherapies, vaccines, and viruses designed to destroy cancer cells that might be effective against prostate cancer could be tested and developed with greater speed. As with breast cancer, people are dying for the lack of better treatments.

---

**READINGS**

## Section 1: Perspectives on Gender and Race

### Gender, Race, and Class in the Delivery of Health Care

#### Susan Sherwin

Susan Sherwin argues that the poor receive inadequate health care under the current system, because they are those made poor by being oppressed by their gender, race, or sexuality. The connection between oppression and illness is damaging and unfair, and the only way to reverse the situation is to replace the current hierarchical and authoritarian medical model, which is dominated by white, middle-class male physicians, by a model reflecting the insights of feminist ethics.

The new model would recognize the social dimensions of health, broaden the basis of expertise in determining health policy, and replace authoritarian structures with egalitarian ones. Further, current emphasis on curing the sick would be replaced by the cheaper alternative of empowering consumers to protect their health by healthy living. Generally, a feminist system would aim to avoid or lessen the contribution that the health-care system makes to maintaining oppression.

#### Oppression and Illness

It is widely recognized throughout the field of biomedical ethics that people's health care needs usually vary inversely with their power and privilege within society. Most bioethical discussions explain these dif-

Susan Sherwin. "Gender, Race, and Class in the Delivery of Health Care," in *No Longer Patient: Feminist Ethics and Health Care,* 1992, pp. 222–240. Reprinted by permission of Temple University Press. (Notes omitted.)

ferences solely in economic terms, observing that health and access to health resources are largely dependent on income levels. Poverty is an important determining factor in a person's prospects for health: being poor often means living without access to adequate nutrition, housing, heat, clean water, clothing, and sanitation, and each of these factors may have a negative impact on health (Lewis 1990). . . . And the poor suffer higher rates of mental illness and addiction than do other segments of the population. Financial barriers also often force the poor to let diseases reach an advanced state before they seek professional help; by the time these individuals do receive care, recovery may be compromised.

It is not sufficient, however, just to notice the effects of poverty on health; it is also necessary to consider who is at risk of becoming the victim of poverty. In a hierarchical society such as the one we live in, members of groups that are oppressed on the basis of gender, race, sexuality, and so forth are the people who are most likely to be poor. Moreover, not only does being oppressed lead to poverty and poverty to poor health but being oppressed is itself also a significant determining factor in the areas of health and health care. Those who are most oppressed in society at large are likely to experience the most severe and frequent health problems and have the least access to adequate medical treatment. . . .

North American society is characteristically sexist, racist, classist, homophobic, and frightened of physical or mental imperfections; we can anticipate, then, that those who are oppressed by virtue of their gender, race, class, sexual orientation, or disabilities—and especially, those who are oppressed in a number of different ways—will experience a disproportional share of illness and will often suffer reduced access to resources. Moreover, the connection between illness and oppression can run in both directions; because serious or chronic illness is often met with fear and hostility, it may also precipitate an individual's or family's slide into poverty and can therefore lead to oppression based on class.

The damaging connections between oppression and illness are profoundly unfair. Because this situation is ethically objectionable, bioethicists have a responsibility to consider ways in which existing medical institutions can be modified to challenge and undermine these connections, rather than contribute to them. Ethical analyses of the distribution of health and health care must take into consideration the role that oppression plays in a person's prospects for health and well-being.

## Patients as Members of Oppressed Groups

. . . Women are the primary consumers of health care, but the care they receive does not always serve their overall health interests. In a report presented to the American Medical Association, Richard McMurray

(1990) reviewed recent studies on gender disparities in clinical decision-making; he found that although women are likely to undergo more medical procedures than do men when they present the same symptoms and condition, they have significantly less access than men do to some of the major diagnostic and therapeutic interventions that are considered medically appropriate for their conditions. In some cases the discrepancies were quite remarkable: for example, despite comparable physical needs, women were 30 percent less likely than men to receive kidney transplants, 50 percent as likely to be referred for diagnostic testing for lung cancer, and only 10 percent as likely to be referred for cardiac catheterization. The studies were unable to identify any biological difference that would justify these discrepancies. In addition, even though biological differences are sometimes significant in the course of various diseases and therapies, McMurray found that medical researchers have largely ignored the study of diseases and medications in women; for instance, cardiovascular disease is the leading cause of death in women in the United States, but research in this area has been almost exclusively conducted on men.

Therefore, as a group, it appears that women are particularly vulnerable to poor health care. Although they receive a great deal of medical treatment, the relevant research data are frequently missing, and specific treatment decisions seem to be biased against them. When women are medically treated, they are often overtreated, that is, subjected to excessive testing, surgery, and prescription drugs (Weaver and Garrett 1983). . . .

In bioethics literature the issue of justice is often raised, but most discussions focus on whether or not everyone has a right to health care and, if so, what services this right might entail. Accessibility is viewed as the principal moral concern, but even where there is universal health insurance (for example, in Canada), the system is not designed to respond to the particular health needs of many groups of women. Being subject to violence, at risk of developing addictions to alcohol or other mood-altering drugs, and lacking adequate resources to obtain a nutritious food supply are all factors that affect people's prospects for health and their ability to promote their own well-being. Such threats to health are a result of the social system, which promotes oppression of some groups by others. Health care alone will not correct all these social effects, but as long as the damage of oppression continues, it is necessary to help its victims recover from some of the harms to their health that occur as a result of their oppressed status.

Bioethicists share with health care professionals and the rest of the community an ethical responsibility to determine how the health needs generated by oppressive structures can best be meet. Medical care per se will not always be the most effective means of restoring or preserving the health of oppressed persons. Investigation of how best to respond to these socially generated needs is a topic that must be added to the traditional agenda of health care ethics.

## The Organization of Health Care

Much of the explanation for the different ways in which health care providers respond to the needs of different social groups can be found in the very structures of the health care delivery system. The dominance structures that are pervasive throughout society are reproduced in the medical context; both within and without the health care delivery system, sex, race, economic class, and able-bodied status are important predictors in determining someone's place in the hierarchy. The organization of the health care system does not, however, merely mirror the power and privilege structures of the larger society; it also perpetuates them. . . .

In the formal institutions of health care delivery, women constitute over 80 percent of paid health care workers, but men hold almost all the positions of authority. Health policy is set by physicians, directors, and legislators, and these positions are filled overwhelmingly by men. Despite recent dramatic increases in female enrollment in medical schools, most physicians are men (78.8 percent in Canada and 84.8 percent in the United States as of 1986); further, female physicians tend to cluster in less influential specialties, such as family practice and pediatrics, and they are seldom in positions of authority within their fields. Most medical textbooks are written by men, most clinical instructors are men, and most hospital directors are men. The professional fields that women do largely occupy in the health care system are ones associated with traditionally female skills, such as nursing, nutrition, occupational and physical therapy, and public health. Women who work in health administration tend to be situated in middle-management positions, where their mediating skills may be desirable but their influence on policy is limited. . . .

When we focus directly on issues of race and economic class, the isolation of health care provider from consumer becomes even more pronounced. Although many members of minority races and plenty of poor people are involved in the delivery of health care, very few hold positions of authority. Working-class and minority employees are concentrated in the nonprofessional ranks of cleaners, nurses' aides, orderlies, kitchen staff, and so forth. Women from these groups generally have the lowest income and status in the whole health care system. They have no opportunity to shape health care policy or voice their concerns about their own health needs or those of persons for whom they are responsible. One result of this unbalanced representation is that there has been virtually no research into the distinct needs of minority women (White 1990). . . .

The gender and racial imbalances in the health care system are not accidental; they are a result of specific barriers designed to restrict access to women and minorities to the ranks of physicians. Regina Morantz-Sanchez (1985) documents how the medical profession organized itself over the last century to exclude and harass women who sought to become doctors, and Margaret Campbell (1973) shows that many of these mechanisms are still with us. Blacks, too, have been subject to systematic barriers, which keep them out of the ranks of physicians. For example, it is necessary to serve as an intern to become licensed to practice medicine, but until the 1960s, few American hospitals would grant internship positions to black physicians; those blacks who did manage to become qualified to practice medicine often encountered hospitals that refused to grant them the opportunity to admit patients (Blount 1990). Because black women must overcome both gender and race barriers, they face nearly insurmountable obstacles to pursuing careers as physicians (Weaver and Garrett 1983; Gamble 1990). Therefore, although blacks make up 12 percent of the population of the United States, they account for only 3 percent of the population of practicing doctors, and black women constitute only 1 percent of the nation's physicians; further, blacks represent only 2 percent of the faculty at medical schools (Gamble 1990). . . .

## Gender, Race, and Class as Ideological Influences in Health Care

Beyond the basic injustice apparent in the differential opportunities and care that result from an unequal health care system, indirect moral costs are also created. The hierarchical organization of our health care system not only reflects the sexist, racist, and classist values of society but also lends support to them.

That the demographic patterns of the health care system are reflections of those found in the larger society compounds their effect. When the patterns of gender, race, and class distribution that are found in health care are repeated in most other major social institutions—including universities, the justice system, the business community, and the civil service—they appear inevitable. In health care, as throughout society, the most prestigious, rewarding, and powerful positions are occupied by privileged white males, who are supported by a vast pyramid of relatively undervalued, white, professional women; unskilled laborers of color have been relegated to the realm of "merely physical" work.

This arrangement is of moral concern not just because of its obvious unfairness but because it provides an ideological foundation for maintaining a hierarchically structured, stratified society. Within the realm of health care, authoritarian structures are rationalized as necessary to the goals of achieving good health. The metaphors that structure participants' experiences within the system appeal explicitly to models of dominance: doctors "command" health care teams, "battle" illnesses, and "lead campaigns" against dangerous life-styles. Their expertise entitles them to give "orders" to workers in the affiliated health professions (nurses, physical therapists, pharmacists, and so forth) and to patients. These arrangements are justified in terms of their end, health. Because the end is of unquestionable value, the means are usually considered acceptable to the degree that they achieve this goal. Thus medicine's worthy goals and remarkable accomplishments are said to demonstrate the benefits of retaining power and privilege for a socially vital elite. That numerous critics have questioned the success of this model in the actual achievement of health has done little to dissuade the medical establishment from encouraging the public to accept its structures as necessary (York 1987). When feminists and other critics challenge the legitimacy of social hierarchies, the medical model can be held up as evidence of the value of hierarchical structures in achieving important social goals. . . .

There are further reasons for concern over the close correspondence between system and social power in an oppressive society. Decisions about illness in members of oppressed groups may be tainted by the social expectations that accompany discriminatory practices. Such decisions often reflect cultural stereo-

types, which themselves derive from unjust social arrangements. At the same time, those decisions may serve to legitimize particular damaging stereotypes and the social divisions that depend on them.

For example, white health care experts (and others) have identified alcoholism as a pervasive problem in the native American community; they have preached abstinence as a response. Generally, these judgments are made without examining the devastation that white culture has wrought on native community values and without extending any support for traditional, native healing options as alternative paths to recovery. Often health care workers have uncritically accepted the stereotypical view of "drunken Indians" and suggested that natives are either weak-willed or have some genetic propensity to alcohol dependency; either way, their misfortune is a reflection of some deficiency within them, not society. Most health professionals are committed to the individualistic medical model, which views diseases as belonging to individuals; although they may acknowledge a role for genetic or sociological factors, they believe that the individual is the proper site for health care treatment.

Other conceptions are available, however, and it is useful to reflect on alternatives in these circumstances. Some native healers suggest that alcoholism in their communities is really a social disease of the community, which should be understood as connected to the brutal separation of their people from their culture. Their account leads to an alternative strategy for recovery and a distinct form of health care; where the medical model treats the individual, native healers believe it is necessary to heal the community. Nevertheless, only the medically authorized response receives approval and support from those with the power to allocate health care resources.

The social harms extend further. Because the authority of health care decision-making is concentrated in nonnative hands, native people who identify themselves as alcoholics are required to adapt to treatment programs that have been designed for a white, urban population. They are deemed to be failures if the programs do not succeed in curing them. Because the problems usually continue, native people are seen to fulfill their culturally generated stereotypes; their severely disadvantaged economic and social position is then explained away by experts who speak authoritatively of native peoples' "natural" propensity to alcohol abuse. As long as health care decision-making resides in the hands of an elite, nonnative few, we can anticipate its continued failure to recognize and address the real needs of the native community. These failures, in turn, support the cultural prejudices that view natives as inferior members of modern society who cannot hope to rise above their designated status on the socioeconomic scale. . . .

The power and authority that society has entrusted to doctors give them the opportunity to destroy many of the patriarchal assumptions about women collectively and the racist, classist, homophobic, and other beliefs about various groups of women that are key to their oppression. Few physicians, however, have chosen to exercise their social power in this way. Many doctors have accepted uncritically the biases of an oppressive society, and some have offered evidence in confirmation of such values. As a group, physicians have held onto their own power and privilege by defending the primacy of the authoritarian medical model as a necessary feature of health care. Most have failed to listen honestly to the alternative perspectives of oppressed people who are very differently situated in society.

The medical model organizes our current attempts at defining and responding to health needs. It has been conceived as a structure that requires a hierarchically organized health care system, in which medical expertise is privileged over other sorts of knowledge. It grants license to an elite class of experts to formulate all matters of health and to determine the means for responding to them. As we have seen, however, there are several serious moral problems with this model. First, it responds differently to the health needs of different groups, offering less and lower-quality care to members of oppressed groups. Second, its structures and presuppositions support the patterns of oppression that shape our society. Finally, it rationalizes the principle of hierarchy in human interactions, rather than one of equality, by insisting that its authoritarian structures are essential to the accomplishment of its specific ends, and it tolerates an uneven distribution of positions within its hierarchy.

## Some Conclusions

We need, then, different models to guide our thinking about ways to organize the delivery of health care. In addition to the many limits to the medical model that have been named in the bioethics literature, the traditional model reflects and perpetuates oppression in society. I conclude by summarizing some feminist suggestions that I believe should be incorporated into alternative models, if they are to be ethically acceptable.

A model that reflects the insights of feminist ethics would expand its conceptions of health and health expertise. It would recognize social as well as physiological dimensions of health. In particular, it would reflect an understanding of both the moral and the health costs of oppression. Thus it would make clear that those who are committed to improving the health status of all members of the population should assume responsibility for avoiding and dismantling the dominance structures that contribute to oppression.

Such a model would require a change in traditional understandings of who has the relevant knowledge to make decisions about health and health policy. Once we recognize the need to include oppression as a factor in health, we can no longer maintain the authoritarian medical model, in which physicians are the experts on all matters of health and are authorized to respond to all such threats. We need also to recognize that experiential knowledge is essential to understanding how oppression affects health and how the damage of oppression can be reduced. Both political and moral understandings may be necessary to address these dimensions of health and health care. Physiological knowledge is still important, but it is not always decisive.

Therefore, a feminist model would resist hierarchical structures and proclaim a commitment to egalitarian alternatives. Not only would these alternatives be more democratic in themselves and hence more morally legitimate, they would also help to produce greater social equality by empowering those who have been traditionally disempowered. They would limit the scope for domination that is available to those now accustomed to power and control. More egalitarian structures would foster better health care and higher standards of health for those who are now oppressed in society; such structures would recognize voices that are now largely unheard and would be in a position to respond to the needs they express.

The current health care system is organized around the central ideal of pursuing a "cure" in the face of illness, wherein "cure" is interpreted with most of the requisite agency belonging to the health care providers. A feminist alternative would recommend that the health care system be principally concerned with empowering consumers in their own health by providing them with the relevant information and the means necessary to bring about the changes that would contribute to their health. The existing health care system, modeled as it is on the dominance structures of an oppressive society, is closed to many innovative health strategies that would increase the power of patients; a feminist model would be user-controlled and responsive to patient concerns.

Such a change in health care organization would require us to direct our attention to providing the necessities of healthy living, rather than trying only to correct the serious consequences that occur when the opportunities for personal care have been denied. Moreover, as an added benefit, a shift to a more democratized notion of health needs may help to evolve a less expensive, more effective health care delivery system; most patients seem to be less committed than are their professional health care providers to a costly high-tech, crisis-intervention focus in health care (York 1987).

A health care system that reflects feminist ideals would avoid or at least lessen the contribution that the system of health care makes in the maintenance of oppression. It would be significantly more egalitarian in both organization and effect than anything that we are now accustomed to. This system not only would be fairer in its provision of health services but would also help to undermine the ideological assumptions on which many of our oppressive practices rest. Such an

alternative is required as a matter of both ethics and health.

### References

Blount, Melissa. 1990. "Surpassing Obstacles: Pioneering Black Women Physicians." In *The Black Women's Health Book: Speaking for Ourselves,* ed. Evelyn C. White. Seattle: Seal Press.

Campbell, Margaret. 1973. "Why Would a Woman Go into Medicine?" *Medical Education in the United States: A Guide for Women.* Old Westbury, N.Y.: Feminist Press.

Gamble, Vanessa Northington. 1990. "On Becoming a Physician: A Dream Not Deferred." In *The Black Women's Health Book: Speaking for Ourselves,* ed. Evelyn C. White. Seattle: Seal Press.

Lewis, Andrea. 1990. "Looking at the Total Picture: A Conversation with Health Activist Beverly Smith." In *The Black Women's Health Book.* See Battle 1990.

McMurray, Richard J. 1990. "Gender Disparities in Clinical Decision-making." Report to the American Medical Association Council on Ethical and Judicial Affairs.

Morantz-Sanchez, Regina Markell. 1985. *Sympathy and Science: Women Physicians in American Medicine.* New York: Oxford University Press.

Weaver, Jerry L., and Sharon D. Garrett. 1983. "Sexism and Racism in the American Health Care Industry: A Comparative Analysis." In *Women and Health.* See Brown.

White, Evelyn C., ed., 1990. *The Black Women's Health Book: Speaking for Ourselves.* Seattle: Seal Press.

York, Geoffrey. 1987. *The High Price of Health: A Patient's Guide to the Hazards of Medical Politics.* Toronto: James Lorimer and Company.

# Bioethics: The Need for a Dialogue with African Americans

## Annette Dula

Annette Dula argues for the importance of expanding bioethics to include the perspectives of various racial and ethnic groups. While she focuses on African Americans, she sees the points she makes as also applying to Hispanics, Native Americans, Asians, and other groups who have had health-care experiences out of the mainstream.

The African-American perspective, according to Dula, has been shaped by the experience of receiving poor-quality care (a situation mostly ignored as a problem by bioethics) and by the emphasis on action and social justice found in the work of black philosophers. By reviewing the history of the birth control movement and the Tuskegee experiment, Dula illustrates the need for an African-American perspective on health care. She then uses the entrance of Blacks into professional psychology and the "white women's movement" to illustrate how the introduction of a new perspective can change social perceptions of a group, weaken stereotypes, and promote justice.

Dula asks that bioethics recognize access to health care as a serious bioethical problem requiring debate and action. She ends by calling for the formation of a community of scholars who will "conduct research and articulate the perspectives of African Americans and other poor and underserved peoples."

## Introduction

. . . I intend to show that the articulation and development of professional bioethics perspectives by minority academics are necessary to expand the narrow margins of debate. Without representation by every sector of society, the powerful and powerless alike, the discipline of bioethics is missing the opportunity to be enriched by the inclusion of a broader range of perspectives. Although I use African-American perspectives as an example, these points apply to other racial and ethnic groups—Hispanics, Native Americans, and Asians—who have suffered similar health care experiences.

In the first section of this chapter, I suggest that an African-American perspective on bioethics has two bases: (1) our health and medical experiences and (2) our tradition of black activist philosophy. In the second section, through examples, I show that an unequal power relationship has led to unethical medical behavior toward blacks, especially regarding reproductive issues. In the third section, I argue that developing a professional perspective not only gives voice to the concerns of those not in the power circle, but also enriches the entire field of bioethics.

## Medical and Health Experiences

The health of a people and the quality of health care they receive reflect their status in society. It should come as little surprise, then, that the health experiences of African Americans differ vastly from those of white people. These differences are well documented. Compared to whites, more than twice as many black babies are born with low birthweight and over twice as many die before their first birthday. Fifty percent more blacks than whites are likely to regard them-

selves as being in fair or poor health. Blacks are included in fewer trials of new drugs—an inequity of particular importance for AIDS patients, who are disproportionately black and Hispanic. The mortality rate for heart disease in black males is twice that for white males; research has shown that blacks tend to receive less aggressive treatment for this condition. More blacks die from cancer, which, unlike the situation in whites, is likely to be systemic by the time it is detected. African Americans live five fewer years than do whites. Indeed, if blacks had the same death rate as whites, 59,000 black deaths a year would not occur. Colin McCord and Harold P. Freeman, who reported that black men in Harlem are less likely to reach the age of 65 than are men in Bangladesh, conclude that the mortality rates of inner cities with largely black populations "justify special consideration analogous to that given to natural-disaster areas" (McCord and Freeman 1990, p. 173).

These health disparities are the result of at least three forces: institutional racism, economic inequality, and attitudinal barriers to access. Institutional racism has roots in the historically unequal power relations between blacks and the medical profession, and between blacks and the larger society. It has worked effectively to keep blacks out of the profession, even though a large percentage of those who manage to enter medicine return to practice in minority communities—where the need for medical professionals is greatest. Today, institutional racism in health care is manifested in the way African Americans and poor people are treated. They experience long waits, are unable to shop for services, and often receive poor quality and discontinuous health care. Moreover, many government programs do not target African Americans as a group. As a result, benefits to racially defined populations are diffused. There is hope: Healthy People 2000 complemented by the Clinton health care proposal can go a long way to reducing these problems.

Black philosopher W. E. B. Du Bois summed up the economic plight of African Americans: "To be poor is hard, but to be a poor race in a land of dollars is the very bottom of hardships" (Du Bois 1961, p. 20). Poor people are more likely to have poor health, and a disproportionate number of poor people are black. African Americans tend to have lower paying jobs and fewer income-producing sources such as investments. Indeed, whites on average accumulate eleven times more wealth than do blacks. Less money also leads to substandard housing—housing that may contain unacceptable levels of lead paint, asbestos insulation, or other environmental hazards. Thus, both inadequate employment and subpar housing available to poor African Americans present health problems that wealthier people are able to avoid. In addition, going to the doctor may entail finding and paying for a babysitter and transportation, and taking time off from work at the risk of being fired, all of which the poor cannot afford.

Attitudinal barriers—perceived racism, different cultural perspectives on health and sickness, and beliefs about the health care system—are a third force that brings unequal health care. Seeking medical help may not have the same priority for poor people as it has for middle-class people. One study in the *Journal of the American Medical Association* revealed that, compared to whites, blacks are less likely to be satisfied with how their physicians treat them, more dissatisfied with their hospital care, and more likely to believe that their hospital stay was too short. In addition, many blacks, like people of other racial and ethnic groups, use home remedies and adhere to traditional theories of illness and healing that lie outside of the mainstream medical model. Institutional racism, economic inequality, and attitudinal barriers, then, contribute to inadequate access to health care for poor and minority peoples. These factors must be seen as bioethical concerns. Bioethics cannot be exclusively medical or even ethical. Rather, it must also deal with beliefs, values, cultural traditions, and the economic, political, and social order. A number of medical sociologists have severely criticized bioethicists for ignoring cultural and societal particularities that limit access to health care.

This inattention to cultural and societal aspects of health care may be attributed in part to the mainstream Western philosophy on which the field of bioethics is built. For example, renowned academic bioethicists such as Robert Veatch, Tom Beauchamp, and Alasdair MacIntyre rely on the philosophical works of Rawls, Kant, and Aristotle. In addition, until recently the mainstream Western philosophic method has been presented primarily as a thinking enterprise, rarely advocating change or societal transformation. Thus, for the most part, Western philosophers have either gingerly approached or neglected altogether to comment on such social injustices as slavery, poverty, racism, sexism, and classism. As pointed out in *Black Issues in Higher Education,* until recently mainstream philosophy was seen as above questions of history and culture.

## Black Activist Philosophy

The second bias for an African-American perspective on bioethics is black activist philosophy. Black philosophy differs from mainstream philosophy in its emphasis on action and social justice. African-American philosophers view the world through a cultural and societal context of being an unequal partner. Many black philosophers believe that academic philosophy devoid of societal context is a luxury that black scholars can ill afford. Moreover, African-American philosophers have purposely elected to use philosophy as a tool not only for naming, defining, and analyzing social situations, but also for recommending, advocating, and sometimes harassing for political and social empowerment—a stance contrary to mainstream philosophic methods. Even though all bioethicists would do well to examine the thinking of such philosophers as Alain Locke, Lucius Outlaw, Anita Allen, Leonard Harris, W. E. B. Du Bois, Bernard Boxill, Angela Davis, Cornel West, William Banner, and Jorge Garcia, references to the work of these African Americans are rarely seen in the bioethics literature.

Although the professionalization of bioethics has frequently bypassed African-American voices, there are a few notable exceptions. Mark Siegler, director of the Center for Clinical Medical Ethics at the University of Chicago, included three African-American fellows in the 1990–91 medical ethics training program; Edmund Pellegrino of the Kennedy Institute for Advanced Ethics co-sponsored three national conferences on African-American perspectives on bioethics; and Howard Brody at Michigan State University is attempting to diversify his medical ethics program. In addition, a number of current publications offer important information for bioethicists. For example, the National Research Council's *A Common Destiny: Blacks and American Society* provides a comprehensive analysis of the status of black Americans, including discussions on health, education, employment, and economic factors, as does the National Urban

League's annual *The State of Black America;* Marlene Gerber Fried's *From Abortion to Reproductive Freedom* presents many ideas of women of color concerning abortion; and several journals (e.g., *Ethnicity and Disease,* published by the Loyola University School of Medicine, and *The Journal of Health Care for the Poor and Underserved*) call particular attention to the health experiences of poor and undeserved people. Finally, literature and narrative as forms of presenting African-American perspectives on bioethics are now being explored.

Clearly, bioethics and African-American philosophy overlap. Both are concerned with distributive justice and fairness, with autonomy and paternalism in unequal relationships, and with both individual and societal ills. African-American philosophy, therefore, may have much to offer bioethics in general and African-American bioethics in particular.

## Mainstream Issues Relevant to African Americans

A shocking history of medical abuse against unprotected people is also grounds for African-American perspectives in bioethics. In particular, reproductive rights issues—questions of family planning, sterilization, and genetic screening—are of special interest to black women.

A critical examination of the U.S. birth control movement reveals fundamental differences in perspectives, experiences, and interests between the white women who founded the movement and African-American women who were affected by it. Within each of three phases, the goals of the movement implicitly or explicitly served to exploit and subordinate African-American as well as poor white women.

The middle of the nineteenth century marked the beginning of the first phase of the birth control movement, characterized by the rallying cry "Voluntary Motherhood!" Advocates of voluntary motherhood asserted that women ought to say "no" to their husbands' sexual demands as a means of limiting the number of their children. The irony, of course, was that, while early white feminists were refusing their husbands' sexual demands, most black women did not have the same right to say "no" to these and other white women's husbands. Indeed, African-American women were exploited as breeding wenches in order to produce stocks of enslaved people for plantation owners. August Meier and Elliott Rudwick comment on slave-rearing as a major source of profit for nearly all slaveholding farmers and planters: "Though most Southern whites were scarcely likely to admit it, the rearing of slaves for profit was a common practice. [A] slave woman's proved or anticipated fecundity was an important factor in determining her market value; fertile females were often referred to as 'good breeders.'"

The second phase of the birth control movement gave rise to the actual phrase "birth control," coined by Margaret Sanger in 1915. Initially, this stage of the movement led to the recognition that reproductive rights and political rights were intertwined; birth control would give white women the freedom to pursue new opportunities made possible by the vote. This freedom allowed white women to go to work while black women cared for their children and did their housework.

This second stage coincided with the eugenics movement, which advocated improvement of the human race through selective breeding. When the white birth rate began to decline, eugenists chastised middle-class white women for contributing to the suicide of the white race: "Continued limitation of offspring in the white race simply invites the black, brown, and yellow races to finish work already begun by birth control, and reduce the whites to a subject race preserved merely for the sake of its skill."

Eugenists proposed a twofold approach for curbing "race suicide": imposing moral obligations on middle-class white women to have large families and on poor immigrant women and black women to restrict the size of theirs. For the second group, geneticists advocated birth control. The women's movement adopted the ideals of the eugenists regarding poor, immigrant, and minority women, and it even surpassed the rhetoric of the eugenists. Margaret Sanger described the relationship between the two groups: "The eugenists wanted to shift the birth-control emphasis from less children for the poor to more children for the rich. We went back of that [*sic*] and sought first to stop the multiplication of the unfit." Thus, while black women have historically practiced birth control, they learned to distrust the birth control movement as espoused by white feminists—a distrust that continues to the present day.

The third stage of the birth control movement began in 1942 with the establishment of the Planned Parenthood Federation of America. Although Planned Parenthood made valuable contributions to the independence, self-esteem, and aspirations of many women, it accepted existing power relations, continuing the eugenic tradition by defining undesirable "stock" by class or income level. Many blacks were suspicious of Planned Parenthood; men, particularly, viewed its policies as designed to weaken the black community politically or to wipe it out genetically. From the beginning of this century, both public and private institutions attempted to control the breeding of those deemed "undesirable." The first sterilization law was passed in Indiana in 1907, setting the stage for not only eugenic, but also punitive sterilization of criminals, the feebleminded, rapists, robbers, chicken thieves, drunkards, and drug addicts. By 1931 thirty states had passed sterilization laws, allowing more than 12,145 sterilizations. By the end of 1958, the sterilization total had risen to 60,926. In the 1950s several states attempted to extend sterilization laws to include compulsory sterilization of mothers of "illegitimate" children. As of 1991, sterilization laws were still in force in twenty-two states. They are seldom enforced, and where they have been, their eugenic significance has been negligible.

Numerous federal and state measures perpetuated a focus on poor women and women of color. Throughout the United States in the 1960s, the federal government began subsidizing family planning clinics designed to reduce the number of people on welfare by checking the transmission of poverty from generation to generation. The number of family planning clinics in a given geographical area was proportional to the number of black and Hispanic residents. In Puerto Rico, a massive federal birth control campaign introduced in 1937 was so successful that by the 1950s, the demand for sterilization exceeded facilities, and by 1965, one-third of the women in Puerto Rico had been sterilized.

In 1972 Los Angeles County Hospital, a hospital catering to large numbers of women of color, reported a sevenfold rise in hysterectomies. Between 1973 and 1976, almost 3,500 Native American women were sterilized at one Indian Health Service hospital in Oklahoma. In 1973 two black sisters from Montgomery, Alabama, 12-year-old Mary Alice Relf and 14-year-old Minnie Lee Relf, were reported to have been surgically sterilized without their parents' consent. An investigation revealed that in the same town, eleven other young girls of about the same age as the Relf sisters had also been sterilized; ten of them were black. During the early 1970s in Aiken, South Carolina, of thirty-four Medicaid-funded deliveries, eighteen included sterilizations, and all eighteen involved young black women. In 1972 Carl

Schultz, director of the Department of Health, Education, and Welfare's Population Affairs Office, acknowledged that the government had funded between 100,000 and 200,000 sterilizations. These policies aroused black suspicions that family planning efforts were inspired by racist and eugenist motives.

The first phase of the birth control movement, then, completely ignored black women's sexual subjugation to white masters. In the second phase, the movement adopted the racist policies of the eugenics movement. The third stage saw a number of government-supported coercive measures to contain the population of poor people and people of color. While blacks perceive birth control per se as beneficial, blacks have historically objected to birth control as a method of dealing with poverty. Rather, most blacks believe that poverty can be remedied only by creating meaningful jobs, raising the minimum wage so that a worker can support a family, providing health care to working and nonworking people through their jobs or through universal coverage, instituting a high-quality day care system for low- or no-income people, and improving educational opportunities.

## Informed Consent

Informed consent is one of the key ethical issues in bioethics. In an unequal patient–provider relationship, informed consent may not be possible. The weaker partner may consent because he or she is powerless, poor, or does not understand the implications of consent. And when members of subordinate groups are not awarded full respect as persons, those in positions of power then consider it unnecessary to obtain consent. The infamous Tuskegee experiment is a classic example. Starting in 1932, over 400 poor and uneducated syphilitic black men in Alabama were unwitting subjects in a Public Health Service experiment, condoned by the surgeon general, to study the course of untreated syphilis. Physicians told the men that they were going to receive special treatment, concealing the fact that the medical procedures were diagnostic rather than therapeutic. Although the effects of untreated syphilis were already known by 1936, the experiment continued for forty years. In 1969 a committee appointed by the Public Health Service to review the Tuskegee study decided to continue it. The Tuskegee experiment did not come to widespread public attention until 1972, when the *Washington Star* documented this breach of medical ethics. As a result, the experiment was halted. Unfortunately, however, the legacy of the experiment lingers on, as several chapters in this volume illustrate.

It may be tempting to assume that such medical abuses are part of the distant past. However, there is evidence that violations of informed consent persist. Of 52,000 Maryland women screened annually for sickle cell anemia between 1978 and 1980, 25 percent were screened without their consent, thus denying these women the benefit of prescreening education or followup counseling, or the opportunity to decline screening. A national survey conducted in 1986 found that 81 percent of women subjected to court-ordered obstetrical interventions (Caesarean section, hospital detention, or intrauterine transfusion) were black, Hispanic, or Asian; nearly half were unmarried; one-fourth did not speak English; and none were private patients. When in 1981, a Texas legislator asked his constituency whether they favored sterilization of women on welfare, a majority of the respondents said that welfare benefits should be tied to sterilizations.

## How a Professional Perspective Makes a Difference

Thus far, I have shown some grounds for African-American perspectives on bioethics, based on black activist philosophy and the unequal health status of African Americans. I have also argued that a history of medical abuse and neglect toward people in an unequal power relationship commands our attention to African-American perspectives on bioethics issues. In this final section, I will argue that a professional perspective can voice the concerns of those not in the power circle. Two examples—black psychology and the white women's movement—illustrate that professional perspectives can make a difference in changing society's perceptions and, ultimately, policies regarding a particular population.

### Black Psychology

Until recently, mainstream psychology judged blacks as genetically and mentally inferior, incapable of abstract reasoning, culturally deprived, passive, ugly, lazy, childishly happy, dishonest, and emotionally immature or disturbed. Mainstream psychology owned these definitions and viewed African Americans through a deficit–deficiency model—a model it had constructed to explain African-American behavior. When blacks entered the profession of psychology, they challenged that deficit model by presenting an

African-American perspective that addressed the dominant group's assessments and changed, to a certain extent, the way society views blacks. Real consequences of black psychologists' efforts to encourage self-definition, consciousness, and self-worth have been felt across many areas: professional training, intelligence and ability testing, criminal justice, and family counseling. Black psychologists have presented their findings before professional conferences, legislative hearings, and policy-making task forces. For example, black psychologists are responsible for the ban in California on using standardized intelligence tests as a criterion for placing black and other minority students in classes for the mentally retarded. The Association of Black Psychologists publishes the *Journal of Black Psychology,* and black psychologists contribute to a variety of other professional journals. As a result of these and other efforts, most respected psychologists no longer advocate the deficit–deficiency model.

### The Women's Movement

The women's movement is another example of a subordinated group defining its own perspectives. The perspectives of white women have historically been defined largely by white men; white women's voices, like black voices, have traditionally been ignored or trivialized. A mere twenty years ago, the question, "Should there be a woman's perspective on health?" was emotionally debated. Although the question is still asked, a respected discipline of women's studies has emerged, with several journals devoted to women's health. Women in increasing numbers have been drawn to the field of applied ethics, specifically to bioethics, and they debate issues such as maternal and child health, rights of women versus rights of the fetus, unnecessary hysterectomies and Caesareans, the doctor–patient relationship, and the absence of women in clinical trials of new drugs. Unfortunately, however, the mainstream women's movement is largely the domain of white women. This, of course, does not mean that black women have not been activists for women's rights; on the contrary, African-American women historically have been deeply involved in fighting both racism and sexism, believing that the two are inseparable. Many black women distrust the movement, criticizing it as racist and self-serving, concerned only with white middle-class women's issues. Black feminists working within the abortion rights movement and with the National Black Women's Health Project, an Atlanta-based self-help and health advocacy organization, are raising their voices to identify issues relevant to African-American women and men in general, and reproductive and health issues in particular. Like black psychologists, these black feminists are articulating a perspective that is effectively promoting pluralism.

## Conclusion

The disturbing health inequities between blacks and whites—differences in infant mortality, average life span, chronic illnesses, and aggressiveness of treatment—suggest that minority access to health care should be recognized and accepted as a *bona fide* concern of bioethics. Opening the debate can only enrich this new field, thereby avoiding the moral difficulties of exclusion. Surely the serious and underaddressed health concerns of a large and increasing segment of our society are an ethical issue that is at least as im-

portant as such esoteric, high-visibility issues as the morality of gestational surrogacy. The front page of the August 5, 1991, *New York Times* headlined an article, "When Grandmother Is Mother, Until Birth." Although interesting and worthy of ethical comment, such sensational headlines undermine the moral seriousness of a situation in which over 37 million poor people do not have access to health care.

There is a basis for developing African-American perspectives on bioethics, and I have presented examples of medical abuse and neglect that suggest particular issues for consideration. Valuable as our advocacy has been, our perspectives have not gained full prominence in bioethics debates. Thus, it is necessary to form a community of scholars to conduct research on the contributions as well as the limitations of perspectives of African-American and other poor and underserved peoples in this important field.

---

## READINGS

## Section 2: Conducting Research

## Women and Underserved Populations: Access to Clinical Trials

### Sara Goering

Sara Goering claims that clinical trials restricted to white male subjects are not generalizable to other populations, who may even be harmed if the trials are used as a basis for treatment. She argues that women and minorities must be included in the studies and counters such arguments against including them as the necessity of avoiding confounding factors, the risk of harming the fetuses of pregnant women, the difficulties of recruiting female and minority subjects, and the potential for exploiting minority populations.

Goering argues that in the interest of acting fairly and not causing harm, these objections must be overcome. So too must the dangers of racism and sexism that always threaten when race and sex differences are explicitly studied.

Reprinted from *"It Just Ain't Fair": The Ethics of Health Care for African Americans,* ed. Annette Dula and Sara Goering (Westport, Conn.: Praeger, 1994), pp. 182–189. © 1994 by Annette Dula and Sara Goering. Reprinted by permission. (References edited.)

### Introduction

Lack of adequate access to health care for traditionally underserved populations (most notably poor ethnic minorities and women) is tied to a lack of medical research focused on their particular needs. The two problems are intricately related—each feeds on the other. Many of the factors that make access to health care difficult for underserved populations (including, for instance, lack of funding, geographical maldistribution of services, inadequate transportation, and cultural or linguistic differences and discrimination) also make it difficult to involve them as subjects in medical research. Although a majority of these barriers to health care could be overcome by balancing current socioeconomic inequities, a growing body of literature suggests that in at least some instances diseases themselves may be manifested differently among the races and sexes, requiring different kinds or levels of treatment. Thus, socioeconomic reparations alone will not remedy the health problems of underserved ethnic groups and women. Without research to assess the particular needs of these groups, access to the existing health care system might not significantly help them and in some cases could even be harmful. . . .

In this [selection] I will show why restricting medical research to studies done with white, middle-aged men as subjects is inappropriate and unjust. I will point to several examples in which such conduct has led to worrisome results. I will also show how the current justifications for the exclusion of minorities and women in research are based on racism and sexism in the medical establishment, and suggest that steps be taken to remedy this situation. Finally, I will offer a word of caution regarding the segregation of races and sexes in research, for the potential for great benefits is tainted with the possibility of serious costs.

## Problems with the White Male Model

A growing body of literature reveals clinical studies in which ethnic and sex differences have a significant effect on the course and kind of treatment. Simply extrapolating data obtained from white middle-aged men is proving not to be the answer to settling these differences. Although they are an easily accessible population to procure as research subjects, white middle-aged men are not a truly representative population, and the seemingly less accessible populations pay the price of misrepresentation.

Techniques and treatments that have been studied on white middle-aged men in a controlled and closely monitored research environment are then unleashed on the much more diverse general population, most often without the security of the clinical setting.

Patients from populations who experience difficulties in getting access to health care may be given a new treatment and never be heard from again, at least not by the same physician. Given that population differences in disease manifestation and treatment do exist, this is a dangerous method of treating underserved populations and may place them in even greater danger than the illness for which they believe they are receiving treatment. In what follows, I will give several examples as evidence of this problem. Clearly, the solution is to target more clinical studies on the particular medical needs of these populations, using members of the groups themselves as subjects.

Thus far, the issue of ethnic and sex differences in disease diagnosis and treatment has been addressed only in obvious cases, such as sickle cell disease among African Americans, Tay-Sachs among Eastern European Jews. . . .  Noteworthy population differences, however, go far beyond these most obvious cases. Consider the following examples.

Studies conducted on white men led the American Heart Association to suggest a diet for all Americans to reduce their cholesterol levels in order to decrease the risk of coronary heart disease. Although they recommended a general reduction in cholesterol intake, they targeted low-density lipoprotein (LDLs) in particular. Further studies, however, have suggested that, although high levels of LDLs are dangerous for men, they are far less threatening for women. In addition, women are much more sensitive to low levels of the so-called good cholesterol, or high-density lipoprotein (HDLs). This means that diets that recommend a general cholesterol reduction are potentially harmful to women.

In another study, African-American men with psychiatric problems traditionally treated with lithium, a drug tested and used successfully on white men, suffered excessive toxic reactions when treated with the drug. It was found that the African-American men as a group had less efficient lithium–sodium countertransport mechanisms than white men. The toxicity of the lithium treatment greatly increased the already high risk of renal failure for the African-American men.

A number of studies have shown that Asian patients reacts more strongly than whites when treated with popranolol, a beta-blocker that reduces heart rate and blood pressure. While this variation was traditionally accounted for by generalized differences in body size and/or weight, new evidence shows that Asians as a group have a much faster metabolism for popranolol than whites and that a smaller percentage of the dosage is inactivated by plasma protein binding in Asians. On the other hand, data show that African-American hypertensive patients do not respond to beta-blockers as well as whites and that the serum concentration of popranolol is lower in African-American patients than in whites who received identical doses.

While the list of studies showing significant differences between populations goes on, its length is not to be outdone by the number of studies continuing to ignore these findings. For instance, an NIH-funded study on the potential prophylactic effects of aspirin on heart disease was conducted entirely on men, although heart disease is the number one killer of women. One reason cited for the exclusion of women as subjects was the lack of available women physicians. (The study was conducted with physicians as subjects.) Others blame the extra time and money that would have been needed to complete the study to significance. . . .

The lack of women in the subject population of this study made it difficult for many doctors to personally prescribe the courses of action that are publicly suggested by organizations such as the American Heart Association. However, after an uproar about the unknown effects of regular aspirin consumption on women, another study was undertaken with female nurses as subjects, with the conclusion that aspirin does indeed reduce the risk of heart attack for women. The fact that these studies rendered similar results for both sexes should not be too quickly generalized to other disorders and treatments.

Recently, for example, concern has arisen about sex differences in response to HIV infection. In order to be considered for most clinical drug trials for AIDS, a person must exhibit "full-blown" AIDS, which includes a broad spectrum of illnesses related to HIV infections. Until recently, many women did not fit this description because their infections had progressed in a different pattern than that strictly recognized as AIDS, resulting in a new diagnosis, AIDS Related Complex (ARC). If HIV affects men and women differently, resulting in varying groups of infections, we ought not limit our studies to the syndrome as it affects men. In 1993 the Centers for Disease Control revised its classification system for HIV infection, in part to address these concerns.

Craig Svensson has investigated the exclusion of African Americans from clinical drug trials, focusing on studies published in *Clinical Pharmacology and Therapeutics* over a three-year period.[1] He found that only ten of fifty published accounts of new drug trials included any racial data, and even in the study of antihypertensive drugs, an area in which differential racial responses to drug treatments have been well-documented, only about half of the researchers gave racial data. Of the antihypertensive studies that included subjects of different races, only one attempted to determine if there was a race-related response difference. Furthermore, in more than half of the trials in which racial data were available, the percentage of African-American subjects was less than the percentage of African Americans in the community and in the U.S. population. Apparently, African Americans were underrepresented in the clinical trials, and as Svensson notes, this "suggests that insufficient data exist to accurately assess the safety and efficacy of many new drugs in blacks."[2]

## Justifications for the Exclusions in Clinical Trials

How do researchers explain this blatant and seemingly unethical exclusion of ethnic minorities and women in medical research? Their reasoning is varied and extensive, covering problems from financing and recruitment to problems with tight experimental control and subject safety. Svensson's study suggests that many researchers simply have not even considered racial health differences a pertinent issue in their research. In what follows, I will address these so-called justifications and show why none of them is truly substantial, and how most of them can be overcome.

Some of the researchers involved claim that using white middle-aged men is necessary because of the need to maintain tight experimental controls and to avoid confounding factors. Clearly, research done on homogeneous groups yields tighter, more exact results. Yet this is precisely the problem at hand. The tighter and more exact the results are, the less they can be safely generalized to the population as a whole. Since the population in general is not homogeneous, why should we take data from one of the homogeneous groups within it and apply it to all the other groups? Surely it would be safer and more beneficial to society as a whole to study representative groups from each population sector and thus to obtain tight and exact data specific to each population's distinct needs.

In defense of the exclusion of women in medical research, many researchers claim that the fluctuating hormonal cycles of women serve as confounding factors in clinical studies. However, as Dresser correctly questions, "Why is it female, but not male, hormones that 'complicate' research?"[3] Why is it that white men must serve as the exclusive prototype? In addition, one wonders why, if the menstrual cycles of women may complicate the experimental results, women are then allowed and even encouraged to abide by the results obtained on men—results that take no account of the potential complications? The fact is, women have distinct hormonal cycles, and if complications are a possibility during clinical trials, then they are also a possibility after drug or treatment approval, when women may be taking a new drug outside the safe confines of the clinical setting.

Another excuse for not using women as subjects in clinical trials deals with the possibility that a woman may become pregnant while participating in the research. In such a case, participation in the experiment may cause complications with the pregnancy, miscarriage, or birth defects. This means that, in effect, "In the name of *potential* protection for *potentially* pregnant women and their fetuses, all women have lost the opportunity to improve and extend their lives." This attempted justification ignores the fact that many potential women subjects may be beyond their reproductive years, not sexually active, or simply taking adequate precautions against pregnancy. To preclude all women from participating is to assume that all women are simply walking wombs who are unreliable in their contraceptive practices. This assumption is a bit ridiculous, particularly when some of the women concerned may be elderly cardiac patients who presumably are not planning pregnancies.

Even if we consider only sexually active fertile women who are in their reproductive years, it seems that we really ought to allow these women themselves to make decisions regarding their participation in clinical trials. Most of the women in this group would no doubt prefer to be informed of the risks and hazards as well as the potential benefits, and then to choose whether to participate. We might also ask why sexually active fertile women of reproductive age are excluded while men of the same class are allowed, and in many

cases encouraged, to participate. Drugs and other treatments that could potentially damage a woman's reproductive system or a fetus might very well also have a detrimental effect on a man's sperm.

Problems associated with the recruitment of minority and women subjects are also often cited as reasons for their exclusion in clinical trials. There are at least several reasons for recruitment problems. First, these difficulties point to much greater problems within the medical system. For instance, a great disparity exists between the numbers of ethnic minorities and women, as compared to white men, studying in medical schools and working as medical researchers and physicians. Therefore, this common subject pool for medical research is nearly devoid of available non-standard (white male) subjects. The long-term answer is to get a more diverse population into the profession. In the short term, however, there are other solutions. Clearly, subjects will have to come from outside the medical system, and the solution to their recruitment will have to address the existing obstacles. Poor women, for example, may need help with child care and transportation in order to participate. This will undoubtedly involve extra financial burdens on the researchers and, in the end, on the taxpaying public, but . . . potential payoffs are surely worth the associated costs.

Second, widespread distrust of the medical establishment was understandably strengthened after the Tuskegee study (in which African-American men with syphilis were deliberately left untreated in order to study the course of the disease; this study started in the 1930s and was not ended until 1972). Following this study, the National Commission for the Protection of Human Research Subjects of Biomedical and Behavioral Research released the Belmont Report, which warned against "vulnerable subjects . . . such as racial minorities . . . being continually sought as research subjects" owing to their availability in research-oriented university and public hospitals. The commission was concerned that less advantaged populations would become guinea pigs for treatments that would in the end be more readily available to the more advantaged groups who weren't involved in the risks and discomforts of the research. While this was and remains a serious concern, researchers may have overcompensated, translating it into a policy of complete exclusion of minorities and women from clinical studies. Today we must understand that ethnic minorities and women have much to gain from participation in clinical studies. As long as their participation is carefully controlled and not abused, they will be able to reap benefits that have for too long accrued almost exclusively to white men.

One potential solution to the recruitment problems is to start with community-based research that comes out of minority practices and clinics in underserved areas. Minority populations will presumably be more likely to trust community health care facilities and physicians than more distant and less personal health care providers. This would also alleviate some of the problems of transportation, accessibility, and linguistic or cultural differences and discrimination in the delivery of health care. . . . However, potential conflicts of interest exist when the provider serves a dual role as researcher and physician.

Finally, there are the inevitable financial difficulties associated with intensified recruitment and more diverse research. These difficulties have been remedied in part by the recent NIH Women's Health Initiative— a ten-year, $500 million study involving three large-scale research projects on women's health issues. This project was launched under the directorship of Bernadine Healy, after several years of NIH guideline revisions regarding the inclusion of women and minorities in research, and a General Accounting Office investigation into the rules, spurred by the Congressional Caucus for Women's Issues. The result is an enormous and lengthy research initiative for women's health issues. Significant financial backing for health issues specific to particular ethnic groups is needed before we can realistically feel that health care equity in clinical studies is being adequately addressed.

## Conclusion

There are, of course, more problems on the horizon. Acknowledging inherent differences between the races and sexes may inadvertently cause a rise in racism and sexism. It may refuel the fires of the once livid nature/nurture debate, which will bring with it all

the misconceptions about superior and inferior genetic abilities associated with eugenics. It may "serve only the interests of those eager to blame the disproportionate share of the burden of poverty and disease borne by minorities on inherent racial traits and genetic defects rather than on societal problems such as poverty, suboptimal health care, or a legacy of racial prejudice."[4] Differences in disease manifestation, treatment, and incidence among population sectors could lead to increases in discrimination and exclusionary hiring practices. Differences between the blood and kidneys of different ethnic groups could lead to white-only or black-only blood banks and organ donor lists, reminiscent of the segregated drinking fountains and restaurants of another era.

On the other hand, failing to acknowledge the differences is also a form of racism, one that is alive and well today, and that is thus perhaps more important than the distant fear. Our society ought to be able to address the inherent differences among its population and embrace them, rather than instinctively labeling them as flaws. As Dresser has said, "Perhaps we have come far enough to recognize such differences without transforming them into tools for maintaining the traditional social hierarchy" (p. 29). The challenge is ours to move forward rather than to stagnate or return to the clearly unjust ways of bygone eras. An ethical medical establishment must ascertain the particular needs of all its patients and must find a way to allow them equity in access to treatment. One of the first steps toward this goal should be the inclusion of nontraditional groups as subjects of medical research.

## Notes

1. C. K. Svensson, "Representation of American Blacks in Clinical Trials of New Drugs," *Journal of the American Medical Association* 261(2) (1989): 263–265.—ED.

2. Svensson, p. 265—ED.

3. R. Dresser, "Wanted: Single, White Male for Medical Research," *Hastings Center Report* 22(1) (1992): 24.—ED.

4. N. Osbourne and M. D. Feit, "The Use of Race in Medical Research," *Journal of the American Medical Association* 267(2) (1992): 275–279.—ED.

# The Dangers of Difference: The Legacy of the Tuskegee Syphilis Study

## Patricia A. King

Patricia King, like Goering (see preceding reading), recognizes that clinical research cannot afford to ignore racial differences. Even so, she points out, focusing on racial differences has injured already stigmatized groups more often than it has helped them.

King proposes that research always begin with the presumption that, with respect to disease, Blacks and Whites are biologically identical. While the presumption may be shown to be wrong in the course of the study, it acknowledges that, historically speaking, more harm has come from imputing racial differences than from ignoring them.

It has been sixty years since the beginning of the Tuskegee syphilis experiment and twenty years since its existence was disclosed to the American public. The social and ethical issues that the experiment poses for medicine, particularly for medicine's relationship with African Americans, are still not broadly understood, appreciated, or even remembered. Yet a significant aspect of the Tuskegee experiment's legacy is that in a racist society that incorporates beliefs about the inherent inferiority of African Americans in contrast with the superior status of whites, any attention to the question of differences that may exist is likely to be pursued in a manner that burdens rather than benefits African Americans.

The Tuskegee experiment, which involved approximately 400 males with late-stage, untreated syphilis and approximately 200 controls free of the disease, is by any measure one of the dark pages in the history of American medicine. In this study of the natural course of untreated syphilis, the participants did not give informed consent. Stunningly, when penicillin was subsequently developed as a treatment for syphilis, measures were taken to keep the diseased participants from receiving it.

Patricia A. King, "The Dangers of Difference," *Hastings Center Report*, Vol. 22, No. 6 (1992), pp. 35–38. Reprinted by permission of the author and publisher. © The Hastings Center. (Most notes omitted.)

Obviously, the experiment provides a basis for the exploration of many ethical and social issues in medicine, including professional ethics, the limitations of informed consent as a means of protecting research subjects, and the motives and methods used to justify the exploitation of persons who live in conditions of severe economic and social disadvantage. At bottom, however, the Tuskegee experiment is different from other incidents of abuse in clinical research because all the participants were black males. The racism that played a central role in this tragedy continues to infect even our current well-intentioned efforts to reverse the decline in health status of African Americans. . . .

## The Dilemma of Difference

In the context of widespread belief in the racial inferiority of blacks that surrounded the Tuskegee experiment, it should not come as a surprise that the experiment exploited its subjects. Recognizing and taking account of racial differences that have historically been utilized to burden and exploit African Americans poses a dilemma. Even in circumstances where the goal of a scientific study is to benefit a stigmatized group or person, such well-intentioned efforts may nevertheless cause harm. If the racial difference is ignored and all groups or persons are treated similarly, unintended harm may result from the failure to recognize racially correlated factors. Conversely, if differences among groups or persons are recognized and attempts are made to respond to past injustices or special burdens, the effort is likely to reinforce existing negative stereotypes that contributed to the emphasis on racial differences in the first place.

This dilemma about difference is particularly worrisome in medicine. Because medicine is pragmatic, it will recognize racial differences if doing so will promote health goals. As a consequence, potential harms that might result from attention to racial differences tend to be overlooked, minimized, or viewed as problems beyond the purview of medicine.

The question of whether (and how) to take account of racial differences has recently been raised in the context of the current AIDS epidemic. The participation of African Americans in clinical AIDS trials has been disproportionately small in comparison to the numbers of African Americans who have been infected with the human immunodeficiency virus. Because of the possibility that African Americans may respond differently to drugs being developed and tested to combat AIDS, those concerned about the care and treatment of AIDS in the African American community have called for greater participation by African Americans in these trials. Ironically, efforts to address the problem of underrepresentation must cope with the enduring legacy of the Tuskegee experiment—the legacy of suspicion and skepticism toward medicine and its practitioners among African Americans.

In view of the suspicion Tuskegee so justifiably engenders, calls for increased participation by African Americans in clinical trials are worrisome. The question of whether to tolerate racially differentiated AIDS research testing of new or innovative therapies, as well as the question of what norms should govern participation by African Americans in clinical research, needs careful and thoughtful attention. A generic examination of the treatment of racial differences in medicine is beyond the scope of this article. However, I will describe briefly what has occurred since disclosure of the Tuskegee experiment to point out the dangers I find lurking in our current policies.

## Inclusion and Exclusion

In part because of public outrage concerning the Tuskegee experiment, comprehensive regulations governing federal research using human subjects were revised and subsequently adopted by most federal agencies. An institutional review board (IRB) must ap-

prove clinical research involving human subjects, and IRB approval is made contingent on review of protocols for adequate protection of human subjects in accordance with federal criteria. These criteria require, among other things, that an IRB ensure that subject selection is "equitable." The regulations further provide that

> [i]n making this assessment the IRB should take into account the purposes of the research and the setting in which the research will be conducted, and should be particularly cognizant of the special problems of research involving vulnerable populations, such as women, mentally disabled persons, or economically or educationally disadvantaged persons.[1]

The language of the regulation makes clear that the concern prompting its adoption was the protection of vulnerable groups from exploitation. The obverse problem—that too much protection might promote the exclusion or underrepresentation of vulnerable groups, including African Americans—was not at issue. However, underinclusion can raise as much of a problem of equity as exploitation.

A 1990 General Accounting Office study first documented the extent to which minorities and women were underrepresented in federally funded research. In response, in December 1990 the National Institutes of Health, together with the Alcohol, Drug Abuse and Mental Health Administration, directed that minorities and women be included in study populations,

> so that research findings can be of benefit to all persons at risk of the disease, disorder or condition under study; special emphasis should be placed on the need for inclusion of minorities and women in studies of diseases, disorders and conditions that disporportionately affect them.[2]

If minorities are not included, a clear and compelling rationale must be submitted.

The new policy clearly attempts to avoid the perils of overprotection, but it raises new concerns. The policy must be clarified and refined if it is to meet the intended goal of ensuring that research findings are of benefit to all. There are at least three reasons for favoring increased representation of African Americans in clinical trials. The first is that there may be biological differences between blacks and whites that might affect the applicability of experimental findings to blacks, but these differences will not be noticed if blacks are not included in sufficient numbers to allow the detection of statistically significant racial differences. The second reason is that race is a reliable index for social conditions such as poor health and nutrition, lack of adequate access to health care, and economic and social disadvantage that might adversely affect potential benefits of new interventions and procedures. If there is indeed a correlation between minority status and these factors, then African Americans and all others with these characteristics will benefit from new information generated by the research. The third reason is that the burdens and benefits of research should be spread across the population regardless of racial or ethnic status. . . .

The third justification carries with it the obvious danger that the special needs or problems generated as a result of economic or social conditions associated with minority status may be overlooked and that, as a result, African Americans and other minorities will be further disadvantaged. The other two justifications are problematic and deserve closer examination. They each assume that there are either biological, social, economic, or cultural differences between blacks and whites. . . .

## The Way Out of the Dilemma

Understanding how, or indeed whether, race correlates with disease is a very complicated problem. Race itself is a confusing concept with both biological and social connotations. Some doubt whether race has biological significance at all. Even if race is a biological fiction, however, its social significance remains.

In the wake of Tuskegee and, in more recent times, the stigma and discrimination that resulted from screening for sickle-cell trait (a genetic condition that occurs with greater frequency among African Americans), researchers have been reluctant to explore associations between race and disease. There is increasing recognition, however, of evidence of heightened resistance or vulnerability to disease along racial lines. Indeed, sickle-cell anemia itself substantiates the view that biological differences may exist. Nonetheless, separating myth from reality in determining the cause of disease and poor health status is not easy. Great caution should be exercised in attempting to validate biological differences in susceptibility to disease in light of this society's past experience with biological differences. Moreover, using race as an index for other conditions that might influence health and well-being is also dangerous. Such practices could emphasize social and economic differences that might also lead to stigma and discrimination.

If all the reasons for increasing minority participation in clinical research are flawed, how then can we promote improvement in health status of African Americans and other minorities through participation in clinical research, while simultaneously minimizing the harms that might flow from such participation? Is it possible to work our way out of this dilemma?

An appropriate strategy should have as its starting point the defeasible presumption that blacks and whites are biologically the same with respect to disease and treatment. Presumptions can be overturned of course, and the strategy should recognize the possibility that biological differences in some contexts are possible. But the presumption of equality acknowledges that historically the greatest harm has come from the willingness to impute biological differences rather than the willingness to overlook them. For some, allowing the presumption to be in any way defeasible is troubling. Yet I do not believe that fear should lead us to ignore the possibility of biologically differentiated responses to disease and treatment, especially when the goal is to achieve medical benefit.

It is well to note at this point the caution sounded by Hans Jonas. He wrote, "Of the new experimentation with man, medical is surely the most legitimate; psychological, the most dubious; biological (still to come), the most dangerous."[3] Clearly, priority should be given to exploring the possible social, cultural, and environmental determinants of disease before targeting the study of hypotheses that involve biological differences between blacks and whites. For example, rather than trying to determine whether blacks and whites respond differently to AZT, attention should first be directed to learning whether response to AZT is influenced by social, cultural, or environmental conditions. Only at the point where possible biological differences emerge should hypotheses that explore racial differences be considered.

A finding that blacks and whites are different in some critical aspect need not inevitably lead to increased discrimination or stigma for blacks. If there indeed had been a difference in the effects of untreated syphilis between blacks and whites such information might have been used to promote the health status of blacks. But the Tuskegee experiment stands as a reminder that such favorable outcomes rarely if ever occur. More often, either racist assumptions and stereotypes creep into the study's design, or findings broken down by race become convenient tools to support policies and behavior that further disadvantage those already vulnerable.

**Notes**

1. 45 *Code of Federal Regulations* §46.111 (a)(3).

2. National Institutes of Health and Alcohol, Drug Abuse and Mental Health Administration, "Special Instructions to Applicants Using Form PHS 398 Regarding Implementation of the NIH/ADAMHA Policy Concerning Inclusion of Women and Minorities in Clinical Research Study Populations," December 1990.

3. Hans Jonas, "Philosophical Reflections on Experimenting with Human Subjects," in *Experimentation with Human Subjects,* ed. Paul A. Freund (New York: George Braziller, 1970), p. 1.

## READINGS

# Section 3: Setting Public Policy

## The Demise of Affirmative Action and the Future of Health Care

### H. Jack Geiger

Jack Geiger argues that the drop in medical school admissions of African Americans and other minorities, due to factors like the rollback of affirmative action and the underfunding of public schools, is the beginning of a "potential public health disaster."

By 2050 minority groups will make up the majority of the population, but who will be their physicians? A diverse population, Geiger says, "requires a diverse, culturally competent physician workforce" able to meet people's needs. Developing such a workforce requires recognizing that medical education is a social good and not merely a prize awarded to favored individuals. Yet our policies appear to be taking our society in the opposite direction.

Just over 50 years ago, fewer than 4000 of the more than 200,000 American physicians were African American. More than a third of all US medical schools were closed to non-Whites. Only 8 graduates of Howard and Meharry, the traditionally Black medical schools, were training in White hospitals. Only 20 predominantly White schools had any African American students. As recently as 30 years ago, 99% of the students in US medical schools other than Howard and Meharry were non-Hispanic Whites. The legacy of that era of injustice, racial segregation, and exclusion is with us now: White males constitute 37% of the US population—but more than 67% of all US physicians.[1]

Progress over the last 30 years has been substantial, but its course has been as erratic and fitful as the nation's overall commitment to racial justice and equity of opportunity. As a result of the civil rights movement and a concerted effort by medical schools,[2] underrepresented minorities (African Americans, Mexican Americans, mainland Puerto Ricans, and Native Americans) reached 10% of the total number of medical students by the mid-1970s, but then began to drop. (Ironically, minority population growth occurred much more rapidly during this period, so that minority underrepresentation in medical schools—despite the enrollment gains—actually increased.) A renewed intensive effort by the Association of American Medical Colleges[3] helped to produce a 36% increase in minority enrollment—to 12%—between 1990 and 1995. But then the assault on affirmative action, a backlash that had produced relatively modest limitations over the preceding 2 decades, resulted in the passage in California of Proposition 209, a voter initiative flatly barring so-called racial or ethnic preferences (even to pursue the goal of diversity) as a factor in admission to the University of California system. (Preferences for athletes, veterans, women, and the children of alumni were not addressed.) In Texas, the decision in *Hopwood*

Original title, "Ethnic Cleansing in the Groves of Academe," *American Journal of Public Health,* Vol. 88, No. 9, (1998), pp. 1299–1300. Reprinted by permission of the American Public Health Assn.

*v. Texas* had the same effect on admission to public universities in that state, Louisiana, and Mississippi.

The data presented by Carlisle et al.[4] in this issue of the Journal show that the damaging effect of such decisions on minority enrollment, while worse regionally, is national in scope. Overall, the admission of underrepresented minorities to the 1997 entering medical school class fell by 9.1%, on the heels of a 5.2% drop in 1996. The states of California, Texas, Mississippi, and Louisiana accounted for 44% of the decline. What is most ominous is that these reversals were concentrated in public institutions: minority enrollment declined at 61% of publicly funded schools, and 9 of the 10 schools with the biggest percentage drops were public. Yet two thirds of all underrepresented minority students attend such institutions. If these trends continue—and there are powerful reasons to believe that they will—we will return to the levels of the 1980s, or worse.

Not everyone, apparently, regards this as a bad thing. In a little-noted and blatantly racist remark to the *New York Times* in 1997, Ward Connerly, regent of the University of California, said, "If you're lying on a gurney, and a black doctor shows up, you're going to get up and crawl out."[5] Such comments rest on an elaborate structure of myths, fallacies, and slurs: that quantitative instruments such as the Scholastic Achievement Test and the Medical College Admission Test are the only meaningful measures of applicant quality; that they are predictive of future clinical and professional performance; that they reflect only "innate ability" or "individual merit" and not, as well, the preparatory resources available to different groups of students; that it is only the playing field that need be level, and not the path that leads to it; that modest differences in mean scores justify an indelible label of "less qualified," even among those who successfully pass all subsequent educational and professional hurdles; and, in the racist extreme, that lower scores indicate genetic inferiority.[6] All of these allegations have been elegantly refuted;[7] still, they persist.

What is perhaps not fully recognized is that these reversals in minority admissions are merely the leading edge of a potential public health disaster. Application to medical school, after all, comes at the end of a long educational pipeline. The public school preparatory route, from kindergarten through high school and college, is equally under assault—most intensely where the majority of the students are minorities, or poor, or immigrants, or come from non-English-speaking homes, or all of the above.

Peter Schrag, in the recently published *Paradise Lost: California's Experience, America's Failure*,[8] offers that state's version of the savage inequalities in public education portrayed nationally by Jonathon Kozol.[9] As the state's demographics changed, Schrag points out, California's public schools, once the envy of the nation, have literally begun to rot. The state now spends $1000 less per child than the national median. It ranks 38th among the states in spending on library books and 45th in spending on computer software, and 54% of its high school teachers don't have enough textbooks for all their students. "There are schools," Schrag reports, "where ceilings are flaking, bare wiring hangs down, and floors buckle; where rotting planks make walkways dangerous. . . . " A million students are housed in "temporary" buildings "which now look more often like migrant camps."[8(pp67–71)] And so, he reports, California public school students now rank 49th in reading and are tied for dead last in mathematics proficiency.

At the next level up, the combined effects of these levels of preparation and Proposition 209 can be seen in admission to the state university's elite campuses at Berkeley and Los Angeles (UCLA). Admission rates for African Americans and Hispanics were cut nearly in half, from 22% last year to 10.5% this year at Berkeley and from 22% to 14% at UCLA. Overall, the university system is now 85% White and Asian. Yet—to use the criteria so favored by affirmative action opponents—roughly 400 of the minority students who "failed to qualify" at Berkeley had perfect high school grade-point averages of 4.0 and Scholastic Achievement Test scores over 1200.

These are not just West Coast phenomena. The trustees of the City University of New York, where the student body is 70% non-White and heavily immigrant, recently voted to deny admission to students who failed any placement test in reading, writing, or mathematics and to prohibit the senior colleges from continuing to offer remediation courses. It is estimated that this change will bar 67% of African American applicants, 70% of Latinos, and 71% of Asians; overall, the senior colleges will lose 13,000 students a year and suffer crippling budget cuts in consequence. One trustee said, "We are *cleaning out* the four-year colleges, and putting remediation where it belongs [italics added]."[10] And at the same time, presumably, putting the minority students where they "belong." Whatever the intent, the effect will be clear. To use the trustee's metaphor, it will be the academic equivalent of ethnic cleansing.

What has all this to do with public health? We have only to look at the demographics. From 1980 to 1995 in the US, the White population increased by 12%, while African Americans increased by 24%, Hispanics by 83%, Native Americans by 57%, and Asians by 163%. By 2050, if not earlier, the members of these minority groups will make up the majority of Americans.[11] Who will provide their medical care—and that of the minority of Whites as well? If present patterns persist, access to care for those in greatest need and at greatest risk will worsen; what are now shameful disparities could become public health failures of staggering magnitude.

The argument is not that minority physicians must be the ones who care for the underserved, the people of color, the poorest and sickest of our populations, though the evidence is overwhelming that this is disproportionately the case at present.[12–14] The argument is, rather, that a diverse population in a democracy requires a diverse, culturally competent physician workforce that is fully prepared—by background, motivation, and training—to meet that population's unique needs. To achieve such a workforce, in turn, requires recognition that medical education—like all education—is a social good, an investment in the commonweal, and not merely a prize to be awarded to favored individual competitors. It is possible to be simultaneously excellent and inclusive. In a diverse and evolving democracy, it is essential.

The evidence presented by Carlisle et al. indicates that we are headed in the opposite direction. We continue in that direction at our own peril, and that of our children, and ultimately that of our society.

## References

1. Nickens HW, Cohen JJ. On affirmative action. *JAMA*. 1996;275:572–574.

2. *Report of the Association of American Medical Colleges Task Force to the Inter-Association Committee on Expanding Education Opportunities for Blacks and Other Minority Students*. Washington, DC: Association of American Medical Colleges; 1970.

3. Nickens HW, Ready TP, Petersdorf RG. Project 3000 by 2000: racial and ethnic diversity in U.S. medical schools. *N Engl J Med*. 1994;331:472–476.

4. Carlisle DM, Gardiner JE, Liu H. The entry of underrepresented minority students into US medical schools: an evaluation of recent trends. *Am J Public Health*. 1998;88:1314–1318.

5. Bearak B. Questions of race run deep for foe of preferences. *New York Times*. July 17, 1997:A1.

6. Hernstein RJ, Murray C. *The Bell Curve: Intelligence and Class Structure in American Life*. New York, NY: Free Press; 1994.

7. *Questions and Answers on Affirmative Action in Medical Education*. Washington, DC: Association of American Medical Colleges; April 1995.

8. Schrag P. *Paradise Lost: California's Experience, America's Failure*. New York, NY: The New Press; 1998.

9. Kozol J. *Savage Inequalities: Children in America's Schools*. New York, NY: Crown Publishers, 1991.

10. Arenson KW. CUNY to tighten admissions policy at 4-year schools. *New York Times*. May 27, 1998:A1.

11. *Population Projections of the U.S. by Age, by Race, and Hispanic Origin: 1992–2050*. Washington, DC: Bureau of the Census; 1992:xviii Table 1.

12. Komaromy M, Grumbach K, Drake M, et al. The role of Black and Hispanic physicians in providing health care for underserved populations. *N Engl J Med*. 1996;334:1304–1328.

13. Cantor JC, Miles EL, Baker LC, Barker DC. Physician service to the underserved: implications for affirmative action in medical education. *Inquiry*. 1996;33(2):167–180.

14. Moy E, Bartman BA. Physician race and care of minority and medically indigent patients. *JAMA* 1995;273:1515–1520.

# Parties to the Social Contract? Justice and Health Care for Undocumented Immigrants

## Kenneth DeVille

Kenneth DeVille argues that in terms of the social-contract view of those who favor excluding undocumented immigrants from access to health care, the immigrants can be understood as parties to the social contract, under which health benefits are distributed. Undocumented immigrants live under the same laws as citizens, pay many of the same taxes, and contribute significantly to the workforce (often at a big discount). Hence, they deserve some share of the benefits of the commonwealth.

DeVille also argues that even in purely utilitarian terms, the commonwealth benefits from the medical treatment of undocumented immigrants. It not only protects citizens from the spread of communicable disease but also encourages pregnant women to seek prenatal care and parents to seek preventive care for their U.S.-born children. Because these children, who are citizens, will be healthier, they will be more likely to contribute to the commonwealth and not become a burden on it.

On November 8, 1994, the voters of California approved by a 59%–41% margin a ballot initiative known as Proposition 187. Proposition 187, currently blocked by a federal restraining order, denies undocumented immigrants access to virtually every form of public welfare, including non-emergency health care, prenatal clinics, public health services and public schools. Physicians, health professionals and employees at public health facilities, welfare offices and schools are required to demand evidence of legal residency and report those persons seeking aid without such proof to the Immigration and Naturalization Service (INS). Supporters of the proposal note that at least 1.6 million undocumented immigrants in California annually consume over three billion dollars worth of scarce social services and constitute an unjustified and unbearable burden on state and U.S. taxpayers. However, the vast support for Proposition 187 may also reflect frustration with a stagnant state economy, high unemployment and a xenophobic fear of demographic and cultural reconquest from the Hispanic south.

Most observers, including even such conservative stalwarts as Jack F. Kemp and William K. Bennett, have declared Proposition 187 unconstitutional and predict that it stands no chance of becoming the law of the land in California or in any other state that may pursue similar remedies. . . .

Regardless of what the courts finally decide, . . . it is important to determine whether Proposition 187 and like policies are just, wise, practical and morally sound, irrespective of their ultimate legal and constitutional status.

## Parties to the Social Contract?

Supporters of Proposition 187 appear to rest their moral claims on an unarticulated version of social contractarianism. Classical social contract tradition, articu-

Original title, "Parties to the Social Contract? Justice, Proposition 187 and Health Care for Undocumented Immigrants," *Trends In Health Care, Law & Ethics,* Vol. 10, No. 1/2 (Winter–Spring 1995), pp. 113–117. Reprinted by permission of Robert Wood Johnson Medical School. (Most notes omitted.)

lated by such thinkers as John Locke, Thomas Hobbes, and Jean-Jacques Rousseau, maintains that individuals create civil societies by joining together for their mutual benefit and protection. According to Locke, individuals establish a society

> by agreeing with other men to join and unite into a community for their comfortable, safe and peaceable living one amongst another, in a secure enjoyment of their properties and a greater security against any that are not of it.[1]

A society, Locke reasons, is free to exclude some individuals and groups outside the social contract from its benefits and protection because ". . . it injures not the freedom of the rest; they are left as they were in the liberty of the state of nature." Therefore, social contract theory does provide some potential support for the contention that some of the society's benefits, including health and welfare services, may be withheld from those who are not parties to the contract. The key question under this analysis becomes who is a party to the social contract.

Proposition 187 is apparently predicated on the implicit assumption that citizenship is an accurate and the exclusive emblem of participation in the social contract. If citizenship is an appropriate guide as to who is a member of the social contract, then it may be reasonable to suggest that society's benefits may be justifiably limited to citizens. However, while this rendering of the social contract lends some support to the withholding of health, education and welfare benefits from undocumented aliens, it is problematic.

Citizenship is not the only, or even the best, means of determining which individuals are parties to the social contract. Locke, Hobbes and Rousseau did not explicitly equate participation in the social contract with the status of citizenship. As importantly, many of our social and legal practices suggest that non-citizens are significant participants in our civil and communal life. For example, American society has decided to distribute social benefits to many non-citizens, most notably, resident aliens. The U.S. Constitution, the central and most enduring document in American public life, grants broad protections to resident aliens—non-citizens. State legislatures, when attempting to deny privileges and benefits to resident aliens, must demonstrate that the restriction is necessary to protect a compelling state interest and that the state goal cannot be accomplished by less restrictive means. Thus, documented aliens—one class of non-citizens—appear to enjoy almost the full benefit of the social contract.

The most obvious distinction is that undocumented aliens are in the country in violation of the law; resident aliens are not. But the relevance of illegality, too, is questionable. Illegal actions typically do not deny the lawbreaker access to the benefits and protection of society. Other lawbreakers are still protected by the Constitution, the civil and the criminal law. Even a convicted murderer, for example, is entitled to the protections of due process, to have his contracts honored, to sue his physician if he is negligently injured and to receive social welfare benefits, if qualified. Similarly, most laws continue to protect those persons who enter or remain in this country illegally. Undocumented aliens have standing to sue for breach of contract or for injuries suffered as a result of tortuous conduct. An illegal immigrant cannot be convicted of a crime in this country without the same due process protections granted native-born citizens. It is true that non-citizens cannot vote nor hold public office, but in many essential respects, a person's legal treatment is unaffected by the legality of his or her presence in the country. Therefore, the legality of an immigrant's presence in the country does not seem to be a satisfactory means of distinguishing him or her from other documented resident aliens.

Because there is no morally relevant difference between citizens and documented resident aliens for most social goods, it is difficult to see how either technical citizenship or legality of entry can be grounds for denying a person access to the goods and protection of the social contract. Even if the illegality of one's presence is justifiable grounds to distinguish between society's differential treatment of documented and undocumented aliens, it cannot justify a different standard of treatment for children. Immigrant children, after all, are not lawbreakers; they were brought into the country by their parents. Proposition 187 applies to undocumented alien minors as well as adults.

In sum, even if one accepts the premises underlying social contract theory, citizenship cannot be the sole determinant of who is a party to that contract. Citizenship is merely a sufficient, but not a necessary, determinant of which individuals should be considered parties to the social contract and are due its benefits. Substantial participation in the life of the commonwealth should be sufficient to justify one's inclusion in the social contract. In many cases immigrants are socially, culturally and economically integrated members of our civil society, even if they are outside of our political community. Undocumented aliens live under the same laws as citizens. They pay many of the same taxes. If they work, they may pay income taxes and social security payments through payroll deduction, even though they can never collect a refund or claim social security retirement benefits. Immigrants contribute to the economy by providing ready, and frequently inexpensive, labor. According to INS officials, approximately 80% of the construction and garment manufacturing companies in Los Angeles and Orange County, California, employ undocumented aliens. During harvest time, illegal immigrants constitute between 33–50% of the nation's farm workers.

But membership in a community is not merely based on economic activity and contribution. In the parts of the country where immigrants are most prevalent—California, Florida, New Mexico, New York and Texas—citizens and non-citizens together weave the tapestry of social and cultural life. Citizens and undocumented non-citizens interact on the streets, in businesses and even in private homes. Immigrants harvest and cook our food, watch and help raise our children, build our buildings, sew our clothes and maintain our lawns. Some immigrants are entrepreneurs and provide employment opportunities for citizens.

In addition, American society has not made an unambiguous decision to exclude undocumented aliens from its social and economic life. Instead, until recently, one could argue that American society and American government have implicitly accepted undocumented aliens' incorporation into civil, if not political, society by weakly enforcing immigration and work laws, by tolerating an inefficient deportation system and by benefitting from, and in some cases exploiting, immigrant labor. And, while social contract theory might justify excluding immigrants from participating in American society, it does not justify denying social goods to groups of individuals who have become accepted and significant participants in society. It is this position that many opponents of Proposition 187, such as Kathleen Brown, former Treasurer of California, have taken. They oppose the categorical denial of social services to undocumented aliens, but recommend substantially more vigilant border patrols, streamlined deportation procedures and the elimination of undocumented immigrants' access to employment. The question of whether more stringent limitations on immigration itself are justified when viewed within the context of the human suffering in Mexico and the considerable interdependence of the two economies is the subject of a related, but discrete, debate. However, one could with consistency favor strict immigration laws and yet oppose the types of remedies embodied in Proposition 187. It is an unsettled question whether undocumented aliens participate sufficiently in the commonwealth, through their employment or otherwise, to suggest that they are fully part of American society and parties to the social contract. But it is a threshold question that must be answered before we can justly consider barring immigrants' access to social welfare benefits. One might draw a justifiable distinction between undocumented aliens who work and participate in society, and those undocumented aliens who enter the country seeking not participation in society but only the benefits of the welfare system. Arguably, the latter are not entitled to public resources. But there is little evidence to suggest that a large number of immigrants come to this country primarily to exploit the welfare system. Therefore, the remedy provided by Proposition 187 is arbitrary and unfairly over-inclusive because it excludes many immigrants who have become integral members of the American community from society's benefits.

## What Social Contract?

Social contractarianism does not justify second-class status for immigrants who have become tacit parties to the social contract. That aside, social contract theory is a weak reed on which to construct a social morality. As many philosophers have observed, the social contract "is an agreement which could only be made by persons who never existed and never could exist," and "isn't worth the paper it's not written on."[2] Social contract theory may be a helpful explanatory framework within which to view some duties and rights, but it frequently fails to resolve many important moral issues.

There are alternative and frequently more compelling ways to view our moral obligations towards others, perspectives that better explain this nation's duty towards immigrants who require health and welfare assistance. Several philosophers, most notably David Hume and Adam Smith, have claimed that humans possess a natural, instinctual "sympathy" for one another. This instinctual sentiment originates in hu-

mans' resemblance to other humans, a natural sociability, and a recognition of shared vulnerability and needs. In his discussion of justice and access to health care, Larry Churchill explains how the human capacity for sympathy is the foundation of moral sensibility. According to Churchill, social contract theory portrays humans as solitary and self-interested when they are instead social and empathetic. He contends that all humans share a common susceptibility—ill health—and have common needs—a modicum of health care. Individuals' perception and recognition of that shared vulnerability and need, serve as the basis of the desire and moral mandate to provide such care.[3] This analysis suggests that undocumented aliens who are part of the American community are justly entitled to some health and welfare benefits, regardless of their formal status as citizens. They are entitled to aid based on the fundamental needs they share in common with other members of their community.

How far the moral community extends beyond the geographic borders of the country is, as suggested earlier, part of the larger debate over national immigration policy. Regardless of how one resolves the general immigration question, however, it is clear that a large number of the undocumented immigrant population presently in the country warrant inclusion in any reasonable conception of the relevant moral community by virtue of their economic, social, cultural and personal interaction with those who live in the same geographic area.

## Justice as Reciprocity?

Undocumented aliens' significant participation in the U.S. economy as producers, consumers and taxpayers also demands moral reciprocity and justifies some access to social benefits in the interest of distributive justice. Individuals deserve an equitable return on the contributions they make to society. Illegal-immigrant contributions to society and the economy suggest that they merit a fair share of society's benefits. An American Civil Liberties Union (ACLU) Immigration Right's Project report concluded that when immigrants (both legal and illegal) participate in the U.S. economy they create more jobs than they fill.

While it is true that immigrants are a substantial drain on public health, education and welfare services, they frequently contribute nearly as much or more to the national economy. A Rand Corporation Study found that immigrants (both legal and illegal) cost Los Angeles County $954 million a year, but paid

$4.3 billion in taxes. Unfortunately, much of that tax revenue was deposited in the federal, not the state treasury, so the burden on California is real and profound. The Texas Office of Immigration and Refugee Affairs calculated that the state's estimated 550,000 illegal immigrants contribute $290 million of net revenue to the Texas economy while costing $456 million a year in health, education, welfare and prison costs, a net loss to the state economy of $166 million. However, many immigrants impose burdens on the state budgets only in the short run, until they are fully integrated into the economic life of the country.

Many American citizens, too, cost states more money in services and benefits than they contribute to state coffers. The federal government commands the lion's share of tax revenues. In addition, all states and all citizens benefit in some way from the participation of undocumented immigrants in the American economy, most directly in the form of increased tax revenues and lower priced consumer goods. Consequently, it may be unjust to require states such as California, Florida, and Texas to bear the financial burden that is represented by immigrants, when other states also garner benefit from the immigrant presence in the country. Precisely what constitutes a just return on the contribution undocumented aliens make to American society is in part an empirical question, and has yet to be resolved. It is clear that their contributions merit more than a complete cessation of all benefits. But whatever return-on-investment is due immigrant participants in this society, the debate could be more accurately and fairly framed not as a conflict between immigrants and citizens, but rather as a discussion of the most appropriate distribution of tax dollars among the states and federal government.

## Good Sense, Good Policy

As James W. Nickel has explained, there are also pragmatic, utilitarian and prudential reasons for providing health care and other benefits for undocumented immigrants. American citizens may benefit greatly from medical treatment rendered to undocumented aliens.[4] Immigrants have traditionally suffered from high rates of communicable illnesses such as tuberculosis, hepatitis, sexually transmitted diseases and infectious and parasitic intestinal diseases. In addition, they often live under conditions that aggravate and spread these illnesses. Without access to health care, health education and immunizations they are more likely to spread those diseases not only to fellow immigrants, but also to the American citizenry. For example, evidence presented at a House of Representatives subcommittee hearing indicated that undocumented aliens were the source of increased leprosy rates in Los Angeles in the late 1970s. By denying preventive care to an at-risk population, Proposition 187 both forecloses an important public health option and endangers the health of American citizens.

Proposition 187 further discourages the seeking of prophylactic treatment for potentially communicable diseases by requiring health workers to report patients who cannot provide documentation of citizenship to the INS. Undocumented immigrants who fear deportation may be less likely to seek care for potentially communicable yet treatable diseases. The reporting requirement poses an additional and special danger for one class of Americans—the citizen-children of undocumented aliens. By the terms of the Fourteenth Amendment, children born in the U.S. to undocumented immigrants are automatically granted citizenship and are due the health and welfare benefits provided other citizens. However, parents may be hesitant to seek health benefits for their children if they fear exposure and deportation. For example, following passage of the California proposition, a Palm Springs pharmacist reportedly required proof of citizenship from a woman filling a prescription for her daughter who was a U.S. citizen. And in Anaheim, Proposition 187 has been blamed for the death of a 12-year-old boy whose illegal-immigrant parents delayed seeking medical treatment out of fear that the hospital would report them to immigration officials.

The Proposition 187 requirement that health professionals report undocumented persons seeking medical attention creates an environment that is inconsistent with the ethos of professional relationships. Patients are inherently vulnerable and rely on physicians for guidance, information and medical judgment. It is a relationship based on trust. Patients expect, and medical professionals have agreed, that physicians, nurses and other allied health professionals are to act in the best interests of their patients, do no harm and take no advantage of this special vulnerability and trust.

The reporting requirement of Proposition 187 violates and undermines several of these foundational assumptions. A physician who reports patients to law enforcement authorities can hardly be said to be acting in their best interests, especially when that exposure is likely to lead to loss of employment, deportation and denial of medical care. The reporting requirement asks physicians to expose their patients to harm, to breach their confidentiality and to subvert the general trust that is central to the therapeutic alliance. One might argue that the law has required physicians to breach patient confidentiality in cases where the public interest is at stake, for example in the treatment of gunshots or contagious diseases. Nevertheless, in its 1994 national meeting, the American Medical Association condemned Proposition 187 not only as a public health threat, but also because, in the words of AMA president Lonnie Bristow, it poses a "breach of physician ethics and patient confidentiality."

Unless more stringent and aggressive limitations on immigration decrease the number of immigrants remaining in the country, the denial of preventive care to undocumented immigrants also risks injuring future citizens and imposes a greater and unnecessary economic burden on the American public. Pregnant immigrant women who eschew prenatal care from fear of deportation or are denied care because of their undocumented status are more likely to deliver premature, underweight infants who may suffer from long-term injuries and disabilities, both physical and mental. These infants, native-born American citizens, will then be eligible for full social welfare and education benefits and may constitute a considerable burden to the American taxpayer. Preventive prenatal care for infants likely to be born as citizens in the U.S. is almost certainly more economically efficient, as well as more humane, than denying pregnant women prenatal care and addressing the child's health complications sometimes long after birth. . . .

## Conclusion

While social contractarianism may support the full exclusion of immigrants from a society, it does not justify second-class status for immigrants who have become implicit, yet genuine, parties to the social contract. In short, it may be legitimate to exclude non-citizens from the country, but it is illegitimate to allow their participation in the social and economic life of the community, exploit their labor and deny them benefits granted other members of the commonweal.

Opponents of more rigorous immigration restrictions might fruitfully argue that the relevant moral community extends beyond this country's geographic boundaries and that Americans are in fact part of a world commonwealth with shared needs, interwoven economies and reciprocal duties. This position, as well as pragmatic concerns, is currently being tested in a national debate as the President and Congress contemplate more scrupulous monitoring of undocumented immigrants. The country may, over the next several months, impose substantially more restrictive immigration regulations, enhance deportation efforts, penalize those who use undocumented laborers and decrease its reliance on immigrant workers. The prudence and morality of these measures cannot be resolved here. And, wise or foolish, just or unjust, if these measures are successful, one can no longer argue that the country has implicitly accepted widespread immigrant inclusion into the social contract. But that time has not yet come. Until it does, social contractarianism, justice, utility and benevolence all demand that immigrants be granted reasonable access to social goods available to the rest of society.

### Notes

1. Locke J. *Second Treatise of Government.* New York: Bobbs- Merrill Co., 1952, chap. VIII, para. 95, pp. 54.
2. Churchill LR. *Rationing Health Care in America: Perceptions and Principles of Justice.* South Bend: University of Notre Dame Press, 1987, p. 45; and Rachels J. *The Elements of Moral Philosophy.* New York: McGraw-Hill, 1993, p. 155.
3. Churchill, *Rationing Health Care, passim,* pp. 50–52; 63–66; and 90–103.
4. Nickel JW. Should Undocumented Aliens Be Entitled to Health Care? *Hastings Cent Rep* 1986; 16(6): 20.

### Decision Scenario 1

Anne Fadiman in *The Spirit Catches You and You Fall Down* follows the experiences of a Hmong family, the Lees, in Merced, California, as they encounter the people and institutions of Western medicine in seeking help for their infant daughter Lisa.

Lisa was diagnosed with a severe seizure disorder. The Lee family, in accordance with Hmong tradition, believed it was caused by spirits called *dabs* catching hold of Lisa and throwing her down, then holding her there, despite her struggles to get up. The only remedy, the Lees thought, was to sacrifice animals and persuade the *dabs* to turn loose of her soul. Once they did, she would be free of seizures forever.

Lisa's physicians at the hospital where she was evaluated prescribed a drug regimen to bring her seizures under control. Her family, however, believing her seizures had nothing to do with anything that could be helped by medications, refused to give her the drugs.

Because Lisa's seizures were left uncontrolled, they became worse over time. Eventually, Lisa suffered irreversible brain damage. Her physicians attributed her worsened condition to her parents' failure to give her the drugs that could have helped her, while her parents attributed it to the drugs her physicians gave her during several hospital stays.

"You can't tell them somebody is diabetic, because their pancreas doesn't work," said one of her physicians. "They don't have a word for pancreas. They don't have an *idea* for pancreas."

1. If Dula's recommendation was put into effect, what impact might it have on reducing the number of such cases as the Lees'?

2. If what Sherwin calls the "hierarchical" model of medicine is rejected, does this mean parents should be allowed to choose what they consider the best treatment for their child, even if this means the child will not receive the treatment Western medicine considers best?

3. When there is conflict between parents of another culture and representatives of Western medicine, what sort of approach might be taken to resolve it?

4. If resolution does not prove possible and a child's life is at stake, should the best interest of the child be given precedence over expressing respect for the cultural beliefs of the parents?

---

## Decision Scenario 2

A study published in 1998 provided the first substantial evidence showing that routine PSA screening for prostate cancer can significantly reduce the number who die from the disease. A group headed by Fernand Labrie studied approximately 46,000 men in Quebec, between the ages of forty-five and eighty, who were divided into two groups. Two-thirds were invited by letter to be tested for prostate cancer; of the 8137 men who underwent annual examinations from 1989 to 1997, 5 men died of the disease—a death rate of 15 per 100,000 man-years. In the group of 38,056 men who were not screened, 137 died—a rate of 48.7 per 100,000 man-years. Thus, the death rate in the unscreened group was 3.5 times higher than the rate in the screened group. Also, 4 of the 5 deaths in the screened group were men who already had advanced prostate cancer at the time of the first screening.

Labrie recommended that all men over age fifty be tested every one to two years, depending on their PSA results. African-American men and those with a family history of prostate cancer should begin testing at age forty. The cost he estimated to be $3000 for each cancer found, less than the comparative cost of mammograms for breast cancer and Pap smears for cervical cancer. Other very large studies have supported Labrie's findings.

1. If insurance companies and public programs like Medicare pay for mammograms and Pap smears, should they be required to pay for prostate cancer–screening tests as well?

2. If research into prostate cancer detection and prevention is funded at a significantly lower level than funding for breast cancer, is this grounds for insisting its funding be increased until the levels are more similar?

3. If research into diseases affecting men has taken precedence over those affecting women (as some critics charge), why has research into prostate cancer lagged behind research into breast cancer?

## Decision Scenario 3

About 65 percent of the breast cancers diagnosed every year are classified as stage 1 or 2. About 75 percent of such "early-stage" cancers fit the American College of Clinical Oncology guidelines for lumpectomy followed by a course of radiation treatments. This "breast-conserving" therapy has been shown by a number of studies over the years to be as effective as mastectomy—complete removal of the breast and underlying tissues—in stage 1 and 2 cancers.

Even so, a 1998 study reported that in a group of some 18,000 women treated for breast cancer in 1994, only 44 percent of those qualifying for breast-conserving therapy received it. Instead, they underwent mastectomies.

Contraindications for lumpectomies (for example, multiple tumors, pregnancy) are recognized as present in 10 percent of women with stage 1 cancers and 30 percent of those with stage 2. Also, national practice guidelines state that age, tumor types, and prognosis should not be used as a basis for physicians' recommending a mastectomy over a lumpectomy.

1. What are some of the possible reasons for physicians' not recommending breast-conserving therapy?

2. If Sherwin's feminist model for delivering health care were adopted, might it be expected to keep situations like this from occurring?

3. If a woman's surgeon tells her she qualifies for a lumpectomy and she insists on a mastectomy, would it be morally acceptable for the surgeon to refuse to perform the surgery? Would this count as "abandoning the patient"?

## Decision Scenario 4

Abner Sims is a forty-six-year-old African American who was diagnosed HIV positive three years ago. Although he did well when he was taking AZT (ZDV), his physician now wants to start him on a course of protease inhibitors. "Some people have done so well, it's no longer possible even to detect the virus in their blood," Sims's doctor tells him. "It's not a cure, but it's the next best thing."

Sims doesn't tell his doctor he won't take the new drug. Instead, he accepts the prescription, then doesn't get it filled. He also stops taking AZT when his supply runs out. When asked why he doesn't want to follow his physician's advice, Sims says, "A black man can't trust what a doctor tells him. If he wants to use that new drug on me, probably it's because he wants another guinea pig. That's what black people are to doctors—guinea pigs." When asked, Sims says he has never heard of the Tuskegee Syphilis Study.

1. Why might Sims be said to be an example of the *Tuskegee effect?* How could he be an example, if he has never heard of the Tuskegee Syphilis Study?

2. How might Sherwin's nonhierarchical, nonauthoritarian approach to health care do a better job of gaining the trust of those like Abner Sims?

3. According to Dula, the African-American perspective is rooted in social action and a commitment to justice. How might that perspective help the medical establishment in dealing with those like Abner Sims?

4. What steps might be taken to encourage Sims and people like him to trust their physicians? What steps might be taken by physicians and the medical establishment to earn the trust of Sims and others?

## Decision Scenario 5

"I'm sick and tired of all these Mexicans sneaking over the border, then expecting us to take care of their medical problems," Claude Murry said.

"Amen," Savi Ra said. "They're citizens of a foreign country, not our people. Let their government take care of them, and our government will take care of us."

"Right," Claude said. "I hate to see my tax dollars spent on treating people who have no business being here. So far as I'm concerned, they're here illegally, and so we owe them nothing."

1. If people are in this country illegally, is it true they can have no legitimate claims against us?

2. Does the fact that illegal immigrants are not citizens mean they are not part of the *social contract,* under which health-care benefits are distributed?

3. Why does DeVille say that from a utilitarian point of view, illegal immigrants ought to be given health care?

4. If Sherwin's feminist model were in operation, is it reasonable to think medical care would be freely available to illegal immigrants?

## Decision Scenario 6

"Of course, he shouldn't have been admitted to medical school," Angela Forester said. "His grades were below the level of those admitted, and so were his MCAT scores."

"So what?" Brux Tai asked. "He's an African American, and there aren't many of those in med school nowadays."

"There would be more African Americans, if those who wanted to go to medical school brought up their GPAs and test scores," Angela snapped. "As an African American, I'm not willing to see exceptions made on the basis of race. It's embarrassing."

1. Why does Geiger think that a decrease in the number of minorities in medical school is the start of a potential public health disaster?

2. Why does Geiger, like Brux Tai, downplay the importance of grades and test scores in determining admissions?

3. What factors does Geiger see as making it difficult for minorities to do as well academically as others?

4. Would Dula and Sherwin endorse Geiger's notion that we have a group of diverse and "culturally competent" physicians?

# Part II

# Controls

## Chapter 5

# Genetic Control

## Chapter Contents

## Classic Case Presentation

### *The Stem-Cell Debate*

Research groups headed by James Thomson of the University of Wisconsin, Madison and John Gearhart of Johns Hopkins University announced in November 1998 that they had succeeded in isolating and culturing human embryonic stem cells. Embryonic stem cells are undifferentiated cells produced after a fertilized egg has divided several times and developed into a blastocyst.

### Embryonic Stem Cells Versus Adult Stem Cells

The *blastocyst,* a hollow ball of cells, contains a little lump called the inner-cell mass consisting of fifteen to twenty embryonic stem cells. As development proceeds, embryonic stem cells differentiate and become specialized. They turn into so-called *adult* stem cells. These are cells that go on to produce the approximately 120 different cell types that form tissues and organs such as the blood, brain, bone, and liver. Adult stem cells have been found in the bone marrow and the brain, but biologists believe that adult stem cells are associated with every organ.

Before embryonic stem cells begin to differentiate, they have the potential to become any of the specialized cells. Afterwards, their fate is determined, and they cannot go back to their previous state. When heart cells divide, for example, they produce only heart cells. (Success in cloning mammals demonstrates, however, that the genetic material in a body cell can be made to return to its default position. Each cell retains the genetic information needed to develop into a complete individual—including all the cell types.)

### Source of Stem Cells

Thomson retrieved embryonic stem cells from surplus embryos produced for fertility treatments. (He obtained consent from the egg and sperm donors.) Gearhart used a different method. A group of cells known as embryonic germ cells form the sperm and ova that transmit genetic information to the next generation, and these cells are protected from the process that turns stem cells into specialized components of tissues and organs. Gearhart retrieved embryonic germ cells from aborted fetuses and cultured them to produce stem cells. Stem cells obtained in this way are apparently no different from the ones obtained directly from blastocysts.

### New Treatment Possibilities

The identification of embryonic stem cells and the ability to culture them are important steps in opening up an amazing new range of possibilities for treating many chronic, debilitating, and life-threatening diseases. Cultures of embryonic stem cells appear to be what biologists call *immortal* cell lines. That is, the cells can replicate for an indefinite number of generations without dying or accumulating genetic errors. This capacity reduces the need to acquire new stem cells with great frequency. Cell lines can be established to supply the needs of researchers and physicians. If scientists learn how to control the system of chemical messengers and receptors that regulate the development of "blank" embryonic stem cells into specialized brain, heart, liver, or pancreas cells, it may be possible to repair those organs by injections of stem cells.

This may make it possible, for example, to treat Parkinson's disease by injecting stem cells into the substantia nigra in the brain to boost the production of the neurotransmitter dopamine. (The lack of dopamine produces the symptoms of the disease.) Or diabetes might be brought under control by inducing the pancreas to incorporate insulin-producing islet cells developed from stem cells.

Because embryonic stem cells have the capacity to become cells of any type, it is possible that they could be used to produce whatever sort of cells are needed to treat a particular disease. Damaged spinal nerves that keep people from walking or even moving their bodies might be repaired, and faulty retinas that cause blindness might be replaced with functional ones.

An even more dramatic prospect is that embryonic stem cells might be used to grow body tissues and even whole organs for transplantation. People could be provided with bone or skin grafts, liver segments, lung lobes, or even new kidneys or hearts. The problems caused by the intractable shortage of transplant organs would simply disappear. (See Chapter 7.)

Growing transplant organs is, at best, a distant dream. By one estimate, about 14,000 genes may be involved in the immensely complicated signal-receptor system governing embryonic development in higher mammals. A better understanding of the system is necessary to orchestrate the development of embryonic stem cells to produce replacement organs. The goal is in sight, however, and that has never been true before.

## Treatments with Adult Stem Cells

The therapeutic promises of embryonic stem cells are, to an extent, paralleled by the promises of adult stem cells. How adult stem cells can be used in treatments is currently being investigated vigorously. Evidence from animal studies suggests, for example, that heart muscle damaged by a heart attack can be treated effectively by an injection of adult stem cells. These cells produce normal heart cells, forming new tissue to replace damaged tissue. Amazingly, the stem cells employed come from the bone marrow, where they ordinarily produce blood cells. No adult stem cells have been found in the heart. Apparently, the bone-marrow cells respond to the biochemical environment of the heart, and it reprograms them to produce heart cells.

Swedish scientists in January 1999 identified *neural stem cells*. These are brain cells that have differentiated to become cavity-lining cells, yet when they divide, their progeny can differentiate into either *glial* (structural) cells or neurons. When the brain is injured, the cavity-lining cells begin reproducing, and the neural stem cells produce glial cells that form scars. If a way could be found to induce the neural stem cells to produce more neurons at the injury site, more brain function might be preserved.

## Rejection Potentially Solved

Embryonic and adult stem cells, like the tissues and organs derived from them, cannot escape the problem of immunological rejection that results from the triggering of an individual's immune response. All cells have protein markers on their surfaces that the immune system recognizes as self or not-self. Hence, an injection of neural stem cells donated by Romano into Walters will result in Walters' immune system attacking the cells as foreign.

The problem of the rejection of tissue and organ transplants is currently dealt with by using powerful immunosuppressive drugs. Good antigen (proteins on the cell surface) matching, which reduces the severity of the immune response, might be achieved by maintaining a bank of stem cells. With a wide range of (say) embryonic stem-cell lines to choose from, transplant physicians could select the cells most compatible with the individual.

A second solution is to find a way to suppress or disguise markers on the surfaces of stem cells so they don't provoke the immune response. But researchers concerned with preventing the rejection of transplant organs have been trying without success to accomplish this for a long time.

The third and most elegant solution is to make use of embryonic stem cells acquired from an embryo created by using the techniques of cloning. This involves removing the nucleus from a donor egg, then replacing it with the DNA taken from a cell of an individual. The egg will contain only the DNA of the donor. Thus, when the egg develops into an embryo and the stem cells are removed, they will be genetically identical with those of the individual contributing the DNA. (This is called *therapeutic cloning,* in contrast with *reproductive cloning.* For more details on cloning, see the Classic Case Presentation in Chapter 6.)

## Regenerative Medicine

Stem cells have the potential to serve as the foundation for treatments that will allow us to repair or replace most, if not all, of our ailing organs. They hold the promise of a secular miracle. They could provide a way to still the tremors of Parkinson's disease, knit together a severed spinal cord, supply the cells needed to produce the enzyme required to metabolize sugar, replace the cells in a malfunctioning retina, and heal a damaged heart. Stem cells could become treatments for diseases like Alzheimer's and Huntington's for which there are no effective therapies. And the list goes on and on.

Stem cells may offer us the chance to redeem from disease and injury the lives of countless numbers of people. In this respect, they may usher in a new era of medicine. Regenerative medicine, therapies that produce new tissues and perhaps whole organs, holds out the promise of cures in dozens of cases where no effective treatments now exist.

## Ethical Issues

The retrieval of embryonic stem cells from human fetuses or embryos raises ethical problems for those who oppose abortion or believe that a fetus or embryo has a special moral status. From this perspective, a fertilized egg (an embryo) has the potential to develop into a human being, and (in a strong version) this makes it entitled to be treated as a person in the moral sense. Because it is wrong to kill an innocent person, it is thus wrong to destroy a human embryo. (See the discussion in Chapter 9.)

Taking embryonic stem cells from an aborted fetus is also seen as morally wrong by the same critics. Because abortion is viewed as a wrongful act, it is considered morally wrong to benefit from it. Also, as with the use of fetal tissue generally, by giving stem cells an instrumental value (in using them to treat a disease, for example), we are tacitly encouraging abortion and endorsing its practice. We are also showing a lack of respect for the fetus, given the special status bestowed on it by its potential to develop into a human being, by treating it as a product or commodity we are free to use to suit our needs.

Those who do not assign a special status to a fetus or embryo typically do not oppose the use of embryonic stem cells. Rather, their concerns resemble ones associated with cloning and genetic manipulation in general. They oppose reproductive cloning, for example, because they think it cheapens human life. To consider another example, genes could be added to embryonic stem cells to produce individuals with some special trait that could be inherited. Potentially, then, the whole human species might be altered by altering stem cells.

Some critics maintain that to choose such a course of action would be dangerous, because of its unforeseen biological and social consequences. Others hold that it would be wrong, because tampering with the human genome would violate our notion of what it is to be human.

## Alternatives to Embryonic Stem Cells

1.  Most critics object to the way embryonic stem cells are acquired, not to the use of the cells. Thus, those who consider the destruction of an embryo to obtain stem cells immoral, may (but not always) consider it legitimate to obtain stem cells from spontaneously aborted fetuses. But those ascribing a different moral status to the human embryo claim this way of getting stem cells is expensive and difficult. Also, because a fetus is spontaneously aborted, the stem cells may be abnormal in some way.

2.  Some critics think research should be restricted to adult stem cells. If they can be used to develop effective treatments, we would not need embryonic stem cells. Hence, there would be no need to destroy human embryos. Most researchers are not satisfied with the prospect of restricting research to adult stem cells. They point out that we don't yet know enough about embryonic stem cells to know whether their therapeutic potential could be equaled by using adult stem cells. Only research with embryonic and adult stem cells will answer this question.

3.  Some who oppose acquiring stem cells from embryos or aborted fetuses would find stem cells produced by a process of parthenogenesis morally acceptable. That is, if an unfertilized human egg could be induced by biochemical means to divide and produce stem cells, the stem cells recovered could be legitimately used.

Because the unfertilized egg would lack the genetic information needed for development, even if implanted into a uterus, it would not be a human embryo and thus would have no special moral status.

## Regulations and Stem-Cell Research

A 1995 law prohibits the use of federal funds to support research in which a human embryo is destroyed, and nine states ban all research involving fetal tissue. The research by Thomson and Gearhart leading to the recovery and culturing of stem cells was not supported by federal grants but by the Geron Corporation, a small biotechnology company. When Gearhart and Thomson announced their success, the question of the moral legitimacy of obtaining and using embryonic stem cells quickly became the topic of a national debate.

The National Conference of Catholic Bishops and other social-conservative groups and politicians opposed spending any federal money on stem-cell research. This included many of the traditional opponents of abortion. They argued, fundamentally, that human embryos have the status of persons, so that retrieving their stem cells, thus killing them, would be morally wrong.

In contrast, many disease-advocacy groups, seeing the possibility of cures by means of stem cells, advocated making stem-cell research eligible for federal funding. Without such funding, they argued, the chances that effective treatments would be found for many diseases would be significantly reduced. Private funding would be inadequate. Also, the United States would fall behind in medical innovation as other countries moved into the research gap that a lack of federal support would produce. Those pressing for going ahead with research included many politicians who ordinarily aligned themselves with the social conservatives.

Many people, politicians included, found it hard to object to removing stem cells from embryos that had been created at reproductive clinics, then not used. Ordinarily, such embryos are discarded. If so, then why not retrieve the stem cells and use them to develop treatments for diseases?

Social conservatives, Roman Catholics in particular, did not find this argument persuasive. So far as they were concerned, it was morally wrong to create and destroy embryos for the purpose of assisted reproduction. Hence, destroying them to acquire stem cells would also be wrong. (Even if the stem cells were used to treat disease, it would be wrong. The morally poisoned tree bears only poisoned fruit.)

President George Bush faced this politically vexed situation in 2001, and in August of that year he announced a policy to guide future federal funding of research involving human embryonic stem cells. The decision he made was to allow research on the (alleged) sixty-four human embryonic stem cell lines already established, but not permit federal funds to be used to acquire new stem cells through the destruction of new embryos. "This allows us to explore the promise and potential of stem cell research without crossing a fundamental moral line, by providing taxpayer funding that would sanction or encourage further destruction of human embryos that have at least the potential for life," he said in announcing his decision. He also established a President's Council on Bioethics to consider the consequences of stem-cell research.

The new policy met with a mixed response. It was denounced by the National Conference of Catholic Bishops as "morally unacceptable," while many researchers and patient advocates viewed the policy as placing an unwarranted restriction on research. Scientists were particularly concerned about limiting research to already established cell lines. No one could say in advance, they pointed out, exactly how many genetically different kinds of stem cells would be adequate for treating diseases.

Yet many observers also welcomed the decision as being less restrictive than they had feared. Many had been afraid the president would respond to the pressure from social conservatives by presenting a policy that would forbid using stem cells, no matter when or how obtained, in federally funded projects.

Perhaps the most unfortunate effect of the policy, in the view of most patient advocates and researchers, is that it forecloses the possibility of therapeutic cloning. Because embryos cannot be destroyed, the process described above of acquiring embryonic stem cells genetically identical with one's own cells cannot be employed.

Advocates of cloning for therapeutic purposes stress that they are not advocating reproductive cloning—that is, producing an embryo that is transferred to someone's uterus and allowed to develop into a child. Critics of cloning generally oppose it for any reason.

In March 2002 the NIH broadened the path for researchers a bit by issuing an interpretation of the federal restrictions on using stem cells. The interpretation holds that scientists can study new stem-cell lines and even create them, so long as the work is not supported by federal money.

Even given this loosening of restrictions, researchers claim their work is severely hampered by the president's policy. Private money for basic research is a scarce commodity, and most progress is made when large amounts of federal grant money is available. Grants drive research, and their lack slows it down.

Also, the federally-approved cell lines have proved to be fewer in number than the president initially suggested, some may be contaminated with non-human cells, and others may be restricted for use because they are the property of private companies.

Some critics of the president's stem-cell policy hoped it might be changed after the bioethics panel he appointed considered the issues and made its report. The Council reported in July 2002 and recommended that while cloning for biomedical research should not be banned outright, a four-year moratorium should be established. This would allow time for public debate to take place and other options to cloning to be explored.

The president's policy bans all cloning, so the Council's recommendation is at odds with it, but the recommendation does not give researchers the free hand to produce stem cells they were hoping for. The panel itself was badly split, with some unwilling to approve cloning for any purpose and others wanting to allow therapeutic or research cloning to proceed with government support and oversight.

Embryonic stem-cell research, including therapeutic cloning, is likely to remain a flashpoint of controversy for the immediate future. While its promises are too powerful to ignore, its opponents consider the destruction of human embryos to acquire stem cells the moral equivalent of murder. Finding an acceptable political compromise will be a long-term challenge.

---

## BRIEFING SESSION

The two great triumphs of nineteenth-century biology were Darwin's formulation of the theory of organic evolution and Mendel's statement of the laws of transmission genetics. One of the twentieth century's outstanding accomplishments was the development of an understanding of the molecular structures and processes involved in genetic inheritance. All three great achievements give rise to moral and social issues of considerable complexity. The theories are abstract, but the problems they generate are concrete and immediate.

Major problems are associated with our increased knowledge of inheritance and genetic change. One class of problems concerns the use we make of the knowledge we possess in dealing with individuals. We know a great deal about the ways genetic diseases are transmitted and the sorts of errors that can occur in human development. We have the means to make reliable predictions about the chances of the occurrence of a disease in a particular case, and we have the medical technology to detect some disorders before birth.

To what extent should we employ this knowledge? One possibility is that we might use it to detect, treat, or prevent genetic disorders. Thus, we might require that everyone submit to screening and counseling before having children. We might require that children be tested either prenatally or immediately after birth. We might recommend or require selective abortions. We might require or recommend for some couples in vitro fertilization, then the selection of embryos free of a disease-producing gene for implantation. Using some combination of these methods, we might be able to bring many genetic diseases under control (although we could never eliminate them) in the way we have brought contagious diseases under control.

Requiring screening and testing suggests another possibility, one that involves taking a broader view of human genetics. Eliminating genetic disease might simply become part of a much more ambitious plan for deliberately improving the entire species. Shall we attempt to control human evolution by formulating policies and practices designed to alter the genetic composition of the human population? Shall we make use of "gene surgery" and recombinant-DNA technology to shape physical and mental attributes of our species? That is, shall we practice some form of eugenics?

Another class of problems has to do with the wider social and environmental consequences of genetic research and technology. Research in molecular genetics concerned with recombinant DNA has already revealed to us ways in which the machinery of cells can be altered in beneficial ways. We are able to make bacteria synthesize such important biological products as human insulin, and we are able to alter bacteria to serve as vaccines against diseases. In effect, recombinant-DNA technology produces life forms that have never existed before. Should biotech industries be allowed to patent such forms in the way new inventions are patented? Or do even altered organisms belong to us all?

Also, what are we to say about the deliberate release of genetically modified organisms into the environment? Is the threat that such organisms pose greater than the benefits they are likely to produce? We have already witnessed the great damage that can be done by pesticides and chemical pollution. Is there any way we can avoid the potential damage that might be caused by genetically engineered organisms?

In the following three sections, we shall focus attention on the issues raised by the actual and potential use of genetic information. Our topics are these: genetic intervention (screening, counseling, and prenatal diagnosis), eugenics, and genetic research (therapy, technology, and biohazards).

## Genetic Intervention: Screening, Counseling, and Diagnosis

Our genes play a major role in making us what we are. Biological programs of genetic information work amazingly well to produce normal, healthy individuals. But sometimes things go wrong, and when they do, the results can be tragic.

Almost 5000 human diseases have been identified as involving genetic factors. Some of the diseases are quite rare, whereas others are relatively common. Some are invariably fatal, whereas others are comparatively minor. Some

respond well to treatment, whereas others do not.

The use of genetic information in predicting and diagnosing diseases has significantly increased during the last few decades. New scientific information, new medical techniques, and new social programs have all contributed to this increase.

Three approaches in particular have been adopted by the medical community as means of acquiring and employing genetic information related to diseases: genetic screening, genetic counseling, and prenatal genetic diagnosis. Each approach has been the source of significant ethical and social issues, but before examining the approaches and the problems associated with them, we need to consider the idea of a genetic disease.

### Genetic Disease

The concept of a "genetic" disease is far from being clear. Roughly speaking, a genetic disease is one in which genes or the ways in which they are expressed are causally responsible for particular biochemical, cellular, or physiological defects. Rather than rely upon such a general definition, it's more useful for understanding genetic diagnosis to consider some of the ways genes may play a role in producing diseases.

**Gene Defects.** The program of information coded into DNA (the genetic material) may in some way be abnormal because of the occurrence of a mutation at some time or other. (That is, a particular gene may have been lost or damaged, or a new gene added.) Consequently, when the DNA code is "read" and its instructions followed, the child that develops will have impairments.

For example, a number of diseases, like phenylketonuria (PKU), are the result of "inborn errors of metabolism." (For an explanation of PKU, see "Genetic Screening" later in the Briefing Session.) The diseases are produced by the lack of a particular enzyme necessary for ordinary metabolic functioning. The genetic coding required for the production of the enzyme is simply not present—the gene for the enzyme is missing.

A missing or defective gene may be due to a new mutation, but more often the condition has been inherited. It has been transmitted to the offspring through the genetic material contributed by the parents. Because defective genes can be passed on in this way, the diseases they produce are themselves described as heritable. (Thus, PKU is a genetically transmissible disease.) The diseases follow regular patterns through generations, and tracing out those patterns has been one of the great accomplishments of modern biology and medicine.

**Developmental Defects.** The biological development of a human being from a fertilized egg to a newborn child is an immensely complicated process. It involves an interplay between both genetic and environmental factors, and the possibility of errors occurring is quite real.

Mistakes that result as part of the developmental process are ordinarily called "congenital." Such defects are not in the original coding (genes) but result either from genetic damage or from the reading of the code. When either happens, the manufacture and assembly of materials required for normal fetal development are affected.

Radiation, drugs, chemicals, and nutritional deficiencies can all cause changes in an otherwise normal process. Also, biological disease agents, such as certain viruses, may intervene in development. They may alter the machinery of the cells, interfere with the formation of tissues, and defeat the carefully programmed processes that lead to a normal child.

Finally, factors internal to fetal development may also alter the process and lead to defects. The most common form of Down syndrome, for example, is caused by a failure of chromosomes to separate normally. The outcome is a child who has failed to develop properly and displays physical anomalies and some degree of mental retardation.

Defects occurring during the developmental process are not themselves the results of inheritance. Consequently, they cannot be passed on to the next generation.

**Genetic Carriers.** Some diseases are produced only when an individual inherits two copies of a gene (two alleles) for the disease from the parents. Parents who possess only one copy of the gene generally show none of the disease's symptoms. However, sometimes a parent may have symptoms of the same kind as are associated with the disease, although much less severe.

In the metabolic disease PKU, for example, individuals who have inherited only one allele (that is, who are heterozygous, rather than homozygous) may show a greater-than-normal level of phenylalanine in their blood. Such people are somewhat deficient in the enzyme required to metabolize this substance, but the level of the substance may not be high enough to cause them any damage. Even so, they are carriers of a gene that, when passed on with another copy of the same gene from the other parent, can cause the disease PKU in their offspring. (As we will see later, this is also true for carriers of sickle-cell trait.) The individual who receives both alleles for PKU obviously has the disease, but what about the parents? The point at which a condition becomes a disease is often uncertain.

**Genetic Predisposition.** It's been suggested that every disease involves a genetic component in some way or other. Even when people are exposed to the same new virus their bodies react differently; some may destroy the virus, while others may become infected. Genetic variations may play a role in these differences. For example, while AIDS researchers noted in the 1980s that some who had been HIV positive for years hadn't developed AIDS, it wasn't until a mutation in the gene called CCR5 was identified that a potential explanation was found. The mutation is present in 10 to 15 percent of Whites and appears to be absent in Blacks and Asians.

In some cases genes play a larger role in producing disease than in others. We have good evidence that hypertension, heart disease, various forms of cancer, and differential responses to environmental agents (such as sunlight, molds, or chemical pollutants) run in families, and the genetic makeup of particular individuals may predispose them to specific diseases.

For example, women who carry the BRCA1 gene are more likely to develop breast cancer at an early age than others in the population. Of course not every woman who carries the gene develops breast cancer. What distinguishes the two groups? Their diet? Possessing other genes? No one knows, and what's true for familial breast cancer is also known to hold for dozens of other diseases.

Even granted the role of genes in producing diseases, it's important to keep in mind that predispositions are not themselves diseases. At best they can be regarded only as causal conditions that, in conjunction with other conditions (likely to be unknown), can produce disease.

The action of genes in disease processes are even more complicated than described here. Nevertheless, our general categories are adequate to allow us to talk about the use made of information in genetic diagnosis.

## Genetic Screening

In 1962 Dr. Robert Guthrie of the State University of New York developed an automated procedure for testing the blood of newborn children for the disease PKU. Although a diagnostic test for PKU had been available since 1934, it was time consuming and labor intensive. The Guthrie test made it practical to diagnose a large number of infants at a relatively low price.

PKU is a serious metabolic disorder. Infants affected are deficient in the enzyme phenylalanine hydroxylase. Because the enzyme is necessary to convert the amino acid phenylalanine into tyrosine as part of the normal metabolic process, a deficiency of the enzyme leads to a high concentration of phenylalanine in the infant's blood. The almost invariable result is severe mental retardation.

If the high level of phenylalanine in an infant's blood is detected very early, the infant can be put on a diet low in that amino acid. Keeping children on the diet until they are around the age of six significantly reduces the severity of the retardation that is otherwise inescapable.

The availability of the Guthrie test and the prospects of saving newborn children from irreparable damage encouraged state legislatures to pass mandatory screening laws. Massachusetts passed the first such law in 1963, and by 1967 similar legislation had been adopted by forty-one states.

The term *genetic screening* is sometimes used to refer to any activity having to do with locating or advising people with genetically connected diseases. We will restrict the term's application here and use it to refer only to public health programs that survey or test target populations with the aim of detecting individuals at risk of disease for genetic reasons.

The Massachusetts PKU law pointed the way for the development of public screening programs. PKU was the first disease tested for, but before long others were added to the list. A number of public health programs now screen particular populations for such conditions as sickle-cell anemia, sickle-cell trait, metabolic disorders, hypothyroidism, and chromosome anomalies. Technological developments make it possible to use a single drop of blood to test for some forty disease conditions in one analysis. New York state developed plans in 2002 to test newborns for all forty.

Although genetic screening is relatively new as a social program, the concept is historically connected with public health measures for the detection and prevention of communicable diseases like tuberculosis and syphilis. (HIV has been added to the list by states and the federal Centers for Disease Control.) If an individual with such a disease is identified, he can receive treatment, but most important, he can be prevented from spreading the disease to other members of the population.

Similarly, it is possible to think of diseases with a genetic basis as resembling contagious diseases. Individuals are affected, and they can pass on the disease. With genetic diseases the potential spread is not horizontal through the population, however, but vertical through the generations.

In terms of this model, public health measures similar to the ones that continue to be effective in the control of contagious diseases might be used to help bring genetic diseases under control. When screening locates an individual with a genetic disorder, then steps can be taken to ensure she receives appropriate therapy. Furthermore, when carriers of genes that produce diseases are identified, they can be warned about their chances of having children that are genetically impaired. Thus, a limited amount of control over the spread of genetic disease can be exercised, and the suffering of at least some individuals can be reduced or eliminated. Public health experts estimate about 3000 babies a year are identified as having diseases in which early intervention can save their lives or prevent serious disabilities.

The justification of laws mandating screening programs can be sought in the power and responsibility of government to see to the welfare of its citizens. Here again, the public health measures employed to control contagion might be looked to as a model. We do not permit the parents of a child to decide on their own whether the child should be vaccinated against measles. We believe that society, operating through its government, has a duty to protect the child. Similarly, some argue that society owes it to the child with PKU to see to it that the condition is discovered as quickly as possible so treatment can be instituted.

Critics of screening programs haven't been convinced that the contagious-disease model is appropriate in dealing with genetic diseases. Because the way in which genetic diseases are spread is so different, only a very small part of the population can be said to suffer any risk at all. By contrast, an epidemic of smallpox may threaten millions of people. Furthermore, some genetic screening programs don't have follow-up or counseling services attached to them, so often

---

## Screening Newborns

**PKU**    Metabolic disorder causing seizures and retardation; 1 in 12,000 newborns.

**MCAD**    Enzyme needed to convert fat to energy is missing; causes seizures, respiratory failure, cardica arrest, and death; 1 in 15,000 newborns.

**Congenital hypothyroidism**    Deficiency of thyroid hormone retards growth and brain development; 1 in 4000 newborns.

**Congenital adrenal hyperplasia**    Defects in the synthesis of the adrenal hormones; can alter sexual development and in severe cases of metabolic disturbance result in death; 1 in 5000 newborns.

**Biotinidase deficiency**    Results in failure to synthesize biotin (a B vitamin), causing seizures, uncontrolled movements, deafness, and mental retardation; 1 in 70,000 births.

**Maple-syrup urine disease (branched-chain ketoaciduria)**    In-born metabolic error causing mental retardation and death; 1 in 250,000 births.

**Galactosemia**    Missing enzyme needed to convert galactose sugar into glucose, causing mental retardation, blindness and death; 1 in 50,000 births.

**Homocystinuria**    Missing enzyme needed to convert galactose sugar into glucose, causing mental retardation, blindness, bone abnormalities, and stroke; 1 in 275,000 births.

**Sickle-cell disease**    Disorder of the red blood cells, causing damage to vital organs resulting in heart attack and stroke, pain, ulceration, and infection; 1 in 400 births among Blacks (including African Americans), 1 in 1000–30,000 among Hispanics.

*Source:* March of Dimes Foundation to Prevent Birth Defects, 2002

---

nothing is done that benefits the participants. By being told they are the carriers of a genetic disease, people may be more harmed than helped by the programs.

In general, whether the benefits of screening programs are sufficient to outweigh the liabilities remains a serious question. In particular, are screening programs so worthwhile that they justify the denial of individual choice entailed by required participation? What if parents don't want to know whether their child has the genes responsible for a particular disease? Is it legitimate for a state, in the interest of protecting the child, to require parents to find this out, whether or not they want to know?

These issues and others related to them are easier to appreciate when considered in the context of particular kinds of screening programs. We'll discuss briefly two programs that have been both important and controversial.

**PKU Screening.**  Screening for PKU was not only the first mass testing program to be mandated by state laws, it's generally agreed it has also been the most successful program.

PKU is a relatively rare disease. It accounts for only about 0.8 percent of mentally retarded people who are institutionalized, and among the infants screened during a year in a state like Massachusetts, only three or four cases of PKU may be discovered. (The incidence is 5.4 per 100,000 infants.) Given this relatively low incidence of the disease, critics have argued that the abrogation of the freedom of choice required by a mandatory program doesn't make the results worthwhile.

This is particularly true, they suggest, because of the difficulties with the testing procedure itself. The level of phenylalanine in the blood may fluctuate so that not all infants with a higher-than-normal level at the time of the test actually have PKU. If they are put on the restricted diet, then they may suffer consequences from the diet that are harmful to their health. Thus, in attempting to protect the health of some infants, a mandatory program may unintentionally injure the health of other infants.

Tests more refined than the Guthrie one are possible. However, their use increases considerably the cost of the screening program, even if they are employed only when the Guthrie test is positive for PKU. From the statistical standpoint of public health, then, the financial cost of preventing a few cases of PKU may be much greater than allowing the cases to remain undetected and untreated.

Furthermore, there are additional hidden social costs. Female infants successfully treated for PKU may grow into adults and have children of their own. Their children run a very high risk of being born with brain damage. The reason for this is not genetic but developmental. The uterine environment of PKU mothers is one high in phenylalanine, and in high concentrations it causes damage to the infant. Thus, one generation may be saved from mental retardation by screening only to cause mental retardation in the next.

**Sickle Cell.**  Sickle-cell disease is a group of genetic disorders involving the hemoglobin in red blood cells. Because of faulty hemoglobin, the cells assume a characteristic sickle shape and do not transport oxygen as well as normal red cells. They are also fragile and break apart more frequently. The result is anemia and, often, the blocking of blood vessels by fragments of ruptured cells. The pain can be excruciating, and infections in tissues that have broken down because of oxygen deprivation can be life threatening. Stroke and heart disease often cause death in the early thirties.

The disease occurs only in those who have inherited both alleles for the disease from their parents. (That is, the gene for the disease is recessive, and those who are homozygous for the gene are the ones who develop the disease.) Those with only one allele for the disease (that is, are heterozygous) are said to have sickle-cell trait. Sickle-cell disease may develop at infancy, or it may manifest itself later in life in painful and debilitating symptoms. Those with sickle-cell trait rarely show any of the more serious clinical symptoms.

In the United States, the disease is most common among African Americans, but it is also found among those of Mediterranean, Caribbean, and Central and South American ancestry. The trait is carried by about 7 to 9 percent of African Americans (about 3 million people), and the disease occurs in about 0.3 percent of the population. Many people with the disease are not severely affected and can live relatively normal lives. However, the disease may also be fatal, and at present there is no cure for it. It can be diagnosed prenatally, however.

In 1970 a relatively inexpensive and accurate test for sickle-cell hemoglobin was developed, making it possible to identify the carriers of sickle-cell trait. This technological development combined with political pressures generated by rising consciousness among African Americans led to the passage of various state laws mandating sickle-cell screening. During 1971 and 1972, twelve states enacted sickle-cell legislation.

The results were socially disastrous. Some laws required African Americans who applied for a marriage license to undergo screening. Because the only way to reduce the incidence of the disease was for two carriers to avoid having children (now embryos may be screened before implantation), many African Americans charged that the mandatory screening laws were a manifestation of a plan for genocide.

Medical reports that carriers of sickle-cell trait sometimes suffer from the pain and disability of sickling crises served as a new basis of discrimination. Some employers and insurance companies began to require tests of African American employees, and as a result some job possibilities were closed off to people with sickle-cell trait.

In 1972, Congress passed the National Sickle-Cell Anemia Control Act. In order to qualify for federal grants under the act, states were required to make sickle-cell screening voluntary, provide genetic counseling, and take steps to protect the confidentiality of participants. The most significant impact of the act was to force states to modify their laws to bring them into conformity with the act's requirements. In response, thirty-four states with sickle-cell screening laws now require universal screening.

The National Genetic Diseases Act, passed in 1976 and funded annually since then, provides testing and counseling for the diagnosis and treatment of a number of genetic diseases. The act further strengthens the commitment to voluntary participation and to guarantees of confidentiality.

The lesson learned from the public controversy over the first sickle-cell screening programs is that genetic information can be used in ways that are harmful to the interests of individuals. Furthermore, the information can be used as a basis for systematic discrimination.

In April 1993, an expert panel assembled by the Agency for Health Care and Policy (a part of the Public Health Service) recommended that all newborns, regardless of race, be screened for sickle cell. In making its recommendations, the panel stressed that sickle cell is not uniquely a disease of African Americans or Blacks and that the general belief that it is can result in failing to see to it that people of non-African origin receive appropriate treatment.

Furthermore, the panel claimed, targeted screening of high-risk groups is not adequate to identify all infants with sickle-cell disease because it is not always possible to know an individual's racial heritage. Targeted screening, according to one study, may miss as many as 20 percent of cases.

What the panel did not point out was that one advantage of universal screening is that it permits individuals needing treatment to be identified without stigmatizing them just by requiring screening. However, whether having the disease or the trait becomes a social stigma is not a matter that can be resolved by an expert panel. It's something that must be dealt with by law, social policy, and public education.

## Genetic Counseling

Much is known about the ways in which a number of genetic diseases are inherited. Those like PKU, sickle cell, and Tay–Sachs follow the laws of Mendelian genetics. Accordingly, given the appropriate information, it is often possible to determine how likely it is that a particular couple will have a child with a certain disease.

Suppose, for example, an African-American couple is concerned about the possibility of having a child with sickle-cell disease. They will be tested to discover whether either or both of them are carriers of sickle-cell trait.

Sickle-cell disease occurs only when two recessive alleles are both present—one inherited from the mother, one from the father. If only one of the parents is a carrier of the trait (is heterozygous), no child will have the disease. If both parents are carriers of the trait, the chances are one out of four that their child will have the disease. (This is determined simply by considering which combinations of the two genes belonging to each parent will produce a combination that is a homozygous recessive. The combination of Ss and Ss will produce ss in only 25 percent of the possible cases.)

Such information can be used to explain to potential parents the risks they might run in having children. But, as the case of sickle-cell disease illustrates, it is often very difficult for individuals to know what to do with such information.

Is a 25 percent risk of having a child with sickle-cell disease sufficiently high that a couple ought to decide to have no children at all? If the couple is opposed to abortion, the question becomes especially crucial. Answering it is made more difficult by the fact that sickle-cell disease varies greatly in severity. A child with the disease may be virtually normal, or doomed to a short life filled with suffering. No one can say in advance of its birth which possibility is more likely.

If a couple isn't opposed to abortion, is a 25 percent risk high enough to warrant a prenatal test? Or perhaps they should avoid the question of abortion by relying on artificial insemination so the embryos could be screened before one is implanted. This would be expensive and probably not covered by insurance.

It is generally agreed that the question of whether or not to have a child when a serious risk is involved is a decision that must be made by the couple. The counselor may provide information about the risk, and—just as important—the counselor may provide information about

medical therapies that are available for a child born with a hereditary disease.

In diseases in which prenatal diagnosis is possible, the option of abortion may be open to potential parents. Here, too, the object of counseling is to see to it that the couple is educated in ways relevant to their needs.

## Prenatal Genetic Diagnosis

A variety of new technological developments now make it possible to secure a great amount of information about the developing fetus while it is still in the uterus. Ultrasound, radiography, and fiber optics allow examination of soft-tissue and skeletal development. Anatomical abnormalities can be detected early enough to permit an abortion to be safely performed, if that is the decision of the woman carrying the fetus.

**Amniocentesis and CVS.**  Yet the most common methods of prenatal diagnosis are amniocentesis and chorionic villus sampling (CVS), which involve direct cell studies. In amniocentesis, the amnion (the membrane surrounding the fetus) is punctured with a needle and some of the amniotic fluid is removed for study. The procedure cannot be usefully and safely performed until fourteen to sixteen weeks into the pregnancy. Until that time, there is an inadequate amount of fluid. The risk to the woman and to the fetus from the procedure is relatively small, usually less than 1 percent. (The risk that the procedure will result in a miscarriage is about 1 in 200.) A recent study shows that if amniocentesis is performed eleven to twelve weeks after conception, there is an increase in foot deformity from 0.1 percent to 1.3 percent in the child.

Chorionic villus sampling involves retrieving hairlike villi cells from the developing placenta. The advantage of the test is that it can be employed six to ten weeks after conception. Although the procedure is as safe as amniocentesis, a 1994 study by the Centers for Disease Control found that infants whose mothers had undergone CVS from 1988 to 1992 had a 0.03 percent risk of missing or undeveloped fingers or toes. The normal risk is 0.05 percent. A later study questioned this finding and found reason to believe that the risk of fetal damage is greater than normal.

Amniocentesis came into wide use only in the early 1960s. At first, it was mostly restricted to testing fetuses in cases in which there was a risk of Rh incompatibility. When the mother lacks a group of blood proteins called the Rh (or Rhesus) factor, and the fetus has it, the immune system of the mother may produce antibodies against the fetus. The result for the fetus may be anemia, brain damage, and even death.

It was soon realized that additional information about the fetus could be gained from further analysis of the amniotic fluid and the fetal cells in it. The fluid can be chemically assayed, and the cells can be grown in cultures for study. An examination of the DNA can show whether there are any known abnormalities that are likely to cause serious physical or mental defects. Some metabolic disorders (such as Tay–Sachs disease) can be detected by chemical analysis of the amniotic fluid. However, some of the more common ones, such as PKU and Huntington's or muscular dystrophy, require an analysis of the genetic material. Because only males have a Y chromosome, it's impossible to examine fetal cells without also discovering the gender of the fetus.

Amniocentesis and CVS do have some hazards attached to them. Accordingly, prenatal genetic diagnosis is not at all regarded as a routine procedure to be performed in every pregnancy. There must be some indication that the fetus is at risk from a genetic or developmental disorder. One indication is the age of the mother. Down syndrome is much more likely to occur in fetuses conceived in women over the age of thirty-five. Because the syndrome is produced by a chromosome abnormality, an examination of the chromosomes in the cells of the fetus can reveal the defect.

A relatively new test for Down syndrome employs a blood sample taken from the pregnant woman. The sample is examined for the presence of three fetal proteins. About sixteen to eighteen weeks after gestation, fetuses with the syndrome are known to produce abnormally small quantities of estriol and alpha fetoprotein and abnormally large amounts of chorionic gonadotropin. The levels of the proteins, plus such factors as the woman's age, can be used to determine the statistical probability of a child with the syndrome.

Genetic screening can also provide an indication of a need to perform amniocentesis. For example, Tay–Sachs disease is a metabolic disorder that occurs 10 times as often among Jews originating in central and eastern Europe (the Ashkenazi) as in the general population. (The disease is invariably fatal and follows a sad course. An apparently normal child progressively develops blindness and brain damage, then dies at an early age.) Carriers of the Tay–Sachs gene can be identified by a blood test, and couples who are both carriers of the trait run a 25 percent risk of having a child with the disease. In such a case, there would be a good reason to perform amniocentesis.

**When Is a Test Justified?**   Our ability to test for the presence of certain genes can give rise to cases some people find particularly troubling. Suppose, for example, a woman with a family history of breast and ovarian cancer wants to know whether the fetus she is carrying has the BRCA1 gene. If the gene is present, she wants to have an abortion, then get pregnant again.

Chances are good that no clinic or testing center would agree to test the fetus for the BRCA1 gene. After all, its presence only increases the probability that a woman will develop breast and ovarian cancer. Unlike, say, the gene for Huntington's disease, the BRCA1 gene doesn't inevitably produce the disease. Hence, a testing center is likely to reject the woman's request, on the grounds that it's unwilling to support anyone's attempt to get a "perfect baby."

Yet the woman, not the center, is the one who has responsibility for her child. Hence, if she wants to have a child that, so far as can be determined by the tests available, is free from the threat of disease, shouldn't she be allowed to seek that aim? What's wrong about trying to have a baby lacking the gene predisposing her to two forms of cancer?

Another controversy has developed as pregnant women younger than thirty-five with no particular risk factors in their background have increasingly sought prenatal screening. The women argue that even though their risk of having a child with a detectable genetic abnormality is small, the financial and emotional consequences of raising an impaired child are so serious that they should be allowed to take advantage of the technology available to minimize even the slight risk.

Opponents of this view point out that the risk of a miscarriage from a diagnostic procedure is around 1 in 200 while the risk of a woman below the age of forty having an impaired child is about 1 in 192. Hence, the chance of losing a normal child to miscarriage is almost as great as the chance of having an impaired child. Further, amniocentesis costs from $1000 to $2500 to perform, and the money spent on such unnecessary screening procedures contributes to the general rise in health-care costs.

Such replies aren't convincing to those advocating wider access to prenatal testing. Some see the issue as one of the right of a woman to make choices affecting her body and her life. For some, the distress caused by a miscarriage is much less than that they would experience by having to raise an impaired child, but in any case, women should be the ones to decide what risks and burdens they are willing to bear. Such decisions should not be made unilaterally by physicians, hospitals, and health-policy planners.

Advocates of access to prenatal testing argue that, as far as increasing the cost of health care is concerned, when the costs of raising an impaired child are considered, the money spent on testing is insignificant. It costs about $100,000 to support a Down syndrome child during just the first year of life, and expenditures in the millions may be required to meet the needs of a severely impaired person over a lifetime. In addition, the potential emotional burden of the parents and other family members must be taken into account, even though they can't be assigned a dollar cost.

Some women want the added feeling of control prenatal screening can provide. The test can give them information that will put them in a position to make a decision about abortion, depending on the test results, or will provide them the peace of mind that comes from knowing their pregnancy is proceeding with only a small likelihood that the developing child will suffer a serious impairment. The general attitude is that the technology to secure relevant information exists, and it should be available to anyone who wants to make use of it. It certainly shouldn't be under the complete control of physicians.

**Selective Abortion.**  In most cases in which prenatal diagnosis indicates that the fetus suffers from a genetic disorder or developmental defect, the only means of avoiding the birth of an impaired child is abortion. Because those who go through the tests required to determine the condition of the fetus are concerned with having a child, abortion performed under such circumstances is called *selective.* That is, the woman decides to have an abortion to avoid producing a child with birth impairments, not just to avoid having a child.

Those who oppose abortion in principle (see Chapter 9) also oppose selective abortion. In the view of some, the fact that a child will be born impaired is in no way a justification for terminating the life of the fetus.

Those prepared to endorse abortion at all typically approve of selective abortion as an acceptable way of avoiding suffering. In their view, it's better that the potential person—the fetus—not become an actual person, full of pain, disease, and disability.

The painful decision between having an abortion or giving birth to an impaired child may be avoided by employing ova, sperm, or embryo screening. This means, however, using the techniques developed in assisted reproduction (see Chapter 6), and the costs in time, frustration, and money can be considerable.

In the last few years, another way to avoid abortion has opened up as the techniques of fetal surgery have been employed to correct at least some abnormal physical conditions. Repairs to the heart, the insertion of shunts to drain off excess brain fluids, and the placement of tubes to inflate collapsed lungs are some of the intrauterine surgical procedures now being performed. Some surgeons believe it may be possible to expose the fetus within the uterus, perform surgery, then close up the amnion again. This would make possible more extensive surgery for a greater variety of conditions.

The present hope is that as new surgical techniques for the treatment of fetuses are perfected and extended, the need to rely on abortion to avoid the birth of impaired children will significantly decline. Of course, surgery cannot, even in principle, provide a remedy for a large number of hereditary disorders. It can do nothing for a child with Tay–Sachs, sickle cell, cystic fibrosis, muscular dystrophy, or PKU.

Helplessness in this regard is balanced by the hope that in future years pharmaceutical and biochemical therapies will be available to employ in cases involving missing enzymes; or perhaps gene therapy will make it possible to insert the proper gene for manufacturing a needed biochemical into the DNA of the cells of a fetus.

**Embryo Selection.**  Potential parents who learn they are carriers of genes responsible for lethal or life-threatening diseases may decide to use the techniques of assisted reproduction to avoid having a child affected with the disease. Their embryos, produced by in vitro fertilization, can be genetically screened, then only those free of the disease-causing genes transferred to the woman's uterus. (See Chapter 6 for a fuller discussion.)

Embryo screening allows couples to avoid the risk their genetic heritage poses for their offspring. Those carrying the Tay–Sachs gene or the gene responsible for cystic fibrosis, for example, can be sure they don't have children with these diseases. It also makes selective abortion unnecessary. (However, some consider destroying embryos, for whatever reason, the moral equivalent of abortion.)

The painful present reality is that for most children born with genetic diseases or defects little can be done. Embryo selection and selective abortion are the primary means of avoiding the birth of a child known to be genetically impaired, and only abortion offers the possibility of avoiding the birth of a child discovered to be developmentally impaired.

## Ethical Difficulties with Genetic Intervention

Genetic screening, counseling, prenatal diagnosis, and embryo selection present bright possibilities for those who believe in the importance of exercising control through rational planning and decision making. They see the prospect of avoiding the birth of children with crippling impairments as one of the triumphs of contemporary medicine.

Furthermore, the additional prospect of wholly eliminating some genetic diseases by counseling and reproductive control holds the promise of an even better future. For example, if people who are carriers of diseases caused by a dominant gene (such as Huntington's) produced no children with the disease, the disease would soon disappear entirely. The gene causing the disease would simply not be passed on to the next generation.

A vision of a world without the misery caused by genetic defects is a motivating factor among those who are strong advocates of programs of genetic intervention. (See the section on Eugenics later in this Briefing Session.) The vision must have its appeal to all who are moved by compassion in the face of suffering. Yet whether or not one shares this vision and is prepared to use it as a basis for social action, serious ethical questions about genetic intervention must be faced.

We've already mentioned some of the issues in connection with particular programs and procedures. We can now add some more general questions to that list. The moral and social issues connected with genetic intervention are woven into a complicated fabric of personal and social considerations, and we can merely sketch the main outline of the pattern.

1. *Is there a right to have children who are likely to be impaired?* Suppose a woman is informed, after an alphafetoprotein (AFP) test and amniocentesis, that the child she's carrying will be born with a neural tube defect. Does she have the right to refuse an abortion and have the child anyway?

    Those opposed to all abortion on the grounds of natural law would favor the woman's having the child. By contrast, a utilitarian might argue that the decision would be wrong. The amount of suffering the potential child might be expected to undergo outweighs any parental loss. For different reasons, a Kantian might endorse this same point of view. Even if we assume the fetus is a person, a Kantian might argue that we are obliged to prevent its suffering.

    Suppose we decide a woman does have a right to have a child that is almost certain to be impaired. If so, then is society obligated to bear the expense of caring for the child? On the natural law view, the answer is almost certainly yes.

    The child, impaired or not, is a human person and, as such, is entitled to the support and protection of society. If we agree that the impaired child is a person, he or she is also a disadvantaged person. Thus, an argument based on Rawls's principles of justice would support the view that the child is entitled to social support.

2. *Is society justified in requiring that people submit to genetic screening, counseling, or prenatal diagnosis?* Children born with genetic diseases and defects require the expenditure of large amounts of public funds. Mandatory diagnosis need not be coupled with mandatory abortion or abstention from bearing children. (A related question is whether society ought to make available genetic testing to all who wish it, regardless of their ability to pay.)

    On utilitarian grounds, it might be argued that society has a legitimate interest in seeing to it that, no matter what people ultimately decide, they should at least have the information about the likelihood that they will produce an impaired child.

    If this view is adopted, then a number of specific medically related questions become relevant. For example, who should be screened? It's impractical and unnecessary to screen everyone. Why should we screen schoolchildren or prisoners, those who are sterile, or those past the age of childbearing?

    This is closely connected with a second question: What should people be screened for? Should everyone be screened for Tay–Sachs disease, even though it's the Jewish population that is most at risk? Should everyone be screened for the cystic-fibrosis gene, even though the disease occurs primarily among Whites?

    Those who accept the contagious-disease model of genetic screening frequently defend it on the utilitarian grounds that screening promotes the general social welfare. However, one might argue that screening can also be justified on deontological grounds. It could be claimed that we owe it to developing fetuses, regarded as persons, to see to it they receive the opportunity for the most effective treatment. For example, it might be said that we have an obligation to provide a PKU child with the immediate therapy required to save him or her from severe mental retardation. The restriction of the autonomy of individuals by requiring screening might be regarded as justified by this obligation. If screening is voluntary, the welfare of the child is made to depend on ignorance and accidental opportunity.

3. *Do physicians have an obligation to inform their patients who are prospective parents*

*about the kinds of genetic tests that are available?* A study of one population of women screened for Tay–Sachs disease showed that none had sought testing on the recommendation of her physician.

If the autonomy of the individual is to be preserved, then it seems clear it is the duty of a physician to inform patients about genetic testing. A physician who disapproves of abortion might be reluctant to inform patients about tests that might encourage them to seek an abortion or embryo screening. Nevertheless, to the extent that abortion is a moral decision, it is a decision properly made by the individual, not by someone acting paternalistically in her behalf.

The duty of a physician to inform patients about the possibility of genetic tests seems quite straightforward. Yet the issue becomes more complicated in light of the next question about truth telling.

4. *Do patients have a right to be informed of all of the results of a genetic test?* Ethical theories based on respect for the autonomy of the individual (such as Kant's and Ross's) suggest that patients are entitled to know what has been learned from the tests.

But what if the test reveals that the fetus carries the gene for a minor genetically transmissible disease or for increased susceptibility to a serious disease? Should the physician risk the patient's deciding to have an abortion merely because she is committed to the ideal of a "perfect" baby? Or is such a decision one for the physician to make?

Furthermore, what about the matter of sex determination? Screening tests can also reveal the gender of the fetus. Are prospective parents entitled to know this information? When an abortion is elective, it's possible for the woman to decide to avoid giving birth to a child of a particular gender. (The same possibility is presented by embryo selection.)

It might be argued on both utilitarian and deontological grounds that the sex of the fetus is information that isn't relevant to the health of the fetus. Accordingly, the physician is under no obligation to reveal the gender. Indeed, the physician may be under an obligation not to reveal the gender to avoid the possibility of its destruction for a trivial reason. But, again, is this really a decision for the physician?

5. *Should public funds be used to pay for genetic tests when an individual is unable to pay?* This is a question that holders of various ethical theories may not be prepared to answer in a simple yes-or-no fashion. Those who oppose abortion on natural law grounds might advocate providing funds only for genetic testing and counseling. That is, they might favor providing prospective parents with information they might use to decide whether to refrain from having children. Yet opponents of abortion might be against spending public money on tests that might encourage the use of abortion to prevent the birth of an impaired child.

The views of Rawls and of utilitarianism might support the use of public funds for genetic testing as part of a more general program of providing for health-care needs. Whether genetic testing programs are funded and what the level of funding might be would then depend on judgments about their expected value in comparison with other health-care programs.

A present ethical and social difficulty is caused by the fact that federal funds may be employed to pay for genetic screening and testing, yet federal money cannot legally be used to pay for abortions. Consequently, it's possible for a woman to discover she is carrying a fetus with a serious genetic disease, wish to have an abortion, yet lack the means to pay for it.

Issues about the confidentiality of test results, informed consent, the use of genetic testing to gather epidemiological information, and a variety of other matters might be mentioned here in connection with genetic intervention. Those that have been discussed are sufficient to indicate that the difficulties presented by genetic intervention are at least as numerous as the benefits it promises.

## Eugenics

Like other organisms, we are the products of millions of years of evolutionary development. This process has taken place through the operation of natural selection on randomly produced genetic mutations. Individual organisms are successful in an evolutionary sense when they contribute a number of genes to the gene pool of their species proportionately greater than the number contributed by others.

Most often, this means that the evolutionarily successful individuals are those with the largest number of offspring. These are the individuals favored by natural selection. That is, they possess the genes for certain properties that are favored by existing environmental factors. (This favoring of properties is natural selection.) The genes of "favored" individuals will thus occur with greater frequency than the genes of others in the next generation. If the same environmental factors continue to operate, these genes will spread through the entire population.

Thanks to Darwin and the biologists who have come after him, we now have a sound understanding of the evolutionary process and the mechanisms by which it operates. This understanding puts us in a position to intervene in evolution. We no longer have to consider ourselves subject to the blind working of natural selection, and if we wish, we can modify the course of human evolution. As the evolutionary biologist Theodosius Dobzhansky expressed the point: "Evolution need no longer be a destiny imposed from without; it may conceivably be controlled by man, in accordance with his wisdom and values."

Those who advocate eugenics accept exactly this point of view. They favor social policies and practices that, over time, offer the possibility of increasing the number of genes in the human population responsible for producing or improving intelligence, beauty, musical ability, and other traits we value.

The aim of increasing the number of favorable genes in the human population is called *positive eugenics*. By contrast, *negative eugenics* aims at decreasing the number of undesirable or harmful genes. Those who advocate negative eugenics are most interested in eliminating or reducing from the population genes responsible for various kinds of genetic diseases.

Both positive and negative eugenics require instituting some sort of control over human reproduction. Several kinds of policies and procedures have been advocated, and we will discuss a few of the possibilities.

### Negative and Positive Eugenics

The discussion of genetic screening, counseling, prenatal genetic diagnosis, and embryo selection makes it unnecessary to repeat here information about the powers we possess for predicting and diagnosing genetic diseases. It is enough to recall that, given information about the genetic makeup and background of potential parents, a large number of genetic diseases can be predicted with a certain degree of probability as likely to occur in a child of such parents. Or the presence of the genes can be determined by genetic analysis of the chromosomes. This is true of such diseases as PKU, sickle cell, hemophilia, Huntington's disease, Tay–Sachs, and muscular dystrophy.

When genetic information isn't adequate for a reliable prediction or direct determination, information about the developing fetus can often be obtained by employing one of several procedures of prenatal diagnosis. Even when information is adequate for a reliable prediction, whether the fetus has a certain disease can be determined by prenatal testing. Thus, in addition to the genetic disorders named previously, prenatal tests can be performed for such developmental defects as neural tube anomalies and Down syndrome. Also, other tests can be performed on ova, sperm, or embryos.

A proponent of negative eugenics might advocate that a screening process for all or some currently detectable genetic diseases or dispositions (or developmental impairments) be required by law. When the probability of the occurrence of a disease is high (whatever figure that might be taken to be), then the potential parents might be encouraged to have no children. Indeed, the law might require that such a couple either abstain from having children or rely on embryo selection and prescribe a penalty for going against the decision of the screening board.

If those carrying the genes for some genetic diseases could be prevented from having children, over time the incidence of the diseases would decrease. In cases when the disease is the result of a dominant gene (as it is in Huntington's disease), the disease would eventually disappear. (It would appear again with new mutations, however.)

When the disease is of the sort that can be detected only after a child is conceived, if the results of a prenatal diagnosis show the developing fetus has a heritable disease, an abortion might be encouraged. Or a couple identified as at risk might be encouraged to seek artificial insemination and embryo testing and transfer.

Short of a law requiring abortion, a variety of social policies might be adopted to make abortion or embryo selection an attractive option. (For example, the cost of an abortion might be paid for by government funds or women choosing abortion might be financially rewarded. Or the costs of embryo selection might be paid for under a federal program.) The aborting of a fetus found to have a transmissible genetic disease would not only prevent the birth of an impaired infant, it would also eliminate a potential carrier of the genes responsible for the disease.

Similarly, the sterilization of people identified as having genes responsible for certain kinds of physical or mental impairments would prevent them from passing on these defective genes. In this way, the number of such genes in the population would be proportionately reduced.

Currently, no state or federal laws make it a crime for couples who are genetically a bad risk to have children. Yet a tendency toward more genetic regulation may be developing. Screening newborns for certain genetic diseases that respond well to early treatment is an established practice. Also, genetic testing programs are frequently offered in communities to encourage people to seek information about particular diseases.

At present, genetic testing (for adults) and counseling are voluntary. They aim at providing information and then leave reproductive decisions up to the individuals concerned. Most often, they are directed toward the immediate goal of decreasing the number of children suffering from birth defects and genetic diseases. Yet genetic testing and counseling might also be viewed as a part of negative eugenics. To the extent they discourage the birth of children carrying deleterious genes, they also discourage the spread of those genes in the human population.

Obviously, genetic testing and genetic counseling programs might also be used to promote positive eugenics. Individuals possessing genes for traits society values might be encouraged to have large numbers of children. In this way, genes for those traits would increase in relative frequency in the population.

No programs of positive eugenics currently operate in the United States. It is easy to imagine, however, how a variety of social and economic incentives (such as government bonuses) might be introduced as part of a plan to promote the spread of certain genes by rewarding favored groups of people for having children.

## Use of Desirable Germ Cells

Developments in reproductive technology have opened up possibilities once considered so remote as to be the stuff of science fiction. Artificial insemination by the use of frozen sperm is already commonplace. So too is the use of donor eggs and embryos. While some of the embryos may be donated by couples who don't need or want them, some are produced in infertility clinics by combining sperm from commercial sperm banks with donor ova. The developing embryos can be divided into several genetically identical embryos, and before long it may be possible to clone a human being from a single body cell.

Those wishing to have a child now have the option of selecting donor eggs or sperm from individuals with traits considered desirable. Alternatively, they may select a frozen embryo on the basis of descriptions of the gamete contributors. They may also turn to physicians who may offer them embryos they've created from sperm and eggs obtained from what they judge to be outstanding traits.

We have available to us right now the means to practice both negative and positive eugenics at the level of both the individual and the society. If we wished, we could encourage groups of individuals to avoid having their own biological children and, instead, make use of the "superior" sperm, ova, and embryos currently offered at sperm banks and infertility centers. In this way, we could increase the number of genes for desirable traits in the population. (See Chapter 6.)

## Ethical Difficulties with Eugenics

Critics have been quick to point out that the proposals mentioned suffer from serious drawbacks. First, negative eugenics isn't likely to make much of a change in the species as a whole. Most hereditary diseases are genetically recessive and so occur only when both parents possess the same defective gene. Even though a particular couple might be counseled (or required) not to have children, the gene will still be widespread in the population among people we would consider wholly normal. For a similar reason, sterilization and even embryo selection would have few long-range effects.

Also, the uncomfortable fact is that geneticists have estimated that, on the average, everyone carries recessive genes for five genetic defects or diseases. Genetic counseling and the use of the techniques of assisted reproduction may help individuals, but negative eugenics doesn't promise much for the population as a whole.

Positive eugenics can promise little more. It's difficult to imagine we would all agree on what traits we'd like to see increased in the human species. But even if we could, it's not clear we'd be able to increase them in any simple way.

For one thing, we have little understanding of the genetic basis of traits such as "intelligence," "honesty," "musical ability," "beauty" and so on. It's clear, however, there isn't just a single gene for them, and the chances are they are the result of a complicated interplay between genetic endowment and social and environmental factors. Consequently, the task of increasing their frequency is quite different from that of, say, increasing the frequency of short-horned cattle. Furthermore, desirable traits may be accompanied by less desirable ones, and we may not be able to increase the first without also increasing the second.

Quite apart from biological objections, eugenics also raises questions of a moral kind. Have we indeed become the "business manager of evolution," as Julian Huxley once claimed? If so, do we have a responsibility to future generations to improve the human race? Would this responsibility justify requiring genetic screening and testing? Would it justify establishing a program of positive eugenics? Affirmative answers to these questions may generate conflicts with notions of individual dignity and self-determination.

Of the ethical theories we have discussed, it seems likely that only utilitarianism might be construed as favoring a program of positive eugenics. The possibility of increasing the frequency of desirable traits in the human species might, in terms of the principle of utility, justify placing restrictions on reproduction. Yet the goal of an improved society or human race might be regarded as too distant and uncertain to warrant the imposition of restrictions that would increase current human unhappiness.

As far as negative eugenics is concerned, the principle of utility could be appealed to in order to justify social policies that would discourage or prohibit parents who are carriers of the genes for serious diseases from having children. The aim here need not be the remote one of improving the human population but the more immediate one of preventing the increase in sorrows and pain that would be caused by an impaired child.

Natural law doctrines of Roman Catholicism forbid abortion, sterilization, and embryo selection. Thus, these means of practicing negative eugenics are ruled out. Also, the natural law view that reproduction is a natural function of sexual intercourse seems, at least prima facie, to rule out negative eugenics as a deliberate policy altogether. It could be argued, however, that voluntary abstinence from sexual intercourse or some other acceptable form of birth control would be a legitimate means of practicing negative eugenics.

Ross's prima facie duty of causing no harm might be invoked to justify negative eugenics. If there is good reason to believe a child is going to suffer from a genetic disease, we may have a duty to prevent the child from being born. Similarly, Rawls's theory might permit a policy that would require the practice of some form of negative eugenics for the benefit of its immediate effects of preventing suffering and sparing all the cost of supporting those with genetic diseases.

It is difficult to determine what sort of answer to the question of negative eugenics might be offered in terms of Kant's ethical principles. Laws regulating conception or forced abortion or sterilization might be considered to violate the dignity and autonomy of individuals. Yet moral agents as rational decision makers require information on which to base their decisions. Thus, programs of genetic screening and counseling might be considered to be legitimate.

# Genetic Research, Therapy, and Technology

By replacing natural selection with artificial selection that is directly under our control, we can, over time, alter the genetic composition of populations of organisms. This has been done for thousands of years by animal and plant breeders, and our improved understanding of genetics allows us to do it today with more effectiveness and certainty of results. Yet such alterations require long periods of time. Molecular genetics holds out the possibility of immediate changes. Bacteria continue to be the major organisms of research, but genetic technology is already being applied to plants and animals. The same technology is now on the verge of being applied to humans.

## Recombinant DNA

The information required for genetic inheritance is coded in the two intertwined strands of DNA (deoxyribonucleic acid) found in plant and animal cells—the double helix. The strands are made up of four kinds of chemical units called nucleotides, and the genetic message is determined by the particular sequence of nucleotides. Three nucleotides in sequence form a triplet codon. Each codon directs the synthesis of a particular amino acid and determines the place it will occupy in making up a protein molecule. Since virtually all properties of organisms (enzymes, organs, eye color, and so on) depend on proteins, the processes directed by DNA are fundamental.

Alterations in the nucleotide sequence in DNA occur naturally as mutations—random changes introduced as "copying errors" when DNA replicates (reproduces) itself. These alterations result in changes in the properties of organisms, because the properties are under the control of DNA. Much research in current molecular genetics is directed toward bringing about desired changes by deliberately manipulating the nucleotide sequences in DNA. The major steps toward this goal have involved the development of techniques for recombining DNA from different sources.

The recombinant process begins by taking proteins known as restriction enzymes from bacteria and mixing them with DNA that has been removed from cells. These enzymes cut open the DNA strands at particular nucleotide locations. DNA nucleotide sequences from another source can then be added, and certain of these will attach to the cut ends. Thus, DNA from distinct sources can be recombined to form a single molecule.

This recombinant DNA can then be made to enter a host cell. The organism most widely employed is the one-celled bacterium *E. coli* that inhabits the human intestine by the billions. In addition to the DNA in the nucleus, *E. coli* also has small circular strands of DNA known as *plasmids*. The plasmid DNA can be recombined with DNA from an outside source and returned to the cell. When the plasmid replicates, it will make copies of both the original nucleotides and the added segments. Thus, a strain of bacteria can be produced that will make limitless numbers of copies of the foreign DNA.

The obvious question is, what benefits might recombinant DNA technology produce? From the standpoint of theory, it might lead to a better understanding of the molecular processes involved in such diseases as cancer, diabetes, and hemophilia. Or it might provide more effective treatment for metabolic diseases like PKU and Tay–Sachs.

From the practical standpoint, recombinant-DNA technology has already led to the development of new breeds of plants able to utilize nitrogen from the air and requiring little or no fertilizer. Specially engineered bacteria might be used to clean up the environment by breaking down currently nonbiodegradable compounds like DDT. Other bacteria might convert petroleum into other useful chemical compounds, including plastics.

The most immediate benefit of recombinant-DNA technology is the use of bacteria modified into chemical factories that produce biological materials of medical importance. A glance at a few of the many recent research developments gives an appreciation of the powerful potential of genetic technology:

- Hypopituitary dwarfism is a condition caused by a deficiency in growth hormone. The hormone itself consists of molecules too large and structurally complex to synthesize in the laboratory, but as early as 1979 researchers employed recombinant-DNA technology to induce bacteria to produce the hormone. It's now available in quantities large enough to be used as a therapy.

- Modified bacteria now produce human insulin in quantities large enough to meet the need of diabetics, some of whom are allergic to swine or bovine insulin.

- Genetically engineered bacteria have been used to produce a vaccine against hepatitis B and against a strain of genital herpes. The clotting factor employed in the treatment of hemophilia has been similarly produced.

- Genetically engineered flu vaccines grown in moth cells may replace some of those currently grown in fertilized chicken eggs, reducing production time from six to nine months to two to three.

- In 1985 the Cetus Corporation was awarded the first patent for an altered form of the protein interleukin-2. Il-2 activates the immune system and is used in the treatment of some cancers. It occurs naturally but in very small amounts; thus, it wasn't possible to use it therapeutically until it was produced in quantity by genetically altered bacteria.

- Researchers have inserted human genes into plants and induced the plants to produce large quantities of medically significant proteins. Antibodies, serum albumin, enkephalins, hormones, and growth factors are among those currently produced.

- Substances occurring in the human body in minute amounts that can be important as drugs when widely available are now being produced in large quantities by genetic engineering. For example, tissue plasminogen activator (TPA), which is produced in blood vessels, dissolves blood clots and is a useful drug in the treatment of heart attacks. Also, blood factor-VIII, a clotting agent, may improve the lives and health of hemophiliacs by reducing their chances of viral infection from donated blood.

- In 1997 researchers genetically engineered mice to serve as an animal model for sickle-cell disease by inserting into the mice human genes for the defective hemoglobin that causes the disease. Having animal models may speed up the testing of new drugs and suggest approaches for an effective treatment.

- Researchers have inserted into mouse embryos human DNA equivalent to an entire chromosome and discovered the DNA is passed on to the next mouse generation. Such research promises to lead to an understanding of the ways in which genes work normally and in disease processes. Further, animals containing segments of human DNA might be induced to produce medically useful products. (See the Classic Case Presentation: "Hello, Dolly" in Chapter 6.)

## Gene Therapy

The rapid advancement in genetic knowledge during the last few years has led to the use of recombinant-DNA techniques in experimental medical therapies. Therapy in which a missing or nonfunctioning gene is inserted into a patient's cells is already being employed. So is the use of altered cells to induce the formation of new blood vessels to treat unhealing leg ulcers and, perhaps soon, coronary artery blockages. (See the Case Presentation: "Gene Therapy" in this chapter for more details.)

The ability to alter the basic machinery of life to correct its malfunctioning is surely the most powerful form of therapy imaginable. The imme-

diate prospects for gene therapy involve the relatively modest, but very dramatic, task of splicing into the DNA of body cells a gene that controls the production of a specific substance. Diseases such as PKU that are caused by the absence of an enzyme might then be corrected by inducing the patient's cells to manufacture that enzyme. Some genetic diseases involve dozens or even hundreds of genes, and often the mechanism by which the genes produce the disease is not understood. Consequently, it's likely to be a long while before most genetic diseases can be treated by gene therapy. Even so, the effective treatment of single-gene disorders is a most promising possibility.

Few special moral or social issues are raised by the use of gene therapy as long as the cells modified are somatic (body) cells. The issues change significantly with the prospect of modifying human germ-line (sex) cells. Somatic-cell changes cannot be inherited, but germ-line cell changes can be. This possibility holds out the benign prospect of eliminating forever a number of genetic diseases. However, we need not wait for germ-line therapy to accomplish this. Embryo testing and selection before implantation, a technology already in common use, would be a simpler way to achieve the same goal.

While germ-line therapy may have no medical use, it points toward a frightening prospect. It offers us a way of "engineering" human beings by tinkering with the sex cells to produce people who meet our predetermined specification. Because we'll discuss this possibility later in the chapter, it's only relevant to note here that the technology required to alter human sex cells doesn't exist at present.

## Biohazards

The issues connected with gene therapy, testing, and screening may be overshadowed in significance by questions concerning dangers inherent in the development of genetic technology and the release of its products into the environment.

The question of whether recombinant-DNA research ought to be halted is no longer a serious social issue. However, this hasn't always been so. In 1974 a group of scientists active in such research issued a report recommending that scientists be asked to suspend work voluntarily on recombinant experiments involving tumor viruses, increased drug resistance in harmful bacteria, and increased toxicity in bacteria. The discussion that ensued resulted in the formulation of guidelines by the National Institutes of Health to regulate research.

The major concern initially was that recombinant techniques might be employed to produce essentially new organisms that would threaten human health. Suppose that the nucleotide sequence for manufacturing a lethal toxin were combined with the DNA of *E. coli.* This usually harmless inhabitant of the intestine might be transformed into a deadly organism that would threaten the existence of the entire human population. (In recent years we've seen how deadly naturally occurring mutant forms of *E. coli* can be when they appear in the food supply.)

Or to take another scenario, perhaps a nucleotide sequence that transforms normal cells into cancerous ones might trigger an epidemic of cancer. Without a thorough knowledge of the molecular mechanisms involved, little could be done to halt the outbreak. Indeed it isn't even clear what would happen if one of the engineered insulin-producing strains of bacteria escaped from the lab and spread through the human population.

These and similar dangers prompted some critics to call for an end to all genetic-engineering research. However, almost two decades of recombinant-DNA research have passed without the occurrence of any biological catastrophes. Most observers regard this as sufficient proof of the essential safety of the research. Yet, in the view of others, the fact that no catastrophes have yet occurred must not be allowed to give us a false sense of security. Almost no one advocates that the research be abandoned, but several molecular geneticists have argued that the very fact that we still do not know enough to estimate the risks involved with a high degree of certainty is a good reason for continuing to control it severely.

Quite apart from the possible hazards associated with genetic engineering, many people continue to be uneasy about the direction of research. A number of biotechnological possibilities are on the horizon, some of which might have far-reaching consequences. As we discussed earlier, gene surgery offers more possibilities than just medical therapy. If undesirable DNA segments can be sliced out of the genetic code and replaced with others, this would permit the "engineering" of human beings to an extent and degree of precision never before imagined.

The eugenic dream of producing people to match an ideal model would be a reality. What would happen then to such traditional and moral values as autonomy, diversity, and the inherent worth of the individual?

The same techniques employed to manufacture the ideal person might also be used to design others to fit special needs. It's not difficult to imagine using genetic surgery to engineer a subhuman race to serve as a slave class for the society. The scenarios of cautionary science fiction might be acted out in our own future.

Further, the technique of asexual reproduction known as cloning might be employed to produce individuals that are exact genetic copies of someone whose DNA has been engineered to suit our needs or ideals. While human cloning is not yet a practical reality, a giant step toward it was taken in 1997 when Ian Wilmut and his colleagues at the Roslin Institute in Scotland cloned a sheep. (See Social Context: "Hello, Dolly" in Chapter 6.)

We might use reproductive technology in combination with genetic engineering to have several children that are copies of ourselves. If the embryos were stored, some of these might be born years apart.

Consider one last possibility. Virtually new organisms might be produced by splicing together DNA from two or more sources. Thus, the world might be faced with creatures of an unknown and unpredictable nature that are not the product of the natural processes of evolution.

It's little wonder molecular biologists have become concerned about the nature and direction of their research. As Robert Sinsheimer says, "Biologists have become, without wanting it, custodians of great and terrible power." Such power in the hands of a tyrannical government could be used with irresistible effectiveness to control its subjects. Societies might create a race of semihuman slaves or armies of genetically engineered soldiers. The possibilities are both fantastic and unlimited.

## Ethical Difficulties with Genetic Research, Therapy, and Technology

The risks involved in gene therapy are not unique ones. In most respects, they exactly parallel those involved in any new medical treatment. Accordingly, it seems reasonable to believe that the same standards of safety and the same consideration for the welfare of the patient that are relevant to the use of other forms of therapy should be regarded as relevant to gene therapy.

The principles of Kant and Ross suggest that the autonomy of the individual must be respected and preserved. The individual ought not to be viewed as an experimental case for testing a procedure that may later prove helpful. If the person is adequately informed, competent to consent, and no alternative therapy is likely to be effective, it would be morally legitimate for the patient to be given the opportunity to benefit from the therapy. However, if the hazards are great or completely unknown, it's doubtful whether the patient would be justified in risking his or her life.

By contrast, on utilitarian principles, if the outcome of gene therapy can be reasonably expected to produce more benefit than harm, its use might be considered justifiable. If we assume a person is likely to die anyway, that in itself might be enough to warrant the use of the therapy. In addition, since each case treated is likely to contribute to increased understanding and to benefit others, this tends to support the use of gene therapy, even in cases in which it is of doubtful help to the individual. (See the

Case Presentation: "Gene Therapy" for a fuller discussion.)

Genetic research and its associated technology present issues much greater in scope than those raised by gene therapy. They are issues that require us to decide what sort of society we want to live in.

Very few responsible people currently believe we should call a halt to research in molecular genetics and forgo the increase in power and understanding it has already brought. However, the possibilities of genetic engineering include ones that are frightening and threatening, ones that could wholly alter our society and destroy some of our most cherished values. These are the possibilities that require us to make decisions about whether or to what extent we want to see them realized.

The natural law view of ethics would not, in general, support any policy of restricting scientific inquiry in the area of molecular genetics. For on this view there is a natural inclination (and hence a natural duty) to seek knowledge. Yet certain types of experiments and gene engineering would be ruled out. Those that aim at altering human beings or creating new species from mixed DNA are most likely to be considered to violate the natural order. On the Roman Catholic view, such a violation of nature would run counter to God's plan and purpose and so be immoral.

The principle of utility might be invoked to justify limiting, directing, or even ending research in molecular genetics. If research or its results are more likely to bring about more harm than benefit, regulation would be called for. Yet if the promise of relieving misery or increasing well-being is great, then some risk that we might also acquire dangerous knowledge in the process might be acceptable.

On the utilitarian view, knowledge may be recognized as a good, but it's only one good among others. Possessing the knowledge to alter human beings in accordance with a eugenic ideal or to create new species means we have to make a decision about whether doing so would result in an overall benefit. That judgment will then be reflected in our social policies and practices.

Such an analysis also seems to be consistent with Rawls's principles. There is not, for Rawls, an absolute right to seek knowledge, nor is there any obligation to employ knowledge that is available. Restriction might well be imposed on scientific research and on the technological possibilities it presents if the good of society seems to demand it.

# SOCIAL CONTEXT: THE HOLY GRAIL OF BIOLOGY: THE HUMAN GENOME PROJECT

The Holy Grail in medieval Christian legend is the lost cup used by Christ at the Last Supper. Because the Grail delivers salvation to whoever possesses it, finding the Grail was the aim in many tales of valorous quests. While deciphering the human genome cannot promise eternal life, it offers the benefits of genetic knowledge, including the possibility of exercising control over our genes and the ways they affect us. This is promise enough to give the Human Gene Project the status of a secular Holy Grail.

## Genome

On June 26, 2000, Francis Collins, Director of the National Genome Research Institute, and J. Craig Venter, president of Celera Genetics, announced that, thanks to the joint work of the two groups, the human genome had been sequenced.

This means that the estimated 3.2 billion base pairs making up human DNA have been identified and sequenced—that is, the precise order of the base pairs has been established. Human DNA is now thought to contain about 30,000 genes. Earlier estimates had put this figure around 100,000, so the lower number came as a considerable surprise. Using the comparison by writer Nicholas Wade, if the complete DNA

sequence was published in the *New York Times,* it would cover 75,490 pages.

This complete set of genes contained in the forty-six chromosomes is known as the *genome.* Metaphorically, it is the total set of coded instructions for assembling a human being that is stored in the nucleus of each cell. About 75 percent of the genome is thought to be (as geneticists say) junk, consisting of repetitive DNA sequences accumulated during evolution and contributing nothing to human development or functioning. Yet biologists are also quick to say that we don't yet know enough to declare the junk DNA absolutely useless. It may contain sequences that in the future we will realize are crucially important.

## Background

In 1985, biologist Robert Sinsheimer began promoting the idea that the entire human genome should be mapped and its genes sequenced. Because the genome was recognized as involving some 3 billion base pairs, the genome project would be on a scale unprecedented in the biological sciences. It would compare with the efforts of physicists to develop the atomic bomb during World War II and with the manned space project in the 1960s.

The size of the genome project made many scientists skeptical about supporting it. Some believed it would drain money away from smaller projects of immediate value in favor of one with only distant and uncertain promise. Also, some feared the genome project would turn out to be too much like the space project, emphasizing the solution to engineering problems more than the advancement of basic science.

Attitudes changed in 1988 when the National Research Council endorsed the genome project and outlined a gradual approach of coordinated research that would protect the interest of the basic sciences. When James Watson (who, along with Francis Crick, worked out the structure of DNA in 1953) agreed to be director of the project, most critics dropped their opposition, and many became enthusiastic participants. Watson headed the project with great success until he resigned in 1993, when the position was taken over by Francis S. Collins.

Mapping and sequencing the human genome was expected to take fifteen to twenty years and cost between $3 and $5 billion. In 1989, Congress approved $31 million to initiate the program, but the project eventually came to cost about $200 million per year, and most biological and medical scientists view the money as well and wisely spent. The project was divided among nine different centers at both national laboratories and universities, and hundreds of scientists participated in the research and contributed to the final product.

The project was expected to be completed by 2005, but in response to a challenge by a commercial enterprise to the federal project and eventual cooperation between the two, the project was completed five years ahead of schedule.

Biologist J. Craig Venter, head of the Celera Corporation, claimed he would begin sequencing in 1999 and finish in 2001. Venter's group took a different approach than the federal project. Celera sequenced millions of DNA fragments, then used a computer program to piece them together on the basis of their overlaps. Unlike the HEP approach, Celera did not break DNA into fragments, then create a map of each piece's location.

The payoff of the genome project is considered by most biological and medical researchers to be of inestimable worth. The information has already provided us with a better understanding of the patterns and processes of human evolution and clarified our degree of genetic relatedness with other organisms.

Most important, the detailed genetic information is giving us a much improved understanding of the relationships between certain genes and particular diseases. This information may eventually permit us to develop gene therapy to such a degree that genetic diseases can be wholly eliminated or their results effectively controlled.

The genome project achieved its goal sooner than even its most avid supporters ever thought possible. In 1993, Daniel Cohen, assembling data from some 129 researchers, published a complete map of human chromosomes. The map was sketchy, but it was four times more detailed than the first chromosomal-linkage map published in 1987. The map made it ten times quicker to locate a particular gene than by using earlier linkage maps. After the Cohen map a number of other maps, based on increasingly more complete data, were published.

Another milestone was reached in 1997 when the team led by David Schlessinger of the Washington University Medical School completed a high-resolution map of the X chromosome. The 160 million base pairs of the chromosome were mapped with markers around every 75,000 pairs. Because a number of sex-linked diseases, such as hemophilia, result from a defective gene on the X chromosome, the map made it easier to locate the genes responsible for them. (Females have two copies of the X chromosome. Males have only one; so if it carries a defective gene, they lack a backup gene to prevent the consequences.)

## Identified Genes

The rapidity with which the genes responsible for a large number of human diseases have been identified has been astounding. A sampling from a list of about a thousand gives some idea of how successful researchers have been in locating actual genes or gene markers for diseases:

*Colon cancer.* For the familial form of colon cancer, a marker was found on the upper end of chromosome 2 for a "repair" gene that corrects minor errors in cellular DNA. In its mutant form, the gene seems to function by triggering hundreds of thousands of mutations in other genes. One in 200 people has the gene; 65 percent of the carriers are liable to develop cancer. The familial form accounts for about 15 percent of all colon tumors. (A blood test is expected to be available soon.)

*Amyotrophic lateral sclerosis.* The familial form of ALS (Lou Gehrig's disease) results from a mutation of a gene on chromosome 21 that codes for the enzyme superoxide dismutase, which plays a role in eliminating free radicals. If they aren't controlled, it's believed they may damage motor neurons, which will then lead to muscle degeneration. The familial form of the disease accounts for only about 10 percent of cases, but those with a family history of the disease can now be screened for the defective gene.

*Type II (adult onset) diabetes.* A still unidentified gene on chromosome 7 codes for glucokinase, an enzyme that stimulates the pancreas to produce insulin. At least twenty-three mutated forms of the gene may cause the disease by encoding for a faulty enzyme that apparently fails to trigger insulin production. A screening test for the mutated genes is available.

*Alzheimer's disease.* The gene ApoE on chromosome 19 codes for a protein that transports cholesterol. People who have both alleles for the form of the protein known as E4 have 8 times the risk of developing Alzheimer's; those with one allele have 2 to 3 times the risk. The gene could account for as many as half of those with the disease, although the causal role of E4 in producing it is not yet known.

*X-linked SCID.* Severe combined immunodeficiency disease (SCID) is caused by a defective gene passed from mothers to sons on the X chromosome. The normal gene codes for part of the receptor of interleukin-2, which serves in the cytokine messenger system that keeps the T-cells of the immune system functioning. Newborns with the mutated gene have few or no T-cells, and even a mild infection is life threatening. The disease occurs in only 1 in every 100,000 births.

(The cells used in the study were from "David," who died in Houston after he was removed from the sterile environment where he had spent almost twelve years of his life and given a bone marrow transplant. Because of the publicity surrounding him, SCIDS is known popularly as "the Bubble Boy disease.")

This list could be multiplied to include spinocerebellar ataxia (a degenerative disease linked to a gene on chromosome 6), Huntington's disease (see the Case Presentation: "Huntington's Disease" in this chapter), Lorenzo's disease (adrenoleukodystrophy, or ALD, which involves the degeneration of the myelin sheath around nerves), Canavan disease (a rare and fatal brain disorder similar to ALD affecting mostly Ashkenazi Jews), achondroplastic dwarfism (the gene FGR3 causes about one-third of the cases of dwarfism), and cystic fibrosis (in which mucus accumulates in the lungs and pancreas; the gene, discovered on chromosome 7, is known to exist in hundreds of mutant forms).

More and more genes associated with particular disorders are likely to be identified in the near future. The map of the genome is a powerful tool for understanding the role of genes that in the past could only be guessed at or located only by determined research and good luck.

## The Proteins Project

The Human Genome Project's achievement of mapping, identifying, and sequencing all the genes in the human body is a major milestone on the way to our acquiring something like a complete understanding of our genetic makeup. Being able to locate a gene and knowing it consists of a certain segment of DNA is a crucial step toward understanding the complex roles of genes, but a knowledge of where genes appear on the map of the genome is incomplete in a crucial way. It has to be accompanied by an understanding of what proteins are determined by the genes and what role those proteins play.

Genes do most of their work through the production of proteins. The proteins interact with other proteins to regulate human development, cell division, physiological functioning, immunological responses, tissue repair, and so on.

An enzyme or hormone that is missing or deficient, for example, is responsible for diseases like Tay–Sachs and diabetes. Indeed, perhaps all diseases can be viewed as involving genetically-based responses. We already know of genes that predispose people to heart disease and breast cancer, and many researchers think it is reasonable to believe there are scores (if not hundreds) of predisposing genes for many other diseases, ranging from schizophrenia to glaucoma.

In the future, we can expect researchers to unravel some of the connections between proteins and diseases. When this happens, we can also hope to see new approaches to diagnosing and treating diseases that have often been mysterious and lacking an effective therapy. Instead of a broad diagnostic category like "breast cancer," for example, the disease may be subdivided into many more specific categories, and each may have its own prognosis and its own therapy.

Indeed, pharmaceutical companies may be able to design drugs that are specific for individuals and their particular genetic makeup. By tailoring an individual treatment to an individual version of a disease, not only could such designer drugs be more effective, they could lack some of the worst side-effects of drugs aimed at a general population of patients. Thus, if Sonia Henty is treated for breast cancer, she will receive drugs designed to treat her genetically characterized disease, and if the drugs hit their target more specifically, she may not suffer the literally sickening effects of wide-spectrum chemotherapy.

When we understand the interplay among genes, development, and environmental factors, we will be well on the way to grasping the causes of diseases. Understanding these causes will put us on the road to finding effective measures to prevent them, treat them, or even cure them.

That is the promise of the secular Holy Grail.

## Case Presentation

### Huntington's Disease: Genetic Testing and Ethical Dilemmas

Huntington's disease (HD) is a particularly cruel and frightening genetic disorder. It has no effective treatment and is invariably fatal. Furthermore, each child of an affected parent has a 50 percent chance of developing the disease.

The disease typically makes its appearance between the ages of thirty-five and forty-five in men and women who have shown no previous symptoms. The signs of its onset may be quite subtle—a certain clumsiness in performing small tasks, a slight slurring of speech, a few facial twitches. But the disease is progressive. Over time the small signs develop into massive physical and mental changes. Walking becomes jerky and unsteady, the face contorts into wild grimaces, the hands repeatedly clench and relax, and the whole body writhes with involuntary muscle spasms. The victim eventually loses the power of speech, becomes disoriented, and gives way to irrational emotional outbursts. Before mental deterioration becomes too advanced, HD victims often kill themselves out of sheer hopelessness and despair. Death may occur naturally from fifteen to twenty years after the beginning of the symptoms. Usually, it results from massive infection and malnutrition—as the disease progresses, the victim loses the ability to swallow normally.

In the United States, at any given time, some 30,000 people are diagnosed as having the disease, and as many as 150,000 more may have the gene responsible for it. The incidence of the disease is only 1 in 10,000, but for the child of someone with the disease, the chances of having it are 1 in 2.

### Gene Identified

The gene causing the disease was identified in 1993 after ten years of intensive research carried out in six laboratories in the United States, England, and Wales. Following the leads provided by genetic markers for the disease, the gene was finally located near the tip of chromosome 4. When researchers sequenced the nucleotides making up the gene, they discovered that the mutation was a trinucleotide repeat. In healthy individuals, the nucleotides CAG are repeated eleven to thirty-four times, whereas in individuals with HD, the repetitions typically range from thirty-seven to eighty-six. Some evidence suggests that higher numbers of repetitions are associated with earlier onset.

When the HD gene was identified, it was expected this would have almost immediate consequences for the development of an effective treatment. This has not turned out to be the case because the mechanism of the gene's action is not yet understood. Furthermore, the gene was expected to be found functioning only in the brain, but in fact radioactive tagging has shown that the gene operates in virtually every tissue of the body, including the colon, liver, pancreas, and testes. The protein the gene codes for is believed to be toxic to neuronal development, but the protein itself has not yet been isolated. (In 1998 it was discovered that the disease involves the formation of a protein plaque in brain cells that destroys them, but this hasn't yet led to a therapy.)

Before the HD gene was identified or a marker for it discovered, the disease was known to be transmitted from generation to generation in the sort of hereditary pattern indicating it is caused by a single gene. However, because the disease makes its appearance relatively late in life, an unsuspecting victim may already have passed on the gene to a child before showing any sign of the disease. In the absence of a genetic test to detect the gene, the individual could not know whether he or she was a carrier.

In 1983 a major step toward the development of such a test was announced by James F. Gusella and his group at Massachusetts General Hospital. The team did not locate the gene itself, but discovered a "genetic marker" indicating its presence. They began by studying the DNA taken from members of a large American family with a history of Huntington's disease, then employed recombinant-DNA techniques to attempt to locate DNA segments that might be associated with the HD gene.

The techniques involved using proteins known as restriction enzymes. A particular enzyme, when mixed with a single strand of DNA, cuts the strand at specific locations known as recognition sites. After the DNA strand has been cut up by restriction enzymes, short sections of radioactive, single-stranded DNA are added to serve as probes. The probes bind to particular segments of the DNA. Because the probes are radioactive, the segments to which they are attached can be identified on photographic film. The various fragments of DNA produced by the restriction enzymes and identified by probes form a pattern that is typical of individuals. Thus, if the pattern of someone who does not have the disease is compared with the pattern of a family member who does, the fragments that include the faulty gene can be identified, even when the gene itself is unknown. The pattern serves as a marker for the presence of the gene.

Gusella's group faced the problem of finding a marker consistently inherited by those with Huntington's disease but not by those free of the disease. This meant identifying perhaps as many as 800 markers and determining whether one could serve as the marker for the HD gene. Incredibly, the team identified a good candidate on its twelfth try. It was a marker found in all members of the family they were studying. Those with the disease had the same form of the marker, while those free of the disease had some other form.

Gusella and other researchers were supported in their work by the Hereditary Disease Foundation. The organization was founded by Milton Wexler after his wife was diagnosed with Huntington's. Wexler hoped a treatment for the disease could be found that might benefit his daughters, Nancy and Alice, who stood a 50 percent chance of developing the disease. Nancy Wexler soon became an active participant in research activities aimed at discovering a genetic marker.

In collaboration with the Hereditary Disease Foundation, plans were made to test Gusella's candidate marker in a large population. It was known that a large family with a high incidence of HD lived along the shores of Lake Maracaibo in Venezuela. Nancy Wexler led a team to this remote location to collect family history and to obtain blood and skin samples for analysis. The lake-dwelling family included some 100 people with the disease and 1100 children with the risk of developing it. Analysis of the samples showed that those with the disease also carried the same form of the marker as their American counterparts. Gusella estimated that the odds were 100 million to 1 that the marker was linked to the HD gene. Subsequent work by Susan Naylor indicated the marker was on chromosome 4. When the gene itself was identified in 1993, this turned out to be correct.

## Genetic Test Available

Once the location of the gene for Huntington's disease was known, a genetic test for its presence was quickly developed. The availability of the test, however, raises a number of serious ethical and social issues. The basic question people with a family history that puts them at risk for the disease must ask is whether they should have the test.

A study conducted in Wales revealed that more than half of those whose parents or relatives were victims of Huntington's disease would not want to have a test that would tell them whether they had the HD gene, even if such a test were available. Considering that the disease cannot be effectively treated and is invariably fatal, this is not a surprise finding.

Nancy Wexler confided to a reporter that she and her sister had assumed that once a test for determining whether they were carrying the HD gene was available, they would take it. However, when they met with their father to work out the details for a test based on a genetic marker, he suddenly said, "What are we doing here? Are we sure we want to do this?" The sisters, Nancy recalled, "had a visceral understanding that either one of us could get bad news and that it would certainly destroy my father."

But do those who are at risk have obligations to others? Because a test is available, is it fair to a potential marriage partner to marry without finding out whether one is a carrier of the HD gene and informing the potential partner of the result? Perhaps he or she may be willing to take the chance that the offspring of an HD parent will not have the disease. Even so, because of the tremendous burden the disease places on the other spouse, the possibility of being tested for the presence of the gene deserves serious consideration.

The decision about whether to have children can also be affected by the knowledge that one partner is a carrier of the HD gene so that there is a 50 percent chance that any child will also develop the disease. Should a potential carrier of the gene impose on the other partner the risk of having a child who will inherit the gene? Should such a risk be imposed on a potential child? The genetic test can determine whether an individual carries the gene. If he or she does, then the couple has knowledge of the relevant facts that will put them in a position to make a decision about having a child.

## Prenatal Test

The test now in use can also be employed in conjunction with amniocentesis to determine whether a developing fetus carries the HD gene. Possessing such information may add a particular difficulty to making an abortion decision for some. A child born with the HD gene will inevitably develop the disease but may not do so for three, four, or even five or more decades.

Is the fact that the child will eventually succumb to the disease reason enough to make an abortion morally obligatory? On the other hand, should the parents even have the fetus tested, if they are not prepared to have it aborted in the event of a positive test for the HD gene?

One disadvantage of the direct testing of the fetus for the presence of the HD gene is that if the fetus is found to have the gene, then the parent with the family history of the disease will know that she or he has the gene also. To avoid this consequence, a so-called nondisclosing prenatal test can be performed. The test employs a gene-probe method to determine how a segment of fetal chromosome 4 compares with segments from grandparents. If the segment resembles that of a healthy grandparent, the child is not likely to have the gene. If it matches that of the grandparent with the disease, there is a 50 percent chance that the child possesses the gene.

This is the same as the risk for a mother or father with one parent who developed the disease. Hence, the potential parent has learned nothing new about his or her own chances of having the gene, and it is this that makes the test nondisclosing. However, if the potential parents do not plan to abort the fetus should they learn that it has a 50 percent chance of possessing the HD gene, there is no reason to perform the test.

## Social Risks

The advent of a standard, inexpensive test for the HD gene raises various other moral and social issues. For example, insurance companies may refuse to provide life or health insurance to those from families with Huntington's disease, unless they prove that they are not carriers of the gene. Employers may refuse to provide health benefits to family members unless they are tested and found to lack the gene. Adoption agencies have requested that infants available for adoption be tested to assure potential adopting families that the children are not at risk for HD. As Nancy Wexler put the point, "In our culture, people assume that knowledge is always good. . . . But our experience with Huntington's has shown that some things may be better left unknown."

Informing someone that he or she carries the gene also has problems associated with it. Such news can be devastating, both to the person and to the person's family. About 10 to 12 percent of HD victims kill themselves, and 30 percent of those at risk say that this is what they will do if they learn they have the disease. Thus, the mere act of conveying the information that someone will later develop the signs of a fatal disease can itself constitute a threat to life. Nancy Wexler has refused to disclose publicly whether she has been tested for the HD gene. "I don't want to influence anyone's decision," she says.

In the best of worlds, an effective means of preventing the onset of Huntington's disease or treating it effectively would be available. Then the moral and social issues associated with a genetic test for it would disappear without having to be resolved. Regrettably, that world still lies in the future.

## SOCIAL CONTEXT: GENETIC TESTING AND SCREENING

The discovery of dozens of new disease-predisposing genes has been followed by the development of new screening tests. Given the increasing sophistication of biotechnology, tests that are now complex and expensive are likely to become simple and cheap quite soon. By using cells from a blood sample in an automated process involving biochip arrays of genetic probes, it should be possible to screen simultaneously for the presence of literally hundreds of genes. Already researchers test for the presence of many genes simultaneously and instantaneously by using a modified form of DNA and mass spectrometry.

While researchers are well on the way to identifying an entire catalogue of genes and their associated diseases, the concept of a genetic disease is not as clear-cut as it may seem. Rarely is it the case that if a person carries a certain gene, she will invariably develop a certain disease. While single-gene disorders like sickle-cell and Huntington's diseases have been the focus of research, they account for only about 2 percent of genetic disorders. Most diseases result from a multiplicity of conditions such as the particular form of a gene (many genes have scores and even hundreds of mutated versions), the pres-

---

## A Sample of DNA Tests Currently Available

| Disease | Description |
| --- | --- |
| Huntington's disease | Progressive neurological disorder, onset in 40s or 50s |
| Polycystic kidney disease | Multiple kidney cysts leading to loss of kidney function |
| Cystic fibrosis | Mucus clogs lungs and pancreas; death in 30s is common |
| Sickle-cell disease | Hemoglobin defect; anemia, strokes, and heart damage |
| Alpha-1-Antitrypsin deficiency | Can cause hepatitis, cirrhosis, and emphysema |
| Familial adenomatous polyposis | Colon polyps by age 35, often leading to cancer |
| Muscular dystrophy | Progressive muscle deterioration |
| Hemophilia | Blood fails to clot properly |
| Tay–Sachs disease | Lipid metabolism disorder causing death in first one to four years of life |
| Retinoblastoma | Cancerous tumor of the eye; most common in childhood |
| Phenylketonuria | Enzyme deficiency producing mental retardation |
| Retinitis pigmentosa | Progressive retinal degeneration leading to blindness |
| Familial breast cancer | 5 to 10 percent of breast cancers |
| Familial hypercholesterolemia | High levels of cholesterol leading to early heart disease |
| Spinocerebellar ataxia | Neurological disorder producing lack of muscle control |

ence or absence of other genes, and the presence or absence of specific environmental factors. Being predisposed to develop a disease raises a number of questions about the value and dangers of genetic screening.

## Individuals and Screening

The ambivalence we all feel about genetic testing is shown by the results of a recent survey. When 500 people were asked if they would like to take a genetic test that would tell them what diseases they would suffer from later in life, 50 percent said they would want to take it, and 49 percent said they wouldn't. We are torn between seeing the value of knowing and the comfort of not knowing.

Information about a genetic predisposition to a particular disease can be beneficial to individuals. It can alert them to the need to seek medical surveillance so they can receive appropriate therapy for the disease, should it develop, at the earliest time. Further, it can make them aware of the need to avoid environmental factors that may trigger the disease. For example, those with the gene for xeroderma pigmentosum are extremely sensitive to ultraviolet radiation, and exposure to it is likely to lead to a form of melanoma that is usually incurable. However, if those with the gene avoid prolonged exposure to sunlight, they have a good chance of avoiding developing melanoma.

By contrast, in the case of some single-gene diseases like Huntington's, knowing one is a carrier of the gene opens up no ways of altering the outcome of the disease. No way of preventing the disease is known, and early intervention makes no difference in the course of the illness. While some might want to know whether they are carriers of the gene in order to make informed decisions about such personal matters as marriage, childbearing, and lifestyle, others might prefer to live their lives without knowing. (See the preceding Case Presentation: "Huntington's Disease" in this chapter.)

Equally difficult issues are associated with screening for the genes known to be associated with familial breast cancer. Mutations in the gene BRCA1, located on chromosome 17, were identified in 1994 as being responsible for the susceptibility to breast cancer and ovarian cancer in a group of families with multiple incidence of the diseases. A "frame-shift mutation" apparently causes the translation of codons to start in the wrong place, producing a nonsense protein. A second gene, BRCA2, located on chromosome 13, that also causes susceptibility to breast cancer was discovered in 1995. More than 200 mutations have been identified on the BRCA genes, but one study suggests it is a mutation in BRCA1 most likely to cause cancer in younger women.

Women who carry the mutated genes are estimated to have an 85 percent chance of developing breast cancer and a 60 percent chance of developing ovarian cancer by age 65. Whether these figures can be generalized to any carrier of the gene is in some dispute, because they are based on samples from families with a history of breast cancer. Critics suggest a more realistic figure for breast cancer for a woman with the BRCA mutation is 56 percent.

The two mutated genes may explain the majority of hereditary breast cancers. (BRCA1 appears responsible for about 50 percent and BRCA2 for 30 to 40 percent.) Yet to the surprise of researchers, no evidence suggests the BRCA1 or BRCA2 gene plays a role in the 90 to 95 percent of "sporadic" breast cancers—ones not known to be due to inherited susceptibility. (The possibility that mutations in other genes are responsible is under investigation.)

But susceptibility to breast cancer means only that a woman is more likely than average to develop the disease. The extent to which she might control the outcome by altering such factors as diet, alcohol consumption, and exercise aren't known. Some evidence suggests the chance of developing cancer might be reduced by a prophylactic double mastectomy. Even so, cancer can still occur in the remaining tissue, and ovarian cancer might remain as likely. While the grounds for recommending that women be screened for the breast cancer genes are shaky, some women may still want to be tested. They might find a psychological value in knowing, and this might have practical consequences, even though not preventive or therapeutic ones.

## Employment

Whether or not individuals find value in knowing their own genetic predispositions to develop diseases, some observers worry that our newly acquired understanding of parts of the human genome may result in opening the way for new forms of discrimination—ones based on genetic predisposition.

This worry is reflected in the responses to the survey mentioned earlier. While individuals may be ambivalent about knowing their own genetic predispositions, they are virtually unanimous in wanting such information kept from employers. In response to the question "Do you think it should be legal for employers to use genetic tests in deciding whom to hire?" only 9 percent of the 500 people surveyed said yes; an overwhelming 87 percent said no.

While individuals may be sure about what they don't want employers to know, employers may believe they have good reasons to know anything likely to affect the health and performance of employees. Because employers have financial responsibilities and legal liabilities with respect to their employees, they may believe they are entitled to all relevant health information.

The way in which genetic screening for disease predisposition becomes entangled with thorny issues of public policy is illustrated by a telling example occurring early in the history of genetic screening. People prone to develop an acute form of anemia after exposure to naphthalene should avoid jobs in which the chemical is employed. In principle, susceptible workers could be assigned to jobs allowing them to avoid being exposed to the chemicals particularly harmful to them.

With such an aim in view, in 1982 some 59 percent of large companies surveyed indicated they either had a genetic screening program or intended to institute one. Their motivation was partly based on economic self-interest; the costs of damage suits and insurance premiums could be lowered by keeping susceptible workers out of danger.

By 1986, however, the majority of plans to screen workers had been abandoned by corporations that had initially favored them. This was mostly in response to criticisms from civil rights groups, women's organizations, and labor unions. The critics pointed out that the results of genetic screening could be used to discriminate against the hiring of entire classes of workers. Because African Americans are more susceptible to environmentally induced anemia, they would be effectively shut out of jobs in which the risk to them was greater than to other workers.

Similarly, because fetuses are likely to be affected by a number of chemicals used in manufacturing, pregnant women would not be hired for a wide variety of jobs. Indeed, the possibility that a woman might be or become pregnant without knowing it might result in the exclusion of women as a group.

As this case illustrates, the possibility of genetic screening in connection with employment presents us with a number of dilemmas of a moral and social kind. We wish to promote equal opportunity for workers, yet we also wish to protect their health and safety. If those genetically predisposed to certain diseases are allowed to compete for jobs that place them at risk, then we are not seeing to their health and safety. Yet if we see to their health, we are not allowing them equal opportunity. Similarly, we wish to promote individual freedom in the society, but at what point do we decide that an individual is taking an unacceptable risk? If we allow someone to risk her health, are we willing to bear the social cost associated with her falling ill?

A worker found to be susceptible to a common manufacturing chemical would be at a clear disadvantage in attempting to get a job and might claim that an employer who required him to take a screening test as a condition of employment was violating his right to privacy. Yet should employers be allowed no protection from the added costs of damage suits and higher insurance premiums caused by a higher rate of illness among susceptible workers?

The Equal Employment Opportunities Commission construes the Americans with Disabilities Act as making it unlawful to use the results of genetic testing to refuse employment. EEO's opinion has not yet been supported by any court rulings, however, and until that happens both employees and employers must make decisions without a definite policy to guide them.

### Insurance

Quite apart from the issues of employment, individuals who are screened for whatever reason and found to be at risk for some genetic diseases may find they can get only very expensive health insurance, if they can get it at all. Insurance companies, for their part, may attempt to make genetic screening for probabilities of certain known disorders a condition of insurability. Are individuals entitled to keep such information about themselves private? Are insurers entitled to know what risk they are taking before insuring an applicant?

While some states have passed laws forbidding insurers to require genetic testing or to use the results of genetic tests as a reason for denying applicants for health insurance, federal laws currently offer little or no protection against genetic discrimination. Recent efforts to pass such legislation have met with strong opposition from the insurance industry.

### Social Issues

In addition to issues connected with employment and insurance, genetic screening opens up the possibility of identifying a class of people that may become regarded as socially undesirable. Being predisposed to a genetic disease may become a stigma in a society that prizes health. Genetic carriers of disease-causing genes might be shunned as marriage partners or find it difficult to make their way into positions of social power

and influence. Regarded as genetic pariahs, they might come to be outcasts in their own society, stigmatized by their biological inheritance.

These are merely some of the difficulties raised by the new possibilities of screening for the genetic predisposition to diseases. The promise of being able to prevent the occurrence of some disease in many individuals is genuine, but we have yet to make an adequate effort to resolve the social and moral issues that fulfilling the promise presents. Until we deal with them satisfactorily, a powerful technology may remain underutilized.

### Screening and Children

Researchers attempting to identify a gene predisposing women to breast cancer conducted their work among families with a high incidence of the disease. During the course of their work, they learned which females in the family had to be carriers of the BRCA1 gene and so had an 85 percent chance of developing the disease. The question they faced was, should they inform the women that they or their children were at such risk?

Some researchers decided they would not volunteer any information and would provide it only to women eighteen or older who asked for it. They refused to divulge any information about children, even when pressed to do so by their parents, because being predisposed to breast cancer is not a condition for which there is a treatment. Also, the researchers reasoned, if a child knew she was predisposed to breast cancer, she might be inclined to think of herself as sick and her breasts as likely to kill her.

Some critics of screening have argued that children should not be included in screening tests, except when there is some direct benefit for them. The acquisition of knowledge is not in itself a justification for screening children, the critics hold, nor is the usefulness of the knowledge in the treatment of others. Screening tests and the results they yield have the potential to damage or destroy a child's self-esteem, causing emotional harm, or altering the way in which the family views the child. In some instances, upon learning that a child is likely to develop a disease, some families have distanced themselves from the child, even to the point of placing the child in a foster home. When the child herself receives no benefit, the threat of such an outcome makes the test unjustifiable.

At least one survey shows, however, that parents often believe children should be aware of their risks for developing a particular disease. Some 61 percent of parents visiting prenatal testing clinics said they should be permitted to have their children tested for Alzheimer's, and 47 percent said that parents should inform the children of the results.

However, another survey of families with members already diagnosed with genetic diseases shows a different result. Survey participants seemed to feel strongly that parents should have their children tested for a disease only when it is a treatable or preventable one. When the disease is neither, as is the case with Alzheimer's, the screening should not be done.

The issue may be complicated in some cases by the recent discovery that a disease that is mild or even asymptomatic in a parent may be much worse in an offspring. This was discovered to be the case with myotonic muscular dystrophy, the most common form of the disease. A segment of DNA on chromosome 19 appears to repeat itself with increasing frequency over generations. Hence, someone who does not have any clinical sign of the disease may pass on the gene to a child, who will develop a devastating form of the disease. It might be argued that if a parent knows that a child is at high risk for developing a life-threatening disease, the parent has a duty to inform the child, although perhaps only after the child has reached a certain level of maturity.

The questions of whether children should be tested and who should decide when and how much they should know are issues that are likely to become more pressing as the number of tests for disease-causing genes increases.

## Case Presentation

### Gene Therapy

On September 14, 1990, at the National Institutes of Health in Bethesda, Maryland, a four-year-old girl became the first patient under an approved protocol to be treated by gene therapy. The child, whose parents initially asked that her identity not be made public, lacked the gene for producing adenosine deaminase (ADA), an enzyme required to keep immune cells alive and functioning.

Her life expectancy was low because without ADA she would almost certainly develop cancers and opportunistic infections that cannot be effectively controlled by conventional treatments. The aim of the therapy was to provide her with cells that would boost her immune system by increasing the production of essential antibodies. During the following months, she received four injections of altered cells.

The treatment, under the direction of W. French Anderson, R. Michael Blaese, and Kenneth Culver, involved taking blood from the patient, isolating the T-cells and then growing a massive number of them. These cells were infected with a weakened retrovirus into which a copy of the human gene for ADA had been spliced. The cells were then injected into the patient in a blood transfusion.

The idea behind the therapy was for the ADA gene to migrate to the cellular DNA, switch on, and begin producing ADA. If the cells produced enough of the enzyme, the child's immune system would not be destroyed. Because most T-cells live for only weeks or months, the process had to be repeated at regular intervals. The girl's parents, from a Cleveland suburb, later revealed their daughter's identity. She is Ashanthi Desilva, and over a decade later, she is alive and doing well. Soon after her treatment, on January 30, 1991, nine-year-old Cynthia Cutshall, became the second person to receive gene therapy.

Laboratory tests showed both children's immune systems were functioning effectively. But the need to replace short-lived T-cells meant Ashanthi and Cynthia had to continue to receive regular injections of altered cells. However, Anderson and his collaborators had always hoped to find a way around this need, and the break came when an NIH group developed a procedure for isolating stem cells from the bone marrow. If enough stem cells could be obtained and genetically altered, when injected back into the patient, the cells might produce enough T-cells for an adequately functioning immune system.

In May 1993, Cynthia's stem cells were harvested, exposed to the retrovirus containing the normal ADA gene, and reinjected. She tolerated the procedure with no apparent ill effects, and later that year essentially the same procedure was repeated with Ashanthi. While the immune systems of both continue to function within the normal range, the evidential value of the experiment is difficult to assess, because both subjects have also been treated with a standard drug regimen. Gene therapy can't be said to have produced a cure for ADA, but advocates of the therapy believe that eventually it will.

## Effectiveness and Risks

More definitive evidence for the effectiveness of gene therapy comes from results of clinical trials conducted at Paris's Necker Hospital in 2000 by Alain Fischer. Fischer's group treated eleven patients (ten infants and a teenager) with severe combined immunodeficiency disease (SCID), a disorder caused by a defect on the X chromosome. (See the discussion in Social Context: "The Holy Grail of Biology" for more details.) Eight of those treated by using a retrovirus to insert new genes were cured. This is an astounding outcome, considering that most children born with the defect die from the disease by the end of their first year. Bone marrow transplants, the standard treatment, are successful only about 75 percent of the time.

Then in 2002 a three-year-old boy in the study who had been considered cured developed leukemia-like symptoms. Then a second child became ill with the same symptoms. The clinical trial in France was immediately halted. Regulatory agencies in the United States were already particularly inclined to caution because of the death of eighteen-year-old Jesse Gelsinger in 1999 (see the Classic Case Presentation in Chapter 1), so the adverse events in France raised the question of whether gene-therapy trials were so unsafe as to be discontinued. The FDA decided to suspend twenty-seven gene-therapy trials involving the technologies used in the French trials, despite the undoubted cures obtained by French investigators.

## Wide Promise

The FDA decision had an immediate impact for many researchers and patients. The promise gene therapy holds for those who suffer from a variety of genetic disorders is enormous. Experimental clinical protocols for the treatment of a wide range of relatively common diseases such as cystic fibrosis, hemophilia, phenylketonuria, sickle-cell anemia, hypercholesterolemia, AIDS, cardiovascular disease, cancer, lupus erythematous, and blood-clotting disorders either have already been initiated or are under consideration. Here are a few examples.

*Parkinson's Disease.* Parkinson's disease, which affects about 400,000 people in the United States, is a progressive disorder in which cells in the part of the brain called the substantia nigra die off, resulting in a lack of the neurotransmitter dopamine. This leads to symptoms such as hand tremors, a stooped posture, and a shuffling walk. As more cells die, the symptoms become progressively worse.

A new treatment aims to slow cell loss by using a modified cold virus to transport copies of the gene for glial cell-derived neurotrophic factors or GDNF into the cells of the substantia nigra. Studies show GDNF can block cell degeneration, and experiments with rats indicate that those treated with GDNF suffered less brain cell death than untreated ones. The therapy will next be tested with primates, and if it is effective, it will then be ready for application to humans.

*Sickle-Cell Disease.* Sickle-cell disease, affecting about 1 in 400 African Americans, is produced by a gene that affects the folding of the two chains making up the hemoglobin molecule. In a developing treatment, molecular fragments called chimeraplasts will be induced to enter red blood cell–producing stem cells in the bone marrow.

If a stem cell takes up the fragment and incorporates it into the nucleus, the cell's own repair system should eliminate the code for the defective hemoglobin chain and substitute that provided by the chimeraplast. If enough stem cells are altered and function, the amount of red blood cells produced should eliminate the tissue damage and strokes that often cause early death in those with the disease.

*Malignant Melanoma.* In one proposed cancer treatment, researchers will make trillions of copies of the gene that codes for the antigen HLA-B7, then inject them directly into the tumors of those with melanoma. The DNA is expected to enter the cells of the tumor, insert itself in the cellular DNA, then trigger the production of HLA-B7. The antigen will then extrude from the cell, causing the cell to be attacked by killer T-cells. Animal experiments suggest the immune system will attack not only tumor cells with the antigen markers, but those around it.

*Leukemia.* A genetic abnormality known as the Philadelphia chromosome triggers cancerous changes in stem cells in the bone marrow. The resulting disease is chronic myelogenous leukemia, which affects about 7000 people a year and is responsible for 20 to 25 percent of all cases of leukemia. The best standard treatment is to inject patients with stem cells from a bone marrow donor. Sometimes, however, a compatible donor can't be located; also, the therapy has a lower level of success in people over fifty-five.

A new gene-based therapy is used to alter the patient's own stem cells by adding an antisense sequence to the cellular DNA. The sequence is designed to block the formation of the protein leading to cancerous growth, thus making the cancer cells behave like normal cells. The sequence will also have attached to it a gene making the altered cells more resistant to the chemotherapeutic drug methotrexate. When a patient receives chemotherapy, the cancerous cells will be killed, while the altered ones will survive and reproduce. The altered stem cells should then produce normal red blood cells. The main difficulty, at present, is to get the stem cells to incorporate the new genes.

*Hypercholesterolemia.* Hypercholesterolemia is a disease in which the excess production of cholesterol often leads to heart attacks and early death. The gene therapy being developed to treat it involves removing part of a patient's liver, then culturing the cells and inserting into them a gene that produces the low-density lipoprotein receptor. The receptor plays an important role in removing cholesterol from the blood. The treated cells are then injected into the patient's liver, where they attach themselves to the liver's capillaries and start producing the

protein of the receptor. Six months after the experimental study was started, the results were so satisfactory that federal approval was given to include more patients in the study.

*Collateral Blood Vessel Growth.* Every year 30,000 to 40,000 people in the United States develop almost complete blockage in the arteries of their legs. Shut off from a blood supply, the tissues in the leg develop ulcers that don't heal, and, eventually, when gangrene sets in, the leg must be amputated to save the person's life. Twenty percent of the patients died in the hospital, and forty percent died within the next year. No drugs are available to increase the blood flow to the legs.

A new treatment uses the gene that codes for vascular endothelial growth factor, or vegF, a protein that stimulates the growth of collateral blood vessels. When billions of vegF genes are injected into leg muscle, about 5 percent of them are incorporated into muscle cells, causing them to start producing the vegF protein. Because the vessel cells beyond the blockage are deprived of blood, their membranes become altered so as to be more receptive to the vegF molecule. When it attaches to the surface of cells, the cells begin to produce tiny new blood vessels that grow around the blockage. While only a few people have been treated with vegF gene therapy, it has shown itself to be effective. Plans are now under way to test the effectiveness of the therapy in heart disease. If vegF can establish collateral circulation in the heart, the need for coronary artery bypass surgery may be reduced or even eliminated. Those too frail or sick to undergo a bypass or even angioplasty might eventually be helped by the new technique.

*Cystic Fibrosis.* In April 1993, a twenty-three-year-old man became the first patient to receive human gene therapy for the treatment of cystic fibrosis. An altered form of the adenovirus was used to transport into his lungs the gene that codes for cystic fibrosis transmembrane conductance regulator. The regulator controls the flow of chloride through body cells. Cystic fibrosis patients lack the regulator gene, and as a result, they suffer severe salt imbalances that cause abnormal mucus excretions in the lungs and pancreas.

The first test of the therapy was evaluated in 1996. While the evidence did not demonstrate that it was effective, most investigators think ultimately it will be. Part of the difficulty is to find a way of getting the gene into the cells of the lungs. If the problems can be solved, gene therapy will offer the 30,000 Americans who suffer from cystic fibrosis a cure for the disease.

*AIDS.* Several experiments are under way utilizing gene therapy to treat AIDS. In one of them, a few CD4 cells, the principal target of the HIV virus, will be taken from an AIDS patient, and a molecule called a "hairpin ribozyme" spliced into their DNA. The ribozyme slices up RNA, and because HIV depends on RNA for replication, cells with altered DNA should prevent the virus from reproducing. If enough altered CD4 cells were present in an HIV-positive individual, the level of infection might be lowered.

Paralleling the development of gene therapy are other treatment strategies based on the technology of recombinant DNA. One of the most promising is the use of drugs to alter the function of genes not behaving normally. The drugs in effect "turn on" a malfunctioning gene so it plays the role it is supposed to. Some promising results in the treatment of thalassemia and sickle-cell anemia have been reported.

Another technique involves transplanting cells into the brain, and it has been used experimentally in the treatment of Parkinson's disease. Researchers in Sweden have reported success in transplanting cells from fetal tissue into the substantia nigra of the brain. Other work also supports the idea that transplant therapy for diseases such as Parkinson's and Alzheimer's will be effective in the not-too-distant future.

## Germ-Line Therapy

The gene therapy in humans currently under development is somatic-cell therapy, where modifications take place in the body cells of patients, not in the sex cells.

This means that even if the therapy can eliminate the disease produced in an individual who has inherited a defective gene, the therapy will do nothing to alter the probability that a child of that person will inherit the same defective gene. To change this circumstance, germ-line cells would have to be altered. That is, the defective gene in an ovum or sperm cell would have to be replaced.

If this were possible, then certain genetic diseases could be eliminated from families. Germ-line therapy would make it unnecessary to perform somatic-cell therapy for each generation of affected individuals. As appealing as this prospect is, at present germ-line therapy has many more technical difficulties associated with it than does somatic-cell therapy. Uniformly encouraging results have not so far been produced in animal research, and even somatic-cell therapy in humans remains a distant prospect.

Moreover, some question the value of germ-line therapy. If the aim is to eliminate heritable diseases from a family, the most direct and effective way to achieve this is to screen embryos and avoid implanting those that carry the flawed gene. This process is currently available at infertility clinics and doesn't involve the risks and uncertainties of tinkering with the DNA of germ cells.

Most of the moral issues discussed in connection with gene therapy have centered around germ-line therapy. It holds out the prospect of genetically engineering sex cells to produce offspring with virtually any set of characteristics desired. This possibility has led many critics to warn that "genetic surgery" may be leading us into a sort of "Brave New World" in which we practice eugenics and manufacture our children to order. (See the Briefing Session in this chapter for a fuller discussion.) However, any dangers posed by germ-line therapy are far from immediate.

While somatic-cell therapy continues to be experimental, some of its forms are likely to become standard therapies within the next two to five years. Other forms will for some time remain experimental, and as such they will raise the same sorts of moral questions typical of any experimental procedure—questions of informed consent, benefit, and risk.

# Section 1: Stem Cells

## Cloning and Stem Cells

### President's Council on Bioethics

While the Council was unanimous in finding "cloning-to-produce-children" unacceptable, it split on "cloning-for-biomedical-research." (These phrases aim for neutrality: some consider "therapeutic cloning" question-begging; others object to "reproductive cloning," holding that all cloning is reproductive.)

Council members presented opposing cases. Those endorsing research cloning state two different positions: one seeing it as involving special moral problems, the other recognizing none. Those opposing research cloning acknowledge it may open up therapeutic possibilities, but argue that it is morally wrong to destroy embryos, even for good reasons.

Ten members of the Council recommend a four-year moratorium on research cloning, as well as a review of all practices involving human embryos. The seven in the minority recommend the regulation of cloned embryos in research.

### The Ethics of Cloning-for-Biomedical-Research

To make clear to all what is at stake in the decision, Council Members have presented, as strongly as possible, the competing ethical cases for and against cloning-for-biomedical-research in the form of first-person attempts at moral suasion. Each case has tried to address what is owed to suffering humanity, to the human embryo, and to the broader society. Within each case, supporters of the position in question speak only for themselves, and not for the Council as a whole.

### A. The Moral Case for Cloning-for-Biomedical-Research

The moral case for proceeding with the research rests on our obligation to try to relieve human suffering, an obligation that falls most powerfully on medical practitioners and biomedical researchers. We who support cloning-for-biomedical-research all agree that it may offer uniquely useful ways of investigating and possibly treating many chronic debilitating diseases and disabilities, providing aid and relief to millions. We

From President's Council on Bioethics, *Human Cloning and Human Dignity: An Ethical Inquiry,* "Executive Summary" (pp. 8–11; 12–14). Pre-Publication version, July, 2002 (*www.bioethics.gov*).

also believe that the moral objections to this research are outweighed by the great good that may come from it. Up to this point, we who support the research all agree. But we differ among ourselves regarding the weight of the moral objections, owing to differences about the moral status of the cloned embryo. These differences are sufficient to warrant distinguishing two different moral positions within the moral case for cloning-for-biomedical-research:

**Position Number One.** Most Council Members who favor cloning-for-biomedical-research do so with serious moral concerns. Speaking only for ourselves, we acknowledge the following difficulties, but think that they can be addressed by setting proper boundaries.

■ *Intermediate Moral Status.* While we take seriously concerns about the treatment of nascent human life, we believe there are sound moral reasons for not regarding the embryo in its earliest stages as the moral equivalent of a human person. We believe the embryo has a developing and intermediate moral worth that commands our special respect, but that it is morally permissible to use early-stage cloned human embryos in important research under strict regulation.

■ *Deliberate Creation for Use.* We believe that concerns over the problem of deliberate creation of cloned embryos for use in research have merit, but when properly understood should not preclude cloning-for-biomedical-research. These embryos would not be "created for destruction," but for use in the service of life and medicine. They would be destroyed in the service of a great good, and this should not be obscured.

- *Going Too Far.* We acknowledge the concern that some researchers might seek to develop cloned embryos beyond the blastocyst stage, and for those of us who believe that the cloned embryo has a developing and intermediate moral status, this is a very real worry. We approve, therefore, only of research on cloned embryos that is strictly limited to the first fourteen days of development—a point near when the primitive streak is formed and before organ differentiation occurs.

- *Other Moral Hazards.* We believe that concerns about the exploitation of women and about the risk that cloning-for-biomedical-research could lead to cloning-to-produce-children can be adequately addressed by appropriate rules and regulations. These concerns need not frighten us into abandoning an important avenue of research.

**Position Number Two.** A few Council Members who favor cloning-for-biomedical-research do not share all the ethical qualms expressed above. Speaking only for ourselves, we hold that this research, at least for the purposes presently contemplated, presents no special moral problems, and therefore should be endorsed with enthusiasm as a potential new means of gaining knowledge to serve humankind. Because we accord no special moral status to the early-stage cloned embryo and believe it should be treated essentially like all other human cells, we believe that the moral issues involved in this research are no different from those that accompany any biomedical research. What is required is the usual commitment to high standards for the quality of research, scientific integrity, and the need to obtain informed consent from donors of the eggs and somatic cells used in nuclear transfer.

### B. The Moral Case Against Cloning-for-Biomedical-Research

The moral case against cloning-for-biomedical-research acknowledges the possibility—though purely speculative at the moment—that medical benefits might come from this particular avenue of experimentation. But we believe it is morally wrong to exploit

and destroy developing human life, even for good reasons, and that it is unwise to open the door to the many undesirable consequences that are likely to result from this research. We find it disquieting, even somewhat ignoble, to treat what are in fact seeds of the next generation as mere raw material for satisfying the needs of our own. Only for very serious reasons should progress toward increased knowledge and medical advances be slowed. But we believe that in this case such reasons are apparent.

- *Moral Status of the Cloned Embryo.* We hold that the case for treating the early-stage embryo as simply the moral equivalent of all other human cells (Position Number Two, above) is simply mistaken: it denies the continuous history of human individuals from the embryonic to fetal to infant stages of existence; it misunderstands the meaning of potentiality; and it ignores the hazardous moral precedent that the routinized creation, use, and destruction of nascent human life would establish. We hold that the case for according the human embryo "intermediate and developing moral status" (Position Number One, above) is also unconvincing, for reasons both biological and moral. Attempts to ground the limited measure of respect owed to a maturing embryo in certain of its developmental features do not succeed, and the invoking of a "special respect" owed to nascent human life seem to have little or no operative meaning if cloned embryos may be created in bulk and used routinely with impunity. If from one perspective the view that the embryo seems to amount to little may invite a weakening of our respect, from another perspective its seeming insignificance should awaken in us a sense of shared humanity and a special obligation to protect it.

- *The Exploitation of Developing Human Life.* To engage in cloning-for-biomedical-research requires the irreversible crossing of a very significant moral boundary: the creation of human life expressly and exclusively for the purpose of its use in research, research that necessarily involves its deliberate destruction. If we permit this research to proceed, we will effectively be endorsing the complete transformation of nascent human life into nothing more than a resource or a tool. Doing so would coarsen our moral sensibilities and make us a different society: one less humble toward that which we cannot fully understand, less willing to extend the boundaries of human respect ever outward, and more willing to transgress moral boundaries once it appears to be in our own interests to do so.

■  *Moral Harm to Society.* Even those who are uncertain about the precise moral status of the human embryo have sound ethical–prudential reasons to oppose cloning-for-biomedical-research. Giving moral approval to such research risks significant moral harm to our society by (1) crossing the boundary from sexual to asexual reproduction, thus approving in principle the genetic manipulation and control of nascent human life; (2) opening the door to other moral hazards, such as cloning-to-produce-children or research on later-stage human embryos and fetuses; and (3) potentially putting the federal government in the novel and unsavory position of mandating the destruction of nascent human life. Because we are concerned not only with the fate of the cloned embryos but also with where this research will lead our society, we think prudence requires us not to engage in this research.

■  *What We Owe the Suffering.* We are certainly not deaf to the voices of suffering patients; after all, each of us already shares or will share in the hardships of mortal life. We and our loved ones are all patients or potential patients. But we are not only patients, and easing suffering is not our only moral obligation. As much as we wish to alleviate suffering now and to leave our children a world where suffering can be more effectively relieved, we also want to leave them a world in which we and they want to live—a world that honors moral limits, that respects all life whether strong or weak, and that refuses to secure the good of some human beings by sacrificing the lives of others. . . .

## The Council's Policy Recommendations

*Majority Recommendation:* Ten Members of the Council recommend *a ban on cloning-to-produce-children combined with a four-year moratorium on cloning-for-biomedical-research. We also call for a federal review of current and projected practices of human embryo research, pre-implantation genetic diagnosis, genetic modification of human embryos and gametes, and related matters, with a view to recommending and shaping ethically sound policies for the entire field.* Speaking only for ourselves, those of us who support this recommendation do so for some or all of the following reasons:

■  By permanently banning cloning-to-produce-children, this policy gives force to the strong ethical verdict against cloning-to-produce-children, unanimous in this Council (and in Congress) and widely supported by the American people. And by enacting a four-year moratorium on the creation of cloned embryos, it establishes an additional safeguard not afforded by policies that would allow the production of cloned embryos to proceed without delay.

■  It calls for and provides time for further democratic deliberation about cloning-for-biomedical-research, a subject about which the nation is divided and where there remains great uncertainty. A national discourse on this subject has not yet taken place in full, and a moratorium, by making it impossible for either side to cling to the status-quo, would force both to make their full case before the public. By banning all cloning for a time, it allows us to seek moral consensus on whether or not we should cross a major moral boundary (creating nascent cloned human life solely for research) and prevents our crossing it without deliberate decision. It would afford time for scientific evidence, now sorely lacking, to be gathered—from animal models and other avenues of human research—that might give us a better sense of whether cloning-for-biomedical-research would work as promised, and whether other morally nonproblematic approaches might be available. It would promote a fuller and better-informed public debate. And it would show respect for the deep moral concerns of the large number of Americans who have serious ethical problems with this research.

■  Some of us hold that cloning-for-biomedical-research can never be ethically pursued, and endorse a moratorium to enable us to continue to make our case in a democratic way. Others of us support the moratorium because it would provide the time and incentive required to develop a system of national regulation that might come into use if, at the end of the four-year period, the moratorium were not reinstated or made permanent. Such a system could not be developed overnight, and therefore even those who support the research but want it regulated should see that at the very least a pause is required. In the absence of a moratorium, few proponents of the research would have much incentive to institute an effective regulatory system. Moreover, the very process of proposing such regulations would clarify the moral and prudential judgments involved in deciding whether and how to proceed with this research.

- A moratorium on cloning-for-biomedical-research would enable us to consider this activity in the larger context of research and technology in the areas of developmental biology, embryo research, and genetics, and to pursue a more comprehensive federal regulatory system for setting and executing policy in the entire area.

- Finally, we believe that a moratorium, rather than a lasting ban, signals a high regard for the value of biomedical research and an enduring concern for patients and families whose suffering such research may help alleviate. It would reaffirm the principle that science can progress while upholding the community's moral norms, and would therefore reaffirm the community's moral support for science and biomedical technology.

The decision before us is of great importance. Our society should take the time to make a judgment that is well-informed, respectful of strongly held views, and representative of the priorities and principles of the American people. We believe this ban-plus-moratorium proposal offers the best available way to a wise and prudent policy.

This position is supported by Council Members Rebecca S. Dresser, Francis Fukuyama, Robert P. George, Mary Ann Glendon, Alfonso Gómez-Lobo, William B. Hurlburt, Leon R. Kass, Charles Krauthammer, Paul McHugh, and Gilbert C. Meilaender.

*Minority Recommendation:* Seven Members of the Council recommend *a ban on cloning-to-produce-children, with regulation of the use of cloned embryos for biomedical research.* Speaking only for ourselves, those of us who support this recommendation do so for some or all of the following reasons:

- By permanently banning cloning-to-produce-children, this policy gives force to the strong ethical verdict against cloning-to-produce-children,

unanimous in this Council (and in Congress) and widely supported by the American people. We believe that a ban on the transfer of cloned embryos to a woman's uterus would be a sufficient and effective legal safeguard against the practice.

- *It approves cloning-for-biomedical-research and permits it to proceed without substantial delay.* This is the most important advantage of this proposal. The research shows great promise, and its actual value can only be determined by allowing it to go forward now. Regardless of how much time we allow it, no amount of experimentation with animal models can provide the needed understanding of *human* diseases. The special benefits from working with stem cells from *cloned* human embryos cannot be obtained using embryos obtained by IVF. We believe this research could provide relief to millions of Americans, and that the government should therefore support it, within sensible limits imposed by regulation.

- It would establish, as a condition of proceeding, the necessary regulatory protections to avoid abuses and misuse of cloned embryos. These regulations might touch on the secure handling of embryos, licensing and prior review of research projects, the protection of egg donors, and the provision of equal access to benefits.

- Some of us also believe that mechanisms to regulate cloning-for-biomedical-research should be part of a larger regulatory program governing all research involving human embryos, and that the federal government should initiate a review of present and projected practices of human embryo research, with the aim of establishing reasonable policies on the matter.

Permitting cloning-for-biomedical-research now, while governing it through a prudent and sensible regulatory regime, is the most appropriate way to allow important research to proceed while insuring that abuses are prevented. We believe that the legitimate concerns about human cloning expressed throughout this report are sufficiently addressed by this ban-plus-regulation proposal, and that the nation should affirm and support the responsible effort to find treatments and cures that might help many who are suffering.

This position is supported by Council Members Elizabeth H. Blackburn, Daniel W. Foster, Michael S. Gazzaniga, William F. May, Janet D. Rowley, Michael J. Sandel, and James Q. Wilson.

# Declaration on the Production and the Scientific and Therapeutic Use of Human Embryonic Stem Cells

## Pontifical Academy for Life

The declaration by the Pontifical Academy sets out the official Roman Catholic position on the moral aspects of acquiring and using human embryonic stem cells. The Academy declares it is not morally legitimate to produce or use human embryos as a source of stem cells, nor is it acceptable to use stem cells from cell lines already established. The Academy endorses the idea of directing research toward using adult stem cells to achieve the benefits that it is hoped embryonic stem cells might achieve.

. . .

Given the nature of this article, the key ethical problems implied by these new technologies are presented briefly, with an indication of the responses which emerge from a careful consideration of the human subject from the moment of conception. It is this consideration which underlies the position affirmed and put forth by the Magisterium of the Church.

The *first ethical problem,* which is fundamental, can be formulated thus: *Is it morally licit to produce and/or use living human embryos for the preparation of ES cells?*

*The answer is negative,* for the following reasons:

1. On the basis of a complete biological analysis, the living human embryo is—from the moment of the union of the gametes—a *human subject* with a well defined identity, which from that point begins its own *coordinated, continuous and gradual development,* such that at no later stage can it be considered as a simple mass of cells.

2. From this it follows that as a *"human individual"* it has the *right* to its own life; and therefore every intervention which is not in favour of the embryo is an act which violates that right. Moral theology has always taught that in the case of *"jus certum tertii"* the system of probabilism does not apply.

3. Therefore, the ablation of the inner cell mass (ICM) of the blastocyst, which critically and irremediably damages the human embryo, curtailing its development, is a *gravely immoral* act and consequently is *gravely illicit.*

Pontifical Academy for Life, Vatican City, August 25, 2000.

4. *No end believed to be good,* such as the use of stem cells for the preparation of other differentiated cells to be used in what look to be promising therapeutic procedures, *can justify an intervention of this kind.* A good end does not make right an action which in itself is wrong.

5. For Catholics, this position is explicitly confirmed by the Magisterium of the Church which, in the Encyclical *Evangelium Vitae,* with reference to the Instruction *Donum Vitae* of the Congregation for the Doctrine of the Faith, affirms: "The Church has always taught and continues to teach that the result of human procreation, from the first moment of its existence, must be guaranteed that unconditional respect which is morally due to the human being in his or her totality and unity in body and spirit: The human being is to be respected and treated as a person from the moment of conception; and therefore from that same moment his rights as a person must be recognized, among which in the first place is the inviolable right of every innocent human being to life."

The *second ethical problem* can be formulated thus: *Is it morally licit to engage in so-called "therapeutic cloning"* by producing cloned human embryos and then destroying them in order to produce ES cells?

*The answer is negative,* for the following reason: Every type of therapeutic cloning, which implies producing human embryos and then destroying them in order to obtain stem cells, is illicit; for there is present the ethical problem examined above, which can only be answered in the negative.

The **third ethical problem** can be formulated thus: *Is it morally licit to use ES cells, and the differentiated cells obtained from them, which are supplied by other researchers or are commercially obtainable?*

*The answer is negative,* since: prescinding from the participation—formal or otherwise—in the morally illicit intention of the principal agent, the case in question entails a proximate material cooperation in the production and manipulation of human embryos on the part of those producing or supplying them.

In conclusion, it is not hard to see the seriousness and gravity of the ethical problem posed by the desire to extend to the field of human research the production and/or use of human embryos, even from an humanitarian perspective.

The possibility, now confirmed, of using **adult stem cells** to attain the same goals as would be sought with embryonic stem cells—even if many further steps in both areas are necessary before clear and conclusive results are obtained—indicates that adult stem cells represent a more reasonable and human method for making correct and sound progress in this new field of research and in the therapeutic applications which it promises. These applications are undoubtedly a source of great hope for a significant number of suffering people.

## Regulated Cloning for Biomedical Research

James Q. Wilson

James Wilson, a member of the President's Council on Bioethics and persuaded of the potential for medical advances by using stem cells, takes a minority view and endorses a policy permitting regulated research on cloned embryos no older than fourteen days.

The more a fertilized egg develops, Wilson holds, the more "claims it exerts on our moral feelings." Some say life begins at conception, yet one-third to one-half of fertilized eggs fail to implant or develop, so at conception there is only a "reasonable chance" at life.

Wilson believes embryos deserve protection to keep researchers from taking the next step. He would forbid implanting cloned embryos and limit the existence of such embryos to fourteen days. He rejects the allegation that allowing research on fertilized eggs will lead to a slippery slope, with scientists pressing for research on older embryos.

I would allow regulated biomedical research on cloned embryos provided the blastocyst is no more than fourteen days old and would not allow implantation in a uterus, human or animal. I take this position because I believe that research on human blastocysts may have substantial medical value in finding ways of improving human life. As our report indicates, such research may help doctors deal with Parkinson's disease, Alzhei-

"Statement of Professor Wilson," from President's Council on Bioethics, *Human Cloning and Human Dignity: An Ethical Inquiry,* "Personal Statements," (pp. 59–63). Pre-Publication version, July, 2002 (*www.bioethics.gov*).

mer's disease, juvenile diabetes, and spinal cord injury. Members of the Council disagree as to how best to do that research.

The group that favors a moratorium on the use of cloned embryos for such research may think that the study of adult stem cells or in vitro fertilized eggs that are not used to impregnate a woman will produce all the knowledge we need to discover whether stem cells have therapeutic value. The other group, of which I am a part, favors regulated research on cloned embryos because it believes that all sources of stem cells, including those produced by blastocysts, must be studied if we are to discover whether great medical advances are possible. That is because the use of cloned blastocysts may be the only important way of overcoming the problems of immune rejection and learning more about genetic diseases. If substantial medical benefit can be had from research, then it is unlikely that those benefits will derive from studying only stem cells derived from adult tissue or from left-over IVF eggs. To follow the policy recommended by the majority of this Council would be to do research with one hand tied behind our backs.

Moreover, I do not think there is any moral difference between a fertilized egg created in an in vitro fertilization clinic and one created by cloning an embryo. Both eggs are deliberately produced by scientific intervention and both (except for the IVF egg used to impregnate a woman) are destroyed.

Having said that there is no moral difference between these two sources of eggs does not mean, I believe, that using either kind of egg does not raise important and difficult moral questions. Every human begins as a fertilized egg, even though not every fertilized egg becomes a human. But the issue before us is not whether any human life should be destroyed but whether every fertilized egg should be preserved. To oppose the willful destruction of any fertilized egg is to oppose in vitro fertilization (since all fertilized eggs beyond that needed for successful implantation will be destroyed). Yet, in vitro procedures have produced (as of 1999) about thirty thousand babies for otherwise infertile couples. Initially, in vitro fertilizations were opposed by many who have since changed their minds, because the great benefits (many healthy new infants) so greatly outweighed the trivial costs (some tiny cells frozen or destroyed).

A fertilized cell has some moral worth, but much less than that of an implanted cell, and that has less than that of a fetus, and that less than that of a viable fetus, and that the same as of a newborn infant. My view is that people endow a thing with humanity when it appears, or even begins to appear, human; that is, when it resembles a human creature. The more a cell resembles a person, the more claims it exerts on our moral feelings. Now this last argument has no religious or metaphysical meaning, but it accords closely, in my view, with how people view one another. It helps us understand why aborting a fetus in the twentieth week is more frightening than doing so in the first, and why so-called partial birth abortions are so widely opposed. And this view helps us understand why an elderly, comatose person lacking the ability to speak or

act has more support from people than a seven-week-old fetus that also lacks the ability to speak or act.

Human worth grows as humanity becomes more apparent. In general, we are profoundly grieved by the death of a newborn, deeply distressed by the loss of a nearly born infant or a late-month miscarriage, and (for most but not all people) worried but not grieved by the abortion of a seven-week-old fetus. Our humanity, and thus the moral worth we assign to people, never leaves us even if many elements of it are later stripped away by age or disease.

This fact becomes evident when we ask a simple question: Do we assign the same moral blame to harvesting organs from a newborn infant and from a seven-day-old blastocyst? The great majority of people would be more outraged by doing the former than by doing the latter. A seven-day-old blastocyst that is no more than one millimeter in diameter and contains only a hundred or so largely undifferentiated cells does not make the same moral claims on us as does a live infant. Unless everyone who makes this distinction is wrong, then the moral status of a blastocyst is vastly less compelling than that of a neonate.

Some people believe that human life begins at conception and ought to be free from any human attack from that moment on. The difficulty with this rejoinder is that a large fraction (perhaps one-third to one-half) of fertilized cells fail to implant in the uterus or, if implanted, fail to develop into an embryo. Knowing this, one who offers this rejoinder would have to say that there is at best only a reasonable chance that life begins at conception.

But even blastocysts and leftover IVF eggs deserve some protection, because if society authorizes their destruction it has taken a dramatic and morally significant step. It has intervened in a profoundly important human process in ways that may lead future generations to take what may then appear to be the easy next steps, such as implanting a cloned embryo in a uterus or killing a fetus to extract some supposedly beneficial substance.

To avoid this, I favor federal regulations that would ban implanting a cloned embryo in any uterus, animal as well as human, and would insist that every cloned embryo raised in a glass dish exist for no more than fourteen days.

There is always some risk that allowing even strongly regulated research will create conditions that lead some scientists to ask for access to fertilized eggs beyond the blastocyst stage. But I do not believe we can object to this by making a generalized slippery slope argument, since virtually every medical procedure that involves entering or affecting the human body would also be liable to such an argument, a conclusion that would leave us (for example) without surgery. The slippery slope argument, stated baldly, would lead us to oppose allowing doctors to removed an inflamed appendix because they might later decide to remove a kidney, and after that a heart, and to oppose as well doctors prescribing a drug that will harm 0.5 percent of its recipients because we suspect that, once they do this, they will later insist on prescribing drugs that harm 1 percent, and then 10 percent, and possibly 50 percent of their patients. There may be good slippery slope arguments, but they cannot rest simply on the phrase "slippery slope"; they must also point clearly to a serious moral hazard and contain some reason for thinking that this hazard will become much more likely if we take the first step.

## READINGS

# Section 2: Genetic Testing

## Pitfalls of Genetic Testing

### Ruth Hubbard and R. C. Lewontin

Ruth Hubbard and R. C. Lewontin argue that most genetic testing has little practical value and can cause unnecessary harm. Because in most cases correlations between DNA patterns and diseases are only statistical, and social, economic, psychological, or other biological factors may also be involved, DNA tests usually help neither patients nor their physicians.

If a woman tests positive for BRCA1 and BRCA2 (the genes "for" breast cancer and ovarian cancer), she is much more likely than others to develop cancer if she is from a "cancer-prone" family. Yet, whatever a woman's family history, no measures to prevent breast or ovarian cancer are known to be effective. Even so, private companies have started developing tests for the genes.

When patients ask about getting tested, what can physicians say? They can point to the tests' uncertainty and to the lack of practical consequences associated with them. They can also make it clear that the results may have devastating consequences for the psychological well-being, family relationships, employability, and insurability of those who are tested. Some patients considering testing may change their minds when they understand the limits of the tests.

Genes have become the preferred way to explain all types of ill health and unwanted behavior. Some of the attributions seem fairly clear-cut, but many are being embraced uncritically and oversold. This situation can be troubling for clinicians, as well as for the general public. It is often hard to be sure that genes do account for someone's complex condition, such as circulatory problems or cancer. But even when such an association seems fairly clear, it is hard to know what practical conclusions to draw. Unfortunately, many of these uncertainties arise from the way genes function, not just from shortcomings of technique.

At present, our increased knowledge about the DNA sequences that constitute genes is transforming the concepts of wild-type, or "normal," genes and their mutations. The relations between such sequences of nucleotides and their clinical manifestations can be complex and unpredictable, even in conditions with mendelian patterns of inheritance. A sequence of bases is designated as the gene "for" a particular trait when it can be correlated with that phenotype, but it turns out that sequences in the same gene can vary

From the *New England Journal of Medicine,* Vol. 334, no. 18 (1996), pp. 1192–1194. © 1996 Massachusetts Medical Society. All rights reserved.

considerably from one person to another. The only differences that are acknowledged as mutations, however, are those associated with noticeable consequences. What this means is that a gene (together with its regulatory regions) is simply the locus of the various DNA sequences that are manifested in a trait and its variant forms. This definition does not imply that the appearance of the same trait in different people corresponds to the presence of an identical sequence of DNA bases. Conversely, although the sequence of bases may offer predictive information—in Tay–Sachs disease, for example—in most cases it does not predict the way a trait will be manifested phenotypically, for two reasons.

First, even for the relatively predictable familial conditions that we designate as mendelian traits, the actual nucleotide sequences—the DNA patterns—are much more variable than the phenotypic manifestations. More than 200 different nucleotide variations appear to produce the symptoms of hemophilia B, for example.[1] And of the many variants that constitute what is called the cystic fibrosis gene, some are associated with phenotypically different symptoms, but the symptoms associated with others are indistinguishable.[2]

Conversely, people with the same DNA pattern can have a range of clinical manifestations, or none at all. An example is autosomal dominant retinitis pigmentosa, a condition in which retinal rod cells typically degenerate over time. One form of this condition has been associated with a gene on chromosome 3 that is involved in coding for rhodopsin, the light-sensitive visual pigment of the retinal rods. Currently, changes in about one fifth of the amino acids in this protein have been linked to autosomal dominant retinitis pigmentosa. In one family containing two sisters with the same mutation, however, one is blind, whereas the other (the older one) drives a truck even at night. Furthermore, in both the autosomal dominant and the recessive forms of retinitis pigmentosa, the rod cells do not degenerate at a uniform rate across the entire retina, and some base changes are typically associated with the destruction of only the lower half of the retina.[3, 4]

Fortunately for the development of molecular genetics, interest in the field was sparked by what we now realize to be the highly unusual case of sickle cell anemia. The transformation of ordinary hemoglobin into sickle cell hemoglobin (hemoglobin S) depends on a change of only one base in what we call the hemoglobin gene. But the simplicity of this one case may have misled researchers and clinicians so that they expect similarly simple correlations between other DNA sequences and the diseases we associate with them. Even for this mutation, however, there is a considerable range in the expression of sickle cell disease among different people, as well as in the same person at different times. The phenotypes depend on a variety of circumstances, including the concentration of hemoglobin in the blood corpuscles, the degree of hydration, the state of constriction of capillaries, and so on. Another point to bear in mind is that the simplicity of the alterations in the base sequence and hemoglobin associated with sickle cell anemia has not yielded therapeutic benefits. And many DNA variants are involved in another hemoglobinopathy, ß-thalassemia.

By current estimates, human beings appear to be heterozygous for about 1/10 of 1 percent of the nucleotides in their DNA. Assuming that there are about 3 billion nucleotides in human chromosomes, each of us is heterozygous for about 3 million of them, and none of us are homozygous for the sequence of bases in any one gene. Only a small fraction of this nucleotide variation is translated into differences in amino acid sequences, although we cannot be sure that it does not have some other effect. Nor do all differences in amino acid sequences have phenotypic importance.

The conclusion we are forced to accept is that even in the case of so-called simple mendelian variations, the relation between the DNA sequence of a gene and the corresponding phenotype is far from simple. When we move from the relatively rare conditions whose patterns of inheritance follow Mendel's laws (such as cystic fibrosis, phenylketonuria, and Huntington's disease) to the more prevalent and usually late-onset conditions that sometimes have familial components (such as diabetes, coronary heart disease, Alzheimer's disease, and certain cancers), the situation becomes even more complicated. In these diseases, the patterns of transmission are unpredictable and seem to depend on various other factors, be they social, economic, psychological, or biologic. The notion that health or illness can be predicted on the basis of DNA patterns becomes highly questionable. For each condition, extensive, population-based research would be needed in order to establish the existence and extent of correlations between specific DNA patterns and overt manifestations over time. Furthermore, the correlations are likely to have only a degree of statistical validity, not absolute validity. Therefore, DNA tests cannot usually help clinicians or benefit patients—and not only because the techniques are still inadequate, but also because biologic phenomena result from multiple and complex interactions.

Serious difficulties arise from the relative ease with which information on DNA sequences can be acquired, when adequate knowledge of its correct interpretation is lacking. This can be seen in relation to the so-called breast-cancer genes *BRCA1* and *BRCA2*. These two DNA sequences have both been linked to increased susceptibility to breast or ovarian cancer. To date, more than 100 variants of *BRCA1* and several variants of *BRCA2* have been identified. Only a few of them, however, have been shown to be associated with tumor growth. They have been found predominantly among the small percentage of women who belong to families in which there is an unusually high incidence of one or both types of cancer or in whom breast cancer develops at an unusually young age. Yet about 90 percent of women with breast or ovarian cancer do not fall into these categories.

We must therefore ask how the predictive tests now being developed on the basis of variants of *BRCA1* are relevant to most women. The fact that a woman from a "cancer-prone" family tests positive for one of the cancer-linked DNA variants does not mean that she will definitely have a tumor, even though her lifetime risk of breast cancer may be as high as 85 percent, and that of ovarian cancer as high as 45 percent. Clearly, other factors are also involved. If the woman tests negative for cancer-linked DNA variants, her risk of having a tumor is similar to that of any woman in the general population. Furthermore, it is not clear what a woman should do if she tests positive, whatever her family history, since there are no effective measures of prevention. "Early detection" is problematic because it is uncertain what is actually being detected, and even such extreme measures as "prophylactic" bilateral mastectomy and oophorectomy provide no assurance that a tumor will not develop in the residual tissue. Given the uncertainty of what being "susceptible" signifies, it is hard to know how to counsel women who are trying to decide whether to be tested for a cancer-associated variant of *BRCA1*. It is also hard to know how to help women integrate the information they may receive from such a test into the context of their lives.[5, 6]

Despite the biologic uncertainties and the potential for discrimination and other social and personal problems, biotechnology companies have begun to develop tests for DNA variants thought to be linked to "cancer susceptibilities." OncorMed, a company in

Maryland, is marketing tests for *BRCA1* and colon cancer directly to physicians. Myriad Genetics in Utah plans to offer a *BRCA1* test, at first only for clinical trials conducted by cancer centers, but for commercial purposes later in 1996. Indeed, Dr. Joseph D. Schulman has just announced that his commercial laboratory, the Genetics and I.V.F. Institute of Fairfax, Virginia, will sell women a test for a *BRCA1* variant that appears to occur with unusual frequency among Jews of Eastern European extraction. Although there is no evidence linking this variant to nonfamilial breast or ovarian cancer, Schulman says he is offering the test because women have a right to know whether they carry the variant. At present, the only thing certain is that each test will bring in $295 to Dr. Schulman's company.[7]

These companies are not required to involve the Food and Drug Administration, because they are using their own reagents and performing the tests in their own laboratories. This means, however, that there has been no external certification of the quality of the procedures or the proper way to interpret the results. (Both the American Society for Human Genetics and the National Breast Cancer Coalition, an advocacy organization, are opposed to susceptibility testing outside controlled clinical trials.)

Physicians are soon likely to confront extremely awkward situations. Worried patients, encouraged by overly optimistic claims by researchers, biotechnology companies, and the media, may want to have genetic tests performed whose validity has not been established. At the same time, physicians may legitimately feel at sea about the meaning, reliability, and predictiveness of the tests. For the foreseeable future, perhaps the best they can do is to alert patients about the underlying uncertainty associated with the tests themselves and their actual prognostic value, and to point out that usually no practical consequences can be drawn from the information gained, however the test comes out. In the meantime, the test results can have disastrous implications for the psychological well-being, family relationships, and employability and insurability of those tested. All the same, some people will want to be tested because they want to know whether they carry a particular variant. Recent studies and testimony, however, show that people's decisions about whether to undergo DNA tests often change when they come to understand more about the wider implications of the tests and the uncertain meaning of the results.[8–12]

The ground is shifting almost from week to week. Physicians need to recognize the limitations of the new information and the commercial pressures behind the speed with which preliminary scientific data are being turned into tests. They should also understand the risks to patients of being stigmatized as "susceptible" by insurers or employers, as well as the psychological and social risks patients run by putting excessive faith in predictions of an often very uncertain future.

## References

1. Giannelli F, Green PM, High KA, et al. Haemophilia B: database of point mutations and short additions and deletions. *Nucleic Acids Res* 1990:18:4053–9.

2. The Cystic Fibrosis Genotype–Phenotype Consortium. Correlation between genotype and phenotype in patients with cystic fibrosis. *N Engl J Med* 1993:329:1308–13.

3. Papermaster DS. Necessary but insufficient. *Nat Med* 1995:1:874–5.

4. Humphries P, Kenna P, Farrar GJ. On the molecular genetics of retinitis pigmentosa. *Science* 1992:256:804–8.

5. Collins, FS. BRCA1—lots of mutations, lots of dilemmas. *N Engl J Med* 1996:334:186–8.

6. Hoskins KF, Stopfer JE, Calzone KA, et al. Assessment and counseling for women with a family history of breast cancer. *JAMA* 1995:273:577–85.

7. Kolata G. Breaking ranks, lab offers test to assess risk of breast cancer. *New York Times.* April 1, 1996:A1, A15.

8. Wertz DC, James SR, Rosenfield JM, Erbe RW. Attitudes toward the prenatal diagnosis of cystic fibrosis: factors in decision making among affected families. *Am J Hum Genet* 1992:50:1077–85.

9. Babul R, Ada S, Kremer B, et al. Attitudes toward direct predictive testing for the Huntington disease gene: relevance for other adult-onset disorders. *JAMA* 1993:270:2321–5.

10. Seachrist L. Testing genes: physicians wrestle with the information that genetic tests provide. *Science News* 1995:148:394–5.

11. Siebert C. Living with toxic knowledge. *New York Times Magazine.* September 17, 1995:50–7, 64, 74, 93–4, 104.

12. Geller G, Bernhardt BA, Helzlsouer K, Holtzman NA, Stefanek M, Wilcox PM. Informed consent and BRCA1 testing. *Nat Genet* 1995:11:364.

# Disowning Knowledge: Issues in Genetic Testing

## Robert Wachbroit

Robert Wachbroit argues against the paternalism associated with genetic testing. Physicians are making nonmedical judgments about what test results it's not good for patients to know because the results might cause them psychological or social harm. Yet, no evidence suggests everyone needs such protection.

In Wachbroit's view, sound scientific reasons may exist for restricting access to some tests (for example, ones for the BRCA1 gene), but those reasons have been obscured by paternalistic assumptions. Informing patients of their condition or withholding the information from them are not the only alternatives. Physicians can tell patients before testing that the test may reveal evidence of an associated condition (such as Alzheimer's) and ask if they want to know the result. (A similar practice is already common in connection with amniocentesis.)

Wachbroit holds, however, that in some situations people have a professional or personal responsibility to know genetic information about themselves, even if they would prefer not to learn it.

Last fall in Chicago, at a conference sponsored by the Alzheimer's Association and the National Institute on Aging, doctors and researchers met to discuss an ethical dilemma that has grown increasingly familiar as advances in diagnostic techniques outstrip the therapeutic abilities of the medical profession. The meeting

Robert Wachbroit, "Disowning Knowledge: Issues in Genetic Testing," *Report from the Institute for Philosophy and Public Policy,* Vol. 16, no. 3 and 4 (1996), pp. 14–18. Reprinted by permission of the author.

focused on the use of a medical test for a particular heart condition—a test that can also, in some cases, predict with 90 percent accuracy whether someone will develop Alzheimer's disease by the age of 80. Should patients tested for the heart condition be told of their risk of contracting Alzheimer's disease, when there is little if anything medicine at present can do to prevent or ameliorate the condition?

Some people, including many of those attending the meeting, believe that the answer to this question is no: if the information is of little therapeutic value, it's of little value to the patient as well. It is wrong to burden the patient with troubling news when there is little or nothing that the physician can do about it.

At this stage in the history of medical practice, we may well be surprised to encounter such a response. Over the past few decades there has been an intense effort to articulate and defend a person's right to be informed of his or her medical condition. Not so long ago, this right was not widely acknowledged. Health professionals generally assumed that, in the case of certain diseases, patients didn't really want to know. Moreover, even if they did want to, they wouldn't really understand the diagnosis; and even if they did want to know and could understand, they would be so psychologically harmed by the information that the result would likely be, if not suicide, then a clinical depression that would interfere with any sort of available care. Over the years the arguments attempting to defend this medical paternalism have been carefully examined and successfully undermined. The very idea of health professionals deciding whether a patient should know his or her medical condition is now routinely criticized in bioethics courses. Nonetheless, the advent of genetic testing appears to have provoked a resurgence of paternalistic thinking, especially in those cases where doctors can detect the genetic condition associated with a particular disease but are as yet unable to prevent or treat that disease.

The association between a genetic condition and a disease, and so the type of information a genetic test reveals, is subject to considerable variation. With results from the test for a specific mutation at the tip of chromosome 4, we can predict with near certainty whether an individual will suffer from Huntington's disease, a severe late-onset neurological disorder, but we can't yet tell when the disease will occur. With information from the test for mutations of the BRCA1 gene, we can, in particular situations, conclude that an individual has a susceptibility to a specific type of breast cancer, but we don't yet know what other conditions must be in place to trigger this susceptibility. With information from the test discussed in Chicago— a test that detects the presence of the apolipoprotein E genotype—we can, in particular situations, conclude that an individual is at an increased risk of contracting Alzheimer's disease, but there is still some controversy about the relative importance of this risk factor.

Recent concern has largely focused on these last two tests. At the Chicago meeting, the issue was the disclosure of certain additional information from a test already administered. In other cases, professional organizations, as well as some advocacy groups, have proposed limits on the very availability of certain genetic tests. It is argued that tests for certain conditions should be restricted to research settings for the time being and not offered routinely or to all.

Are these proposals based on medical paternalism? Or can restrictions on genetic testing be defended on other grounds? I wish to examine possible justifications for limiting testing, distinguishing between those that are paternalistic and those that are not. I shall then consider the reasons and responsibilities that might influence patients in deciding whether to be tested or to receive genetic information.

## Grounds for Restrictions

A discussion of reasons for restricting genetic testing should begin by acknowledging that there is no *right* to genetic testing. A right to be informed of test results (assuming that such a right exists) would not entail a right to *be* tested. And a "right to health care" (in the usual ways that phrase is understood) is not taken to include a right to have every diagnostic test, including genetic tests, performed. But though there is no right to genetic testing, a decision to withhold or restrict certain tests should be based on good public reasons (as opposed to private, economic reasons). This is especially true in the case of genetic tests, since in many cases genetic testing facilities, e.g., those connected with teaching hospitals, are supported, directly or indirectly, with public funds.

Reasons for restricting certain kinds of genetic tests can be divided into two broad categories. One set of reasons focuses on the *time and resources* that would be lost by the inappropriate use of genetic testing. Given the current state of knowledge, the results obtained from certain tests may include such a high number of false-positives or false-negatives, or be so difficult to interpret, that performing these tests would be a waste of the health professional's or laboratory's time, diverting resources from tests that are diagnostically more useful. For example, research has revealed a large number of possible mutations in BRCA1. Unless a woman's family history implicates a particular mutation in the occurrence of breast cancer, there is no point in testing her for that mutation; whatever the test result may be, it will not be interpretable. Thus, a decision not to offer BRCA1 testing to all women would be defensible on the grounds that widespread testing would needlessly draw upon society's limited resources of expertise and technology. Where the best available evidence shows that a given procedure would yield no meaningful information, it is entirely appropriate, so the argument goes, to restrict that procedure.

The second set of grounds for restricting the availability of genetic tests focuses on claims about the *social or psychological harms* that individuals might suffer from knowing their test results, where these harms are not offset by any corresponding medical benefit. Indeed, in many cases these harms are considered to be so palpable and the medical benefits so clearly nonexistent that it is assumed people would not want to know their genetic condition even if they had the opportunity.

One widely cited harm of knowing one's genetic condition arises from the prospect of discrimination in employment or insurance coverage. Someone with a known genetic condition indicating a susceptibility to breast cancer might be denied a job or a promotion, or denied health or life insurance, because she is regarded as a health risk and therefore as too great an economic risk. This concern about discrimination chiefly provides a reason why *third parties* should not be given access to an individual's genetic information. Yet an individual may well decide to forgo this information in order to maintain deniability. For example, suppose an insurance contract requires the individual to tell all she knows about her genetic condition, so that discovering that any information was withheld would constitute grounds for dismissing later claims. A person in this situation might well decide to remain ignorant, since she can't be penalized for withholding information she doesn't have.

However, a person can maintain ignorance of her genetic condition only up to a point, since genetic tests are not the only source of information about that condition. Standard family medical histories can sometimes tell a good deal, and claiming ignorance of this history may not be possible. If an individual suffers from Huntington's disease, then his or her children have a 50 percent probability of contracting it as well. If a woman's sister, mother, and aunt suffer from breast cancer, then it is likely that the woman is at greater risk than the general population of contracting breast cancer herself. Furthermore, genetic information is not always bad news. Someone who appears to be at risk for a certain disease because of her family history could discover, and so presumably assure an employer or insurer, that she is in fact not at risk because her test result was negative. Nevertheless, we should acknowledge that there can be perverse incentives to be ignorant, especially in the absence of appropriate laws regarding "genetic discrimination" or regulations regarding insurance and preexisting conditions.

A completely different harm that is associated with genetic information has to do with the psychological burden of knowing. Indeed, one writer refers to such information as "toxic knowledge." Unlike concerns about employment discrimination or insurance, fears about the burden of knowing speak directly to the question of the desirability of self-knowledge. For some people, the discovery that they have a genetic condition that places them at an especially high risk of suffering certain diseases could so depress them that the quality, joy, and purpose of their lives would evaporate. Moreover, even if the results of a genetic test were negative, some people might experience the reaction commonly known as "survivor's guilt," as they contemplate the prospects of their less fortunate siblings or other relatives.

The applicability of this reason will vary from person to person. Some people might be able to handle bad news calmly and move on, while others might become irrevocably incapacitated. We are individuals in how we each deal with the disappointments and tragedies in our lives. Genetic knowledge might be extremely toxic for one individual but less so for another. Presumably, however, if a person does raise this issue in his own case, it probably applies.

## Deciding for the Patient

It is this last set of reasons, when invoked to justify limits on the availability of genetic testing, that suggests a resurgent paternalism with respect to medical information. They involve explicit judgments by medical professionals about what would be good for the patient, where the "good" (i.e., the avoidance of certain social and psychological harms) extends beyond matters of medical expertise. Whatever force they may have as reasons an *individual* might give for not wanting to know genetic information, their persuasiveness weakens considerably when they are offered by third parties as reasons for restrictions on genetic testing. While certain people might be psychologically devastated by their test results, there is no evidence to support the assumption that most people will be so devastated; indeed, such an assumption flies in the face of our commonsense knowledge of people's differences. Similarly, the likelihood that people will confront employment discrimination or insurance problems, and the seriousness with which they regard such a prospect, will vary with circumstances. It is therefore paternalistic to cite these concerns as grounds for restricting genetic testing.

The same can be said of arguments that the results of genetic tests are too complex or ambiguous for patients to understand. Test results may identify risk factors rather than yield predictions; the information may consist of probabilities rather than certainties. In other medical contexts, however, the complexity of information is not accepted as an excuse for taking decisions out of the patient's hands. For example, we require physicians to obtain informed consent before they engage in an intervention. However complex the relevant information might be, usefully communicating it to the patient is a challenge to which the professional must rise.

A rejection of the paternalistic arguments does not yield the conclusion that all genetic tests should be available to the public. As we have seen, restrictions on the availability of certain genetic tests, or of any medical procedure, need not be based on paternalism. For example, none of these comments affects the legitimacy or persuasiveness of the scientific reasons for restricting certain tests.

Unfortunately, some of the professional organizations and advocacy groups seeking to restrict genetic testing have allowed an admixture of paternalism to enter into what would otherwise be sound scientific arguments. Instead of simply pointing out that a test for BRCA1 mutations can yield no useful information about most women, they express worries about the "fear" and "panic" that widespread testing might provoke. The first objection to indiscriminate testing is valid; the second is not. By including arguments that would in other contexts be rejected as unwarranted medical paternalism, these organizations have inadvertently ceded the moral high ground to the for-profit laboratories that have rushed in to perform these tests. Whether the labs can provide testing with the appropriate care and counseling is an open question. But efforts to regulate or even comment upon their services are likely to be ineffectual so long as the laboratories can self-righteously affirm the patient's "right to know" against the paternalism of their critics.

Similarly, when the researchers in Chicago tried to formulate a policy regarding the disclosure of test results, paternalistic assumptions clouded the issue. It was agreed that a cardiac test yielding information about the risk of Alzheimer's disease poses an ethical problem for the physician, who must either inform patients of their condition or withhold that information. But there is another alternative: the physician can tell patients, before testing for one condition, that information about another condition will be available. Whether or not to be informed becomes the patient's decision. Indeed, this option is standard in communicating the results of various medical tests, including results where disease is not at issue. The obstetrician performing amniocentesis doesn't typically agonize over whether to inform the couple of the fetus's sex. The couple are simply asked whether they want to know. And in our society at this time, the patient's desire to know or not to know is taken to settle the matter.

## A Responsibility to Know

It is mainly those who wish to know their genetic condition who are likely to object to paternalistic restrictions on genetic testing. We cannot assume, however, that most people would fall into this category. In one recent study, only 43 percent of research subjects who were offered the BRCA1 test agreed to have it performed. Many who refused the test cited the concerns about employment and insurance that I have already described, while others pointed to the psychological distress that knowledge might bring.

If the challenge to medical paternalism is based on the notion that people should be free to make their own choices with respect to information, then in general the decision not to know should be as fully respected as the decision to know. No one would be in favor of frog-marching people to a genetics lab, having them tested, and then compelling them to listen to the results. The widely acknowledged right people have to refuse treatment surely includes a right to refuse diagnostic tests. If some people simply don't want their decisions about how they live their lives to depend upon genetic information, it would seem that they have no reason, and certainly no obligation, to know.

Nevertheless, there are many circumstances in which people might have a moral responsibility to know—a responsibility that grows out of their professional or personal obligations. The case for professional obligations, though limited, is fairly clear. The same reasoning that supports drug testing of individuals in particular professions—air traffic controller, train conductor, airline pilot—also supports claiming that these individuals have an obligation to know their genetic information. If an individual might have a condition that, if manifested, would interfere with his job performance in such a way as to endanger other people, that person has an obligation to know and monitor that condition, whether he wants to or not.

Since most of us are not employed in such professions, however, this obligation attaches to relatively few people. Moreover, most genetic conditions are unlikely to have an impact on the safety of other people. It is difficult to argue that an airline pilot's refusal to know whether she is at special risk of contracting breast cancer would endanger the lives of the passengers.

The ways in which personal obligations may generate a responsibility to know one's genetic condition have not been given comparable attention, even though they are more widely applicable. Most of us are enmeshed in a network of personal obligations and commitments—to families, dependents, loved ones. In many cases, with information about our medical condition, we can more effectively discharge our obligations, or at least avoid measures that, under the circumstances, may be futile. Consider the case of a 50-year-old parent of minor children who refuses to know whether he is at high risk of contracting Alzheimer's disease within the next ten years. His refusal to know might be irresponsible; it might amount to a failure to engage fully in the (not just financial) planning that is part of a parent's commitment to his children. Whether one has a moral responsibility to know one's genetic condition, and the strength of that responsibility, will depend upon the particulars of the situation. In all likelihood, however, a person's *responsibility* to know will not depend upon the strength of his or her *desire* to know or not to know.

The idea of having a responsibility to know can seem jarring at first. We are drawn to a picture of an individual, faced with the prospect of knowing, weighing how that knowledge would affect her personally. The thought that someone ought to know seems to go against our cultural assumptions, as if such an obligation were an unwelcome interference in the private relationship a person has with her own life. The problem with this picture of solitary individuals contemplating whether to know about their future is that it fits so few of us.

How should the responsibility of knowing be balanced against the possible burden and cost of knowing? There is probably little of use that can be said at this level of generality, since much will depend on the circumstances. The 50-year-old who has minor children, by birth or adoption, is in a different situation from the footloose 20-year-old. In any event it should be clear that if we are to make responsible decisions about accepting or refusing medical information, we must begin by acknowledging that these decisions affect others as well as ourselves.

## Section 3: Genetic Counseling

### Genetic Dilemmas and the Child's Right to an Open Future

#### Dena S. Davis

Dena Davis asks whether genetic counselors must assist couples who wish to have a child who will be deaf or an achondroplastic dwarf. Taking deafness as an example, she argues that although counselors are professionally committed to an ethic of patient autonomy, they may reject such a request, on the ground that it would limit the future autonomy of any child that might be born.

Davis compares the situation with one in which Jehovah's Witnesses refuse to consent to a lifesaving blood transfusion for their child and one in which Amish parents remove their children from school after the eighth grade. While courts have allowed the second, Davis sees both as unjustifiably denying children an "open future."

Whether deafness is considered a disability in a culture, being born deaf significantly restricts the choices open to a child. Thus, if it is chosen before birth by the child's parents, it must be considered a harm. For this reason, genetic counselors should not help parents produce deaf children.

The profession of genetic counseling is strongly characterized by a respect for patient autonomy that is greater than in almost any other area of medicine. When moral challenges arise in the clinical practice of genetics, they tend to be understood as conflicts between the obligation to respect patient autonomy and other ethical norms, such as doing good and avoiding harm. Thus, a typical counseling dilemma exists when a person who has been tested and found to be carrying the gene for Tay–Sachs disease refuses to share that information with siblings and other relatives despite the clear benefits to them of having that knowledge, or when a family member declines to participate in a testing protocol necessary to help another member discover his or her genetic status.

This way of looking at moral issues in genetic counseling often leaves both the counselors and commentators frustrated, for two reasons. First, by elevating respect for patient autonomy above all other values, it may be difficult to give proper weight to other factors, such as human suffering. Second, by privileging patient autonomy and by defining the patient as the person or couple who has come for counseling, there seems no "space" in which to give proper attention to the moral claims of the future child who is the endpoint of many counseling interactions.

These difficulties have been highlighted of late by the surfacing of a new kind of genetic counseling request: parents with certain disabilities who seek help in trying to assure that they will have a child who shares their disability. The two reported instances are in families affected by achondroplasia (dwarfism) and by hereditary deafness. This essay will focus on deafness.

Such requests are understandably troubling to genetic counselors. Deeply committed to the principle of giving clients value-free information with which to make their own choices, most counselors nonetheless make certain assumptions about health and disability—for example, that it is preferable to be a hearing person rather than a deaf person. Thus, counselors

typically talk of the "risk" of having a child with a particular genetic condition. Counselors may have learned (sometimes with great difficulty) to respect clients' decisions not to find out if their fetus has a certain condition or not to abort a fetus which carries a genetic disability. But to respect a parental value system that not only favors what most of us consider to be a disability, but actively expresses that preference by attempting to have a child with the condition, is "the ultimate test of nondirective counseling."[1]

To describe the challenge primarily as one that pits beneficence (concern for the child's quality of life) against autonomy (concern for the parents' right to decide about these matters) makes for obvious difficulties. These are two very different values, and comparing and weighing them invites the proverbial analogy of "apples and oranges." After all, the perennial critique of a principle-based ethics is that it offers few suggestions for ranking principles when duties conflict. Further, beneficence and respect for autonomy are values that will always exist in some tension within genetic counseling. For all the reasons I list below, counselors are committed to the primacy of patient autonomy and therefore to nondirective counseling. But surely, most or all of them are drawn to the field because they want to help people avoid or at least mitigate suffering.

Faced with the ethical challenge of parents who wish to ensure children who have a disability, I suggest a different way to look at this problem. Thinking this problem through in the way I suggest will shed light on some related topics in genetics as well, such as sex selection. I propose that, rather than conceiving this as a conflict between autonomy and beneficence, we recast it as a conflict between parental autonomy and the child's future autonomy: what Joel Feinberg has called "the child's right to an open future."

## New Challenges

The Code of Ethics of the National Society of Genetic Counselors states that its members strive to:

■   Respect their clients' beliefs, cultural traditions, inclinations, circumstances, and feelings.

Dena S. Davis, "Genetic Dilemmas and the Child's Right to an Open Future," *Hastings Center Report,* Vol. 27, no. 2 (1997): 7–15. Reprinted by permission.

■    Enable their clients to make informed independent decisions, free of coercion, by providing or illuminating the necessary facts and clarifying the alternatives and anticipated consequences.[2]

Considering the uncertain and stochastic nature of genetic counseling, and especially in light of the difficulty physicians experience in sharing uncertainty with patients, it is remarkable that medical geneticists have hewed so strongly to an ethic of patient autonomy. This phenomenon can be explained by at least five factors: the desire to disassociate themselves as strongly as possible from the discredited eugenics movement;[3] an equally strong desire to avoid the label of "abortionist," a realistic fear if counselors are perceived as advocates for abortion of genetically damaged fetuses;[4] the fact that few treatments are available for genetic diseases; an awareness of the intensely private nature of reproductive decisions; and the fact that genetic decisions can have major consequences for entire families.[5] As one counselor was quoted, "I am not going to be taking that baby home—they will."[6]

The commitment to patient autonomy faces new challenges with the advances arising from the Human Genome Project. The example of hereditary deafness is reported by Walter E. Nance, who writes:

> It turns out that some deaf couples feel threatened by the prospect of having a hearing child and would actually prefer to have a deaf child. The knowledge that we will soon acquire [due to the Human Genome Project] will, of course, provide us with the technology that could be used to assist such couples in achieving their goals. This, in turn, could lead to the ultimate test of nondirective counseling. Does adherence to the concept of nondirective counseling actually require that we assist such a couple in terminating a pregnancy with a hearing child or is this nonsense?[7]

Several issues must be unpacked here. First, I question Nance's depiction of deaf parents as feeling "threatened" by the prospect of a hearing child. From Nance's own depiction of the deaf people he encounters, it is at least as likely that deaf parents feel that a deaf child would fit into their family better, especially if the parents themselves are "deaf of deaf" or if they already have one or more deaf children. Or perhaps the parents feel that Deafness (I use the capital "D," as Deaf people do, to signify Deafness as a culture) is an asset—tough at times but worthwhile in the end—like belonging to a racial or religious minority.

Second, I want to avoid the issue of abortion by discussing the issue of "deliberately producing a deaf child" as distinct from the question of achieving that end by aborting a hearing fetus. The latter topic is important, but it falls outside the purview of this paper. I will focus on the scenario where a deaf child is produced without recourse to abortion. We can imagine a situation in the near future where eggs or sperm can be scrutinized for the relevant trait before fertilization, or the present situation in which preimplantation genetic diagnosis after in vitro fertilization allows specialists to examine the genetic makeup of the very early embryo before it is implanted.

Imagine a Deaf couple approaching a genetic counselor. The couple's goals are to learn more about the cause(s) of their own Deafness, and, if possible, to maximize the chance that any pregnancy they embark upon will result in a Deaf child. Let us suppose that the couple falls into the 50 percent of clients whose Deafness has a genetic origin.[8] The genetic counselor who adheres strictly to the tenets of client autonomy will respond by helping the couple to explore the ways in which they can achieve their goal: a Deaf baby. But as Nance's depiction of this scenario suggests, the counselor may well feel extremely uneasy about her role here. It is one thing to support a couple's decision to take their chances and "let Nature take its course," but to treat as a goal what is commonly considered to be a risk may be more pressure than the value-neutral ethos can bear. What is needed is a principled argument against such assistance. This refusal need not rise to a legal prohibition, but could become part of the ethical norms and standard of care for the counseling profession.[9]

The path I see out of this dilemma relies on two steps. First, we remind ourselves why client autonomy is such a powerful norm in genetic counseling. Clients come to genetic counselors with questions that are simultaneously of the greatest magnitude and of the greatest intimacy. Clients not only have the right to bring their own values to bear on these questions, but in the end they must do so because they—and their children—will live with the consequences. As the President's Commission said in its 1983 report on Screening and Counseling for Genetic Conditions:

> The silence of the law on many areas of individual choice reflects the value this country places on pluralism. Nowhere is the need for freedom to pursue divergent conceptions of the good more deeply felt than in decisions concerning reproduction. It would be a cruel irony, therefore, if technological advances undertaken in the name of providing information to expand the range of individual choices resulted in unantici-

pated social pressures to pursue a particular course of action. Someone who feels compelled to undergo screening or to make particular reproductive choices at the urging of health care professionals or others or as a result of implicit social pressure is deprived of the choice-enhancing benefits of the new advances. The Commission recommends that those who counsel patients and those who educate the public about genetics should not only emphasize the importance of preserving choice but also do their utmost to safeguard the choices of those they serve.[10]

Now let us take this value of respect for autonomy and put it on both sides of the dilemma. Why is it morally problematic to seek to produce a child who is deaf? Being deaf does not cause one physical pain or shorten one's life span, two obvious conditions which it would be prima facie immoral to produce in another person. Deaf people might (or might not) be less happy on average than hearing people, but that is arguably a function of societal prejudice. The primary argument against deliberately seeking to produce deaf children is that it violates the child's own autonomy and narrows the scope of her choices when she grows up; in other words, it violates her right to an "open future."

## The Child's Right to an Open Future

Joel Feinberg begins his discussion of children's rights by noticing that rights can ordinarily be divided into four kinds. First, there are rights that adults and children have in common (the right not to be killed, for example). Then, there are rights that are generally possessed only by children (or by "childlike" adults). These "dependency-rights," as Feinberg calls them, derive from the child's dependence on others for such basics as food, shelter, and protection. Third, there are rights that can only be exercised by adults (or at least by children approaching adulthood), for example, the free exercise of religion. Finally, there are rights that Feinberg calls "rights-in-trust," rights which are to be "saved for the child until he is an adult." These rights can be violated by adults now, in ways that cut off the possibility that the child, when it achieves adulthood, can exercise them. A striking example is the right to reproduce. A young child cannot physically exercise that right, and a teenager might lack the legal and moral grounds on which to assert such a right. But clearly the child, when he or she attains adulthood, will have that right, and therefore the child now has the right not to be sterilized, so that the child may ex-

ercise that right in the future. Rights in this category include a long list: virtually all the important rights we believe adults have, but which must be protected now to be exercised later. Grouped together, they constitute what Feinberg calls "the child's right to an open future."[11]

Feinberg illustrates this concept with two examples. The first is that of the Jehovah's Witness child who needs a blood transfusion to save his life but whose parents object on religious grounds. In this case, the parents' right to act upon their religious beliefs and to raise their family within the religion of their choice conflicts with the child's right to live to adulthood and to make his own life-or-death decisions. As the Supreme Court said in another (and less defensible) case involving Jehovah's Witnesses:

> Parents may be free to become martyrs themselves. But it does not follow that they are free in identical circumstances to make martyrs of their children before they have reached the age of full and legal discretion when they can make that decision for themselves.[12]

The second example is more controversial. In 1972, in a famous Supreme Court case, a group of Old Order Amish argued that they should be exempt from Wisconsin's requirement that all children attend school until they are either sixteen years old or graduate from high school.[13] The Amish didn't have to send their children to public school, of course; they were free to create a private school of their own liking. But they framed the issue in the starkest manner: to send their children to any school, past eighth grade, would be antithetical to their religion and their way of life, and might even result in the death of their culture.

The case was framed as a freedom of religion claim on the one hand, and the state's right to insist on an educated citizenry on the other. And within that frame, the Amish won. First, they were able to persuade the Court that sending their children to school after eighth grade would potentially destroy their community, because it

> takes them away from their community, physically and emotionally, during the crucial and formative adolescent period. During this period, the children must acquire Amish attitudes favoring manual work and self-reliance and the specific skills needed to perform the adult role of an Amish farmer or housewife. In the Amish belief higher learning tends to develop values they reject as influences that alienate man from God. (p. 211)

Second, the Amish argued that the state's concerns—that children be prepared to participate in the political and economic life of the state—did not apply in this case. The Court listened favorably to expert witnesses who explained that the Amish system of home-based vocational training—learning from your parent—worked well for that community, that the community itself was prosperous, and that few Amish were likely to end up unemployed. The Court said:

> the value of all education must be assessed in terms of its capacity to prepare the child for life . . . It is one thing to say that compulsory education for a year or two beyond the eighth grade may be necessary when its goal is the preparation of the child for life in modern society as the majority live, but it is quite another if the goal of education can be viewed as the preparation of the child for life in the separated agrarian community that is the keystone of the Amish faith. (p. 222)

What only a few justices saw was that the children themselves were largely ignored in this argument. The Amish wanted to preserve their way of life. The state of Wisconsin wanted to make sure that its citizens could vote wisely and make a living. No justice squarely faced the question of whether the liberal democratic state owes all its citizens, especially children, a right to a basic education that can serve as a building block if the child decides later in life that she wishes to become an astronaut, a playwright, or perhaps to join the army. As we constantly hear from politicians and educators, without a high school diploma one's future is virtually closed. By denying them a high school education or its equivalent, parents are virtually ensuring that their children will remain housewives and agricultural laborers. Even if the children agree, is that a choice parents ought to be allowed to make for them?

From my perspective, the case was decided wrongly. If Wisconsin had good reasons for settling on high school graduation or age sixteen as the legal minimum to which children are entitled, then I think that the Amish children were entitled to that minimum as well, despite their parents' objections. In deciding the issue primarily on grounds that the Amish were not likely to create problems for the state if allowed to keep their children out of school, the Court reflected a rather minimalist form of liberalism. In fact, the abiding interest of this case for many political philosophers lies in the deep conflict it highlights between two different concepts of liberalism: commitment to autonomy and commitment to diversity. William Galston, for example, argues that:

A standard liberal view (or hope) is that these two principles go together and complement one another: the exercise of autonomy yields diversity, while the fact of diversity protects and nourishes autonomy. By contrast, my . . . view is that these principles do not always, perhaps even do not usually, cohere; that in practice, they point in quite different directions in currently disputed areas such as education . . . Specifically: the decision to throw state power behind the promotion of individual autonomy can weaken or undermine individuals and groups that do not and cannot organize their affairs in accordance with that principle without undermining the deepest sources of their identity.[14]

Galston claims that "properly understood, liberalism is about the protection of diversity, not the valorization of choice . . . To place an ideal of autonomous choice . . . at the core of liberalism is in fact to narrow the range of possibilities available within liberal societies" (p. 523).

One can see this conflict quite sharply if one returns to the work of John Stuart Mill. On the one hand, there is probably no philosopher who gives more weight to the value of individual choice than does Mill. In *On Liberty,* he claims that the very measure of a human being is the extent to which he makes life choices for himself, free of societal pressure:

> The human faculties of perception, judgment, discriminative feeling, mental activity, and even moral preference, are exercised only in making a choice. He who does anything because it is the custom makes no choice.[15]

Mill would abhor a situation like that of the Amish communities in *Yoder,* which unabashedly want to give their children as few choices as possible. But, on the other hand, it is clear from both common sense and from Mill's own statements that in order for people to have choices about the pattern of their lives (and to be inspired to create new patterns) there must be more than one type of community available to them. To quote Mill again, "There is no reason that all human existence should be constructed on some one or some small number of patterns" (p. 64). As we look at the last three centuries of American history, we see what an important role different community "patterns" have played, from the Shakers to the Mormons to Bronson Alcott's Fruitlands to the communal experiments of the 1960s. If those patterns are to exhibit the full range of human endeavor and experiment, they must include communities that are distinctly antiliberal. Not only does the panoply of widely different communities enrich our culture, but it also provides a welcome for those who do not fit into the mainstream. As Mill says, "A man cannot get a coat or pair of shoes to fit him unless they are either made to his measure, or he has a whole warehouseful to choose from: and is it easier to fit him with a life than with a coat[?]" (p. 64). Some of us are geniuses who make our lives to "fit our measure," others are happy enough to fit into the mainstream, but for others, the availability of a "warehouseful" of choices increases the possibility of finding a good fit. And for some, a good fit means an authoritarian community based on tradition, where one is freed from the necessity of choice. Thus Galston is correct in pointing to the paradox: if the goal of a liberal democracy is to actively promote something like the greatest number of choices for the greatest number of individuals, this seems to entail hostility toward narrow-choice communities like the Amish. But if the Amish, because of that hostility, fail to flourish, there will be fewer choices available to all.

The compromise I promote is that a liberal state must tolerate even those communities most unsympathetic to the liberal value of individual choice. However, this tolerance must exist within a limiting context, which is the right of individuals to choose which communities they wish to join and to leave if they have a mind to. Even Galston begins with the presumption that society must "defend . . . the liberty not to be coerced into, or trapped within, ways of life. Accordingly, the state must safeguard the ability of individuals to shift allegiances and cross boundaries."[16] Thus, I argue that the autonomy of the individual is ethically prior to the autonomy of the group. Both ideals have powerful claims on us, but when group rights would extinguish the abilities of the individuals within them to make their own life choices, then the liberal state must support the individual against the group. This is especially crucial when the individual at issue is a child, who is particularly vulnerable to adult coercion and therefore has particular claims on our protection.

Unfortunately, it is precisely where children are concerned that groups are understandably most jealous of their prerogatives to guide and make decisions. The Amish are an example of a group guarding its ability to shape the lives of its children; Deaf parents wishing to ensure Deaf children are an example of families pursuing the same goals. Of course, groups and families ought to—in fact, they must—strive to shape the values and lives of the children in their care;

not to do so leads to social and individual pathology. But when that shaping takes the form of a radically narrow range of choices available to the child when she grows up, when it impinges substantially on the child's right to an open future, then liberalism requires us to intervene to support the child's future ability to make her own choices about which of the many diverse visions of life she wishes to embrace.

But I concede one problem with this point of view. As a liberal who believes that the state should not dictate notions of "the good life," Feinberg believes that the state must be neutral about the goals of education, skewing the question neither in favor of the Amish lifestyle nor in favor of the "modern," technological life most Americans accept. The goal of education is to allow the child to make up its own mind from the widest array of options; the best education is the one which gives the child the most open future. A neutral decision would assume only that education should equip the child with the knowledge and skills that will help him choose whichever sort of life best fits his native endowment and matured disposition. It should send him out into the adult world with as many open opportunities as possible, thus maximizing his chances for self-fulfillment.[17]

The problem here is that an education which gave a child this array of choices would quite possibly make it impossible for her to choose to remain Old Order Amish. Her "native endowment and matured disposition" might now have taken her away from the kind of personality and habits that would make Amish life pleasant. Even if she envies the peace, warmth, and security that a life of tradition offers, she may find it impossible to turn her back on "the world," and return to her lost innocence. To quote the Amish, she may have failed irreversibly to "acquire Amish attitudes" during "the crucial and formative adolescent period." This problem raises two issues. First, those of us who would make arguments based on the child's right to an open future need to be clear and appropriately humble about what we are offering. Insisting on a child's right to a high school education may open a future wider than she otherwise could have dreamed, but it also may foreclose one possible future: as a contented member of the Amish community. Second, if the Amish are correct in saying that taking their children out of school at grade eight is crucial for the child's development into a member of the Amish community, then there is no "impartial" stance for the state to take. The state may well be impartial about whether the "better life" is to be found within or without the Amish community, but it cannot act in an impartial fashion. Both forcing the parents to send their children to school or exempting them from the requirement has likely consequences for the child's continued existence within the community when she grows up and is able to make a choice. Feinberg seeks to avoid this second problem by claiming that the neutral state would act to

> let all influences . . . work equally on the child, to open up all possibilities to him, without itself influencing him toward one or another of these. In that way, it can be hoped that the chief determining factor in the grown child's choice of a vocation and life-style will be his own governing values, talents, and propensities. (pp. 134–35)

The problem with this is that, as I understand the Amish way of life, being Amish is precisely not to make one's life choices on the basis of one's own "talents and propensities," but to subordinate those individual leanings to the traditions of the group. If one discovers within oneself a strong passion and talent for jazz dancing, one ought to suppress it, not nurture it.

## Is Creating a Deaf Child a Moral Harm?

Now, as we return to the example of the couple who wish to ensure that they bear only deaf children, we have to confront two distinctly different issues. The first is, in what sense is it ever possible to do harm by giving birth to a child who would otherwise not have been born at all? The second is whether being deaf rather than hearing is in fact a harm.

The first issue has been well rehearsed elsewhere.[18] The problem is, how can it be said that one has harmed a child by bringing it into the world with a disability, when the only other choice was for the child not to have existed at all? In the case of a child whose life is arguably not worth living, one can say that life itself is a cruelty to the child. But when a child is born in less than ideal circumstances, or is partially disabled in ways that do not entail tremendous suffering, there seems no way to argue that the child herself has been harmed. This may appear to entail the conclusion, counter to our common moral sense, that therefore no harm has been done. "A wrong action must be bad for someone, but [a] choice to create [a] child with its handicap is bad for no one."[19]

All commentators agree that there is no purely logical way out of what Dan Brock calls the "wrongful handicap" conundrum (p. 272). However, most commentators also agree that one can still support a moral critique of the parents' decision. Bonnie Steinbock and Ron McClamrock argue for a principle of "parental responsibility" by which being a good parent entails refraining from bringing a child into the world when one cannot give it "even a decent chance at a good life."[20] Brock, following Parfit, distinguishes same person from same number choices. In same person choices, the same person exists in each of the alternative courses of action the agent chooses, but the person may exist more or less harmed. In same number choices, "the choice affects who, which child, will exist."[21] Brock claims that moral harms can exist in both instances, despite the fact that in same number choices the moral harm cannot be tied to a specific person. Brock generates the following principle:

> Individuals are morally required not to let any possible child . . . for whose welfare they are responsible experience serious suffering or limited opportunity if they can act so that, without imposing substantial burdens or costs on themselves or others, any alternative possible child . . . for whose welfare they would be responsible will not experience serious suffering or limited opportunity. (pp. 272–73)

While agreeing with Brock, Steinbock, and others, I locate the moral harm differently, at least with respect to disabled persons wishing to reproduce themselves in the form of a disabled child. Deliberately creating a child who will be forced irreversibly into the parents' notion of "the good life" violates the Kantian principle of treating each person as an end in herself and never as a means only. All parenthood exists as a balance between fulfillment of parental hopes and values and the individual flowering of the actual child in his or her own direction. The decision to have a child is never made for the sake of the child—for no child then exists. We choose to have children for myriad reasons, but before the child is conceived those reasons can only be self-regarding. The child is a means to our ends: a certain kind of joy and pride, continuing the family name, fulfilling religious or societal expectations, and so on. But morally the child is first and foremost an end in herself. Good parenthood requires a balance between having a child for our own sakes and being open to the moral reality that the child will exist for her own sake, with her own talents and weaknesses, propensities and interests, and with her own life to make. Parental practices that close exits virtually forever are insufficiently attentive to the child as end in herself. By closing off the child's right to an open future, they define the child as an entity who exists to fulfill parental hopes and dreams, not her own.

Having evaded the snares of the wrongful handicap conundrum, we must tackle the second problem: is being deaf a harm? At first glance, this might appear as a silly question. Ethically, we would certainly include destroying someone's hearing under the rubric of "harm"; legally, one could undoubtedly receive compensation if one were rendered deaf through someone else's negligence. Many Deaf people, however, have recently been claiming that Deafness is better understood as a cultural identity than as a disability. Particularly in the wake of the Deaf President Now revolution at Gallaudet University in 1988, Deaf people have been asserting their claims not merely to equal access (through increased technology) but also to equal respect as a cultural minority. As one (hearing) reporter noted:

> So strong is the feeling of cultural solidarity that many deaf parents cheer on discovering that their baby is deaf. Pondering such a scene, a hearing person can experience a kind of vertigo. The surprise is not simply the unfamiliarity of the views; it is that, as in a surrealist painting, jarring notions are presented as if they were commonplace.[22]

From this perspective, the use of cochlear implants to enable deaf children to hear, or the abortion of deaf fetuses, is characterized as "genocide."[23] Deaf pride advocates point out that as Deaf people they lack the ability to hear, but they also have many positive gains: a cohesive community, a rich cultural heritage built around the various residential schools, a growing body of drama, poetry, and other artistic traditions, and, of course, what makes all this possible, American Sign Language.[24] Roslyn Rosen, the president of the National Association of the Deaf, is Deaf, the daughter of Deaf parents, and the mother of Deaf children. "I'm happy with who I am," she says, "and I don't want to be 'fixed.' Would an Italian-American rather be a WASP? In our society everyone agrees that whites have an easier time than blacks. But do you think a black person would undergo operations to become white?"[25]

On the other side of the argument is evidence that deafness is a very serious disability. Deaf people have incomes thirty to forty percent below the national average.[26] The state of education for the deaf is unacceptable by anyone's standards; the typical deaf student graduates from high school unable to read a newspaper.[27]

However, one could also point to the lower incomes and inadequate state of education among some racial and ethnic minorities in our country, a situation we do not (or at least ought not) try to ameliorate by eradicating minorities. Deaf advocates often cite the work of Nora Ellen Groce, whose oral history of Martha's Vineyard, *Everyone Here Spoke Sign Language*, tells a fascinating story. For over two hundred years, ending in the middle of the twentieth century, the Vineyard experienced a degree of hereditary deafness exponentially higher than that of the mainland. Although the number of deaf people was low in non-comparative terms (one in 155), the result was a community in which deaf people participated fully in the political and social life of the island, had an economic prosperity on par with their neighbors, and communicated easily with the hearing population, for "everyone here spoke sign language." So endemic was sign language for the general population of the island that hearing islanders often exploited its unique properties even in the absence of deaf people. Old-timers told Groce stories of spouses communicating through sign language when they were outdoors and did not want to raise their voices against the wind. Or men might turn away and finish a "dirty" joke in sign when a woman walked into the general store. At church, deaf parishioners gave their testimony in sign.

As one Deaf activist said, in a comment that could have been directly related to the Vineyard experience, "When Gorbachev visited the U.S., he used an interpreter to talk to the President. Was Gorbachev disabled?"[28] Further, one might argue that, since it is impossible to eradicate deafness completely even if that were a worthy goal, the cause of deaf equality is better served when parents who are proud to be Deaf deliberately have Deaf children who augment and strengthen the existing population. Many of the problems that deaf people experience are the result of being born, without advance warning, to hearing parents. When there is no reason to anticipate the birth of a deaf child, it is often months or years before the child is correctly diagnosed. Meanwhile, she is growing up in a world devoid of language, unable even to communicate with her parents. When the diagnosis is made, her parents first must deal with the emotional shock, and then sort through the plethora of conflicting advice on how best to raise and educate their child. Most probably, they have never met anyone who is deaf. If they choose the route recommended by most Deaf activists and raise their child with sign language, it will take the parents years to learn the language. Meanwhile, their child has missed out on the crucial development of language at the developmentally appropriate time, a lack that is associated with poor reading skills and other problems later (p. 43).

Further, even the most accepting of hearing parents often feel locked in conflict with the Deaf community over who knows what is best for their child. If Deafness truly is a culture rather than a disability, then raising a deaf child is somewhat like white parents trying to raise a black child in contemporary America (with a background chorus of black activists telling them that they can't possibly make a good job of it!). Residential schools, for example, which can be part of the family culture for a Deaf couple, can be seen by hearing parents as Dickensian nightmares or, worse, as a "cultlike" experience in which their children will be lost to them forever.

By contrast, deaf children born to Deaf parents learn language (sign) at the same age as hearing children. They are welcomed into their families and inculcated into Deaf culture in the same way as any other children. Perhaps for these reasons, by all accounts the Deaf of Deaf are the acknowledged leaders of the Deaf Pride movement, and the academic crème de la crème. In evaluating the choice parents make who deliberately ensure that they have Deaf children, we must remember that the statistics and descriptions of deaf life in America are largely reflective of the experience of deaf children born to hearing parents, who make up the vast majority of deaf people today.

But if Deafness is a culture rather than a disability, it is an exceedingly narrow one. One factor that does not seem clear is the extent to which children raised with American Sign Language as their first language ever will be completely comfortable with the written word. (Sign language itself has no written analogue and has a completely different grammatical structure from English.) At present, the conflicted and politicized state of education for the deaf, along with the many hours spent (some would say "wasted") on attempting to teach deaf children oral skills, makes it impossible to know what is to blame for the dismal reading and writing skills of the average deaf person. Some deaf children who are raised with sign language from birth do become skilled readers. But there is reason to question whether a deaf child may have very limited access to the wealth of literature, drama, and poetry that liberals would like to consider every child's birthright.

Although Deaf activists rightly show how many occupations are open to them with only minor technological adjustments, the range of occupations will always be inherently limited. It is not likely that the world will become as Martha's Vineyard, where everyone knew sign. A prelingually deafened person not only cannot hear, but in most instances cannot speak well enough to be understood. This narrow choice of vocation is not only a harm in its own sake but also is likely to continue to lead to lower standards of living. (Certainly one reason why the Vineyard deaf were as prosperous as their neighbors was that farming and fishing were just about the only occupations available.)

## Either Way, a Moral Harm

If deafness is considered a disability, one that substantially narrows a child's career, marriage, and cultural options in the future, then deliberately creating a deaf child counts as a moral harm. If Deafness is considered a culture, as Deaf activists would have us agree, then deliberately creating a Deaf child who will have only very limited options to move outside of that culture, also counts as a moral harm. A decision, made before a child is even born, that confines her forever to a narrow group of people and a limited choice of careers, so violates the child's right to an open future that no genetic counseling team should acquiesce in it. The very value of autonomy that grounds the ethics of genetic counseling should preclude assisting parents in a project that so dramatically narrows the autonomy of the child to be.

## Coda

Although I rest my case at this point, I want to sketch out some further ramifications of my argument. Are there other, less obvious, ways in which genetic knowledge and manipulation can interfere with the child's right to an open future?

The notion of the child's right to an open future can help in confronting the question of whether to test children for adult-onset genetic diseases, for example Huntington disease.[29] It is well known that the vast majority of adults at risk for Huntington disease choose not to be tested. However, it is not uncommon for parents to request that their children be tested; their goals may be to set their minds at rest, to plan for the future, and so on. On one account, parental authority to make medical decisions suggests that clinicians should accede to these requests (after proper counseling about possible risks). A better account, in my opinion, protects the child's right to an open future by preserving into adulthood his own choice to decide whether his life is better lived with that knowledge or without.[30]

Finally, a provocative argument can be made that sex selection can be deleterious to the child's right to an open future. I am ignoring here all the more obvious arguments against sex selection, even when accomplished without abortion. Rather, I suspect that parents who choose the sex of their offspring are more likely to have gender-specific expectations for those children, expectations that subtly limit the child's own individual flowering. The more we are able to control our children's characteristics (and the more time, energy, and money we invest in the outcome), the more invested we will become in our hopes and dreams for them. It is easy to sympathize with some of the reasons why parents might want to ensure a girl or boy. People who already have one or two children of one sex can hardly be faulted for wanting to "balance" their families by having one of each. And yet, this ought to be discouraged. If I spent a great deal of time and energy to get a boy in the hope of having a football player in the family, I think I would be less likely to accept it with good grace if the boy hated sports and spent all his spare time at the piano. If I insisted on having a girl because I believed that as a grandparent I would be more likely to have close contact with the children of a daughter than of a son, I think I would find it much harder to raise a girl who saw motherhood as a choice rather than as a foregone conclusion. Parents whose preferences are compelling enough for them to take active steps to control the outcome, must, logically, be committed to certain strong gender-role expectations. If they want a girl that badly, whether they are hoping for a Miss America or the next Catherine McKinnon, they are likely to make it difficult for the actual child to resist their expectations and to follow her own bent.

## Acknowledgments

The author is grateful to the Cleveland-Marshall Fund for financial support while writing this article, and to Samuel Gorovitz, Eric Juengst, Thomas H. Murray, Lisa Parker, and Matthew Silliman for their comments on earlier drafts.

## References

1. Walter E. Nance, "Parables," in *Prescribing Our Future: Ethical Challenges in Genetic Counseling*, ed. Dianne M. Bartels, Bonnie S. LeRoy, and Arthur L. Caplan (New York Aldine De Gruyter, 1993), p. 92.

2. National Society of Genetic Counselors, Code of Ethics, reprinted in *Prescribing Our Future*, pp. 169–71.

3. James R. Sorenson, "Genetic Counseling: Values That Have Mattered," *Prescribing Our Future*, p. 11; Arthur L. Caplan, "The Ethics of Genetic Counseling," *Prescribing Our Future*, p. 161.

4. Charles Bosk, "Workplace Ideology," *Prescribing Our Future*, pp. 27–28.

5. Dianne M. Bartels, "Preface," *Prescribing Our Future*, pp. ix–xiii.

6. Barbara Katz Rothman, *The Tentative Pregnancy: Prenatal Diagnosis and the Future of Motherhood* (New York: Viking Press, 1986), p. 41.

7. Nance, "Parables," p. 92.

8. D. Lindhout, P. G. Frets, and M. C. Niermeijer, "Approaches to Genetic Counseling," *Annals of the New York Academy of Sciences* 630 (1991): 223–29, at 224.

9. Jeffrey R. Botkin, "Fetal Privacy and Confidentiality," *Hastings Center Report* 25, no. 3 (1995): 32–39.

10. President's Commission for the Study of Ethical Problems in Biomedical and Behavioral Research, *Screening and Counseling for Genetic Conditions: A Report on the Ethical, Social, and Legal Implications of Genetic Screening, Counseling, and Education Programs* (Washington, D.C.: Government Printing Office, 1983), p. 56.

11. Joel Feinberg, "The Child's Right to an Open Future," in *Whose Child? Children's Rights, Parental Authority, and State Power*, ed. William Aiken and Hugh LaFollette (Totowa, N.J.: Littlefield, Adams & Co., 1980), pp. 124–53.

12. Prince v. Massachusetts, 321 U.S. 158 (1944), at 170.

13. Wisconsin v. Yoder, 406 U.S. 205 (1972).

14. William Galston, "Two Concepts of Liberalism," *Ethics* 105, no. 3 (1995): 516–34, at 521.

15. John Stuart Mill, *On Liberty* (New York: W. W. Norton, 1975), p. 55.

16. Galston, "Two Concepts of Liberalism," p. 522.

17. Feinberg, "The Child's Right," pp. 134–35.

18. Cynthia Cohen, "'Give Me Children or I Shall Die!' New Reproductive Technologies and Harm to Children," *Hastings Center Report* 26, no. 2 (1996): 19–29.

19. Dan Brock, "The Non-Identity Problem and Genetic Harms," *Bioethics* 9, no. 3/4 (1995): 269–75, at 271.

20. Bonnie Steinbock and Ron McClamrock, "When Is Birth Unfair to the Child?" *Hastings Center Report* 24, no. 6 (1994): 15–21, at p. 17.

21. Brock, "The Non-Identity Problem," p. 272.

22. Edward Dolnick, "Deafness as Culture," *The Atlantic Monthly* 272/3 (1993): 37–53.

23. Amy Elizabeth Brusky, "Making Decisions for Deaf Children Regarding Cochlear Implants: The Legal Ramifications of Recognizing Deafness as a Culture Rather than a Disability," *Wisconsin Law Review* (1995): 235–70.

24. John B. Christiansen, "Sociological Implications of Hearing Loss," *Annals of the New York Academy of Science* 630 (1991): 230–35.

25. Dolnick, "Deafness as Culture," p. 38.

26.   Nora Ellen Groce, *Everyone Here Spoke Sign Language: Hereditary Deafness on Martha's Vineyard* (Cambridge: Harvard University Press, 1985), p. 85.

27.   Andrew Solomon, "Defiantly Deaf," *New York Times Magazine*, 28 August 1994: 40–45 et passim.

28.   Dolnick, "Deafness as Culture," p. 43.

29.   I am grateful to Thomas H. Murray and Ronald M. Green for bringing this topic to my attention.

30.   "The Genetic Testing of Children," *Journal of Medical Genetics* 31 (1994): 785–97.

## READINGS

# Section 4: Genetic Testing and Reproductive Decisions

## Genetics and Reproductive Risk: Can Having Children Be Immoral?

### Laura M. Purdy

Laura Purdy argues that it can sometimes be immoral to have children when we know (or should know) that our offspring may have a genetic disease. Purdy supports this claim by arguing for three interconnected theses: (1) We have a duty to provide every child with a normal opportunity for a good life; (2) we do not harm possible children by preventing them from existing; (3) the duty to provide a normal opportunity for a good life takes precedence over a potential parent's right to reproduce.

Purdy maintains that this duty not to reproduce when there is a high likelihood of passing on a debilitating genetic disease applies most strictly to those who are unwilling to have prenatal testing and selective abortions. If a couple is willing to have the potential child tested for the presence of the genetic disease and to abort if that test is positive, Purdy argues it is permissible for them to attempt to conceive genetically related offspring. But for those who are unwilling to have selective abortions, Purdy maintains there is a strong moral duty for them not to conceive children in some cases.

Is it morally permissible for me to have children?[1] A decision to procreate is surely one of the most significant decisions a person can make. So it would seem that it ought not to be made without some moral soul-searching.

There are many reasons why one might hesitate to bring children into this world if one is concerned about their welfare. Some are rather general, like the deteriorating environment or the prospect of poverty. Others have a narrower focus, like continuing civil war in Ireland, or the lack of essential social support for childrearing persons in the United States. Still others may be relevant only to individuals at risk of passing harmful diseases to their offspring.

There are many causes of misery in this world, and most of them are unrelated to genetic disease. In the general scheme of things, human misery is most efficiently reduced by concentrating on noxious social and political arrangements. Nonetheless, we shouldn't ignore preventable harm just because it is confined to a relatively small corner of life. So the question arises: can it be wrong to have a child because of genetic risk factors?[2]

Unsurprisingly, most of the debate about this issue has focused on prenatal screening and abortion:

much useful information about a given fetus can be made available by recourse to prenatal testing. This fact has meant that moral questions about reproduction have become entwined with abortion politics, to the detriment of both. The abortion connection has made it especially difficult to think about whether it is wrong to prevent a child from coming into being since doing so might involve what many people see as wrongful killing; yet there is no necessary link between the two.

Clearly, the existence of genetically compromised children can be prevented not only by aborting already existing fetuses but also by preventing conception in the first place. Worse yet, many discussions simply assume a particular view of abortion, without any recognition of other possible positions and the difference they make in how people understand the issues. For example, those who object to aborting fetuses with genetic problems often argue that doing so would undermine our conviction that all humans are in some important sense equal.[3] However, this position rests on the assumption that conception marks the point at which humans are endowed with a right to life. So aborting fetuses with genetic problems looks morally the same as killing "imperfect" people without their consent.

This position raises two separate issues. One pertains to the legitimacy of different views on abortion. Despite the conviction of many abortion activists to the contrary, I believe that ethically respectable views can be found on different sides of the debate, including one that sees fetuses as developing humans without any serious moral claim on continued life. There is no space here to address the details, and doing so would be once again to fall into the trap of letting the abortion question swallow up all others. Fortunately, this issue need not be resolved here. However, opponents of abortion need to face the fact that many thoughtful individuals do not *see* fetuses as moral persons. It follows that their reasoning process and hence the implications of their decisions are radically different from those envisioned by opponents of prenatal screening and abortion. So where the latter see genetic abortion as murdering people who just don't measure up, the former see it as a way to prevent the development of persons who are more likely to live miserable lives. This is consistent with a world view that values persons equally and holds that each deserves high quality life. Some of those who object to genetic abortion appear to be oblivious to these psychological and logical facts. It follows that the nightmare scenarios

they paint for us are beside the point: many people simply do not share the assumptions that make them plausible.

How are these points relevant to my discussion? My primary concern here is to argue that conception can sometimes be morally wrong on grounds of genetic risk, although this judgment will not apply to those who accept the moral legitimacy of abortion and are willing to employ prenatal screening and selective abortion. If my case is solid, then those who oppose abortion must be especially careful not to conceive in certain cases, as they are, of course, free to follow their conscience about abortion. Those like myself who do not see abortion as murder have more ways to prevent birth.

## Huntington's Disease

There is always some possibility that reproduction will result in a child with a serious disease or handicap. Genetic counselors can help individuals determine whether they are at unusual risk and, as the Human Genome Project rolls on, their knowledge will increase by quantum leaps. As this knowledge becomes available, I believe we ought to use it to determine whether possible children are at risk *before* they are conceived.

I want in this paper to defend the thesis that it is morally wrong to reproduce when we know there is a high risk of transmitting a serious disease or defect. This thesis holds that some reproductive acts are wrong, and my argument puts the burden of proof on those who disagree with it to show why its conclusions can be overridden. Hence it denies that people should be free to reproduce mindless of the consequences.[4] However, as moral argument, it should be taken as a proposal for further debate and discussion. It is not, by itself, an argument in favor of legal prohibitions of reproduction.[5]

There is a huge range of genetic diseases. Some are quickly lethal; others kill more slowly, if at all. Some are mainly physical, some mainly mental; others impair both kinds of function. Some interfere tremendously with normal functioning, others less. Some are painful, some are not. There seems to be considerable agreement that rapidly lethal diseases, especially those, like Tay–Sachs, accompanied by painful deterioration, should be prevented even at the cost of abortion. Conversely, there seems to be substantial agreement that relatively trivial problems, especially cosmetic ones, would not be legitimate grounds for abortion.[6] In short, there are cases ranging from low risk of mild disease or disability to high risk of serious disease or disability. Although it is difficult to decide where the duty to refrain from procreation becomes compelling, I believe that there are some clear cases. I have chosen to focus on Huntington's disease to illustrate the kinds of concrete issues such decisions entail. However, the arguments presented here are also relevant to many other genetic diseases.[7]

The symptoms of Huntington's disease usually begin between the ages of thirty and fifty. It happens this way:

> Onset is insidious. Personality changes (obstinacy, moodiness, lack of initiative) frequently antedate or accompany the involuntary choreic movements. These usually appear first in the face, neck, and arms, and are jerky, irregular, and stretching in character. Contractions of the facial muscles result in grimaces, those of the respiratory muscles, lips, and tongue lead to hesitating, explosive speech. Irregular movements of the trunk are present; the gait is shuffling and dancing. Tendon reflexes are increased. . . . Some patients display a fatuous euphoria; others are spiteful, irascible, destructive, and violent. Paranoid reactions are common. Poverty of thought and impairment of attention, memory, and judgment occur. As the disease progresses, walking becomes impossible, swallowing difficult, and dementia profound. Suicide is not uncommon.[8]

The illness lasts about fifteen years, terminating in death.

Huntington's disease is an autosomal dominant disease, meaning that it is caused by a single defective gene located on a non-sex chromosome. It is passed from one generation to the next via affected individuals. Each child of such an affected person has a fifty percent risk of inheriting the gene and thus of eventually developing the disease, even if he or she was born before the parent's disease was evident.[9]

Until recently, Huntington's disease was especially problematic because most affected individuals did not know whether they had the gene for the disease until well into their childbearing years. So they had to decide about childbearing before knowing whether they could transmit the disease or not. If, in time, they did not develop symptoms of the disease, then their children could know they were not at risk for the disease. If unfortunately they did develop symptoms, then each of their children could know there was a fifty percent chance that they, too, had inherited the gene. In both cases, the children faced a period of prolonged anxiety as to whether they would develop the disease. Then, in the 1980s, thanks in part to an energetic campaign by Nancy Wexler, a genetic marker was found that, in certain circumstances, could tell people with a relatively high degree of probability whether or not they had the gene for the disease.[10] Finally, in March 1993, the defective gene itself was discovered.[11] Now individuals can find out whether they carry the gene for the disease, and prenatal screening can tell us whether a given fetus has inherited it. These technological developments change the moral scene substantially.

How serious are the risks involved in Huntington's disease? Geneticists often think a ten percent risk is high.[12] But risk assessment also depends on what is at stake: the worse the possible outcome the more undesirable an otherwise small risk seems. In medicine, as elsewhere, people may regard the same result quite differently. But for devastating diseases like Huntington's this part of the judgment should be unproblematic: no one wants a loved one to suffer in this way.[13]

There may still be considerable disagreement about the acceptability of a given risk. So it would be difficult in many circumstances to say how we should respond to a particular risk. Nevertheless, there are good grounds for a conservative approach, for it is reasonable to take special precautions to avoid very bad consequences, even if the risk is small. But the possible consequences here *are* very bad: a child who may inherit Huntington's disease has a much greater than average chance of being subjected to severe and prolonged suffering. And it is one thing to risk one's own welfare, but quite another to do so for others and without their consent.

Is this judgment about Huntington's disease really defensible? People appear to have quite different opinions. Optimists argue that a child born into a family afflicted with Huntington's disease has a reasonable chance of living a satisfactory life. After all, even children born of an afflicted parent still have a fifty percent chance of escaping the disease. And even if afflicted themselves, such people will probably enjoy some thirty years of healthy life before symptoms appear. It is also possible, although not at all likely, that some might not mind the symptoms caused by the disease. Optimists can point to diseased persons who have lived fruitful lives, as well as those who seem genuinely glad to be alive. One is Rick Donohue, a sufferer from the Joseph family disease. "You know, if my mom hadn't had me, I wouldn't be here for the life I have had. So there is a good possibility I will have children."[14] Optimists therefore conclude that it would be a shame if these persons had not lived.

Pessimists concede some of these facts, but take a less sanguine view of them. They think a fifty percent risk of serious disease like Huntington's appallingly high. They suspect that many children born into afflicted families are liable to spend their youth in dreadful anticipation and fear of the disease. They point out that Rick Donohue is still young, and has not experienced the full horror of his sickness. It is also well-known that some young persons have such a dilated sense of time that they can hardly envision themselves at thirty or forty, so the prospect of pain at that age is unreal to them.[15]

More empirical research on the psychology and life history of sufferers and potential sufferers is clearly needed to decide whether optimists or pessimists have a more accurate picture of the experiences of individuals at risk. But given that some will surely realize pessimists' worst fears, it seems unfair to conclude that the pleasures of those who deal with the situation simply cancel out the suffering of those others when that suffering could be avoided altogether.

I think that these points indicate that the morality of procreation in situations like this demands further investigation. I propose to do this by looking first at the position of the possible child, then at that of the potential parent.

## Possible Children and Potential Parents

The first task in treating the problem from the child's point of view is to find a way of referring to possible future offspring without seeming to confer some sort of morally significant existence upon them. I will follow the convention of calling children who might be born in the future but who are not now conceived "possible" children, offspring, individuals, or persons.

Now, what claims about children or possible children are relevant to the morality of childbearing in the circumstances being considered? Of primary importance is the judgment that we ought to try to provide every child with something like a minimally satisfying life. I am not altogether sure how best to formulate this standard but I want clearly to reject the view that it is morally permissible to conceive individuals so long as we do not expect them to be so miserable that they wish they were dead.[16] I believe that this kind of moral minimalism is thoroughly unsatisfactory and that not many people would really want to live in a world where it was the prevailing standard. Its lure is

that it puts few demands on us, but its price is the scant attention it pays to human well-being.

How might the judgment that we have a duty to try to provide a minimally satisfying life for our children be justified? It could, I think, be derived fairly straightforwardly from either utilitarian or contractarian theories of justice, although there is no space here for discussion of the details. The net result of such analysis would be the conclusion that neglecting this duty would create unnecessary unhappiness or unfair disadvantage for some persons.

Of course, this line of reasoning confronts us with the need to spell out what is meant by "minimally satisfying" and what a standard based on this concept would require of us. Conceptions of a minimally satisfying life vary tremendously among societies and also within them. *De rigeur* in some circles are private music lessons and trips to Europe, while in others providing eight years of schooling is a major accomplishment. But there is no need to consider this complication at length here since we are concerned only with health as a prerequisite for a minimally satisfying life. Thus, as we draw out what such a standard might require of us, it seems reasonable to retreat to the more limited claim that parents should try to ensure something like normal health for their children. It might be thought that even this moderate claim is unsatisfactory since in some places debilitating conditions are the norm, but one could circumvent this objection by saying that parents ought to try to provide for their children health normal for that culture, even though it may be inadequate if measured by some outside standard.[17] This conservative position would still justify efforts to avoid the birth of children at risk for Huntington's disease and other serious genetic diseases in virtually all societies.[18]

This view is reinforced by the following considerations. Given that possible children do not presently exist as actual individuals, they do not have a right to be brought into existence, and hence no one is maltreated by measures to avoid the conception of a possible person. Therefore, the conservative course that avoids the conception of those who would not be expected to enjoy a minimally satisfying life is at present the only fair course of action. The alternative is a laissez-faire approach which brings into existence the lucky, but only at the expense of the unlucky. Notice that attempting to avoid the creation of the unlucky does not necessarily lead to *fewer* people being brought into being; the question boils down to taking steps to bring those with better prospects into existence, instead of those with worse ones.

I have so far argued that if people with Huntington's disease are unlikely to live minimally satisfying lives, then those who might pass it on should not have genetically related children. This is consonant with the principle the greater the danger of serious problems, the stronger the duty to avoid them. But this principle is in conflict with what people think of as the right to reproduce. How might one decide which should take precedence?

Expecting people to forego having genetically related children might seem to demand too great a sacrifice of them. But before reaching that conclusion we need to ask what is really at stake. One reason for wanting children is to experience family life, including love, companionship, watching kids grow, sharing their pains and triumphs, and helping to form members of the next generation. Other reasons emphasize the validation of parents as individuals within a continuous family line, children as a source of immortality, or perhaps even the gratification of producing partial replicas of oneself. Children may also be desired in an effort to prove that one is an adult, to try to cement a marriage, or to benefit parents economically.

Are there alternative ways of satisfying these desires? Adoption or new reproductive technologies can fulfill many of them without passing on known genetic defects. Replacements for sperm have been available for many years via artificial insemination by donor. More recently, egg donation, sometimes in combination with contract pregnancy,[19] has been used to provide eggs for women who prefer not to use their own. Eventually it may be possible to clone individual humans, although that now seems a long way off. All of these approaches to avoiding the use of particular genetic material are controversial and have generated much debate. I believe that tenable moral versions of each do exist.[20]

None of these methods permits people to extend both genetic lines, or realize the desire for immortality or for children who resemble both parents; nor is it clear that such alternatives will necessarily succeed in proving that one is an adult, cementing a marriage, or providing economic benefits. Yet, many people feel these desires strongly. Now, I am sympathetic to William James's dictum regarding desires: "Take any demand, however slight, which any creature, however weak, may make. Ought it not, for its own sole sake to be satisfied? If not, prove why not."[21] Thus a world where more desires are satisfied is generally better

than one where fewer are. However, not all desires can be legitimately satisfied since, as James suggests, there may be good reasons—such as the conflict of duty and desire—why some should be overruled.

Fortunately, further scrutiny of the situation reveals that there are good reasons why people should attempt—with appropriate social support—to talk themselves out of the desires in question or to consider novel ways of fulfilling them. Wanting to see the genetic line continued is not particularly rational when it brings a sinister legacy of illness and death. The desire for immortality cannot really be satisfied anyway, and people need to face the fact that what really matters is how they behave in their own lifetime. And finally, the desire for children who physically resemble one is understandable, but basically narcissistic, and its fulfillment cannot be guaranteed even by normal reproduction. There are other ways of proving one is an adult, and other ways of cementing marriages— children don't necessarily do either. Children, especially prematurely ill children, may not provide the expected economic benefits anyway. Non-genetically related children may also provide benefits similar to those that would have been provided by genetically related ones, and expected economic benefit is, in many cases, a morally questionable reason for having children.

Before the advent of reliable genetic testing, the options of people in Huntington's families were cruelly limited. On the one hand, they could have children, but at the risk of eventual crippling illness and death for them. On the other, they could refrain from childbearing, sparing their possible children from significant risk of inheriting this disease, perhaps frustrating intense desires to procreate—only to discover, in some cases, that their sacrifice was unnecessary because they did not develop the disease. Or they could attempt to adopt or try new reproductive approaches.

Reliable genetic testing has opened up new possibilities. Those at risk who wish to have children can get tested. If they test positive, they know their possible children are at risk. Those who are opposed to abortion must be especially careful to avoid conception if they are to behave responsibly. Those not opposed to abortion can responsibly conceive children, but only if they are willing to test each fetus and abort those who carry the gene. If individuals at risk test negative, they are home free.

What about those who cannot face the test for themselves? They can do prenatal testing and abort fetuses who carry the defective gene. A clearly positive test also implies that the parent is affected, although negative tests do not rule out that possibility. Prenatal testing can thus bring knowledge that enables one to avoid passing the disease to others, but only, in some cases, at the cost of coming to know with certainty that one will indeed develop the disease. This situation raises with peculiar force the question of whether parental responsibility requires people to get tested.

Some people think that we should recognize a right "not to know." It seems to me that such a right could be defended only where ignorance does not put others at serious risk. So if people are prepared to forgo genetically related children, they need not get tested. But if they want genetically related children then they must do whatever is necessary to ensure that affected babies are not the result. There is, after all, something inconsistent about the claim that one has a right to be shielded from the truth, even if the price is to risk inflicting on one's children the same dread disease one cannot even face in oneself.

In sum, until we can be assured that Huntington's disease does not prevent people from living a minimally satisfying life, individuals at risk for the disease have a moral duty to try not to bring affected babies into this world. There are now enough options available so that this duty needn't frustrate their reasonable desires. Society has a corresponding duty to facilitate moral behavior on the part of individuals. Such support ranges from the narrow and concrete (like making sure that medical testing and counseling is available to all) to the more general social environment that guarantees that all pregnancies are voluntary, that pronatalism is eradicated, and that women are treated with respect regardless of the reproductive options they choose.

## Notes

1. This paper is loosely based on "Genetic Diseases: Can Having Children Be Immoral?" originally published in *Genetics Now*, ed. John L. Buckley (Washington, DC: University Press of America, 1978) and subsequently anthologized in a number of medical ethics texts. Thanks to Thomas Mappes and David DeGrazia for their helpful suggestions about updating the paper.

2. I focus on genetic considerations, although with the advent of AIDS the scope of the general question here could be expanded. There are two reasons for sticking to this relatively narrow formulation. One is that dealing with a smaller chunk of the problem may help us think more clearly, while realizing that some conclusions may nonetheless be relevant to the larger problem. The other is the peculiar capacity of some genetic problems to affect ever more individuals in the future.

3. For example, see Leon Kass, "Implications of Prenatal Diagnosis for the Human Right to Live," *Ethical Issues in Human Genetics*, eds. Bruce Hilton et al. (New York: Plenum Press, 1973).

4. This is, of course, a very broad thesis. I defend an even broader version in "Loving Future People," *Reproduction, Ethics and the*

*Law*, ed. Joan Callahan (Bloomington: Indiana University Press, forthcoming).

5. Why would we want to resist legal enforcement of every moral conclusion? First, legal action has many costs, costs not necessarily worth paying in particular cases. Second, legal enforcement would tend to take the matter in question out of the realm of debate and treat it as settled. But in many cases, especially where mores or technology are rapidly evolving, we don't want that to happen. Third, legal enforcement would undermine individual freedom and decision-making capacity. In some cases, the ends envisioned are important enough to warrant putting up with these disadvantages, but that remains to be shown in each case.

6. Those who do not see fetuses as moral persons with a right to life may nonetheless hold that abortion is justifiable in these cases. I argue at some length elsewhere that lesser defects can cause great suffering. Once we are clear that there is nothing discriminatory about failing to conceive particular possible individuals, it makes sense, other things being equal to avoid the prospect of such pain if we can. Naturally, other things rarely are equal. In the first place, many problems go undiscovered until a baby is born. Secondly, there are often substantial costs associated with screening programs. Thirdly, although women should be encouraged to consider the moral dimensions of routine pregnancy, we do not want it to be so fraught with tension that it becomes a miserable experience. (See "Loving Future People.")

7. It should be noted that failing to conceive a single individual can affect many lives: in 1916, nine hundred and sixty-two cases could be traced from six seventeenth-century arrivals in America. See Gordon Rattray Taylor, *The Biological Time Bomb* (New York, 1968), p. 176.

8. *The Merck Manual* (Rathway, N. J.: Merck, 1972), pp. 1363, 1346. We now know that the age of onset and severity of the disease is related to the number of abnormal replications of the glutamine code on the abnormal gene. See Andrew Revkin, "Hunting Down Huntington's," *Discover*, December 1993, p. 108.

9. Hyrnie Gordon, "Genetic Counseling," *JAMA*, Vol. 217, no. 9 (August 30, 1971), p. 1346.

10. See Revkin, "Hunting Down Huntington's," pp. 99–108.

11. "Gene for Huntington's Disease Discovered," *Human Genome News*, Vol. 5, no. 1 (May 1993), p. 5.

12. Charles Smith, Susan Holloway, and Alan E. H. Emery, "Individuals at Risk in Families—Genetic Disease," *Journal of Medical Genetics*, Vol. 8 (1971), p. 453.

13. To try to separate the issue of the gravity of the disease from the existence of a given individual, compare this situation with how we would asses a parent who neglected to vaccinate an existing child against a hypothetical viral version of Huntington's.

14. The *New York Times*, September 30, 1975, p. 1, col. 6. The Joseph family disease is similar to Huntington's disease except that the symptoms start appearing in the twenties. Rick Donohue was in his early twenties at the time he made this statement.

15. I have talked to college students who believe that they will have lived fully and be ready to die at those ages. It is astonishing how one's perspective changes over time, and how ages that one once associated with senility and physical collapse come to seem the prime of human life.

16. The view I am rejecting has been forcefully articulated by Derek Parfit, *Reasons and Persons* (Oxford: Oxford University Press, 1984). For more discussion, see "Loving Future People."

17. I have some qualms about this response since I fear that some human groups are so badly off that it might still be wrong for them to procreate, even if that would mean great changes in their cultures. But this is a complicated issue that needs its own investigation.

18.  Again, a troubling exception might be the isolated Venezuelan group Nancy Wexler found where, because of inbreeding, a large portion of the population is affected by Huntington's. See Revkin, "Hunting Down Huntington's."

19.  Or surrogacy, as it has been popularly known. I think that "contract pregnancy" is more accurate and more respectful of women. Eggs can be provided either by a woman who also gestates the fetus or by a third party.

20.  The most powerful objections to new reproductive technologies and arrangements concern possible bad consequences for women. However, I do not think that the arguments against them on these grounds have yet shown the dangers to be as great as some believe. So although it is perhaps true that new reproductive technologies and arrangements shouldn't be used lightly, avoiding the conceptions discussed here is well worth the risk. For a series of viewpoints on this issue, including my own "Another Look at Contract Pregnancy," See Helen B. Holmes, *Issues in Reproductive Technology 1: An Anthology* (New York: Garland Press, 1992).

21.  *Essays in Pragmatism,* ed. A. Castell (New York: 1948), p. 73.

# Implications of Prenatal Diagnosis for the Human Right to Life

## Leon R. Kass

Leon Kass expresses concern that the practice of "genetic abortion" will strongly affect our attitudes toward all who are "defective" or abnormal. Those who escape the net of selective abortion might receive less care and might even come to think of themselves as second-class specimens. Furthermore, on Kass's view, genetic abortion might encourage us to accept the general principle that defectives of any kind ought not to be born. This in turn would threaten our commitment to the basic moral principle that each person, despite any physical or mental handicap, is the inherent equal of every other person.

Kass presents six criteria that he suggests ought to be satisfied to justify the abortion of a fetus for genetic reasons. In the remainder of his paper, he focuses on the question raised by the last criterion: According to what standards should we judge a fetus with genetic abnormalities unfit to live? As candidates for such standards, Kass examines the concepts of social good, family good, and the "healthy and sound" fetus. He finds difficulty with all, and in the end he professes himself unable to provide a satisfactory justification for genetic abortion. Kass's difficulty with the "healthy and sound" fetus as a standard puts his general position in conflict with that taken by Laura Purdy. What Purdy regards as a relatively clearcut criterion, Kass views as a relatively vague and arbitrary social standard.

I wish to focus on the special ethical issues raised by the abortion of "defective" fetuses (so-called "abortion for fetal indications"). I shall consider only the cleanest cases, those cases where well-characterized genetic diseases are diagnosed with a high degree of certainty by means of amniocentesis, in order to sidestep the

Reprinted from *Ethical Issues in Human Genetics: Genetic Counseling and the Use of Genetic Knowledge,* edited by Bruce Hilton, Daniel Callahan, Maureen Harris, Peter Condliffe, and Burton Berkely (New York: Plenum, 1973), pp. 186–199. A revised version of this essay ("Perfect Babies: Prenatal Diagnosis and the Equal Right to Life") appears in Kass's book, *Toward a More Natural Science: Biology and Human Affairs* (New York: Free Press, 1985). (Notes omitted.)

added moral dilemmas posed when the diagnosis is suspected or possible, but unconfirmed. However, many of the questions I shall discuss could also be raised about cases where genetic analysis gives only a statistical prediction about the genotype of the fetus, and also about cases where the defect has an infectious or chemical rather than a genetic cause (e.g. rubella, thalidomide). . . .

. . . Precisely because the quality of the fetus is central to the decision to abort, the practice of genetic abortion has implications which go beyond those raised by abortion in general. What may be at stake here is the belief that all human beings possess equally and independent of merit certain fundamental rights, one among which is, of course, the right to life.

To be sure, the belief that fundamental human rights belong equally to all human beings has been but an ideal, never realized, often ignored, sometimes shamelessly. Yet it has been perhaps the most powerful moral idea at work in the world for at least two centuries. It is this idea and ideal that animates most of the current political and social criticism around the globe. It is ironic that we should acquire the power to detect and eliminate the genetically unequal at a time when we have finally succeeded in removing much of the stigma and disgrace previously attached to victims of congenital illness, in providing them with improved care and support, and in preventing, by means of education, feelings of guilt on the part of their parents. One might even wonder whether the development of amniocentesis and prenatal diagnosis may represent a backlash against these same humanitarian and egalitarian tendencies in the practice of medicine, which, by helping to sustain to the age of reproduction persons with genetic disease has itself contributed to the increasing incidence of genetic disease, and with it, to increased pressures for genetic screening, genetic counseling, and genetic abortion.

No doubt our humanitarian and egalitarian principles and practices have caused us some new difficulties, but if we mean to weaken or turn our backs on them, we should do so consciously and thoughtfully. If, as I believe, the idea and practice of genetic abortion points in that direction, we should make ourselves aware of it. And if, as I believe, the way in which genetic abortion is described, discussed, and justified is perhaps of even greater consequence than its practice for our notions of human rights and of their equal possession by all human beings, we should pay special attention to questions of language and in particular, to the question of justification. Before turning full attention to these matters, two points should be clarified.

First, my question "What decision, and why?" is to be distinguished from the question "Who decides, and why?" There is a tendency to blur this distinction and to discuss only the latter, and with it, the underlying question of private freedom versus public good. I will say nothing about this, since I am more interested in exploring what constitutes "good," both public and private. Accordingly, I would emphasize that the moral question—What decision, and why?—does not disappear simply because the decision is left in the hands of each pregnant woman. It is the moral question she faces. I would add that the moral health of the community and of each of its members is as likely to be affected by the aggregate of purely private and voluntary decisions on genetic abortions as by a uniform policy imposed by statute. We physicians and scientists especially should refuse to finesse the moral question of genetic abortion and its implications and to take refuge behind the issue, "Who decides?" For it is we who are responsible for choosing to develop the technology of prenatal diagnosis, for informing and promoting this technology among the public, and for the actual counseling of patients.

Second, I wish to distinguish my discussion of what ought to be done from a descriptive account of what in fact is being done, and especially from a consideration of what I myself might do, faced with the difficult decision. I cannot know with certainty what I would think, feel, do, or want done, faced with the knowledge that my wife was carrying a child branded with Down's syndrome or Tay–Sachs disease. But an understanding of the issues is not advanced by personal anecdote or confession. We all know that what we and others actually do is often done out of weakness, rather than conviction. It is all-too-human to make an exception in one's own case (consider, e.g., the extra car, the "extra" child, income tax, the draft, the flight from cities). For what it is worth, I confess to feeling more than a little sympathy with parents who choose abortions for severe genetic defect. Nevertheless, as I shall indicate later, in seeking for reasons to justify this practice, I can find none that are in themselves fully satisfactory and none that do not simultaneously justify the killing of "defective" infants, children, and adults. I am mindful that my arguments will fall far from the middle of the stream, yet I hope that the oarsmen of the flagship will pause and row more slowly, while we all consider whither we are going.

## Genetic Abortion and the Living Defective

The practice of abortion of the genetically defective will no doubt affect our view of and our behavior toward those abnormals who escape the net of detection and abortion. A child with Down's syndrome or with hemophilia or with muscular dystrophy born at a time when most of his (potential) fellow sufferers were destroyed prenatally is liable to be looked upon by the community as one unfit to be alive, as a second-class (or even lower) human type. He may be seen as a person who need not have been, and who would not have been, if only someone had gotten to him in time.

The parents of such children are also likely to treat them differently, especially if the mother would have wished but failed to get an amniocentesis because of ignorance, poverty, or distance from the testing station, or if the prenatal diagnosis was in error. In such cases, parents are especially likely to resent the child. They may be disinclined to give it the kind of care they might have before the advent of amniocentesis and genetic abortion, rationalizing that a second-class specimen is not entitled to first-class treatment. If pressed to do so, say by physicians, the parents might refuse, and the courts may become involved. This has already begun to happen.

In Maryland, parents of a child with Down's syndrome refused permission to have the child operated on for an intestinal obstruction present at birth. The physicians and the hospital sought an injunction to require the parents to allow surgery. The judge ruled in favor of the parents, despite what I understand to be the weight of precedent to the contrary, on the grounds that the child was Mongoloid; that is, had the child been "normal," the decision would have gone the other way. Although the decision was not appealed to and hence not affirmed by a higher court, we can see through the prism of this case the possibility that the new powers of human genetics will strip the blindfold from the lady of justice and will make official the dangerous doctrine that some men are more equal than others.

The abnormal child may also feel resentful. A child with Down's syndrome or Tay–Sachs disease will probably never know or care, but what about the child with hemophilia or with Turner's syndrome? In the past decade, with medical knowledge and power over the prenatal child increasing and with parental authority over the postnatal child decreasing, we have seen the appearance of a new type of legal action, suits for wrongful life. Children have brought suit against their parents (and others) seeking to recover damages for physical and social handicaps inextricably tied to their birth (e.g., congenital deformities, congenital syphilis, illegitimacy). In some of the American cases, the courts have recognized the justice of the child's claim (that he was injured due to parental negligence), although they have so far refused to award damages, due to policy considerations. In other countries, e.g., in Germany, judgments with compensation have gone for the plaintiffs. With the spread of amniocentesis and genetic abortion, we can only expect such cases to increase. And here it will be the soft-hearted rather than the hard-hearted judges who will establish the doctrine of second-class human beings, out of compassion for the mutants who escaped the traps set out for them.

It may be argued that I am dealing with a problem which, even if it is real, will affect very few people. It may be suggested that very few will escape the traps once we have set them properly and widely, once people are informed about amniocentesis, once the power to detect prenatally grows to its full capacity, and once our "superstitious" opposition to abortion dies out or is extirpated. But in order even to come close to this vision of success, amniocentesis will have to become part of every pregnancy—either by making it mandatory, like the test for syphilis, or by making it "routine medical practice," like the Pap smear. Leaving aside the other problems with universal amniocentesis, we would expect that the problem for the few who escape is likely to be even worse precisely because they will be few.

The point, however, should be generalized. How will we come to view and act toward the many "abnormals" that will remain among us—the retarded, the crippled, the senile, the deformed, and the true mutants—once we embark on a program to root out genetic abnormality? For it must be remembered that we shall always have abnormals—some who escape detection or whose disease is undetectable *in utero*, others a result of new mutations, birth injuries, accidents, maltreatment, or disease—who will require our care and protection. The existence of "defectives" cannot be fully prevented, not even by totalitarian breeding and weeding programs. Is it not likely that our principle with respect to these people will change from "We try harder" to "Why accept second best?" The idea of "the unwanted because abnormal child" may become a self-fulfilling prophecy, whose consequences may be worse than those of the abnormality itself.

## Genetic and Other Defectives

The mention of other abnormals points to a second danger of the practice of genetic abortion. Genetic abortion may come to be seen not so much as the prevention of genetic disease, but as the prevention of birth of defective or abnormal children—and, in a way, understandably so. For in the case of what other diseases does preventive medicine consist in the elimination of the patient-at-risk? Moreover, the very language used to discuss genetic disease leads us to the easy but wrong conclusion that the afflicted fetus or person is rather than has a disease. True, one is partly defined by his genotype, but only partly. A person is more than his disease. And yet we slide easily from the language of possession to the language of identity, from "He has hemophilia" to "He is a hemophiliac," from "She has diabetes" through "She is diabetic" to "She is a diabetic," from "The fetus has Down's syndrome" to "The fetus is a Down's." This way of speaking supports the belief that it is defective persons (or potential persons) that are being eliminated, rather than diseases.

If this is so, then it becomes simply accidental that the defect has a genetic cause. Surely, it is only because of the high regard for medicine and science, and for the accuracy of genetic diagnosis, that genotypic defectives are likely to be the first to go. But once the principle, "Defectives should not be born," is established, grounds other than cytological and biochemical may very well be sought. Even ignoring racialists and others equally misguided—of course, they cannot be ignored—we should know that there are social scientists, for example, who believe that one can predict with a high degree of accuracy how a child will turn out from a careful, systematic study of the socio-economic and psycho-dynamic environment into which he is born and in which he grows up. They might press for the prevention of socio-psychological disease, even of "criminality," by means of prenatal environmental diagnosis and abortion. I have heard a rumor that a crude, unscientific form of eliminating potential "phenotypic defectives" is already being practiced in some cities, in that submission to abortion is allegedly being made a condition for the receipt of welfare payments. "Defectives should not be born" is a principle without limits. We can ill-afford to have it established.

Up to this point, I have been discussing the possible implications of the practice of genetic abortion for our belief in and adherence to the idea that, at least in fundamental human matters such as life and liberty, all men are to be considered as equals, that for these matters we should ignore as irrelevant the real qualitative differences amongst men, however important these differences may be for other purposes. Those who are concerned about abortion fear that the permissible time of eliminating the unwanted will be moved forward along the time continuum, against newborns, infants, and children. Similarly, I suggest that we should be concerned lest the attack on gross genetic inequality in fetuses be advanced along the continuum of quality and into the later stages of life.

I am not engaged in predicting the future; I am not saying that amniocentesis and genetic abortion will lead down the road to Nazi Germany. Rather, I am suggesting that the principles underlying genetic abortion simultaneously justify many further steps down that road. . . .

Perhaps I have exaggerated the dangers; perhaps we will not abandon our inexplicable preference for generous humanitarianism over consistency. But we should indeed be cautious and move slowly as we give serious consideration to the question "What price the perfect baby?"

## Standards for Justifying Genetic Abortion

. . . According to what standards can and should we judge a fetus with genetic abnormalities unfit to live, i.e., abortable? It seems to me that there are at least three dominant standards to which we are likely to repair.

The first is societal good. The needs and interest of society are often invoked to justify the practices of prenatal diagnosis and abortion of the genetically abnormal. The argument, full blown, runs something like this. Society has an interest in the genetic fitness of its members. It is foolish for society to squander its precious resources ministering to and caring for the unfit, especially for those who will never become "productive," or who will never in any way "benefit" society. Therefore, the interests of society are best served by the elimination of the genetically defective prior to their birth.

The societal standard is all-too-often reduced to its lowest common denominator: money. Thus one physician, claiming that he has "made a cost–benefit analysis of Tay–Sachs disease," notes that "the total cost of carrier detection, prenatal diagnosis and termination of at-risk pregnancies for all Jewish individuals in the United States under 30 who will marry is $5,730,281. If the program is set up to screen only one married partner, the cost is $3,122,695. The hospital costs for the 990 cases of Tay–Sachs disease in these individuals would produce over a thirty-year period in the United States is $34,650,000." Another physician, apparently less interested or able to make such a precise audit has written: "Cost–benefit analyses have been made for the total prospective detection and monitoring of Tay–Sachs disease, cystic fibrosis (when prenatal detection becomes available for cystic fibrosis) and other disorders, and in most cases, the expenditures for hospitalization and medical care far exceed the cost of prenatal detection in properly selected risk populations, followed by selective abortion." Yet a third physician has calculated that the costs to the state of caring for children with Down's syndrome is more than three times that of detecting and aborting them. (These authors all acknowledge the additional non-societal "costs" of personal suffering, but insofar as they consider society, the costs are purely economic.)

There are many questions that can be raised about this approach. First, there are questions about the accuracy of the calculations. Not all the costs have been reckoned. The aborted defective child will be "re-placed" by a "normal" child. In keeping the ledger, the "costs" to society of his care and maintenance cannot be ignored—costs of educating him, or removing his wastes and pollutions, not to mention the "costs" in non-replaceable natural resources he consumes. Who is the greater drain on society's precious resources, the average inmate of a home for the retarded or the aver-age graduate of Harvard College? I am not sure we know or can even find out. Then there are the costs of training the physicians and genetic counselors, equip-ping their laboratories, supporting their research, and sending them and us to conferences to worry about what they are doing. An accurate economic analysis seems to me to be impossible, even in principle. And even if it were possible, one could fall back on the words of that ordinary language philosopher, Andy Capp, who, when his wife said that she was getting re-ally worried about the cost of living, replied: "Sweet-'eart, name me one person who wants t'stop livin' on account of the cost."

A second defect of the economic analysis is that there are matters of social importance that are not re-ducible to financial costs, and others that may not be quantifiable at all. How does one quantitate the costs of real and potential social conflict, either between children and parents, or between the community and the "deviants" who refuse amniocentesis and continue to bear abnormal children? Can one measure the ef-fect on racial tensions of attempting to screen for and prevent the birth of children homozygous (or het-erozygous) for sickle cell anemia? What numbers does one attach to any decreased willingness or ability to take care of the less fortunate, or to cope with difficult problems? And what about the "costs" of rising expec-tations? Will we become increasingly dissatisfied with anything short of the "optimum baby"? How does one quantify anxiety? humiliation? guilt? Finally, might not the medical profession pay an unmeasurable price if genetic abortion and other revolutionary activities

bring about changes in medical ethics and medical practice that lead to the further erosion of trust in the physician?

An appeal to social worthiness or usefulness is a less vulgar form of the standard of societal good. It is true that great social contributions are unlikely to be forthcoming from persons who suffer from most seri-ous genetic diseases, especially since many of them die in childhood. Yet consider the following remarks of Pearl Buck (1968) on the subject of being a mother of a child retarded from phenylketonuria:

"My child's life has not been meaningless. She has in-deed brought comfort and practical help to many peo-ple who are parents of retarded children or are themselves handicapped. True, she has done it through me, yet without her I would not have had the means of learning how to accept the inevitable sor-row, and how to make that acceptance useful to oth-ers. Would I be so heartless as to say that it has been worthwhile for my child to be born retarded? Cer-tainly not, but I am saying that even though gravely retarded it has been worthwhile for her to have lived.

"It can be summed up, perhaps, by saying that in this world where cruelty prevails in so many aspects of our life, I would not add the weight of choice to kill rather than to let live. A retarded child, a handicapped person, brings its own gift to life, even to the life of normal human beings. That gift is comprehended in the lessons of patience, understanding, and mercy, lessons which we all need to receive and to practice with one another, whatever we are."

The standard of potential social worthiness is lit-tle better in deciding about abortion in particular cases than is the standard of economic cost. To drive the point home, each of us might consider retrospectively whether he would have been willing to stand trial for his life while a fetus, pleading only his worth to society as he now can evaluate it. How many of us are not so-cially "defective" and with none of the excuses possi-ble for a child with phenylketonuria? If there is to be human life at all, potential social worthiness cannot be its entitlement.

Finally, we should take note of the ambiguities in the very notion of societal good. Some use the term "society" to mean their own particular political com-munity, others to mean the whole human race, and still others speak as if they mean both simultaneously, following that all-too-human belief that what is good for me and mine is good for mankind. Who knows what is genetically best for mankind, even with respect to Down's syndrome? I would submit that the genetic heritage of the human species is largely in the care of persons who do not live along the amniocentesis frontier. If we in the industrialized West wish to be really serious about the genetic future of the species, we would concentrate our attack on mutagenesis, and especially on our large contribution to the pool of environmental mutagens.

But even the more narrow use of society is ambiguous. Do we mean our "society" as it is today? Or do we mean our "society" as it ought to be? If the former, our standards will be ephemeral, for ours is a faddish "society." (By far the most worrisome feature of the changing attitudes on abortion is the suddenness with which they changed.) Any such socially determined standards are likely to provide too precarious a foundation for decisions about genetic abortion, let alone for our notions of human rights. If we mean the latter, then we have transcended the societal standard, since the "good society" is not to be found in "society" itself, nor is it likely to be discovered by taking a vote. In sum, societal good as a standard for justifying genetic abortion seems to be unsatisfactory. It is hard to define in general, difficult to apply clearly to particular cases, susceptible to overreaching and abuse (hence, very dangerous), and not sufficient unto itself if considerations of the good community are held to be automatically implied.

A second major alternative is the standard of parental or familial good. Here the argument of justification might run as follows. Parents have a right to determine, according to their own wishes and based upon their own notions of what is good for them, the qualitative as well as the quantitative character of their families. If they believe that the birth of a seriously deformed child will be the cause of great sorrow and suffering to themselves and to their other children and a drain on their time and resources, then they may ethically decide to prevent the birth of such a child, even by abortion.

This argument I would expect to be more attractive to most people than the argument appealing to the good of society. For one thing, we are more likely to trust a person's conception of what is good for him than his notion of what is good for society. Also, the number of persons involved is small, making it seem less impossible to weigh all the relevant factors in determining the good of the family. Most powerfully, one can see and appreciate the possible harm done to healthy children if the parents are obliged to devote most of their energies to caring for the afflicted child.

Yet there are ambiguities and difficulties perhaps as great as with the standard of societal good. In first

place, it is not entirely clear what would be good for the other children. In a strong family, the experience with a suffering and dying child might help the healthy siblings learn to face and cope with adversity. Some have even speculated that the lack of experience with death and serious illness in our affluent young people is an important element in their difficulty in trying to find a way of life and in responding patiently yet steadily to the serious problems of our society (Cassell, 1969). I suspect that one cannot generalize. In some children and in some families, experience with suffering may be strengthening, and in others, disabling. My point here is that the matter is uncertain, and that parents deciding on this basis are as likely as not to be mistaken.

The family or parental standard, like the societal standard, is unavoidably elastic because "suffering" does not come in discontinuous units, and because parental wishes and desires know no limits. Both are utterly subjective, relative, and notoriously subject to change. Some parents claim that they could not tolerate having to raise a child of the undesired sex; I know of one case where the woman in the delivery room, on being informed that her child was a son, told the physician that she did not even wish to see it and that he should get rid of it. We may judge her attitude to be pathological, but even pathological suffering is suffering. Would such suffering justify aborting her normal male fetus?

Or take the converse case of two parents, who for their own very peculiar reasons, wish to have an abnormal child, say a child who will suffer from the same disease as grandfather or a child whose arrested development would preclude the threat of adolescent rebellion and separation. Are these acceptable grounds for the abortion of "normals"?

Granted, such cases will be rare. But they serve to show the dangers inherent in talking about the parental right to determine, according to their wishes, the quality of their children. Indeed, the whole idea of parental rights with respect to children strikes me as problematic. It suggests that children are like property, that they exist for the parents. One need only look around to see some of the results of this notion of parenthood. The language of duties to children would be more in keeping with the heavy responsibility we bear in affirming the continuity of life with life and in trying to transmit what wisdom we have acquired to the next generation. Our children are not our children. Hopefully, reflection on these matters could lead to a greater appreciation of why it is people do and should have children. No better consequence can be hoped for from the advent of amniocentesis and other technologies for controlling human reproduction.

If one speaks of familial good in terms of parental duty, one could argue that parents have an obligation to do what they can to ensure that their children are born healthy and sound. But this formulation transcends the limitation of parental wishes and desires. As in the case of the good society, the idea of "healthy and sound" requires an objective standard, a standard in reality. Hard as it may be to uncover it, this is what we are seeking. Nature as a standard is the third alternative.

The justification according to the natural standard might run like this. As a result of our knowledge of genetic diseases, we know that persons afflicted with certain diseases will never be capable of living the full life of a human being. Just as a no-necked giraffe could never live a giraffe's life, or a needle-less porcupine would not attain true "porcupine-hood," so a child or fetus with Tay–Sachs disease or Down's syndrome, for example, will never truly be human. They will never be able to care for themselves, nor have they even the potential for developing the distinctively human capacities for thought or self-consciousness. Nature herself has aborted many similar cases, and has provided for the early death of many who happen to get born. There is no reason to keep them alive; instead, we should prevent their birth by contraception or sterilization if possible, and abortion if necessary.

The advantages of this approach are clear. The standards are objective and in the fetus itself, thus avoiding the relativity and ambiguity in societal and parental good. The standard can be easily generalized to cover all such cases and will be resistant to the shifting sands of public opinion.

This standard, I would suggest, is the one which most physicians and genetic counselors appeal to in their heart of hearts, no matter what they say or do about letting the parents choose. Why else would they have developed genetic counseling and amniocentesis? Indeed, the notions of disease, of abnormal, of defective, make no sense at all in the absence of a natural norm of health. This norm is the foundation of the art of the physician and of the inquiry of the health scientist. Yet, as Motulsky and others [1971] . . . have pointed out, the standard is elusive. Ironically, we are gaining increasing power to manipulate and control our own nature at a time in which we are increasingly confused about what is normal, healthy, and fit.

Although possibly acceptable in principle, the natural standard runs into problems in application when attempts are made to fix the boundary between potentially human and potentially not human. Professor Lejeune (1970) has clearly demonstrated the difficulty, if not the impossibility, of setting clear molecular, cytological, or developmental signposts for this boundary. Attempts to induce signposts by considering the phenotypes of the worst cases is equally difficult. Which features would we take to be the most relevant in, say, Tay–Sachs disease, Lesch–Nyhan syndrome, Cri du chat, Down's syndrome? Certainly, severe mental retardation. But how "severe" is "severe"? As . . . I argued earlier, mental retardation admits of degree. It too is relative. Moreover it is not clear that certain other defects and deformities might not equally foreclose the possibility of a truly or fully human life. What about blindness or deafness? Quadriplegia? Aphasia? Several of these in combination? Not only does each kind of defect admit of a continuous scale of severity, but it also merges with other defects on a continuous scale of defectiveness. Where on this scale is the line to drawn after mental retardation? blindness? muscular dystrophy? cystic fibrosis? hemophilia? diabetes? galactosemia? Turner's syndrome? XYY? club foot? Moreover, the identical two continuous scales—kind and severity—are found also among the living. In fact, it is the natural standard which may be the most dangerous one in that it leads most directly to the idea that there are second-class human beings and sub-human human beings.

But the story is not complete. The very idea of nature is ambiguous. According to one view, the one I have been using, nature points to or implies a peak, a perfection. According to this view, human rights depend upon attaining the status of humanness. The fetus is only potential; it has no rights, according to this view. But all kinds of people fall short of the norm: children, idiots, some adults. This understanding of nature has been used to justify not only abortion and infanticide, but also slavery.

There is another notion of nature, less splendid, more humane and, though less able to sustain a notion of health, more acceptable to the findings of modern science. Animal nature is characterized by impulses of self-preservation and by the capacity to feel pleasure and to suffer pain. Man and other animals are alike on this understanding of nature. And the right to life is ascribed to all such self-preserving and suffering creatures. Yet on this understanding of nature, the fetus—even a defective fetus—is not potential, but actual. The right to life belongs to him. But for this reason, this understanding of nature does not provide and may even deny what it is we are seeking, namely a justification for genetic abortion, adequate unto itself, which does not simultaneously justify infanticide, homicide, and enslavement of the genetically abnormal.

There is a third understanding of nature, akin to the second, nature as sacrosanct, nature as created by a Creator. Indeed, to speak about this reminds us that there is a fourth possible standard for judgments about genetic abortion: the religious standard. I shall leave the discussion of this standard to those who are able to speak of it in better faith.

Now that I am at the end, the reader can better share my sense of frustration. I have failed to provide myself with a satisfactory intellectual and moral justification for the practice of genetic abortion. Perhaps others more able than I can supply one. Perhaps the pragmatists can persuade me that we should abandon the search for principled justification, that if we just trust people's situational decisions or their gut reactions, everything will turn out fine. Maybe they are right. But we should not target the sage observation of Bertrand Russell: "pragmatism is like a warm bath that heats up so imperceptibly that you don't know when to scream." I would add that before we submerge ourselves irrevocably in amniotic fluid, we take note of the connection to our own baths, into which we have started the hot water running.

### References

Buck, P. S. (1968). Foreword to *The Terrible Choice: The Abortion Dilemma.* New York: Bantam Books, pp. ix–xi.

Cassell, E. (1969). "Death and the Physician," *Commentary* (June), pp. 73–79.

Lejeune, J. (1970). *American Journal of Human Genetics,* 22, p. 121.

Lincoln, A. (1854). In *The Collected Works of Abraham Lincoln,* R. P. Basler, editor. New Brunswick, N.J.: Rutgers University Press, Vol. II, p. 222.

Motulsky, A. G., G. R. Fraser, and J. Felsenstein (1971). In Symposium on Intrauterine Diagnosis, D. Bergsma, editor. *Birth Defects: Original Article Series,* Vol. 7, No. 5.

Neel, J. (1972). In *Early Diagnosis of Human Genetic Defects: Scientific and Ethical Considerations,* M. Harris, editor. Washington, D.C.: U.S. Government Printing Office, pp. 366–380.

### READINGS

# Section 5: Gene Therapy

## Germ-Line Therapy and the Medical Imperative

### Ronald Munson and Lawrence H. Davis

Ronald Munson and Lawrence Davis point out that although germ-line gene therapy has the potential to eliminate hundreds of genetic diseases, critics claim that it is morally unacceptable. The authors examine three objections: (1) Germ-line therapy violates the rights of future persons to an unaltered genetic inheritance; (2) eliminating or adding genetic traits will produce conflicts between individuals and society and exacerbate social and economic inequalities; (3) tampering with the basic structure of humans is "playing God" and may produce results we are not competent to predict or control.

Munson and Davis maintain that none of the objections justifies prohibiting germ-line gene therapy. Moreover, they argue that medicine has a "therapeutic imperative" that imposes on it a prima facie obligation to pursue therapies that promise to promote human health effectively. Because germ-line gene therapy holds such a promise, medicine has a prima facie obligation to pursue it.

. . . Gene therapy refers to the use of recombinant DNA techniques to treat diseases involving missing or impaired genes. It is still in the experimental stages with only a handful of patients at the National Institutes of Health currently undergoing the therapy. Within this decade, however, two types of gene therapy—gene augmentation and gene modification—are likely to become established modes of treatment (see Verma 1990). Gene augmentation, in which a normal copy of a gene is inserted into a cell to direct the synthesis of a protein that would normally be produced by the missing or defective gene, is the only approach so far attempted in humans. Gene modification, in which an impaired gene is corrected by splicing in a gene at a specific location in the cellular DNA but not otherwise altering the cell's genome, has been demonstrated in several mammalian species. Gene surgery, which involves excising an impaired gene and replacing it with a normal copy, remains a distant—although real—possibility.

Although even the experimental use of gene therapy is recent, its possibilities have been discussed extensively for more than a decade, and critics have raised a number of objections to it or some aspects of it (President's Commission 1982; OTA 1984; Nichols 1988; Walters 1991). NIH committees overseeing the research and many other observers now approve of somatic cell therapy as long as safeguards needed in any experimental procedure are followed and protocols pass appropriate review. No similar consensus has been reached, however, regarding the application of gene therapy to cells in the germ line—ova, sperm, and cells that give rise to them. This is partly because of the enormous technical difficulties facing germ-line gene therapy. But it is also because germ-line gene therapy strikes many as involving especially difficult moral issues. In this paper we examine the most important of these. We argue that none presents an insurmountable moral obstacle to germ-line gene therapy. To the contrary, we will argue that medicine has a positive duty to proceed with its development.

## The Limits and Possibilities of Somatic Cell and Germ-Line Therapy

Gene therapy is likely to have the most impact in treating diseases caused by single gene defects, especially autosomal recessive disorders (Nichols 1988;

From the *Kennedy Institute of Ethics Journal*, Vol. 2, no. 2, 137–158, June 1992. Reprinted by permission.

Anderson 1990; Holtzman 1989). This accounts for many conditions, including sickle-cell disease, Tay–Sachs disease, phenylketonuria, and cystic fibrosis. The hundreds of diseases caused by chromosomal disorders (e.g., Down Syndrome) or by an interaction between genes and the environment during fetal development (e.g., neural tube defects) are not obvious prospects. But the estimated 4,000 monogenic diseases cause 7 percent of neonatal deaths, affect 1 percent of newborns, and are responsible for almost 10 percent of childhood deaths. About half of these diseases cause early death, and almost three-quarters of the rest produce severe impairments that make ordinary life virtually impossible (Nichols 1988, p. 9).

The thrust of efforts to find ways to treat these diseases so far has involved somatic cell therapy. Hence, even if the therapy can treat or eliminate a disease from an individual who has inherited a faulty gene, it will do nothing to alter the probability that the person's offspring will inherit the same defective gene. For example, someone with Huntington's disease has a 50–50 chance of passing on the gene causing the disease. Even if somatic cell therapy could eliminate the way the gene is expressed, the 50–50 chance of passing it on would remain.

Alteration of germ-line cells might change this. For dominant conditions, the aim would be to remove the defective gene from a person's gametes (ova or sperm cells) or their precursors, and replace it with one that would function normally. For recessive conditions, it might suffice to insert a gene that would function normally. Or instead of this "gametocyte therapy," the cells of an already-conceived pre-embryo might be similarly treated ("pre-embryo transformation"). Success of either of these forms of germ-line gene therapy would mean that neither the individuals resulting from treated gametes or pre-embryo, nor their progeny, would inherit the disorder (Fowler et al. 1989).

If germ-line gene therapy were possible, practical, and widely employed, hundreds of genetic diseases might be eliminated from families. In each case, it would be possible for the disease to occur again through mutation, but the risk would be no greater than in the population at large, and the total number of cases needing somatic cell or other therapy would be greatly reduced. Horrible diseases like Lesch–Nyhan, PKU, and Tay–Sachs would simply disappear as a nightmarish heritage in certain family lines. . . . We would reach the goal described over a decade ago by Joseph Fletcher:

The ultimate goal of [gene therapy] is not to ameliorate the ills of patients prenatally or postnatally, but to start people off healthy and free of disease through the practice of medicine preconceptively. . . . It aims to control people's initial genetic design and constitution—their genotypes—by gene surgery and by genetic design. (1974, p. 56)

## Moral Objections to Germ-Line Gene Therapy

Against Fletcher's vision, some argue that there is a morally relevant distinction between somatic and germ-line therapy, and that germ-line therapy is a morally unacceptable means of achieving the goal of eradicating genetic disease.

But what wrong can be alleged about germ-line therapy? Its distinguishing feature is its impact on future generations. (In some cases, somatic cell therapy can also have an effect on future generations, but this is not the aim of the treatment—see Lappé 1991, pp. 623f., 627, 629f.) Somehow, this feature has led to a widespread feeling that the procedure is morally questionable. However, the moral doubts are often only hinted at in a rhetorical fashion and are not carefully articulated. Part of what we want to do here is to state those doubts as clearly and persuasively as we can so that we can lay them to rest definitively.

We think all the doubts about germ-line therapy express the single basic worry that it is illegitimate "tampering." The three lines of objection that have played important roles in the public debate see this as tampering with the rights of individuals, with the social order, and with the order of nature itself. We will present and examine each of these in turn, emphasizing the third. In no case will we find an insurmountable moral barrier to the development and use of germ-line therapy.

### 1. Germ-Line Therapy and Individual Rights

The Parliamentary Assembly of the Council of Europe (1982b) refers to a person's right to a genome that has not been "tampered" with:

[The Assembly r]ecommends that the Committee of Ministers: . . . provide for explicit recognition in the European Convention on Human Rights of the right to a genetic inheritance which has not been artificially interfered with, except in accordance with certain principles which are recognized as being fully compatible with respect for human rights (as, for example, in the field of therapeutic applications) . . .

The basis for this alleged right is none too clear, even if we do not question (as many would) the very idea of a right possessed by as-yet-unconceived individuals. Prior to the passage quoted, the recommendation invokes the "rights to life and to human dignity protected by Articles 2 and 3 of the European Convention on Human Rights," and claims that these "imply" the right to a pristine genetic inheritance. We fail to see the "implication." For philosophers like Kant, human dignity is equated with our dignity as rational beings, and not with the whole of our biological nature as homo sapiens. Thus as rational beings, we are ends in ourselves, and have a right not to be treated as mere means to the ends of others (Kant [1785] 1959, p. 47). This may entail that others ought not to interfere (unjustifiably) with our pursuit of our own legitimate ends. It does not entail that others ought not to have interfered with our chances to have been conceived, say, with genes for hazel eye color. . . .

Another possible basis mentioned by Mauron and Thévoz (1991) is Hans Jonas's view that we have "an ontological responsibility toward the preservation of the 'image of man.'" We reject this view, although we cannot discuss it here. We conclude then that the alleged right to an untouched genome has no basis and in fact there is no such right. . . .

Less dramatically, germ-line therapy involves "tampering" with a person's body, so it may easily infringe on several genuine and important individual rights. Yet all forms of gene therapy—indeed, all forms of therapy—can be viewed as doing this. For example, procedures like coronary-artery bypass surgery could violate a person's autonomy and right not to be subjected to harm or to the risk of harm. We offer protection against such violation and legitimate the "tampering" by requiring the individual's "informed consent." Perhaps this would suffice for germ-line therapy as well.

A critic might object that this is a bad analogy because germ-line therapy can affect the descendants of the recipient, too. As many writers have emphasized, this feature makes it impossible to secure the informed consent of all the individuals affected (see, for example, Fletcher 1983; Lappé 1991).

This is undeniably true. However we are aware of no persuasive reasons for thinking that non-existent potential progeny or members of future generations have (as yet) any autonomy that could be tampered with. So there is nothing to protect by requiring their "informed consent." Thus, we see no point in lamenting the impossibility of our obtaining it.

We are less certain about whether those in this group of potential offspring and descendants have the right not to be harmed or subjected to risk of harm. But we are certain that insofar as they have such rights—or, more simply, insofar as we are obligated not to subject them to harm or (extra) risk of harm—neither the rights nor the obligations are absolute.

Some may claim that even if these rights and obligations are not absolute, they still are strong enough so that in practice, germ-line gene therapy would rarely if ever be permissible. This seems implied by the "Declaration of Inuyama" adopted by the Council for International Organizations of Medical Sciences (CIOMS 1991): "There would have to be confidence that, when treatment affecting future generations is undertaken, descendants of those so treated would still agree with the decision generations later."

Similarly, Berger and Gert (1991, p. 679) would limit germ-line therapy to "cases in which the benefits to the person receiving the initial treatment is [sic] so great that it outweighs the risks not only for him but also for all of his descendants" since "the genetic make-up of an unlimited number of people" is affected. We cannot confidently predict what the conditions of life or people's values will be generations from now, so we cannot confidently predict our remote descendants' agreement with our decisions, nor can we judge precisely about benefits and risks to infinitely many of our descendants, so germ-line gene therapy would rarely if ever meet the requirements set by these statements.

But these statements are too strong. The first seems unduly influenced by the idea of informed consent, which we have already argued is irrelevant in this context. And the second views our actions as more momentous than they probably are. We should bear in mind that a remote future generation may be able to reverse a genetic change we introduce that turns out disadvantageous (Moseley 1991, p. 644). And as several authors have pointed out, we regularly make decisions that we know will affect future generations—including the very decision to have children—without acknowledging requirements as strong as these (Moseley 1991, pp. 642ff.; Lappé 1991, p. 631; and cf. Zimmerman 1991, p. 597). It is implausible that this practice is wrong, even if we have not been as responsible as we should be in our actions (including reproduction) affecting future generations. . . . Whatever exactly the rights of offspring and descendants, the promise of good enough consequences—say, the eradication of Lesch–Nyhan disease—could outweigh

a sufficiently uncertain threat of harm and justify "tampering" with those rights.

If germ-line therapy involves illegitimate tampering, it is not illegitimate tampering with the rights of those directly affected or their descendants.

### 2. Germ-Line Therapy and Conflicts of Interest

H. J. J. Leenen (1988, p. 79) has pointed out another area of concern. The introduction of germ-line therapy as an option could lead to clashes between parental autonomy and the interests of present society or groups within society. For example, suppose a woman refused to agree to a demand by society or an insurance company that to become a parent she must have germ-line therapy to prevent her offspring from inheriting her gene for Huntington's disease. Should she be forced to submit?

Fletcher and Anderson (1992) ask about clashes of a different sort: "Can genetic diagnosis and therapy be equitably distributed, so as not primarily to benefit elites? Will germ-line therapy invest too-radical power in the hands of few?" Similarly, Zimmerman (1991, pp. 606–7) cites fears that germ-line therapy will lead to the development of nontherapeutic "enhancement" procedures, so that parents having the means will use it to guarantee themselves above-average children: "[T]he distribution of desirable biological traits among different socioeconomic and ethnic groups would become badly skewed, resulting de facto in exacerbated social and economic inequality" (Zimmerman 1991, p. 607; see also Anderson 1989).

Concerns like these suggest that germ-line therapy threatens to open a Pandora's box of new moral conflicts and dilemmas, and therefore some people would avoid it. Even making it available, would be a kind of "tampering" with the social order. But the problems are no different in kind from conflicts and dilemmas we already face. For example, should we require those with Huntington's disease in their family history to be tested for the gene and allow them to reproduce only when the result is negative (Purdy 1988)? Or, to take a different kind of case, should we legally require a pregnant woman to act in ways that will not subject the fetus to greater than normal risks? Doing so would mean, at the least, that she should not smoke, consume alcohol, or use nonprescribed drugs (Mathieu 1991), and might also mean she should eat a proper diet and exercise regularly.

The examples could be multiplied, but these two are enough to show that Pandora's box is already open. Similarly, we should remember that problems of fair distribution of scarce resources are hardly unprecedented. We already have the kind of social and moral difficulties in our society to which germ-line therapy would give rise. Introduction of the therapy, then, would not be an illegitimate "tampering" with the social order.

### 3. Germ-Line Therapy as "Playing God"

The novel feature of germ-line therapy is that by it we modify the very genetic structure that as-yet-unconceived individuals are to have. This seems both more serious and potentially more sinister than any other medical therapies or public health measures. An individual's genetic structure, after all, determines the kind of being an individual will be, apart from and prior to the influence of both the biological and social environment. It determines whether the creature that develops is a bird or a beaver, a horse or a human. Hence, changing the genetic makeup of germ cells is tampering with the very order of nature. In the popular phrase, it is "playing God."

As rhetorically effective as this phrase may be in encouraging a negative attitude toward germ-line therapy, it is not at all clear just what is wrong with "playing God" in this particular way. Three attempts to explain are worth considering. (See also the President's Commission's 1982 report, *Splicing Life*, pp. 53–60.)

**a. Germ-Line Therapy as a Prelude to Eugenics.** Some argue that what begins as genetic "tampering" aimed at obliterating disease will lead to positive eugenics—"tampering" aimed at improving our children and the whole of humanity. As our understanding of the genetic basis of socially desirable traits like musical talent, mathematical insight, and athletic skill increases, we will be able to engineer human beings to meet our specifications. But trying to do this would be wrong (apart from the questions of fair distribution already mentioned) because, as Paul Ramsey (1970, p. 124) puts it, "Man [is not] wise enough to make himself a successful self-modifying system or wise enough to begin doctoring the species." (See also Anderson 1989.)

At least two problems weaken the force of this objection. First, the objection is only to genetic modification in the service of positive eugenics. Even if Ramsey is right about our lacking the wisdom to turn ourselves into a "self-modifying system," it does not follow that there is anything intrinsically wrong with employing germ-line therapy to eliminate diseases.

And as for the worry that negative eugenics will lead to positive eugenics, we may note that the potential for practicing positive eugenics has been with us at least since the time we recognized that there is a connection between the traits of offspring and those of their parents. We have resisted virtually all efforts and proposals to make use of selective breeding to shape the human species to satisfy an articulated ideal (Ludmerer 1972). Perhaps our experience with attempts at eugenics fits the description that Mauron and Thévoz give of the whole history of bioethical issues:

> [T]he slippery slope really looks more like a ramshackle staircase: once in a while, we trip down a few steps. This makes us wake up, take stock of ethical shortcomings and climb up the stairs by appropriate measures such as societal regulation. (1991, p. 658)

While it is true that germ-line engineering offers an easier and more effective way to exert control over the human gene pool, we have no reason to suppose that just because we possessed the technology we would employ it. It is simply not true that as a society we have always done whatever it is possible to do. . . .

. . . Our second problem for Ramsey, then, is that it is not obvious that we lack the wisdom to "doctor" ourselves in the manner indicated. In truth, we do not know yet whether we have it or not. After we have had experience modifying the genome of other organisms and predicting the outcome, when we have learned the possible drawbacks and the chances of success in modifications performed on humans, then perhaps we can judge our wisdom. We can imagine ways of making ourselves better than we are now, but the unanswered questions concern how much and what kinds of risk we will be willing to take and what sort of price we will be willing to pay to improve ourselves. These questions cannot be answered usefully in a vacuum. (For other discussion of the acceptability of positive eugenics, see Mauron and Thévoz 1991, pp. 651–52.)

**b. Germ-Line Therapy and Unpredictable Losses.** Even if gene therapy remains confined to therapeutic applications, some raise the question "whether something important may be lost as disease genes are eliminated" (Cavalieri 1983, p. 473). On one interpretation, this worry is illustrated by the following sort of case. Suppose we are successful in eliminating sickle-cell disease from the human population by removing the disease causing gene and substituting a gene producing normal red blood cells. As it happens, those with sickle-cell trait (i.e., those who are heterozygous for the gene) are more resistant to falciparum malaria. Hence, if we eliminated the gene, we would also be eliminating potential benefits its possession bestows.

The objection takes it for granted that eliminating this potential benefit would be obviously wrong. Yet what it fails to consider is that, since we know about the connection between sickle-cell disease and resistance to malaria, we might decide that eliminating a lethal disease like sickle-cell is worth the loss of a relative immunity to malaria. This would be a reasonable decision, especially since we have effective ways of controlling and treating malaria, but lack adequate treatments for sickle-cell disease.

However, a critic might ask, "How many other connections might there be between diseases and important biological capacities that we don't even realize we have but would be lost forever if we rushed to eradicate the diseases by germ-line therapy?" It would be better not to "tamper" with something whose full significance we cannot hope to appreciate in advance.

Critics who invoke the hazard of an unforeseen disaster cannot be satisfied completely. No one can guarantee that an unexpected hazard might not result from germ-line gene therapy. However, we are not totally ignorant of the nature of genes and of the evolutionary process, and there is no reason to fear that germ-line therapy is more likely to produce an unanticipated disaster than is somatic cell therapy or any other use of recombinant DNA technology. These matters must be assessed in individual cases on the basis of acquired knowledge and experience. When the potential benefits of germ-line therapy are considered, rejecting its use on the basis of potential but unknown hazards is not justifiable.

### c. Germ-Line Therapy as Threatening "Humanity."

The previous question about "whether something important may be lost" by the use of germ-line therapy refers to specific biological capacities. However, the question may be understood as having to do with the impossible-to-specify cluster of capacities and features that make us human. Thus, germ-line therapy might be said to be wrong because "tampering" with our humanity is wrong.

As we observed in our discussion of eugenics, germ-line gene therapy is unlikely to compromise the humanity of its products. "Humanity" may be understood just as membership in our biological species, or it may be interpreted as something more subtle, perhaps as our distinctive kind of consciousness or capacities to think and feel. Either way, it is unreasonable to think that the possession of the defective genes that would be eliminated by germ-line therapy—or the absence of genes that would be added—is essential to being human.

Even straightforward examples of nontherapeutic enhancement would not endanger the humanity of its products (cf. Anderson 1989, p. 685). By operating on a person's gametocytes so that her or his descendants would be prone to low cholesterol levels or unusual musical talent, we would not render these descendants nonhuman. Even if such a procedure tended to have genetic effects beyond those specifically planned and desired this would not alter matters. After all, mutations have been occurring throughout human history without compromising the humanity of those in whom they occurred. The human species, like any other, is not a fixed Platonic idea, but an ever-changing population of genes.

Nonetheless, the human species might change. First, it is possible that over many generations genetic changes, some introduced by gene therapy and some occurring by mutation, might accumulate in the gene pool of the human population. Alone, each change might be relatively unimportant, yet the total impact might be that the population embodying these changes is no longer human. In biological terms, phyletic evolution would have occurred. A second possibility is that genetic intervention, by accident or design, might produce immediate and wholesale changes in the progeny of some individuals.

Leon Kass evidently has the first possibility in mind:

> It may . . . mark the end of *human* life as we and all other humans have known it. It is possible that the non-human life which may take our place will be superior, but I think it most unlikely and certainly not demonstrable. In either case, we are ourselves human beings; therefore, we have a proprietary interest in our survival, and our survival *as human beings*. (1972, p. 61)

We can call this the homo superior objection to germ-line gene therapy.

H. J. J. Leenen is concerned with a variant of the second possibility, which we can call the cyborg objection:

> In my opinion . . . the science of genetics with human cells has to remain within human boundaries. . . . the creation of animal–human creatures and of plant–human combinations is inadmissible. This is not to say that the same holds for hybrids, which cannot develop. When scientists transgress the boundaries of

what is human, they place themselves outside human society. (1988, p. 75)

Each of these authors views the production of nonhumans from humans with evident dismay. What is striking in these passages is that neither gives a cogent explanation why he feels this way, or why the feeling is justified.

Leenen perhaps is thinking of cyborgs, the monsters of ancient mythology or modern science fiction. Bringing such creatures into existence would be a great evil—to others, to the unhappy creatures themselves, or to both. But that is because these creatures are depicted as subhuman, and/or active enemies of humans. If animal– or plant–human combinations remain favorably disposed toward their human ancestors, why should the scientists who originally produce them be considered "outside human society"? (cf. President's Commission (1982, pp. 57–60), which also considers "hybrids," and assumes they would be inferior to us). Suppose for example that through genetic modification our offspring and their descendants were equipped with chlorophyll-bearing patches on their skin and the capacity for photosynthesis. The resulting partial or complete independence of the usual food chain might be a good thing on the whole, even if we had to classify them all as nonhuman.

Kass's position is that even if our nonhuman descendants are superior to us, their existence would be contrary to our "proprietary interest" in our "survival as human beings." He claims the existence of this interest is a consequence simply of the fact that we are human. But this claim is a blatant non sequitur. From the fact that we are human, it does not follow that we have an interest in our survival as humans, nor that we have any interest in survival at all. Compare: we (the authors) are Missourians and Americans. We have some interest in our survival as Americans, but none to speak of in our survival as Missourians. Of course Kass is speaking of collective survival. But we have no strong feeling about the survival of Missouri, nor of our descendants (or anyone else's) as Missourians. We do care about the survival of the United States, but we could accept its replacement by something "superior," to use Kass's term. By the same token, we would accept our descendants being citizens of this replacement.

In short, for Kass's argument to work, he needs a premise articulating just what it is about being human that he thinks gives us all a "proprietary interest" in survival as such. This he has conspicuously failed to supply.

Perhaps the thought underlying the objections of Kass, Leenen, and others to tampering with our humanity is something like this. We are Americans and Missourians contingently but humans necessarily. To have a sense of self-worth, then, we need to feel that being human is a good thing to be, that a life lived within the limits of what is humanly possible is [potentially] a good kind of life to lead. There may be "superior" things actual or possible, but there is nothing unsatisfactory about being human. If our offspring will ultimately be nonhuman, then something of value which we exemplify will cease to be. If we choose to bring it about that our offspring are nonhuman, then we seem to be rendering a final negative judgment on our humanity. Tampering with the genetic structure that makes us human is wrong, then, because it conflicts with our sense of our own value.

In reply to this argument, it may be denied that a sense of self-worth requires such an attitude toward one's humanity. Nonetheless such attitudes are common, and may often play the role described. One further example may be the view of Hans Ruh as presented by Mauron and Thévoz (1991, p. 656), "that we ought to transmit to future generations . . . the capability to live a genuinely human life (with its ups and downs)." What is wrong with transmitting the capability to live a superior kind of life, with more "ups" and fewer "downs"?

We concede that people like Leenen and Kass, on our analysis of their position, do have a legitimate concern. But we insist that this attachment to our humanity cannot be adequate grounds for opposition to germ-line gene therapy. First, both of the scenarios described whereby nonhumans would result from the procedure are exceedingly remote. Especially if applications of the techniques are limited to the therapeutic for the foreseeable future, the "end of human life as we know it" that worries Kass could not be a serious threat for thousands of years, if ever (cf. OTA 1984, p. 32). Nor is there any reason to think a clearly nonhuman being could or would be produced deliberately by even the most enthusiastic advocates of positive eugenics. The bare conceivability of these disasters surely does not warrant refusing to develop the techniques for eliminating genetic diseases. Second, if we imagine future circumstances in which the end of humanity because of these techniques was an immediate threat, we might find that alternatives were worse. Being remembered by whatever nonhumans succeed us may be better than simple extinction without a trace. In any case, this sort of concern need affect our values and present day practical reasoning no more than speculation about the ultimate "cosmic crunch" or heat death of the universe.

This completes our examination of reasons for thinking it wrong to tamper with our genetic structure by performing germ-line gene therapy. We have found no cogent objection. The claim that "we are not wise enough" is at best premature. The worry that something of great value depends on the genes that we would remove is without foundation. The concern that germ-line gene therapy, or nontherapeutic use of the techniques employed in it, may pose a threat to our humanity or our feelings about our humanity, cannot be taken seriously as offsetting the value of eliminating genetic diseases.

In sum, all three objections are open to the same counterobjection: It may be wrong for us not to tamper with our genetic structure. Faced with the reality of genetic diseases, how can we justify not developing and employing a promising remedy? Are we wise enough to see a compelling reason for not doing so? Can we be sure that we will never face even worse dangers, against which skill in manipulating genes in germ-line cells would be our only protection? Conceivably, a day might come when our very survival as humans would depend on our ability to use complex techniques for which germ-line gene therapy is only the beginning. Why are the objections any more plausible than this counterobjection? (Mauron and Thévoz (1991, p. 660) point out that if we had foresworn recombinant DNA research since the Berg Moratorium, we would know less about AIDS today than we do; perhaps we would not even have been able to identify the HIV virus as the agent of AIDS.)

The objections take for granted that by tampering with our genetic natures, we are likely to cause more trouble than we prevent. What evidence supports this rather than its exact opposite? Occasionally, mention is made of the "wisdom of evolution" (see, for example, Cavalieri 1983, p. 472; President's Commission 1982, p. 62). But even if some "wisdom" can be found in the mechanism by which natural selection has left us susceptible to genetic diseases, it cannot be supposed that this "wisdom" is a reliable guide for us (cf. President's Commission 1982, pp. 62–63).

A more likely support for the objections is the common belief that our genetic nature is the design of a good and wise Being. His wisdom can be relied upon; if our design permits genetic diseases, there must be a good reason, which we cannot expect to

fathom. Moreover, common belief also suggests that He has a right and an interest in our survival as humans which would be violated if we engineered our eventual replacement by another species. On this analysis, all the objections reduce to the claim: Germline gene therapy is wrong because it is tampering with His handwork.

None of the objectors cited express themselves in these terms, and none would, not even the ones who share the belief in a good and wise Designer of humanity. The parallel to "If God wanted us to fly He would have given us wings" is too obvious and unanswerable. This sort of theological appeal cannot be correct, whether or not God exists. But we have seen that the objections as actually expressed do not work either. Germ-line gene therapy cannot be branded as illegitimate "tampering" with the order of nature.

## Medicine and the Therapeutic Imperative

We wish now to go beyond the moral legitimacy of this therapy and argue—still on the assumptions noted—that medicine itself has a prima facie duty to pursue and employ germ-line gene therapy. Sometimes, a certain course of action is morally right, although no one has an obligation to take it. For example, it would be right for physicians to work one day a month without fees in community clinics, but they have no moral duty to do so, either individually or collectively. However, in contrast, we want to claim that members of the medical professions would be collectively derelict if research aimed at the therapeutic use of germ-line gene therapy were neglected without good reason.

We should stress that our claim is only for the existence of a collective obligation, a duty falling on medicine as an enterprise. Very likely, if we are right and our assumptions are correct, then this collective obligation will entail some individual obligations on specific persons or groups of persons. But without a detailed examination of the structure, membership, and existing practices of the medical enterprise, these individual obligations cannot be determined. For a somewhat parallel example, suppose it were argued that the American people had a collective obligation to provide shelter for its homeless; exactly which members of the "American people" had precisely which specific obligations toward this end would be a matter for a wholly different argument, depending on the structure and existing practices of our governmental and other bodies, and many other factors. We shall not attempt this "wholly different argument" for the case of medicine, and so shall not say how the collective obligation differentially affects physicians, medical researchers, public health officials, and others affiliated with the medical enterprise. Our interest is rather in the prima facie duty itself, and its basis in the nature of medicine.

Many assume unreflectively that medicine is a science, and many also think that science is "value-neutral" in some sense. These views may lead one to conclude that "medicine" cannot have any duty at all, prima facie or actual. At most, individual physicians or researchers have obligations to heal or develop therapies because of general moral principles, such as beneficence. (The arguments of Zimmerman (1991, p. 591) and Fletcher and Anderson (1992) may be read this way.) We believe that medicine itself has an obligation.

We escape the reasoning of the preceding paragraph by denying that medicine is a science. (For a detailed defense of this position, see Munson 1981.) We begin our argument by contrasting medicine with science in the respect most relevant here, the idea of what it is most concerned with. . . .

Medicine, like science, pursues knowledge, but not in a disinterested way. Indeed, it is antithetical to the character of medicine as an enterprise to seek knowledge as an inherent or self-justifying good. Medicine's concern with knowledge is unequivocally instrumental or conditional. Medicine is joined so closely with science in inquiry and experiment, because it is by means of scientific understanding that medicine can most effectively secure its end of promoting human health.

Not all aspects of medicine involve the basic theories and concepts of the natural sciences. Clinical medicine, in particular, involves complicated human interactions, and part of the "art" of medicine involves "taking care" of patients without the guidance of established theories and proven rules. Nevertheless, science is one of contemporary medicine's major means of working to promote the welfare of patients as a population.

An enterprise is successful when it achieves its aims. Loosely speaking, science does its job when it provides persuasive reasons for accepting empirical theories about the nature and character of the world. The success of medicine cannot be judged by any comparable epistemic criterion. Rather, the basic standard of evaluation must be practical or instrumental success with respect to its specific aim.

In seeking to meet health needs, medicine can be described as a quest for control over the factors affecting health. Understanding (knowledge) is important to medicine because it leads to control. Yet where understanding is lacking, medicine will seek control by relying on low-level empirical rules validated by practical success.

A consequence of medicine's aim of meeting health needs is that medicine possesses a therapeutic obligation imposed by its own character. That is, basic to medicine as an enterprise is the prima facie duty to treat those who are ill in ways that will help them achieve the degree of health of which they are capable.

Treatment by drugs or surgery, diet or exercise, is one way in which medicine exercises control over disease, but the therapeutic obligation can also be regarded as involving an obligation to prevent the occurrence of disease. Although the success of a treatment might be most dramatic, preventing a disease altogether might be seen as the most effective form of control. Medicine aims at promoting human health by exercising control over disease, and since elimination is the most effective form of control, elimination of disease is the ultimate aim of medicine.

The eradication of smallpox from the world's population exemplifies the realization of this aim in a particular instance. The elimination of the disease was announced by the World Health Organization in 1979, and certainly the disappearance of the disease is to be preferred over all forms of therapy, no matter how effective. To our knowledge, no one argued that it would be morally wrong to eradicate smallpox through vaccination and other public health measures.

What is true of infectious diseases like smallpox is, of course, also true of genetic diseases. Somatic cell therapy promises to become a valuable means of controlling them and minimizing the suffering they cause. Once again, however, complete control would go beyond prevention or effective treatment in individual cases.

Germ-line gene therapy offers us the chance to rid ourselves completely (except for new mutations) of many serious genetic diseases for which there is no effective treatment. Given medicine's aim of seeing to the health of people and its instrumental character, it is this ideal that medicine is obligated to pursue. Social circumstances (such as a lack of resources to conduct research) and unavoidable difficulties (such as not being able to solve the technical problems of safely and effectively altering sex cells) may make the road leading to germ-line gene therapy a long one.

Nevertheless, the prima facie duty to pursue this ideal remains.

## Conclusion

The more than 4,000 genetic diseases involving a defect in a single gene cause thousands of deaths, an incalculable amount of suffering, and staggering economic costs. We have shown that the objections most often raised to germ-line gene therapy are not so persuasive as to stand in the way of using it to treat diseases. And we have shown that the character of medicine imposes on medical professionals a prima facie duty to pursue the development and use of germ-line gene therapy.

The diseases are so serious and the promise of the therapy so great, that it would be wrong to give in to the objections that have been raised to gene therapy. If they are allowed to prevail, then the social and scientific support needed to realize the therapeutic possibilities of gene therapy may never materialize. This outcome would be as wrong and almost as serious as if we had failed to develop and use antibiotics or vaccines.

We thank Robert Cook-Deegan and LeRoy Walters for extremely valuable comments on an earlier version of this paper. Ronald Munson gratefully acknowledges the support of a University of Missouri—St. Louis Faculty Research Fellowship.

## References

Anderson, W. French. 1989. Human Gene Therapy: Why Draw a Line? *The Journal of Medicine and Philosophy* 14:681–93.

———. 1990. Genetics and Human Malleability. *Hastings Center Report* 20 (1): 21–24.

Berger, Edward M., and Gert, Bernard M. 1991. Genetic Disorders and the Ethical Status of Germ-line Gene Therapy. *The Journal of Medicine and Philosophy* 16: 667–83.

Cavalieri, Liebe F. 1983. Testimony at a Hearing before the Subcommittee and Oversight Committee on Science and Technology, U.S. House of Representatives, 16–18 November 1982. In *Human Genetic Engineering*, Committee Print No. 170, pp. 470–76. Washington, DC: U.S. Government Printing Office.

CIOMS [Council for International Organizations of Medical Sciences]. 1991. *Human Genome Mapping, Genetic Screening and Gene Therapy: Ethical Issues.* Proceedings of the XXIVth CIOMS Conference: Human Genome Mapping, Genetic Screening and Therapy, ed. Z. Bankowski and A. M. Capron. Geneva.

Council of Europe, Parliamentary Assembly. 1982a. Report on genetic engineering presented by the Legal Affairs Committee, J. P.

Elmquist rapporteur. Document 4832 of the 33rd Ordinary Session, 18 January. Strasbourg, France.

———. 1982b. Recommendation 934 "On Genetic Engineering." Strasbourg, France.

Fletcher, John C. 1983. Moral Problems and Ethical Issues in Prospective Human Gene Therapy. *Virginia Law Review* 69: 538–40.

Fletcher, John C., and Anderson, W. French. 1992. Germ-Line Gene Therapy: A New Stage of Debate. *Law, Medicine, and Health Care* 20 (1–2). forthcoming.

Fletcher, Joseph. 1974. *The Ethics of Genetic Control.* New York: Doubleday.

Fowler, Gregory; Juengst, Eric T.; and Zimmerman, Burke K. 1989. Germ-line Gene Therapy and the Clinical Ethos of Medical Genetics. *Theoretical Medicine* 10:151–65.

Holtzman, Neil A. 1989. *Proceed with Caution.* Baltimore, MD: The Johns Hopkins University Press.

Kant, Immanuel. [1785] 1959. *Foundations of the Metaphysics of Morals.* Trans. Lewis White Beck. Indianapolis: The Bobbs Merrill Company, Inc.

Kass, Leon, 1972. New Beginnings in Life. In *The New Genetics*, ed. Michael Hamilton, pp. 15–63. Grand Rapids, MI: Eerdmans.

Lappé, Marc. 1991. Ethical Issues in Manipulating The Human Germ Line. *The Journal of Medicine and Philosophy* 16: 621–39.

Leenen, H. J. J. 1988. Genetic Manipulation with Human Beings. *Medicine and Law* 7:71–79.

Ludmerer, Kenneth M. 1972. *Genetics and American Society: A Historical Appraisal.* Baltimore, MD: The Johns Hopkins University Press.

Mathieu, Deborah. 1991. *Preventing Prenatal Harm: Should the State Intervene?* Dordrecht, Holland: Kluwer Academic Publishers.

Mauron, Alex, and Thévoz, Jean-Marie, 1991. Germ-line Engineering: A Few European Voices. *The Journal of Medicine and Philosophy* 16: 649–66.

Moseley, Ray. 1991. Commentary: Maintaining the Somatic/Germ-line Distinction: Some Ethical Drawbacks. *The Journal of Medicine and Philosophy* 16: 641–47.

Munson, Ronald. 1981. Why Medicine Cannot Be a Science. *The Journal of Medicine and Philosophy* 6: 183–208.

Nichols, Eve K. 1988. *Human Gene Therapy.* Cambridge, MA: Harvard University Press.

OTA. 1984. *Human Gene Therapy—A Background Paper.* Washington, DC: Office of Technology Assessment.

President's Commission for the Study of Ethical Problems in Medicine and Biomedical and Behavioral Research. 1982. *Splicing Life: A Report on the Social and Ethical Issues of Genetic Engineering with Human Beings.* Washington, DC: U.S. Government Printing Office.

Purdy, L. M. 1988. Genetic Diseases: Can Having Children Be Immoral? In *Intervention and Reflection: Basic Issues in Medical Ethics*, ed. Ronald Munson, pp. 364–71. Belmont, CA: Wadsworth Publishing Co.

Ramsey, Paul. 1970. *Fabricated Man.* New Haven: Yale University Press.

Walters, LeRoy. 1991. Human Gene Therapy: Ethics and Public Policy. *Human Gene Therapy* 2: 115–22.

Verma, Inder M. 1990. Gene Therapy. *Scientific American* 172: 68–72.

Zimmerman, Burke K. 1991. Human Germ-line Therapy: The Case for Its Development and Use. *The Journal of Medicine and Philosophy* 16: 593–612.

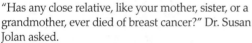

### Decision Scenario 1

"Research with embryonic stem cells must go forward," Tina Cuella said. "We owe it to people with spinal cord injuries, Parkinson's, diabetes, and a hundred other diseases who might be helped by treatments using stem cells."

"Do you also favor taking hearts, livers, and kidneys from living infants and giving them to other people?" Howard Lain asked. "Because that's exactly like what you're doing when you destroy an embryo to get stem cells."

"That's ridiculous. An embryo isn't like a baby."

1. Why, according to the Pontifical Academy, is it morally wrong to destroy a human embryo?

2. What status is ascribed to the embryo by those endorsing Position One in the Bioethics Council report? What status is assigned by those endorsing Position Two?

3. Explain the conflict between Wilson's claim that a fertilized egg merely has a "reasonable chance at life" and the position taken by those of the Council endorsing "The Moral Case Against Cloning-for-Biomedical-Research." State the rest of their case.

4. What, according to members opposed to research cloning, are the limits on what we owe to the sick?

5. Why does Wilson reject the slippery slope argument against research using embryos?

### Decision Scenario 2

"Has any close relative, like your mother, sister, or a grandmother, ever died of breast cancer?" Dr. Susan Jolan asked.

"No one," Lola A'tibe said. "But I want to be tested for the gene anyway. I'm forty years old and very health conscious, so I'd like to do everything I can to protect myself from breast cancer."

"I understand your motive," Dr. Jolan said. "I'll arrange for you to be tested for both the BRCA1 and BRCA2 genes as soon as possible."

1. Would Hubbard and Lewontin say that Dr. Jolan had responded properly to her patient's concerns? Why or why not?

2. Private companies are developing tests that can be administered to whoever wants them and can pay for them. Why do Hubbard and Lewontin object to this service?

3. If a woman is found to be the carrier of one of the mutated genes that causes breast cancer, this does not mean she will develop breast cancer. It does mean she is at greater risk than other women. Is this the sort of information a woman might find worth having?

## Decision Scenario 3

"Dr. Gress, two of the people we tested for heart disease also turned out positive for the APOe gene," Clara Chang said. "Do we have an obligation to notify them they are at risk of developing Alzheimer's?"

"Absolutely not," Charles Gress said. "We have an obligation *not* to notify them. What good would it do for them to know they're at risk for a disease that can't be prevented and can't be treated? It would only cause them distress and unhappiness."

1. Is Dr. Gress's position compatible with the views of Hubbard and Lewontin?

2. Does the fact that the knowledge was acquired accidentally as part of a research program and not at the request of the individuals relieve the investigators of any obligation to inform the test subjects of any genetic discoveries about them?

3. Would Wachbroit consider Dr. Gress's position paternalistic? If so, how might he recommend that the genetic information about individual patients be handled?

4. Wachbroit holds that sometimes patients have a duty to know their genetic status, even if they would prefer not to. Might an investigator have a duty to inform a patient of his status, even if the patient has said he doesn't want to know the outcome of a test?

## Decision Scenario 4

"Carl and I wouldn't know how to raise a regular child," Olivia Padrone said. "We know what it's like to be dwarves, and we could help a child who was a dwarf."

"So you want me to help arrange for the amnio, then counsel you on the results?" Dallas Stratford asked.

"Exactly, we want a child just like us," Olivia said. "We're proud of being dwarves, and we're both active in getting people to recognize that our culture and way of life is as good as anyone else's. Having a regular child would betray our ideals and be false to our view of life."

"I don't know what to say," Dallas said. "Usually, people want to avoid having a child with the mutation that produces dwarfism."

1. Genetic counselors have been "value neutral," not recommending that a woman have an abortion, no matter what tests revealed about the fetus. Yet their neutrality is challenged when a woman is willing to abort a normal child to have a child who has a specific birth "defect," such as dwarfism, deafness, or blindness. According to Dena Davis, are there circumstances in which value neutrality should be set aside?

2. On what grounds, according to Davis, might a counselor turn down the request of someone for help in having a child with a particular "defect"?

3. If dwarfism, deafness, or blindness is a way of life and a culture, is it wrong to discourage the birth of more people who belong to the culture?

## Decision Scenario 5

In 1983 a group of Orthodox Jews in New York and Israel initiated a screening program with the aim of eliminating from their community diseases transmitted as recessive genes. The group called itself Dor Yeshorim, "the generation of the righteous."

Because Orthodox Jews do not approve of abortion in most instances, the program does not employ prenatal testing. Instead, high school students are given a blood test to determine if they carry the genes for Tay–Sachs, cystic fibrosis, or Gaucher's disease. Each student is given a six-digit identification number, and if two students consider dating, they are encouraged to call a hotline. They are told either that they are "compatible" or that they each carry a recessive gene for one of the three diseases. Couples who are carriers are offered genetic counseling.

During 1993, 8000 people were tested, and eighty-seven couples who were considering marriage decided against it, after they learned that they were both carriers of recessive genes. The test costs $25, and the program is supported in part by funds from the Department of Health and Human Services. Some view the Dor Yeshorim program as a model that might be followed by other groups or by society in general.

The tests were initially only for Tay–Sachs, but over time the other two diseases were added. Current plans are to continue to add tests for even more diseases. However, some critics regard it as a mistake to have moved from testing for almost invariably lethal, untreatable diseases like Tay–Sachs to testing for cystic fibrosis. Individuals may feel pressured into being tested, and those who are carriers of one or more disease-predisposing genes may become unmarriageable social outcasts. Considering that genes for most diseases manifest themselves in various degrees of severity, many individuals may suffer social rejection for inadequate reasons. For example, Gaucher's disease, which involves an enzyme defect producing anemia and an enlarged liver and spleen, manifests itself only after age forty-five in half the diagnosed cases. Further, although the disease may be fatal, it often is not, and the symptoms can be treated.

1. Is the Dor Yeshorim screening program a form of eugenics? If so, does this make it unacceptable?

2. Is the program a good model for a national screening program? If not, why not?

3. Is it reasonable to screen for nonlethal genetic diseases?

4. What are the dangers inherent in any screening program?

5. Would Purdy's arguments tends to support a mandatory testing program? Explain your position.

## Decision Scenario 6

"I'm sorry I wasn't able to bring you better news," Dr. Valery Mendez said.

Timothy Schwartz shook his head. "We gambled and lost," he said. "We can't say we didn't know what we were doing."

"That doesn't make it much easier," Judith Schwartz said. "When you said we were both Tay–Sachs carriers, I thought, 'Well, it won't happen to us.' But I was wrong. What about this new test? Can we really trust the results?"

"I'm afraid so," said Dr. Mendez. "The fetal cells taken during amniocentesis were cultured, and the chromosome study showed that the child you're carrying will have Tay–Sachs."

"What do you recommend?" Mr. Schwartz asked.

"It's not for me to recommend. I can give you some information—tell you the options—but you've got to make your own decision."

"Is abortion the only solution?" Mrs. Schwartz asked.

"If you call it a solution," Mr. Schwartz said.

"The disease is almost invariably fatal," Dr. Mendez said. "And there is really no effective treatment for it. A lot of people think there may be in the future, but that doesn't help right now."

"So what does it involve?" Mr. Schwartz asked.

"At first your child will seem quite normal, but that's only because it takes time for a particular chemical to build up in the brain. After the first year or so, the child will start to show signs of deterioration. He'll start losing his sight. Then, as brain damage progresses, he'll lose control over his muscles, and eventually he will die."

"And we just have to stand by and watch that happen?" Mrs. Schwartz asked.

"Nothing can be done to stop it," Dr. Mendez said. "It's a terrible and sad disease."

"We certainly do want to have a child," Mr. Schwartz said. "But we don't want to have one that is going to suffer all his life. I don't think I could stand that."

1. In this case, how persuasive is Kass's argument that genetic abortion constitutes a threat to the principle that all persons are of equal value?

2. Can Purdy's argument that every child deserves a normal opportunity for a good life be used to justify requiring abortion in a case such as this?

3. Dena Davis uses the notion of a child's right to an "open future" as grounds for refusing to assist deaf parents in having a deaf child. Couldn't this same notion be used to justify recommending that a woman pregnant with a fetus carrying the Tay–Sach gene have an abortion?

4. Kass contends that none of the three standards he examines can allow us to justify selective abortion. State and evaluate his arguments.

5. How unfavorably must the odds be against having a normal child before (according to Purdy) parents have a duty not to reproduce? In what way is the seriousness of the disease at issue relevant to the odds?

## Decision Scenario 7

"I don't see the problem," Harold Lucas said. "We have the opportunity to eliminate at least one form of hereditary blindness forever."

"I'm not exactly in favor of blindness," Amy Lamont said. "I know many blind people have a hard time in our society."

"So, let's slice out the defective gene that causes it, and splice in one that does the job right," Lucas said. "With germ-line therapy we can modify the sex cell of the carriers and get rid of that form of the disease."

Lamont shook her head. "It sounds humane, but it's not so easy as that," she said. "Wanting to eliminate blindness suggests there's something wrong with blind people and that it's better for them not to be born."

"I think it's better for them not to be born *blind*."

"Also, getting rid of that gene means modifying human beings," Amy Lamont said. "If we start doing that, I don't know when we would stop. We might do anything at all with them."

"You're afraid of some kind of wild eugenics scheme?"

"That's one problem," Lamont said. "My objection is deeper than that, though. I don't like the idea of tampering with human life and human destiny. To change ourselves deliberately is, I think, to make us something less than human."

1. Rephrase Lamont's arguments so they are explicit.

2. Does wanting to eliminate hereditary blindness imply that blind people are less worthy or less human than sighted people? Why or why not?

3. Is Lamont's objection to eliminating hereditary blindness a slippery slope argument? If so, how? If not, why not?

4. Do Munson and Davis endorse Lamont's objection that germ-line therapy would be wrong because it alters the human genome? Explain.

5. How useful is it to consider the elimination of blindness therapeutic and any change going beyond the "normal" range of human abilities enhancement?

## Chapter 6

# Reproductive Control

## Chapter Contents

## Classic Case Presentation

### Hello, Dolly: The Advent of Reproductive Cloning

On February 3, 1997, Ian Wilmut of the Roslin Institute in Edinburgh, Scotland, made public the information that he and his research group had successfully produced a clone of an adult sheep. The younger genetic twin, the clone they named Dolly, had been born about seven months earlier and appeared to be healthy and normal in every respect.

The procedure Wilmut followed had a cookbook simplicity but was scientifically highly sophisticated. He took cells from the mammary tissue of a Finn Dorset ewe and got them to stop going through the ordinary process of cell division by culturing them in a medium with a low level of nutrients. Retrieving egg cells from a Scottish Blackface ewe, he removed their nuclei (hence the DNA), then mixed them with the mammary cells. By passing a weak current of electricity through the mixture, Wilmut got some of the egg cells and mammary cells to fuse together. He then used a second pulse of electricity to activate the machinery responsible for cell division.

Six days later, some of the fused cells had divided, becoming embryos in the way a fertilized egg develops into an embryo. Using the technology of embryo transfer, Wilmut succeeded in implanting one of the embryos in the uterus of a third sheep, another Blackface ewe. At the end of her pregnancy, the ewe gave birth to a lamb that was the genetic twin of the Finn Dorset sheep that supplied the mammary cells.

Wilmut and his group made 277 tries at fusing the body cells with the enucleated cells, but they managed to produce only 29 embryos that lasted longer than six days, the usual time in vitro fertilization specialists allow for a fertilized egg to develop into an embryo before transferring it into the uterus. Of the embryos Wilmut implanted, Dolly was the sole success.

The great majority of biologists were amazed at Wilmut's achievement. While they acknowledged that the DNA in the nucleus of a body cell contains a complete set of genes and so, in principle, could be used to produce another genetically identical individual, they didn't believe our understanding of cells was detailed enough actually to do it. The view accepted by most researchers was that once a cell finds its place in the body, it switches off all the genes it contains, except those it needs to do its job and to reproduce itself. But to become an embryo, the genes must be switched on again. When the embryo is implanted in a uterus, they must be able to orchestrate the stunningly complicated process of development, changing the embryo into an offspring.

Wilmut demonstrated that what the majority of scientists considered only a distant possibility could be achieved in a relatively straightforward fashion. Placing the mammary cells in a culture low in nutrients seemed to return them to the state when their genetic potential is still open, and the pulse of electricity seemed to trigger them into dividing and developing. Wilmut showed it wasn't necessary to understand the underlying biology of the process to control it. Under the right conditions, the DNA would reprogram itself to initiate and direct development.

## Established as Real

Wilmut's achievement was initially greeted with skepticism by some in the research community. Cloning was demonstrated as a phenomenon beyond doubt, however, in July 1998. Ryuzo Yanagimachi and his team at the University of Hawaii reported that they had produced more than fifty mouse clones. Some of the mice, moreover, were clones of clones.

Yanagimachi's technique was a variation of Wilmut's. Using the genetic material from a mouse cumulus cell in the resting phase, he injected it into an enucleated mouse egg, then used chemicals to get the cell to divide. The cell was then implanted into a surrogate mother and allowed to develop into a mouse. In one experiment, tan mice were used as genetic donors, black mice as egg donors, and white mice as gestational surrogates. The clones were all tan.

After Yanagimachi's demonstration, doubt about the reality of cloning evaporated. Scientists have now succeeded in cloning cows, goats, pigs, and cats. The first cat was cloned in 2002 only because researchers at Texas A&M failed (as others had) to clone a dog. Called cc, for "carbon copy" or "copycat," the kitten was the only successful result of attempts using eighty-seven cloned embryos transferred to gestational surrogates.

## Drawbacks

Despite cc's name, she really isn't an exact copy of her biological mother, a two-year-old calico cat named Rainbow. Although the two are genetically identical, the color and pattern of cc's coat is different. Coat color results from the separation and distribution of pigmented cells. This takes place during development and is not completely determined by genes.

While cc is apparently healthy and normal, some cloned animals have not been so fortunate. A number die soon after birth, while others suffer from a variety of birth anomalies. Developmental delays, defective hearts, underdeveloped lungs, neurological deficits, and faulty immune systems are the more common flaws. Some cloned mice appear normal, then as they grow, they become extremely fat. Developing calves become oversized and die prematurely.

Scientists don't know exactly what happens to cause these adverse results. Apparently, however, cloning promotes the occurrence of random changes. During normal reproduction, both egg and sperm mature before they combine, but in cloning, eggs are harvested and the DNA in cells combined with them must all be reprogrammed during a period of minutes or hours. During the process, researchers think, genes are altered and random errors occur. These cause unpredictable problems that can crop up at any time during development or after birth.

That cloning works at all is surprising to some researchers, given what needs to happen to make it possible. Still, even under the best laboratory conditions and in skilled hands, only about 3 percent of attempts at cloning mammals are successful. Only about one attempt in a hundred results in a viable calf.

When Dolly was born, some scientists speculated that it was likely she would age prematurely. The cell from which the nuclear DNA was removed had already undergone a number of cell divisions and, given that cells divide only about fifty times before they die, perhaps the clock for Dolly had already been ticking before she was born. Experience with cloned animals, however, has so far not shown that they age prematurely.

## Practical Uses

1. Cloning is expected to be the foundation of what is now called *pharming*—the use of animals to produce drugs. The Roslin Institute is an agricultural research center, and a third of Wilmut's funding came from PLP Therapeutics, a biotechnology firm. Wilmut's aim, as well as PLP's, is to produce a flock of sheep genetically engineered to give milk containing such medically valuable and expensive substances as blood-clotting factor, insulin, and human growth hormone. If a single sheep able to secrete one of these substances in her milk could be created, cells from her could be cloned into a herd. Cloning would make it possible to produce whatever number of animal drug factories are needed, insuring us a supply of useful substances at lower prices.

2. The interest in cloning cattle is to produce a line that has properties that are valued for commercial reasons. A cow that produces substantially more milk than usual, for example, could be cloned to produce a herd of dairy cows. The milk yield from such a herd would significantly reduce the cost of milk production and boost profits.

3. The research that produced cc, the cloned cat, was supported by Genetics Saving and Clone, a biotech company that aims to profit from cloning valued pets. The company is already storing, for a fee, DNA samples from pets, with the expectation that cloning technology will soon be adequate to producing a genetic replica of a beloved pet. Dogs were the first target, but when cloning them turned out to be intractable, the company turned to cats.

   Critics object to the whole idea of the enterprise, pointing out that in the United States alone millions of dogs and cats are destroyed each year as an unwanted surplus. Thus, it is pointlessly cruel to create even more. Those who believe they will get an identical version of their cat or dog are simply mistaken. Cc's coat color was different from her mother's, and very likely her behavior and personality will also be different. Developmental factors, including environmental ones, are likely to result in a very different animal.

4. In 2002 Immerge Biotherapeutics and PPL Therapeutics independently announced that they had succeeded in cloning pigs from which the gene encoding the sugar GAL had been "knocked out." The GAL molecule on the surface of cells triggers hyperacute rejection in humans. (The molecule is not expressed in primates.) Thus, the hope is that the production of pigs lacking this molecule will make it more likely that pig organs can be used as transplants in humans.

5. Advanced Cell Technologies announced in 2002 that it had cloned cow eggs and, when the embryos had developed into fetuses, had removed kidney cells and transferred them to a spongelike matrix. The cells developed into what researchers described as a small kidney. When the kidney was implanted into the cow contributing the DNA, it produced a small amount of urine. While no one sees this as an acceptable procedure for use with human cells, it demonstrates the possibility of growing transplant organs without relying on stem cells. (For the controversy over stem cells, see the Classic Case Presentation: "The Stem-Cell Debate" in Chapter 5.)

6. The possibility of using human embryonic stem cells to treat diseases, repair organs, and even grow whole organs makes cloning outstandingly important. Embryonic stem cells are obtained from embryos. If someone with (say) diabetes needed stem cells for treatment, to overcome the problem of tissue rejection, her DNA could be used to replace the nucleus in a donor egg. When the egg formed a blastocyst, the stem cells could be removed. They would be a perfect genetic match with her own tissue. This is an example of *therapeutic cloning*. That is, the cloning is for the purpose of getting materials for treatment, not for the purpose of reproduction. Because embryos must be destroyed to secure the stem cells, those who consider human embryos to have the status of persons regard even therapeutic cloning as a serious moral wrong.

## What About Humans?

Most of the public discussion has focused on human *reproductive cloning*. People have been quick to realize that if a sheep and other mammals have been cloned, there seems to be no technical reason a human can't be also.

Assuming the procedure were perfected, here are a few of the possibilities it opens up:

1. When one of a couple carries a gene responsible for a devastating illness like Tay–Sachs disease, the couple could decide to have a child using only the genetic material from the noncarrier.

2. Women who have entered menopause as a result of chemotherapy, had their ovaries removed for therapeutic reasons, or are postmenopausal could still have a genetically connected child by employing the DNA from their somatic cells. The child would be a genetically identical twin, as well as an offspring.

3. Similarly, men who are sterile for any reason or who no longer are capable of producing undamaged sperm (as a result of cancer surgery or radiation treatments, for example) may still father a child.

4. The parents of a dying child could decide to have another child who will be a genetically identical replacement.

5. A woman could decide to use the DNA of a dying (or just dead) partner to have a child who would be the partner's genetic twin. A man could achieve the same end by finding a woman who would agree to be a gestational surrogate.

6. A "family" could be made up of several offspring who are genetically identical with the mother or the father. The father would also be a

twin brother and the mother a twin sister, although separated by years.

These possibilities, which many regard as potential benefits, are shadowed by other possibilities that some see as offering serious objections to human cloning.

1.  Those who are rich and egocentric might decide to clone themselves for no reason except to perpetuate their unique combination of genes.

2.  Dictators or powerful political leaders could replace themselves with a clone, thus promoting an indefinite continuation of their influence.

3.  The cellular DNA from popular figures such as athletes and movie stars might become marketed as commodities. Or because cloning would make "popular" DNA valuable, it might be stolen and used to produce children without the consent of an unwitting and unwilling donor.

Some fears about cloning seem to reflect the mistaken belief that the clone of an individual will grow up to be exactly the same as the individual—a sort of photocopy. But of course genetic identity doesn't result in exact similarity. We already know that identical twins, even when brought up in the same family, may turn out to be quite distinct in personality, interests, and motivations.

A child who develops in a different uterine environment, then grows up in a world filled with different people, practices, events, and experiences, is quite unlikely to be exactly like the person cloned. Even individuals can become "different people" with experience and education.

The most serious objection to human reproductive cloning at the moment is that it would lead to so many tragic outcomes. With a success rate with mice hovering around a mere 3 percent, the number of failed pregnancies is not likely to be better. Also, the chance of children being born with either lethal or seriously debilitating impairments is unacceptably high. We know from cloned mammals that unpredictable genetic and developmental errors occur.

No serious researcher thinks it would be anything but premature and morally indefensible to attempt to clone a human at the moment. Even if it is not wrong in principle, it would be wrong to produce children who would most likely be severely impaired, assuming they didn't die shortly after birth.

But what of the future? In what circumstances, if any, would the cloning of humans be legitimate? Are we willing to take the risks involved in its development? Are we prepared to accept the alterations in our society that successful human cloning would produce?

## Politics

Research involving cloning human embryos has been controversial from the start. On February 4, 1997, the day after Ian Wilmut announced the cloning of Dolly, President Clinton asked the National Bioethics Advisory Committee to report to him in ninety days "with recommendations on possible federal actions" to prevent the "abuse" of cloning. Meanwhile, on March 4, the president issued an Executive Order banning the use of federal funds to support research leading to the cloning of humans. On June 9, the committee made its report to the president, and he immediately called for legislation banning cloning "for the purpose of creating a child."

Human cloning for the purpose of reproduction continues to be denounced, even in principle, by many, and researchers in the area have repeatedly asserted they have no plans to carry out experiments like the ones that have produced other mammals. The fundamental practical interest in cloning is with therapeutic cloning—the creation of human embryos to acquire stem cells to treat diseases and injuries.

The potential of stem cells to cure diseases is so significant that it has split social conservatives. Many who once joined to oppose abortion are now divided on the question of whether an early human embryo before it is implanted in a uterus should be regarded as equivalent to a fetus. (See the Classic Case Presentation on stem cells in Chapter 5.) Those who think not are often willing to support therapeutic cloning, although they condemn reproductive cloning.

In August 2001 President George Bush announced he was prepared to allow human embryonic stem-cell research supported by federal funds to continue on stem cells that had already been recovered from embryos. Federal money could not be used, however, to create new embryos. Thus, the decision left no room for even therapeutic cloning.

The president also appointed a President's Council "to monitor stem cell research, to recommend appropriate guidelines and regulations and to consider all of the medical and ethical ramifications of biomedical innovation." The Council reported in July 2002 and recommended the continuation of the ban on reproductive cloning. It also called for a four-year moratorium on cloning for the purpose of biomedical research. (See the President's Council's report in Chapter 5.)

## BRIEFING SESSION

"Oh, brave new world that has such people in it!" exclaims Miranda in Shakespeare's *The Tempest*.

This is the line from which Aldous Huxley took the title for his dystopian novel *Brave New World*. A dystopia is the opposite of a utopia, and the future society depicted by Huxley is one we're invited to view with shock and disapproval.

In Huxley's dystopia, "pregnancy" is a dirty word, sex is purely recreational, and children are produced according to explicit genetic standards in the artificial wombs of state "hatcheries." Furthermore, one's genetic endowment determines the social position and obligations one has within the society, and everyone is conditioned to believe the role she finds herself in is the best one to have.

In significant ways, that future society is now. The new and still-developing technologies of human reproduction have reached a stage in which the innovations imagined by Huxley in 1932 to make such a society possible are well within the limits of feasibility.

We have no state hatcheries and no artificial uteruses. But we do have sperm banks, donor ova, artificial insemination, frozen embryos, and surrogate pregnancies. We have it within our power to remove an ovum from a woman's body, fertilize it, then place it in her uterus so it may develop into a child. We can remove one or more of the cells of a growing embryo and allow them to develop into separate embryos. Because we have the power to clone mammals, producing a genetically identical twin, we most likely also have the power to clone humans.

The new technology of human-assisted reproduction is so powerful it differs only in degree from that of Huxley's dystopian world. What we have yet to do is to employ the technology as part of a deliberate social policy to re-

structure our world along the lines imagined by Huxley.

Yet the potentiality is there. Perhaps more than anything else, it is the bleak vision of such a mechanistic and dehumanized future that has motivated much of the criticism of current reproductive technology. The "brave new world" of Huxley is one in which traditional values associated with reproduction and family life, values based on individual autonomy, have been replaced by values of a purely social kind. In such a society, it is the good of the society or the species, not the good of individuals, that is the touchstone of justification.

The possible loss of personal values is a legitimate and serious concern. The technologies of human reproduction are sometimes viewed as machines that may be employed to pave the road leading to a world of bleakness and loss. Yet it is important to remember that these same technologies also promise to enhance the lives of those presently living and prevent potential suffering and despair.

Thousands of women (as well as a lesser number of men) unable to have children may find it possible to do so through the use of reproductive technology. It offers a means of conception when biological dysfunction makes the normal means unlikely or impossible. Women past the age of ovulation or who have lost their ovaries to surgery and men with a low sperm count are among those who have an opportunity where not long ago none existed.

These are all potentialities that have become actualities. But in the view of some, current methods merely mark a beginning, and the possibilities inherent in reproductive technology still remain relatively unrealized. It may be possible before long, for example, to avoid sexual reproduction and use in vitro fertilization and surrogate pregnancy to reproduce clones of an individual. The technology is so powerful that, if we wish, we can employ it to change the basic fabric and pattern of our society.

Should we do that? Or will the use of the technology promote the development of a dystopia? One way of thinking about these general questions is to turn once more to Huxley.

In 1962 Huxley published a utopian novel entitled *Island.* Like the society in *Brave New World,* Huxley's ideal society also relies on the principles of science, but they are used to promote autonomy and personal development. For over a hundred years, the society on the island of Pala has shaped itself in accordance with the principles of reason and science. Living is communal, sexual repression is nonexistent, children are cared for by both biological parents and other adults, drugs are used to enhance perceptual awareness, and social obligations are assigned on the basis of personal interest and ability.

Reproductive technology is one of the means the society uses to achieve its ends. It practices contraception, eugenics, and artificial insemination. Negative eugenics to eliminate genetic diseases is considered only rational. But more than this, by the use of DF and AI (Deep Freeze and Artificial Insemination), sperm from donors with superior genetic endowments is available for the use of couples who wish to improve their chances of having a child with special talents or higher-than-usual intelligence.

Huxley's ideal society is not above criticism, even from those sympathetic toward the values he endorses. Yet *Brave New World* is such a powerful cautionary tale of what might happen if science were pressed into the service of repressive political goals that it makes it difficult to imagine other possible futures in which some of the same technology plays a more benign role. *Island* is an attempt to present such an alternative future, so in thinking about the possibilities inherent in reproductive technology, fairness demands that we also consider Palinese society and not restrict our attention to the world of soma and state hatcheries.

## IVF, GIFT, ZIFT, and Other Techniques

The birth of Louise Brown in 1978 (see the Case Presentation in this chapter) was a major media event. Photographs, television coverage, inter-

views, and news stories presented the world with minute details of the lives of the people involved and close accounts of the procedures leading to Louise's conception.

Despite the unprecedented character of the event, few people seemed surprised by it. The idea of a "test-tube baby" was one already familiar from fiction and folklore. Medieval alchemists were thought capable of generating life in their retorts, and hundreds of science fiction stories depicted a future in which the creation of life in the laboratory was an ordinary occurrence. Thus, in some ways, the birth of Louise Brown was seen as merely a matter of science and medicine catching up with imagination. Indeed, they didn't quite catch up, for the "test tube" contained sperm and an egg, not just a mixture of chemicals.

While it's doubtful the public appreciated the magnitude of the achievement that resulted in the birth of Louise Brown, it was one of considerable significance. The first embryo transfer was performed in rabbits in 1890, but it wasn't until the role of hormones in reproduction, the nutritional requirements of developing cells, and the reproductive process itself were better understood that it became possible to consider seriously the idea of fertilizing an egg outside the mother's body and then returning it for ordinary development. By 2002 considerably more than 100,000 babies worldwide had been born through the use of in vitro fertilization or some other form of assisted reproduction.

### IVF

*In vitro* is a Latin phrase that means "in glass," and in embryology, it is used in contrast with *in utero,* or "in the uterus." Ordinary human fertilization takes place in utero (strictly speaking, in the fallopian tubes) when a sperm cell unites with an ovum. In vitro fertilization, then, is fertilization that is artificially performed outside the woman's body—in a test tube, so to speak.

The ovum that produced Louise Brown was fertilized in vitro. But the remainder of the process involved *embryo transfer.* After the ovum from her mother's body was fertilized and had become an embryo, it was transferred—returned for in utero development.

Robert Edwards and Patrick Steptoe, who were responsible for developing and performing the techniques that led to the birth of Louise Brown, followed a process that, allowing for technical improvements, is basically the same as the one still employed.

The patient is given a reproductive hormone to cause ova to ripen. Several mature eggs are extracted from the ovarian follicles and placed in a nutrient solution to which sperm is then added. With luck, sperm cells penetrate several ova, fertilizing them. The fertilized eggs are transferred to another nutrient solution where they undergo cell division. The embryo (also called a zygote or, by some, pre-embryo) is then transferred to the woman, who has been given injections of hormones to prepare her uterus to receive it.

Numerous modifications and extensions of Steptoe and Edwards's techniques have been introduced since 1978. It's now common to employ a nonsurgical procedure for securing ova. After hormones stimulate the ovarian follicles, ultrasound is used to locate the follicles, and a hollow needle is inserted through the vaginal wall and into a follicle. Fluid is withdrawn and egg cells identified under the microscope. They are then fertilized with the sperm, cultured, and the resulting embryos implanted.

Also, it's now not unusual to implant two, three, or even as many as ten fertilized ova at a time. (Implanting more than four is coming to be viewed as not good medical practice.) This makes it more likely that at least one will attach to the uterine wall and so eliminates the need for a woman to have eggs removed another time. Yet the practice also has the disadvantage of increasing the chances of multiple births. (See the Case Presentation: "Septuplets: The Perils of Multiple Pregnancies" later in this chapter.)

## GIFT, ZIFT, IVC, ULER, PZD, ICSI, DNA Transfer, and CD

*Gamete intrafallopian transfer* or GIFT uses some of the same manipulative techniques as IVF. It involves inserting both ova and sperm into the fallopian tubes through a small abdominal incision so if fertilization takes place, it does so inside the woman's body. Some regard the procedure as being more "natural" than in vitro fertilization.

*Zygote intrafallopian transfer* or ZIFT involves culturing eggs and sperm outside the body, then placing the zygotes into a woman's fallopian tubes. If the transfer is done at a particular developmental stage, it is called *pronuclear stage tubal transfer* or PROST. Both are variants of *tubal embryo transfer* or TET and reflect the view that the fallopian tubes provide the most protective environment for embryo development.

*Intravaginal culture* or IVC is another attempt at naturalness. Ova are placed in a tube to which sperm cells are added, and the tube is then inserted into the vagina and kept next to the cervix by a diaphragm. Normal sexual intercourse can take place with the tube in place. Two days later, the tube is removed, the contents decanted, and any fertilized ova transferred into the uterus.

*Uterine lavage embryo retrieval* or ULER is a method for assisting pregnancy in a woman with a functioning uterus but who is either incapable of ovulation or for some reason (e.g., she knows she is the carrier of a lethal gene) doesn't wish to use her own ova. An ovulating woman is inseminated with donor sperm, then after around five days, the fertilized egg is washed out of the uterus (this is the lavage) before it becomes implanted in the uterine wall. Once retrieved, the embryo is implanted in the woman being assisted. Because fertilization takes place in vivo, instead of in vitro, a potential difficulty is that the embryo may not be washed out before it becomes embedded in the uterine wall. If this happens, the donor must then decide whether to have an abortion.

*Partial zona dissection* or PZD involves using microtechniques to drill holes in the *zona*, or protective membrane surrounding an ovum, to facilitate the passage of sperm into the interior. This increases the chances of fertilization by reducing the egg's resistance to penetration, which is particularly useful when the sperm involved may be constitutionally weak.

*Intracytoplasmic sperm injection* or ICSI is a technique that can help 50 to 60 percent of infertile men become fathers. Sperm are examined microscopically and one that seems best shaped and most active is injected directly into the egg cell.

*DNA transfer* involves replacing the nucleus of an older egg with one taken from a younger donor egg. The aim is to take advantage of the cellular mechanisms of the younger egg, while keeping the maternal genetic material.

*Cytoplasmic donation* or CD involves removing the cytoplasm from a younger donor egg and injecting it into an older egg. Some data indicate this will increase the developmental success of the recipient egg.

New techniques to assist reproduction are being developed at a rapid rate. That so many are available means that if one technique doesn't work, a woman may try another. Yet having so many possibilities makes it difficult for some women who wish to become pregnant to give up the attempt, even after repeated failure.

## Need, Success Rates, and Costs of Assisted Reproduction

In 1995 (the latest year for which data are available) the U.S. population included 60.2 million women of reproductive age. Some 6.1 million of them, almost 10 percent, were infertile. By some estimates, at least 4 million men are infertile, and one in nine married couples have difficulty conceiving a child. In 1995 alone about 600,000 infertile women sought assistance at the over 300 clinics specializing in treating infertility.

The Centers for Disease Control reported in 2000 the results of its study (the most recent) of the effectiveness of assisted reproductive technology as employed in 360 infertility clinics. Attempts to produce pregnancy involve one-month cycles, and during 1998 the clinics intervened in 61,650 cycles. The interventions resulted in 15,372 live births (some of them multiple), for a success rate of 24.9 percent.

About 30.5 percent of the women treated got pregnant, and 81.6 percent of the pregnancies resulted in live births. (These figures exclude the use of donor eggs or frozen embryos.) Single births occurred in 62 percent of the cases, twins in 32 percent, and triplets or more in 6 percent.

According to these figures, the chance of a woman's becoming pregnant with the help of reproductive technology is roughly the same (by some estimates) as that of a normal, healthy couple attempting conception during the woman's regular monthly cycle. But of course not all the pregnancies result in births, and almost three-quarters of the women treated in infertility programs never become pregnant.

The financial cost of an attempt to become pregnant can be staggering. Each fertilization cycle costs from $10,000 to $11,000, and most women who get pregnant go through three or four cycles before pregnancy occurs. Only fifteen states require insurers to cover infertility treatments, and many people go deeply in debt to pay for them. By some estimates the money spent on fertility-related medical services exceeds $3 billion to $5 billion a year.

Cost is not the only drawback to assisted reproduction. Both the consequences of the methods and the methods themselves are associated with a variety of moral and social difficulties.

### Multiple Births

One of the hazards of assisted reproduction is that the fertility drugs given to women to speed up the production of ova can increase the chances that the women will become pregnant with multiple fetuses. Also, if in vitro fertilization is employed, the practice of transferring several embryos into a woman's fallopian tubes to improve the probability that at least one will implant in the uterus may result in the implanting of several embryos.

Unless selective abortion (called *fetal reduction*) is performed, a pregnancy with multiple fetuses puts the pregnancy at risk for miscarriage. A woman carrying quadruplets has a 25 percent chance of a miscarriage in the first trimester; a woman carrying quintuplets has a 50 percent chance.

Also, even if a miscarriage doesn't occur, a multiple pregnancy puts the infants at risk. Normal pregnancies last about forty weeks, but multiple pregnancies rarely go full term. Triplets are born at around 33.5 weeks and quadruplets after 31 weeks. Because of their prematurity, babies born as multiples often suffer from such problems as blindness, stroke, brain damage, and impaired motor skills.

The number of women taking fertility drugs has almost tripled in the last decade, rising from about 1 million to 2.7 million, and the number of multiple births has *quadrupled* in the last twenty-five years. In 1995, 4973 children were born in groups of three or more. Triplets were most common, but already three sets of sextuplets have been born, and no doubt more are on the way.

Should women who become pregnant with multiple fetuses be permitted to decide to try to carry them all to term? Should infertility specialists be restricted in the use they make of fertility drugs? The costs of carrying multiples includes a social cost along with the personal costs of the parents. Should our society insist on selective reduction? (See the Case Presentation: "Septuplets" in this chapter for more details.)

## Freezing Embryos

An important development in the technology of assisted reproduction is the perfection of techniques for freezing embryos. Evidence to date indicates embryos can be stored in a frozen condition and then unfrozen and implanted without any damage to the chromosomes. One advantage of the procedure is that it eliminates

the need for a woman to undergo the lengthy and uncomfortable process required to secure additional ova. If a woman fails to become pregnant at a first attempt, an embryo saved from the initial fertilization can be employed in another effort.

The technique also makes it possible to delay an embryo transplant until the potential mother has reached the most favorable time in her menstrual cycle. Furthermore, because embryos survive storage better than ova, when a woman who wants to preserve her option to have a child undergoes chemotherapy, she may have her ova fertilized and the embryos preserved.

Each year around 25,000 embryos are frozen at fertility clinics. Not all the embryos are implanted, and this raises what many consider to be the serious question of what should be done with them. What if a couple storing their embryos get divorced? What if both die? What if the woman changes her mind about wanting to be pregnant? What if no surrogate is found?

Because more embryos are usually stored than are used to produce a pregnancy, what should be done with the leftovers? Fertility clinics typically offer the options of having excess embryos destroyed, used for research, or offered to an infertile couple. Sometimes, though, couples cannot be traced, and centers are unwilling to give away an embryo without their permission. When embryos are unclaimed in this way or the bills for storage are left unpaid, frozen embryos are usually destroyed simply by being allowed to thaw. (A frozen embryo is only a tiny speck, because development is at the four- to eight-cell stage.)

A British law requires the destruction of unclaimed embryos after five years. The law took effect in August of 1996, and in the face of some protest about 3300 frozen embryos were destroyed. The courts had refused to set aside the law, and the prime minister ignored appeals that he intervene. Protesters held a vigil outside Westminster Cathedral, and the Vatican newspaper denounced the destruction as a "prenatal massacre."

Another layer of complexity has been added by the practice at some fertility centers of creating embryos from donated eggs and sperm from commercial sperm banks. The rationale is that donor eggs are scarce, and when more are available than are needed in a particular case, they shouldn't be wasted. Having on hand a collection of embryos that don't belong to any person or couple allows the centers to offer what fertility specialists call *embryo adoption.* This means a woman or couple can choose ("adopt") an embryo for transfer on the basis of a description of the social and educational background and physical characteristics of the gamete donors. A couple can thus try for a resemblance between them and their potential child.

Some critics are troubled by the move from the creation of embryos to help particular people to the production of embryos on the speculation that someone who wants one may appear at the clinic. The practice is open to the charge that reproductive technology is a step nearer to treating human embryos as commercial products to be offered to discriminating consumers. At present there are no national regulations or guidelines for dealing with frozen embryos. Fertility centers set their own policies, and as might be expected, the rules followed by various centers are far from uniform.

The current controversy over embryonic stem cells has focused attention on unused embryos. Those who oppose the use of embryonic stem cells usually do so on the ground that acquiring them typically means destroying human embryos, which they consider to have the moral status of a person. By contrast, those favoring the use of embryonic stem cells argue that it is legitimate to retrieve them from unwanted embryos. Otherwise the embryos will discarded, and the potential to use the stem cells to help cure diseases will be lost.

## Gestational Surrogates and Donor Ova

This is perhaps the most dramatic possibility opened up by in vitro fertilization. A woman whose uterus has been removed, making her incapable of normal pregnancy, can contribute an ovum that, after being fertilized in vitro, is implanted in the uterus of a second woman whose uterus has been prepared to receive it. The "host" or gestational surrogate then carries the baby to term.

In a similar procedure, when a woman is incapable of producing ova, as the result either of disease, injury, or normal aging, a donor ovum may be fertilized in vitro then implanted in her uterus, and she then carries the child to term. Thus, postmenopausal women or many women once considered hopelessly barren may now become pregnant and give birth to a baby, even though they are genetically unrelated to the child.

Gestational surrogacy is a relatively new practice, and it opens up a number of possibilities that may have significant social consequences. That women past the natural age of childbearing can now become mothers is a stunning possibility that has already given rise to ethical and policy questions. (For a discussion, see Social Context: Postmenopausal Motherhood.) Second, women using the services of a gestational surrogate do so at present because they are unable to bear children themselves. However, it is only a short step from being unable to bear children to being *unwilling* to bear children.

Thus, it is easy to imagine that some women might choose to free themselves from the rigors of pregnancy by hiring a gestational surrogate. The employer would be the source of the ovum, which would then be fertilized in vitro and implanted as an embryo in the uterus of the surrogate. Women who could afford to do so could have their own genetic children without ever having to be pregnant.

Although a few have advocated using "genetically superior" women as a source of ova and "less superior" women as gestational surrogates, it is unlikely such a program will ever be endorsed by society. (See the Briefing Session in Chapter 5 for the difficulties in determining genetic "superiority.") Nevertheless, such practices are entirely possible, and it's likely they will continue to excite discussion.

The possibilities inherent in the use of gestational surrogacy, donor ova, and IVF mentioned so far are all currently employed or easily implemented. By contrast, the development of "baby factories" or "hatcheries" similar to those described in *Brave New World* is technologically unlikely, judged by current science and medicine. Machines would have to serve the function now served by the uterus, and designing such machines would require knowing enough about the needs of the developing fetus to reproduce that function. At present, it's not possible even to state all the problems that would have to be solved.

## Criticisms of Assisted Reproduction Practices

While admitting the present and potential values of reproductive technology in assisting women who want to have children, many critics think it has been oversold. Despite their hopes, the majority of women who must rely on it don't become pregnant. Also, women aren't always properly informed about their chances. A particular clinic may have a success rate of 25 percent, but for a woman in her early forties, the rate may be only a 1 to 2 percent chance per month of trying. (Only about 25 percent of those who seek assistance overcome their infertility.)

Critics also point out that the expense of trying to become pregnant can be quite high. Each attempt costs about $10,000 or more, and several attempts are usually required for success. Further, the procedures involve anxiety and discomfort. While the risk of injury and infection isn't great, it is real. In addition, the safety of the fertility drugs used to trigger ovulation and to prepare the uterus for implantation has been questioned. Also, there is a possibility the high hormone levels in the blood the drugs produce may increase a woman's risk of breast cancer.

An increase in the use of "donated" eggs raises serious issues about donors. All are young women, many are college students, and most are motivated to contribute their eggs for money. A typical fee is around $2000, and some women contribute two or more times. Sperm donors (see further on) usually receive only about $50, but egg donors must spend more time, experience discomfort, and run risks to their own health. They must agree to be injected with drugs to stimulate their ovaries (which may produce nausea and fatigue) and have frequent blood tests and ultrasound scans to determine when the ova are ready. They must then be anesthetized and the eggs retrieved from their follicles.

Donated ova are a scarce commodity, and some fertility clinics and programs make an effort to recruit donors so ova will be available for their clients. Some critics regard the situation as one in which young women in need lack the protection of the law and risk being exploited by those in a financial position to offer them money. As matters stand, only the moral principles of those who recruit donors regulate the practice.

## Benefits of IVF and Other Forms of Assisted Reproduction

Assisted reproduction is complicated, expensive, and requires a great investment of skill, knowledge, and resources. An obvious question is, What is to be gained by it? That is, what benefits might justify the use of the technically difficult and expensive medical procedures involved?

The most direct and perhaps the most persuasive answer is that assisted reproduction makes it possible for many people to have children who wouldn't otherwise be able to do so. For those people, this is a decisive consideration. Research shows that more than 10 percent of married couples in the United States are infertile—that is, they have attempted to conceive a child for a year or longer without success. As noted earlier, infertility affects 6.1 million women and an estimated 4 million men. In 1995 alone more than 1 million people sought professional help in conceiving a child.

Assisted reproduction isn't a solution to all problems of fertility, but it's the only solution possible in a large number of cases. Figures show that as many as 45 percent of all cases of female infertility are caused by abnormal or obstructed fallopian tubes. Although normal ova are produced, they cannot move down the tubes to be fertilized. In some cases, tissue blocking the tubes may be removed, or the tubes reconstructed. In other cases, however, the tubes may be impossible to repair or may be entirely absent. (Only 40 to 50 percent of infertile women can be helped through surgery.) This means that the only way in which these women can expect to have a child of their own is by means of some sort of assisted reproduction. This is also true when the woman has no uterus or is post-menopausal and must rely on a donated ovum. Thus, technology offers a realistic possibility of becoming parents to many people who once had no hope of having a child.

Critics of assisted reproduction often claim there is no *right* to have a child and suggest that those unable to conceive should simply accept the fact and perhaps adopt a child. Proponents don't justify assisted reproduction in terms of rights, however. They refer primarily to the strong desire some people have to become parents, and some point out that assisted reproduction, as it is most often employed, is nothing more than a means of facilitating a natural function that can't be carried out because of some sort of biological failure.

## Ethical and Social Difficulties

Several aspects of the technology of assisted reproduction and the way it is being employed are regarded by some people as troublesome. Briefly, we will consider a few sources of unease not mentioned earlier.

1.  *Destroyed Embryos.* Ova removed for fertilization may not all be used. Although they may be mixed with sperm and several become fertilized, only a few embryos are selected for implantation. The others may be simply discarded. Unclaimed and unused frozen embryos may be treated the same way. For those who believe that human life begins at conception, the destruction of embryos may be viewed as tantamount to

abortion. Thus, the destruction may be regarded as destroying innocent human life.

Others, who are not prepared to ascribe personhood to an embryo, may still be troubled by its pointless destruction. They may believe its potential to develop into a human being at least requires that it be treated with concern and respect. Those who subscribe to such views might argue that the only legitimate form of assisted reproduction is one in which the effort is made to fertilize only a single ovum. A failure in fertilization would then be similar to the failure that occurs naturally, and what would be eliminated would be the necessity of destroying fertilized eggs that cannot be implanted.

2.  *Danger to the Fetus.* Some critics worry that the use of reproductive technology like IVF, GIFT, or frozen embryos may pose risks to the fetus and to the person it may become. But experience has taken the teeth out of this objection. The rate of birth impairments in children born using established forms of reproductive technology is about 3 percent, virtually the same as that of ordinary births.

So far there is no evidence that children conceived by means of assisted reproduction differ in any way from other children. Where a new technology like cloning is concerned, however, this objection may still have bite. So far the necessary animal experiments haven't been done to establish a cloning procedure as reliable and safe.

3.  *Eugenics.* The use of reproductive technology may encourage the development of eugenic ideas about improving the species. Rather than having children of their own, would-be parents might be motivated to seek out ova (and sperm) from people who possess physical and intellectual characteristics that are particularly admired. Thus, even without an organized plan of social eugenics (see Chapter 5), individuals might

be tempted to follow their own eugenic notions. This includes the tendency to try to have "the perfect baby," and this cheapens human life by promoting the view that human babies are commodities produced to order.

4. *Sex Selection.* Similarly, would-be parents might be inclined to exercise the potential for control over the sex of their offspring. Only males contain both an X and a Y chromosome, and their presence is detectable in the cells of the developing embryo. Determination of the sex of the embryo would allow the potential parents to decide whether they wish to have a male or female child. Consequently, a potential human being (the developing fetus) might be destroyed for what is basically a trivial reason.

5. *Weakening of Family.* Reproductive technology may promote a social climate in which having children becomes severed from the family. The procedures emphasize the mechanics of conception and so minimize the significance of the shared love and commitments of the parents of a child conceived by intercourse.

    Similarly, the technology dilutes the notion of parenthood by making possible peculiar relationships. For example, as many as five people may become involved in having a child, for a couple can use donor sperm and donor eggs and rely on the services of a surrogate for pregnancy. Because there is no clear sense in which the child belongs to any of them, parenthood is radically severed from conception.

Obviously, these difficulties are not ones likely to be considered equally serious by everyone. Those who do not believe life begins at conception will hardly be troubled by the discarding of unimplanted embryos. Research and experience will likely reduce the risks of new and still unused technologies like cloning. Sex choice is possible now by the use of amniocentesis, so it's not a problem unique to reproductive technol-

ogy, and the same is true of the implementation of eugenic ideas.

Finally, whether assisted reproduction actually leads to a weakening of the values associated with the family is partly an empirical question that only additional experience will show. Even if childbearing does become severed from current family structure, it still must be shown this is in itself something of which we ought to disapprove. It's not impossible that alternative social structures for childbearing and child rearing might be superior to ones currently dominant in Western culture.

## Cloning and Twinning

Cloning involves producing individuals that are exact genetic copies of the donor from whom the DNA was obtained. Some animal cells have been cloned for more than five decades, but it wasn't until 1997 that the first mammal was cloned. Nothing in principle seems to stand in the way of cloning a human, but if human cloning became a practical reality, it would present serious moral and social issues. (See the Classic Case Presentation: "Hello, Dolly.")

Many of the issues raised in a speculative way by cloning are raised in a more immediate way by the procedure known as *twinning*. In 1993 Jerry Hall and Robert Stillman took 17 two- to eight-cell human embryos, separated the *blastomeres* (the individual cells) and coated them with artificial *zona pellucida* (the protective coat surrounding egg cells), then placed them in various nutrient solutions. The outcome was the production of forty-eight new embryos from the original ones.

The cells continued to divide, but development stopped after six days, partly because the embryos were abnormal—the original ones were chosen just because they were defective. The work was purely experimental, and it was never intended that the embryos would be implanted.

The immediate advantage of the techniques developed by Hall and Stillman (as well as many others) is to increase the supply of implantable embryos for couples with fertility problems. If a couple's embryos produced by in vitro fertilization can be used to produce several embryos, these can be used in repeated implantation attempts. Thus, the woman does not have to undergo repetitions of the unpleasant, expensive, and somewhat risky procedures involved in triggering ovulation, then retrieving ova for in vitro fertilization. Regarded from this point of view, for some couples the techniques may make having a child easier, cheaper, and less time-consuming.

The process used by Hall and Stillman was, strictly speaking, not actually cloning, which requires taking a somatic cell from a developed organism, extracting the DNA, then growing an embryo from it. Even so, the process of twinning they employed showed it would take very little more technically to use the techniques of assisted reproduction and produce a number of genetically identical humans.

Such techniques, when combined with the freezing of embryos, open up a number of social possibilities as surprising and controversial as those cloning would make possible:

1.  The production of several identical embryos would make a market in embryos possible. If a child had already been born and could be shown to have desirable qualities, the couple who had produced the embryos might sell them at high prices. It would then be possible for someone to have a child genetically identical to the one with the desirable qualities.

2.  Parents could have a family in which all their children are genetic copies of one another. The oldest and the youngest would have the same genetic endowment. If several gestational mothers were employed, it would be possible to produce a dozen or more genetically identical children of the same age.

3.  A couple might have a child, while also freezing an embryo twin as a spare. If the child should die, then the genetic twin could be grown from the embryo. The twin would be as much like the lost child as genetics makes possible.

4.  If embryo twins were frozen and stored, they could be implanted in a gestational mother years apart. Thus, one twin might be sixty years old, while the other is only six.

5.  Twins of an individual might be stored so that if the person needed something like a bone marrow or kidney transplant, the twin could be implanted in a gestational surrogate and allowed to develop. The tissue match from the twin would be perfect, and the problem of rejection would not arise.

The issues raised by twinning differ little from those raised by cloning, and twinning is already a practical reality. Some of the uses are so benign as to be hardly debatable, while others may result in such a cheapening or commercialization of human life as to be undesirable options.

## Artificial Insemination

In 1909, an unusual letter appeared in the professional journal *Medical World*. A. D. Hard, the author of the letter, claimed that when he was a student at Jefferson Medical College in Philadelphia, a wealthy businessman and his wife consulted a physician on the faculty about their inability to conceive a child. A detailed examination showed the man was incapable of producing sperm. The case was presented for discussion in a class of which Hard was a member. According to Hard, the class suggested semen should be taken from the "best-looking member of the class" and used to inseminate the wife.

The letter claimed this was done while the woman was anesthetized and that neither the husband nor the wife was told about the process. The patient became pregnant and gave birth to a son. The husband was then told how the pregnancy was produced, and, although he was pleased with the result, he asked that his wife not be informed.

The event described by Hard took place in 1884, and Hard was probably "the best-looking member of the class."

The Philadelphia case is usually acknowledged to be the first recorded instance of the artificial insemination of donor sperm in a human patient. However, the process itself has a much longer history. Arab horsemen in the fourteenth century apparently inseminated mares with semen-soaked sponges, and in the eighteenth century the Italian physiologist Spallansani documented experiments in which he fertilized dogs, reptiles, and frogs.

## The Procedure

Artificial insemination has become one of the basic techniques of assisted reproduction. It's initiated when the woman's body temperature indicates that ovulation is to take place in one or two days, then is repeated once or twice more until her body temperature shows that ovulation is completed. Typically, three inseminations are performed during a monthly cycle.

The procedure is simple. The patient is usually placed in a position so that her hips are raised. A semen specimen, collected earlier through masturbation or taken from a sperm bank, is placed in a syringe attached to a catheter. The catheter is inserted into the cervical canal and the semen slowly injected into the uterus. The patient then stays in her position for fifteen or twenty minutes to increase the chances that the sperm will fertilize an ovum.

The overall success rate of artificial insemination is about 85 to 90 percent. Success on the first attempt is quite rare, and the highest rate occurs in the third month. In unusual cases, efforts may be made every month for as long as six months or a year. Such efforts are continued, however, only when a detailed examination shows that the woman is not suffering from some unrecognized problem preventing her from becoming pregnant.

When sperm taken from donors is used, the rate of congenital abnormalities is a little lower than that for the general population. There is no evidence that manipulating the sperm causes any harm. Some physicians prefer to employ fresh, rather than frozen, sperm to minimize the amount of environmental change the sperm is subjected to. Other physicians, however, claim that frozen sperm is to be preferred, for it provides an opportunity for screening out defective sperm or chromosome abnormalities.

## Reasons for Seeking Artificial Insemination

Artificial insemination may be sought for a variety of reasons. When a couple is involved, the reasons are almost always associated with factors that make it impossible for the couple to conceive a child in the usual sexual way. About 10 percent of all married couples are infertile, and 40 percent of those cases are due to factors involving the male.

In some instances, the male may be unable to produce any sperm at all (a condition called asospermia), or the number of sperm he produces may be too low to make impregnation of the female likely (a condition called oligospermia). In other cases, while adequate numbers of sperm cells may be produced, they may not function normally. They may not be sufficiently motile to make their way past the vaginal canal and through the opening to the uterus. Hence, their chances of reaching and penetrating an ovum are slight. Finally, the male may suffer from a neurological condition that makes ejaculation impossible or from a disease (such as diabetes) that renders him impotent.

If the female cannot ovulate, or if her fallopian tubes are blocked so that ova cannot descend, artificial insemination can accomplish nothing. (See the earlier section on in vitro fertilization.) Yet there are factors affecting the female that artificial insemination can be helpful in overcoming. For example, if the female has a vaginal environment that is biochemically inhospitable to sperm, the artificial insemination may be successful. Because the sperm need not pass through the vagina, they have a better chance of surviving. Also, if the female has a small cervix (the opening to the uterus) or if her uterus is in an abnormal position, then artificial insemination may be used to deliver the sperm to an advantageous position for fertilization, a position they otherwise might not reach.

A couple might also seek artificial insemination for genetic reasons. Both may be carriers of a recessive gene for a genetic disorder (Tay–Sachs disease, for example) or the male may be the carrier of a dominant gene for a genetic disorder (Huntington's disease, for example). In either case, the couple may not want to run the statistical risk of their child's being born with a genetic disease, yet may also not be willing to accept prenatal testing and abortion. To avoid the possibility they fear, they may choose to make use of artificial insemination with sperm secured from a donor.

The traditional recipient of artificial insemination is a married woman who, in consultation with her husband, has decided to have a child. Some physiological or physical difficulty in conceiving leads them to turn to artificial insemination. But the traditional recipient is no longer the only recipient.

Those seeking to have the procedure performed now include single women who wish to have a child but do not wish to have it fathered in the usual fashion. The number of such inseminations may increase in the future if the notion of being a single parent continues to be met with acceptance or approval within our society. The increase may be quite rapid if the attitudes of physicians, in particular, change. At present, single women who wish to become mothers are likely to be discouraged, and some physicians and infertility centers won't accept them as candidates for artificial insemination.

## Types of Artificial Insemination

Artificial insemination can be divided into types in accordance with the source of the sperm employed. Artificial insemination (homologous) or AIH uses sperm obtained from the male partner. Artificial insemination (heterologous) or AID uses sperm from a sperm donor. The use of semen obtained from a donor is the most frequent of AI procedures and gives rise to most of the social and legal issues surrounding the practice.

Artificial insemination (confused) or CAI employs a mixture of sperm from the male partner and sperm obtained from a donor. CAI has no particular biological advantage, but it offers a couple a degree of psychological support. Because they cannot be sure that it was not sperm from the male partner that resulted in conception, they may be more inclined to accept the child as the product of their union. The role of the third-party sperm donor is thus psychologically minimized.

## Sperm Donors

Sperm donors are typically selected from medical or college student volunteers. Commercial sperm banks may recruit widely, but generally an effort is made to employ as donors people in excellent health with a high level of intellectual ability. Their family histories are reviewed to reduce the possibility of transmitting a genetic disorder, and their blood type is checked to determine its compatibility with that of the AID recipient. Such general physical features of the donor as body type, hair and eye color, and complexion are matched in a rough way with those of the potential parents. To be a donor, an individual must also be known to be fertile. This means he must already be a biological parent or that he must fall within the normal range in several semen analyses.

Donors are typically paid for their services. What is more, their identity is kept secret from the recipient and her husband. A coding system is ordinarily used both to preserve the anonymity of the donor and to ensure that the same donor is used in all inseminations.

Sperm contributed by a donor might be employed in an insemination within one to three hours after the semen is obtained. As mentioned earlier, some physicians prefer to use freshly obtained sperm in the procedure. But sperm may also be maintained in a frozen condition and, after being restored to the proper temperature, used in the same way as fresh sperm. Sperm banks are no more than freezers containing racks of coded plastic tubes holding donated sperm.

The semen stored in sperm banks is not necessarily that of anonymous donors. For a variety of reasons, individuals may wish to have their sperm preserved and pay a fee to a sperm-bank operator for this service. For example, a man planning a vasectomy or one expecting to become sterile because of a progressive disease may store his sperm in the event that he may later want to father a child.

## Issues in Artificial Insemination

Artificial insemination presents a variety of moral, legal, and social issues that have not been addressed in a thorough fashion. Legal scholars have explored some of the consequences that AI has for traditional legal doctrines of paternity, legitimacy, and inheritance. They have also made recommendations for formulating new laws (or reformulating old ones) to take into account the reality of the practice of AI.

Others who have written about AI have focused mostly on its potential for altering the relationship between husbands and wives and for producing undesirable social changes. Many of the objections to assisted reproduction in general have also been offered to AI. For example, it's been argued that AI will take the love out of sexual procreation and make it a purely mechanical process, that AI will promote eugenics and so denigrate the worth of babies that fall short of some ideal, and that AI is just another step down the road toward the society of *Brave New World.*

Some of the issues that need close attention from philosophers concern individual rights and responsibilities. For example, does a man who has served as a sperm donor have any special moral responsibilities? He certainly must have some responsibilities. For example, it would be wrong for him to lie about any genetic diseases in his family history. But does he have any responsibilities to the child that is produced by AI employing his sperm? If donating sperm is no different from donating blood, then perhaps he does not. But is such a comparison apt?

Can a child born as a result of AI legitimately demand to know the name of his biological father? We need not assume mere curiosity might motivate such a request. Someone could need to know his family background in order to determine how likely it is that a potential child might have a genetic disorder. Perhaps the current practice of maintaining the anonymity of sperm donors is not one that can stand critical scrutiny.

Should a woman be allowed to order sperm donated by someone who approximates her concept of an ideal person? Should she be able to request a donor from a certain ethnic group, with particular eye and hair color, certain minimum or maximum height, physical attractiveness, with evidence of intelligence, and so on? At present, the physician who performs the procedure also makes the choice of the donor. But why should the physician be granted the right to make the selection? One might argue that allowing the physician to exercise such a power violates the autonomy of the AI recipient.

A number of other ethical questions are easily raised about AI: Does any woman (married or single, of any age) have the right to demand AI? Should a physician make AID available to a married woman even if her husband is opposed?

Other questions concerning the proper procedures to follow in the practice of AI are also of considerable significance. For example, how thoroughly must sperm donors be screened for genetic defects? What standards of quality must sperm as a biological material be required to satisfy? What physical, educational, or general social traits (if any) should individual donors possess? Should records be maintained and shared through an established network to prevent the marriage or mating of individuals born from AID with the same biological father?

At present, these questions have been answered only by individual physicians or clinics, if at all. There are no general medical or legal policies governing the practice of AI. Even if present practices are adequate, most people would agree there is a need to develop uniform policies to regulate AI.

Obviously, we have touched upon only a few of the ethical and social issues that the practice of artificial insemination generates. Indeed, at the moment, it is not wholly clear even what the more significant issues may be.

### Ova Donors

The use of donor ova presents virtually the same set of issues as those raised by artificial insemination. In addition, as mentioned earlier, unlike AI, egg donation raises questions about the exploitation of donors. They are typically young women who agree to donate ova because they want to earn the several thousand dollars fertility clinics are willing to pay.

To earn the money, they must put themselves through an uncomfortable process involving treatment with powerful drugs and the retrieval of the eggs by a small surgical incision or a needle puncture. The risk to their health is small but real. Critics point out that women willing to submit themselves to the process must be young and are likely to be naive and vulnerable. A need for money will thus make them ripe for exploitation. Paying money to someone for performing a service does not in itself constitute exploitation, however, and critics could make a stronger case if they were able to show how women are harmed by the practice.

## Surrogate Pregnancy

A *gestational surrogate* (see the previous discussion) is a "host mother," a woman who is implanted with an embryo produced from the ovum of another woman. *Surrogate mothers* are women who agree to become pregnant by means of artificial insemination. The surrogate mother carries the baby to term, then turns the baby over for adoption to the couple or individual with whom she made the agreement.

Surrogate mothers are typically sought by couples who wish to have a child with whom at least the man has a genetic link and who have been unsuccessful in conceiving one themselves. Also, a woman unable to conceive but wanting a child may also arrange for the services of a surrogate mother by using donor sperm.

Various legal complications surround surrogate pregnancy, and at least eighteen states have passed laws regulating surrogacy arrangements. Some laws, like those in Michigan and New Jersey, make it illegal for couples to adopt a child born to a surrogate mother. The aim is to discourage surrogacy.

When surrogacy arrangements are allowed, a major problem is to find a way to pay women who agree to be surrogates. Adoption laws forbid the selling of children or even the payment of money to one of the biological parents in connection with adoption. The child must be freely surrendered. Because a child born to a surrogate mother is, in the absence of laws to the contrary, legally her child, the child must be adopted by the couple securing her services. How then can the surrogate mother be paid?

Some women have simply volunteered to be surrogate mothers so the issue of payment would not arise. In general, however, the difficulty has been resolved by paying the mother to compensate her for her inconvenience and the loss of her time. Technically, then, she is not being paid for conceiving and bearing a child, nor is she being paid for the child who is handed over for adoption. Hence, laws against selling a child are not violated, and the surrogate is paid from $10,000 to $25,0000.

A second problem is finding a way to permit surrogacy, while avoiding turning it into a commercial operation resembling the breeding of horses or show dogs. Surrogacy is often arranged by an attorney acting as a broker on behalf of a couple who want a child. The attorney finds the surrogate and draws up a contract between her and the couple. (The contract can include such items as a prorated fee if the surrogate miscarries or a requirement that the surrogate have an abortion if prenatal tests reveal a fetal abnormality.) The surrogate must agree to relinquish her maternal rights and not stand in the way of adoption by the contracting couple. For arranging the surrogacy, as well as for drawing up the contract, the broker receives a fee of $15,000 to $25,000.

Despite the claim that a surrogate is being paid for her time and inconvenience, some critics charge that surrogacy arrangements are no more than "baby selling." To avoid this appearance, New York state passed a law with the aim of removing the profit motive from surrogacy arrangements and making them completely noncommercial. The state kept it legal for a woman to become a surrogate but made it illegal to pay a broker to handle the arrangements. Further, the state made it illegal to pay a surrogate for anything more than her medical expenses. A contract agreeing to pay a fee to a broker or to a woman acting as a surrogate would have no legal standing in court.

Some of the same reasons offered to justify assisted reproduction can also be offered for surrogate pregnancy. Fundamentally, couples who wish to have a child of their own but are unable to do so because of some uncorrectable medical difficulty experienced by the woman view surrogate pregnancy as the only hope remaining to them. Some rule out adoption because of the relative shortage of available infants, and some simply want a genetic connection between them and the child. Many people are quite desperate to have a child of their own.

Some critics have charged that surrogate pregnancy is no more than a specialized form of prostitution. A woman, in effect, rents out her body for a period of time and is paid for doing so. Such a criticism rests on the assumption that prostitution is morally wrong, and this is a claim at least some would deny is correct. Furthermore, the criticism fails to take into account the differences in aims. Some surrogate mothers have volunteered their services with no expectation of monetary reward, and some women have agreed to be surrogate mothers at the request of their sister, friend, daughter, or son. Even those who are paid mention that part of their motivation is to help those couples who so desperately want a child. Far from condemning surrogate mothers as acting immorally, it is possible to view at least some as acting in a morally heroic way by contributing to the good of others through their actions.

Perhaps the most serious objection to surrogate mothers is that they are likely to be re-

cruited from the ranks of those most in need of money. Women of upper- and middle-income groups are not likely to serve as surrogate mothers. Women with low-paying jobs or no jobs at all are obviously the prime candidates for recruiters. It might be charged, then, that women who become surrogate mothers are being exploited by those who have money enough to pay for their services.

Merely paying someone in need of money to do something does not constitute exploitation, however. To make such a charge stick, it would be necessary to show that women who become surrogate mothers are under a great deal of social and economic pressure and have no other realistic options. Furthermore, it could be argued that, within limits, individuals have a right to do with their bodies as they choose. If a woman freely decides to earn money by serving as a surrogate mother, then we have no more reason to object to her decision than we would have to object to a man's decision to earn money by working as a laborer.

As the population ages and women with careers postpone having children, the employment of surrogate mothers is likely to increase. The practice is now well established, but the ethical and social issues are far from being resolved to the general satisfaction of our society.

## Ethical Theories and Reproductive Control

One of the themes of Mary Shelley's famous novel *Frankenstein* is that it is both wrong and dangerous to tamper with the natural forces of life. It is wrong because it disturbs the natural order of things, and it is dangerous because it unleashes forces beyond human control. The "monster" that is animated by Dr. Victor Frankenstein stands as a warning and reproach to all who seek to impose their will on the world through the powers of scientific technology.

The fundamental ethical question about the technology of human reproductive control is whether it ought to be employed at all. Is it simply wrong for us to use our knowledge of human biology to exercise power over the processes of human reproduction?

The natural law view, as represented by currently accepted doctrines of the Roman Catholic Church, suggests that all the techniques for controlling human reproduction that we have discussed here are fundamentally wrong.

Children may ordinarily be expected as a result of sexual union within marriage. However, if no measures are wrongfully taken to frustrate the possibility of their birth (contraception, for example), then a married couple has no obligation to attempt to conceive children by means such as artificial insemination or in vitro fertilization. Certainly, they have no reason to resort to anything as extreme as cloning or using donor embryos.

Indeed, many of the technological processes are themselves inherently objectionable. Artificial insemination, for example, requires male masturbation, which is prima facie wrong, since it is an act that can be considered to be unnatural, given the natural end of sex. AI, even when semen from the husband is used, tends to destroy the values inherent in the married state. It makes conception a mechanical act.

In vitro fertilization is open to the same objections. In addition, the process itself involves the destruction of fertilized ova. On the view that human conception takes place at the moment of fertilization, this means that the discarding of unimplanted embryos amounts to the destruction of human life.

On the utilitarian view, no reproductive technology is in itself objectionable. The question that has to be answered is whether the use of any particular procedure, in general or in a certain case, is likely to lead to more good than not. In general, it is reasonable to believe that a utilitarian would be likely to approve of all the procedures we've discussed here.

A rule utilitarian, however, might oppose any or all of the procedures. If there is strong evidence to support the view that the use of reproductive technology will lead to a society in which the welfare of its members will not be served, then a rule utilitarian would be on firm ground in arguing that reproductive technology ought to be abandoned.

According to Ross's ethical theory, we have prima facie duties of beneficence. That is, we have an obligation to assist others in bettering their lives. This suggests that the use of reproductive technology may be justified as a means to promote the well-being of others. For example, if a couple desires to have a child but is unable to conceive one, then either in vitro fertilization procedures or artificial insemination might be employed to help them satisfy their shared desire. Twinning might be used to increase the number of embryos, and even cloning seems prima facie unobjectionable.

Kantian principles don't seem to supply grounds for objecting to assisted reproduction or reproductive technology in general as inherently wrong. However, the maxim involved in each action must always be one that satisfies the categorical imperative. Consequently, some instances of in vitro fertilization, artificial insemination, twinning, and cloning would no doubt be morally wrong.

The technology of reproduction is a reality of ordinary life. So far it has made our society into neither a dystopia nor a utopia. It's just one set of tools among the many that science and medicine have forged.

Yet the tools are powerful ones, and we should beware of allowing familiarity to produce indifference. The moral and social issues raised by reproductive technology are just as real as the technology. So far we have not treated some of them with the seriousness they deserve.

## Case Presentation

### Louise Brown: The First "Test-Tube Baby"

Under other circumstances, the birth announcement would have been perfectly ordinary, the sort appearing in newspapers every day: *Born to John and Lesley Brown: a baby girl, Louise, 5 lbs. 12 ozs., 11:47 P.M., July 25, 1978, Oldham (England) General Hospital.*

But the birth of Louise Brown was far from being an ordinary event, and the announcement of its occurrence made headlines throughout the world. For the first time in history, a child was born who was conceived outside the mother's body under controlled laboratory conditions. Louise Brown was the world's first "test-tube baby."

For John and Lesley Brown, the birth of Louise was a truly marvelous event. "She's so small, so beautiful, so perfect," her mother told a reporter. Her father said, "It was like a dream. I couldn't believe it."

The joy of the Browns was understandable. From the time of their marriage in 1969 they had both very much wanted to have a child. Then they discovered that Lesley Brown was unable to conceive because of blocked Fallopian tubes—the ova would not descend so fertilization could not occur. In 1970, she had surgery to correct the condition, but the procedure was unsuccessful.

The Browns decided they would adopt a child, because they couldn't have one of their own. After two years on a waiting list, they gave up that plan. But the idea of having their own child was rekindled when a nurse familiar with the work of embryologist Robert Edwards and gynecologist Patrick Steptoe referred the Browns to them.

For the previous twelve years, Steptoe and Edwards had been working on the medical and biochemical techniques required for embryo transfer. Steptoe developed techniques for removing a ripened ovum from a woman's ovaries, then reimplanting it in the uterus after it has been fertilized. Edwards improved the chemical solutions needed to keep ova functioning and healthy outside the body and perfected a method of external fertilization with sperm.

Using their techniques, Steptoe and Edwards had successfully produced a pregnancy in one of their patients in 1975, but it had resulted in a miscarriage. They continued to refine their procedures and were confident their techniques could produce a normal pregnancy that would result in a healthy baby.

They considered Lesley Brown a superb candidate for an embryo transfer. She was in excellent general health, at thirty-one she was within the usual age range for pregnancy, and she was highly fertile. In 1976, Steptoe did an exploratory operation and found her Fallopian tubes were not functional and could not be surgically repaired. He removed them so he would have unimpeded access to the ovaries.

In November 1977, Mrs. Brown was given injections of a hormone to increase the maturation rate of her egg cells. Then, in a small private hospital in Old-

ham, Dr. Steptoe performed a minor surgical procedure. Using a laparoscope to guide him—a tube with a built-in eyepiece and light source that is inserted through a tiny slit in the abdomen—he extracted an ovum with a suction needle from a ripened follicle.

The ovum was then placed in a small glass vessel containing biochemical nutrients and sperm secured from John Brown. Once the egg was fertilized, it was transferred to another nutrient solution. More than fifty hours later, the ovum had reached the eight-cell stage of division. Guided by their previous experience and research, Steptoe and Edwards had decided that it was at this stage an ovum should be returned to the womb. Although in normal human development the ovum has divided to produce sixty-four or more cells before it completes its descent down the Fallopian tube and becomes attached to the uterine wall, they had learned that attachment is possible at an earlier stage. The stupendous difficulties in creating and maintaining the proper biochemical environment for a multiplying cell made it reasonable to reduce the time outside the body as much as possible.

Lesley Brown had been given another series of hormone injections to prepare her uterus. Two and a half days after the ovum was removed, the fertilized egg—an embryo—was reimplanted. Using a laparoscope and a hollow plastic tube (a *cannula*), Dr. Steptoe introduced the small sphere of cells into Mrs. Brown's uterus. It successfully attached itself to the uterine wall.

Lesley Brown's pregnancy proceeded normally. But, because of the special nature of her case, seven weeks before the baby was due she entered the Oldham Hospital maternity ward so she could be continuously monitored. About a week before the birth was expected, the baby was delivered by Cesarean section. Mrs. Brown had developed toxemia, a condition associated with high blood pressure that can lead to stillbirth.

The baby was normal, and all concerned were jubilant. "The last time I saw the baby it was just eight cells in a test tube," Dr. Edwards said. "It was beautiful then, and it's still beautiful now." After the delivery, Dr. Steptoe said, "She came out crying her head off, a beautiful normal baby."

John Brown almost missed the great event, because no one on the hospital staff had bothered to tell him his wife was scheduled for the operation. Only when he had been gone from the hospital for about two hours and called to talk to his wife did he find out what was about to happen.

He rushed back and waited anxiously until a nurse came out and said, "You're the father of a wonderful little girl." As he later told a reporter, "Almost before I knew it, there I was holding our daughter in my arms."

Like many ordinary fathers, he ran down the halls of the hospital telling people he passed, "It's a girl! I've got a baby daughter."

To calm down, he went outside and stood in the rain. It was there a reporter from a London newspaper captured Mr. Brown's view of the event. "The man who deserves all the praise is Dr. Steptoe," he said. "What a man to be able to do such a wonderful thing."

On July 25, 1998, Louise Brown turned twenty. While working part-time in a fast-food restaurant, she was studying to become a school nurse. Despite dire predictions of opponents of in vitro fertilization, Louise didn't turn out to be either grossly abnormal or psychologically scarred. The main feature distinguishing her from most twenty-somethings turns out to be her trust fund composed of earnings from a book by her parents and various television projects over the years.

"I want to have my own children, whatever it takes," she told a reporter from London's *Daily Mail*. "I would use the in vitro method if I couldn't have a baby."

## Case Presentation

### Septuplets: The Perils of Multiple Pregnancies

Shortly before noon on November 19, 1997, in the small town of Cheerlessly, Iowa, a twenty-nine-year-old woman named Bobbi McCaughey gave birth by cesarean section to seven babies.

Mrs. McCaughey (pronounced McCoy) had set a world record for the number of live babies born in a single pregnancy. The family was immediately bathed in the glare of worldwide media attention, and for a while they became emblems of the American family—hard-working, religious, and committed to the welfare of their children. Bobbi McCaughey was admired for her courage and fortitude for coping so well with a difficult thirty-one week pregnancy.

To help prevent a miscarriage, she had been confined to bed in the nineteenth week, and for the last months, she had been hospitalized. While all the babies had a lower than normal birth weight, ranging

from 2.5 to 3.4 pounds, with the help of the more than forty obstetricians, neonatologists, pediatricians, and other specialists who attended the birth, the babies all survived. Some suffered difficulties, but eventually even they were pulled to safety by aggressive medical management.

### Fertility Drugs and Multiple Births

Because the McCaugheys had experienced difficulty conceiving their first child, Mikayla, when they were ready to have another they sought help from an infertility clinic. Bobbi McCaughey was treated with Pergonal to increase her chances of becoming pregnant, which she soon did.

Pergonal is one of several fertility drugs associated with multiple pregnancies. The drugs increase the likelihood of pregnancy by causing more than one egg to be released per menstrual cycle, but this also increases the likelihood that more than one egg will be fertilized.

Early in Mrs. McCaughey's pregnancy, her physician informed the couple she was carrying seven fetuses and recommended some of them be terminated. The elimination procedure, called *selective reduction*, involves deliberately destroying and removing fetuses and is performed to increase the chances that the remaining fetuses will develop into healthy babies. The McCaugheys rejected the recommendation on the ground that their religious beliefs made abortion unacceptable. "God gave us those babies," Mrs. McCaughey told a reporter. "He wants us to raise them."

While Mrs. McCaughey's pregnancy set a record, it is only one of an increasing number of multiple pregnancies. During the period 1988 to 1997, the number of women taking fertility drugs almost tripled, rising from about 1 million to 2.7 million. Not coincidentally, the number of multiple births has *quadrupled* over the last thirty years. In 1995 (the latest year with complete figures), 4973 children were born in groups of three or more. Triplets were most common, but already three sets of sextuplets have been born, and no doubt more are on the way.

### Dangers

A multiple pregnancy increases the risk of a miscarriage. Mark Evans, a fertility expert at Wayne State Hospital, estimates that a woman pregnant with quadruplets has a 25 percent chance of a miscarriage in the first trimester; a woman pregnant with quintuplets has a 50 percent chance. Cases of pregnancies with a larger number of fetuses are too few to permit significant generalizations.

The risk of losing all fetuses to a miscarriage was sadly illustrated by the case of Mary Atwood in England. Pregnant with eight fetuses, she arranged to sell her story to a tabloid, with the amount she would be paid dependent on the number of surviving babies. All eight were lost in a miscarriage.

Even when a miscarriage doesn't occur, multiple pregnancies rarely reach the end of a full forty-week term. Triplets are born after an average of 33.5 weeks and quadruplets after 31 weeks. The result is that babies born as multiples often suffer from one or more of the many problems of prematurity: retinal damage causing blindness, bleeding into the brain producing permanent brain damage, retardation, learning disabilities, impaired motor skills, chronic lung problems, or cerebral palsy.

### Irresponsible?

The McCaugheys were lucky with their seven babies, but they and their fertility specialists aren't without critics. Some believe the specialists should have stopped the fertility drugs sooner and perhaps prevented the release of so many eggs. Others think the specialists should have required the McCaugheys to agree to a selective reduction of multiple fetuses before starting Mrs. McCaughey's treatment. Also, when it became apparent how many fetuses were present, they should have pressed the McCaugheys harder to eliminate some of them.

Critics also see the McCaugheys as having acted irresponsibly. If they weren't prepared to accept selective reduction, they shouldn't have sought help from an infertility clinic. Also, because they were lucky enough to have a good outcome, their example may suggest multiple pregnancies are now safe and reliable and thus others may be encouraged to believe they can safely have multiple babies.

### Costs

Further, the cost of medical care for Mrs. McCaughey and her children has been estimated at around $1.5 million. This is money the McCaugheys can't afford to pay, and it must be picked up in some way by the health-care system and the society. With so much medical need unmet, society cannot afford to indulge the wishes of others like the McCaugheys.

Infertility specialists discourage multiple pregnancies. Their aim is to assist a woman in having one or at most two healthy babies. A multiple pregnancy carried to term is viewed not so much as a mark of success as a sign of failure. But because infertility clinics are almost completely self-regulated, the penalty for the failure is borne by the woman, her babies, the family, and society, but not by the clinic treating her. If the number of multiple births continues to rise, however, infertility clinics will be under increasing pressure either to reduce the number or to become subject to government regulation. While multiple births can sometimes be occasions for joy, they are too often times of trouble and tragedy.

## Social Context: Postmenopausal Motherhood

In late 1996 sixty-three-year-old Arceli Keh gave birth to a healthy baby girl. This made her the oldest woman ever to become a first-time mother.

This highly unusual event was not an accident of nature, but the result of deliberate planning and technological manipulation. Even so, Dr. Richard Paulson, the physician at the University of Southern California infertility clinic who treated Keh, hadn't known her true age. She had lied to her previous doctors, and the age on her chart was recorded as fifty.

Fifty was already five years over the clinic's limit for in vitro fertilization, but Keh was in excellent health and did well on tests for strength and endurance. Paulson approved her for IVF, and by the time he discovered her true age, she was pregnant with an embryo formed by a donor egg fertilized with sperm provided by her sixty-year-old husband Isagani Keh.

The Kehs, who had immigrated from the Philippines, lived in Highland, California, about sixty miles east of Los Angeles. Although they had been married sixteen years, they had been unsuccessful in conceiving a child.

"I wasn't trying to make history," Arceli told a reporter for the London newspaper *The Express*.

"We are working people," she said. "I only retired to have my baby." Isagani was still working as a carpenter to help pay the more than $60,000 they spent on the procedures resulting in the birth of their daughter, whom they named Cynthia.

Keh was the oldest postmenopausal woman to bear a child, but she wasn't the first. On Christmas Day, 1993, a fifty-nine-year-old British woman, identified only as Jennifer F., gave birth to twins. Jennifer F. was married and highly successful in business, but even though she was a millionaire, there came a time when she realized she regretted not having a child. By then she had undergone menopause, making it impossible for her to conceive.

Refusing to surrender her dream, Jennifer F. visited a National Health Service fertility clinic in London and asked for help. She wanted to be made pregnant with an embryo produced from her husband's sperm and a donor egg. Physicians at the clinic declined to perform the procedure, telling her she was too old to cope with the physical and emotional stress required to be a mother.

Determined to do everything possible to have a child, Jennifer F. then went to the clinic operated by Severino Antinori in Rome. Antinori agreed to accept her as a patient and performed the in vitro fertilization and embryo transfer procedure. Antinori claims he has assisted more than fifty women over the age of fifty to become pregnant.

Although both Arceli Keh and Jennifer F. attracted much media attention, other postmenopausal women had earlier become pregnant and borne children. In 1993 Geraldine Wesoloski, fifty-three, gave birth to a baby who was both her child and her grandchild. She was the gestational surrogate for her son, Mark, and his wife Susan. As a result of an accident, Susan had undergone a hysterectomy, but she and Mark were able to provide the embryo that was then transferred to Wesoloski.

A year earlier, Mary Shearing, also fifty-three, gave birth to twin girls. She was made pregnant with embryos produced by donated eggs and sperm from her thirty-two-year-old husband. Even though Mary Shearing was no longer ovulating, she and her husband had decided to have a child of their own.

Since 1987 it has been technologically possible for a postmenopausal woman to become pregnant with donor eggs, and during the last few years, the number of older (usually first-time) mothers has been increasing. In the United States in 2000, there were 255 births to women between the ages of 50 and 54, a significant increase from the 174 in 1999. (Statistics on births to women over the age of fifty-four are not collected by the Centers for Disease Control.)

The increase may be due partly to changes in the policies of infertility clinics. Until recently, most clinics in the United States would not accept as patients women past their early or mid-forties. Experts suspected that older women would not only have a low success rate but that they would be putting their health at greater risk. A large study released in 2002 provides grounds to question both claims.

The study was carried out at the University of Southern California and involved seventy-seven postmenopausal women treated at the university's reproductive clinic from 1991 to 2001; forty-two of the women gave birth. The study showed that healthy women in their fifties have rates of pregnancy using donor eggs that are comparable to those of younger women. Further, although older women face higher rates of pregnancy-induced diabetes and hypertension, the conditions are temporary. Older women are, however, more likely to have a cesarean section than younger women.

**Con.** While clinics are making it easier for postmenopausal women to attempt motherhood, critics argue that, given the scarcity of donor eggs, they ought to be reserved for younger women. It is best for a child, critics claim, to have physically and mentally active parents. Older parents may be unable to keep up with the demands of growing children, and the children will thus be cheated by not having parents who do things with them. Also, older parents are more likely to die, leaving behind young children still in need of guidance and financial support.

**Pro.** Defenders of granting access to fertility services to older women argue it is pure gender bias to deny them the possibility of having a child. Men often father children well into their old age and are often admired for doing so. Charlie Chaplin was seventy-three when he had his last child, and Senator Strom Thurmond had four children during his sixties and seventies. The actor Tony Randall became a father for the first time when he was seventy-seven. By contrast, a woman no longer ovulating, even with a younger husband, has no way to have a child without relying on assisted reproduction.

Also, just because a woman is relatively young does not mean she will be a better mother. On the contrary, it seems likely an older woman with more psychological and financial security will be a better parent than many young women. Besides, younger women do not have to prove they will be good mothers before they are allowed to have children, so why should older women? Finally, babies born to older women using eggs obtained from younger women do just as well as babies born to younger women, and now the evidence suggests that older mothers are not risking their health to a significant extent.

The number of women past menopause wishing to become pregnant is never expected to become great. Even so, the conflict between those who argue that older women are entitled to access to assisted reproduction and those who argue access should be denied to them is likely to continue. Now that a number of children have been born to older mothers, some relevant factual questions about safety have been settled. Yet ethical and social questions about post-menopausal motherhood still remain.

## SOCIAL CONTEXT: FATHER SHOPPING: SPERM BY MAIL

Several commercial sperm banks now offer potential mothers the opportunity to browse through a catalogue of sperm donors and choose the one they prefer. One has a web site providing detailed information about a donor's medical history, appearance, and interests, while another, with the permission of its donors, includes photographs and donor profiles online.

A California web site employs a search function to allow shoppers to specify donor characteristics ranging from blood type and race to level of education, hair color, and appearance. The computer then searches its data banks for particular donors that meet the specifications.

Some sperm banks also offer ways of allowing donors to reveal aspects of their personality. While preserving their anonymity, the banks give them the option of writing a personal essay or letter about themselves that can be read by a prospective recipient and, later, by a child conceived by the use of the sperm. Donors are sometimes even asked to indicate their willingness to meet their biological child in the future, if the child requests it.

The frozen sperm from the favored recipient chosen by the potential recipient can be ordered and shipped by mail, but the ordering must be done by a physician. Both the physician and the patient must sign a consent form.

## Case Presentation

### Baby M and Mary Beth Whitehead: Surrogate Pregnancy in Court

On March 30, 1986, Elizabeth Stern, a professor of pediatrics, and her husband William accepted from Mary Beth Whitehead a baby who had been born four days earlier. The child's biological mother was Whitehead, but she had been engaged by the Sterns as a surrogate mother. Even so, it was not until almost exactly a year later that the Sterns were able to claim legal custody of the child.

The Sterns, working through the Infertility Center of New York, had first met with Whitehead and her husband Richard in January of 1985. Whitehead, who already had a son and a daughter, had indicated her willingness to become a surrogate mother by signing up at the Infertility Center. "What brought her there was empathy with childless couples who were infertile," her attorney later stated. Her own sister had been unable to conceive.

According to court testimony, the Sterns considered Mrs. Whitehead a "perfect person" to bear a child for them. Mr. Stern said it was "compelling" for him to have children, for he had no relatives "anywhere in the world." He and his wife planned to have children, but they put off attempts to conceive until his wife completed her medical residency in 1981. In 1979, however, she was diagnosed as having an eye condition indicating she probably had multiple sclerosis. When she learned the symptoms of the disease might be worsened by pregnancy and that she might become temporarily or even permanently paralyzed, the Sterns "decided the risk wasn't worth it." It was this decision that led them to the Infertility Center and to Mary Beth Whitehead.

The Sterns agreed to pay Whitehead $10,000 to be artificially inseminated with Mr. Stern's sperm and to bear a child. Whitehead would then turn the child over to the Sterns, and Elizabeth Stern would be allowed to adopt the child legally. The agreement was drawn up by a lawyer specializing in surrogacy. Mr. Stern later testified that Whitehead seemed perfectly pleased with the agreement and expressed no interest in keeping the baby she was to bear. "She said she would not come to our doorstep," he said. "All she wanted from us was a photograph each year and a little letter on what transpired that year."

### Birth and Strife

The baby was born on March 27, 1986. According to Elizabeth Stern, the first indication Whitehead might not keep the agreement was her statement to the Sterns in the hospital two days after the baby's birth. "She said she didn't know if 'I can go through with it,'" Dr. Stern testified. Although Whitehead did turn the baby over to the Sterns on March 30, she called a few hours later. "She said she didn't know if she could live any more," Elizabeth Stern said. She called again the next morning and asked to see the baby, and she and her sister arrived at the Sterns' house before noon.

According to Elizabeth Stern, Whitehead told her she "woke up screaming in the middle of the night" because the baby was gone, her husband was threatening to leave her, and she had "considered taking a bottle of Valium." Stern quoted Whitehead as saying, "I just want her for a week, and I'll be out of your lives forever." The Sterns allowed Mrs. Whitehead to take the baby home with her.

Whitehead then refused to return the baby and took the infant with her to her parents' home in Florida. The Sterns obtained a court order, and on July 31 the child was seized from Whitehead. The Sterns were granted temporary custody. Then Mr. Stern, as the father of the child, and Mrs. Whitehead, as the mother, each sought permanent custody from the Superior Court of the State of New Jersey.

### Trial

The seven-week trial attracted national attention, for the legal issues were without precedent. Whitehead was the first to challenge the legal legitimacy of a surrogate agreement in a U.S. court. She argued the agreement was "against public policy" and violated New Jersey prohibitions against selling babies. In contrast, Mr. Stern was the first to seek a legal decision to uphold the "specific performance" of the terms of a surrogate contract. In particular, he argued Whitehead should be ordered to uphold her agreement and to surrender her parental rights and permit his wife to become the baby's legal mother. In addition to the contractual issues, the judge had to deal with the "best interest" of the child as required by New Jersey child-custody law. In addition to being a vague concept, the "best interest" standard had never been applied in a surrogacy case.

On March 31, 1987, Judge Harvey R. Sorkow announced his decision. He upheld the legality of the surrogate-mother agreement between the Sterns and Whitehead and dismissed all arguments that the contract violated public policy or prohibitions against selling babies.

Immediately after he read his decision, Judge Sorkow summoned Elizabeth Stern into his chambers and allowed her to sign documents permitting her to adopt the baby she and her husband called Melissa. The court decision effectively stripped Mary Beth Whitehead of all parental rights concerning this same baby, the one she called Sara.

### Appeal

The Baby M story did not stop with Judge Sorkow's decision. Whitehead's attorney appealed the ruling to the New Jersey Supreme Court, and on February 3, 1988, the seven members of the court, in a unanimous decision, reversed Judge Sorkow's ruling on the surrogacy agreement.

The court held that the agreement violated the state's adoption laws, because it involved a payment for a child. "This is the sale of a child, or at the very least, the sale of a mother's right to her child," Chief Justice Wilentz wrote. The agreement "takes the child from the mother regardless of her wishes and her maternal fitness . . . ; and it accomplishes all of its goals through the use of money."

The court ruled that surrogacy agreements might be acceptable if they involved no payment and if a surrogate mother voluntarily surrendered her parental rights. In the present case, though, the court regarded paying for surrogacy as "illegal, perhaps criminal, and potentially degrading to women."

The court let stand the award of custody to the Sterns, because "their household and their personalities promise a much more likely foundation for Melissa to grow and thrive." Mary Beth Whitehead, having divorced her husband three months earlier, was romantically involved with a man named Dean Gould and was pregnant at the time of the court decision.

Despite awarding custody to the Sterns, the court set aside the adoption agreement signed by Elizabeth Stern. Whitehead remained a legal parent of Baby M, and the court ordered a lower court hearing to consider visitation rights for the mother.

The immediate future of the child known to the court and to the public as Baby M was settled. Neither the Sterns nor Mary Beth Whitehead had won exactly what they had sought, but neither had they lost all.

## Case Presentation

### The Calvert Case: A Gestational Surrogate Changes Her Mind

Disease forced Crispina Calvert of Orange County, California to have a hysterectomy, but only her uterus was removed by surgery, not her ovaries. She and her husband, Mark, wanted a child of their own, but without a uterus Crispina would not be able to bear it. For a fee of $10,000 they arranged with Anna Johnson to act as a surrogate.

Unlike the more common form of surrogate pregnancy, Johnson would have no genetic investment in the child. The ovum that would be fertilized would not be hers. Mary Beth Whitehead, the surrogate in the controversial Baby M case, had received artificial insemination. Thus, she made as much genetic contribution to the child as did the biological father.

Johnson, however, would be the gestational surrogate. In an in vitro fertilization process, ova were ex-

tracted from Crispina Calvert and mixed with sperm from Mark. An embryo was implanted in Anna Johnson's uterus, and a fetus began to develop.

Johnson's pregnancy proceeded in a normal course, but in her seventh month she announced she had changed her mind about giving up the child. She filed suit against the Calverts to seek custody of the unborn child. "Just because you donate a sperm and an egg doesn't make you a parent," said Johnson's attorney. "Anna is not a machine, an incubator."

"That child is biologically Chris and Mark's," said the Calverts' lawyer. "That contract is valid."

Critics of genetic surrogate pregnancy are equally critical of gestational surrogate pregnancy. Both methods, some claim, exploit women, particularly poor women. Further, in gestational pregnancy the surrogate is the one who must run the risks and suffer the discomforts and dangers of pregnancy. She has a certain biological claim to be the mother, because it was her body that produced the child according to the genetic information supplied by the implanted embryo.

Defenders of surrogate pregnancy respond to the first criticism by denying surrogates are exploited. They enter freely into a contract to serve as a surrogate for pay, just as anyone might agree to perform any other service for pay. Pregnancy has hazards and leaves its marks on the body, but so do many other paid occupations. As far as gestational surrogacy is concerned, defenders say, since the surrogate makes no genetic contribution to the child, in no reasonable way can she be regarded as the child's parent.

The Ethics Committee of the American Fertility Society has endorsed a policy opposing surrogate pregnancy "for non-medical reasons." The apparent aim of the policy is to permit the use of gestational surrogate pregnancy in cases like that of Mrs. Calvert, while condemning it when its motivation is mere convenience or an unwillingness to be pregnant. When a woman is fertile but, because of diabetes, uncontrollable hypertension, or some other life-threatening disorder, is unable to bear the burden of pregnancy, then gestational surrogacy would be a legitimate medical option.

### Birth and Resolution

The child carried by Anna Johnson, a boy, was born on September 19, and for a while, under a court order, Johnson and the Calverts shared visitation rights. Then, in October, 1990, a California Superior Court denied Johnson the parental right she had sought. Justice R. N. Parslow awarded complete custody of the child to the Calverts and terminated Johnson's visitation rights.

"I decline to split the child emotionally between two mothers," the judge said. He said Johnson had nurtured and fed the fetus in the way a foster parent might take care of a child, but she was still a "genetic stranger" to the boy and could not claim parenthood because of surrogacy.

Justice Parslow found the contract between the Calverts and Johnson to be valid, and he expressed doubt about Johnson's contention that she had "bonded" with the fetus she was carrying. "There is substantial evidence in the record that Anna Johnson never bonded with the child till she filed her lawsuit, if then," he said. While the trial was in progress, Johnson had been accused of planning to sue the Calverts from the beginning to attempt to make the case famous so she could make money from book and movie rights.

"I see no problem with someone getting paid for her pain and suffering," Parslow said. "There is nothing wrong with getting paid for nine months of what I understand is a lot of misery and a lot of bad days. They are not selling a baby; they are selling pain and suffering."

The Calverts were overjoyed by the decision.

## READINGS

# Section 1: Assisted Reproduction

## Instruction on Respect for Human Life in Its Origin and on the Dignity of Procreation: Replies to Certain Questions of the Day

### Congregation for the Doctrine of the Faith

This "Instruction" was issued on February 22, 1987. It was approved and ordered published by Pope John Paul II and thus may be taken as representing the official position of the Roman Catholic Church on the issues addressed.

The document takes the position that a number of current or potential practices connected with reproductive technology are morally illegitimate. Included are the following:

- Prenatal diagnosis by amniocentesis or ultrasound for the purpose of identifying impaired fetuses so that abortion can be performed

- Therapeutic intervention that may cause a risk to a fetus disproportionate to a potential benefit

- Experimentation on a living embryo that is not directly therapeutic

- Keeping alive human embryos for experimental or commercial purposes

- Destroying human embryos produced by in vitro techniques for the purpose of either research or procreation

- Cross-species fertilization involving human and animal gametes

- The gestation of a human embryo in an animal uterus or an artificial uterus

- The use of human genetic material in procedures like cloning, parthenogenesis, and twin fission (the splitting of gametes)

- Attempts to manipulate genetic material for the purpose of sex selection or to promote desirable characteristics

- Artificial insemination involving unmarried individuals or the artificial insemination of an unmarried woman or a widow, even if the sperm is that of her deceased husband
- Acquiring sperm by means of masturbation
- Surrogate motherhood

Some techniques and practices, according to the document, are morally legitimate. Included are the following:

- Medical intervention to remove the causes of infertility
- The prescription of drugs to promote fertility
- Prenatal diagnosis with the aim of promoting the welfare of the fetus
- Prenatal therapeutic intervention (including genetic manipulation) with the aim of healing the developing embryo or fetus
- Prenatal research that is limited to monitoring or observing the embryo

The document also makes a number of specific recommendations to governments to establish laws and policies governing reproductive technologies. It asks that civil laws be passed to prohibit the donation of sperm or ova between unmarried people. Laws should "expressly forbid" the use of living embryos for experimentation and protect them from mutilation and destruction. Further, legislation should prohibit "embryo banks, postmortem insemination and 'surrogate motherhood.'"

Some Roman Catholic theologians disagreed sharply with parts of the document. "The document argues that a child can be born only from a sexual act," Richard McCormick pointed out. "The most that can be argued is that a child should be born within a marriage from a loving act. Sexual intercourse is not the only loving act." Some suggested that individuals would make up their own minds on the issues, quite apart from the Vatican position. The significance of the document to non-Catholics is that the positions taken and the arguments for them are likely to affect the character of the discussion about reproductive technology and have an impact on legislation that will place restraints on research and practices many currently consider legitimate.

Notes and references are omitted in this excerpt.

## Part 1: Respect for Human Embryos

Careful reflection on this teaching of the Magisterium and on the evidence of reason . . . enables us to respond to the numerous moral problems posed by technical interventions upon the human being in the first phases of his life and upon the processes of his conception.

### 1. What Respect Is Due to the Human Embryo, Taking into Account His Nature and Identity?

*The human being must be respected—as a person—from the very first instant of his existence.*

The implementation of procedures of artificial fertilization has made possible various interventions upon embryos and human fetuses. The aims pursued are of various kinds: diagnostic and therapeutic, scientific and commercial. From all of this, serious problems arise. Can one speak of a right to experimentation upon human embryos for the purpose of scientific research? What norms or laws should be worked out with regard to this matter? The response to these problems presupposes a detailed reflection on the nature and specific identity—the word "status" is used—of the human embryo itself. . . .

This Congregation is aware of the current debates concerning the beginning of human life, concerning the individuality of the human being and concerning the identity of the human person. The Congregation recalls the teaching found in the Declaration on Procured Abortion: "From the time that the ovum is fertilized, a new life is begun which is neither that of the father nor of the mother: it is rather the life of a new human being with his own growth. It would never be made human if it were not human already. To this perpetual evidence . . . modern genetic science brings valuable confirmation. It has demonstrated that, from the first instant, the programme is fixed as to what this living being will be: a man, this individual-man with his characteristic aspects already well determined. Right from fertilization is begun the adventure of a human life, and each of its great capacities requires time . . . to find its place and to be in a position to act." This teaching remains valid and is further confirmed, if confirmation were needed, by recent findings of human biological science which recognize that in the zygote* resulting from fertilization the biological identity of a new human individual is already constituted. . . .

Thus the fruit of human generation, from the first moment of its existence, that is to say from the moment the zygote has formed, demands the unconditional respect that is morally due to the human being in his bodily and spiritual totality. The human being is to be respected and treated as a person from the moment of conception; and therefore from that same moment his rights as a person must be recognized, among which in the first place is the inviolable right of every innocent human being to life.

The doctrinal reminder provides the fundamental criterion for the solution of the various problems posed by the development of the biomedical sciences in this field: since the embryo must be treated as a person, it must also be defended in its integrity, tended and cared for, to the extent possible, in the same way as any other human being as far as medical assistance is concerned.

### 2. Is Prenatal Diagnosis Morally Licit?

If prenatal diagnosis respects the life and integrity of the embryo and the human fetus and is directed towards its safeguarding or healing as an individual, then the answer is affirmative.

For prenatal diagnosis makes it possible to know the condition of the embryo and of the fetus when still in the mother's womb. It permits, or makes it possible

---

*The zygote is the cell produced when the nuclei of the two gametes have fused.

to anticipate earlier and more effectively, certain therapeutic, medical or surgical procedures.

Such diagnosis is permissible, with the consent of the parents after they have been adequately informed, if the methods employed safeguard the life and integrity of the embryo and the mother, without subjecting them to disproportionate risks. But this diagnosis is gravely opposed to the moral law when it is done with the thought of possibly inducing an abortion depending upon the results: a diagnosis which shows the existence of a malformation or a hereditary illness must not be the equivalent of a death-sentence. Thus a woman would be committing a gravely illicit act if she were to request such a diagnosis with the deliberate intention of having an abortion should the results confirm the existence of a malformation or abnormality. The spouse or relatives or anyone else would similarly be acting in a manner contrary to the moral law if they were to counsel or impose such a diagnostic procedure on the expectant mother with the same intention of possibly proceeding to an abortion. So too the specialist would be guilty of illicit collaboration if, in conducting the diagnosis and in communicating its results, he were deliberately to contribute to establishing or favoring a link between prenatal diagnosis and abortion.

In conclusion, any directive or program of the civil and health authorities or of scientific organizations which in any way were to favor a link between prenatal diagnosis and abortion, or which were to go as far as directly to induce expectant mothers to submit to prenatal diagnosis planned for the purpose of eliminating fetuses which are affected by malformations or which are carriers of hereditary illness, is to be condemned as a violation of the unborn child's right to life and as an abuse of the prior rights and duties of the spouses.

### 3. Are Therapeutic Procedures Carried Out on the Human Embryo Licit?

As with all medical interventions on patients, *one must uphold as licit procedures carried out on the human embryo which respect the life and integrity of the embryo and do not involve disproportionate risks for it but are directed towards its healing, the improvement of its condition of health, or its individual survival.*

Whatever the type of medical, surgical or other therapy, the free and informed consent of the parents is required, according to the deontological rules, followed in the case of children. The application of this moral principle may call for delicate and particular precautions in the case of embryonic or fetal life. . . .

### 4. How Is One to Evaluate Morally Research and Experimentation on Human Embryos and Fetuses?

*Medical research must refrain from operations on live embryos, unless there is a moral certainty of not causing harm to the life or integrity of the unborn child and the mother, and on condition that the parents have given their free and informed consent to the procedure.* It follows that all research, even when limited to the simple observation of the embryo, would become illicit were it to involve risk to the embryo's physical integrity or life by reason of the methods used or the effects induced.

As regards experimentation, and presupposing the general distinction between experimentation for purposes which are not directly therapeutic and experimentation which is clearly therapeutic for the subject himself, in the case in point one must also distinguish between experimentation carried out on embryos which are still alive and experimentation carried out on embryos which are dead. *If the embryos are living, whether viable or not, they must be respected just like any other human person; experimentation on embryos which is not directly therapeutic is illicit.*

No objective, even though noble in itself, such as a foreseeable advantage to science, to other human beings or to society, can in any way justify experimentation on living human embryos or fetuses, whether viable or not, either inside or outside the mother's womb. The informed consent ordinarily required for clinical experimentation on adults cannot be granted by the parents, who may not freely dispose of the physical integrity or life of the unborn child. Moreover, experimentation on embryos and fetuses always involves risk, and indeed in most cases it involves the certain expectation of harm to their physical integrity or even their death. . . .

In the case of experimentation that is clearly therapeutic, namely, when it is a matter of experimental forms of therapy used for the benefit of the embryo itself in a final attempt to save its life, and in the absence of other reliable forms of therapy, recourse to drugs or procedures not yet fully tested can be licit. . . .

### 5. How Is One to Evaluate Morally the Use for Research Purposes of Embryos Obtained by Fertilization "In Vitro"?

Human embryos obtained in vitro are human beings and subjects with rights: their dignity and right to life must be respected from the first moment of their existence. *It is immoral to produce human embryos destined to be exploited as disposable "biological material."*

In the usual practice of in vitro fertilization, not all of the embryos are transferred to the woman's body; some are destroyed. Just as the Church condemns induced abortion, so she also forbids acts against the life of these human beings. *It is a duty to condemn the particular gravity of the voluntary destruction of human embryos obtained "in vitro" for the sole purpose of research, either by means of artificial insemination or by means of "twin fission."* By acting in this way the researcher usurps the place of God; and, even though he may be unaware of this, he sets himself up as the master of the destiny of others inasmuch as he arbitrarily chooses whom he will allow to live and whom he will send to death and kills defenseless human beings.

Methods of observation or experimentation which damage or impose grave and disproportionate risks upon embryos obtained in vitro are morally illicit for the same reasons. Every human being is to be respected for himself, and cannot be reduced in worth to a pure and simple instrument for the advantage of others. *It is therefore not in conformity with the moral law deliberately to expose to death human embryos obtained "in vitro."* In consequence of the fact that they have been produced in vitro, those embryos which are not transferred into the body of the mother and are called "spare" are exposed to an absurd fate, with no possibility of their being offered safe means of survival which can be licitly pursued.

### 6. What Judgment Should Be Made on Other Procedures of Manipulating Embryos Connected with the "Techniques of Human Reproduction"?

Techniques of fertilization in vitro can open the way to other forms of biological and genetic manipulation of human embryos, such as attempts or plans for fertilization between human and animal gametes and the gestation of human embryos in the uterus of animals, or the hypothesis or project of constructing artificial uteruses for the human embryos. *These procedures are contrary to the human dignity proper to the embryo, and at the same time they are contrary to the right of every person to be conceived and to be born within marriage and from marriage. Also, attempts or hypotheses for obtaining a human being without any connection with sexuality through "twin fission," cloning or parthenogenesis are to be considered contrary to the moral law, since they are in opposition to the dignity both of human procreation and of the conjugal union.*

The *freezing of embryos,* even when carried out in order to preserve the life of an embryo—cryopreservation—*constitutes an offense against the respect due to human beings* by exposing them to grave risks of death or harm to their physical integrity and depriving them, at least temporarily, of maternal shelter and gestation, thus placing them in a situation in which further offenses and manipulation are possible.

*Certain attempts to influence chromosomic or genetic inheritance are not therapeutic but are aimed at producing human beings selected according to sex or other predetermined qualities. These manipulations are contrary to the personal dignity of the human being and his or her integrity and identity.* Therefore in no way can they be justified on the grounds of possible beneficial consequences for future humanity. Every person must be respected for himself: in this consists the dignity and right of every human being from his or her beginning.

## Part II: Interventions upon Human Procreation

By "artificial procreation" or "artificial fertilization" are understood here the different technical procedures directed towards obtaining a human conception in a manner other than the sexual union of man and woman. This Instruction deals with fertilization of an ovum in a test-tube (in vitro fertilization) and artificial insemination through transfer into the woman's genital tracts of previously collected sperm.

A preliminary point for the moral evaluation of such technical procedures is constituted by the consideration of the circumstances and consequences which those procedures involve in relation to the respect due the human embryo. Development of the practice of in vitro fertilization has required innumerable fertilizations and destructions of human embryos. Even today, the usual practice presupposes a hyper-ovulation on the part of the woman: a number of ova are withdrawn, fertilized and then cultivated in vitro for some days. Usually not all are transferred into the genital tracts of the woman; some embryos, generally called "spare," are destroyed or frozen. On occasion, some of the implanted embryos are sacrificed for various eugenic, economic or psychological reasons. Such deliberate destruction of human beings or their utilization for different purposes to the detriment of their integrity and life is contrary to the doctrine on procured abortion already recalled.

The connection between in vitro fertilization and the voluntary destruction of human embryos occurs too often. This is significant: through these procedures, with apparently contrary purposes, life and death are subjected to the decision of man, who thus sets himself up as the giver of life and death by decree. This dynamic of violence and domination may remain unnoticed by those very individuals who, in wishing to utilize this procedure, become subject to it themselves. The facts recorded and the cold logic which links them must be taken into consideration for a moral judgment on IVF and ET (in vitro fertilization and embryo transfer): the abortion-mentality which has made this procedure possible, thus leads, whether one wants it or not, to man's domination over the life and death of his fellow human beings and can lead to a system of radical eugenics.

Nevertheless, such abuses do not exempt one from a further and thorough ethical study of the techniques of artificial procreation considered in themselves, abstracting as far as possible from the destruction of embryos produced in vitro.

The present Instruction will therefore take into consideration in the first place the problems posed by heterologous artificial fertilization (II, 1–3),* and subsequently those linked with homologous artificial fertilization (II, 4–6).[†]

Before formulating an ethical judgment on each of these procedures, the principles and values which determine the moral evaluation of each of them will be considered.

### A. Heterologous Artificial Fertilization

**1. Why Must Human Procreation Take Place in Marriage?** *Every human being is always to be accepted as a gift and blessing of God. However, from the moral*

---

*By the term heterologous artificial fertilization or procreation, the Instruction means techniques used to obtain a human conception artificially by the use of gametes coming from at least one donor other than the spouses who are joined in marriage. Such techniques can be of two types:

a. Heterologous IVF and ET: the technique used to obtain a human conception through the meeting in vitro of gametes taken from at least one donor other than the two spouses joined in marriage.

b. Heterologous artificial insemination: the technique used to obtain a human conception through the transfer into the genital tracts of the woman of the sperm previously collected from a donor other than the husband.

[†]By artificial homologous fertilization or procreation, the Instruction means the technique used to obtain a human conception using the gametes of the two spouses joined in marriage. Homologous artificial fertilization can be carried out by two different methods:

a. Homologous IVF and ET: the technique used to obtain a human conception through the meeting in vitro of the gametes of the spouses joined in marriage.

b. Homologous artificial insemination: the technique used to obtain a human conception through the transfer into the genital tracts of a married woman of the sperm previously collected from her husband.

*point of view a truly responsible procreation vis-a-vis the unborn child must be the fruit of marriage.*

For human procreation has specific characteristics by virtue of the personal dignity of the parents and of the children: the procreation of a new person, whereby the man and the woman collaborate with the power of the Creator, must be the fruit and the sign of the mutual self-giving of the spouses, of their love and of their fidelity. *The fidelity of the spouses in the unity of marriage involves reciprocal respect of their right to become a father and a mother only through each other.*

The child has the right to be conceived, carried in the womb, brought into the world and brought up within marriage: it is through the secure and recognized relationship to his own parents that the child can discover his own identity and achieve his own proper human development.

The parents find in their child a confirmation and completion of their reciprocal self-giving: the child is the living image of their love, the permanent sign of their conjugal union, the living and indissoluble concrete expression of their paternity and maternity.

By reason of the vocation and social responsibilities of the person, the good of the children and of the parents contributes to the good of civil society; the vitality and stability of society require that children come into the world within a family and that the family be firmly based on marriage.

The tradition of the Church and anthropological reflection recognize in marriage and in its indissoluble unity the only setting worthy of truly responsible procreation.

**2. Does Heterologous Artificial Fertilization Conform to the Dignity of the Couple and to the Truth of Marriage?**  Through IVF and ET and heterologous artificial insemination, human conception is achieved through the fusion of gametes of at least one donor other than the spouses who are united in marriage. *Heterologous artificial fertilization is contrary to the unity of marriage, to the dignity of the spouses, to the vocation proper to parents, and to the child's right to be conceived and brought into the world in marriage and from marriage. . . .*

*These reasons lead to a negative moral judgment concerning heterologous artificial fertilization: consequently fertilization of a married woman with the sperm of a donor different from her husband and fertilization with the husband's sperm of an ovum not coming from his wife are morally illicit. Furthermore, the artificial fertilization of a*

*woman who is unmarried or a widow, whoever the donor may be, cannot be morally justified.*

The desire to have a child and the love between spouses who long to obviate a sterility which cannot be overcome in any other way constitute understandable motivations; but subjectively good intentions do not render heterologous artificial fertilization conformable to the objective and inalienable properties of marriage or respectful of the rights of the child and of the spouses.

**3. Is "Surrogate"\* Motherhood Morally Licit?** *No, for the same reasons which lead one to reject heterologous artificial fertilization: for it is contrary to the unity of marriage and to the dignity of the procreation of the human person.*

Surrogate motherhood represents an objective failure to meet the obligations of maternal love, of conjugal fidelity and of responsible motherhood; it offends the dignity and the right of the child to be conceived, carried in the womb, brought into the world and brought up by his own parents; it sets up, to the detriment of families, a division between the physical, psychological and moral elements which constitute those families.

**B. Homologous Artificial Fertilization**

Since heterologous artificial fertilization has been declared unacceptable, the question arises of how to evaluate morally the process of homologous artificial fertilization: IVF and ET and artificial insemination between husband and wife. First a question of principle must be clarified.

**4. What Connection Is Required from the Moral Point of View Between Procreation and Conjugal Act?**  . . . In reality, the origin of a human person is the result of an act of giving. The one conceived must be

---

\*By "surrogate mother" the Instruction means:

a. the woman who carries in pregnancy an embryo implanted in her uterus and who is genetically a stranger to the embryo because it has been obtained through the union of the gametes of "donors." She carries the pregnancy with a pledge to surrender the baby once it is born to the party who commissioned or made the agreement for the pregnancy.

b. the woman who carries in pregnancy an embryo to whose procreation she has contributed the donation of her own ovum, fertilized through insemination with the sperm of a man other than her husband. She carries the pregnancy with a pledge to surrender the child once it is born to the party who commissioned or made the agreement for the pregnancy.

the fruit of his parents' love. He cannot be desired or conceived as the production of an intervention of medical or biological techniques; that would be equivalent to reducing him to an object of scientific technology. No one may subject the coming of a child into the world to conditions of technical efficiency which are to be evaluated according to standards of control and dominion.

*The moral relevance of the link between the meanings of the conjugal act and between the goods of marriage, as well as the unity of the human being and the dignity of his origin, demand that the procreation of a human person be brought about as the fruit of the conjugal act specific to the love between spouses.* The link between procreation and the conjugal act is thus shown to be of great importance on the anthropological and moral planes, and it throws light on the positions of the Magisterium with regard to homologous artificial fertilization.

**5.  Is Homologous "In Vitro" Fertilization Morally Licit?**  The answer to this question is strictly dependent on the principles just mentioned. Certainly one cannot ignore the legitimate aspirations of sterile couples. For some, recourse to homologous IVF and ET appears to be the only way of fulfilling their sincere desire for a child. The question is asked whether the totality of conjugal life in such situations is not sufficient to insure the dignity proper to human procreation. It is acknowledged that IVF and ET certainly cannot supply for the absence of sexual relations and cannot be preferred to the specific acts of conjugal union, given the risks involved for the child and the difficulties of the procedure. But it is asked whether, when there is no other way of overcoming the sterility which is a source of suffering, homologous in vitro fertilization may not constitute an aid, if not a form of therapy, whereby its moral licitness could be admitted.

The desire for a child—or at the very least an openness to the transmission of life—is a necessary prerequisite from the moral point of view for responsible human procreation. But this good intention is not sufficient for making a positive moral evaluation of in vitro fertilization between spouses. The process of IVF and ET must be judged in itself and cannot borrow its definitive moral quality from the totality of conjugal life of which it becomes part nor from the conjugal acts which may precede or follow it.

It has already been recalled that, in the circumstances in which it is regularly practiced, IVF and ET involves the destruction of human beings, which is something contrary to the doctrine on the illicitness of abortion previously mentioned. But even in a situation in which every precaution were taken to avoid the death of human embryos, homologous IVF and ET dissociates from the conjugal act the actions which are directed to human fertilization. For this reason the very nature of homologous IVF and ET also must be taken into account, even abstracting from the link with procured abortion.

Homologous IVF and ET is brought about outside the bodies of the couple through actions of third parties whose competence and technical activity determine the success of the procedure. Such fertilization entrusts the life and identity of the embryo into the power of doctors and biologists and establishes the domination of technology over the origin and destiny of the human person. Such a relationship of domination is in itself contrary to the dignity and equality that must be common to parents and children.

Conception in vitro is the result of the technical action which presides over fertilization. *Such fertilization is neither in fact achieved nor positively willed as the expression and fruit of specific acts of the conjugal union. In homologous IVF and ET, therefore, even if it is considered in the context of "de facto" existing sexual relations, the generation of the human person is objectively deprived of its proper perfection: namely, that of being the result and fruit of a conjugal act* in which the spouses can become "co-operators with God for giving life to a new person." . . .

Certainly, homologous IVF and ET fertilization is not marked by all that ethical negativity found in extra-conjugal procreation; the family and marriage continue to constitute the setting for the birth and upbringing of the children. Nevertheless, in conformity with the traditional doctrine relating to the goods of marriage and the dignity of the person, *the Church remains opposed from the moral point of view to homologous "in vitro" fertilization. Such fertilization is in itself illicit and in opposition to the dignity of procreation and of the conjugal union, even when everything is done to avoid the death of the human embryo.*

Although the manner in which human conception is achieved with IVF and ET cannot be approved, every child which comes into the world must in any case be accepted as a living gift of the divine Goodness and must be brought up with love.

**6.  How Is Homologous Artificial Insemination to Be Evaluated from the Moral Point of View?**  *Homologous artificial insemination within marriage cannot be admitted except for those cases in which the technical means is not a substitute for the conjugal act but serves to* *facilitate and to help so that the act attains its natural purpose.*

The teaching of the Magisterium on this point has already been stated. This teaching is not just an expression of particular historical circumstances but is based on the Church's doctrine concerning the connection between the conjugal union and procreation and on a consideration of the personal nature of the conjugal act and of human procreation. "In its natural structure, the conjugal act is a personal action, a simultaneous and immediate cooperation on the part of the husband and wife, which by the very nature of the agents and the proper nature of the act is the expression of the mutual gift which, according to the words of Scripture, brings about union 'in one flesh.'" Thus moral conscience "does not necessarily proscribe the use of certain artificial means destined solely either to the facilitating of the natural act or to insuring that the natural act normally performed achieves its proper end." If the technical means facilitates the conjugal act or helps it to reach its natural objectives, it can be morally acceptable. If, on the other hand, the procedure were to replace the conjugal act, it is morally illicit.

Artificial insemination as a substitute for the conjugal act is prohibited by reason of the voluntarily achieved dissociation of the two meanings of the conjugal act. Masturbation, through which the sperm is normally obtained, is another sign of this dissociation: even when it is done for the purpose of procreation, the act remains deprived of its unitive meaning: "It lacks the sexual relationship called for by the moral order, namely the relationship which realizes 'the full sense of mutual self-giving and human procreation in the context of true love.'" . . .

### 7. The Suffering Caused by Infertility in Marriage.
*The suffering of spouses who cannot have children or who are afraid of bringing a handicapped child into the world is a suffering that everyone must understand and properly evaluate.*

On the part of the spouses, the desire for a child is natural: it expresses the vocation to fatherhood and motherhood inscribed in conjugal love. This desire can be even stronger if the couple is affected by sterility which appears incurable. Nevertheless, marriage does not confer upon the spouses the right to have a child, but only the right to perform those natural acts which are per se ordered to procreation.

*A true and proper right to a child would be contrary to the child's dignity and nature. The child is not an object to which one has a right, nor can be considered as an object of ownership: rather, a child is a gift, "the supreme gift" and the most gratuitous gift of marriage, and is a living testimony of the mutual giving of his parents. For this reason, the child has the right, as already mentioned, to be the fruit of the specific act of the conjugal love of his parents; and he also has the right to be respected as a person from the moment of his conception.*

Nevertheless, whatever its cause or prognosis, sterility is certainly a difficult trial. The community of believers is called to shed light upon and support the suffering of those who are unable to fulfill their legitimate aspiration to motherhood and fatherhood. Spouses who find themselves in this sad situation are called to find in it an opportunity for sharing in a particular way in the Lord's Cross, the source of spiritual fruitfulness. Sterile couples must not forget that "even when procreation is not possible, conjugal life does not for this reason lose its value. Physical sterility in fact can be for spouses the occasion for other important services to the life of the human person, for example, adoption, various forms of educational work, and assistance to other families and to poor or handicapped children."

Many researchers are engaged in the fight against sterility. While fully safeguarding the dignity of human procreation, some have achieved results which previously seemed unattainable. Scientists therefore are to be encouraged to continue their research with the aim of preventing the causes of sterility and of being able to remedy them so that sterile couples will be able to procreate in full respect for their own personal dignity and that of the child to be born . . .

# The Right to Lesbian Parenthood

## Gillian Hanscombe

Gillian Hanscombe sees the possibility of becoming a single parent as a major advantage of reproductive technology. She argues that homosexual parents are entitled to the same treatment from physicians and institutions as heterosexual ones. The objection that lesbian women should not be allowed to reproduce by artificial insemination is not one that can be supported by relevant evidence, Hanscombe claims. No studies have demonstrated that lesbian mothering is any different from heterosexual mothering or that children of lesbian mothers "fall victim to negative psychosexual developmental influences." She mentions instances of what she considers to be groundless prejudice against lesbian women by the medical establishment.

Anyone daring to address the subject of human rights faces both an appalling responsibility and being accused of an unnatural arrogance of utterance. I accept these risks not because I think myself expert on the subject of human rights, but because my experience is that human rights in the domain of parenthood are so very often denied existence.

I refer to a large minority in our population, that of lesbian women and gay men. Even at the most conservative estimate—which is that at least 1 in 20 adult people are homosexual—a group comprising 5 per cent—we are dealing with a group larger than the 4 per cent ethnic minorities group which already receives, as indeed it deserves to do, special attention. Lesbian women and gay men have to date, in all matters of social policy, been traditionally regarded as a deviant group.

It is the case, nonetheless, that the pathologising of this group is increasingly questioned, not only by members of the gay community themselves, but also by the agencies of our institutional life: that is, by medical practitioners, by teachers and social workers, and by working parties of religious and/or political orientation.

I am the co-author of a book about lesbian mothers.[1] It is written for the general public, rather than for specialists, but is nevertheless the only book to date on the subject which I know of. It records the experiences of a selected group of lesbian mothers—selected to range over the varieties of social existence these parents and their children experience—from divorced women to single women who have deliberately chosen to conceive their children by artificial insemination by donor (AID).

The question asked by many heterosexual professionals who are charged with the theory or practice of social policy, is whether lesbian women, for example, should be (a) allowed, and (b) aided, to become mothers.

Objections to lesbian women being *allowed* to reproduce can only be social, since no physiological studies seeking to find physical differences between lesbian and non-lesbian women have ever succeeded in demonstrating such a difference.

Social objections fall into two categories: (a) the extent to which the psychopathology of the lesbian mother is assumed or demonstrated to deviate negatively from the norm. No studies to date have demonstrated that lesbian mothering is either significantly different from heterosexual mothering or that the lesbian mother is psychologically inadequately equipped to mother;[2] (b) the extent to which the children of lesbian mothers are assumed to fall victim to negative psychosexual developmental influences. No study to date has succeeded in demonstrating such a phenomenon.[3]

There remains social objections issuing from prejudice, which in turn issues from ignorance. Since the medical profession forms a professional part of our social policy-making institutional life, it is required that medical practitioners do not form judgments based on ignorance. A mere assumption that because, historically, lesbian women have been pathologised this

Reprinted by permission of *Journal of Medical Ethics*, Vol. 9 (1983): 133–135.

somehow proves that they are "not normal" (and that in a negative sense) is, of course, unacceptable.

A good way of thinking about this is to begin with what is known about female sexuality. In the first place, it is clear that women, unlike men, are able to separate their sexual practice from their reproductive practice. It is possible, that is, for a woman (a) to become sexually aroused and reach orgasm without any possibility that she will become pregnant and (b) for a woman to be inseminated—either naturally or artificially—and become pregnant whether or not, at the same time, she experiences any sexual pleasure. Whatever might be thought, therefore, about lesbian sexual practice, it is clear that lesbian women are able to conceive and bear children in the same way as non-lesbian women do.

Hence, attempting not to allow them to do so would be highly problematic, even apart from the massive dilemma—were such a decision taken—of not being able to enforce the sanction. Contrary to popular prejudice, it is the case that lesbian women, like other women, are quite capable of engaging in sexual intercourse with a man and, like other women, often solely for the reason that they intend to become pregnant.

Prejudice is not only rife within what are called the "helping professions," it is rife, too, in the courts. Lesbian mothers in dispute with husbands almost all lose custody of their children solely on the grounds of their lesbianism.[4] Because of this, as well as for many other reasons, young women in the last decade have turned increasingly to the alternative of AID. They have found, by and large, that medical practitioners are not willing to provide AID for them, again solely on the grounds of their lesbianism. They have decided, increasingly, in response to this attitude, to conduct AID by themselves, with the assistance of sympathetic men. This is neither technically difficult nor is it illegal. Many AID daughters and sons of lesbian women are now in our nurseries and schools.

There are over two million lesbian mothers in the United States. Calculations for Britain are well-nigh impossible, owing to the professional nonrecognition of the existence of the group, together with the mothers' reticence in the face of prejudice. They are rightly anxious to conceal their sexuality since, like nearly all mothers, they love their children and will not willingly give them up, either to the courts or to any other social agency.

We might consider one case in particular. A lesbian woman, of middle-class background and professional standing in her own right, decided that she wanted to become a mother. It was, for her, a natural fulfillment of her womanhood, just as it is for millions of other women.

She became pregnant, deliberately, but unfortunately suffered a miscarriage, accompanied by much distress and depression. The usual practice of the hospital treating her was that, following the customary D & C, the patient should report to her own general practitioner. This she did, some six weeks later, wanting very much to know whether there were any clinical reasons why she might suffer further miscarriages. She asked the GP whether the hospital had sent her report.

"Yes, why?" came the reply.

"I want to know whether there is anything wrong with me which explains why I lost the baby," the woman explained.

"Why do you want to know?" persisted the GP.

"Because if there isn't, I want to become pregnant again," said the woman. "It was so dreadful losing the baby that I wouldn't knowingly go through it again. But if I can have a normal, full-term pregnancy, I want to try."

"But you can't have a baby," replied the GP, appalled; "you're not married!"

"What's that got to do with it?" asked the woman. And so ensued an embarrassing session of moralistic instruction from the GP to the silent woman. Her question remained unanswered.

She asked a friend who was a GP in a different area to write to the hospital for the information. This was done. There was no clinical reason for the miscarriage and the woman was pronounced normal and healthy.

The woman became pregnant again. But instead of feeling she could be cared for by her GP, she felt forced to opt for ante-natal care in the impersonal atmosphere of the hospital, where hundreds of women attended the clinic and where the same practitioner hardly ever appeared twice. At each visit, she was seen by different staff, which was comfortless but which at least ensured minimal questioning.

When she was nearly three months pregnant, the sister-in-charge said she must see the social worker. It was "hospital policy." But only, of course, for the unmarried. The woman felt angry and hurt, but didn't want to be accused of "making trouble." The social worker was sympathetic. "Just for the record, do you want your baby?" she asked. "Just for the record," the woman replied, "I planned my baby."

After delivery, she and her baby were not placed in an ordinary ward, but in one where mothers with handicapped babies were placed, together with mothers who had not had normal deliveries. In addition, she was "strongly advised" to stay for the full period, rather than go home after 48 hours. And yet both she and her baby were fit and healthy.

This mother keeps away from the "helping professionals." She is not open with her present GP, her child's school or the para-medical services, either about the circumstances of her child's birth or about her own sexuality. When she is offered contraception during her cervical smear tests, she simply declines it, not daring to explain that she is one of thousands of lesbian women who don't need it.

This woman is a proud and independent mother.[5] And her story is only one among scores. There is the mother who was refused AID by her local medical services and who then answered an advertisement in a lonely hearts column in order to find a man who would make her pregnant. She chartered her ovulation cycle, and when she was fertile, dated the man, who only and clearly wanted casual sex. Her "experiment" worked and she bore a healthy child. There is the mother who came home from work one day to find a weeping partner who had to tell her that both her children—a son aged nine and a daughter aged seven—had been taken into care, because someone had told the social worker that the two women were lesbians.[6]

Hardly any histories of lesbian mothers and their children are on the record. But they are amongst us and they deserve the same care from professional caregivers as do other mothers and their children.

There are, too, gay men who parent and there are lesbian women and gay men who, though not biological parents themselves, are necessarily involved in childcare by virtue of their partners' parenthood. And there are men who donate semen for the insemination of women who take on themselves the responsibility of conception in order to exercise their rights to reproduce and bring up children. None of the considered and intricate planning undertaken by all these people is mentioned in the vast literature about the family, either in professional or popular publications. Hardly any of this material finds its way into discussions and seminars about family policy, about education, about poverty and so on.

In addition, cruel and heartless lobbying from powerful religious and political quarters—aimed against the human rights of adult homosexual women and men—is ongoing, despite its lack of scientific objectivity. Such pressure is also richly funded. The onus is therefore on the rational, well-informed and compassionate professionals in our caring institutions to consider how they will respond to those of our number born to homosexual parents. Removing the right to reproduce is both immoral and impractical. Neglecting the need of parents for normal support is both discriminatory and cruel. Removing their children from the natural custody of their parents—merely on grounds of the parents' sexuality—is a monstrous interference, with consequences for the children which are no better than the fate of children who are unwanted by their natural mothers. What is needed is education, not legislation.

There are no data—scientific, psychological, or social—which could support the thesis that homosexual people should not have the right to reproduce and to bring up their children. There are only differing opinions and prejudices, which are not capable of sustaining the rigorous intellectual analysis upon which any given body of knowledge must rest. Hitler didn't like homosexuals. Or the handicapped. Or Jews. His answer was to attempt to exterminate them. Our cruelties are not so extreme. What we do is simply to ignore groups of people whose existence troubles us.

I submit, humbly but confidently, that using an argument to exclude adult people from parenthood which is based solely on the definition of an individual's sexual practice, is untenable and uncivilized. Adult people have in their gift the right to dispose of their own reproductive potential as they themselves think suitable. And the rest of us share, all of us, in the responsibility to care for all those committed to parenting and for the children for whom they care.

### References and Notes

1. Hanscombe, G. E., Forster, J. *Rocking the cradle*. London: Peter Owen, 1981 and Sheba Feminist Publishers, 1982.
2. Green, R. Sexual identity of 37 children raised by homosexual or transexual parents. *American Journal of Psychiatry* 1978; 6: 692–697.
3. See projects comparing the psychosexual development of lesbians' children with that of single non-lesbians' children, undertaken by Michael Rutter, Susan Golombok and Ann Spencer, of the Institute of Psychiatry in London. Not all the data is yet published—to my present knowledge—but see reference (1) 85–87.
4. In February of this year the Court of Appeal ruled in favour of a lesbian mother retaining custody of her two daughters. The case made newspaper headlines, not least because such rulings have been so rare.
5. Identity and details withheld.
6. Identities and details withheld.

# "Give Me Children or I Shall Die!" New Reproductive Technologies and Harm to Children

## Cynthia B. Cohen

Cynthia Cohen points to evidence suggesting that the use of reproductive technologies produces serious deficits in a small number of children and asks whether, if this is so, it would be wrong to continue to use them. Cohen focuses on the "Interest in Existing" argument, which holds that producing deficits wouldn't necessarily be wrong because, except in extreme cases, it's better to be alive than not exist.

A flaw in the argument, Cohen claims, is that it assumes children are waiting in a world of nonexistence, where they are worse off than if they were born. A second flaw is that the argument justifies the use of technology to produce any harm in children, as long as it is not so bad as to make death preferable (produce a "wrongful life"). Cohen argues that this is to view the nonexistence of not being born (which is neither good nor bad) as the same as the nonexistence produced by death (which may be preceded by devastating or serious deficits).

Cohen addresses the issue of what counts as a serious deficiency and claims such judgments must be made in specific circumstances in particular cultures. She ends by considering how obligations to actual children differ from those to potential children and why potential parents must make informed choices about using reproductive technologies. (Compare Cohen's views with those of Laura Purdy and Dena Davis in the preceding chapter.)

"Be fruitful and multiply," God urged newly created humans. Those who take this command to heart cherish the opportunity to procreate and nurture children, to pass on their individual traits and family heritage to their offspring. Having children, for many, is a deeply significant experience that offers overall meaning for their lives. Not all who wish to do so, however, can fulfill the biblical injunction to multiply. Those who cannot often experience a terrible sense of loss. Rachel, in Genesis, felt such despair over her failure to conceive that she cried out to Jacob, "Give me children, or I shall die!" Some who echo her cry today turn to the new reproductive technologies.

There are ethical limits, however, to what may be done to obtain long-sought offspring. Having a deep desire and even a need for something does not justify doing anything whatsoever to obtain it. If the means

used to bring children into the world were to create substantial harm to others or to these very children, this would provide strong moral reason not to employ them. It would be wrong, for instance, for infertile couples to place women at risk of substantial harm by enticing those who are not in peak physical condition to "donate" eggs with handsome sums of money. By the same token, it would be wrong to use reproductive technologies to create children if this bore a significant chance of producing serious disease and impairments in these very children. Questions are being raised about whether in vitro fertilization (IVF) and other reproductive technologies do, in fact, create serious illness and deficits in a small but significant proportion of children who are born of them. If these technologies were found to do so, it would be wrong to forge ahead with their use.

Yet advocates of procreative liberty reject this seemingly inescapable conclusion. They contend that even if children were born with serious disorders traceable to their origin in the new reproductive technologies, this would not, except in rare cases, provide

Cynthia B. Cohen, "'Give Me Children or I Shall Die!' New Reproductive Technologies and Harm to Children," *Hastings Center Report*, Vol. 26, no. 2 (1996): 19–27. Reprinted by permission of the publisher.

moral reason to refrain from using them. Those who conclude otherwise, they maintain, do not understand the peculiar sort of substantial harm to which children born of these novel reproductive means are susceptible. Surely, John Robertson and like-minded thinkers claim, it is better to be alive—even with serious disease and deficits—than not. And these children would not be alive, but for the use of the new reproductive techniques. Therefore, they argue, these children cannot be substantially harmed by the use of these means to bring them into the world. Only if they are caused by these technologies to suffer devastating illness that makes life worse than nonexistence can they be said to be substantially harmed by them.

This startling claim raises intriguing questions. What do we mean by substantial harm—particularly when children who might experience it have not yet been conceived? What degree of disease and suffering that a child would experience as a result of the application of these novel means of conception would make it wrong to use them? Would it be wrong if the child's life would be so terrible that nonexistence would be better? Few conditions would be excluded by this standard. Would it be wrong if the child's life would not be awful, but would include major physical impairments, severe mental disability, and/or considerable pain and suffering?

In responding to such questions, we must consider the possibility that different standards of substantial harm may apply to children at the time when we consider conceiving them and after conception and birth. If so, we must develop a standard of substantial harm that applies to children who might be conceived that is distinct from one that applies to those already born—and must explain how children who are not born can be harmed. We must also address the concern that decisions not to conceive children because they would have serious deficits devalue the lives of those already living who were born with such deficits. Finally, we must grapple with the question of what parents and infertility specialists ought to do in the current state of inadequate knowledge about the effects of the new reproductive technologies on the children who result from their use.

## The Harm to Children Argument

To ask what it means to attribute substantial harm to children who result from the new reproductive technologies is not just to pose an interesting abstract question. Studies indicate this may be a very practical, real question, as they raise the possibility that these technologies may create serious deficits in some proportion of the children born of them. To get a sense of the harms at issue, let us consider the claims of critics of the use of these technologies about their effect on the children born of them.

A primary harm that they attribute to the use of the new reproductive technologies is physical damage. Few long-term studies have been undertaken of the kinds and rates of physical diseases and abnormalities incurred by children born of the new reproductive technologies. Moreover, the evidence these investigations provide is conflicting. Australia is the only country that has kept statistics on the condition at birth *and* subsequent progress of children born of IVF since the inception of this technique in the late 1970s. Data from that country indicate that these children are two or three times more likely to suffer such serious diseases as spina bifida and transposition of the great vessels (a heart abnormality). The Australian data also suggest that some drugs used to stimulate women's ovaries to produce multiple oocytes in preparation for IVF increase the risk of serious birth impairments in the resulting children. Other investigations and commentators support this finding.[1] Still other reports, however, suggest that there is no increase in disorders at birth among children resulting from the use of the new reproductive technologies.[2] One small American follow-up study of the health status of children born of IVF and gamete intrafallopian transfer (GIFT) could find no significant differences in the rate of physical or neurological abnormalities in children born of techniques of assisted conception.[3] No controlled study to date, however, has incorporated an adequate sample size or sufficiently long follow-up monitoring period to determine accurately the risk of physical disorders associated with children born of IVF.

And little is known about the physiological impact on children who result from such other procedures as embryo freezing, gamete donation, zona drilling, and intracytoplasmic sperm injection.

It is well known that the higher rate of multiple births in IVF due to the implantation of several embryos in the uterus at a time contributes to an increased rate of preterm and low birth-weight babies. This, in turn, is associated with a higher incidence of perinatal, neonatal, and infant mortality in children conceived by IVF than those conceived coitally.[4] In France, for instance, the rates of prematurity and intrauterine growth retardation among IVF births in a two-year period were 16 percent and 14 percent respectively, whereas the expected rates for the general population were 7 percent and 3 percent.[5] An analysis of IVF outcome data from France between 1986 and 1990 indicated that perinatal mortality among IVF births also was higher than that in the general population, even when data were stratified according to gestational number. French neonatologists who had worked to prevent low birth weight, congenital anomalies, and genetic disorders among newborns observed that "[n]ow, we suddenly find our NICU filled with high-risk newborns . . . [as a result of the expansion of IVF services]."

Critics also express concern that the new reproductive technologies may jeopardize the psychological and social welfare of the children who result from them, particularly when they involve third parties in donor or surrogacy arrangements and depend on secrecy.[6] These children, they hypothesize, will view themselves as manufactured products, rather than distinctive individuals born of love between a man and a woman.[7] They will be denied the stable sense of identity that comes from knowing their biological heritage and family lineage should their rearing parents differ from their genetic parents.[8] Moreover, the social stigma these children will experience when others learn that they were conceived by these novel means will increase their difficulties, opponents contend. Little research is available on the effect of the use of assisted reproduction on the psychosocial development of the resulting children. In the first controlled study of family relationships and the psychological development of children created by the new reproductive technologies, no group differences in the emotions, behavior, or relationships with parents between children born of assisted reproduction and children conceived naturally or adopted could be found.[9]

One commentator summarizes the issues of harm raised by the use of the new reproductive technologies as follows:

> The technology for both IVF and GIFT as well as adjunct technologies such as zona drilling, embryo freezing, and gamete donation have not been accompanied by careful scrutiny and analysis of the risks involved. Indeed, even when risks are clearly established (as with multiple pregnancy), there has been no discernible attempt to reduce these risks by altering procedures and protocols. There also has been an appalling lack of follow-up studies to determine the long-term health, psychological, and social consequence of these procedures.[10]

In view of the current lack of systematic knowledge about difficulties these methods may create in children born of them, opponents of the new reproductive technologies maintain it is wrong to use them. Those who resort to these techniques, they claim, bear the burden of proof of their safety. They have an obligation to establish whether these ever-increasing methods of assisted reproduction do, in fact, harm a small but significant proportion of children before they are used. For ease of reference, we will call their claims the Harm to Children Argument against the use of the new reproductive technologies.

## The Interest in Existing Argument

The basic response to the Harm to Children Argument by several proponents of the use of the new reproductive technologies,[11] of whom John Robertson is a respected spokesperson, is that even if children born of the new reproductive technologies were to suffer serious impairments as a result of their origin, this would not necessarily render it wrong to use these techniques. We might call this response the Interest in Existing Argument: since it is, in almost all cases, better to be alive than not, and these children would not be alive but for the employment of these techniques, using them to bring these children into the world is justified. Robertson writes:

> [A] higher incidence of birth defects in such offspring would not justify banning the technique in order to protect the offspring, because without these techniques these children would not have been born at all. Unless their lives are so full of suffering as to be worse than no life at all, a very unlikely supposition, the defective children of such a union have not been harmed if they would not have been born healthy.[12]

Only where "from the perspective of the child, viewed solely in light of his interests as he is then situated, any life at all with the conditions of his birth would be so harmful to him that from his perspective he would prefer not to live,"[13] could it be said to be a substantial harm to have been brought into existence by means of the new reproductive technologies.

Robertson here implicitly distinguishes between *devastating harm*—harm that brings such suffering into a person's life that this life is worse than no life at all—[and] *serious harm*—harm that does not render life worse than death, but that includes such detriments as major physical impairments, severe mental disability, and/or considerable pain and suffering. He labels only the former *substantial harm*. Indeed, at certain points, Robertson maintains that children damaged by their origin in the new reproductive technologies cannot be said to suffer harm at all, since their birth is an overriding benefit.

The Harm to Children Argument is logically flawed, Robertson and like-minded thinkers maintain, because the benefit of life that children born of these techniques receive outweighs almost any detriment they might experience as a result of their origins. Robertson notes:

> Preventing harm would mean preventing the birth of the child whose interests one is trying to protect. Yet a child's interests are hardly protected by preventing the child's existence. If the child has no way to be born or raised free of that harm, a person is not injuring the child by enabling her to be born in the circumstances of concern.[14]

It is not open to children damaged by the use of the new reproductive technologies to live free of impairment, since they could not have existed without the use of these technologies. The alternative for them would have been not to live at all, a state which is not in their interests. Consequently, according to the Interest in Existing Argument, it is, in almost all instances, in the interests of children who might be born of the new reproductive technologies to be brought into the world by these means, even if this would risk serious harm to them.

This argument applies only to children who suffer harm that is a necessary result of the use of these techniques. Thus, if it were claimed that contract surrogacy creates psychological harm for a child because the biological mother and rearing parents would be in a constant state of conflict with each other, the Interest in Existing Argument could not be used in response. This is because the warring trio could behave in a different manner less likely to cause this sort of harm to the child. According to advocates of the Interest in Existing Argument it was not a necessary condition of the child's very existence that the conflict among these various parents occur.

## The Harm of Not Existing

The Interest in Existing Argument assumes that children with an interest in existing are waiting in a spectral world of nonexistence where their situation is less desirable than it would be were they released into this world. This presupposition is revealed by such observations as "a child's interests are hardly protected by preventing the child's existence" and that it is a disadvantage to such children that they "have no way of being born." In the Interest in Existing Argument children who might be conceived are pictured as pale preexisting entities with an interest in moving into the more full-blooded reality of this world. Their admission into this realm is thwarted by the failure to use available new reproductive technologies. This failure negates their interest in existing and thereby harms them.

Before a person exists, however, he or she does not reside in some other domain. Prior to conception, there is *no one who waits to be brought into this world*. Joel Feinberg argues, "Since it is necessary to *be* if one is to *be better off*, it is a logical contradiction to say that someone could be better off though not in existence."[15] To say that it was good for someone already in existence to have been born does not imply that his existence in this world is better than his life in some other realm. Nor does it imply that if he had not been caused to exist, this would have been bad for him.[16] Although a wealth of possible children can be conceived, their interests cannot be diminished if they are not. Therefore, it cannot be coherently argued that it is "better" for children to be created by means of the new reproductive technologies, even when this would result in serious disorders to them, since there is no alternative state in which their lot could be worse.

Part of the confusion at the heart of the Interest in Existing Argument stems from an incoherence found in tort actions for "wrongful life," to which this argument has an acknowledged debt. In these suits, children born with impairments claim that their current condition is worse than the state of nonexistence they would have had were it not for negligence on the part of physicians, hospitals, or testing laboratories. The wrong done to them, they contend, is not that their impaired condition was negligently caused, but that their very existence was negligently caused. This, they maintain, is a serious injury, since they would have been better off not being born at all. They ask for compensation for the injury of being brought into this world.

In an early wrongful life case, *Gleitman v. Cosgrove,* a child born with impairments whose mother had been told erroneously that her exposure to German measles during pregnancy would not harm the fetus, brought suit for damages for the injury of being born.[17] The traditional method of measuring damages in tort is to compare the condition of the plaintiff before and after an injury and to compensate for the difference. When the putative wrong done to the plaintiff is to have been brought into existence in an impaired state, the court must measure the difference between nonexistence and existence with impairments. In *Gleitman*, the court found it "logically impossible" to "weigh the value of life with impairments against the nonexistence of life itself." We cannot, according to the court, conceptualize a world in which the plaintiff did not exist and ask what benefits and burdens he experienced in that world in order to compare it with his situation in this world.

Even so, the *Gleitman* court concluded that the value of life, no matter how burdened, outweighs the disvalue of not existing, and that damages therefore could not be awarded to the child for "wrongful life." In drawing this conclusion, the court implicitly compared the world of existence with that of nonexistence and declared the former always preferable to the latter. Yet this is precisely the step the court had said it could not take. Similarly, in another leading case, *Berman v. Allan*, the court ruled against recognition of a "wrongful life" claim on grounds that "life—whether experienced with or without a major physical handicap—is more precious than non-life."[18] These courts were concerned that awarding damages for being alive would diminish the high value that the law places on human life. This public policy concern, however, caused them to lapse into incoherence. They claimed that the world of existence cannot be measured against that of nonexistence. However, if existence is better than nonexistence, as they also declared, nonexistence must be conceptually accessible in some sense so that an intelligible comparison can be made between it and existence.

Proponents of the Interest in Existing Argument adopt the two-world view underlying the logically impossible thesis of the early wrongful life cases when they claim that children are harmed if they are not brought out of the world of nonexistence into the world of existence. This leaves them with two problems: (1) explaining how to conceptualize and comprehend nonexistence and (2) justifying the claim that it is better to exist than not. Moreover, their dependence on the wrongful life decisions causes them to overlook an essential feature of their opponents' argument. The Harm to Children Argument is a *before-the-fact* one that applies to the time when a decision must be made about whether to employ the new reproductive technologies. *At this time, unlike the wrongful life cases, no child exists who could be harmed.* The Harm to

Children Argument holds that at this preconception time, the morally right decision is not to use such technologies until further research establishes the degree of harm this might do to children who result. The Interest in Existing Argument, however, is an after-the-fact argument meant to apply at a time when children are already born. It must be used as a response to those who object to having already brought children into the world. Since the harm posited by the critics has not yet occurred when the decision is made whether to employ them, it is not an adequate response to say that without these technologies the resulting children would not have been born.[19] That is precisely what is at issue—*whether these children ought to have been conceived and born.*

A further difficulty is that the Interest in Existing Argument justifies allowing the new reproductive technologies to create almost any harm to children conceived as a result of their use—as long as this is not devastating harm in which death is preferable to life with it. As Bonnie Steinbock and Ron McClamrock observe, "Very few lives meet the stringent conditions imposed by the wrongful life analysis. . . . Even the most dismal sorts of circumstances of opportunity (including, for example . . . an extremely high chance of facing an agonizing death from starvation in the early years of life, severe retardation plus quadriplegia) fail to be covered"[20] by the standard of devastating harm. Yet it would strike many as ethically objectionable to proceed with reproductive techniques should such serious, but not devastating harms result from them in a significant proportion of cases.

## The "Wrongful Life" Standard of Substantial Harm

Those who present the Interest in Existing Argument, adopting the standard applied in wrongful life cases, describe substantial harm as that which, in Robertson's words, puts one in a condition that renders life so "horrible"[21] and so "full of unavoidable suffering" (p. 169) that it is worse than "no life at all."[22] Robertson does not give a more precise definition of substantial harm, nor does he present specific examples of conditions which fall under that rubric in his discussion of harm to children and the new reproductive technologies. Feinberg expands on the "wrongful life" standard of substantial harm:

> Surely in most cases of suffering and impairment we think of death as even worse. This is shown by the widespread human tendency to "cling to life at all

costs." And even for severe genetic handicaps and inherited maladies, most competent persons who suffer from them will not express regret that they were born in the first place. . . . In the most extreme cases, however, I think it is rational to prefer not to have come into existence at all, and while I cannot prove this judgment, I am confident that most people will agree that it is at least plausible. I have in mind some of the more severely victimized sufferers from brain malformation, spina bifida, Tay–Sachs disease, polycystic kidney disease, Lesch–Nyhan syndrome, and those who, from whatever cause, are born blind and deaf, permanently incontinent, severely retarded, and in chronic pain or near-total paralysis, with life-expectancies of only a few years.[23]

To talk about death, both Feinberg and Robertson assume, is the same as to talk about "not coming into existence at all." They assimilate nonexistence before life and nonexistence after having lived. This is a mistake. *Nonexistence before coming into being* and *nonexistence after having lived* are two distinct concepts.

Lucretius observed that we do not express concern about nonexistence before creation, but we do fear our nonexistence after death. Why is this? The reason we perceive death as bad, Thomas Nagel proposes, is that it causes us to have fewer goods of this life than we would have had if we had continued to live.[24] Frances Kamm further observes that it is not only the absence of future goods in this life that leads us to fear death, but that death "takes away what already was and would have continued to be."[25] Preconception nonexistence, however, does not deprive us of what was ours already. In it there is no particular individual whose life ends and who thereby loses out on life's goods. Consequently, nonexistence before conception and birth does not seem as bad as death. We are indifferent to it.

Several other features of death that are also not characteristic of preconception nonexistence contribute to our assessment of it as bad. Death, for instance, happens to a person, whereas preconception nonexistence does not include an event in which nonexistence happens to a person. Death reveals our vulnerability in that through it a person is destroyed and deprived of life's goods. If a person does not exist, in contrast, this does not reflect negatively on "his" or "her" capacities.[26] Because of significant differences between them, preconception and posthumous nonexistence are qualitatively distinct concepts that are not interchangeable. Death has characteristics that lead us to evaluate it as bad, whereas preconception nonexistence strikes us as neither good nor bad.

Do we, too, fall into the trap of positing a shadowy world of nonexistence by distinguishing between preconception and posthumous nonexistence? We do not claim that either of these forms of nonexistence is a metaphysical locale. Instead, we view both as logical constructs built out of what we know about being alive. For both Nagel and Kamm, the meaning of death is derived from what we know about our existence in this world. The same is true of preconception nonexistence. Although the multitude of children whom it is possible for us to bring into the world do not exist, we can conceptualize certain things about them and what their lives would be like were we to conceive and bear them. We can also comprehend certain things about the negation of their existence were they to be born. That is, we can understand what they would lose if we decided not to conceive them and bring them into the world. Thus, we can meaningfully compare preconception nonexistence with life. We can consider children who might be brought into existence and ask whether we ought to conceive them without having to postulate a separate sphere of nonexistence in which they wait as we ponder the question.

While we can make sense of the notion of preconception nonexistence, can we also intelligibly claim that children who have not yet been conceived can have interests? It might be argued that those who do not exist cannot have interests and that therefore possible children can have no interest in not being conceived and brought into the world with serious disorders. Yet possible children can have interests, if these are taken in the sense of what contributes to their good, rather than as psychological states. We can conceive of what would promote their welfare were they to be brought into the world. To deny them such interests is mistakenly to reason by analogy with the dead. It has been supposed that the dead can have no interests because we cannot perform any actions that will affect the condition of their lives.[27] We cannot causally impinge on them for better or worse, it has been argued, for their lives have been completed. But this is not the case with possible children. We can affect them causally for better or worse by our present actions. Thus, we can ascribe to possible children certain interests that can be thwarted or fulfilled by actions that we take.

The interests of children who might be born of the new reproductive technologies are not adequately captured by the "wrongful life" standard. The comparison that parents and physicians must make when they assess whether use of these technologies would negatively affect the good of children who might result is not between *death* and the condition of these children were they to be born with certain deficits. The appropriate comparison is between *preconception nonexistence* and their condition were they to be born with certain deficits. If preconception nonexistence, unlike death, is neither good nor bad, then any life that will be worse than it *will not have to be as bad as the life of devastating deficits set out in the wrongful life standard*. A life with serious, but not devastating deficits, could be bad and therefore worse than preconception nonexistence, which is neither good nor bad. Therefore, we must modify the wrongful life standard of substantial harm to indicate that if new reproductive technologies were shown to cause a significant proportion of children born of them to suffer either devastating *or* serious deficits, they would cause substantial harm to these children and consequently ought not be used.

## The Inadequate Opportunity for Health Standard of Substantial Harm

How are we to identify the serious deficits that—along with devastating deficits—would constitute substantial harm to these children? The boundary between moderate, serious, and devastating deficits is sufficiently blurred that reasonable people can disagree about where it lies in particular cases. Many would disagree with Feinberg that children knowingly conceived with such disorders as spina bifida, blindness, deafness, severe retardation, or permanent incontinence should be considered to be suffering from devastating deficits that make their lives worse than death. However, they might well view these disorders as amounting to serious deficits that make their lives worse than preconception nonexistence. What is needed is a conceptual framework that marks off those deficits that have such a negative impact on children that reasonable people would agree that knowingly to conceive children with these disorders would be to impose substantial harm on them in the vast majority of cases.

Laura Purdy suggests that we cause substantial harm to future children and therefore ought not knowingly conceive them "when there is a high risk of transmitting a serious disease or defect [of a sort that would deny them] a normal opportunity for health."[28] At points in Purdy's discussion, as when she states that "every parent should try to ensure normal health for his child," she can be taken to mean that having an abnormal state of health would constitute a disorder

sufficiently serious to warrant not conceiving a child who would have it. On this approach, children with a particular biological, chemical, or mental state different from the norm would be said to lack "normal health" and therefore to suffer from a "serious disease or defect" that would justify not conceiving them. Yet it would not strike us as wrong knowingly to conceive children who are not "normal" because they have myopia or albinism. Normality does not appear to provide an adequate standard for deciding that a disorder is a serious deficit that substantially harms a child knowingly conceived with it.

At other points, however, Purdy seems to suggest that the focus for defining a serious deficit that falls under the substantial harm rubric should be on the failure to provide an adequate opportunity for a healthy life, as this is defined within a culture. Here she seems on the right track, for notions of health and disease—for better and for worse—are embedded within a society. What constitutes health and what represents a serious falling away from it varies from culture to culture and changes from time to time. As the notion of health and of an adequate opportunity for health vary according to the cultural context and conditions, so, too, does the meaning of a serious disease or deficit. Moreover, access to health services and the resulting opportunity for health—or lack of it—also affect what is meant by health, serious disorder, and substantial harm.

In our society, children who are color-blind are considered to have only a mild deficit and no diminution of their opportunity for health. However, in certain African cultures in which the capacity to distinguish a great variety of shades of green is needed to function at a minimal level for survival, color blindness is a serious deficit. Children born with this condition in such cultures do not have an adequate opportunity for health because their condition cannot be remedied. Thus, cultural values affect the meanings of health and of serious disorders. Stanley Hauerwas observes that "disease descriptions and remedies are relative to a society's values and needs. Thus 'retardation' might not 'exist' in a society which values cooperation more than competition and ambition."[29] Further, medical practices in different cultures reflect different views of what constitutes health and serious disorders. In Germany children with blood pressure that differs from the norm for their age on both the high and low end are suspected to be at risk of serious disease, whereas in America only high blood pressure is considered an indicator of serious disease.

What makes a disorder serious, however, is not only a matter of cultural needs, expectations, constructions, and practices. Some children are born with remediable conditions that are transformed into serious deficits when they are not ameliorated due to circumstances of injustice and neglect within a culture. The child born with spina bifida to poor parents in the hills of Appalachia has a minimal opportunity for health and a more serious disorder than the child born with this same condition to professional parents in Los Angeles. It might not be unfair to a child knowingly to conceive him or her with paralysis of the lower limbs if that child, once born, would have access to support structures giving him or her adequate mobility.[30] Nor would we have grounds for considering it wrong for parents knowingly to conceive a blind child if that child would receive compensatory education and ameliorative instruments enabling him or her to have an adequate opportunity for health within a society.

This relativity of the notion of health and of an adequate opportunity for health means that no definition of serious disease or disorder amounting to substantial harm that would apply across all cultures, times, and places can be given. Instead, the assessment of serious disease amounting to substantial harm must be made under specific circumstances within particular cultures. It must be defined not only in terms of a given physical or mental condition that damages a child's ability to function within a culture, but also in terms of the failure or inability of a culture to provide a child with access to ameliorative resources.

Sidney Callahan maintains that a principle of proportionality should be applied when making decisions concerning reproduction.[31] This would mean that the lower the risk and gravity of impairment to the child and the more would-be parents, family, and the institutional structures of a society are able and willing to ameliorate the impairment, the less the likelihood that a child would suffer a serious deficit and the more ethically justifiable it would be to conceive him or her. Should the probability and gravity of impairment be great, however, and the would-be parents, family, and social structure unwilling or unable to provide ameliorative measures for the child with such impairment, the higher the likelihood the child would suffer a serious deficit and the less ethically justifiable it would be to conceive that child. We do not end up with a black letter definition of a deficit serious enough to be termed substantial harm on this approach, but one that requires us to consider the nature of the disorder from which the child would suffer, the circumstances into which the child would be brought, and the ameliorative resources available for that child. Under current circumstances in our culture in which children born with disabling disorders have inadequate support, it would be morally questionable, at least, knowingly to conceive a child suffering from some of the deficits listed by Feinberg above.

## Obligations to Actual and Possible Children

Although we consider it ethically necessary to provide treatment to keep children alive who have serious illnesses, we do not consider it ethically necessary knowingly to conceive children with those same disorders. Why is this? Why do we assume that our obligations to children who already exist differ from our obligations to children whom we might conceive?

The difference between an actual and possible child and between our evaluations of preconception nonexistence and death help to explain this distinction. Since we view death as an evil in relation to being alive, we tend to maintain that once children are born, only if they suffer devastating harms that make life worse than death would we be justified in not doing what we can to prevent their death. Being alive is better than being dead, except in rare circumstances. However, we do not believe that we have an obligation to do everything we can to conceive and bring into the world possible children who would suffer serious or devastating illness as a result. This is because no one exists who is wronged by not being conceived and also because preconception nonexistence does not strike us as being either bad or good. To fail to actualize a possible child, therefore, does not put that child in a worse situation or wrong that child.

Furthermore, we have no obligation to conceive children if this would detrimentally affect the good of the family or culture into which they would be born. We have no obligation, for instance, to conceive a sixth child if we believe our family can only function adequately with five. And we need not bring children into the world when this would contribute to a problem of overpopulation or of limited resources. It is morally acceptable, indeed, some would say, morally required, that *before* we bring children into the world, we consider not only their well-being were they to be born, but the good of those who would be affected by their birth. *After* birth, however, the interest in existing of the living child comes into play and morally outweighs remnants of a parental or societal interest in not having had that child.

These conclusions may appear to intimate that the lives of children born with serious or even devastating disorders are not valued or valuable. This conclusion does not follow from the preceding argument. Should parents, after receiving convincing evidence that use of the new reproductive technologies would harm the resulting children, decide against employing them, this could say one of two things to living children with serious or devastating disorders. It could suggest that it would have been better for their families if a different child had been born without these disorders and she was not. Or it could imply that it would have been better for this child to have been born without these disorders.[32] The first implication suggests that it would be better for others if children with these disorders were not born, whereas the second maintains that it would be better for the children themselves if they had not been born with them. The first implies that it is regrettable that these children are alive instead of "normal" children. The second implies that it is regrettable that these children have these disorders. The second implication is the one on which we tend to act. This is exhibited by efforts we make to avoid serious or devastating disorders in children during pregnancy and to treat and care for children with such disorders after they are born. All of this suggests that it is not the children we disvalue, but the disorders that they have sustained. Consequently, it is not necessarily a reproach to disabled children who are already born if decisions are made against knowingly conceiving children who would have the same disabilities.

It is, however, a reproach to us and to our social institutions that once children with serious and devastating disorders are born, we provide woefully insufficient services and resources to them and their families. Does this contradict the claim that we value living children with disabilities and have their interests at heart? Hauerwas provides one perceptive explanation of our ambivalent and complex attitude toward those who live with serious disabilities in the course of discussing those who are developmentally delayed. He observes:

> After all, what we finally seek is not simply to help the retarded better negotiate their disability but to be like us: not retarded. Our inability to accomplish that frustrates and angers us, and sometimes the retarded themselves become the object of our anger. We do not like to be reminded of the limits of our power, and we do not like those who remind us.[33]

We wish to remedy the disabilities with which children may be born, but find it difficult to cope with the recognition of our own vulnerability that they inadvertently call forth. Therefore, we relegate them to a separate domain within the world of existence where we believe unknown others will assist them to meet the special challenges they face. This is uncharitable and unjust. We have a responsibility to overcome our misplaced frustration about being unable to render those who have serious or devastating disorders more like those who do not. We have a responsibility to assist them to make their own way in the world unhampered by our irrational fears.

## Taking Harms Seriously

The biblical injunction to multiply does not exhort us to do anything whatsoever to have children. It would be wrong to have children if it were known before conception that the means used to bring this about could inflict serious or devastating deficits on those very children. Yet the logic of the Interest in Existing Argument leads its proponents to brush aside the question whether these technologies might create such serious impairments. The thrust of this argument is that use of the new reproductive technologies provides its own justification—it produces children. This claim disregards the welfare of these children. Moreover, it creates a barrier to more extensive and detailed investigations of the effect of the new reproductive technologies on children born of them.

On the approach presented here, if it were known ahead of time that children conceived with the assistance of the new reproductive technologies would not have an adequate opportunity for health, it would be wrong to use them. Assessment of when and whether this would be the case would be carried out in light of the personal, familial, and social circumstances into which these children would be born. This means that would-be parents who consider resorting to the new reproductive technologies must be informed about the risks these techniques would present to the children born as a result of their use, the means available for ameliorating deficits these children might experience, and what social support would be available should they lack the resources to address such deficits on their own. Only then can they decide whether they ought to proceed with these techniques. To implement this recommendation, evidence for and against the contention that the new reproductive technologies cause serious or devastating physical, psychological, or social harm to the resulting children should be investigated more thoroughly than at present. Because of limited knowledge of the possible effects of these measures on their children, those who repeat Rachel's cry today face an agonizingly difficult decision when they consider whether to use the new reproductive technologies.

## Acknowledgments

I am indebted to the faculty and Senior Research Fellows of the Kennedy Institute of Ethics at Georgetown University for their perceptive comments on an earlier draft of this paper and to Michael E. McClure and James L. Mills of the National Institute of Child Health and Human Development for providing extremely helpful references and insights related to medical studies of the status of children born of assisted conception. These individuals are not responsible for the conclusions drawn here.

## References

1. National Perinatal Statistics Unit, Fertility Society of Australia, *In Vitro Fertilization Pregnancies. Australia and New Zealand 1979–1985*, Sydney, Australia, 1987; Paul L. Lancaster, "Congenital Malformations after In-Vitro Fertilisation," [letter] *Lancet* 2 (1987): 1392–93; see also AIHW National Perinatal Statistics Unit, Fertility Society of Australia, *Assisted Conception in Australia and New Zealand 1990* (Sydney: AIHW National Perinatal Statistics Unit, 1992); Gail Vines, "Shots in the Dark for Infertility," *New Scientist* 140 (1993): 13–15; Lene Koch, "Physiological and Psychosocial Risks of the New Reproductive Technologies," in *Tough Choices: In Vitro Fertilization and the Reproductive Technologies*, ed. Patricia Stephenson and Marsden G. Wagner (Philadelphia: Temple University Press, 1993), pp. 122–34.

2. U. B. Wennerholm et al., "Pregnancy Complications and Short-Term Follow-Up of Infants Born after In Vitro Fertilization and Embryo Transfer," *Acta Obstetrica et Gynecologicia Scandinavica* 70 (1991): 565–73; B. Rizk et al., "Perinatal Outcome and Congenital Malformations in In-Vitro Fertilization Babies from the Bourn-Hallam Group," *Human Reproduction* 6 (1991): 1259–64; S. Friedler, S. Mashiach, N. Laufer, "Births in Israel Resulting from In-Vitro Fertilization/Embryo Transfer, 1982–1989: National Registry of the Israeli Association for Fertility Research," *Human Reproduction* 7 (1992): 1159–63; Society for Assisted Reproductive Technology, American Society for Reproductive Medicine, Assisted Reproductive Technology in the United States and Canada, "1993 Results Generated from the American Society for Reproductive Medicine/Society for Assisted Reproductive Technology Registry," *Fertility and Sterility* 64 (1995): 13–21.

3. Norma C. Morin et al., "Congenital Malformations and Psychosocial Development in Children Conceived by In Vitro Fertilization," *Journal of Pediatrics* 115 (1989): 222–27.

4. V. Beral et al., " Outcome of Pregnancies Resulting from Assisted Conception," *British Medical Bulletin* 46, no. 3 (1990): 753–68; I. Craft and T. al-Shawaf, "Outcome and Complications of Assisted Reproduction," *Current Opinion in Obstetrics and Gynecology* 3 (1991): 668–73; Rizk et al., "Perinatal Outcome and Congenital Malformations in In-Vitro Fertilization Babies from the Bourn-Hallam Group"; P. Doyle, V. Beral, and N. Maconochie, "Preterm Delivery, Low Birthweight and Small-for-Gestational-Age in Liveborn Singleton Babies Resulting from In-Vitro Fertilization," *Human Reproduction* 7 (1992): 425–28; Friedler et al., "Births in Israel," pp. 1160–63.

5. Jean-Pierre Relier, Michele Couchard, and Catherine Huon, "The Neonatologist's Experience of In Vitro Fertilization Risks,"

*Tough Choices*, pp. 135–143; see also P. Rufat et al., "Task Force Report on the Outcome of Pregnancies and Children Conceived by In Vitro Fertilization (France: 1987 to 1989)," *Fertility and Sterility* 61 (1994): 324–30; FIVNAT (French In Vitro National), "Pregnancies and Births Resulting from In Vitro Fertilization: French National Registry, Analysis of Data 1986 to 1990," *Fertility and Sterility* 64 (1995): 746–56.

6. Cynthia B. Cohen, "Reproductive Technologies: Ethical Issues," in *Encyclopedia of Bioethics*, ed. Warren Thomas Reich (New York: Simon and Schuster Macmillan, 1995), vol. 4, pp. 2233–41; A. Baran and R. Pannor, *Lethal Secrets: The Shocking Consequences and Unsolved Problems of Artificial Insemination* (New York: Warner Books, 1989); D. N. Mushin, J. Spensley, M. Barreda-Hanson, "In Vitro Fertilization Children: Early Psychosocial Development," *Journal of In Vitro Fertilization and Embryo Transfer* 4 (1986): 247–52.

7. Margaret Radin, "Market-Inalienability," *Harvard Law Review* 100 (1987): 1921–36; Sidney Callahan, "The Ethical Challenges of the New Reproductive Technologies," in *Medical Ethics: A Guide for Health Professionals*, ed. J. Monagle and David Thomas (Rockville, Md.: Aspen, 1988), pp. 26–37.

8. Leon Kass, *Toward a More Natural Science: Biology and Human Affairs* (New York: Free Press, 1985), p. 113; Lisa Sowle Cahill, "The Ethics of Surrogate Motherhood: Biology, Freedom, and Moral Obligation," *Law, Medicine and Health Care* 16, nos. 1–2 (1988): 65–71, at 69; Cynthia B. Cohen, "Parents Anonymous," in *New Ways of Making Babies: The Case of Egg Donation*, ed. Cynthia B. Cohen (Bloomington: Indiana University Press, 1996), forthcoming.

9. Susan Golombok et al., "Parents and Their Children Happy with Assisted Conception," [letter] *British Medical Journal* 307 (1994): 1032.

10. Lene Koch, "Physiological and Psychosocial Risks of the New Reproductive Technologies," p. 128.

11. Ruth F. Chadwick, "Cloning," *Philosophy* 57 (1982): 201–9; John A. Robertson, "Procreative Liberty and the Control of Conception, Pregnancy, and Childbirth," *University of Virginia Law Review* 69 (1983): 405–462, at 434; John A. Robertson, "Embryos, Families, and Procreative Liberty: The Legal Structure of the New Reproduction," *Southern California Law Review* 59 (1986): 942–1041, at 958, 988; John A. Robertson, "Procreative Liberty, Embryos, and Collaborative Reproduction: A Legal Perspective," in *Embryos, Ethics, and Women's Rights: Exploring the New Reproductive Technologies*, ed. E. F. Baruch, A. F. Adamo, Jr., J. Seager (New York: Howarth Press, 1988), pp. 179–94; John A. Robertson, "The Question of Human Cloning," *Hastings Center Report* 24, no. 3 (1994): 6–14; John A. Robertson, *Children of Choice: Freedom and the New Reproductive Technologies* (Princeton, N.J.: Princeton University Press, 1994), pp. 75–76, 110–11, 122–23, 152, 169–70; Ruth Macklin, "Splitting Embryos on the Slippery Slope," *Kennedy Institute of Ethics Journal* 4 (1994): 209–25, at 219–20.

12. Robertson, "Procreative Liberty and the Control of Conception, Pregnancy, and Childbirth," p. 434.

13. Robertson, *Children of Choice*, pp. 75–76.

14. Robertson, *Children of Choice*, pp. 75–76.

15. Joel Feinberg, "Wrongful Life and the Counterfactual Element in Harming," *Social Philosophy and Policy* 4 (1988): 145–78, at 158.

16. Derek Parfit, *Reasons and Persons* (Oxford: Oxford University Press, 1985), p. 487.

17. *Gleitman v. Cosgrove*, 49 N.J. 22, 227 A. 2d 689 (1967).

18. *Berman v. Allan*, 80 N.J. 421, 404 A. 2d 8 (1979).

19. Robertson, *Children of Choice*, pp. 75, 117; "Embryos, Families, and Procreative Liberty," pp. 958, 988.

20. Bonnie Steinbock and Ron McClamrock, "When Is Birth Unfair to the Child?" *Hastings Center Report* 24, no. 6 (1994): 16–22, at 17.

21. Robertson, *Children of Choice*, pp. 82, 85.

22. Robertson, "Procreative Liberty and the Control of Conception, Pregnancy, and Childbirth," p. 434.

23. Feinberg, "Wrongful Life," p. 159.

24. Thomas Nagel, "Death," in *Mortal Questions* (Cambridge: Cambridge University Press: 1979), pp. 1–10.

25. Frances M. Kamm, *Morality, Mortality, Volume I. Death and Whom to Save from It* (New York: Oxford University Press, 1993), p. 40.

26. Kamm, *Morality, Mortality*, pp. 40–41.

27. Joan Callahan, "On Harming the Dead," *Ethics* 97 (1987): 341–52; Ernest Partridge, "Posthumous Interests and Posthumous Respect," *Ethics* 91 (1981): 243–64.

28. Laura Purdy, "Genetic Diseases: Can Having Children Be Immoral?" in *Genetics Now: Ethical Issues in Genetic Research*, ed.

John Buckly, Jr. (Washington, D.C.: University Press of America, 1978), pp. 25–39, at 25.

29. Stanley Hauerwas, "Suffering the Retarded: Should We Prevent Retardation?" in *Suffering Presence: Theological Reflections on Medicine, the Mentally Handicapped, and the Church*, ed. Stanley Hauerwas (Notre Dame: University of Notre Dame Press, 1986), pp. 159–81.

30. Steinbock and McClamrock, "When Is Birth Unfair to the Child?" and Sidney Callahan, "An Ethical Analysis of Responsible Parenthood," in *Genetic Counseling: Facts, Values, and Norms*, ed. Alexander M. Capron, Marc Lappé, Robert F. Murray (New York: Alan R. Liss, 1979), pp. 217–38.

31. Callahan, "An Ethical Analysis of Responsible Parenthood."

32. Mary Warnock, "Ethical Challenges in Embryo Manipulation," *British Medical Journal* 304 (1992): 1045–49, at 1047.

33. Hauerwas, "Suffering the Retarded," p. 176.

# Medical Miracle or Medical Mischief? The Saga of the McCaughey Septuplets

## Arlene Judith Klotzko

Arlene Klotzko reviews the McCaughey case and, despite the media representation of it, characterizes it as resulting from the failure of medical judgment or medical management. Contrary to public opinion, the McCaugheys did not face a choice between multiple pregnancy and abortion, because the multiple pregnancy could have been avoided. Such pregnancies result from the misuse of fertility drugs, perhaps as an outcome of the entrepreneurial nature of infertility clinics in the United States.

Klotzko concludes by raising, but not answering, six questions about infertility treatments she finds morally troubling. They concern the role of the media, the stigmatization of infertility as a disease, the matter of eligibility, the question of cost, the matter of consent to selective reduction, and selective reduction itself.

The story of the McCaughey septuplets is a quintessentially American story, combining many ingredients of modern life. The oftentimes uncritical celebration of dramatic, medical technological breakthroughs, the romanticization of life in Middle America, and the growing influence of fundamentalist Christianity, along with its close relative, the anti-abortion movement. And in the later stages of the story, the growing visibility of bioethics and bioethicists.

Arlene Judith Klotzko, "Medical Miracle or Medical Mischief? The Saga of the McCaughey Septuplets," *Hastings Center Report*, Vol. 28, no. 3 (1998), 5–8. Reprinted with permission of The Hastings Center.

On 19 November, after thirty-one weeks gestation, the seven babies—dubbed "the magnificent seven" by wide-eyed reporters—were born within six minutes. Their weights ranged from two pounds five ounces to three pounds four ounces. A team of forty nurses, respiratory therapists, perinatologists, neonatologists, and anesthesiologists officiated at the delivery. All the septuplets were placed on ventilator support for some days, but by the end of November they were breathing on their own.

The birth that captured and held the attention of the American media took place at Iowa Methodist Medical Center, just ten miles from the small midwestern town of Carlisle, Iowa, population 3,240.

Carlisle is the home of Bobbi McCaughey, a twenty-nine-year-old seamstress, and her husband, Kenny, twenty-seven, a billing clerk at a local automobile dealership. They shared their small two-bedroom house with a daughter, Mikayla, aged two. Since the septuplets' birth, the Governor of Iowa made good his promise to build them a new—and much larger—house.

This was the most generous of a bewildering assortment of gifts showered upon the family, including seven years of cable TV, university scholarships for all the children, ten years of portrait photographs, and a lifetime supply of Pampers. And there were more meaningful and less tangible gifts. According to *Time* magazine (1 December 1997), the response of the other inhabitants of Carlisle "bespoke a neighborliness that seems to have vanished from much of America. . . . A brigade of neighbors and friends has coordinated meal preparation, laundry, transportation, baby sitting, and house cleaning. They say it takes a village to raise children,' says city administrator Neil Ruddy. 'We just didn't know it would be our village.'" Lonely city sophisticates on both coasts turned green with envy.

Bobbi had been born with a malfunctioning pituitary gland that produced too little follicle stimulating hormone (FSH) that normally prompts a few eggs to mature every month. She wanted very much to have a child and sought fertility treatment. After one year without success, her doctors prescribed a stronger drug, Metrodin, which is rich in FSH. Mikayla, a single child, was the result. When the little girl was sixteen months old, the McCaugheys decided that she should have a brother or sister. Reluctant to wait a year, they asked that Metrodin be administered without delay.

What happened next is somewhat unclear. There have been conflicting reports, but it seems that Bobbi was given a shot of human chorionic gonadotropin (HCG), which helped release her eggs and enabled them to unite with her husband's sperm. Bobbi became pregnant on the first try and six weeks later an ultrasound revealed that she was carrying seven fetuses. A failure of medical judgment—or at least medical management—seems to have occurred, but much of the media resolutely kept its eyes off this aspect of the story.

Most Americans believe that the McCaugheys faced an inevitable choice between the risks of this multiple pregnancy and what was for this family, as fundamentalist Christians, the morally untenable option of selective abortion. But abortion is a retrospective solution, and prospective remedies are always better. This multiple pregnancy simply did not have to happen. Good medical practice mandates ultrasound scans for women who have taken fertility drugs in order to monitor accurately the number of eggs they produce. If the number is too high and the risks of multiple pregnancy too great, the patient should be advised to refrain from sexual activity and try again later.

Moreover, when the ultrasound scan reveals a large number of eggs, in vitro fertilization (IVF) can be used. Bobbi McCaughey's physicians could have removed some of her eggs, fertilized them outside her body, and then implanted a maximum of three embryos. In some ways—as wonderful as it most certainly is that Bobbi McCaughey and her children are doing so well—the birth of septuplets should be seen not as a great success of modern medical technology, but as a failure.

Dr. Mark Sauer, Chief of Reproductive Endocrinology at Columbia Presbyterian Medical Center in New York, told the *Washington Post* (21 November 1977) that "it would have been obvious that her ovaries had overreacted to the drug. . . . She must have had a dozen or more eggs going, and if she was being monitored correctly they had to know she was grossly overstimulated before she got her HCG shot." Voices such as his were drowned out, however, as the celebration of a happy outcome for the McCaughey family quickly metamorphosed into a celebration of technology.

Two days after the birth, critical voices were raised once more. Bioethicists participated in two of the three major Sunday news programs. Dr. Sauer appeared as well, characterizing the birth of the septuplets as an example of the overzealous use of fertility drugs. This inappropriate use, he said, has resulted in widespread iatrogenic fetal reduction. And a shocking number of multiple births—since 1972, the number of multiple births in the United States has quadrupled.

It has resulted, as well, in mothers and babies being exposed to great—and avoidable—risk. Ovarian overstimulation carries dangers of swelling and bleeding of the ovaries and severe fluid retention. In rare cases this can lead to heart failure. Women carrying multiple fetuses are at risk for potentially fatal blood clots during pregnancy and delivery. Children born in numbers greater than three often suffer from illnesses including chronic lung disease, strokes, mental retardation, and blindness. Once medical management has failed, however, the only remedy is selective reduction.

Selective abortion, as this practice is usually called in the United States, inspires a great deal of controversy. There is a large measure of irony here as well. As Dr. Sauer said, the practice is an emblem of medical failure. But that failure is due in no small part to the absence of a comprehensive regulatory scheme for IVF and embryo research in the United States. And the cause of that effect is the political power of the anti-abortion movement. Human IVF has developed in the private sector. Several hundred clinics operate with no government money and little government oversight. Guidelines have been developed by the industry, but compliance is voluntary. There is also a set of ethical considerations, published by The American Society for Reproductive Medicine in 1994.

It could well be that this entrepreneurial atmosphere has in itself encouraged the inappropriate use of fertility drugs. In the American culture—where the customer is always right—the customer in this case wants to become pregnant. And if possible, she will choose the clinic that has the highest pregnancy rate. One way of securing a competitive advantage is to overuse fertility drugs. In the United States the costs of fertility treatments are usually not covered by insurance; they must be borne by the patient. Thus there is even more pressure for a quick success—and, as a result, more and more multiple births.

In many respects, the situation in Britain provides an interesting and illuminating comparison. In the United Kingdom assisted reproduction is regulated by the Human Fertilisation and Embryology Act. The Act's Code of Practice for physicians providing infertility treatment limits the number of embryos that can be implanted to three. Any more would pose unacceptable dangers for mother and babies. But there are gaps in even the best legislative scheme. The administration of fertility drugs is not covered by U.K. legislation. Hence the infamous case of Mandy Allwood, a case that both shocked and fascinated the British public in 1996.

Even though she had conceived naturally several times, Mandy applied for and was given fertility drugs. After an ultrasound revealed the presence of an unsafe number of eggs, she ignored her physician's advice not to have intercourse. Mandy became pregnant with eight fetuses. She refused to have selective abortion, but it soon became apparent that her decision probably had a pecuniary rather than a moral basis. Reportedly, a tabloid—the *News of the World*—had agreed to pay her £1,000,000 if all eight babies were born. But Mandy could not sustain her pregnancy and after nineteen weeks she lost all eight fetuses. She had literally gambled and lost.

Bobbi McCaughey gambled as well, but according to both the family and the media, she had a powerful ally. As *Time* magazine put it, "The McCaughey's faith, plus a gamble on fertility drugs, won them a seven-figure jackpot." *People* magazine (8 December 1997) said that, "defying the medical odds, Bobbi and Kenny McCaughey clung to their faith and were rewarded—times seven." This religious vocabulary was certainly apt for the McCaugheys. Fundamentalist Christian religion is central to their lives, and to the life of the town of Carlisle. And it is not out of place in much—but not all—of contemporary America.

Ronald Dworkin has described the profound ambivalence of Americans on the subject of religion. Despite a constitutionally mandated separation of church and state, the United States is among the most religious of modern western democracies. And in the tone of its most powerful religious groups, by far the most fundamentalist. With its opposition to abortion and to euthanasia, the Catholic church has played an important role, as have fundamentalist Christians—particularly in regard to abortion, fetal tissue research, and embryo research. For the McCaugheys, selective reduction "just wasn't an option," Kenny told reporters. "We were trusting in the Lord for the outcome."

For those of a more secular turn of mind, several troublesome moral issues are raised by this case. And they are certainly not peculiar to the American scene.

First, the role and responsibility of the media, a role that was pivotal in the Allwood case. The offer of one million pounds from the *News of the World* may well have affected her decision not to have selective reduction. But more often, as in the McCaughey case, the media plays a less direct role. When they report a story such as this one in a way that emphasizes the positive side and de-emphasizes the risks, they are behaving irresponsibly. Indeed, the celebratory tenor of the septuplet coverage raises a real danger that giving birth to seven babies all at once will be seen as the medical state of the art to be emulated for fame or for profit.

Second, the stigmatization of infertility as a disease and not, as Tristram Engelhardt might call it, an unfortunate result of life's lottery. If Bobbi McCaughey was willing to go to such lengths to become a mother, are those with less strength of purpose or less success somehow flawed?

Third, the matter of eligibility and access. Mandy Allwood had conceived naturally several times and Bobbi McCaughey already had one child. What are morally permissible criteria for eligibility? And who decides? In the United States it is the market. Fertility drugs seem to be the poor person's remedy, while IVF is reserved for those with means or very good insurance. The McCaugheys are economically in the lower middle class. One can only wonder about the care Bobbi McCaughey would have received at a more state of the art—and expensive—program.

In Britain, in theory, the physician decides who should have treatment. The Code of Practice of the Human Fertilisation and Embryology Act gives broad discretion to physicians to make eligibility determinations based on the best interests of potential children. But the so-called "internal market" may be distorting the process. Fertility clinics in the United Kingdom provide services according to contractual arrangements made with the particular patient's local or regional health authority. Some contracts contain criteria that are more stringent than others. Thus while some women must be infertile or at least childless to qualify for treatment, others need not meet such qualifications. Such discrepancies seem both arbitrary and grossly unfair.

Fourth, the question of cost—both human and economic. The former relates to the risk of harm to mother and baby, the latter to the identity of the payer. In the United Kingdom patients have IVF on the National Health Service, but also privately. Should the identity of the payer—the state or private funds—change the moral calculus in regard to eligibility? If the government pays, thus expending a communal resource, should eligibility be restricted to those who are childless or married? In the United States, although the costs of fertility treatment are seldom covered by insurance, the exorbitant cost of caring for multiple premature newborns—in this case estimated at upwards of $1,500,000—is a covered expense. Society must bear these costs in one way or another. Do people have the right to inflict costs like these on others?

Fifth, some difficult informed consent questions. Many practitioners consider selective reduction to be a fall-back position to be used when fertility treatment goes wrong. What is to be done if the patient, like the McCaugheys, simply refuses? Is it morally permissible to build this decision into the informed consent process and if the woman will not acquiesce in advance, deny her treatment? Can a document be drafted that would lock a patient into agreeing to selective reduction if there were a certain number of embryos? For both legal and ethical reasons, certainly not.

Sixth, the question of the propriety of selective reduction itself. If we could save some lives only by taking others, could it somehow be more ethical to allow all to perish? It certainly seems not, but selective reduction is performed in circumstances in which there is no way to know which fetus is more likely to be normal or to flourish. Does this veil of ignorance make selective reduction more morally problematic than abortion for reasons of defect?

What are the circumstances in which we should allow or even recommend selective reduction? Should this option be limited to situations of great risk to mother or baby, or can its use be more discretionary? In the United States the right to an abortion is a fundamental right under the Constitution and cannot be infringed upon in any way during the first trimester of pregnancy. The current abortion law in Britain is also quite broad. But what of morally troublesome cases like the recent instance, in Britain, of selective reduction of a twin for social reasons—for the convenience of an upper middle class working mother?

Finally, it is crucial that the humanity in human interest stories such as the tale of the McCaughey septuplets does not obscure the key moral issues. There are many. They are compelling. And they must be addressed. Bioethicists have been seen, but have they really been heard?

### Acknowledgments

My thanks to Alan Fleischman, Senior Vice President, New York Academy of Medicine, for his helpful comments and suggestions. And to Elizabeth Graham, Senior Information Officer, the Wellcome Centre for Medical Science, London, for her research assistance.

# Section 2: Surrogate Pregnancy

## Surrogate Motherhood as Prenatal Adoption

### Bonnie Steinbock

Bonnie Steinbock reviews the Baby M case and maintains that the court decision was inconsistent in considering the best interest of the child. The aim of legislation, she claims, should be to minimize potential harms and prevent cases like that of Baby M from happening again. This can be so only if surrogacy is not intrinsically wrong.

   This leads Steinbock to examine three lines of argument and attempt to show that neither paternalism of the sort outlined by Gerald Dworkin (see Chapter 2) nor such considerations as threats of exploitation, loss of dignity, or harm to the child are adequate to show that surrogacy is inherently objectionable. In Steinbock's view, regulating surrogacy—and protecting liberty—is preferable to prohibiting it.

The recent case of "Baby M" has brought surrogate motherhood to the forefront of American attention. Ultimately, whether we permit or prohibit surrogacy depends on what we take to be good reasons for preventing people from acting as they wish. A growing number of people want to be, or hire, surrogates; are there legitimate reasons to prevent them? Apart from its intrinsic interest, the issue of surrogate motherhood provides us with an opportunity to examine different justifications for limiting individual freedom.

   In the first section, I examine the Baby M case, and the lessons it offers. In the second section, I examine claims that surrogacy is ethically unacceptable because it is exploitive, inconsistent with human dignity, or harmful to the children born of such arrangements. I conclude that these reasons justify restrictions on surrogate contracts, rather than an outright ban.

### I. Baby M

Mary Beth Whitehead, a married mother of two, agreed to be inseminated with the sperm of William Stern, and to give up the child to him for a fee of $10,000. The baby (whom Mrs. Whitehead named Sara, and the Sterns named Melissa) was born on

From "Surrogate Motherhood as Prenatal Adoption," by Bonnie Steinbock, *Law, Medicine and Health Care*, Vol. 16, no. 1 (1988), 44–50. Reprinted by permission.

March 27, 1986. Three days later, Mrs. Whitehead took her home from the hospital, and turned her over to the Sterns.

   Then Mrs. Whitehead changed her mind. She went to the Sterns' home, distraught, and pleaded to have the baby temporarily. Afraid that she would kill herself, the Sterns agreed. The next week, Mrs. Whitehead informed the Sterns that she had decided to keep the child, and threatened to leave the country if court action was taken.

   At that point, the situation deteriorated into a cross between the Keystone Kops and Nazi storm troopers. Accompanied by five policemen, the Sterns went to the Whitehead residence armed with a court order giving them temporary custody of the child. Mrs. Whitehead managed to slip the baby out of a window to her husband, and the following morning the Whiteheads fled with the child to Florida, where Mrs. Whitehead's parents lived. During the next three months, the Whiteheads lived in roughly twenty different hotels, motels, and homes to avoid apprehension. From time to time, Mrs. Whitehead telephoned Mr. Stern to discuss the matter: He taped these conversations on advice of counsel. Mrs. Whitehead threatened to kill herself, to kill the child, and falsely to accuse Mr. Stern of sexually molesting her older daughter.

   At the end of July 1986, while Mrs. Whitehead was hospitalized with a kidney infection, Florida police raided her mother's home, knocking her down, and seized the child. Baby M was placed in the custody of Mr. Stern, and the Whiteheads returned to New Jersey, where they attempted to regain custody. After a long and emotional court battle, Judge Harvey R. Sorkow ruled on March 31, 1987, that the surrogacy contract was valid, and that specific performance was justified in the best interests of the child. Immediately after reading his decision, he called the Sterns into his chambers so that Mr. Stern's wife, Dr. Elizabeth Stern, could legally adopt the child.

This outcome was unexpected and unprecedented. Most commentators had thought that a court would be unlikely to order a reluctant surrogate to give up an infant merely on the basis of a contract. Indeed, if Mrs. Whitehead had never surrendered the child to the Sterns, but had simply taken her home and kept her there, the outcome undoubtedly would have been different. It is also likely that Mrs. Whitehead's failure to obey the initial custody order angered Judge Sorkow, and affected his decision.

The decision was appealed to the New Jersey Supreme Court, which issued its decision on February 3, 1988. Writing for a unanimous court, Chief Justice Wilentz reversed the lower court's ruling that the surrogacy contract was valid. The court held that a surrogacy contract which provides money for the surrogate mother, and which includes her irrevocable agreement to surrender her child at birth, is invalid and unenforceable. Since the contract was invalid, Mrs. Whitehead did not relinquish, nor were there any other grounds for terminating, her parental rights. Therefore, the adoption of Baby M by Mrs. Stern was improperly granted, and Mrs. Whitehead remains the child's legal mother.

The Court further held that the issue of custody is determined solely by the child's best interests, and it agreed with the lower court that it was in Melissa's best interests to remain with the Sterns. However, Mrs. Whitehead, as Baby M's legal as well as natural mother, is entitled to have her own interest in visitation considered. The determination of what kind of visitation rights should be granted to her, and under what conditions, was remanded to the trial court.

The distressing details of this case have led many people to reject surrogacy altogether. Do we really want police officers wrenching infants from their mothers' arms, and prolonged custody battles when surrogates find they are unable to surrender their children, as agreed? Advocates of surrogacy say that to reject the practice wholesale, because of one unfortunate instance, is an example of a "hard case" making bad

policy. Opponents reply that it is entirely reasonable to focus on the worst potential outcomes when deciding public policy. Everyone can agree on at least one thing: This particular case seems to have been mismanaged from start to finish, and could serve as a manual of how not to arrange a surrogate birth.

First, it is now clear that Mary Beth Whitehead was not a suitable candidate for surrogate motherhood. Her ambivalence about giving up the child was recognized early on, although this information was not passed on to the Sterns.[1] Second, she had contact with the baby after birth, which is usually avoided in "successful" cases. Typically, the adoptive mother is actively involved in the pregnancy, often serving as the pregnant woman's coach in labor. At birth, the baby is given to the adoptive, not the biological, mother. The joy of the adoptive parents in holding their child serves both to promote their bonding, and to lessen the pain of separation of the biological mother.

At Mrs. Whitehead's request, no one at the hospital was aware of the surrogacy arrangement. She and her husband appeared as the proud parents of "Sara Elizabeth Whitehead," the name on her birth certificate. Mrs. Whitehead held her baby, nursed her, and took her home from the hospital—just as she would have done in a normal pregnancy and birth. Not surprisingly, she thought of Sara as her child, and she fought with every weapon at her disposal, honorable and dishonorable, to prevent her being taken away. She can hardly be blamed for doing so.[2]

Why did Dr. Stern, who supposedly had a very good relation with Mrs. Whitehead before the birth, not act as her labor coach? One possibility is that Mrs. Whitehead, ambivalent about giving up her baby, did not want Dr. Stern involved. At her request, the Sterns' visits to the hospital to see the newborn baby were unobtrusive. It is also possible that Dr. Stern was ambivalent about having a child. The original idea of hiring a surrogate was not hers, but her husband's. It was Mr. Stern who felt a "compelling" need to have a child related to him by blood, having lost all his relatives to the Nazis.

Furthermore, Dr. Stern was not infertile, as was stated in the surrogacy agreement. Rather, in 1979 she was diagnosed by two eye specialists as suffering from optic neuritis, which meant that she "probably" had multiple sclerosis. (This was confirmed by all four experts who testified.) Normal conception was ruled out by the Sterns in late 1982, when a medical colleague told Dr. Stern that his wife, a victim of multiple sclerosis, had suffered a temporary paralysis during pregnancy. "We decided the risk wasn't worth it," Mr. Stern said.[3]

Mrs. Whitehead's lawyer, Harold J. Cassidy, dismissed the suggestion that Dr. Stern's "mildest case" of multiple sclerosis determined their decision to seek a surrogate. He noted that she was not even treated for multiple sclerosis until after the Baby M dispute had started. "It's almost as though it's an afterthought," he said.[4]

Judge Sorkow deemed the decision to avoid conception "medically reasonable and understandable." The Supreme Court did not go so far, noting that "her anxiety appears to have exceeded the actual risk, which current medical authorities assess as minimal."[5] Nonetheless the court acknowledged that her anxiety, including fears that pregnancy might precipitate blindness and paraplegia, was "quite real." Certainly, even a woman who wants a child very much, may reasonably wish to avoid becoming blind and paralyzed as a result of pregnancy. Yet is it believable that a woman who really wanted a child would decide against pregnancy *solely* on the basis of *someone else's* medical experience? Would she not consult at least one specialist on her *own* medical condition before deciding it wasn't worth the risk? The conclusion that she was at best ambivalent about bearing a child seems irresistible.

This possibility conjures up many people's worst fears about surrogacy: That prosperous women, who do not want to interrupt their careers, will use poor and educationally disadvantaged women to bear their children. I will return shortly to the question of whether this is exploitive. The issue here is psychological: What kind of mother is Dr. Stern likely to be? If she is unwilling to undergo pregnancy, with its discomforts, inconveniences, and risks, will she be willing to make the considerable sacrifices which good parenting requires? Mrs. Whitehead's ability to be a good mother was repeatedly questioned during the trial. She was portrayed as immature, untruthful, hysterical, overly identified with her children, and prone to smothering their independence. Even if all this is true—and I think that Mrs. Whitehead's inadequacies were exaggerated—Dr. Stern may not be such a prize either. The choice for Baby M may have been between a highly strung, emotional, over-involved mother, and a remote, detached, even cold one.

The assessment of Mrs. Whitehead's ability to be a good mother was biased by the middle-class prejudices of the judge and mental health officials who testified. Mrs. Whitehead left school at 15, and is not conversant with the latest theories on child rearing:

She made the egregious error of giving Sara teddy bears to play with, instead of the more "age-appropriate," expert-approved pans and spoons. She proved to be a total failure at patty-cake. If this is evidence of parental inadequacy, we're all in danger of losing our children.

The Supreme Court felt that Mrs. Whitehead was "rather harshly judged" and acknowledged the possibility that the trial court was wrong in its initial award of custody. Nevertheless, it affirmed Judge Sorkow's decision to allow the Sterns to retain custody, as being in Melissa's best interests. George Annas disagrees with the "best interests" approach. He points out that Judge Sorkow awarded temporary custody of Baby M to the Sterns in May 1986 without giving the Whiteheads notice or an opportunity to obtain legal representation. That was a serious wrong and injustice to the Whiteheads. To allow the Sterns to keep the child compounds the original unfairness: " . . . justice requires that reasonable consideration be given to returning Baby M to the permanent custody of the Whiteheads."[6]

But a child is not a possession, to be returned to the rightful owner. It is not fairness to all parties that should determine a child's fate, but what is best for her. As Chief Justice Wilentz rightly stated, "The child's interests comes first: We will not punish it for judicial errors, assuming any were made."[7]

Subsequent events have substantiated the claim that giving custody to the Sterns was in Melissa's best interests. After losing custody, Mrs. Whitehead, whose husband had undergone a vasectomy, became pregnant by another man. She divorced her husband and married Dean R. Gould last November. These developments indicate that the Whiteheads were not able to offer a stable home, although the argument can be made that their marriage might have survived, but for the strains introduced by the court battle, and the loss of Baby M. But even if Judge Sorkow had no reason to prefer the Sterns to the Whiteheads back in May 1986, he was still right to give the Sterns custody in March 1987. To take her away then, at nearly eighteen months of age, from the only parents she had ever known, would have been disruptive, cruel, and unfair to her.

Annas's preference for a just solution is premised partly on his belief that there is no "best interest" solution to this "tragic custody case." I take it that he means that however custody is resolved, Baby M is the loser. Either way, she will be deprived of one parent. However, a best interests solution is not a perfect solution. It is simply the solution which is on balance best for the child, given the realities of the situation. Applying this standard, Judge Sorkow was right to give the Sterns custody, and the Supreme Court was right to uphold the decision.

The best interests argument is based on the assumption that Mr. Stern has at least a *prima facie* claim to Baby M. We certainly would not consider allowing a stranger who kidnapped a baby, and managed to elude the police for a year, to retain custody on the grounds that he was providing a good home to a child who had known no other parent. However, the Baby M case is not analogous. First, Mr. Stern is Baby M's biological father and, as such, has at least some claim to raise her, which no non-parental kidnapper has. Second, Mary Beth Whitehead agreed to give him their baby. Unlike the miller's daughter in *Rumpelstiltskin*, the fairy tale to which the Baby M case is sometimes compared, she was not forced into the agreement. Because both Mary Beth Whitehead and Mr. Stern have *prima facie* claims to Baby M, the decision as to who should raise her should be based on her present best interests. Therefore we must, regretfully, tolerate the injustice to Mrs. Whitehead, and try to avoid such problems in the future.

It is unfortunate that the Court did not decide the issue of visitation on the same basis as custody. By declaring Mrs. Whitehead Gould the legal mother, and maintaining that she is entitled to visitation, the Court has prolonged the fight over Baby M. It is hard to see how this can be in her best interests. This is no ordinary divorce case, where the child has a relation with both parents which it is desirable to maintain. As Mr. Stern said at the start of the court hearing to determine visitation, "Melissa has a right to grow and be happy and not be torn between two parents."[8]

The court's decision was well-meaning but internally inconsistent. Out of concern for the best interests of the child, it granted the Sterns custody. At the same time, by holding Mrs. Whitehead Gould to be the legal mother, with visitation rights, it precluded precisely what is most in Melissa's interest, a resolution of the situation. Further, the decision leaves open the distressing possibility that a Baby M situation could happen again. Legislative efforts should be directed toward ensuring that this worse-case scenario never occurs.

## II. Should Surrogacy Be Prohibited?

On June 27, 1988, Michigan became the first state to outlaw commercial contracts for women to bear children for others. Yet making a practice illegal does not necessarily make it go away: Witness black market adoption. The legitimate concerns which support a ban on surrogacy might be better served by careful regulation. However, some practices, such as slavery, are ethically unacceptable, regardless of how carefully regulated they are. Let us consider the arguments that surrogacy is intrinsically unacceptable.

### A. Paternalistic Arguments

These arguments against surrogacy take the form of protecting a potential surrogate from a choice she may later regret. As an argument for banning surrogacy, as opposed to providing safeguards to ensure that contracts are freely and knowledgeably undertaken, this is a form of paternalism.

At one time, the characterization of a prohibition as paternalistic was a sufficient reason to reject it. The pendulum has swung back, and many people are willing to accept at least some paternalistic restrictions on freedom. Gerald Dworkin points out that even Mill made one exception to his otherwise absolute rejection of paternalism: He thought that no one should be allowed to sell himself into slavery, because to do so would be to destroy his future autonomy.

This provides a narrow principle to justify some paternalistic interventions. To preserve freedom in the long run, we give up the freedom to make certain choices, those which have results which are "far-reaching, potentially dangerous and irreversible."[9] An example would be a ban on the sale of crack. Virtually everyone who uses crack becomes addicted and, once addicted, a slave to its use. We reasonably and willingly give up our freedom to buy the drug, to protect our ability to make free decisions in the future.

Can a Dworkinian argument be made to rule out surrogacy agreements? Admittedly, the decision to give up a child is permanent, and may have disastrous effects on the surrogate mother. However, many decisions may have long-term, disastrous effects (e.g., postponing childbirth for a career, having an abortion, giving a child up for adoption). Clearly we do not want the state to make decisions for us in all these matters. Dworkin's argument is rightly restricted to paternalistic interferences which protect the individual's autonomy or ability to make decisions in the future. Surrogacy does not involve giving up one's autonomy, which distinguishes it from both the crack and selling-oneself-into-slavery examples. Respect for individual freedom requires us to permit people to make choices which they may later regret.

## B. Moral Objections

Four main moral objections to surrogacy were outlined in the Warnock Report.[10]

1.  It is inconsistent with human dignity that a woman should use her uterus for financial profit.

2.  To deliberately become pregnant with the intention of giving up the child distorts the relationship between mother and child.

3.  Surrogacy is degrading because it amounts to child-selling.

4.  Since there are some risks attached to pregnancy, no woman ought to be asked to undertake pregnancy for another in order to earn money.

We must all agree that a practice which exploits people or violates human dignity is immoral. However, it is not clear that surrogacy is guilty on either count.

**1. Exploitation.** The mere fact that pregnancy is *risky* does not make surrogate agreements exploitive, and therefore morally wrong. People often do risky things for money; why should the line be drawn at undergoing pregnancy? The usual response is to compare surrogacy and kidney-selling. The selling of organs is prohibited because of the potential for coercion and exploitation. But why should kidney-selling be viewed as intrinsically coercive? A possible explanation is that no one would do it, unless driven by poverty. The choice is both forced and dangerous, and hence coercive.

The situation is quite different in the case of the race car driver or stuntman. We do not think that they are *forced* to perform risky activities for money: They freely choose to do so. Unlike selling one's kidneys, these are activities which we can understand (intellectually, anyway) someone choosing to do. Movie stuntmen, for example, often enjoy their work, and derive satisfaction from doing it well. Of course they "do it for the money," in the sense that they would not do it without compensation; few people are willing to work "for free." The element of coercion is missing, however, because they enjoy the job, despite the risks, and could do something else if they chose.

The same is apparently true of most surrogates. "They choose the surrogate role primarily because the fee provides a better economic opportunity than alternative occupations, but also because they enjoy being pregnant and the respect and attention that it draws."[11] Some may derive a feeling of self-worth from an act they regard as highly altruistic: Providing a couple with a child they could not otherwise have. If these motives are present, it is far from clear that the surrogate is being exploited. Indeed, it seems objectionably paternalistic to insist that she is.

**2. Human Dignity.** It may be argued that even if womb-leasing is not necessarily exploitive, it should still be rejected as inconsistent with human dignity. But why? As John Harris points out, hair, blood and other tissue is often donated or sold; what is so special about the uterus?[12]

Human dignity is more plausibly invoked in the strongest argument against surrogacy, namely, that it is the sale of a child. Children are not property, nor can they be bought or sold. It could be argued that surrogacy is wrong because it is analogous to slavery, and so is inconsistent with human dignity.

However, there are important differences between slavery and a surrogate agreement. The child born of a surrogate is not treated cruelly or deprived of freedom or resold; none of the things which make slavery so awful are part of surrogacy. Still, it may be thought that simply putting a market value on a child is wrong. Human life has intrinsic value; it is literally priceless. Arrangements which ignore this violate our deepest notions of the value of human life. It is profoundly disturbing to hear the boyfriend of a surrogate say, quite candidly in a television documentary on surrogacy, "We're in it for the money."

Judge Sorkow accepted the premise that producing a child for money denigrates human dignity, but he denied that this happens in a surrogate agreement. Mrs. Whitehead was not paid for the surrender of the child to the father: She was paid for her willingness to be impregnated and carry Mr. Stern's child to term. The child, once born, is his biological child. "He cannot purchase what is already his."

This is misleading, and not merely because Baby M is as much Mrs. Whitehead's child as Mr. Stern's. It is misleading because it glosses over the fact that the surrender of the child was part—indeed, the whole point—of the agreement. If the surrogate were paid merely for being willing to be impregnated and carrying the child to term, then she would fulfill the contract upon giving birth. She could take the money *and* the child. Mr. Stern did not agree to pay Mrs. Whitehead merely to *have* his child, but to provide him with a child. The New Jersey Supreme Court held that this violated New Jersey's laws prohibiting the payment or acceptance of money in connection with adoption.

One way to remove the taint of baby-selling would be to limit payment to medical expenses associated with the birth or incurred by the surrogate during pregnancy (as is allowed in many jurisdictions, including New Jersey, in ordinary adoptions). Surrogacy could be seen, not as baby-selling, but as a form of adoption. Nowhere did the Supreme Court find any legal prohibition against surrogacy when there is no payment, and when the surrogate has the right to change her mind and keep the child. However, this solution effectively prohibits surrogacy, since few women would become surrogates solely for self-fulfillment or reasons of altruism.

The question, then, is whether we can reconcile paying the surrogate, beyond her medical expenses, with the idea of surrogacy as prenatal adoption. We can do this by separating the terms of the agreement, which include surrendering the infant at birth to the biological father, from the justification for payment. The payment should be seen as compensation for the risks, sacrifice, and discomfort the surrogate undergoes during pregnancy. This means that if, through no fault on the part of the surrogate, the baby is stillborn, she should still be paid in full, since she has kept her part of the bargain. (By contrast, in the Stern–Whitehead agreement, Mrs. Whitehead was to receive only $1,000 for a stillbirth.) If, on the other hand, the surrogate changes her mind and decides to keep the child, she would break the agreement, and would not be entitled to any fee, or compensation for expenses incurred during pregnancy.

### C.  The Right of Privacy

Most commentators who invoke the right of privacy do so in support of surrogacy. However, George Annas makes the novel argument that the right to rear a child you have borne is also a privacy right, which cannot be prospectively waived. He says:

> [Judge Sorkow] grudgingly concedes that [Mrs. Whitehead] could not prospectively give up her right to have an abortion during pregnancy. . . . This would be an intolerable restriction on her liberty and under *Roe* v. *Wade,* the state has no constitutional authority to enforce a contract that prohibits her from terminating her pregnancy.
>
> But why isn't the same logic applicable to the right to rear a child you have given birth to? Her constitutional rights to rear the child she has given birth to are even stronger since they involve even more intimately, and over a lifetime, her privacy rights to reproduce and rear a child in a family setting.[13]

Absent a compelling state interest (such as protecting a child from unfit parents), it certainly would be an intolerable invasion of privacy for the state to take children from their parents. But Baby M has two parents, both of whom now want her. It is not clear why only people who can give birth (i.e., women) should enjoy the right to rear their children.

Moreover, we do allow women to give their children up for adoption after birth. The state enforces those agreements, even if the natural mother, after the prescribed waiting period, changes her mind. Why should the right to rear a child be unwaivable before, but not after birth? Why should the state have the constitutional authority to uphold postnatal, but not prenatal, adoption agreements? It is not clear why birth should affect the waivability of this right, or have the constitutional significance which Annas attributes to it.

Nevertheless, there are sound moral and policy, if not constitutional, reasons to provide a postnatal waiting period in surrogate agreements. As the Baby M case makes painfully clear, the surrogate may underestimate the bond created by gestation, and the emotional trauma caused by relinquishing the baby. Compassion requires that we acknowledge these feelings, and not deprive a woman of the baby she has carried because, before conception, she underestimated the strength of her feelings for it. Providing a waiting period, as in ordinary postnatal adoptions, will help protect women from making irrevocable mistakes, without banning the practice.

Some may object that this gives too little protection to the prospective adoptive parents. They cannot be sure that the baby is theirs until the waiting period is over. While this is hard on them, a similar burden is placed on other adoptive parents. If the absence of a guarantee serves to discourage people from entering surrogacy agreements, that is not necessarily a bad thing, given all the risks inherent in such contracts. In addition, this requirement would make stricter screening and counseling of surrogates essential, a desirable side effect.

### D.  Harm to Others

Paternalistic and moral objections to surrogacy do not seem to justify an outright ban. What about the effect on the offspring of such contracts? We do not yet have solid data on the effects of being a "surrogate child." Any claim that surrogacy creates psychological problems in the children is purely speculative. But what if we did discover that such children have deep feelings of worthlessness from learning that their natural mothers deliberately created them with the intention of giving them away? Might we ban surrogacy as posing an unacceptable risk of psychological harm to the resulting children?

Feelings of worthlessness are harmful. They can prevent people from living happy, fulfilling lives. However, a surrogate child, even one whose life is miserable because of these feelings, cannot claim to have been harmed by the surrogate agreement. Without the agreement, the child would never have existed. Unless she is willing to say that her life is not worth living because of these feelings, that she would be better off never having been born, she cannot claim to have been harmed by being born of a surrogate mother.

Children can be *wronged* by being brought into existence, even if they are not, strictly speaking, *harmed*. They are wronged if they are deprived of the minimally decent existence to which all citizens are entitled. We owe it to our children to see that they are not born with such serious impairments that their most basic interests will be doomed in advance. If being born to a surrogate is a handicap of this magnitude, comparable to being born blind or deaf or severely mentally retarded, then surrogacy can be seen as wronging the offspring. This would be a strong reason against permitting such contracts. However, it does not seem likely. Probably the problems arising from surrogacy will be like those faced by adopted children and children whose parents divorce. Such problems are not trivial, but neither are they so serious that the child's very existence can be seen as wrongful.

If surrogate children are neither harmed nor wronged by surrogacy, it may seem that the argument for banning surrogacy on grounds of its harmfulness to the offspring evaporates. After all, if the children themselves have no cause for complaint, how can anyone else claim to reject it on their behalf? Yet it seems extremely counter-intuitive to suggest that the risk of emotional damage to the children born of such arrangements is not even relevant to our deliberations. It seems quite reasonable and proper—even morally obligatory—for policymakers to think about the possible detrimental effects of new reproductive technologies, and to reject those likely to create physically or emotionally damaged people. The explanation for this must involve the idea that it is wrong to bring people into the world in a harmful condition, even if they are not, strictly speaking, harmed by having been brought into existence. Should evidence emerge that surrogacy produces children with serious psychological problems, that would be a strong reason for banning the practice.

There is some evidence on the effect of surrogacy on the other children of the surrogate mother. One woman reported that her daughter, now 17, who was 11 at the time of the surrogate birth," . . . is still having problems with what I did, and as a result she is still angry with me." She explains, "Nobody told me that a child could bond with a baby while you're still pregnant. I didn't realize then that all the times she listened to his heartbeat and felt his legs kick that she was becoming attached to him."[14]

A less sentimental explanation is possible. It seems likely that her daughter, seeing one child given away, was fearful that the same might be done to her. We can expect anxiety and resentment on the part of children whose mothers give away a brother or sister. The psychological harm to these children is clearly relevant to a determination of whether surrogacy is contrary to public policy. At the same time, it should be remembered that many things, including divorce, remarriage, and even moving to a new neighborhood, create anxiety and resentment in children. We should not use the effect on children as an excuse for banning a practice we find bizarre or offensive.

## Conclusion

There are many reasons to be extremely cautious of surrogacy. I cannot imagine becoming a surrogate, nor would I advise anyone else to enter into a contract so fraught with peril. But the fact that a practice is risky, foolish, or even morally distasteful is not sufficient reason to outlaw it. It would be better for the state to regulate the practice, and minimize the potential for harm, without infringing on the liberty of citizens.

### Notes

1. Had the Sterns been informed of the psychologist's concerns as to Mrs. Whitehead's suitability to be a surrogate, they might have ended the arrangement, costing the Infertility Center its fee. As Chief Justice Wilentz said, "It is apparent that the profit motive got the better of the Infertility Center." In the matter of Baby M, Supreme Court of New Jersey, A–39, at 45.

2. "[W]e think it is expecting something well beyond normal human capabilities to suggest that this mother should have parted with her newly born infant without a struggle. . . . We . . . cannot conceive of any other case where a perfectly fit mother was expected to surrender her newly born infant, perhaps forever, and was then told she was a bad mother because she did not." *Id.* at 79.

3. Father recalls surrogate was "perfect." *New York Times*, January 6, 1987, B2.

4. *Id.*

5.   In the matter of Baby M, *supra* note 1, at 8.

6.   Annas, G. J.: Baby M: babies (and justice) for sale. *Hastings Center Report* 17 (3): 15, 1987.

7.   In the matter of Baby M, *supra* note 1, at 75.

8.   Anger and Anguish at Baby M Visitation Hearing, *New York Times*, March 29, 1988, 17.

9.   Dworkin, G.: Paternalism. In Wasserstrom, R. A., ed.: *Morality and the Law*. Belmont, Calif., Wadsworth, 1971; reprinted in Feinberg, J., Gross, H., eds., *Philosophy of Law,* 3rd ed. Wadsworth, 1986, p. 265.

10.   Warnock, M., chair: *Report of the committee of inquiry into human fertilisation and embryology*. London: Her Majesty's Stationery Office, 1984.

11.   Robertson, J. A.: Surrogate mothers: not so novel after all. *Hastings Center Report* 13 (5): 29,1983. Citing Parker, P.: Surrogate mother's motivations: initial findings. *American Journal of Psychiatry* (140): 1, 1983.

12.   Harris, J.: *The Value of Life*. London: Routledge & Kegan Paul, 1985, 144.

13.   Annas, *supra* note 6.

14.   Baby M case stirs feelings of surrogate mothers. *New York Times*, March 2, 1987, B1.

# Is Women's Labor a Commodity?

## Elizabeth S. Anderson

Elizabeth Anderson argues that commercial surrogacy should not be allowed. The practice of paying women to be surrogate mothers involves a "commodification" of both children and women. It treats women and their children as things to be used, instead of as persons deserving respect. Hence, surrogacy contracts should be unenforceable, and those who arrange them should be subject to criminal penalties.

Anderson holds that the introduction of market values and norms into a situation previously based on respect, consideration, and unconditional love has the effect of harming children and degrading and exploiting women. The values of the market contribute to a tendency to view children as property. When this happens, they are no longer valued unconditionally (as is the case with parental love), but are valued only because they possess characteristics with a market value.

Market values require that surrogate mothers repress whatever parental love they may feel for their children. Hence, the feelings of women are manipulated, degraded, and denied legitimacy. Further, women are exploited by having the personal feelings that incline them to become surrogates turned into something that can be marketed as part of a commercial enterprise.

In the past few years the practice of commercial surrogate motherhood has gained notoriety as a method for acquiring children. A commercial surrogate mother is anyone who is paid money to bear a child for other people and terminate her parental rights, so that the others may raise the child as exclusively their own. The growth of commercial surrogacy has raised with new urgency a class of concerns regarding the proper scope of the market. Some critics have objected to commercial surrogacy on the ground that it improperly treats children and women's reproductive capacities as commodities.[1] The prospect of reducing children to consumer durables and women to baby factories surely inspires revulsion. But are there good reasons behind the revulsion? And is this an accurate description of what commercial surrogacy implies? This article offers a theory about what things are properly regarded as commodities which supports the claim that commercial surrogacy constitutes an unconscionable commodification of children and of women's reproductive capacities.

From *Philosophy & Public Affairs,* Vol. 19, no. 1 (1990): 71–87, 91–92. © 1990 by Princeton University Press. Reprinted by permission.

## What Is a Commodity?

The modern market can be characterized in terms of the legal and social norms by which it governs the production, exchange, and enjoyment of commodities. To say that something is properly regarded as a commodity is to claim that the norms of the market are appropriate for regulating its production, exchange, and enjoyment. To the extent that moral principles or ethical ideals preclude the application of market norms to a good, we may say that the good is not a (proper) commodity.

Why should we object to the application of a market norm to the production or distribution of a good? One reason may be that to produce or distribute the good in accordance with the norm is to *fail to value it in an appropriate way*. Consider, for example, a standard Kantian argument against slavery, or the commodification of persons. Slaves are treated in accordance with the market norm that owners may use commodities to satisfy their own interests without regard for the interests of the commodities themselves. To treat a person without regard for her interests is to fail to respect her. But slaves are persons who may not be merely used in this fashion, since as rational beings they possess a dignity which commands respect. In Kantian theory, the problem with slavery is that it treats beings worthy of *respect* as if they were worthy merely of *use*. "Respect" and "use" in this context denote what we may call different *modes of valuation*. . . .

These considerations support a general account of the sorts of things which are appropriately regarded as commodities. Commodities are those things which are properly treated in accordance with the norms of the modern market. We can question the application of market norms to the production, distribution, and enjoyment of a good by appealing to ethical ideals which support arguments that the good should be valued in some other way than use. Arguments of the latter sort claim that to allow certain market norms to govern our treatment of a thing expresses a mode of valuation not worthy of it. If the thing is to be valued appropriately, its production, exchange, and enjoyment must be removed from market norms and embedded in a different set of social relationships.

## The Case of Commercial Surrogacy

Let us now consider the practice of commercial surrogate motherhood in the light of this theory of commodities. Surrogate motherhood as a commercial enterprise is based upon contracts involving three parties: the intended father, the broker, and the surrogate mother. The intended father agrees to pay a lawyer to find a suitable surrogate mother and make the requisite medical and legal arrangements for the conception and birth of the child, and for the transfer of legal custody to himself.[2] The surrogate mother agrees to become impregnated with the intended father's sperm, to carry the resulting child to term, and to relinquish her parental rights to it, transferring custody to the father in return for a fee and medical expenses. Both she and her husband (if she has one) agree not to form a parent–child bond with her child and to do everything necessary to effect the transfer of the child to the intended father. At current market prices, the lawyer arranging the contract can expect to gross $15,000 from the contract, while the surrogate mother can expect a $10,000 fee.[3]

The practice of commercial surrogacy has been defended on four main grounds. First, given the shortage of children available for adoption and the difficulty of qualifying as adoptive parents, it may represent the only hope for some people to be able to raise a family. Commercial surrogacy should be accepted as an effective means for realizing this highly significant good. Second, two fundamental human rights support commercial surrogacy: the right to procreate and freedom of contract. Fully informed autonomous adults should have the right to make whatever arrangements they wish for the use of their bodies and the reproduction of children, so long as the children themselves are not harmed. Third, the labor of the surrogate mother is said to be a labor of love. Her altruistic acts should be permitted and encouraged.[4] Finally, it is argued that commercial surrogacy is no different in its ethical implications from many already accepted practices which separate genetic, gestational, and social parenting, such as artificial insemination by donor, adoption, wet-nursing, and day care. Consistency demands that society accept this new practice as well.[5]

In opposition to these claims, I shall argue that commercial surrogacy does raise new ethical issues, since it represents an invasion of the market into a new sphere of conduct, that of specifically women's labor—that is, the labor of carrying children to term in pregnancy. When women's labor is treated as a commodity, the women who perform it are degraded. Furthermore, commercial surrogacy degrades children by reducing their status to that of commodities. Let us consider each of the goods of concern in surrogate motherhood—the child, and women's reproductive labor—to see how the commercialization of parenthood affects people's regard for them.

## Children as Commodities

The most fundamental calling of parents to their children is to love them. Children are to be loved and cherished by their parents, not to be used or manipulated by them for merely personal advantage. Parental love can be understood as a passionate, unconditional commitment to nurture one's child, providing it with the care, affection, and guidance it needs to develop its capacities to maturity. This understanding of the way parents should value their children informs our interpretation of parental rights over their children. Parents' rights over their children are trusts, which they must always exercise for the sake of the child. This is not to deny that parents have their own aspirations in raising children. But the child's interests beyond subsistence are not definable independently of the flourishing of the family, which is the object of specifically parental aspirations. The proper exercise of parental rights includes those acts which promote their shared life as a family, which realize the shared interests of the parents and the child.

The norms of parental love carry implications for the ways other people should treat the relationship between parents and their children. If children are to be loved by their parents, then others should not attempt to compromise the integrity of parental love or work to suppress the emotions supporting the bond between parents and their children. If the rights to children should be understood as trusts, then if those rights are lost or relinquished, the duty of those in charge of transferring custody to others is to consult the best interests of the child.

Commercial surrogacy substitutes market norms for some of the norms of parental love. Most importantly, it requires us to understand parental rights no longer as trusts but as things more like property rights—that is, rights of use and disposal over the things owned. For in this practice the natural mother deliberately conceives a child with the intention of giving it up for material advantage. Her renunciation of parental responsibilities is not done for the child's sake, nor for the sake of fulfilling an interest she shares with the child, but typically for her own sake (and possibly, if "altruism" is a motive, for the intended parents' sakes). She and the couple who pay her to give up her parental rights over her child thus treat her rights as a kind of property right. They

thereby treat the child itself as a kind of commodity, which may be properly bought and sold.

Commercial surrogacy insinuates the norms of commerce into the parental relationship in other ways. Whereas parental love is not supposed to be conditioned upon the child having particular characteristics, consumer demand is properly responsive to the characteristics of commodities. So the surrogate industry provides opportunities to adoptive couples to specify the height, I.Q., race, and other attributes of the surrogate mother, in the expectation that these traits will be passed on to the child.[6] Since no industry assigns agents to look after the "interests" of its commodities, no one represents the child's interests in the surrogate industry. The surrogate agency promotes the adoptive parents' interests and not the child's interests where matters of custody are concerned. Finally, as the agent of the adoptive parents, the broker has the task of policing the surrogate (natural) mother's relationship to her child, using persuasion, money, and the threat of a lawsuit to weaken and destroy whatever parental love she may develop for her child.[7]

All of these substitutions of market norms for parental norms represent ways of treating children as commodities which are degrading to them. Degradation occurs when something is treated in accordance with a lower mode of valuation than is proper to it. We value things not just "more" or "less," but in qualitatively higher and lower ways. To love or respect someone is to value her in a higher way than one would if one merely used her. Children are properly loved by their parents and respected by others. Since children are valued as mere use-objects by the mother and the surrogate agency when they are sold to others, and by the adoptive parents when they seek to conform the child's genetic makeup to their own wishes, commercial surrogacy degrades children insofar as it treats them as commodities.[8]

One might argue that since the child is most likely to enter a loving home, no harm comes to it from permitting the natural mother to treat it as property. So the purchase and sale of infants is unobjectionable, at least from the point of view of children's interests.[9] But the sale of an infant has an expressive significance which this argument fails to recognize. By engaging in the transfer of children by sale, all of the parties to the surrogate contract express a set of attitudes toward children which undermine the norms of parental love. They all agree in treating the ties between a natural mother and her children as properly loosened by a monetary incentive. Would it be any wonder if a child born of a surrogacy agreement feared resale by parents who have such an attitude? And a child who knew how anxious her parents were that she have the "right" genetic makeup might fear that her parents' love was contingent upon her expression of these characteristics.[10]

The unsold children of surrogate mothers are also harmed by commercial surrogacy. The children of some surrogate mothers have reported their fears that they may be sold like their half-brother or half-sister, and express a sense of loss at being deprived of a sibling.[11] Furthermore, the widespread acceptance of commercial surrogacy would psychologically threaten all children. For it would change the way children are valued by people (parents and surrogate brokers)— from being loved by their parents and respected by others, to being sometimes used as objects of commercial profit-making.[12]

Proponents of commercial surrogacy have denied that the surrogate industry engages in the sale of children. For it is impossible to sell to someone what is already his own, and the child is already the father's own natural offspring. The payment to the surrogate mother is not for her child, but for her services in carrying it to term.[13] The claim that the parties to the surrogate contract treat children as commodities, however, is based on the way they treat the *mother's* rights over her child. It is irrelevant that the natural father also has some rights over the child; what he pays for is exclusive rights to it. He would not pay her for the "service" of carrying the child to term if she refused to relinquish her parental rights to it. That the mother regards only her labor and not her child as requiring compensation is also irrelevant. No one would argue that the baker does not treat his bread as property just because he sees the income from its sale as compensation for his labor and expenses and not for the bread itself, which he doesn't care to keep.[14]

Defenders of commercial surrogacy have also claimed that it does not differ substantially from other already accepted parental practices. In the institutions of adoption and artificial insemination by donor (AID), it is claimed, we already grant parents the right to dispose of their children.[15] But these practices differ in significant respects from commercial surrogacy. The purpose of adoption is to provide a means for placing children in families when their parents cannot or will not discharge their parental responsibilities. It is not a sphere for the existence of a supposed parental right to dispose of one's children for profit. Even AID does not sanction the sale of fully formed human beings.

The semen donor sells only a product of his body, not his child, and does not initiate the act of conception.

Two developments might seem to undermine the claim that commercial surrogacy constitutes a degrading commerce in children. The first is technological: the prospect of transplanting a human embryo into the womb of a genetically unrelated woman. If commercial surrogacy used women only as gestational mothers and not as genetic mothers, and if it was thought that only genetic and not gestational parents could properly claim that a child was "theirs," then the child born of a surrogate mother would not be hers to sell in the first place. The second is a legal development: the establishment of the proposed "consent–intent" definition of parenthood.[16] This would declare the legal parents of a child to be whoever consented to a procedure which leads to its birth, with the intent of assuming parental responsibilities for it. This rule would define away the problem of commerce in children by depriving the surrogate mother of any legal claim to her child at all, even if it was hers both genetically and gestationally.[17]

There are good reasons, however, not to undermine the place of genetic and gestational ties in these ways. Consider first the place of genetic ties. By upholding a system of involuntary (genetic) ties of obligation among people, even when the adults among them prefer to divide their rights and obligations in other ways, we help to secure children's interests in having an assured place in the world, which is more firm than the wills of their parents. Unlike the consent–intent rule, the principle of respecting genetic ties does not make the obligation to care for those whom one has created (intentionally or not) contingent upon an arbitrary desire to do so. It thus provides children with a set of preexisting social sanctions which give them a more secure place in the world. The genetic principle also places the children in a far wider network of associations and obligations than the consent–intent rule sanctions. It supports the roles of grandparents and other relatives in the nurturing of children, and provides children with a possible focus of stability and an additional source of claims to care if their parents cannot sustain a well-functioning household.

In the next section I will defend the claims of gestational ties to children. To deny these claims, as commercial surrogacy does, is to deny the significance of reproductive labor to the mother who undergoes it and thereby to dehumanize and degrade the mother herself. Commercial surrogacy would be a corrupt practice even if it did not involve commerce in children.

## Women's Labor as a Commodity

Commercial surrogacy attempts to transform what is specifically women's labor—the work of bringing forth children into the world—into a commodity. It does so by replacing the parental norms which usually govern the practice of gestating children with the economic norms which govern ordinary production processes. The application of commercial norms to women's labor reduces the surrogate mothers from persons worthy of respect and consideration to objects of mere use.

Respect and consideration are two distinct modes of valuation whose norms are violated by the practices of the surrogate industry. To respect a person is to treat her in accordance with principles she rationally accepts—principles consistent with the protection of her autonomy and her rational interests. To treat a person with consideration is to respond with sensitivity to her and to her emotional relations with others, refraining from manipulating or denigrating these for one's own purposes. . . .

The application of economic norms to the sphere of women's labor violates women's claims to respect and consideration in three ways. First, by requiring the surrogate mother to repress whatever parental love she feels for the child, these norms convert women's labor into a form of alienated labor. Second, by manipulating and denying legitimacy to the surrogate mother's evolving perspective on her own pregnancy, the norms of the market degrade her. Third, by taking advantage of the surrogate mother's noncommercial motivations without offering anything but what the norms of commerce demand in return, these norms leave her open to exploitation. The fact that these problems arise in the attempt to commercialize the labor of bearing children shows that women's labor is not properly regarded as a commodity.

The key to understanding these problems is the normal role of the emotions in noncommercialized pregnancies. Pregnancy is not simply a biological process but also a social practice. Many social expectations and considerations surround women's gestational labor, marking it off as an occasion for the parents to prepare themselves to welcome a new life into their family. For example, obstetricians use ultrasound not simply for diagnostic purposes but also to encourage maternal bonding with the fetus.[18] We can

all recognize that it is good, although by no means inevitable, for loving bonds to be established between the mother and her child during this period.

In contrast with these practices, the surrogate industry follows the putting-out system of manufacturing. It provides some of the raw materials of production (the father's sperm) to the surrogate mother, who then engages in production of the child. Although her labor is subject to periodic supervision by her doctors and by the surrogate agency, the agency does not have physical control over the product of her labor as firms using the factory system do. Hence, as in all putting-out systems, the surrogate industry faces the problem of extracting the final product from the mother. This problem is exacerbated by the fact that the social norms surrounding pregnancy are designed to encourage parental love for the child. The surrogate industry addresses this problem by requiring the mother to engage in a form of emotional labor.[19] In the surrogate contract, she agrees not to form or to attempt to form a parent–child relationship with her offspring.[20] Her labor is alienated, because she must divert it from the end which the social practices of pregnancy rightly promote—an emotional bond with her child. The surrogate contract thus replaces a norm of parenthood, that during pregnancy one create a loving attachment to one's child, with a norm of commercial production, that the producer shall not form any special emotional ties to her product. . . .

Commercial surrogacy is also a degrading practice. The surrogate mother, like all persons, has an independent evaluative perspective on her activities and relationships. The realization of her dignity demands that the other parties to the contract acknowledge rather than evade the claims which her independent perspective makes upon them. But the surrogate industry has an interest in suppressing, manipulating, and trivializing her perspective, for there is an ever-present danger that she will see her involvement in her pregnancy from the perspective of a parent rather than from the perspective of a contract laborer.

How does this suppression and trivialization take place? The commercial promoters of surrogacy commonly describe the surrogate mothers as inanimate objects: mere "hatcheries," "plumbing," or "rented property"—things without emotions which could make claims on others.[21] They also refuse to acknowledge any responsibility for the consequences of the mother's emotional labor. Should she suffer psychologically from being forced to give up her child, the father is not liable to pay for therapy after her pregnancy, although he is liable for all other medical expenses following her pregnancy.[22]

The treatment and interpretation of surrogate mothers' grief raises the deepest problems of degradation. Most surrogate mothers experience grief upon giving up their children—in 10 percent of cases, seriously enough to require therapy.[23] Their grief is not compensated by the $10,000 fee they receive. Grief is not an intelligible response to a successful deal, but rather reflects the subject's judgment that she has suffered a grave and personal loss. Since not all cases of grief resolve themselves into cases of regret, it may be that some surrogate mothers do not regard their grief, in retrospect, as reflecting an authentic judgment on their part. But in the circumstances of emotional manipulation which pervade the surrogate industry, it is difficult to determine which interpretation of her grief more truly reflects the perspective of the surrogate mother. By insinuating a trivializing interpretation of her emotional responses to the prospect of losing her child, the surrogate agency may be able to manipulate her into accepting her fate without too much fuss, and may even succeed in substituting its interpretation of her emotions for her own. Since she has already signed a contract to perform emotional labor—to express or repress emotions which are dictated by the interests of the surrogate industry—this might not be a difficult task.[24] A considerate treatment of the mothers' grief, on the other hand, would take the evaluative basis of their grief seriously.

Some defenders of commercial surrogacy demand that the provision for terminating the surrogate mother's parental rights in her child be legally enforceable, so that peace of mind for the adoptive parents can be secured.[25] But the surrogate industry makes no corresponding provision for securing the peace of mind of the surrogate. She is expected to assume the risk of a transformation of her ethical and emotional perspective on herself and her child with the same impersonal detachment with which a futures trader assumes the risk of a fluctuation in the price of pork bellies. By applying the market norms of enforcing contracts to the surrogate mother's case, commercial surrogacy treats a moral transformation as if it were merely an economic change.[26]

The manipulation of the surrogate mother's emotions which is inherent in the surrogate parenting contract also leaves women open to grave forms of exploitation. A kind of exploitation occurs when one party to a transaction is oriented toward the exchange of "gift" values, while the other party operates in accordance with the norms of the market exchange of commodities. Gift values, which include love, gratitude, and appreciation of others, cannot be bought or obtained through piecemeal calculations of individual advantage. Their exchange requires a repudiation of a self-interested attitude, a willingness to give gifts to others without demanding some specific equivalent good in return each time one gives. The surrogate mother often operates according to the norms of gift relationships. The surrogate agency, on the other hand, follows market norms. Its job is to get the best deal for its clients and itself, while leaving the surrogate mother to look after her own interests as best as she can. The situation puts the surrogate agencies in a position to manipulate the surrogate mothers' emotions to gain favorable terms for themselves. For example, agencies screen prospective surrogate mothers for submissiveness, and emphasize to them the importance of the motives of generosity and love. When applicants question some of the terms of the contract, the broker sometimes intimidates them by questioning their character and morality: if they were really generous and loving they would not be so solicitous about their own interests.[27] . . .

Many surrogate mothers see pregnancy as a way to feel "adequate," "appreciated," or "special." In other words, these women feel inadequate, unappreciated, or unadmired when they are not pregnant.[28] Lacking the power to achieve some worthwhile status in their own right, they must subordinate themselves to others' definitions of their proper place (as baby factories) in order to get from them the appreciation they need to attain a sense of self-worth. But the sense of self-worth one can attain under such circumstances is precarious and ultimately self-defeating. For example, those who seek gratitude on the part of the adoptive parents and some opportunity to share the joys of seeing their children grow discover all too often that the adoptive parents want nothing to do with them.[29] For while the surrogate mother sees in the arrangement some basis for establishing the personal ties she needs to sustain her emotionally, the adoptive couple sees it as an impersonal commercial contract, one of whose main advantages to them is that all ties between them and the surrogate are ended once the terms of the contract are fulfilled.[30] To them, her presence is a threat to marital unity and a competing object for the child's affections.

These considerations should lead us to question the model of altruism which is held up to women by the surrogacy industry. It is a strange form of altruism which demands such radical self-effacement, alienation from those whom one benefits, and the subordination of one's body, health, and emotional life to the independently defined interests of others.[31]

The primary distortions which arise from treating women's labor as a commodity—the surrogate mother's alienation from loved ones, her degradation, and her exploitation—stem from a common source. This is the failure to acknowledge and treat appropriately the surrogate mother's emotional engagement with her labor. Her labor is alienated, because she must suppress her emotional ties with her own child, and may be manipulated into reinterpreting these ties in a trivializing way. She is degraded, because her independent ethical perspective is denied, or demoted to the status of a cash sum. She is exploited, because her emotional needs and vulnerabilities are not treated as characteristics which call for consideration, but as factors which may be manipulated to encourage her to make a grave self-sacrifice to the broker's and adoptive couple's advantage. These considerations provide strong grounds for sustaining the claims of women's labor to its "product," the child. The attempt to redefine parenthood so as to strip women of parental claims to the children they bear does violence to their emotional engagement with the project of bringing children into the world.

## Commercial Surrogacy, Freedom, and the Law

In the light of these ethical objections to commercial surrogacy, what position should the law take on the practice? At the very least, surrogate contracts should not be enforceable. Surrogate mothers should not be forced to relinquish their children if they have formed emotional bonds with them. Any other treatment of women's ties to the children they bear is degrading.

But I think these arguments support the stronger conclusion that commercial surrogate contracts should be illegal, and that surrogate agencies who arrange such contracts should be subject to criminal penalties. Commercial surrogacy constitutes a degrading and harmful traffic in children, violates the dignity of women, and subjects both children and women to a serious risk of exploitation. . . .

If commercial surrogate contracts were prohibited, this would be no cause for infertile couples to lose hope for raising a family. The option of adoption is still available, and every attempt should be made to open up opportunities for adoption to couples who do not

meet standard requirements—for example, because of age. While there is a shortage of healthy white infants available for adoption, there is no shortage of children of other races, mixed-race children, and older and handicapped children who desperately need to be adopted. Leaders of the surrogate industry have proclaimed that commercial surrogacy may replace adoption as the method of choice for infertile couples who wish to raise families. But we should be wary of the racist and eugenic motivations which make some people rally to the surrogate industry at the expense of children who already exist and need homes.

The case of commercial surrogacy raises deep questions about the proper scope of the market in modern industrial societies. I have argued that there are principled grounds for rejecting the substitution of market norms for parental norms to govern the ways women bring children into the world. Such substitutions express ways of valuing mothers and children which reflect an inferior conception of human flourishing. When market norms are applied to the ways we allocate and understand parental rights and responsibilities, children are reduced from subjects of love to objects of use. When market norms are applied to the ways we treat and understand women's reproductive labor, women are reduced from subjects of respect and consideration to objects of use. If we are to retain the capacity to value children and women in ways consistent with a rich conception of human flourishing, we must resist the encroachment of the market upon the sphere of reproductive labor. Women's labor is *not* a commodity.

### Notes

The author thanks David Anderson, Steven Darwall, Ezekiel Emanuel, Daniel Hausman, Don Herzog, Robert Nozick, Richard Pildes, John Rawls, Michael Sandel, Thomas Scanlon, and Howard Wial for helpful comments and criticisms.

1.  See, for example, Gena Corea, *The Mother Machine* (New York: Harper and Row, 1985), pp. 216, 219; Angela Holder, "Surrogate Motherhood: Babies for Fun and Profit," *Case and Comment* 90 (1985): 3–11; and Margaret Jane Radin, "Market Inalienability," *Harvard Law Review* 100 (June 1987): 1849–1937.

2.  State laws against selling babies prevent the intended father's wife (if he has one) from being a party to the contract.

3.  See Katie Marie Brophy, "A Surrogate Mother Contract to Bear a Child," *Journal of Family Law* 20 (1981–82): 263–91, and Noel Keane, "The Surrogate Parenting Contract," *Adelphia Law Journal* 2 (1983): 45–53, for examples and explanations of surrogate parenting contracts.

4.  Mary Warnock, *A Question of Life* (Oxford: Blackwell, 1985), p. 45. This book reprints the Warnock Report on Human Fertilization and Embryology, which was commissioned by the British

government for the purpose of recommending legislation concerning surrogacy and other issues. Although the Warnock Report mentions the promotion of altruism as one defense of surrogacy, it strongly condemns the practice overall.

5. John Robertson, "Surrogate Mothers: Not So Novel After All," *Hastings Center Report*. October 1983, pp. 28–34; John Harris, *The Value of Life* (Boston: Routledge and Kegan Paul, 1985).

6. See "No Other Hope for Having a Child," *Time*, 19 January 1987, pp. 50–51. Radin argues that women's traits are also commodified in this practice. See "Market Inalienability," pp. 1932–35.

7. Here I discuss the surrogate industry as it actually exists today. I will consider possible modifications of commercial surrogacy in the final section below.

8. Robert Nozick has objected that my claims about parental love appear to be culture-bound. Do not parents in the Third World, who rely on children to provide for the family subsistence, regard their children as economic goods? In promoting the livelihood of their families, however, such children need not be treated in accordance with market norms—that is, as commodities. In particular, such children usually remain a part of their families and hence can still be loved by their parents. But insofar as children are treated according to the norms of modern capitalist markets, this treatment is deplorable wherever it takes place.

9. See Elizabeth Landes and Richard Posner, "The Economics of the Baby Shortage," *Journal of Legal Studies* 7 (1978): 323–48, and Richard Posner, "The Regulation of the Market in Adoptions," *Boston University Law Review* 67 (1987): 59–72

10. Of course, where children are concerned it is irrelevant whether these fears are reasonable. One of the greatest fears of children is separation from their parents. Adopted children are already known to suffer from separation anxiety more acutely than children who remain with their natural mothers, for they feel that the original mother did not love them. In adoption, the fact that the child would be even worse off if the mother did not give it up justifies her severing of ties and can help to rationalize this event to the child. But in the case of commercial surrogacy, the severing of ties is done not for the child's sake, but for the parents' sakes. In the adoption case there are explanations for the mother's action which may quell the child's doubts about being loved which are unavailable in the case of surrogacy.

11. Kay Longcope, "Surrogacy: Two Professionals on Each Side of Issue Give Their Argument for Prohibition and Regulation," *Boston Globe*, 23 March 1987, pp. 18–19; and Iver Peterson, "Baby M Case: Surrogate Mothers Vent Feelings, *New York Times*, 2 March 1987, pp. B1, B4.

12. Herbert Krimmel, "The Case Against Surrogate Parenting," *Hastings Center Report*, October 1983, pp. 35–37.

13. Judge Sorkow made this argument in ruling on the famous case of Baby M. See *In Re Baby M*, 217 N.J. Super 313. Reprinted in *Family Law Reporter* 13 (1987): 2001–30. Chief Justice Wilentz of the New Jersey Supreme Court overruled Sorkow's judgment. See *In the Matter of Baby M*, 109 N.J. 396, 537 A. 2d 1227 (1988).

14. Sallyann Payton has observed that the law does not permit the sale of parental rights, only their relinquishment or forced termination by the state, and these acts are subject to court review for the sake of the child's best interests. But this legal technicality does not change the moral implications of the analogy with baby-selling. The mother is still paid to do what she can to relinquish her parental rights and to transfer custody of the child to the father. Whether or not the courts occasionally prevent this from happening, the actions of the parties express a commercial orientation to children which is degrading and harmful to them. The New Jersey Supreme Court ruled that surrogacy contracts are void precisely because they assign custody without regard to the child's best interests. See *In the Matter of Baby M*, p. 1246.

15. Robertson, "Surrogate Mothers: Not So Novel After All, p. 32; Harris, *The Value of Life*, pp. 144–45.

16. See Philip Parker, "Surrogate Motherhood: The Interaction of Litigation, Legislation and Psychiatry," *International Journal of Law and Psychiatry* 5 (1982): 341–54.

17. The consent–intent rule would not, however, change the fact that commercial surrogacy replaces parental norms with market norms. For the rule itself embodies the market norm which acknowledges only voluntary, contractual relations among people as having moral force. Whereas familial love invites children into a network of unwilled relationships broader than those they have with their parents, the willed contract creates an exclusive relationship between the parents and the child only.

18. I am indebted to Dr. Ezekiel Emanuel for this point.

19. One engages in emotional labor when one is paid to express or repress certain emotions. On the concept of emotional labor and its consequences for workers, see Arlie Hochschild, *The Managed Heart* (Berkeley and Los Angeles: University of California Press, 1983).

20. Noel Keane and Dennis Breo, *The Surrogate Mother* (New York: Everest House, 1981), p. 291; Brophy, "A Surrogate Mother Contract," p. 267. The surrogate's husband is also required to agree to this clause of the contract.

21. Corea, *The Mother Machine*, p. 222.

22. Keane and Breo, *The Surrogate Mother*, p. 292.

23. Kay Longcope, "Standing Up for Mary Beth," *Boston Globe*, 5 March 1987, p. 83; Daniel Goleman, "Motivations of Surrogate Mothers," *New York Times*, 20 January 1987, p. C1; Robertson, "Surrogate Mothers: Not So Novel After All," pp. 30, 34 n. 8. Neither the surrogate mothers themselves nor psychiatrists have been able to predict which women will experience such grief.

24. See Hochschild, *The Managed Heart*, for an important empirical study of the dynamics of commercialized emotional labor.

25. Keane and Breo, *The Surrogate Mother*, pp. 236–37.

26. For one account of how a surrogate mother who came to regret her decision viewed her own moral transformation, see Elizabeth Kane: *Birth Mother: The Story of America's First Legal Surrogate Mother* (San Diego: Harcourt Brace Jovanovich, 1988). I argue below that the implications of commodifying women's labor are not significantly changed even if the contract is unenforceable.

27. Susan Ince, "Inside the Surrogate Industry," in *Test-Tube Women*, ed. Rita Ardith, Ranate Duelli Klein, and Shelley Minden (Boston: Pandora Press, 1984), p. 110.

28. The surrogate broker Noel Keane is remarkably open about reporting the desperate emotional insecurities which shape the lives of so many surrogate mothers, while displaying little sensitivity to the implications of his taking advantage of these motivations to make his business a financial success. See especially Keane and Breo, *The Surrogate Mother*, pp. 247ff.

29. See, for example, the story of the surrogate mother Nancy Barrass in Arlene Fleming, "Our Fascination with Baby M," *New York Times Magazine*, 29 March 1987, p. 38.

30. For evidence of these disparate perspectives, see Peterson, "Baby M Case: Surrogate Mothers Vent Feelings," p. B4.

31. The surrogate mother is required to obey all doctor's orders made in the interests of the child's health. (See Brophy, "A Surrogate Mother Contract"; Keane, "The Surrogate Parenting Contract"; and Ince, "Inside the Surrogate Industry.") These orders could include forcing her to give up her job, travel plans, and recreational activities. The doctor could confine her to bed, and order her to submit to surgery and take drugs. One can hardly exercise an autonomous choice over one's health if one could be held in breach of contract and liable for $35,000 damages for making a decision contrary to the wishes of one's doctor.

# Section 3: Human Cloning

## The Wisdom of Repugnance

Leon R. Kass

Leon Kass argues that the repulsion many people feel about the possibility of human cloning springs from a recognition that it violates our nature as embodied, engendered, and engendering beings and the social relations we have because of that nature. First, cloning would distort the cloned person's sense of individuality and social identity. Second, like IVF and prenatal genetic testing, cloning would transform procreation into manufacture and children into commodities. Third, cloning would encourage parents to regard children as property.

In contrast to those who see cloning as simply another technique, like AI and IVF, for helping individuals exercise their "right" to reproduce, Kass regards cloning as a significant slide down the slippery slope toward the "sperm to term" production of genetically designed children. In view of all these considerations, Kass urges an international legal ban on human cloning.

. . . "Offensive. " "Grotesque." "Revolting." "Repugnant." "Repulsive." These are the words most commonly heard regarding the prospect of human cloning. Such reactions come both from the man or woman in the street and from the intellectuals, from believers and atheists, from humanists and scientists. Even Dolly's creator has said he "would find it offensive" to clone a human being.

People are repelled by many aspects of human cloning. They recoil from the prospect of mass production of human beings, with large clones of look-alikes, compromised in their individuality, the idea of father–son or mother–daughter twins; the bizarre prospects of a woman giving birth to and rearing a genetic copy of herself, her spouse or even her deceased father or mother; the grotesqueness of conceiving a child as an exact replacement for another who has died; the utilitarian creation of embryonic genetic duplicates of oneself, to be frozen away or created when necessary, in case of need for homologous tissues or organs for transplantation; the narcissism of those who would clone themselves and the arrogance of others who think they know who deserves to be cloned or which genotype any child-to-be should be thrilled to receive; the Frankensteinian hubris to create human life and increasingly to control its destiny; man

From *The New Republic*, 2 June 1997, pp. 17–26. Reprinted by permission of the author.

playing God. Almost no one finds any of the suggested reasons for human cloning compelling; almost everyone anticipates its possible misuses and abuses. Moreover, many people feel oppressed by the sense that there is probably nothing we can do to prevent it from happening. This makes the prospect all the more revolting.

Revulsion is not an argument; and some of yesterday's repugnances are today calmly accepted— though, one must add, not always for the better. In crucial cases, however, repugnance is the emotional expression of deep wisdom, beyond reason's power fully to articulate it. Can anyone really give an argument fully adequate to the horror which is father–daughter incest (even with consent), or having sex with animals, or mutilating a corpse, or eating human flesh, or even just (just!) raping or murdering another human being?

Would anybody's failure to give full rational justification for his or her revulsion at these practices make that revulsion ethically suspect? Not at all. On the contrary, we are suspicious of those who think that they can rationalize away our horror, say, by trying to explain the enormity of incest with arguments only about the genetic risks of inbreeding.

The repugnance at human cloning belongs in this category. We are repelled by the prospect of cloning human beings not because of the strangeness or novelty of the undertaking, but because we intuit and feel, immediately and without argument, the violation of things that we rightfully hold dear. Repugnance, here as elsewhere, revolts against the excesses of human willfulness, warning us not to transgress what is unspeakably profound. Indeed, in this age in which everything is held to be permissible so long as it is freely done, in which our given human nature no longer commands respect, in which our bodies are regarded as mere instruments of our autonomous rational wills, repugnance may be the only voice left that speaks up to defend the central core of our humanity. Shallow are the souls that have forgotten how to shudder.

The goods protected by repugnance are generally overlooked by our customary ways of approaching all new biomedical technologies. The way we evaluate cloning ethically will in fact be shaped by how we characterize it descriptively, by the context into which we place it, and by the perspective from which we view it. The first task for ethics is proper description. And here is where our failure begins.

Typically, cloning is discussed in one or more of three familiar contexts, which one might call the technological, the liberal and the meliorist. Under the first, cloning will be seen as an extension of existing techniques for assisting reproduction and determining the genetic makeup of children. Like them, cloning is to be regarded as a neutral technique, with no inherent meaning or goodness, but subject to multiple uses, some good, some bad. The morality of cloning thus depends absolutely on the goodness or badness of the motives and intentions of the cloners: as one bioethicist defender of cloning puts it, "the ethics must be judged [only] by the way the parents nurture and rear their resulting child and whether they bestow the same love and affection on a child brought into existence by a technique of assisted reproduction as they would on a child born in the usual way."

The liberal (or libertarian or liberationist) perspective sets cloning in the context of rights, freedoms and personal empowerment. Cloning is just a new option for exercising an individual's right to reproduce or to have the kind of child that he or she wants. Alternatively, cloning enhances our liberation (especially women's liberation) from the confines of nature, the vagaries of chance, or the necessity for sexual mating. Indeed, it liberates women from the need for men altogether, for the process requires only eggs, nuclei and (for the time being) uteri—plus, of course, a healthy dose of our (allegedly "masculine") manipulative science that likes to do all these things to mother nature and nature's mothers. For those who hold this outlook, the only moral restraints on cloning are adequately informed consent and the avoidance of bodily harm. If no one is cloned without her consent, and if the clonant is not physically damaged, then the liberal conditions for licit, hence moral, conduct are met. Worries that go beyond violating the will or maiming the body are dismissed as "symbolic"—which is to say, unreal. . . .

The meliorist perspective embraces valetudinarians and also eugenicists. The latter were formerly more vocal in these discussions, but they are now generally happy to see their goals advanced under the less threatening banners of freedom and technological growth. These people see in cloning a new prospect for improving human beings—minimally, by ensuring the perpetuation of healthy individuals by avoiding the risks of genetic disease inherent in the lottery of sex, and maximally, by producing "optimum babies," preserving outstanding genetic material, and (with the help of soon-to-come techniques for precise genetic engineering) enhancing inborn human capacities on many fronts. Here the morality of cloning as a means is justified solely by the excellence of the end, that is, by the outstanding traits or individuals cloned— beauty, or brawn, or brains. . . .

The technical, liberal and meliorist approaches all ignore the deeper anthropological, social and, indeed, ontological meanings of bringing forth new life. To this more fitting and profound point of view, cloning shows itself to be a major alteration, indeed, a major violation, of our given nature as embodied, gendered and engendering beings—and of the social relations built on this natural ground. Once this perspective is recognized, the ethical judgment on cloning can no longer be reduced to a matter of motives and intentions, rights and freedoms, benefits and harms, or even means and ends. It must be regarded primarily as a matter of meaning: Is cloning a fulfillment of human begetting and belonging? Or is cloning rather, as I contend, their pollution and perversion? To pollution and perversion, the fitting response can only be horror and revulsion; and conversely, generalized horror and revulsion are prima facie evidence of foulness and violation. The burden of moral argument must fall entirely on those who want to declare the widespread repugnances of humankind to be mere timidity or superstition.

Yet repugnance need not stand naked before the bar of reason. The wisdom of our horror at human cloning can be partially articulated, even if this is finally one of those instances about which the heart has its reasons that reason cannot entirely know. . . .

## The Perversities of Cloning

Cloning creates serious issues of identity and individuality. The cloned person may experience concerns about his distinctive identity not only because he will be in genotype and appearance identical to another human being, but, in this case, because he may also be twin to the person who is his "father" or "mother"—if one can still call them that. What would be the psychic burdens of being the "child" or "parent" of your twin? The cloned individual moreover, will be saddled with a genotype that has already lived. He will not be fully a surprise to the world. People are likely always to compare his performances in life with that of his alter ego. True, his nurture and his circumstance in life will be different; genotype is not exactly destiny. Still, one must also expect parental and other efforts to shape this new life after the original—or at least to view the child with the original version always firmly in mind. Why else did they clone from the star basketball player, mathematician and beauty queen—or even dear old dad—in the first place?. . .

Troubled psychic identity (distinctiveness), based on all-too-evident genetic identity (sameness), will be made much worse by the utter confusion of social identity and kinship ties. For, as already noted, cloning radically confounds lineage and social relations, for "offspring" as for "parents." As bioethicist James Nelson has pointed out, a female child cloned from her "mother" might develop a desire for a relationship to her "father," and might understandably seek out the father of her "mother," who is after all also her biological twin sister. Would "Grandpa," who thought his paternal duties concluded, be pleased to discover that the clonant looked to him for paternal attention and support?

Social identity and social ties of relationship and responsibility are widely connected to, and supported by, biological kinship. Social taboos on incest (and adultery) everywhere serve to keep clear who is related to whom (and especially which child belongs to which parents), as well as to avoid confounding the social identity of parent-and-child (or brother-and-sister) with the social identity of lovers, spouses and co-parents. True, social identity is altered by adoption (but as a matter of the best interest of already living children: we do not deliberately produce children for adop-

tion). True, artificial insemination and in vitro fertilization with donor sperm, or whole embryo donation, are in some way forms of "prenatal adoption"—a not altogether unproblematic practice. Even here, though, there is in each case (as in all sexual reproduction) a known male source of sperm and a known single female source of egg—a genetic father and a genetic mother—should anyone care to know (as adopted children often do) who is genetically related to whom.

In the case of cloning, however, there is but one "parent." The usually sad situation of the "single-parent child" is here deliberately planned, and with a vengeance. In the case of self-cloning, the "offspring" is, in addition, one's twin; and so the dreaded result of incest—to be parent to one's sibling—is here brought about deliberately, albeit without any act of coitus. Moreover, all other relationships will be confounded. What will father, grandfather, aunt, cousin, sister mean? Who will bear what ties and what burdens? What sort of social identity will someone have with one whole side—"father's" or "mother's"—necessarily excluded? It is no answer to say that our society, with its high incidence of divorce, remarriage, adoption, extramarital childbearing and the rest, already confounds lineage and confuses kinship and responsibility for children (and everyone else), unless one also wants to argue that this is, for children, a preferable state of affairs.

Human cloning would also represent a giant step toward turning begetting into making, procreation into manufacture (literally, something "handmade"), a process already begun with in vitro fertilization and genetic testing of embryos. With cloning, not only is the process in hand, but the total genetic blueprint of the cloned individual is selected and determined by the human artisans. To be sure, subsequent development will take place according to natural processes; and the resulting children will still be recognizably human. But we here would be taking a major step into making man himself simply another one of the man-made things. Human nature becomes merely the last part of nature to succumb to the technological project, which turns all of nature into raw material at human disposal, to be homogenized by our rationalized technique according to the subjective prejudices of the day.

How does begetting differ from making? In natural procreation, human beings come together, complementarily male and female, to give existence to another being who is formed, exactly as we were, *by what we are*: living, hence perishable, hence aspiringly erotic, human beings. In clonal reproduction, by contrast, and in the more advanced forms of manufacture to which it leads, we give existence to a being not by what we are but by what we intend and design. As with any product of our making, no matter how excellent, the artificer stands above it, not as an equal but as a superior, transcending it by his will and creative prowess. Scientists who clone animals make it perfectly clear that they are engaged in instrumental making; the animals are, from the start, designed as means to serve rational human purposes. In human cloning, scientists and prospective "parents" would be adopting the same technocratic mentality to human children: human children would be their artifacts.

Such an arrangement is profoundly dehumanizing, no matter how good the product. Mass-scale cloning of the same individual makes the point vividly; but the violation of human equality, freedom and dignity are present even in a single planned clone. And procreation dehumanized into manufacture is further degraded by commodification, a virtually inescapable result of allowing babymaking to proceed under the banner of commerce. Genetic and reproductive biotechnology companies are already growth industries, but they will go into commercial orbit once the Human Genome Project nears completion. Supply will create enormous demand. Even before the capacity for human cloning arrives, established companies will have invested in the harvesting of eggs from ovaries obtained at autopsy or through ovarian surgery, practiced embryonic genetic alteration, and initiated the stockpiling of prospective donor tissues. Through the rental of surrogate-womb services, and through the buying and selling of tissues and embryos, priced according to the merit of the donor, the commodification of nascent human life will be unstoppable.

Finally, and perhaps most important, the practice of human cloning by nuclear transfer—like other anticipated forms of genetic engineering of the next generation—would enshrine and aggravate a profound and mischievous misunderstanding of the meaning of having children and of the parent–child relationship. When a couple now chooses to procreate, the partners are saying yes to the emergence of new life in its novelty, saying yes not only to having a child but also, tacitly, to having whatever child this child turns out to be. In accepting our finitude and opening ourselves to our replacement, we are tacitly confessing the limits of our control. In this ubiquitous way of nature, embracing the future by procreating means precisely that we are relinquishing our grip, in the very activity of taking up

our own share in what we hope will be the immortality of human life and the human species. This means that our children are not *our* children: they are not our property, not our possessions. Neither are they supposed to live our lives for us, or anyone else's life but their own. To be sure, we seek to guide them on their way, imparting to them not just life but nurturing, love, and a way of life; to be sure, they bear our hopes that they will live fine and flourishing lives, enabling us in small measure to transcend our own limitations. Still, their genetic distinctiveness and independence are the natural foreshadowing of the deep truth that they have their own and never-before-enacted life to live. They are sprung from a past, but they take an uncharted course into the future.

Much harm is already done by parents who try to live vicariously through their children. Children are sometimes compelled to fulfill the broken dreams of unhappy parents; John Doe Jr. or the III is under the burden of having to live up to his forebear's name. Still, if most parents have hopes for their children, cloning parents will have expectations. In cloning, such overbearing parents take at the start a decisive step which contradicts the entire meaning of the open and forward-looking nature of parent–child relations. The child is given a genotype that has already lived, with full expectation that this blueprint of a past life ought to be controlling of the life that is to come. Cloning is inherently despotic, for it seeks to make one's children (or someone else's children) after one's own image (or an image of one's choosing) and their future according to one's will. In some cases, the despotism may be mild and benevolent. In other cases, it will be mischievous and downright tyrannical. But despotism—the control of another through one's will—it inevitably will be.

## Meeting Some Objections

The defenders of cloning, of course, are not wittingly friends of despotism. Indeed, they regard themselves mainly as friends of freedom: the freedom of individuals to reproduce, the freedom of scientists and inventors to discover and devise and to foster "progress" in genetic knowledge and technique. They want large-scale cloning only for animals, but they wish to preserve cloning as a human option for exercising our "right to reproduce"—our right to have children, and children with "desirable genes." As law professor John Robertson points out, under our "right to reproduce" we already practice early forms of unnatural, artificial and extramarital reproduction, and we already practice early forms of eugenic choice. For this reason, he argues, cloning is no big deal.

We have here a perfect example of the logic of the slippery slope, and the slippery way in which it already works in this area. Only a few years ago, slippery slope arguments were used to oppose artificial insemination and in vitro fertilization using unrelated sperm donors. Principles used to justify these practices, it was said, will be used to justify more artificial and more eugenic practices, including cloning. Not so, the defenders retorted, since we can make the necessary distinctions. And now, without even a gesture at making the necessary distinctions, the continuity of practice is held by itself to be justificatory.

The principle of reproductive freedom as currently enunciated by the proponents of cloning logically embraces the ethical acceptability of sliding down the entire rest of the slope—to producing children ectogenetically from sperm to term (should it become feasible) and to producing children whose entire genetic makeup will be the product of parental eugenic planning and choice. If reproductive freedom means the right to have a child of one's own choosing, by whatever means, it knows and accepts no limits.

But, far from being legitimated by a "right to reproduce," the emergence of techniques of assisted reproduction and genetic engineering should compel us to reconsider the meaning and limits of such a putative right. In truth, a "right to reproduce" has always been a peculiar and problematic notion. Rights generally belong to individuals, but this is a right which (before cloning) no one can exercise alone. Does the right then inhere only in couples? Only in married couples? Is it a (woman's) right to carry or deliver or a right (of one or more parents) to nurture and rear? Is it a right to have your own biological child? Is it a right only to attempt reproduction, or a right also to succeed? Is it a right to acquire the baby of one's choice?

The assertion of a negative "right to reproduce" certainly makes sense when it claims protection against state interference with procreative liberty, say, through a program of compulsory sterilization. But surely it cannot be the basis of a tort claim against nature, to be made good by technology, should free efforts at natural procreation fail. Some insist that the right to reproduce embraces also the right against state interference with the free use of all technological means to obtain a child. Yet such a position cannot be sustained: for reasons having to do with the means employed, any community may rightfully prohibit sur-

rogate pregnancy, or polygamy, or the sale of babies to infertile couples, without violating anyone's basic human "right to reproduce." When the exercise of a previously innocuous freedom now involves or impinges on troublesome practices that the original freedom never was intended to reach, the general presumption of liberty needs to be reconsidered.

We do indeed already practice negative eugenic selection, through genetic screening and prenatal diagnosis. Yet our practices are governed by a norm of health. We seek to prevent the birth of children who suffer from known (serious) genetic diseases. When and if gene therapy becomes possible, such diseases could then be treated, in utero or even before implantation—I have no ethical objection in principle to such a practice (though I have some practical worries), precisely because it serves the medical goal of healing existing individuals. But therapy, to be therapy, implies not only an existing "patient." It also implies a norm of health. In this respect, even germline gene "therapy," though practiced not on a human being but on egg and sperm, is less radical than cloning, which is in no way therapeutic. But once one blurs the distinction between health promotion and genetic enhancement, between so-called negative and positive eugenics, one opens the door to all future eugenic designs. "To make sure that a child will be healthy and have good chances in life": this is Robertson's principle, and owing to its latter clause it is an utterly elastic principle, with no boundaries. Being over eight feet tall will likely produce some very good chances in life, and so will having the looks of Marilyn Monroe, and so will a genius-level intelligence. . . .

## Ban the Cloning of Humans

What, then, should we do? We should declare that human cloning is unethical in itself and dangerous in its likely consequences. In so doing, we shall have the backing of the overwhelming majority of our fellow Americans, and of the human race, and (I believe) of most practicing scientists. Next, we should do all that we can to prevent the cloning of human beings. We should do this by means of an international legal ban if possible, and by a unilateral national ban, at a minimum. Scientists may secretly undertake to violate such a law, but they will be deterred by not being able to stand up proudly to claim the credit for their technological bravado and success. Such a ban on clonal baby-making, moreover, will not harm the progress of basic genetic science and technology. On the contrary, it will reassure the public that scientists are happy to proceed without violating the deep ethical norms and intuitions of the human community. . . .

The president's call for a moratorium on human cloning has given us an important opportunity. In a truly unprecedented way, we can strike a blow for the human control of the technological project, for wis-dom, prudence and human dignity. The prospect of human cloning, so repulsive to contemplate, is the occasion for deciding whether we shall be slaves of unregulated progress, and ultimately its artifacts, or whether we shall remain free human beings who guide our technique toward the enhancement of human dignity.

## Cloning Human Beings: Ethical Considerations

National Bioethics Advisory Commission

The National Bioethics Advisory Commission (NBAC) considers six areas of ethical concern associated with the prospect of cloning humans: safety; harms to individuality; threats to the family; threats to social values like love, nurturing, loyalty, and respect; commodifying life; and eugenic "improvements." After examining arguments in each area, the NBAC concludes that the lack of safety makes human cloning unacceptable at this time. Moreover, even if cloning were safe, enough concerns remain unresolved to make it unwise to proceed. Even so, the NBAC refuses to recommend banning cloning as inherently unethical.

### [Ethical Considerations]

. . . The unique prospect, vividly raised by Dolly, is the creation of a new individual genetically identical to an existing (or previously existing) person—a "delayed" genetic twin. This prospect has been the source of the overwhelming public concern about such cloning. While the creation of embryos for research purposes alone always raises serious ethical questions, the use of somatic cell nuclear transfer to create embryos raises no new issues in this respect. The unique and distinctive ethical issues raised by the use of somatic cell nuclear transfer to create children relate to, for example, serious safety concerns, individuality, family integrity, and treating children as objects. Consequently, the Commission focused its attention on the use of such techniques for the purpose of creating an embryo which would then be implanted in a woman's uterus and brought to term. It also expanded its analysis of this particular issue to encompass activities in both the public and private sector.

*Cloning Human Beings: Report and Recommendations of the National Bioethics Advisory Commission*, Rockville, Md., June 1997, pp. 64–75, 79–85. (Notes have been renumbered and moved to the end.)

### 1. Potential for Physical Harms

. . . It is important to recognize that the technique that produced Dolly the sheep was successful in only 1 of 277 attempts. If attempted in humans, it would pose the risk of hormonal manipulation in the egg donor; multiple miscarriages in the birth mother; and possibly severe developmental abnormalities in any resulting child. Clearly the burden of proof to justify such an experimental and potentially dangerous technique falls on those who would carry out the experiment. Standard practice in biomedical science and clinical care would never allow the use of a medical drug or device on a human being on the basis of such a preliminary study and without much additional animal research. Moreover, when risks are taken with an innovative therapy, the justification lies in the prospect of treating an illness in a patient, whereas, here no patient is at risk until the innovation is employed. Thus, no conscientious physician or Institutional Review Board should approve attempts to use somatic cell nuclear transfer to create a child at this time. For these reasons, prohibitions are warranted on all attempts to produce children through nuclear transfer from a somatic cell at this time.

Even on this point, however, NBAC has noted some difference of opinion. Some argue, for example, that prospective parents are already allowed to conceive, or to carry a conception to term, when there is a significant risk—or even certainty—that the child will suffer from a serious genetic disease. Even when others think such conduct is morally wrong, the parents' right to reproductive freedom takes precedence. Since many of the risks believed to be associated with somatic cell nuclear transfer may be no greater than those associated with genetic disorders, some contend that such cloning should be subject to no more restriction than other forms of reproduction (Brock, 1997).

And, as in any new and experimental clinical procedure, harms cannot be accurately determined until trials are conducted in humans. Law professor John Robertson noted before NBAC on March 13, 1997, that:

> "The first transfer [into a uterus] of a human [embryo] clone [will occur] before we know whether it will succeed. [Some have argued therefore] that the first transfers are somehow unethical . . . experimentation on the resulting child, because one does not know what is going to happen, and one is . . . possibly leading to a child who could be disabled and have developmental difficulties. . . . [But the] child who would result would not have existed but for the procedure at issue, and [if] the intent there is actually to benefit that child by bringing it into being. . . . [this] should be classified as experimentation for [the child's] benefit and thus it would fall within recognized exceptions. . . . We have a very different set of rules for experimentation intended to benefit [the experimental subject]" (Robertson, 1997).

But the argument that somatic cell nuclear transfer cloning experiments are "beneficial" to the resulting child rest on the notion that it is a "benefit" to be brought into the world as compared to being left unconceived and unborn. This metaphysical argument, in which one is forced to compare existence with non-existence, is problematic. Not only does it require us to compare something unknowable—non-existence—with something else, it also can lead to absurd conclusions if taken to its logical extreme. For example, it would support the argument that there is no degree of pain and suffering that cannot be inflicted on a child, provided that the alternative is never to have been conceived. Even the originator of this line of analysis rejects this conclusion.[1]

In addition, it is true that the actual risks of physical harm to the child born through somatic cell nuclear transfer cannot be known with certainty unless and until research is conducted on human beings. It is likewise true that if we insisted on absolute guarantees of no risk before we permitted any new medical intervention to be attempted in humans, this would severely hamper if not halt completely the introduction of new therapeutic interventions, including new methods of responding to infertility. The assertion that we should regard attempts at human cloning as "experimentation for [the child's] benefit" is not persuasive.

## 2.  Cloning and Individuality

In addition to physical harms, many worry about psychological harms associated with such cloning. One of the forms of psychological harm most frequently mentioned is the possible loss of a sense of uniqueness.

Many argue that somatic cell nuclear transfer cloning creates serious issues of identity and individuality and forces us to reconsider how we define ourselves. In his testimony before NBAC March 13, 1997, Gilbert Meilaender commented on the importance of genetic uniqueness not only for individuals but in the eyes of their parents:

> "Our children begin with a kind of genetic independence of us, their parents. They replicate neither their father nor their mother. That is a reminder of the independence that we must eventually grant to them and for which it is our duty to prepare them. To lose even in principle this sense of the child as gift will not be good for children" (Meilaender, 1997).

The concept of creating a genetic twin, although separated in time, is one aspect of somatic cell nuclear transfer cloning that most find both troubling and fascinating. The phenomenon of identical twins has intrigued human cultures across the globe, and throughout history (Schwartz, 1996). It is easy to understand why identical twins hold such fascination. Common experience demonstrates how distinctly different twins are, both in personality and in personhood. At the same time, observers cannot help but imbue identical bodies with some expectation that identical persons occupy those bodies, since body and personality remain intertwined in human intuition. With the prospect of somatic cell nuclear transfer cloning comes a scientifically inaccurate but nonetheless instinctive fear of multitudes of identical bodies, each housing personalities that are somehow less than distinct, less unique, and less autonomous than usual.

Is there a moral or human right to a unique identity, and if so would it be violated by this manner of human cloning? For such somatic cell nuclear transfer cloning to violate a right to a unique identity, the relevant sense of identity would have to be genetic identity, that is a right to a unique unrepeated genome.

Even with the same genes, two individuals—for example homozygous twins—are distinct and not identical, so what is intended must be the various properties and characteristics that make each individual qualitatively unique and different than others. Does having the same genome as another person undermine that unique qualitative identity?

Along these lines of inquiry some question whether reproduction using somatic cell nuclear transfer would violate what philosopher Hans Jonas called a right to ignorance, or what philosopher Joel Feinberg called a right to an open future, or what Martha Nussbaum called the quality of "separateness" (Jonas, 1974; Feinberg, 1980; Nussbaum, 1990). Jonas argued that human cloning, in which there is a substantial time gap between the beginning of the lives of the earlier and later twin, is fundamentally different from the simultaneous beginning of the lives of homozygous twins that occur in nature. Although contemporaneous twins begin their lives with the same genetic inheritance, they also begin their lives or biographies at the same time, in ignorance of what the twin who shares the same genome will by his or her choices make of his or her life. To whatever extent one's genome determines one's future, each life begins ignorant of what that determination will be, and so remains as free to choose a future as are individuals who do not have a twin. In this line of reasoning, ignorance of the effect of one's genome on one's future is necessary for the spontaneous, free, and authentic construction of a life and self.

A later twin created by cloning, Jonas argues, knows, or at least believes he or she knows, too much about him or herself. For there is already in the world another person, one's earlier twin, who from the same genetic starting point has made the life choices that are still in the later twin's future. It will seem that one's life has already been lived and played out by another, that one's fate is already determined, and so the later twin will lose the spontaneity of authentically creating and becoming his or her own self. One will lose the sense of human possibility in freely creating one's own future. It is tyrannical, Jonas claims, for the earlier twin to try to determine another's fate in this way.

And even if it is a mistake to believe such crude genetic determinism according to which one's genes determine one's fate, what is important for one's experience of freedom and ability to create a life for oneself is whether one thinks one's future is open and undetermined, and so still to be largely determined by one's own choices. One might try to interpret Jonas' objec-

tion so as not to assume either genetic determinism, or a belief in it. A later twin might grant that he or she is not destined to follow in his or her earlier twin's footsteps, but that nevertheless the earlier twin's life would always haunt the later twin, standing as an undue influence on the latter's life, and shaping it in ways to which others' lives are not vulnerable.

In a different context, and without applying it to human cloning, Feinberg has argued for a child's right to an open future. This requires that others raising a child not close off the future possibilities that the child would otherwise have by constructing his or her own life. One way this right to an open future would be violated is to deny even a basic education to a child, and another way might be to create the child as a later twin so that he or she will believe its future has already been set by the choices made and the life lived by the earlier twin.

On the other hand, all of these concerns are not only quite speculative, but are directly related to certain specific cultural values. Someone created through the use of somatic cell nuclear transfer techniques may or may not believe that their future is relatively constrained. Indeed, they may believe the opposite. In addition, quite normal parenting usually involves many constraints on a child's behavior that children may resent. Moreover, Feinberg's argument does not apply, if the belief is false and it can be shown to be false.

Thus, a central difficulty in evaluating the implications for somatic cell nuclear transfer cloning of a right either to ignorance or to an open future, is whether the right is violated merely because the later twin may be likely to believe that its future is already determined, even if that belief is clearly false and supported only by the crudest genetic determinism. Moreover, what such a twin is likely to believe will depend on the facts that emerge and what scientists and ethicists claim.

### 3. Cloning and the Family

Among those concerns that are not focused on arguments about harm to the child are a set of worries about use of such cloning as a means of control. There are concerns, for example, about possibly generating large numbers of people whose life choices are limited by their own constrained self-image or by the constraining expectations of others. From this image of less-than-autonomous children comes the fear, however misplaced, of technology creating armies of cloned soldiers, each diminished in his or her physical individuality and thereby diminished in their psychological autonomy. Similarly, this expectation of diminished autonomy underlies the eugenic arguments that have led many to speculate about the possibility of cloning "desirable" or "evil" people, ranging from actors to dictators of various stripes to distinguished religious leaders. Complicating matters even further, this misplaced belief in the ability of genes to fully determine behavior and personality amplifies the image, so that in the end one imagines being able to make either armies of complacent workers, crazed soldiers, brilliant musicians, or beatific saints.

Although such fears are based . . . on gross misunderstandings of human biology and psychology, they are nonetheless fears that have been voiced. In addition, these same concerns also manifest themselves in fears that underlie the characterization of somatic cell nuclear transfer cloning as a form of "making" children rather than "begetting" children. With cloning, the total genetic blueprint of the cloned individual is selected and determined by the human artisans. This, according to Kass:

"... would be taking a major step into making man himself simply another one of the man made things. Human nature becomes merely the last part of nature to succumb to the technological project which turns all of nature into raw material at human disposal. . . . As with any product of our making, no matter how excellent, the artificer stands above it, not as an equal but as a superior, transcending it by his will and creative prowess" (Kass, 1997).

For many, this kind of relationship is inconsistent with an ideal of parenting, in which parents embrace not only the similarities between themselves and their children but also the differences, and in which they accept not only the developments they sought to bring about through care and teaching but also the serendipitous developments they never planned for or anticipated (Rothenberg, 1997).

Of course, parents already exercise great control over their offspring, through means as varied as contraception to control of the timing and spacing of births, to genetic screening and use of donor gametes to avoid genetic disorders, to organized medical and educational interventions to guide physical and intellectual development. These interventions exist along a spectrum of control over development. Somatic cell nuclear transfer cloning, some fear, offers the possibility of virtually complete control over one important aspect of a child's development, his or her genome, and it is the completeness of this control, even if only over this partial aspect of human development that is

alarming to many people and invokes images of manufacturing children according to specification. The lack of acceptance this implies for children who fail to develop according to expectations, and the dominance it introduces into the parent–child relationship, is viewed by many as fundamentally at odds with the acceptance, unconditional love, and openness characteristic of good parenting. Meilaender addressed both the mystery of reproduction and fears about it veering toward a means of production in his testimony before NBAC:

"But whatever we say of [other reproductive technologies], surely human cloning would be a new and decisive turn on the road. Far more emphatically a kind of production. Far less a surrender to the mystery of the genetic lottery which is the mystery of the child who replicates neither Father nor Mother but incarnates their union. Far more an understanding of the child as a product of human will" (Meilaender, 1997).

Questions are raised, as well, about the effect such interventions will have on a particular child. Will the child himself or herself feel less independent from the nucleus donor than a child ordinarily would from a parent? Will the knowledge of how one's genetic profile developed in another person at another time leave the child feeling that his character is as predetermined as his eye or hair color? Even if the child feels completely independent of the nucleus donor, will others regard the child as a copy or a successor to that donor? If so, will such expectations on the part of others warp the child's emerging self-understanding?

Finally, some critics of such cloning are concerned that the legal or social status of the child arising from nuclear transfer of somatic cells may be uncertain. For some, the disparity between the child's genetic and social identity threatens the stability of the family. Is the child who results from somatic cell nuclear transfer the sibling or the child of its parents? The child or the grandchild of its grandparents? From this perspective the child's psychological and social well-being may be in doubt or even endangered. Ambiguity over parental roles may undermine the child's sense of identity. It may be harder for a child to achieve independence from a parent who is also his or her twin.

At the same time, others are not persuaded by such objections. Children born through assisted reproductive technologies may also have complicated relationships to genetic, gestational, and rearing parents. Skeptics of this point of view note that there is no evidence that confusion over family roles has harmed children born through assisted reproductive technologies, although the subject has not been carefully studied.

## 4. Potential Harms to Important Social Values

Those with grave reservations about somatic cell nuclear transfer cloning ask us to imagine a world in which cloning human beings via somatic cell nuclear transfer were permitted and widely practiced. What kind of people, parents, and children would we become in such a world? Opponents fear that such cloning to create children may disrupt the interconnected web of social values, practices, and institutions that support the healthy growth of children. The use of such cloning techniques might encourage the undesirable attitude that children are to be valued according to how closely they meet parental expectations, rather than loved for their own sake. In this way of looking at families and parenting, certain values are at the heart of those relationships, values such as love, nurturing, loyalty, and steadfastness. In contrast, a world in which such cloning were widely practiced would give, the critics claim, implicit approval to vanity, narcissism, and avarice. To these critics, changes that undermine those deeply prized values should be avoided if possible. At a minimum, such undesirable changes should not be fostered by public policies.

On the other hand, others are not persuaded by these objections. First, many social observers point out that if strongly held moral values are in decline, there are likely many complex reasons for this, which would not be addressed by a ban on cloning in this fashion. Furthermore, skeptics argue that people can, and do, adapt in socially redeeming ways, to new technologies. In their view, a child born through somatic cell nuclear transfer could be loved and accepted like any other child, and not disrupt important family and kinship relations.

The strength of public reaction, however, reflects a deep concern that somehow many important social values could be harmed in a society where such cloning were widely used. In his testimony before the Commission on March 13, 1997, bioethicist Leon Kass summarized many of the widely held concerns regarding the possibility of cloning human beings via somatic cell nuclear transfer when he noted:

"Almost no one sees any compelling reason for human cloning. Almost everyone anticipates its possible misuses and abuses. Many feel oppressed by the sense that there is nothing we can do to prevent it from happening and this makes the prospect seem all the more revolting. Revulsion is surely not an argument. . . . But . . . in crucial cases repugnance is often the emotional bearer of deep wisdom beyond reason's power fully to articulate it" (Kass, 1997).

But some people, however, argue against relying on moral intuition to set public policy. While it is certainly true that repugnance may be the bearer of wisdom, it may also be the bearer of simple and thoughtless prejudice. In her testimony before NBAC on March 14, 1997, bioethicist Ruth Macklin challenged the inclination to take as axiomatic the proposition that to be born as a result of using these techniques is to be harmed or at least to be wronged:

"Intuition has never been a reliable epistemological method, especially since people notoriously disagree in their moral intuitions. . . . If objectors to cloning can identify no greater harm than a supposed affront to the dignity of the human species, that is a flimsy basis on which to erect barriers to scientific research and its applications" (Macklin, 1997).

Nevertheless, opponents assert that this new type of cloning tempts human beings to transgress moral boundaries and to grasp for powers that are properly outside human control. Ancient Greek literature and many Biblical interpretations emphasize that human beings occupy a moral position between other forms of life and the divine. In particular, humans should not consider themselves as omnipotent over nature. From this perspective, respecting limits is to respect the appropriate place of humankind in the universe and to ensure that technology is not allowed to push aside critical social and moral commitments. This view need not be tied to a single religious doctrine, a particular view of God, or even a belief in God. However, these objections are often expressed in religious terms. For example, critics talk of how the ability to create children through somatic cell nuclear transfer may tempt us to seek immortality, to usurp the role of God, or to violate divine commands.

On the other hand, some observers do not see this type of cloning as dramatically new or extreme, especially when compared to other assisted reproductive technologies. Robertson notes:

"In an important sense cloning is not the most radical thing on the horizon. Much more significant, I think, would be the ability to actually alter or manipulate the genome of offspring. Cloning takes a genome as it is . . . and might replicate it . . . [T]hat is much less ominous than having an ability to take a given genome and either add or take out a gene which could then lead to a child being born with characteristics other than it would have had with the genome it started with" (Robertson, 1997).

Finally, critics have also raised questions about an inappropriate use of scarce resources. The generation of children through somatic cell nuclear transfer would divert scarce resources, including the skills of researchers and clinicians, from more pressing social and medical needs. These considerations about allocation of resources are particularly pertinent if public funds would be involved. In the words of theologian Nancy Duff:

"When considering research into human cloning we must look at the responsible use of limited resources. . . . It is mandatory to ask whether other research projects will serve a greater number of people than research on human cloning and take the answer to that seriously" (Duff, testimony, 1997).

### 5. Treating People as Objects

Some opponents of somatic cell nuclear cloning fear that the resulting children will be treated as objects rather than as persons. This concern often underlies discussions of whether such cloning amounts to "making" rather than "begetting" children, or whether the child who is created in this manner will be viewed as less than a fully independent moral agent. In sum, will being cloned from the somatic cell of an existing person result in the child being regarded as less of a person whose humanity and dignity would not be fully respected?

One reason this discussion can be hard to capture and to articulate is that certain terms, such as "person," are used differently by different people. What is common to these various views, however, is a shared understanding that being a "person" is different from being the manipulated "object" of other people's desires and expectations. Writes legal scholar Margaret Radin,

"The person is a subject, a moral agent, autonomous and self-governing. An object is a non-person, not treated as a self-governing moral agent. . . . [By] 'objectification of persons,' we mean, roughly, what Kant would not want us to do."[3]

That is, to objectify a person is to act towards the person without regard for his or her own desires or well-being, as a thing to be valued according to externally imposed standards, and to control the person rather than to engage her or him in a mutually respectful relationship. Objectification, quite simply, is treating the child as an object—a creature less deserv-

ing of respect for his or her moral agency. Commodification is sometimes distinguished from objectification and concerns treating persons as commodities, including treating them as a thing that can be exchanged, bought or sold in the marketplace. To those who view the intentional choice by another of one's genetic makeup as a form of manipulation by others, somatic cell nuclear transfer cloning represents a form of objectification or commodification of the child.

Some may deny that objectification is any more a danger in somatic cell nuclear transfer cloning than in current practices such as genetic screening or, in the future perhaps, gene therapy. These procedures aim either to avoid having a child with a particular condition, or to compensate for a genetic abnormality. But to the extent that the technology is used to benefit the child by, for example, allowing early preventive measures with phenylketonuria, no objectification of the child takes place.

When such cloning is undertaken not for any purported benefit of the child himself or herself, but rather to satisfy the vanity of the nucleus donor, or even to serve the need of someone else, such as a dying child in need of a bone marrow donor, then some would argue that it goes yet another step toward diminishing the personhood of the child created in this fashion. The final insult, opponents argue, would come if the child created through somatic cell nuclear transfer is regarded as somehow less than fully equal to the other human beings, due to his or her diminished physical uniqueness and the diminished mystery surrounding some aspects of his or her future, physical development.

### 6. Eugenic Concerns

The desire to improve on nature is as old as humankind. It has been played out in agriculture through the breeding of special strains of domesticated animals and plants. With the development of the field of genetics over the past 100 years came the hope that the selection of advantageous inherited characteristics—called eugenics, from the Greek eugenes meaning wellborn or noble in heredity—could be as beneficial to humankind as selective breeding in agriculture.

The transfer of directed breeding practices from plants and animals to human beings is inherently problematic, however. To begin, eugenic proposals require that several dubious and offensive assumptions be made. First, that most, if not all people would mold their reproductive behavior to the eugenic plan; in a country that values reproductive freedom, this outcome would be unlikely absent compulsion. Second, that means exist for deciding which human traits and characteristics would be favored, an enterprise that rests on notions of selective human superiority that have long been linked with racist ideology.

Equally important, the whole enterprise of "improving" humankind by eugenic programs oversimplifies the role of genes in determining human traits and characteristics. Little is known about correlation between genes and the sorts of complex, behavioral characteristics that are associated with successful and rewarding human lives; moreover, what little is known indicates that most such characteristics result from complicated interactions among a number of genes and the environment. While cows can be bred to produce more milk and sheep to have softer fleece, the idea of breeding humans to be superior would belong in the realm of science fiction even if one could conceive how to establish the metric of superiority, something that turns not only on the values and prejudices of those who construct the metric but also on the sort of a world they predict these specially bred persons would face.

Nonetheless, at the beginning of this century eugenic ideas were championed by scientific and political leaders and were very popular with the American public. It was not until they were practiced in such a grotesque fashion in Nazi Germany that their danger became apparent. Despite this sordid history and the very real limitations in what genetic selection could be expected to yield, the lure of "improvement" remains very real in the minds of some people. In some ways, creating people through somatic cell nuclear transfer offers eugenicists a much more powerful tool than any before. In selective breeding programs, such as the "germinal choice" method urged by the geneticist H. J. Muller a generation ago (Kevles, 1995), the outcome depended on the usual "genetic lottery" that occurs each time a sperm fertilizes an egg, fusing their individual genetic heritages into a new individual. Cloning, by contrast, would allow the selection of a desired genetic prototype which would be replicated in each of the "offspring," at least on the level of the genetic material in the cell nucleus.

It might be enough to object to the institution of a program of human eugenic cloning—even a voluntary program—that it would rest on false scientific premises and hence be wasteful and misguided. But that argument might not be sufficient to deter those people who want to push the genetic traits of a population in a particular direction. While acknowledging that a particular set of genes can be expressed in a variety of ways and therefore that cloning (or any other form of eugenic selection) does not guarantee a particular phenotypic manifestation of the genes, they might still argue that certain genes provide a better starting point for the next generation than other genes.

The answer to any who would propose to exploit the science of cloning in this way is that the moral problems with a program of human eugenics go far beyond practical objections of infeasibility. Some objections are those that have already been discussed in connection with the possible desire of individuals to use somatic cell nuclear transfer that the creation of a child under such circumstances could result in the child being objectified, could seriously undermine the value that ought to attach to each individual as an end in themselves, and could foster inappropriate efforts to control the course of the child's life according to expectations based on the life of the person who was cloned.

In addition to such objections are those that arise specifically because what is at issue in eugenics is more than just an individual act, it is a collective program. Individual acts may be undertaken for singular and often unknown or even unknowable reasons, whereas a eugenics program would propagate dogma about the sorts of people who are desirable and those who are dispensable. That is a path that humanity has tread before, to its everlasting shame. And it is a path to whose return the science of cloning should never be allowed to give even the slightest support. . . .

## Consideration of Exceptional Cases

Even as a matter of ethics, rather than of law, it is quite possible to argue against a wholesale condemnation of somatic cell nuclear transfer cloning of human beings. Some circumstances have been identified in which the choice to create a child in this manner would be understandable, or even, as some have argued, desirable. Consider the following examples:

■ A couple wishes to have children, but both adults are carriers of a lethal recessive gene. Rather than risk the one in four chance of conceiving a child who will suffer a short and painful existence, the couple considers the alternatives: to forgo rearing children; to adopt; to use prenatal diagnosis and selective abortion; to use donor gametes free of the recessive trait; or to use the cells of one of the adults and attempt to clone a child. To avoid donor gametes and selective abortion, while maintaining a genetic tie to their child, they opt for cloning.

■ A family is in a terrible accident. The father is killed, and the only child, an infant, is dying. The mother decides to use some cells from the dying infant in an attempt to use somatic cell nuclear transfer to create a new child. It is the only way she can raise a child who is the biological offspring of her late husband.

■ The parents of a terminally ill child are told that only a bone marrow transplant can save the child's life. With no other donor available, the parents attempt to clone a human being from the cells of the dying child. If successful, the new child will be a perfect match for bone marrow transplant, and can be used as a donor without significant risk or discomfort. The net result: two healthy children, loved by their parents, who happen to be identical twins of different ages.

In each of these examples, the impulse to attempt such cloning can be understood. In the first example, the possible complications caused by having a child who is genetically identical to one of the parents is weighed against the value of avoiding selective abortion or of keeping the marital relationship free of the ghost of an anonymous sperm or egg donor. In the second, the psychological complexities of bearing a "replacement" child are weighed against the grief of losing not only a husband but also the possibility of a child who will grow up as a physical reminder of that love. While some may argue that neither case is compelling, because infertility and grief are part of human existence, the intensely personal nature of that infertility or grief argues for an equally personal decision about how to respond. The third case makes what is probably the strongest possible case for cloning a human being, as it demonstrates how this technology could be used for lifesaving purposes. Indeed, the tragedy of allowing the sick child to die because of a moral or political objection to such cloning overall merely points up the difficulty of making policy in this area.

Some would argue that what is more important in these scenarios is how the resulting child will be viewed. Macklin argues that:

"The ethics of these situations must be judged by the way in which the parents nurture and rear the resulting child and whether they bestow the same love and affection on a child brought into existence by a technique of assisted reproduction as they would on a child born in the usual way" (Macklin, 1997).

It may be that a policy which prohibited the creation of children though somatic cell nuclear transfer cloning would ban a handful of scenarios for which some people feel sympathy. Nonetheless, it may be necessary to forbid the practice overall in order to protect other crucial societal values. . . .

## Conclusions

In the summary, the Commission reached several conclusions in considering the appropriateness of public policies regarding the creation of children through somatic cell nuclear transfer. First and foremost, creating children in this manner is unethical at this time because available scientific evidence indicates that such techniques are not safe at this time. Even if concerns about safety are resolved, however, significant concerns remain about the negative impact of the use of such a technology on both individuals and society. Public opinion on this issue may remain divided. Some people believe that cloning through somatic cell nuclear transfer will always be unethical because it undermines important social values and will always risk causing psychological or other harms to the resulting child. In addition, although the Commission acknowledged that there are cases for which the use of such cloning might be considered desirable by some people, overall these cases were insufficiently compelling to justify proceeding with the use of such techniques. Finally, the Commission was not persuaded by objections to a prohibition against such cloning which were based, in part, on the expectation that its use is unlikely to be widespread and, in part, on the belief that many of the assumed harms are purely speculative.

Finally, many scenarios of creating children through somatic cell nuclear transfer are based on the serious misconception that selecting a child's genetic makeup is equivalent to selecting the child's traits or accomplishments. A benefit of more widespread discussion of such cloning would be a clearer recognition that a person's traits and achievements depend heavily on education, training, and the social environment, as well as on genes. Should this type of cloning proceed, however, any children born as a result of this technique should be treated as having the same rights and moral status as any other human being.

Clearly, there is a need for further public deliberation on the serious moral concerns raised by the prospect of cloning human beings. As the Commission proceeded in its review, the members learned from listening to the public and to each other. Many important issues remain unresolved, such as the nature and scope of our moral interest in the freedom to make procreative choices, and whether that freedom should encompass creating a child through somatic cell nuclear transfer cloning. The Commission believes that it is essential to try to understand the diverse reactions to such cloning and the ethical arguments for and against various policies regarding its use. This report is only the beginning of a public process to assess the impact of this new technology.

## References

Annas, G. J., "Regulatory models for human embryo cloning: The free market, professional guidelines, and government restrictions," *Kennedy Institute of Ethics Journal* (4)3:235–249, 1994.

Brock, D., "Cloning Human Beings: An Assessment of the Ethical Issues Pro and Con," paper prepared for NBAC, 1997.

Brock, D. W., "The non-identity problem and genetic harm," *Bioethics* 9:269-275, 1995.

Cahill, L., Testimony presented to the National Bioethics Advisory Commission, March 13, 1997.

Chadwick, R. F., "Cloning," *Philosophy* 57:201–209, 1982.

Coleman, "Playing God or playing scientist: A constitutional analysis of laws banning embryological procedures," *27 Pacific Law Journal* 1331, 1996.

Duff, N., "Theological Reflections on Human Cloning," Testimony presented to the National Bioethics Advisory Commission, March 13, 1997.

Etzioni, A., *The Moral Dimension* (New York: The Free Press, 1990).

Feinberg, J., "The child's right to an open future, " in *Whose Child? Children's Rights, Parental Authority, and State Power*, W. Aiken and H. LaFollette (eds.) (Totowa, NJ: Rowman and Littlefield, 1980).

Glendon, M. A., *Rights Talk* (New York: The Free Press, 1991).

Gutmann, A., and D. Thompson, *Democracy and Disagreement* (Cambridge, MA: Belknap Press, 1996).

Jonas, H., *Philosophical Essays: From Ancient Creed to Technological Man* (Englewood Cliffs, NJ: Prentice-Hall, 1974).

Kass, L., "Why We Should Ban the Cloning of Human Beings," Testimony presented to the National Bioethics Advisory Commission, March 13, 1997.

Kevles. D. J., *In the Name of Eugenics* (Cambridge, MA: Harvard University Press, 1995).

Macklin, R., "Why We Should Regulate—But Not Ban—the Cloning of Human Beings," Testimony presented to the National Bioethics Advisory Commission, March 14, 1997.

Macklin, R., "Splitting embryos on the slippery slope: Ethics and public policy," *Kennedy Institute of Ethics Journal* 4:209–226, 1994.

Meilaender, G., "Remarks on Human Cloning to the National Bioethics Advisory Commission," Testimony presented to the National Bioethics Advisory Commission, March 13, 1997.

Mill, J. S., *On Liberty* (Indianapolis, IN: Bobbs-Merrill Publishing, 1859).

National Institutes of Health, *Report of the Human Embryo Research Panel* (Bethesda, MD: National Institutes of Health, 1994).

Nussbaum, M. C. "Aristotelian social democracy," in *Liberalism and the Good* 203, R. Bruce Douglass et al. (eds.), pp. 217–226, 1990.

Parfit, D., *Reasons and Persons* (Oxford: Oxford University Press, 1984).

Posner, R., *Sex and Reason* (Cambridge, MA: Harvard University Press, 1992).

Radin, M., "Reflections on Objectification," *65 Southern California Law Review* 341 (November 1991).

Radin, M., "The Colin Ruagh Thomas O'Fallon Memorial Lecture on Personhood," *74 Oregon Law Review* 423 (Summer 1995).

Rhodes, R., "Clones, harms, and rights," *Cambridge Quarterly of Healthcare Ethics* 4:285-290, 1995.

Robertson, J. A., "A Ban on Cloning and Cloning Research Is Unjustified," Testimony Presented to the National Bioethics Advisory Commission, March 14, 1997.

Robertson J. A., "The question of human cloning," *Hasting Center Report* 24:6–14, 1994.

Robertson, "The scientist's right to research: A constitutional analysis, *51 Southern California Law Review 1203,* 1997.

Rothenberg, K., Testimony before the Senate Committee on Labor and Human Resources, March 12, 1997.

Schwartz, H., *The Culture of Copy* (New York: Zone Books, 1996).

## Notes

1.  There is one argument that has been used by several commentators to undermine the apparent significance of potential harms to a child created through somatic cell nuclear transfer (Chadwick, 1982; Robertson, 1994, 1997; Macklin, 1994). The point derives from a general problem, called the non-identity problem, posed by the philosopher Derek Parfit and not originally directed to human cloning (Parfit, 1984). This view argues that all the problems of having been born via such cloning are not net harms to the resulting child because they are not worse than no life at all. Parfit does not accept the above argument as sound. Instead, he believes that if one could have a different child without these burdens (for example, by using a different method of reproduction) there is as strong a moral reason to do so (Brock, 1995).

2.  Moral philosophers think about personhood when they construct and deploy their views of human choice and moral agency. For Kantians, personhood is about free will and reason. From the point of view of Kantian moral personality, all of us are identical as persons. Philosophers of mind think about personhood when they try to figure out what constitutes personal identity. For many of these philosophers, personal identity means having a continuous life story that incorporates a past and a future for oneself. From the point of view of personal identity, all of us are different, unique, as persons. Psychoanalysts think about personhood when they relate the constants of human life and development to broad personality structures. From the psychoanalytic point of view, each of us manifests the same dynamic personality structures, yet no two of us do so in exactly the same way; we are all the same and also all different. Welfare rights activists and human rights activists may think about personhood: what is the minimum of necessary resources for a fully human life? Some medical ethicists think about personhood while trying to decide at what point does life cease to be a human life worth living? Political theorists at times think about personhood in the context of trying to understand what are the basics of individuality that the state should recognize or underwrite? Parents think about personhood: what part do I play in making possible the fullest kind of humanness for my children?" (Radin, 1995).

3.  "Kantian ethical thought," writes Radin, "distinguishes morally between persons and objects. Rational beings possessing free will (persons) are autonomous; the moral law requires that persons be treated as ends, not means. Objects in the natural world that are not rational beings possessing free will are not

persons, and may appropriately be used as means by persons. Kant's view requires that persons, moral agents, not be treated as objects manipulated at the will of persons. Kant presented his basic principles of ethics in *Immanuel Kant, Groundwork of the*

*Metaphysics of Morals* (1785), translated by H. J. Paton in *The Moral Law* (1948)." [Margaret Radin, "Reflections on Objectification." *65 Southern California Law Review* 341 (November 1991), at footnote 4.]

---

## Decision Scenario 1

"You've got to help us," Clarence Woody said. "Keith is . . . . was . . . . our only child, and he meant the world to us. When the police came and told us he was dead, all Sara and I could think of was how we could get him back."

"But you can't get him back," Dr. Alma Lieu said. "Even if we prepared one of his cells and implanted it in your wife's uterus, the baby wouldn't be Keith."

"But he would be his genetic twin," Clarence said. "He would be as close as we can get to replacing our son." His eyes filled with tears. "Won't you help us?"

1. On what grounds does Kass object to cloning a human?

2. Assuming the safety of the cloned person is not in question, would the National Bioethics Advisory Commission endorse the moral legitimacy of cloning in such a case as this?

3. Does the cloning of a human necessarily lead to the commodification of human life, as Kass suggests?

4. How persuasive in a case like this is Kass's objection that cloning is "repugnant" to us because it violates our nature as biological and social organisms?

---

## Decision Scenario 2

"You realize that the drugs we'll be using in preparing you for implanting the embryos will involve a slight but significant risk to any child you might have?" Dr. Aaron asked.

"I certainly didn't," Stephanie Dalata said. "You mean I might have a child with a birth defect?"

"You might," Dr. Aaron said. "Or one who is premature or has a low birth weight. Or if we implant four embryos, all four of them might develop, and all the babies would be at risk."

"I don't think you should go through with the treatments," Alice Stimmons said. "If assisted reproduction is going to produce a child with a serious birth defect, it's wrong."

"I'm going to go ahead anyway," Stephanie Dalata said. "I think it's better for a child to have even serious defects than not exist at all."

1. Dalata apparently endorses the "Interest in Existing" argument. State the argument clearly and concisely.

2. What flaws does Cohen find in this argument?

3. Cohen does not mention that even births that don't involve assisted reproduction are associated with risks of serious and perhaps devastating harm to the child. Do her objections to the "Interest in Existing" argument also apply to ordinary sexual (nonassisted-reproduction) pregnancies?

4. Dr. Aaron warns Ms. Dalata that if he implants four embryos, all four might develop. State and discuss the six issues about infertility treatments and multiple births Klotzko raises.

## Decision Scenario 3

"I'm sorry we can't help you," Patricia Spring said. "But what you want is simply against our policy."

Charles Blendon and Carla Neuman didn't try to hide their disappointment. The San Diego Reproductive Clinic had been their last hope. They badly wanted to have a child, but Carla's fallopian tubes had been surgically removed as part of a successful effort to treat precancerous growths.

"In fact," Patricia Spring continued, "you don't meet at least two of our criteria."

"We can afford to pay," Charles said.

"That's not it. First of all, Carla is forty-five, and we set forty as the upper limit. And second, you two aren't married, and we require that the donor and the patient be husband and wife."

"Who makes those rules?" Carla asked. "If we want to have a child, that's our business and nobody else's."

"The clinic makes the rules, " Patricia Spring said. "You see, there is an increasing number of birth defects in older women. There are sound medical reasons for our criteria."

"But what if we're willing to take the risk?" Charles asked.

"You can't take a risk that's likely to affect a child."

"But I'm willing to have tests," Carla said. "And neither of us is against abortion. If there's something wrong with the fetus, then I'll have an abortion."

"And what sort of medical basis is there for the marriage requirement?" Charles asked. "It seems to me that the clinic is just imposing its own moral standards on Carla and me."

"Look," Patricia Spring said, "I know you're both upset and disappointed. But the clinic operates in a community, and our criteria reflect both good medical judgment and the standards of the community."

1. Is the clinic justified in setting an age limit on the women it will accept as patients? If so, why?

2. How might a rule utilitarian justify the clinic's requirement that a couple be married in order for the woman to be accepted as a patient?

3. If the clinic receives public funds, would that provide any reason to believe its services should be open to everyone?

4. On what grounds might the Vatican "Instruction" and Anderson object to the very existence of such a clinic? Is such a clinic consistent with Steinbock's views?

## Decision Scenario 4

In January 1985 the British High Court took custody of a five-day-old girl, the first child known to be born in Britain to a woman paid to be a surrogate mother.

An American couple, known only as "Mr. and Mrs. A," were reported to have paid about $7500 to a twenty-eight-year-old woman who allowed herself to be artificially inseminated with sperm from Mr. A. The woman, Kim Cotton, was prevented from turning the child over to Mr. and Mrs. A by a court order issued because of the uncertainty over the legal status of a surrogate mother.

The court permitted "interested parties, including the natural father" to apply for custody of the child. Mr. A applied, and Judge Sir John Latey ruled that the couple could take the baby girl out of the country because they could offer her the chance of "a very good upbringing."

1. Are there moral reasons that might have made the court hesitate before turning over the child to her biological father? For example, could it be persuasively argued that Kim Cotton was in effect selling her baby to Mr. and Mrs. A?

2. Kim Cotton agreed to be a surrogate mother for the sake of the money. Is surrogate pregnancy a practice that tends to exploit the poor? Or is it a legitimate way to earn money by providing a needed service? How might Steinbock respond to these questions?

3. Is serving as a surrogate mother essentially the same as prostitution? If it is not, then what are the relevant differences?

4. On what grounds do the Vatican "Instruction" and Anderson oppose the practice of surrogate pregnancy? How persuasive are the arguments?

---

## Decision Scenario 5

Dr. Charles Davis quickly scanned the data sheet on his desk, then looked at the woman seated across from him. Her name was Nancy Callahan. She was twenty-five years old and worked as a print conservator at an art museum.

I see you aren't married," Dr. Davis said.

"That's right," Nancy Callahan said. "That's basically the reason I'm here." When Dr. Davis looked puzzled, she added, "I still want to have a child."

Dr. Davis nodded and thought for a moment. Nancy Callahan was the first unmarried person to come to the Bayside Fertility Clinic to request AID. As the legal owner and operator of the clinic, as well as the chief of medical services, Dr. Davis was the one ultimately responsible for the clinic's policies.

"You're not engaged or planning to get married?"

"No, but I don't want to rule out the possibility that I will want to get married someday."

"Don't you know anybody you would want to have a child with in the ordinary sexual way?"

"I might be able to find someone," Nancy Callahan said. "But you see, I don't want to get involved with anybody right now. I'm ready to be a mother, but I'm not ready to get into the kind of situation that having a child in what you call 'the ordinary sexual way' would require."

"It's just somewhat unusual," Dr. Davis said.

"But it's not illegal, is it?"

"No," Dr. Davis said. "It's not illegal."

"So what's the problem? I'm healthy. I'm financially sound and mentally stable, and I'm both able and eager to accept the responsibility of being a mother."

"It's just that at the moment the policy of our clinic requires that patients be married and that both husband and wife agree to the insemination procedure."

"But there's nothing magical about a policy," Nancy Callahan said. "It can be changed for good reasons, can't it?"

"Perhaps so," said Dr. Davis.

1. Suppose that Ms. Callahan is a lesbian. Should this be a relevant consideration in deciding whether she should receive AID? Why, according to Hanscombe, should it not be?

2. What utilitarian argument can be advanced in favor of the clinic's policy?

3. Does the Vatican's natural law view support such a policy?

4. How might it be argued that respect for Ms. Callahan's autonomy makes it wrong to deny her the service she requests, while providing it to a married woman? Is Steinbock's position consistent with the clinic's policy?

## Decision Scenario 6

"I'm going to sell my sperm for the simple reason that I need the money," John Lolton said. "It's no big deal."

"I think it is," Jane Cooper said. "You seem to think it's like selling your blood, but it isn't. If somebody is transfused with your blood, that's an end to things. But if a woman is inseminated with your sperm, a child may result."

"I don't have any responsibilities for what people do with my sperm," Lolton replied. "It's just a product."

"Not so," Cooper said. "It's a product all right, but if it's used in artificial insemination, that means that you're the father of a child. And if you're the father of a child, that means you have to be willing to accept responsibility for that child."

"That is absolute nonsense," Lolton said.

1. If sperm is just a product, is Lolton correct in saying that he has no responsibilities for its use?

2. State as explicitly as possible Cooper's argument that a sperm donor is responsible for any child resulting from AI using his donated sperm.

3. We expect biological parents to take responsibility for their offspring. Can a departure from this standard be justified when the child is born as a result of donated sperm or egg?

4. According to the Vatican "Instruction," are there instances in which AI is morally licit? What is the moral status of a child conceived by AI?

5. Ova as well as sperm may be donated. Although women get paid more, on what grounds might one argue that they are exploited while men are not?

## Decision Scenario 7

"I'm curious," Lois Ramer said. "What happens to the eggs you take from me that get fertilized but not implanted?"

"We donate them to other women," Dr. Martha Herman said.

"Oh," Lois Ramer said, sounding surprised. "I don't want that to happen."

"Why is that?"

"Because they belong to my husband and me, and implanting them into other women would be like giving our children away."

"But an egg isn't a person," Dr. Herman said.

1. Is it necessary to think a fertilized egg is equivalent to a person to agree with Lois Ramer's objection? Construct an argument supporting her position.

2. What position does the Vatican "Instruction" take on the question of the status of an egg that is fertilized for the purpose of implantation, but then not used?

3. If every egg fertilized was implanted, would this make the procedure of embryo transfer morally legitimate according to the Vatican "Instruction"?

# Part III

# Resources

Chapter **7**

# Scarce Medical Resources

## Chapter Contents

# Classic Case Presentation

## Selection Committee for Dialysis

In 1966 Brattle, Texas, proper had a population of about 10,000 people. In Brattle County there were 20,000 more people who lived on isolated farms deep within the pine forests, or in crossroads towns with a filling station, a feed store, one or two white frame churches, and maybe twenty or twenty-five houses. Brattle was the market town and county seat, the place all the farmers, their wives, and children went to on Saturday afternoon.

It was also the medical center because it had the only hospitals in the county. One of them, Conklin Clinic, was hardly more than a group of doctors' offices. But Crane Memorial Hospital was quite a different sort of place. Occupying a relatively new three-story brick building in downtown Brattle, the hospital offered new equipment, a well-trained staff, and high-quality medical care.

This was mostly due to the efforts of Dr. J. B. Crane, Jr. The hospital was dedicated to the memory of his father, a man who had practiced medicine in Brattle County for almost fifty years. Before Crane became a memorial hospital, it was Crane Clinic. But J. B. Crane, Jr., after returning from Johns Hopkins Medical School, was determined to expand the clinic and transform it into a modern hospital. The need was there, and private investors were easy to find. Only a year after his father's death, Dr. Crane was able to offer Brattle County a genuine hospital.

It was only natural that, when the County Commissioner decided that Brattle County should have a dialysis machine, he would turn to Dr. Crane's hospital. The machine was bought with county funds, but Crane Memorial Hospital would operate it under a contract agreement. The hospital was guaranteed against loss by the county, but the hospital was also not permitted to make a profit on dialysis. Furthermore, although access to the machine was not restricted to county residents, residents were to be given priority.

Dr. Crane was not pleased with this stipulation. "I don't like to have medical decisions influenced by political considerations," he told the Commissioner. "If a guy comes in and needs dialysis, I don't want to tell him that he can't have it because somebody else who doesn't need it as much is on the machine and that person is a county resident."

"I don't know what to tell you," the Commissioner said. "It was county tax money that paid for the machine, and the County Council decided that the people who supplied the money ought to get top priority."

"What about the kind of case that I mentioned?" Dr. Crane asked.

"What about somebody who could wait for dialysis who is a resident as opposed to somebody who needs it immediately who's not a resident?"

"We'll just leave that sort of case to your discretion," the Commissioner said. "People around here have confidence in you and your doctors. If you say they can wait, then they can wait. I know you won't let them down. Of course, if somebody died while some outsider was on the machine . . . well, that would be embarrassing for all of us, I guess."

Dr. Crane was pleased to have the dialysis machine in his hospital. Not only was it the only one in Brattle County, but none of the neighboring counties had even one. Only the big hospitals in places like Dallas, Houston, and San Antonio had the machines. It put Crane Memorial up in the top rank.

Dr. Crane was totally unprepared for the problem when it came. He hadn't known there were so many people with chronic renal disease in Brattle County. But when news spread that there was a kidney machine available at Crane Memorial Hospital, twenty-three people applied for the dialysis program. Some were Dr. Crane's own patients or patients of his associates on the hospital staff. But a number of them were referred to the hospital by other physicians in Brattle and surrounding towns. Two of them were from neighboring Lopez County.

Working at a maximum, the machine could accommodate fourteen patients. But the staff decided that maximum operation would be likely to lead to dangerous equipment malfunctions and breakdowns. They settled on ten as the number of patients that should be admitted to the program.

Dr. Crane and his staff interviewed each of the program's applicants, reviewed their medical history, and got a thorough medical workup on each. They persuaded two of the patients to continue to commute to Houston, where they were already in dialysis. In four cases, renal disease had already progressed to the point that the staff decided that the patients could not benefit sufficiently from the program to make them good medical risks. In one other case, a patient suffering intestinal cancer and in generally poor health was rejected as a candidate. Two people were not in genuine need of dialysis but could be best treated by a program of medication.

That left fourteen candidates for the ten positions. Thirteen were from Brattle County and one from Lopez County.

"This is not a medical problem," Dr. Crane told the Commissioner. "And I'm not going to take the responsibility of deciding which people to condemn to death and which to give an extra chance at life."

"What do you want me to do?" the Commissioner asked. "I wouldn't object if you made the decision. I mean, you wouldn't have to tell everybody about it. You could just decide."

"That's something I won't do," Dr. Crane said. "All of this has to be open and aboveboard. It's got to be fair. If I decide, then everybody will think I am favoring my own patients or just taking the people who can pay the most money."

"I see what you mean. If I appoint a selection committee, will you serve on it?"

"I will. As long as my vote is the same as everybody else's."

"That's what I'll do, then," the Commissioner said.

The Brattle County Renal Dialysis Selection Committee was appointed and operating within the week. In addition to Dr. Crane, it was made up of three people chosen by the Commissioner. Amy Langford, a Brattle housewife in her mid-fifties whose husband owned the largest automobile and truck agency in Brattle County, was one member. The Reverend David Johnson was another member. He was the only African American on the committee and the pastor of the largest predominantly African-American church in Brattle. The last member was Jacob Sims, owner of a hardware store in the nearby town of Silsbee. He was the only member of the committee not from the town of Brattle.

"Now I'm inclined to favor this fellow," said Mr. Sims at the selection committee's first meeting. "He's twenty-four years old, he's married, and he has a child two years old."

"You're talking about James Nelson?" Mrs. Langford asked. "I had some trouble with him. I've heard that he used to drink a lot before he got sick, and from the looks of his record he's had a hard time keeping a job."

"That's hard to say," said Reverend Johnson. "He works as a pulp-wood hauler, and people who do that change jobs a lot. You just have to go where the work is."

"That's right," said Mr. Sims. "One thing, though. I can't find any indication of his church membership.

He says he's a Methodist, but I don't see where he's told us what his church is."

"I don't either," said Mrs. Langford." And he's not a member of the Masons or the Lions Club or any other sort of civic group. I wouldn't say he's made much of a contribution to this community."

"That's right," said Reverend Johnson. "But let's don't forget that he's got a wife and baby depending on him. That child is going to need a father."

"I think he is a good psychological candidate," said Dr. Crane. "That is, I think if he starts the program he'll stick to it. I've talked with his wife, and I know she'll encourage him."

"We should notice that he's a high school dropout," Mrs. Langford said. "I don't think we can ever expect him to make much of a contribution to this town or to the county."

"Do you want to vote on this case?" asked Mr. Sims, the chairman of the committee.

"Let's talk about all of them, then go back and vote," Reverend Johnson suggested.

Everyone around the table nodded in agreement. The files were arranged by date of application, and Mr. Sims picked up the next one from the stack in front of him.

"Alva Algers," he said. "He's a fifty-three-year-old lawyer with three grown children. His wife is still alive, and he's still married to her. He's Secretary of the Layman's Board of the Brattle Episcopal Church, a member of the Rotary Club and the Elks. He used to be a scoutmaster."

"From the practical point of view," said Dr. Crane, "he would be a good candidate. He's intelligent and educated and understands what's involved in dialysis."

"I think he's definitely the sort of person we want to help," said Mrs. Langford. "He's the kind of person that makes this a better town. I'm definitely in favor of him."

"I am too," said Reverend Johnson. "Even if he does go to the wrong church."

"I'm not so sure," said Mr. Sims. "I don't think fifty-three is old—I'd better not, because I'm fifty-two myself. Still, his children are grown; he's led a good life. I'm not sure I wouldn't give the edge to some younger fellow."

"How can you say that?" Mrs. Langford said. "He's got a lot of good years left. He's a person of good character who might still do a lot for other people. He's not like that Nelson, who's not going to do any good for anybody except himself."

"I guess I'm not convinced that lawyers and members of the Rotary Club do a lot more good for the community than drivers of pulp-wood trucks," Mr. Sims said.

"Perhaps we ought to go on to the next candidate," Reverend Johnson said.

"We have Mrs. Holly Holton, a forty-three-year-old housewife from Mineral Springs," Mr. Sims said.

"That's in Lopez County, isn't it?" Mrs. Langford asked. "I think we can just reject her right off. She didn't pay the taxes that bought the machine, and our county doesn't have any responsibility for her."

"That's right," said Reverend Johnson.

Mr. Sims agreed, and Dr. Crane raised no objection.

"Now," said Mr. Sims, "here's Alton Conway. I believe he's our only African-American candidate."

"I know him well," said Reverend Johnson. "He owns a dry-cleaning business, and people in the black community think very highly of him."

"I'm in favor of him," Mrs. Langford said. "He's married and seems quite settled and respectable."

"I wouldn't want us to take him just because he's black," Reverend Johnson said. "But I think he's got a lot in his favor."

"Well," said Mr. Sims, "unless Dr. Crane wants to add anything, let's go on to Nora Bainridge. She's a thirty-year-old divorced woman whose eight-year-old boy lives with his father over in Louisiana. She's a waitress at the Pep Cafe."

"She is a very vital woman," said Dr. Crane. "She's had a lot of trouble in her life, but I think she's a real fighter."

"I don't believe she's much of a churchgoer," said Reverend Johnson. "At least she doesn't give us a pastor's name."

"That's right," said Mrs. Langford. "And I just wonder what kind of morals a woman like her has. I mean, being divorced and working as a waitress and all."

"I don't believe we're trying to award sainthood here," said Mr. Sims.

"But surely moral character is relevant," said Mrs. Langford.

"I don't know anything against her moral character," said Mr. Sims. "Do you?"

"I'm only guessing," said Mrs. Langford. "But I wouldn't say that a woman of her background and apparent character is somebody we ought to give top priority to."

"I don't want to be the one to cast the first stone," said Reverend Johnson. "But I wouldn't put her at the top of our list either."

"I think we had better be careful not to discriminate against people who are poor and uneducated," said Dr. Crane.

"I agree," said Mrs. Langford. "But surely we have to take account of a person's worth."

"Can you tell us how we can measure a person's worth?" asked Mr. Sims.

"I believe I can," Mrs. Langford said. "Does the person have a steady job? Is he or she somebody we would be proud to know? Is he a churchgoer? Does he or she do things for other people? We can see what kind of education the person has had, and consider whether he is somebody we would like to have around."

"I guess that's some of it, all right," said Mr. Sims. "But I don't like to rely on things like education, money, and public service. A lot of people just haven't had a decent chance in this world. Maybe they were born poor or have had a lot of bad luck. I'm beginning to think that we ought to make our choices just by drawing lots."

"I can't approve of that," said Reverend Johnson. "That seems like a form of gambling to me. We ought to choose the good over the wicked, reward those who have led a virtuous life."

"I agree," Mrs. Langford said. "Choosing by drawing straws or something like that would mean we are just too cowardly to make decisions. We would be shirking our responsibility. Clearly, some people are more deserving than others, and we ought to have the courage to say so."

"All right," said Mr. Sims. "I guess we'd better get on with it, then. Simon Gootz is a forty-eight-year-old baker. He's got a wife and four children. Owns his own bakery—probably all of us have been there. He's Jewish."

"I'm not sure he's the sort of person who can stick to the required diet and go through the dialysis program," Dr. Crane said.

"I'll bet his wife and children would be a good incentive," said Mrs. Langford.

"There's not a Jewish church in town," said Reverend Johnson. "So of course we can't expect him to be a regular churchgoer."

"He's an immigrant," said Mr. Sims. "I don't believe he has any education to speak of, but he did start that bakery and build it up from nothing. That says a lot about his character."

"We can agree he's a good candidate," said Mrs. Langford.

"Let's just take one more before we break for dinner," Mr. Sims said. "Rebecca Scarborough. She's a sixty-three-year-old widow. Her children are all grown and living somewhere else."

"She's my patient," Dr. Crane said. "She's a tough and resourceful old woman. I believe she can follow orders and stand up to the rigors of the program, and her health in general is good."

Reverend Johnson said, "I just wonder if we shouldn't put a lady like her pretty far down on our list. She's lived a long life already, and she hasn't got anybody depending on her."

"I'm against that," Mrs. Langford said. "Everybody knows Mrs. Scarborough. Her family has been in this town for ages. She's one of our most substantial citizens. People would be scandalized if we didn't select her."

"Of course, I'm not from Brattle," said Mr. Sims. "And maybe that's an advantage here, because I don't see that she's got much in her favor except being from an old family."

"I think that's worth something," said Mrs. Langford.

"I'm not sure it's enough, though," said Reverend Johnson.

After dinner at the Crane Memorial Hospital cafeteria, the selection committee met again to discuss the seven remaining candidates. It was past ten o'clock before their final decisions were made. James Nelson, the pulp-wood truck driver, Holly Holton, the housewife from Mineral Springs, and Nora Bainridge, the waitress, were all rejected as candidates. Mrs. Scarborough was rejected also. The lawyer, Alva Algers, the dry cleaner, Alton Conway, and the baker, Simon Gootz, were selected to participate in the dialysis program. Others selected were a retired secondary school teacher, an assembly-line worker at the Rigid Box Company, a Brattle County Sheriff's Department patrolman, and a twenty-seven-year-old woman file clerk in the office of the Texas Western Insurance Company.

Dr. Crane was glad that the choices were made so the program could begin operation. But he was not pleased with the selection method and resolved to talk to his own staff and with the County Commissioner about devising some other kind of selection procedure.

Without giving any reasons, Mr. Sims sent a letter to the County Commissioner resigning from the Renal Dialysis Selection Committee. Mrs. Langford and Reverend Johnson also sent letters to the Commissioner. They thanked him for appointing them to the committee and indicated their willingness to continue to serve.

---

## BRIEFING SESSION

Few of us have as much as we desire of the world's goods. Usually, this is because we don't have enough money to pay for everything we want. We have to make choices. If we wish to spend a month in Paris, we can't afford a new car. Even when an abundance of goods is available, we can't buy everything we want. Sometimes, even when we have the money, we can't buy some item because the supply is inadequate or nonexistent. A computer manufacturer, for example, might not be turning out a new laptop fast enough to meet the demand. Or, to take a different sort of case, we can't buy fresh figs in Minnesota in January, because they simply aren't available.

In some circumstances, we can't acquire an item because its supply is limited and our society has decided that it falls into the category of things that require more than money to acquire. The item may be rationed on the basis of priorities. During wartime, for example, the military is supplied with all the food it needs, and food for civilians is rationed. Thus, even those able to pay for a pound of butter may not be permitted to buy it.

Medical goods and services include medications, care by physicians, visits to the emergency room, stays in hospitals, surgical operations, MRIs, diagnostic laboratory tests, in vitro fertilization, bone-marrow transplants, blood transfusions, genetic screening . . . and so on. Not everyone who wants these goods and services or even everyone who needs them can get them. To acquire them in our society, except in special circumstances, you must have the means of paying for them. This means having cash or adequate insurance coverage or being covered by a government entitlement program. You can't get so much as a CT scan, unless you can demonstrate your ability to pay. (Emergency services to get you medically stable must be provided by hospitals receiving federal money.)

In the case of some medical goods and services, however, the need and ability to pay are not enough. That was the way it was with dialysis machines at the beginning. That's the way it sometimes is when there is a shortage of a crucial drug. That's the way it always is when we have to decide who gets the next donor liver, heart, or kidney that becomes available.

These are decisions about distributing scarce resources. Most of this chapter will focus on the distribution of transplant organs. Aside from the distribution of health care itself, which is addressed in the next chapter, parceling out donated organs to people likely to die unless they receive them is the most pressing medical distribution problem in our society. The issues that arise in distributing transplant organs are not in principle different from those that arise in connection with any scarce commodity.

Transplant organs are of particular concern, however. Not only because they can save and extend lives and so ought not be wasted, but because we have no way of eliminating the shortage. We can't simply crank up production, the way we can with drugs and diagnostic equipment. Nor is there an equivalent of building more hospitals or training more physicians and nurses.

## Transplants, Kidneys, and Machines

The story of Robin Cook's novel *Coma* takes place in a large Boston hospital at the present time. What sets the novel apart from dozens of others with similar settings and characters is the fact that the plot hinges on the operations of a large-scale black market in transplant organs. For enormous fees, the criminals running the operation will supply corneas, kidneys, or hearts to those who can pay.

Cook claims that the inspiration for his novel came from an advertisement in a California newspaper. The anonymous ad offered to sell for $5000 any organ that a reader wanted to buy. In this respect, Cook's novel seems rooted firmly in the world we know today and not merely a leap into the speculative realms of science fiction.

Organ transplants have attracted a considerable amount of attention in the last few years. Not only are transplants dramatic, often offering last-minute salvation from an almost certain death, but the very possibility of organ transplants is bright with promise. We can easily imagine a future in which any injured or diseased organ can be replaced almost as easily as the parts on a car. The present state of biomedical technology makes this more than a distant dream, although not a current reality. Kidneys, hearts, lungs, livers, intestines, and pancreases are now transplanted as a matter of routine, and perhaps before long the list will be extended to include ovaries, testes, spleen, gall bladder, esophagus, and stomach. The basic problem with organ transplants is the phenomenon of tissue rejection by the immune system.

### Controlling Rejection

Alien proteins trigger the body's defense mechanisms. In pioneering work with kidneys, the proteins in the transplanted tissues were matched as carefully as possible with those of the recipient; then powerful immunosuppressive drugs were used in an effort to allow the host body to accommodate itself to the foreign tissue. These drugs left the body open to infections that it could normally cope with without much difficulty.

Use of the drug cyclosporine dramatically improved the success of organ transplants when it was first used almost three decades ago. Cyclosporine selectively inhibits only part of the immune system and leaves enough of it functional to fight off most of the infections that were once fatal to large numbers of transplant recipients. Also, although tissue matching is important, particularly for kidneys, matches do not have to be as close as before and may be dispensed with altogether.

Now 90 to 96 percent of transplanted kidneys function after one year; in the 1970s only about 50 percent did. Since 1970, the one-year survival rate for children with liver transplants has increased from 38 percent to more than 75 percent, and there is good reason to believe that if children survive for as long as one year, they have a genuine chance to live a normal life. About 82 percent of heart transplant recipients now live for at least one year, a major increase from the 20 percent of the 1970s. Lung and heart–lung transplants have a success rate of about 54 percent.

Some new drugs promise to be even more effective than cyclosporine in controlling acute rejection. One of the drugs, FK-506, was approved by the FDA in 1994, and some data suggest that up to 8 percent more adult liver-transplant patients and 15 percent more pediatric patients survive with the drug than with cyclosporine. Although the drug was approved only for liver transplants, some studies of patients receiving it for transplanted kidneys, bone marrow, and intestines indicate it may also be more effective than cyclosporine in those cases.

## Allocation and Scarcity

Because of the relatively high rate of success in organ transplants, the need for organs (kidneys in particular) is always greater than the supply. (The black-market operation in Cook's novel is not wholly unrealistic.) In such a situation, where scarcity and need conflict, it is frequently necessary to decide who among the candidates for a transplant will receive an available organ.

Relatively objective considerations such as the "goodness" of tissue matching, the size of the organ, and the general medical condition of the candidates may rule out some individuals. But it does happen that choices have to be made. Who should make such choices? Should they be made by a physician, following her own intuitions? Should they be made by a committee or board? If so, who should be on the committee? Should a patient have an advocate to speak for his interest—someone to "make a case" for his

receiving the transplant organ? Should the decision be made in accordance with a set of explicit criteria? If so, what criteria are appropriate? Are matters such as age, race, gender, and place of residence irrelevant? Should the character and accomplishments of the candidates be given any weight? Should people be judged by their estimated "worth to the community"? Should the fact that someone is a parent be given any weight?

What if one is a smoker, an alcoholic, or obese? Are these to be considered "medical" or "behavioral" risk factors that may legitimately be employed to eliminate someone as a candidate for a transplant? Or, on the other hand, are these to be treated as aspects of people's chosen "lifestyle" that cannot be used as a basis for denying them an organ needed to save their lives?

These are just some of the questions relevant to the general issue of deciding how to allocate medical goods in situations in which the available supply is surpassed by a present need. Transplant organs are an example of one type of goods. (See Social Context: "Acquiring and Allocating Transplant Organs" in this chapter.) Even so, most of the ethical issues raised by the distribution of organs also arises when we have to consider how we're going to parcel out such goods and services as hospital beds, physician consultations, nursing care, physical therapy, medications, diagnostic MRIs, chemotherapy, coronary angiography, or any of the hundreds of other resources used in delivering medical care. All resources, economists remind us, are limited, and so we must always face the problem of how to distribute them. It was a shortage of machines, rather than organ transplantation, that first called public attention to the issue of medical resource allocation.

## Seattle and Kidney Machines

This occurred most dramatically in the early 1960s when the Artificial Kidney Center in Seattle, Washington, initiated an effective large-scale treatment program for people with renal diseases. Normal kidneys filter waste products from the blood that have accumulated as a result of ordinary cellular metabolism—salt, urea, creatinine, potassium, uric acid, and other substances. These waste products are sent from the kidneys to the bladder, where they are then secreted as urine. Kidney failure, which can result from one of a number of diseases, allows waste products to build up in the blood. This can cause high blood pressure and even heart failure, tissue edema (swelling), and muscular seizure. If unremedied, the condition results in death.

When renal failure occurs, hemodialysis is a way of cleansing the blood of waste products by passing it through a cellophane-like tube immersed in a chemical bath. The impurities in the blood pass through the membrane and into the chemical bath by osmosis, and the purified blood is then returned to the patient's body.

At the beginning of the Seattle program, there were many more candidates for dialysis than units ("kidney machines") to accommodate them. As a response to this situation, the Kidney Center set up a committee to select patients who would receive treatment. (See the Classic Case Presentation in this chapter for an account of how such a committee might work.) In effect, the committee was offering to some a better chance for life than they would have without access to dialysis equipment.

As other centers and hospitals established renal units, they faced the same painful decisions that Seattle had. Almost always there were many more patients needing hemodialysis than there was equipment available to treat them. It was partly in response to this situation that Section 299-1 of Public Law 92-603 was passed by Congress in 1972. Those with end-stage renal disease who require hemodialysis or kidney transplants are now guaranteed treatment under Medicare.

## Dialysis Costs and Decisions

More than 300,000 patients are now receiving dialysis paid for by Medicare. Present costs are over $10 billion per year, and the patient load is increasing by about 50,000 per year. Dialysis saves lives, but the cost is high.

Although the average cost of each treatment session has dropped from $150 in 1973 to $115 in 1997, many more groups of patients now have dialysis than were treated earlier. In particular, the treatment population now includes many more elderly and diabetic people than was envisioned when the dialysis program was established.

Quite apart from the cost, which is about four times higher than originally expected, dialysis continues to present moral difficulties. Resources are still finite, so, while virtually everyone needing dialysis can be accomodated, physicians face the problem of deciding whether everyone should be referred. If a physician believes a patient isn't likely to gain benefits from dialysis sufficient to justify the expense or isn't likely to show up for appointments, should she recommend the patient for dialysis anyway? Not to do so may mean death for the patient in the near future, yet the social cost (measured in terms of the expense of equipment and its operation, hospital facilities, and the time of physicians, nurses, and technicians) may be immense—$100,000 or more per year for a single person.

Nor does dialysis solve all problems for patients with terminal kidney diseases. Although time spent on the machine varies, some patients spend five hours, three days per week, attached to the machine. Medical and psychological problems are typical even when the process works at its most efficient. Prolonged dialysis can produce neurological disorders, severe headaches, gastrointestinal bleeding, and bone diseases. Psychological and physical stress is always present, and particularly before dialysis treatments, severe depression is common. One study showed that 5 percent of dialysis patients take their own lives, and "passive suicide," resulting from dropping out of treatment programs, is the third most common cause of death among older dialysis patients. (The overall death rate for those on dialysis is about 25 percent per year. The worst outlook is for diabetics starting dialysis at age 55 or older. After one year, only 18 percent are still alive.) For these reasons, strong motivation, psychological stability, age, and a generally sound physical condition are factors considered important in deciding whether to admit a person to dialysis.

The characteristics required to make someone a "successful" dialysis patient are to some extent "middle-class virtues." A patient must not only be motivated to save his life, but he must also understand the need for the dialysis, be capable of adhering to a strict diet, show up for scheduled dialysis sessions, and so on. As a consequence, where decisions about whether to admit a patient to dialysis are based on estimates of the likelihood of the patient's doing what is required, members of the white middle class appear to have a definite edge over others. Selection criteria that are apparently objective may actually involve hidden class or racial bias.

Various ways of dealing with both the costs and the personal problems presented by dialysis are currently under discussion. In the view of some, increasing the number of kidney transplants would do the most to improve the lives of patients and to reduce the cost of the kidney program. (This would have the result of increasing even more the demand for transplant organs. See the Social Context: "Acquiring and Allocating Transplant Organs" later in this chapter for a discussion of proposals for doing this.) Others have pressed for training more patients to perform home dialysis, which is substantially cheaper than dialysis performed in clinics or hospitals. However, those who are elderly, live alone, or lack adequate facilities are not likely to be able to use and maintain the complicated equipment involved. Other things being equal, should such people be given priority for transplants?

## Microallocation Versus Macroallocation

Some critics have questioned the legitimacy of the dialysis program and pointed to it as an example of social injustice. While thousands of people have benefited from the program, why should kidney disease be treated differently from other diseases? Why should the treatment of

kidney disease alone be federally funded? Why shouldn't society also pay for the treatment of those afflicted with cancer or neurological disorders? Perhaps only the development of a new national health-care policy will render this criticism irrelevant.

The problems of transplants and dialysis involve decisions that affect individuals in a direct and immediate way. For example, a person either is or is not accepted into a dialysis program. As we will see in the next chapter, there are a number of broader social issues connected with providing and distributing medical resources. But our concern here is with decisions involving the welfare of particular people in specific situations in which demand exceeds supply. The basic question becomes, Who shall get it and who shall go without?

Any commodity or service that can be in short supply relative to the need for it raises the issue of fair and justifiable distribution. Decisions that control the supply itself—that determine, for example, what proportion of the federal budget will be spent on medical care—are generally referred to as macroallocation decisions. These are the large-scale decisions that do not involve individuals in a direct way. Similarly, deciding what proportion of the money allocated to health care should be spent on dialysis is a macroallocation decision.

By contrast, microallocation decisions directly impinge on individuals. Thus, when one donor heart is available and six people in need of a transplant make a claim on it, the decision as to who gets the heart is a microallocation decision. In Chapter 8, in discussing paying for health care, we will focus more on macroallocation, but here we will be concerned mostly with microallocation. (The distinction between macroallocation and microallocation is often less clear than the explanation here suggests. After all, decision making occurs at many levels in the distribution of resources, and the terms "macro" and "micro" are relative ones.)

The examples we have considered have been restricted to transplant organs and dialysis machines, but, as mentioned earlier, the question of fair distribution can be raised just as appropriately about other medical goods and services. This includes cardiac resuscitation teams, microsurgical teams, space in burn units or intensive-care wards, hospital beds, drugs and vaccines, medical-evacuation helicopters, operating rooms, physicians' time, and all other medical commodities that are in limited supply with respect to the demand for them. (See the Case Presentation: "Drug Lottery" later in this chapter.)

Earlier, in connection with transplants, we considered some of the more specific questions that have to be asked about distribution. The questions generally fall into two categories: Who shall decide? What criteria or standards should be employed in making the allocation decision? These are questions that must be answered whenever there is scarcity relative to needs and wants.

## Ethical Theories and the Allocation of Medical Resources

Discussions of the distribution of limited medical resources frequently compare such a situation to the plight of a group of people adrift in a lifeboat. If some are sacrificed, the others will have a much better chance of surviving. But who should be sacrificed?

One answer to this question is that no one should be. Simply by virtue of being human, each person in the lifeboat has an equal worth. Any action that involved sacrificing someone for the good of the others in the boat would not be morally defensible. This suggests that the only right course of action would be simply to do nothing.

This point of view may be regarded as compatible with Kant's ethical principles. Because each individual may be considered to have inherent value, considerations such as talent, intelligence, age, social worth, and so on are morally irrelevant. Accordingly, there seem to be no grounds for distinguishing those who are to be sacrificed from those who may be saved. In the medical context, this would mean that when

there are not enough goods and services to go around, then no one should receive them.

This is not a result dictated by Kant's principles, however. One might also argue that the fact that every person is equal to every other in dignity and worth does not require the sacrifice of all. A random procedure—such as drawing straws—might be used to determine who is to have an increased chance of survival. In such a case, each person is being treated as having equal value, and the person who loses might be regarded as exercising autonomy by sacrificing him- or herself.

The maxim underlying the sacrifice would, apparently, be one that would meet the test of the categorical imperative. Any rational person might be expected to sacrifice himself in such a situation and under the conditions in which the decision was made. In the case of medical resources, a random procedure would seem to be a morally legitimate procedure.

Both the natural law view and Ross's would seem to support a similar line of argument. Although we all have a duty, on these views, to preserve our lives, this does not mean that we do not sometimes have to risk them. Just such a risk might be involved in agreeing to abide by the outcome of a random procedure to decide who will be sacrificed and who saved.

Utilitarianism does not dictate a specific answer to the question of who, if anyone, should be saved. It does differ radically in one respect, however, from those moral views that ascribe an intrinsic value to each human life. The principle of utility suggests that we ought to take into account the consequences of sacrificing some people rather than others. Who, for example, is more likely to make a contribution to the general welfare of the society, an accountant or a nurse? This approach opens the way to considering the "social worth" of people and makes morally relevant such characteristics as education, occupation, age, record of accomplishment, and so on.

To take this approach would require working out a set of criteria to assign value to various properties of people. Those to be sacrificed would be those whose point total put them at the low end of the ranking. Here, then, a typical "calculus of utilities" would be relied on to solve the decision problem. The decision problem about the allocation of medical resources would follow exactly the same pattern.

This approach is not one required by the principle of utility, however. Some might argue that a policy formulated along those lines would have so many harmful social consequences that some other solution would be preferable. Thus, a utilitarian might argue that a better policy would be one based on some random process. In connection with medical goods and services, a "first-come, first-served" approach might be superior. (This is a possible option for rule utilitarianism. It could be argued that an act utilitarian would be forced to adopt the first approach.)

Rawls's principles of justice seem clearly to rule out distributing medical resources on the criterion of "social worth." Where special benefits are to be obtained, those benefits must be of value to all and open to all. It is compatible with Rawls's view, of course, that there should be no special medical resources. But if there are, and they must be distributed under conditions of scarcity, then some genuinely fair procedure, such as random selection, must be the procedure used.

No ethical theory that we have considered gives a straightforward answer to the question of who shall make the selection. Where a procedure is random or first-come, first-served, the decision-making process requires only establishing the right kind of social arrangements to implement the policy. Only when social worth must be judged and considered as a relevant factor in decision making does the procedure assume importance. (This is assuming that medical decisions about appropriateness—decisions that establish a class of candidates for the limited resources—have already been made.)

A utilitarian answer as to who shall make the allocation decision might be that the decision should be made by those who are in a good position to judge the likelihood of an individual's contributing to the welfare of the society as a whole. Since physicians are not uniquely qualified to make such judgments, leaving decisions to an individual physician or a committee of physicians would not be the best approach. A better one would perhaps be to rely on a committee composed of a variety of people representative of the society.

Many more questions of a moral kind connected with the allocation of scarce resources arise than have been mentioned here. We have not, for example, considered whether an individual should be allowed to make a case for receiving resources. Nor have we examined any of the problems with employing specific criteria for selection (such as requiring that a person be a resident of a certain community or state; the Classic Case Presentation in this chapter illustrates such a selection process). We have, however, touched upon enough basic issues to make it easy to see how other appropriate questions might be asked.

## SOCIAL CONTEXT: ACQUIRING AND ALLOCATING TRANSPLANT ORGANS

Organ transplantation is perhaps the most dramatic example of how contemporary medical technology can extend or improve the lives of tens of thousands of people. Developments in surgical techniques, improvements in organ preservation, and the advent of new immuno-suppressive drugs have made organ transplantation into a standard surgical therapy.

Yet behind the wonder and drama of transplant surgery lies the troubling fact that the need for transplant organs seriously and chronically outstrips the supply. Thus, against a background of a chronic shortage, physicians, surgeons, and committees must make judgments that will offer an opportunity for some, while destroying the last vestige of hope for others.

While transplanting kidneys began as early as the 1950s, the list of organs now transplanted with a significant degree of success has been expanded over the last twenty years to include corneas, bone marrow, bone and skin grafts, livers, lungs, pancreases, intestines, and hearts. All involve special problems, but we will limit discussion to solid organs—those like the heart and liver that are complete functional units.

Worldwide, more than 150,000 kidney transplants have been performed, and about 93 percent of the organs are still functioning one year later. (Some recipients are still alive after more than thirty years.) Thomas Starzl and his team successfully transplanted the first liver in 1967, and the survival rate after three years is about 75 percent. Also in 1967, Christian Barnard transplanted a human heart, and now around 75 percent of the procedures are considered successful. Lung transplants, though still a relatively new procedure, have a 55 percent three-year survival rate. New techniques of management and the development of drugs to suppress part of the immune response have done much to increase the success rate of transplants, but additional improvements will probably require improvements in the ability to control tissue rejection. (See the Briefing Session for more details.)

## Costs

A major social and moral difficulty of transplant surgery is that it is extremely expensive. For example, a kidney transplant may cost about $40,000, a heart transplant about $150,000, and a liver transplant in the range of $200,000 to $300,000. The immunosuppressive drugs needed to prevent the rejection of a transplanted organ cost from $10,000 to $20,000 a year, and they must be taken for the remainder of the patient's life. Despite the high costs of transplantation, it may offer cost savings over dialysis and medical treatments. Further, combined costs constitute less than 1 percent of all health-care costs.

Questions have been raised in recent years about what restrictions, if any, should be placed on access to transplants. Should society deny them to everyone, pay for all who need them but cannot afford them, or pay for only some who cannot pay? (For a discussion of some of these issues, see Chapter 8.) Medicare, Medicaid, and most, but not all, insurance companies pay for organ transplants and at least part of the continuing drug and treatment costs. The End-Stage Renal Disease Program covers kidney transplants for everyone, yet people needing any other sort of transplant who don't qualify for public programs and lack appropriate insurance must find some way of raising the money. Otherwise, hospitals are not likely to provide them with an organ. Every transplant candidate, in Starzl's phrase, must pass a wallet biopsy to qualify.

## Availability

The second major problem, after cost, is the availability of donor organs. The increase in the number of transplant operations performed during the last twenty-five years has produced a chronic scarcity of organs. While in 1996 over 20,000 people received transplants at the nation's 278 transplant centers, more than 3000 more died waiting for organs. On the last day of 1996 (the last year for which figures are available), 50,407 were on the transplant waiting list, and during the year there was a total of 33,000 new registrations. For every organ transplanted, two more people enter the waiting list, and those on the waiting list currently die at a rate of ten a day.

Those in need of a kidney or pancreas can rely on dialysis and insulin injections to treat their diseases, but those in need of a liver, heart, or lung have limited alternative treatments available. Artificial livers remain experimental, and left ventricular-assist devices can help only some heart patients. For those waiting for livers, lungs, or hearts, the lack of a suitable transplant organ spells almost certain death. Given the currently limited supply of organs, we face two key questions: How can the supply be increased? How are those who will actually receive organs to be selected from the pool of candidates?

## Increasing Supply

An obvious answer to the first question is that the supply of organs can be increased by increasing donations. Exactly how many organs that could be used for transplant aren't retrieved from those declared dead is unclear. According to one estimate, between 6900 and 10,700 potential donors are available, but because of such factors as the next of kin's not being asked to donate or refusing to donate or because of the circumstances of death or condition of the organs, only about 37 to 57 percent of potential donors become actual donors.

## Required Request and Required Response Laws

The federal Uniform Anatomical Gift Act of 1984 served as a model for state laws, and virtually all states have enacted laws to promote the increase of organ donation. Some have "required response" laws requiring people to declare when renewing their driver's license whether they wish to become organ donors, and most make it easy for people to decide to become donors by printing organ donation cards on the backs of driver's licenses. State laws based on the act spell out a person's right to donate all or part of his body and to designate a person or institution as a recipient. Starting in 1997, a new federal law mandates that organ donor cards be included with tax refund checks.

Even with the support of such laws, physicians and hospital administrators have been reluctant to intrude on a family's grief by asking that a deceased patient's organs be donated for use as transplants. Even if a patient has signed an organ donation card, the permission of the immediate family is required, in most cases, before the organs can be removed. In 1991, a federal appeals court ruled in favor of an Ohio woman who argued that the coroner who had removed her husband's corneas during an autopsy and donated them to the Cincinnati Eye Bank had violated her property rights. Her property interest in her husband's body was found to be protected under the due process clause of the Fourteenth Amendment.

In an attempt to overcome the reluctance of physicians to request organ donations, a 1986 federal law requires that hospitals receiving Medicare or Medicaid payments (97 percent of the nation's hospitals) identify patients who could become organ donors at death. The law also requires that hospitals discuss organ donations with the families of such patients and inform them of their legal power to authorize donations. Although this "required request" law has been in effect for about ten years, because of difficulties in administering it, including overcoming the reluctance of physicians to approach worried or bereaved families, the law has led to only a modest (about 10 percent) increase in the supply of transplant organs.

## Non–Heart Beating Donors

An approach devised recently at the University of Pittsburgh involves acting on the requests of patients (or their representatives) to remove their organs when their hearts stop beating, even though they may not yet be brain-dead. (See Chapter 11 for a discussion of criteria for determining death.) Hence, someone on a respirator wanting to be weaned off the machine may ask that her organs be used for transplant, should the withdrawal result in her death. The respirator is removed in an operating room, and at least three minutes after the patient's heart has stopped beating, the transplant organs are removed. In practice, most donor candidates are not like the one described. They have suffered severe brain damage but are not brain-dead, and permission has been obtained from their families.

Critics of the practice have raised questions about using the cessation of heartbeat as a proper criterion for death. (Perhaps the patient could be resuscitated. Is three minutes long enough to wait?) Some have also wondered if the practice doesn't put pressure on mentally competent, but seriously ill, patients to give up the struggle for their lives by volunteering to become organ donors. Similarly, critics have charged, by providing a rationalization, the practice may make it too easy for the parents or other representatives of comatose patients on life support to decide to withdraw support and end the person's life.

## Organ Protection Before Obtaining Consent

Another innovative but controversial approach employed by some medical centers involves injecting organ-protective drugs and preservatives into patients who die in an emergency room or en route. The organs are not removed from the body (although some surgical steps may be taken), but by making sure the organs have a good blood supply and so are protected from damage, physicians gain additional time to seek permission from the families. Otherwise, the organs would deteriorate and be useless for transplantation.

Critics of this practice claim that hospitals do not always wait to determine that a patient is dead before injecting these drugs. Thus, physicians can cause harm to still-living patients. Others claim the practice borders on desecration and denies dignity to individuals whose dead bodies are subjected to an invasive procedure without their prior consent. Further, critics say, we have no generally accepted ideas about what it is legitimate to do to a newly dead body to provide benefit to others.

Defenders of the practice say it gives families time to recover from the shock of learning about the death of a loved one and allows them to make a more considered decision. In this respect, the practice is more humane than asking a family for permission to take an organ from a loved one right at the time they learn of the loved one's death. Also, taking steps to preserve the organs of a dead body enables us to use them to save the lives of others.

Using organs from non–heart beating cadavers and preserving the organs of the newly dead before securing consent to use them are both practices that aim to provide a way to fill the gap between the number of transplant organs obtainable from brain-dead individuals and the number needed by those awaiting transplant. While 10,000 to 12,000 people are declared brain-dead every year, 60,000 are in need of transplants.

## Selling Organs

Another possibility for increasing the organ supply is to permit organs to be offered for sale on the open market. Before death, an individual might arrange payment for the posthumous use of one or more of his organs. Or after his death, his survivors might sell his organs to those needing them. In a variation of this proposal, donors or their families might receive tax credits, or a donor might be legally guaranteed that if a family member or friend required a transplant organ, that person would be given priority in the distribution. Under either plan, there would be a strong incentive to make organs available for transplant.

The public reaction to any plan for marketing organs has been strongly negative. People generally regard the prospect of individuals in need of transplants bidding against one another in an "organ auction" as ghoulish and morally repugnant, and this attitude extends to all forms of the market approach. (A government-regulated market with fixed prices is likely to be preferable to a genuine open market.) In 1984, the National Organ Transplantation Act made the sale of organs for transplant illegal in the United States. At least twenty other countries, including Canada, Britain, and most of Europe, have similar laws.

A third possibility would be to allow living individuals to sell their nonvital organs to those in need of transplants. Taking hearts and livers from living people would be illegal as it would involve homicide by the surgeon who removed them. However, kidneys occur in pairs, and we already permit individuals to donate one of their kidneys—indeed, we celebrate those who do. It is only a short step from the heroic act of giving away a kidney to the commercial act of selling one.

Kidney donors must undergo surgery that involves incurring a twelve-inch incision, the removal of a rib, and three to six weeks of recuperation. Donors face odds of 1 in 20,000 of dying from surgical complications, but the risk of dying as a result of having only one kidney is extremely small. People with one kidney are slightly more likely to develop high blood pressure than those with two.

Allowing the sale of an organ would be in keeping with the generally acknowledged principle that people ought to be free to do as they wish with their own bodies. We already permit the sale of blood, plasma, bone marrow, ova, and sperm. The decisive disadvantage to allowing such transactions as a matter of social policy, however, is that it would be the poor who would be most likely to suffer from it.

It is all too easy to imagine a mother wishing to improve the lives and opportunities of her children deciding to sell a kidney to help make that possible. That the economically advantaged should thrive by literally exploiting the bodies of the poor seems morally repulsive to most people. (The 1984 Organ Transplant Act was in direct response to the operations of the International Kidney Exchange, which was established in Virginia for the purpose of selling kidneys from living donors. The donors were predominantly indigent.) It is no answer to object that someone should be permitted to do as he wishes with his body to provide for the welfare of his family. If selling a kidney and putting his own life and health at risk is the only option open to someone with that aim, this in itself constitutes a prima facie case for major social reform.

## "Everyone Makes a Fee, Except for the Donor"

Despite strong public sentiment against selling organs, a telephone poll conducted by the United Network for Organ Sharing and the National Kidney Foundation showed that 48 percent of the people interviewed favored some form of "donor compensation." Under the Transplant Act, there can be none.

The law does permit payments associated with removing, preserving, transporting, and storing human organs. As a result, a large industry has developed around organ transplants. Sixty-nine procurement organizations, operating in federally defined geographical regions, collect organs from donors and transport them to the 278 hospitals with transplant facilities.

A procurement agency may be paid about $25,000 for its services. This includes ambulance trips to pick up and deliver the organ, fees to the hospital for the use of the operating room where the organ is removed, costs of tissue matching and blood testing, and overhead expenses for the agency and its personnel.

In addition, costs involved in a transplant may include fees paid to local surgeons to prepare the patient for organ removal and fees paid to a surgical team coming into town to remove the organ. Such fees typically amount to several thousand dollars.

Hospitals pay for the organs they receive, but they pass on their costs and more. Hospitals charge, as a rough average, $16,000 to $18,000 for a kidney or a heart and $20,000 to $22,000 for a liver. According to one study, hospitals may mark up the cost of an organ by as much as 200 percent to cover costs that patients are unable to pay or that exceed the amount the government will reimburse. A donor of several organs can produce considerable income for the transplanting hospital.

Some critics of current transplant practices have pointed out that everyone makes a fee from donated organs except for the donor. Yet matters show little sign of changing. A representative of the National Kidney Foundation proposed to a congressional committee that the law be changed to allow a relatively small amount of money (perhaps $2000) to be given to the families of organ donors as a contribution to burial expenses. The recommendation was not acted on, and similar proposals are no more likely to meet with success.

Given current transplant practices, it is understandable why donor families can sometimes become bitter. When Judy Sutton's daughter Susan killed herself, Mrs. Sutton donated Susan's heart and liver and so helped save the lives of two people. Mrs. Sutton then had to borrow the money to pay for Susan's funeral. "Susan gave life even in death," Mrs. Sutton told a reporter. "It's wrong that doctors make so much money off donors. Very wrong."

## Presumed Consent

A possibility widely discussed as a means of increasing the number of transplant organs is the adoption of a policy of "presumed consent." That is, a state or federal law would allow hospitals to take it for granted that a recently deceased person has tacitly consented to having any needed organs removed, unless the person had indicated otherwise or unless the family objects. The burden of securing consent would be removed from physicians and hospitals, but the burden of denying consent would be imposed on individuals or their families. To withdraw consent would require a positive action.

A policy of presumed consent has been adopted by several European countries. Critics of the policy point out that this has not, in general, done much to reduce the shortage of transplant organs in those countries. Although legally empowered to remove organs without a family's permission, physicians continue to be reluctant to do so. It is doubtful that a policy of presumed consent would be any more successful in this country. Also, if families are to be given the opportunity to deny consent, they must be notified of the death of the patient, and in many cases this would involve not only complicated practical arrangements, but also considerable loss of time. Thus, it is doubtful that presumed consent would do a great deal to increase the number of usable transplant organs.

## Altruistic Donation

In the view of many observers, the present system of organ procurement by voluntary donation for altruistic reasons is the best system. It appeals to the best in people, rather than to greed and self-interest, it avoids exploiting the poor, and it's efficient. Families who donate organs can gain some satisfaction from knowing that the death of a loved one brought some benefit to others.

## Living Donors

Some centers have relaxed or eliminated rules requiring that a living donor belong to the same family as the recipient. This allows those who wish to act in a generous and commendable fashion to directly benefit a friend, a coworker, or (in principle) a complete stranger. In 1995 over 3000 people received a kidney from a living donor. The majority of kidneys were donated by siblings (46 percent) or came from parents (22 percent), but they were also donated by spouses, children, and other relatives.

Kidneys are no longer the only organs transplanted from living donors. A healthy liver rapidly regenerates, and liver segments have been transplanted with great success. More recently, lung segments have been added to the list. Kidneys from living donors have a better success rate than ones from cadavers, but it is too early to tell whether this holds for liver and lung segments. Also, the history of using living kidney donors shows that the risk to donors is slight, with death as a result of the surgery occurring in about 3 in 10,000 cases. Experience with liver and lung segment donors isn't sufficiently extensive to be statistically meaningful, but the early data suggest they too pose little risk to the donor.

While the use of living donors can help reduce the chronic scarcity of some organs, the practice is not without critics. Thomas Starzl, the developer of liver transplants, refuses to use living donors, because too often the person in a family who "volunteers" to be a donor does so only because of the pressures of family dynamics. In effect, Starzl charges, consent cannot be voluntary. Those favoring the practice argue that Starzl's criticism is not a reason to reject the use of living donors so much as it is a reason to design a system of securing consent that will protect vulnerable individuals.

The chronic shortage of transplant organs can probably not be relieved by any one of the proposals mentioned here. Some combination of them might come close to solving the problem. Most likely, however, we must wait for a technological solution. If genetic engineering made it possible to breed pigs with organs invisible to the human immune system, the shortage of transplant organs would be ended. Not all moral problems would be solved, however, for some already question the breeding and use of animals solely to serve human wants and needs.

## Organ Allocation

Whatever the future may promise, the fact remains that at present there is a limited supply of transplant organs, and the demand far exceeds the supply. Thus, the key question today is, How are organs to be distributed when they become available? Currently, no national policies or procedures supply a complete answer to this question. Usually, with some exceptions, such decisions are made in accordance with policies adopted by particular regional or hospital-based transplant programs.

Typically, a transplant center employs a screening committee made up of surgeons, physicians, nurses, social workers, and a psychologist to determine whether a candidate for a transplant should be admitted to the waiting list. Medical need—whether the candidate might benefit from the transplant—is the first consideration, but it is far from the only one. A committee's decisions may also be based on the patient's general medical condition, age, and ability to pay for the operation, as well as whether he has the social support needed to assist him during recovery, shows evidence of being able to adhere to a lifetime regimen of antirejection drugs, and he belongs to the constituency that the center is committed to serving. Factors like race and gender are considered irrelevant, but in practice the individual's "social worth" (education, occupation, accomplishments) may also be taken into account.

Some large transplant centers employ a scoring system that involves assigning values to

a list of what the center considers relevant factors. Those with the highest score are accepted as candidates and given a priority ranking. If their medical condition worsens, they may later be moved up in the ranking. At most centers this process is done in a more informal fashion.

### Guidelines for Distribution

Once a patient is admitted to a center's waiting list, the allocation rules of the federally funded United Network for Organ Sharing (UNOS) also apply. UNOS policies stipulate the ways in which organs are distributed. Until recently, when an organ became available within one of the nine UNOS regions of the country, the institutions in the region had first claim on it, without respect to the needs of patients in other regions. In practice few organs ever left the region in which they were donated. In a recent move, UNOS now stipulates that an organ must go to a patient with the greatest need, no matter what the region, assuming the organ can be transported in good condition to the patient.

The policy is likely to have the effect of creating something like a national waiting list. Proponents say it will get more organs to the patients who need them most, while critics charge it will mean the greatest number of organs will go to the largest transplant centers, because the largest number of patients in acute need are there. Consequently, a number of centers will have to close. Some observers view this positively, for not all of the 278 centers do enough transplants to gain the experience needed to offer patients the best outcomes possible.

Some of the factors considered by transplant centers in admitting a patient to the waiting list have been criticized by many as morally irrelevant to deciding who is to receive a transplant organ. A patient's social worth and ability to pay are rejected by most critics, but opinion is divided over how much weight should be given to factors such as alcoholism, drug abuse, and poor health habits. Because of the shortage of organs, people needing transplants as a result of "lifestyle diseases" caused in part by obesity, smoking, or alcohol abuse would automatically be excluded as transplant candidates by some. By contrast, others would ask only that such people demonstrate a willingness to change their behavior. At present, transplant centers have much leeway in deciding which candidates they will accept.

A good example of an effort to formulate acceptable guidelines for making decisions about allocating organs is the Massachusetts Task Force on Organ Transplantation. The group issued a unanimous report that included the following recommendations:

1. Transplant surgery should be provided "to those who can benefit most from it in terms of probability of living for a significant period of time with a reasonable prospect for rehabilitation."

2. Decisions should not be based on "social worth" criteria.

3. Age may be considered as a factor in the selection process, but only to the extent that age is relevant to life expectancy and prospects for rehabilitation. Age must not be the only factor considered.

4. If not enough organs are available for all those who might benefit from them, final selections should be made by some random process (for example a lottery or first-come, first-served basis).

5. Transplants should be provided to residents of New England on the basis of need, regardless of their ability to pay, as long as this does not adversely affect health-care services with a higher priority. Those who are not residents of New England should be accepted as transplant candidates only after they have demonstrated their ability to pay for the procedure.

Organ transplantation continues to face two crucial problems: the chronic shortage of organs and the inability of some people needing a transplant to pay for one. The shortage problem might eventually be solved by developments in bio-

technology, but the financial problem could be solved immediately by a change in social policy.

## Case Presentation

### Sandra Jensen Gets a Transplant

Sandra Jensen was born with a deformed heart, but it wasn't until she was thirty-five that it began to make her so sick that she needed a heart–lung transplant to extend her life. She was young and otherwise healthy, but transplant centers at both Stanford University and the University of California, San Diego rejected her as a candidate.

Sandra Jensen also had Down syndrome, and the transplanters doubted she had sufficient intelligence to care for herself after the surgery. She would have to follow the complicated routine of taking doses of dozens of medications daily that is the lot of every transplant recipient. If she failed to adhere to the post-operative requirements, she would die, and the organs that might have saved the life of one or two other people would be wasted.

William Bronston, a state rehabilitation administrator and a friend of Jensen, became her advocate. He pointed out that she had demonstrated a high level of intellectual functioning. She was a high school graduate who worked with people with Down syndrome, and she had lived on her own for several years. She spoke for the disabled in California and attended the Washington signing by George H. Bush of the Americans with Disabilities Act in 1990.

Thanks to strong lobbying by Bronston and the threat of adverse publicity, Stanford reversed its decision. On January 23, 1996, in a five-hour operation, Ms. Jensen became the first seriously mentally retarded person in the United States to receive a major organ transplant.

More than a year later, on May 4, 1997, after her health began deteriorating, Ms. Jensen entered Sutter General Hospital in San Francisco. She had been admitted to the hospital several times before because of her reaction to the immunosuppressive drug. But this time was the last, and she died there on May 25, 1997. "Every day was always precious and lived well by her," her friend William Bronston said.

Prompted by Ms. Jensen's struggle to be accepted for a transplant, the California Assembly passed a bill to prohibit transplant centers from discriminating against impaired people needing a transplant.

# Case Presentation

## The Ayalas' Solution: Having a Child to Save a Life

Anissa Ayala was fifteen years old in 1988 when she was diagnosed with chronic myelogenous leukemia. She received radiation and chemotherapy treatments to destroy diseased bone marrow and blood cells, but the usual outcome of such treatments is that the bone marrow is left unable to produce an adequate number of normal blood cells.

Anissa's parents, Mary and Andy Ayala, were informed that without a bone marrow transplant of stem cells her survival chances were virtually zero, while with a transplant she would have a 70 to 80 percent chance.

Tests showed that neither the Ayalas nor their nineteen-year-old son, Airon, had bone marrow sufficiently compatible for them to be donors for Anissa. They turned to a public registry to assist them and during the next two years searched for a donor. The odds of a match between two nonrelated people is only 1 in 20,000, and as time passed and no one was found, the Ayalas began to feel increasingly desperate. Anissa's health had stabilized, yet that condition couldn't be counted on to last forever.

The Ayalas decided that the only way they could do more to help save their daughter's life was to try to have another child. Anissa's physician tried to discourage them, pointing out that the odds were only one in four that the child would have the right tissue type to be a stem-cell donor. Furthermore, the possibility that they could conceive another child was doubtful. Andy Ayala was forty-five years old and had had a vasectomy performed sixteen years earlier. Mary Ayala was forty-two, well past the period of highest fertility. Nevertheless, the Ayalas decided to go ahead with their plan, and as the first step Andy Ayala had surgery to repair the vasectomy.

Against all the odds, Mary Ayala became pregnant. When it became known that the Ayalas planned to have a child because their daughter needed compatible bone marrow, they became the subjects of intense media attention and received much harsh criticism. Some said that they were treating the baby they expected to have as a means only and not as a person of unique worth. One commentator described their actions as "outrageous." Others said they were taking a step down the path that would lead to conceiving children merely to be sources for tissues and organs.

A few opposed this outpouring of criticism by noting that people decide to have children for many and complex reasons and sometimes for no reason at all. No one observed that a reason for having a child need not determine how one regards the child. Also, those who condemned the Ayalas often emphasized the "child-as-an-organ-bank" notion but never mentioned the relative safety of a bone marrow transplant.

The Ayalas were hurt by the criticisms. Mary Ayala said she had wanted a third child for a number of years but had been unable to get her husband to agree. Andy Ayala admitted that he wouldn't have wanted another child if Anissa hadn't become ill, but he said he also had in mind the comfort a child would bring to the family if Anissa should die. The whole family said they would want and love the child, whether or not its bone marrow was a good match for Anissa's.

In February 1990 the Ayalas found they had beat the odds once more. Tests of the developing fetus showed that the stem cells were nearly identical with Anissa's. During an interview after the results were known, Anissa Ayala said "A lot of people think 'How can you do this? How can you be having this baby for your daughter?' But she's my baby sister and we're going to love her for who she is, not for what she can give me."

Then, on April 6, in a suburban Los Angeles hospital, more than a week before the predicted date, Mary Ayala gave birth to a healthy six-pound baby girl. The Ayalas named her Marissa Eve. Anissa's physician, pediatric oncologist Patricia Konrad, collected and froze blood from the baby's umbilical cord. Umbilical blood contains a high concentration of stem cells, and she wanted the blood available should Anissa need it before Marissa was old enough to be a donor.

When Marissa Eve was fourteen months old and had reached an adequate weight, she was given general anesthesia and marrow was extracted from her hipbone. After preparation, the donated marrow was injected into one of Anissa's veins. The procedure was successful, and the stem cells migrated to Anissa's marrow and began to multiply. Anissa's own bone marrow began to produce normal blood cells.

In 1993 Anissa married Bryan Espinosa, and Marissa Eve was the flower girl at the wedding.

Radiation treatments destroyed Anissa's chances of having a child of her own, but she claims that the bond between her and Marissa Eve is especially close. "Marissa is more than a sister to me," Anissa told reporter Anni Griffiths Belt. "She's almost like my child too."

"I was struck by the extraordinary bond between the sisters," Belt said. "The fact is, neither one would be alive today without the other."

---

# SOCIAL CONTEXT: FETAL-CELL IMPLANTS

Parkinson's disease often begins with tremors and a mild stiffening of the limbs that is followed, usually over a period of years, by a gradual but progressive loss of muscle control. Although remaining intellectually lucid, people with the disease are often unable to walk, use the toilet, wash, or even eat without assistance.

Their behavior also has a peculiar and disturbing off/on aspect. Someone may be walking or talking when, without the least warning, he freezes during the action. Some find this feature of the disease so disconcerting that they become recluses, fearful of freezing in midmotion in public or in a dangerous place. Over 1.5 million people, most of them over sixty, are estimated to suffer from the disease. In 1996 what might be the gene responsible for the disease was traced to chromosome 4, but the gene itself has not been identified.

The disease is causally connected with the dying off of cells in a darkly pigmented part of the brain called the *substantia nigra*. These cells produce dopamine, a neurotransmitter essential in conveying impulses to brain cells that control muscle movements. A major therapeutic advance in the treatment of Parkinsonism occurred with the introduction of the drug L-dopa. L-dopa is a biochemical precursor of dopamine, and when the body converts the drug to dopamine, people often make an amazing recovery from the effects of the disease. Unfortunately, within a few years L-dopa ceases to be effective, and the old problems of rigidity, "freezing," and general loss of muscle control return.

In 1987, Ignacio Madrazo reported in Mexico that he had successfully transplanted cells from the adrenal cortex of two Parkinson patients into the caudate nucleus area of their brains. The adrenal gland is known to produce dopamine, and Madrazo described his patients as making substantial functional recoveries that he expected to continue over the long term. (Five years previously, Swedish researchers performed a similar operation but reported that their patients made only slight and transitory improvements.) Madrazo's results were never reported in a scientific journal, and although scientists made efforts to repeat the work, no one was successful. Thus, early hopes for adrenal-cell transplants as an effective treatment for Parkinsonism were disappointed.

Then in February 1990, matters began to look hopeful again. Olle Lindvall of University Hospital in Lund, Sweden, reported in *Science* that he and his research team had implanted fetal brain cells into the brain of a forty-nine-year-old man with severe Parkinson's disease. The cells were injected into the left putamen, an area known to be the site of numerous dopamine pathways.

The man's symptoms were significantly relieved. Previously, even with medication, he had spent more than half his time in a frozen "off" position, but within three months after the implant, he had only one or two brief "off" periods each day. (The man's course was followed from eleven months before the surgery, and it was still being followed at the time of publication five months afterward.) Most important, brain-imaging methods indicated that the fetal cells were continuing to function and to produce dopamine.

Lindvall's team had been working on the problem since 1979, and the team's reputation, experimental procedures, and data convinced most of the biomedical community that their results were reliable. Other researchers indicated that they had experiments under way that were likely to confirm Lindvall's results.

The Swedish procedure involved taking neural tissue from four fetuses eight to nine weeks old. Fetal brain tissue offers the possibility of a better biological match than cells even from an individual's own adrenal gland. Further, neural fetal tissue seems to be unlikely to provoke an autoimmune response and cause graft-host rejection. Treating Parkinsonism with fetal-cell implants is an exciting therapeutic possibility that may benefit hundreds of thousands of sufferers. Furthermore, the treatment points the way toward the development of other therapies involving fetal tissues.

Fetal liver cells may be used to generate new bone marrow to treat those suffering from leukemia, sickle-cell anemia, thalassemia, aplastic anemia, or radiation sickness. (Robert Gale employed fetal liver cells to treat some victims of the Chernobyl disaster, although without success.) Alzheimer's disease and Huntington's disease may yield to treatments involving fetal neural cells. Fetal heart tissue may be used to replace damaged heart muscle, and the bodies of the more than 2 million insulin-dependent (Type-I) diabetics may someday be able to produce their own insulin, if implants of islet cells from fetal pancreatic tissue should be successful.

In 1997 scientists at the Veterans Affairs Medical Center in Gainesville, Florida, initiated a clinical trial involving treating ten patients with spinal cord injuries with injections of cells from fetal spinal cord tissue. The hope is that the fetal cells will reproduce and fill in the gaps in the spinal cavity where nerves have been destroyed. Adult neural tissue does not regenerate, but fetal neural tissue still has the capacity to grow. Animal studies, as well as experiments performed in Russia and Sweden hold out the hope that the new neural tissue will make it possible for some patients to regain some control over their bodies. Tissue from five to eight fetuses will be required to treat each patient. About 10,000 people are paralyzed by spinal cord injuries each year, and no therapy has yet been shown to reverse paralysis.

The potential therapeutic marvels promised by fetal cells hold out the only hope for literally millions of people suffering from a wide range of diseases. However, fetal-cell implants and their use in research and therapy have also produced serious moral and social issues we have yet to resolve.

The most vexed issue is that of induced abortion as the source of fetal tissue. Opponents of elective abortion argue that research and therapy using fetal tissue both condone and encourage abortion. According to a National Right to Life Committee representative, the medical use of fetal tissue will "offer an additional rationalization to those who defend the killings."

Also, both opponents and advocates of elective abortion express concern over the possibility that some women might deliberately conceive a child, then have an abortion for the sole purpose of obtaining the fetal tissue. The tissue could then either be used to help some member of the woman's family or sold as a commodity. Although a 1988 amendment to the National Organ Transplant Act prohibits the sale of fetal organs and tissue, the success of fetal-cell therapy could lead to a repeal. Some have suggested that fetal tissue, like blood, bone marrow, ova, and sperm, can be considered a renewable resource. The potential for a fetal-tissue market exists, and some have speculated that the current law may only encourage the establishment of an off-shore source of supply. People will seek out illegal sources of supplies of fetal tissue in much the same way they seek illegal sources of drugs they believe are crucial to their survival.

Some critics see the possibility that women might be exploited. The idea that women might be put under pressure by social expectations or by their friends, husbands, or families to have an abortion to provide fetal tissue needed to treat an ailing relative is not farfetched. Further, if there were a market in fetal tissue, women might be under pressure to produce a fetus to secure money needed to support themselves or their families. (It should be kept in mind, though, that even in the absence of pressure, a woman might choose to sell or donate fetal tissue for a variety of reasons.)

While the Catholic Church condemns induced abortion, it condones the use of fetal tissue, at least that obtained from spontaneous abortions, within certain limits. The "fetal organ donor" must be treated with the same respect as any other organ donor, and it is necessary to be certain the donor is dead. This requirement presents a difficulty, however, for the standards for fetal brain death are far from clear.

About 1.25 million abortions are performed each year, and most fetal tissue used in research is obtained from those performed during the first four months of pregnancy. Although the matter is in dispute, some researchers regard tissue from eight- to nine-week-old fetuses as preferable, while some claim older tissue is better. In either case, social and economic pressure on a woman to delay an abortion may start to build and the best interest of the woman may be compromised by the need for mature fetal tissue. Instead of using a drug like RU-486 to inhibit the implantation of a fertilized ovum or instead of having an early abortion, a woman might carry the fetus until a time dictated by needs other than her own health.

The possibility of using only spontaneously aborted fetuses is dimmed by the fact that up to 60 percent show chromosomal abnormalities or other defects that might affect the tissue recipient. But one way of addressing the abortion objection to the use of fetal tissue is to employ cells from a single fetus, grow them in cultures, then harvest them as needed. This would eliminate the need for a large number of mature fetuses and make the research and treatment more independent of abortion.

Another possibility is to use the techniques of molecular biology to clone cells taken from an individual patient. If the cells can be made to multiply in sufficient quantity, the patient can be treated with his own cells. The problem of an immune reaction would be eliminated, and cell therapy would be severed from abortion.

Because fetal cells are now available and not dependent on technological development, people suffering from Parkinson's disease, spinal-cord injuries, and other disorders that might be helped by fetal-cell implants are understandably not eager to see research in this area delayed. For a great number, the development of a future technology that will disconnect cell therapy and abortion will come too late to help.

In 1987, the Department of Health and Human Services suspended the support of research projects using fetal tissue obtained through induced abortions. After two reviews of the issues, a special panel of the National Institutes of Health decided in 1988 that the use of fetal tissue for research and treatment can be morally legitimate. The panel separated the question of elective abortion from that of the use of fetal tissue and took no position on the moral status of abortion. The panel also recommended that women not be permitted to donate fetal tissue for the treatment of their friends or family.

In April 1989, NIH, following most of the recommendations of its panel, issued guidelines for the use of fetal tissue in research and experimental therapy. The ban on the use of such tissue initiated during the Reagan administration was continued by the Bush administration, however, and federal funds could not be used for human fetal-tissue implants. In addition, at least seven states passed laws forbidding the use of fetal tissue obtained from induced abortions. Many researchers objected to these restrictions. Some claimed that the restrictions were immoral because they seriously impeded the development of effective treatments for devastating diseases. Others used funds from private foundations to continue their research.

Despite objections from the research community, the ban on federal financing of studies using cells from aborted fetuses remained in effect until it was lifted by President Clinton in one of his first official acts. In January 1994, the National Institute of Neurological Disorders announced grants of $4.5 million to three institutions to study the effects of fetal-cell implants in Parkinson's patients.

One of the grants was awarded to researchers at the University of Colorado, in Denver. During the ban, the researchers, operating on private financing, injected fetal brain cells into sixteen patients with Parkinson's disease. The outcome was that about one-third of the patients improved significantly, one-third improved some, and one-third showed no measurable improvement.

Patients with diseases that might be relieved by fetal-cell therapy, as well as their families, are eager to see it developed as rapidly as possible. Some are angered by what they see as an unjustified delay in federal research funding. Others are angered by what they see as an endorsement of abortion.

## Case Presentation

### Drug Lottery: The Betaseron Shortage

Multiple sclerosis (MS) is a neurological disorder affecting almost 300,000 Americans. Its symptoms include fatigue, dizziness, slurred speech, vision loss, numbness, tingling sensations, and muscle spasticity that affects coordination and makes walking difficult. The disease strikes adults from twenty to forty years old. It is progressive and, in extreme cases, can lead to paralysis.

About one-third of those with the disease have a form known as relapsing–remitting multiple sclerosis. They can live free of symptoms for months, then have an attack during which their symptoms return, and they may be confined to a wheelchair for weeks. Typically, the symptoms are worse than they were during the last episode, and as the attacks continue to occur, people become progressively more disabled.

The hopes of some sufferers were raised in 1993 when the FDA announced its approval of a new drug that had been shown in clinical trials to reduce the frequency of attacks by about 30 percent in early stages of the relapsing–remitting form. What's more, magnetic resonance imaging indicated that brain changes associated with the symptoms were fewer than those seen in untreated patients. The drug was a genetically engineered form of interferon known as interferon beta IB with the trade name Betaseron. An injectable drug, it promised to help an estimated 100,000 to 175,000 people with multiple sclerosis. It was the first drug that promised to slow the

course of the disease, rather than merely treat its symptoms.

By the fall of 1993, immediately after FDA approval, MS patients throughout the country were pressuring their physicians to prescribe the drug for them. Most physicians were happy to do so, but the problem was there wasn't enough Betaseron to meet the needs of the patients who might benefit from it. Berlex Laboratories, its developer, had been caught by surprise by FDA's fast-track approval process and so was not in a position to manufacture large quantities of the drug rapidly. Further, because Betaseron can be manufactured only in a fermentation process using genetically engineered E. coli bacteria, its production could not be speeded up to meet demand.

Berlex's response to the situation was to establish a lottery, the first of its kind, as a means of determining who would receive the drug. The lottery was open only to those with relapsing–remitting multiple sclerosis who were certified by their doctors to be in the earlier stages of the disease and able to walk at least 100 yards unassisted. Some 67,000 people applied for the drug by the September 15 deadline, and another 7000 applied after the deadline.

As people applied, they were assigned randomly to positions on a waiting list by a computer program. Enough doses of the drug were available to help 17,000 people immediately. Those receiving higher numbers would have to wait for additional supplies to be manufactured.

Berlex was especially concerned that those treated with Betaseron receive an uninterrupted course of the drug. "A lot of patients on and off therapy is no good for anybody," Jeffrey Latts, a Berlex vice president said. "We felt it was better for some patients to get continuous therapy rather than intermittent therapy."

Before announcing the lottery, Berlex officials talked with patient groups, drug distribution experts, and physicians. Patients tended to favor a lottery, but physicians were generally not happy with the idea of giving up control over choosing which patients might benefit from the drug.

"We felt it was important to keep this process completely clean," Latts said about the lottery. "I personally can guarantee that no one got moved up, no matter how influential. We said, 'No, Governor, we can't,' and 'I'm sorry, Senator, it's not possible.' We heard rumors that someone was offering to pay for a lower number, but we have records of what number went to what patient where."

Despite Berlex's commitment to fairness, some patients did receive Betaseron without going through the lottery. Some 3500 doses of the drug were sent to 100 medical centers, and the centers decided how to distribute them. "I feel guilty I was chosen and other people weren't," said a fifty-seven-year-old lawyer who was one of those who got the drug without entering the lottery. "But not guilty enough not to take it. When you've had MS for many years, you just look for some ray of hope."

Some patients not meeting the lottery guidelines pressured their physicians into certifying them as in the early stages of the disease, permitting them to qualify for the lottery. An even larger number objected to being excluded from the lottery, claiming that they had as much right as anyone to get whatever benefit they could from Betaseron. Most physicians, however, rejected this point of view. They considered it wrong to give the drug to patients for whom it had not been proved effective, when there was an inadequate supply of the drug for patients for whom its effectiveness had been demonstrated.

Along with the lottery, Berlex Laboratories introduced a second program with the aim of assuring access to Betaseron by those who might benefit from it. The cost of the drug was $989 a month, putting it out of the financial reach of many people. To address this problem Berlex provided the drug free to those who were uninsured and earned less than $20,000 a year. For those uninsured and earning up to $50,000, it employed a sliding scale of charges. Medicaid and most private insurance companies paid for the drug, but Medicare did not. To encourage patients to adhere to the best treatment schedule, Berlex committed itself to providing free drugs to all patients for the eleventh and twelfth months.

By 1994 the shortage of Betaseron was over. While some physicians and patients were unhappy with the lottery approach, most observers considered it the best model to follow in the event of future drug shortages. Given that many new drugs are likely to be the product of genetic engineering, the next shortage may not lie far in the future.

## READINGS

## Section 1: Allocation Principles

## The Allocation of Exotic Medical Lifesaving Therapy

### Nicholas Rescher

Nicholas Rescher makes a useful distinction between two kinds of criteria: criteria of inclusion (for the selection of candidates) and criteria of comparison (for selection of recipients). Rescher argues that three areas need to be considered in establishing a class of candidates: (1) constituency (is the person a member of the community the institution is designed to serve?); (2) progress of science (can new knowledge be gained from the case?); and (3) success (is the treatment of the person likely to be effective?).

Five factors, Rescher claims, ought to be considered in deciding upon recipients of the goods or services: (1) the likelihood of successful treatment compared with others in the group; (2) the life expectancy of the person; (3) the person's family role, (4) the potential of the person in making future contributions; and (5) the person's record of services or contributions.

Rescher argues that it is necessary to have a rational selection system, but he admits that the exact manner in which a system takes into account relevant factors cannot be fixed and exact. In his view, which is basically a utilitarian one, an acceptable selection system might be one that makes use of point ratings of the factors mentioned above. This would establish a smaller group, but as a final step, he suggests, the best procedure might well be to make use of a chance factor (such as a lottery) to choose recipients.

## I. The Problem

Technological progress has in recent years transformed the limits of the possible in medical therapy. However, the elevated state of sophistication of modern medical technology has brought the economists' classic problem of scarcity in its wake as an unfortunate side product. The enormously sophisticated and complex equipment and the highly trained teams of experts requisite for its utilization are scarce resources in relation to potential demand. The administrators of the great medical institutions that preside over these scarce resources thus come to be faced increasingly with the awesome choice: *Whose life to save?*

A (somewhat hypothetical) paradigm example of this problem may be sketched within the following set of definitive assumptions: We suppose that persons in some particular medically morbid condition are "mortally afflicted": It is virtually certain that they will die within a short time period (say ninety days). We assume that some very complex course of treatment (e.g., a heart transplant) represents a substantial probability of life prolongation for persons in this mortally afflicted condition. We assume that the facilities available in terms of human resources, mechanical instrumentalities, and requisite materials (e.g., hearts in the case of heart transplant) make it possible to give a certain treatment—this "exotic (medical) lifesaving therapy," or ELT for short—to a certain, relatively small number of people. And finally we assume that a substantially greater pool of people in the mortally afflicted condition is at hand. The problem then may be formulated as follows: How is one to select within the pool of afflicted patients the ones to be given the ELT treatment in question; how to select those "whose lives are to be saved"? Faced with many candidates for an ELT process that can be made available to only a few, doctors and medical administrators confront the decision of who is to be given a chance at survival and who is, in effect, to be condemned to die.

As has already been implied, the "heroic" variety of spare-part surgery can pretty well be assimilated to this paradigm. One can foresee the time when heart

Reprinted from *Ethics* 79 (April 1969), by permission of the University of Chicago Press and the author. © 1969 the University of Chicago Press. (Notes omitted.)

transplantation, for example, will have become pretty much a routine medical procedure, albeit on a very limited basis, since a cardiac surgeon with the technical competence to transplant hearts can operate at best a rather small number of times each week and the elaborate facilities for such operations will most probably exist on a modest scale. Moreover, in "spare-part" surgery there is always the problem of availability of the "spare parts" themselves. A report in one British newspaper gives the following picture: "Of the 150,000 who die of heart disease each year [in the U.K.], Mr. Donald Longmore, research surgeon at the National Heart Hospital [in London] estimated that 22,000 might be eligible for heart surgery. Another 30,000 would need heart and lung transplants. But there are probably only between 7,000 and 14,000 potential donors a year." Envisaging this situation in which at the very most something like one in four heart-malfunction victims can be saved, we clearly confront a problem in ELT allocation.

A perhaps even more drastic case in point is afforded by long-term haemodialysis, an ongoing process by which a complex device—an "artificial kidney machine"—is used periodically in cases of chronic renal failure to substitute for a nonfunctional kidney in "cleaning" potential poisons from the blood. Only a few major institutions have chronic haemodialysis units, whose complex operation is an extremely expensive proposition. For the present and foreseeable future the situation is that "the number of places available for chronic haemodialysis is hopelessly inadequate."

The traditional medical ethos has insulated the physician against facing the very existence of this problem. When swearing the Hippocratic Oath, he commits himself to work for the benefit of the sick in "whatsoever house I enter." In taking this stance, the physician substantially renounces the explicit choice of saving certain lives rather than others. Of course, doctors have always in fact had to face such choices on the battlefield or in times of disaster, but there the issue had to be resolved hurriedly, under pressure, and in circumstances in which the very nature of the case effectively precluded calm deliberation by the decision maker as well as criticism by others. In sharp contrast, however, cases of the type we have postulated in the present discussion arise predictably, and represent choices to be made deliberately and "in cold blood."

It is, to begin with, appropriate to remark that this problem is not fundamentally a medical problem. For when there are sufficiently many afflicted candidates for ELT then—so we may assume—there will also be more than enough for whom the purely medical grounds for ELT allocation are decisively strong in any individual case, and just about equally strong throughout the group. But in this circumstance a selection of some afflicted patients over and against others cannot *ex hypothesi* be made on the basis of purely medical considerations.

The selection problem, as we have said, is in substantial measure not a medical one. It is a problem *for* medical men, which must somehow be solved by them, but that does not make it a medical issue—any more than the problem of hospital building is a medical issue. As a problem it belongs to the category of philosophical problems—specifically a problem of moral philosophy or ethics. Structurally, it bears a substantial kinship with those issues in this field that revolve about the notorious whom-to-save-on-the-lifeboat and whom-to-throw-to-the-wolves-pursuing-the-sled questions. But whereas questions of this just-indicated sort are artificial, hypothetical, and farfetched, the ELT issue poses a genuine policy question for the responsible administrators in medical institutions, indeed a question that threatens to become commonplace in the foreseeable future.

Now what the medical administrator needs to have, and what the philosopher is presumably *ex officio* in a position to help in providing, is a body of *rational guidelines* for making choices in these literally life-or-death situations. This is an issue in which many interested parties have a substantial stake, including the responsible decision maker who wants to satisfy his conscience that he is acting in a reasonable way. Moreover, the family and associates of the man who is turned away—to say nothing of the man himself—have the right to an acceptable explanation. And indeed even the general public wants to know that what is being done is fitting and proper. All of these interested parties are entitled to insist that a reasonable code of operating principles provides a defensible rationale for making the life-and-death choices involved in ELT.

## II. The Two Types of Criteria

Two distinguishable types of criteria are bound up in the issue of making ELT choices. We shall call these *Criteria of Inclusion* and *Criteria of Comparison,* respectively. The distinction at issue here requires some explanation. We can think of the selection as being made by a two-stage process: (1) the selection from among all possible candidates (by a suitable screening process) of a group to be taken under serious consideration as candidates for therapy, and then (2) the actual singling out, within this group, of the particular individuals to whom therapy is to be given. Thus the first process narrows down the range of comparative choices by eliminating en bloc whole categories of potential candidates. The second process calls for a more refined case-by-case comparison of those candidates that remain. By means of the first set of criteria one forms a selection group; by means of the second set, an actual selection is made within this group.

Thus what we shall call a "selection system" for the choice of patients to receive therapy of the ELT type will consist of criteria of these two kinds. Such a system will be acceptable only when the reasonableness of its component criteria can be established.

## III. Essential Features of an Acceptable ELT Selection System

To qualify as reasonable, an ELT selection must meet two important "regulative" requirements: it must be *simple* enough to be readily intelligible, and it must be *plausible,* that is, patently reasonable in a way that can be apprehended easily and without involving ramified subtleties. Those medical administrators responsible for ELT choices must follow a modus operandi that virtually all the people involved can readily understand to be acceptable (at a reasonable level of generality, at any rate). Appearances are critically important here. It is not enough that the choice be made in a *justifiable* way; it must be possible for people—*plain* people—to "see" (i.e., understand without elaborate teaching or indoctrination) that *it is justified,* insofar as any mode of procedure can be justified in cases of this sort.

One "constitutive" requirement is obviously an essential feature of a reasonable selection system: all of its component criteria—those of inclusion and those of comparison alike—must be reasonable in the sense of being *rationally defensible.* The ramifications of this requirement call for detailed consideration. But one of its aspects should be noted without further ado: it must be *fair*—it must treat relevantly like cases alike, leaving no room for "influence" or favoritism, etc.

## IV. The Basic Screening Stage: Criteria of Inclusion (and Exclusion)

Three sorts of considerations are prominent among the plausible criteria of inclusion/exclusion at the basic screening stage: the constituency factor, the progress-of-science factor, and the prospect-of-success factor.

### A. The Constituency Factor

It is a "fact of life" that ELT can be available only in the institutional setting of a hospital or medical institute or the like. Such institutions generally have normal clientele boundaries. A veterans' hospital will not concern itself primarily with treating non-veterans, a children's hospital cannot be expected to accommodate the "senior citizen," an army hospital can regard college professors as outside its sphere. Sometimes the boundaries are geographic—a state hospital may admit only residents of a certain state. There are, of course, indefensible constituency principles—say race or religion, party membership, or ability to pay; and there are cases of borderline legitimacy, e.g., sex. A medical institution is justified in considering for ELT only persons within its own constituency, provided this constituency is constituted upon a defensible basis. Thus the haemodialysis selection committee in Seattle "agreed to consider only those applications who were residents of the state of Washington. They justified this stand on the grounds that since the basic research . . . had been done at . . . a state-supported institution—the people whose taxes had paid for the research should be its first beneficiaries."

While thus insisting that constituency considerations represent a valid and legitimate factor in ELT selection, I do feel there is much to be said for minimizing their role in life-or-death cases. Indeed a refusal to recognize them at all is a significant part of medical tradition, going back to the very oath of Hippocrates. They represent a departure from the ideal arising with the institutionalization of medicine, moving it away from its original status as an art practiced by an individual practitioner.

### B. The Progress-of-Science Factor

The needs of medical research can provide a second valid principle of inclusion. The research interests of the medical staff in relation to the specific nature of the cases at issue is a significant consideration. It may be important for the progress of medical science—and thus of potential benefit to many persons in the future—to determine how effective the ELT at issue is with diabetics or persons over sixty or with a negative RH factor. Considerations of this sort represent another type of legitimate factor in ELT selection. A very definitely *borderline* case under this head would revolve around the question of a patient's willingness to pay, not in monetary terms, but in offering himself as an experimental subject, say by contracting to return at designated times for a series of tests substantially unrelated to his own health, but yielding data of importance to medical knowledge in general.

### C. The Prospect-of-Success Factor

It may be that while the ELT at issue is not without *some* effectiveness in general, it has been established to be highly effective only with patients in certain specific categories (e.g., females under forty of a specific blood type). This difference in effectiveness—in the absolute or in the probability of success—is (we assume) so marked as to constitute virtually a difference in kind rather than in degree. In this case, it would be perfectly legitimate to adopt the general rule of making the ELT at issue available only or primarily to persons in this substantial-promise-of-success category. (It is on grounds of this sort that young children and persons over fifty are generally ruled out as candidates for haemodialysis.)

We have maintained that the three factors of constituency, progress of science, and prospect of success represent legitimate criteria of inclusion for ELT selection. But it remains to examine the considerations which legitimate them. The legitimating factors are in the final analysis practical or pragmatic in nature. From the practical angle it is advantageous—indeed to some extent necessary that the arrangements governing medical institutions should embody certain constituency principles. It makes good pragmatic and utilitarian sense that progress-of-science considerations should be operative here. And, finally, the practical aspect is reinforced by a whole host of other considerations—including moral ones—in supporting the prospect-of-success criterion. The workings of each of these factors are of course conditioned by the ever-present element of limited availability. They are operative only in this context, that is, prospect of success is a legitimate consideration at all only because we are dealing with a situation of scarcity.

## V. The Final Selection Stage: Criteria of Selection

Five sorts of elements must, as we see it, figure primarily among the plausible criteria of selection that are to be brought to bear in further screening the group constituted after application of the criteria of inclusion: the relative-likelihood-of-success factor, the life-expectancy factor, the family role factor, the potential-contributions factor, and the services rendered factor. The first two represent the *biomedical* aspect, the second three the *social* aspect.

### A. The Relative-Likelihood-of-Success Factor

It is clear that the relative likelihood of success is a legitimate and appropriate factor in making a selection within the group of qualified patients that are to receive ELT. This is obviously one of the considerations that must count very significantly in a reasonable selection procedure.

The present criterion is of course closely related to item C of the preceding section. There we were concerned with prospect-of-success considerations categorically and en bloc. Here at present they come into play in a particularized case-by-case comparison among individuals. If the therapy at issue is not a once-and-for-all proposition and requires ongoing treatment, cognate considerations must be brought in. Thus, for example, in the case of a chronic ELT procedure such as haemodialysis it would clearly make sense to give priority to patients with a potentially reversible condition (who would thus need treatment for only a fraction of their remaining lives).

### B. The Life-Expectancy Factor

Even if the ELT is "successful" in the patient's case he may, considering his age and/or other aspects of his general medical condition, look forward to only a very short probable future life. This is obviously another factor that must be taken into account.

### C. The Family Role Factor

A person's life is a thing of importance not only to himself but to others—friends, associates, neighbors, colleagues, etc. But his (or her) relationship to his immediate family is a thing of unique intimacy and significance. The nature of his relationship to his wife, children, and parents, and the issue of their financial and psychological dependence upon him, are obviously matters that deserve to be given weight in the ELT selection process. Other things being anything like equal, the mother of minor children must take priority over the middle-aged bachelor.

### D. The Potential Future-Contributions Factor (Prospective Service)

In "choosing to save" one life rather than another, "the society," through the mediation of the particular medical institution in question—which should certainly look upon itself as a trustee for the social interest—is clearly warranted in considering the likely pattern of future *services to be rendered* by the patient (adequate recovery assumed), considering his age, talent, training, and past record of performance. In its allocations of ELT, society "invests" a scarce resource in one person as against another and is thus entitled to look to the probable prospective "return" on its investment.

It may well be that a thoroughly egalitarian society is reluctant to put someone's social contribution into the scale in situations of the sort at issue. One popular article states that "the most difficult standard would be the candidate's value to society," and goes on to quote someone who said: "You can't just pick a brilliant painter over a laborer. The average citizen would be quickly eliminated." But what if it were not a brilliant painter but a brilliant surgeon or medical researcher that was at issue? One wonders if the author of the *obiter dictum* that one "can't just pick" would still feel equally sure of his ground. In any case, the fact that the standard is difficult to apply is certainly no reason for not attempting to apply it. The problem of ELT selection is inevitably burdened with difficult standards.

Some might feel that in assessing a patient's value to society one should ask not only who if permitted to continue living can make the greatest contribution to society in some creative or constructive way, but also who by dying would leave behind the greatest burden on society in assuming the discharge of their residual responsibilities. Certainly the philosophical utilitarian would give equal weight to both these considerations. Just here is where I would part ways with orthodox utilitarianism. For—though this is not the place to do so—I should be prepared to argue that a civilized society has an obligation to promote the furtherance of positive achievements in cultural and related areas even if this means the assumption of certain added burdens.

## E. The Past Services-Rendered Factor (Retrospective Service)

A person's services to another person or group have always been taken to constitute a valid basis for a claim upon this person or group—of course a moral and not necessarily a legal claim. Society's obligation for the recognition and reward of services rendered—an obligation whose discharge is also very possibly conducive to self-interest in the long run—is thus another factor to be taken into account. This should be viewed as a morally necessary correlative of the previously considered factor of *prospective* service. It would be morally indefensible of society in effect to say: "Never mind about services you rendered yesterday—it is only the services to be rendered tomorrow that will count with us today." We live in very future-oriented times, constantly preoccupied in a distinctly utilitarian way with future satisfactions. And this disinclines us to give much recognition to past services. But parity considerations of the sort just adduced indicate that such recognition should be given *on grounds of equity*. No doubt a justification for giving weight to services rendered can also be attempted along utilitarian lines. ("The reward of past services rendered spurs people on to greater future efforts and is thus socially advantageous in the long-run future.") In saying that past services should be counted "on grounds of equity"—rather than "on grounds of utility"—I take the view that even if this utilitarian defense could somehow be shown to be fallacious, I should still be prepared to maintain the propriety of taking services rendered into account. The position does not rest on a utilitarian basis and so would not collapse with the removal of such a basis.

As we have said, these five factors fall into three groups: the biomedical factors *A* and *B*, the familial factor *C*, and the social factors *D* and *E*. With items *A* and *B* the need for a detailed analysis of the medical considerations comes to the fore. The age of the patient, his medical history, his physical and psychological condition, his specific disease, etc., will all need to be taken into exact account. These biomedical factors represent technical issues: they call for the physicians' expert judgment and the medical statisticians' hard data. And they are ethically uncontroversial factors—their legitimacy and appropriateness are evident from the very nature of the case.

Greater problems arise with the familial and social factors. They involve intangibles that are difficult to judge. How is one to develop subcriteria for weighing the relative social contributions of (say) an architect or a librarian or a mother of young children? And they involve highly problematic issues. (For example, should good moral character be rated a plus and bad a minus in judging services rendered?) And there is something strikingly unpleasant in grappling with issues of this sort for people brought up in times greatly inclined towards maxims of the type "Judge not!" and "Live and let live!" All the same, in the situation that concerns us here such distasteful problems must be faced, since a failure to choose to save some is tantamount to sentencing all. Unpleasant choices are intrinsic to the problem of ELT selection; they are of the very essence of the matter.

But is reference to all these factors indeed inevitable? The justification for taking account of the medical factors is pretty obvious. But why should the social aspect of services rendered and to be rendered be taken into account at all? The answer is that they must be taken into account not from the *medical* but from the *ethical* point of view. Despite disagreement on many fundamental issues, moral philosophers of the present day are pretty well in consensus that the justification of human actions is to be sought largely and primarily—if not exclusively—in the principles of utility and of justice. But utility requires reference of services to be rendered and justice calls for a recognition of services that have been rendered. Moral considerations would thus demand recognition of these two factors. (This, of course, still leaves open the question of whether the point of view provides a valid basis of action: Why base one's actions upon moral principles—or, to put it bluntly—Why be moral? The present paper is, however, hardly the place to grapple with so fundamental an issue, which has been canvassed in the literature of philosophical ethics since Plato.)

## VI. More Than Medical Issues Are Involved

An active controversy has of late sprung up in medical circles over the question of whether non-physician laymen should be given a role in ELT selection (in the specific context of chronic haemodialysis). One physician writes: "I think that the assessment of the candidates should be made by a senior doctor on the [dialysis] unit but I am sure that it would be helpful to him—both in sharing responsibility and in avoiding personal pressure if a small unnamed group of people [presumably including laymen] officially made the final decision. I visualize the doctor bringing the data to the group, explaining the points in relation to each case, and obtaining their approval of his order of priority."

Essentially this procedure of a selection committee of laymen has for some years been in use in one of the most publicized chronic dialysis units, that of the Swedish Hospital of Seattle, Washington. Many physicians are apparently reluctant to see the choice of allocation of medical therapy pass out of strictly medical hands. Thus in a recent symposium on the "Selection of Patients for Haemodialysis," Dr. Ralph Shakman writes: "Who is to implement the selection? In my opinion it must ultimately be the responsibility of the consultants in charge of the renal units . . . I can see no reason for delegating this responsibility to lay persons. Surely the latter would be better employed if they could be persuaded to devote their time and energy to raise more and more money for us to spend on our patients." Other contributors to this symposium strike much the same note. Dr. F. M. Parsons writes: "In an attempt to overcome . . . difficulties in selection some have advocated introducing certain specified lay people into the discussions. Is it wise? I doubt whether a committee of this type can adjudicate as satisfactorily as two medical colleagues, particularly as successful therapy involves close cooperation between doctor and patient." And Dr. M. A. Wilson writes in the same symposium: "The suggestion has been made that lay panels should select individuals for dialysis from among a group who are medically suitable. Though this would relieve the doctor-in-charge of a heavy load of responsibility, it would place the burden on those who have no personal knowledge and have to base their judgments on medical or social reports. I do not believe this would result in better decisions for the group or improve the doctor–patient relationship in individual cases."

But no amount of flag waving about the doctor's facing up to his responsibility—or prostrations before the idol of the doctor–patient relationship and reluctance to admit laymen into the sacred precincts of the conference chambers of medical consultations—can obscure the essential fact that ELT selection is not a wholly medical problem. When there are more than enough places in an ELT program to accommodate all who need it, then it will clearly be a medical question to decide who does have the need and which among these would successfully respond. But when an admitted gross insufficiency of places exists, when there are ten or fifty or one hundred highly eligible candidates for each place in the program, then it is unrealistic to take the view that purely medical criteria can furnish a sufficient basis for selection. The question of ELT selection becomes serious as a phenomenon of scale—because, as more candidates present themselves, strictly medical factors are increasingly less adequate as a selection criterion precisely because by numerical category-crowding there will be more and more cases whose "status is much the same" so far as purely medical considerations go.

The ELT selection problem clearly poses issues that transcend the medical sphere because—in the nature of the case—many residual issues remain to be dealt with once *all* of the medical questions have been faced. Because of this there is good reason why laymen as well as physicians should be involved in the selection process. Once the medical considerations have been brought to bear, fundamental social issues remain to be resolved. The instrumentalities of ELT have been created through the social investment of scarce resources, and the interests of the society deserve to play a role in their utilization. As representatives of their social interests, lay opinions should function to complement and supplement medical views once the proper arena of medical considerations is left behind. Those physicians who have urged the presence of lay members on selection panels can, from this point of view, be recognized as having seen the issue in proper perspective.

One physician has argued against lay representation on selection panels for haemodialysis as follows: "If the doctor advises dialysis and the lay panel refuses, the patient will regard this as a death sentence passed by an anonymous court from which he has no right of appeal." But this drawback is not specific to the use of a lay panel. Rather, it is a feature inherent in every *selection* procedure, regardless of whether the selection is done by the head doctor of the unit, by a panel of physicians, etc. No matter who does the selecting among patients recommended for dialysis, the feelings of the patient who has been rejected (and knows it) can be expected to be much the same, provided that he recognizes the actual nature of the choice (and is not deceived by the possibly convenient but ultimately poisonous fiction that because the selection was made by physicians it was made entirely on medical grounds).

In summary, then, the question of ELT selection would appear to be one that is in its very nature heavily laden with issues of medical research, practice, and administration. But it will not be a question that can be resolved on solely medical grounds. Strictly social issues of justice and utility will invariably arise in this area—questions going outside the medical area in whose resolution medical laymen can and should play a substantial role.

## VII. The Inherent Imperfection (Non-Optimality) of Any Selection System

Our discussion to this point of the design of a selection system for ELT has left a gap that is a very fundamental and serious omission. We have argued that five factors must be taken into substantial and explicit account:

A.   *Relative likelihood of success.* Is the chance of the treatment's being "successful" to be rated as high, good, average, etc.?

B.   *Expectancy of future life.* Assuming the "success" of the treatment, how much longer does the patient stand a good chance (75 per cent or better) of living—considering his age and general condition?

C.   *Family role.* To what extent does the patient have responsibilities to others in his immediate family?

D.   *Social contributions rendered.* Are the patient's past services to his society outstanding, substantial, average, etc.?

E.   *Social contributions to be rendered.* Considering his age, talents, training, and past record of performance, is there a substantial probability that the patient will—*adequate recovery being assured*—render in the future services to his society that can be characterized as outstanding, substantial, average, etc.?

This list is clearly insufficient for the construction of a reasonable selection system, since that would require not only *that these factors be taken into account* (somehow or other), but—going beyond this—would *specify a specific set of procedures for taking account of them.* The specific procedures that would constitute such a system would have to take account of the interrelationship of these factors (e.g., B and E), and to set out exact guidelines as to the relevant weight that is to be given to each of them. This is something our discussion has not as yet considered.

In fact, I should want to maintain that there is no such thing here as a single rationally superior selection system. The position of affairs seems to me to be something like this: (1) It is necessary (for reasons already canvassed) to have a system, and to have a system that is rationally defensible, and (2) to be rationally defensible, this system must take the factors A–E into substantial and explicit account. But (3) the exact manner in which a rationally defensible system takes account of these factors cannot be fixed in any one specific way on the basis of general considerations. Any of the variety of ways that give A–E "their due" will be acceptable and viable. One cannot hope to find within this range of workable systems some

one that is optimal in relation to the alternatives. There is no one system that does "the (uniquely) best"—only a variety of systems that do "as well as one can expect to do" in cases of this sort.

The situation is structurally very much akin to that of rules of partition of an estate among the relations of a decedent. It is important *that there be* such rules. And it is reasonable that spouse, children, parents, siblings, etc., be taken account of in these rules. But the question of the exact method of division—say that when the decedent has neither living spouse nor living children then his estate is to be divided, dividing 60 per cent between parents, 40 per cent between siblings versus dividing 90 per cent between parents, 10 per cent between siblings—cannot be settled on the basis of any general abstract considerations of reasonableness. Within broad limits, *a variety* a resolutions are all perfectly acceptable—so that no one procedure can justifiably be regarded as "the (uniquely) best" because it is superior to all others.

## VIII. A Possible Basis for a Reasonable Selection System

Having said that there is no such thing as *the optimal* selection system for ELT, I want now to sketch out the broad features of what I would regard as *one acceptable* system.

The basis for the system would be a point rating. The scoring here at issue would give roughly equal weight to the medical considerations (*A* and *B*) in comparison with the extramedical considerations (*C* = family role, *D* = services rendered, and *E* = services to be rendered), also giving roughly equal weight to the three items involved here (*C*, *D*, and *E*). The result of such a scoring procedure would provide the essential starting point of our ELT selection mechanism. I deliberately say "starting point" because it seems to me that one should not follow the results of this scoring in an *automatic* way. I would propose that the actual selection should only be guided but not actually be dictated by this scoring procedure, along lines now to be explained.

## IX. The Desirability of Introducing an Element of Chance

The detailed procedure I would propose—not of course as optimal (for reasons we have seen), but as eminently acceptable—would combine the scoring procedure just discussed with an element of chance. The resulting selection system would function as follows:

1. First the criteria of inclusion of Section IV above would be applied to constitute a *first phase selection group*—which (we shall suppose) is substantially larger than the number *n* of persons who can actually be accommodated with ELT.

2. Next the criteria of selection of Section V are brought to bear via a scoring procedure of the type described in Section VIII. On this basis a *second phase selection group* is constituted which is only *somewhat* larger—say by a third or a half—than the critical number *n* at issue.

3. If this second phase selection group is relatively homogeneous as regards rating by the scoring procedure—that is, if there are no really major disparities within this group (as would be likely if the initial group was significantly larger than *n*)—then the final selection is made by *random* selection of *n* persons from within this group.

This introduction of the element of chance—in what could be dramatized as a "lottery of life and death"—must be justified. The fact is that such a procedure would bring with it three substantial advantages.

First, as we have argued above (in Section VII), any acceptable selection system is inherently non-optimal. The introduction of the element of chance prevents the results that life-and-death choices are made by the automatic allocation of an admittedly imperfect selection method.

Second, a recourse to chance would doubtless make matters easier for the rejected patient and those who have a specific interest in him. It would surely be quite hard for them to accept his exclusion by relatively mechanical application of objective criteria in whose implementation subjective judgment is involved. But the circumstances of life have conditioned us to accept the workings of chance and to tolerate the element of luck (good or bad): human life is an inherently contingent process. Nobody, after all, has an absolute right to ELT—but most of us would feel that we have "every bit as much right" to it as anyone else in significantly similar circumstances. The introduction of the element of chance assures a like handling of like cases over the widest possible area that seems reasonable in the circumstances.

Third (and perhaps least), such a recourse to random selection does much to relieve the administrators of the selection system of the awesome burden of ultimate and absolute responsibility.

These three considerations would seem to build up a substantial case for introducing the element of chance into the mechanism of the system for ELT selection in a way limited and circumscribed by other weightier considerations, along some such lines as those set forth above.

It should be recognized that this injection of *man–made* chance supplements the element of *natural* chance that is present inevitably and in any case (apart from the role of chance in singling out certain persons as victims for the affliction at issue). As F. M. Parsons has observed: "any vacancies [in an ELT program—specificlly haemodialysis] will be filled immediately by the first suitable patients, even though their claims for therapy may subsequently prove less than those of other patients refused later." Life is a chancy business and even the most rational of human arrangements can cover this over to a very limited extent at best.

---

**READINGS**

# Section 2: Acquiring Transplant Organs

## The Donor's Right to Take a Risk

### Ronald Munson

Ronald Munson asks whether, given the risk to themselves, we should permit people to donate a liver lobe and whether, by operating on a donor for the benefit of a recipient, surgeons are violating the dictum "Do no harm." He claims that, while autonomy warrants consent, we must take measures to guarantee that consent is both informed and freely given. So far as benefit is concerned, Munson maintains, when consent is valid, living donors can be viewed as benefiting themselves, as well as the recipients of their gift.

Mike Hurewitz, a 57-year-old journalist, died at Mount Sinai Hospital in Manhattan on Sunday [January 13, 2002] after an operation to remove part of his liver for transplant. The recipient, his younger brother, is apparently doing well. The procedure of liver-lobe transplantation, hardly more than a decade old, can save lives, but it can also lead to disaster. The case of the Hurewitz brothers illustrates both. The risk of death for a donor may be as high as 1 in 100. Yet even when the magic works, when donor and recipient survive, the procedure raises troubling questions. The death of Mike Hurewitz gives those questions a sharper edge.

Given the risk and the potential for family pressure, should we permit people to become liver donors? Are physicians violating the "do no harm" rule by operating on healthy donors, causing them pain and risking their lives, yet bringing them no medical benefit?

These questions have urgency because for end-stage liver disease, we have no effective treatment other than transplantation. The lives of people in kidney failure can be extended considerably by dialysis, and those with heart failure can often be sustained by an implantable pump, but we have no machines capable of taking over the liver's functions.

The lack of an alternative results in a high demand for cadaver livers. About 19,000 people are now on the waiting list for those organs, but only 5,000 will get transplants, and about 2,000 die each year waiting for livers.

Until the advent of liver transplants from live donors, a patient who could not get a liver was doomed. Now there is hope. In this procedure, the liver segments in the donor and the recipient grow back to full size in about a month. The success of liver-segment transplantation, first used in treating children, has led surgeons to begin using adults as donors for other adults.

That the benefits of liver transplantation seem totally one-sided raises questions about whether a

From the *New York Times*, 19 January 2002.

donor is giving informed consent. Our society recognizes the autonomy of individuals, which means letting people decide which risks they take. Most parents, given a chance to save the life of a desperately ill child, would willingly gamble their own. Some people might risk themselves for a sister, husband or close friend, while others might decide otherwise.

For consent to be legitimate, it must be both informed and freely given. A potential donor must be educated about the pain and risks, including death, that the surgery involves. Most important, potential donors must be protected from the overt and subtle pressures of friends and relatives. They must be free to say no as well as yes.

One way to ensure that the interests of prospective donors are recognized is to create a federal agency that would make certain that hospitals meet minimum standards when employing these new therapies and would monitor how hospital review boards screen potential donors. The boards also need to be able to shield potential donors from coercion. For example, in cases when an individual decides against becoming a donor, a board should simply inform the intended recipient that the potential donor is "not suitable" without further explanation.

But even when consent is valid, are doctors harming liver donors while bringing them no benefit? That might be true, but only under an overly narrow understanding. As a Massachusetts court reasoned in 1957, a teenager who donated a kidney to his twin brother was not only saving his brother's life, but also promoting his own emotional well-being and health, which would be adversely affected if his brother died. When informed consent is valid, living donors can be viewed as exercising their autonomy and doctors can legitimately be viewed as helping both patient and donor.

Until we can develop machines, employ animal organs or grow new livers using stem cells, we are dependent on transplants, including living donor transplants. We must rely on the courage of people like Mike Hurewitz. They are moral heroes; they must not be made medical dupes.

# Conscription of Cadaveric Organs for Transplantation: Let's at Least Talk About It

## Aaron Spital and Charles A. Erin

Aaron Spital and Charles Erin observe that the scarcity of transplant organs results in the death of many people who could be saved and that a major barrier to acquiring organs is the refusal of families of the recently dead to donate their organs. The authors argue for the adoption of a new policy—the *conscription* of organs. All useable organs should be taken, without consent, and used for transplantation. Spital and Erin address objections and defend the view that consent is not ethically required and that conscription, which can save lives, is ethically preferable to all current and proposed practices.

Among patients with end-stage renal disease (ESRD), those who receive kidney transplants enjoy a better quality and longer duration of life compared with those who are treated with dialysis.[1] Renal transplantation is also less costly than dialysis.[2] Clearly then, from the point of view of both the patient and society, renal transplantation is the best therapy for ESRD. For patients with irreversible failure of other vital organs, transplantation, which now has high success rates,[3] offers the only hope for long-term survival.

Unfortunately, the ability to deliver this medical miracle is limited by a severe shortage of transplantable organs. In most developed countries, the rate at which people with end-stage organ disease (ESOD) are being added to transplant waiting lists greatly exceeds the rate at which organs are being donated.[4,5] This has led to long and steadily lengthening lists of potential recipients waiting and hoping for organs to become available for life-saving transplants. For example, in the United States, as of June 2001, almost 77,000 people were registered on the national transplant waiting list.[6] The result is a tragic situation in which people with ESOD are dying not because modern medicine does not know how to treat them, but rather because we have been unable to procure enough organs for all who need them. Compounding this tragedy is the fact that many usable organs are being buried instead of being transplanted because of the relatively low efficiency of cadaveric organ procurement (the major source of transplantable organs).[7,8]

Reprinted from *American Journal of Kidney Diseases,* Vol 39, No 3 (March), 2002: pp 611–615, with permission from Elsevier. ©2002 National Kidney Foundation.

If we are to remedy this tragic situation we need to ask what is wrong with our current system for procuring cadaveric organs for transplantation and what can we do to improve it? To answer these questions, we need to briefly review the procurement systems currently in use.

### Problems with Current Cadaveric Organ Procurement Systems and Proposed Improvements

Cadaveric organ procurement now involves three basic steps: (1) identification of a potential organ donor; (2) maintaining the potential donor in good physiological condition to preserve organ function; and (3) obtaining consent to remove organs for transplantation, usually from the family, after brain death has been declared. (To our knowledge, all developed countries require consent before organs can be removed from recently deceased individuals.) While failure at any of these steps will result in donor loss, the major barrier to procurement is failure to obtain consent.[4,8–10]

Two systems for obtaining consent are currently in place.[4,11] Some countries, including the United Kingdom, Canada, and the United States, practice so-called "opting-in." This requires explicit consent from the decedent before death or from the decedent's family after death; in practice, the decision is almost always made by the family, because even when a donor card or other similar document is available, very few centers will honor it without permission from the next of kin.[12] Many other European countries follow an "opting-out" approach in which the organs of recently deceased people may be removed for transplantation unless the decedent has voiced her objection pre-mortem or her family objects at the time of her death. This system is also called (erroneously, we believe) "presumed consent."[13] It should be noted that most countries with presumed consent laws still consult with and honor the wishes of the family before removing organs from recently deceased individuals.[4,14]

It is not our purpose here to argue the relative merits of these two approaches but rather to point out that under both systems many life-saving organs are lost because of family refusal. For example, in the United States, despite great efforts to increase consent rates, about 50% of families say no when asked for permission to remove organs from recently deceased loved ones.[8,10] Similar results were reported in a recent study from France (an opting-out country).[9] Clearly, if the consent barrier could be eliminated, many more organs for transplantation would become available.

Several proposals designed to increase consent rates have been suggested. These include providing financial[15,16] or nonfinancial incentives (such as priority status for transplantation for people agreeing to donate after death),[17] and mandated choice, which would require every adult to make a binding decision for him or herself regarding posthumous organ donation.[18] The envisioned benefits of these approaches have been discussed in the literature. But despite growing interest in them, especially financial incentives, all are controversial and have been sharply criticized.[19–22] Furthermore, it is highly unlikely that any of them would approach the 100% efficiency of cadaveric organ procurement that patients with ESOD so desperately need. However, there is another alternative that would likely achieve this seemingly unreachable goal but which is rarely mentioned in reviews of this subject[5,23,24]—conscription of all usable cadaveric organs.

## A Proposal for Conscription of Cadaveric Organs

Under conscription, all usable organs would be removed from recently deceased people and made available for transplantation; consent would be neither required nor requested and, with the possible exception of people with religious objections, opting-out would not be possible.[25,26] No doubt this proposal will initially evoke shock, mockery, and even outrage among those who believe that consent is an absolute requirement for cadaveric organ procurement. But the ethical basis for this widely held view is far from clear. Indeed, perhaps because the idea that consent is nec-

essary has been so readily accepted as a given, few authors have seen the need to justify this point of view.[27] We believe that this is a mistake. We will argue that careful consideration of the relevant issues will show that consent for cadaveric organ removal is not ethically required and that conscription is actually preferable. This conclusion is based on an assessment of the envisioned advantages and disadvantages of conscription of cadaveric organs.

### Advantages of Conscription of Cadaveric Organs for Transplantation

The most important advantage of conscription is that the number of cadaveric organs made available to patients with ESOD would increase dramatically. No longer would large numbers of precious life-saving organs be buried or burned instead of transplanted because, under conscription, the efficiency of cadaveric organ procurement would approach 100%. From the point of view of efficiency, no other approach to organ procurement can even come close. As a result of the increased number of transplantable organs that conscription would provide, the lives of many more people with ESOD would be improved and extended.

Another advantage to conscription is that it is simpler and less costly than other approaches to organ procurement.[15] Under conscription there would be no need to convince people to donate their organs, no need to train requestors to obtain and document informed consent, no need for donor registries, no need for complex regulatory mechanisms that would be required to avoid abuses under plans for financial incentives, and no need to spend resources to induce people to participate.

A third advantage to conscription is that because consultation with the family would no longer occur, this plan would eliminate the added stress that uncomfortable staff members and devastated families now experience when confronting the possibility of organ donation. And the current need to seek some form of family approval often results in delays that can jeopardize the quality of organs. Obviously, this would not occur under conscription.

A final advantage of conscription is that it satisfies the ethical principle of distributive justice, which refers to fair and equitable distribution of benefits and burdens.[28] Under conscription all people would share the burden of providing organs after death and all would stand to benefit should the need arise. This contrasts with current procurement systems in which people can choose not to donate their organs and yet compete equally for an organ with more generous people who choose to give. And in contrast to proposals for financial incentives, there would be no risk of exploitation of the poor for the benefit of the rich.

### Disadvantages of Conscription of Cadaveric Organs and Responses to Them

A major concern about conscription of cadaveric organs is that it violates the ethical principle of respect for individual autonomy. However, it makes little sense to speak of autonomy of a dead person.[29,30] As Jonsen[30] points out, "consent is ethically important because it manifests and protects the moral autonomy of persons . . . [and] it is a barrier to exploitation and harm. These purposes are no longer relevant to the cadaver which has no autonomy and cannot be harmed." On the other hand, it has been argued that people have critical interests[31] that persist after death,[32] and Childress[33] asserts that "people can be wronged even when they are not harmed (e.g., by having their will thwarted after their deaths) . . . " We are not convinced that this is true,[13,34] but even if it is, as will soon be discussed, this concern is not sufficient to reject conscription.

Another disadvantage of conscription is that it may harm the interests of surviving family members who are opposed to organ procurement. Many people have strong feelings about how the body of a recently deceased loved one should be handled. And as Boddington[35] points out, "So much does the death of a group member affect those still alive, and so heavily imbued with spiritual, religious, and cultural significance are the rituals of death in human societies, that there are good grounds for respecting claims of the group [i.e., the family] for autonomy over these matters."

It appears then that conscription has the potential to harm families and perhaps "wrong" the decedent. It may therefore violate the ethical principle of non-maleficence which states that one should not intentionally inflict harm.[28] However, it is important to remember that this principle is not absolute and may be justifiably overridden when the expected benefit of an action exceeds the harm inflicted.[28] In our view, this would apply to conscription of cadaveric organs for transplantation. However strong are the interests of the family, and even if there are individual interests that survive after death, it is hard to see how they could possibly be as important as the lives of desperately ill patients with ESOD who will die without an organ transplant. Preservation of life is perhaps the paramount principle of medical ethics.[36] Consistent with this view, Jonsen[30] argues, "respecting the former beliefs of the decedent or observing cultural practices about burial, while important, would seem to yield before the significant value of therapy for those suffering from serious illness." On this point Harris[32] is even stronger: "If we can save or prolong the lives of living people and can only do so at the expense of the sensibilities of others, it seems clear to me that we should. For the alternative involves the equivalent of sacrificing people's lives so that others will simply *feel* better or not feel so bad, and this seems nothing short of outrageous." And consider that a military draft is widely accepted during wartime even though the death of a young son would be much more painful for families than would the drafting of organs from a relative who is already dead.[11,26]

A final concern about conscription of cadaveric organs is that it would generate outrage among the public. While initially there probably would be public resistance to this plan, some authors believe it might not be as great as one might think.[27] Furthermore, we and others[32] believe that eventually people would get used to the idea, especially once they realize that everyone stands to benefit from the practice. Support for this prediction comes from the observation that there already exist widely accepted coercive practices that require participation of all citizens regardless of their wishes. These include forced taxation, a military draft in wartime, mandatory autopsy in cases of suspected foul play, and required vaccination of children attending public schools.[26] But even if the public remained opposed to conscription, this would still not be a sufficient reason for abandoning the plan. As already alluded to, the state may act coercively in order to protect itself and the lives of its constituents. As noted by Silver,[26] "Even if the Court were to conclude that an individual's decision regarding the disposition of her dead body is protected by the right of privacy, it would likely uphold the proposed organ draft on the ground that it promotes a state interest of sufficient importance to warrant an intrusion into constitutionally protected decisionmaking. State interests in obtaining evidence and in public health already override the individual's 'liberty' to be disposed of as she pleases. Surely, state interests in preserving life are more important than these other state interests and the invasion no more severe."

The possibility of religious objection is a sensitive and important issue. But it should be noted that even the protection of religious interests is not absolute.[25] For example, these interests are not sufficient to prevent compulsory autopsy. Are not the reasons for conscription of cadaveric organs at least as compelling as those for autopsy?

## A Final Argument Supporting Conscription of Cadaveric Organs for Transplantation

Peters[17] and others claim that consenting to posthumous organ removal should not be considered an act of charity but rather "a moral duty of substantial stringency." Peters[17] argues that because there is no risk of harming cadavers, and because their organs may be life-saving, posthumous organ donation is an example of an easy rescue of an endangered person. Based on this reasoning, he concludes that everyone is "under a moral obligation to *now* explicitly consent to the posthumous taking of his or her own organs for this lifesaving purpose."[17] Unfortunately, left to their own devices, not enough people meet this obligation. Conscription of cadaveric organs could then be justified as necessary to ensure that all citizens do what they should have done on their own but did not. "Good Samaritan" laws provide precedent for this approach.

## Conclusion

The severe shortage of organs is the major barrier to transplantation today and the situation is growing steadily worse. This crisis has led many workers in the field to propose and try new approaches in the hope of improving the efficiency of cadaveric organ procurement. All of them are beset by logistical and ethical problems, but only conscription can achieve an efficiency rate that approaches 100%. Because the stakes are so high we should aim for nothing less. A strong burden of proof falls upon those who would oppose conscription to justify why any non–life-threatening interest should be given greater weight than those of patients with ESOD, many of whom will continue to die unless conscription of cadaveric organs becomes routine. If we can conscript young men into the military at the risk of losing their lives in the name of protecting the welfare of our citizens, then surely we can conscript organs from cadavers that cannot be harmed for the same purpose. No doubt there will be many people who do not agree, but before rejecting the idea out of hand, let's at least talk about it.

## Acknowledgment

We wish to thank Sam Spital for his careful review of the manuscript and his very helpful comments.

## References

1.  Wolfe RA, Ashby VB, Milford EL, et. al: Comparison of mortality in all patients on dialysis, patients on dialysis awaiting transplantation, and recipients of a first cadaveric transplant. N Engl J Med 341:1725–1730, 1999

2.  US Renal Data System: Excerpts From the USRDS 2000 Annual Data Report: Atlas of End-Stage Renal Disease in the United States. Am J Kidney Dis 36:S163-S176, 2000 (suppl 2)

3.  Lin HM, Kauffman M, McBride MA, et al: Center-specific graft and patient survival rates. 1997 United Network for Organ Sharing (UNOS) Report. JAMA 280:1153–1160, 1998.

4.  Cohen B, Wight C: A European perspective on organ procurement. Transplantation 68:985–990, 1999

5.  Hou S: Expanding the kidney donor pool: Ethical and medical considerations. Kidney Int 58:1820–1836, 2000

6.  www.unos.org/Newsroom/critdata_main.htm

7.  Evans RW, Orians CE, Ascher NL: The potential supply of organ donors. An assessment of the efficiency of organ procurement in the United States. JAMA 267:239–246, 1992

8.  Gortmaker SL, Beasley CL, Brigham LE, et al: Organ donor potential and performance: Size and nature of the organ donor shortfall. Crit Care Med 24:432–439, 1996

9.  Durand-Zaleski I, Waissman R, Lang P, Weil B, Foury M, Bonnet F: Nonprocurement of transplantable organs in a tertiary care hospital. Transplantation 62:1224–1229, 1996

10. Siminoff LA, Arnold RM, Caplin AL, Virnig BA, Seltzer DL: Public policy governing organ and tissue procurement in the United States. Ann Intern Med 123:10–17, 1995

11. Spital A: Obtaining consent for organ donation: What are our options? Balliere's Clin Annesth 13:179–193, 1999

12. Wendler D, Dickert N: The consent process for cadaveric organ procurement, How does it work? How can it be improved? JAMA 285:329–333, 2001

13. Erin CA: Presumed consent, contracting out, and conscription of the dead. BSHI 36:4–7, 1999

14. Matesanz R: Cadaveric organ donation: Comparison of legislation in various countries of Europe. Nephrol Dial Transplant 13:1632–1635, 1998

15. Barnett AH, Kaserman DL: The shortage of organs for transplantation: Exploring the alternatives. Issues Law Med 9:117–137, 1993

16. Council on Ethical and Judicial Affairs, American Medical Association: Financial incentives for organ procurement. Ethical aspects of future contracts for cadaveric donors. Arch Intern Med 155:581–589, 1995

17. Peters DA: A unified approach to organ donor recruitment, organ procurement, and distribution. J Law Health 3:157–3187, 1989–90

18. Spital, A: Mandated choice for organ donation: Time to give it a try. Ann Intern Med 125:66–69, 1996

19. Dossetor J: Kidney vending: "Yes!" or "No!" Am J Kidney Dis 35:1002–1018, 2000

20. Klassen AC, Klassen DK: Who are the donors in organ donation? The family's perspective in mandated choice. Ann Intern Med 125:70–73, 1996

21. Menikoff J: Organ swapping. Hastings Center Report 29:28–33 1999

22. Gillon R: On giving preference to prior volunteers when allocating organs for transplantation. J Med Ethics 21:195–196, 1995

23. Gridelli B, Remuzzi G: Strategies for making more organs available for transplantation. N Engl J Med 343:404–410, 2000

24. Hauptman PJ, O'Connor KJ: Procurement and allocation of solid organs for transplantation. N Engl J Med 336:422–431, 1997

25. Compulsory removal of cadaver organs. Columbia Law Rev 69:693–705, 1979

26. Silver T: The case for a post-mortem organ draft and a proposed model organ draft act. Boston Univ Law Rev 68:681–728, 1988

27. Emson HE: The ethics of human cadaver organ transplantation: A biologist's viewpoint. J Med Ethics 13:124–126, 1987

28. Beauchamp TL, Childress JF: Principles of Biomedical Ethics (ed 4). Oxford, UK, Oxford University Press, 1994, pp. 194, 327

29. Murray TH, Youngner SJ: Organ salvage policies. A need for better data and more insightful ethics. JAMA 272:814–815, 1994

30. Jonsen AR: Transplantation of fetal tissue: An ethicist's viewpoint. Clin Res 36:215–219, 1988

31. Dworkin R: Life's Dominion: An Argument About Abortion and Euthanasia. London, UK, Harper Collins, 1993, pp. 199–213

32. Harris J: Wonderwoman and Superman. The Ethics of Human Biotechnology. Oxford, UK, Oxford University Press, 1992, pp. 100–103

33. Childress JF: Ethical criteria for procuring and distributing organs for transplantation. J Health Politics Policy Law 14:87–113, 1989

34. Erin CA: Some comments on the ethics of consent to the use of ovarian tissue from aborted fetuses and dead women, in Harris J, Holm S (eds): The Future of Human Reproduction. Ethics, Choice, and Regulation. Oxford, UK, Clarendon, 1998, pp. 162–175

35. Boddington P: Organ donation after death—Should I decide, or should my family? J Appl Philosophy 15:69–81, 1998

36. Dukeminier J, Sanders D: Organ transplantation: A proposal for routine salvaging of cadaver organs. N Engl J Med 279:413–419, 1968

# Take My Kidney, Please

## Michael Kinsley

Michael Kinsley examines the issue of whether we should permit the sale of transplant organs. How far, he asks, are we willing to pursue the logic of capitalism? Kinsley shows that, in the final analysis, when we react with horror to the spectacle of a man forced to sell a kidney to pay for his daughter's operation, we are actually reacting to the injustices of life.

Even Margaret Thatcher's devotion to the free market has some limits, it seems. Reacting to newspaper reports that poor Turkish peasants are being paid to go to London and give up a kidney for transplant, the British Prime Minister said that "the sale of kidneys or any organs of the body is utterly repugnant." Emergency legislation is now being prepared for swift approval by Parliament to make sure that capitalism does not perform its celebrated magic in the market for human organs.

Commercial trade in human kidneys does seem grotesque. But it's a bit hard to say why. After all, the moral logic of capitalism does not stop at the epidermis. That logic holds, in a nutshell, that if an exchange is voluntary, it leaves both parties better off. In one case, a Turk sold a kidney for £2,500 ($4,400) because

From *Time*, March 13, 1989, p. 88. Copyright © 1989 TIME Inc. Reprinted by permission.

he needed money for an operation for his daughter. Capitalism in action: one person had $4,400 and wanted a kidney, another person had a spare kidney and wanted $4,400, so they did a deal. What's more, it seems like an advantageous deal all around. The buyer avoided a lifetime of dialysis. The seller provided crucial help to his child, at minimum risk to himself. (According to the *Economist*, the chance of a kidney donor's dying as a result of the loss is 1 in 5,000.)

Nevertheless, the conclusion that such trade is abhorrent is not even controversial. Almost everyone agrees. Is almost everyone right? This question of how far we are willing to push the logic of capitalism will be thrust in our faces increasingly in coming years. Medical advances are making it possible to buy things that were previously unobtainable at any price. (The Baby M. "womb renting" case is another example.) Meanwhile, the communications and transportation revolutions are breaking down international borders, making new commercial relations possible between the comfortably rich and the desperately poor. On what basis do we say to a would-be kidney seller, "Sorry, this is one deal you just can't make"?

One widely accepted category of forbidden deals involves health and safety regulations: automobile standards, bans on food additives, etc. Although we quarrel about particular instances, only libertarian cranks reject in principle the idea that government sometimes should protect people from themselves. But it is no more dangerous to sell one of your kidneys than it is to give one away to a close relative—a transaction we not only allow but admire. On health grounds alone, you can't ban the sale without banning the gift as well. Furthermore, the sale of a kidney is not necessarily a foolish decision that society ought to protect you from. To pay for a daughter's operation, it seems the opposite.

But maybe there are some things money just shouldn't be allowed to buy, sensibly or otherwise. Socialist philosopher Michael Walzer added flesh to this ancient skeleton of sentiment in his 1983 book, *Spheres of Justice*. Walzer argued that a just society is not necessarily one with complete financial equality—a hopeless and even destructive goal—but one in which the influence of money is not allowed to dominate all aspects of life. By outlawing organ sales, you are indeed keeping the insidious influence of money from leaching into a new sphere and are thereby reducing the power of the rich. Trouble is, you are also reducing opportunity for the poor.

The grim trade in living people's kidneys would not be necessary if more people would voluntarily offer their kidneys (and other organs) when they die. Another socialist philosopher, Richard Titmuss, wrote a famous book two decades ago called *The Gift Relationship*, extolling the virtues of donated blood over purchased blood and, by extension, the superiority of sharing over commerce. Whatever you may think of Titmuss's larger point, the appeal of the blood-donor system as a small testament to our shared humanity is undeniable. Perhaps we should do more to encourage organ donation at death for the same reason. On the

other hand, however cozy and egalitarian it might seem, a system that supplied all the kidneys we need through voluntary donation would be no special favor to our Turkish friend, who would be left with no sale and no $4,400. Why not at least let his heirs sell his kidneys when he dies? A commercial market in cadaver organs would wipe out the sale of live people's parts a lot more expeditiously than trying to encourage donations.

The logic of capitalism assumes knowledgeable, reasonably intelligent people on both sides of the transaction. Is this where the kidney trade falls short? At $4,400, the poor Turk was probably underpaid for his kidney. But in an open, legal market with protections against exploitation, he might have got more. At some price, the deal would make sense for almost anyone. I have no sentimental attachment to my kidneys. Out of prudence, I'd like to hang on to one of them, but the other is available. My price is $2 million.

Of course, I make this offer safe in the knowledge that there will always be some poor Turk ready to undercut me. So maybe, because of who the sellers inevitably will be, the sale of kidneys is by its very nature exploitation. A father shouldn't have to sacrifice a kidney to get a necessary operation for his daughter. Unfortunately, banning the kidney sale won't solve the problem of paying for the operation. Nor can the world yet afford expensive operations for everyone who needs one. And leaving aside the melodrama of the daughter's operation, we don't stop people from doing things to support their families—working in coal mines, for example—that reduce their life expectancies more than would the loss of a kidney. In fact, there are places in the Third World where even $4,400 can do more for a person's own life expectancy than a spare kidney.

The horror of kidney sales, in short, is a sentimental reaction to the injustice of life—injustice that the transaction highlights but does not increase. This is not a complaint. In fact, it may even be the best reason for a ban on such transactions. That kind of sentiment ought to be encouraged.

# Ethics of Paid Organ Donation

## Kishore D. Phadke and Urmila Anandh

Kishore Phadke and Urmila Anandh observe that, although organ sales are prohibited in all countries, society in general has shifted toward regarding transplant organs as commodities that can be bought. In developing countries like India, laws against organ sales are not enforced, and the practice has popular support. The authors call for the medical profession to refuse to be a part of "this unscrupulous trade," which exploits the poor, discourages altruistic giving, commercializes the body, and undercuts human dignity.

## Introduction

Paid organ donors are the most prevalent source of kidney donors in India at present. Though no official transplant registries exist, it is estimated that more than 60% of kidney donations are paid. Organ donation, specifically paid organ donation, in a developing country such as India raises many ethical and moral issues. It also hampers the development of a viable living-related and cadaver organ donor program. In India, where there are strong family ties, organ donation, especially for children from living relatives, is negatively influenced by the availability of paid donors. India, which is on the threshold of scientific and medical achievements, is a country of many contrasts—the most striking being the stark financial and social inequalities. Because of this, organ donation is often unrelated and paid for despite the legislation banning "Commerce in Transplantation" (Human Organ Transplantation Act, Government of India, 1994), making it a criminal offense. There are instances of alleged removal of organs without the knowledge of the donor and exploitation of the donor by the "middleman."[1] Also, there have been reports in the medical literature of multiple complications in the recipients, including life threatening infection.[2] By and large, unrelated donors are commercial paid donors. Often the true history of these donors is hidden. Their general health is poorer. Reliable data about these transplants do not exist. Despite the existing problems, there have always been strong proponents of paid organ donation, often raising issues of great concern.[3] The concept of paid organ donation is not limited to India, but is prevalent in many other developing countries. The developed world is also witnessing a tendency towards drifting into the marketing of organs.[4, 5]

There is a universal consensus that in living-related organ donation, the benefits of organ donation far outweigh the risk to the donor. There has been adequate evidence to suggest that kidney donation is medically safe.[6] Although there is pain, anxiety and some risk involved with the nephrectomy procedure, the benefits to the recipient and the psychological, spiritual, and emotional advantage to the donor, along

From *Pediatric Nephrology* May 2002, Vol. 17, pp. 309–311.

with the fact that kidney donation increases self-esteem,[7] justify the act of kidney donation. What is more important, is that the donor has made an informed decision, with a clear understanding of the risks and benefits, to donate his/her kidney, based on altruistic motives and not on coercion. Thus, in living-related kidney donations, the principle of non-maleficence is outweighed by other tenets of ethics, namely autonomy and beneficence.

The perspective changes when we talk about selling or vending the organ, considering the organ as marketable commodity in contrast to giving the organ as a gift. As the waiting list of patients requiring organ transplantation grows, there is a subtle but noticeable shift in society towards accepting organs as a commodity, which can be paid for. In the next few paragraphs, we discuss arguments for and against paid organ donation.

## The Issue of Altruism and Autonomy

It is argued that as altruism has failed to supply enough organs, resulting in many patients waiting for a kidney, the option of paid organ donation should be explored. Maybe the sale of body parts is a necessary social evil and hence our concerns should focus not on some philosophic imperative such as altruism, but on our collective responsibility of maximizing life-saving organ recovery.[8]

However, the above argument appears at once as an easy way out with tremendous moral and ethical implications for society. By advocating financial incentives (it is difficult to fix a price), a deliberate conflict is created between altruism and self-interest, reducing freedom to make a gift. The concept that human organs are spare parts that can be bought and sold can adversely influence respect for the human body and human dignity. It puts organ sale in the same category of paid human body transactions as prostitution and slavery.[9] When organs are "thingified," these marketing practices can lead to serious erosion of cherished values in society. This issue has been highlighted in Iran, where the selling of organs is allowed. It has been shown that in almost all instances, the donor–recipient relationship becomes pathological. Fifty-one percent of donors hated the recipients and 82% were unsatisfied with their behavior.[10] Some sections of society may be treated as saleable commodities rather than as human beings. The medical profession compromises its deontological commitments (that all individuals have a value beyond price) by adopting a mainly utilitarian ethic (maximizing the good for the largest number).[11] The medical profession also has a moral obligation to use its influence to change the cultural behavior of society. For example, if female feticide is the cultural behavior of society, the medical profession, instead of accepting it, should make active efforts to bring about a behavioral change in society. It should be remembered that, once a moral barrier is broken, it is difficult to contain abuses in society, even by regulation or law.

On the face of it, the act of selling an organ may seem justifiable on the principle of autonomy. However, it should be noted that human autonomy has limitations. This is because "no man is an island entire of itself; every man is a piece of the continent, a part of the main." The act of selling should be considered as arising out of narcissism—too much self-focussing rather than mere execution of autonomy.

It is usually the poor who donate and poverty is perhaps the most significant factor in making a person vulnerable to coercion.[12]

Since the consent for kidney sale can be considered to be under coercion, it cannot be accepted as a valid consent.

### Can and Should Paid Organ Donation Be Regulated?

It has been suggested that the concerns relating to malfunction of the organ trade, such as exploitation by middlemen or brokers, may be addressed organizationally through a centralized coordinated organ bank or "National Commission for Kidney Purchase—NCKP."[7]

Rewarded gifting or compensation (tax rebates, burial grants, future medical coverage, tuition subsidies for children) to the donors has been suggested. Although paid organ donation in an ideal situation (i.e. without exploitation, with justice to everyone and transparent) may be acceptable, we have reservations as to whether the regulation and implementation of regulatory law on this subject is a possibility at all in a developing country such as India. In many developing countries, including India, a great degree of societal and governmental dysfunction exists. Rampant corruption colors almost every monetary transaction. Vigilance against wrong and unjust practices in relation to the existent laws is grossly inadequate. Sufficient legal resources, checks, controls and balances for such a system to keep it from getting on the slippery slope of commercialism do not exist. The boundaries between pure compensation and incentives for organ donation with potential for inducement, manipulation, coercion and exploitation will be difficult to define and monitor in developing countries. Only the rich who can afford to buy kidneys will derive benefits, thus violating the principle of justice. Organ donation will be practiced with a neglect of beliefs, sentiments and emotions. It will be practiced in backstreet clinics without adequate facilities for postoperative care.[13] This practice will only enhance high morbidity and mortality among recipients who have bought living-unrelated donor kidneys.[14] The slippery slope of commercialism is no ethical illusion but a recurrent reality in India.

Cadaver organ transplantation is in its infancy in the developing world, and, legalizing paid organ donation will kill the cadaver program without any increase in the number of transplants.[15,16]

Also, paid organ donation should not be looked upon as a measure of alleviating the poverty of individuals. There are 3.5 billion poor people worldwide and there are better ways to address poverty issues, which include providing fresh drinking water, adequate sewage facilities, and immunization programs.

### Are the Issues Different in the Developed World?

We feel it is logical to think that universalistic ethics promoting human life and dignity transcend time, space, national boundaries and boundaries of social circumstances. The differences in expression of fundamental ethical principles merely reflect inequities in resources between first and third world countries. Complex modes of moral reasoning and considerations of ethics of rights, as well as social responsibilities, everywhere should guide the practice of modern medicine everywhere. The regulatory forces may be considered to be better developed in the developed world, making regulated sale of organs an achievable proposition. It is suggested though, that the principle of minimizing ethical risk should be pursued, wherein, promotion of living-related donor programs, cadaver programs and xenotransplantation should be explored to the fullest extent before embarking on commercialization of transplantation. The business nature of organ donation and neglect of altruism will alter the attitudes of society towards medical professionals, with the development of suspicion and loss of respect. This may be considered an unhealthy trend.

## Conclusions

The question of organ shortage and the problem of patients awaiting the availability of organs will continue to exist. Offering paid organ donation as a solution to this problem raises many ethical and moral issues. WHO guidelines issued in 1989 clearly state that "commercialization of human organs and tissues should be prevented, if necessary by penal sanctions. National and International measures should be adopted to prevent the utilization of organs and tissues obtained through the exploitation of the economic needs of the donor or their relatives." As of now, no regulatory body has endorsed paid organ donation. The organ trade is likely to take unfair advantage of poor people and poor countries. Paid organ donation will exploit the poor, commercialize the human body, deter altruism, and retard the progress of living-related, cadaver and animal organ donor programs. In a society that acknowledges gift giving and resource sharing, there is no place for organ marketing. "Even if it is banned, it will go on anyway" is a very inadequate reason to support it. It is high time that health professionals stop turning a blind eye, becoming accomplices to the unscrupulous and illegal organ trade. It is our plea that the medical community, ethicists, etc., address the issue in its totality before they think of legalizing the organ trade.

## References

1. Chugh KS, Jha V (1996) Commerce in transplantation in third world countries. Kidney Int 49:1181–1186

2. Sever MS, Ecer T, Ayedin AE, Turkman A, Kallicallan I, Uysal V, Erakay H. Calangu S, Carin M, Eldegez U (1994) Living unre-

lated (unpaid) kidney transplantation in third world countries: high risk of complications besides the ethical problem. Nephrol Dial Transplant 9:350–354

3. Radcliffe R, Daar AS, Guttman RD, Hoffenberg R, Kennedy I, Lock M, Sells RA, Tilney N (1998) The case for allowing kidney sales: International forum for transplant ethics. Lancet 351: 1951–1952

4. Cameron JS, Hoffenberg R (1999) Ethics and the International Society of Nephrology: paid organ donation and the use of executed prisoners as donors. Kidney Int 55:724–732

5. Miller RB (1999) Ethics of paid organ donation and the use of executed prisoners as donors: a dialectic with Professors Cameron and Hoffenberg. Kidney Int 55:733–737

6. Ferhman-Ekholm I, Elinder C, Stenbeck M, Tyden G, Growth C (1997) Kidney donors live longer. Transplantation 64:976–978

7. Wesley L, Fauchald P, Talseth T, Jacobson A, Flatmark A (1993) Donors enjoy more self-esteem. Nephrol Dial Transplant 8:1146–1148

8. Thomas GP (1991) Life or death: the issue of payment in cadaver organ donation. JAMA 265:1302–1305

9. Levine DJ (2000) Kidney vending: yes or no; Nephrology Ethics Forum. Am J Kidney Dis 35:1002–1018

10. Zargooshi J (2001) Iranian kidney donors: motivations and relations with recipients. J Urol 165:386–392

11. Veatch RM (2000) An ethical framework. In: Veatch RM (ed) Transplantation ethics. Georgetown University Press, Washington, USA, pp 28–39

12. Marshall PA, Thomasma DC, Daar AS (1996) Market human organs: the autonomy paradox. Theor Med 17:1–18

13. Chugh KS, Jha V (2000) Problems and outcome of living unrelated donor transplants in the developing countries. Kidney Int 57: Suppl 74:S131–S135

14. Salahudeen AK, Woods HF, Pingle A, Nur-El-Huda-Suleyman A, Shakuntal K, Nandakumar M, Yahya TM, Daar AS (1990) High mortality among recipients of bought living unrelated donor kidneys. Lancet 336:725–728

15. Thiel G (1997) Emotionally related living kidney donation: pros and cons. Nephrol Dial Transplant 12:1820–1824

16. Braumand B (1999) Living donors: the Iran experience. Nephrol Dial Transplant 12:1830–1831

---

**READINGS**

## Section 3: Allocating Transplant Organs

## The Prostitute, the Playboy, and the Poet: Rationing Schemes for Organ Transplantation

### George J. Annas

George Annas takes a position on transplant selection that introduces a modification of the first-come, first-served principle. He reviews four approaches to rationing scarce medical resources—market, selection committee, lottery, and customary—and finds each has disadvantages so serious as to make them all unacceptable. An acceptable approach, he suggests, is one that combines efficiency, fairness, and a respect for the value of life. Because candidates should both want a transplant and be able to derive significant benefits from one, the first phase of selection should involve a screening process that is based exclusively on medical criteria that are objective and as free as possible of judgments about social worth.

Since selection might still have to be made from this pool of candidates, it might be done by social-worth criteria or by lottery. However, social-worth criteria seem arbitrary, and a lottery would be unfair to those who are in more immediate need of a transplant—ones who might die quickly without it. After reviewing the relevant considerations, a committee operating at this stage might allow those in immediate need of a transplant to be moved to the head of a waiting list. To those not in immediate need, organs would be distributed in a first-come, first-served fashion. Although absolute equality is not embodied in this process, the procedure is sufficiently flexible to recognize that some may have needs that are greater (more immediate) than others.

In the public debate about the availability of heart and liver transplants, the issue of rationing on a massive scale has been credibly raised for the first time in United States medical care. In an era of scarce resources, the eventual arrival of such a discussion was, of course, inevitable.[1] Unless we decide to ban heart and liver transplantation, or make them available to everyone, some rationing scheme must be used to choose among potential transplant candidates. The debate has existed throughout the history of medical ethics. Traditionally it has been stated as a choice between saving one of two patients, both of whom require the immediate assistance of the only available physician to survive.

National attention was focused on decisions regarding the rationing of kidney dialysis machines when they were first used on a limited basis in the late 1960s. As one commentator described the debate within the medical profession:

> "Shall machines or organs go to the sickest, or to the ones with most promise of recovery; on a first-come, first-served basis; to the most 'valuable' patient (based on wealth, education, position, what?); to the one with the most dependents; to women and children first; to those who can pay; to whom? Or should lots be cast, impersonally and uncritically?"[2]

In Seattle, Washington, an anonymous screening committee was set up to pick who among competing candidates would receive the life-saving technology. One lay member of the screening committee is quoted as saying:

Reprinted by permission of the author and *The American Journal of Public Health*, Vol. 75, no. 2, 1985, pp. 187–189.

> "The choices were hard . . . I remember voting against a young woman who was a known prostitute. I found I couldn't vote for her, rather than another candidate, a young wife and mother. I also voted against a young man who, until he learned he had renal failure, had been a ne'er do-well, a real playboy. He promised he would reform his character, go back to school, and so on, if only he were selected for treatment. But I felt I'd lived long enough to know that a person like that won't really do what he was promising at the time."[3]

When the biases and selection criteria of the committee were made public, there was a general negative reaction against this type of arbitrary device. Two experts reacted to the "numbing accounts of how close to the surface lie the prejudices and mindless cliches that pollute the committee's deliberations," by concluding that the committee was "measuring persons in accordance with its own middle-class values." The committee process, they noted, ruled out "creative nonconformists" and made the Pacific Northwest "no place for a Henry David Thoreau with bad kidneys."[4]

To avoid having to make such explicit, arbitrary, "social worth" determinations, the Congress, in 1972, enacted legislation that provided federal funds for virtually all kidney dialysis and kidney transplantation procedures in the United States.[5] This decision, however, simply served to postpone the time when identical decisions will have to be made about candidates for heart and liver transplantation in a society that does not provide sufficient financial and medical resources to provide all "suitable" candidates with the operations.

There are four major approaches to rationing scarce medical resources: the market approach; the selection committee approach; the lottery approach; and the "customary" approach.[1]

## The Market Approach

The market approach would provide an organ to everyone who could pay for it with their own funds or private insurance. It puts a very high value on individual rights, and a very low value on equality and fairness. It has properly been criticized on a number of bases, including that the transplant technologies have been developed and are supported with public funds, that medical resources used for transplantation will not be available for higher priority care, and that financial success alone is an insufficient justification for demanding a medical procedure. Most telling is its complete lack of concern for fairness and equity.[6]

A "bake sale" or charity approach that requires the less financially fortunate to make public appeals for funding is demeaning to the individuals involved, and to society as a whole. Rationing by financial ability says we do not believe in equality, but believe that a price can and should be placed on human life and that it should be paid by the individual whose life is at stake. Neither belief is tolerable in a society in which income is inequitably distributed.

## The Committee Selection Process

The Seattle Selection Committee is a model of the committee process. Ethics Committees set up in some hospitals to decide whether or not certain handicapped newborn infants should be given medical care may represent another.[7] These committees have developed because it was seen as unworkable or unwise to explicitly set forth the criteria on which selection decisions would be made. But only two results are possible, as Professor Guido Calabresi has pointed out: either a pattern of decision-making will develop or it will not. If a pattern does develop (e.g., in Seattle, the imposition of middle-class values), then it can be articulated and those decision "rules" codified and used directly, without resort to the committee. If a pattern does not develop, the committee is vulnerable to the charge that it is acting arbitrarily, or dishonestly, and therefore cannot be permitted to continue to make such important decisions.[1]

In the end, public designation of a committee to make selection decisions on vague criteria will fail because it too closely involves the state and all members of society in explicitly preferring specific individuals over others, and in devaluing the interests those others have in living. It thus directly undermines, as surely as the market system does, society's view of equality and the value of human life.

## The Lottery Approach

The lottery approach is the ultimate equalizer which puts equality ahead of every other value. This makes it extremely attractive, since all comers have an equal chance at selection regardless of race, color, creed, or financial status. On the other hand, it offends our notions of efficiency and fairness since it makes no distinctions among such things as the strength of the desires of the candidates, their potential survival, and their quality of life. In this sense it is a mindless method of trying to solve society's dilemma which is caused by its unwillingness or inability to spend enough resources to make a lottery unnecessary. By making this macro spending decision evident to all, it also undermines society's view of the pricelessness of human life. A first-come, first-served system is a type of natural lottery since referral to a transplant program is generally random in time. Nonetheless, higher income groups have quicker access to referral networks and thus have an inherent advantage over the poor in a strict first-come, first-served system.[8,9]

## The Customary Approach

Society has traditionally attempted to avoid explicitly recognizing that we are making a choice not to save individuals lives because it is too expensive to do so. As long as such decisions are not explicitly acknowledged, they can be tolerated by society. For example, until recently there was said to be a general understanding among general practitioners in Britain that individuals over age 55 suffering from end-stage kidney disease not be referred for dialysis or transplant. In 1984, however, this unwritten practice became highly publicized, with figures that showed a rate of new cases of end-stage kidney disease treated in Britain at 40 per million (versus the US figure of 80 per million) resulting in 1500–3000 "unnecessary deaths" annually.[10] This has, predictably, led to movements to enlarge the National Health Service budget to expand dialysis services to meet this need, a more socially acceptable solution than permitting the now publicly recognized situation to continue.

In the U.S., the customary approach permits individual physicians to select their patients on the basis of medical criteria or clinical suitability. This, however, contains much hidden social worth criteria. For example, one criterion, common in the transplant literature, requires an individual to have sufficient family support for successful aftercare. This discriminates against individuals without families and those who have become alienated from their families. The criterion may be relevant, but it is hardly medical.

Similar observations can be made about medical criteria that include IQ, mental illness, criminal records, employment, indigence, alcoholism, drug addiction, or geographical location. Age is perhaps more difficult, since it may be impressionistically related to outcome. But it is not medically logical to assume that an individual who is 49 years old is necessarily a better medical candidate for a transplant than one who is 50 years old. Unless specific examination of the characteristics of older persons that make them less desirable candidates is undertaken, such a cut off is arbitrary, and thus devalues the lives of older citizens. The same can be said of blanket exclusions of alcoholics and drug addicts.

In short, the customary approach has one great advantage for society and one great disadvantage: it gives us the illusion that we do not have to make choices; but the cost is mass deception, and when this deception is uncovered, we must deal with it either by universal entitlement or by choosing another method of patient selection.

## A Combination of Approaches

A socially acceptable approach must be fair, efficient, and reflective of important social values. The most important values at stake in organ transplantation are fairness itself, equity in the sense of equality, and the value of life. To promote efficiency, it is important that no one receive a transplant unless they want one and are likely to obtain significant benefit from it in the sense of years of life at a reasonable level of functioning.

Accordingly, it is appropriate for there to be an initial screening process that is based *exclusively* on medical criteria designed to measure the probability of a successful transplant, i.e., one in which the patient survives for at least a number of years and is rehabilitated. There is room in medical criteria for social worth judgments, but there is probably no way to avoid this completely. For example, it has been noted that "in many respects social and medical criteria are inextricably intertwined" and that therefore medical criteria might "exclude the poor and disadvantaged because health and socioeconomic status are highly interdependent."[11] Roger Evans gives an example. In the End Stage Renal Disease Program, "those of lower socio-

economic status are likely to have multiple comorbid health conditions such as diabetes, hepatitis, and hypertension" making them both less desirable candidates and more expensive to treat.[11]

To prevent the gulf between the haves and have nots from widening, we must make every reasonable attempt to develop medical criteria that are objective and independent of social worth categories. One minimal way to approach this is to require that medical screening be reviewed and approved by an ethics committee with significant public representation, filed with a public agency, and made readily available to the public for comment. In the event that more than one hospital in a state or region is offering a particular transplant service, it would be most fair and efficient for the individual hospitals to perform the initial medical screening themselves (based on the uniform, objective criteria), but to have all subsequent nonmedical selection done by a method approved by a single selection committee composed of representatives of all hospitals engaged in a particular transplant procedure, as well as significant representation of the public at large.

As this implies, after the medical screening is performed, there may be more acceptable candidates in the "pool" than there are organs or surgical teams to go around. Selection among waiting candidates will then be necessary. This situation occurs now in kidney transplantation, but since the organ matching is much more sophisticated than in hearts and livers (permitting much more precise matching of organ and recipient), and since dialysis permits individuals to wait almost indefinitely for an organ without risking death, the situations are not close enough to permit use of the same matching criteria. On the other hand, to the extent that organs are specifically tissue- and size-matched and fairly distributed to the best matched candidate, the organ distribution system itself will resemble a natural lottery.

When a pool of acceptable candidates is developed, a decision about who gets the next available, suitable organ must be made. We must choose between using a conscious, value-laden, social worth selection criterion (including a committee to make the actual choice), or some type of random device. In view of the unacceptability and arbitrariness of social worth criteria being applied, implicitly or explicitly, by committee, this method is neither viable nor proper. On the other hand, strict adherence to a lottery might create a situation where an individual who has only a one-in-four chance of living five years with a transplant (but who could survive another six months without one) would get an organ before an individual who could survive as long or longer, but who will die within days or hours if he or she is not immediately transplanted. Accordingly, the reasonable approach seems to be to allocate organs on a first-come, first-served basis to members of the pool but permit individuals to "jump" the queue if the second level selection committee believes they are in immediate danger of death (but still have a reasonable prospect for long-term survival with a transplant) and the person who would otherwise get the organ can survive long enough to be reasonably assured that he or she will be able to get another organ.

The first-come, first-served method of basic selection (after a medical screen) seems the preferred method because it most closely approximates the randomness of a straight lottery without the obviousness of making equity the only promoted value. Some unfairness is introduced by the fact that the more wealthy and medically astute will likely get into the pool first, and thus be ahead in line, but this advantage should decrease sharply as public awareness of the system grows. The possibility of unfairness is also inherent in permitting individuals to jump the queue, but some flexibility needs to be retained in the system to permit it to respond to reasonable contingencies.

We will have to face the fact that should the resources devoted to organ transplantation be limited (as they are now and are likely to be in the future), at some point it is likely that significant numbers of individuals will die in the pool waiting for a transplant. Three things can be done to avoid this: (1) medical criteria can be made stricter, perhaps by adding a more rigorous notion of "quality" of life to longevity and prospects for rehabilitation; (2) resources devoted to transplantation and organ procurement can be increased; or (3) individuals can be persuaded not to attempt to join the pool.

Of these three options, only the third has the promise of both conserving resources and promoting autonomy. While most persons medically eligible for a transplant would probably want one, some would not—at least if they understood all that was involved, including the need for a lifetime commitment to daily immunosuppression medications, and periodic medical monitoring for rejection symptoms. Accordingly, it makes public policy sense to publicize the risks and side effects of transplantation, and to require careful explanations of the procedure be given to prospective patients before they undergo medical screening. It is likely that by the time patients come to the transplant center they have made up their minds and would do

almost anything to get the transplant. Nonetheless, if there are patients who, when confronted with all the facts, would voluntarily elect not to proceed, we enhance both their own freedom and the efficiency and cost-effectiveness of the transplantation system by screening them out as early as possible.

## Conclusion

Choices among patients that seem to condemn some to death and give others an opportunity to survive will always be tragic. Society has developed a number of mechanisms to make such decisions more acceptable by camouflaging them. In an era of scarce resources and conscious cost containment, such mechanisms will become public, and they will be usable only if they are fair and efficient. If they are not so perceived, we will shift from one mechanism to another in an effort to continue the illusion that tragic choices really don't have to be made, and that we can simultaneously move toward equity of access, quality of services, and cost containment without any challenges to our values. Along with the prostitute, the playboy, and the poet, we all need to be involved in the development of an access model to extreme and expensive medical technologies with which we can live.

## Notes

1.  Calabresi G, Bobbitt P: *Tragic Choices*. New York: Norton, 1978.

2.  Fletcher J: Our shameful waste of human tissue. In: Cutler DR (ed): *The Religious Situation*. Boston: Beacon Press, 1969; 223–252.

3.  Quoted in Fox R, Swazey J: *The Courage to Fail*. Chicago: Univ of Chicago Press, 1974; 232.

4.  Sanders & Dukeminier: Medical advance and legal lag: haemodialysis and kidney transplantation. *UCLA L Rev* 1968; 15: 357.

5.  Rettig RA: The policy debate on patient care financing for victims of end stage renal disease. *Law & Contemporary Problems* 1976; 40: 196.

6.  President's Commission for the Study of Ethical Problems in Medicine: *Securing Access to Health Care*. US Govt Printing Office, 1983; 25.

7.  Annas GJ: Ethics committees on neonatal care: substantive protection or procedural diversion? *Am J Public Health* 1984; 74: 843–845.

8.  Bayer R: Justice and health care in an era of cost containment: allocating scarce medical resources. *Soc Responsibility* 1984; 9: 37–52.

9.  Annas GJ: Allocation of artificial hearts in the year 2002: *Minerva v National Health Agency. Am J Law Med* 1977; 3: 59–76.

10. Commentary: UK's poor record in treatment of renal failure. *Lancet*, July 7, 1984; 53.

11. Evans R: Health care technology and the inevitability of resource allocation and rationing decisions, Part 11. *JAMA* 1983; 249: 2208, 2217.

# Alcoholics and Liver Transplantation

Carl Cohen, Martin Benjamin, and the Ethics and Social Impact Committee of the Transplant and Health Policy Center, Ann Arbor, Michigan

Carl Cohen, Martin Benjamin, and their associates examine the moral and medical arguments for excluding alcoholics as candidates for liver transplants and conclude that neither kind of argument justifies a categorical exclusion.

The moral argument holds that alcoholics are morally blameworthy for their condition. Thus, when resources are scarce, it is preferable to favor an equally sick nonblameworthy person over a blameworthy one. The authors maintain that if this argument were sound, it would require physicians to examine the moral character of all patients before allocating scarce resources. But this is not feasible, and such a policy could not be administered fairly by the medical profession.

The medical argument holds that because of their bad habits, alcoholics have a lower success rate with transplants. Hence, scarce organs should go to others more likely to benefit. The authors agree that the likelihood of someone following a treatment regimen should be considered, but they maintain that the consideration must be given case by case.

We permit transplants in cases where the prognosis is the same or worse, and the categorical exclusion of alcoholics is unfair. We cannot justify discrimination on the grounds of alleged self-abuse, "unless we are prepared to develop a detailed calculus of just deserts for health care based on good conduct."

Alcoholic cirrhosis of the liver—severe scarring due to the heavy use of alcohol—is by far the major cause of end-stage liver disease.[1] For persons so afflicted, life may depend on receiving a new, transplanted liver. The number of alcoholics in the United States needing new livers is great, but the supply of available livers for transplantation is small. *Should those whose end-stage liver disease was caused by alcohol abuse be categorically excluded from candidacy for liver transplantation?* This question, partly medical and partly moral, must now be confronted forthrightly. Many lives are at stake.

Reasons of two kinds underlie a widespread unwillingness to transplant livers into alcoholics: First, there is a common conviction—explicit or tacit—that alcoholics are morally blameworthy, their condition the result of their own misconduct, and that such blameworthiness disqualifies alcoholics in unavoidable competition for organs with others equally sick but blameless. Second, there is a common belief that because of their habits, alcoholics will not exhibit satisfactory survival rates after transplantation, and that,

From *JAMA*, March 13, 1991, Vol. 265, pp. 1299–1301. Reprinted by permission.

therefore, good stewardship of a scarce lifesaving resource requires that alcoholics not be considered for liver transplantation. We examine both of these arguments.

## The Moral Argument

A widespread condemnation of drunkenness and a revulsion for drunks lie at the heart of this public policy issue. Alcoholic cirrhosis—unlike other causes of end-stage liver disease—is brought on by a person's conduct, by heavy drinking. Yet if the dispute here were only about whether to treat someone who is seriously ill because of personal conduct, we would not say—as we do not in cases of other serious diseases resulting from personal conduct—that such conduct disqualifies a person from receiving desperately needed medical attention. Accident victims injured because they were not wearing seat belts are treated without hesitation; reformed smokers who become coronary bypass candidates partly because they disregarded their physicians' advice about tobacco, diet, and exercise are not turned away because of their bad habits. But new livers are a scarce resource, and transplanting a liver into an alcoholic may, therefore, result in death for a competing candidate whose liver disease was wholly beyond his or her control. Thus we seem driven, in this case unlike in others, to reflect on the weight given to the patient's personal conduct. And heavy drinking—unlike smoking, or overeating, or failing to wear a seat belt—is widely regarded as morally wrong.

Many contend that alcoholism is not a moral failing but a disease. Some authorities have recently reaffirmed this position, asserting that alcoholism is "best regarded as a chronic disease."[2] But this claim cannot be firmly established and is far from universally believed. Whether alcoholism is indeed a disease, or a moral failing, or both, remains a disputed matter surrounded by intense controversy.[3-9]

Even if it is true that alcoholics suffer from a somatic disorder, many people will argue that this disorder results in deadly liver disease only when coupled with a weakness of will—a weakness for which part of the blame must fall on the alcoholic. This consideration underlies the conviction that the alcoholic needing a transplanted liver, unlike a nonalcoholic competing for the same liver, is at least partly responsible for his or her need. Therefore, some conclude, the alcoholic's personal failing is rightly considered in deciding upon his or her entitlement to this very scarce resource.

Is this argument sound? We think it is not. Whether alcoholism is a moral failing, in whole or in part, remains uncertain. But even if we suppose that it is, it does not follow that we are justified in categorically denying liver transplants to those alcoholics suffering from end-stage cirrhosis. We could rightly preclude alcoholics from transplantation only if we assume that qualification for a new organ requires some level of moral virtue or is canceled by some level of moral vice. But there is absolutely no agreement—and there is likely to be none—about what constitutes moral virtue and vice and what rewards and penalties they deserve. The assumption that undergirds the moral argument for precluding alcoholics is thus unacceptable. Moreover, even if we could agree (which, in fact, we cannot) upon the kind of misconduct we would be looking for, the fair weighting of such a consideration would entail highly intrusive investigations into patients' moral habits—investigations universally thought repugnant. Moral evaluation is wisely and rightly excluded from all deliberations of who should be treated and how.

Indeed, we do exclude it. We do not seek to determine whether a particular transplant candidate is an abusive parent or a dutiful daughter, whether candidates cheat on their income taxes or their spouses,

or whether potential recipients pay their parking tickets or routinely lie when they think it is in their best interests. We refrain from considering such judgments for several good reasons: (1) We have genuine and well-grounded doubts about comparative degrees of voluntariness and, therefore, *cannot pass judgment fairly.* (2) Even if we could assess degrees of voluntariness reliably, we *cannot know what penalties different degrees of misconduct deserve.* (3) *Judgments of this kind could not be made consistently in our medical system*—and a fundamental requirement of a fair system in allocating scarce resources is that it treat all in need of certain goods on the same standard, without unfair discrimination by group.

If alcoholics should be penalized because of their moral fault, then all others who are equally at fault in causing their own medical needs should be similarly penalized. To accomplish this, we would have to make vigorous and sustained efforts to find out whose conduct has been morally weak or sinful and to what degree. That inquiry, as a condition for medical care or for the receipt of goods in short supply, we certainly will not and should not undertake.

The unfairness of such moral judgments is compounded by other accidental factors that render moral assessment especially difficult in connection with alcoholism and liver disease. Some drinkers have a greater predisposition for alcohol abuse than others. And for some who drink to excess, the predisposition to cirrhosis is also greater; many grossly intemperate drinkers do not suffer grievously from liver disease. On the other hand, alcohol consumption that might be considered moderate for some may cause serious liver disease in others. It turns out, in fact, that the disastrous consequences of even low levels of alcohol consumption may be much more common in women than in men.[10] Therefore, penalizing cirrhotics by denying them transplant candidacy would have the effect of holding some groups arbitrarily to a higher standard than others and would probably hold women to a higher standard of conduct than men.

Moral judgments that eliminate alcoholics from candidacy thus prove unfair and unacceptable. The alleged (but disputed) moral misconduct of alcoholics with end-stage liver disease does not justify categorically excluding them as candidates for liver transplantation.

## Medical Argument

Reluctance to use available livers in treating alcoholics is due in some part to the conviction that, because alcoholics would do poorly after transplant as a result of their bad habits, good stewardship of organs in short supply requires that alcoholics be excluded from consideration.

This argument also fails, for two reasons: First, it fails because the premise—that the outcome for alcoholics will invariably be poor relative to other groups—is at least doubtful and probably false. Second, it fails because, even if the premise were true, it could serve as a good reason to exclude alcoholics only if it were an equally good reason to exclude other groups having a prognosis equally bad or worse. But equally low survival rates have not excluded other groups; fairness therefore requires that this group not be categorically excluded either.

In fact, the data regarding the post-transplant histories of alcoholics are not yet reliable. Evidence gathered in 1984 indicated that the 1-year survival rate for patients with alcoholic cirrhosis was well below the survival rate for other recipients of liver transplants, excluding those with cancer.[11] But a 1988 report, with a larger (but still small) sample number, shows remarkably good results in alcoholics receiving transplants: 1-year survival is 73.2%—and of 35 carefully selected (and possibly nonrepresentative) alcoholics who received transplants and lived 6 months or longer, only two relapsed into alcohol abuse.[12] Liver transplantation, it would appear, can be a very sobering experience. Whether this group continues to do as well as a comparable group of nonalcoholic liver recipients remains uncertain. But the data, although not supporting the broad inclusion of alcoholics, do suggest that medical considerations do not now justify categorically excluding alcoholics from liver transplantation.

A history of alcoholism is of great concern when considering liver transplantation, not only because of the impact of alcohol abuse upon the entire system of the recipient, but also because the life of an alcoholic tends to be beset by general disorder. Returning to heavy drinking could ruin a new liver, although probably not for years. But relapse into heavy drinking would quite likely entail the inability to maintain the routine of multiple medication, daily or twice-daily, essential for immunosuppression and survival. As a class, alcoholic cirrhotics may therefore prove to have substantially lower survival rates after receiving transplants. All such matters should be weighed, of course. But none of them gives any solid reason to exclude alcoholics from consideration categorically.

Moreover, even if survival rates for alcoholics selected were much lower than normal—a supposition

now in substantial doubt—what could fairly be concluded from such data? Do we exclude from transplant candidacy members of other groups known to have low survival rates? In fact we do not. Other things being equal, we may prefer not to transplant organs in short supply into patients afflicted, say, with liver cell cancer, knowing that such cancer recurs not long after a new liver is implanted.[13,14] Yet in some individual cases we do it. Similarly, some transplant recipients have other malignant neoplasms or other conditions that suggest low survival probability. Such matters are weighed in selecting recipients, but they are insufficient grounds to categorically exclude an entire group. This shows that the argument for excluding alcoholics based on survival probability rates alone is simply not just.

## The Arguments Distinguished

In fact, the exclusion of alcoholics from transplant candidacy probably results from an intermingling, perhaps at times a confusion, of the moral and medical arguments. But if the moral argument indeed does not apply, no combination of it with probable survival rates can make it applicable. Survival data, carefully collected and analyzed, deserve to be weighed in selecting candidates. These data do not come close to precluding alcoholics from consideration. Judgments of blameworthiness, which ought to be excluded generally, certainly should be excluded when weighing the impact of those survival rates. Some people with a strong antipathy to alcohol abuse and abusers may, without realizing it, be relying on assumed unfavorable data to support a fixed moral judgment. The arguments must be untangled. Actual results with transplanted alcoholics must be considered without regard to moral antipathies.

The upshot is inescapable: there are no good grounds at present—moral or medical—to disqualify a patient with end-stage liver disease from consideration for liver transplantation simply because of a history of heavy drinking.

## Screening and Selection of Liver Transplant Candidates

In the initial evaluation of candidates for any form of transplantation, the central questions are whether patients (1) are sick enough to need a new organ and (2) enjoy a high enough probability of benefiting from this limited resource. At this stage the criteria should be noncomparative.[15,16] Even the initial screening of patients must, however, be done individually and with great care.

The screening process for those suffering from alcoholic cirrhosis must be especially rigorous—not for moral reasons, but because of factors affecting survival, which are themselves influenced by a history of heavy drinking—and even more by its resumption. Responsible stewardship of scarce organs requires that the screening for candidacy take into consideration the manifold impact of heavy drinking on long-term transplant success. Cardiovascular problems brought on by alcoholism and other systematic contraindications must be looked for. Psychiatric and social evaluation is also in order, to determine whether patients understand and have come to terms with their condition and whether they have the social support essential for continuing immunosuppression and follow-up care.

Precisely which factors should be weighed in this screening process have not been firmly established. Some physicians have proposed a specified period of alcohol abstinence as an "objective" criterion for selection—but the data supporting such a criterion are far from conclusive, and the use of this criterion to exclude a prospective recipient is at present medically and morally arbitrary.[17,18]

Indeed, one important consequence of overcoming the strong presumption against considering alcoholics for liver transplantation is the research opportunity it presents and the encouragement it gives to the quest for more reliable predictors of medical success. As that search continues, some defensible guidelines for case-by-case determination have been devised, based on factors associated with sustained recovery from alcoholism and other considerations related to liver transplantation success in general. Such guidelines appropriately include (1) refined diagnosis by those trained in the treatment of alcoholism, (2) acknowledgment by the patient of a serious drinking problem, (3) social and familial stability, and (4) other factors experimentally associated with long-term sobriety.[19]

The experimental use of guidelines like these, and their gradual refinement over time, may lead to more reliable and more generally applicable predictors. But those more refined predictors will never be developed until prejudices against considering alcoholics for liver transplantation are overcome.

Patients who are sick because of alleged self-abuse ought not be grouped for discriminatory treatment—unless we are prepared to develop a detailed calculus of just deserts for health care based on good conduct. Lack of sympathy for those who bring serious disease upon themselves is understandable, but the temptation to institutionalize that emotional response must be tempered by our inability to apply such considerations justly and by our duty *not* to apply them unjustly. In the end, some patients with alcoholic cirrhosis may be judged, after careful evaluation, as good risks for a liver transplant.

## Objection and Reply

Providing alcoholics with transplants may present a special "political" problem for transplant centers. The public perception of alcoholics is generally negative. The already low rate of organ donation, it may be argued, will fall even lower when it becomes known that donated organs are going to alcoholics. Financial support from legislatures may also suffer. One can imagine the effect on transplantation if the public were to learn that the liver of a teenager killed by a drunken driver had been transplanted into an alcoholic patient. If selecting even a few alcoholics as transplant candidates reduces the number of lives saved overall, might that not be good reason to preclude alcoholics categorically?

No. The fear is understandable, but excluding alcoholics cannot be rationally defended on that basis. Irresponsible conduct attributable to alcohol abuse should not be defended. No excuses should be made for the deplorable consequences of drunken behavior, from highway slaughter to familial neglect and abuse. But alcoholism must be distinguished from those consequences; not all alcoholics are morally irresponsible, vicious, or neglectful drunks. If there is a general failure to make this distinction, we must strive to overcome that failure, not pander to it.

Public confidence in medical practice in general, and in organ transplantation in particular, depends on the scientific validity and moral integrity of the policies adopted. Sound policies will prove publicly defensible. Shaping present health care policy on the basis of distorted public perceptions or prejudices will, in the long run, do more harm than good to the process and to the reputation of all concerned.

Approximately one in every 10 Americans is a heavy drinker, and approximately one family in every three has at least one member at risk for alcoholic cirrhosis.[3] The care of alcoholics and the just treatment of them when their lives are at stake are matters a democratic policy may therefore be expected to act on with concern and reasonable judgment over the long run. The allocation of organs in short supply does present vexing moral problems: if thoughtless or shallow moralizing would cause some to respond very negatively to transplanting livers into alcoholic cirrhotics, that cannot serve as good reason to make such moralizing the measure of public policy.

We have argued that there is now no good reason, either moral or medical, to preclude alcoholics categorically from consideration for liver transplantation. We further conclude that it would therefore be unjust to implement that categorical preclusion simply because others might respond negatively if we do not.

### Notes

1. Consensus conference on liver transplantation. NIH. *JAMA.* 1983: 250: 2961–2964.

2. Klerman F. L. Treatment of alcoholism. *N Engl J Med.* 1989: 320: 394–396.

3. Vaillant G. E. *The Natural History of Alcoholism.* Cambridge, Mass: Harvard University Press: 1983.

4. Jellinek E. M. *The Disease Concept of Alcoholism.* New Haven, Conn: College and University Press: 1960.

5. Rose R. M. and Barret J. E., eds. *Alcoholism: Origins and Outcome.* New York, NY: Raven Press: 1988.

6. *Alcohol and Health: Sixth Special Report to the Congress.* Washington, DC: US Dept of Health and Human Services: 1987. DHHS publication ADM 87-1519.

7. Fingarette H. Alcoholism: the mythical disease. *Public Interest.* 1988: 91: 3–22.

8. Madsen W. Thin thinking about heavy drinking. *Public Interest.* 1989: 95: 112–118.

9. Fingarette H. A rejoinder to Madsen. *Public Interest.* 1989: 95: 118–21.

10. Berglund M. Mortality in alcoholics related to clinical state at first admission: a study of 537 deaths. *Acta Psychiatr Scand.* 1984: 70: 407–416.

11. Scharschmidt B. F. Human liver transplantation: analysis of data on 540 patients from four centers. *Hepatology.* 1984: 4: 95–111.

12. Starzl T. E., Van Thiel D., and Tzakis A. G. et al. Orthotopic liver transplantation for alcoholic cirrhosis. *JAMA.* 1988: 260: 2542–2544.

13. Gordon R. D., Iwatsuki S., and Tzakis A. G. et al. The Denver-Pittsburgh Liver Transplant Series. In: Terasaki P. I. ed. *Clinical Transplants.* Los Angeles, Calif: UCLA Tissue-Typing Laboratory: 1987: 43–49.

14. Gordon R. D., Iwatsuki S., and Esquivel C. O. Liver transplantation. In: Cerilli C. I. ed. *Organ Transplantation and Replacement.* Philadelphia, PA: J. B. Lippincott: 1988: 511–534.

15. Childress J. F. Who shall live when not all can live? *Soundings.* 1970: 53: 339–362.

16. Starzl T. E., Gordon R. D., and Tzakis S. et al. Equitable allocation of extrarenal organs: with special reference to the liver. *Transplant Proc.* 1988: 20: 131–138.

17. Schenker S., Perkins H. S., and Sorrell M. F. Should patients with end-stage alcoholic liver disease have a new liver? *Hepatology.* 1990: 11: 314–319.

18. *Allen v. Mansour A.* US District Court for the Eastern District of Michigan. Southern Division. 1986: 86–73429.

19. Beresford T. P., Turcotte J. G., and Merion R. et al. A rational approach to liver transplantation for the alcoholic patient. *Psychosomatics* 1990: 31: 241–254.

---

### Decision Scenario 1

"We think Natasha's got about a 60 percent chance of surviving, if we can transplant her with a lung," Dr. Mary Wicker said. "We've got her listed with UNOS, but the chance of getting a lung in time varies from slight to none."

"Can you use my lungs?" Sara Besinny asked. "She's my only child. I'd give my life for even a 10 percent chance."

"We couldn't take your whole lung," Dr. Wicker said. "That would kill you, and we can't do that. But you may be eligible to donate a segment. Segments have been used successfully at this hospital and elsewhere. But somebody needs to talk to you about the risks and make sure you understand what donating a lung segment means."

1. Should Besinny be allowed to risk her life, if the chance Natasha would be helped is less than fifty-fifty?

2. Why does Munson think we should permit people to become living donors, despite the risks to themselves?

3. Why, in Munson's view, are transplant surgeons not causing harm to living donors by operating on them, even though the point of the surgery is to benefit someone else?

## Decision Scenario 2

"We haven't been able to get in touch with his wife or any family member," nurse Becky Small told Dr. Sam Long. "Dr. Soon has declared him dead, but we've left him on the respirator."

"Call the organ procurement people," Dr. Long said. "Tell them we've got a twenty-four-year-old head-trauma victim with usable heart, kidneys, lungs, and liver, and they should arrange for surgical teams to remove them."

"Don't we have to get the consent of at least somebody in the family?" Becky asked.

"Not anymore," Dr. Long said. "We're operating under the new policy of conscription."

1. What is organ conscription?

2. Why, according to Spital and Erin, is conscription ethically preferable to the present policy of requiring explicit consent?

3. Critics of conscription may object that it involves an unjustified "taking" of organs and thus is a violation of the due process clause of the Constitution. Evaluate this criticism.

4. Why do Spital and Erin think that consent is not "ethically required" for using cadaveric organs?

## Decision Scenario 3

Colin Benton, a British citizen, died in the summer of 1988 of renal disease after a kidney transplant failed. Benton's widow later revealed that the donor kidney had been obtained from a Turkish citizen who traveled to London for the surgery. The kidney donor was paid the equivalent of around $4400. When asked why he had sold the organ, the man explained that he needed the money to pay for medical treatment for his daughter. It was this case that led the British Parliament to outlaw organ sales.

1. On what grounds do Phadke and Anandh consider it wrong for society to allow people to sell organs?

2. What view of selling an organ might be taken by a natural law theorist? For such a theorist, is there a moral distinction between donating a kidney out of benevolence and selling one for financial gain?

3. If a father has no other way to raise money for surgery necessary to preserve the life of his child, would it be morally permissible for him to sell a kidney? Should we hold him morally blameworthy if, given the opportunity, he refused to do so?

4. Is selling one's kidney different in any morally relevant way from selling one's labor under potentially hazardous conditions (for example, mining coal)?

## Decision Scenario 4

The microsurgical team at Benton Public Hospital consisted of twenty-three people. Five were surgeons, three were anesthesiologists, three were internists, two were radiologists, and the remaining members were various sorts of nurses and technicians.

Early Tuesday afternoon on a date late in March, the members of the team that had to be sterile were scrubbing while the others were preparing to start operating on Mr. Hammond Cox. Mr. Cox was a fifty-nine-year-old unmarried African American who worked as a janitor in a large apartment building. While performing his duties Mr. Cox had caught his hand in the mechanism of a commercial trash compactor. The bones of his wrist had been crushed and blood vessels severed.

The head of the team, Dr. Herbert Lagorio, believed it was possible to restore at least partial functioning to Mr. Cox's hand. Otherwise, the hand would have to be amputated.

Mr. Cox had been drunk when it happened. When the police ambulance brought him to the emergency room, he was still so drunk that a decision was made to delay surgery for almost an hour to give him a chance to burn up some of the alcohol he had consumed. As it was, administering anesthesia to Mr. Cox would incur a greater-than-average risk. Furthermore, blood tests had shown that Mr. Cox already suffered from some degree of liver damage. In both short- and long-range terms, Mr. Cox was not a terribly good surgical risk.

Dr. Lagorio was already scrubbed when Dr. Carol Levine, a resident in emergency medicine, had him paged.

"This had better be important," he told her. "I've got a patient prepped and waiting."

"I know," Dr. Levine said. "But they just brought in a thirty-five-year-old white female with a totally severed right hand. She's a biology professor at Columbia and was working late in her lab when some maniac looking for drugs came in and attacked her with a cleaver."

"What shape is the hand in?"

"Excellent. The campus cops were there within minutes, and there was ice in the lab. One of the cops had the good sense to put the hand in a plastic bag and bring it with her."

"Is she in good general health?"

"It seems excellent," Dr. Levine said.

"This is a real problem."

"You can't do two cases at once?"

"No way. We need everybody we've got to do one."

"How about sending her someplace else?"

"No place else is set up to do what has to be done."

"So what are you going to do?"

1. Does a first-come, first-served criterion like that defended by Annas require that Mr. Cox receive the surgery?

2. Do Rescher's guidelines provide a way to make the choice?

3. Can the chance of a successful outcome in each case be used as a criterion without violating the notion that all people are of equal inherent worth?

4. Should the fact that Mr. Cox's injury is the consequence of his own negligence be considered in determining to whom Dr. Lagorio ought to devote his attention? How are Cohen et al. likely to stand on this question?

5. In your view, who should have the potential benefits of the surgery? Give reasons to support your view.

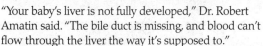

### Decision Scenario 5

"Your baby's liver is not fully developed," Dr. Robert Amatin said. "The bile duct is missing, and blood can't flow through the liver the way it's supposed to."

Clarissa Austin nodded to show she understood something was wrong with her child. She had already made up her mind to do whatever she had to do to see to it that her baby was all right.

"That means the liver can't do its job and that the blood is backing up," Dr. Amatin went on. "Surgery really can't correct a problem like his."

"Can you give him a new liver?"

Dr. Amatin avoided answering the question directly. "A transplant is his best hope," he said. "If we can surgically remove the malformed liver and attach a new one, the baby has a very good chance of living."

"I'll be happy to give my permission, if that's what you're waiting for," Clarrisa said.

"It's not that simple," Dr. Amatin said. He looked uncomfortable. "It really comes down to a matter of money."

"I don't have much money," Clarissa said. "You know I'm on Medicaid, and I don't have any insurance."

"Medicaid will pay for the surgery, but not for an organ, and that's the only way we can get one."

"How much does a liver cost?"

"I've got a family right now that says it wants $15,000 for the liver of their baby. She died this morning."

"I can't get money like that," Clarissa said.

"I can ask them to come up and talk to you. Maybe they would take less, or maybe you could work out some kind of deferred payment with them."

"What if I can't?"

Dr. Amatin shook his head. "I can't arrange for a transplant without an organ that size, and I suspect they will try to find somebody else to sell it to."

"That don't seem fair," Clarissa said. "Just because I haven't got the money, my baby is going to die."

1. Does the possibility of such situations demonstrate that the present policy of relying on donated organs is a superior one?

2. Why do Phadke and Anandh object to selling organs? Do their objections apply to all kinds of organ sales—for example, to a government-regulated market with set prices, as well as to a free market? If it's all right to give away organs, why should it be thought wrong to sell them?

3. What other organ-procurement policy, besides voluntary donation and organ sales, might be worth considering as a means to increase the number of transplant organs available?

4. Is Ms. Austin correct in saying that it would be unfair for her child not to have the organ because she cannot afford to pay the asking price? After all, surely it is not unfair for her child not to have, say, a silver drinking cup because she cannot afford to pay the asking price.

5. On what grounds does Annas object to the market approach? What position might Kinsley take?

6. Phadke and Anandh claim organ sales will promote the "commodification" of the human body. What, if anything, is wrong with that?

---

## Decision Scenario 6

Dr. Sarah Brandywine hurried into Dr. Kline's inner office. Dr. Kline was transplant coordinator at Midwestern General Hospital, and he was expecting her. She had called him for an appointment as soon as she had realized the dimension of the problem with Mr. Wardell.

"So tell me about Mr. Wardell," Dr. Kline said, nodding toward the chair beside his desk.

"He's a fifty-one-year-old man who came to the hospital two days ago because he was frightened by the jaundice and ascites he developed over the course of the last week," Dr. Brandywine said. "He had been experiencing fatigue and loss of appetite several weeks prior to the jaundice. His liver is swollen and lumpy."

"Sounds like cirrhosis," Dr. Kline said. "I'm sure you did liver function tests, but what about a biopsy?"

"We did both yesterday, and I called you right after the final results. There's so much scarring that Mr. Wardell has little liver function left." She shook her head. "I want to put him on the transplant list."

"What's the cause of his disease?"

"It's alcohol induced."

"No way." Dr. Kline shook his head. "No livers for alcoholics. No ifs, ands, or buts about it."

"This is a man with two kids." Dr. Brandywine tried to keep her voice level. "One's twelve, and the other is eight. Their mother died two years ago, and their dad is all they've got left."

"Oh, God, the kids make it particularly sad." Dr. Kline's voice took on a pained expression. "But look, 30,000 people a year die from alcoholic cirrhosis, and we can't treat them all."

"I know we can't, but can't we treat some?" Dr. Brandywine leaned forward. "Is being an alcoholic enough for an automatic turndown?"

"I'm afraid so." Dr. Kline nodded. "These are people who created their own problem. There are far from being enough livers to go around, so it's only fair for us to put folks with problems not of their own making on the list and to leave others off."

"But, look, this guy's got two kids depending on him." Sarah squeezed her hands into fists. "If I can get him into a rehab program, can we promise him the chance at a liver then?" She quickly added. "Not a guaranteed liver, but a chance at one."

"The answer's still no." Dr. Kline paused. "I'm not saying alcoholics can't be reformed, but I am saying they're bad risks. If we give a transplant to somebody whose liver was destroyed by biliary cirrhosis, we're likely to get a good, long-term survival. But if we transplant somebody who's been drinking for the last ten or twenty years, we're not likely to get good, long-term results. The guy may promise to stop drinking, and maybe he'll do it for a while. But chances are good that, within a few years, he's going to be back in the hospital with liver failure again, and alcohol is going to be the cause."

"I admit the numbers are against me." Dr. Brandywine inhaled deeply, then let her breath out in a long whoosh. "There's nothing I can say to convince you?"

"We can't afford to risk wasting a liver," Dr. Kline said. "That's what I've got to convince you of." He shook his head. "It breaks my heart to think about Mr. Wardell's children, but I've got to think about the parents with cirrhosis who aren't alcoholics."

1. State explicitly the two arguments against liver transplants for alcoholics that Dr. Kline invokes.

2. Why should so-called lifestyle factors be considered relevant in making transplant decisions? By the same reasoning, shouldn't we deny heart transplants to people who, through overeating and lack of exercise, have allowed themselves to become fat? Why should alcoholics be held to a higher standard than others needing transplants?

3. How would Cohen et al. respond to Dr. Kline's argument? What might Dr. Kline say in response to their criticisms?

4. If you were responsible for determining whether there would be a categorical exclusion of alcoholics from receiving liver transplants, what would you decide? How would you justify that decision?

Chapter **8**

# Paying for Health Care

## Chapter Contents

## Classic Case Presentation

### *Robert Ingram: Dilemma of the Working Poor*

Robert Ingram (as I'll call him) was fifty-two years old and very worried about himself, a result of two months of having episodes of sharp, stabbing pains on the left side of his chest. When the pains came, he felt cold and sweaty, and although he tried to ignore them, he found he had to stop what he was doing and wait until they passed.

He hadn't mentioned the pains to Jeri, his wife, right at first. He half-expected and half-hoped they would simply go away, but they hadn't. Eventually he'd had to tell her, when the stabbing came at home while he was moving a large upholstered chair with a broken frame out to the trash. She'd seen him put the chair down and put his hand on his chest.

When he told her how long he'd been having the pains, she'd made him call up Lane Clinic for an appointment. He hadn't wanted to miss most of a day's work. He operated Bob's Express, which picked up car and truck parts from the smaller supply houses and delivered them to mechanics and garages within a twenty-mile radius. He'd founded the business only a year ago, after working as a mechanic himself for almost thirty years.

He had hoped to be able to expand, but there weren't as many deliveries to make as he'd counted on. The big supply houses had their own distribution system, and he had to scramble to get business from the wrecking yards and the rebuilders.

He was making enough money to pay the operating expenses and the rent, but not much more. All he had to show for his work was one Chevy Silverado pickup and a ten-year-old Ford station wagon. He had one part-time employee, Phil Archer. Jeri took the phone orders from their home office, and he and Phil made the rounds. He was his own boss, and that's what he and Jeri most liked about the business. He worked hard, but he didn't have to answer to anybody.

On Wednesday, the day of his appointment, he asked Phil to work the whole day. He drove the Ford to the clinic, so he'd be able to go directly from there to Ace Distributors and pick up the shirttail full of parts he knew he had to deliver. If anybody called with more orders for Ace, he could get them too.

Dr. Tran was a short, thin, Asian man who looked young enough to be a teenager. But he seemed to know

exactly what he was doing. He moved the stethoscope over Robert's chest, listening to his heart. He had him walk across the room, then listened to it again.

Dr. Tran asked about Robert's parents and grandparents. Robert told him both grandfathers had died of heart attacks in their late fifties. One of his grandmothers was still alive, but the other had also died of a heart attack.

Then Dr. Tran asked questions about the chest pain. How long had he had it? What did it feel like? How long did it last? Did anything in particular seem to bring it on? Did he ever get it while sleeping? Did it start when he was carrying grocery bags or simply walking? Did the pain seem to radiate down his left arm? Did his arm feel numb? Did the last two fingers tingle?

Robert did his best to answer all the questions, but he didn't see the point to them. He was almost sorry he'd come. It was easy to believe nothing was seriously wrong with him while he was sitting on the edge of the examining table talking to Dr. Tran. He needed to be making his deliveries. Otherwise, Phil would get hopelessly behind. Late deliveries could lose customers.

Dr. Tran finished his examination and asked Robert to get dressed and have a seat in the chair beside the small built-in desk. Dr. Tran left the room for ten minutes or so, then returned. He took the swivel chair beside the desk.

"I'm worried that you may be on the verge of a heart attack," Dr. Tran told Robert. "You may already have had one or more small attacks."

"Wouldn't I have known it?" Robert could hardly believe what he was hearing.

"Not necessarily," Dr. Tran said. "The blood gets blocked for a moment, some tissue dies. You feel pain, then it's over." He paused. "But what concerns me most is that your coronary arteries may be significantly blocked by plaque, and if that's so, the outcome could be devastating."

"You mean I could die."

"Exactly," Dr. Tran said. "We need to know what shape your heart's in, so I want you to have a coronary angiogram. I'm going to refer you to a cardiologist, and she may want you to have ultrasound as well."

Seeing Robert's blank look, Dr. Tran explained what was involved in the angiogram, then talked about the images sonography could produce.

"Do you really need to take a look at my heart like that?" Robert asked. "Couldn't you just let it go at listening?"

"We need to find out if you've got some blocked coronary arteries," Dr. Tran said. "We also need to get some sense of how your valves are working and what size your heart is. Otherwise, we'd just be guessing and basing a treatment on what we thought was happening. Technology lets us go beyond that."

Dr. Tran leaned forward and touched Robert's knee.

"Don't worry. Angiography is quite safe, really. And the ultrasound amounts to nothing at all."

"But what will they *cost?*"

"I'm not sure exactly," Dr. Tran said. "Probably in the neighborhood of $5000 to $7000. Maybe more if Dr. Goode needs for you to spend the night at the hospital."

"Then it's all out of the question," Robert said. "I don't have the money."

"Your insurance will cover both procedures."

"I don't have insurance, Doctor." Robert shook his head. "I run my own business, and I put all my money into keeping it going. I can't even mortgage my house, because it's rented."

"You're not old enough to qualify for Medicare," Dr. Tran said. "Do you own some property or jewelry? Something you can sell?"

"All I own is a broken-down station wagon and part of a pickup truck. I still owe money on the truck. Maybe I could sell it for enough to pay it off and pay for those tests you want me to have."

"If the tests show what I think they might," Dr. Tran said, "you'll need coronary artery bypass surgery. That will cost in the neighborhood of $30,000. Perhaps as much as $50,000, depending on complications and hospital stays."

"That's just laughable," Robert said. "No way I could raise $30,000. Not even if my life depended on it."

"I suspect it does," Dr. Tran said. "But selling your truck would have the advantage of qualifying you for Medicaid. In this state, if you have assets under $3000, you qualify."

"But if I sold my truck, I'd have to go out of business," Robert said. "I wouldn't have any way to earn a living, and my wife's sickly. She can't work a regular job, because of her headaches."

"Don't you have some family you could borrow from?"

"Maybe I could borrow $1000 from Jeri's mother, but she lives on Social Security. And there's nobody else. The few friends we have haven't got any more money than we do."

"I don't know what to say."

"Can't you just give me some pills?"

"I don't see any alternative," Dr. Tran said. "But I'm uncomfortable doing it, because I don't know exactly what we're up against. Like I told you, you could be on the verge of having a heart attack. We could help you with the right tests and, if necessary, the right sort of surgery. But as it is. . . . "

"I'll just have to take my chances," Robert said. "Until I'm either rich enough or poor enough to get the right treatment."

---

## BRIEFING SESSION

Some historians of medicine estimate that it was not until the middle 1930s that the intervention of a physician in the treatment of an illness was likely to affect the outcome in a substantial way. The change was brought about by the discovery and development of antibiotic agents such as penicillin and sulfa drugs. They made it possible, for the first time, both to control infection and to provide specific remedies for a variety of diseases. Additional advances in treatment modalities, procedures, and technology have helped establish contemporary medicine as an effective enterprise.

Before these dramatic changes occurred, there was little reason for anyone to be particularly concerned with the question of the distribution of medical care within society. The situation in the United States has altered significantly, and a number of writers have recently argued that everyone ought to be guaranteed at least some form of medical care. In part this is a reflection of the increased effectiveness of contemporary medicine, but it is also no doubt due to a growing awareness of the serious difficulties faced by disadvantaged groups within society.

The previous chapter focused on one aspect of the problem of the distribution of medical resources—that of allocating limited resources among competing individuals in a particular situation. Here we need to call attention to some of the broader social issues. These issues transcend moral decisions about particular people and raise questions about the basic aims and obligations of society.

A great number of observers believe that the United States is currently faced with a health-care crisis. Some of the reasons supporting this belief, as well as some proposed solutions, are outlined in the Social Context parts of this chapter, and we need not repeat them here. But one element of the crisis is often said to be the lack of any program to provide health care for everyone in the society. That people should be forced to do without needed health care for primarily financial reasons has seemed to some a morally intolerable state of affairs.

This point of view has frequently been based on the claim that everyone has a right to health care. Thus, it has been argued, society has a duty to provide that care; if it does not, then it is sanctioning a situation that is inherently wrong. To remedy the situation requires redesigning the health-care system and present practices to see to it that all who need health care have access to it.

The language of "rights" is very slippery. To understand and evaluate arguments that involve claiming (or denying) rights to health care, it is important to understand the nature of the claim. The word "rights" is used in several distinct ways, and a failure to be clear about the use in any given case leads only to unproductive confusion.

The following distinctions may help capture some of the more important sorts of things that people have in mind when they talk about rights.

## Claim-Rights, Legal Rights, and Statutory Rights

Suppose I own a copy of the book *Fan Mail.* If so, then I may be said to have a right to do with the book whatever I choose. Other people may be said to have a duty to recognize my right in appropriate ways. Thus, if I want to read the book, burn it, or sell it, others have a duty not to interfere with me. If I loan the book to someone, then he or she has a duty to return it.

Philosophers of law generally agree that a *claim-right* to something serves as a ground for other people's duties. A claim-right, then, always entails a duty or duties on the part of someone else.

Generally speaking, *legal rights* are claim-rights. Someone has a legal right when someone else has a definable duty, and legal remedies are available when the duty is not performed. Either the person can be forced to perform the duty, or damages of some sort can be collected for failure to perform. If I pay someone to put a new roof on my house by a certain date, she has contracted a duty to perform the work we have agreed to. If the task is not performed, then I can turn to the legal system for enforcement or damages.

*Statutory rights* are claim-rights that are explicitly recognized in legal statutes or laws. They impose duties on certain classes of people under specified conditions. A hospital contractor, for example, has a duty to meet certain building codes. If he fails to meet them, he is liable to legal penalties. But not all legal rights are necessarily statutory rights. Such considerations as "customary and established practices" may sometimes implicitly involve a legally enforceable claim-right.

## Moral Rights

A *moral right,* generally speaking, is one that is stated in or derived from the principles of a moral theory. More specifically, to say that someone has a moral right to certain goods or manner of treatment is to say that others have a moral duty to see to it that she receives what she has a right to. A moral right is a certain kind of claim-right. Here, though, the source of justification for the right and for the corresponding duty lies in moral principles and not in the laws or practices of a society.

According to Ross, for example, people have a duty to treat other people benevolently. This is a duty that is not recognized by our legal system. We may, if we wish, treat others in a harsh and unsympathetic manner and in doing so violate no law.

Of course, many rights and duties that are based upon the principles of moral theories are also embodied in our laws. Thus, to take Ross again as an example, we have a prima facie duty not to injure or kill anyone. This duty, along with its correlative right to be free from injury or death at the hands of another, is reflected in the body of statutory law and common law that deals with bodily harm done to others and with killing.

The relationship between ethical theories and the laws of a society is complicated and controversial. The fundamental question is always the extent to which laws should reflect or be based upon an ethical theory. In a society such as ours, it does not seem proper that an ethical theory accepted by only a part of the people should determine the laws that govern us all. It is for this reason that some object to laws regulating sexual activity, pornography, and abortion. These are considered best regarded as a part of personal morality.

At the same time, however, it seems that we must rely upon ethical theories as a basis for evaluating laws. Unless we are prepared to say that what is legal is, in itself, what is right, we must recognize the possibility of laws that are bad or unjust. But what makes a law bad? A possible answer is that a law is bad when it violates a right derived from the principles of an ethical theory. Similarly, both laws and social practices may be criticized for failing to recognize a moral right. An ethical theory, then, can serve as a basis for a demand for the reform of laws and practices.

Clearly there is no sharp line separating the moral and the legal. Indeed, virtually all of the moral theories we discuss in Part V have been used by philosophers and other thinkers as the basis for principles applying to society as a whole. Within such frameworks as utilitarianism, natural law theory, and Rawls's theory of a just society, legal and social institutions are assigned roles and functions in accordance with more general moral principles.

## Political Rights

Not everyone attempts to justify claims to rights by referring such claims directly to a moral theory. Efforts are frequently made to provide justification by relying upon principles or commitments that are generally acknowledged as basic to our society. (Of course, to answer how these are justified may force us to invoke moral principles.) Our society, for example, is committed to individual autonomy and equality, among other values. It is by reference to commitments of this sort that we evaluate proposals and criticize practices.

From this point of view, to recognize health care as a right is to acknowledge it as a *political right.* This means showing that it is required by our political commitments or principles. Of course, this may also mean resolving any conflicts that may arise from other rights that also seem to be demanded by our principles. But this is a familiar state of affairs. We are all aware that the constitutional guarantee of freedom of speech, for example, is not absolute and unconditional. It can conflict with other rights or basic commitments, and we look to the courts to provide us with guidelines to resolve the conflicts.

## Health Care as a Right

With the distinctions that we have discussed in mind, let us return now to the question of a general right to health care. What can those who make such a claim be asserting?

Obviously everyone in our society is free to seek health care and, when the proper arrangements are made, to receive it. That is, health care is a service available in society, and people may avail themselves of it. At the same time, however, no physician or hospital has a duty to provide health care that is sought. The freedom to seek does not imply that others have a duty to provide what we seek.

There is not in our society a legally recognized claim-right to health care. Even if I am sick, no one has a legal duty to see to it that I receive treatment for my illness. (Hospitals receiving federal money have a legal duty to treat people faced with life-threatening emergencies until they are stabilized.) I may request care, or I may attempt to persuade a physician that it is his or her moral duty to provide me with care. But I have no legal right to health care, and, if someone refuses to provide it, I cannot seek a legal remedy.

I may, of course, contract with a physician, clinic, or hospital for care, either in general or for a certain ailment. If I do this, then the other party acquires a legally enforceable duty to provide me the kind of care that we agreed upon. Contracting for health care, in this respect, is not relevantly different from contracting for a new roof on my house.

Those who assert that health care is a right cannot be regarded as making the obviously false claim that there is a legal right to care. Their claim, rather, must be interpreted as one of a moral or political sort. They might be taken as asserting something like "Everyone in our society ought to be entitled to health care, regardless of his or her financial condition."

Anyone making such a claim must be prepared to justify it by offering reasons and evidence in support of it. The ultimate source of the justification is most likely to be the principles of a moral theory. For example, Kant's principle that every person is of inherent and equal worth might be used to support the claim that every person has an equal right to medical care, simply by virtue of being a person.

Justification might also be offered in terms of principles that express the aims and commitments of the society. A society that endorses justice and equality, one might argue, must be prepared to offer health care to all, if it offers it to anyone.

However justification is offered, to claim that health care is a right is to go beyond merely expressing an attitude. It is to say more than something like "Everyone would like to have health care" or "Everyone needs health care."

The language of "rights" is frequently used in a rhetorical way to encourage us to recognize the wants and needs of people—or even other organisms, such as animals and trees. This is a perfectly legitimate way of talking. But, at bottom, to urge that something be considered a right is to make a claim requiring justification in terms of some set of legal, social, or moral principles.

## Objections

Why not recognize health care for all as a right? Virtually everyone would admit that in the abstract it would be a good thing. If this is so, then why should anyone wish to oppose it? Briefly stated, arguments against a right to health care are most frequently of two kinds.

First, those who subscribe to a position sometimes called "medical individualism" argue that to recognize a right to health care would have the consequence of violating the rights of physicians and other medical practitioners. Physicians, they claim, would be required to employ their intelligence, knowledge, and skills in a way dictated by society. Thus, physicians would be deprived of their autonomy and, in a very real sense, made slaves of the state.

Second, some critics have pointed out that, while it is possible to admit health care to the status of a right, we must also recognize that health care is only one social good among others. Education, transportation, housing, legal assistance, and so on are other goods that are also sought and needed by members of our society. It is impossible to admit all of these (and perhaps others) to the status of rights, for the society simply cannot afford to pay for them.

The first line of argument, medical individualism, fails to recognize that the health-care situation is perhaps best regarded as one in which there is a conflict of rights (between patients and providers) and not just one in which the rights of physicians are being restricted.

The second line of argument does not necessarily lead to the conclusion that we should not recognize a right to health care. It does serve to warn us that we must be careful to specify exactly what sort of right—if any—we want to support. Do we want to claim, for example, that everyone has a right to a certain minimum of health care? Or do we want to claim that everyone has a right to equal health care (whatever anyone can get, everyone can demand)?

Furthermore, this line of argument warns us that we have to make decisions about what we, as a society, are willing to pay for. Would we, for example, be willing to give up all public support for education in order to use the money for health care? Probably not. But we might be willing to reduce the level of support for education in order to increase that for health care. Whatever we decide, we have to face up to the problem of distributing our limited resources. This is an issue that is obviously closely connected with what sort of right to health care (or, really, the right to what sort of health care) we are prepared to endorse.

The need for health care by those unable to purchase it calls attention to fundamental issues about rights, values, and social goals. If we are to recognize a right to health care, we must be clear about exactly what this involves.

Are we prepared to offer only a "decent minimum"? Does justice require that we make available to all whatever is available to any? Are we prepared to restrict the wants of some people in order to satisfy the basic needs of all people?

Such questions are of more than academic interest, and they concern more than just a handful of patients and physicians. How they are resolved will affect us all, directly and indirectly, through the character of our society. We are the richest nation in the history of the world, yet we have not solved the problem of providing needed medical care to all our citizens.

## SOCIAL CONTEXT: COSTS OF CARE

It was one of the most effective political ads of all time.

Harry and Louise, a forty-something couple, are sitting at the kitchen table browsing through the stacks of paper of the 1994 Clinton health plan. "Things are going to change, and not all for the better," says an announcer in a voice-over. "The government may force us to pick from a few health care plans designed by government bureaucrats."

Looking at Harry, Louise says, "Having choices we don't like is no choice at all."

The ad, which was sponsored by the Health Insurance Association of America, tapped into the worries and anxieties felt by millions of Americans as they contemplated the prospect of abandoning the old and familiar fee-for-service medical care system funded mostly by private insurance. If the Clinton plan passed into law, they would then find themselves in a system of managed competition in which they would be required to choose from a variety of medical plans with varying price tags. Although the insurance companies would administer the plans, the plans themselves would need to meet federal requirements and be subject to government oversight.

Due in large part to the Harry and Louise ad, the reforms of the Clinton plan were defeated politically. Ironically, the old fee-for-service system that Harry and Louise appeared to favor virtually disappeared within a couple of years after the ad had done its work. In 1988 about 71 percent of employees in the United States were enrolled in traditional medical insurance plans, but by 2001 more than 93 percent were enrolled in managed-care plans. Since then, the fee-for-service medical system has virtually disappeared.

The plans now available aren't ones designed by a government bureaucracy of the sort feared by Harry and Louise. But so far as "having choices we don't like" is concerned, rather than being able to choose from a large variety of health-care plans, most Americans' choices are limited to the few offered to them by their employer.

Employers, concerned about profits, negotiate with managed-care companies to offer plans that are relatively inexpensive. The companies, focused on their own profits, try to lower the costs of the health care they deliver through the physicians, hospitals, testing laboratories, and clinics with whom they have contracts.

Has the movement to managed care and the radical change in the way that most Americans receive and pay for their health care resolved the crisis that prompted the efforts at reform that so disturbed Harry and Louise? Not really.

Indeed, dissatisfactions with the managed-care system have driven people to demand other alternatives. Also, hospitals and doctors' groups, unwilling to agree to the fees and restrictions imposed by insurers have started to negotiate with insurers to promote their own interests.

These changes have led to higher costs to insurance companies and to newer versions of managed care in which controls over care have been reduced. The result is that the cost of medical treatment is again on the rise. Managed care has not so much failed as we have refused to accept the rationing that it requires to reduce costs.

### Crisis

A crisis exists in a social institution when factors are present that tend to destroy it or render it ineffective in achieving its goals. Two major factors are present in the American health-care system that put it in a state of crisis: the increasing cost to the society of health care and the failure to deliver at least a decent minimum of health care to everyone who needs it.

Despite the widespread expectation that managed care plus a combination of legislative approaches would deal with the crisis, this has not happened. The way in which most Americans now receive health care has been drastically altered, but the crisis continues. We'll examine briefly a few of the key factors producing it, then consider some solutions that have been offered.

### Current Costs

In 1960 health spending in the United States amounted to some $27 billion. In 1970 it rose to $75 billion, and in 1983 it increased to $356 billion. Despite the coming of widespread managed care plans starting around 1994, spending continued to increase. By 1996 U.S. health-care costs had climbed to an astounding $1 trillion. This was 4.4 percent more than in 1995; even so, it was the smallest increase in thirty-seven years.

By 2000 spending on health care topped the scale at $1.3 trillion. This was an increase of 6.9 percent over 1993, the year major health-care reform was first proposed. Health-care costs now account for 13.3 percent of the nation's gross domestic product, up .1 percent from 1999 and 1.1 percent from 1998.

The 2000 costs of $1.3 trillion represents spending an average of $4637 on each person. Spending in earlier years reflects the continuing increase: $2966 in 1991; $4001 in 1997; and $4377 in 1999. Economists project that by 2010 costs will rise to $1.87 trillion. (Canada now spends 9.3 percent of its GDP on health care, about $2000 per capita; for the United Kingdom, the figures are 6.9 percent and $1569.)

Salaries in health care and insurance premiums have mirrored these increases. But the major reason for the increase during the last few years economists believe to be opposition to the strictures of managed care by physicians and patients.

### Managed Care Avoided

The spread of managed care initially succeeded in bringing costs under control. This was done by instituting policies—some controversial, others objectionable, and nearly all disliked—governing treatments and drugs that would be paid for, access to medical specialists, and length of hospital stays. Although such controls reduced medical costs at first, by 1998 they began to rise again, and the figures for 2001 (the most recent available) show the trend has continued.

When given the choice, consumers in growing numbers prefer a form of managed care that has fewer restrictions than the older plans that required vigilant "gatekeepers" to restrict the tests and treatment options physicians could choose. Traditional health maintenance organizations (HMOs), with their rigid regulations, are now no longer the preferred model for health-care delivery.

The second factor in the weakening of managed care is the product of the new negotiating strengths of health-care providers. Consolidations of hospitals and the organization of physicians into practice groups have given health-care providers more bargaining power when dealing with insurers. They can negotiate higher payments for services and greater autonomy in decision making.

## Hospital Care and Drugs

In 2000, national health care spending increased almost $84 billion over the 1999 amount. Hospital care and prescription drugs account for 45 percent of the increase. The cost of hospital care rose by about $10 billion to $412 billion, while the cost of drugs increased by almost $18 billion to some $122 billion.

Drugs have become the focus of much debate about health reform. From 1995–2000, the cost of drugs doubled, and from 1990–2000, the cost tripled. The increase was about 15 percent a year from 1996 to 2000. From 2001 to 2002, costs increased 17.1 percent. Drug manufacturers cite the costs of research for producing new and effective drugs, while critics point to new "me-too" drugs that are no more than expensive variations on old drugs. The new drugs, they say, are often no more effective than the older and cheaper ones. That people want them is often due to consumer advertising on television. Thus, Xela is perceived as being superior to Zola merely because of heavy promotion. In this respect, health-care costs are being driven up with little or no improvement in anybody's health.

## Why Do Costs Rise?

Various explanations have been given for the rising costs of health care. Economists point out that in medicine a surplus of services does not drive prices down. Instead, it may drive up demand. The availability of laboratories, high-technology equipment, hospital beds, and a variety of medical services increases the probability that they will be used.

While managed care can exert some control over demand, the control cannot be total. Managed-care plans must compete for contracts, and the plan that offers the most services at the lowest prices has a competitive advantage. Also, with hospitals and physicians' groups now at the negotiating table, insurers and their business clients can no longer make take-it-or-leave-it offers to health-care providers.

Apart from the way the health-care system operates, other factors having to do with a changing population and the state of medicine itself are responsible to some extent for increasing costs. Here are a few of them:

- Children born during the baby boom of the 1940s are reaching late middle age, so the median age of the population has increased. An aging population requires more, as well as more expensive, medical care than a younger population.

- Advancements in medical technology now make it possible to provide a greater number of services to hospitalized patients. Hence, more people are likely to be hospitalized in order to receive the services. Similarly, while sophisticated medical tests, such as CT scans, sonograms, and endoscopic examinations can now be done on an outpatient basis, that very fact may increase the likelihood of their use.

- Also, surgical procedures like knee or cataract operations that once would have been performed in a hospital may now be performed on outpatients. Yet any possible savings are offset by the increase in the number of the procedures performed.

- Improvements in medicine and surgery now make it possible to provide therapies for diseases that once would not have been treated. The availability of such treatments means increasing the hospital population, and the success of such treatments means that more people will be alive who can benefit from additional care.

- The treatments themselves are likely to be expensive. Surgery, radiation, chemotherapy, and bone marrow transplants may all be used in treating breast cancer. A liver transplant may cost $100,000, and the combination drug therapy now used in the treatment of AIDS can cost from $12,000 to $20,000 a year.

The very success of medicine creates, in a sense, the need for more medicine. Americans have traditionally refused to accept less effective medical treatments when more effective ones are available, even though the best treatments come with a higher price tag.

Similarly, Americans have taken a more interventionist approach toward dealing with disease, and most people, when faced with a serious illness, choose an aggressive approach to treating it. This, too, usually costs more money. Also, Americans have an unwillingness to accept the explicit rationing of resources that would involve, for example, denying heart transplants to people in their eighties or mammograms to women in their forties. No doubt the whole complex of American attitudes about health care is responsible to a large degree for the amount spent on care in our society.

### The Need for Health-Care Reform

While efforts over the past two decades have improved access to health care for low-income and minority groups, a significant portion of this population is still not receiving needed care.

The number of people without medical insurance has reached 44 million (almost 19 percent of the population), up from 29 million in 1979. Because people leave and enter the insurance rolls, some analysts estimate that as many as 50 to 60 million people are uninsured for at least some of the time during the year. Half those without insurance are children or families with children. Children themselves make up about 25 percent of the uninsured.

The 1994 Clinton health plan was a proposal to provide access to at least basic health care for everyone. In rejecting the plan, Congress showed an unwillingness to pass any kind of comprehensive national health plan that would address the problems of the uninsured. Those with no sort of medical insurance, as well as those with inadequate coverage, did not disappear when the comprehensive health plan was defeated. Indeed, since that time, despite a period of high employment, a strong economy, and new laws intended to extend health benefits, the number of people without health insurance has continued to rise. The number has increased steadily since 1987, and the recent downturn in the economy is likely to speed up the increase. Why do so many people lack medical coverage? The answers are diverse and complex.

### Lost Jobs, New Jobs, Smaller Companies

The economy generated about 14 million new jobs from 1993 to 2000, but the economic downturn beginning that year meant that people who had been counting on their employer to provide them with health insurance found themselves out of a job and responsible for paying the full cost of their policies. For many, the cost was more than they could afford, and they allowed their coverage to lapse. (See the discussion of the Kassebaum-Kennedy plan on the next page for details on how that plan was supposed to help.) They joined the ranks of the uninsured. In 2001, 1.4 million Americans lost their health insurance due to the economic downturn.

Even when the economy was booming, most new jobs were in small companies not likely to offer group health insurance. Such employers often say they can't afford to pay even part of the insurance premiums for their employees and still make a profit. Employers are not required by law to offer health insurance, and often they do so only as a fringe benefit to attract the workforce they want. With a downturn in business, the need to attract employees lessens, and employers may eliminate health insurance as part of the job package. Insurance premiums rose 11 percent in 2001 and an additional 15 percent in 2002.

Some employers also say employees prefer higher wages to health insurance. Because employees usually have to contribute to paying insurance premiums in a group plan, those in low-wage jobs frequently say they can't afford health insurance, even when an employer pays part of the cost. A worker making $800 a month who has to pay even as little as $75 a month for insurance coverage is left with a substantially reduced income.

Finally, even if an employee is in a group health plan, the plan may not cover the employee's spouse or children. If it doesn't, the family is then faced with paying for private policies that most of them simply can't afford. In 2002, 30 million people in families headed by a worker lacked any health-care coverage. Lack of insurance has now become a middle-class problem.

## Failure of Kassebaum–Kennedy Law

After the political defeat of the Clinton health proposal, various laws were passed with the aim of helping groups of vulnerable people get health-care coverage and assisting working people in keeping their health insurance. Generally, the laws have not worked as their framers and advocates intended.

The Kassebaum–Kennedy law of 1996 was supposed to allow people to change jobs without losing their health insurance. Before the law was passed, an insurance company could drop its coverage on an employee who left a group health plan to take another job. If that happened, someone with a preexisting condition, such as asthma or heart disease, might find it impossible to locate an insurance company willing to insure her. For this reason, many people reported they couldn't risk changing jobs, because they would lose their insurance. Those who got fired from their jobs often automatically lost their insurance.

The Kassebaum–Kennedy law guarantees that people leaving a job with group insurance will, regardless of any preexisting condition, be covered by the group insurance of another employer, if the employer offers group insurance.

The General Accounting Office recently reported to Congress, however, that the law is not working as intended. While the law requires insurers to give policies to individuals who leave their jobs, it does not regulate the fees the insurer can charge. One study showed that some insurance companies charged an individual $10,000 to $15,000 or more a year for a policy. One company charged "high risk" people five times the usual rate.

Critics say insurers get rid of the people they don't want—those who may cost them money—by charging them so much they cannot afford to pay. The law's failure thus leaves people who lose or change jobs in the same position as before. Moreover, the law applies only to those who already have group coverage. Those without it may simply be turned down by insurance companies, who have no obligation to accept them as risks.

## Failure of Children's Program

The aim of the 1997 Children's Health Insurance Program (CHIP) was to provide health benefits for the country's 20 million (or more) uninsured children. The initial legislation provided $24 billion to be spent over five years in a joint federal-state program.

So far, however, the program has left the problem of uninsured children relatively unsolved. Many who qualify for Medicaid are simply not enrolled. In January 1998 the federal government estimated that the number was 3 million, and in May the estimate was increased to almost 5 million.

One reason the program has not been successful is that parents are not aware they can get health coverage for their children, coverage generally better than that provided by private insurers. Parents who work at low-paying jobs may earn enough to disqualify them from Medicaid coverage, but not their children. Similarly, while welfare laws limit the time an adult may be on welfare and eligible for Medicaid, the same limits do not apply to their children. Parents may mistakenly assume that they must qualify for Medicaid for their children to qualify. State officials don't always check to see whether the children are eligible, even though their parents aren't.

CHIP is funded jointly by the federal government and the states. When the money a state allocates for the program runs out, then even children who qualify for medical care might not receive it. Their wait for the next round of funding may have serious consequences for them. Some states have allocated relatively small amounts for the program, so many children never get treated. Also, with so many states now in economic difficulty and under the obligation to balance their budgets, many are talking about cutting support for CHIP, eliminating some services, and tightening the eligibility rules. Thus, many poor children with medical needs are likely to go without the necessary care.

### Not Poor Enough

Not all those who are uninsured can qualify for Medicaid coverage, even if they are poor. According to federal statistics, 43.3 percent of people defined as poor in terms of income were covered by Medicaid at some time during 1997. However, Medicaid is a joint federal-state program, and some states set the level of income required for qualification so low that it is below the federal poverty line.

Childless adults, in particular, find it quite difficult to qualify for Medicaid in several states. Having assets in excess of $3000 to $4000 may be enough to disqualify someone. Hence, to secure medical care, people may be required to divest themselves of virtually all their assets. Many, for the sake of dignity, are unwilling to impoverish themselves to qualify for Medicaid, and so they choose to go without needed care.

### Lack of Care and Delayed Care

The lack of medical coverage suggests that many people in need of medical care fail to get it. Some studies show that more than 10 percent of the population receive no care at all and that more than 4 million people seriously in need of care are forced to do without it.

Evidence also indicates that when uninsured people are admitted to hospitals, they are discharged earlier and receive fewer diagnostic and therapeutic procedures than those who have insurance. Some see results of this kind as proof that the United States has already moved to at least a two-tier medical system in which the poor are provided with second-class care, while those able to pay receive the best care available.

Studies also show that the underinsured often delay seeking medical treatment. The frequent result is that a disease that could have been treated effectively and inexpensively at an early stage must subsequently be treated with greater expense and less effectiveness.

### Rational Fear

The fear of being in medical need and not being able to get care has become a specter haunting many Americans. People rarely suffer from not being able to buy new cars or better clothes, but when they cannot afford health care, they may pay a permanent and serious price.

Their worry may be quite rational. Anyone out of a job and unable to afford health insurance risks not being able to get needed medical treatment in the event of a serious illness or accident. The American dream can quickly turn into a peculiarly American nightmare—the best of treatments is in sight, but not within reach.

## SOCIAL CONTEXT: SOLVING THE PROBLEM?

The failure of our society to guarantee an adequate level of health care (a "decent minimum") to everyone needing it continues to be the major force behind efforts to establish a national health plan that would provide universal coverage. Few people, including legislators, doubt that the United States needs some sort of plan.

While many hoped that managed care would move in the direction of solving the problem, this has not turned out to be the case. Costs are still increasing, and so are the number of people who cannot afford medical care.

Managed care generated a new set of problems. People were (and some still are) unhappy with the extent to which their medical choices were limited, and physicians were displeased with restrictions on their discretion. The need of managed care companies to make a profit can also seriously compromise the quality of medical care and weaken the trust between physicians and their patients.

Dissatisfaction with restrictive health maintenance organizations (HMOs) has undermined the attempt to reduce medical costs by rationing care. We no longer have the old fee-for-service system, but for higher fees people can choose managed care plans that place fewer restrictions on them and their physicians.

The present system, as a result, is still one that offers two kinds of medicine—one for the rich and one for the poor. And it too often happens that the medicine for the poor is none at all.

## Proposed Solutions

The intense national debate about health care in 1994 produced a number of proposals for radically reforming the ways in which medical care is financed and delivered. All the proposals addressed the conjoined issues of increasing costs and the need to provide greater access to health care, but the proposals differed significantly in advocating ways in which costs might be controlled and in recommending how and to what extent access might be provided.

## Managed Competition

People in a geographical region would be clustered into state-based pools or "health alliances." The pools would include the uninsured, people now paying for their own insurance, and those working for small companies. Companies with many employees would, in effect, constitute their own health alliance.

The health alliances (and large companies) would bargain with the representatives of various health plans (including those operated by private, for-profit insurance companies) to obtain a standard set of basic benefits for reasonable rates.

The plan would offer universal care, and everyone would have access to the same basic insurance. However, group members would be offered the choice of several plans. People without resources would have no option but to choose one of the basic plans. Tax incentives would encourage all members to choose lower-cost plans, but if members could pay extra, they would get extra coverage or privileges (for example, consulting a physician who is not in the health plan).

Physicians, hospitals, and insurers would join together to form provider groups. The provider groups would offer health plans to the health alliances. Most plans would probably be like those now offered by HMOs, in which for a set yearly fee the HMO undertakes to provide all needed medical care. The provider groups would compete with one another to offer plans to attract the most patients. Plans would be judged in terms of price and quality. Hence, the mechanism of competition should keep prices as low as possible, while providing as much quality as possible. The role of government would be to supervise the process, guarantee the quality of care, and make sure that the poor are enrolled in alliances.

The managed-competition plan could be financed in a variety of ways. Under the 1994 Clinton proposal, it would be paid for by a combination of taxes, employee premiums, and an "employer mandate" (that is, an insurance premium paid by employers). Small businesses and the poor (including the working poor) would be subsidized by the government.

*Advantages.* Managed competition offers universal coverage, portability of insurance (people can move from one health alliance to another without losing insurance), and comprehensiveness (coverage for all medically necessary conditions). In addition, managed competition promises to control costs, while also providing high-quality medical care.

*Criticisms.* Most people are happy with the care they receive under the present system and managed competition would force them into a new and untried system. The HMO-type plans would require people to choose physicians from an approved list, and people would be forced to deal with a "gatekeeper" to gain access to specialists.

Provider groups, forced to lower prices in response to competition, might reduce the quality of care they give to patients. Even with government oversight, the pressure on investor-owned groups to make a profit is likely to lead to undertreatment, undertesting, and a delay in referring patients to needed specialists.

The awkward structure of a health–alliance/provider–group system would only add to the already high costs of paperwork. The almost 25 percent of health costs now spent on administration could be better spent on improving care. If private investors (insurance companies) were removed from the system, savings would be even greater.

The system is completely untried, and as a result, it is not clear that the savings from implementing it would be as great as they need to be to control health costs. Also, from a practical perspective, how would the system handle rural areas, where there can be no competition because there are few physicians? What could be done about plans that attract a disproportionately large number of older or sicker patients?

These criticisms are not necessarily unanswerable. They are some of the questions raised about the 1994 managed-competition health plan proposal.

### Single-Payer Plan

All citizens and legal residents would be automatically enrolled in a program of national health insurance established by the federal government and administered by the states. Everyone would be provided with a basic minimum of medical care and allowed to choose personal physicians. Private insurance premiums could be replaced by a combination of taxes that would include payroll taxes on employers and a tax on employee's income. Private insurers would offer policies for benefits not covered in the basic-services packages.

*Advantages.* The single-payer plan offers universal coverage, portability of insurance, access to medical care, and comprehensiveness. It offers the possibility of controlling costs, while providing high-quality medical care. It reduces overhead expenses, preserves people's freedom to choose physicians, and breaks the control that the insurance industry has on American medical care. The emphasis on primary care and prevention would not only save money, but also lead to a general improvement in the health of the nation.

The single-payer system is the simplest and most direct way of providing for universal cover-

age. Further, it has a proven track record in Canada.

*Criticisms.* The change is too radical to be accepted by Americans, and it involves the government too deeply in health care. There is no reason to believe that the system will control costs adequately, and it is likely to lead to long delays in treatment and even a rationing system. The emphasis on primary care would eventually result in slowing the advance in American medical technology.

### Managed Care

Managed care is the name given to medical care that is provided in such a way that costs are controlled by restricting access to the more expensive forms of testing and treatment. Typically, patients are limited to seeing specific physicians and being admitted to particular hospitals. In principle, emphasis is placed on preventive care, and patients receive only the testing and therapies that they genuinely require.

The current American system has become predominantly a managed-care system as businesses have steadily moved away from group health insurance plans that pay fees-for-service.

The earliest and most popular form of managed care is the health maintenance organization. An HMO is a medical plan in which a fixed annual fee is paid to an organized group of physicians and hospitals ("health-care providers"). The group then undertakes to supply the individual with most kinds of needed medical services, at no additional charge.

By 2002, 93 percent of all insured people were enrolled in some managed-care plan. Managed care has become so popular with businesses because it offers them a chance to reduce the medical costs they must pay by negotiating fees with the provider group. The provider group agrees to supply medical care in accordance with specific rules. These rules are designed to avoid unnecessary tests and procedures, because the profit of the provider group is determined by the money remaining after the expenses of patients have been paid.

Patients are penalized for going "out of network" to other physicians and hospitals, and physicians must follow strict rules in approving or denying care. Often, there is a personal financial incentive for the physician not to refer a patient to a specialist. In every case, the primary-care physician serves as a "gatekeeper," controlling the patient's access to specialized testing and care.

*Advantages.* Better patient care is claimed to result from HMOs because they encourage patients to consult a physician at the beginning of an illness, rather than waiting until it grows serious. This is advantageous both to the patient and the HMO, which can avoid spending a larger part of its budget treating the patient's more serious condition.

The managed-care concept can be employed in various forms. Some HMOs have actual physical locations, while others are "HMOs without walls." Preferred provider organizations (PPOs) have the advantage of allowing individuals to choose their physicians from a list of those who have entered into the arrangement. In this way, a major complaint against HMOs—that the individual is required to receive care from a group and has no physician of his own—is avoided. A range of plans, some more expensive than others and allowing more flexibility can be offered. Those willing to pay more can expect better medical service.

Managed care, in the view of some analysts, offers the best approach to providing universal coverage. As an approach to medical care, it is compatible with a number of plans for providing care—including the two previously discussed.

Managed care can reduce health-care costs for particular groups by restricting access to secondary and tertiary health care. Further, by emphasizing preventive care and keeping out-of-pocket expenses low, people are encouraged to consult physicians more often. The outcomes of treatment rules are typically researched, with the result that a rational basis for decisions can be established.

*Criticisms.* Economists question whether managed care provides overall savings on health care. Contracts negotiated with providers may be so low that they result in physicians and hospitals shifting some of the cost of a managed-care patient to patients with more insurance benefits.

Both managers and physicians have an incentive to encourage physicians to provide less-than-optimal care to maximize profits. Patients may be dissatisfied with the care they receive and yet not be able to do much about it. For example, an HMO may refuse to pay for the long-term use of an expensive drug to treat an enlarged prostate, but be willing to pay for prostate surgery. The choice is not left up to the patient. Acting as gatekeepers, physicians (often, in practice, their staff) are empowered to turn down requests for medical services or consultations.

Disability-rights groups have asserted strongly that the disabled should have access to the best specialists, even if they are not part of the network. Also, anecdotal evidence suggests that many individuals accustomed to taking charge of their own medical care become highly dissatisfied with managed care.

Physicians have often been critical of managed care. Some have felt that the rules imposed on them by the managers of particular plans do not allow them to practice medicine in the best way. Even when they do not disagree with the rules, some say that they find the rules irksome, narrow, and demeaning.

Physicians have also complained of being excluded from membership in managed-care organizations. If the physicians do not follow the rules, they may be dropped from a group without recourse. Or if they are in an area dominated by managed-care groups, they might wish to join one or more of the groups, yet be turned down. This could be financially and professionally disastrous for them.

Some critics point out that the initial success of managed care in reducing medical costs was the result of two factors that have now changed. First, physicians and hospitals were not organized into groups that could bargain effectively with insurers. Thus, the insurers often extracted lower prices, because the health-care providers had no realistic option to agreeing to fees set by insurers.

Second, employees had to accept the insurance plan offered by their employer, even if it was a highly restrictive plan. Bitter criticisms of such plans, illustrated with horror stories of treatment denials, soon made it clear that Americans were not willing to accept a rigid plan. Some made avoiding such a plan a consideration in employment decisions. With increased demand for employees beginning in the 1990s, companies often had to offer medical plans with less restrictive options to attract workers.

## Incremental Solutions

The debates over health care in 1994 left many people pessimistic about the possibility of a wholesale change in American health care. Neither the political nor the public will to make the change seemed present. Others became convinced that there was no need to make wholesale changes and that the problems of increasing costs and access to care could be solved merely by altering some aspects of the current system.

The American Medical Association, with a membership of 42 percent of licensed physicians in the United States, abandoned its ambitious plan for health-care reform that would include universal coverage and recommended that the nation "search for ways to expand access to care with an incremental reform approach." Then-executive vice president James Todd said, "Our goal of universal coverage has not changed, it's just that we need to find ways of getting there in an incremental fashion."

The following are among the numerous proposals being discussed for patching up the present system of health care:

1. **Subsidies.** To deal with the uninsured and the underinsured, provide direct government subsidies to pay for the cost of their insurance. Critics fear that such a program would encourage employers to reduce even further the insurance coverage they provide their workers. Why should a business pay for a high level of benefits, if the government will make up the difference between the cost of care covered by insurance and the cost billed to the patient?

2. **Standard benefits.** Insurers should be required to offer a minimal level of benefits. In this way, those who are underinsured would be covered. Critics see such a step as an unwarranted interference with market forces.

3. **Insurance regulations.** Insurers should be required to cover people with preexisting conditions. They should also be required to make insurance portable without increasing the premium cost, so that people can take their coverage with them when they change jobs or become unemployed.

4. **Community rating.** Insurers currently charge different rates to different segments of the population. The rates are based on the expected frequency of diseases in the various segments. Thus, the old pay higher rates than the young. Community rating would even out premiums to reflect the average cost of insuring the whole community.

   Critics claim that this would unfairly penalize young people and lead many of them to drop their insurance. Indeed, something like this happened in 1993 when the State of New York ended rate variation based on age. Rates went down for people in their sixties, while rising for the young and healthy. A half million younger people canceled their insurance. The result was that the premiums of those remaining sharply increased because those left in the pool were, on the average, sicker than before.

5. **State experiments.** Several states have already attempted innovative health-care plans for their citizens. In 2001 a referendum in Maine endorsed (52 percent to 48) a measure to make the state the first to offer universal health coverage for its citizens. (The proposal was opposed by the insurance industry, which funded "Harry-

and-Louise"-style attack ads.) Several other states are discussing the possibility. A large number of states have worked out plans for providing care for some people unable to pay.

Critics point out that having a variety of state health-care programs will make it difficult for companies that do business across the country to operate. They will be faced with a patchwork of laws and regulations. Furthermore, state programs may become so entrenched that they stand in the way of eventually achieving a needed national reform.

6. **Extend Medicare.** In 2002 the Bush administration authorized the extension of Medicare coverage to pay for the treatment of Alzheimer's disease. Until that happened, reimbursements for the cost of mental-health care, physical therapy, hospice care, and home-health care for Alzheimer's patients were usually automatically denied. Although the cost is expected to be several billion dollars, a significant part of it is expected to be defrayed by allowing patients to remain at home longer, saving on the costs of institutionalization.

The broadening of Medicare to cover special segments of the population could be a way of incrementally extending health care until everyone in the society has some form of coverage. For example, everyone becomes eligible for Medicare at age 65, but it is often during their fifties that people are likely to become unemployable and unable to afford health insurance. This is also the time when they are more likely to need medical care than in earlier decades. By lowering the Medicare age limit by ten years, millions of the uninsured and underinsured would qualify for needed care.

The main criticism of this proposal is that it would shift to taxpayers an even heavier Medicare burden. Many critics already see the Medicare system as requiring too much money, and in implementing the Balanced Budget Act of 1997, the agency has significantly reduced payments to physicians and hospitals. Indeed, reductions have been so severe that some physicians no longer are willing to accept Medicare patients, claiming that the fees paid to them by Medicare are lower than their costs. Hospitals also say that they lose money on Medicare patients. Extending Medicare, then, would require a significant change of political attitude in our society. Congress would have to be willing to provide the money to fund the system adequately to cover its new responsibilities.

Faced with the failure of complete health reform, yet recognizing the nagging persistence of a host of problems, most analysts and politicians are willing to endorse some small-scale changes. Their attitude is summed up in health economist Uwe Reinhardt's statement about incremental change: "It's like fixing a car, and in some ways this car is going to get worse, but it will still carry you some miles."

The crisis in health care has not abated, yet the system has not collapsed either. Significant reform probably lies in the future, but meanwhile, we must deal with today.

## Case Presentation

### *The Canadian System as a Model for the United States?*

The United States remains the only nation in the industrialized Western world in which parents worry about being able to pay for the medical care needed by their child, workers worry about losing their medical coverage by changing jobs, people without jobs worry about paying for medical insurance, and husbands and wives worry about going bankrupt to pay for the long-term care needed by an ailing spouse.

#### A Single-Payer System?

During the course of debate in recent years, some critics have pointed to these failings of the present health-care system and recommended that it be replaced by a so-called single-payer system. Under such a system, universal coverage would be provided to all citizens, regardless of their ability to pay, and the single payer would be the federal government.

"Socialized medicine" was the phrase once used to condemn all single-payer systems. The phrase was a label suggesting something like political heresy. How could a capitalist society adopt a plan exempting medical care from the rules of the market economy? Medical care, like house painting, was a service one could purchase from a provider for an agreed upon fee. The physician-provider, like the painter-provider, was an independent economic agent, and to suggest otherwise would be to recommend the practice of socialism.

Of course, those unable to pay a physician's fee would have to do without the service. A charitable organization or a benevolent physician might provide treatment for some truly in need. This wasn't something to be counted on, and in neither case was need a basis for demanding the service. Clearly, just as you couldn't expect a painter to paint your house without pay, so you couldn't expect a physician to provide you with medical care for nothing. Nor did anyone expect the government to pick up the bill. The role of the government in a market economy is not to provide some citizens with free goods, whether it is painting their houses or providing them with medical care.

## Changing Attitudes

For decades this view dominated public discussions about national health programs. Critics of a proposed program hardly had to do more than apply the label "socialized medicine" to it to bring discussion to a close. Then attitudes began to change for a complex of reasons, including the spiraling cost of health care, the increasing power and value of medical intervention, and the growing number of citizens needing care but lacking insurance.

The introduction of the Medicare program in 1965 provided care to millions of people, many of whom would have received no medical assistance at all. Medicare also helped change the thinking of many people. They came to realize that a social insurance plan like Medicare was not "socialized medicine" and that a plan for universal medical care might be offered along the same lines.

Other factors have also encouraged many to look with favor on the introduction of a single-payer plan. The steady increase in the number of citizens lacking health insurance and unable to pay for even basic medical care is the most dramatic. The number of people in this predicament is estimated at 44 million, and the number has been growing at a rate of 1 million per year.

Even people with medical insurance are willing to consider other ways of supporting health care, for they do not feel secure. Most are aware, either from news accounts or personal experience, that their coverage may not be adequate to pay for their medical needs and that they may be forced to do without care or go into debt to pay for it.

People also fear that their policies might be canceled because their medical expenses are too high or their insurer sees them as too much of a risk. Some fail even to get needed medical attention out of fear that their insurer will cancel their policy. The loss of insurance because of a rate increase after a change in jobs or unemployment is also feared. Those who suffer from a "preexisting condition," such as diabetes, may find it impossible to buy insurance or, if they can, to afford the extraordinarily high premiums that are likely.

Factors such as these may have been responsible for prompting 75 percent of Americans surveyed to say they favor a government program to make sure people have some sort of medical insurance. In an earlier survey, 75 percent said they were in favor of abandoning the private fee-for-service medical system in favor of some form of government-backed national health system.

Many proponents of a single-payer system consider the Canadian system a model for what the American health-care system should become. At least at first sight, Canada and the United States seem much alike in relevant respects. They are both democracies with partially regulated, free-market economies. Furthermore, both have a central, federal government, as well as a number of independent provincial or state governments. These similarities suggest that the Canadian experience with its health-care system might provide detailed guidance for reforming the United States system.

## The Canadian Health-Care System

Canada established universal health insurance coverage in 1971. It did not nationalize hospitals or make physicians government employees, as did Great Britain. Rather, it eliminated most forms of private medical insurance and enrolled citizens in a government plan administered by the ten provinces. The plan is paid for by a variety of federal and provincial taxes. The system is not "socialized medicine." It is, rather, a form of tax-based insurance and does not differ in principle from the United States' Social Security or Medicare.

In addition to physician services, diagnostic testing, hospitalization, and surgery, the plan provides for long-term care, prescription drugs for those over sixty-five, and mental-health care. Benefits vary slightly among provinces, and private insurance is used only to bridge the gaps in provincial coverage.

## Principles of the Health Act

The details of insurance coverage are decided by each province, but every plan adopted must conform to the five principles spelled out in the Canadian Health Act:

1. Universality. Every citizen is covered.

2. Portability. People can move to another province, change jobs, or be unemployed and retain their coverage.

3. Accessibility. Everyone has access to physicians, hospitals, and other elements of the health-care system.

4. Comprehensiveness. Medically necessary treatments must be covered.

5. Public administration. The system is publicly operated and publicly accountable.

The first four of these principles are often mentioned as ones that should guide reform of the United States' system. However, suggestions that the fifth one be adopted have occasioned much controversy.

## Canadian Citizens as Patients

Every Canadian citizen is guaranteed access to a physician, and she may see any primary-care physician she chooses. If hospitalization, testing, or surgery is necessary, then the government insurance plan will pay for it without any direct cost to the patient.

Patients do not receive bills, fill out claim forms, make copayments, or wait for reimbursement. Instead, they need only show their identification card to receive medical services. Their physician bills the insurance plan of the province, and payment is made within two to four weeks. Paperwork is kept at a minimum, and this helps lower administrative costs.

## Popularity and Effectiveness of the Program

The medical system is highly popular with Canadian citizens. In a 1992 survey, 7 out of 10 said they receive good or excellent care, and 9 out of 10 said the health-care system "is one of the things that makes Canada the best country in the world in which to live." Only 3 percent of Canadians in another poll said that they would "prefer a health-care system like that in the United States." Over the last ten years, Canadians have become less pleased with their system (as we will see later), but they are by no means ready to exchange it for an American model.

Various objective measures of health care show that the Canadian system has been successful. The infant mortality rate of 7.1 per 1000 live births is superior to the U.S. rate of 8.9. The Canadian life expectancy is 78.6 years (from 1997), while life expectancy in the United States is 76.5 years. Cost control also has been successful under the plan. In 1999, Canada spent about 9.3 percent of its national income for medical care; the United States spent 13.1 percent. In 1971, the year Canadian Medicare became universal, the proportions were 7.3 percent and 7.4 percent, respectively. This suggests that the Canadians have been able to provide both universal coverage and high-quality care, while successfully controlling costs.

## Canadian Physicians

Canadian physicians, like U.S. physicians, practice in their own offices and provide care for the patients who choose to consult them. The significant difference is that Canadian physicians must charge for their services according to a fee schedule. The schedule is negotiated by the Ministry of Health and the Provincial Medical Association. Canadian physicians were initially bitterly opposed to the universal health-care system. Many now approve of it, though, for it has turned out to have aspects they like. Although they cannot charge as much as physicians in the United States, they need not contend with the paperwork burden. Nor do they have to argue with insurance representatives who challenge their judgment about a needed medical service.

Physicians' fees in the United States are more than double that of Canadian fees. Canadian physicians have been able to maintain incomes equal to two-thirds that of U.S. physicians. The reason the incomes are not lower is that Canadian physicians see more patients.

Canada has 100 primary-care or family physicians per 100,000 people. The United States has 20. Even when pediatricians, gynecologists, internists, and family and general practitioners are considered, only 30 percent of physicians in the United States offer primary care to their patients. Provincial plans encourage patients to seek a referral to a specialist from a general practitioner. If a specialist sees a patient without a referral, the specialist can bill only for the same amount as a general practitioner would charge. (As sometimes happens, the specialist calls the general practitioner only after the patient has seen her.)

The preponderance of Canadian physicians committed to primary care means that it is possible to emphasize disease prevention. In the long run, this may help prevent the need for costly treatments. Furthermore, primary-care physicians are not as likely to order expensive diagnostic testing as are specialists.

## Coverage and Costs

Per capita, Canada spends less than half what the United States does on health care. For that money, it covers, for the entire population of the country, hospitalization, physician visits, rehabilitation therapy, most dental work, prescription drugs for the poor and those over sixty-five, and most laboratory tests.

The United States has no coverage standards for insurance, so many people who are insured have uneven coverage. In addition, the 19 percent of the U.S. population that is uninsured receives little or no health care.

## Drawbacks of the System

The Canadian system has aspects that can be viewed as negative. One of the ways in which costs are kept down is to restrict investment in high-cost medical technology. The United States has 1500 cardiac catheterization labs (166 people per unit), while Canada has 31 (816 people per unit). Canada has 12 magnetic resonance imagers (2108 people per unit), while the United States has 1375 (182 people per unit). Similarly, Canada has increased the number of general practitioners and pediatricians, but it has cut back the number of people in medical specialties. Canada has only 11 heart surgery units, while the United States has 793.

## Restricted Access

The strength of the Canadian system is its emphasis on basic care and prevention. Its weakness is the restricted access it permits to specialized care, equipment, and procedures. Patients may have to wait from three to six months for heart surgery, a hip replacement, or a bed in a cancer unit. Care is not explicitly rationed, but it is organized so that those with a greater need are given higher priorities. In fairness, the restrictions on care may not be as serious as critics sometimes claim. Government statistics show that the majority of Canadians receive medical care within seven days of requesting it. Hundreds of therapeutic and diagnostic procedures—general surgery, endoscopy, thyroid function tests, X rays, ultrasound, amniocentesis, EKGs, and so on—are performed regularly and with little or no waiting.

Canadian physicians are definitely more sparing in the use of MRIs and other high technology, and patients must wait longer to receive whatever benefits it offers than in the United States. The only other option, defenders of the system say, is to waste resources by unnecessarily duplicating equipment. By not taking this path, Canada has avoided the dizzying cost increases that plague the United States.

Restrictions on care can go too far, and in a 2000 survey of 3000 Canadians, 93 percent said that improving health care should be the government's top priority. Another poll found that 74 percent of the people supported the introduction of user fees that would reduce the demand on the medical system and reduce waiting times.

During the 1990s the federal government also cut revenue sharing with the provinces. This resulted in closing or merging a number of hospitals. Also, places in Canadian medical schools were reduced. In Canada the ratio of medical students to people is 1 per 20,000, while in the United States and Britain it is 1 per 13,000.

Despite these cutbacks, demand on the system has continued to grow. Like the United States, Canada has an aging population, and within thirty years the number of people over sixty-five is expected to double to 25 percent. The increasing demand for medical services has meant that Canada has moved in the direction of a two-tier system. Ninety percent of Canadians live within 100 miles of the U.S. border, and those who can afford to, often travel to the United States to receive services like hip replacements, MRIs, chemotherapy, and prostate or heart bypass surgery they might have to wait months for in Canada. Ironically, the treatments may even be administered by a Canadian physician who has immigrated to the United States for the prospect of making more money.

The emergence of this double-tier system has provoked harsh comments from defenders of the Canadian system. In their view, those who travel to the United States for medical treatment are, in effect, buying a place at the head of the line. This violates the sense of social equality the Canadian system aims to reflect.

By contrast, others point to people's need to go to the United States for medical services as evidence for revising Canadian health policy. It should allow, they argue, private hospitals to open in Canada to serve Canadian citizens who are willing and able to pay for treatments. But others see this as offering American profit-making hospitals a wedge for undermining the health-care system.

In 2002, a long-awaited Canadian government report addressed the issue of the emerging two-tier system and the problems that make it seem attractive to some. The report recommends that the federal government increase its spending on health care by roughly 25 percent over the next three years, an increase of about $4 billion. This would stabilize the system by reducing waiting times, extending services to those in rural areas, provide more services to the elderly, and pay for medications required by those with chronic diseases.

Critics of the report charged that it should have called for fundamental changes in the system, instead of merely asking for additional federal funding. Some favored shifting some of the cost burden onto individual patients, in effect adding copayments for services received. Otherwise, the federal government may be faced with a deficit, or money needed for education, housing, and highways might have to go to fund health care.

## A Canadian System for the United States?

Would the single-payer Canadian system work in the United States? Some observers who know both systems well express doubts. According to economist Victor Fuchs, "There is reason to doubt that the quality of our civil services is up to the quality of the Canadian civil services. There is also reason to question whether the organization and degree of discipline in the [medical] profession is as strong as in Canada. We are very much individualists, and that includes physicians."

Similar doubts have been expressed by David Woods, who sees the different systems of health care as expressions of "national character." "Canada's system is a centralized public enterprise, cautious and based upon ingrained notions (or delusions) of egalitarianism. America's system is decentralized, market-driven, entrepreneurial, and with 37 [now 39] million citizens uninsured by it, certainly unequal in terms of access."

Further, access to specialized care and technology is highly restricted in the Canadian system, something Americans would find particularly galling. Also, Canadians have indicated a greater willingness to pay much higher taxes, both explicit and hidden, to guarantee universal access than have Americans.

Despite these doubts and criticisms, many continue to believe that a single-payer system, with attributes of the Canadian system, would solve a significant number of the problems that plague the present system:

1.  The money now spent on private insurance, with its high administrative costs and spotty coverage for individuals, when combined with Medicaid and Medicare funds, could be used to extend basic coverage to all citizens. The problems of what to do about the uninsured and the underinsured would disappear.

2.  People would no longer have to worry about having their policies canceled, exceeding the limits of their coverage, or being uninsurable because of a preexisting medical condition.

3.  Universal access would encourage individuals to get medical help early, and rapid intervention would lead to cost savings from prevention and early detection and treatment.

4.  The single payer would be able to negotiate with physicians, hospitals, laboratories, and pharmaceutical companies to hold down prices.

The big financial losers in a single-payer system are private health insurance companies. The role they play is reduced to that of offering policies covering treatments not included in the single-payer plan. To a lesser extent, physicians, hospitals, and suppliers also stand to lose more financially in the change to a single-payer system. However, erosions in income due to HMOs and other forms of managed care have already taken place in all sectors of the health economy.

What physicians might expect to gain from a switch to a single-payer system is freedom from some of the more rigid and time-consuming utilization review processes of managed care. In this respect, physicians may be able to regain some of the autonomy that some claim has been declining steadily as third-party payers have taken a more active role in determining what procedures and treatments they are willing to pay for.

What remains unanswered is the basic question of whether the virtues of the Canadian single-payer system could be reproduced in the United States and whether the United States would be satisfied with a system that, for many people, is more restrictive than the one they are accustomed to. The Canadian system has flaws—the long waiting times for testing and treatment, in particular—nevertheless, it is one the United States ought to consider carefully, with an eye to altering its own system, if not forsaking it.

As T. R. Marmor and John Godfrey observe, "Canada is the country closest to ours in wealth, geography, ethnic diversity, and patterns of medical practice. If we cannot learn from Canada, we cannot learn from any country."

Perhaps aspects of the Canadian system combined with aspects of the American system might offer a way to support and deliver medical care so that those unable to pay could receive at least a decent minimum. The United States already has a two-tier (or even multi-tier) system of health care, but what it lacks is a way of providing for the medical needs of those who are uninsured (or underinsured) without forcing them into indigence.

## Case Presentation

### Employer-Mandated Health Insurance: The Hawaiian Example

Hawaii's Prepaid Health Care Act was passed in 1974 and took effect in 1975. The act requires all employers, no matter their size, to provide health insurance coverage for their workers. Part-time employees working less than twenty hours per week are the only ones who need not be included in the coverage.

Workers can be compelled to pay a share of the insurance premium up to 50 percent of its cost or 1.5 percent of their wages, whichever figure is lower. Some employers require that their workers contribute to the cost of their insurance up to the legal maximum, while others pay the entire premium as a job benefit. Also, although employers are not required to do so, most companies pay part or all of the costs of health insurance for their workers' families.

As a result of the act and its influence, about 96 percent of the 1.2 million Hawaiians have health coverage—a figure unrivaled by any other state. (Before 1975, 17 percent of Hawaiians had no health insurance.) Unemployed and seasonal workers are covered by state medical subsidies. The coverage required includes physician and hospital bills, but it need not include the costs of prescription medications, vision care, or dental care.

Hawaii's twenty years of experience with virtually universal health-care coverage for its citizens has pro-

duced generally satisfying results. Most important, by placing emphasis on primary and preventive care, the Hawaiian system has improved the overall health of the state's people. For example, despite the high rate of breast cancer in Hawaii, the early detection of tumors, which is the direct result of including mammography in health coverage, has permitted the state to achieve the lowest rate of mortality from the disease.

General measurements of health that focus on a variety of determinants also confirm the success of Hawaii's approach. The American Public Health Association rated the overall health of Hawaiians as better than that of people in any other state. The Centers for Disease Control put Hawaii either at or near the top of the list of states in lowering infant mortality, increasing longevity, and lowering rates of premature death from cancer, lung disease, and heart disease.

Hawaii's almost-universal coverage of its citizens has also had consequences for controlling increases in health-care costs. Insurance premiums in Hawaii are 30 percent lower than the cost for comparable coverage on the mainland. Indeed, insurance cost is about the only commodity that is cheaper in Hawaii than in other parts of the United States. Part of the control of costs may be the result of the Hawaiian system's emphasis on preventive measures and the detection of diseases at early stages when the cost of treatment may be both cheaper and more effective.

Commercial, for-profit insurers chose to stay out of the Hawaiian market, rather than give up their freedom to decide which applicants they were willing to accept. As a result, the competition for customers mostly has been between Hawaii Medical Service Association (the Blue Cross organization with about 50 percent of the market) and the Kaiser Permanente HMO (with about 20 percent). Competition between them has helped keep prices down, while also encouraging primary and preventive care. The larger insurers have also done much to control cost by exerting pressure on physicians and hospitals to keep rates low.

Another cost-saving aspect of the Hawaiian plan is that the pool of workers covered by a given insurance plan is not drawn from a single workplace but from the entire population. By spreading the risk in a large pool, the cost per person of paying for even an expensive medical service is kept low.

Most of the 17 percent of people who lacked health insurance before 1975 worked for small factories, shops, or restaurants. Most large businesses already provided their employees with insurance coverage. The Prepaid Health Care Act had a more direct effect on small businesses because for the first time they were required to pay a large portion of the insurance premium for their workers. Nevertheless, this did not force companies out of business. Nor did it result in an increase in unemployment. Most businesses in Hawaii have simply come to accept the requirements of the act as one more item in the cost of doing business.

Indeed, despite the fact that the insurance that businesses must provide is mandated, businesses, in general, express approval of the requirement. The state's economy is mostly run by small businesses, with more than 90 percent of businesses employing fifty or fewer people. In a U.S. Chamber of Commerce survey of its members (who are typically in small businesses), Hawaii was the only state in which a majority of members favored compulsory health insurance. Many small businesses that pay the whole premium see insurance coverage as an inducement to help them keep valued workers.

Large businesses in Hawaii also express general approval of mandated insurance. The president of Hawaiian Electric put the point this way: "Probably speaking for most big businesses, we support the idea of the Prepaid Health Care Act. As a company we are very much focused on the preventive end. In the long run, it will save us money."

But businesses have not been happy with every aspect of mandated care. In particular, they have been concerned about whether the state government would keep costs that businesses must pay within reasonable limits. Grounds for this concern arose most dramatically when the state legislature decided to add benefits to workers' insurance and found themselves unable to do so without engaging in some creative lawmaking.

Federal laws make it impossible for the state to raise the level of workers' contributions to health-care premiums that was set when the law was passed in 1974. Because the legislature could not require employees to pay more, they changed the state's insurance laws to require that all health insurers and HMOs add mental health and drug and alcohol treatment, mammograms, well-baby care, and in vitro fertilization to their coverage. The result of this maneuver was to pass on the cost of the benefits to businesses. This provoked resentment in many in business, because it seemed that there was no limit on what sort of coverage the legislature might decide to force them to pay for.

Hawaii's transition to its present system was made easier by a number of factors. The population is small, the climate is healthful, and because of the large number of workers in unions, the state has a long tradition of generous medical coverage for employees. Also, Hawaii has an historically low rate of unemployment, so insurers have had little need to shift costs incurred by the uninsured to the insured. Further, Hawaii has always had a much larger number of primary-care physicians than specialists. This encourages the sort of preventive care that produces an above-average number of office visits, yet also results in lower rates of surgery and hospitalization.

Hawaii has maintained the relatively high proportion of primary-care physicians to specialists, but similar ratios are not found in most other states. This alone would make it difficult for them to switch to a system in which primary-care physicians play the predominant role. Also, Hawaii's geographic isolation makes it difficult for businesses dissatisfied with the health-care plan to relocate. On the mainland, it is a relatively simple matter to move a business across a state line to avoid the demands of a state-based health-care system.

Whether an employer-mandated insurance plan similar to the one that has been successful in Hawaii would be successful in other states or in the country as a whole remains very much a matter of dispute. At the very least, however, Hawaii stands as an example of how a mandated plan operates and provides us with an opportunity to examine its strengths and limits.

## READINGS

# Section 1: Justice and Health Care

## An Ethical Framework for Access to Health Care

*President's Commission for the Study of Ethical Problems in Medicine*

The commission claims that the role played by health care in enabling people to live full and satisfying lives gives it a special importance. The crucial role of health care explains why it ought to be accessible in an equitable fashion to everyone in the society. After reviewing various meanings of "equitable access," the commission concludes that fairness is satisfied if everyone has access to "an adequate level of care."

The commission stops short of endorsing a "right" to health care. It holds, rather, that society has a moral obligation to provide everyone with access to adequate care. The government, as one social institution among others, is not solely or even primarily responsible for providing the access. It might be achieved by a pluralistic approach that relies on both the private and public sectors. Ultimately, though, it is the government that has a duty to see to it that society's moral obligation to provide care is satisfied.

. . . Most Americans believe that because health care is special, access to it raises special ethical concerns. In part, this is because good health is by definition important to well-being. Health care can relieve pain and suffering, restore functioning, and prevent death; it can enhance good health and improve an individual's opportunity to pursue a life plan; and it can provide valuable information about a person's overall health. Beyond its practical importance, the involvement of health care with the most significant and awesome events of life—birth, illness, and death—adds a symbolic aspect to health care: it is special because it signifies not only mutual empathy and caring but the mysterious aspects of curing and healing.

Furthermore, while people have some ability—through choice of life-style and through preventive measures—to influence their health status, many health problems are beyond their control and are therefore undeserved. Besides the burdens of genetics, environment, and chance, individuals become ill because of things they do or fail to do—but it is often difficult for an individual to choose to do otherwise or even to know with enough specificity and confidence what he or she ought to do to remain healthy. Finally, the incidence and severity of ill health is distributed very unevenly among people. Basic needs for housing and food are predictable, but even the most hardworking and prudent person may suddenly be faced with overwhelming needs for health care. Together, these considerations lend weight to the belief that health care is different from most other goods and services. In a society concerned not only with fairness and equality of opportunity but also with the redemptive powers of science, there is a felt obligation to ensure that some level of health services is available to all.

From President's Commission for the Study of Ethical Problems in Medicine and Biomedical and Behavioral Research, Securing Access to Health Care, Vol. 1 (1983), pp. 11–12, 16–21, 22–23, 30–32, 34–37 (Notes and references omitted.)

There are many ambiguities, however, about the nature of this societal obligation. What share of health costs should individuals be expected to bear, and what responsibility do they have to use health resources prudently? Is it society's responsibility to ensure that every person receives care or services of as high quality and as great extent as any other individual? Does it require that everyone share opportunities to receive all available care or care of any possible benefit? If not, what level of care is "enough"? And does society's obligation include a responsibility to ensure both that care is available and that its costs will not unduly burden the patient?

The resolution of such issues is made more difficult by the spectre of rising health care costs and expenditures. Although the finitude of national resources demands that trade-offs be made between health care and other social goods, there is little agreement about which choices are most acceptable from an ethical standpoint. In this chapter, the Commission attempts to lay an ethical foundation for evaluating both current patterns of access to health care and the policies designed to address remaining problems in the distribution of health care resources. . . .

## The Special Importance of Health Care

Although the importance of health care may, at first blush, appear obvious, this assumption is often based on instinct rather than reasoning. Yet it is possible to step back and examine those properties of health care that lead to the ethical conclusion that it ought to be distributed equitably.

### Well-Being

Ethical concern about the distribution of health care derives from the special importance of health care in promoting personal well-being by preventing or relieving pain, suffering, and disability and by avoiding loss of life. The fundamental importance of the latter is obvious: pain and suffering are also experiences that people have strong desires to avoid, both because of the intrinsic quality of the experience and because of their effects on the capacity to pursue and achieve other goals and purposes. Similarly, untreated disability can prevent people from leading rewarding and fully active lives.

Health, insofar as it is the absence of pain, suffering, or serious disability, is what has been called a primary good, that is, there is no need to know what a particular person's other ends, preferences, and values are in order to know that health is good for that individual. It generally helps people carry out their life plans, whatever they may happen to be. This is not to say that everyone defines good health in the same way or assigns the same weight or importance to different aspects of being healthy, or to health in comparison with the other goods of life. Yet though people may differ over each of these matters, their disagreement takes place within a framework of basic agreement on the importance of health. Likewise, people differ in their beliefs about the value of health and medical care and their use of it as a means of achieving good health, as well as in their attitudes toward the various benefits and risks of different treatments.

### Opportunity

Health care can also broaden a person's range of opportunities, that is, the array of life plans that is reasonable to pursue within the conditions obtaining in society. In the United States equality of opportunity is a widely accepted value that is reflected throughout public policy. The effects that meeting (or failing to meet) people's health needs have on the distribution of opportunity in a society become apparent if diseases are thought of as adverse departures from a normal level of functioning. In this view, health care is that which people need to maintain or restore normal functioning or to compensate for inability to function normally. Health is thus comparable in importance to education in determining the opportunities available to people to pursue different life plans.

### Information

The special importance of health care stems in part from its ability to relieve worry and to enable patients to adjust to their situation by supplying reliable information about their health. Most people do not understand the true nature of a health problem when it first develops. Health professionals can then perform the worthwhile function of informing people about their conditions and about the expected prognoses with or without various treatments. Though information sometimes creates concern, often it reassures patients either by ruling out a feared disease or by revealing the self-limiting nature of a condition and, thus, the lack of need for further treatment. Although health care in many situations may thus not be necessary for good physical health, a great deal of relief from unnecessary concern—and even avoidance of pointless or potentially harmful steps—is achieved by health care in the form of expert information provided to worried patients. Even when a prognosis is unfavorable and health professionals have little treatment to offer, accurate information can help patients plan how to cope with their situation.

### The Interpersonal Significance of Illness, Birth, and Death

It is no accident that religious organizations have played a major role in the care of the sick and dying and in the process of birth. Since all human beings are vulnerable to disease and all die, health care has a special interpersonal significance: it expresses and nurtures bonds of empathy and compassion. The depth of a society's concern about health care can be seen as a measure of its sense of solidarity in the face of suffering and death. Moreover, health care takes on special meaning because of its role in the beginning of a human being's life as well as the end. In spite of all the advances in the scientific understanding of birth, disease, and death, these profound and universal experiences remain shared mysteries that touch the spiritual side of human nature. For these reasons a society's commitment to health care reflects some of its most basic attitudes about what it is to be a member of the human community.

## The Concept of Equitable Access to Health Care

The special nature of health care helps to explain why it ought to be accessible, in a fair fashion, to all. But if this ethical conclusion is to provide a basis for evaluating current patterns of access to health care and proposed health policies, the meaning of fairness or equity in this context must be clarified. The concept of equitable access needs definition in its two main aspects: the level of care that ought to be available to all and the extent to which burdens can be imposed on those who obtain these services.

### Access to What?

"Equitable access" could be interpreted in a number of ways: equality of access, access to whatever an individual needs or would benefit from, or access to an adequate level of care.

**Equity as Equality.** It has been suggested that equity is achieved either when everyone is assured of receiving an equal quantity of health care dollars or when people enjoy equal health. The most common characterization of equity as equality, however, is as providing everyone with the same level of health care. In this view, it follows that if a given level of care is available to one individual it must be available to all. If the initial standard is set high, by reference to the highest level of care presently received, an enormous drain would result on the resources needed to provide other goods. Alternatively, if the standard is set low in order to avoid an excessive use of resources, some beneficial services would have to be withheld from people who wished to purchase them. In other words, no one would be allowed access to more services or services of higher quality than those available to everyone else, even if he or she were willing to pay for those services from his or her personal resources.

As long as significant inequalities in income and wealth persist, inequalities in the use of health care can be expected beyond those created by differences in need. Given people with the same pattern of preferences and equal health care needs, those with greater financial resources will purchase more health care. Conversely, given equal financial resources, the different patterns of health care preferences that typically exist in any population will result in a different use of health services by people with equal health care needs. Trying to prevent such inequalities would require interfering with people's liberty to use their income to purchase an important good like health care while leaving them free to use it for frivolous or inessential ends. Prohibiting people with higher incomes or stronger preferences for health care from purchasing more care than everyone else gets would not be feasible, and would probably result in a black market for health care.

**Equity as Access Solely According to Benefit or Need.** Interpreting equitable access to mean that everyone must receive all health care that is of any benefit to them also has unacceptable implications. Unless health is the only good or resources are unlimited, it would be irrational for a society—as for an individual—to make a commitment to provide whatever

health care might be beneficial regardless of cost. Although health care is of special importance, it is surely not all that is important to people. Pushed to an extreme, this criterion might swallow up all of society's resources, since there is virtually no end to the funds that could be devoted to possibly beneficial care for diseases and disabilities and to their prevention.

Equitable access to health care must take into account not only the benefits of care but also the cost in comparison with other goods and services to which those resources might be allocated. Society will reasonably devote some resources to health care but reserve most resources for other goals. This, in turn, will mean that some health services (even of a lifesaving sort) will not be developed or employed because they would produce too few benefits in relation to their costs and to the other ways the resources for them might be used.

It might be argued that the notion of "need" provides a way to limit access to only that care that confers especially important benefits. In this view, equity as access according to need would place less severe demands on social resources than equity according to benefit would. There are, however, difficulties with the notion of need in this context. On the one hand, medical need is often not narrowly defined but refers to any condition for which medical treatment might be effective. Thus "equity as access according to need" collapses into "access according to whatever is of benefit."

On the other hand, "need" could be even more expansive in scope than "benefit." Philosophical and economic writings do not provide any clear distinction between "needs" and "wants" or "preferences." Since the term means different things to different people, "access according to need" could become "access to any health service a person wants." Conversely, need could be interpreted very narrowly to encompass only a very minimal level of services—for example, those "necessary to prevent death."

**Equity as an Adequate Level of Health Care.** Although neither "everything needed" nor "everything beneficial" nor "everything that anyone else is getting" are defensible ways of understanding equitable access, the special nature of health care dictates that everyone have access to *some* level of care: enough care to achieve sufficient welfare, opportunity, information, and evidence of interpersonal concern to facilitate a reasonably full and satisfying life. That level can be termed "an adequate level of health care." The difficulty of sharpening this amorphous notion into a workable foundation for health policy is a major problem in the United States today. This concept is not new; it is implicit in the public debate over health policy and has manifested itself in the history of public policy in this country. In this chapter, the Commission attempts to demonstrate the value of the concept, to clarify its content and to apply it to the problems facing health policymakers.

Understanding equitable access to health care to mean that everyone should be able to secure an adequate level of care has several strengths. Because an adequate level of care may be less than "all beneficial care" and because it does not require that all needs be satisfied, it acknowledges the need for setting priorities within health care and signals a clear recognition that society's resources are limited and that there are other goods besides health. Thus, interpreting equity as access to adequate care does not generate an open-ended obligation. One of the chief dangers of interpretations of equity that require virtually unlimited resources for health care is that they encourage the view that equitable access is an impossible ideal. Defining equity as an adequate level of care for all avoids an impossible commitment of resources without falling into the opposite error of abandoning the enterprise of seeking to ensure that health care is in fact available for everyone.

In addition, since providing an adequate level of care is a limited moral requirement, this definition also avoids the unacceptable restriction on individual liberty entailed by the view that equity requires equality. Provided that an adequate level is available to all, those who prefer to use their resources to obtain care that exceeds that level do not offend any ethical principle in doing so. Finally, the concept of adequacy, as the Commission understands it, is society-relative. The content of adequate care will depend upon the overall resources available in a given society, and can take into account a consensus of expectations about what is adequate in a particular society at a particular time in its historical development. This permits the definition of adequacy to be altered as societal resources and expectations change.

### With What Burdens?

It is not enough to focus on the care that individuals receive; attention must be paid to the burdens they must bear in order to obtain it—waiting and travel time, the cost and availability of transport, the financial cost of the care itself. Equity requires not only that adequate care be available to all, but also that these burdens not be excessive.

If individuals must travel unreasonably long distances, wait for unreasonably long hours, or spend most of their financial resources to obtain care, some will be deterred from obtaining adequate care, with adverse effects on their health and well-being. Others may bear the burdens, but only at the expense of their ability to meet other important needs. If one of the main reasons for providing adequate care is that health care increases welfare and opportunity, then a system that required large numbers of individuals to forgo food, shelter, or educational advancement in order to obtain care would be self-defeating and irrational.

The concept of acceptable burdens in obtaining care, as opposed to excessive ones, parallels in some respects the concept of adequacy. Just as equity does not require equal access, neither must the burdens of obtaining adequate care be equal for all persons. What is crucial is that the variations in burdens fall within an acceptable range. As in determining an adequate level of care, there is no simple formula for ascertaining when the burdens of obtaining care fall within such a range. Yet some guidelines can be formulated. To illustrate, since a given financial outlay represents a greater sacrifice to a poor person than to a rich person, "excessive" must be understood in relation to income. Obviously everyone cannot live the same distance from a health care facility, and some individuals choose to locate in remote and sparsely populated areas. Concern about an inequitable burden would be appropriate, however, when identifiable groups must travel a great distance or long time to receive care—though people may appropriately be expected to travel farther to get specialized care, for example, than to obtain primary or emergency care. . . .

### A Societal Obligation

Society has a moral obligation to ensure that everyone has access to adequate care without being subject to excessive burdens. In speaking of a societal obligation the Commission makes reference to society in the broadest sense—the collective American community. The community is made up of individuals, who are in turn members of many other, overlapping groups, both public and private: local, state, regional, and national units; professional and workplace organizations; religious, educational, and charitable organizations; and family, kinship, and ethnic groups. All these entities play a role in discharging societal obligations.

The Commission believes it is important to distinguish between society, in this inclusive sense, and government as one institution among others in society. Thus the recognition of a collective or societal obligation does not imply that government should be the only or even the primary institution involved in the complex enterprise of making health care available. It is the Commission's view that the societal obligation to ensure equitable access for everyone may best be fulfilled in this country by a pluralistic approach that relies upon the coordinated contributions of actions by both the private and public sectors.

Securing equitable access is a societal rather than a merely private or individual responsibility for several reasons. First, while health is of special importance for human beings, health care—especially scientific health care—is a social product requiring the skills and efforts of many individuals; it is not something that individuals can provide for themselves solely through their own efforts. Second, because the need for health care is both unevenly distributed among persons and highly unpredictable and because the cost of securing care may be great, few individuals could secure adequate care without relying on some social mechanism for sharing the costs. Third, if persons generally deserved their health conditions or if the need for health care were fully within the individual's control, the fact that some lack adequate care would not be viewed as an inequity. But differences in health status, and hence differences in health care needs, are largely undeserved because they are, for the most part, not within the individual's control. . . .

In light of the special importance of health care, the largely undeserved character of differences in health status, and the uneven distribution and unpredictability of health care needs, society has a moral obligation to ensure adequate care for all. Saying that the obligation is societal (rather than merely individual) stops short, however, of identifying who has the ultimate responsibility for ensuring that the obligation is successfully met.

## Who Should Ensure That Society's Obligation Is Met?

. . .

### A Role for Government

The extent of governmental involvement in securing equitable access to care depends on the extent to which the market and private charity achieve this objective. . . . Although it is clear that—even for those with adequate resources—the purchase of health care differs from other market transactions, the market

(which includes private health insurance) is capable of providing many people with an adequate level of health care. However, when the market and charity do not enable individuals to obtain adequate care or cause them to endure excessive burdens in doing so, then the responsibility to ensure that these people have equitable access to health care resides with the local, state, and Federal governments.

**Locating Responsibility.**  Although it is appropriate that all levels of government be involved in seeing that equitable access to health care is achieved, the *ultimate* responsibility for ensuring that this obligation is met rests with the Federal government. The Commission believes it is extremely important to distinguish between the view that the Federal government ought to provide care and the view that the Federal government is ultimately responsible for seeing that there is equitable access to care. It is the latter view that the Commission endorses. It is not the purpose of this Report to assign the precise division of labor between public and private provision of health care. Rather, the Commission has attempted here only to locate the ultimate responsibility for ensuring that equitable access is attained.

A view that has gained wide acceptance in this country is that the government has a major responsibility for making sure that certain basic social goods, such as health care and economic security for the elderly, are available to all. Over the past half-century, public policy and public opinion have increasingly reflected the belief that the Federal government is the logical mechanism for ensuring that society's obligation to make these goods available is met. In the case of health care, this stance is supported by several considerations. First, the obligation in question is society-wide, not limited to particular states or localities; it is an obligation of all to achieve equity for all. Second, government responsibility at the national level is needed to secure reliable resources. Third, only the Federal government can ultimately guarantee that the burdens of providing resources are distributed fairly across the whole of society. Fourth, meeting society's obligation to provide equitable access requires an "overview" of efforts. Unless the ultimate responsibility has been clearly fixed for determining whether the standard of equitable access is being met, there is no reason to believe it will be achieved.

**The Limitations of Relying upon the Government.**  Although the Commission recognizes the necessity of government involvement in ensuring equity of access, it believes that such activity must be carefully crafted and implemented in order to achieve its intended purpose. Public concern about the inability of the market and of private charity to secure access to health care for all has led to extensive government involvement in the financing and delivery of health care. This involvement has come about largely as a result of ad hoc responses to specific problems: the result has been a patchwork of public initiatives at the local, state, and Federal level. These efforts have done much to make health care more widely available to all citizens, but . . . they have not achieved equity of access.

To a large extent, this is the result of a lack of consensus about the nature of the goal and the proper role of government in pursuing it. But to some degree, it may also be the product of the nature of government activity. In some instances, government programs (of all types, not just health-related) have not been designed well enough to achieve the purposes intended or have been subverted to serve purposes explicitly not intended.

In the case of health care, it is extremely difficult to devise public strategies that, on the one hand, do not encourage the misuse of health services and, on the other hand, are not so restrictive as to unnecessarily or arbitrarily limit available care. There is a growing concern, for example, that government assistance in the form of tax exemptions for the purchase of employment-related health insurance has led to the overuse of many services of only very marginal benefit. Similarly, government programs that pay for health care directly (such as Medicaid) have been subject to fraud and abuse by both beneficiaries and providers. Alternatively, efforts to avoid misuse and abuse have at times caused local, state, and Federal programs to suffer from excessive bureaucracy, red tape, inflexibility, and unreasonable interference in individual choice. Also, as with private charity, government programs have not always avoided the unfortunate effects on the human spirit of "discretionary benevolence," especially in those programs requiring income or means tests.

It is also possible that as the government role in health care increases, the private sector's role will decrease in unforeseen and undesired ways. For example, government efforts to ensure access to nursing home care might lead to a lessening of support from family, friends, and other private sources for people who could be cared for in their homes. Although these kinds of problems do not inevitably accompany governmental involvement, they do occur and their presence provides evidence of the need for thoughtful and careful structuring of any government enterprise.

### *A Right to Health Care?*

Often the issue of equitable access to health care is framed in the language of rights. Some who view health care from the perspective of distributive justice argue that the considerations discussed in this chapter show not only that society has a moral obligation to provide equitable access, but also that every individual has a moral right to such access. The Commission has chosen not to develop the case for achieving equitable access through the assertion of a right to health care. Instead it has sought to frame the issues in terms of the special nature of health care and of society's moral obligation to achieve equity, without taking a position on whether the term "obligation" should be read as entailing a moral right. The Commission reaches this conclusion for several reasons: first, such a right is not legally or Constitutionally recognized at the present time; second, it is not a logical corollary of an ethical obligation of the type the Commission has enunciated; and third, it is not necessary as a foundation for appropriate governmental actions to secure adequate health care for all. . . .

**Moral Obligations and Rights.**  The relationship between the concept of a moral right and that of a moral obligation is complex. To say that a person has a moral right to something is always to say that it is that person's due, that is, he or she is morally entitled to it. In contrast, the term "obligation" is used in two different senses. All moral rights imply corresponding obligations, but, depending on the sense of the term that is being used, moral obligations may or may not imply corresponding rights. In the broad sense, to say that society has a moral obligation to do something is to say that it ought morally to do that thing and that failure to do it makes society liable to serious moral criticism. This does not, however, mean that there is a corresponding right. For example, a person may have a moral obligation to help those in need, even though the needy cannot, strictly speaking, demand that person's aid as something they are due.

The government's responsibility for seeing that the obligation to achieve equity is met is independent of the existence of a corresponding moral right to health care. There are many forms of government involvement, such as enforcement of traffic rules or taxation to support national defense, to protect the environment, or to promote biomedical research, that do not presuppose corresponding moral rights but that are nonetheless legitimate and almost universally recognized as such. In a democracy, at least, the people may assign to government the responsibility for seeing that important collective obligations are met, provided that doing so does not violate important moral rights.

As long as the debate over the ethical assessment of patterns of access to health care is carried on simply by the assertion and refutation of a "right to health care," the debate will be incapable of guiding policy. At the very least, the nature of the right must be made clear and competing accounts of it compared and evaluated. Moreover, if claims of rights are to guide policy they must be supported by sound ethical reasoning and the connections between various rights must be systematically developed, especially where rights are potentially in conflict with one another. At present, however, there is a great deal of dispute among competing theories of rights, with most theories being so abstract and inadequately developed that their implications for health care are not obvious. Rather than attempt to adjudicate among competing theories of rights, the Commission has chosen to concentrate on what it believes to be the more important part of the question: what is the nature of the societal obligation, which exists whether or not people can claim a corresponding right to health care, and how should this societal obligation be fulfilled?

## Meeting the Societal Obligation

### How Much Care Is Enough?

Before the concept of an adequate level of care can be used as a tool to evaluate patterns of access and efforts to improve equity, it must be fleshed out. Since there is no objective formula for doing this, reasonable people can disagree about whether particular patterns and policies meet the demands of adequacy. The Commission does not attempt to spell out in detail what adequate care should include. Rather it frames the terms in which those who discuss or critique health care issues can consider ethics as well as economics, medical science, and other dimensions.

**Characteristics of Adequacy.** First, the Commission considers it clear that health care can only be judged adequate in relation to an individual's health condition. To begin with a list of techniques or procedures, for example, is not sensible: A CT scan for an accident victim with a serious head injury might be the best way to make a diagnosis essential for the appropriate treatment of that patient; a CT scan for a person with headaches might not be considered essential for adequate care. To focus only on the technique, therefore,

rather than on the individual's health and the impact the procedure will have on that individual's welfare and opportunity, would lead to inappropriate policy.

Disagreement will arise about whether the care of some health conditions falls within the demands of adequacy. Most people will agree, however, that some conditions should not be included in the societal obligation to ensure access to adequate care. A relatively uncontroversial example would be changing the shape of a functioning, normal nose or retarding the normal effects of aging (through cosmetic surgery). By the same token, there are some conditions, such as pregnancy, for which care would be regarded as an important component of adequacy. In determining adequacy, it is important to consider how people's welfare, opportunities, and requirements for information and interpersonal caring are affected by their health condition.

Any assessment of adequacy must consider also the types, amounts, and quality of care necessary to respond to each health condition. It is important to emphasize that these questions are implicitly comparative: the standard of adequacy for a condition must reflect the fact that resources used for it will not be available to respond to other conditions. Consequently, the level of care deemed adequate should reflect a reasoned judgment not only about the impact of the condition on the welfare and opportunity of the individual but also about the efficacy and the cost of the care itself in relation to other conditions and the efficacy and cost of the care that is available for them. Since individual cases differ so much, the health care professional and patient must be flexible. Thus adequacy, even in relation to a particular health condition, generally refers to a range of options.

**The Relationship of Costs and Benefits.** The level of care that is available will be determined by the level of resources devoted to producing it. Such allocation should reflect the benefits and costs of the care provided. It should be emphasized that these "benefits," as well as their "costs," should be interpreted broadly, and not restricted only to effects easily quantifiable in monetary terms. Personal benefits include improvements in individuals' functioning and in their quality of life, and the reassurance from worry and the provision of information that are a product of health care. Broader social benefits should be included as well, such as strengthening the sense of community and the belief that no one in serious need of health care will be left without it. Similarly, costs are not merely the funds spent for a treatment but include other less tangible and quantifiable adverse consequences, such as diverting funds away from other socially desirable endeavors including education, welfare, and other social services. There is no objectively correct value that these various costs and benefits have or that can be discovered by the tools of cost/benefit analysis. Still, such an analysis, as a recent report of the Office of Technology Assessment noted, "can be very helpful to decisionmakers because the process of analysis gives structure to the problem, allows an open consideration of all relevant effects of a decision, and forces the explicit treatment of key assumptions." But the valuation of the various effects of alternative treatments for different conditions rests on people's values and goals, about which individuals will reasonably disagree. In a democracy, the appropriate values to be assigned to the consequences of policies must ultimately be determined by people expressing their values through social and political processes as well as in the marketplace.

**Approximating Adequacy.** The intention of the Commission is to provide a frame of reference for policymakers, not to resolve these complex questions. Nevertheless, it is possible to raise some of the specific issues that should be considered in determining what constitutes adequate care. It is important, for example, to gather accurate information about and compare the costs and effects, both favorable and unfavorable, of various treatment or management options. The options that better serve the goals that make health care of special importance should be assigned higher value. As already noted, the assessment of costs must take two factors into account: the cost of a proposed option in relation to alternative forms of care that would

achieve the same goal of enhancing the welfare and opportunities of the patient, and the cost of each proposed option in terms of foregone opportunities to apply the same resources to social goals other than that of ensuring equitable access.

Furthermore, a reasonable specification of adequate care must reflect an assessment of the relative importance of many different characteristics of a given form of care for a particular condition. Sometimes the problem is posed as: What *amounts* of care and what *quality* of care? Such a formulation reduces a complex problem to only two dimensions, implying that all care can readily be ranked as better or worse. Because two alternative forms of care may vary along a number of dimensions, there may be no consensus among reasonable and informed individuals about which form is of higher overall quality. It is worth bearing in mind that adequacy does not mean the highest possible level of quality or strictly equal quality any more than it requires equal amounts of care; of course, adequacy does require that everyone receive care that meets standards of sound medical practice.

Any combination of arrangements for achieving adequacy will presumably include some health care delivery settings that mainly serve certain groups, such as the poor or those covered by public programs. The fact that patients receive care in different settings or from different providers does not itself show that some are receiving inadequate care. The Commission believes that there is no moral objection to such a system so long as all receive care that is adequate in amount and quality and all patients are treated with concern and respect. . . .

---

# Is There a Right to a Decent Minimum of Health Care?

## Allen E. Buchanan

After Allen Buchanan analyzes the notion of what it is to have a right, he then argues that we don't need to demonstrate that there is a "right to health care" to require our government to guarantee a "decent minimum" of care for everybody.

Buchanan claims that the combined weight of four arguments is sufficient to show that the government has an obligation to provide a decent minimum: (1) previous injustices support providing care to African Americans and others; (2) public health goals support a moral (maybe even a constitutional) obligation to provide "equal protection"; (3) national defense and the need for a workforce require a decent minimum; (4) the duty of charity, which helps provide a decent minimum, must sometimes be enforced by the government.

## The Assumption That There Is a Right to a Decent Minimum

A consensus that there is (at least) a right to a decent minimum of health care pervades recent policy debates and much of the philosophical literature on health care. Disagreement centers on two issues. Is there a more extensive right than the right to a decent minimum of health care? What is included in the decent minimum to which there is a right? . . .

Though the concept of a right is complex and controversial, for our purposes a partial sketch will do. To say that a person has a right to something, X, is first of all to say that A is entitled to X, that X is due to him or her. This is not equivalent to saying that if A were granted X it would be a good thing, even a morally good thing, or that X is desired by or desirable for A. Second, it is usually held that valid right-claims, at least in the case of basic rights, may be backed by sanctions, including coercion if necessary (unless doing so would produce extremely great disutility or grave moral evil), and that (except in such highly exceptional circumstances) failure of an appropriate authority to apply the needed sanctions is itself an injustice. Recent rights-theorists have also emphasized a third feature of rights, or at least of basic rights or rights in the strict sense: valid right-claims 'trump' appeals to what would maximize utility, whether it be the utility of the right-holder, or social utility. In other words, if A has a right to X, then the mere fact that infringing A's right would maximize overall utility or even A's utility is not itself a sufficient reason for infringing it.[1] Finally, a universal (or general) right is one which applies to all persons, not just to certain individuals or classes because of their involvement in special actions, relationships, or agreements.

The second feature—enforceability—is of crucial importance for those who assume or argue that there is a universal right to a decent minimum of health care. For, once it is granted that there is such a right and that such a right may be enforced (absent any extremely weighty reason against enforcement), the claim that there is a universal right provides the moral basis for using the coercive power of the state to assure a decent minimum for all. Indeed, the surprising absence of attempts to justify a coercively backed decent minimum policy by arguments that do *not* aim at establishing a universal right suggests the following

From President's Commission, *Securing Access to Health Care*, Vol. II. Washington, D.C. U.S. Government Printing Office, 1983.

hypothesis: advocates of a coercively backed decent minimum have operated on the assumption that such a policy must be based on a universal right to a decent minimum. The chief aim of this article is to show that this assumption is false.

I think it is fair to say that many who confidently assume there is a (universal) right to a decent minimum of health care have failed to appreciate the significance of the first feature of our sketch of the concept of a right. It is crucial to observe that the claim that there is a right to a decent minimum is much stronger than the claim that everyone *ought* to have access to such a minimum, or that if they did it would be a good thing, or that any society which is capable, without great sacrifice, of providing a decent minimum but fails to do so is deeply morally defective. None of the latter assertions implies the existence of a right, if this is understood as a moral entitlement which ought to be established by the coercive power of the state if necessary. . . .

## The Need for a Supporting Theory

. . . The concept of a right to a decent minimum of health care is inadequate as a moral basis for a coercively backed decent minimum policy in the absence of a coherent and defensible theory of justice. . . . A theoretical grounding for the right to a decent minimum of health care is indispensable. . . .

My suggestion is that the combined weight of arguments from special (as opposed to universal) rights to health care, harm-prevention, prudential arguments of the sort used to justify public health measures, and two arguments that show that effective charity shares features of public goods (in the technical sense) is sufficient to do the work of an alleged universal right to a decent minimum of health care.

### Arguments from Special Rights

The right-claim we have been examining (and find unsupported) has been a *universal* right-claim: one that attributes the same right to all persons. *Special* right-claims, in contrast, restrict the right in question to certain individuals or groups.

There are at least three types of arguments that can be given for special rights to health care. First, there are arguments from the requirements of rectifying past or present institutional injustices. It can be argued, for example, that American blacks and native Americans are entitled to a certain core set of health-care services owing to their history of unjust treatment by government or other social institutions, on the grounds that these injustices have directly or indirectly had detrimental effects on the health of the groups in question. Second, there are arguments from the requirements of compensation to those who have suffered unjust harm or who have been unjustly exposed to health risks by the assignable actions of private individuals or corporations—for instance, those who have suffered neurological damage from the effects of chemical pollutants.

Third, a strong moral case can be made for special rights to health care for those who have undergone exceptional sacrifices for the good of society as a whole—in particular those whose health has been adversely affected through military service. The most obvious candidates for such compensatory special rights are soldiers wounded in combat.

### Arguments from the Prevention of Harm

The content of the right to a decent minimum is typically understood as being more extensive than those traditional public health services that are usually justified on the grounds that they are required to protect the citizenry from certain harms arising from the interactions of persons living together in large numbers. Yet such services have been a major factor—if not *the* major factor—in reducing morbidity and mortality rates. Examples include sanitation and immunization. The moral justification of such measures, which constitute an important element in a decent minimum of health care, rests upon the widely accepted Harm (Prevention) Principle, not upon a right to health care.

The Harm Prevention argument for traditional public health services, however, may be elaborated in a way that brings them closer to arguments for a universal right to health care. With some plausibility one might contend that once the case has been made for expending public resources on public health measures, there is a moral (and perhaps Constitutional) obligation to achieve some standard of *equal protection* from the harms these measures are designed to prevent. Such an argument, if it could be made out, would imply that the availability of basic public health services should not vary greatly across different racial, ethnic, or geographic groups within the country.

### Prudential Arguments

Prudent arguments for health-care services typically emphasize benefits rather than the prevention of

harm. It has often been argued, in particular, that the availability of certain basic forms of health care make for a more productive labor force or improve the fitness of the citizenry for national defense. This type of argument, too, does not assume that individuals have moral rights (whether special or universal) to the services in question.

It seems very likely that the combined scope of the various special health-care rights discussed above, when taken together with harm prevention and prudential arguments for basic health services and an argument from equal protection through public health measures, would do a great deal toward satisfying the health-care needs which those who advocate a universal right to a decent minimum are most concerned about. In other words, once the strength of a more pluralistic approach is appreciated, we may come to question the popular dogma that policy initiatives designed to achieve a decent minimum of health care for all must be grounded in a universal moral right to a decent minimum. This suggestion is worth considering because it again brings home the importance of the methodological difficulty encountered earlier. Even if, for instance, there is wide consensus on the considered judgment that the lower health prospects of inner city blacks are not only morally unacceptable but an injustice, it does not follow that this injustice consists of the infringement of a universal right to a decent minimum of health care. Instead, the injustice might lie in the failure to rectify past injustices or in the failure to achieve public health arrangements that meet a reasonable standard of equal protection for all.

### Two Arguments for Enforced Beneficence

The pluralistic moral case for a legal entitlement to a decent minimum of health care (in the absence of a universal moral right) may be strengthened further by non-rights-based arguments from the principle of beneficence.[2] The possibility of making out such arguments depends upon the assumption that some principles may be justifiably enforced even if they are not principles specifying valid right-claims. There is at least one widely recognized class of such principles requiring contribution to the production of 'public goods' in the technical sense (for example, tax laws requiring contribution to national defense). It is characteristic of public goods that each individual has an incentive to withhold his contribution to the collective goal even though the net result is that the goal will not be achieved. Enforcement of a principle requiring all individuals to contribute to the goal is necessary to overcome the individual's incentive to withhold contribution by imposing penalties for his own failure to contribute and by assuring him that others will contribute. There is a special subclass of principles whose reinforcement is justified not only by the need to overcome the individual's incentive to withhold compliance with the principle but also to ensure that individuals' efforts are appropriately *coordinated.* For example, enforcing the rule of the road to drive only on the right not only ensures a joint effort toward the goal of safe driving but also coordinates individuals' efforts so as to make the attainment of that goal possible. Indeed, in the case of the 'rule of the road' a certain kind of coordinated joint effort is the public good whose attainment justifies enforcement. But regardless of whether the production of a public good requires the solution of a coordination problem or not, there may be no *right* that is the correlative of the coercively backed obligation specified by the principle. There are two arguments for enforced beneficence, and they each depend upon both the idea of coordination and on certain aspects of the concept of a public good.

Both arguments begin with an assumption reasonable libertarians accept: there is a basic moral obligation of charity or beneficence to those in need. In a society that has the resources and technical knowledge to improve health or at least to ameliorate important health defects, the application of this requirement of beneficence includes the provision of resources for at least certain forms of health care. If we are sincere, we will be concerned with the efficacy of our charitable or beneficent impulses. It is all well and good for the libertarian to say that voluntary giving *can* replace the existing array of government entitlement programs, but this *possibility* will be cold comfort to the needy if, for any of several reasons, voluntary giving falters.

Social critics on the left often argue that in a highly competitive acquisitive society such as ours it is naive to think that the sense of beneficence will win out over the urgent promptings of self-interest. One need not argue, however, that voluntary giving fails from weakness of the will. Instead one can argue that even if each individual recognizes a moral duty to contribute to the aid of others and is motivationally capable of acting on that duty, some important forms of

beneficence will not be forthcoming because each individual will rationally conclude that he should not contribute.

Many important forms of health care, especially those involving large-scale capital investment for technology, cannot be provided except through the contributions of large numbers of persons. This is also true of the most important forms of medical research. But if so, then the beneficent individual will not be able to act effectively, in isolation. What is needed is a coordinated joint effort.

**First Argument.** There are many ways in which I might help others in need. Granted the importance of health, providing a decent minimum of health care for all, through large-scale collective efforts, will be a more important form of beneficence than the various charitable acts A, B, and C, which I might perform *independently,* that is, whose success does not depend upon the contributions of others. Nonetheless, if I am rationally beneficent I will reason as follows: either enough others will contribute to the decent minimum project to achieve this goal, even if I do not contribute to it; or not enough others will contribute to achieve a decent minimum, even if I do contribute. In either case, my contribution will be wasted. In other words, granted the scale of the investment required and the virtually negligible size of my own contribution, I can disregard the minute possibility that my contribution might make the difference between success and failure. But if so, then the rationally beneficent thing for me to do is not to waste my contribution on the project of ensuring a decent minimum but instead to undertake an independent act of beneficence; A, B, or C—where I know my efforts will be needed and efficacious. But if everyone, or even many people, reason in this way, then what we each recognize as the most effective form of beneficence will not come about. Enforcement of a principle requiring contributions to ensuring a decent minimum is needed.

The first argument is of the same form as standard public goods arguments for enforced contributions to national defense, energy conservation, and many other goods, with this exception. In standard public goods arguments, it is usually assumed that the individual's incentive for not contributing is self-interest and that it is in his interest not to contribute because he will be able to partake of the good, if it is produced, even if he does not contribute. In the case at hand, however, the individual's incentive for not contributing to the joint effort is not self-interest, but rather his desire to maximize the good he can do for others with a given amount of his resources. Thus if he contributes but the goal of achieving a decent minimum for all would have been achieved without his contribution, then he has still failed to use his resources in a maximally beneficent way relative to the options of either contributing or not to the joint project, even though the goal of achieving a decent minimum is attained. The rationally beneficent thing to do, then, is not to contribute, even though the result of everyone's acting in a rationally beneficent way will be a relatively ineffective patchwork of small-scale individual acts of beneficence rather than a large-scale, coordinated effort.

**Second Argument.** I believe that ensuring a decent minimum of health care for all is more important than projects A, B, or C, and I am willing to contribute to the decent minimum project, but only if I have assurance that enough others will contribute to achieve the threshold of investment necessary for success. Unless I have this assurance, I will conclude that it is less than rational—and perhaps even morally irresponsible—to contribute my resources to the decent minimum project. For my contribution will be wasted if not enough others contribute. If I lack assurance of sufficient contributions by others, the rationally beneficent thing for me to do is to expend my 'beneficence budget' on some less-than-optimal project A, B, or C, whose success does not depend on the contribution of others. But without enforcement, I cannot be assured that enough others will contribute, and if others reason as I do, then what we all believe to be the most effective form of beneficence will not be forthcoming. Others may fail to contribute either because the promptings of self-interest overpower their sense of beneficence, or because they reason as I did in the First Argument, or for some other reason.

Both arguments conclude that an enforced decent minimum principle is needed to achieve coordinated joint effort. However, there is this difference. The Second Argument focuses on the *assurance problem,* while the first does not. In the Second Argument all that is needed is the assumption that rational beneficence requires assurance that enough others will contribute. In

the First Argument the individual's reason for not contributing is not that he lacks assurance that enough others will contribute, but rather that it is better for him not to contribute regardless of whether others do not.

Neither argument depends on an assumption of conflict between the individual's moral motivation of beneficence and his inclination of self-interest. Instead the difficulty is that in the absence of enforcement, individuals who strive to make their beneficence most effective will thereby fail to benefit the needy as much as they might.

A standard response to those paradoxes of rationality known as public goods problems is to introduce a coercive mechanism which attaches penalties to noncontribution and thereby provides each individual with the assurance that enough others will reciprocate so that his contribution will not be wasted and an effective incentive for him to contribute even if he has reason to believe that enough others will contribute to achieve the goal without his contribution. My suggestion is that the same type of argument that is widely accepted as a justification for enforced principles requiring contributions toward familiar public goods provides support for a coercively backed principle specifying a certain list of health programs for the needy and requiring those who possess the needed resources to contribute to the establishment of such programs, even if the needy have no *right* to the services those programs provide. Such an arrangement would serve a dual function: it would coordinate charitable efforts by focusing them on one set of services among the indefinitely large constellation of possible expressions of beneficence, and it would ensure that the decision to allocate resources to these services will become effective. . . .

### Notes

1.  Ronald Dworkin, *Taking Rights Seriously* (Cambridge, MA: Harvard University Press, 1977), pp. 184–205.

2.  For an exploration of various arguments for a duty of beneficence and an examination of the relationship between justice and beneficence, in general and in health care, see Allen E. Buchanan, "Philosophical Foundations of Beneficence," *Beneficence and Health Care,* ed. Earl E. Shelp (Dordrecht, Holland: Reidel Publishing Co., 1982).

## Section 2: Managed Care and Rationing

### The Doctor as Double Agent

Marcia Angell

Marcia Angell argues that the sole duty of the physician should be to act in the patient's interest. Until the 1980s this was the doctor's recognized role; as health care became more effective and more costly, however, doctors also became agents of society, acting to protect its resources. Angell illustrates her claim by describing ways HMOs encourage doctors to withhold care that, as agents only for their patients, they would have prescribed.

Angell poses five objections to the doctor's current double role: (1) It is based on the false premise that health care is costly because resources are scarce; (2) using doctors to ration resources falsely assumes that what is saved in one case will be put to better use in another; (3) having the doctor as the patient's agent only assures us that our basic right to life is being preserved; (4) doctors have no special knowledge of what treatment is worth the cost, so their rationing decisions are arbitrary and unfair; (5) the role of double agent violates sick people's need for their doctor to act only to heal them.

Angell concludes, on the basis of there considerations, that we should preserve the traditional role of the physician as an agent for the patient alone.

In earlier times—that is, before 1980—it was generally agreed that the doctor's sole obligation was to take care of each patient. The doctor was the patient's fiduciary or agent, and the doctor was to act only in the patient's interest. Now all that has changed. Many of us—economists, governmental officials, corporate executives, and yes, even ethicists, and yes, even many doctors themselves—now believe that doctors have other obligations that compete with their obligation to the patient. In particular, they believe that doctors have acquired an obligation to save resources for society. Doing so requires doctors to practice with one eye on costs, which may mean sometimes denying beneficial care that they would surely have provided in earlier times.

According to the new view, doctors are no longer simply agents for their patients. They are now agents for society's needs as well. They are, in short, double agents, expected to decide whether the benefits of

This article is based on the annual Edmund D. Pellegrino Lecture at the Kennedy Institute of Ethics. *Kennedy Institute of Ethics Journal,* Vol. 3, no. 3 (1993), pp. 279–286. © 1993 by The Johns Hopkins University Press. Reprinted with permission of the Johns Hopkins University Press.

treatment to their patients are worth the costs to society. Many distinguished ethicists have enthusiastically embraced this new ethic (Callahan 1990; Morreim 1991). To them, keeping an eye on the price tag means saving scarce resources for other, more important uses.

How did this extraordinary shift in our view of doctors' obligations come about? Is it just coincidence that it began with our first realization—roughly in the mid-1970s—that our seemingly endless resources were in fact finite? And is it just coincidence that it accorded with the wishes of the third-party payers—who discovered during the 1980s that they had severe and growing budgetary problems? In short, can it be that the ethical underpinnings of the practice of medicine have been scrapped in a single decade for financial reasons? Is economics driving ethics?

I'll begin with my conclusions. I believe that doctors *are* now asked to be double agents and that their dual obligation is a recent construct, which arose out of the economic difficulties of the large third-party payers. I will argue that we embrace this new ethic at our peril. Even if we as a society decide that health care should take a smaller piece of the national economic pie, there are ways to do this that do not entail rebuilding—and perhaps destroying—almost overnight, the ethical underpinnings of the profession.

## Historical Review

First, a quick review of how we got here. This requires an economic analysis, since my thesis is that economics is now driving ethics. The economic history of health care in the United States can be divided into three phases. First, there was the phase of the true market, lasting until roughly World War II. Patients paid doctors out-of-pocket for their medical care. If the price was too high, the doctor was confronted with an unhappy patient. Even after private insurance companies began to flourish in the 1930s, the premiums were still paid out-of-pocket and so patients continued to feel the costs, although the pain was blunted. Fortunately, medical care was fairly inexpensive. Unfortunately, it was also relatively ineffective, compared with the power of modern medicine.

The second phase was marked by the entry of big business into the health care picture. Big business began to offer health insurance as a fringe benefit in order to evade the wage and price controls in effect during World War II. Offering health insurance was tantamount to increasing wages, and furthermore, it was not taxed. The connection between employment and health insurance was thus an historical accident that haunts us still. But the important effect of this connection for the discussion here is that it insulates patients from the costs of medical care. Neither doctors nor patients had to worry any longer about the costs of medical care. With the enactment of Medicare and Medicaid in 1966, this insulation from costs spread to the poor and, most importantly, to the elderly—a politically powerful group. By the end of the 1960s, anything resembling a true market in health care had vanished. Nearly everyone was covered by third-party payers—government, business, and private insurance companies. And medical care was becoming both more expensive and more effective. Despite the increasing costs, the third parties happily paid the charges, with few questions asked.

The third phase began with the realization that health care costs were consistently rising far more rapidly than the GNP. Now that patients and doctors and hospitals were insulated from accountability, there were no limits on the expansion of the health care industry in this country. It was open-ended and nearly risk-free, absorbing an ever greater share of our domestic spending. While national expenditures for other social goods, such as education, stagnated or declined, expenditures for health care rose rapidly—from roughly 6 percent of the GNP in 1965 to nearly 10 percent in 1980 to 13 percent in 1991 (Stoline and Weiner 1993).

Not only was there nothing to stop the inflation, but there were features that virtually guaranteed it. These included the piecework, fee-for-service reimbursement system that is greatly skewed toward high-technology procedures and specialists. Doctors, of course, act as both providers and purchasing agents, so these highly paid specialists could easily generate their own business. For example, the cardiologist who recommends coronary angiography to a patient also bills for it.

## Cost Containment

In the 1970s, the Arab oil embargo made Americans realize that our resources were finite. Health care costs began to occupy the attention of some experts and policymakers. By the 1980s, it became clear to nearly everyone that we could not indefinitely sustain rising health care costs, and for the first time, efforts were made to control them. "Cost containment" crept into the lexicon, and by the end of the 1980s the *New England Journal of Medicine* probably received more manuscripts about cost containment than about cancer. The efforts to control costs were spearheaded by the major third parties—government and big business. They were responding essentially to budgetary problems, not to moral problems. They went about cost containment in a number of ad hoc, uncoordinated ways, as briefly mentioned below. None of them was notably successful. In fact health care costs rose even faster— I believe, *because* of cost containment efforts, not despite them.

Regulation by third parties, including managed care, simply led to the growth of an expensive and intrusive new bureaucracy. Efforts to foster competition led to increased marketing, not to lower prices. And attempts to limit demand through higher deductibles and copayments simply shifted costs and limited care, primarily to the most vulnerable. Efforts by insurers to avoid risks also shifted costs. In general, savings to one part of the system were costs to another. In fact, the dominant characteristic of the American health care system is that there is no system. There is just a hodgepodge of arrangements, existing independently, often working at cross purposes, and generating enormous administrative costs. Indeed, administrative costs—billing, marketing, underwriting, claims processing, utilization review—now consume more than 20 cents of the health care dollar (Woolhandler and Himmelstein 1991).

Why do I recapitulate this sorry history of the economics of the American health care system? I do so because it is important to understand the context in which doctors are being invited to act as double agents. They are invited to do so in an open-ended, inherently inflationary system (or, rather, non-system) that spends roughly 40 percent more per citizen on health care than the next most expensive health care system in the world and at least twice as much on administrative costs. Further, this system is embedded in a society that routinely spends billions and billions on such goods as tobacco, television ads, and cosmetics. Clearly, we as a society aren't facing scarcity; instead we are facing the inefficient and frivolous use of vast resources.

### Saving for Third Parties

What precisely is the doctor supposed to do as double agent? In a nutshell, doctors are supposed to tailor their care of patients to save money for third parties. For example, under the DRG system of hospital reimbursement for Medicare patients, doctors are supposed to be agents for the hospital, discharging patients as rapidly as possible and keeping services to a minimum so that the hospital can game the system. In many HMOs doctors are expected to keep costs as low as possible, and some HMOs even directly reward doctors with bonuses when the HMO comes out ahead. They may also withhold a portion of doctors' salaries if they refer patients to specialists too often or use too many tests and procedures. Thus, doctors are agents for the HMO and have a direct incentive to undertreat their patients, just as in the fee-for-service system they have an incentive to overtreat them. Other forms of managed care also deter doctors from delivering care. Those that require utilization review often make it so complicated and difficult to get approval for hospitalization or procedures that the doctor is reluctant even to try. And it should be noted that nearly all medical care these days is managed in one way or another, by which I mean it is subject to efforts of insurers to limit care.

In essence, then, doctors are increasingly being asked, in one way or another, to save money for a third party—and sometimes for themselves—by scrimping on the medical care they deliver. But the pressure is seldom described in these terms. Instead, it is described as practicing "cost-effective" medicine. "Cost-effective" is the new watchword. It used to be a technical term that referred to the least expensive of two equally effective alternatives, or to the most effective of two equally costly ones. Now it is simply a shorthand for any attempt to save money. The word sounds fine, and who can object to it?

### Justification for Double Agents

But how can we justify asking doctors to deprive their patients of care, including clearly beneficial care that in other circumstances they would not hesitate to provide? Just as the problem is new, so are the ethical justifications.

First, it is claimed that limiting care is what society wishes, and that the medical profession has an obligation not only to accept the will of society but to further it. Doctors are simply anticipating and delivering what is expected of them by the body politic, despite the fact that individual patients may want something else when they are sick.

Second, it is argued that because third parties now pay for nearly all medical care, they have gained a legitimate voice—indeed, the overriding voice—in how much medical care patients should receive. I find this a peculiarly American argument. Essentially the message is that whoever pays the piper calls the tune. The purest example of this view is the Oregon plan for rationing the care received by Medicaid patients. This is often described as a decision to allocate scarce resources rationally and justly, but it is, of course, nothing of the sort. It is instead a matter of taxpayers deciding to limit the care received by the poor, on the grounds that the taxpayers are funding it. Those who drew up the priority list of medical services are not those to whom it would apply. Even if we were to accept the idea that paying for medical care confers the right to limit it, we should remember that most patients do in fact still pay for their medical care, just as they always did. They simply pay in advance and indirectly, through their work or their taxes. The third parties are not using their own money.

The third justification for doctors to be double agents is the most compelling. It appeals to the doctor as good citizen or, more dramatically, to the doctor as occupant of a metaphorical lifeboat with limited supplies. According to this view, resources saved in denying patients expensive medical care could be used to provide less expensive care to a larger number of patients. Or it could be used for even more important public purposes, such as education. This line of argument has been put forward most persuasively by Dan Callahan (1990) who contends that Americans have overvalued individual health care compared with other social goods.

## Arguments Against Double Agents

Despite these justifications, I see five serious problems with the view that doctors should act to contain costs, patient by patient. First and most simply, this view of the role of doctors is based on the premise that resources in our health care system are in fact scarce. But, of course, they aren't. The mere fact that we spend so much more on health care than all other advanced nations is proof that our health care resources are plentiful. Given that in 1990 we spent about $2,566 on every man, woman, and child in the United States, and Canada spent only $1,770, we can hardly claim inadequate resources (Schieber, Poullier, and Greenwald 1992). And since Americans and Canadians are subject to the same ailments and have roughly the same outcomes, we must assume that our system is grossly inefficient. Clearly, the answer to an inefficient system is not to stint on care, but rather to restructure the system to make it more efficient.

Second, enlisting doctors as ad hoc rationers presumes that resources saved by denying health care would be put to better use. But in our system there is absolutely no reason to think that it would. As Norman Daniels (1986) has pointed out, in the United Kingdom or Canada, resources saved by denying care would be used for presumably more valuable health care, but that is not the case here. In the U.S., we do not have a closed system in which funds taken from one form of health care are diverted to another that is deemed to be more important. Instead, funds not used for health care may find their way into any sector of the larger economy, to be used for anything—e.g., defense, education, farm subsidies, or personal savings. Furthermore, even funds that remain within the health care system might not be used for more effective care; instead, money saved on, say, heart transplantation may very well find its way to a hospital's public relations office or to higher salaries for administrators. Under these circumstances, it is very difficult to sustain an ethical argument for doctors acting as double agents. The only principled way to ration health care is to close the system and establish limits that apply to everyone—not just to the poor.

Third, asking doctors to be double agents overlooks an important symbolic function of health care. Our society was founded on the principle that individuals enjoy a set of basic rights that cannot be denied them. As medicine has become increasingly effective in preserving life, medical care has come to be counted among these rights. Thus, doctors are seen to preserve a basic human right, namely life, just as criminal lawyers are seen to preserve liberty by defending their clients. Lawyers do not decide part way through a trial to call it quits because it's just too expensive to go on with it. In both situations, there has been a consensus that the single-minded focus on the patient or the client serves the broader interests of society. This argument is particularly compelling in a society as unequal as ours. People will tolerate the vast inequities in income and privilege in this country only if they feel assured that their irreducible set of rights is truly protected. It has been suggested that high technology medicine may serve precisely such a reassuring function in our society. And public opinion polls tend to support this view (Blendon 1991). The public, in contrast to the third-party payers, does not feel that we are spending too much on health care, only that we are not getting our money's worth.

Fourth, when doctors act as double agents, they are merely acting on their own particular prejudices. They are deciding that this or that medical service costs too much. This is not a medical judgment, but a political or philosophical one. Another doctor (or a plumber or electrician) might make quite a different judgment. This is no way to allocate health care.

And fifth and perhaps most important, the doctor as double agent is not honest. Sick people need and expect their doctors' single purpose to be to heal them. The doctor–patient relationship would not survive a candid statement by the doctor that only care that seems to the doctor to be worth the money will be provided. Anything short of full efforts to heal the individual patient, then, must involve a hidden agenda—an ethically indefensible position.

## Conclusion

In sum, we should be loath to abandon or modify the patient-centered ethic, and we should be wary of ethical justifications for doing so. Unfortunately, history shows us that ethics in practice are often highly malleable, *justifying* political decisions rather than *informing* them. Necessity is the mother of invention, in ethics as well as in other aspects of life. For example, in 1912, when the AMA thought salaried practice was a threat to the autonomy of the profession, its Code of Ethics pronounced it unethical for physicians to join group practices. Now, some 80 years later, we are again hearing that it is a matter of ethics for the medical profession to carry out what is essentially a political agenda. But ethics should be a little more stable than that. Ethics should be based on fundamental moral principles governing our behavior and obligations toward one another. If a doctor is ethically committed to care for the individual patient, that commitment should not be abridged lightly. And it should not be nullified by a budgetary crunch. Doctors should continue to care for each patient unstintingly, even while they join with other citizens to devise a more efficient and just health care system. To control costs effectively will in my view require a coherent national health care system, with a global cap and a single payer (Angell 1993). Only in this way can we have an affordable health care system that does not require doctors to be double agents.

### References

Angell, Marcia. 1993. How Much Will Health Care Reform Cost? *New England Journal of Medicine* 328: 1778–79.

Blendon, Robert J. 1991. The Public View of Medicine. *Clinical Neurosurgery* 37: 2563–65.

Callahan, Daniel. 1990. *What Kind of Life? The Limits of Medical Progress.* New York: Simon & Schuster.

Daniels, Norman. 1986. Why Saying No to Patients in the United States Is So Hard: Cost Containment, Justice, and Provider Autonomy. *New England Journal of Medicine* 314: 1380–83.

Morreim, E. Haavi. 1991. *Balancing Act: The New Medical Ethics of Medicine's Economics.* Boston: Kluwer Academic Publishers.

Schieber, George J.; Poullier, Jean-Pierre; and Greenwald, Leslie M. 1992. U.S. Health Expenditure Performance: An International Comparison and Data Update. *Health Care Financing Review* 13 (4): 1–15.

Stoline, Anne M., and Weiner, Jonathan P. 1993. *The New Medical Marketplace: A Physician's Guide to the Health Care System in the 1990s.* Baltimore: Johns Hopkins University Press.

Woolhandler, Steffie, and Himmelstein, David. 1991. The Deteriorating Administrative Efficiency of the U.S. Health Care System. *New England Journal of Medicine* 324: 1253–58.

# Wanted: A Clearly Articulated Social Ethic for American Health Care

Uwe E. Reinhardt

Uwe Reinhardt argues that U.S. policy deliberately rations children's health care according to parents' ability to pay for it either directly or through insurance. Those in the uninsured group receive only 60 percent of health services received by the insured and have worse outcomes for the same conditions. Even so, policymakers give priority to "maximization of wealth" over "maximization of utility," with the result that poor children of one generation are allowed to suffer so that all children in future generations may be better off.

Reinhardt sees this ranking of priorities as unjust for two reasons. First, it is not chosen from a position of Rawlsian ignorance, so policymakers know that their families won't fall into the lowest tiers of national income. Second, those who oppose government-subsidized health insurance for low-income families enjoy employer-provided health insurance subsidized through federal tax preferences. If medical savings accounts are permitted, this subsidy to high-income families will be enlarged, reinforcing the rationing of children's health care in accordance with parents' ability to pay.

Throughout the past 3 decades, Americans have been locked in a tenacious ideological debate whose

From *JAMA,* November 5, 1997, Vol. 278, no. 17, pp. 1446–1447. Reprinted by permission.

essence can be distilled into the following pointed question: As a matter of national policy, and to the extent that a nation's health system can make it possible, should the child of a poor American family have the same chance of avoiding preventable illness or of being cured from a given illness as does the child of a rich American family?

The "yeas" in all other industrialized nations had won that debate hands down decades ago, and these nations have worked hard to put in place health insurance and health care systems to match that predominant sentiment. In the United States, on the other hand, the "nays" so far have carried the day. As a matter of conscious national policy, the United States always has and still does openly countenance the practice of rationing health care for millions of American children by their parents' ability to procure health insurance for the family or, if the family is uninsured, by their parents' willingness and ability to pay for health care out of their own pocket or, if the family is unable to pay, by the parents' willingness and ability to procure charity care in their role as health care beggars.

At any moment, over 40 million Americans find themselves without health insurance coverage, among them some 10 million children younger than 18 years. All available evidence suggests that this number will grow.[1] America's policymaking elite has remained unfazed by these statistics, reciting the soothing mantra that "to be uninsured in these United States does not means to be without care." There is, to be sure, some truth to the mantra. Critically ill, uninsured Americans of all ages usually receive adequate if untimely care under an informal, albeit unreliable, catastrophic health insurance program operated by hospitals and many physicians, largely on a voluntary basis. Under that informal program, hospitals and physicians effectively become insurance underwriters who provide succor to hard-stricken uninsured and who extract the premium for that insurance through higher charges to paying patients. The alarming prospect is that the more effective the techniques of "managed care" will be in controlling the flow of revenue to physicians and hospitals, the more difficult it will be to play this insurance scheme otherwise known as the "cost shift." It can be expected that, within the next decade, the growing number of the nation's uninsured will find themselves in increasingly dire straits.

But these straits have never been smooth for the uninsured, notwithstanding the soothing mantra cited earlier. Empirical research must have convinced policymakers long ago that our nation rations health care, health status, and life-years by ability to pay.

It is known that other socioeconomic factors (such as income, family status, location, and so on) being equal, uninsured Americans receive, on average, only about 60% of the health services received by equally situated insured Americans.[2] This appears to

be true even for the subgroup of adults whose health status is poor or only fair.[3] Studies have shown that uninsured Americans relying on the emergency departments of heavily crowded public hospitals experience very long waits before being seen by a physician, sometimes so long that they leave because they are too sick to wait any longer.[4-6] Studies have found that after careful statistical control for a host of socioeconomic and medical factors, uninsured Americans tend to die in hospitals from the same illness at up to triple the rate that is observed for equally situated insured Americans[7] and that, over the long run, uninsured Americans tend to die at an earlier age than do similarly situated insured Americans.[8] Indeed, before the managed care industry cut the fees paid physicians sufficiently to make fees paid by Medicaid look relatively attractive to physicians and hospitals, even patients insured by that program found it difficult to find access to timely care. In one study, in which research assistants approached private medical practices pretending to be Medicaid patients in need of care, 63% of them were denied access because the fees paid by Medicaid were then still paltry relative to the much higher fees from commercial insurers.[9]

If the champions of the uninsured believe that the assembly and dissemination of these statistics can move the nation's policymaking elite to embrace universal coverage, they may be in for a disappointment. The working majority of that elite not only are unperturbed by these statistics, but they believe that rationing by price and ability to pay actually serves a greater national purpose. In that belief they find ample support in the writing of distinguished American academics. Commenting critically on the State Children's Health Insurance Program enacted by Congress in August 1997 as part of its overall budget bill, for example, Richard Epstein, author of the recently published *Mortal Peril: Our Inalienable Right to Health Care?*,[10] warns darkly that the new federal plan "introduces large deadweight administrative costs, invites overuse of medical care and reduces parental incentives to prevent accidents or illness." Summing up, he concludes: "We could do better with less regulation and less subsidy. *Scarcity matters, even in health care*" (italics added).[11]

Clearly, the scarcity Epstein would like to matter in health care would impinge much more heavily on the poor than it would on members of his own economic class, as Epstein surely is aware. In his view, by the way, Epstein finds distinguished company in former University of Chicago colleague Milton Friedman, the widely celebrated Nobel laureate in economics, who had proposed in 1991 that for the sake of economic efficiency, Medicare and Medicaid be abolished altogether and every American family have merely a catastrophic health insurance policy with a deductible of $20,000 per year or 30% of the previous 2 years' income, whichever is lower.[12] Certainly, Epstein and Friedman would be content to let price and family income ration the health care of American children. They rank prominently among the "nays."

In his book, Epstein frames the debate over the right to health care as a choice between the "maximization of social wealth" as a national objective and the "maximization of utility," by which he means human happiness. "Under wealth maximization," he writes, "individual preferences count only if they are backed by dollars. Preferences, however genuine, that are unmediated by wealth just do not count."[10 (p32)] One implication of resource allocation with the objective of wealth maximization is that a physician visit to the healthy infant of a rich family is viewed as a more valuable activity than is a physician visit to the sick child of a poor family. If one does not accept that relative valuation, then one does not favor wealth maximization as the binding social objective.

Although conceding that wealth maximization does imply a harsh algorithm for the allocation of scarce resources, Epstein nevertheless appears to embrace it, even for health care. Establishing positive legal rights to health care regardless of ability to pay, he argues, could well be counterproductive in the long run, because it detracts from the accumulation of wealth. "Allowing wealth to matter [in the allocation of health] is likely to do far better in the long run than any policy that insists on allocating health care without regard to ability to pay. To repeat, any effort to redistribute from rich to poor in the present generation necessarily entails the redistribution from the future to the present generation."[13] Applying his proposition to the question posed at the outset of this commentary, the argument seems to be that poor children in one generation can properly be left to suffer, so that all children of future generations may be made better off than they otherwise would have been.

One need not share Epstein's social ethic to agree with him that, over the long run, a nation that allocates resources generously to the unproductive frail, whether rich or poor, is likely to register a relatively slower growth of material wealth than does a nation that is more parsimonious vis-à-vis the frail.[10(p114)] Nor does one need to share his social ethic to admire him for his courage to expose his conviction so boldly for open debate. Deep down, many members of this nation's policymaking elite, including many pundits who inspire that elite, and certainly a working majority of Congress, share Epstein's view, although only rarely do they have the temerity to reveal their social ethic to public scrutiny. Although this school of thought may not hold a numerical majority in American society, they appear to hold powerful sway over the political process as it operates in this country.[14] In any event, they have for decades been able to preserve a status quo that keep millions of American families uninsured, among them about 10 million children.

At the risk of violating the American taboo against class warfare, it is legitimate to observe that virtually everyone who shares Epstein's and Friedman's distributive ethic tends to be rather comfortably ensconced in the upper tiers of the nation's income distribution. Their prescriptions do not emanate from behind a Rawlsian[15] veil of ignorance concerning their own families' station in life. Furthermore, most well-to-do Americans who strongly oppose government-subsidized health insurance for low-income families and who see the need for rationing health care by price and ability to pay enjoy the full protection of government-subsidized, employer-provided, private health insurance that affords their families comprehensive coverage with out-of-pocket payments that are trivial relative to their own incomes and therefore spare their own families the pain of rationing altogether. The government subsidy in these policies flows from the regressive tax preference traditionally accorded employment-based health insurance in this country, whose premiums are paid out of pretax income.[16] This subsidy was estimated to have amounted to about $70 billion in 1991, of which 26% accrued to high-income households with annual incomes over $75,000.[17] The subsidy probably is closer to $100 billion now—much more than it would cost for every uninsured American to afford the type of coverage enjoyed by insured Americans. In fairness it must be stated that at least some critics of government-financed health insurance—Epstein among them—argue against this tax preference as well.[10(p182)] But that untoward tax preference has widespread supporters among members of Congress of all political stripes, and also in the executive suites of corporate America.

This regressive tax preference would only be enlarged further under the medical savings accounts (MSAs) now favored by organized American medicine. Under that concept, families would purchase catastrophic health insurance policies with annual deductibles of $3000 to $5000 per family, and they would finance their deductible out of MSAs into which they could deposit $3000 to $5000 per year out of the family's pretax income. In terms of absolute, after-tax dollars, this construct effectively would make the out-of-pocket cost of a medical procedure much lower for high-income families (in high marginal tax brackets) than it would for low-income families. It is surely remarkable to see such steadfast support in the Congress for this subsidy for the well-to-do, in a nation that claims to lack the resources to afford every mother and child the peace of mind and the health benefits that come with universal health insurance, a privilege mothers and children in other countries have long taken for granted. Unwittingly, perhaps, by favoring this regressive scheme to finance health care, physicians take a distinct stand on the preferred distributive ethic for American health care. After all, can it be doubted that the MSA construct would lead to rationing children's health care by income class?

Typically, the opponents of universal health insurance cloak their sentiments in actuarial technicalities or in the mellifluous language of the standard economic theory of markets,[18] thereby avoiding a debate on ideology that truly might engage the public. It is time, after so many decades, that the rival factions in America's policymaking elite debate openly their distinct visions of a distributive ethic for health care in this country, so that the general public can decide by which of the rival elites it wishes to be ruled. A good start in that debate could be made by answering forthrightly the pointed question posed at the outset.

## Notes

1. Thorpe KE. *The Rising Number of Uninsured Workers: An Approaching Crisis in Health Care Financing*. Washington, DC: The National Coalition on Health Care; September 1997.

2. *Behavioral Assumptions for Estimating the Effects of Health Care Proposals*. Washington, DC: Congressional Budget Office; November 1993; Table 3:viii.

3. Long SH, Marquis MS. *Universal Health Insurance and Uninsured People: Effects on Use and Costs: Report to Congress*. Washington, DC: Office of Technology Assessment and Congressional Research Service, Library of Congress; August 5, 1994; Figure 1:4.

4. Kellerman AL. Too sick to wait. *JAMA*. 1991;266:1123–1124.

5. Baker DW, Stevens CD, Brook RH. Patients who leave a public hospital emergency department without being seen by a physician. *JAMA*. 1991;266:1091–1096.

6. Bindman AB, Grumbach D, Keane D, Rauch L, Luce JM. Consequences of queuing for care at a public hospital emergency department. *JAMA*. 1991;266:1091–1096.

7. Hadley J, Steinbergt EP, Feder J. Comparison of uninsured and privately insured hospital patients. *JAMA*. 1991;265:374–379.

8. Franks P, Clancy CM, Gold MR. Health insurance and mortality: evidence from a national cohort. *JAMA*. 1993;270:737–741.

9. The ultimate denial: rationing is a reality. *Issue Scan: Q Rep Health Care Issues Trends From Searle*. 1994;4(2):5.

10. Epstein RA. *Mortal Peril: Our Inalienable Right to Health Care?* New York, NY: Addison-Wesley; 1997.

11. Epstein RA. Letter to the editor. *The New York Times*. August 10, 1997:14.

12. Friedman M. Gammon's law points to health care solution. *The Wall Street Journal*. November 12, 1991:A19.

13. Reinhardt UE. Abstracting from distributional effects, this policy is efficient. In: Barer M, Getzen T, Stoddard G, eds. *Health, Health Care, and Health Economics: Perspectives on Distribution*. London, England: John Wiley & Sons Ltd; 1997:1–53.

14. Taylor H, Reinhardt UE. Does the system fit? *Health Manage Q*. 1991;13(3):2–10.

15. Rawls J. *A Theory of Justice*. Cambridge, Mass: Harvard University Press; 1971.

16. Reinhardt UE. Reorganizing the financial flows in American health care. *Health Aff (Millwood)*. 1993;12(suppl):172–193.

17. Butler SM. A policymaker's guide to the health care crisis, I. *Heritage Talking Points*. Washington, DC: The Heritage Foundation; February 12, 1992:5.

18. Reinhardt UE. Economics. *JAMA*. 1996;275:1802–1804.

## READINGS

# Section 3: Alternatives to the Present System

## The Forgotten Domestic Crisis

### Marcia Angell

Marcia Angell claims that the "fatal flaw" in the American health-care system is that "we treat health care as a commodity." Ability to pay, not need, becomes the condition for receiving it, and insurers try to avoid high-cost patients. Thus, about half of health-care dollars go for administration and never reach hospitals and doctors, who must then spend more dealing with multiple insurers. Piecemeal changes in the system lead to the dilemma that providing access to services makes cost rise, while lowering costs reduces access to services.

Angell argues that a national single-payer system, something like an expanded Medicare and financed through a special tax on income, could bring down costs and extend benefits to the entire population. If we were to spend the same amount on health care as we now do, we wouldn't be faced with the long waiting lists found in Canada and Britain, because they spend far less than we do. By eliminating waste and profiteering, Angell claims, we can afford to pay for everyone.

If it weren't for the steady beat of war drums, health care would be front and center in the political debate. And war or no war, politicians will not be able to avoid it much longer. As John Breaux of Louisiana, one of the most conservative Senate Democrats, recently told the press, "the system is collapsing around us."

That is not hyperbole. Private health insurance premiums are rising at an unsustainable average of about 13 percent per year—and as much as 25 percent in some areas of the country. Coverage is shrinking, as more employers decide to cap their contributions to health insurance plans and workers find they cannot pay their rapidly expanding share. And with the rise in unemployment, more people are losing what limited coverage they had. Last month, the Census Bureau reported that nearly 1.5 million Americans lost their insurance in 2001.

The fatal flaw in the system is that we treat health care as a commodity. That has been the case for a long time, but the effects were masked during the economic boom of the 1990's. Now, with the recession, the irrationality of that approach is exposed.

When health care becomes a commodity, the criterion for receiving it is ability to pay, not medical need. Private insurers and providers compete with one another to avoid getting stuck with high-cost patients, so they can keep more of their revenues. But this game of hot potato takes a lot of oversight and paperwork. In fact, the hallmark of the system is the extent to which health funds are diverted to overhead and profits.

Look at what happens to the health-care dollar as it wends its way from employers to the doctors and hospitals that provide medical services. Private insurers regularly skim off the top 10 percent to 25 percent of premiums for administrative costs, marketing and

profits. The remainder is passed along a gantlet of satellite businesses—insurance brokers, disease-management and utilization-review companies, lawyers, consultants, billing agencies, information management firms and so on. Their function is often to limit services in one way or another. They, too, take a cut, including enough for their own administrative costs, marketing and profits. As much as half the health-care dollar never reaches doctors and hospitals—who themselves face high overhead costs in dealing with multiple insurers.

One more absurdity of our market-based system: the pressure is to increase total health-care expenditures, not reduce them. Presumably, as a nation we want to constrain the growth of health costs. But that's simply not what health-care businesses do. Like all businesses, they want more, not fewer, customers—but only if they can pay.

All piecemeal attempts to improve the system—while keeping it market-based—have run into the following dilemma: if access to services is expanded, costs rise; if costs are lowered, access is cut. That's the way it is. The only way to avoid this dilemma is to change the system entirely.

What we need is a national single-payer system that would eliminate unnecessary administrative costs, duplication and profits. In many ways, this would be tantamount to extending Medicare to the entire population. Medicare is, after all, a government-financed single-payer system embedded within our private, market-based system. It's by far the most efficient part of our health-care system, with overhead costs of less than 3 percent, and it covers virtually everyone over the age of 65. Medicare is not perfect, but it's the most popular part of the American health-care system.

Many people believe a single-payer system is a good idea, but that we can't afford it. The truth is that we can no longer afford not to have such a system. We now spend more than $5,000 a year on health care for each American—more than twice the average of other advanced countries. But nearly half that amount is wasted. We now pay for health care in multiple ways—through our paychecks, the prices of goods and services, taxes at all levels of government, and out-of-pocket fees. It makes more sense to pay only once, perhaps through a new tax on income earmarked for health care (in the same way Medicare is financed through payroll taxes).

It is sometimes argued that innovative technologies would be scarce in a national single-payer system, so we would have long waiting lists. This misconception is based on the fact that there are indeed waits for elective procedures in some countries with national health systems like Great Britain and Canada. But that's because they spend far less on health care then we do. If they were to put the same amount of money as we do into their systems, there would be no waits. For them, the problem is not the system; it's the money. For us, it's not the money; it's the system. We already spend enough for an excellent universal system.

A single-payer system is not socialized medicine. Although a new national program—like Medicare—would be publicly financed, the doctors and hospitals would not work for the government, but would remain private. Some fear onerous government regulations from a national payment system, but surely nothing could be more onerous for patients and providers than the multiple, intrusive regulations imposed on them by the private insurance industry today.

We live in a country that tolerates enormous disparities in income, material possessions and social privilege. That may be inevitable in a free-market economy. But those disparities should not extend to essential services like education, clean water and air and protection from crime, all of which we already acknowledge are public responsibilities. The same should be true for medical care—particularly since we can well afford to provide it for everyone if we end the waste and profiteering of our market-based system.

## The Benefits of Privatization

Victor Dirnfeld

Victor Dirnfeld argues that Canada's universal medical coverage should be supplemented by a regulated, private, not-for-profit system of insurance. Cutbacks in funding have raised concern about the accessibility and quality of care, so affordable private insurance would help relieve the demand that is straining the public system. Because a parallel private system would be regulated and not profit driven, it would escape the drawbacks of the U.S. system.

A dual system would be just, because most people would remain within the public system, rather than abandoning it to the poor and allowing it to deteriorate. Yet, it would be beneficial because it would provide both those who buy private insurance and those who remain in the public system improved access to better health care.

When it was introduced through the Medical Care Act in December 1966, Canadian medicare was a bold and innovative measure based on the desirable concept of providing essential medical coverage for all of the citizens of Canada. However, in the 30 years since it was born, because of the excesses of planners and dream-

From the *Canadian Medical Association Journal*, August 15, 1996: 155 (4), pp. 407–410. © 1996 Canadian Medical Association. Reprinted by permission.

ers, medicare, like other social programs, has grown too comprehensive and too costly to be funded by the public purse. The result has been a decade-long deceleration in the growth of transfer payments from the federal to the provincial governments for health, post-secondary education and social assistance. In April of 1996, these transfer payments began to decrease substantially, with the provinces slated to receive an estimated $18 billion less during the next 4 years than they had during the previous 4 years.

Even before these cuts in transfer payments, the massive debt loads that had been accumulated by almost every provincial government had necessitated considerable cutbacks in health care funding. The effects of these cutbacks included closure of hospitals and of beds in some of the hospitals that remained open, elimination of some programs and significant curtailment of others (for instance, special care units, coronary angiography and angioplasty, prosthetic surgery for hips and knees, and cataract removal and lens implantations), and stagnation of programs that needed to grow to keep pace with a growing and aging population (such as radiation oncology) or with improved technology (such as computed tomography, magnetic resonance imaging and use of newer-generation implantable pacemakers). Physicians are now faced not only with their patients' diminished access to needed and appropriate care but also with inadequate levels of nursing staff in acute care wards. The problem has grown to such proportions that, for the first time, concern about the deteriorating quality of care is being expressed by responsible and respected physicians from both academic–tertiary care centres and community hospitals (CMA Quality of Care Committee, Ottawa: unpublished data, 1996).[1]

Canadians are beginning to experience the effects of the "restructuring" and "downsizing" of the health care system. Polls of both the public and the medical profession show a high degree of concern about lack of accessibility and deterioration of quality of care, with 65% of members of the public responding to one poll (Canadian Attitudes Towards Health Care Funding, Insight Canada Research for the CMA, Ottawa: unpublished data, 1995), 87% of those responding to another (CBC Prime Time News, Toronto: unpublished data, 1995), 65% of physicians responding to one poll (Focus Canada poll, Environics Research Group, Toronto: unpublished data, 1994) and 83% of those responding to another (British Columbia Medical Association (BCMA)/Government of British Columbia Medical Services Commission Public Education poll, Angus Reid, Vancouver: unpublished data, 1995) indicating concern about these issues.

As a solution to the perceived and actual underfunding of the public medicare system, many have proposed a parallel, private system of medical care funded by a not-for-profit, regulated system of insurance. Such insurance schemes existed across the country and covered almost half of the population (85% in British Columbia) before medicare was introduced; a substantial balance of the population was covered by commercial insurance in 1965.[2] "Regulated" means that the insurance scheme would have to accept all applications for coverage (with premiums appropriately adjusted for actuarial risk), which would eliminate any possibility of "cream skimming" or selecting only low-risk clients. The pooled risk would allow for a premium structure that would be affordable for most wage-earners, as are premiums for a similar scheme in Australia, where more than 1 million people with annual earnings of less than Can$23 000 are covered. The Australian scheme is supported by a labour-socialist government, according to the Australia Liberal/National Coalition Health Care Policy presented in 1996.

This kind of insurance system—that is, a universal, public medicare system to which all taxpayers contribute a proportion of their taxes (and, in some jurisdictions, premiums), paralleled by a private, regulated, not-for-profit insurance plan—exists in every Western industrialized nation in the world except the United States and Canada. This system works effectively in other countries because the private option serves to decrease waiting lists for public facilities, thereby improving access for those using the public system. The private system offers a standard of care to which the public system must aspire, because the two systems can be directly compared.[3] Without a parallel, private system, the public system delivers care according to what the government payer dictates—and that can mean, as it has in Canada, rationing and decreasing quality of care. The cost-effectiveness of a private system has been demonstrated. According to unpublished data obtained from the British Columbia Ministry of Health in 1995, the cost of performing a procedure in a public hospital is double that in a private facility.

Experience worldwide has shown that 10% to 15% of the public opts for a private system.[4,5] Therefore, there has been no significant movement of the best physicians and nurses from the public system to the private one, because there is not enough work in the private system alone to support them. In any case, governments across Canada report an excess of nurses and physicians in the public system; if this claim is correct, their movement to the private system should not cause concern or alarm. Physicians in British Columbia are committed, as a mater of policy, to provide the necessary level of service to maintain a comprehensive public medicare system. Given the consistently high degree of support for medicare among Canadian physicians, it is safe to assume that physicians across the country would make a similar commitment.

There are already parallel public and private systems of social services in Canada, of which the most obvious example is the educational system. The existence of both public and private school systems is well accepted by the Canadian public, and, where they exist, private schools are not the exclusive domain of the rich. Healthy, privately donated subsidies, particularly to private religious schools of all denominations, provide substantial financial support for those who cannot afford full fees.

Criticism of a parallel, private system is usually grounded in the politics of fear and envy. Opponents often draw comparisons with the U.S. system. Horror stories about American citizens who are underinsured, uninsured or locked into jobs in order to be covered by health insurance are used liberally to frighten Canadian citizens. Raising the spectre of managed care, now the practice in many U.S. health maintenance organizations, is the new tactic to frighten Canadian physicians. However, no Canadian physician who supports a parallel, private Canadian system endorses the adoption of the U.S. system. Canadian physicians strongly support public medicare, and they always will.

The politics of envy involve suggestions that the rich could buy quicker and better care under a parallel, private system. Better that all be doomed to the lowest common denominator of care than that preferential access be allowed, these critics say. However, the coverage under a regulated, not-for-profit insurance scheme would be available to average wage-earners—blue-collar or white-collar, unionized or self-employed—at a cost that would probably be lower than the cost of insuring a car. The rich have always been able to buy their care; they can afford to travel to wherever prompt care, and the latest medical technology and equipment, are available, either in their own communities or elsewhere, and pay for such care. Canadians spend $1 billion for health care in the United States each year, an amount that represents a loss of 10 000 health care jobs. These jobs could have been retained in Canada if a parallel, private, not-for-profit, regulated insurance system had been permitted.

Canadian medicare has resulted in the tyranny of a monopsony (single payer), which has led to rationing through the use of queues, to decreasing accessibility and to diminishing quality. Disability and even deaths are resulting from the underfunding of the system. In British Columbia during the past year, the waiting list for elective surgery grew substantially (by more than 35% in one major Vancouver hospital),[6] and there are waiting lists of many months for coronary angiography and angioplasty at tertiary care centres. British Columbia residents represent about one third of the patients receiving radiation therapy, paid for by the British Columbia government, at one U.S. hospital,[7] and 50% of patients attending an in-vitro fertilization clinic at the University of Washington in Seattle are from British Columbia. A study conducted by the London School of Economics and published in January 1996 showed that, in the United Kingdom, dissatisfaction with the quality of service, rather than with the concept of public provision, drives people to the private sector for their health care.[8] In regions of the United Kingdom with long waiting lists, there is more individually purchased private insurance. The authors also pointed to the increased costs of new medical technology, the rarity of labour-saving technological progress in medical care delivery and the demographic implications of longer lifespans and greater consumption of medical care among older people—factors that "will imply a greater role of private insurance as the distance between services available publicly and privately grows." This likely describes our future in Canada as well.

Choice is a cherished value. Denial of choice, in medical care as in other areas of human experience, is unacceptable to many. Critics of a parallel, private system state that, by adopting universal medicare, Canadians decided to forgo choice in favour of a single-payer system. What these critics ignore is that the promise made when medicare was introduced—that accessibility and quality of care would meet a high standard—is now broken. The terms and conditions under which Canadians originally decided to forgo choice no longer apply, and increasing numbers of Canadians now support the availability of alternatives such as those that would be embodied in a parallel, private system. A public poll by Angus Reid, commissioned by the CMA, showed that approximately 50% of respondents supported a private system.[9] A similar public poll conducted in British Columbia in May 1996 showed that 49% of respondents supported private health care facilities.[10] These polls showed that support for a private system had almost doubled since a poll taken in 1992.[11] In a CBC News-World poll released on Mar. 30, 1996, respondents were asked, "Do private clinics threaten the public health care system?" and 72% said that they did not.

Over the past several years, most Canadian physicians have also supported a parallel, private system—60% of physicians polled across Canada, 68% of those in Ontario (Focus Canada poll, Environics Research Group, Toronto: unpublished data, 1995) and 78% of those in British Columbia.[12] Physicians have been frustrated by their inability to provide needed services for their patients because of cutbacks in funding. They have worked hard to make the system more efficient and to apply new techniques and technologies innovatively and creatively to increase throughput and to improve accessibility. However, they have also experienced personal professional penalties. Cutbacks in operating-room times have affected surgeons of all types, anesthetists and interventional cardiologists; hospital and bed closures have affected family physicians, emergency physicians and cognitive specialists. The tyranny of a single-payer system also denies physicians a choice. Some of them—often Canada's best—have voted with their feet and gone to the United States. Their numbers are increasing and cannot be dismissed lightly. This same tyranny of a single-payer system allows governments to use the ultimate weapon—legislation—to abrogate valid contracts that they had previously negotiated with physicians in their province (Ontario, Alberta and British Columbia are recent examples).

There are strong arguments supporting a parallel, private system in the Canadian context of a universal, public medicare system. A private, not-for-profit, regulated insurance scheme would be fair and affordable. It would improve access to medical care for patients who purchase private insurance and, by freeing public resources, for those who remain in the public system.

The argument that the administrative costs of a public system are much lower than those of a private system applies only if a public system is compared with the U.S. system.[13] The difference is much less when a public system is compared with the parallel,

private, not-for-profit, regulated system in all other Western countries. Furthermore, the cost of a public system in disability, lowered quality of life and impaired quality of care outweighs the small increase in administrative costs for a parallel, private, not-for-profit, regulated system, which is supported by citizens and health care professionals alike.

### References

1. Canadian Press. Surgery delays prompt call for 2-tier plan. *Vancouver Sun* 1995 Sept 21; Sect A:6.

2. Jackman M. The regulation of private health care under the Canada Health Act and Canadian Charter. *Constitutional Forum* 1995;6:54–60.

3. Belien P. Overview of the lessons about the role of the market from European health care systems [presentation]. Health Care Dilemma Conference; 1995 Nov 7; Toronto.

4. Organization for Economic Cooperation and Development. *The Reform of Health Care Systems: A Review of Seventeen OECD Countries.* Paris: The Organization, 1994.

5. Prewo W. Reorganizing the European welfare systems [presentation]. Pre-Social Summit Symposium; 1995 Jan 20; Copenhagen, Denmark.

6. Noble I. Line-up for surgery grows. *North Shore News* [North Vancouver] 1996 Apr 19:3.

7. Crawley M. Two hospitals deny Liberals' health-care "horror stories." *Vancouver Sun* 1996 May 7; Sect B:3.

8. Besley T, Hall J, Preston I. *Private Health Insurance and the State of the NHS.* London, England: Institute for Fiscal Studies, London School of Economics, 1996.

9. Canadian Medical Association. *Taking the Pulse: The CMA Physician Resource Survey.* Ottawa: The Association, 1996:76.

10. Barrett T. Voters oppose NDP spending: an Angus Reid poll suggests most voters would rather the government reduce debt, even if it means cutting back on services. Social services viewed as good place to cut spending. *Vancouver Sun* 1996 May 7; Sect A:1,9.

11. Toulin A. A different view on health care. *Financial Post* [Toronto] 1992 May 4:14.

12. Surveying the issues—BC doctors speak their mind. *BCMA News* 1994 Sept/Oct(special ed):3-5.

13. Evans RG, Lomas J, Barer ML, Labelle RJ, Fooks C. Stoddard GL, et al. Controlling health expenditures—the Canadian reality. *N Engl J Med* 1989;320:571–7.

---

### Decision Scenario 1

"You need to bring Tim back in about two weeks and let me have another look at him," Dr. Jane Mallory said. "I suspect he's got a form of inflammatory bowel disease, and I want to see how he does with the drugs and diet. If we can't get the disease under control, he might have to have surgery."

"I'm sorry, Doctor," Mr. Hinshaw said. "I just don't have the money. My insurance policy at work covers me, but my wife and kids aren't covered."

1. Reinhardt would consider Tim's case and others like it the result of government policies that delib-

erately ration health care to poor children. On what grounds does he hold this view? On what grounds does he consider such a rationing scheme unfair?

2. On what grounds does Buchanan hold that the government has a duty to see to it that everyone receives a "decent minimum" of health care? Why does he reject the notion of health care as a universal right?

3. Would the President's Commission require society to provide care for cases like Tim's, even though his family can't pay for it? Does the commission endorse a right to health care?

## Decision Scenario 2

"We can offer you a couple of options," Dr. Kenton said. "

"Whatever will make the pain stay away," Bill Czahz said.

"We can do coronary artery bypass surgery. Two arteries are involved, so for you it would be a double bypass."

"This isn't something experimental?"

"No, it's a well-established procedure with a good safety record. About 80 percent who have surgery get rid of their angina."

"I don't much like the idea of being cut, but I'd do most anything to stop those chest pains."

"The other option is that we can treat you medically. We can try you on some drugs and see how you do, put you on a diet, and keep a close watch on you. People we treat this way do a little bit better in terms of living longer than those treated surgically. That's a little misleading, though, because those who have surgery usually have worse cases of the disease."

"What about the angina pains?" Mr. Czahz asked.

"There's the problem. Medical treatment can do something about the pains, but it's really not as effective as surgery."

"So I'll take the surgery."

"Aren't you on health stamps?" Dr. Kenton asked.

"That's right."

"We've got a problem then. You see, health stamps won't cover the cost of bypass surgery. It's an optional procedure under the HHS guidelines, and they won't kick in the extra money to pay for it."

"So I have to make up the difference myself?"

"That's right," Dr. Kenton said. "You're going to have to come up with about five thousand in cash."

"Dr. Kenton, there's no way I can do that."

"Okay, then. I just wanted you to know what the possibilities were. We can put you on a treatment program, and I'm sure you'll do just fine."

"But what about the angina pain?"

"We'll do what we can," Dr. Kenton said.

1. A health-stamp (or voucher) program might operate by granting a fixed amount of money to each person below a certain income level. This would permit someone to shop around for the best health-care bargain he or she could afford. What are the advantages and disadvantages of such a program?

2. Would the President's Commission see the voucher system applied here as providing adequate health care?

3. Is a two-tiered health-care system compatible with the single-payer system supported by Angell? With the system advocated by Dirnfeld?

4. Would Angell (in "The Doctor as Double Agent") endorse the role played by Dr. Kenton?

## Decision Scenario 3

The cashier's office of Archway Memorial Hospital is, even for the wealthy and best educated, a place of frustration. Bills are presented in the form of long computer printouts, covered with unfamiliar names referring to supplies, medical treatment, and diagnostic tests. Associated with each item is a price that seems absurdly high.

For someone without medical insurance, being faced with such a bill is more than confusing—it's frightening. And that was just the situation that Marvin Baldesi found himself in.

"Your age makes you ineligible for Medicare," said Ms. Kearney, the Archway billing officer. "And you say you aren't covered by a private insurance plan?"

"That's right," said Mr. Baldesi. "I own my own business. My wife and me, we run a small upholstery shop. We decided we couldn't afford to keep up our insurance."

"Normally, we wouldn't have admitted you," said Ms. Kearney. "It's only because you came in as an acute emergency that you were allowed to run up such a bill." She paused. "You're going to need some follow-up treatments, too."

Mr. Baldesi looked down to keep from meeting Ms. Kearney's eyes. He felt embarrassed. He had always paid his bills, and now this woman didn't bother to disguise the fact that she saw him as a deadbeat.

"Do you have any savings?" Ms. Kearney asked.

"About fifty dollars. Just enough to keep the account open."

"Then it looks to me like you've only got two choices," Ms. Kearney said. "You've got to borrow the money or declare yourself bankrupt. If you do that, once you've exhausted your assets, you'll be eligible for Medicaid."

"But the bill is almost fifty thousand dollars," Mr. Baldesi said. "I can't borrow money like that. My family and friends don't have it, and no bank would loan it to me without collateral."

"Then you'll have to get a lawyer and declare bankruptcy."

"But I'll lose my business. My credit will be ruined, and I won't be able to get the materials I need from suppliers. Isn't there any other way?"

"I don't know of any," said Ms. Kearney. "But that's not really my problem. But Archway has to be paid. You received our services, and we have to have the money for them."

1. Is Mr. Baldesi's predicament possible in the United States today? If Angell's plan were implemented, would it eliminate such cases? How would Archway Hospital get paid?

2. How should Mr. Baldesi's bills be covered according to the President's Commission?

3. Archway (through Ms. Kearney) is asserting its claim as an agent in a market economy. How would Mr. Baldesi's emergency care be dealt with under the Canadian system?

4. Suppose Mr. Baldesi's illness is connected with his failure to give up smoking and drinking, even though advised to do so by his physician. Would this lead you to view his situation any differently?

## Decision Scenario 4

When the pain began, Alan Warfard was certain he was having a heart attack. The pain lasted more than an hour, and when it was finally over he was weak and exhausted. He knew there was something seriously wrong with him, and as soon as he was able, he called his next-door neighbor and asked her to drive him to Southwest Hospital.

"You have no insurance coverage, except for Medicare?" the man at the admitting desk asked Mr. Warfard. "No private insurance at all?"

"Just Medicare," Mr. Warfard said.

"Can you show us any financial records, such as savings-account passbooks, to establish that you are able to pay your charges here?"

"I live on my Social Security check, and I don't have a savings account."

"Do you have any relatives willing to sign a statement assuming financial responsibility for your treatment here?"

"I'm afraid not," Mr. Warfard said. "But I don't see what the problem is. I told you—I'm covered by Medicare. Isn't that enough?"

The admitting clerk shook his head. "I'm afraid it's not. We don't know what your treatment is likely to cost, and we don't know whether Medicare would pay for all of it. You know, they pay only a certain amount, and you might run up bills above that. This is a private hospital, and I'm afraid that, without your being able to guarantee that you can pay us, I can't admit you for treatment."

"But I'm sick," Mr. Warfard said. "what am I supposed to do, just go home and die?"

"That's not really our concern," the clerk said. "But I suggest you see if you can get yourself admitted to a public hospital. Taking care of people like you is their responsibility."

The phrase "people like you" stung Mr. Warfard's pride. After all those years of paying his taxes and being a good citizen, how could he be dismissed so easily?

1. The problem of underinsurance is not confined to those who receive Medicare. Is a situation such as this consistent with the recommendations of the President's Commission to guarantee a decent minimum of health care to all citizens?

2. Why does Buchanan think our government should see to it that Mr. Warfard gets the medical care he needs?

3. Essential to Angell's argument (as well as the arguments of others) is the idea that health care is special in a way that makes it inappropriate to commodify it and subject it to market forces. If there is something special about health care, what is it and why should it be exempt from the usual economic forces that govern buying and selling in a market economy?

4. If Dirnfeld's proposal were accepted, might Canadian hospitals become as reluctant to accept patients without supplemental private insurance as their U.S. counterparts?

---

## Decision Scenario 5

"Let me see if I understand you correctly," Mrs. Burgone said. "I need a liver transplant, but I'm not allowed to have such an operation?"

"That's correct," Dr. Popp said. "The National Health policy stipulates that transplant surgery cannot be performed on patients over the age of seventy."

Mrs. Burgone shook her head. "But I don't expect National Health to pay for it. I'm able to pay for it myself."

"That doesn't matter. It's a matter of social policy, not medicine. The idea is that we can't afford, as a society, to do everything for every patient. You might be able to pay for such an operation, but not everybody can. Then society would have to pay for those who can't afford it, and society can't afford to do that. Con-sequently, to be fair, the operation is denied to everyone above the age of seventy."

"That doesn't seem fair to me," Mrs. Burgone said. "How can it be fair to condemn someone to pain and a greater risk of death when a way of changing this is available?"

1. Is this sort of system consistent with the position taken by the President's Commission?

2. Would a single-payer system solve the problem posed here, or are such problems the consequence of single-payer systems?

3. Does Buchanan's "decent minimum" necessarily require organ transplants?

## Decision Scenario 6

"Let me explain it to you, Mr. Faust," Charles Young said. "Although your wife is covered by Medicare, we cannot pay for the care she is receiving in the nursing home. As an Alzheimer's patient, she's getting custodial care, and that is explicitly excluded from Medicare coverage. Do you have any insurance?"

"My wife and I both have coverage through my job. But the benefits office told me exactly the same thing. My policy doesn't cover long-term, chronic, or custodial care."

"I'm sorry to hear that," Young said. "That means that you'll have to pay the total cost of the care yourself."

"Where can a sales rep get that kind of money?" Mr. Faust said. "A nursing home will cost me forty or fifty thousand dollars a year. If I sell our house and use all our savings, I could pay for maybe a year or two, but then I wouldn't have anything to live on myself. Where could I live? How could I eat?"

"The only alternative is to divest yourself of your assets so that you cannot be held legally responsible for paying for your wife's care. Then you and she can both get assistance under the Medicaid program."

"Then I have to literally become a pauper before I can get any help?"

"I'm sorry to say that's true."

1. Should a national health-care program pay for the custodial care required by patients with Alzheimer's and similar diseases?

2. Should family members (adult children or grandchildren) be required by law to help pay the health-care expenses of other family members?

3. Should people with incomes adequate to cover the cost of their health care or to buy private insurance be ineligible to participate in a national health insurance plan?

4. We expect people to pay for the goods and services they receive. Since Mrs. Faust is receiving goods and services in getting custodial care, would it be unfair to expect her husband to pay for them?

# Part IV

# Terminations

# Chapter 9

# *Abortion*

## Chapter Contents

## Classic Case Presentation

### *When Abortion Was Illegal: Mrs. Sherri Finkbine and the Thalidomide Tragedy*

*Background Note: The following case concerns an event that took place before the U.S. Supreme Court decision in* Roe v. Wade *was handed down in 1973. That decision had the effect of legalizing abortion in the United States. Before the decision, most state laws permitted abortion only for the purpose of saving the life of the mother. The case presented here illustrates the kinds of problems faced by many women who sought an abortion for other reasons.*

In 1962 Mrs. Sherri Finkbine was the mother of four normal children and was pregnant. Her health was good, but she was having some trouble sleeping. Rather than talking with her doctor, she simply took some of the tranquilizers that her husband had brought back from a trip to Europe. The tranquilizers were widely used there, and, like aspirin, they could simply be bought over the counter.

Subsequently, Mrs. Finkbine read an article that told of the great increase in the number of deformed children being born in Europe. Some of the children's arms and legs failed to develop or developed only in malformed ways; other children were blind and deaf or had seriously defective internal organs. The birth defects had been traced to the use in pregnancy of a supposedly harmless and widely used tranquilizer. Its active ingredient was thalidomide.

Mrs. Finkbine was worried enough to ask her doctor to find out if the pills she had been taking contained thalidomide. They did. When he learned this, her doctor told her, "The odds are so against you that I am recommending termination of pregnancy." He explained that getting approval for an abortion should not be difficult. She had good medical reasons, and all she had to do was explain them to the three-member medical board of Phoenix. Mrs. Finkbine agreed with her doctor's advice. But then she began to think that maybe it was her duty to inform other women who may have been taking thalidomide about its disastrous consequences. She called a local newspaper and told her story to the editor. He agreed not to use her name, but on a front page, bordered in black, he used the headline "BABY-DEFORMING DRUG MAY COST WOMAN HER CHILD HERE."

The story was picked up by the wire services, and it was not long before Mrs. Finkbine's identity became known. The medical board had already approved her request for an abortion, but because of the great publicity her case received they canceled their approval. The State of Arizona abortion statute legally sanctioned abortion only when it was required to save the life of the mother. The board was afraid that their decision might be challenged in court and that the decision could not stand up to the challenge.

Mrs. Finkbine became the object of a great outpouring of antiabortion feelings. *Il Osservatore Romano,* the official Vatican newspaper, condemned Mrs. Finkbine and her husband as murderers. Although she received some letters of support, others were abusive. One writer said: "I hope someone takes the other four children and strangles them, because it is all the same thing." Another wrote from the perspective of the fetus: "Mommy, please dear Mommy, let me live. Please, please, I want to live. Let me love you, let me see the light of day, let me smell a rose, let me sing a song, let me look into your face, let me say Mommy."

Although Mrs. Finkbine tried to obtain a legal abortion outside her own state, she was unable to do so. Eventually, she went to Sweden. After a rigorous investigation by a medical board, Mrs. Finkbine was given an abortion in a Swedish hospital.

Mrs. Finkbine saw her own problem as solved at last. But she continued to have sympathy with those thousands of potential parents of thalidomide children who lacked the money to follow the course of action she had been forced to take by abortion laws she considered to be restrictive and inhumane.

## BRIEFING SESSION

Hardly more than three decades ago, most Americans considered abortion a crime so disgusting that it was rarely mentioned in public. Back-alley abortionists with dirty hands and unclean instruments were real enough, but they were also the villains of cautionary tales to warn women against being tempted into the crime. Abortion was the dramatic stuff of novels and movies portraying "girls in trouble" or women pushed to the brink. To choose to have an abortion was to choose to be degraded.

The Supreme Court decision in *Roe v. Wade* changed all that in 1973. The decision had the effect of legalizing abortion, and since then abortion has gained an ambivalent acceptance from a majority of the population. Yet controversy over the legitimacy of abortion continues to flare. Indeed, no other topic in medical ethics has attracted more attention or so polarized public opinion. The reason is understandable. In the abortion question, major moral, legal, and social issues are intertwined to form a problem of great subtlety and complexity.

Before focusing on some of the specific issues raised by abortion, it is useful to have in hand some of the relevant factual information about human developmental biology and the techniques of abortion.

## Human Development and Abortion

Fertilization occurs when an ovum is penetrated by a sperm cell and the nuclei of the two unite to form a single cell containing forty-six chromosomes. This normally occurs in the fallopian tube (or oviduct), a narrow tube leading from the ovary into the uterus (womb). The fertilized ovum—zygote, or conceptus—continues its passage down the fallopian tube, and during its two- to three-day passage it undergoes a number of cell divisions that increase its size. (Rarely, the zygote does not descend but continues to develop in the fallopian tube, producing an ectopic pregnancy. Because the tube is so small, the pregnancy has to be terminated surgically.) After reaching the uterus, a pear-shaped organ, the zygote floats free in the intrauterine fluid. Here it develops into a *blastocyst,* a ball of cells surrounding a fluid-filled cavity.

By the end of the second week, the blastocyst becomes embedded in the wall of the uterus. At this point and until the end of the eighth week, it is known as an embryo. During the fourth and fifth weeks, organ systems begin to develop, and the external features take on a definitely human shape. During the eighth week, brain activity usually becomes detectable. At this time, the embryo comes to be known as a fetus.

Birth generally occurs about nine months after fertilization or, to be more accurate, around forty-plus weeks. It is customary to divide this time into three three-month (thirteen week) periods or trimesters. At present, pregnancy cannot be diagnosed with certainty by ordinary methods until ten to fourteen days after a woman has missed her menstrual period.

More sensitive pregnancy tests make it possible to detect pregnancy as soon as the embryo is implanted in the uterus, seven to ten days after fertilization. Also, improvements in ultrasound imaging allow the gestational sac surrounding the embryo to be detected in its earliest stages. Hence, a woman may be found to be pregnant even before she has missed an expected period.

Abortion is the termination of pregnancy. It can occur because of internal biochemical factors or as a result of physical injury to the woman. Terminations from such causes are usually referred to as "spontaneous abortions," but they are also commonly called miscarriages.

Abortion can also be a deliberate process resulting from human intervention. The methods used in contemporary medicine depend to a great extent on the stage of the pregnancy. The earliest intervention involves the use of drugs (like RU-486 or the hormones in birth control pills) to prevent the embedding of the blastocyst in the uterine wall.

Because the new tests and ultrasound make it possible to detect pregnancy as early as a week or ten days after fertilization, a pregnancy can be terminated at that point. A physician dilates (widens) the cervix (the narrow opening to the uterus), then uses a hand-operated syringe to suction out the contents of the uterus.

Subsequent intervention during the first trimester (up to about twelve weeks) commonly employs the same technique of uterine or vacuum aspiration. After the cervix is dilated, a small tube is inserted into the uterus, and its contents are emptied by suction. The procedure is known as dilation and evacuation. The classical abortion procedure is dilation and curettage. The cervix is dilated and its contents are gently scraped out by the use of a curette, a spoon-shaped surgical instrument. The procedure has been almost wholly replaced by evacuation in developed countries.

After twelve weeks, when the fetus is too large to make the other methods practical, the most common abortion technique involves dilating the cervix and extracting the fetus. (See the Social Context: The "Partial-Birth Abortion" Controversy later in this chapter for discussion.)

These facts about pregnancy and abortion put us in a position to discuss some of the moral problems connected with them. We won't be able to untangle the skein of issues wrapped around the abortion question. We'll only attempt to state a few of the more serious ones and to indicate the lines of argument that have been offered to support positions taken with respect to them; afterward we'll sketch out some possible responses that might be offered on the basis of the ethical theories we discuss in Part V: Foundations of Bioethics.

## The Status of the Fetus

It is crucial for the application of the principles of any moral theory that we have a settled opinion about the objects and subjects of morality. Although principles are generally stated with respect to rational individuals, every theory recognizes that there are people who in fact cannot be considered rational agents. For example, mental and physical incapacities may diminish or destroy rationality. But ethical theories generally recognize that we still have duties to people who are so incapacitated.

The basic problem that this raises is: Who or what is to be considered a person? Are there characteristics that we can point to and say that it is by virtue of possessing these characteristics that an individual must be considered a person and thus accorded moral treatment?

The abortion issue raises this question most particularly with regard to the fetus. (We will use the term "fetus," for the moment, to refer to the developing organism at any stage.) Just what is the status of the fetus in the world? We must find a satisfactory answer to this question, some writers have suggested, before we can resolve the general moral problem of abortion.

Let's consider the possible consequences of answering the question one way or the other. First, if a fetus is a person, it has a serious claim to life. We must assert the claim on its behalf, for, like an unconscious person, the fetus is unable to do so. The claim of the fetus as a person must be given weight and respect in deliberating about any action that would terminate its life. Perhaps only circumstances as extreme as a threat to the life of the mother would justify abortion.

Assuming the fetus is a person, then an abortion would be a case of killing and something not to be undertaken without reasons sufficient to override the fetus's claim to life. In effect, only conditions of the same sort that would justify our killing an adult person (for example, self-defense) would justify our killing a fetus. Thus, the moral burden in every case would be to demonstrate that abortion is not a case of wrongful killing.

By contrast, if a fetus is not a person in a morally relevant sense, the abortion need not be considered a case of killing equivalent to the killing of an adult. In one view, it might be said that an abortion is not essentially different from an appendectomy. According to this way of thinking, a fetus is no more than a complicated clump of organic material, and its removal involves no serious moral difficulty.

In another view, it could be argued that, even though the fetus is not a person, it is a potential person, and thus is a significant and morally relevant property. The fetus's very potentiality makes it unique and distinguishes it from a diseased appendix or a cyst or any other kind of organic material. Thus, because the fetus can become a person, abortion does present a moral problem. A fetus can be destroyed only for serious reasons. Thus, preventing a person from coming into existence must be justified to an extent comparable to the justification required for killing a person. (Some have suggested that the justification does not have to be identical because the fetus is only a potential person. The justification we might present for killing a person would thus serve only as a guide for those that might justify abortion.)

So far we have used the word "fetus," and this usage tends to obscure the fact that human development is a process with many stages. Perhaps it is only in the later stages of development that the entity becomes a person. But exactly when might this happen?

The difference between a fertilized ovum and a fully developed baby just a few minutes before birth are considerable. The ovum and the blastocyst seem just so much tissue. But the embryo and the fetus present more serious claims to being persons. Should abortion be allowed until the fetus becomes visibly human, or until the fetus shows heartbeat and brain waves, or until the fetus can live outside the uterus (becomes viable)?

The process of development is continuous, and so far it has proved impossible to find differences between stages that can be generally accepted as morally relevant. Some writers on abortion have suggested that it is useless to look for such differences, because any place where the line is drawn will be arbitrary. Others have claimed that it is possible to draw the line by relying on criteria that can be rationally defended. A few have even argued that a reasonable set of criteria for determining who shall be considered a person might even deny the status to infants.

## Pregnancy, Abortion, and the Rights of Women

Pregnancy and fetal development are normal biological processes, and most women who choose to have a child carry it to term without unusual difficulties. However, it is important to keep in mind that even a normal pregnancy involves changes and stresses that are uniquely burdensome. Once the process of fetal growth is initiated, a woman's entire physiology is altered by the new demands placed on it and by the biochemical changes taking place within her body. For example, metabolic rate increases, the thyroid gland grows larger, the heart pumps more blood to meet fetal needs, and a great variety of hormonal changes take place. The growing fetus physically displaces the woman's internal organs and alters the size and shape of her body.

As a result of such changes, the pregnant woman may suffer a variety of ailments. More common ones include severe nausea and vomiting ("morning sickness"), muscle cramps, abdominal pain, anemia, tiredness, and headaches. For many women such complaints are relatively mild or infrequent, while for others they are severe or constant. Nausea and vomiting can lead to dehydration and malnutrition so serious as to be life-threatening. Women who suffer from diseases like diabetes are apt to face special health problems as a result of pregnancy.

Partly because of hormonal changes, women are also more likely to experience psychological difficulties when pregnant, such as emotional lability (mood swings), severe depression, and acute anxiety. Such conditions are often accompanied by quite realistic concerns about the loss of freedom associated with becoming a parent, compromised job status, loss of sexual attractiveness due to the change in body shape, and the pains and risks of childbirth.

The woman who intends to carry a child to term is also likely to have to alter her behavior in many ways. She may have to curtail the time she spends working, take a leave of absence, or even quit her job. Any career plans she has are likely to suffer. She may be unable to participate in social activities to the extent she previously did, and forced to give up some entirely. In addition, if she recognizes an obligation to the developing fetus and is well informed, she may have to alter her diet, stop smoking, and strictly limit the amount of alcohol she consumes.

In summary, the physical and emotional price paid by a woman for a full-term pregnancy is high. Even a normal pregnancy, one that proceeds without any special difficulties, exacts a toll of discomfort, stress, restricted activity, and worry.

Women who wish to have a child are generally willing to undergo the rigors of pregnancy to satisfy this desire. But is it a woman's duty to nurture and carry to term an unwanted child? Pregnancies resulting from rape and incest are the kinds of dramatic cases frequently mentioned to emphasize the seriousness of the burden imposed on women. But the question is also important when the conditions surrounding the pregnancy are more ordinary.

Suppose that a woman becomes pregnant unintentionally and decides that having a child will be harmful to her career or her way of life. Or suppose she simply does not wish to subject herself to the pains of pregnancy. Does a woman have a moral duty to see to it that the developing child comes to be born?

A number of writers have taken the position that women have an exclusive right to control their own reproductive function. In their view, such a right is based upon the generally recognized right to control what is done to our bodies. Since pregnancy is something that involves a woman's body, the woman concerned may legitimately decide whether to continue the pregnancy or terminate it. The decision is hers alone, and social or legal policies that restrict the free exercise of her right are unjustifiable.

Essentially the same point is sometimes phrased by saying that women own their bodies. Because their bodies are their own "property," women alone have the right to decide whether to become pregnant and, if pregnant unintentionally, whether to have an abortion.

Critics have pointed out that this general line of argument, taken alone, does not support the strong conclusion that women should be free from all constraints in making abortion decisions. Even granting that women's bodies are their own property, we nevertheless recognize restrictions on exercising property rights. We have no right to shoot trespassers, and we cannot endanger our neighbors by burning down our house. Similarly, if any legitimate moral claims can be made on behalf of the fetus, then the right of women to decide whether to have an abortion may not be unrestricted.

Some philosophers (Judith Jarvis Thomson, for example) have taken the view that, although women are entitled to control their bodies and make abortion decisions, the decision to have an abortion must be supported by weighty reasons. They have suggested that, even if we grant that a fetus is a person, its claim to life cannot be given unconditional precedence over the woman's claim to control her own life. She is entitled to autonomy and the right to arrange her life in accordance with her own concept of the good. It would be wrong for her to destroy the fetus for a trivial reason, but legitimate and adequate reasons for taking the life of the fetus might be offered.

Others, by contrast, have argued that when a woman becomes pregnant she assumes an obligation for the life of the fetus. It is, after all, completely dependent on her for its continued existence. She has no more right to take its life in order to seek her own best interest than she has to murder someone whose death may bring benefits to her.

## Therapeutic Abortion

Abortion is sometimes required to save the life of the mother or in order to provide her with medical treatment considered essential to her health. Abortion performed for such a purpose is ordinarily regarded as a case of self-defense. For this reason, it is almost universally considered to be morally unobjectionable. (Strictly speaking, the Roman Catholic view condemns abortion in all of its forms. It does approve of providing medical treatment for the mother, even if this results in the death of the fetus, but the death of the fetus must never be intended.)

If the principle of preserving the life and health of the mother justifies abortion, then what conditions fall under that principle? If a woman has cancer of the uterus and her life can be saved only by an operation that will result in the death of the fetus, then this clearly falls under the principle. But what about psychological conditions? Is a woman's mental health relevant to deciding whether an abortion is justified? What if a psychiatrist believes that a woman cannot face the physical rigors of pregnancy or bear the psychological stresses that go with it without developing severe psychiatric symptoms? Would such a judgment justify an abortion? Or is the matter of psychological health irrelevant to the abortion issue?

Consider, too, the welfare of the fetus. Suppose that prenatal tests indicate that the developing child suffers from serious abnormalities. (This was the case of the "thalidomide babies.") Is abortion for the purpose of preventing the birth of such children justifiable?

It might be argued that it is not, that an impaired fetus has as much right to its life as an impaired person. We do not, after all, consider it legitimate to kill people who become seriously injured or suffer from diseases that render them helpless. Rather, we care for them and work to improve their lives—at least we ought to.

Some might argue, however, that abortion in such cases is not only justifiable, but a duty. It is our duty to kill the fetus to spare the person that it will become a life of unhappiness and suffering. We might even be said to be acknowledging the dignity of the fetus by doing what it might do for itself if it could—what any rational creature would do. Destroying such a fetus would spare future pain to the individual and his or her family and save society from an enormous expense. Thus, we have not only a justification to kill such a fetus, but also the positive obligation to do so.

In this chapter, we will not deal explicitly with the issues that are raised by attempting to decide whether it is justifiable to terminate the life of an impaired fetus. Because such issues are directly connected with prenatal genetic diagnosis and treatment, we discuss them more fully in Chapter 6. Nonetheless, in considering the general question of the legitimacy of abortion, it is important to keep such special considerations in mind.

## Abortion and the Law

Abortion in our society has been a legal issue as well as a moral issue. Until the Supreme Court decision in *Roe v. Wade,* nontherapeutic abortion was illegal in virtually all states. The *Webster* decision (see the Social Context: Crucial Legal and Policy Decisions) is a recent indication that the Court is willing to accept more state restrictions than previously, but even so abortions are far

from being illegal. However, even though groups still lobby for a constitutional amendment to protect a fetus's "right to life" and prohibit elective abortion, the position has little popular support.

The rightness or wrongness of abortion is a moral matter, one whose issues can be resolved only by appealing to a moral theory. Different theories may yield incompatible answers, and even individuals who accept the same theory may arrive at different conclusions.

Such a state of affairs raises the question of whether the moral convictions or conclusions of some people should be embodied in laws that govern the lives of all people in the society. The question can be put succinctly: Should the moral beliefs of some people serve as the basis for laws that will impose those beliefs on everyone?

This question cannot be answered in a straightforward way. To some extent, which moral beliefs are at issue is a relevant consideration. So too are the political principles that we are willing to accept as basic to our society. Every ethical theory recognizes that there is a scope of action that must be left to individuals as moral agents acting freely on the basis of their own understanding and perceptions. Laws requiring the expression of benevolence or gratitude, for example, seem peculiarly inappropriate.

Yet, one of the major aims of a government is to protect the rights of its citizens. Consequently, a society must have just laws that recognize and enforce those rights. In a very real way, then, the moral theory we hold and the conclusions arrived at on the basis of it will determine whether we believe that certain types of laws are justified. They are justified when they protect the rights recognized in our moral theories—when political rights reflect moral rights. (See the Briefing Session in Chapter 7 for a fuller discussion of moral rights and their relation to political rights.)

An ethical theory that accords the status of a person to a fetus is likely to claim also that the laws of the society should recognize the rights of the fetus. A theory that does not grant the fetus this position is not likely to regard laws forbidding abortion as justifiable.

# Ethical Theories and Abortion

Theories like those of Mill, Kant, Ross, and Rawls attribute to individuals autonomy or self-direction. An individual is entitled to control his or her own life, and it seems reasonable to extend this principle to apply to one's own body. If so, then a woman should have the right to determine whether or not she wishes to have a child. If she is pregnant with an unwanted child, then, no matter how she came to be pregnant, she might legitimately decide on an abortion. Utilitarianism also suggests this answer on consequential grounds. In the absence of other considerations, if it seems likely that having a child will produce more unhappiness than an abortion would, then an abortion would be justifiable.

If the fetus is considered to be a person, however, the situation is different for some theories. The natural law view holds that the fetus is an innocent person and that direct abortion is never justifiable. Even if the pregnancy is due to rape, the fetus cannot be held at fault and made to suffer through its death. Even though she may not wish to have the child, the mother has a duty to preserve the life of the fetus.

For deontological theories like those of Kant and Ross, the situation becomes more complicated. If the fetus is a person, it has an inherent dignity and worth. It is an innocent life that cannot be destroyed except for the weightiest moral reasons. Those reasons may include the interests and wishes of the woman, but deontological theories provide no clear answer as to how those are to be weighed.

For utilitarianism, by contrast, even if the fetus is considered a person, the principle of utility may still justify an abortion. Killing a person is not, for utilitarianism, inherently wrong. (Yet it is compatible with rule utilitarianism to argue that permitting elective abortion as a matter of policy would produce more unhappiness than forbidding abortion altogether. Thus, utilitarianism does not offer a definite answer to the abortion issue.)

As we have already seen, both utilitarianism and deontological theories can be used to justify therapeutic abortion. When the mother's life or health is at stake, the situation may be construed as one of self-defense. Both Kant and Ross recognize that we each have a right to protect ourselves, even if it means taking the life of another person. For utilitarianism, preserving one's life is justifiable, for being alive is a necessary condition for all forms of happiness.

We have also indicated that abortion "for the sake of the fetus" can be justified by both utilitarianism and deontological theories. If by killing the fetus we can spare it a life of suffering, minimize the sufferings of its family, and preserve the resources of the society, then abortion is legitimate on utilitarian grounds. In the terms of Kant and Ross, destroying the fetus might be a way of recognizing its dignity. If we assume that it is a person, then by sparing it a life of indignity and pain we are treating it in the way that a rational being would want to be treated.

The legitimacy of laws forbidding abortion is an issue that utilitarianism would resolve by considering their effects. If such laws promote the general happiness of the society, then they are justifiable. Otherwise, they are not. In general, Kant, Ross, Rawls, and natural law theory recognize intrinsic human worth and regard as legitimate laws protecting that worth, even if those holding this view are only a minority of the society. Thus, laws discriminating against blacks and women, for example, would be considered unjust on the basis of these theories. Laws enforcing equality, by contrast, would be considered just.

But what about fetuses? The Roman Catholic interpretation of natural law would regard the case as exactly the same. As full human persons, they are entitled to have their rights protected by law. Those who fail to recognize this are guilty of moral failure, and laws permitting abortion are the moral equivalent of laws permitting murder.

For Kant and other deontologists, the matter is less clear. As long as there is substantial doubt about the status of the fetus, it is not certain that it is legitimate to demand that the rights of fetuses be recognized and protected by law. It is clear that the issue of whether or not the fetus is considered a person is most often taken as the crucial one in the abortion controversy.

The battle over abortion is certain to continue in the courts, streets, media, and classrooms. The issues are of great social importance, yet highly personal and explosively emotional. The best hope for a resolution continues to rest with the condemnation of violence and an emphasis on the traditional strategies of verbal persuasion, rational argument, and the appeal to basic moral principles.

The following Social Context pieces and the Case Presentations illustrate not only the conflict of opposing views, but the willingness of most people to attempt to find a nuanced response to the many issues presented by abortion.

# SOCIAL CONTEXT: HOW AMERICANS VIEW ABORTION: TOLERANT AMBIVALENCE

January 2002 marked the thirtieth anniversary of the Supreme Court decision legalizing abortion in the United States. Yet even after three decades, abortion has not become a standard, uncontroversial medical procedure.

Although more than a million abortions are performed every year, Americans remain ambivalent and divided on its moral acceptability. In some respects, abortion has become even less accepted than it was a decade or more ago.

## Poll Results Show Mixed Feelings

The country's mixed feelings about abortion are revealed in a January 2000 poll by the Gallup Organization. When people were asked, "With respect to the abortion issue, would you consider yourself to be pro-choice or pro-life?" those answering pro-life rose to 44 percent from the previous 33 percent of 1995. Those describing themselves as pro-choice declined from 56 to 48 percent.

| Percent Describing Themselves as | | |
|---|---|---|
| | 1995 | 2000 |
| Pro-life | 33 | 44 |
| Pro-choice | 56 | 48 |

*Source:* Gallup Organization, January 2000

This shift was not accompanied by a significant increase in the number wanting to see abortion outlawed. Only 17 to 19 percent endorsed this view, while 51 percent said abortion should be legal under some circumstances. Another 28 percent said it should be legal in any circumstance.

These new results are similar to those of a *New York Times/CBS News* poll taken on the twenty-fifth anniversary of the *Roe v. Wade* decision. (See the Social Context: Crucial Legal and Policy Decisions for a discussion of this and other court rulings.) The poll provides us with the most detailed picture available of American attitudes about abortion.

Half the population considers abortion "the same thing as murder," but even so, 32 percent of those in this group think abortion is "sometimes the best course of action in a bad situation." While 60 percent of the respondents said they thought the Supreme Court ruling establishing a woman's constitutional right to an abortion was good on the whole, almost 80 percent supported a mandatory waiting period and, in the case of minors, parental consent. People were split almost evenly on the question of whether the abortion dispute is about a woman's ability to control her body or about the life of the fetus. While 45 percent said it is about the life of the fetus, 44 percent said it is about a woman's controlling her body.

Despite favoring regulations, nearly 60 percent of those polled thought the government should stay out of abortion decisions. While the idea of a constitutional amendment banning abortion was seen as a political possibility by abortion opponents in the 1980s, more than

75 percent of those polled reject the notion. The clearest message sent by these results seems to be that people believe a decision about having an abortion ought to be thought of as a private moral matter and not a public legal one.

## Abortion for Any Reason?

While abortion rights advocates have long held that women should be free to have an abortion for any reason they believe adequate, the poll results suggest the view is no longer as widely shared as it once was. Almost half (49 percent) of those who had a view on why women have abortions considered the reasons "not serious enough." This was up from the 41 percent of a 1989 poll. In 1989 also, 50 percent of the people surveyed said they didn't think a woman's not wanting to marry the man by whom she became pregnant was a good enough reason to have an abortion. By 1998, the figure had increased to 62 percent.

| Abortion Should . . . | |
| --- | --- |
| not be permitted | 22% |
| be generally available | 32% |
| be available with strict limits | 45% |

*Source:* N.Y. Times/CBS News Poll 1998

## Time of Fetal Development

The time of fetal development has become an important consideration in weighing the legitimacy of abortion for most people. In 1989 half the respondents in a poll thought abortions during the first trimester (first three months) of pregnancy should be permitted, and by 1998 the percentage had risen to 61. However, only 15 percent thought abortion should be allowed in the second trimester, and that figure fell to 7 percent for the last three months.

Time also seems to be a relevant factor for most people in determining the acceptability of drug-induced abortion. In fact, 65 percent of those asked said they would consider a drug that prevents a fertilized egg from becoming implanted in the uterus a form of birth control and not abortion at all. Only 20 percent said they would regard such intervention as abortion. Similarly, while 50 percent of those asked favored "chemical abortion" using a drug like RU-486 (employed in the first seven weeks of pregnancy) as an alternative to surgical abortion, 36 percent opposed it.

## Women and Men

The views of women and men, as represented by the poll results, are virtually the same with respect to the availability of abortion and to the extent that access to abortion should be restricted or forbidden. Thirty-two percent of women and 31 percent of men believe it should be generally available. While 44 percent of women and 45 percent of men favor strict limits, only 21 percent of women and 23 percent of men think abortion should not be permitted.

## Age and Religion

Nor does age seem to matter much. While 21 percent of those eighteen to twenty-nine years old say they believe abortion should not be permitted, the figure rises to 23 percent for those thirty to forty-four, drops to 20 percent for those forty-five to sixty-four, then increases to only 25 percent for those sixty-five or older.

While Roman Catholics are usually perceived as wholly opposed to abortion for everyone, 74 percent said they thought it should be available either generally or under strict limits. The corresponding figure for Protestants was 76 percent. A relatively low 26 percent of Catholics and 24 percent of Protestants believed abortion should not be permitted at all.

However, those who said religion was "extremely important" or "very important" in their daily lives were also most likely to think (43 percent and 23 percent respectively) that abortion shouldn't be allowed. This view was endorsed by only 9 percent of those who said religion was not so important in their daily lives.

## Education

The survey found that the more educated the respondents, the less likely they were to be completely opposed to abortion. Of those without a high school diploma, 28 percent said abortion should not be permitted, but the figure fell to 24 percent for high school graduates. For those with some college it fell to 19 percent, then to 18 percent for those with college degrees.

---

## Abortion Rates

### Age (1994)

| | | | |
|---|---|---|---|
| Under 15 | 1% | 30–34 | 14% |
| 15–19 | 19% | 35–39 | 7% |
| 20–24 | 37% | 40– | 2% |
| 25–29 | 20% | | |

### Race and Ethnicity (1995)

| | |
|---|---|
| White/Hispanic | 60% |
| African American | 38% |
| Other | 2% |

### Previous Children (1995)

| | | | |
|---|---|---|---|
| None | 44% | 3 | 8% |
| 1 | 27% | 4+ | 3% |
| 2 | 18% | | |

### As result of rape or incest

1%

### Number of Abortions (1994)

| | | | |
|---|---|---|---|
| First | 52% | Third | 11% |
| Second | 29% | Fourth + | 8% |

*Source:* Centers for Disease Control and Prevention

---

## Reasons

Over the years since the *Roe v. Wade* decision, the public's attitude toward abortion has remained relatively consistent on several possible reasons for having one. About 80 percent of those surveyed believe a woman should be able to obtain an abortion if her health is signifi-cantly endangered by the pregnancy. About 75 percent believe she should also be able to get an abortion if there is "a strong chance of a serious defect in the baby."

Only 43 percent believe the family having a low income and not being able to afford another child is a good enough reason for an abortion, and the figure drops to 39 percent if the woman is married and simply doesn't want any more children.

## New Medical Technology

To a considerable extent, the ambivalence about abortion and the public clash of opinions about its moral legitimacy are due to the development of new reproductive and life-sustaining technology, as well as to an increase in awareness of the character of the fetus.

When a genetic disease like Tay–Sachs is present in a family, in vitro fertilization and the selection of an embryo free of the disease for implantation can avoid a problem that might lead to abortion. While for some, discarding unused embryos created by in vitro fertilization is equivalent to abortion, most people are more comfortable with the idea of destroying embryos than of aborting a fetus.

Reproductive technology has also made more familiar the concept of "selectively reducing" one or more developing fetuses in a multiple pregnancy resulting from the use of fertility drugs. For some, selective reduction is simply abortion by another name, but for others it is a procedure necessary to give the remaining fetuses a better chance to develop normally.

Also, as the statistics mentioned earlier show, the majority of people aren't troubled by preventing pregnancy by treatment with a "morning after" drug or by using a drug like RU-486 to stop pregnancy from occurring. This may be because most people do not think of a fertilized egg as a fetus until development in the uterus is well under way. Thus, they do not equate it with a baby.

The other relevant development in technology is the ability to keep alive babies that are so premature that in important aspects they are still developing fetuses. A baby is considered full-term if it is born forty weeks after conception, but a state-of-the-art neonatal unit staffed with trained and experienced people can save the lives of infants who have had only twenty-three or twenty-four weeks of development.

These babies often do not do well and suffer serious lifelong problems. Even so, the fact that such small babies can survive outside the uterus has led many people to become more restrained in their endorsement of abortion or to favor restrictions on when it can be performed. After all, the second trimester ends at around twenty-five weeks. (See the discussion of the *Webster* decision later in this chapter.)

### Number of Abortions

In 1990 the number of women who had an abortion was 1.6 million. By 1995 the figure was down to 1,210,833, and by 1997 it was 1.328 million. Thus, from 1990 to 1997 (the last year with complete figures), abortion declined 17.4 percent.

The reasons for the decline are unclear, but some believe it is connected with the aging of the population, the wider availability of contraception, and fewer unwanted pregnancies. Others think the decline reflects a change of attitude toward abortion, as well as changes in society (antiabortion protests, shrinking number of abortion providers, stiffer regulation) that make it more difficult for a woman to secure an abortion.

While the number of abortions is likely to vary slightly from year to year, experts think it is unlikely any increase will reach the 1990 high point. Some suggest that a less-accepting attitude toward abortion will keep the number lower than might be expected otherwise.

### The Middle Position

The abstract and absolute positions represented by statements like "A woman has a right to choose to have an abortion for any reason at all" and "A fertilized egg is as much a person as a born child and has just as much right to life" have become less representative of the beliefs of most people over the last three decades. The majority of people tend toward the view that the most reasonable position on abortion lies somewhere between these extremes.

To sum up in a phrase, Americans appear to think abortion should be "safe, legal, and rare." But of course agreement to such a general proposition doesn't translate into agreements about what restrictions are appropriate. While abstract positions may have blurred for most people, debates over particular policies remain as divisive and acrimonious as they ever were.

---

## SOCIAL CONTEXT: THE "PARTIAL-BIRTH ABORTION" CONTROVERSY

In 1995 debate began to rage around abortion performed after twenty weeks of gestation, often focusing on a specific surgical procedure used to terminate a pregnancy. Technically known as intact dilation and extraction, the procedure was named "partial-birth abortion" by those opposed to abortion.

The debate, now abating, is characterized to an unusual extent by a lack of information and a reliance on misinformation by participants on both sides. Instead of laying out the issues as the opponents present them, it is more useful to begin by considering some of the facts relevant to evaluating the various positions taken.

### Late-Term Abortion

While abortion opponents often portray "abortion doctors" as employing brutal procedures to destroy viable fetuses in order to satisfy the whims of pregnant women, those favoring abortion rights present women as opting for such measures in only rare and extreme cases. The best estimates available suggest that neither picture is accurate.

More than half (52.2 percent) of all abortions are performed less than nine weeks after conception, and about a quarter (24.7 percent) are performed in weeks nine and ten. Indeed, 98.9 percent of all abortions are performed within twenty weeks of conception. Thus, late-term abortion, defined as abortion after twenty weeks, is relatively rare, accounting for only 1.1 percent of all abortions.

No statistics are available on the reasons women have late-term (instead of early) abortions. The best information comes from the congressional testimony of physicians who perform abortions. They suggest that one group of women have abortions because their own health is threatened by pregnancy. For example, the pregnancy may have triggered an autoimmune disease or the woman may have developed cancer and need treatment with chemotherapy and radiation.

A second group of women have late-term abortions because the fetus has developed a severe defect. For example, ultrasound may reveal that the growing child's cerebral hemispheres have failed to develop. If the pregnancy continues, the child that is born will not only lack all cognitive capacity, but will die within a few days or weeks.

The third and largest group are those who have failed to get an early abortion for a variety of mostly social reasons. The group includes teenagers in psychological denial about being pregnant until they (or a parent) had to face the undeniable fact. Also included are indigent women, who may be homeless, mentally retarded, or socially unskilled. Drug users, who engage in their own form of denial, are included in this third group, as are women with menstrual periods so irregular they don't suspect they are pregnant until several months have passed.

Proponents of abortion rights tend to overlook this third group and focus, instead, on the other two. Being able to cite the pressing need of a pregnant woman to save her life or the cruelty of forcing a pregnant woman to carry to term a fetus with a serious developmental defect makes it easier for them to defend their case.

Opponents of abortion, by contrast, tend to discuss late-term abortion as if it were the general rule, rather than very much the statistical exception. When 98.9 percent of all abortions are

performed before twenty weeks, it is misleading to condemn all abortion by focusing on the 1.1 percent as representative. They also tend to ignore powerful reasons for having a late-term abortion, preferring to use cases producing the strongest negative emotional response.

## Fetal Viability

Abortion opponents have focused on fetal viability as the crucial grounds for outlawing late-term abortion. In making their case, they have suggested that late abortions involve killing babies that otherwise would live and thrive. This has made the debate over late-term abortion particularly contentious, for determinations of viability cannot be made in definite and reliable ways.

Perinatologists (specialists in newborns) say that too many factors are involved in determining viability to allow anyone to make reliable generalizations about which fetuses will live and which will die at any given stage of development. In addition to characteristics such as a fetus's weight and the developmental stage of the organs, factors like the health of the mother, her socioeconomic status, and her access to health care also play a role. So do the race and gender of the fetus. In development, a white fetus lags a week behind a black one of the same age, and a male fetus lags the same amount behind a female.

The viability of a fetus is also connected with the state of medical technology and management. At the time of the *Roe v. Wade* decision in 1973, fetal viability was around twenty-six weeks, but now it is closer to twenty-four, with twenty-two weeks being possible. A *micropremie* weighs 500 to 600 grams (a bit over a pound) and is hardly larger than the palm of a man's hand. Babies of this age and size, even if they survive, are likely to have irreversible physical and mental deficits.

The American College of Obstetrics and Gynecology estimates that fewer than 4 percent of babies are born during weeks twenty-three to twenty-five of the normal forty week gestation period, but their survival is conditional on the factors mentioned. Even with aggressive intervention and intensive care, some experts doubt

## Timing of Abortions

| Weeks | Number | Percentage |
|-------|--------|------------|
| >9 | 798,850 | 52.2 |
| 9–10 | 377,570 | 24.7 |
| 11–12 | 181,960 | 11.9 |
| 13–15 | 94,060 | 6.2 |
| 16–20 | 60,040 | 3.9 |
| 21–22 | 10,340 | |
| 23–24 | 4,940 | 1.1 |
| 25–26 | 850 | |
| 26+ | 32 | |
| | 1,528,930 | |

*Source:* Estimates by Alan Gutmacher Institute based on survey, Centers for Disease Control, and National Center for Health Statistics Data, 1997.

that more than about 1 percent of even twenty-five-week-old fetuses would survive. Some hospitals and state laws make twenty-three or twenty-four weeks the cutoff point for elective abortions, while others follow a more restrictive policy and make twenty weeks the limit. After the cutoff, a factor like the health and safety of the mother or a fetal abnormality must be present to justify an abortion.

How viable a fetus is and how likely one is to survive without serious and permanent mental and physical deficits is a clinical judgment that can only be made case by case. A claim to the effect that thousands or even hundreds of viable fetuses are destroyed by abortion is not supported by the evidence.

### Methods

Opponents of abortion have focused attention on a method to perform late-term abortion known as intact dilation and extraction. The procedure involves using a drug to dilate (widen) the pregnant woman's cervix, then manipulating the fetus by hand until it can be pulled though the birth canal. Usually, to ease the passage and

make the procedure easier on the woman, the fetal brain is extracted by suction so the skull can be collapsed (fenestrated). It is this procedure abortion opponents have called *"partial-birth abortion,"* a name coined for rhetorical purposes and not one used in medicine.

Intact dilation and extraction may also be performed by injecting digoxin into the uterus to stop the fetal heart. After the death of the fetus, the woman is induced into labor with a hormone injection, and the fetus is delivered vaginally. Some obstetricians consider this form of the procedure too psychologically stressful for the woman. Others believe it is sufficiently well tolerated to make it the preferred method.

The third or classic method of dilation and extraction does not involve removing an intact fetus. After a woman's cervix is dilated, instruments are used to dismember the fetus and extract the parts through the birth canal. The fetus is either killed by a prior injection or by the process itself. Ultrasound may be used to guide the instruments, and the procedure may take twenty minutes or longer.

Surgeons who prefer intact dilation and extraction point to the time and risks associated with the classic procedure. The woman's uterus may be damaged by an instrument or punctured by a sharp bone fragment. It is safer for the woman, if the intact fetus is pulled out by hand.

About 86 percent of abortions performed after twenty weeks are done by one of these three procedures. "Any procedure done at this stage is pretty gruesome," said one high-risk pregnancy specialist.

### Legislation

In 1996 Congress passed legislation banning late-term abortion, along with intact dilation and extraction, but it was vetoed by President Clinton on the ground that the bill made no provision for protecting the health of the pregnant woman.

A second attempt at passing legislation began a year later. The House passed a bill by a margin large enough (295 to 136) to override a presidential veto. The Senate passed (64 to 36) a similar ban, yet it was short of the votes needed to survive a veto. President Clinton announced he would veto any bill that did not allow an abortion to protect the health of a pregnant woman, but both the House and Senate bills would protect only the life of the pregnant woman. Abortion opponents claimed that allowing an exception for health would virtually be equivalent to no regulation at all, given the nebulous nature of claims about health, particularly mental health.

The final version of the Senate bill was revised to reflect the proposal framed and endorsed by the American Medical Association. In the first endorsement of any position on abortion, the AMA proposal made it clear that dilation and *evacuation,* the procedure most often used in early abortions, was not banned. Also, the proposal protected physicians from criminal penalties, if they had to perform a dilation and extraction because of unforeseen circumstances during a delivery. Finally, the proposal allowed physicians accused of violating the ban to appear before a state medical board, instead of a trial court.

In contrast with the AMA, the American College of Obstetricians and Gynecologists and the American Academy of Pediatrics both opposed any ban on dilation and extraction. Some saw a danger in the AMA's position, suggesting that it invited politicians to make decisions about what medical procedures are appropriate.

## State Laws

Impatient with the slowness of Congress in passing a law banning "partial-birth abortion," by 1997 about 22 states had passed their own laws. By 1998, however, at least half of those laws had been ruled unconstitutional by the courts. The most common flaw was that the language of the laws was so broad it would also apply to abortions performed before the fetus could possibly be viable. Also, like the original bill passed by Congress, the laws made no exception to protect the pregnant woman's health.

In 1995 the Ohio legislature passed a law banning all abortion past the point of fetal viability. Viability was presumed to occur twenty-four weeks after conception. The only exception to

the ban was for abortions a physician decided needed to be performed to "prevent the death of the pregnant woman or a serious risk of the substantial and irreversible impairment of a major bodily function of the pregnant woman."

The law also included a provision making it a crime for a physician to end a pregnancy "by purposely inserting a suction device into the skull of a fetus to remove its brain."

In *Voinovich v. Women's Medical Professional Corporation,* a case brought to challenge the law, the U.S. Sixth Circuit Court of Appeals in Cincinnati ruled that the law unconstitutionally restricted a woman's right to abortion by defining the prohibited procedure so broadly that it had the consequence of banning the most common method of performing a surgical abortion during the second trimester.

The ruling was appealed to the Supreme Court. In a 1998 decision (6 to 3), the Court refused to hear the case, letting the Appeals Court decision stand. In the dissenting opinion, Justice Thomas made clear that the dissenters' concern was not with late-term abortion, but with whether the prohibition of late-term abortion except to protect the life and health of the mother can limit the health protected to physical health and exclude mental. In the 1973 decision *Roe v. Bolton,* the Court had held that "emotional" and "psychological" factors may be considered by physicians in deciding whether an abortion after fetal viability is necessary to preserve the health of the pregnant woman.

A 2000 ruling by the United States Supreme Court on a Nebraska law resulted in nullifying more than thirty state laws prohibiting late-term abortion. The 1997 Nebraska law banned "an abortion procedure in which the person performing the abortion partially delivers vaginally a living unborn child before killing the unborn child and completing the delivery." The phrase "partial delivery" was defined as "deliberately and intentionally delivering into the vagina a living unborn child or a substantial proportion thereof."

The Supreme Court held in a 5-to-4 vote that the government cannot prohibit physicians from employing an abortion procedure that may be the most medically appropriate way of terminating some pregnancies. The Nebraska law, the Court decided, did not contain provisions for protecting the health and safety of the mother. Justice Stevens wrote in the majority opinion that it was "impossible for me to understand how a state has any legitimate interest in requiring a doctor to follow any procedure other than the one he or she reasonably believes will best protect the woman" in exercising her constitutional right to abortion.

The Supreme Court decision effectively declared that all legislation, state or federal, aimed at regulating abortion by specifying what procedures are illegitimate is unconstitutional. Whether this will put an end to efforts to prohibit late-term abortion is uncertain.

Many observers believe there was never a need for laws banning late-term abortion. In keeping with the *Roe v. Wade* decision granting states the power to regulate abortion to protect the interest of the fetus after the first trimester and in keeping with the *Webster* decision (see Social Context: Crucial Legal and Policy Decisions), more than forty states have laws banning abortion after fetal viability has occurred. The problem of determining viability is vexing and perhaps unsolvable, but an additional law banning late-term abortion, even if constitutional, would not help resolve the problem.

Advocates for abortion rights and even some opponents of abortion have expressed the view that the controversy over late-term abortion is primarily a way to keep abortion issues at the forefront of political discussion and to pressure politicians to modify their endorsement of elective abortion. Some have also seen the controversy as a way to raise money for all anti-abortion activities.

While these analyses may be inaccurate, or even cynical, it seems fair to say that the debate over late-term abortion introduced no new ethical issues into the discussion. The old problems remain as complex and perhaps intractable as before.

# Social Context: Crucial Legal and Policy Decisions

## *Roe v. Wade*

Norma McCorvey of Dallas was unmarried, poor, and pregnant. She wished to have an abortion, but under Texas law, abortion was a criminal offense, except when required to save the woman's life. California law was less restrictive, and McCorvey believed she could get an abortion there, but she lacked money for travel and expenses. Unwillingly, she bowed to legal and economic necessity and carried the fetus to term. She then gave up the newborn child for adoption.

When McCorvey was later approached by a public interest attorney and asked if she would agree to be the plaintiff in a class-action suit against Henry Wade, the district attorney of Dallas County, challenging the constitutionality of the Texas abortion law, she readily consented. Federal courts ruled that the Texas statute was void, but Wade appealed to the Supreme Court.

Because McCorvey wished her identity to be protected by a pseudonym, the 1973 Supreme Court decision in the case was titled *Roe v. Wade*. In a 7-to-2 decision, written by Justice Harry A. Blackmun, the Court found the Texas law unconstitutional. In doing so, the court effectively decriminalized abortion, for abortion laws in most other states differed little from the Texas statute.

The *Roe* decision did not require that abortion be unregulated, but it placed limits on the restrictions states could impose. According to the ruling, during the first twelve weeks (the first trimester) of pregnancy, states cannot restrict a woman's decision about abortion. During the second trimester, states may restrict abortion to protect the health of the woman. In the final trimester, because the fetus may be considered viable, states may limit abortions to those necessary to preserve the health of the woman.

After the *Roe* decision, abortions became easily obtainable by most women who wanted them. Yet the decision also triggered a firestorm of controversy between proponents of relatively unregulated choice ("prochoice" advocates) and opponents of so-called abortion on demand ("prolife" or "right-to-life" advocates) that shows no sign of dying down. While those who favor making abortion a matter of individual decision were pleased by the *Roe* decision, those morally opposed to abortion were not.

Many, if not most, who believe abortion is morally wrong also think it should be illegal, except in very special cases. Within the limits of regulation imposed by the *Roe* decision, opponents of abortion have taken various legal measures to attempt to slow or halt its practice. They have become politically active and have often succeeded in getting laws passed that impose requirements on abortion that make it difficult to get one. As this has happened, advocates of personal choice have often charged that the laws are unconstitutional and have filed suits that have frequently ended up before the Supreme Court.

## Supreme Court Decisions After *Roe v. Wade*

The conflict over abortion has been expressed, in part, in a continuing series of legal skirmishes that have produced a number of Supreme Court decisions seeking to define abortion rights and limits. To get some sense of the way in which laws, regulations, and practices have changed since the *Roe* decision in 1973, it is instructive to review a few Court decisions briefly and consider in more detail the ones that have most influenced the direction of public policy on abortion.

*Roe v. Bolton* (1973). The Court rejected the requirement that abortions had to be performed in hospitals, thus opening the way for abortion clinics. The Court also found that emotional and psychological factors connected with the health of the pregnant woman could be considered by physicians in deciding whether an abortion after the first trimester was justifiable.

*Planned Parenthood v. Danforth* (1976). The Missouri law requiring a husband's consent for an abortion was struck down. Also, parents of

minor, unmarried girls were found not to have an absolute veto over their daughter's decision to have an abortion.

*Maher v. Roe* (1977). The Court decided states do not have a constitutional obligation to pay for abortions for the poor. Hence, the Court left it up to states to decide whether they wished to include funding for abortion as part of their contribution to the Medicaid program.

*Harris v. McRae* (1980). The Court upheld the Hyde Amendment, the federal law banning the use of federal Medicaid funds to pay for abortions. Hence, those wanting an abortion and unable to pay for it would have to depend on money from other sources. (States, however, have no constitutional obligation to provide money for abortions.)

*City of Akron v. Akron Center for Reproductive Health* (1983). The Court struck down a law requiring that women wanting an abortion receive counseling that includes the statement that "the unborn child is a human life from the moment of conception," then wait at least twenty-four hours before reaffirming their decision.

*Webster v. Reproductive Health Services* (1989). The Missouri law in the *Webster* case is similar to laws the Court had previously held to be void. However, the law was carefully crafted by prolife advocates to avoid the specific difficulties that had led the Court to reject them. While the preamble of the law asserts that "life begins at conception," at issue were three provisions restricting abortion.

1. Public employees, including physicians and nurses, are forbidden to perform an abortion, except when necessary to save a woman's life.

2. Public hospitals, clinics, or other tax-supported facilities cannot be used to perform abortions not necessary to save a woman's life, even if no public funds are involved.

3. Physicians are required to perform tests to determine the viability of a fetus, if they

have reason to believe the woman has been pregnant for at least twenty weeks.

On July 3, 1989, the Supreme Court in a 5-to-4 decision upheld the constitutionality of the law. Chief Justice William Rehnquist, writing the majority opinion, held that the Court did not have to rule against the claim that life begins at conception, for such language is only an expression of a permissible value judgment. Furthermore, "Nothing in the Constitution requires States to enter or remain in the business of performing abortions. Nor . . . do private physicians and their patients have some kind of constitutional right of access to public facilities for the performance of abortions."

So far as viability is concerned, Rehnquist saw a problem, not with the Missouri law, but with *Roe v. Wade*'s "rigid trimester analysis of the course of a pregnancy." That is, he found the law more sensitive to the issue of viability than the trimester rule, which holds that the state can regulate abortion in the second trimester to protect a woman's health and regulate it more stringently, down to prohibiting it, in the last trimester. Furthermore, "the key elements" of *Roe v. Wade* are "not found in the text of the Constitution or in any place else one would expect to find a constitutional principle."

Justice Harry A. Blackmun, the author of the majority opinion in *Roe v. Wade,* wrote the dissenting opinion in *Webster*. He made clear that he regarded the Court's decision as an outright attack on *Roe.* Rehnquist, he argued, failed to consider the case for viability on appropriate grounds—namely, the right to privacy or autonomy, on which *Roe* was decided. Instead, he misread the Missouri law in a way that seemed to conflict with the trimester structure established in *Roe* to balance the state's interest in maternal health and potential life against the right to privacy.

The hope of abortion opponents was that the Court would use the *Webster* case to overturn *Roe v. Wade.* The Court stopped short of doing that, but the *Webster* decision made it clear that the Court was willing to approve restrictions on abortion of a sort that it had held unconstitutional until then. Various new state and local regulations were formulated and passed into law.

*Planned Parenthood v. Casey* **(1992).** The Pennsylvania Abortion Control Act was one of those pieces of legislation framed with the intention of making abortions more difficult to secure. It included the following restrictions:

1. A physician must inform a woman seeking an abortion about the procedure and its risks, the stage of the pregnancy, and the alternative of carrying the fetus to term.

2. The woman must wait at least twenty-four hours after receiving this information before having an abortion.

3. A girl under the age of eighteen must secure the informed consent of at least one parent before having an abortion, and a parent must accompany the girl to counseling. Alternatively, consent may be sought from a court.

4. A married woman must (except under certain circumstances) sign a statement that she has notified her husband of her intention to have an abortion.

The 5-to-4 Court ruling upheld most sections of the Pennsylvania law, but it rejected the provision requiring a married woman to notify her husband of her intention to have an abortion.

However, in the view of some observers, the most important outcome of the *Casey* decision was that it reaffirmed what it called the "essence" of the constitutional right to an abortion, while also introducing a new legal standard for testing the constitutional legitimacy of regulations governing abortions. The Court considered the provisions of the Pennsylvania law in terms of whether they had the purpose or result of imposing an "undue burden" on a woman seeking an abortion. In the Court's definition, a burden is "undue" if it places a "substantial obstacle in the path of a woman seeking an abortion before the fetus attains viability." Only the spousal notification requirement, in the Court's view, imposed such a burden.

The undue-burden standard makes it clear that, in the opinion of the Court, laws that attempt to prohibit abortions outright or those that attempt to reduce the frequency of abortions by making them extraordinarily difficult to obtain are unconstitutional.

In its decision, the Court explicitly endorsed *Roe v. Wade* as having established "a rule of law and a component of liberty that we cannot renounce." The majority held that *Roe* has acquired a "rare precedential force" and could be repudiated only "at the cost of both profound and unnecessary damage to the Court's legitimacy and to the nation's commitment to the rule of law."

Until the *Webster* decision, abortion was considered a fundamental right that could not be restricted, except to serve a compelling state interest. This meant that during the first two trimesters of pregnancy, almost all restrictions were considered unconstitutional. After *Webster,* it seemed to many that the way was open for more and heavier regulation of abortion. However, although the "undue-burden" standard introduced in *Casey* permits considerable regulation during this period, it does not allow opponents of abortion to regulate the practice so heavily as to make it virtually unavailable.

### Madsen v. Women's Health Center (1994).

In 1993 a Florida circuit court issued an injunction to protect access to the clinic operated by the Aware Woman Center for Choice in Melbourne, Florida. Demonstrators from Operation Rescue and related organizations were made subject to the injunction. The order imposed a 300-foot protected zone around the clinic, forbade the display of signs that could be seen from inside the clinic, and barred demonstrators from making excessive noise.

The case was appealed, and in a 6-to-3 ruling the Supreme Court upheld the basic provisions of the injunction. It approved an approximately thirty-six-foot buffer zone to keep protesters away from the clinic's entrance and parking lot and off a public right-of-way. The

buffer zone "burdens no more speech than necessary to accomplish the government's interest," Justice Rehnquist wrote.

### Schenck v. Pro-Choice Network (1997).

In a New York state case in which a group opposed to abortion appealed an injunction ordering them to cease blockading the entrances to a clinic and stop harassing and intimidating the women seeking an abortion, the Supreme Court in a 6-to-3 decision upheld the lower court's decision to keep the protesters from blocking doorways and driveways.

The Court struck down (8 to 3) a section of the New York law that established a "floating" fifteen-foot buffer zone between protesters and people entering or leaving a clinic, because the indefinite character of the zone raised the prospect of suppressing more speech than necessary to protect the state's interest in public safety. Yet the Court upheld (6 to 3) a section of the injunction allowing only two protesters at a time to come within a fixed fifteen-foot buffer zone to talk to women in a nonthreatening way and to "cease and desist" and to withdraw outside the zone if asked to do so.

The Court's tacit endorsement of a fixed buffer zone around abortion clinics is significant, because about 300 of the 900 abortion clinics in the country are protected by buffer zones spelled out in court injunctions. Both the Florida and New York rulings are considered important indicators of the Court's view of the Freedom of Access to Clinic Entrances Act. It is designed to provide federal remedies, including criminal penalties, to restrict violent protests at abortion clinics.

### Hill v. Colorado (2000).

The Court held in a 6-to-3 ruling that a Colorado law aimed at protecting abortion clinic physicians, patients, and visitors from harassment by protestors did not violate the protestors' First Amendment rights to free expression. The law holds that within one hundred feet of any health-care facility no one can approach anyone closer than eight feet to talk or pass out leaflets, unless the person approached permits it.

## Federal Policies

President George W. Bush, on his first full day in office, issued an executive order that would cut off federal funds to international family planning programs that provide abortions or even abortion counseling. Thus, Bush reinstated the ban first imposed during the Reagan administration and lifted only by President Clinton.

Some critics consider the need for the order debatable. Legislation passed in 1999 restoring U.S. financing of the United Nations already contained a clause prohibiting the United States Agency for International Development from using money to promote or provide abortions. Nevertheless, the ban made clear the position the Bush administration planned to take on abortion. With world population now standing at 6 billion and increasing by 60 to 80 million a year, even some opposed to abortion worry that withholding funds from family-planning organizations will make it difficult to achieve the goal of stabilizing the population and thus relieving the pressure on natural resources.

Such stability would require a fertility rate of 2.1 children per woman, but most undeveloped countries have a much higher rate. In sub-Saharan Africa, for example, women frequently have six or more children. Also, an estimated 45 percent of pregnancies worldwide are either unwanted or unintended.

The Bush administration's policy on abortion has also come into conflict with the demands of scientists and disease-advocacy groups that embryonic stem cells be made available for research. Because embryonic stem cells can be acquired only by destroying a human embryo, many opponents of abortion object to their use. Others, however, distinguish between an embryo and a fetus and see no incompatibility between opposing abortion and favoring the use of stem cells.

The potential of stem cells to treat injuries and diseases for which now we have no effective therapies (e.g., spinal-cord damage and Parkinson's disease) has both split traditional abortion allies and broadened the debate. (See Chapter 5.)

The administration, finally, issued administrative rules in September 2002 that define a fetus as a child eligible to receive care under the federally sponsored Children's Health Insurance Program. "Child" is defined in the rules as "an individual under the age of nineteen, including the period from conception to birth." While the Secretary of Health and Human Services claimed that the definition was to help ensure that low-income pregnant women receive prenatal care, critics complained it was a cynical move to court political favor of prolife groups. Merely extending coverage to pregnant women would have been enough.

## SOCIAL CONTEXT: RU-486—THE "ABORTION PILL"

Sandra Crane, as we'll call her, decided she had missed her period. She was thirty-one years old, and ordinarily her menstrual cycle was as regular as the calendar. Since she was now a week overdue, she felt sure she was pregnant.

The feeling was familiar. She had two children already, six-year-old Jennifer and two-year-old Thomas. She and her husband had decided they weren't going to have any more. They had discussed the matter, and she resolved that if she became pregnant, she would seek medical help to end her pregnancy.

The next morning Sandra Crane consulted her gynecologist, and a day later she received a phone call informing her that she was pregnant. She explained that she wanted the pregnancy ended as soon as possible, and was told to return to the clinic, where she was given two tablets to swallow—a 600-milligram dosage of the drug RU-486.

Two days later, as directed, Sandra returned to the clinic and took a 400-milligram dosage of misoprostol (a prostaglandin), a drug to make her uterus contract. Later, she began to experience cramping and bleeding, but soon the uterine lining was expelled. She felt some discomfort, but the process differed little from an unusually heavy menstrual period.

After a day of rest, she felt almost her usual self again. Two weeks later, she returned to the clinic for an examination to make sure the abortion was complete.

RU-486, or mifepristone, was developed by the French endocrinologist Etienne-Émile Baulieu. The drug works by blocking the action of progesterone, the hormone that prepares the uterine wall for the implantation of the fertilized egg. The dose of prostaglandins then induces uterine contractions that expel the sloughed-off lining, including the zygote. To be most effective, the drug must be taken during the first five to seven weeks of pregnancy. Physicians urge that the drug be taken as early as possible, but some researchers suggest that its use might be extended even to the tenth week of pregnancy.

If RU-486 is taken early in pregnancy, it blocks the action of progesterone, and as a result, a fertilized egg will not be able to follow its usual course of implanting itself in the uterine wall. Hence, the drug also has the possibility of serving as a "morning-after pill" for preventing pregnancy, even after fertilization. But the drug's major use lies in its power to induce an abortion chemically.

In initial testing, 100 women volunteers less than a month pregnant were given RU-486. Of these, 85 percent aborted within four days, without reporting the pain or psychological difficulties that can accompany surgical abortion. The later use of prostaglandin injections in conjunction with the drug increased the speed of the process. An oral dose of prostaglandins later replaced the injection. Women tolerated

this better, and the price was significantly lower.

Additional clinical trials in France and the use of the drug by more than 200,000 women showed it to be safe and 95.5 percent effective. With the use of the oral prostaglandins, the effectiveness rises to 96.9 percent. Some women taking the drug bleed excessively and a proportion do not abort as expected (about 3 percent, according to a French study) and require surgical intervention. For these reasons, the drug is intended for use only under close medical supervision. All in all, however, the evidence shows that the use of the drug is safer and cheaper than surgical abortion. It is now used by more than 70 percent of French women seeking an abortion and no more than seven weeks pregnant.

Recent studies of RU-486 indicate that it may be of value in preventing endometriosis (a major cause of infertility) and fibroid tumors, which often require a hysterectomy. Thus, the drug may have a role in aiding women in getting pregnant, as well as in preventing or ending pregnancies. Other studies suggest that the drug may help prevent breast cancer and Cushing's syndrome (a metabolic disorder).

### The Conflict

The drug was developed in 1980 by the pharmaceutical company Roussel-Uclaf and approved for use in France in September 1988. A month later, in response to a boycott of the company's products by abortion opponents, Roussel took the drug off the market. This provoked public protests, and Health Minister Claude Evin notified the company that if it did not release the drug the government, which owned 36.25 percent of the company, would permanently transfer the patent to another company. "From the moment the governmental approval of the drug was granted, RU-486 became the moral property of women, not just the property of the drug company," Evin said. Two days later the company resumed marketing the drug.

## The United States

Roussel licensed the drug for use in China, Sweden, and Britain. Initial plans to market the drug in the United States were abandoned because of opposition from right-to-life groups. Opponents of abortion generally consider RU-486 as no more than a biochemical means for producing an abortion and so oppose its use. According to the president of the National Right-to-Life Coalition, RU-486 represents "chemical warfare against an entire class of innocent humans."

The National Right-to-Life Coalition (NRL) and other groups opposed to abortion informed drug companies that they would boycott all of a company's products if it tried to market an abortion-inducing drug. "Our basic position is that death drugs designed to kill unborn babies have no place in America," the NRL education director said.

Baulieu, the drug's developer, claims that fears of such reprisals have kept RU-486 from being distributed worldwide. Indeed, the fear of boycotts of Roussel and Hoechst, the German pharmaceutical company that is its majority stockholder, led the company to decide against trying to get approval to sell the drug in the United States. Fear of the response of the prolife movement also kept U.S. drug companies from applying to the Food and Drug Administration (FDA) for approval.

Baulieu also charges that Roussel should not have put approval of the drug for international use in the hands of the World Health Organization (WHO). The WHO, he claims, has delayed its approval because it is so financially dependent on the United States that a reprisal in the form of a withdrawal of U.S. funds would severely cripple its operations.

"I believe the key to the future of RU-486 lies in the United States," Baulieu said at a news conference. He said that because of the drug's simplicity, it could dramatically reduce the number of illegal abortions and related maternal deaths throughout the world. "How can we ignore that 500 women a day die as a result of badly executed abortions?" he asked. "At present, things are so bad in the Third World that anything that improves the situation is welcome. I think it is our moral duty to act."

Louise B. Tyrer of Planned Parenthood similarly characterized the lack of availability of the drug, calling it "discriminatory to women" and "a threat to their safety and health." In her view and in the opinion of prochoice advocates, "Women should have a choice between medical and surgical abortion."

In April 1993, the situation changed when Roussel-Uclaf agreed to license the drug and the technology used to make it to the Population Council, a nonprofit research organization. The council agreed to find a manufacturer, establish a clinical trial, and then apply to the FDA to license the drug for use in the United States.

In 1996 the Council presented data from the French studies to the FDA. The agency gave its preliminary approval of the drug, pronouncing it safe and effective and making it legal to manufacture, sell, and prescribe it in the United States. Still, no company could be found willing to make the drug.

In 1998 the Council published data produced by its own tests of the drug. The results were similar to those of the French. The study was conducted from September 1994 to September 1995 and involved 2121 woman from ages eighteen to thirty-five who were given the drug at seventeen clinics. The drug was most effective in the 849 women who were no more than forty-nine days pregnant. For 92 percent of them, drugs alone terminated the pregnancy. Only 1 percent were still pregnant after taking the drugs, and the remainder had surgical abortions because of heavy bleeding.

The Population Council, working with a group of private investors, made arrangements with Danco Laboratories, a small pharmaceutical company, to produce RU-486 under the trade name Mifeprex. All that was required was final FDA approval.

## Approval

On September 28, 2000, the FDA at last recognized RU-486, or Mifeprex, as safe and effective, and made it a legitimate prescription drug. Danco promised to have supplies of the drug available to physicians by the end of October. Although the FDA had considered placing unusually severe restrictions on the use of the drug, in the end it decided any physician qualified to determine the length of a pregnancy and practicing within one hour of facilities able to offer a surgical abortion could administer the drug in the office.

Reactions to the approval were predictably mixed. George W. Bush denounced the FDA as "wrong," and abortion opponents, calling the drug a "baby poison," vowed to lobby for legislation to prohibit its use. Prochoice advocates celebrate the approval, saying it would allow women to keep their abortion decisions private. Also, women living in rural areas without easy access to surgical abortion would now have a safe option. A survey by the Kaiser Family Foundation found that 44 percent of physicians involved in women's health care would be at least "somewhat likely" to prescribe Mifeprex.

### In Practice

Most of the hopes that prochoice advocates pinned on getting mifepristone (RU-486) approved have not materialized. Many physicians still prefer the speed and reliability of surgical abortions. A procedure takes only a few minutes, then the patient is on the way to recovery. RU-486 is limited to use during the first seven weeks of pregnancy, and, once given the drug, the woman must return to the office two more times. The process takes about three weeks.

Many physicians, furthermore, who thought they were likely to prescribe the drug to patients wanting a medical abortion have come to realize that abortion is typically regulated by a bewildering complexity of state laws. Some states require that a physcian performing abortions must have an ultrasound machine, life-support equipment, and an operating suite available. Other laws stipulate the standard the facility must satisfy—the hall width, temperature of the running water, and amount of ventilation.

Thirteen states require counseling before an abortion is performed and dictate a waiting period. Some states require that the fetal tissue be inspected, while others demand it be disposed of by cremation or burial. While the laws of some states regulate abortion in general, those in other states specifically mention drug-induced abortion.

It is not surprising, given the circumstances, that the availability of a drug to produce abortion has had little impact so far on the practice of abortion. Most abortions are still performed in clinics by the same people who provided them before, and most of those people still prefer the surgical method. To what extent the situation would be different without state laws passed over the last three decades to discourage abortion is a matter of speculation.

## SOCIAL CONTEXT: THE "MORNING-AFTER PILL"

About 3.5 million unwanted pregnancies occur each year. Although some 1 million of them are terminated by abortion, a great number of women end up having children they don't want. Many of these unwanted pregnancies could be prevented by contraceptive drugs that are taken *after* intercourse.

Emergency contraception is a way to prevent pregnancy by delaying or inhibiting ovulation, inhibiting fertilization, or preventing a fertilized egg from implanting itself in the uterine wall. The drugs that can function in this way are already available as birth control pills.

Although the Federal Drug Administration has reviewed these drugs and found them safe and effective in preventing pregnancy and invited manufacturers to submit proposals for relabeling the drugs for use as emergency contraception, so far drug companies have not made any submissions. Even so, because the drugs already have FDA approval, they can be legitimately prescribed by a physician for emergency use. (RU-486 can also prevent pregnancy if used early enough. See the previous Social Context.)

Eight brands of birth control pills can be used for emergency contraception. Seven contain a combination of the hormones estrogen and progestin. If one of these pills is taken within seventy-two hours of having sex and a second pill is taken twelve hours afterward, the chance of preventing pregnancy is 75 percent. Statistically, 8 of 100 women engaging in unprotected sex during the second or third week of their menstrual cycle will become pregnant. If they take the birth control pills as described, only two will.

The second type of birth control pill contains levonorgestrel (a progestin). One dose taken forty-eight hours after sex and a second dose twelve hours later will also reduce by 75 percent the chance of pregnancy.

Emergency contraception can also be achieved mechanically by the insertion of the copper-T IUD (intrauterine device) by a physician. The IUD effectively blocks the migration of the fertilized egg into the uterus. It is more than 99 percent effective in preventing pregnancy.

The major side-effects of the double dose of birth control pills is nausea and vomiting. One- to two-thirds of women taking the pills experience nausea for about two days, and some 12 to 22 percent have episodes of vomiting. An anti-nausea drug taken at the same time as the contraceptives can reduce the side-effects.

Because there is no way to tell when an egg becomes fertilized after intercourse, emergency contraception blurs the line between contraception and abortion. A majority of Americans have no objections either to contraception or to early abortion, so to them emergency contraception is a favored way to prevent an unwanted pregnancy.

Even the National Right to Life Committee, a group opposed to abortion, does not condemn emergency contraception outright. "Some chemical compounds may work to either prevent fertilization or kill the developing human being which has begun to grow," the group said in an official comment. The statement went on to recommend that a woman consult her physician to see whether in the physician's "best medical judgment" taking the pill would prevent fertilization or cause an abortion.

Washington, Alaska, California, and Oregon are among those states now operating pilot programs providing "morning-after" pills without a prescription. Washington's laws allow a pharmacist to acquire from a physician the right to dispense certain prescription drugs when, in the pharmacist's judgment, they are needed. More than 30,000 women have now received the pills, known as Plan B, under the law.

In France a similar drug can be dispensed by a nurse. Norway was the first country to make a drug like Plan B available over the counter, but it has since been followed by Great Britain.

## READINGS

## Section 1: The Status of the Fetus

### An Almost Absolute Value in History

John T. Noonan Jr.

John Noonan argues that at the moment of fertilization a developing human being becomes a person. Noonan reviews some distinctions used by abortion proponents who maintain that personhood is achieved at a later stage of development (viability, experience, and social visibility) and concludes that they are all illegitimate. Noonan argues that conception is the decisive moment of humanization because it is then that the new being receives a genetic code from its parents.

The basic principle that should govern our attitude toward the fetus, Noonan claims, is a theological and humanistic one: Do not injure your fellow man without a sufficient reason. Thus, abortion is never right except to save the mother's life. Abortion is immoral because it "violates the rational humanistic tenet of the equality of human lives."

The most fundamental question involved in the long history of thought on abortion is: How do you determine the humanity of a being? To phrase the question that way is to put in comprehensive humanistic terms what the theologians either dealt with as an explicitly theological question under the heading of "ensoulment" or dealt with implicitly in their treatment of abortion. The Christian position as it originated did not depend on a narrow theological or philosophical concept. It had no relation to theories of infant baptism. It appealed to no special theory of instantaneous ensoulment. It took the world's view on ensoulment as that view changed from Aristotle to Zacchia. There was, indeed, theological influence affecting the theory of ensoulment finally adopted, and, of course, ensoulment itself was a theological concept, so that the position was always explained in theological terms. But the theological notion of ensoulment could easily be translated into humanistic language by substituting "human" for "rational soul"; the problem of knowing when a man is a man is common to theology and humanism.

If one steps outside the specific categories used by the theologians, the answer they gave can be analyzed as a refusal to discriminate among human beings on the basis of their varying potentialities. Once conceived, the being was recognized as man because he had man's potential. The criterion for humanity, thus, was simple and all-embracing: If you are conceived by human parents, you are human.

The strength of this position may be tested by a review of some of the other distinctions offered in the contemporary controversy over legalizing abortion. Perhaps the most popular distinction is in terms of viability. Before an age of so many months, the fetus is not viable, that is, it cannot be removed from the

Reprinted by permission of the publisher from *The Morality of Abortion: Legal and Historical Perspectives*, edited by John T. Noonan Jr., pp. 51-59. Cambridge, Mass.: Harvard University Press. Copyright © 1970 by the President and Fellows of Harvard College. (Notes omitted.)

mother's womb and live apart from her. To that extent, the life of the fetus is absolutely dependent on the life of the mother. This dependence is made the basis of denying recognition to its humanity.

There are difficulties with this distinction. One is that the perfection of artificial incubation may make the fetus viable at any time: It may be removed and artificially sustained. Experiments with animals already show that such a procedure is possible. This hypothetical extreme case relates to an actual difficulty; there is considerable elasticity to the idea of viability. Mere length of life is not an exact measure. The viability of the fetus depends on the extent of its anatomical and functional development. The weight and length of the fetus are better guides to the state of its development than age, but weight and length vary. Moreover, different racial groups have different ages at which their fetuses are viable. Some evidence, for example, suggests that Negro fetuses mature more quickly than white fetuses. If viability is the norm, the standard would vary with race and with many individual circumstances.

The most important objection to this approach is that dependence is not ended by viability. The fetus is still absolutely dependent on someone's care in order to continue existence; indeed a child of one or three or even five years of age is absolutely dependent on another's care for existence; uncared for, the older fetus or the younger child will die as surely as the early fetus detached from the mother. The unsubstantial lessening in dependence at viability does not seem to signify any special acquisition of humanity.

A second distinction has been attempted in terms of experience. A being who has had experience, has lived and suffered, who possesses memories, is more human than one who has not. Humanity depends on formation by experience. The fetus is thus "unformed" in the most basic human sense.

This distinction is not serviceable for the embryo which is already experiencing and reacting. The embryo is responsive to touch after eight weeks and at least at that point is experiencing. At an earlier stage the zygote is certainly alive and responding to its environment. The distinction may also be challenged by the rare case where aphasia has erased adult memory: has it erased humanity? More fundamentally, this distinction leaves even the older fetus or the younger child to be treated as an unformed inhuman thing. Finally, it is not clear why experience as such confers humanity. It could be argued that certain central experiences such as loving or learning are necessary to make a man human. But then human beings who have failed to love or to learn might be excluded from the class called man. . . .

Finally, a distinction is sought in social visibility. The fetus is not socially perceived as human. It cannot communicate with others. Thus, both subjectively and objectively, it is not a member of society. As moral rules are rules for the behavior of members of society to each other, they cannot be made for behavior toward what is not yet a member. Excluded from the society of men, the fetus is excluded from the humanity of men.

By force of the argument from the consequences, this distinction is to be rejected. It is more subtle than that founded on an appeal to physical sensation, but it is equally dangerous in its implications. If humanity depends on social recognition, individuals or whole groups may be dehumanized by being denied any status in their society. Such a fate is fictionally portrayed in *1984* and has actually been the lot of many men in many societies. In the Roman empire, for example, condemnation to slavery meant the practical denial of most human rights; in the Chinese Communist world, landlords have been classified as enemies of the people and so treated as nonpersons by the state. Humanity does not depend on social recognition, though often the failure of society to recognize the prisoner, the alien, the heterodox as human has led to the destruction of human beings. Anyone conceived by a man and a woman is human. Recognition of this condition by society follows a real event in the objective order, however imperfect and halting the recognition. Any attempt to limit humanity to exclude some group runs the risk of furnishing authority and precedent for excluding other groups in the name of the consciousness or perception of the controlling group in society.

A philosopher may reject the appeal to the humanity of the fetus because he views "humanity" as a secular view of the soul and because he doubts the existence of anything real and objective which can be identified as humanity. One answer to such a philosopher is to ask how he reasons about moral questions without supposing that there is a sense in which he

and the others of whom he speaks are human. Whatever group is taken as the society which determines who may be killed is thereby taken as human. A second answer is to ask if he does not believe that there is a right and wrong way of deciding moral questions. If there is such a difference, experience may be appealed to: to decide who is human on the basis of the sentiment of a given society has led to consequences which rational men would characterize as monstrous.

The rejection of the attempted distinctions based on viability and visibility, experience and feeling, may be buttressed by the following considerations: Moral judgments often rest on distinctions, but if the distinctions are not to appear arbitrary *fiat*, they should relate to some real difference in probabilities. There is a kind of continuity in all life, but the earlier stages of the elements of human life possess tiny probabilities of development. Consider for example, the spermatozoa in any normal ejaculate: There are about 200,000,000 in any single ejaculate, of which one has a chance of developing into a zygote. Consider the oocytes which may become ova: there are 100,000 to 1,000,00 oocytes in a female infant, of which a maximum of 390 are ovulated. But once spermatozoa and ovum meet and the conceptus is formed, such studies as have been made show that roughly in only 20 percent of the cases will spontaneous abortion occur. In other words, the chances are about 4 out of 5 that this new being will develop. At this stage in the life of the being there is a sharp shift in probabilities, an immense jump in potentialities. To make a distinction between the rights of spermatozoa and the rights of the fertilized ovum is to respond to an enormous shift in possibilities. For about twenty days after conception the egg may split to form twins or combine with another egg to form a chimera, but the probability of either event happening is very small.

It may be asked, What does a change in biological probabilities have to do with establishing humanity? The argument from probabilities is not aimed at establishing humanity but at establishing an objective discontinuity which may be taken into account in moral discourse. As life itself is a matter of probabilities, as most moral reasoning is an estimate of probabilities, so it seems in accord with the structure of reality and the nature of moral thought to found a moral judgment on the change in probabilities at conception. The appeal to probabilities is the most commonsensical of arguments, to a greater or smaller degree all of us based our actions on probabilities, and in morals, as in law, prudence and negligence are often measured by the account one has taken of the probabilities. If the chance is 200,000,000 to 1 that the movement in the bushes into which you shoot is a man's, I doubt if many persons would hold you careless in shooting; but if the chances are 4 out of 5 that the movement is a human being's, few would acquit you of blame. Would the argument be different if only one out of ten children conceived came to term? Of course this argument would be different. This argument is an appeal to probabilities that actually exist, not to any and all states of affairs which may be imagined.

The probabilities as they do exist do not show the humanity of the embryo in the sense of a demonstration in logic any more than the probabilities of the movement in the bush being a man demonstrate beyond all doubt that the being is a man. The appeal is a "buttressing" consideration, showing the plausibility of the standard adopted. The argument focuses on the decisional factor in any moral judgment and assumes that part of the business of a moralist is drawing lines. One evidence of the nonarbitrary character of the line drawn is the difference of probabilities on either side of it. If a spermatozoon is destroyed, one destroys a being which had a chance of far less than 1 in 200 million of developing into a reasoning being, possessed of the genetic code, a heart and other organs, and capable of pain. If a fetus is destroyed, one destroys a being already possessed of the genetic code, organs, and sensitivity to pain, and one which had an 80 percent chance of developing further into a baby outside the womb who, in time, would reason.

The positive argument for conception as the decisive moment of humanization is that at conception the new being receives the genetic code. It is this genetic information which determines his characteristics, which is the biological carrier of the possibility of human wisdom, which makes him a self-evolving being. A being with a human genetic code is man.

This review of current controversy over the humanity of the fetus emphasizes what a fundamental question the theologians resolved in asserting the inviolability of the fetus. To regard the fetus as possessed of equal rights with other humans was not, however, to decide every case where abortion might be employed. It did decide the case where the argument was that the fetus should be aborted for its own good. To say a being was human was to say it had a destiny to decide for itself which could not be taken from it by another man's decision. But human beings with equal rights often come in conflict with each other, and some decision must be made as whose claims are to prevail. Cases of conflict involving the fetus are different only in two respects: the total inability of the fetus to speak for itself and the fact that the right of the fetus regularly at stake is the right to life itself.

The approach taken by the theologians to these conflicts was articulated in terms of "direct" and "indirect." Again, to look at what they were doing from outside their categories, they may be said to have been drawing lines or "balancing values." "Direct" and "indirect" are spatial metaphors; "line-drawing" is another. "To weigh" or "to balance" values is a metaphor of a more complicated mathematical sort hinting at the process which goes on in moral judgments. All the metaphors suggest that, in the moral judgments made, comparisons were necessary, that no value completely controlled. The principle of double effect was no doctrine fallen from heaven, but a method of analysis appropriate where two relative values were being compared. In Catholic moral theology, as it developed, life even of the innocent was not taken as an absolute. Judgments of acts affecting life issued from a process of weighing. In the weighing, the fetus was always given a value greater than zero, always a value separate and independent from its parents. This valuation was crucial and fundamental in all Christian thought on the subject and marked it off from any approach which considered that only the parents' interests needed to be considered.

Even with the fetus weighed as human, one interest could be weighed as equal or superior: that of the mother in her own life. The casuists between 1450 and 1895 were willing to weigh this interest as superior. Since 1895, that interest was given decisive weight only in the two special cases of the cancerous uterus and the ectopic pregnancy. In both of these cases the fetus itself had little chance of survival even if abortion were not performed. As the balance was once struck in favor of the mother whenever her life was endangered, it could be so struck again. The balance reached between 1895 and 1930 attempted prudentially and pastorally to forestall a multitude of exceptions for interests less than life.

The perception of the humanity of the fetus and the weighing of fetal rights against other human rights constituted the work of the moral analysts. But what spirit animated abstract judgments? For the Christian community it was the injunction of Scripture to love your neighbor as yourself. The fetus as human was a neighbor; his life had parity with one's own. The commandment gave life to what otherwise would have been only rational calculation.

The commandment could be put in humanistic as well as theological terms: do not injure your fellow man without reasons. In these terms, once the humanity of the fetus is perceived, abortion is never right except in self-defense. When life must be taken to save life, reason alone cannot say that a mother must prefer a child's life to her own. With this exception, now of great rarity, abortion violates the rational humanist tenet of the equality of human lives.

For Christians the commandment to love had received a special imprint in that the exemplar proposed of love was the love of the Lord for his disciples. In the light given by this example, self-sacrifice carried to the point of death seemed in the extreme situations not without meaning. In the less extreme cases, preference for one's own interests to the life of another seemed to express cruelty or selfishness irreconcilable with the demands of love.

# A Defense of Abortion

## Judith Jarvis Thomson

Judith Jarvis Thomson, in this very influential article, avoids the problem of determining when the fetus become a person. For the sake of argument only, she grants the conservative view that the fetus is a person from the moment of conception. She points out, however, that the conservative argument using this claim as a premise actually involves an additional unstated premise. The argument typically runs: The fetus is an innocent person; therefore, killing a fetus is always wrong. The argument requires that we assume that killing an innocent person is always wrong. But, Thomson claims, killing an innocent person is sometimes allowable. This is most clearly so when self-defense requires it.

Using several moral analogies, Thomson attempts to show that a fetus's right to life does not consist in the right not to be killed, but in the right not to be killed unjustly. The fetus's claim to life is not an absolute one that must always be granted unconditional precedence over the interests of its mother. Thus, abortion is not always permissible, but neither is it always impermissible. When the reasons for having an abortion are trivial, then abortion is not legitimate. When the reasons are serious and involve the health or welfare of the woman, then abortion is justifiable.

Most opposition to abortion relies on the premise that the fetus is a human being, a person, from the moment of conception. The premise is argued for, but, as I think, not well. Take, for example, the most common argument. We are asked to notice that the development of a human being from conception through birth into childhood is continuous; then it is said that to draw a line, to choose a point in this development and say "before this point the thing is not a person, after this point it is a person" is to make an arbitrary choice,

Judith Jarvis Thomson, "A Defense of Abortion," *Philosophy & Public Affairs* 1, no. 1 (Fall 1971). Copyright © 1971 by Princeton University Press. Reprinted by permission of Princeton University Press. (Notes edited.)

a choice for which in the nature of things no good reason can be given. It is concluded that the fetus is, or anyway that we had better say it is, a person from the moment of conception. But this conclusion does not follow. Similar things might be said about the development of an acorn into an oak tree, and it does not follow that acorns are oak trees, or that we had better say they are. Arguments of this form are sometimes called "slippery slope arguments"—the phrase is perhaps self-explanatory—and it is dismaying that opponents of abortion rely on them so heavily and uncritically.

I am inclined to agree, however, that the prospects for "drawing a line" in the development of the fetus look dim. I am inclined to think also that we shall probably have to agree that the fetus has already become a human person well before birth. Indeed, it comes as a surprise when one first learns how early in its life it begins to acquire human characteristics. By the tenth week, for example, it already has a face, arms and legs, fingers and toes; it has internal organs, and brain activity is detectable.[1] On the other hand, I think that the premise is false, that the fetus is not a person from the moment of conception. A newly fertilized ovum, a newly implanted clump of cells, is no more a person than an acorn is an oak tree. But I shall not discuss any of this. For it seems to me to be of great interest to ask what happens if, for the sake of argument, we allow the premise. How, precisely, are we supposed to get from there to the conclusion that abortion is morally impermissible? Opponents of abortion commonly spend most of their time establishing that the fetus is a person, and hardly any time explaining the step from there to the impermissibility of abortion. Perhaps they think the step too simple and obvious to require much comment. Or perhaps instead they are simply being economical in argument. Many of those who defend abortion rely on the premise that the fetus is not a person, but only a bit of tissue that will become a person at birth; and why pay out more arguments than you have to? Whatever the explanation, I suggest that the step they take is neither easy nor obvious, that it calls for closer examination than it is commonly given, and that when we do give it this closer examination we shall feel inclined to reject it.

I propose, then, that we grant that the fetus is a person from the moment of conception. How does the argument go from here? Something like this, I take it. Every person has a right to life. So the fetus has a right to life. No doubt the mother has a right to decide what shall happen in and to her body; everyone would grant that. But surely a person's right to life is stronger and more stringent than the mother's right to decide what happens in and to her body, and so outweighs it. So the fetus may not be killed; an abortion may not be performed.

It sounds plausible. But now let me ask you to imagine this. You wake up in the morning and find yourself in bed with an unconscious violinist. A famous unconscious violinist. He has been found to have a fatal kidney ailment, and the Society of Music Lovers has canvassed all the available medical records and found that you alone have the right blood type to help. They have therefore kidnapped you, and last night the violinist's circulatory system was plugged into yours, so that your kidneys can be used to extract poisons from his blood as well as your own. The director of the hospital now tells you, "Look, we're sorry the Society of Music Lovers did this to you—we would never have permitted it if we had known. But still, they did it, and the violinist is now plugged into you. To unplug you would be to kill him. But never mind, it's only for nine months. By then he will have recovered from his ailment, and can safely be unplugged from you." Is it morally incumbent on you to accede to this situation? No doubt it would be very nice of you if you did, a great kindness. But do you *have* to accede to it? What if it were not nine months, but nine years? Or longer still? What if the director of the hospital says, "Tough luck, I agree, but now you've got to stay in bed, with the violinist plugged into you, for the rest of your life. Because remember this. All persons have a right to life, and violinists are persons. Granted you have a right to decide what happens in and to your body, but a person's right to life outweighs your right to decide what happens in and to your body. So you cannot ever be unplugged from him." I imagine you would regard this as outrageous, which suggests that something really is wrong with that plausible-sounding argument I mentioned a moment ago.

In this case, of course, you were kidnapped; you didn't volunteer for the operation that plugged the violinist into your kidneys. Can those who oppose abortion on the ground I mentioned make an exception for pregnancy due to rape? Certainly. They can say that all persons have a right to life, but that some have less of a right to life than others, in particular, that those who came into existence because of rape have less. But these statements have a rather unpleasant sound. Surely the question of whether you have a right to life at all, or how much of it you have, shouldn't turn on the question of whether or not you are a product of a rape. And in fact the people who oppose abortion on the ground I mentioned do not make this distinction, and hence do not make an exception in case of rape.

Nor do they make an exception for a case in which the mother has to spend the nine months of her pregnancy in bed. They would agree that would be a great pity, and hard on the mother; but all the same, all persons have a right to life, the fetus is a person, and so on. I suspect, in fact, that they would not make an exception for a case in which, miraculously enough, the pregnancy went on for nine years, or even for the rest of the mother's life.

Some won't even make an exception for a case in which continuation of the pregnancy is likely to shorten the mother's life; they regard abortion as impermissible even to save the mother's life. Such cases are nowadays very rare, and many opponents of abortion do not accept this extreme view. All the same, it is a good place to begin: a number of points of interest come out in respect to it.

## 1.

Let us call the view that abortion is impermissible even to save the mother's life "the extreme view." I want to suggest that it does not issue from the argument I mentioned earlier without the addition of some fairly powerful premises. Suppose a woman has become pregnant, and now learns that she has a cardiac condition such that she will die if she carried the baby to term. What may be done for her? The fetus, being a person, has a right to life, but as the mother is a person too, so has she a right to life. Presumably they have an equal right to life. How is it supposed to come out that an abortion may not be performed? If mother and child have an equal right to life, shouldn't we perhaps flip a coin? Or should we add to the mother's right to life her right to decide what happens in and to her body, which everybody seems to be ready to grant—the sum of her rights now outweighing the fetus's right to life?

The most familiar argument here is the following. We are told that performing the abortion would be directly killing[2] the child, whereas doing nothing would not be killing the mother, but only letting her die. Moreover, in killing the child, one would be killing an innocent person, for the child has committed no crime, and is not aiming at his mother's death. And then there are a variety of ways in which this might be continued. (1) But as directly killing an innocent person is always and absolutely impermissible, an abortion may not be performed. Or, (2) as directly killing an innocent person is murder, and murder is always and absolutely impermissible, an abortion may not be performed.[3] Or, (3) as one's duty to refrain from directly killing an innocent person is more stringent than one's duty to keep a person from dying, an abortion may not be performed. Or, (4) if one's only options are directly killing an innocent person or letting a person die, one must prefer letting the person die, and thus an abortion may not be performed.[4]

Some people seem to have thought that these are not further premises which must be added if the conclusion is to be reached, but they follow from the very fact that an innocent person has a right to life.[5] But

this seems to me to be a mistake, and perhaps the simplest way to show this is to bring out that while we must certainly grant that innocent persons have a right to life, the theses in (1) through (4) are all false. Take (2) for example. If directly killing an innocent person is murder, and thus is impermissible, then the mother's directly killing the innocent person inside her is murder, and thus is impermissible. But it cannot seriously be thought to be murder if the mother performs an abortion on herself to save her life. It cannot seriously be said that she *must* refrain, that she *must* sit passively by and wait for her death. Let us look again at the case of you and the violinist. There you are, in bed with the violinist, and the director of the hospital says to you, "It's all most distressing, and I deeply sympathize, but you see this is putting an additional strain on your kidneys, and you'll be dead within the month. But you *have* to stay where you are all the same. Because unplugging you would be directly killing an innocent violinist, and that's murder, and that's impermissible." If anything in the world is true, it is that you do not commit murder, you do not do what is impermissible, if you reach around to your back and unplug yourself from that violinist to save your life.

The main focus of attention in writings on abortion has been on what a third party may or may not do in answer to a request from a woman for an abortion. This is in a way understandable. Things being as they are, there isn't much a woman can safely do to abort herself. So the question asked is what a third party may do, and what the mother may do, if it is mentioned at all, is deduced, almost as an afterthought, from what it is concluded that third parties may do. But it seems to me that to treat the matter in this way is to refuse to grant to the mother that very status of person which is so firmly insisted on for the fetus. For we cannot simply read off what a person may do from what a third party may do. Suppose you find yourself trapped in a tiny house with a growing child. I mean a very tiny house, and a rapidly growing child—you are already up against the wall of the house and in a few minutes you'll be crushed to death. The child on the other hand won't be crushed to death; if nothing is done to stop him from growing he'll be hurt, but in the end he'll simply burst open the house and walk out a free man. Now I could well understand it if a bystander were to say, "There's nothing we can do for you. We cannot choose between your life and his, we cannot be the ones to decide who is to live, we cannot intervene." But it cannot be concluded that you too can do nothing, that you cannot attack it to save your life. However innocent the child may be, you do not have to wait passively while it crushes you to death. Perhaps a pregnant woman is vaguely felt to have the status of house, to which we don't allow the right of self-defense. But if the woman houses the child, it should be remembered that she is a person who houses it.

I should perhaps stop to say explicitly that I am not claiming that people have a right to do anything whatever to save their lives. I think, rather, that there are drastic limits to the right of self-defense. If someone threatens you with death unless you torture someone else to death, I think you have not the right, even to save your life, to do so. But the case under consideration here is very different. In our case there are only two people involved, one whose life is threatened, and one who threatens it. Both are innocent: the one who is threatened is not threatened because of any fault, the one who threatens does not threaten because of any fault. For this reason we may feel that we bystanders cannot intervene. But the person threatened can.

In sum, a woman surely can defend her life against the threat to it posed by the unborn child, even if doing so involves its death. And this shows not merely that the theses in (1) through (4) are false; it shows also that the extreme view of abortion is false, and so we need not canvass any other possible ways of arriving at it from the argument I mentioned at the outset.

## 2.

The extreme view could of course be weakened to say that while abortion is permissible to save the mother's life, it may not be performed by a third party, but only by the mother herself. But this cannot be right either. For what we have to keep in mind is that the mother and the unborn child are not like two tenants in a small house which has, by an unfortunate mistake, been rented to both: the mother *owns* the house. The fact that she does adds to the offensiveness of deducing that the mother can do nothing from the supposition that third parties can do nothing. Certainly it lets us see that a third party who says "I cannot choose between you" is fooling himself if he thinks this is impartiality. If Jones has found and fastened on a certain coat, which he needs to keep him from freezing, but which Smith also needs to keep him from freezing, then it is not impartiality that says "I cannot choose between you" when Smith owns the coat. Women have said again and again "This body is *my* body!" and

they have reason to feel angry, reason to feel that it has been like shouting into the wind. Smith, after all, is hardly likely to bless us if we say to him, "Of course it's your coat, anybody would grant that it is. But no one may choose between you and Jones who is to have it."

We should really ask what it is that says "no one may choose" in the face of the fact that the body that houses the child is the mother's body. It may be simply a failure to appreciate this fact. But it may be something more interesting, namely the sense that one has a right to refuse to lay hands on people, even where justice seems to require that somebody do so. Thus justice might call for somebody to get Smith's coat back from Jones, and yet you have a right to refuse to be the one to lay hands on Jones, a right to refuse to do the physical violence to him. This, I think, must be granted. But then what should be said is not "no one may choose," but only "*I* cannot choose," and indeed not even this, but "*I* will not *act*," leaving it open that somebody else can or should, and in particular that anyone in a position of authority, with the job of securing people's rights, both can and should. So this is no difficulty. I have not been arguing that any given third party must accede to the mother's request that he perform an abortion to save her life, but only that he may.

I suppose that in some view of human life the mother's body is only on loan to her, the loan not being one which gives her any prior claim to it. One who held this view might well think it impartiality to say "I cannot choose." But I shall simply ignore this possibility. My own view is that if a human being has any just, prior claim to anything at all, he has a just, prior claim to his own body. And perhaps this needn't be argued for here anyway, since, as I mentioned, the arguments against abortion we are looking at do grant that the woman has a right to decide what happens in and to her body.

But although they do grant it, I have tried to show that they do not take seriously what is done in granting it. I suggest the same thing will reappear even more clearly when we turn away from cases in which the mother's life is at stake, and attend, as I propose we now do, to the vastly more common cases in which a woman wants an abortion for some less weighty reason than preserving her own life.

## 3.

Where the mother's life is not at stake, the argument I mentioned at the outset seems to have a much stronger pull. "Everyone has a right to life, so the unborn person has a right to life." And isn't the child's right to life weightier than anything other than the mother's own right to life, which she might put forward as ground for an abortion?

This agreement treats the right to life as if it were unproblematic. It is not, and this seems to me to be precisely the source of the mistake.

For we should now, at long last, ask what it comes to, to have a right to life. In some views having a right to life includes having a right to be given at least the bare minimum one needs for continued life. But suppose that what in fact *is* the bare minimum a man needs for continued life is something he has no right at all to be given? If I am sick unto death, and the only thing that will save my life is the touch of Henry Fonda's cool hand on my fevered brow, then all the same, I have no right to be given the touch of Henry Fonda's cool hand on my fevered brow. It would be frightfully nice of him to fly in from the West Coast to provide it. It would be less nice, though no doubt well meant, if my friends flew out to the West Coast and carried Henry Fonda back with them. But I have no right at all against anybody that he should do this for me. Or again, to return to the story I told earlier, the fact that for continued life the violinist needs the continued use of your kidneys does not establish that he has a right to be given the continued use of your kidneys. He certainly has no right against you that *you* should give him continued use of your kidneys. For nobody has any right to use your kidneys unless you give him this right—if you do allow him to go on using your kidneys, this is a kindness on your part, and not something he can claim from you as his due. Nor has he any right against anybody else that *they* should give him continued use of your kidneys. Certainly he had no right against the Society of Music Lovers that they should plug him into you in the first place. And if you now start to unplug yourself, having learned that you will otherwise have to spend nine years in bed with him, there is nobody in the world who must try to prevent you, in order to see to it that he is given something he has a right to be given.

Some people are rather stricter about the right to life. In their view, it does not include the right to be given anything, but amounts to, and only to, the right not to be killed by anybody. But here a related difficulty arises. If everybody is to refrain from killing that violinist, then everybody must refrain from doing a great many different sorts of things. Everybody must refrain from slitting his throat, everybody must refrain from shooting him—and everybody must refrain from unplugging you from him. But does he have a right

against everybody that they shall refrain from unplugging you from him? To refrain from doing this is to allow him to continue to use your kidneys. It could be argued that he has a right against us that *we* should allow him to continue to use your kidneys. That is, while he had no right against us that we should give him the use of your kidneys, it might be argued that he anyway has a right against us that we shall not now intervene and deprive him of the use of your kidneys. I shall come back to third-party inteventions later. But certainly the violinist has no right against you that *you* shall allow him to continue to use your kidneys. As I said, if you do allow him to use them it is a kindness on your part, not something you owe him.

The difficulty I point to here is not peculiar to the right to life. It reappears in connection with all the other natural rights, and it is something which an adequate account of rights must deal with. For present purposes it is enough just to draw attention to it. But I would stress that I am not arguing that people do not have a right to life—quite to the contrary, it seems to me that the primary control we must place on the acceptability of an account of rights is that it should turn out in that account to be a truth that all persons have a right to life. I am arguing only that having a right to life does not guarantee having either a right to be given the use of or a right to be allowed continued use of another person's body—even if one needs it for life itself. So the right to life will not serve the opponents of abortion in the very simple and clear way in which they seem to have thought it would.

## 4.

There is another way to bring out the difficulty. In the most ordinary sort of case, to deprive someone of what he has a right to is to treat him unjustly. Suppose a boy and his small brother are jointly given a box of chocolates for Christmas. If the older boy takes the box and refuses to give his brother any of the chocolates, he is unjust to him, for the brother has been given a right to half of them. But suppose that, having learned that otherwise it means nine years in bed with that violinist, you unplug yourself from him. You surely are not being unjust to him, for you gave him no right to use your kidneys, and no one else can have given him any such right. But we have to notice that in unplugging yourself, you are killing him; and violinists, like everybody else, have a right to life, and thus in the view we were considering just now, the right not to be killed. So here you do what he supposedly has a right you shall not do, but you do not act unjustly to him in doing it.

The emendation which may be made at this point is this: the right to life consists not in the right not to be killed, but rather in the right not to be killed unjustly. This runs a risk of circularity, but never mind: it would enable us to square the fact that the violinist has a right to life with the fact that you do not act unjustly toward him in unplugging yourself, thereby killing him. For if you do not kill him unjustly, you do not violate his right to life, and so it is no wonder you do him no injustice.

But if this emendation is accepted, the gap in the argument against abortion stares us plainly in the face: it is by no means enough to show that the fetus is a person, and to remind us that all persons have a right to life—we need to be shown also that killing the fetus violates its right to life, i.e., that abortion is unjust killing. And is it?

I suppose we may take it as a datum that in a case of pregnancy due to rape the mother has not given the unborn person a right to the use of her body for food and shelter. Indeed, in what pregnancy could it be supposed that the mother has given the unborn person such a right? It is not as if there were unborn persons drifting about the world, to whom a woman who wants a child says "I invite you in."

But it might be argued that there are other ways one can have acquired a right to the use of another person's body than by having been invited to use it by that person. Suppose a woman voluntarily indulges in intercourse, knowing of the chance it will issue in pregnancy, and then she does become pregnant; is she not in part responsible for the presence, in fact the very existence, of the unborn person inside? No doubt she did not invite it in. But doesn't her partial responsibility for its being there itself give it a right to the use of her body?[6] If so, then her aborting it would be more like the boy's taking away the chocolates, and less like your unplugging yourself from the violinist—doing so would be depriving it of what it does have a right to, and thus would be doing it an injustice.

And then, too, it might be asked whether or not she can kill it even to save her own life: If she voluntarily called it into existence, how can she now kill it, even in self-defense?

The first thing to be said about this is that it is something new. Opponents of abortion have been so concerned to make out the independence of the fetus, in order to establish that it has a right to life, just as its mother does, that they have tended to overlook the possible support they might gain from making out that the fetus is *dependent* on the mother, in order to establish that she has a special kind of responsibility for it, a responsibility that gives it rights against her which are not possessed by any independent person—such as an ailing violinist who is a stranger to her.

On the other hand, this argument would give the unborn person a right to its mother's body only if her pregnancy resulted from a voluntary act, undertaken in full knowledge of the chance a pregnancy might result from it. It would leave out entirely the unborn person whose existence is due to rape. Pending the availability of some further argument, then, we would be left with the conclusion that unborn persons whose existence is due to rape have no right to the use of their mothers' bodies, and thus that aborting them is not depriving them of anything they have a right to and hence is not unjust killing.

And we should also notice that it is not at all plain that this argument really does go even as far as it purports to. For there are cases and cases, and the details make a difference. If the room is stuffy, and I therefore open a window to air it, and a burglar climbs in, it would be absurd to say, "Ah, now he can stay, she's given him a right to the use of her house—for she is partially responsible for his presence there, having voluntarily done what enabled him to get in, in full knowledge that there are such things as burglars, and that burglars burgle." It would be still more absurd to say this if I had had bars installed outside my windows, precisely to prevent burglars from getting in, and a burglar got in only because of a defect in the bars. It remains equally absurd if we imagine it is not a burglar who climbs in, but an innocent person who blunders or falls in. Again, suppose it were like this: people-seeds drift about in the air like pollen, and if you open your windows, one may drift in and take root in your carpets or upholstery. You don't want children, so you fix up your windows with fine mesh screens, the very best you can buy. As can happen, however, and on very, very rare occasions does happen, one of the screens is defective, and a seed drifts in and takes root. Does the person-plant who now develops have a right to the use of your house? Surely not—despite the fact that you voluntarily opened your windows, you knowingly kept carpets and upholstered furniture, and you knew that screens were sometimes defective. Someone may argue that you are responsible for its rooting, that it does have a right to your house, because after all you could have lived out your life with bare floors and furniture, or with sealed windows and doors. But this won't do—for by the same token anyone can avoid a pregnancy due to rape by having a hysterectomy, or anyway by never leaving home without a (reliable!) army.

It seems to me that the argument we are looking at can establish at most that there are some cases in which the unborn person has a right to the use of its mother's body, and therefore *some* cases in which abortion is unjust killing. There is room for much discussion and argument as to precisely which, if any. But I think we should sidestep this issue and leave it open, for at any rate the argument certainly does not establish that all abortion is unjust killing.

## 5.

There is room for yet another argument here, however. We surely must all grant that there may be cases in which it would be morally indecent to detach a person from your body at the cost of his life. Suppose you learn that what the violinist needs is not nine years of your life, but only one hour: all you need do to save his life is to spend one hour in that bed with him. Suppose also that letting him use your kidneys for that one hour would not affect your health in the slightest. Admittedly you were kidnapped. Admittedly you did not give anyone permission to plug him into you. Nevertheless it seems to me plain you *ought* to allow him to use your kidneys for that hour—it would be indecent to refuse.

Again, suppose pregnancy lasted only an hour, and constituted no threat to life or health. And suppose that a woman becomes pregnant as a result of rape. Admittedly she did not voluntarily do anything to bring about the existence of a child. Admittedly she did nothing at all which would give the unborn person a right to the use of her body. All the same it might well be said, as in the newly amended violinist story, that she *ought* to allow it to remain for that hour—that it would be indecent of her to refuse.

Now some people are inclined to use the term "right" in such a way that it follows from the fact that you ought to allow a person to use your body for the hour he needs, that he has a right to use your body for the hour he needs, even though he has not been given that right by any person or act. They may say that it follows also that if you refuse, you act unjustly toward him. This use of the term is perhaps so common that it cannot be called wrong; nevertheless it seems to me to be an unfortunate loosening of what we would do better to keep a tight rein on. Suppose that box of

chocolates I mentioned earlier had not been given to both boys jointly, but was given only to the older boy. There he sits, stolidly eating his way through the box, his smaller brother watching enviously. Here we are likely to say, "You ought not to be so mean. You ought to give your brother some of those chocolates." My own view is that it just does not follow from the truth of this that the brother has any right to any of the chocolates. If the boy refuses to give his brother any, he is greedy, stingy, callous—but not unjust. I suppose that the people I have in mind will say it does follow that the brother has a right to some of the chocolates, and thus that the boy does act unjustly if he refuses to give his brother any. But the effect of saying this is to obscure what we should keep distinct, namely the difference between the boy's refusal in this case and the boy's refusal in the earlier case, in which the box was given to both boys jointly, and in which the small brother thus had what was from any point of view clear title to half.

A further objection to so using the term "right" that from the fact that A ought to do a thing for B, it follows that B has a right against A that A do it for him, is that it is going to make the question of whether or not a man has a right to a thing turn on how easy it is to provide him with it; and this seems not merely unfortunate, but morally unacceptable. Take the case of Henry Fonda again. I said earlier that I had no right to the touch of his cool hand on my fevered brow, even though I needed it to save my life. I said it would be frightfully nice of him to fly in from the West Coast to provide me with it, but that I had no right against him that he should do so. But suppose he isn't on the West Coast. Suppose he has only to walk across the room, place a hand briefly on my brow—and lo, my life is saved. Then surely he ought to do it, it would be indecent to refuse. Is it to be said, "Ah, well, it follows that in this case she has a right to the touch of his hand on her brow, and so it would be an injustice in him to refuse"? So that I have a right to it when it is easy for him to provide it, though no right when it's hard? It's rather a shocking idea that anyone's rights should fade away and disappear as it gets harder and harder to accord them to him.

So my own view is that even though you ought to let the violinist use your kidneys for the one hour he needs, we should not conclude that he has a right to do so—we should say that if you refuse, you are, like the boy who owns all the chocolates and will give none away, self-centered and callous, indecent in fact, but not unjust. And similarly, that even supposing a case in which a woman pregnant due to rape ought to allow the unborn person to use her body for the hour he needs, we should not conclude that he has a right to do so; we should conclude that she is self-centered, callous, indecent, but not unjust, if she refuses. The complaints are no less grave; they are just different. However, there is no need to insist on this point. If anyone does wish to deduce "he has a right" from "you ought," then all the same he must surely grant that there are cases in which it is not morally required of you that you allow that violinist to use your kidneys, and in which he does not have the right to use them, and in which you do not do him an injustice if you refuse. And so also for mother and unborn child. Except in such cases as the unborn person has a right to demand it—and we were leaving open the possibility that there may be such cases—nobody is morally *required* to make large sacrifices, of health, of all other interests and concerns, of all other duties and commitments, for nine years, or even for nine months, in order to keep another person alive.

## 6.

We have in fact to distinguish between two kinds of Samaritan: the Good Samaritan and what we might call the Minimally Decent Samaritan. The story of the Good Samaritan, you will remember, goes like this:

> A certain man went down from Jerusalem to Jericho, and fell among thieves, which stripped him of his raiment, and wounded him, and departed, leaving him half dead.
>
> And by chance there came down a certain priest that way: and when he saw him, he passed by on the other side.
>
> And likewise a Levite, when he was at the place, came and looked on him, and passed by on the other side.
>
> But a certain Samaritan, as he journeyed, came where he was; and when he saw him he had compassion on him.
>
> And went to him, and bound up his wounds, pouring in oil and wine, and set him on his own beast, and brought him to an inn, and took care of him.
>
> And on the morrow, when he departed, he took out two pence, and gave them to the host, and said unto him, "Take care of him, and whatsoever thou spendest more, when I come again, I will repay thee." (Luke 10:30–35)

The Good Samaritan went out of his way, at some cost to himself, to help one in need of it. We are not told what the options were, that is, whether or not the priest and the Levite could have helped by doing less than the Good Samaritan did, but assuming they could have, then the fact they did nothing at all shows they were not even Minimally Decent Samaritans, not because they were not Samaritans, but because they were not even minimally decent.

These things are a matter of degree, of course, but there is a difference, and it comes out perhaps most clearly in the story of Kitty Genovese, who, as you will remember, was murdered while thirty-eight people watched or listened, and did nothing at all to help her. A Good Samaritan would have rushed out to give direct assistance against the murderer. Or perhaps we had better allow that it would have been a Splendid Samaritan who did this, on the ground that it would have involved a risk of death for himself. But the thirty-eight not only did not do this, they did not even trouble to pick up a phone to call the police. Minimally Decent Samaritanism would call for doing at least that, and their not having done it was monstrous.

After telling the story of the Good Samaritan, Jesus said, "Go, and do thou likewise." Perhaps he meant that we are morally required to act as the Good Samaritan did. Perhaps he was urging people to do more than is morally required of them. At all events it seems plain that it was not morally required of any of the thirty-eight that he rush out to give direct assistance at the risk of his own life, and that it is not morally required of anyone that he give long stretches of his life—nine years or nine months—to sustaining the life of a person who has no special right (we were leaving open the possibility of this) to demand it.

Indeed, with one rather striking class of exceptions, no one in any country in the world is *legally* required to do anywhere near as much as this for anyone else. The class of exceptions is obvious.

My main concern here is not the state of law in respect to abortion, but it is worth drawing attention to the fact that in no state in this country is any man compelled by law to be even a Minimally Decent Samaritan to any person; there is no law under which charges could be brought against the thirty-eight who stood by while Kitty Genovese died. By contrast, in most states in this country women are compelled by law to be not merely Minimally Decent Samaritans, but Good Samaritans to unborn persons inside them. This doesn't by itself settle anything one way or the other, because it may well be argued that there should be laws in this country—as there are in many European countries—compelling at least Minimally Decent

Samaritanism.[7] But it does show that there is a gross injustice in the existing state of the law. And it shows also that the groups currently working against liberalization of abortion laws, in fact working toward having it declared unconstitutional for a state to permit abortion, had better start working for the adoption of Good Samaritan laws generally, or earn the charge that they are acting in bad faith.

I should think, myself, that Minimally Decent Samaritan laws would be one thing, Good Samaritan laws quite another, and in fact highly improper. But we are not here concerned with the law. What we should ask is not whether anybody should be compelled by law to be a Good Samaritan, but whether we must accede to a situation in which somebody is being compelled—by nature, perhaps—to be a Good Samaritan. We have, in other words, to look now at third-party interventions. I have been arguing that no person is morally required to make large sacrifices to sustain the life of another who has no right to demand them, and this even where the sacrifices do not include life itself; we are not morally required to be Good Samaritans or anyway Very Good Samaritans to one another. But what if a man cannot extricate himself from such a situation? What if he appeals to us to extricate him? It seems to me plain that there are cases in which we can, cases in which a good Samaritan would extricate him. There you are, you were kidnapped, and nine years in bed with that violinist lie ahead of you. You have your own life to lead. You are sorry, but you simply cannot see giving up so much of your life to the sustaining of his. You cannot extricate yourself, and ask us to do so. I should have thought that—in light of his having no right to the use of your body—it was obvious that we do not have to accede to your being forced to give up so much. We can do what you ask. There is no injustice to the violinist in our doing so.

## 7.

Following the lead of the opponents of abortion, I have throughout been speaking of the fetus merely as a person, and what I have been asking is whether or not the argument we began with, which proceeds only from the fetus's being a person, really does establish its conclusion. I have argued that it does not.

But of course there are arguments and arguments, and it may be said that I have simply fastened on the wrong one. It may be said that what is important is not merely the fact that the fetus is a person, but that it is a person for whom the woman has a spe-

cial responsibility issuing from the fact that she is its mother. And it might be argued that all my analogies are therefore irrelevant—for you do not have that special kind of responsibility for that violinist, Henry Fonda does not have that special kind of responsibility for me. And our attention might be drawn to the fact that men and women both *are* compelled by law to provide support for their children.

I have in effect dealt (briefly) with this argument in section 4 above; but a (still briefer) recapitulation now may be in order. Surely we do not have any such "special responsibility" for a person unless we have assumed it, explicitly or implicitly. If a set of parents do not try to prevent pregnancy, do not obtain an abortion, but rather take it home with them, then they have assumed responsibility for it, they have given it rights, and they cannot *now* withdraw support from it at the cost of its life because they now find it difficult to go on providing for it. But if they have taken all reasonable precautions against having a child, they do not simply by virtue of their biological relationship to the child who comes into existence have a special responsibility for it. They may wish to assume responsibility for it, or they may not wish to. And I am suggesting that if assuming responsibility for it would require large sacrifices, then they may refuse. A Good Samaritan would not refuse—or anyway, a Splendid Samaritan, if the sacrifices that had to made were enormous. But then so would a Good Samaritan assume responsibility for that violinist; so would Henry Fonda, if he is a Good Samaritan, fly in from the West Coast and assume responsibility for me.

## 8.

My argument will be found unsatisfactory on two counts by many of those who want to regard abortion as morally permissible. First, while I do argue that abortion is not impermissible, I do not argue that it is always permissible. There may well be cases in which carrying the child to term requires only Minimally Decent Samaritanism of the mother, and this is a standard we must not fall below. I am inclined to think it a merit of my account precisely that it does *not* give a general yes or a general no. It allows for and supports our sense that, for example, a sick and desperately frightened fourteen-year-old schoolgirl, pregnant due to rape, may *of course* choose abortion, and that any law which rules this out is an insane law. And it also allows for and supports our sense that in other cases resort to abortion is even positively indecent. It would be indecent in the woman to request an abortion, and indecent in a doctor to perform it, if she is in her seventh month, and wants the abortion just to avoid the nuisance of postponing a trip abroad. The very fact that the arguments I have been drawing attention to treat all cases of abortion, or even all cases of abortion in which the mother's life is not at stake, as morally on a par ought to have made them suspect at the outset.

Second, while I am arguing for the permissibility of abortion in some cases, I am not arguing for the right to secure the death of the unborn child. It is easy to confuse these two things in that up to a certain point in the life of the fetus it is not able to survive outside the mother's body; hence removing it from her body guarantees its death. But they are importantly different. I have argued that you are not morally required to spend nine months in bed, sustaining the life of that violinist; but to say that is by no means to say that if, when you unplug yourself, there is a miracle and he survives, you then have a right to turn around and slit his throat. You may detach yourself even if this costs him his life; you have no right to be guaranteed his death, by some other means, if unplugging yourself does not kill him. There are some people who will feel dissatisfied by this feature of my argument. A woman may be utterly devastated by the thought of a child, a bit of herself, put out for adoption and never seen or heard of again. She may therefore want not merely that the child be detached from her, but more, that it die. Some opponents of abortion are inclined to regard this as beneath contempt—thereby showing insensitivity to what is surely a powerful source of despair. All the same, I agree that the desire for the child's death is not one which anybody may gratify, should it turn out to be possible to detach the child alive.

At this place, however, it should be remembered that we have only been pretending throughout that the fetus is a human being from the moment of con-

ception. A very early abortion is surely not the killing of a person, and so is not dealt with by anything I have said here.

### Notes

1. Daniel Callahan, *Abortion: Law, Choice and Morality* (New York, 1970), p. 373. This book gives a fascinating survey of the available information on abortion. The Jewish tradition is surveyed in David M. Feldman, *Birth Control in Jewish Law* (New York, 1968). Part 5, the Catholic tradition in John T. Noonan, Jr., "An Almost Absolute Value in History," in *The Morality of Abortion,* ed. John T. Noonan, Jr. (Cambridge, Mass., 1970).

2. The term "direct" in the arguments I refer to is a technical one. Roughly, what is meant by "direct killing" is either killing as an end in itself, or killing as a means to some end, for example, the end of saving someone else's life. See note 5 below, for an example of its use.

3. Cf. *Encyclical Letter of Pope Pius XI on Christian Marriage,* St. Paul Editions (Boston, n.d.), p. 32: "However much we may pity the mother whose health and even life is gravely imperiled in the performance of the duty allotted to her by nature, nevertheless what could ever be a sufficient reason for excusing in any way the direct murder of the innocent? This is precisely what we are dealing with here." Noonan (*The Morality of Abortion,* p. 43) reads this as follows: "What cause can ever avail to excuse in any way the direct killing of the innocent? For it is a question of that."

4. The thesis in (4) is in an interesting way weaker than those in (1), (2), and (3): they rule out abortion even in cases in which both mother *and* child will die if the abortion is not performed. By contrast, one who held the view expressed in (4) could consistently say that one needn't prefer letting two persons die to killing one.

5. Cf. the following passage from Pius XII, *Address to the Italian Catholic Society of Midwives:* "The baby in the maternal breast has the right to life immediately from God.—Hence there is no man, no human authority, no science, no medical, eugenic, social, economic or moral 'indication' which can establish or grant a valid juridical ground for a direct deliberate disposition of an innocent human life, that is a disposition which looks to its destruction either as an end or as a means to another end perhaps in itself illicit.—The baby, still not born, is a man in the same degree and for the same reason as the mother" (quoted in Noonan, *The Morality of Abortion,* p. 45).

6. The need for a discussion of this argument was brought home to me by members of the Society for Ethical and Legal Philosophy, to whom this paper was originally presented.

7. For a discussion of the difficulties involved, and a survey of the European experience with such laws, see *The Good Samaritan and the Law,* ed. James M. Ratcliffe (New York, 1966).

# On the Moral and Legal Status of Abortion

## Mary Anne Warren

Mary Anne Warren takes an even stronger position than Thomson (see preceding article), arguing that a woman's right to have an abortion is unrestricted. She attempts to show that there is no adequate basis for holding that the fetus has "a significant right to life" and that, whatever right can be appropriately granted to the fetus, it can never override a woman's right to protect her own interest and well-being. Accordingly, the laws that restrict access to abortion are an unjustified violation of a woman's rights.

Warren is critical of both Noonan (see earlier article) and Thomson. Noonan, she claims, fails to demonstrate that whatever is genetically human (the fetus) is also morally human (a person). Thomson, Warren argues, is mistaken in believing that it is possible both to grant that the fetus is a person and to produce a satisfactory defense of the right to obtain an abortion. Contrary to Thomson's aim, her central argument supports the right to abortion only in cases in which the woman is in no way responsible for her pregnancy.

Like Noonan, Warren conceives the basic issue in abortion to be the question of what properties something must possess to be a person in the moral sense. She offers five traits she believes anyone would accept as central and argues that the fetus, at all stages of development, possesses none of them. Since the fetus is not a person, it is not entitled to the full range of moral rights. That the fetus has the potential to become a person may give it a prima facie right to life, but the rights of an actual person always outweigh those of a potential person.

We will be concerned with both the moral status of abortion, which for our purposes we may define as the act which a woman performs in voluntarily terminating, or allowing another person to terminate, her pregnancy, and the legal status which is appropriate for this act. I will argue that, while it is not possible to produce a satisfactory defense of a woman's right to obtain an abortion without showing that a fetus is not a human being, in the morally relevant sense of that term, we ought not to conclude that the difficulties involved in determining whether or not a fetus is human make it impossible to produce any satisfactory solution to the problem of the moral status of abortion. For it is possible to show that, on the basis of intuitions which we may expect even the opponents of abortion to share, a fetus is not a person, hence not the sort of entity to which it is proper to ascribe full moral rights.

Of course, while some philosophers would deny the possibility of any such proof, [1] others will deny that there is any need for it, since the moral permissibility of abortion appears to them to be too obvious to require proof. But the inadequacy of this attitude should be evident from the fact that both the friends and foes of abortion consider their position to be morally self-evident. Because proabortionists have never adequately come to grips with the conceptual issues surrounding abortion, most if not all, of the arguments which they advance in opposition to laws restricting access to abortion fail to refute or even weaken the

Reprinted from *The Monist* 57, no. 1, LaSalle, Illinois 61301, with permission.

traditional antiabortion argument, i.e., that a fetus is a human being, and therefore abortion is murder.

These arguments are typically of one of two sorts. Either they point to the terrible side effects of the restrictive laws, e.g., the deaths due to illegal abortions, and the fact that it is poor women who suffer the most as a result of these laws, or else they state that to deny a woman access to abortion is to deprive her of her right to control her own body. Unfortunately, however, the fact that restricting access to abortion has tragic side effects does not, in itself, show that the restrictions are unjustified, since murder is wrong regardless of the consequences of prohibiting it; and the appeal to the right to control one's body, which is generally construed as a property right, is at best a rather feeble argument for the permissibility of abortion. Mere ownership does not give me the right to kill innocent people whom I find on my property, and indeed I am apt to be held responsible if such people injure themselves while on my property. It is equally unclear that I have any moral right to expel an innocent person from my property when I know that doing so will result in his death . . .

. . . . John Noonan is correct in saying that "the fundamental question in the long history of abortion is, How do you determine the humanity of a being?" [2] He summarizes his own antiabortion argument, which is a version of the official position of the Catholic Church, as follows:

. . . it is wrong to kill humans, however poor, weak, defenseless, and lacking in opportunity to develop their potential they may be. It is therefore morally wrong to kill Biafrans. Similarly, it is morally wrong to kill embryos.[3]

Noonan bases his claim that fetuses are human upon what he calls the theologians' criterion of humanity: that whoever is conceived of human beings is human. But although he argues at length for the appropriateness of this criterion, he never questions the assumption that if a fetus is human then abortion is wrong for exactly the same reason that murder is wrong.

Judith Thomson is, in fact, the only writer I am aware of who has seriously questioned this assumption; she has argued that, even if we grant the anti-abortionist his claim that a fetus is a human being, with the same right to life as any other human being, we can still demonstrate that, in at least some and perhaps most cases, a woman is under no moral obligation to complete an unwanted pregnancy.[4] Her argument is worth examining, since if it holds up it may enable us to establish the moral permissibility of abortion without becoming involved in problems about what entitles an entity to be considered human, and accorded full moral rights. To be able to do this would be a great gain in the power and simplicity of the proabortion position, since, although I will argue that these problems can be solved at least as decisively as can any other moral problem, we should certainly be pleased to be able to avoid having to solve them as part of the justification of abortion.

On the other hand, even if Thomson's argument does not hold up, her insight, i.e., that it requires arguments to show that if fetuses are human then abortion is properly classified as murder, is an extremely valuable one. The assumption she attacks is particularly invidious, for it amounts to the decision that it is appropriate, in deciding the moral status of abortion, to leave the rights of the pregnant woman out of consideration entirely, except possibly when her life is threatened. Obviously, this will not do; determining what moral rights, if any, a fetus possesses is only the first step in determining the moral status of abortion. Step two, which is at least equally essential, is finding a just solution to the conflict between whatever rights the fetus may have, and the rights of the woman who is unwillingly pregnant. While the historical error has been to pay far too little attention to the second step, Ms. Thomson's suggestion is that if we look at the second step first we may find that a woman has a right to obtain an abortion *regardless* of what rights the fetus has.

Our own inquiry will also have two stages. In Section I, we will consider whether or not it is possible to establish that abortion is morally permissible even on the assumption that a fetus is an entity with a full-fledged right to life. I will argue that in fact this cannot be established, at least not with the conclusiveness which is essential to our hopes of convincing those who are skeptical about the morality of abortion, and that we therefore cannot avoid dealing with the question of whether or not a fetus really does have the same right to life as a (more fully developed) human being.

In Section II, I will propose an answer to this question, namely, that a fetus cannot be considered a member of the moral community, the set of beings with full and equal moral rights, for the simple reason that it is not a person, and that it is personhood, and not genetic humanity, i.e., humanity as defined by Noonan, which is the basis for membership in this community. I will argue that a fetus, whatever its stage of development, satisfies none of the basic criteria of personhood, and is not even enough *like* a person to be accorded even some of the same rights on the basis of this resemblance. Nor, as we will see, is a fetus's *potential* personhood a threat to the morality of abortion, since, whatever the rights of potential people may be, they are invariably overridden in any conflict with the moral rights of actual people.

## I

We turn now to Professor Thomson's case for the claim that even if a fetus has full moral rights, abortion is still morally permissible, at least sometimes, and for some reasons other than to save the woman's life. Her argument is based upon a clever, but I think faulty, thinking. She asked us to picture ourselves waking up one day, in bed with a famous violinist. Imagine that you have been kidnapped, and your bloodstream hooked up to that of the violinist, who happens to have an ailment which will certainly kill him unless he is permitted to share your kidneys for a period of nine months. No one else can save him, since you alone have the right type of blood. He will be unconscious all that time, and you will have to stay in bed with him, but after the nine months are over he may be unplugged, completely cured, that is provided that you have cooperated.

Now then, she continues, what are your obligations in this situation? The antiabortionist, if he is consistent, will have to say that you are obligated to stay in bed with the violinist: for all people have a right to life, and violinists are people, and therefore it would be murder for you to disconnect yourself from him and

let him die.[5] But this is outrageous, and so there must
be something wrong with the same argument when it
is applied to abortion. It would certainly be commendable of you to agree to save the violinist, but it is absurd to suggest that your refusal to do so would be
murder. His right to life does not obligate you to do
whatever is required to keep him alive; nor does it justify anyone else forcing you to do so. A law which required you to stay in bed with the violinist would
clearly be an unjust law, since it is no proper function
of the law to force unwilling people to make huge sacrifices for the sake of other people toward whom they
have no such prior obligation.

Thomson concludes that, if this analogy is an apt
one, then we can grant the antiabortionist his claim
that a fetus is a human being, and still hold that it is at
least sometimes the case that a pregnant woman has
the right to refuse to be a Good Samaritan towards the
fetus, i.e., to obtain an abortion. For there is a great
gap between the claim that *x* has a right to life, and
the claim that *y* is obligated to do whatever is necessary to keep *x* alive, let alone that he ought to be
forced to do so. It is *y's* duty to keep *x* alive only if he
has somehow contracted a *special* obligation to do so;
and a woman who is unwillingly pregnant, e.g., who
was raped, has done nothing which obligates her to
make the enormous sacrifice which is necessary to
preserve the conceptus.

This argument is initially quite plausible, and in
the extreme case of pregnancy due to rape it is probably conclusive. Difficulties arise, however, when we try
to specify more exactly the range of cases in which
abortion is clearly justifiable even on the assumption
that the fetus is human. Professor Thomson considers
it a virtue of her argument that it does not enable us to
conclude that abortion is *always* permissible. It would,
she says, be "indecent" for a woman in her seventh
month to obtain an abortion just to avoid having to
postpone a trip to Europe. On the other hand, her argument enables us to see that "a sick and desperately
frightened schoolgirl pregnant due to rape may *of
course* choose abortion, and that any law which rules
this out is an insane law" (p. 65). So far, so good; but
what are we to say about the woman who becomes
pregnant not through rape but as a result of her own
carelessness, or because of contraceptive failure, or
who gets pregnant intentionally and then changes her
mind about wanting a child? With respect to such
cases, the violinist analogy is of much less use to the
defender of the woman's right to obtain an abortion.

Indeed, the choice of a pregnancy due to rape, as
an example of a case in which abortion is permissible

even if a fetus is considered a human being, is extremely significant; for it is only in the case of pregnancy due to rape that the woman's situation is
adequately analogous to the violinist case for our intuitions about the latter to transfer convincingly. The
crucial difference between a pregnancy due to rape
and the normal case of an unwanted pregnancy is that
in the normal case we cannot claim that the woman is
in no way responsible for her predicament; she could
have remained chaste, or taken her pills more faith-
fully, or abstained on dangerous days, and so on. If on
the other hand, you are kidnapped by strangers, and
hooked up to a strange violinist, then you are free of
any shred of responsibility for the situation, on the basis of which it would be argued that you are obligated
to keep the violinist alive. Only when her pregnancy is
due to rape is a woman clearly just as nonresponsible.[6]

Consequently, there is room for the antiabortionist to argue that in the normal case of unwanted pregnancy a woman has, by her own actions, assumed
responsibility of the fetus. For if *x* behaves in a way
which he could have avoided, and which he knows involves, let us say, a 1 percent chance of bringing into
existence a human being, with a right to life, and does
so knowing that if this should happen then that human being will perish unless *x* does certain things to
keep him alive, then it is by no means clear that when
it does happen *x* is free of any obligation to what he
knew in advance would be required to keep that human being alive.

The plausibility of such an argument is enough to
show that the Thomson analogy can provide a clear
and persuasive defense of a woman's right to obtain
an abortion only with respect to those cases in which
the woman is in no way responsible for her pregnancy,
e.g., where it is due to rape. In all other cases, we
would almost certainly conclude that it was necessary
to look carefully at the particular circumstances in order to determine the extent of the woman's responsibility, and hence the extent of her obligation. This is an
extremely unsatisfactory outcome, from the viewpoint
of the opponents of restrictive abortion laws, most of
whom are convinced that a woman has a right to obtain an abortion regardless of how and why she got
pregnant.

Of course a supporter of the violinist analogy
might point out that it is absurd to suggest that forget-
ting her pill one day might be sufficient to obligate a
woman to complete an unwanted pregnancy. And indeed it *is* absurd to suggest this. As we will see, the
moral right to obtain an abortion is not in the least
dependent upon the extent to which a woman is

responsible for her pregnancy. But unfortunately, once we allow the assumption that a fetus has full moral rights, we cannot avoid taking this absurd suggestion seriously. Perhaps we can make this point more clear by altering the violinist story just enough to make it more analogous to a normal unwanted pregnancy and less to a pregnancy due to rape, and then seeing whether it is still obvious that you are not obligated to stay in bed with the fellow.

Suppose, then, that violinists are peculiarly prone to the sort of illness the only cure for which is the use of someone else's bloodstream for nine months, and that because of this there has been formed a society of music lovers who agree that whenever a violinist is stricken they will draw lots and the loser will, by some means, be made the one and only person capable of saving him. Now then, would you be obligated to co-operate in curing the violinist if you had voluntarily joined this society, knowing the possible conse-quences, and then your name had been drawn and you had been kidnapped? Admittedly, you did not promise ahead of time that you would, but you did de-liberately place yourself in a position in which it might happen that a human life would be lost if you did not. Surely this is at least a prima facie reason for suppos-ing that you have an obligation to stay in bed with the violinist. Suppose that you had gotten your name drawn deliberately; surely *that* would be quite a strong reason for thinking that you had such an obligation.

It might be suggested that there is one important disanalogy between the modified violinist case and the case of an unwanted pregnancy, which makes the woman's responsibility significantly less, namely, the fact that the fetus *comes into existence* as the result of the woman's actions. This fact might give her a right to refuse to keep it alive, whereas she would not have had this right had it existed previously, independently, and then as a result of her actions become dependent upon her for its survival.

My own intuition, however, is that *x* has no more right to bring into existence, either deliberately or as a foreseeable result of actions he could have avoided, a being with full moral rights (*y*), and then refuse to do what he knew beforehand would be required to keep that being alive, than he has to enter into an agree-ment with an existing person, whereby he may be called upon to save that person's life, and then refuse to do so when so called upon. Thus *x*'s responsibility for *y*'s existence does not seem to lessen his obligation to keep *y* alive, if he is also responsible for *y*'s being in a situation in which only he can save him.

Whether or not this intuition is entirely correct, it brings us back once again to the conclusion that once we allow the assumption that a fetus has full moral rights it becomes an extremely complex and difficult question whether and when abortion is justifiable. Thus the Thomson analogy cannot help us produce a clear and persuasive proof of the moral permissibility of abortion. Nor will the opponents of the restrictive laws thank us for anything less; for their conviction (for the most part) is that abortion is obviously *not* a morally serious and extremely unfortunate, even though sometimes justified act, comparable to killing in self-defense or to letting the violinist die, but rather is closer to being a morally neutral act, like cutting one's hair.

The basis of this conviction, I believe, is the real-ization that a fetus is not a person, and thus does not have a full-fledged right to life. Perhaps the reason why this claim has been so inadequately defended is that it seems self-evident to those who accept it. And so it is, insofar as it follows from what I take to be per-fectly obvious claims about the nature of personhood, and about the proper grounds for ascribing moral rights, claims which ought, indeed, to be obvious to both the friends and foes of abortion. Nevertheless, it is worth examining these claims, and showing how they demonstrate the moral innocuousness of abor-tion, since this apparently has not been adequately done before.

## II

The question which we must answer in order to pro-duce a satisfactory solution to the problem of the moral status of abortion is this: How are we to define the moral community, the set of beings with full and equal moral rights, such that we can decide whether a human fetus is a member of this community or not? What sort of entity, exactly, has the inalienable rights to life, liberty, and the pursuit of happiness? Jefferson attributed these rights to all *men*, and it may or may not be fair to suggest that he intended to attribute them *only* to men. Perhaps he ought to have attributed them to all human beings. If so, then we arrive, first, at Noonan's problem of defining what makes a being human, and, second, at the equally vital question which Noonan does not consider, namely, What rea-son is there for identifying the moral community with the set of all human beings, in whatever way we have chosen to define that term?

## 1. On the Definition of "Human"

One reason why this vital second question is so frequently overlooked in the debate over the moral status of abortion is that the term "human" has two distinct, but not often distinguished, senses. This fact results in a slide of meaning, which serves to conceal the fallaciousness of the traditional argument that since (1) it is wrong to kill innocent human beings, and (2) fetuses are innocent human beings, then (3) it is wrong to kill fetuses. For if "human" is used in the same sense in both (1) and (2) then, whichever of the two senses is meant, one of these premises is question-begging. And if it is used in two different senses then of course the conclusion doesn't follow.

Thus, (1) is a self-evident moral truth,[7] and avoids begging the question about abortion, only if "human being" is used to mean something like "a full-fledged member of the moral community." (It may or may not also be meant to refer exclusively to members of the species *Homo sapiens.*) We may call this the *moral* sense of "human." It is not to be confused with what we will call the *genetic* sense; i.e., the sense in which *any* member of the species is a human being, and no member of any other species could be. If (1) is acceptable only if the moral sense is intended, (2) is non-question-begging only if what is intended is the genetic sense.

In "Deciding Who Is Human," Noonan argues for the classification of fetuses with human beings by pointing to the presence of the full genetic code, and the potential capacity for rational thought (p. 135). It is clear that what he needs to show, for his version of the traditional argument to be valid, is that fetuses are human in the moral sense, the sense in which it is analytically true that all human beings have full moral rights. But, in the absence of any argument showing that whatever is genetically human is also morally human, and he gives none, nothing more than genetic humanity can be demonstrated by the presence of the human genetic code. And, as we will see, the *potential* capacity for rational thought can at most show that an entity has the potential for *becoming* human in the moral sense.

## 2. Defining the Moral Community

Can it be established that genetic humanity is sufficient for moral humanity? I think that there are very good reasons for not defining the moral community in this way. I would like to suggest an alternative way of defining the moral community, which I will argue for only to the extent of explaining why it is, or should be, self-evident. The suggestion is simply that the moral community consists of all and *only* people, rather than all and only human beings;[8] and probably the best way of demonstrating its self-evidence is by considering the concept of personhood, to see what sorts of entity are and are not persons, and what the decision that a being is or is not a person implies about its moral rights.

What characteristics entitle an entity to be considered a person? This is obviously not the place to attempt a complete analysis of the concept of personhood, but we do not need such a fully adequate analysis just to determine whether and why a fetus is or isn't a person. All we need is a rough and approximate list of the most basic criteria of personhood, and some idea of which, or how many, of these an entity must satisfy in order to properly be considered a person.

In searching for such criteria, it is useful to look beyond the set of people with whom we are acquainted, and ask how we would decide whether a totally alien being was a person or not. (For we have no right to assume that genetic humanity is necessary for personhood.) Imagine a space traveler who lands on an unknown planet and encounters a race of beings utterly unlike any he has ever seen or heard of. If he wants to be sure of behaving morally toward these beings, he has to somehow decide whether they are people, and hence have full moral rights, or whether they are the sort of thing which he need not feel guilty about treating as, for example, a source of food.

How should he go about making this decision? If he has some anthropological background, he might look for such things as religion, art, and the manufacturing of tools, weapons, or shelters, since these factors have been used to distinguish our human from our prehuman ancestors, in what seems to be closer to the moral than the genetic sense of "human." And no doubt he would be right to consider the presence of such factors as good evidence that the alien beings were people, and morally human. It would, however, be overly anthropocentric of him to take the absence of these things as adequate evidence that they were not, since we can imagine people who have progressed beyond, or evolved without ever developing, these cultural characteristics.

I suggest that the traits which are most central to the concept of personhood, or humanity in the moral sense, are, very roughly, the following:

1.  consciousness (of objects and events external and/or internal to the being), and in particular the capacity to feel pain;

2.   reasoning (the developed capacity to solve new and relatively complex problems);

3.   self-motivated activity (activity which is relatively independent of either genetic or direct external control);

4.   the capacity to communicate, by whatever means, messages of an indefinite variety of types, that is, not just with an indefinite number of possible contents, but on indefinitely many possible topics;

5.   the presence of self-concepts, and self-awareness, either individual or racial, or both.

Admittedly, there are apt to be a great many problems involved in formulating precise definitions of these criteria, let alone in developing universally valid behavioral criteria for deciding when they apply. But I will assume that both we and our explorer know approximately what (1)–(5) mean, and that he is also able to determine whether or not they apply. How, then, should he use his findings to decide whether or not the alien beings are people? We needn't suppose that an entity must have *all* of these attributes to be properly considered a person; (1) and (2) alone may well be sufficient for personhood, and quite probably (1)–(3), if "activity" is construed so as to include the activity of reasoning.

All we need to claim, to demonstrate that a fetus is not a person, is that any being which satisfies *none* of (1)–(5) is certainly not a person. I consider this claim to be so obvious that I think anyone who denied it, and claimed that a being which satisfied none of (1)–(5) was a person all the same, would thereby demonstrate that he had no notion at all of what a person is—perhaps because he had confused the concept of a person with that of genetic humanity. If the opponents of abortion were to deny the appropriateness of these five criteria, I do not know what further arguments would convince them. We would probably have to admit that our conceptual schemes were indeed irreconcilably different, and that our dispute could not be settled objectively.

I do not expect this to happen, however, since I think that the concept of a person is one which is very nearly universal (to people), and that it is common to both proabortionists and antiabortionists, even though neither group has fully realized the relevance of this concept to the resolution of their dispute. Furthermore, I think that on reflection even the antiabortionists ought to agree not only that (1)–(5) are central to the concept of personhood, but also that it is a part of this concept that all and only people have full moral rights. The concept of a person is in part a moral concept; once we have admitted that *x* is a person we have recognized, even if we have not agreed to respect, *x's* right to be treated as a member of the moral community. It is true that the claim that *x* is a *human being* is more commonly voiced as part of an appeal to treat *x* decently than is the claim that *x* is a person, but this is either because "human being" is here used in the sense which implies personhood, or because the genetic and moral sense of "human" have been confused.

Now if (1)–(5) are indeed the primary criteria of personhood, then it is clear that genetic humanity is neither necessary nor sufficient for establishing that an entity is a person. Some human beings are not people, and there may well be people who are not human beings. A man or woman whose consciousness has been permanently obliterated but who remains alive is a human being which is no longer a person; defective human beings, with no appreciable mental capacity, are not and presumably never will be people; and a fetus is a human being which is not yet a person, and which therefore cannot coherently be said to have full moral rights. Citizens of the next century should be prepared to recognize highly advanced, self-aware robots or computers, should such be developed, and intelligent inhabitants of other worlds, should such be found, as people in the fullest sense, and to respect their moral rights. But to ascribe full moral rights to an entity which is not a person is as absurd as to ascribe moral obligations and responsibilities to such an entity.

### 3. Fetal Development and the Right to Life

Two problems arise in the application of these suggestions for the definition of the moral community to the determination of the precise moral status of a human fetus. Given that the paradigm example of a person is a normal adult being, then (1) How like this paradigm, in particular how far advanced since conception, does a human being need to be before it begins to have a right to life by virtue, not of being fully a person as of yet, but of being *like* a person? and (2) To what extent, if any, does the fact that a fetus has the *potential* for becoming a person endow it with some of the same rights? Each of these questions requires some comment.

In answering the first question, we need not attempt a detailed consideration of the moral rights of organisms which are not developed enough, aware enough, intelligent enough, etc., to be considered people, but which resemble people in some respects. It does seem reasonable to suggest that the more like a person, in the relevant respects, a being is, the stronger is the case for regarding it as having a right to life, and indeed the stronger its right to life is. Thus we ought to take seriously the suggestion that, insofar as "the human individual develops biologically in a continuous fashion . . . the rights of a human person might develop in the same way."[9] But we must keep in mind that the attributes which are relevant in determining whether or not an entity is enough like a person to be regarded as having some of the same moral rights are no different from those which are relevant to determining whether or not it is fully a person—i.e., are no different from (1)–(5)—and that being genetically human, or having recognizably human facial and other physical features, or detectable brain activity, or the capacity to survive outside the uterus, are simply not among these relevant attributes.

Thus it is clear that even though a seven- or eight-month fetus has features which makes it apt to arouse in us almost the same powerful protective instinct as is commonly aroused by a small infant, nevertheless it is not significantly more personlike than is a very small embryo. It is *somewhat* more personlike; it can apparently feel and respond to pain, and it may even have a rudimentary form of consciousness, insofar as its brain is quite active. Nevertheless, it seems safe to say that it is not fully conscious, in the way that an infant of a few months is, and that it cannot reason, or communicate messages of indefinitely many sorts, does not engage in self-motivated activity, and has no self-awareness. Thus, in the *relevant* respects, a fetus, even a fully developed one, is considerably less personlike than is the average mature mammal, indeed the average fish. And I think that a rational person must conclude that if the right to life of a fetus is to be based upon its resemblance to a person, then it cannot be said to have any more right to life then, let us say, a newborn guppy (which also seems to be capable of feeling pain), and that a right of that magnitude could never override a woman's right to obtain an abortion, at any stage of her pregnancy.

There may, of course, be other arguments in favor of placing legal limits upon the stage of pregnancy in which an abortion may be performed. Given the relative safety of the new techniques of artificially inducing labor during the third trimester, the danger to the woman's life or health is no longer such an argument. Neither is the fact that people tend to respond to the thought of abortion in the later stages of pregnancy with emotional repulsion, since mere emotional responses cannot take the place of moral reasoning in determining what ought to be permitted. Nor, finally, is the frequently heard argument that legalizing abortion, especially late in the pregnancy, may erode the level of respect for human life, leading, perhaps, to an increase in unjustified euthanasia and other crimes. For this threat, if it is a threat, can be better met by educating people to the kinds of moral distinctions which we are making here than by limiting access to abortion (which limitation may, in its disregard for the rights of women, be just as damaging to the level of respect for human rights).

Thus, since the fact that even a fully developed fetus is not personlike enough to have any significant right to life on the basis of its personlikeness shows that no legal restrictions upon the stage of pregnancy in which an abortion may be performed can be justified on the grounds that we should protect the rights of the older fetus; and since there is no other apparent justification for such restrictions, we may conclude that they are entirely unjustified. Whether or not it would be *indecent* (whatever that means) for a woman in her seventh month to obtain an abortion just to avoid having to postpone a trip to Europe, it would not, in itself, be *immoral*, and therefore it ought to be permitted.

### 4. Potential Personhood and the Right to Life

We have seen that a fetus does not resemble a person in any way which can support the claim that it has even some of the same rights. But what about its *potential*, the fact that if nurtured and allowed to develop naturally it will very probably become a person? Doesn't that alone give it at least some right to life? It is hard to deny that the fact that an entity is a potential person is a strong prima facie reason for not destroying it; but we need not conclude from this that a potential person has a right to life, by virtue of that potential. It may be that our feeling that it is better, other things being equal, not to destroy a potential person is better explained by the fact that potential people are still (felt to be) an invaluable resource, not to be lightly squandered. Surely, if every speck of dust were a potential person, we would be much less apt to conclude that every potential person has a right to become actual.

Still, we do not need to insist that a potential person has no right to life whatever. There may well be something immoral, and not just imprudent, about wantonly destroying potential people, when doing so isn't necessary to protect anyone's rights. But even if a potential person does have some prima facie right to life, such a right could not possibly outweigh the right of a woman to obtain an abortion, since the rights of any actual person invariably outweigh those of any potential person, whenever the two conflict. Since this may not be immediately obvious in the case of a human fetus, let us look at another case.

Suppose that our space explorer falls into the hands of an alien culture, whose scientists decide to create a few hundred thousand or more human beings, by breaking his body into its component cells, and using these to create fully developed human beings, with, of course, his genetic code. We may imagine that each of these newly created men will have all of the original man's abilities, skills, knowledge, and so on, and also have an individual self-concept, in short that each of them will be a bona fide (though hardly unique) person. Imagine that the whole project will take only seconds, and that its chances of success are extremely high, and that our explorer knows all of this, and also knows that these people will be treated fairly. I maintain that in such a situation he would have every right to escape if he could, and thus to deprive all of these potential people of their potential lives; for his right to life outweighs all of theirs together, in spite of the fact that they are all genetically human, all innocent, and all have a very high probability of becoming people very soon, if only he refrains from acting.

Indeed, I think he would have a right to escape even if it were not his life which the alien scientists planned to take, but only a year of his freedom, or, indeed, only a day. Nor would he be obligated to stay if he had gotten captured (thus bringing all these people-potentials into existence) because of his own carelessness, or even if he had done so deliberately, knowing the consequences. Regardless of how he got captured, he is not morally obligated to remain in captivity for *any* period of time for the sake of permitting any number of potential people to come into actuality, so great is the margin by which one actual person's right to liberty outweighs whatever right to life even a hundred thousand potential people have. And it seems reasonable to conclude that the rights of a woman will outweigh by a similar margin whatever

right to life a fetus may have by virtue of its potential personhood.

Thus, neither a fetus's resemblance to a person, nor its potential for becoming a person provides any basis whatever for the claim that it has any significant right to life. Consequently, a woman's right to protect her health, happiness, freedom, and even her life,[10] by terminating an unwanted pregnancy, will always override whatever right to life it may be appropriate to ascribe to a fetus, even a fully developed one. And thus, in the absence of any overwhelming social need for every possible child, the laws which restrict the right to obtain an abortion, or limit the period of pregnancy during which an abortion may be performed, are a wholly unjustified violation of a woman's most basic moral and constitutional rights.[11]

### Notes

1. For example, Roger Wertheimer, who in "Understanding the Abortion Argument" (*Philosophy and Public Affairs*, 1, No. 1 [Fall, 1971], 67–95), argues that the problem of the moral status of abortion is insoluble, in that the dispute over the status of the fetus is not a question of fact at all, but only a question of how one responds to the facts.

2. John Noonan, "Abortion and the Catholic Church: A Summary History," *Natural Law Forum*, 12 (1967), 125.

3. John Noonan, "Deciding Who Is Human," *Natural Law Forum*, 13 (1968), 134.

4. "A Defense of Abortion."

5. Judith Thomson, "A Defense of Abortion," *Philosophy and Public Affairs*, 1, No. 1 (Fall, 1971), 47–66.

6. We may safely ignore the fact that she might have avoided getting raped, e.g., by carrying a gun, since by similar means you might likewise have avoided getting kidnapped, and in neither case does the victim's failure to take all possible precautions against a highly unlikely event (as opposed to reasonable precautions against a rather likely event) mean that he is morally responsible for what happens.

7. Of course, the principle that it is (always) wrong to kill innocent human beings is in need of many other modifications, e.g., that it may be permissible to do so to save a greater number of other innocent human beings, but we may safely ignore these complications here.

8. From here on, we will use "human" to mean genetically human, since the moral sense seems closely connected to, and perhaps derived from, the assumption that genetic humanity is sufficient for membership in the moral community.

9. Thomas L. Hayes, "A Biological View," *Commonweal*, 85 (March 17, 1967), 677–78; quoted by Daniel Callahan, in *Abortion, Law, Choice, and Morality* (London: Macmillan & Co., 1970).

10. That is, insofar as the death rate, for the woman, is higher for childbirth than for early abortion.

11. My thanks to the following people, who were kind enough to read and criticize an earlier version of this paper: Herbert Gold, Gene Glass, Anne Lauterbach, Judith Thomson, Mary Mothersill, and Timothy Binkley.

# Why Abortion Is Immoral

## Don Marquis

Don Marquis offers what he considers to be an essentially new argument to establish the basic wrongness of abortion. The reason murder is wrong, according to Marquis, is that it deprives a person of the value of his or her future. Because a fetus, if not aborted, can be assumed to have a future like ours that is also of value, abortion, like any other kind of killing, can be justified only by the most compelling reasons. Contraception, by contrast, is not wrong, because there is no identifiable individual to be deprived of a future.

The view that abortion is, with rare exceptions, seriously immoral has received little support in the recent philosophical literature. No doubt most philosophers affiliated with secular institutions of higher education believe that the anti-abortion position is either a symptom of irrational religious dogma or a conclusion generated by seriously confused philosophical argument. The purpose of this essay is to undermine this general belief. This essay sets out an argument that purports to show, as well as any argument in ethics can show, that abortion is, except possibly in rare cases, seriously immoral, that it is in the same moral category as killing an innocent adult human being . . .

## I

. . . [A] necessary condition of resolving the abortion controversy is a more theoretical account of the wrongness of killing. After all, if we merely believe, but do not understand, why killing adult human beings such as ourselves is wrong, how could we conceivably show that abortion is either immoral or permissible?

## II

In order to develop such an account, we can start from the following unproblematic assumption concerning our own case: it is wrong to kill *us*. Why is it wrong? Some answers can be easily eliminated. It might be said that what makes killing us wrong is that a killing brutalizes the one who kills. But the brutalization con-

Don Marquis, "Why Abortion Is Immoral," *The Journal of Philosophy* 86, no. 4 (April 1989), pp. 183, 189-198, 201-202. Reprinted by permission. (Notes omitted.)

sists of being inured to the performance of an act that is hideously immoral; hence, the brutalization does not explain the immorality. It might be said that what makes killing us wrong is the great loss others would experience due to our absence. Although such hubris is understandable, such an explanation does not account for the wrongness of killing hermits, or those whose lives are relatively independent and whose friends find it easy to make new friends.

A more obvious answer is better. What primarily makes killing wrong is neither its effect on the murderer nor its effect on the victim's friends and relatives, but its effect on the victim. The loss of one's life is one of the greatest losses one can suffer. The loss of one's life deprives one of all the experiences, activities, projects, and enjoyments that would otherwise have constituted one's future. Therefore, killing someone is wrong, primarily because the killing inflicts (one of) the greatest possible losses on the victim. To describe this as the loss of life can be misleading, however. The change in my biological state does not by itself make killing me wrong. The effect of the loss of my biological life is the loss to me of all those activities, projects, experiences, and enjoyments which would otherwise have constituted my future personal life. These activities, projects, experiences, and enjoyments are either valuable for their own sakes or are means to something else that is valuable for its own sake. Some parts of my future are not valued by me now, but will come to be valued by me as I grow older and as my values and capacities change. When I am killed, I am deprived both of what I now value which would have been part of my future personal life, but also what I would come to value. Therefore, when I die, I am deprived of all of the value of my future. Inflicting this loss on me is ultimately what makes killing me wrong.

This being the case, it would seem that what makes killing *any* adult human being prima facie seriously wrong is the loss of his or her future. . . .

The claim that what makes killing wrong is the loss of the victim's future is directly supported by two considerations. In the first place, this theory explains why we regard killing as one of the worst of crimes. Killing is especially wrong, because it deprives the victim of more than perhaps any other crime. In the second place, people with AIDS or cancer who know they are dying believe, of course, that dying is a very bad thing for them. They believe that the loss of a future to them that they would otherwise have experienced is what makes their premature death a very bad thing for them. A better theory of the wrongness of killing would require a different natural property associated with killing which better fits with the attitudes of the dying. What could it be?

The view that what makes killing wrong is the loss to the victim of the value of the victim's future gains additional support when some of its implications are examined. In the first place, it is incompatible with the view that it is wrong to kill only beings who are biologically human. It is possible that there exists a different species from another planet whose members have a future like ours. Since having a future like that is what makes killing someone wrong, this theory entails that it would be wrong to kill members of such a species. Hence, this theory is opposed to the claim that only life that is biologically human has great moral worth, a claim which many anti-abortionists have seemed to adopt. This opposition, which this theory has in common with personhood theories, seems to be a merit of the theory.

In the second place, the claim that the loss of one's future is the wrong-making feature of one's being killed entails the possibility that the futures of some actual nonhuman mammals on our own planet are sufficiently like ours that it is seriously wrong to kill them also. Whether some animals do have the same right to life as human beings depends on adding to the account of the wrongness of killing some additional account of just what it is about my future or the futures of other adult human beings which makes it wrong to kill us. No such additional account will be offered in this essay. Undoubtedly, the provision of such an account would be a very difficult matter. Undoubtedly, any such account would be quite controversial. Hence, it surely should not reflect badly on this sketch of an elementary theory of the wrongness of killing that it is indeterminate with respect to some very difficult issues regarding animal rights.

In the third place, the claim that the loss of one's future is the wrong-making feature of one's being killed does not entail, as sanctity of human life theories do, that active euthanasia is wrong. Persons who are severely and incurably ill, who face a future of pain and despair, and who wish to die will not have suffered a loss if they are killed. It is, strictly speaking, the value of a human's future which makes killing wrong in this theory. This being so, killing does not necessarily wrong some persons who are sick or dying. Of course, there may be other reasons for a prohibition of active euthanasia, but that is another matter. Sanctity-of-human-life theories seem to hold that active euthanasia is seriously wrong even in an individual case where there seems to be good reason for it independently of public policy considerations. This consequence is most implausible, and it is a plus for the claim that the loss of a future of value is what makes killing wrong that it does not share this consequence.

In the fourth place, the account of the wrongness of killing defended in this essay does straightforwardly entail that it is prima facie seriously wrong to kill children and infants, for we do presume that they have futures of value. Since we do believe that it is wrong to kill defenseless little babies, it is important that a theory of the wrongness of killing easily account for this. Personhood theories of the wrongness of killing, on the other hand, cannot straightforwardly account for the wrongness of killing infants and young children. Hence, such theories must add special ad hoc accounts of the wrongness of killing the young. The plausibility of such ad hoc theories seems to be a function of how desperately one wants such theories to work. The claim that the primary wrong-making feature of a killing is the loss to the victim of the value of its future accounts for the wrongness of killing young children and infants directly; it makes the wrongness of such acts as obvious as we actually think it is. This is a further merit of this theory. Accordingly, it seems that this value of a future-like-ours theory of the wrongness of killing shares strengths of both sanctity-of-life and personhood accounts while avoiding weaknesses of both. In addition, it meshes with a central intuition concerning what makes killing wrong.

The claim that the primary wrong-making feature of a killing is the loss to the victim of the value of its future has obvious consequences for the ethics of abortion. The future of a standard fetus includes a set of experiences, projects, activities, and such which are identical with the futures of adult human beings and are identical with the future of young children. Since the reason that is sufficient to explain why it is wrong to kill human beings after the time of birth is a reason that also applies to fetuses, it follows that abortion is prima facie seriously morally wrong.

This argument does not rely on the invalid inference that, since it is wrong to kill persons, it is wrong to kill potential persons also. The category that is morally central to this analysis is the category of having a valuable future like ours; it is not the category of personhood. The argument to the conclusion that abortion is prima face seriously morally wrong proceeded independently of the notion of person or potential person or any equivalent. . . .

Of course, this value of a future-like-ours argument, if sound, shows only that abortion is prima facie wrong, not that it is wrong in any and all circumstances. Since the loss of the future to a standard fetus, if killed, is, however, at least as great a loss as the loss of the future to a standard adult human being who is killed, abortion, like ordinary killing, could be justified only by the most compelling reasons. The loss of one's life is almost the greatest misfortune that can happen to one. Presumably abortion could be justified in some circumstances, only if the loss consequent on failing to abort would be at least as great. Accordingly, morally permissible abortions will be rare indeed unless, perhaps, they occur so early in pregnancy that a fetus is not yet definitely an individual. Hence, this argument should be taken as showing that abortion is presumptively very seriously wrong, where the presumption is very strong—as strong as the presumption that killing another adult human being is wrong.

## III

How complete an account of the wrongness of killing does the value of a future-like-ours account have to be in order that the wrongness of abortion is a consequence? This account does not have to be an account of the necessary conditions for the wrongness of killing. Some persons in nursing homes may lack valuable human futures, yet it may be wrong to kill them for other reasons. Furthermore, this account does not obviously have to be the sole reason killing is wrong where the victim did have a valuable future. This analysis claims only that, for any killing where the victim did have a valuable future like ours, having that future by itself is sufficient to create the strong presumption that the killing is seriously wrong.

One way to overturn the value of a future-like-ours argument would be to find some account of the wrongness of killing which is at least as intelligible and which has different implications for the ethics of abortion. Two rival accounts possess at least some degree of plausibility. One account is based on the obvious fact that people value the experience of living and wish for that valuable experience to continue. Therefore, it might be said, what makes killing wrong is the discontinuation of that experience for the victim. Let us call this the *discontinuation account.* Another rival account is based upon the obvious fact that people strongly desire to continue to live. This suggests that what makes killing us so wrong is that it interferes with the fulfillment of a strong and fundamental desire, the fulfillment of which is necessary for the fulfillment of any other desires we might have. Let us call this the *desire account.*

Consider first the desire account as a rival account of the ethics of killing which would provide the basis for rejecting the anti-abortion position. Such an account will have to be stronger than the value of a future-like-ours account of the wrongness of abortion if it is to do the job expected of it. To entail the wrongness of abortion, the value of a future-like-ours account has only to provide a sufficient, but not a necessary, condition for the wrongness of killing. The desire account, on the other hand, must provide us also with a necessary condition for the wrongness of killing in order to generate a pro-choice conclusion on abortion. The reason for this is that presumably the argument from the desire account moves from the claim that what makes killing wrong is interference with a very strong desire to the claim that abortion is not wrong because the fetus lacks a strong desire to live. Obviously, this inference fails if someone's having the desire to live is not a necessary condition of its being wrong to kill that individual.

One problem with the desire account is that we do regard it as seriously wrong to kill persons who have little desire to live or who have no desire to live or, indeed, have a desire not to live. We believe it is seriously wrong to kill the unconscious, the sleeping, those who are tired of life, and those who are suicidal. The value-of-a-human-future account renders standard morality intelligible in these cases; these cases appear to be incompatible with the desire account.

The desire account is subject to a deeper difficulty. We desire life, because we value the goods of this life. The goodness of life is not secondary to our desire for it. If this were not so, the pain of one's own premature death could be done away with merely by an appropriate alteration in the configuration of one's desires. This is absurd. Hence, it would seem that it is the loss of the goods of one's future, not the interference with the fulfillment of a strong desire to live, which accounts ultimately for the wrongness of killing. . . .

The discontinuation account looks more promising as an account of the wrongness of killing. It seems just as intelligible as the value of a future-like-ours account, but it does not justify an anti-abortion position. Obviously, if it is the continuation of one's activities, experiences, and projects, the loss of which makes killing wrong, then it is not wrong to kill fetuses for that reason, for fetuses do not have experiences, activities, and projects to be continued or discontinued. Accordingly, the discontinuation account does not have the anti-abortion consequences that the value of a future-like-ours account has. Yet, it seems as intelligible as the value of a future-like-ours account, for when we think of what would be wrong with our being killed, it does seem as if it is the discontinuation of what makes our lives worthwhile which makes killing us wrong.

Is the discontinuation account just as good an account as the value of a future-like-ours account? The discontinuation account will not be adequate at all, if it does not refer to the *value* of the experience that may be discontinued. One does not want the discontinuation account to make it wrong to kill a patient who begs for death and who is in severe pain that cannot be relieved short of killing. (I leave open the question of whether it is wrong for other reasons.) Accordingly, the discontinuation account must be more than a bare discontinuation account. It must make some reference to the positive value of the patient's experience. But, by the same token, the value of a future-like-ours account cannot be a bare future account either. Just having a future surely does not itself rule out killing the above patient. This account must make some reference to the value of the patient's future experience and projects also. Hence, both accounts involve the value of experiences, projects, and activities. So far we still have symmetry between the accounts.

The symmetry fades, however, when we focus on the time period of the value of the experiences, etc., which has moral consequences. Although both accounts leave open the possibility that the patient in our example may be killed, this possibility is left open only in virtue of the utterly bleak future for the patient. It makes no difference whether the patient's immediate past contains intolerable pain, or consists of being in a coma (which we can imagine is a situation of indifference), or consists in a life of value. If the patient's future is a future of value, we want our account to make it wrong to kill the patient. If the patient's future is intolerable, whatever his or her immediate past, we want our account to allow killing the patient. Obviously, then, it is the value of that patient's future which is doing the work in rendering the morality of killing the patient intelligible.

This being the case, it seems clear that whether one has immediate past experiences or not does no work in the explanation of what makes killing wrong. The addition the discontinuation account makes to the value of a human future is otiose. Its addition to the value-of-a-future account plays no role at all in rendering intelligible the wrongness of killing. Therefore, it can be discarded with the discontinuation account of which it is a part.

## IV

The analysis of the previous section suggests that alternative general accounts of the wrongness of killing are either inadequate or unsuccessful in getting around the anti-abortion consequences of the value of a future-like-ours argument. A different strategy for avoiding these anti-abortion consequences involves limiting the scope of the value of a future argument. More precisely, the strategy involves arguing that fetuses lack a property that is essential for the value-of-a-future argument (or for any anti-abortion argument) to apply to them.

One move of this sort is based upon the claim that a necessary condition of one's future being valuable is that one values it. Value implies a valuer. Given this one might argue that, since fetuses cannot value their futures, their futures are not valuable to them. Hence, it does not seriously wrong them deliberately to end their lives.

This move fails, however, because of some ambiguities. Let us assume that something cannot be of value unless it is valued by someone. This does not entail that my life is of no value unless it is valued by me. I may think, in a period of despair, that my future is of no worth whatsoever, but I may be wrong because others rightly see value—even great value—in it. Furthermore, my future can be valuable to me even if I do not value it. This is the case when a young person attempts suicide, but is rescued and goes on to significant human achievements. Such young people's futures are ultimately valuable to them, even though such futures do not seem to be valuable to them at the moment of attempted suicide. A fetus's future can be valuable to it in the same way. Accordingly, this attempt to limit the anti-abortion argument fails. . . .

## V

In this essay, it has been argued that the correct ethic of the wrongness of killing can be extended to fetal life and used to show that there is a stronger presumption that an abortion is morally impermissible. If the ethic of killing adopted here entails, however, that contraception is also seriously immoral, then there would appear to be a difficulty with the analysis of this essay.

But this analysis does not entail that contraception is wrong. Of course, contraception prevents the actualization of a possible future of value. Hence it follows from the claim that futures of value should be maximized that contraception is prima facie immoral. This obligation to maximize does not exist, however; furthermore, nothing in the ethics of killing in this paper entails that it does. The ethics of killing in this essay would entail that contraception is wrong only if something were denied a human future of value by contraception. Nothing at all is denied such a future by contraception, however.

Candidates for a subject of harm by contraception fall into four categories: (1) some sperm or other, (2) some ovum or other, (3) a sperm and an ovum separately, and (4) a sperm and an ovum together. Assigning the harm to some sperm is utterly arbitrary, for no reason can be given for making a sperm the subject of harm rather than an ovum. Assigning the harm to some ovum is utterly arbitrary, for no reason can be given for making an ovum the subject of harm rather than a sperm. One might attempt to avoid these problems by insisting that contraception deprives both the sperm and the ovum separately of a valuable future like ours. On this alternative, too many futures are lost. Contraception was supposed to be wrong, because it deprived us of one future of value, not two. One might attempt to avoid this problem by holding that contraception deprives the combination of sperm and ovum of a valuable future like ours. But here the definite article misleads. At the time of contraception, there are hundreds of millions of sperm, one (released) ovum and millions of possible combinations of all of these. There is no actual combination at all. Is the subject of the loss to be a merely possible combination? Which one? This alternative does not yield an actual subject of harm either. Accordingly, the immorality of contraception is not entailed by the loss of a future-like-ours argument simply because there is no nonarbitrarily identifiable subject of the loss in the case of contraception.

## VI

The purpose of this essay has been to set out an argument of the serious presumptive wrongness of abortion subject to the assumption that the moral permissibility of abortion stands or falls on the moral status of the fetus. Since a fetus possesses a property, the possession of which in adult human beings is sufficient to make killing an adult human being wrong, abortion is wrong. . . .

---

# The Morality of Abortion and the Deprivation of Futures

## Mark T. Brown

Mark Brown rejects Donald Marquis's argument that abortion is wrong for the same reason killing an adult is wrong—it deprives the person of a future of value. Brown claims the argument trades on the ambiguity of "future of value," which may mean either "potential future of value" or "self-represented future of value."

The first interpretation implies we commit homicide whenever we fail to provide someone with whatever he needs to live, but not to provide someone with necessities (e.g., medical care) is not necessarily to treat him unjustly. A fetus could have a presumptive right to life only if women had no right to control their bodies. Marquis's argument fails for it "implausibly" assigns people "welfare rights to valuable futures" and "liberty rights not to be killed."

While the second interpretation makes Marquis's argument deductively valid, it cannot be sound (i.e., have all true premises), because the fetus lacks the neurological development required for imagining a future. Marquis's argument gains its force only by trading on the ambiguity of "future of value."

In an influential essay entitled "Why abortion is wrong," Donald Marquis presents an argument which purports to derive the immorality of abortion from a deceptively simple but intuitively compelling claim: it is presumptively wrong to kill us, competent adult human beings, because doing so destroys our most valuable possession, a future of value.[1] Marquis claims that killing actual persons is wrong because it unjustly deprives the victim of his or her future; that the fetus has a future similar in morally relevant respects to the future lost by a competent adult homicide victim, and that, as consequence, abortion is justifiable only in the same special and extreme circumstances in which killing competent adult human beings is justifiable. Marquis presents the gist of the Future Like Ours (FLO) argument in this way:

> . . . we can start from the following unproblematic assumption: it is wrong to kill us . . . when I am killed I am deprived of all the value of my future. Inflicting this loss on me is ultimately what makes killing me wrong. The future of a standard fetus includes a set of experiences, projects, activities and such which are identical with the futures of adult human beings and the futures of young children. Since the reason that is sufficient to explain why it is wrong to kill human beings after the time of birth is a reason that also applies to fetuses, it follows that abortion is prima facie seriously wrong.[2]

The Future Like Ours argument has been criticised on the grounds that it ignores the point of view of the pregnant woman; that it is incompatible with contraception and abstinence; and that it understates the explanatory resources of the competing personhood theory while overstating its own explanatory power.[3] These objections make a powerful cumulative case that something is amiss in FLO, but none come to grips with the metaphysical thesis at the heart of the argument: the claim that actual persons possess a future of value. What exactly does it mean to have a future of value?

From *Journal of Medical Ethics* 26, no. 2 (April 2000), pp. 103–105.

The expression is ambiguous. It could mean that actual persons have a potential future of value in the sense that given favourable conditions they are likely to have a worthwhile life; or it could mean that actual persons have a self-represented future of value in the sense that they can construct mental representations of valuable futures. The FLO argument turns upon this ambiguity. The expression occurs twice in the argument, first in the claim that homicide is presumptively wrong because it deprives its victim of a future of value, and second in the claim that both actual persons and fetuses have a future of value. The Future Like Ours argument would be valid if "future of value" were used consistently to mean either "potential future of value" or "self-represented future of value," and FLO would be sound if one or the other interpretation supported both the moral claim and the metaphysical claim, but if any interpretation which makes the argument valid renders it unsound, then FLO must be rejected. I first argue that the potential future of value interpretation is unsound because it is not presumptively seriously wrong to deprive someone of a potential future of value. I then argue that the self-represented future of value interpretation is unsound because the fetus does not represent its future. The essay concludes with an analysis of the intuitive appeal of the Future Like Ours argument.

## I

The Future Like Ours argument might be salvaged if homicide were presumptively wrong because it deprives a human being of a potential future of value, whether or not that human being ever imagined his or her future. In this case, the expression "a future of value" could be used consistently throughout the argument: killing persons is presumptively wrong because it deprives them of their potential future of value; a fetus has a potential future of value; thus killing a fetus is presumptively wrong. The second premise is plausible. In most cases the course of a pregnancy can be foreseen with enough confidence to predict that the fetus will be born as an infant who has the capacity to enjoy a life qualitatively similar to the lives of actual persons.

The first premise is implausible, in part because a potential future of value interpretation implies welfare rights which most people would reject in other spheres of life. If deprivation of potential futures of value is presumptively a form of culpable homicide, then culpable homicide is committed whenever a person is denied access to what he or she needs to live. A homeless man who dies of exposure, an elderly woman whose unheated apartment precipitates a fatal case of pneumonia, an injured child who dies for want of a suitable blood transfusion would all be homicide victims. Each case is tragic in its own way, but it is far from clear that these persons' rights have been violated. Persons can die in ways which do not violate their rights.[4] This is not to say that no harm is done when a potential future of value is foreclosed. On the contrary, to prevent a person from acting upon a highly reliable anticipated future imposes upon them significant opportunity costs, but it does not necessarily treat him or her unjustly. Only if the person had a right to the favourable circumstances which make possible a potential future of value would depriving him or her of that future be presumptively wrong.

For example, the future quality of life of many actual persons depends critically upon whether they receive prompt and effective medical treatment. Many persons with end stage renal disease could expect bright futures if they were to receive a kidney transplant, but neither medical need nor therapeutic benefit entitles these persons to medical services. Patients have a right to life-enhancing medical interventions because they subscribe to a health care plan which covers the procedure or because they are citizens of a country which maintains a functioning system of universal health care or for some other reason, but they do not have a right to medical services, or to any other external good, simply because they would have a better future if someone were to provide for their needs.

The potential future of value of the fetus is no less dependent upon favourable external circumstances. Since the fetus will become a person who has the capacity to enjoy its life and derive meaning from it only if it has access to the reproductive system of a woman, abortion would be presumptively wrong only if women had no presumptive right to control access to their reproductive systems. The fetus certainly needs its uterine environment if it is to realise its potential, but persons do not in general have a right to satisfy their needs at the expense of the autonomy, bodily integrity and wellbeing of another person. If I need a

bone marrow transplant in order to realise my potential future of value, I do not thereby gain a right to your bone marrow, even if you are my mother. Perhaps pregnancy creates more stringent duties than motherhood, but if so, an argument is needed to establish this claim, an argument notably absent from Marquis's presentation of the Future Like Ours argument.

A defender of FLO might object at this point that abortion kills the fetus and that killing a person does violate his or her rights in all but the most extreme circumstances, even if depriving him or her of life-sustaining services need not, but this is not a distinction that can be drawn within a potential future of value interpretation of FLO. Someone who has been killed and someone who has been denied access to life support have been deprived equally of their potential futures. The potential future of value interpretation fails because the moral premise if true implausibly entitles persons to welfare rights to valuable futures in addition to liberty rights not to be killed. A self-represented future of value interpretation is needed to distinguish between the right not to be killed and the right to valuable futures.

## II

The Future Like Ours argument would be valid if the expression "a future of value" consistently meant "a self-represented future of value." Substituting in, the argument would look like this: killing persons is presumptively wrong because it deprives them of their self-represented future; fetuses have self-represented futures; thus, killing fetuses is presumptively wrong. The first premise is plausible. At any moment a person can project a representation of a self which extends over time, a self understood from the perspective of the present, reconstructed from present remnants of the past and projected from the present into many possible futures. Persons care about their self-represented futures and their memories, their self-represented past, because this self-conception defines who they are and confers meaning and significance upon what they think and do. In contrast with potential futures, self-represented futures do not depend upon outside agencies for their realisation. The value of a self-represented future resides within the person herself, as a feature of a richly complex mental life. Killing a person deprives her of this future: her hopes and dreams are dashed, her goals unfulfilled, her sins unforgiven, longed for reunions and reconciliations never occur. All of this happens in the present, to a person able to unite in a moment of self-consciousness a personal past, present and future. One reason why killing persons violates their rights, but depriving them of life support need not, is that killing persons deprives them of a future and a past which is rightfully their own because it is something they themselves have created.

Even if killing a person is presumptively wrong because it deprives its victim of his self-represented future, this cannot be a reason why it is wrong to kill a fetus because the fetus does not construct mental representations of its future. The neurological and embryological evidence of this issue is clear.[5] Higher order cognitive functioning of the type implicated in planning and memory is dependent upon massive cortical/sub-cortical conductivity. Sub-cortical thalamic fibres first begin to form synapses with cortical neurons at about twenty-five weeks' gestation and only at some point well after birth does conductivity reach a critical threshold sufficient for self-awareness. A third trimester fetus may be sentient but there is no medical reason to think it is capable of self-consciousness.

The Future Like Ours argument rests upon two substantive claims: (1) killing persons is presumptively wrong because it deprives them of a future of value; and (2) fetuses have futures of value. The plausibility of the first claim depends upon the intuition that persons suffer significant harm when prevented from experiencing their self-represented future, but since the fetus does not represent its future it cannot be harmed in this way. The plausibility of the second claim depends upon the proposition that both the fetus and actual persons have a potential future of value, but unless one has a right to the conditions under which this potential can be realised, neither homicide nor abortion are presumptively wrong for this reason. The self-represented future of value interpretation underwrites the moral claim about the wrongness of homicide but militates against the metaphysical claim that persons and fetuses are relevantly similar; the potential future of value interpretation uncovers a genuine commonality between persons and fetuses but not one which can support the moral claim that abortion is presumptively seriously wrong. We may conclude that the Future Like Ours argument retains its force only if one equivocates on the concept of a future of value. . . .

### Notes

1. Marquis D. "Why abortion is immoral." *Journal of Philosophy* 1989, 86-4: 183–202.

2. See reference 1: 189, 190, 202.

3. Cudd A. "Sensationalized philosophy: a reply to Marquis's Why abortion is immoral." *The Journal of Philosophy* 1990;87,5: 262–4. Norcross A. "Killing, abortion, and contraception." *The Journal of Philosophy* 1990;87,5:268–77. Paske G. "Abortion and the neo-natal right to life: a critique of Marquis's futurist argument." In Pojman L, Beckwith F, eds. *The abortion controversy.* Boston: Jones and Bartlett, 1994: 343–53. Similar criticisms were levelled against FLO by an anonymous referee for this journal.

4. Here I draw upon Thomson JJ. "A defense of abortion." *Philosophy and Public Affairs* 1971;1,1:47–56, and the enormous literature this essay has elicited over the years.

5. Flower M. "Neuromaturation of the human fetus." *Journal of Medicine and Philosophy* 1985;10:237–51. Grobstein C. *Science and the unborn.* New York: Basic Books, 1988: 55, 130.

---

## READINGS

# Section 2: Feminist Perspectives

## Abortion Through a Feminist Ethic Lens

Susan Sherwin

Susan Sherwin sees the abortion controversy as part of the larger struggle for women's liberation. She argues that the power to control the incidence, timing, and frequency of childbearing is central to the control of most other things in a woman's life. Only the woman herself is in a position to weigh all the relevant factors necessary to determine whether abortion is the best response to the situation.

The fetus is morally significant, but its status is dependent upon its relation to the pregnant woman. Patterns of male sexual dominance mean that women often have little control over their sexual lives, and because women cannot rely on birth control alone to avoid pregnancy, abortion must be available if they are to be genuinely liberated from male dominance.

. . . [M]ost feminists believe that a pregnant woman is in the best position to judge whether abortion is the appropriate response to her circumstances. Since she is usually the only one able to weigh all the relevant factors, most feminists reject attempts to offer any general abstract rules for determining when abortion is morally justified . . . Although I think that it is possible for a woman to make a mistake in her judgment on this matter (i.e., it is possible that a woman may come to believe that she was wrong about her decision to continue or terminate a pregnancy), the intimate nature of this sort of decision makes it unlikely that anyone else is in a position to arrive at a more reliable conclusion; it is, therefore, improper to grant others the authority to interfere in women's decisions to seek abortions.

Feminist analysis regards the effects of unwanted pregnancies on the lives of women individually and collectively as a central element in the moral evaluation of abortion. Even without patriarchy, bearing a child would be a very important event in a woman's life. It involves significant physical, emotional, social, and (usually) economic changes for her. The ability to exert control over the incidence, timing, and frequency of childbearing is often tied to her ability to control most other things she values. Since we live in a patriarchal society, it is especially important to ensure that women have the authority to control their own reproduction. Despite the diversity of opinion among feminists on most other matters, virtually all feminists seem to agree that women must gain full control over their own reproductive lives if they are to free themselves from male dominance. Many perceive the commitment of the political right wing to opposing abortion as part of a general strategy to reassert patriarchal control over women in the face of significant feminist influence (Petchesky 1980, p. 112).

Women's freedom to choose abortion is also linked with their ability to control their own sexuality. Women's subordinate status often prevents them from refusing men sexual access to their bodies. If women cannot end the unwanted pregnancies that result from male sexual dominance, their sexual vulnerability to particular men can increase, because caring for an(other) infant involves greater financial needs and reduced economic opportunities for women. As a result, pregnancy often forces women to become dependent on men. Since a woman's dependence on a man is assumed to entail that she will remain sexually loyal to him, restriction of abortion serves to channel women's sexuality and further perpetuates the cycle of oppression.

In contrast to most non-feminist accounts, feminist analyses of abortion direct attention to the question of how women get pregnant. Those who reject abortion seem to believe that women can avoid unwanted pregnancies by avoiding sexual intercourse. Such views show little appreciation for the power of sexual politics in a culture that oppresses women. Existing patterns of sexual dominance mean that women often have little control over their sexual lives. They may be subject to rape by strangers, or by their husbands, boyfriends, colleagues, employers, customers, fathers, brothers, uncles, and dates. Often, the sexual coercion is not even recognized as such by the participants, but is the price of continued "good will"—popularity, economic survival, peace, or simple acceptance. Few women have not found themselves in circumstances where they do not feel free to refuse a man's demands for intercourse, either because he is holding a gun to her head or because he threatens to be emotionally hurt if she refuses (or both). Women are socialized to be compliant and accommodating, sensitive to the feelings of others, and frightened of physical power; men are socialized to take advantage of every opportunity to engage in sexual intercourse and to use sex to express dominance and power. Under such circumstances, it is difficult to argue that women could simply "choose" to avoid heterosexual activity if they wish to avoid pregnancy. Catherine MacKinnon neatly sums it up: "the logic by which women are supposed to consent to sex [is]: preclude the alternatives, then

Susan Sherwin, "Abortion Through a Feminist Ethic Lens," *Dialogue* 30, 1991, pp. 329-331, 334-335, 336, 338-339. (Notes omitted.)

call the remaining option 'her choice'" (MacKinnon 1989, p. 192).

Nor can women rely on birth control alone to avoid pregnancy. There simply is no form of reversible contraception available that is fully safe and reliable. The pill and the IUD are the most effective means offered, but both involve significant health hazards to women and are quite dangerous for some. No woman should spend the 30 to 40 years of her reproductive life on either form of birth control. Further, both have been associated with subsequent problems of involuntary infertility, so they are far from optimum for women who seek to control the timing of their pregnancies.

The safest form of birth control involves the use of barrier methods (condoms or diaphragms) in combination with spermicidal foams or jelly. But these methods also pose difficulties for women. They may be socially awkward to use: young women are discouraged from preparing for sexual activity that might never happen and are offered instead romantic models of spontaneous passion. (Few films or novels interrupt scenes of seduction for the fetching of contraceptives.) Many women find their male partners unwilling to use barrier methods of contraception and they do not have the power to insist. Further, cost is a limiting factor for many women. Condoms and spermicides are expensive and are not covered under most health care plans. There is only one contraceptive option which offers women safe and fully effective birth control: barrier methods with the back-up option of abortion.

From a feminist perspective, a central moral feature of pregnancy is that it takes place in *women's bodies* and has profound effects on *women's* lives. Gender-neutral accounts of pregnancy are not available; pregnancy is explicitly a condition associated with the female body. Because the need for abortion is experienced only by women, policies about abortion affect women uniquely. Thus, it is important to consider how proposed policies on abortion fit into general patterns of oppression for women. Unlike non-feminist accounts, feminist ethics demands that the effects on the oppression of women be a principal consideration when evaluating abortion policies. . . .

## A Feminist View of the Fetus

Because the public debate has been set up as a competition between the rights of women and those of fetuses, feminists have often felt pushed to reject claims of fetal value in order to protect women's claims. Yet, as Addelson (1987) has argued, viewing abortion in this way "tears [it] out of the context of women's lives" (p. 107). There are other accounts of fetal value that are more plausible and less oppressive to women.

On a feminist account, fetal development is examined in the context in which it occurs, within women's bodies rather than in the imagined isolation implicit in many theoretical accounts. Fetuses develop in specific pregnancies which occur in the lives of particular women. They are not individuals housed in generic female wombs, nor are they full persons at risk only because they are small and subject to the whims of women. Their very existence is relational, developing as they do within particular women's bodies, and their principal relationship is to the women who carry them.

On this view, fetuses are morally significant, but their status is relational rather than absolute. Unlike other human beings, fetuses do not have any independent existence; their existence is uniquely tied to the support of a specific other. Most non-feminist commentators have ignored the relational dimension of fetal development and have presumed that the moral status of fetuses could be resolved solely in terms of abstract metaphysical criteria of personhood. They imagine that there is some set of properties (such as genetic heritage, moral agency, self-consciousness, language use, or self-determination) which will entitle all who possess them to be granted the moral status of persons (Warren 1973, Tooley 1972). They seek some particular feature by which we can neatly divide the world into the dichotomy of moral persons (who are to be valued and protected) and others (who are not entitled to the same group privileges); it follows that it is a merely empirical question whether or not fetuses possess the relevant properties.

But this vision misinterprets what is involved in personhood and what it is that is especially valued about persons. Personhood is a social category, not an isolated state. Persons are members of a community; they develop as concrete, discrete, and specific individuals. To be a morally significant category, personhood must involve personality as well as biological integrity. It is not sufficient to consider persons simply as Kantian atoms of rationality; persons are all embodied, conscious beings with particular social histories. . . .

No human, and especially no fetus, can exist apart from relationships; feminists' views of what is valuable about persons must reflect the social nature of their existence. Fetal lives can neither be sustained nor destroyed without affecting the women who support them. Because of a fetus's unique physical status—*within* and dependent on a particular woman—the responsibility and privilege of determining its specific social status and value must rest with the woman carrying it. Fetuses are not persons because they have not developed sufficiently in social relationships to be persons in any morally significant sense (i.e., they are not yet second persons). Newborns, although just beginning their development into persons, are immediately subject to social relationships, for they are capable of communication and response in interaction with a variety of other persons. Thus, feminist accounts of abortion stress the importance of protecting women's right to continue as well as to terminate pregnancies as each sees fit.

## Feminist Politics and Abortion

. . . Feminist analysis addresses the context as well as the practice of abortion decisions. Thus, feminists also object to the conditions which lead women to abort wanted fetuses because there are not adequate financial and social supports available to care for a child. Because feminist accounts value fetuses that are wanted by the women who carry them, they oppose practices which force women to abort because of poverty or intimidation. Yet, the sorts of social changes necessary if we are to free women from having abortions out of economic necessity are vast; they include changes not only in legal and health-care policy, but also in housing, child care, employment, etc. (Petchesky 1980, p. 112). Nonetheless, feminist ethics defines reproductive freedom as the condition under which women are able to make truly voluntary choices about their reproductive lives, and these many dimensions are implicit in the ideal.

Clearly, feminists are not "pro-abortion," for they are concerned to ensure the safety of each pregnancy to the greatest degree possible; wanted fetuses should not be harmed or lost. Therefore, adequate pre- and post-natal care and nutrition are also important elements of any feminist position on reproductive freedom. Where anti-abortionists direct their energies to trying to prevent women from obtaining abortions, feminists seek to protect the health of wanted fetuses. They recognize that far more could be done to protect and care for fetuses if the state directed its resources at supporting women who continue their pregnancies, rather than draining away resources in order to police women who find that they must interrupt their pregnancies. Caring for the women who carry fetuses is not only a more legitimate policy than is regulating them; it is probably also more effective at insuring the health and well-being of more fetuses.

Feminist ethics also explores how abortion policies fit within the policies of sexual domination. Most feminists are sensitive to the fact that many men support women's right to abortion out of the belief that women will be more willing sexual partners if they believe they can readily terminate an unwanted pregnancy. Some men coerce their partners into obtaining abortions the women may not want. Feminists understand that many women oppose abortion for this very reason, being unwilling to support a practice that increases women's sexual vulnerability (Luker 1984, pp. 209–15). Thus, it is important that feminists develop a coherent analysis of reproductive freedom that includes sexual freedom (as women choose to define it). That requires an analysis of sexual freedom that includes women's right to refuse sex; such a right can only be assured if women have equal power to men and are not subject to domination by virtue of their sex.

In sum, then, feminist ethics demands that moral discussions of abortion be more broadly defined than they have been in most philosophic discussions. Only by reflecting on the meaning of ethical pronouncements on actual women's lives and the connections between judgments on abortion and the conditions of domination and subordination can we come to an adequate understanding of the moral status of abortion in our society. As Rosalind Petchesky (1980) argues, feminist discussion of abortion "must be moved beyond the framework of a 'woman's right to choose' and connected to a much broader revolutionary movement that addresses all of the conditions of women's liberation" (p. 113).

### References

Addelson, Kathryn Pyne. 1987. "Moral Passages." In *Women and Moral Theory*. Edited by Eva Feder Kittay and Diana T. Meyers. Totowa, NJ: Rowman & Littlefield.

Luker, Kristin. 1984. *Abortion and the Politics of Motherhood*. Berkeley: University of California Press.

MacKinnon, Catherine. 1989. *Toward a Feminist Theory of the State*. Cambridge, MA: Harvard University Press.

Petchesky, Rosalind Pollack. 1980. "Reproductive Freedom: Beyond 'A Woman's Right to Choose.'" In *Women: Sex and Sexuality*. Edited by Catharine R. Stimpson and Ethel Spector Person. Chicago: University of Chicago Press.

Tooley, Michael. 1972. "Abortion and Infanticide." *Philosophy and Public Affairs*, 2, 1 (Fall): 37–65.

Warren, Mary Anne. 1973. "On the Moral and Legal Status of Abortion." *The Monist*, 57: 43–61.

# A Case for Pro-life Feminism

## Sidney Callahan

Sidney Callahan offers four claims as representing the prochoice feminist case for the moral legitimacy of abortion: (1) the right to control one's body; (2) the necessity of autonomy in personal responsibility; (3) the value of fetal life is contingent on the mother's investment; (4) the right of women to social equality.

Callahan reviews the support for the claims, then argues against each. In her view, (1) the fetus is an immature form of human life, so the right to control one's body does not extend to using the power to end a dependent life; (2) a woman's status as a human owes as much to her connection with the human community and its implicit obligations as to personal autonomy. She further claims that (3) human life has intrinsic value from conception and is not dependent on the wants or decisions of others. Finally, Callahan contends (4) that for women to attain equality they need more social support and an increase in self-confidence and self-esteem. Women would benefit in these respects from a "feminization of sexuality" that rejects the aggressive male-orientation that has been harmful to women and children by promoting pornography, venereal disease, sexual abuse, adolescent pregnancy, divorce, and abortion.

The abortion debate continues. In the latest and perhaps most crucial development, pro-life feminists are contesting pro-choice feminist claims that abortion rights are prerequisites for women's full development and social equality. The outcome of this debate may be decisive for the culture as a whole. Pro-life feminists, like myself, argue on good feminist principles that women can never achieve the fulfillment of feminist goals in a society permissive toward abortion.

These new arguments over abortion take place within liberal political circles. This round of intense intra-feminist conflict has spiraled beyond earlier right-versus-left abortion debates, which focused on "tragic choices," medical judgments, and legal compromises. Feminist theorists of the pro-choice position now put forth the demand for unrestricted abortion rights as a moral imperative and insist upon women's right to complete reproductive freedom. They morally justify the present situation and current abortion practices. Thus it is all the more important that pro-life feminists articulate their different feminist perspective.

These opposing arguments can best be seen when presented in turn. Perhaps the most highly de-

From *Commonweal* 25, April 1986, pp. 232-238. Copyright © 1986 Commonweal Foundation. Reprinted by permission.

veloped feminist arguments for the morality and legality of abortion can be found in Beverly Wildung Harrison's *Our Right to Choose* (Beacon Press, 1983) and Rosalind Pollack Petchesky's *Abortion and Woman's Choice* (Longman, 1984). Obviously it is difficult to do justice to these complex arguments, which draw on diverse strands of philosophy and social theory and are often interwoven in pro-choice feminists' own version of a "seamless garment." Yet the fundamental feminist case for the morality of abortion, encompassing the views of Harrison and Petchesky, can be analyzed in terms of four central moral claims: (1) the moral right to control one's own body; (2) the moral necessity of autonomy and choice in personal responsibility; (3) the moral claim for the contingent value of fetal life; (4) the moral right of women to true social equality.

### 1. The Moral Right to Control One's Own Body

Pro-choice feminism argues that a woman choosing an abortion is exercising a basic right of bodily integrity granted in our common law tradition. If she does not choose to be physically involved in the demands of a pregnancy and birth, she should not be compelled to be so against her will. Just because it is her body which is involved, a woman should have the right to terminate any pregnancy, which at this point in medical history is tantamount to terminating fetal life. No one can be forced to donate an organ or submit to other invasive physical procedures for however good a cause. Thus no woman should be subjected to "compulsory pregnancy." And it should be noted that in pregnancy much more than a passive biological process is at stake.

## 2. The Moral Necessity of Autonomy and Choice in Personal Responsibility

Beyond the claim for individual *bodily* integrity, the pro-choice feminists claim that to be a full adult *morally,* a woman must be able to make responsible life commitments. To plan, choose, and exercise personal responsibility, one must have control of reproduction. A woman must be able to make yes or no decisions about a specific pregnancy, according to her present situation, resources, prior commitments and life plan. Only with such reproductive freedom can a woman have the moral autonomy necessary to make mature commitments, in the area of family, work, or education . . .

## 3. The Moral Claim for the Contingent Value of Fetal Life

Pro-choice feminist exponents like Harrison and Petchesky claim that the value of fetal life is contingent upon the woman's free consent and subjective acceptance. The fetus must be invested with maternal valuing in order to become human. This process of "humanization" through personal consciousness and "sociality" can only be bestowed by the woman in whose body and psychosocial system a new life must mature. The meaning and value of fetal life are constructed by the woman; without this personal conferral there only exists a biological, physiological process. Thus fetal interests or fetal rights can never outweigh the woman's prior interest and rights. If a woman does not consent to invest her pregnancy with meaning or value, then the merely biological process can be freely terminated. Prior to her own free choice and conscious investment, a woman cannot be described as a "mother" nor can a "child" be said to exist.

Moreover, in cases of voluntary pregnancy, a woman can withdraw consent if fetal genetic defects or some other problem emerges at any time before birth. Late abortion should thus be granted without legal restrictions. Even the minimal qualifications and

limitations on women embedded in *Roe* v. *Wade* are unacceptable—repressive remnants of patriarchal unwillingness to give power to women.

## 4. The Moral Right of Women to Full Social Equality

Women have a moral right to full social equality. They should not be restricted or subordinated because of their sex. But this morally required equality cannot be realized without abortion's certain control of reproduction. Female social equality depends upon being able to compete and participate as freely as males can in the structures of educational and economic life. If a woman cannot control when and how she will be pregnant or rear children, she is at a distinct disadvantage, especially in our male-dominated world.

Psychological equality and well-being is also at stake. Women must enjoy the basic right of a person to the free exercise of heterosexual intercourse and full sexual expression, separated from procreation. No less than males, women should be able to be sexually active without the constantly inhibiting fear of pregnancy. Abortion is necessary for women's sexual fulfillment and the growth of uninhibited feminine self-confidence and ownership of their sexual powers.

But true sexual and reproductive freedom means freedom to procreate as well as to inhibit fertility. Pro-choice feminists are also worried that women's freedom to reproduce will be curtailed through the abuse of sterilization and needless hysterectomies. Besides the punitive tendencies of a male-dominated health-care system, especially in response to repeated abortions or welfare pregnancies, there are other economic and social pressures inhibiting reproduction. Genuine reproductive freedom implies that day care, medical care, and financial support would be provided mothers, while fathers would take their full share in the burdens and delights of raising children.

Many pro-choice feminists identify feminist ideals with communitarian, ecologically sensitive approaches to reshaping society. Following theorists like Sara Ruddick and Carol Gilligan, they link abortion rights with the growth of "maternal thinking" in our heretofore patriarchal society. Maternal thinking is loosely defined as a responsible commitment to the loving nurture of specific human beings as they actually exist in socially embedded interpersonal contexts. It is a moral perspective very different from the abstract, competitive, isolated, and principled rigidity so characteristic of patriarchy.

How does a pro-life feminist respond to these arguments? Pro-life feminists grant the good intentions of their pro-choice counterparts but protest that the pro-choice position is flawed, morally inadequate, and inconsistent with feminism's basic demands for justice. Pro-life feminists champion a more encompassing moral ideal. They recognize the claims of fetal life and offer a different perspective on what is good for women. The feminist vision is expanded and refocused.

## 1. From the Moral Right to Control One's Own Body to a More Inclusive Ideal of Justice

The moral right to control one's own body does apply to cases of organ transplants, mastectomies, contraception, and sterilization; but it is not a conceptualization adequate for abortion. The abortion dilemma is caused by the fact that 266 days following a conception in one body, another body will emerge. One's own body no longer exists as a single unit but is engendering another organism's life. This dynamic passage from conception to birth is genetically ordered and universally found in the human species. Pregnancy is not like the growth of cancer or infestation by a biological parasite: it is the way every human being enters the world. Strained philosophical analogies fail to apply: having a baby is not like rescuing a drowning person, being hooked up to a famous violinist's artificial life-support system, donating organs for transplant—or anything else.

As embryology and fetology advance, it becomes clear that human development is a continuum. Just as astronomers are studying the first three minutes in the genesis of the universe, so the first moments, days, and weeks at the beginning of human life are the subject of increasing scientific attention. While neonatology pushes the definition of viability ever earlier, ultrasound and fetology expand the concept of the patient in utero. Within such a continuous growth process, it is hard to defend logically any demarcation point after conception as the point at which an immature form of human life is so different from the day before or the day after, that it can be morally or legally discounted as a non-person. Even the moment of birth can hardly differentiate a nine-month fetus from a newborn. It is not surprising that those who countenance late abortions are logically led to endorse selective infanticide.

The same legal tradition which in our society guarantees the right to control one's own body firmly recognizes the wrongfulness of harming other bodies, however immature, dependent, different looking, or powerless. The handicapped, the retarded, and newborns are legally protected from deliberate harm. Pro-life feminists reject the suppositions that would except the unborn from this protection.

After all, debates similar to those about the fetus were once conducted about feminine personhood. Just as women, or blacks, were considered too different, too underdeveloped, too "biological," to have souls or to possess legal rights, so the fetus is now seen as "merely" biological life, subsidiary to a person. A woman was once viewed as incorporated into the "one flesh" of her husband's person; she too was a form of bodily property. In all patriarchal unjust systems, lesser orders of human life are granted rights only when wanted, chosen, or invested with value by the powerful.

Fortunately, in the course of civilization there has been a gradual realization that justice demands the powerless and dependent be protected against the uses of power wielded unilaterally. No human can be treated as a means to an end without consent. The fetus is an immature, dependent form of human life which only needs time and protection to develop. Surely, immaturity and dependence are not crimes.

In an effort to think about the essential requirements of a just society, philosophers like John Rawls recommend imagining yourself in an "original position," in which your position in the society to be created is hidden by a "veil of ignorance." You will have to weigh the possibility that any inequalities inherent in that society's practices may rebound upon you in the worst, as well as in the best, conceivable way. This thought experiment helps ensure justice for all.

Beverly Harnson argues that in such an envisioning of society everyone would institute abortion rights in order to guarantee that if one turned out to be a woman one would have reproductive freedom. But surely in the original position and behind the "veil of ignorance," you would have to contemplate the possibility of being the particular fetus to be aborted. Since everyone has passed through the fetal stage of development, it is false to refuse to imagine oneself in this state when thinking about a potential world in which justice would govern. Would it be just that an embryonic life—in half the cases, of course, a female life—be sacrificed to the right of a woman's control over her own body? A woman may be pregnant without consent and experience a great many penalties, but a fetus killed without consent pays the ultimate penalty. . . .

As the most recent immigrants from non-person-hood, feminists have traditionally fought for justice for themselves and the world. Women rally to feminism as a new and better way to live. Rejecting male aggression and destruction, feminists seek alternative, peaceful, ecologically sensitive means to resolve conflicts while respecting human potentiality. It is a chilling inconsistency to see pro-choice feminists demanding continued access to assembly-line, technological methods of fetal killing—the vacuum aspirator, prostaglandins, and dilation and evacuation. It is a betrayal of feminism, which has built the struggle for justice on the bedrock of women's empathy. After all, "maternal thinking" receives its name from a mother's unconditional acceptance and nurture of dependent, immature life. It is difficult to develop concern for women, children, the poor and the dispossessed—and to care about peace—and at the same time ignore fetal life.

## 2. From the Necessity of Autonomy and Choice in Personal Responsibility to an Expanded Sense of Responsibility

A distorted idea of morality overemphasizes individual autonomy and active choice. Morality has often been viewed too exclusively as a matter of human agency and decisive action. In moral behavior persons must explicitly choose and aggressively exert their wills to intervene in the natural and social environments. The human will dominates the body, overcomes the given, breaks out of the material limits of nature. Thus if one does not choose to be pregnant or cannot rear a child, who must be given up for adoption, then better to abort the pregnancy. Willing, planning, choosing one's moral commitments through the contracting of one's individual resources becomes the premier model of moral responsibility.

But morality also consists of the good and worthy acceptance of the unexpected events that life presents. Responsiveness and responsibility to things unchosen are also instances of the highest human moral capacity. Morality is not confined to contracted agreements of isolated individuals. Yes, one is obligated by explicit contracts freely initiated, but human beings are also obligated by implicit compacts and involuntary relationships in which persons simply find themselves. To be embedded in a family, a neighborhood, a social system, brings moral obligations which were never entered into with informed consent.

Parent–child relationships are one instance of implicit moral obligations arising by virtue of our being part of the interdependent human community. A woman, involuntarily pregnant, has a moral obligation to the now-existing dependent fetus whether she explicitly consented to its existence or not. No pro-life feminist would dispute the forceful observations of pro-choice feminists about the extreme difficulties that bearing an unwanted child in our society can entail. But the stronger force of the fetal claim presses a woman to accept these burdens; the fetus possesses rights arising from its extreme need and the interdependency and unity of human kind. The woman's moral obligation arises both from her status as a human being embedded in the interdependent human community and her unique life-giving female reproductive power. To follow the pro-choice feminist ideology of insistent individualistic autonomy and control is to betray a fundamental basis of the moral life.

## 3. From the Moral Claim of the Contingent Value of Fetal Life to the Moral Claim for the Intrinsic Value of Human Life

The feminist pro-choice position which claims that the value of the fetus is contingent upon the pregnant woman's bestowal—or willed, conscious "construction"—of humanhood is seriously flawed. The inadequacies of this position flow from the erroneous premises (1) that human value and rights can be granted by individual will; (2) that the individual woman's consciousness can exist and operate in an *a priori* isolated fashion; and (3) that "mere" biological, genetic human life has little meaning. Pro-life feminism takes a very different stance to life and nature.

Human life from the beginning to the end of development *has* intrinsic value, which does not depend on meeting the selective criteria or tests set up by powerful others. A fundamental humanist assumption is at stake here. Either we are going to value embodied human life and humanity as a good thing, or take some variant of the nihilist position that assumes human life is just one more random occurrence in the universe such that each instance of human life must explicitly be justified to prove itself worthy to continue. When faced with a new life, or an involuntary pregnancy, there is a world of difference in whether one first asks, "Why continue?" or "Why not?" Where is the burden of proof going to rest? The concept of "compulsory pregnancy" is as distorted as labeling life "compulsory aging."

In a sound moral tradition, human rights arise from human needs, and it is the very nature of a right, or valid claim upon another, that it cannot be denied, conditionally delayed, or rescinded by more powerful others at their behest. It seems fallacious to hold that in the case of the fetus it is the pregnant woman alone who gives or removes its right to life and human status solely through her subjective conscious investment or "humanization." Surely no pregnant woman (or any other individual member of the species) has created her own human nature by an individually willed act of consciousness, nor for that matter been able to guarantee her own human rights. An individual woman and the unique individual embryonic life within her can only exist because of their participation in the genetic inheritance of the human species as a whole. Biological life should never be discounted. Membership in the species, or collective human family, is the basis for human solidarity, equality, and natural human rights.

## 4. The Moral Right of Women to Full Social Equality from a Pro-life Feminist Perspective

Pro-life feminists and pro-choice feminists are totally agreed on the moral right of women to the full social equality so far denied them. The disagreement between them concerns the definition of the desired goal and the best means to get there. Permissive abortion laws do not bring women reproductive freedom, social equality, sexual fulfillment, or full personal development. . . .

Women's rights and liberation are pragmatically linked to fetal rights because to obtain true equality, women need (1) more social support and changes in the structure of society, and (2) increased self-confidence, self-expectations, and self-esteem. Society in general, and men in particular, have to provide women more support in rearing the next generation, or our devastating feminization of poverty will continue. But if a woman claims the right to decide by herself whether the fetus becomes a child or not, what does this do to paternal and communal responsibility? Why should men share responsibility for child support or childrearing if they cannot share in what is asserted to be the woman's sole decision? Furthermore, if explicit intentions and consciously accepted contracts are necessary for moral obligations, why should men be held responsible for what *they* do not voluntarily choose to happen? By pro-choice reasoning, a man who does not want to have a child, or whose contraceptive fails, can be exempted from the responsibilities of fatherhood and child support. Traditionally, many men have been laggards in assuming parental responsibility and support for their children;

ironically, ready abortion, often advocated as a response to male dereliction, legitimizes male irresponsibility and paves the way for even more male detachment and lack of commitment.

For that matter, why should the state provide a system of day-care or child support, or require workplaces to accommodate women's maternity and the needs of childrearing? Permissive abortion, granted in the name of women's privacy and reproductive freedom, ratifies the view that pregnancies and children are a woman's private individual responsibility. More and more frequently, we hear some versions of this old rationalization: if she refuses to get rid of it, it's her problem. A child becomes a product of the individual woman's freely chosen investment, a form of private property resulting from her own cost–benefit calculation. The larger community is relieved of moral responsibility.

With legal abortion freely available, a clear cultural message is given: conception and pregnancy are no longer serious moral matters. With abortion as an acceptable alternative, contraception is not as responsibly used; women take risks, often at the urging of male sexual partners. Repeat abortions increase, with all their psychological and medical repercussions. With more abortion there is more abortion. Behavior shapes thought as well as the other way round. One tends to justify morally what one has done; what becomes commonplace and institutionalized seems harmless. Habituation is a powerful psychological force. Psychologically it is also true that whatever is avoided becomes more threatening; in phobias it is the retreat from anxiety-producing events which reinforces future avoidance. Women begin to see themselves as too weak to cope with involuntary pregnancies. Finally, through the potency of social pressure and the force of inertia, it becomes more and more difficult, in fact almost unthinkable, not to use abortion to solve problem pregnancies. Abortion becomes no longer a choice but a "necessity." . . .

Fully accepting our bodies as ourselves, what should women want? I think women will only flourish when there is a feminization of sexuality, very different from the current cultural trend toward masculinizing female sexuality. Women can never have the self-confidence and self-esteem they need to achieve feminist goals in society until a more holistic, feminine model of sexuality becomes the dominant cultural ethos. To say this affirms the view that men and women differ in the domain of sexual functioning, although they are more alike than different in other personality characteristics and competencies. For those of us committed to achieving sexual equality in the culture, it may be hard to accept the fact that sexual differences make it imperative to talk of distinct male and female models of sexuality. But if one wants to change sexual roles, one has to recognize pre-existing conditions. A great deal of evidence is accumulating which points to biological pressures for different male and female sexual functioning.

Males always and everywhere have been more physically aggressive and more likely to fuse sexuality with aggression and dominance. Females may be more variable in their sexuality, but since Masters and Johnson, we know that women have a greater capacity than men for repeated orgasm and a more tenuous path to arousal and orgasmic release. Most obviously, women also have a far greater sociobiological investment in the act of human reproduction. On the whole, women as compared to men possess a sexuality which is more complex, more intense, more extended in time, involving higher investment, risks, and psychosocial involvement.

Considering the differences in sexual functioning, it is not surprising that men and women in the same culture have often constructed different sexual ideals. In Western culture, since the nineteenth century at least, most women have espoused a version of sexual functioning in which sex acts are embedded within deep emotional bonds and secure long-term commitments. Within these committed "pair bonds" males assume parental obligations. In the idealized Victorian version of the Christian sexual ethic, culturally endorsed and maintained by women, the double standard was not countenanced. Men and women did not need to marry to be whole persons, but if they did engage in sexual functioning, they were to be equally chaste, faithful, responsible, loving, and parentally concerned. Many of the most influential women in the nineteenth-century women's movement preached and lived this sexual ethic, often by the side of exemplary feminist men. While the ideal has never been universally obtained, a culturally dominant demand for monogamy, self-control, and emotionally bonded and committed sex works well for women in every stage of their sexual life cycles. When love, chastity, fidelity, and commitment for better or worse are the ascendant cultural prerequisites for sexual functioning, young girls and women expect protection from rape and seduction, adult women justifiably demand male support in childrearing, and older women are more protected from abandonment as their biological attractions wane. . . .

In pro-choice feminism, a permissive, erotic view of sexuality is assumed to be the only option. Sexual intercourse with a variety of partners is seen as "inevitable" from a young age and as a positive growth experience to be managed by access to contraception and abortion. Unfortunately, the pervasive cultural conviction that adolescents, or their elders, cannot exercise sexual self-control, undermines the responsible use of contraception. When a pregnancy occurs, the first abortion is viewed in some pro-choice circles as a *rite de passage.* Responsibly choosing an abortion supposedly ensures that a young woman will take charge of her own life, make her own decisions, and carefully practice contraception. But the social dynamics of a permissive, erotic model of sexuality, coupled with permissive laws, work toward repeat abortions. Instead of being empowered by their abortion choices young women having abortions are confronting the debilitating reality of *not* bringing a baby into the world; *not* being able to count on a committed male partner; *not* accounting oneself strong enough, or the master of enough resources, to avoid killing the fetus. Young women are hardly going to develop the self-esteem, self-discipline, and self-confidence necessary to confront a male-dominated society through abortion.

The male-oriented sexual orientation has been harmful to women and children. It has helped bring us epidemics of venereal disease, infertility, pornography, sexual abuse, adolescent pregnancy, divorce, displaced older women, and abortion. Will these signals of something amiss stimulate pro-choice feminists to rethink what kind of sex ideal really serves women's best interests? While the erotic model cannot encompass commitment, the committed model can—happily—encompass and encourage romance, passion, and playfulness. In fact, within the security of long-term commitments, women may be more likely to experience sexual pleasure and fulfillment. . . .

New feminist efforts to rethink the meaning of sexuality, femininity, and reproduction are all the more vital as new techniques for artificial reproduction, surrogate motherhood, and the like present a whole new set of dilemmas. In the long run, the very long run, the abortion debate may be merely the opening round in a series of far-reaching struggles over the role of human sexuality and the ethics of reproduction. Significant changes in the culture, both positive and negative in outcome, may begin as local storms of controversy. We may be at one of those vaguely realized thresholds when we had best come to full attention. What kind of people are we going to be? Pro-life feminists pursue a vision for their sisters, daughters, and granddaughters. Will their great-granddaughters be grateful?

# Section 3: Late-Term Abortion

## Thomson, the Right to Life, and Partial-Birth Abortion

### Peter Alward

Peter Alward argues that J. J. Thomson's attempt to reconcile a woman's right to an abortion with the fetus's right to life does not establish the "robust right to abortion" usually assumed. Thomson argues (see her article "A Defense of Abortion" in Section 1) that if a woman becomes pregnant without her consent, the fetus does not have a right to the continued use of her body, even if it needs it to survive.

Alward claims that, on this view, granting the fetus has a right to life, an abortion that involves depriving the fetus of what it needs to survive that belongs to it (and not to the woman) is morally impermissible. Thus, a common technique used in late-term abortion (suctioning out the brain) is ruled out, as are abortions involving feticide. Thomson's argument, accordingly, does not establish as much as has been claimed for it.

I have always found Judith Jarvis Thomson's arguments in "A Defense of Abortion" to be very persuasive.[1] I have even been convinced of her most controversial conclusion, that the termination of a pregnancy which resulted from contraceptive failure is morally permissible, even if the fetus is a person with a full right to life. But recently, as I taught Thomson's article to a group of undergraduates for the nth time, it occurred to me that there is a worrisome gap in her argument. In particular, I have come to believe that it follows from Thomson's own principles that employing an abortion technique which does not merely remove the fetus from the womb, but which more directly kills it, is morally impermissible, even if removing it from the womb would have otherwise caused its death. If this is right, then Thomson must conclude that many abortion techniques commonly in use today are morally impermissible, at least when the pregnant woman's life is not at stake.

## I

Thomson's defence of abortion rights proceeds as follows. Suppose someone wakes up to find that, while asleep, she has been attached to a famous violinist

Reprinted from *Journal of Medical Ethics*, 28, no. 2 (April 2002), pp. 99–101, with permission from the BMJ Publishing Group.

whose circulatory system has been plugged into hers. He needs to remain attached to the woman for nine months, and if unplugged in the interim, will die. Thomson argues that despite the fact that continued use of the woman's body is the bare minimum the violinist needs to survive, the violinist lacks the right to such use. After all, the woman did not consent to being used in this way. As a result, she would not violate the violinist's right to life by unplugging him. Thomson points out that this situation is relevantly analogous to one in which a woman has become pregnant, without consenting to being in such a state. And she concludes on this basis that the fetus does not have the right to continued use of the woman's body despite the fact that it is the bare minimum the fetus needs to survive, even if the fetus is a full moral person with a full right to life. The pregnant woman would not violate this right if she had an abortion in such circumstances.

## II

One way to cause a person's death is to deprive her of the bare minimum she needs to survive. There are, of course, two ways to go about doing this: discontinuing a person's receipt of what she needs, and refraining from providing her with the same in the first place. So, for example, if Sarah needed to be hooked up to a respirator in order to survive, one could cause her death either by disconnecting her from the respirator after she had already been hooked up to it, or by refraining from connecting her to it in the first place.

According to Thomson, one violates a person's right to life by causing her death in this way only if she was entitled to the bare minimum she needed to survive. (Thomson argues that even if a person were not entitled to what she needed, it might still be morally reprehensible, albeit not unjust, to cause her death by depriving her of it. In particular, it would be reprehensible if providing for her needs would only require that one behave as a "minimally decent samaritan." For present purposes, I am going to restrict my attention to cases in which much greater sacrifices are required.) We never get from Thomson a precise account of the conditions which have to [be] met in order for someone to be entitled to the bare minimum she needs, but there are certain tolerably clear cases:

Case #1: Suppose Sarah needs to be hooked up to a respirator in order to survive, and suppose Sarah owns the respirator. In these circumstances, Sarah would be entitled to the bare minimum she needs to survive and to deprive her of it would be to violate her right to life.

Case #2: Suppose Sarah needs to be hooked up to a respirator in order to survive, and suppose Fred owns the respirator. Suppose that Fred freely enters into an agreement with Sarah to provide her with the use of the respirator for as long as she needs it. In these circumstances, Sarah would be entitled to the use of the respirator, at least as long as she keeps up her side of the bargain.

Case # 3: Suppose Sarah needs to be hooked up to a respirator in order to survive, and suppose Fred owns the respirator. Suppose that Fred has entered into no agreement with Sarah to provide her with the use of the respirator, and has engaged in no behaviour which could constitute tacit consent to her use of it. In such circumstances, Sarah would not be entitled to the use of the respirator, and even if depriving her of it caused her death, doing so would not violate her right to life.

The hard cases are those in which the owner of the needed goods in some sense tacitly consents to their use by those in need. It's not entirely clear whether Sarah would be entitled to the use of Fred's respirator if, for example, Fred carelessly left it on Mary's front lawn for a couple of days and Sarah proceeded to connect herself to it in the interim. But I do think that Thomson has made a good case for thinking that a woman who gets pregnant as a result of contraceptive failure has not given tacit consent to the fetus for use of her body, and hence the fetus is not entitled to such use.

## III

Things are, as always, however, more complicated than they seem at first glance. A person typically (always?) needs many things to survive, and to deprive someone of any one of these things would cause her death. Suppose, for example, that Sarah needed to be hooked up to both a respirator and a dialysis machine in order to survive. In such circumstances, one could cause Sarah's death either by depriving her of the use of the respirator or by depriving her of the use of the dialysis machine.

As above, one violates Sarah's right to life by causing her death by one of these means only if she was entitled to the use of the machine of which she was deprived. Now it might turn out that Sarah is entitled to the use of one of the machines but not the other. After all, she might own the dialysis machine while Fred owns the respirator (and has made no agreement with Sarah allowing her to use it). Or Fred might own both machines, but has agreed to allow Sarah to use only the dialysis machine. And if either scenario were true, causing Sarah's death by depriving her of the dialysis machine would violate her right to life, whereas causing her death by depriving her of the respirator does not violate her rights.

## IV

Now let's suppose that Sarah is currently hooked up to both the respirator and the dialysis machine, and if either machine is disconnected, she will die. As before, let's suppose Sarah is entitled to the use of the dialysis machine but not entitled to the use of the respirator. And let's suppose that Fred decides to retrieve the respirator, denying Sarah continued use of it, as he is well within his rights to do. (As before, we'll assume that allowing Sarah continued use of the respirator would require more of Fred than minimally decent samaritanhood.) Broadly speaking, there are four procedures (of interest, for present purposes) by means of which he (or his agent) might go about doing this:

Procedure #1: First, Fred detaches Sarah from the respirator. (Fred leaves her connected to the dialysis machine.) Second, Sarah dies.

Procedure #2: First, Fred detaches Sarah from the respirator. Second, he detaches her from the dialysis machine. Third, Sarah dies.

Procedure #3: First, Fred detaches Sarah from the respirator. Second, Sarah dies. Third, Fred detaches Sarah from the dialysis machine.

Procedure #4: First, Fred detaches Sarah from the dialysis machine. Second, he detaches her from the respirator. Third, Sarah dies. (Note: it does not matter if the order of steps two and three is reversed.)

What I want to do now is to consider a number of cases. These cases differ in the procedures available to Fred. I am, for now, going to assume that none of these procedures will be more or less beneficial or detrimental to Fred's health (or general wellbeing) than any other, and that his life and/or health will not be at risk if he fails to retrieve the respirator.

Case #1: All four procedures are available to Fred. Nothing is preventing Fred retrieving his respirator by means of any procedure he chooses.

In these circumstances, it is fairly clear that Fred ought to use procedure #1 to retrieve his respirator. The use of procedures #2 and #4 would violate Sarah's right to life and so ought to be avoided. Procedure #3 would not involve a violation of Sarah's right to life because she would be detached from the dialysis machine only after she was dead. But Fred does not need to disconnect Sarah from the dialysis machine in order to retrieve the respirator (procedure #1 is available after all). And there may be other moral grounds for refraining from doing so, such as its being disrespectful of the dead.

Case #2: Procedure #1 is unavailable to Fred. Procedures #2–4 are available. He can detach Sarah from the respirator without detaching her from the dialysis machine, but he cannot retrieve the respirator without detaching her from the dialysis machine as well. (Let's suppose that the tubes and wires are inextricably tangled.)

In these circumstances, it is fairly clear that it is permissible for Fred to use only procedure #3. Once again, procedures #2 and #4 would violate Sarah's right to life and should be avoided. One might argue that since procedure #3 is permissible, procedure #2 is permissible as well. After all, the only difference is that you kill someone who is going to die very soon in any event. But this is akin to claiming that the deathbed homicide of a rich heiress would be permissible because she is, well, on her deathbed.

Case #3: Procedures #1–3 are unavailable. Only procedure #4 is available.

In these circumstances, it would be impermissible for Fred to retrieve his respirator from Sarah. To do so would violate her right to life and, other things being equal, a right to life outweighs any property right. Now it could be argued that the claim that the right to life outweighs property rights entails that property could be taken away from people to save lives. One might resist by claiming that it is only the negative right to life that outweighs property rights. But even if this manoeuvre is ultimately unsatisfactory, this implication should not worry us too much. After all, it would come into play only if the only way to save lives involved seizing private property. Moreover, considerations of justice would presumably prevent too great a burden in this regard from falling on any single property owner.

It is worth noting how this relates back to the issue of abortion. Fred is intended to be analogous to the pregnant woman and the respirator is analogous to the pregnant woman's womb. Sarah is meant to be analogous to the fetus and the dialysis machine is analogous to the internal organs of the fetus. The fetus needs both continued use of the pregnant woman's womb and continued proper functioning of its organs in order to survive. I in no way mean to suggest that the pregnant woman's womb is in any sense property of the fetus.

## V

But now let's suppose that these procedures are not equal with respect to Fred's wellbeing: some of them are more detrimental to Fred's health than others. To make this concrete, let's suppose that Fred's respirator is a double and that both he and Sarah are hooked up to it. Moreover, let's suppose all four procedures are available to Fred, but (a) procedure #1 is complicated and likely to damage the respirator and (b) the only way to implement procedure #3 would involve shutting down the respirator, which would likely result in Fred's death as well as Sarah's.

The first thing to note is that unless Fred's life or health is at serious risk, none of this makes any difference. Remember, Fred has a fifth choice: he can always leave Sarah attached to the respirator. And unless leaving Sarah attached poses a serious risk to Fred's life, the fact that procedures #1 and #3 would pose a serious risk does not give good ground for using procedure #2 or #4, and thereby violating Sarah's right to life.

But what if leaving Sarah attached to the respirator did pose an imminent risk to Fred's life? In my view, Thomson has successfully defended the thesis that one can in self defence violate the right to life of an innocent person. (If one finds the notion of a morally permissible violation of rights unpalatable, we can speak instead of the performance of an act that in ordinary circumstances would involve a violation of rights.) And if this is right, then it would clearly be permissible for Fred to use procedure #2 or #4 to disconnect Sarah, given the risks involved in using either of the other procedures, or in leaving Sarah attached to the respirator.

## VI

Consider now the procedure used in interuterine cranial decompression abortions (or ICD abortions), popularly, and notoriously, referred to as "partial birth" abortions.

1. the cervix is dilated;

2. the fetus is partially removed from the womb, feet first;

3. a sharp object is inserted into the back of the fetus's head and then removed;

4. a vacuum tube is inserted through the resulting hole and the brain is removed;

5. the head of the fetus contracts, allowing the fetus to be more easily removed from the womb, and the fetus then is removed.

Clearly, this procedure is a variation of procedure #4 discussed above. The fetus needs both the use of the pregnant woman's body and a functioning brain in order to survive. And while depriving the fetus of continued use of the woman's body would not violate its right to life (unless the woman has in some way consented to this use), depriving the fetus of a functioning brain would constitute a violation of its right to life. After all, if anything is the property of a person, his or her brain is. (If one objects to taking a person's bodily organs to be her property, the argument can be recast in terms of a right to bodily integrity. While this would make the analogy with the case of Fred and Sarah weaker, the argument would still retain its plausibility.) And so the ICD procedure deprives the fetus of something which the fetus needs and to which it is entitled, before depriving it of use of the woman's body to which it lacks entitlement. The upshot is that, if we accept Thomson's defence of abortion, the ICD abortion technique is morally impermissible unless the life or health of the pregnant woman is a serious risk and any other alternatives pose a serious danger as well.

But suppose that the fetus is going to die anyhow and available alternative procedures subject the pregnant woman to greater risks. In such circumstances utilitarian considerations would incline in favour of the ICD procedure. There are two comments I wish to make regarding this point. First, at best it would permit only limited use of the ICD procedure. And second, it is far from clear that utilitarian considerations justify violating the right to life of even a dying person.

Now one might argue that this is all moot: given that ICD abortions are performed late in pregnancy (during the fifth month of gestation or later), Thomson's own commitments imply that it is impermissible. There are (at least) three ways one might argue from Thomson's commitments to the conclusion that ICD abortions are impermissible. First, one might argue that by refraining from having an abortion for five months, the pregnant woman has tacitly consented to the fetus's continued use of her body. And hence, an abortion by any means would be impermissible. But even if you think a woman could give tacit consent in this way, there are obvious cases in which a pregnant woman who waits at least five months before having an abortion clearly has not done so. Consider, for example, a poor woman in a state in which there is no public funding for abortions, there are no nearby abortion clinics, and there is a 24 hour waiting period for having an abortion. Refraining from getting an abortion because your circumstances make it very difficult for you to do so could not plausibly be considered to suffice for tacit consent of the relevant sort.

Second, one might argue that even though ICD abortions do not involve a violation of the fetus's right to life, once one is in the late stages of pregnancy, carrying a fetus to term requires only minimally decent samaritanism of the pregnant woman. Thomson says: "[it] would be indecent in the woman to request an abortion, and indecent in the doctor to perform it, if she is in her seventh month, and wants the abortion just to avoid the nuisance of postponing a trip abroad."[2] And, hence, an abortion by any means at this late date would be impermissible (or at least indecent). The trouble here, of course, it that it is far from clear that carrying a fetus to term for as long as four months requires only minimally decent samaritanism of the pregnant woman. And, of course, it is far from clear that it requires only minimally decent samaritanism of women who have more serious reasons for wanting an abortion, even if continuing the pregnancy does not pose a serious risk to life or health.

And third, Thomson argues only for a right to have an abortion and not for a right to secure the death of a fetus.[2] And so long as there is an alternative procedure which would allow the fetus to survive outside the womb, an ICD abortion is impermissible. And given that ICD abortions occur late in pregnancy, there is an alternative procedure: remove the fetus by caesarean section and place it in an incubator. But what Thomson fails to note is that even if there is no procedure which would allow the fetus to survive outside the womb (and, arguably, at five months there is no procedure which would reliably do so), or if the only such procedure subjected the pregnant woman to serious risks, an ICD abortion would still be impermissible (unless, of course, continuing the pregnancy was, itself, to risk serious harm).

## VII

The upshot of all of this seems to be that, if one accepts Thomson's defence of abortion, how an abortion is performed makes a moral difference. If the pregnant woman's life is not at stake, then, no procedure which causes the fetus's death by any means except its removal from the woman's body is morally permissible. And, as we have seen, this implies that the ICD abortion procedure is morally impermissible. Moreover, similar considerations rule out all late abortions involving feticide. Now, of course, such restrictions are simply unacceptable to people who want to defend robust abortion rights. But I think it is clear that Thomson's strategy will not yield a ground for such a robust right. Unless some other approach can be found for reconciling the fetus's putative right to life with robust abortion rights, the personhood issue must be faced head on.

### References

1. Thomson JJ. "A defense of abortion." [See above.] Originally published in *Philosophy and Public Affairs* 1971; 1:47–66.
2. See reference 1: *Philosophy and Public Affairs:* 65.

## Decision Scenario 1

For months doctors told eleven-year-old Visna (as we'll call her) and her parents that her abdominal pains were nothing but indigestion. Then in July 1998 the truth finally emerged—Visna was twenty-seven weeks pregnant.

Visna's family had emigrated from India to the Detroit suburb of Sterling Heights, Michigan, only the previous summer. Her parents found factory jobs and rented a two-bedroom apartment, and Visna shared one of the rooms with Hari, her sixteen-year-old brother. Sometime during the winter after their arrival in the United States, Visna told her parents that Hari had raped her, but this emerged only after Visna, who had turned twelve, was found to be pregnant.

As soon as Visna's parents learned her condition, they made plans to take her to Kansas for an abortion. Visna would have to have a late-term abortion, and because Michigan law bans almost all abortions after twenty-four weeks, her family would have to take her out of state. But their plans were frustrated when they were leaked to a family court judge. Charges of

parental negligence were filed by prosecutors against her parents, and the court immediately removed Visna from her family and made her a ward of the state.

At a court hearing, Visna's doctor argued that if her pregnancy were allowed to continue, it could cause her both physical and psychological damage. A psychologist testified that, because Visna was a Hindu, if she were forced to have an illegitimate child, it would make her unfit for marriage by another Hindu. Her parents also expressed their worry that if Visna had a child, the child might suffer from genetic abnormalities and, in particular, might be mentally retarded, because her brother was the father.

At the end of the hearing, the prosecution announced it was convinced pregnancy might endanger Visna's life and dropped the negligence charge against her parents. Visna was reunited with her family, and her parents pursued their original plan of taking her to Kansas. In Wichita, Dr. George Tiller, who had been shot in 1993 by a prolife activist, stopped the fetus's heart and used drugs to induce labor, thus performing a "partial-birth" abortion.

1. Why does Alward believe Thomson's argument fails to establish the moral legitimacy of late-term abortion?

2. Would Callahan's "prolife feminist" position permit abortion in a case like Visna's?

3. Could Sherwin's feminist position on abortion justify a general policy of late-term abortion?

4. Can grounds be found in Marquis's view of abortion for allowing late-term abortions?

5. Although late-term abortions may present no problem for Warren, infanticide might. Are there circumstances in which Warren would allow infanticide?

---

## Decision Scenario 2

It happened after a concert. Sixteen-year-old Mary Pluski had gone with three of her friends to hear Bruce Springsteen at Chicago's Blanton Auditorium. After the concert, in a crowd estimated at 11,000, Mary became separated from the other three girls. She decided that the best thing to do was to meet them at the car.

But when she got to the eight-story parking building, Mary realized she wasn't sure what level they had parked on. She thought it might be somewhere in the middle so she started looking on the fourth floor. While she was walking down the aisles of cars, two men in their early twenties, one white and the other black, stopped her and asked if she was having some kind of trouble.

Mary explained the situation to them, and one of the men suggested that they get his car and drive around inside the parking building. Mary hesitated, but both seemed so polite and genuinely concerned to help that she decided to go with them.

Once they were in the car, however, the situation changed. They drove out of the building and toward the South Side. Mary pleaded with them to let her out of the car. Then, some seven miles from the auditorium, the driver stopped the car in a dark area behind a vacant building. Mary was then raped by both men.

Mary was treated at Allenworth Hospital and released into the custody of her parents. She filed a complaint with the police, but her troubles were not yet over. Two weeks after she missed her menstrual period, tests showed that Mary was pregnant.

"How do you feel about having this child?" asked Sarah Ruben, the Pluski family physician.

"I hate the idea," Mary said. "I feel guilty about it, though. I mean, it's not the child's fault."

"Let me ask a delicate question," said Dr. Ruben. "I know from what you've told me before that you and your boyfriend have been having sex. Can you be sure this pregnancy is not really the result of that?"

Mary shook her head. "Not really. I use my diaphragm, but I know it doesn't give a hundred percent guarantee."

"That's right. Now, does it make any difference to you who the father might be, so far as a decision about terminating the pregnancy is concerned?"

"If I were sure it was Bob, I guess the problem would be even harder," Mary said.

"There are some tests we can use to give us that information," Dr. Ruben said. "But that would mean waiting for the embryo to develop into a fetus. It would be easier and safer to terminate the pregnancy now."

Mary started crying. "I don't want a child," she said. "I don't want any child. I don't care who's the father. It was forced on me, and I want to get rid of it."

"I'll make the arrangements," said Dr. Ruben.

1. What reasons would Sherwin offer in defense of Mary Pluski's right to have an abortion?

2. Would Noonan consider abortion immoral in this case?

3. Suppose the fetus is a person; would the maxim in this case satisfy the categorical imperative?

4. Does Mary's uncertainty about the father add any special moral difficulties?

5. Would Marquis consider abortion immoral in this case? Why does Brown think Marquis's argument fails?

## Decision Scenario 3

Clare Macwurter was twenty-two years old chronologically, but mentally she remained a child. As a result of her mother's prolonged and difficult labor, Clare had been deprived of an adequate blood–oxygen supply during her birth. The consequence was that she suffered irreversible brain damage.

Clare enjoyed life and was generally a happy person. She couldn't read, but she liked listening to music and watching television, although she could rarely understand the stories. She was physically attractive and, with the help of her parents, she could care for herself.

Clare was also interested in sex. When she was seventeen, she and a fellow student at the special school they attended had been caught having intercourse. Clare's parents had been told about the incident, but after Clare left the school the following year, they took no special precautions to ensure that Clare would not become sexually involved with anyone. After all, she stayed at home with her mother every day, and, besides, it was a matter they didn't much like to think about.

The Macwurters were both surprised and upset when Clare became pregnant. At first they couldn't imagine how it could have happened. They recalled that on several occasions Clare had been sent to stay at the house of Mr. Macwurter's brother and his wife while Mrs. Macwurter went shopping.

John Macwurter at first denied that he had had anything to do with Clare's pregnancy. But during the course of a long and painful conversation with his brother, he admitted that he had had sexual relations with Clare.

"I wasn't wholly to blame," John Macwurter said. "I mean, I know I shouldn't have done it. But still, she was interested in it too. I didn't really rape her. Nothing like that."

The Macwurters were at a loss about what they should do. The physician they consulted told them that Clare would probably have a perfectly normal baby. But of course Clare couldn't really take care of herself, much less a baby. She was simply unfit to be a mother. Mrs. Macwurter, for her part, was not eager to assume the additional responsibilities of caring for another child. Mr. Macwurter would be eligible to retire in four more years and the couple had been looking forward to selling their house and moving back to the small town in Oklahoma where they had first met and then married. The money they had managed to save, plus insurance and a sale of their property, would permit them to place Clare in a long-term care facility after their deaths. Being responsible for another child would both ruin their plans and jeopardize Clare's future well-being.

"I never thought I would say such a thing," Mrs. Macwurter told her husband, "but I think we should arrange for Clare to have an abortion."

"That's killing," Mr. Macwurter said.

"I'm not so sure it is. I don't really know. But even if it is, I think it's the best thing to do."

Mrs. Macwurter made the arrangements with Clare's physician for an abortion to be performed. When Mr. Macwurter asked his brother to pay for the operation, John Macwurter refused. He explained that he was opposed to abortion and so it would not be right for him to provide money to be used in that way.

1. Could Thomson's defense of abortion be employed here to show that the proposed abortion is permissible?

2. Why would Noonan oppose abortion here? What alternatives might he recommend? What if it were likely that the baby would be impaired? Would this alter the situation for Noonan?

3. Do the traits Warren lists as central to the concept of personhood require that we think of Clare Macwurter as not being a person in a morally relevant sense?

4. Why would Marquis oppose this abortion?

## Decision Scenario 4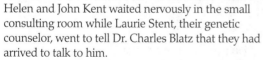

Mrs. Lois Bishop (as we will call her) learned that she was carrying twins at the same time she learned one of the twins had Down syndrome.

"There's no question in my mind," she said. "I want to have an abortion. I had the tests done in the first place to do what I could to guarantee that I would have a normal, healthy child. I knew from the first that there was a possibility that I would have to have an abortion, so I'm prepared for it."

Her obstetrician, Dr. George Savano, nodded. "I understand that," he said. "You are certainly within your rights to ask for an abortion, and I can arrange for you to have one. But there is another possibility, an experimental one, that you might want to consider as an option."

The possibility consisted of the destruction of the abnormally developing fetus. In the end, it was the possibility that Mrs. Bishop chose. A long, thin needle was inserted through Mrs. Bishop's abdomen and guided into the heart of the fetus. A solution was then injected directly into the fetal heart.

Although there was a risk that Mrs. Bishop would have a miscarriage, she did not. The surviving twin

continued to develop normally, and Mrs. Bishop had an uneventful delivery. The child, a boy, is now over five years old.

Dr. Savano was criticized by some physicians as "misusing medicine," but he rejects such charges. Mrs. Bishop also has no regrets, for if the procedure had not been performed, she would have been forced to abort both twins.

1. What sort of utilitarian argument might be offered to justify Dr. Savano's experimental procedure in this case?

2. Would Marquis consider the destruction of the fetus with Down syndrome immoral? After all, it may be argued that persons with Down syndrome do not have "a future like ours."

3. The procedure leads to the death of a developing fetus, so one might say that it is morally equivalent to abortion. Are there any morally relevant factors that distinguish this case from more ordinary cases involving abortion?

## Decision Scenario 5

Helen and John Kent waited nervously in the small consulting room while Laurie Stent, their genetic counselor, went to tell Dr. Charles Blatz that they had arrived to talk to him.

"I regret that I have some bad news for you," Dr. Blatz told them. "The karyotyping that we do after amniocentesis shows a chromosomal abnormality."

He looked at them, and Helen felt she could hardly breathe. "What is it?" she asked.

"It's a condition known as trisomy-21, and it produces a birth defect we call Down syndrome. You may have heard of it under the old name of mongolism."

"Oh, God," John said. "How bad is it?"

"Such children are always mentally retarded," Dr. Blatz said. "Some are severely retarded and others just twenty or so points below average. They have some

minor physical deformities, and they sometimes have heart damage. They typically don't live beyond their thirties, but by and large they seem happy and have good dispositions."

Helen and John looked at each other with great sadness. "What do you think we should do?" Helen asked. "Should I have an abortion, and then we could try again?"

"I don't know," John said. "I really don't know." You've had a hard time being pregnant these last five months, and you'd have to go through that again. Besides, there's no guarantee this wouldn't happen again."

"But this won't be the normal baby we wanted," Helen said. "Maybe in the long run we'll be even unhappier than we are now."

1. Explain the nature of the conflict between the positions taken by Noonan and Warren that arises in this case.

2. If one accepts Thomson's view, what factors are relevant to deciding whether an abortion is justifiable in this instance?

3. Does feminist ethics suggest any way of dealing with this situation? Does care ethics?

4. Would Callahan consider a decision to have an abortion justifiable?

---

## Decision Scenario 6

Ruth Perkins is twenty-four years old, and her husband, Carl Freedon, is four years older. Both are employed, Ruth as an executive for Laporte Gas Transmission and Carl as a systems analyst at a St. Louis bank. Their combined income is over $240,000 a year.

Perkins and Freedon live up to their income. They have an eleven-room house with a tennis court in a high-priced suburb, they both dress well, and Carl is a modest collector of sports cars (three MG-TDs). Both like to travel, and they try to get out of the country at least twice a year—Europe for a month in the summer and Mexico or the Caribbean for a couple of weeks during the winter.

Perkins and Freedon have no children. They agreed when they were married that children would not be a part of their plan for life together. They were distressed when Ruth became pregnant and at first refused to face the problem. They worried about it for several months, considering arguments for and against abortion. At last they decided that Ruth should have an abortion.

"I don't see why I have to go through with this interview," Ruth said to the woman at the Morton Hospital Counseling Center.

"It's required of all who request an abortion," the counselor explained. "We think it's better for a person to be sure what she is doing so she won't regret it later."

"My husband and I are certain," Ruth said. "A child doesn't fit in at all with our lifestyle. We go out a lot, and we like to do things. A child would just get in the way."

"A child can offer many pleasures," the woman said.

"I don't doubt it. If some want them, that's fine with me. We don't. Besides, we both have careers that we're devoted to. I'm not about to quit my job to take care of a child, and the same is true of my husband."

"How long have you been pregnant?"

Ruth looked embarrassed. "Almost six months," she said. "Carl and I weren't sure what we wanted to do at first. It took a while for us to get used to the idea."

"You don't think you waited too long?"

"That's stupid," Ruth said. She could hardly keep her voice under control. "I didn't mean that personally. But Carl and I have a right to live our lives the way we want. So far as we are concerned a six-month fetus is not a person. If we want to get rid of it, that's our business."

"Would you feel the same if it were a child already born?"

"I might," Ruth said. "I mean, a baby doesn't have much personality or anything, does it?"

"I take it you're certain you want the abortion."

"Absolutely. My husband and I think it's the right thing for us. If others think we're wrong . . . well, it's their right to think what they please."

1. How might Warren's arguments be used to support Perkins's position?

2. Could someone who accepts Thomson's arguments consider abortion justified in this case?

3. What position might Sherwin take on Perkins's decision to have an abortion in this case?

4. Does Alward's criticism of Thomson's argument support the claim that late-term abortion is necessarily wrong?

5. If Brown's criticism of Marquis is correct, does this mean that abortion for any reason is justified?

## Chapter 10

# Impaired Infants and Medical Futility

## Chapter Contents

# Classic Case Presentation

## Baby Owens: Down Syndrome and Duodenal Atresia

On a chilly December evening in 1976, Dr. Joan Owens pushed through the plateglass doors of Midwestern Medical Center and walked over to the admitting desk. Dr. Owens was a physician in private practice and regularly visited Midwestern to attend to her patients.

But this night was different. Dr. Owens was coming to the hospital to be admitted as a patient. She was pregnant, and shortly after 9:00 she began having periodic uterine contractions. Dr. Owens recognized them as the beginnings of labor pains. She was sure of this not only because of her medical knowledge but also because the pains followed the same pattern they had before her other three children were born.

While her husband, Phillip, parked the car, Dr. Owens went through the formalities of admission. She was not particularly worried, for the birth of her other children had been quite normal and uneventful. But the pains were coming more frequently now, and she was relieved when she completed the admission process and was taken to her room. Phillip came with her, bringing her small blue suitcase of personal belongings.

At 11:30 that evening, Dr. Owens gave birth to a 4.5-pound baby girl. The plastic bracelet fastened around her wrist identified her as Baby Owens.

## Bad News

Dr. Owens was groggy from exhaustion and from the medication she had received. But when the baby was shown to her, she saw at once that it was not normal. The baby's head was misshapen and the skin around her eyes strangely formed.

Dr. Owens recognized that her daughter had Down syndrome.

"Clarence," she called to her obstetrician. "Is the baby mongoloid?"

"We'll talk about it after your recovery," Dr. Clarence Ziner said.

"Tell me now," said Dr. Owens. "Examine it!"

Dr. Ziner made a hasty examination of the child. He had already seen that Dr. Owens was right and was doing no more than making doubly certain. A more careful examination would have to be made later.

When Dr. Ziner confirmed Joan Owens's suspicion, she did not hesitate to say what she was think-

ing. "Get rid of it," she told Dr. Ziner. "I don't want a mongoloid child."

Dr. Ziner tried to be soothing. "Just sleep for a while now," he told her. "We'll talk about it later."

Four hours later, a little after 5:00 in the morning and before it was fully light, Joan Owens woke up. Phillip was with her, and he had more bad news to tell. A more detailed examination had shown that the child's small intestine had failed to develop properly and was closed off in one place—the condition known as duodenal atresia. It could be corrected by a relatively simple surgical procedure, but until surgery was performed the child could not be fed. Phillip had refused to consent to the operation until he had talked to his wife. Joan Owens had not changed her mind: She did not want the child.

"It wouldn't be fair to the other children to raise them with a mongoloid," she told Phillip. "It would take all of our time, and we wouldn't be able to give David, Sean, and Melinda the love and attention they need."

"I'm willing to do whatever you think best," Phillip said. "But what can we do?"

"Let the child die," Joan said. "If we don't consent to the surgery, the baby will die soon. And that's what we have to let happen."

Phillip put in a call for Dr. Ziner, and, when he arrived in Joan's room, they told him of their decision. He was not pleased with it.

"The surgery has very low risk," he said. "The baby's life can almost certainly be saved. We can't tell how retarded she'll be, but most DS children get along quite well with help from their families. The whole family will grow to love her."

"I know," Joan said. "And I don't want that to happen. I don't want us to center our lives around a defective child. Phillip and I and our other children will be forced to lose out on many of life's pleasures and possibilities."

"We've made up our minds," Phillip said. "We don't want the surgery."

"I'm not sure the matter is as simple as that," Dr. Ziner said. "I'm not sure we can legally just let the baby die. I'll have to talk to the director and the hospital attorney."

## Applying for a Court Order

At 6:00 in the morning, Dr. Ziner called Dr. Felix Entraglo, the director of Midwestern Medical Center, and Isaac Putnam, the head of the center's legal staff. They agreed to meet at 9:00 to talk over the problem presented to them by the Owenses.

They met for two hours. It was Putnam's opinion that the hospital would not be legally liable if Baby Owens were allowed to die because her parents refused to give consent for necessary surgery.

"What about getting a court order requiring surgery?" Dr. Entraglo asked. "That's the sort of thing we do when an infant requires a blood transfusion or immunization and his parents' religious beliefs make them refuse consent."

"This case is not exactly parallel," said Mr. Putnam. "Here we're talking about getting a court to force parents to allow surgery to save the life of a defective infant. The infant will still be defective after the surgery, and I think a court would be reluctant to make a family undergo significant emotional and financial hardships when the parents have seriously deliberated about the matter and decided against surgery."

"But doesn't the child have some claim in this situation?" Dr. Ziner asked.

"That's not clear," said Mr. Putnam. "In general, we assume that parents will act for the sake of their child's welfare, and when they are reluctant to do so we look to the courts to act for the child's welfare. But in a situation like this . . . who can say? Is the Owens baby really a person in any legal or moral sense?"

"I think I can understand why a court would hesitate to order surgery," said Dr. Entraglo. "What sort of life would it be for a family when they had been pressured into accepting a child they didn't want? It would turn a family into a cauldron of guilt and resentment mixed in with love and concern. In this case, the lives of five normal people would be profoundly altered for the worse."

"So we just stand by and let the baby die?" asked Dr. Ziner.

"I'm afraid so," Dr. Entraglo said.

### The Final Days

It took twelve days for Baby Owens to die. Her lips and throat were moistened with water to lessen her suffering, and in a small disused room set apart from the rooms of patients, she was allowed to starve to death.

Many nurses and physicians thought it was wrong that Baby Owens was forced to die such a lingering death. Some thought it was wrong for her to have to die at all, but such a protracted death seemed needlessly cruel. Yet they were cautioned by Dr. Entraglo that anything done to shorten the baby's life would

probably constitute a criminal action. Thus, fear of being charged with a crime kept the staff from administering any medication to Baby Owens.

The burden of caring for the dying baby fell on the nurses in the obstetrics ward. The physicians avoided the child entirely, and it was the nurses who had to see to it that she received her water and was turned in her bed. This was the source of much resentment among the nursing staff, and a few nurses refused to have anything to do with the dying child. Most kept their ministrations to an absolute minimum.

But one nurse, Sara Ann Moberly, was determined to make Baby Owens's last days as comfortable as possible. She held the baby, rocked her, and talked soothingly to her when she cried. Doing all for the baby that she could do soothed Sara Ann as well.

But even Sara Ann was glad when Baby Owens died. "It was a relief to me," she said. "I almost couldn't bear the frustration of just sitting there day after day and doing nothing that could really help her."

## BRIEFING SESSION

If we could speak of nature in human terms, we would often say that it is cruel and pitiless. Nowhere does it seem more heartless than in the case of babies born into the world with severe physical impairments and deformities. The birth of such a child transforms an occasion of expected joy into one of immense sadness. It forces the child's parents to make a momentous decision at a time when they are least prepared to reason clearly: Should they insist that everything be done to save the child's life? Or should they request that the child be allowed an easeful death?

Nor can physicians and nurses escape the burden that the birth of such a child delivers. Committed to saving lives, can they condone the death of that child? What will the physician say to the parents when they turn to him or her for advice? No one involved in the situation can escape the moral agonies that it brings.

To see more clearly what the precise moral issues are in such cases, we need to consider some of the factual details that may be involved in them. We need also to mention other kinds of moral considerations that may be relevant to deciding how an impaired newborn child is to be dealt with by those who have the responsibility to decide.

## Genetic and Congenital Impairments

The development of a child to the point of birth is an unimaginably complicated process, and there are many ways in which it can go wrong. Two kinds of errors are most frequently responsible for producing impaired children: genetic errors and congenital errors.

1.   *Genetic errors.* The program of information that is coded into DNA (the genetic material) may be in some way abnormal because of the occurrence of a mutation. Consequently, when the DNA blueprint is "read" and its instructions followed, the child that develops will be impaired. The defective gene may have been inherited, or it may be due to a new mutation.

2.   *Congenital errors. Congenital* means only "present at birth," and, since genetic defects have results that are present at birth, the term is misleading. Ordinarily, however, the phrase is used to designate errors that result during the developmental process. The impairment, then, is not in the original blueprint (genes) but results either from genetic damage or from the reading of the blueprint. The manufacture and assembly of the materials that constitute the child's development are affected. We know that many factors can influence fetal development. Radiation (such as X rays), drugs (such as thalidomide), chemicals (such as mercury), and nutritional deficiencies (folic acid deficiency) can all cause changes in an otherwise normal process. Also, biological disease agents, such as viruses or spirochetes, may intervene in development. They may alter the machinery of the cell, interfere with the formation of tissues, and defeat the carefully programmed process that leads to a normal child.

## Specific Impairments

Once an impaired child is born, the medical and moral problems are immediate. Let us consider now some of the defects commonly found in newborn children. Our focus will be more on what they are than on what caused them, for, as far as the moral issue is concerned, how the child came to be impaired is of no importance.

### Down Syndrome

This is a chromosomal disorder first identified in 1866 by the English physician J. L. H. Down. Normally, humans have twenty-three pairs of chromosomes, but Down syndrome results from the presence of an extra chromosome. The condition is called trisomy-21, for, instead of a twenty-first pair of chromosomes, the affected person has a twenty-first triple. (Less often, the syndrome is produced when the string of chromosomes gets twisted and chromosome pair number 21 sticks to number 15.)

In ways not wholly understood, the normal process of development is altered by the extra chromosome. The child is born with retardation and various physical abnormalities. Typically, these are relatively minor and include such features as a broad skull, a large tongue, and an upward slant of the eyelids. It is this last feature that led to the name "mongolism" for the condition, a name no longer in use in medicine.

Down syndrome occurs in about 1 of every 1000 births. It occurs most frequently in women over the age of thirty-five, although it is not known why this should be. In 1984 researchers discovered that certain chromosomes sometimes contain an extra copy of a segment known as the *nucleolar organizing region.* This abnormality seems linked to Down syndrome, and families in which either parent has the abnormality are twenty times more likely to have an affected child. Researchers hope to use this information to develop a reliable screening test.

There is no cure for Down syndrome—no way to compensate for the abnormality of the development process. Those with the defect generally have an IQ of about 50 to 80 and require the care and help of others. They can be taught easy tasks, and despite their impairment, those with Down syndrome usually seem to be quite happy people.

## Spina Bifida

Spina bifida is a general name for birth defects that involve an opening in the spine. In development, the spine of the child fails to fuse properly, and often the open vertebrae permit the membrane covering the spinal cord to protrude to the outside. The membrane sometimes forms a bulging, thin sac that contains spinal fluid and nerve tissue. When nerve tissue is present, the condition is called *myelomeningocele*. This form of spina bifida is a very severe one.

Complications arising from spina bifida must often be treated surgically. The opening in the spine must be closed, and in severe cases, the sac must be removed and the nerve tissue inside placed within the spinal canal. Normal skin is then grafted over the area. The danger of an infection of the meninges (meningitis) is great; thus, treatment with antibiotics is also necessary.

Furthermore, a child with spina bifida is also likely to require orthopedic operations to attempt to correct the deformities of the legs and feet that occur because of muscle weakness and lack of muscular control due to nerve damage. The bones of such children are thin and brittle, and fractures are frequent.

A child born with spina bifida is virtually always paralyzed to some extent. Generally, the paralysis is below the waist. Because of the nerve damage, the child will have limited sensation in the lower part of the body. This means she will have no control over her bladder or bowels. The lack of bladder control may result in infection of the bladder, urinary tract, and kidneys because the undischarged urine may serve as a breeding place for microorganisms. Surgery may help with the problem of lack of control of the bladder and bowels.

Spina bifida occurs in between 1 and 10 per 1000 births. For reasons not understood, the rate in white families of low socioeconomic status is three times higher than that in families of higher socioeconomic status. The rate in the black population is less than half of that in the white population. A recent study also shows that women who took multivitamins during pregnancy ran less than half the risk of having an affected child than those who did not, but the significance of this result remains uncertain. Some have suggested that doses of folic acid will prevent the defect from occurring. Spina bifida is almost always accompanied by hydrocephaly.

## Hydrocephaly

This term literally means "water on the brain." When, for whatever reasons, the flow of fluid through the spinal canal is blocked, the cerebrospinal fluid produced within the brain cannot escape. Pressure buildup from the fluid can cause brain damage, and if it is not released the child will die. Although hydrocephaly is frequently the result of spina bifida, it can have several causes and can occur late in a child's development. Treatment requires surgically inserting a thin tube, or shunt, to drain the fluid from the skull to the heart or abdomen where it can be absorbed. The operation can save the baby's life, but physical and mental damage is frequent. Placing the shunt and getting it to work properly are difficult tasks that may require many operations. If hydrocephaly accompanies spina bifida, it is treated first.

## Anencephaly

This term literally means "without brain." In this invariably fatal condition, the cerebral hemispheres of the brain are totally absent. The defect is related to spina bifida, for in some forms the bones of the skull are not completely formed and leave an opening through which brain material bulges to the outside. There is never hope for improvement by any known means.

## Esophageal Atresia

In medical terms, an atresia is the closing of a normal opening or canal. The esophagus is the muscular tube that extends from the back of the throat to the stomach. Sometimes the tube forms without an opening, or it does not completely develop so that it does not extend to the stomach. The condition must be corrected by surgery in order for the child to get food into its stomach. The chances of success in such surgery are very high.

## Duodenal Atresia

The duodenum is the upper part of the small intestine. Food from the stomach empties into it. When the duodenum is closed off, food cannot pass through and be digested. Surgery can repair this condition and is successful in most cases.

## Problems of Extreme Prematurity

A normal pregnancy lasts approximately forty weeks. Infants born after only twenty-six weeks of growth or less typically fail to live. Those born in the weeks after that time have extremely low birth weights. About half of those weighing from 1 to 1.5 pounds fail to survive, and those that do have a multiplicity of problems resulting from the fact that their bodies have simply not had the time to develop adequately to cope with the demands of life outside the uterus.

The undeveloped lungs of premature infant are inefficient and prone to infections. The mechanical ventilation needed to assist their breathing may result in long-term lung damage. Extremely premature infants are subject to cerebral hemorrhages ("brain bleeds") that may lead to seizures, blindness, deafness, retardation, and a variety of less noticeable disabilities. For a discussion of extremely premature infants and the moral issues they present with respect to withholding or withdrawing treatment, see the Social Context following the Briefing Session.

# Testing for Impairments

Genetic impairments are inherited; they are the outcome of the genetic endowment of the child. A carrier of defective genes who has children can pass on the genes. Congenital impairments are not inherited and cannot be passed on.

With proper genetic counseling, individuals belonging to families in which certain diseases "run" can assess the risk that their children might be impaired by examining patterns of inheritance. Also, some genetic diseases can be diagnosed before birth (or even in the embryo) by detecting the presence of the gene. (See Chapter 8 for a discussion of screening for genetic diseases.) Some developmental anomalies, such as the chromosomal abnormality resulting in Down syndrome, can be detected by examining genetic material during fetal development. Large abnormalities in the developing fetus (such as anencephaly, or "missing brain") can often be detected by the use of images produced by ultrasound (sonography).

The most common methods of prenatal diagnosis are amniocentesis and chorionic villus sampling, which involve direct cell studies. In amniocentesis, the amnion (the membrane surrounding the fetus) is punctured with a needle, and some of the amniotic fluid is removed for study. The procedure cannot be usefully and safely performed until fourteen to sixteen weeks into the pregnancy. Until that time, the amount of fluid is inadequate.

The risk to the woman and to the fetus from the procedure is relatively small, usually less than 1 percent. (The risk that the procedure will result in a miscarriage is about 1 in 200.) A recent study shows that if amniocentesis is performed eleven to twelve weeks after conception, there is a small increase in the probability that the child will have a deformed foot.

Chorionic villus sampling (CVS) involves retrieving hairlike villi cells from the developing placenta. The advantage of the test is that it can be employed six to ten weeks after conception. Although the procedure is as safe as amniocentesis, a 1994 study by the Centers for Disease

Control found that infants whose mothers had undergone CVS from 1988 to 1992 had a 0.03 percent risk of missing or undeveloped fingers or toes. A later study questioned this finding and found no reason to believe that the risk of fetal damage is greater than normal.

Amniocentesis came into wide use only in the early 1960s. At first, it was mostly restricted to testing fetuses in cases in which there was a risk of Rh incompatibility. When the mother lacks a group of blood proteins called the Rh (or Rhesus) factor and the fetus has it, the immune system of the mother may produce antibodies against the fetus. The result for the fetus may be anemia, brain damage, and even death.

It was soon realized that additional information about the fetus could be gained from further analysis of the amniotic fluid and the fetal cells in it. The fluid can be chemically assayed, and the cells can be grown in cultures for study. An examination of the DNA can show whether any known abnormalities are likely to cause serious physical or mental defects.

Some metabolic disorders (such as Tay–Sachs disease) can be detected by chemical analysis of the amniotic fluid. However, some of the more common ones, such as PKU, Huntington's chorea, and muscular dystrophy, require an analysis of the genetic material. Because only males have a Y chromosome, it's impossible to examine fetal cells without also discovering the gender of the fetus.

Amniocentesis and CVS do pose slight hazards. Accordingly, neither is regarded as a routine procedure to be performed in every pregnancy. There must be some indication that the fetus is at risk from a genetic or developmental disorder. One indication is the age of the mother. Down syndrome is much more likely to occur in fetuses conceived in women over the age of thirty-five. Because the syndrome is produced by a chromosome abnormality, an examination of the chromosomes in the cells of the fetus can reveal the defect.

A new test for Down syndrome employs a blood sample taken from the pregnant woman. The sample is examined for the presence of three fetal proteins. About sixteen to eighteen weeks after gestation, fetuses with Down syndrome are known to produce abnormally small quantities of estriol and alphafetoprotein and abnormally large amounts of chorionic gonadotropin. The levels of the proteins, plus such factors as the woman's age, can be used to determine the statistical probability of a child with the syndrome. The risks of amniocentesis and CVS are avoided.

Tests are also available for some other developmental impairments. A blood test for the presence of the substance alphafetoprotein can indicate the likelihood of the neural tube defects characteristic of spina bifida. Ultrasound can then be used to confirm or detect these or other developmental anomalies.

An estimated 6 percent of all live births, some 200,000 infants a year, require intensive neonatal care. The afflictions singled out for special mention are those that are most often the source of major moral problems. Those correctable by standard surgical procedures present no special moral difficulties. But even they are often involved with other impairments, such as Down syndrome, that make them important factors in moral deliberations.

## Ethical Theories and the Problem of Birth Impairments

A great number of serious moral issues are raised by impaired newborns. Should they be given only ordinary care, or should special efforts be made to save their lives? Should they be given no care and allowed to die? Should they be killed in a merciful manner? Who should decide what is in the interest of the child? Might acting in the interest of the child require not acting to save the child's life?

A more basic question that cuts even deeper than these concerns the status of the newborn. It is virtually the same as the question raised in Chapter 9 about the fetus. Namely, are severely impaired newborns persons? It might be argued that some infants are so severely impaired that they should not be considered persons in a relevant moral sense. Not only do they lack the capacity to function, but they lack even the potentiality for ordinary psychological and social development. In this respect, they are worse off than most maturing fetuses.

If this view is accepted, then the principles of our moral theories do not require that we act to preserve the lives of impaired newborns. We might, considering their origin, be disposed to show them some consideration and treat them benevolently—perhaps in the same way we might deal with animals that are in a similarly hopeless condition. We might kill them or allow them to die as a demonstration of our compassion.

One major difficulty with this view is that it is not at all clear which impaired infants could legitimately be considered nonpersons. Birth defects vary widely in severity, and, unless one is prepared to endorse infanticide generally, it is necessary to have defensible criteria for distinguishing among newborns. Also, one must defend a general concept of a person that would make it reasonable to regard human offspring as occupying a different status.

By contrast, it might be claimed that the fact that a newborn is a human progeny is sufficient to consider it a person. Assuming that this is so, the question becomes, How ought we to treat a severely impaired infant person? Just because they are infants, impaired newborns cannot express wishes, make claims, or enter into deliberations. All that is done concerning them must be done by others.

A utilitarian might decide that the social and personal cost (the suffering of the infant, the anguish of the parents and family, the monetary cost to society) of saving the life of such an infant is greater than the social and personal benefits that can be expected. Accordingly, such a child should not be allowed to live, and it should be killed as painlessly as possible to minimize its suffering. Yet a rule utilitarian might claim, on the contrary, that the rule "Save every child where possible" would, in the long run, produce more utility than disutility.

The natural law position of Roman Catholicism is that even the most defective newborn is a human person. Yet this view does not require that extraordinary means be used to save the life of such a child. The suffering of the family, great expense, and the need for multiple operations would be reasons for providing only ordinary care. Ordinary care does not mean that every standard medical procedure that might help should be followed. It means only that the defective newborn should receive care of the same type provided for a normal infant. It would be immoral to kill the child or to cause its death by withholding all care.

If the infant is a person, then Kant would regard it as possessing an inherent dignity and value. But the infant in its condition lacks the capacity to reason and to express its will. How, then, should we, acting as its agents, treat him? Kant's principles provide no clear-cut answer. The infant does not threaten our own existence, and we have no grounds for killing him. But, it could be argued, we should allow the child to die. We can imaginatively put ourselves in the place of the infant. Although it would be morally wrong to will our own death (which, Kant claimed, would involve a self-defeating maxim), we might express our autonomy and rationality by choosing to refuse treatment that would prolong a painful and hopeless life. If this is so, then we might act in this way on behalf of the defective child. We might allow the child to die. Indeed, it may be our duty to do so. A similar line of argument from Ross's viewpoint might lead us to decide that, although we have a prima facie duty to preserve the child's life, our actual duty is to allow him to die.

Another basic question remains: Who is to make the decision about how an impaired newborn is to be treated? Traditionally, the assumption has been that this is a decision best left to the infant's parents and physicians. Because they can be assumed to have the highest concern for her welfare and the most knowledge about her condition and prospects, they are the ones who should have the primary responsibility for deciding her fate. If there is reason to believe that they are not acting in a responsible manner, then it becomes the responsibility of the courts to guarantee that the interests of the infant are served.

Hardly any responsible person advocates heroic efforts to save the lives of infants who are most severely impaired, and hardly anyone advocates not treating infants with relatively simple and correctable impairments. The difficult cases are those that fall somewhere along the continuum. Advances in medical management and technology can now save the lives of many infants who earlier would have died relatively quickly, and yet we still lack the power to provide those infants with a life that we might judge to be worthwhile. Yet a failure to treat such infants does not invariably result in their deaths, and a failure to provide them with early treatment may mean that they are even more impaired than they would be otherwise.

No one believes that we currently have a satisfactory solution to this dilemma. It is important to keep in mind that it is not a purely intellectual problem. The context in which particular decisions are made is one of doubt and confusion and genuine anguish.

## SOCIAL CONTEXT: THE DILEMMA OF EXTREME PREMATURITY

When Jan Anderson went into labor, she was twenty-three weeks pregnant—seventeen weeks short of the normal forty-week pregnancy. "They told me I had a beautiful baby boy," she said. But her son, Aaron, weighed only a little more than 750 grams (about 1.5 pounds), and when she finally saw him, he was in the neonatal intensive-care unit. He was attached to a battery of monitors, intravenous lines, and a respirator. Surrounding him were people checking his heart and respiration rates, monitoring his blood gases, siphoning the mucus from his mouth and underdeveloped lungs, and injecting a variety of medications needed to keep his condition stable.

"It was pretty scary," Ms. Anderson, a single woman, told reporter Gina Kolata.

Aaron spent four months in the hospital before Ms. Anderson was allowed to take him home. Aaron's life was preserved, but despite all the treatment he received, he was left with permanent disabilities. By age two, he was quadriplegic and virtually blind, had cerebral palsy, and was perhaps mentally impaired.

### Size of the Problem

Every year at least 287,000 babies are born at least six weeks prematurely, and about 45,000 of them weigh less than 1600 grams (about 3.5 pounds). Thanks to the development of new procedures and new drugs for treating premature infants, almost 85 percent live long enough to leave the hospital (though many must return), and about 20 percent have no lasting major physical or mental impairment.

The more premature an infant and the lower the birth weight, the more likely it is that the infant will die soon after birth or be severely

## Prematurity and Viability

| Weeks of Gestation | Survival Rate (%) |
| --- | --- |
| 21 | 14.8 |
| 22 | 24.8 |
| 23 | 41.7 |
| 24 | 57.2 |
| 25 | 68.9 |
| 26 | 78.4 |
| 27 | 84.8 |
| 28 | 89.2 |
| 29 | 92.2 |
| 30 | 94.7 |
| 40 | 99.7 |

*Source:* National Center for Health Care Statistics (1989–1991).

physically and mentally impaired. About half of premature infants in the 500- to 750-gram (1- to 1.5-pound) range fail to survive. From 25 to 33 percent of babies under 750 grams have irreversible neurological damage. The figure rises to between 40 and 50 percent for those with a birth weight between 500 and 600 grams. About 5 to 10 percent of these very-low-birth-weight babies will have cerebral palsy, and a similar percentage will have IQs below 70, where 100 is average.

Survival rate is closely connected with gestation time. The technological limit for preserving the lives of premature infants is about twenty-three to twenty-four weeks. Estimates of an infant's developmental stage may be off by a week or so because it's impossible to be certain when conception took place. Premature girls have about a one-week developmental advantage over boys, and black infants have the same advantage over white infants. Thus, a white boy may be about two weeks behind in development when compared with a black girl.

## Underdeveloped

Premature babies have not spent enough time in the uterus, and as a result, they are physiologically underdeveloped. The more premature the infant, the more underdeveloped it is. Birth weight, generally, is an index of developmental prematurity. Extremely premature neonates are "fetal infants" that have spent hardly more than half of the forty-week gestation period in their mother's uterus.

Extremely premature infants are liable to life-threatening disorders. Many have problems eating, digesting food, and absorbing nutrients. Their lungs are small and brittle and fill up with secretions, making it impossible for them to breathe normally. They must be put on a mechanical ventilator, and they tend to suffer from respiratory infections.

Poor prenatal development also makes smaller infants prone to cerebral hemorrhages or "brain bleeds" that can result in a variety of devastating consequences. Infants that have had brain bleeds are prone to seizure disorders,

blindness, low vision, deafness, mental retardation, and various more subtle mental difficulties that may show up only years later.

At present more than half of the babies in the 500- to 700-gram range survive, but a mere fifteen years ago, babies born weighing less than about 700 grams rarely lived. Before the early 1970s, prior to the advent of neonatal intensive-care units (NICUs), a child with a birth weight under 900 grams (about 2 pounds) would not be likely to live for long.

Because of aggressive intervention and the use of new drugs and technology, the survival rates of even the most premature infants have risen steadily over the last two decades. Laboratories can now perform dozens of biochemical tests on a few drops of blood, instead of the full vial testing previously required. Newly developed artificial pulmonary surfactants can increase the breathing capacity of an infant's lungs and shorten the time a respirator is needed.

Most important, a twelve-year study published in 1994 showed great value in the use of corticosteroids to treat pregnant women who are likely to give birth during the period from twenty-four to thirty-four weeks of gestation. The drug stimulates fetal development and speeds up the maturation of the lungs. The steroid therapy may reduce by as much as one-third the amount of time a premature infant must remain in intensive care.

As intervention strategies and technologies have improved, the need for them has increased. Babies born prematurely to women who have had no prenatal care and "crack babies" born prematurely to drug-using mothers have placed heavy demands on NICUs.

## After Prematurity

A 2000 study showed that 57.5 percent of normal-birth-weight siblings graduated from high school by age nineteen, but only 15.2 percent of their low-birth-weight siblings did. Graduating from high school is taken as an indicator of the likelihood of future economic and social success.

In another study published in 2000, Saroi Saigal followed 150 babies born two to three months prematurely between 1977 and 1982 until their teens. The children weighed from one pound, two ounces to two pounds, four ounces at birth. She found that at age eight half were receiving special educational help, compared with 10 percent of a population controlled for gender, age, and social class. Twenty-five percent, compared to 6 percent, had repeated a grade in school. Less than half of those in the lowest birth-weight category scored in the normal range on intelligence and achievement tests.

Of the 150 teenagers, 42 had neurological or sensory disorders, such as cerebral palsy, blindness, and deafness. The others, although lacking such deficits, still scored significantly lower on the tests than the control group.

Evidence now strongly suggests that premature infants who survive cannot be counted on to outgrow their initial problems. While some will, the majority will not.

The attitude of those who survive prematurity, however, may be positive. A 1996 study surveyed 150 surviving adolescents about the quality of their lives. Researchers found that, although 27 percent of the group was disabled, they rated their quality of life about as high as a comparison group who had been born after full-term development. Only one of the 150 considered death preferable to his present condition.

## Costs

However, the new success in "saving babies" has not come without financial costs. The cost of keeping alive a premature infant runs about $3000 per day. A very-low-birth-weight neonate may have to remain in intensive care for weeks or even months. The most premature infants may run up bills of more than $500,000. Despite having the highest treatment costs, these infants are also the ones least likely to benefit from the care they are given.

Moreover, the cost of the care is most likely to be born by the taxpayer, for the mothers of the greatest number of very-low-birth-weight babies are often uninsured and unemployed women whose medical care is covered by the federal- and state-funded Medicaid program. Most of these women have received no prenatal care, and many are drug users.

Some critics believe that too much money is being spent on trying to save infants who are not likely to gain significant benefits. According to Michael Rie, a neonatologist at the University of Kentucky, "The hundred highest users of Medicaid dollars in each state are preemies who end up for months on ventilators and end up with cerebral bleeds and extremely lousy outcomes." It costs three times as much to care for an infant under 750 grams as it does to care for a victim of serious burns in a burn unit. It costs 20 percent more to care for such an infant than it does to pay for heart transplant surgery. Most hospitals spend more money on very young patients than they do on the very old, the group often singled out in discussions of medical costs as consuming a disproportionate amount of health-care funds. Concern with medical costs led the state of Oregon to formulate criteria for Medicaid spending, with the result that the treatment of very-low-birth-weight infants was given low priority. The criteria take into account both the seriousness of a disorder and the outcome that might be expected if the disorder is treated. Thus, a life-threatening disease that can be treated with a high degree of success at little cost (such as antibiotic treatment for tuberculosis) is given a high place on the funding list. In contrast, even a serious medical condition, but one with little chance of being improved by treatment, is assigned a low priority. Intensive-care service for newborns under 500 grams was ranked 708 on a list of 709 items.

## Divergence of Views

Not everyone thinks that the Oregon decision can be adequately defended. Indeed, the basic moral question about extremely low-birth-weight infants is whether they ought to be treated at all. Some neonatologists regard the treatment of all infants as a moral obligation. They resuscitate fully any infant showing the slightest signs of life at delivery, regardless of its gestational age or weight. They believe this is the right course of action, even though they know that surviving infants will be likely to have severe mental and physical impairments.

Other neonatologists view the outcome of extraordinary efforts as likely to be so grim as to make resuscitation an unacceptable option. As one NICU physician states the policy at his hospital for dealing with infants weighing less than 500 grams, "We generally keep them warm and let them expire by themselves. These are not viable babies, and it's crazy to do anything more."

Because of these differences in beliefs about the right way to act, a premature infant may be the object of an all-out medical effort to save her life at one hospital, while at another hospital she might be provided only the care needed to keep her comfortable.

The same divergence of views about withholding treatment is found in the question of discontinuing treatment. Some clinicians say that they would go to court to secure an order, if a parent asked that a respirator sustaining an infant be turned off. Other clinicians view the matter as one concerning the best interest of the child. As one put the point in a hypothetical case, "If a baby survives a major head bleed, we'll tell the parents he'll almost surely be damaged and he's suffering a great deal and we don't think we should do anything more."

Perhaps partly because of the development of NICUs and partly because of a misimpression of federal regulations, there has been an increased tendency for physicians to make the basic decisions about whether a premature infant is treated and the extent and limit of the treatment. Parents sometimes say that they were not even consulted about their child's treatment. Indeed, some report that, although they did not want their child treated or wanted treatment discontinued, their wishes were disregarded by physicians, who did whatever they thought best.

### Parent's Decision?

This was the experience of Jan Anderson. Believing that the outcome of her premature baby's

treatment would not be a good one, she twice asked Aaron's physicians to turn off the ventilator. But no one would even discuss the possibility with her. According to Ms. Anderson, one physician screamed at her, "We're trying to save your child, not kill him."

After four months of hospitalization, Aaron went home, but he was a virtually blind quadriplegic, with cerebral palsy and perhaps a permanent mental impairment. Although Ms. Anderson loves him and takes care of him, she says that if she had been given the opportunity, she would have discontinued her baby's life support when he was born. She also says that if she were pregnant and went into labor again at twenty-three weeks, then "I would make sure there was no discussion about saving the child." In her view, "There is no need for anyone to suffer like this."

Some physicians no doubt believe that it is their duty to preserve the lives of premature infants, no matter what the parents of the child might think. However, it is the parents who usually must bear the financial, family, and emotional burdens that a severely impaired child imposes. The courts have often shared this view and allowed the final decision about treatment to rest with the parents. (See Classic Case Presentation: "Baby Owens" and Social Context: "The Baby Doe Cases" in this chapter.) Some physicians apparently still guide their conduct by the so-called Baby Doe laws passed in 1985. These federal regulations were initially interpreted to require that all newborns, regardless of their degree of impairment or the likelihood of their survival, receive lifesaving treatment and support. Physicians were threatened with federal prosecution for not following strict guidelines issued by the surgeon general. However, a series of court decisions stripped away the enforcement provisions of the regulations, and the older practice of making treatment decisions on a case-by-case basis has become acceptable once again.

Insurance companies typically pay the bills for premature infants that receive treatment in NICUs. Hence, physicians do not have to allow financial costs to play a major role in making treatment decisions. This may incline them to ignore the lifelong expenses that will have to be borne somehow by the family. Physicians can go on to the next case, but parents must remain with their child, no matter what the child's condition and prospects. Again, since parents must bear the burden, they have a good claim to be included in the decision-making process.

Does an NICU physician have an incentive, other than the best interest of a patient, to initiate or continue treatment of a low-birth-weight infant? One rarely mentioned reason for aggressive treatment is that neonatologists want to explore the limits of the modes of treatment and the technology currently used. By understanding the limits, it may be possible to take steps to extend them so that smaller and smaller premature infants can be kept alive. Hence, some neonatologists, motivated by an interest in research, may not give parents an adequate opportunity to take part in treatment decisions.

In fairness, however, parents do not always want to be included in the decision-making process. Some prefer to turn over to physicians all responsibility involving initiating or withdrawing medical treatment. Furthermore, physicians themselves do not always know when aggressive treatment is appropriate. They must make recommendations and decisions in an environment of crisis about a patient whose condition is in a constant state of change.

Some neonatologists and philosophers argue that hospital ethics committees should play a crucial role in deciding how premature infants should be treated. Such committees, having no vested interest in the outcome of a decision, could weigh the issues more objectively than either the neonatologist or the parents.

# SOCIAL CONTEXT: THE BABY DOE CASES

In Bloomington, Indiana, in 1982, a child was born with Down syndrome and esophageal atresia. The parents and the physicians of the infant, who became known as Baby Doe, decided

against the surgery that was needed to open the esophagus and allow the baby to be fed. The decision was upheld by the courts, and six days after birth Baby Doe died of starvation and dehydration.

A month later, in May 1982, the secretary of Health and Human Services (HHS) notified hospitals that any institution receiving federal funds could not lawfully "withhold from a handicapped infant nutritional sustenance or medical or surgical treatment required to correct a life-threatening condition if (1) the withholding is based on the fact that the infant is handicapped and (2) the handicap does not render treatment or nutritional sustenance contraindicated."

## Baby Doe Hotline

Ten months later, acting under instructions from President Reagan, an additional and more detailed regulation was issued. Hospitals were required to display a poster in NICUs and pediatric wards indicating that "discrimination" against handicapped infants was a violation of federal law. The poster also listed a toll-free, twenty-four-hour "hotline" number for reporting suspected violations. In addition, the regulations authorized representatives of HHS to take "immediate remedial action" to protect infants. Further, hospitals were required to permit HHS investigators access to the hospital and to relevant patient records.

A group of associations, including the American Academy of Pediatrics, brought suit against HHS in an attempt to stop the regulations from becoming legally effective. Judge Gerhard Gesell of the U.S. District Court ruled, in April 1983, that HHS had not followed the proper procedures in putting the regulations into effect and so they were invalid. In particular, the regulations were issued without notifying and consulting with those affected by them, a procedure that is legally required to avoid arbitrary bureaucratic actions. The judge held that, although HHS had considered relevant factors in identifying a problem, it had failed to consider the effects of the use of the hotline number. An "anonymous tipster" could cause "the sudden descent of Baby

Doe squads" on hospitals, and "monopolizing physician and nurse time, and making hospital charts and records unavailable during treatment, can hardly be presumed to produce quality care of the infant."

Furthermore, Judge Gesell held, the main purpose of the regulations was apparently to "require physicians treating newborns to take into account wholly medical risk–benefit considerations and to prevent parents from having any influence upon decisions as to whether further medical treatment is desirable." The regulations explored no other ways to prevent "discriminatory medical care." In his conclusion, Judge Gesell held that federal regulations dealing with imperiled newborns should "reflect caution and sensitivity" and that "wide public comment prior to rule-making is essential."

HHS responded to the court decision by drafting another regulation (July 5, 1983) that attempted to resolve the procedural objection that invalidated the first. Sixty days was allowed for the filing of written comments. Since the substance of the regulation was virtually the same, the proposal was widely contested, and on January 12, 1984, another set of regulations was published. They too became an object of controversy.

### Baby Jane Doe

Meanwhile, a second Baby Doe case had become the focus of public attention and legal action. On October 11, 1983, an infant who became known as Baby Jane Doe was born in Port Jefferson (Long Island), New York. Baby Jane Doe suffered from meningomyelocele, anencephaly, and hydrocephaly. (See Briefing Session, this chapter, for an explanation of these conditions.) Her parents were told that without surgery she might live from two weeks to two years, but with surgery she might survive twenty years. However, she would be severely retarded, epileptic, paralyzed, and likely to have constant urinary and bladder infections. The parents consulted with neurologists, a Roman Catholic priest, nurses, and social workers. They decided surgery was not in the best interest of the child and opted, instead, for the use of antibiotics to pre-

vent infection of the exposed spinal nerves. "We love her very much," her mother said, "and that's why we made the decision we did."

Lawrence Washburn Jr., a lawyer who for a number of years had initiated lawsuits on behalf of the unborn and impaired, somehow learned that Baby Jane Doe was being denied surgery and entered a petition on her behalf before the New York State Supreme Court. Because Washburn was not related to the infant, his legal standing in the case was questionable, and the court appointed William Weber to represent the interest of Baby Jane Doe. After a hearing, the judge ruled that the infant was in need of surgery to preserve her life and authorized Weber to consent.

This decision was reversed on appeal. The court held that the parents' decision was in the best interest of the infant. Hence, the state had no basis to intervene. The ruling was then appealed to the New York Court of Appeals and upheld. The court held that the parents' right to privacy was invaded when a person totally unrelated and with no knowledge of the infant's condition and treatment entered into litigation in an attempt to challenge the discharge of parental responsibility. However, the main grounds for allowing the ruling to stand were procedural, for the suit had not followed New York law requiring that the state intervene in the treatment of children through the family court.

In the cases of both Baby Doe and Baby Jane Doe, the federal government went to court to demand the medical records of the infants. The government charged that decisions against their treatment represented discrimination against the handicapped. However, the courts consistently rejected the government's demands. In June 1985, the Supreme Court agreed to hear arguments to decide whether the federal laws that protect the handicapped against discrimination also apply to the treatment of imperiled newborns who are denied life-prolonging treatment.

### Final Regulations

On May 15, 1985, the third anniversary of the death of Baby Doe, HHS's final "Baby Doe" regulation went into effect. The regulation was an implementation of an amendment to the Child Abuse Prevention and Treatment Act that was passed into law in October 1985 and the result of negotiations among some nineteen groups representing right-to-life advocates, the disabled, the medical professions, and members of Congress.

The regulation extended the term "medical neglect" to cover cases of "withholding of medically indicated treatment from a disabled infant with a life-threatening condition." Withholding treatment, but not food and water, was not "medical neglect" in three kinds of cases:

1. The infant is chronically and irreversibly comatose.

2. The provision of such treatment would merely prolong dying, not be effective in ameliorating or correcting all the infant's life-threatening conditions, or otherwise be futile in terms of the survival of the infant.

3. The provision of such treatment would be virtually futile in terms of the survival of the infant, and the treatment itself under such circumstances would be inhumane.

The regulation defined "reasonable medical judgment" as "a medical judgment that would be made by a reasonably prudent physician knowledgeable about the case and the treatment possibilities with respect to the medical conditions involved." State child-protection service agencies were designated as the proper organizations to see to it that infants were not suffering "medical neglect," and, in order to receive any federal funds, such agencies were required to develop a set of procedures to carry out this function. Parents, physicians, and hospitals were thus no longer the direct subjects of the regulation.

### Supreme Court Decision

On June 9, 1986, the Supreme Court, in a 5-to-3 ruling with one abstention, struck down the Baby Doe regulations. The Court held that there was no evidence that hospitals had discriminated against impaired infants or had refused treatments sought by parents. Accordingly, there was no basis for federal intervention.

Justice John Paul Stevens, in the majority opinion, stressed that no federal law requires hospitals to treat impaired infants without parental consent. Nor does the government have the right "to give unsolicited advice either to parents, to hospitals, or to state officials who are faced with difficult treatment decisions concerning handicapped children." Furthermore, state child-protection agencies "may not be conscripted against their will as the foot soldiers in a Federal crusade."

Hospitals and those directly involved in neonatal care were generally relieved by the Supreme Court decision. In their arguments before the Court, they had claimed that federal "Baby Doe squads arriving within hours after birth" had second-guessed the agonizing decisions made by parents and physicians and that this had "a devastating impact on the parents."

The Court decision once again placed the responsibility for making decisions about withholding life-sustaining treatment from imperiled newborns on families and physicians acting in consultation. Some hospitals use review committees to recommend whether infants ought to be treated, but what powers these committees should have and who should be on them continues to be a matter of dispute.

## Case Presentation

### Baby K: An Anencephalic Infant and a Mother's Request

The female child known in court records as Baby K was born in 1993 at Fairfax Hospital in Falls Church, Virginia. She was born with the catastrophic impairment called anencephaly. Her brain lacked both cerebral hemispheres, and she would never be capable of even a rudimentary form of thought. Only her brain stem was intact, and it would keep her breathing for a while.

The standard treatment for anencephalic infants is to make them comfortable, provide them with nourishment, then wait until their organ systems fail and death ensues. Death usually comes within a few hours, days, or weeks from respiratory failure, because the brain stem does not adequately regulate breathing.

Baby K remained alive much longer than most babies with her impairment, primarily because of her mother's insistence that the baby's periodic respiratory crises be treated aggressively, including the use of a mechanical ventilator to breathe for her. The mother was described in one court document as "acting out of a firm Christian faith that all life should be protected."

Baby K, at the age of sixteen months, did not live at home with her mother but in an extended-care facility so that she could receive the constant attention needed. She left the nursing home only to have respiratory treatment at Fairfax Hospital. After her second admission, the hospital went to the federal district court to seek a ruling that it would not violate any state or federal law by refusing to provide Baby K with additional treatment. Physicians at the hospital held that further treatment would be futile, and a hospital ethics committee decided that withholding aggressive treatment would be legitimate. Nevertheless, the court ruled that the hospital had to provide the care required to preserve the infant's life.

## Ruling Appealed

The hospital appealed the district court ruling to the U.S. Court of Appeals. The appeal was supported by Baby K's father (who was not married to her mother) and by a court-appointed guardian. However, the court ruled 2-to-1 that the 1986 Federal Emergency Medical Treatment and Active Labor Act required the hospital to provide treatment for Baby K. The court held that, although providing assisted breathing for an anencephalic infant might not be expected to produce a medical benefit, the law as passed by Congress made no exceptions for situations in which the "required treatment would exceed the prevailing standard of medical care."

The appeals court's extension of the Emergency Medical Treatment Act to the Baby K case surprised most observers. The law was passed to keep private hospitals from "dumping" to public facilities patients with emergency problems (including pregnant women in labor) but no money and no health insurance to pay for the cost of their care. (The act is usually referred to as an antidumping law.) However, payment was not an issue in the Baby K case, for her mother was fully insured as a member of the Kaiser Permanente health maintenance organization.

According to the mother's attorney, Ellen Flannery, the court simply applied the law in a straightforward manner. "There's no dispute that the appropriate treatment for acute respiratory distress is ventilation," she said. "The care is not physiologically futile. It will achieve the result required by the mother, and that is to stabilize the baby." The physicians in the case, she claimed, based their decision on judgment about the quality of life such a child might have, and the law does not address such issues.

Others saw the consequences of extending the law as threatening the power of physicians, hospitals, and ethics committees to have a say in decisions about treating infants with profound birth anomalies. Arthur Kohrman, head of the American Academy of Pediatrics ethics committee, was quoted as saying that "this is a profoundly important case, because it strips away the ability of physicians to act as moral agents and turns them into instruments of technology. [Anencephalic] babies are born dying, and the issue is not prolonging their death but supporting it in a humane and dignified way."

Robert Veatch, head of the Kennedy Institute for Bioethics, testifying on behalf of the mother, expressed the view that courts should not defer their judgment to that of physicians. "These are religious and philosophical judgments on which physicians have no more expertise than parents," he said. The impact that the extension of the antidumping law to cases of severe birth impairment may have on treatment decisions is not yet obvious. As the appeals court pointed out, Congress made no exceptions with respect to providing care above the accepted standard in cases judged to be futile. The law might be amended by Congress to include exceptions.

## Potential Results

If the law is not amended, decisions to provide no more than standard treatment for impaired infants may turn out to have no effect in particular cases. When emergency medical attention is requested by a parent, the emergency treatment law may require that an earlier decision about limiting treatment be set aside.

## Section 1: The Status of Impaired Infants

# Examination of Arguments in Favor of Withholding Ordinary Medical Care from Defective Infants

John A. Robertson

John Robertson defends a conservative natural law position in criticizing two arguments in favor of withholding "necessary but ordinary" medical care from impaired infants. He rejects the claim made by Michael Tooley that infants are not persons and argues that, on the contrary, there is no nonarbitrary consideration that requires us to protect the past realization of conceptual capability but not its potential realization.

The second argument that Robertson considers is one to the effect that we have no obligation to treat defective newborns when the cost of doing so greatly outweighs the benefits (a utilitarian argument). In criticism, Robertson claims that we have no way of judging this. Life itself may be of sufficient worth to an impaired person to offset his or her suffering, and the suffering and cost to society are not sufficient to justify withholding care.

## 1. Defective Infants Are Not Persons

Children born with congenital malformations may lack human form and the possibility of ordinary, psychosocial development. In many cases mental retardation is or will be so profound, and physical incapacity so great, that the term "persons" or "humanly alive" have odd or questionable meaning when applied to them. In these cases the infants' physical and mental defects are so severe that they will never know anything but a vegetative existence, with no discernible personality, sense of self, or capacity to interact with others. Withholding ordinary medical care in such cases, one may argue, is justified on the ground that these infants are not persons or human beings in the ordinary or legal sense of the term, and therefore do not possess the right of care that persons possess.

Central to this argument is the idea that living products of the human uterus can be classified into offspring that are persons, and those that are not. Conception and birth by human parents does not automatically endow one with personhood and its ac-

companying rights. Some other characteristic or feature must be present in the organism for personhood to vest, and this the defective infant arguably lacks. Lacking that property, an organism is not a person or deserving to be treated as such.

Before considering what "morally significant features" might distinguish persons from nonpersons, and examining the relevance of such features to the case of the defective infant, we must face an initial objection to this line of inquiry. The objection questions the need for any distinction among human offspring because of

> the monumental misuse of the concept of "humanity" in so many practices of discrimination and atrocity throughout history. Slavery, witchhunts and wars have all been justified by their perpetrators on the grounds that they held their victims to be less than fully human. The insane and criminal have for long periods been deprived of the most basic necessities for similar reasons, and been excluded from society. . . .
>
> . . . Even when entered upon with the best of intentions, and in the most guarded manner, the enterprise of basing the protection of human life upon such criteria and definitions is dangerous. To question someone's humanity or personhood is a first step to mistreatment and killing.

Hence, according to this view, human parentage is a necessary and sufficient condition for personhood, whatever the characteristics of the offspring, because qualifying criteria inevitably lead to abuse and untold suffering to beings who are unquestionably human. Moreover, the human species is sufficiently different from other sentient species that assigning its members greater rights on birth alone is not arbitrary.

This objection is indeed powerful. The treatment accorded slaves in the United States, the Nazi denial of personal status to non-Aryans, and countless other incidents, testify that man's inhumanity to man is indeed greatest when a putative nonperson is involved. Arguably, however, a distinction based on gross physical form, profound mental incapacity, and the very existence of personality or selfhood, besides having an empirical basis in the monstrosities and mutations known to have been born to women is a basic and fundamental one. Rather than distinguishing among the particular characteristics that persons might attain through the contingencies of race, culture, and class, it merely separates out those who lack the potential for assuming any personal characteristics beyond breathing and consciousness.

This reply narrows the issue: should such creatures be cared for, protected, or regarded as "ordinary" humans? If such treatment is not warranted, they may be treated as nonpersons. The arguments supporting care in all circumstances are based on the view that all living creatures are sacred, contain a spark of the divine, and should be so regarded. Moreover, identifying those human offspring unworthy of care is a difficult task and will inevitably take a toll on those whose humanity cannot seriously be questioned. At this point the argument becomes metaphysical or religious and immune to resolution by empirical evidence, not unlike the controversy over whether a fetus is a person. It should be noted, however, that recognizing all human offspring as persons, like recognizing the fetus to be a person, does not conclude the treatment issue.

Although this debate can be resolved only by reference to religious or moral beliefs, a procedural solution may reasonably be considered. Since reasonable people can agree that we ordinarily regard human offspring as persons, and further, that defining categories of exclusion is likely to pose special dangers of abuse, a reasonable solution is to presume that all living human offspring are persons. This rule would be subject to exception only if it can be shown beyond a reasonable doubt that certain offspring will never possess the minimal properties that reasonable persons ordinarily associate with human personality. If this burden cannot be satisfied, then the presumption of personhood obtains.

For this purpose I will address only one of the many properties proposed as a necessary condition of personhood—the capacity for having a sense of self—and consider whether its advocates present a cogent account of the nonhuman. Since other accounts may be more convincingly articulated, this discussion will neither exhaust nor conclude the issue. But it will illuminate the strengths and weaknesses of the personhood argument and enable us to evaluate its application to defective infants.

Michael Tooley has recently argued that a human offspring lacking the capacity for a sense of self lacks the rights to life or equal treatment possessed by other persons. In considering the morality of abortion and infanticide, Tooley considers "what properties a thing must possess in order to have a serious right to life," and he concludes that:

> [h]aving a right to life presupposes that one is capable of desiring to continue existing as a subject of experiences and other mental states. This in turn presupposes both that one has the concept of such a continuing entity and that one believes that one is oneself such an entity. So an entity that lacks such a consciousness of itself as a continuing subject of mental states does not have a right to life.

However, this account is at first glance too narrow, for it appears to exclude all those who do not presently have a desire "to continue existing as a subject of experiences and other mental states." The sleeping or unconscious individual, the deranged, the conditioned, and the suicidal do not have such desires, though they might have had them or could have them in the future. Accordingly, Tooley emphasizes the capability of entertaining such desires, rather than their actual existence. But it is difficult to distinguish the capability for such desires in an unconscious, conditioned, or emotionally disturbed person from the capability existing in a fetus or infant. In all cases the capability is a future one; it will arise only if certain events occur, such as normal growth and development in the case of the infant, and removal of the disability in the other cases. The infant, in fact, might realize its capability long before disabled adults recover emotional balance or consciousness.

To meet this objection, Tooley argues that the significance of the capability in question is not solely its future realization (for fetuses and infants will ordinarily realize it), but also its previous existence and exercise. He seems to say that once the conceptual capability has been realized, one's right to desire continued existence permanently vests, even though the present capability for desiring does not exist, and may be lost for substantial periods or permanently. Yet, what nonarbitrary reasons require that we protect the past realization of conceptual capability but not its potential realization in the future? As a reward for its past realization? To mark our reverence and honor for someone who has realized that state? Tooley is silent on this point.

Another difficulty is Tooley's ambiguity concerning the permanently deranged, comatose, or conditioned. Often he phrases his argument in terms of a temporary suspension of the capability of conceptual thought. One wonders what he would say of someone permanently deranged, or with massive brain damage, or in a prolonged coma. If he seriously means that the past existence of a desire for life vests these cases with the right to life, then it is indeed difficult to distinguish the comatose or deranged from the infant profoundly retarded at birth. Neither will ever possess the conceptual capability to desire to be a continuing subject of experiences. A distinction based on reward or desert seems arbitrary, and protection of life applies equally well in both cases. Would Tooley avoid this problem by holding that the permanently comatose and deranged lose their rights after a certain point because conceptual capacity will never be regained? This would permit killing (or at least withholding of care from) the insane and comatose—doubtless an unappealing prospect. Moreover, we do not ordinarily think of the insane, and possibly the comatose, as losing personhood before their death. Although their personality or identity may be said to change, presumably for the worse, or become fragmented or minimal, we still regard them as specific persons. If a "self" in some minimal sense exists here then the profoundly retarded, who at least is conscious, also may be considered a self, albeit a minimal one. Thus, one may argue that Tooley fails to provide a convincing account of criteria distinguishing persons and nonpersons. He both excludes beings we ordinarily think of as persons—infants, deranged, conditioned, possibly the comatose—and fails to articulate criteria that convincingly distinguish the nonhuman. But, even if we were to accept Tooley's distinction that beings lacking the potential for desire and a sense of self are not persons who are owed the duty to be treated by ordinary medical means, this would not appear to be very helpful in deciding whether to treat the newborn with physical or mental defects. Few infants, it would

seem, would fall into this class. First, those suffering from malformations, however gross, that do not affect mental capabilities would not fit the class of nonpersons. Second, frequently even the most severe cases of mental retardation cannot be reliably determined until a much later period; care thus could not justifiably be withheld in the neonatal period, although this principle would permit nontreatment at the time when nonpersonality is clearly established. Finally, the only group of defective newborns who would clearly qualify as nonpersons is anencephalics, who altogether lack a brain or those so severely brain-damaged that it is immediately clear that a sense of self or personality can never develop. Mongols, myelomeningoceles, and other defective infants from whom ordinary care is now routinely withheld would not qualify as nonpersons. Thus, even the most coherent and cogent criteria of humanity are only marginally helpful in the situation of the defective infant. We must therefore consider whether treatment can be withheld on grounds other than the claim that such infants are not persons.

## 2. No Obligation to Treat Exists When the Costs of Maintaining Life Greatly Outweigh the Benefits

If we reject the argument that defective newborns are not persons, the question remains whether circumstances exist in which the consequences of treatment as compared with nontreatment are so undesirable that the omission of care is justified. As we have seen, the doctrine of necessity permits one to violate the criminal law when essential to prevent the occurrence of a greater evil. The circumstances, however, when the death of a nonconsenting person is a lesser evil than his continuing life are narrowly circumscribed, and do not include withholding care from defective infants. Yet many parents and physicians deeply committed to the loving care of the newborn think that treating severely defective infants causes more harm than good, thereby justifying the withholding of ordinary care. In their view the suffering and diminished quality of the child's life do not justify the social and economic costs of treatment. This claim has a growing commonsense appeal, but it assumes that the utility or quality of one's life can be measured and compared with other lives, and that health resources may legitimately be allocated to produce the greatest personal utility. This argument will now be analyzed from the perspective of the defective patient and others affected by his care.

### a. The Quality of the Defective Infant's Life

Comparisons of relative worth among persons, or between persons and other interests, raise moral and methodological issues that make any argument that relies on such comparisons extremely vulnerable. Thus the strongest claim for not treating the defective newborn is that treatment seriously harms the infant's own interests, whatever may be the effect on others. When maintaining his life involves great physical and psychosocial suffering for the patient, a reasonable person might conclude that such a life is not worth living. Presumably the patient, if fully informed and able to communicate, would agree. One then would be morally justified in withholding lifesaving treatment if such action served to advance the best interests of the patient.

Congenital malformations impair development in several ways that lead to the judgment that deformed retarded infants are "a burden to themselves." One is the severe physical pain, much of it resulting from repeated surgery that defective infants will suffer. Defective children also are likely to develop other pathological features, leading to repeated fractures, dislocations, surgery, malfunctions, and other sources of pain. The shunt, for example, inserted to relieve hydrocephaly, a common problem in defective children, often becomes clogged, necessitating frequent surgical interventions.

Pain, however, may be intermittent and manageable with analgesics. Since many infants and adults experience great pain, and many defective infants do not, pain alone, if not totally unmanageable, does not sufficiently show that a life is so worthless that death is preferable. More important are the psychosocial deficits resulting from the child's handicaps. Many defective children never can walk even with prosthesis, never interact with normal children, never appreciate growth, adolescence, or the fulfillment of education and employment, and seldom are even able to care for themselves. In cases of severe retardation, they may be left with a vegetative existence in a crib, incapable of choice or the most minimal responses to stimuli. Parents or others may reject them, and much of their time will be spent in hospitals, in surgery, or fighting the many illnesses that beset them. Can it be said that such a life is worth living?

There are two possible responses to the quality-of-life argument. One is to accept its premises but to question the degree of suffering in particular cases, and thus restrict the justification for death to the most extreme cases. The absence of opportunities for schooling, career, and interaction may be the fault of social attitudes and the failings of healthy persons, rather than a necessary result of congenital malformations. Psychosocial suffering occurs because healthy, normal persons reject or refuse to relate to the defective, or hurry them to poorly funded institutions. Most nonambulatory, mentally retarded persons can be trained for satisfying roles. One cannot assume that a nonproductive existence is necessarily unhappy; even social rejection and nonacceptance can be mitigated. Moreover, the psychosocial ills of the handicapped often do not differ in kind from those experienced by many persons. With training and care, growth, development, and a full range of experiences are possible for most people with physical and mental handicaps. Thus, the claim that death is a far better fate than life cannot in most cases be sustained.

This response, however, avoids meeting the quality-of-life argument on its strongest grounds. Even if many defective infants can experience growth, interaction, and most human satisfactions if nurtured, treated, and trained, some infants are so severely retarded or grossly deformed that their response to love and care, in fact their capacity to be conscious, is always minimal. Although mongoloid and nonambulatory spina bifida children may experience an existence we would hesitate to adjudge worse than death, the profoundly retarded, nonambulatory blind, deaf infant who will spend his few years in the back-ward cribs of a state institution is clearly a different matter.

To repudiate the quality-of-life argument, therefore, requires a defense of treatment in even these extreme cases. Such a defense would question the validity of any surrogate or proxy judgments of the worth or quality of life when the wishes of the person in question cannot be ascertained. The essence of the quality-of-life argument is a proxy's judgment that no reasonable person can prefer the pain, suffering, and loneliness of, for example, life in a crib at an IQ level of 20, to an immediate, painless death.

But in what sense can the proxy validly conclude that a person with different wants, needs, and interests, if able to speak, would agree that such a life were worse than death? At the start one must be skeptical of the proxy's claim to objective disinterestedness. If the proxy is also the parent or physician, as has been the case in pediatric euthanasia, the impact of treatment on the proxy's interests, rather than solely on those of the child, may influence his assessment. But even if the proxy were truly neutral and committed only to caring for the child, the problem of egocentricity and knowing another's mind remains. Compared with the situation and life prospects of a "reasonable man," the child's potential quality of life indeed appears dim. Yet a standard based on healthy, ordinary development may be entirely inappropriate to this situation. One who has never known the pleasures of mental operation, ambulation, and social interaction surely does not suffer from their loss as much as one who has. While one who has known these capacities may prefer death to a life without them, we have no assurance that the handicapped person, with no point of comparison, would agree. Life, and life alone, whatever its limitations, might be of sufficient worth to him.

One should also be hesitant to accept proxy assessments of quality-of-life because the margin of error in such predictions may be very great. For instance, while one expert argues that by a purely clinical assessment he can accurately forecast the minimum degree of future handicap an individual will experience, such forecasting is not infallible, and risks denying care to infants whose disability might otherwise permit a reasonably acceptable quality-of-life. Thus given the problems in ascertaining another's wishes, the proxy's bias to personal or culturally relative interests, and the unreliability of predictive criteria, the quality-of-life argument is open to serious question. Its strongest appeal arises in the case of a grossly deformed, retarded, institutionalized child, or one with incessant unmanageable pain, where continued life is itself torture. But these cases are few, and cast doubt on the utility of any such judgment. Even if the judgment occasionally may be defensible, the potential danger of quality-of-life assessments may be a compelling reason for rejecting this rationale for withholding treatment.

### b. The Suffering of Others

In addition to the infant's own suffering, one who argues that the harm of treatment justifies violation of the defective infant's right to life usually relies on the psychological, social, and economic costs of maintaining his existence to family and society. In their view the minimal benefit of treatment to persons incapable of full social and physical development does not justify the burdens that care of the defective infant imposes on parents, siblings, health professionals, and other patients. Matson, a noted pediatric neurosurgeon, states:

> [I]t is the doctor's and the community's responsibility to provide [custodial] care and to minimize suffering, but, at the same time, it is also their responsibility not to prolong such individual, familial, and community suffering unnecessarily, and not to carry out multiple procedures and prolonged, expensive, acute hospital-

ization in an infant whose chance for acceptable growth and development is negligible.

Such a frankly utilitarian argument raises problems. It assumes that because of the greatly curtailed orbit of his existence, the costs or suffering of others [are] greater than the benefit of life to the child. This judgment, however, requires a coherent way of measuring and comparing interpersonal utilities, a logical–practical problem that utilitarianism has never surmounted. But even if such comparisons could reliably show a net loss from treatment, the fact remains that the child must sacrifice his life to benefit others. If the life of one individual, however useless, may be sacrificed for the benefit of any person, however useful, or for the benefit of any number of persons, then we have acknowledged the principle that rational utility may justify any outcome. As many philosophers have demonstrated, utilitarianism can always permit the sacrifice of one life for other interests, given the appropriate arrangement of utilities on the balance sheet. In the absence of principled grounds for such a decision, the social equation involved in mandating direct, involuntary euthanasia becomes a difference of degree, not kind, and we reach the point where protection of life depends solely on social judgments of utility.

These objections may well be determinative. But if we temporarily bracket them and examine the extent to which care of the defective infant subjects others to suffering, the claim that inordinate suffering outweighs the infant's interest in life is rarely plausible. In this regard we must examine the impact of caring for defective infants on the family, health professionals, and society-at-large.

**The Family.** The psychological impact and crisis created by birth of a defective infant is devastating. Not only is the mother denied the normal tension release from the stresses of pregnancy, but both parents feel a crushing blow to their dignity, self-esteem, and self-confidence. In a very short time, they feel grief for the loss of the normal expected child, anger at fate, numbness, disgust, waves of helplessness, and disbelief. Most feel personal blame for the defect, or blame their spouse. Adding to the shock is fear that social position and mobility are permanently endangered. The transformation of a "joyously awaited experience into one of catastrophe and profound psychological threat" often will reactivate unresolved maturational conflicts. The chances for social pathology—divorce, somatic complaints, nervous and mental disorders—increase and hard-won adjustment patterns may be permanently damaged.

The initial reactions of guilt, grief, anger, and loss, however, cannot be the true measure of family suffering caused by care of a defective infant, because these costs are present whether or not the parents choose treatment. Rather, the question is to what degree treatment imposes psychic and other costs greater than would occur if the child were not treated. The claim that care is more costly rests largely on the view that parents and family suffer inordinately from nurturing such a child.

Indeed, if the child is treated and accepted at home, difficult and demanding adjustment must be made. Parents must learn how to care for a disabled child, confront financial and psychological uncertainty, meet the needs of other siblings, and work through their own conflicting feelings. Mothering demands are greater than with a normal child, particularly if medical care and hospitalization are frequently required. Counseling or professional support may be nonexistent or difficult to obtain. Younger siblings may react with hostility and guilt, older with shame and anger. Often the normal feedback of child growth that renders the turmoil of childrearing worthwhile develops more slowly or not at all. Family resources can be depleted (especially if medical care is needed), consumption patterns altered, or standards of living modified. Housing may have to be found closer to a hospital, and plans for further children changed. Finally, the anxieties, guilt, and grief present at birth may threaten to recur or become chronic.

Yet, although we must recognize the burdens and frustrations of raising a defective infant, it does not necessarily follow that these costs require nontreatment, or even institutionalization. Individual and group counseling can substantially alleviate anxiety, guilt, and frustration, and enable parents to cope with underlying conflicts triggered by the birth and the adaptations required. Counseling also can reduce psychological pressures on siblings, who can be taught to recognize and accept their own possibly hostile feelings and the difficult position of their parents. They may even be taught to help their parents care for the child.

The impact of increased financial costs also may vary. In families with high income or adequate health insurance, the financial costs are manageable. In others, state assistance may be available. If severe financial problems arise or pathological adjustments are likely, institutionalization, although undesirable for the child, remains an option. Finally, in many cases, the experience of living through a crisis is a deepening and enriching one, accelerating personality maturation, and giving one a new sensitivity to the needs of spouse, siblings, and others. As one parent of a defective child states: "In the last months I have come closer to people and can understand them more. I have met them more deeply. I did not know there were so many people with troubles in the world."

Thus, while social attitudes regard the handicapped child as an unmitigated disaster, in reality the problem may not be insurmountable, and often may not differ from life's other vicissitudes. Suffering there is, but seldom is it so overwhelming or so imminent that the only alternative is death of the child.

**Health Professionals.**  Physicians and nurses also suffer when parents give birth to a defective child, although, of course, not to the degree of the parents. To the obstetrician or general practitioner the defective birth may be a blow to his professional identity. He has the difficult task of informing the parents of the defects, explaining their causes, and dealing with the parents' resulting emotional shock. Often he feels guilty for failing to produce a normal baby. In addition the parents may project anger or hostility on the physician, questioning his professional competence or seeking the services of other doctors. The physician also may feel that his expertise and training are misused when employed to maintain the life of an infant whose chances for a productive existence are so diminished. By neglecting other patients, he may feel that he is prolonging rather than alleviating suffering.

Nurses, too, suffer role strain from care of the defective newborn. Intensive-care-unit nurses may work with only one or two babies at a time. They face the daily ordeals of care—the progress and relapses—and often must deal with anxious parents who are themselves grieving or ambivalent toward the child. The situation may trigger a nurse's own ambivalence about death and mothering, in a context in which she is actively working to keep alive a child whose life prospects seem minimal.

Thus, the effects of care on physicians and nurses are not trivial, and must be intelligently confronted in medical education or in management of a pediatric unit. Yet to state them is to make clear that they can but weigh lightly in the decision of whether to treat a defective newborn. Compared with the situation of the parents, these burdens seem insignificant, are short term, and most likely do not evoke such profound emotions. In any case, these difficulties are hazards of the profession—caring for the sick and dying will always produce strain. Hence, on these grounds alone it is difficult to argue that a defective person may be denied the right to life.

**Society.**  Care of the defective newborn also imposes societal costs, the utility of which is questioned when the infant's expected quality of life is so poor. Medical resources that can be used by infants with a better prognosis, or throughout the health-care system generally, are consumed in providing expensive surgical and intensive-care services to infants who may be severely retarded, never lead active lives, and die in a few months or years. Institutionalization imposes costs on taxpayers and reduces the resources available for those who might better benefit from it, while reducing further the quality of life experienced by the institutionalized defective.

One answer to these concerns is to question the impact of the costs of caring for defective newborns. Precise data showing the costs to taxpayers or the trade-offs with health and other expenditures do not exist. Nor would ceasing to care for the defective necessarily lead to a reallocation within the health budget that would produce net savings in suffering or life; in fact, the released resources might not be reallocated for health at all. In any case, the trade-offs within the health budget may well be small. With advances in prenatal diagnosis of genetic disorders, many deformed infants who would formerly require care will be aborted beforehand. Then, too, it is not clear that the most technical and expensive procedures always constitute the best treatment for certain malformations. When compared with the almost seven percent of the GNP now spent on health, the money in the defense budget, or tax revenues generally, the public resources required to keep defective newborns alive seem marginal, and arguably worth the commitment to life that such expenditures reinforce. Moreover, as the Supreme Court recently recognized, conservation of the taxpayer's purse does not justify serious infringement of fundamental rights. Given legal and ethical norms against sacrificing the lives of nonconsenting others, and the imprecisions in diagnosis and prediction concerning the eventual outcomes of medical care, the social-cost argument does not compel nontreatment of defective newborns.

---

# Ethical Issues in Aiding the Death of Young Children

## H. Tristram Engelhardt Jr.

H.T. Engelhardt contends that children are not persons in the full sense. They must exist in and through their families. Thus, parents, in conference with a physician who provides information, are the appropriate ones to decide whether to treat an impaired newborn when (1) there is not only little likelihood of a full human life but also the likelihood of suffering if the life is prolonged or (2) the cost of prolonging the life is very great.

Engelhardt further argues that it is reasonable to speak of a *duty* not to treat an impaired infant when this will only prolong a painful life or would only lead to a painful death. He bases his claim on the legal notion of a "wrongful life." This notion suggests that there are cases in which nonexistence would be better than existence under the conditions in which a person must live. Life can thus be seen as an injury, rather than as a gift.

Euthanasia in the pediatric age group involves a constellation of issues that are materially different from

This article first appeared in the book *Beneficent Euthanasia*, edited by Marvin Kohl, published by Prometheus Books, Buffalo, N.Y., 1975, and is reprinted by permission. (Notes and references omitted.)

those of adult euthanasia. The difference lies in the somewhat obvious fact that infants and young children are not able to decide about their own futures and thus are not persons in the same sense that normal adults are. While adults usually decide their own fate, others decide on behalf of young children.

Although one can argue that euthanasia is or should be a personal right, the sense of such an argument is obscure with respect to children. Young children do not have any personal rights, at least none that they can exercise on their own behalf with regard to the manner of their life and death. As a result, euthanasia of young children raises special questions concerning the standing of the rights of children, the status of parental rights, the obligations of adults to prevent the suffering of children, and the possible effects on society of allowing or expediting the death of seriously defective infants.

What I will refer to as the euthanasia of infants and young children might be termed by others infanticide, while some cases might be termed the withholding of extraordinary life-prolonging treatment. One needs a term that will encompass both death that results from active intervention and death that ensues when one simply ceases further therapy. In using such a term, one must recognize that death is often not directly but only obliquely intended. That is, one often intends only to treat no further, not actually to have death follow, even though one knows death will follow.

Finally, one must realize that deaths as the result of withholding treatment constitute a significant proportion of neonatal deaths. For example, as high as 14 percent of children in one hospital have been identified as dying after a decision was made not to treat further, the presumption being that the children would have lived longer had treatment been offered.

Even popular magazines have presented accounts of parental decisions not to pursue treatment. These decisions often involve a choice between expensive treatment with little chance of achieving a full, normal life for the child and "letting nature take its course," with the child dying as a result of its defects. As this suggests, many of these problems are products of medical progress. Such children in the past would have died. The quandaries are in a sense an embarrassment of riches; now that one *can* treat such defective children, *must* one treat them? And, if one need not treat such defective children, may one expedite their death?

I will here briefly examine some of these issues. First, I will review differences that contrast the euthanasia of adults to euthanasia of children. Second, I will review the issue of the rights of parents and the status of children. Third, I will suggest a new notion, the concept of the "injury of continued existence," and draw out some of its implications with respect to a duty to prevent suffering. Finally, I will outline some important questions that remain unanswered even if

the foregoing issues can be settled. In all, I hope more to display the issues involved in a difficult question than to advance a particular set of answers to particular dilemmas.

For the purpose of this paper, I will presume that adult euthanasia can be justified by an appeal to freedom. In the face of imminent death, one is usually choosing between a more painful and more protracted dying and a less painful or less protracted dying, in circumstances where either choice makes little difference with regard to the discharge of social duties and responsibilities. In the case of suicide, we might argue that, in general, social duties (for example, the duty to support one's family) restrain one from taking one's own life. But in the face of imminent death and in the presence of the pain and deterioration of a fatal disease, such duties are usually impossible to discharge and are thus rendered moot. One can, for example, picture an extreme case of an adult with a widely disseminated carcinoma, including metastases to the brain, who because of severe pain and debilitation is no longer capable of discharging any social duties. In these and similar circumstances, euthanasia becomes the issue of the right to control one's own body, even to the point of seeking assistance in suicide. Euthanasia is, as such, the issue of assisted suicide, the universalization of a maxim that all persons should be free, *in extremis,* to decide with regard to the circumstances of their death.

Further, the choice of positive euthanasia could be defended as the more rational choice: the choice of a less painful death and the affirmation of the value of a rational life. In so choosing, one would be acting to set limits to one's life in order not to live when pain and physical and mental deterioration make further rational life impossible. The choice to end one's life can be understood as a noncontradictory willing of a smaller set of states of existence for oneself, a set that would not include a painful death. That is, adult euthanasia can be construed as an affirmation of the rationality and autonomy of the self.

The remarks above focus on the active or positive euthanasia of adults. But they hold as well concerning what is often called passive or negative euthanasia, the refusal of life-prolonging therapy. In such cases, the patient's refusal of life-prolonging therapy is seen to be a right that derives from personal freedom, or at least from a zone of privacy into which there are no good grounds for social intervention.

Again, none of these considerations apply directly to the euthanasia of young children, because they cannot participate in such decisions. Whatever else pediatric, in particular neonatal, euthanasia involves, it surely involves issues different from those of adult euthanasia. Since infants and small children cannot commit suicide, their right to assisted suicide is difficult to pose. The difference between the euthanasia of young children and that of adults resides in the difference between children and adults. The difference, in fact, raises the troublesome question of whether young children are persons, or at least whether they are persons in the sense in which adults are. Answering that question will resolve in part at least the right of others to decide whether a young child should live or die and whether he should receive life-prolonging treatment.

## The Status of Children

Adults belong to themselves in the sense that they are rational and free and therefore responsible for their actions. Adults are *sui juris*. Young children, though, are neither self-possessed nor responsible. While adults exist in and for themselves, as self-directive and self-conscious beings, young children, especially newborn infants, exist for their families and those who love them. They are not, nor can they in any sense be, responsible for themselves. If being a person is to be a responsible agent, a bearer of rights and duties, children are not persons in a strict sense. They are, rather, persons in a social sense: others must act on their behalf and bear responsibility for them. They are, as it were, entities defined by their place in social roles (for example, mother–child, family–child) rather than beings that define themselves as persons, that is, in and through themselves. Young children live as persons in and through the care of those who are responsible for them, and those responsible for them exercise the children's rights on their behalf. In this sense children belong to families in ways that most adults do not. They exist in and through their family and society.

Treating young children with respect has, then, a sense different from treating adults with respect. One can respect neither a newborn infant's or very young child's wishes nor its freedom. In fact, a newborn infant or young child is more an entity that is valued highly because it will grow to be a person and because it plays a social role as if it were a person. That is, a small child is treated as if it were a person in social roles such as mother–child and family–child relationships, though strictly speaking the child is in no way capable of claiming or being responsible for the rights

imputed to it. All the rights and duties of the child are exercises and "held in trust" by others for a future time and for a person yet to develop.

Medical decisions to treat or not to treat a neonate or small child often turn on the probability and cost of achieving that future status—a developed personal life. The usual practice of letting anencephalic children (who congenitally lack all or most of the brain) die can be understood as a decision based on the absence of the possibility of achieving a personal life. The practice of refusing treatment to at least some children born with meningomyelocele can be justified through a similar, but more utilitarian, calculus. In the case of anencephalic children one might argue that care for them as persons is futile since they will never be persons. In the case of a child with meningomyelocele, one might argue that when the cost of cure would likely be very high and the probable lifestyle open to attainment very truncated, there is not a positive duty to make a large investment of money and suffering. One should note that the cost here must include not only financial costs but also the anxiety and suffering that prolonged and uncertain treatment of the child would cause the parents.

This further raises the issue of the scope of positive duties not only when there is no person present in a strict sense, but when the likelihood of a full human life is also very uncertain. Clinical and parental judgment may and should be guided by the expected lifestyle and the cost (in parental and societal pain and money) of its attainment. The decision about treatment, however, belongs properly to the parents because the child belongs to them in a sense that it does not belong to anyone else, even to itself. The care and raising of the child falls to the parents, and when considerable cost and little prospect of reasonable success are present, the parents may properly decide against life-prolonging treatment.

The physician's role is to present sufficient information in a usable form to the parents to aid them in making a decision. The accent is on the absence of a positive duty to treat in the presence of severe inconvenience (costs) to the parents; treatment that is very costly is not obligatory. What is suggested here is a general notion that there is never a duty to engage in extraordinary treatment and that "extraordinary" can be defined in terms of costs. This argument concerns children (1) whose future quality of life is likely to be seriously compromised and (2) whose present treatment would be very costly. The issue is that of the circumstances under which parents would not be obliged to take on severe burdens on behalf of their children or those circumstances under which society would not be so obliged. The argument should hold as well for those cases where the expected future life would surely be of normal quality, though its attainment would be extremely costly. The fact of little likelihood of success in attaining a normal life for the child makes decisions to do without treatment more plausible because the hope of success is even more remote and therefore the burden borne by parents or society becomes in that sense more extraordinary. But very high costs themselves could be a sufficient criterion, though in actual cases judgments in that regard would be very difficult when a normal life could be expected.

The decisions in these matters correctly lie in the hands of the parents, because it is primarily in terms of the family that children exist and develop—until children become persons strictly, they are persons in virtue of their social roles. As long as parents do not unjustifiably neglect the humans in those roles so that the value and purpose of that role (that is, child) stands to be eroded (thus endangering other children), society need not intervene. In short, parents may decide for or against the treatment of their severely deformed children.

However, society has a right to intervene and protect children for whom parents refuse care (including treatment) when such care does not constitute a severe burden and when it is likely that the child could be brought to a good quality of life. Obviously, "severe burden" and "good quality of life" will be difficult to define and their meanings will vary, just as it is always difficult to say when grains of sand dropped on a table constitute a heap. At most, though, society need only intervene when the grains clearly do not constitute a heap, that is, when it is clear that the burden is light and the chance of a good quality of life for the child is high. A small child's dependence on his parents is so essential that society need intervene only when the absence of intervention would lead to the role "child" being undermined. Society must value mother–child and family–child relationships and should intervene only in cases where (1) neglect is unreasonable and therefore would undermine respect and care for children, or (2) where societal intervention would prevent children from suffering unnecessary pain.

## The Injury of Continued Existence

But there is another viewpoint that must be considered: that of the child or even the person that the child might become. It might be argued that the child has a right not to have its life prolonged. The idea that forcing existence on a child would be wrong is a difficult notion, which, if true, would serve to amplify the foregoing argument. Such an argument would allow the construal of the issue in terms of the perspective of the child, that is, in terms of a duty not to treat in circumstances where treatment would only prolong suffering. In particular, it would at least give a framework for a decision to stop treatment in cases where, though the costs of treatment are not high, the child's existence would be characterized by severe pain and deprivation.

A basis for speaking of continuing existence as an injury to the child is suggested by the proposed legal concept of "wrongful life." A number of suits have been initiated in the United States and in other countries on the grounds that life or existence itself is, under certain circumstances, a tort or injury to the living person. Although thus far all such suits have ultimately failed, some have succeeded in their initial stages. Two examples may be instructive. In each case the ability to receive recompense for the injury (the tort) presupposed the existence of the individual, whose existence was itself the injury. In one case a suit was initiated on behalf of a child against his father alleging that his father's siring him out of wedlock was an injury to the child. In another case a suit on behalf of a child born of an inmate of a state mental hospital impregnated by rape in that institution was brought against the state of New York. The suit was brought on the grounds that being born with such historical antecedents was itself an injury for which recovery was due. Both cases presupposed that nonexistence would have been preferable to the conditions under which the person born was forced to live.

The suits for tort for wrongful life raise the issue not only of when it would be preferable not to have been born but also of when it would be *wrong* to cause a person to be born. This implies that someone should have judged that it would have been preferable for the child never to have had existence, never to have been in the position to judge that the particular circumstances of life were intolerable. Further, it implies that the person's existence under those circumstances should have been prevented and that, not having been prevented, life was not a gift but an injury. The concept of tort for wrongful life raises an issue concerning the responsibility for giving another person existence, namely the notion that giving life is not always necessarily a good and justifiable action. Instead, in certain circumstances, so it has been argued, one may have a duty *not* to give existence to another person. This concept involves the claim that certain qualities of life have a negative value, making life an injury, not a gift; it involves, in short, a concept of human accountability and responsibility for human life. It contrasts with the notion that life is a gift of God and thus similar to other "acts of God" (that is, events for which no man is accountable). The concept thus signals the fact that humans can now control reproduction and that where rational control is possible humans are accountable. That is, the expansion of human capabilities has resulted in an expansion of human responsibilities such that one must now decide when and under what circumstances persons will come into existence.

The concept of tort for wrongful life is transferable in part to the painfully compromised existence of children who can only have their life prolonged for a short, painful, and marginal existence. The concept suggests that allowing life to be prolonged under such circumstances would itself be an injury of the person whose painful and severely compromised existence would be made to continue. In fact, it suggests that there is a duty not to prolong life if it can be determined to have a substantial negative value for the person involved. Such issues are moot in the case of adults, who can and should decide for themselves. But small children cannot make such a choice. For them it is an issue of justifying prolonging life under circumstances of painful and compromised existence. Or, put differently, such cases indicate the need to develop social canons to allow a decent death for children for whom the only possibility is protracted, painful suffering.

I do not mean to imply that one should develop a new basis for civil damages. In the field of medicine, the need is to recognize an ethical category, a concept of wrongful continuance of existence, not a new legal right. The concept of injury for continuance of existence, the proposed analogue of the concept of tort for wrongful life, presupposes that life can be of a negative value such that the medical maxim *primum non nocere* ("first do no harm") would require not sustaining life.

The idea of responsibility for acts that sustain or prolong life is cardinal to the notion that one should not under certain circumstances further prolong the life of a child. Unlike adults, children cannot decide with regard to euthanasia (positive or negative), and if more than a utilitarian justification is sought, it must be sought in a duty not to inflict life on another person in circumstances where that life would be painful and futile. This position must rest on the facts that (1) medicine now can cause the prolongation of the life of

seriously deformed children who in the past would have died young and that (2) it is not clear that life so prolonged is a good for the child. Further, the choice is made not on the basis of costs to the parents or to society but on the basis of the child's suffering and compromised existence.

The difficulty lies in determining what makes life not worth living for a child. Answers could never be clear. It seems reasonable, however, that the life of children with diseases that involve pain and no hope of survival should not be prolonged. In the case of Tay–Sachs disease (a disease marked by a progressive increase in spasticity and dementia usually leading to death at age three or four), one can hardly imagine that the terminal stages of spastic reaction to stimuli and great difficulty in swallowing are at all pleasant to the child (even insofar as it can only minimally perceive its circumstances). If such a child develops aspiration pneumonia and is treated, it can reasonably be said that to prolong its life is to inflict suffering. Other diseases give fairly clear portraits of lives not worth living: for example, Lesch–Nyhan disease, which is marked by mental retardation and compulsive self-mutilation.

The issue is more difficult in the case of children with disease for whom the prospects for normal intelligence and a fair lifestyle do exist, but where these chances are remote and their realization expensive. Children born with meningomyelocele present this dilemma. Imagine, for example, a child that falls within Lorber's fifth category (an IQ of sixty or less, sometimes blind, subject to fits, and always incontinent). Such a child has little prospect of anything approaching a normal life, and there is a good chance of its dying even with treatment. But such judgments are statistical. And if one does not treat such children, some will still survive and, as John Freeman indicates, be worse off if not treated. In such cases one is in a dilemma. If one always treats, one must justify extending the life of those who will ultimately die anyway and in the process subjecting them to the morbidity of multiple surgical procedures. How remote does the prospect of a good life have to be in order not to be worth great pain and expense? It is probably best to decide, in the absence of a positive duty to treat, on the basis of the cost and suffering to parents and society. But, as Freeman argues, the prospect of prolonged or even increased suffering raises the issue of active euthanasia.

If the child is not a person strictly, and if death is inevitable and expediting it would diminish the child's pain prior to death, then it would seem to follow that, all else being equal, a decision for active euthanasia would be permissible, even obligatory. The difficulty lies with "all else being equal," for it is doubtful that active euthanasia could be established as a practice without eroding and endangering children generally, since, as John Lorber has pointed out, children cannot speak in their own behalf. Thus although there is no argument in principle against the active euthanasia of small children, there could be an argument against such practices based on questions of prudence. To put it another way, even though one might have a duty to hasten the death of a particular child, one's duty to protect children in general could override that first duty. The issue of active euthanasia turns in the end on whether it would have social consequences that refraining would not, on whether (1) it is possible to establish procedural safeguards for limited active euthanasia and (2) whether such practices would have a significant adverse effect on the treatment of small children in general. But since these are procedural issues dependent on sociological facts, they are not open to an answer within the confines of this article. In any event, the concept of the injury of continued existence provides a basis for the justification of the passive euthanasia of small children—a practice already widespread and somewhat established in our society—beyond the mere absence of a positive duty to treat.

## Conclusion

Though the lack of certainty concerning questions such as the prognosis of particular patients and the social consequence of active euthanasia of children prevents a clear answer to all the issues raised by the euthanasia of infants, it would seem that this much can be maintained: (1) Since children are not persons strictly but exist in and through their families, parents are the appropriate ones to decide whether or not to treat a deformed child when (a) there is not only little likelihood of full human life but also great likelihood of suffering if the life is prolonged, or (b) when the cost of prolonging life is very great. Such decisions must be made in consort with a physician who can accurately give estimates of cost and prognosis and who will be able to help the parents with the consequences of their decision. (2) It is reasonable to speak of a duty not to treat a small child when such treatment will only prolong a painful life or would in any event lead to a painful death. Though this does not by any means answer all the questions, it does point out an important fact—that medicine's duty is not always to prolong life doggedly but sometimes is quite the contrary.

# Life-and-Death Decisions in the Midst of Uncertainty

## Robert F. Weir

Robert Weir argues for a position midway between those of Robertson and Engelhardt. He agrees with Robertson that decisions about extremely premature or impaired infants ought not be based on considerations of economic, social, or emotional costs, but he also agrees with Engelhardt that infants are not persons in the full sense. Accordingly, in some cases we may reasonably decide that it is not in the best interest of the infant to be treated.

In Weir's view, neonates not suffering from severe neurological impairments are "potential persons," and as such, they possess basic human rights, including the right not to be killed. However, all infants, including those lacking the potential to become persons in the full sense, are entitled to have their "best interest" considered, and Weir provides eight criteria for determining the best interest of an infant. In accordance with these criteria, an infant's interest may sometimes be served best by withholding treatment and allowing the child to die. Physicians and parents, Weir maintains, ought to make treatment decisions based exclusively on the benefits and burdens of treatment to the infant.

A Neonatal Intensive Care Unit (NICU) is characterized by premature and disabled patients with life-threatening conditions, highly trained medical and nursing specialists, state-of-the-art medical technology, an endless stream of medical consultants, parents grappling with frightening possibilities, and numerous decisions that have to be made in the midst of impenetrable uncertainty. Whether made while looking down at an imperiled baby, in consultation with the baby's parents, or in a conference room near the NICU, many of these decisions are crucial because a baby will continue to live or will die as a consequence of the decisions. . . .

## Do Neonates Count as Persons?

. . . To the extent that there is consensus among philosophers on the concept of personhood, that consensus focuses on the intrinsic rather than the extrinsic qualities of persons. Most philosophers agree on at least the core properties or traits of personhood, if not on all of their applications. Joel Feinberg, in his discussion of "commonsense personhood," puts forth the consensus view of personhood as being the possession of three necessary and jointly sufficient properties: consciousness, self-awareness, and at least minimum rationality. Such properties, for him and many others, represent "person-making characteristics."

The possession of personhood, therefore, has to do with neurological development and, at least among human beings, the absence of profound neurological dysfunction or impairment. The answer to the question of whether neonates are to be counted as persons depends on three interrelated factors:

1. How much neurological development is required for personhood;

2. How much neurological impairment is necessary to rule out personhood; and

3. Whether any significance is to be placed on the principle of potentiality as it applies to personhood.

In my judgment, there are three basic positions regarding the personhood of neonates (and other human beings whose personhood may be questioned), and the positions are distinguishable largely because of their handling of the factors of neurological develop-

ment, neurological impairment, and potential personhood. The first position holds that *all neonates,* whether normal or neurologically impaired, *are nonpersons.* . . .

The second position stands at the other end of a philosophical and political spectrum, and represents a very common view of neonates held by many physicians, nurses, and other people as well. . . .

The third position stands between the other positions, differing from the first position's insufficient claims and the second position's excessive claims regarding the personhood of human newborns. This position, which holds that *most neonates are potential persons,* can be compared with the alternative views on the basis of its four claims:

1. Personhood is a moral category attaching to beings (of any species) with certain characteristics, principally cognitive capacities;

2. Neonates lack the intrinsic qualities that make a human into a person, as do fetuses;

3. Having the potential to become a person through the normal course of development does count, and neonates without severe neurological impairment (and fetuses having exhibited brain activity) have this potential; and

4. All *potential* persons have a *prima facie* claim to the moral benefits of personhood, including the right not to be killed, because they will subsequently acquire an *actual* person's moral and legal right to life.

The last of these positions, in my view, is the correct way of describing the ontological status of neonates. This position is preferable to the neonates-are-not-persons view of some philosophers, because it grants more than a species value to human newborns—and avoids the major weakness of having to allow, in principle, for the indiscriminate termination of an indeterminate number of neonatal lives, whether these lives are cognitively impaired, physically disabled, or normal. The third position is also preferable to the neonates-are-actual-persons view (especially as put forth by several prolife groups), because it takes the philosophical and psychological concept of personhood seriously—and avoids the major weakness of having to say, in principle, that a baby has no more claim to the moral benefits of personhood than an early human embryo does.

Robert F. Weir, "Life and Death in the Midst of Uncertainty," in *Compelled Compassion,* ed. Arthur Caplan, Robert Blank, and Janna Merrick, Totowa, N.J.: Humana Press, 1992, pp. 1, 9–12, 14–19, 21–22, 27–30. (Notes and references omitted.)

## What Is the Best Ethical Option for Making Decisions to Initiate, Continue, or Abate Life-Sustaining Treatment?

. . . The options range from very conservative to very liberal, and they differ from one another regarding the substantive and, to a lesser extent, the procedural aspects of making life-and-death decisions for nonautonomous young patients.

The most conservative of these ethical options is the ethical perspective that was enacted into public policy by the Reagan administration through the "Baby Doe" regulations and subsequent Child Abuse regulations. Incensed that one "Baby Doe" (the 1982 Bloomington, Indiana, case) had died who could have lived with surgical intervention and concerned that other disabled infants were unnecessarily being allowed to die in other hospitals, the leaders of the Reagan administration went to great lengths to advocate the ethical perspective held by Surgeon General C. Everett Koop, and many of the administration's prolife supporters.

This ethical position holds that there is one and only one acceptable moral reason for not sustaining an infant's life, namely, the medical futility in a very limited number of cases of trying to do so. According to this ethical perspective, decisions not to sustain a severely disabled infant's life are acceptable only when such an infant is irretrievably dying (or, for some persons holding this position, an infant whose condition is some form of permanent unconsciousness). Therefore, the only cases in which such decisions by physicians or parents are justifiable are those unusual cases in which there is actually no moral decision to make: God, nature, fate, the roll of the genetic "dice," or some force beyond our control prevents medical efforts at sustaining life from working.

The most liberal option is a position that carries significant weight in some philosophical circles, but not, as we have already discussed, among physicians and others who are more oriented toward a practical, empirically based view of reality. This position, in sharp contrast to the first position, is based on the ontological status of the young lives at risk in critical care units rather than on the severity of their medical conditions. Instead of calling for life-sustaining treatment to be administered to all neonates or young children who are not dying (or permanently unconscious), the philosophers holding this position (e.g., Michael Tooley, Mary Anne Warren, and Peter Singer) argue that physicians and parents are obligated only to provide life-sustaining treatment for neonates and young children who count as persons. The catch is, as we have

seen, that according to this perspective no neonates meet the criteria for personhood, and no moral weight is placed on the potential they may have to become persons later in the course of their development. An unresolved problem for these philosophers—and one of the reasons that this position will never become public policy—is that of defining the "magic moment" beyond the neonatal period when young children do meet the criteria for personhood and are thus protected from having their lives arbitrarily terminated.

The third position is the first of three positions that reside closer to the middle of the philosophical spectrum than either of the views just discussed. The physicians, philosophers, and other individuals who hold this view do not believe that all nondying neonates should be given life-sustaining treatment, nor do they believe that the lives of neonates can be terminated morally on the basis of a definitional point about personhood. Rather, they are convinced that the most important aspect of decisions not to sustain some infants' lives is the procedural question of who should make these difficult decisions. The correct answer to that question, according to the advocates of this position, is that the appropriate decision maker is the parent or parents of the neonate or young child whose life is threatened by his or her medical condition, even though the current federal regulations do not permit this kind of parental discretion. Since the parents of a disabled infant are the ones who stand to gain or lose the most, depending on what happens to the infant, it is they—instead of the physicians, an ethics committee, or anybody else—who should have the right to make the life-or-death decision in all cases over which there is some disagreement about whether a disabled infant should continue to live with or die in the absence of life-sustaining treatment.

Advocates of a fourth ethical position are convinced that quality-of-life judgments are unavoidable in cases of severe neurological or physiological malformation, in spite of what the federal regulations say to the contrary. All of the responsible parties in cases of serious neonatal abnormalities are morally obligated—and should be legally permitted—to raise important questions about the most likely future ahead of these children if their lives are to be prolonged with medical treatment. Of fundamental importance in such cases is not only the question of whether a given child can be salvaged with the abnormalities he or she has, but also what kind of life he or she is most likely to have with those abnormalities. The most important abnormalities to consider are neurological in nature. If a neurological disorder is sufficiently serious that pediatric neurologists and neonatologists project a life with severe disabilities for the child, virtually all persons holding a quality-of-life position would find the abatement of life-sustaining treatment in such a case to be morally justifiable.

The fifth position is held by individuals who are convinced that life-sustaining treatment should be provided to normal and disabled neonates whenever such treatment is in their best interests, and that life-sustaining treatment should be abated in the care of severely premature or severely disabled neonates (and other young children) whenever such treatment is judged not to be in their best interests.

Persons holding this position tend to be in agreement with quality-of-life advocates whose projections of a given child's future focus *entirely* on that child's likely abilities and disabilities, not on the child's impact on anybody else or ability to attain somebody else's minimal standard of acceptability for personal human life. By contrast, persons having a best-interests position disagree with quality-of-life advocates who tend to compare mentally and physically abnormal children with normal children, emphasize the problems that disabled children cause for their families and society, and try to protect families and society from having to deal with disabled children who cannot meet some arbitrary standard of acceptability. Like all advocates of the quality-of-life position, proponents of the best-interests position hold a view that is more liberal than the current federal regulations.

The best-interests position, in my judgment, is the preferable ethical perspective to take in regard to difficult decisions about initiating, continuing, or abating life-sustaining treatment with any patients having life-threatening medical conditions. Neonatal and other young pediatric patients are no exception. They, like other nonautonomous patients, should receive life-sustaining treatment whenever the decision makers are convinced that the treatments available provide a balance of benefit to burden for the child. Such decisions should focus on the child's medical condition, concern suffering and irremediable handicap rather than projected social worth, and involve comparative judgments about the continuation of the child's injurious existence as opposed to the child's nonexistence.

## What Does "Best Interests" Mean When Patients Are Neonates?

Even though widely supported in theory, the best-interests position is not without problems. Some of the advocates of the position admit that the concept of the patient's best interests is inherently vague, especially when the patient is a neonate. Nevertheless, they argue that the concept is helpful in decision making about life-sustaining treatment for neonates, because it focuses the decision-making process on precisely the human lives that ought to be the primary focus of concern.

Some of the critics of the best-interests position, at least as it applies to neonates, think that the conceptual foundation on which it stands is fundamentally flawed. Martin Benjamin argues that neonates simply do not yet possess the cognitive awareness, much less the specific wants and purposes, that are necessary for ascribing to them an interest in continued life. Howard Brody is convinced that any attempt to apply the concept of best interests to infants is bound to fail, because the concept is either incoherent or inadequate as a guide for tough clinical decisions. He argues that, even if infants can intelligibly be said to have interests, such interests would be unknowable by adult decision makers. . . .

. . . One's "interests" consist of relationships, activities, and things in which one has a stake and on which one places value. To have interests (as opposed to sensations or instincts) normally requires as necessary conditions that one be conscious, aware of oneself, and able cognitively to have wants and purposes. In other words, to have interests normally requires that one be a person.

Yet, as Joel Feinberg points out in a discussion of fetal interests, it is plausible to ascribe *future* interests to a "prepersonal fetus." Even though a fetus "presumably has no actual interests," it can correctly be said to have future interests on the assumption that it will at some future point in its normal development (at birth or subsequent to birth) become a person and, thus, the possessor of actual interests. In a similar manner, the law recognizes that fetuses can have "contingent rights," such as the right to property, that will become actual rights the moment the fetus becomes a baby. Any contingent right of a fetus is instantly voided if the fetus dies before birth.

The same kind of reasoning about interests can be used in analyzing the interests that are ascribable to neonates, even by philosophers who claim that all neonates are nonpersons. For even if neonates as nonpersons cannot correctly be said to be the possessors of actual interests, they can be said to have future interests (assuming that they will at some future point become persons) that can be interfered with or damaged by decisions or actions by adults long before these developing human lives become persons. For example, a neonate with myelomeningocele could reasonably be said to have a future interest in physical mobility, but come to realize later in life that a decision by physicians or parents during the neonatal period not to have the lesion surgically corrected had preempted that future interest from being actualized.

An alternative conceptual framework for discussing the interests of neonates was presented earlier, namely the philosophical view that neonates without severe neurological impairments are to be regarded as potential persons. In this framework, an analysis of the interests of neonates does not involve the ascription of future interests to them because they are thought likely to become persons at some "magic moment" in the future, but ascribes future interests to them because they have the potential to become the possessors of interests through the normal course of their development.

The point is a fundamental one. Just as potentiality is an important aspect of the concept of personhood, so potentiality is an important feature of a philosophical understanding of interests (but not of legal rights). Interests change from time to time after one becomes a person, with some interests intensifying over time, others waning, and others appearing as though newly born. For that reason, a discussion of the future interests of any given neonate becomes problematic if one can only project the actual interests that child will have when he or she meets the criteria for personhood at some future point in time. By contrast, the principle of potentiality, as it applies both to the possession of personhood and the possession of interests, permits one reasonably to ascribe to any given neonate the most general and basic kinds of interests that most individuals tend to have as they develop from young children to older children and on through the various phases of personal life. . . .

When applied to neonates, the concept of "best interests" can obviously not refer to the specific wants and purposes any given neonate may have in continued life, much less to the specific wants and purposes that the neonate may have later in life. However, the concept of "best interests" can be used to capture the most fundamental future interest that persons have when they are patients, namely, an interest in not being harmed on balance during the course of medical treatment. For most patients in most clinical situations, this vital interest in not being harmed on balance means that they prefer continued life to death—unless intractable pain and other suffering have made continued life more harmful than the prospect of death. To ascribe this general and basic interest to

neonates is to claim that all neonates lacking severe neurological impairment can reasonably be said to have this future interest in not being harmed, an interest that will become actualized as they become persons during the normal course of their development.

. . . [T]he toughest aspect of using the concept of best interests in decision making in NICUs is determining the factors that should be considered in any given case. How can physicians and parents assess the beneficial and detrimental aspects of medical treatment in a case? How can they decide if life-sustaining treatment is in a neonate's best interests or is contrary to those interests?

My suggestion is to regard the patient's-best-interests standard as having eight variables. In neonatal (and other young pediatric) cases, the variables are as follows:

1. Severity of the patient's medical condition;
2. Availability of curative or corrective treatment;
3. Achievability of important medical goals;
4. Presence of serious neurological impairments;
5. Extent of the infant's suffering;
6. Multiplicity of other serious medical problems;
7. Life expectancy of the infant; and
8. Proportionality of treatment-related benefits and burdens to the infant.

The last of these variables is, in many respects, a summation of the preceding variables. For decision makers in such cases, a consideration of the benefits of the treatment (both short-term and long-term) to the patient is the "bottom line" for determining whether life-sustaining treatment or the abatement of life-sustaining treatment is in a particular neonate's best interests. In making this assessment, decision makers arrive at a subjective judgment that includes objective factors, but is not finally reducible to quantifiable information. For to decide in rare clinical situations that treatment is, on balance, harmful to the infant rather than beneficial is to make a moral judgment. . . .

## Should Life-Sustaining Treatment for Neonates and Other Young Children Ever Be Abated for Economic Reasons?

Neonatologists and other pediatric specialists place considerable importance on providing good patient care. In terms of the patient's-best-interests position, this emphasis on the medical needs and interests of individual patients is the morally preferable perspective for pediatricians and other physicians to have. According to this view, the needs and interests of each patient related to continued life correctly outweigh any competing interests of parents, siblings, or society. Simply put, no neonate or other young , nonautonomous patient should die merely because their medical and hospital care is expensive, even when the physicians and parents in a given case know that the family's income and insurance cannot cover the costs involved in the patient's care.

In the last few years, however, a number of factors have combined to create uncertainty about this basic moral premise for the provision of medical care, especially as it applies to cases of extremely premature or severely disabled neonates. Physicians, hospital administrators, and other concerned persons often question the importance that should be placed on the economic aspects of sustaining the lives of some neonates and other young children, especially when these lives predictably will be characterized by severe mental and physical disabilities. Case discussions in NICUs, PICUs, and specialized chronic care units for young children increasingly have comments and questions by staff physicians, residents, nurses, social workers, and ethicists regarding the costs of the ongoing treatment and who will have to pay for those costs. . . .

. . . [A] factor contributing to uncertainty about the role of economics in neonatal cases pertains to the escalating costs of the care needed by extremely premature or severely disabled newborns. This uncertainty is brought about not only by an awareness of the escalating costs of providing care for these babies, but also by the realization that efforts to provide comparative cost figures for neonatal care have proven less than satisfactory, that the application of diagnosis-related group (DRG) categories has not worked well in NICUs, and that the cost-effectiveness of neonatal care for low-birth-weight neonates is still questionable. . . .

Studies published in recent years all document the increasing cost of providing care for disabled neonates and young children in chronic care units. For example, one study from Canada (using 1978 Canadian dollars) found that the costs of intensive care for infants weighing less than 1000 grams averaged $102,500 per survivor. A study from Australia (using 1984 Australian dollars) determined that the total direct cost for level-III, high-dependency care in one hospital was $690 per day. Studies in the United States, varying greatly in methodology, have found the total cost for selected survivors or neonatal intensive care in a Boston hospital to range from $14,600 to $40,700, for long-term survivors in a Washington, DC, pediatric hospital to be

$182,500 for a year, and for extremely low-birthweight survivors of NICUs in six medical centers to range from $72,110 to $524,110, with a mean cost of care per infant of $158,800 for 137 days.

. . . [Another] factor has been the increased recognition that the financial pressures created by expensive neonatal and pediatric treatment can greatly damage and sometimes destroy families. For example, a 1988 Minnesota followup study of disabled infants and their families had a number of disturbing findings: the proportion of families with young children, but lacking health insurance is increasing, 16% of the families in the study pay the entire cost of their health insurance, middle-income families have not qualified for state financial assistance, several of the families have filed for bankruptcy, and at least one family still owes a hospital and physicians over $300,000 for the care of their young child. The report concludes: "Families should not have to lose their homes, mortgage their future, or neglect other children's needs to pay for the care of a chronically ill or disabled child."

A related, but different factor has to do with the long-term costs of providing medical, nursing, and surgical care for severely disabled children who remain in hospitals for months and years. Sometimes called "boarder babies," these children have complicated, chronic medical conditions, are usually dependent on mechanical ventilation and other technological assistance for survival, and frequently come from low-income, single-parent families that simply cannot afford (in terms of money and time) to have the child at home.

If no other institutional home can be arranged (usually because of the cost and technology involved), and if foster parents are not a realistic option, such children may reside for several years in a specialized chronic care unit in the hospital in which they were born. When that happens, the children become living symbols of a "second generation" type of problem brought about by the successes of neonatal intensive care: They are survivors of the NICU, but remain captives of medical technology in an institution that nobody would choose to call home. . . .

Given the uncertainty generated by these variables, what should be done? For two of the ethical positions described earlier, the answer is reasonably simple: revise or ignore the federal regulations, abate life-sustaining treatment more quickly on the basis of (1) parental discretion or (2) projected quality of life for the neonates involved (including the impact of a neonate's later life on others), and thus cut down on the costs in NICUs, to families, and to institutions.

To go that way, for that reason, would be a mistake. The economic aspects of neonatal intensive care would become a dominant factor in decision making by parents and physicians, and many premature and disabled neonates would have their lives cut short to save money. To establish a policy that would encourage parents to make life-and-death decisions in individual cases as a money-saving strategy for themselves (or for physicians to do the same to save money for their hospitals) is not the best policy for addressing the very real problem of escalating costs for neonatal intensive care, especially if that policy is to be guided by the ethical principles of beneficence, nonmaleficence, and justice.

There is, in my judgment, a better alternative. That alternative is a combination of:

1. Continued use of the patient's-best-interests standard in clinical settings, including increased emphasis on the eight variables that comprise the standard;

2. The establishment of a national policy, based on sound clinical evidence, that would restrict the use of neonatal intensive care in terms of infants' birthweights; and

3. The establishment of a national health insurance program that would pay for the catastrophic health-care expenses generated by providing care for extremely premature severely disabled newborns.

The results of this combined approach would be threefold. A more consistent application of the best-interests standard would result in an increased number of decisions, as difficult as they are, by parents and physicians to discontinue life-sustaining treatment in individual cases. Such decisions would not be made to save money, but would be based on an honest conclusion that the treatment available, although capable of sustaining a neonate's life, is contrary to the infant's best interests.

In addition, the establishment of a national policy that would limit life-sustaining treatment to neonates over a certain birthweight (e.g., 600 grams) would not only cut down on the enormously high costs of caring for extremely low-birthweight infants, but could also be defended, depending on the rationale and details of the policy, as meeting the requirements of justice. Such a policy would surely not solve all of the problems of uncertainty in NICUs, but could provide a measure of greater certainty, if based on a consensus among neonatologists, in establishing a minimum weight limit for neonates who would be given life-sustaining treatment.

Finally, by establishing a national insurance program, the federal government would help pay for the enormous costs that are involved in neonatal intensive care and specialized chronic-care units for young children. For the federal government to mandate that virtually all neonates, unless dying or permanently unconscious, be kept alive, and then to make no serious effort to help parents and institutions pay for that expensive care is unjust. In the absence of such a program, parents and physicians will continue to be faced with the task of making life-and-death decisions for newborns in the midst of great uncertainty—including whether the family will be destroyed financially by costs of the medical care.

## READINGS

# Section 2: Other Perspectives

## Avoiding Anomalous Newborns

### Michael L. Gross

Michael Gross focuses on the Baby Messenger case and examines two protocols used to decide how to "avoid" impaired newborns: (1) meeting threshold criteria for treatment (Denmark); (2) choosing late-term abortion (Israel). Each protocol offers an "ethically sound" way to deal with "the economic and social expense of anomalous newborns." Both protocols, Gross claims, are compatible with the principles of economic justice, utility, and respect for autonomy and so could be adopted in the United States.

The case of baby Messenger, a severely ill preterm infant removed by his parents from ventilator support and allowed to die, serves to illustrate treatment options when infants are threatened by extremely premature birth. In most cases, alternative courses of action are defined within acceptable treatment protocols of impaired newborns. These include a "stastistical" approach whereby treatment is withheld from infants defined as underweight and/or immature, an "initiate and reevaluate" approach whereby aggressive treatment is begun and then reevaluated relative to the infant's progress and parents' wishes, and a "treat until certainty" approach whereby each infant is treated until death or discharge.

Each of these approaches has attendant virtues and vices in the context of American neonatal care. But the Messenger case can also be used to examine prevailing norms and policies of different countries. Policymakers in Denmark, a country that accepts the statistical approach, view the ethical dimension of this case differently from those in the UK and the US where an "initiate and reevaluate" approach is accepted. Each of these treatment options remains, nevertheless, a neonatal protocol. In each case, no decision is taken until after the baby is born. However, in the Israeli context, this case takes an entirely different turn. Israel's unrestrictive abortion policy may well permit the option of a late-term abortion thereby obviating any impaired infant protocol. The situation is exacerbated because neonatal policy in Israel conforms largely to the "wait until certainty" approach. In all instances, a closer look at the Messenger case illustrates the conundrum of abortion and neonatal care in a cross-national context.

## Saving Baby Messenger

Admitted for premature labour at twenty-five weeks gestation, Messenger was informed that her baby stood a 50–75% chance of mortality and a 20–40% chance of severe cerebral haemorrhage and neurological damage should he survive. The consulting neonatalogist also indicated a significant possibility of respiratory complications. With these statistics in mind, the parents instructed the attending physician not to undertake extraordinary efforts to save the life of the newborn. The neonatalogist, in turn, instructed her as-

Michael L. Gross, "Avoiding Anomalous Newborns: Preemptive Abortion, Treatment Thresholds and the Case of Baby Messenger," reprinted from *Journal of Medical Ethics,* August 2000 (vol. 26, no. 4), 242–248, with permission from the BMJ Publishing Group.

sistant to intubate the baby only if he was "vigorous" and "active." Although the baby weighed only 780 grams and was hypotonic and hypoxic these instructions were ignored, and the baby was resuscitated, intubated and incubated. The father, agonised that his instructions were not followed, removed his son from life-support, allowing him to die in his parents' arms.[1]

This case, in which Messenger was charged with manslaughter and acquitted, generated a great deal of discussion regarding alternative avenues of neonatal care, parental rights, and the responsibility of the attending physician to honour parental requests to terminate care. By and large, the ethical discussion is limited by the legal options available in the United States where the case occurred, and is restricted therefore to the relative merits of the "initiate and reevaluate" and "wait until certainty" protocols. Reviewing the Messenger case, most commentators—considering both the infant's best interests and the need for implied or explicit consent—emphasise the need to consider parental interests while allowing parents greater say about the decision to terminate life-support.[2–5] However, two additional options deserve further exploration. First, a statistical approach stipulating thresholds below which young, immature infants would not be resuscitated merits review. Often dismissed by American commentators as fundamentally antithetical to American bioethics, this approach has been adopted by the Danish Council of Ethics. Second, there is room to discuss late-term abortion as a radically different solution to the Messenger case. Given the high mortality rate and significant possibility of impairment, would it not make sense to allow parents the option of abortion, thereby preempting the need for any other neonatal policy?

## Statistical Non-treatment as a Solution to the Messenger Case

In contrast to a strict statistical protocol that denies treatment to all members of a specific class of very extremely low birthweight (ELBW) infants, the Danish Council of Ethics endorses a modified threshold protocol that combines a minimum gestational age, a maturality criterion and respect for parental wishes.[6] Under this protocol, infants younger than 24 or 25 weeks will not be aggressively treated. However, this threshold is modified by two conditions. First, mature infants, even those younger than 24 or 25 weeks may be revived if this can be accomplished using "low technology modalities" and minimal handling to induce respiration.[7,8]

Second, the threshold is further modified by considerations of parental wishes. Viability is a function of the care a child can expect to receive from his parents, and is substantially impaired if the parents are unable or unwilling to provide the intensive care a preterm infant requires. As a result the threshold and maturity criterion may be overridden both by parents wishing to care for a child that fails to meet the criterion or by parents requesting to withhold treatment from a newborn that meets the threshold requirement. Under these guidelines, baby Messenger need not have been resuscitated. Even had the neonatalogist decided that the gestational threshold had been met, the baby's immediate condition following birth did not meet the maturity criterion. This, together with the parents refusal of ventilator support, should deter resuscitation. There is no real dilemma.

There are two distinct principles behind the council's recommendations—the infant's best interests and economic justice:

> The basis for the [modified threshold] recommendation is that the panel considers the 35% occurrence of severe handicaps in children born after a pregnancy term of 24–25 full weeks to be high in relation to the number of surviving infants; the panel also takes into account the comparison of the expenditure incurred with the possible alternative applications for that amount.[9]

From this perspective sanctity of life is tempered by the infant's best interests and societal cost. On the one hand, a 35% risk of severe impairment is simply one that no parent, physician or policy-maker is prepared to inflict on a newborn. On the other, the possibility that the parents may bear the life-long emotional and financial cost of raising a handicapped child is not offset by the likelihood that the child may none the less lead a relatively normal life. While this seems a reasonable decision for parents to make, it also means, by extension, that large numbers of healthy infants are sacrificed to avoid fewer numbers of handicapped infants. While 35 out of every 100 ELBW infants denied treatment would have been severely handicapped, the vast majority would have been normal or only moderately impaired. This outcome seems patently unjust unless tempered by other factors. Such a decision at the social level can only be justified if the attendant cost of neonatal care outweighs the lives of 65 relatively normal children (of every 100 denied treatment). This occurs if the money could be put to better use, i.e. saving more lives. The economic claim is pivotal. There is little interest in devoting resources either to lowering the 35% figure or to saving increasingly younger infants:

> It seems reasonable to exercise reticence in the treatment of extremely preterm infants in order to benefit the slightly less premature, since the prospects of better results increase with age and fewer resources are consumed, allowing more to be helped.[10]

Given the high costs of neonatal care, economic considerations are difficult to assail. Unlike an individual parent's decision to withhold treatment from an ELBW infant, comprehensive policy to do so must be anchored in considerations of economic justice. This is a problem all public health systems grapple with as different groups vie for scarce resources. Interestingly, the council has compartmentalised the recipients of justice. The claims of ELBW newborns are not balanced against adults or other children, but against other premature infants. Under such a modified utilitarian plan one can presumably distribute resources equally between morally relevant groups (such as the elderly, premature, or terminally ill) while cost–benefit calculus can determine resource distribution within each group. This tempers the inherent defect of utilitarian justice that may medically impoverish certain groups in the interests of maximising overall utility.

## One Obvious Objection

In this way, a threshold policy answers to the demands of economic justice, the (modified) demands of utility and some measure of equality as well. Parental discretion allays fears of heavyhanded paternalism while allowing determined parents to care for infants below the threshold or withhold treatment from those above it. Considerations of maturity partially resolve the problem of outliers, as some potentially viable infants are treated regardless of gestational age.

So what's wrong with a modified threshold policy? One obvious objection suggests that the statistical approach denies patients reasonable prognostic certainty. By denying all infants resuscitation the healthy are discarded with the handicapped. Would it not be more just and equally cost-effective if all infants were resuscitated and then evaluated with an eye towards terminating treatment for those most severely afflicted?

As attractive as this argument is, it easily undermines other treatment protocols as well. A typical American response might argue that failure to provide resuscitation is draconian, casting a net that denies a healthy life to viable infants as well. But there is no way to ensure that healthy infants won't die under any policy short of "treat until certainty." While resuscitation may offer the possibility that greater numbers of healthy infants survive, it ultimately falls to the same argument levelled at threshold protocols. Reevaluation and subsequent treatment decisions are based on probability figures no less than the decision to deny treatment at birth. The outcomes of high-grade haemorrhages, for example, might be equally indeterminate as those facing ELBW infants. Why not resuscitate and wait to evaluate the outcomes? But how far down the road should one reevaluate, two weeks, two months, two years? Is it then possible to discontinue treatment for a two- or three-year-old, while in the meantime creating a large pool of handicapped children? The argument based on relative prognostic certainty cannot work. It merely creates a slippery slope one might like to avoid. Resuscitation with the intent to reevaluate and, if necessary, discontinue treatment also blurs the distinction between withholding and withdrawing treatment. The oft-repeated claim that the two are ethically indistinguishable is not universally true. It certainly gives the Danish Council of Ethics pause for reflection while a hard distinction between the two suffuses Israeli case law and practice. Certainly the two are psychologically dissimilar. Parents asked to terminate life-support are not in the same position as those asked to acquiesce to withholding treatment. A threshold policy turns on this difference by making non-treatment the subject of presumed consent: unless parents choose otherwise no treatment is provided. Parental autonomy is affirmed but only covertly, in a manner similar to some European organ donation protocols. Ethically, presumed consent avoids what the council terms the "autonomy trap": the tendency to place too much responsibility on the shoulders of ill-prepared parents. Economically, this policy avoids the costs of extensive resuscitation. Only the most motivated and informed parents are apt to come forward, whether it be on the basis of a decision to care for a severely handicapped infant or to withhold treatment from an infant that might otherwise be treated. It is therefore not at all obvious that an "initiate and reevaluate" protocol affords similar cost-effectiveness as a threshold policy or is as ethically compelling.

## Presumed Consent

Finally it has been suggested that a threshold protocol smacks of sinister social planning that is antithetical to American individualism.[5] But it is not immediately clear how this policy negates individualism. One might argue that the threshold approach does not really respect parental autonomy. But the force of this argument leans heavily on a ratified American vision of autonomy that is coming under increasing attack.[11] In many ways, a modified threshold policy maintains respect for autonomy, albeit a gentler autonomy, largely by removing active decision making from the hands of the parents and relying on presumed consent. Additionally, one might argue that the statistical approach ignores the "ability of outliers' to survive or the willingness of some parents to cope with tragic circumstances."[12] These are reasonable objections but they do not accurately reflect a modified policy tempered by considerations of maturity and parental discretion. Nor do they have much to do with individualism.

Individualism (or more specifically, "individuality") is, to cite Mill, inextricably linked to development and is best achieved when human beings are allowed to achieve the necessary moral, intellectual and practical development to become good citizens.[13] The conditions necessary for continued human development form the basis of the modern welfare state. Oddly enough, American individualism denies its citizens basic health care, certainly one of the most necessary conditions for development. Does a threshold policy of neonatal care similarly deny one the conditions for development? On a very basic level the answer is yes, if it denies life to potentially healthy newborns. But this argument ultimately collapses into those already discussed and discarded. First, any treatment protocol that allows termination of life-support prior to absolute certainty will deny some the chance of a normal life. Second, health care systems are designed not only to provide life for the greatest number but also quality of life for the greatest number. There is no reason to assume that threshold protocols curtail medical services so crucial for personal development. On the contrary, a threshold policy enhances the availability of funds for other health care needs by eliminating an expense that benefits relatively few children.

Finally, one may object that threshold protocols return us to the ever-present slippery slope: if we refuse to treat a large class of newborns, what will prohibit us from aborting late-term fetuses whose odds of survival are similar to those of baby Messenger? What indeed?

## Preemptive Abortion as a Solution to the Messenger Case

Following US jurisprudence, American commentators often define abortion as the "expulsion of an embryo or fetus before it is viable."[14] This makes it difficult to speak of "late-term" abortions, for in the American sense these are not abortions at all, but acts of feticide. From this perspective it is therefore necessary to distinguish between abortion as the termination of a pregnancy and abortion as the termination of a fetus. The former is a constitutionally protected right in the US, while the latter is justified only under rare conditions of fetal best interest.[15]

Abortion in Israel, on the other hand, is broadly defined as termination of pregnancy without regard to gestational age or fetal viability and, at later stages, inevitably includes fetal termination. Abortion at all stages of pregnancy is freely available for any of the following conditions: maternal age (<17 or >40 years of age), premarital pregnancy (or pregnancy resulting from rape or incest), danger to the mother's physical or mental health and/or fetal birth defects. Requests for abortion must be approved by a hospital committee. Abortion law is similar in Denmark while provisions in the UK specify "severe" fetal anomalies. In spite of the flexibility of the law, late-term (third trimester) abortions are generally avoided in the UK and Denmark. Israel, on the other hand, has one of the highest rates of late-term abortion in the world.[16]

The purpose here is not to explore the merits of late-term abortion policy (as discussed elsewhere[16]) but to reflect on the feasibility of preemptive abortion: terminating a normal fetus similar to the Messengers' in order to avoid dealing with the possibility of a severely malformed newborn. The issue is brought in the Israeli context, not because preemptive abortion is practised, but because it has been raised as an ethically problematic possibility that might be allowed under current abortion regulations. Moreover, neonatal treatment protocols in Israel reflect the "treat until certainty" approach. In the event of spontaneous delivery, any live, viable newborn would be treated aggressively. As a result, preemptive abortion is the only way to avoid a malformed newborn when faced with severely premature birth. Under this scenario a woman in Messenger's position would be allowed the option of fetal termination when it was determined that she faced the probability of delivering an anomalous infant. The immediate justification for a late-term abortion focuses on the high probability of severe deformity facing the infant. The immediate objection, on the other hand, focuses on the health of the fetus: in utero s/he is completely normal.

The justification for abortion unpacks to include the same kind of probability calculations that inform a threshold or "initiate and reevaluate" protocol. If one accepts a 35% chance of severe disability as a reason-able threshold to withhold treatment, or the Messenger statistics as a reasonable threshold to withdraw treatment, then why not accept these same probabilities to justify a late-term abortion? What is the difference between a late-term fetus and an early-term infant? If the answer is none then the two must be treated equally. One will not arbitrarily abort fetuses with minor anomalies anymore than one will discontinue treatment for minimally ill newborns nor will one save either with major anomalies. Regardless of the difficulties of defining minor or major anomalies, there is little doubt that the Messenger case represents a high probability of a severely handicapped child. An anomaly that is grounds for withholding life-support must also be grounds for aborting the same fetus.

Absent any crucial difference between the fetuses and newborns any reluctance not to treat the two cases similarly is difficult to understand. Nevertheless, many nations, Denmark, the United States and Great Britain for example, permit one to terminate life-support in the case of anomalous newborns but are reluctant to abort a fetus (in this case the very same fetus) facing similar probabilities of impairment. There is no room for the decision making process that emerges from most analyses of the Messenger case: a carefully balanced consideration of the baby's best interests and deference to parents' desires based on the interests and costs of those who must raise the child.

## Subtle Shift

The sources of this confusion are not clear. It may reflect a misguided quest for reasonable prognostic certainty on the assumption that birth itself may afford some better prognostic perspective or it may reflect influential religious norms. On the latter view, fetal life is sacrosanct while selective non-treatment of newborns is subsumed under the general, permissible practice of withholding or withdrawing medical treatment from any patient. Notice, however, how this reasoning produces a subtle shift in fetal/newborn status. Late-term fetuses and preterm infants no longer enjoy similar status. Instead, the former is elevated with respect to the latter, giving fetuses greater protection than newborns. Similarly, the US Supreme Court protects fetal life to a degree to which it does not protect the neonate. Without this move it is impossible to justify any cogent opposition to a threshold policy or preemptive abortion in those cases of fetuses or newborns facing similar odds of survival.

As it happens the case is somewhat easier to resolve in Israel. There, the status of the late-term fetus and newborn are not identical, for legal and moral personhood are only conferred at birth. Prior to birth, the mother's discretion is paramount. Nevertheless, Israeli law will not allow capricious abortion: the fetus must be malformed, even if the effects of the anomaly are difficult to determine. But in this case the fetus is not malformed. Is there then any ethical relevance to the fact that the fetus in utero is normal, the proximate cause of his anomaly only his impending birth? This is not only an Israeli dilemma. The dilemma also arises in those cultures which view the status of the late-term fetus and the newborn as identical. Any difference in treatment between prenatal and neonatal baby Messenger must reflect some fundamental difference between the two. Can this be found in the distinction between an observed anomaly and an impending anomaly?

Although each anomaly is qualitatively distinct it is currently technologically impossible to separate the fetus's condition in utero from those of his or her imminent birth. Were this possible, alternative justifications would have to be provided for terminating a late-term healthy fetus. One attempt to do so, based on "our duty to avoid bringing unwanted children into a community that is not prepared to accommodate them" has met with considerable resistance.[17,18] Absent this technology, the Messenger baby is absolutely certain to face the odds cited by the consulting neonatalogist: an unavoidable, impending anomaly is extensionally equivalent to an observed anomaly.

Decision making is now relatively straightforward. If fetal and newborn status is similar, the factors informing the decision to abort are identical to those informing termination of neonatal life-support: right to life, quality of life and utility. On the one hand, fetal right to life and reasonable medical care are subject to the same considerations of futility and/or low cost–benefit ratio as that of a newborn. In spite of fetal rights and personhood, we should permit preemptive abortion under the same conditions that we may discontinue life-support. On the other hand, if withholding or withdrawing life-support can be justified by considerations of the infant's and/or family's best interests, so must preemptive abortion.

If the newborn and fetal status are not similar one can still reason from intuitively sound cases of observed fetal anomaly that justify late-term abortion.

Severe spina bifida or hydrocephalus are conditions with a high probability of poor outcomes. A decision to abort such a fetus in the third trimester reflects legitimate considerations of fetal and parental best interests.[19] Absent any significant difference between

the probable outcomes of these observed anomalies and the threat posed by extremely premature birth, preemptive abortion is justified.

### Active Euthanasia

If the latent nature of the anomaly fails to repudiate preemptive abortion, perhaps the difference lies in the form of abortion. In Israel, live abortuses are precluded as late-term abortion is accomplished by intracardial injection of potassium chloride. If the status of the fetus and the newborn are similar, isn't this similar to the lethal injection of a newborn? Condemning the latter also condemns the former. One cannot abort baby Messenger because it moves us unjustifiably close to active euthanasia.

To work through this objection it is important to understand why one might want to terminate a fetus. Considerations of a mother's health may not be a relevant factor, for this usually only justifies termination of pregnancy. Fetal death is a separate act that must be justified in its own right. Most often, justification for fetal termination is anchored in fetal best interests. This can occur in two cases. First, fetal termination is justifiable when the fetus is afflicted with a disease, such as Tay–Sachs, from which it will certainly die. Second, it is justified when a fetus suffers from an affliction, such as Lesch Nynan syndrome, that makes life worse than death. Because these anomalies can often be diagnosed in the second trimester, late-term abortion is relatively rare. Nevertheless, it is important to notice how these justifications for fetal termination place the fetus in a different category from the newborn. To terminate similarly afflicted newborns by lethal injection is nothing short of murder in most nations. While one could withhold or withdraw treatment, any form of active euthanasia is prohibited. As a result of these considerations it is apparent that the status of the late-term fetus is inferior to that of the preterm newborn. There are, therefore, cases that justify fetal termination by lethal injection. Would they extend to the Messenger case?

Once fetal personhood is discounted to allow for the use of lethal injection in cases of certain death or severe malformation accompanied by pain and suffering, the door cracks open for other considerations as well. While in each of these cases, death or suffering is certain, the decision ultimately reflects the parent's assessment of the infant's best interests. This occurs in innumerable other instances as well, where one encounters a high probability of certain death or intense suffering. Parents diagnosed with Tay–Sachs carrier status in the days before fetal screening might legitimately opt for late-term abortion. So might a parent facing the birth of a child with neural tube defects whose probabilities of morbidity are no better than those facing the Messengers. Assuming no significant distinction between an observed and impending anomaly, there is no consistent way to deny preemptive abortion to parents facing the Messenger dilemma unless one absolutely prohibits the use of fatal fetal injection based on the general prohibition of its use among persons, while at the same time reasserting fetus/newborn parity.[20,21]

Preemptive abortion may, nevertheless, fly in the face of deeply held intuitions about the sanctity of life and the natural repugnance associated with lethal injection. Would it not be easier to allow nature to take its course and simply allow spontaneous labour to culminate in delivery thereby avoiding the intentional killing of a fetus, whatever its status? This might be true were spontaneous delivery the only decision to be taken by parents or physicians. The fact remains, however, that soon after delivery one must still decide to withhold, terminate or continue some form of treatment. As suggested above, these options can be equally problematic. If, as in the Israeli case, personhood is attained only at a child's birth then anything less than aggressive treatment may be as repugnant as lethal injection. Moreover, it must be remembered that a conservative "initiate and reevaluate" management strategy confers no better vantage point from which to predict a patient's outcome; prognostic certainty remains equally elusive at any stage in the treatment of malformed children. Finally, preemptive abortion and threshold protocols largely allay the anguish of bearing and raising a severely impaired child. These considerations should not be discounted.

## Concluding Comments

When examined in an international, cross-cultural context, bioethical dilemmas yield alternative policy directions that are not always apparent in their original context. There is no easy way to face the possibility of anomalous newborns, but might not the alternatives analyzed here, preemptive abortion and threshold protocols, provide feasible policy options as bioethics evolves in those countries discussed above?

In Denmark, thresholds are largely justified by the economic imperative to ration scarce medical resources and the ethical imperative to alleviate parental distress while safeguarding parental autonomy through presumed consent. For the time being the two go hand in hand, but one can easily imagine a situation where some technological advance would allow one to guarantee the health of a premature infant, thereby alleviating emotional costs but exacerbating economic expense. At this point it appears that budgetary considerations are paramount:

> . . . . the [threshold] approach has the strength of not stimulating endeavors to become increasingly better at saving increasingly young fetuses. . . . It is thus instrumental—indirectly, at least—in maintaining a level of skepticism about techno-crazed fantasies of engineering "the artificial womb."[10]

In spite of this admonition, there is some evidence to suggest that Danish physicians may be moving away from a modified threshold approach towards an "initiate and reevaluate" strategy for managing ELBW infants.[22] While this trend remains to be confirmed Norup suggests that it may partially be explained by some of the factors whose importance the Council of Ethics, ironically, sought to dispel: increased survival rates of ever smaller infants and a blurring of the distinction between withdrawing and withholding treatment, thereby making it increasingly palatable to begin and later withdraw treatment.

In Israel on the other hand, preemptive abortion would most likely be only a stopgap measure. Given the current bioethical climate in Israel where fertility and aggressive treatment are both overriding norms, Israelis would probably opt for any measure, including an artificial womb, that would let parents avoid a late-term abortion while insuring a normal newborn. Preemptive abortion is not a budgetary imperative but a treatment option to relieve parents of the anguish of dealing with an anomalous newborn. If other measures are available, so much the better. Nevertheless, the Danish Council of Ethics raises an issue that cannot be ignored: when is enough enough insofar as neonatal care is concerned?

Recent research has not produced unequivocal answers. Some suggest, for example, that resuscitation followed by evaluation postpones median time to death by only two days.[23] However, resuscitation also saved 20% of the 23- and 24-week-old newborns in this particular sample, newborns that most likely would not have been resuscitated under Danish guidelines and possibly aborted under current Israeli regulations. Although neonatalogists continue to argue that "medical resources allocated to non-survivors remain low,"[24] this misses the point that threshold protocols and preemptive abortion are driven by the material and emotional costs associated with raising the surviving anomalous newborn.

Policy decisions ultimately come down to ethics and economics. In spite of the possibility of improved neonatal technology the Danish council prefers not to invest in this direction, leaving resources to serve a greater number of citizens. Israelis, on the other hand, may be willing to wait for advanced technology to ensure greater fertility rates and alleviate the distress caused by aborting a normal late-term fetus. The American dilemma is more pronounced. They have no special interest in population growth, nor are they oblivious to rising health care costs. While they should be prime candidates for threshold protocols or preemptive abortion, both options are largely proscribed by state and federal law. Nevertheless, one of ethic's prime functions is to counsel the law and if the arguments supporting each of these two policies are persuasive then there are good reasons for placing these issues on the public agenda.

### References and Notes

1. Paris JJ. "Parental right to determine whether to use aggressive treatment for an early gestational age infant: the Messenger case." *Medicine and Law* 1997;16:679–85.

2. Clark FI. "Making sense of state vs. Messenger." *Pediatrics* 1996;97,4:579–83.

3. Messenger G. "No sense making sense of state vs. Messenger." *Pediatrics* 1997;99,2: 306.

4. Harrison H. "Commentary: the Messenger case." *Journal of Perinatalogy* 1996;16,4:299–301.

5. Paris JJ, Schreiber MD. "Parental discretion in refusal of treatment for newborns: a real but limited right." *Clinics in Perinatalogy* 1996;23,3:573–81.

6. Danish Council of Ethics, "Debate outline: extreme prematurity, ethical aspects." Copenhagen: *Eurolingua*, 1995:28–9.

7. See reference 6:19–21.

8. Jakobson T, Gronvall J, Petersen S, Andersen GE. "'Minitouch' treatment of very-low-birthweight infants." *Acta Paediatrica* 1993;82,3:934–8.

9. See reference 6: 28.

10. See reference 6: 36.

11. Gross ML. "Autonomy and paternalism in communitarian society: patient rights in Israel." *Hastings Center Report* 1999;29,4:13–20.

12. See reference 5: 577.

13. Mill JS. *On liberty*. In: Collini S, ed. *On liberty and other writings*. Cambridge: Cambridge University Press, 1989: ch 3: 56.

14. *The American Heritage Stedman's Medical Dictionary*. Boston: Houghton Mifflin, 1995:3.

15. Mahowald MB. "Concepts of abortion and their relevance to the abortion debate." *Southern Journal of Philosophy*. 1982; Summer: 195–207.

16. Gross NIL. "After feticide: coping with late-term abortion in Israel, Western Europe and the United States." *Cambridge Quarterly of Healthcare Ethics* 1999;8,4:449–62.

17. Callahan J. "Ensuring a stillborn: the ethics of fetal lethal injection in late abortion." *Journal of Clinical Ethics* 1995;6,3:254–63.

18. Fletcher JC. "On learning from mistakes." *Journal of Clinical Ethics* 1995;6,3: 264–70.

19. Abortion of late term fetuses with a high probability of severe anomaly is not without controversy. However, resistance is highest in those nations that grant fetal/newborn parity. See reference 16.

20. Isada NB, Pryde PG, Johnson MP, Hallak M, Blessed WB, Evans MI. "Fetal intracardiac potassium chloride injection to avoid the hopeless resuscitation of an abnormal abortus: I Clinical issues." *Obstetrics and Gynecology* 1992;80:296–9.

21. See references 17 and 18 and also Fletcher JC, Isada NB, Pryde PG, Johnson MP, Evans MI. "Fetal intracardiac potassium chloride injection to avoid the hopeless resuscitation of an abnormal abortus: II Ethical issues." *Obstetrics and Gynecology* 1992;80:310–13. These discussions address fetal injection in late, second trimester pregnancies. While Fletcher, for example, supports using fetal injection in second trimester pregnancies he is reluctant to support third trimester abortions. Callahan, however, is less restrained.

22. Norup M. "Treatment of extremely premature infants: a survey of attitudes among Danish Physicians." *Acta Paediatrica* 1998; 87:896–902.

23. Doron MW, Veness-Meehan KA, Margolis LH, Holoman EM, Stiles AD. "Delivery room resuscitation decisions for extremely premature infants." *Pediatrics* 1998;102:574–82.

24. Meadow W, Reimshisel T, Lantos J. "Birth weight-specific mortality for extremely low birth weight infants vanishes by four days: epidemiology and ethics in the neonatal intensive care unit." *Pediatrics* 1996;97:636–43.

## READINGS

# Section 3: Medical Futility

## Medical Futility

### Nancy S. Jecker and Roberta A. Pagon

Nancy Jecker and Roberta Pagon argue that *futility* and *inhumanity* have medical and moral meanings and can be useful in deciding whether to provide or withdraw medical intervention. "Quantitative futility," they say, applies to situations in which a treatment's chance of providing benefit to a patient is small, whereas "qualitative futility" applies to ones in which the quality of the outcome of even a successful treatment is poor (for example, preserving permanent unconsciousness). A treatment is "inhumane" if it causes or continues suffering but brings the patient no benefit or if it continues a patient's existence but the existence is not humanly meaningful.

The authors analyze the case of Michael, a premature infant with severe central nervous system impairment and multiple medical problems. (Three other cases are omitted in this selection.) When Michael was three-and-a-half months old, life support was withdrawn, and he was allowed to die. Should some of the possible medical steps discussed with his parents have been taken? The authors conclude that the interventions discussed would have been inhumane (caused pain without benefit) and qualitatively futile (been successful but not improved Michael's life). Continuing his treatment would be futile, so withdrawing life support was appropriate.

. . . In this [selection] we wrestle with the problems of futility and inhumanity in medical decision-making. We propose that these terms have clear medical and moral meanings, and that they can serve as useful guides in the care of hopelessly ill newborns. We argue that certain psychological and ethical responses to cruelty or injustice in the neonatal intensive care unit (ICU) are warranted and useful. Others only heighten the anguish and compound the difficulties of medical decisions. Finally, we explore the problem of invoking futility and inhumanity under conditions of future uncertainty. We offer reasons for resisting a propensity of "give the patient the benefit of the doubt," by using all modalities at one's disposal. . . .

## Defining Futility and Inhumanity

Despite misinterpretations of federal regulations and uncertainty regarding health professionals' ethical role, there are clearly cases where aggressive interventions are bad medicine. Neither legal nor ethical principles require provision of life-sustaining medical treatment to all imperiled infants. Nor does the law or ethics require individual providers to act contrary to conscience. Yet conscience is not self-certifying, and claims of conscientiousness should lead us to test conscience's leaning in the light of moral standards. We explore two standards of special relevance to imperiled newborns.

Reprinted by permission of the publishers from *Ethics and Perinatology*, ed. Ammon Goldworth, William Silverman, David K. Stevenson, Ernlé W. D. Young, and Rodney Rivers, pp. 49–56. New York: Oxford University Press. Copyright © 1995. (Notes omitted.)

First is the standard of medical futility. It connotes that medical treatment is wasteful; even our best efforts will be useless and ineffective. Futile situations elicit feelings of hopelessness and pointlessness; health providers who persist with futile efforts may feel a loss of professional purpose because their activities are leading nowhere. The second standard of inhumanity elicits quite different responses. It suggests that medical interventions provided without benefit rob patients of their very humanity. Inhumanity implies that medical care aimlessly prolongs a patient's pain or suffering, making the use of medical technologies a torture or punishment. Inhumanity suggests a failure to empathize with the sufferings of patients.

Yet to what, more specifically, do futility and inhumanity refer? We propose, first, that medical care can be futile in two distinct senses. Following Schneiderman *et al.* we distinguish between quantitative and qualitative medical futility. Quantitative medical futility refers to situations in which the *likelihood* of a medical benefit's resulting from an intervention is extremely small. For example, treatment should be regarded as futile where there is less than one chance in one hundred of success. Qualitative medical futility indicates that the *quality* of outcome associated with an intervention is extremely poor. For instance, treatment that merely preserves permanent unconsciousness or total dependence on intensive medical care is qualitatively futile.

Inhumane medical treatment also refers to two quite different situations. First, medical treatment is inhumane where it aimlessly prolongs an already pain-wracked existence, or where it inflicts new pain or discomfort without benefiting the patient. For example, medical interventions are inhumane if they create intervals of nausea, retching, pain, or depression, or if they require invasion and injury of the body, without promising to help the patient. A second sense of inhumanity denotes circumstances where life-prolonging medical interventions are applied to patients who lack the capacities that make continued existence *humanly* meaningful. Although such an existence is not painful, it can be undignified by virtue of falling sadly short of what human life ordinarily includes. Treatment that is inhumane in this second way may serve to continue the life of a patient who lacks "indicators of humanhood." These include such qualities as consciousness, intelligent communication of thoughts and feelings, motor activity, and capacities of cognition and recognition. When such attributes are absent, and when an individual shows no evidence of enjoying life, treatment is inhumane. For instance, it is inhumane to prolong the life of a conscious stroke victim with the locked-in syndrome who has no control of motor activity and, hence, no means of controlling his or her environment or communicating voluntarily.

Ordinarily, health providers anticipate that interventions will yield some benefit for the patient; hence determinations of medical inhumanity involve a careful weighing of the burden of treatment against its estimated benefits. Where the chance of realizing a benefit for the patient is poor, the burden of treatment should be mild or abbreviated. An example is Trisomy 18, in which the odds of survival are very poor and humane medical care is confined to warmth, oral fluids, and sedation. As the chance of benefits to the patient increase, the burden of treatment can increase within limits, although it should not be prolonged indefinitely. For instance, in cases of severe trauma the chances of recovery are high, and full intervention is applied, despite the fact that it may be quite painful and dehumanizing initially.

Both kinds of inhumane treatment bear a resemblance to qualitative futility. Like inhumanity, qualitative futility refers to interventions where the quality of outcome associated with an intervention includes unrelenting pain or the absence of basic human capacities. However, qualitatively futile care differs from inhumane care because futility refers only to the extreme low end of a quality-of-life continuum. For example, unnecessary abdominal surgery may be inhumane, without being qualitatively futile. Similarly, ineffective chemotherapy that produces skin rashes, hair loss, and vomiting may be inhumane, but it does not indicate a quality of outcome that is below a minimally acceptable threshold. In other words, although a person experiences pain or discomfort, the existence

associated with such interventions is well worth having.

Inhumane treatment also bears a likeness to quantitative futility. For an intervention to be inhumane, it must have little or no chance of benefiting the patient. By contrast, an invasive or burdensome medical treatment that promises to benefit the patient and improve the patient's condition is not inhumane. For this reason, it is not inhumane to invade and injure the body through surgery, or to prescribe medicines with untoward side-effects, when these hold out a reasonable promise of helping the patient. Nor is it inhumane to ventilate mechanically a comatose patient who has a reasonable prospect of recovery of consciousness. However, such actions would be inhumane if they are clearly not beneficial. A second noteworthy point is that treatment may be quantitatively futile without being inhumane. For example, it is futile in the quantitative sense to prescribe antibiotics for a cold, but it is not inhumane. Likewise, putting a cast around a bone that is injured but not broken is ineffective; however, it does not inflict suffering or indignity on the patient. . . .

## Decision-Making Under Uncertainty

. . . Acknowledging medical uncertainty leads some to argue that physicians should "give the patient the benefit of the doubt" and err on the side of treatment. Others, doubting the wisdom of this approach, worry that aggressive medical interventions may only perpetuate a meaningless or painful existence. What are the values implicit in these alternative strategies? What additional options exist?

To address these questions, it is useful to place the general problem of making medical decisions under conditions of uncertainty in broader perspective. One response to medical uncertainty calls for listing the various treatment alternatives and ranking each according to its worst possible outcome. According to this approach, the treatment one selects should be the one whose worst outcome is *superior* to the worst outcome of the other alternatives. The ethical basis for this approach is that physicians have a special ethical duty to avoid harming patients. Where some harms are unavoidable, this duty requires minimizing harm by choosing the outcome that is least bad.

Applying this general approach yields three more specific strategies. Each reflects a different position about how "worst possible outcome" should be defined. One strategy requires collecting statistical data that enables an across-the-board determination that certain categories of infants are unlikely to benefit from treatment; treatment is then not initiated on infants fitting that profile. This approach judges the worst possible outcome as saving an infant who will be severely impaired, and seeks to avoid this by identifying such infants in advance and excluding them from treatment. The trade-off this approach accepts is that some babies will die who could have thrived, although doctors and parents will never know which individual babies they were. One limitation of this approach is that statistical information about the outcomes of treatment for different patient-groups may be unavailable.

A second option involves beginning treatment for every infant that is potentially viable, and continuing active care until it becomes clearer that a particular infant will either die or lead a life of an unacceptable quality. In contrast to the first strategy, this second strategy assumes that the worse outcome consists of not making an effort to save an infant who would have survived and enjoyed a reasonable quality of life.

A final strategy also requires beginning treatment for every infant, but allows parents the option of terminating care before it becomes certain that a particular infant will either die or be devastatingly disabled. This approach takes an intermediate route and avoids identifying either saving a meaningless existence or failing to save a meaningful existence as the worst outcome. Instead, it solicits the input of family members in coming to terms with the "gray area" of medical uncertainty. Parents are asked to provide information about which outcome *they* regard as the worst possible.

Is it worse to fail to rescue a viable infant whose life would be worth having, or is it worse to rescue a child who will go on to lead a painful and unwelcome existence? The advantage of the third option, which calls for individualized decision-making, is that it allows parents to participate in this determination. Although no one is entitled to insist on treatment that is clearly futile or inhumane, in situations of uncertainty about the outcome of medical interventions, parents should be intimately involved in the decision-making process. . . .

### Case [Study]

Michael was born at thirty-one weeks' gestation to his twenty-eight-year-old married mother. The pregnancy had been unplanned. At approximately twenty weeks' gestation an ultrasound examination revealed massive abdominal ascites, compression of the thorax, and polyhydramnios. It was felt at this time that the fetus was non-viable. Pregnancy termination was declined by the family, but stillbirth was anticipated. At thirty-one weeks' gestation, the mother went into spontaneous labor and an emergency cesarean section was performed. Michael was delivered in another city and remained there for nine days before being transferred to our institution. At birth he was severely compromised, requiring intubation, and cardiopulmonary resuscitation with intracardiac injections of epinephrine. Respiration was not established until 1000 cc of fluid had been removed from his abdomen. It was unclear how much asphyxia had occurred.

Michael was diagnosed to have the *prune belly syndrome*, a condition in which there is massive distention of the abdomen secondary to bladder-outlet obstruction. It appeared that Michael had posterior urethral valves which had blocked urine outflow from the bladder *in utero* until a time that they had "ruptured," presumably secondary to increased bladder pressure. Because his bladder was dilated and flaccid, a suprapubic cystostomy tube was placed shortly after birth in order to drain his bladder. Renal function was abnormal initially, but subsequently improved. At six weeks of age he underwent fulguration of the posterior urethral valves following an episode of urinary retention. Because of abnormal-appearing ("echogenic") kidneys, the urologists were unable to give a clear long-term prognosis for renal function. One urologist anticipated that renal failure would occur at some point, perhaps late in adolescence, requiring either transplantation or dialysis; however, another urologist was more optimistic about the long-term outlook.

Michael had respiratory failure requiring intubation immediately after delivery. He remained on a ventilator throughout his entire hospitalization. He appeared to have little primary lung disease, because he was ventilated with low-pressure settings and low levels of inspired oxygen; however, he had a small chest and no abdominal musculature, and it appeared that he lacked adequate diaphragmatic muscles to support independent respiration. At three months of age an attempt at extubation failed after several hours. Subsequently, a thoracic splint was placed in order to try to improve his chest-wall mechanics, and another brief trial of extubation was attempted two weeks later, which also failed within hours. The attending neonatologist and the attending pediatric pulmonologist felt that Michael had virtually no hope of being able to breathe independently and that he would require long-term mechanical ventilation via a tracheostomy. Because Michael was unable to gag or cough secondary to central nervous system dysfunction, the neonatologist and pulmonologist felt that the high risk for aspiration and recurrent pneumonia made him an unsuitable candidate for long-term ventilation.

Michael had evidence of prenatal neurologic compromise in that he had polyhydramnios, which is often an indication of inadequate sucking and swallowing *in utero* and, at the same time, had fixed joints (arthrogryposis), which can be caused by inadequate limb movement secondary to central nervous system dysfunction. In addition, he had a markedly abnormal neurologic examination, with no gag, no cough, severe hearing loss, and no visual tracking. He had no interaction with his environment, except to respond to pain. He had one seizure, and was treated with phenobarbital, which was in the therapeutic range and was not felt to contribute to his neurologic depression. Two cranial ultrasound examinations were normal. The attending neonatologist and a pediatric consultant from the Birth Defects and Neurodevelopmental Service were uncertain whether Michael's abnormal central nervous system examination was attributable to prenatal causes or perinatal asphyxia or both. Both doctors agreed, however, that he had severe neurologic impairment and that over time he had shown no neurologic recovery.

Michael's parents had difficulty adjusting to the various prognoses which had been offered. Because the family had been led to believe that Michael would be stillborn and that urologic surgery would be futile, they had wished no urologic intervention at the time of his admission. The hospital staff described the parents as angry and frustrated about the uncertainty of their son's prognosis. The parents had a strong extended social support network, including family and church members. They had little contact with the social work service, and had declined an offer of more extensive contact.

Because Michael was a poor tracheostomy candidate, the physicians and family decided unanimously to refrain from performing the tracheostomy and to discontinue ventilatory support when Michael was three and a half months old. Michael died shortly after life-support was withdrawn. Subsequently, an anonymous caller asked that the decision to withdraw life-support be reviewed by the Ethics Committee. The caller voiced two concerns about the decision to discontinue ventilatory support. First, Michael was medically stable at the time the ventilator was withdrawn.

This suggested to the caller that the ventilator was not a futile intervention. Second, the caller expressed the related concern that it appeared inconsistent and arbitrary for the medical team to switch from aggressively treating Michael one day to withdrawing all treatment the following day. The underlying issue here appeared to be that some decline in the patient's medical situation should ordinarily occur prior to a judgment of futility. Otherwise, a futility judgment simply reflects a change in the physician's psychological attitude toward the patient, rather than a change in the patient's physical condition.

**Case Discussion.** In this situation there was doubt that a tracheostomy would achieve the goal of facilitating mechanical ventilation and removing secretions. It does not follow, however, that treatment would be quantitatively futile. Quantitative futility requires that the odds of success are not only doubtful, but extremely poor. Certainly mechanical ventilation had been successful up to the time of the final decision. Let us suppose, for the purposes of discussion, that although there was a chance that the intervention would not succeed, there was also a reasonable chance that it would be effective. If we make these assumptions, can we conclude that tracheostomy and mechanical ventilation were not futile in the quantitative sense? Not before considering a further question: Would the physiological effects of treatment benefit Michael? Tracheostomy and artificial ventilation were quantitatively futile if they had an extremely slim chance of *benefiting* Michael in any way. Thus quantitative futility could not be ruled out even if it could be shown that these procedures would produce a favorable physiological *effect*.

The question of whether life-prolonging procedures would benefit Michael leads us to the related concerns of qualitative futility and medical inhumanity. In assessing these issues, two questions are central. First, was the quality of outcome associated with treatments, such as tracheostomy and ventilator support, inhumane in the sense of undignified? A second and related question is whether treatment is qualitatively futile i.e., whether the quality of outcome associated with treatment falls clearly below a minimally decent level. Let us consider these questions in turn. Did Michael possess qualities that enabled him to live a humanly meaningful existence? His severe neurologic impairment had so far shown no signs of improvement, and Michael had no interaction with his

environment except to pain. Although there was disagreement about Michael's long-term prognosis, let us
suppose that Michael's neurologic depression would
neither improve nor worsen. In this case his permanent inability to communicate and to interact with the
environment in any way suggests to us that medical
care was inhumane. Mechanical ventilation and tracheostomy could achieve the effect of prolonging
Michael's life, but would not enable Michael to lead a
dignified and interactive life.

Turning next to qualitative futility, can we say that
Michael's quality of existence is *so* poor that it is
futile? . . . Michael was not in constant pain; [h]owever,
he lacked capacities to recognize others or enjoy interacting with them or his environment. In light of these
evaluations, we make the following assessments. First,
the procedures in question were inhumane in another
sense: they inflicted pain and discomfort without con-
ferring a benefit on Michael. Second, even supposing
that the tracheostomy and respirator could keep
Michael's blood oxygenated, they had little or no
chance of benefiting Michael. Thus, the procedures
were futile in the sense of qualitative futility.

We conclude that the physicians' and parents' decision to withdraw ventilator support and forgo a tracheostomy were ethically supported. The quality of
outcome associated with these life-prolonging procedures did not benefit the patient.

**Case Resolution.** The Ethics Committee's retrospective consideration of Michael's care reaffirmed
the appropriateness of the medical team's prior treatment decisions. It also had a positive effect on addressing the anonymous caller's concerns about how
medical decisions were made in this case. Although
Michael was medically stable and his situation un-
changed at the time the ventilator was withdrawn,
what had changed was that the medical team had reevaluated Michael's medical condition and the value
of this treatment. They had arrived at a reasoned decision that continuing treatment was futile. Although
treatment succeeded in physiologically stabilizing
Michael, it did not benefit him in any broader
sense. . . .

### Concluding Remarks

In this [selection] we have clarified the meanings of
medical futility and inhumanity and discussed their
ethical implications. We have argued that physicians
are not required to offer, nor are patients entitled to
receive, medical treatments that are futile or inhumane. Yet we have also indicated that in situations of
significant medical uncertainty there should be a (re-
buttable) presumption in favor of family decision-
making.

## Medical Futility: Commentary

### Norman C. Fost

Norman Fost rejects Jecker and Pagon's contention that futility and inhumanity
have clear medical and moral meanings and can play a useful role in treatment
decisions. Fost holds that the concepts are "vague, arbitrary, and potentially hazardous" to patients, particularly critically ill newborns.

Fost reviews the concepts to show they are vague and can be ambiguous.
When used as grounds for withholding treatment, they can be self-fulfilling. Also,
they prevent future patients from benefiting from what might be learned from
the aggressive treatment of cases now regarded as futile.

Fost holds that just as the attempt to use a distinction between ordinary and
extraordinary means fails as a way to make treatment decisions, the two concepts also fail. Neither can be applied without relying on "personal value preferences." Finally, difficulty in applying the concepts involves more than uncertainty

about a diagnosis or prognosis. Both can be known, while how to treat remains in doubt.

Fost claims that, in the case of Michael, talk about the futility and inhumanity of intervention detracts from the central question, which is whether his life is worth living. Fost sees a danger in allowing "physicians to medicalize a subjective value judgment by labeling treatment as futile or inhumane."

In their paper "Medical futility: decision-making in the context of probability and uncertainty," Nancy Jecker and Roberta Pagon keep their promise to "wrestle with the problems of futility and inhumanity in medical decision-making." As in most professional wrestling-matches, the conclusion is apparent at the outset, and is clearly stated: ". . . that these terms have clear medical moral meanings, and that they can serve as useful guides in the care of hopelessly ill newborns." I have never understood professional wrestling, so it is not surprising that I would not have predicted the conclusion of their match. That is, I do not find the concepts of futility and inhumanity to be clear or useful. On the contrary, I find them vague, arbitrary, and potentially hazardous, not just to clear thinking but to the welfare of patients, particularly critically ill newborns of the sort they describe in their detailed case discussion. . . .

### The Definition of "Futility"

Since Jecker and Pagon intend that the concept of futility should not just be illuminating but practical, applicable to real cases and real laws, they offer definitions that presumably should allow the concepts to be applied in a consistent way. But the definition relies on other words, whose meaning is even less clear and less susceptible to consistent application.

Consider first their definition of *quantitative* medical futility. This, we are told, refers to a situation in which the "likelihood of a medical benefit . . . is *extremely small*" (italics added), for example < 1:100. Why is 1:101 futile but 1:99 not? Why is 1:1000 futile? The numbers seem to be plucked from the air, with no rational basis. Since reasonable people will disagree about which numbers are the appropriate ones, the authors (or any other defenders of their favorite num-

Reprinted by permission of the publishers from *Ethics and Perinatology*, ed. Amnon Goldworth, William Silverman, David K. Stevenson, Ernlé W. D. Young, and Rodney Rivers, pp. 72–77. New York: Oxford University Press. Copyright © 1995. (Notes and references omitted.)

ber) owe us an explanation of why treatment with a 1:100 chance of success should be considered futile. Since they do not offer us the completed syllogism, we can only surmise. One candidate explanation would be the following.

Perhaps the authors mean that even if the treatment were effective in 1 in 100 tries, it would not be worth it; the costs, broadly defined, of treating 99 patients without benefit would not be outweighed by the admitted benefit of success in 1 patient. But why is that not worth it? How does one determine how much cost is too much to achieve a defined benefit? The answer to that could be determined in a quasi-objective way; through careful cost–benefit analysis. But that creates more problems.

First, cost–benefit analysis would obviously be different for each condition, depending on the cost of the intervention, the value of the benefit, the severity of the condition, and other factors. PKU screening has a favorable cost–benefit ratio even though the "chance of success" is less than 1:10000 for each patient subjected to screening. In contrast, a very expensive intervention might have an unfavorable cost–benefit ratio even if success occurred 1:50 times. Finally, the definition of success or benefit is necessarily subjective. For some patients, survival for a year would be considered a benefit, even though the patient's productivity during that time might not be sufficient to conclude that the treatment costs were worth the benefits in objective terms. In summary, Jecker and Pagon's quantitative sense of medical futility necessarily involves qualitative judgments.

The concept of qualitative futility—meaning "that the quality of outcome is extremely poor"—is more obviously dependent on subjective and personal notions of what benefits are worth certain costs. For some cases, such as the celebrated Wanglie family, treatment which preserves the patient in a state of permanent unconsciousness is not futile. For their own personal reasons, they considered life itself to be a value, and their doctors could not deny that the treatment was medically effective in prolonging that life. Jecker and Pagon's other example of qualitative futility—total dependence on intensive medical care—is even more arbitrary. "Intensive medical care" is not a self-defining term, and even treatments which everyone might consider intensive—such as home ventilator care—are hardly futile in all cases. Many patients totally dependent on such care find life worth living, with benefits that clearly outweigh the burdens in their own value system.

If there were any candidate condition for qualitatively futile medical care it would probably be the persistent vegetative state [PVS]; i.e. there would probably be widespread support for the view that a patient or family asking for treatment in that situation was acting unreasonably. It is important to remember that many patients diagnosed as being in PVS are misdiagnosed. Even whole-brain death, a condition with much clearer criteria and much simpler methods of ascertainment, is commonly misunderstood and misdiagnosed. If the chance of error were high, a request for continued treatment in the face of a *diagnosis* of PVS might not be so unreasonable. That is, continued treatment might not be futile. Jecker and Pagon may have intended to say that treatment for a patient *actually* in PVS might be considered futile; but the Wanglies and others obviously disagreed. It is unclear how one would determine the "correct" definition of futility in such cases.

Because of considerations such as these some observers have concluded that futility can only be defined tautologically or that it should be abandoned as a useful concept in deciding whether or not continued treatment is indicated. Wolf, for example, concluded that futility could only be defined narrowly, as "failing to achieve a defined purpose." Lantos *et al.,* writing in 1988, found futility to be a useful concept in arguing that certain newborns should not be resuscitated. By 1989, Lantos had concluded that futility was an ambiguous concept, with "little consensus about how futility should be determined in practice."

## The Definition of "Inhumane"

If futility cannot be defined without reference to subjective and arbitrary values, then "inhumane medical treatment" would seem even less viable as a moral construct in guiding decision-making. Jecker and Pagon's concept of inhumane treatment includes interventions which prolong the lives of patients who ". . . [fall] sadly short of what human life ordinarily includes"; i.e., patients who lack "indicators of humanhood." The futility of trying to define humanhood has

been much discussed. Joseph Fletcher, who expended considerable thought on the subject, excluded children with Down syndrome from the class of humans, a judgment which was strongly repudiated by the President's Commission, among others. The authors quote Fletcher's article, without criticism, as supportive of their own views.

Their example is illustrative: in the context of discussing treatment of patients who "lack indicators of humanhood" they conclude, "It is inhumane to prolong the life of a conscious stroke patient with the locked-in syndrome." While it is unclear how one would know such a patient were conscious, I infer that even if such a patient were thinking the most brilliant and creative and human-like thoughts, he/she would be "not human."

Perhaps they only meant the patient lacked the indicators of humanhood; that actually, he/she would be human. But if this is ambiguous to me, it may be ambiguous to others. It may be that some patients, perhaps most, would not want to be treated if permanently in such a state; but it is not clear that such a person is not human, or if not, why he/she would not qualify as a human. Defining such a person out of the class of humans would seem, at the least, arbitrary. Some would consider it inhumane.

## Labels as Self-Fulfilling Prophecies

Using such concepts as "futile" and "inhumane" involves dangers beyond the arbitrariness of the terms as applied in practice. They may also be self-fulfilling prophecies, as illustrated by the authors' discussion of trisomy 18. They consider treatment of such a child, other than comfort measures, to be inhumane because "the chance of realizing a benefit for the patient is poor." Withholding definitive treatment from such patients will usually guarantee early death, since they are commonly afflicted with life-threatening anomalies. But neonatologists have long been confronted with children who were considered non-viable.

In the 1960s, when I was an intern, a 1000-gram infant was considered non-viable, presumably because few if any in the hospital in which I worked had survived to discharge. Intensive treatment would presumably have been considered either futile or inhumane in Jecker and Pagon's terms. As a result, in my hospital, medically necessary treatment was routinely withheld, and such infants commonly died. In other hospitals, other doctors were more aggressive—a policy eventually resulting in the present situation, in which most such infants are expected to survive. I do not mean to beg the questions of whether such treatment was morally warranted in 1960; whether appropriate safeguards existed for protection of infants from experimental treatment; or whether it is ever appropriate to "volunteer" a non-consenting patient for experimental treatment that is unlikely to benefit him/her, but which may result in clear benefits for future patients. I only wish to make the point that labeling a situation futile or inhumane may predictably lead to decisions that will result in the patient's death, when a long and prosperous life may be more available than the decision-maker suspects.

There are many illustrations of this problem. New syndromes, such as Reye's syndrome and AIDS, are commonly diagnosed only in their most severe forms in the first cases. This selection bias may lead to the false conclusion that the outcome is worse than appears when a wider range of cases is included. The median life expectancy of a patient with HIV infection has mushroomed from 2 years to 10 years unrelated to advances in treatment, simply because diagnostic advances and better case-finding have resulted in earlier diagnosis, and diagnosis of patients with milder forms of the infection. What was once considered hopeless (futile?) has often become progressively hopeful. Labelling the patients as hopeless, and treatment as futile, can preclude discovery of the possibility of change.

### The Lesson of the Ordinary/ Extraordinary Debate

The authors acknowledge that there will always be uncertainty. What, then, is the value of labelling a treatment as futile or inhumane? If it will virtually always be the case that futile does not mean "definitely unlikely to succeed," but only "probably," then choices must be made.

Leon Kass taught us nearly twenty years ago that technology cannot do moral work. He was discussing the then-popular, now discredited, concept of "extraordinary means." Some writers of the day seemed to believe that, in the case of some treatments, we didn't have to decide whether we had a duty to use them; we only had to decide whether they met the definition of extraordinary means. If the intervention could be labelled as extraordinary, there was, by definition, no duty to use it. This concept arose from, and was most widely advocated by, Roman Catholic writers, following the teaching of Pope Pius XII in the course of discussing a Catholic physician's duty to use a respirator.

History has shown us how elusive and evanescent those definitions were. Even if we conceded that a respirator constituted extraordinary means, whatever that meant at the time, few would consider it so today.

More important, even if it were extraordinary, in secular discussion an argument would be needed to explain why there was no duty to use it. Similarly, we now understand that some treatments that are quite ordinary, such as provision of food and water through a nasogastric tube, need not always be administered.

Just as the concept of extraordinary means failed to provide answers regarding when there is a duty to treat, the concepts of futility and inhumanity will fail for the same reasons. They cannot be defined, or have not to date, in any operational way that is not subject to personal value preferences. Because applying them will always involve uncertainty and choices, they will not help us avoid the untidy work of analyzing each case.

### Uncertainty Is Not the Only Problem

After offering these terms, the authors acknowledge that uncertainty will make it difficult to apply them in the perinatal setting. Uncertainty is only one reason that defining treatment as "futile" will not be dispositive. Consider, for example, the unusual case in which there is absolute certainty as to the diagnosis and prognosis. Certain patients who have been properly diagnosed as brain dead might qualify. When evaluated by competent clinicians, using widely agreed upon criteria, brain death should be one of the simplest diagnoses in all of medicine. When properly diagnosed, the prognosis is as certain as anything.* But even when there is complete certainty as to the hopelessness of recovery, there are still choices to be made regarding continuation of "life" support.

Several reasons could be proposed for maintaining the vegetative functions in such a patient. First, he may be a source of organs or tissues for transplantation. Second, as Gaylin suggested many years ago, maintenance of the living body might serve many other social purposes, including drug-testing; manufacture of useful biologic materials such as antibodies; experiments on human physiology; or as a "cadaver" for trainees to practice procedures. A family member or a physician might find some of these social purposes powerful reasons for maintaining mere biologic existence in a brain-dead patient. The certainty of the

---

*I hasten to remind the reader that, as simple as it is, many highly skilled and experienced doctors just don't get it.

diagnosis of brain death would not therefore end the discussion of whether treatment should continue; rather, it would make such discussion possible.

## Case [Study]: Michael

The case illustrate[s] the imprecision and hazards of applying the concept of futility in the real world. In [this] case, a fetus, later to be known as Michael, was labelled as non-viable at 20 weeks' gestation. In other words, continuation of the pregnancy was considered futile from his perspective, presumably meaning he would not be able to survive outside the uterus.* But wait! Nine days after birth Michael is alive, if not well. Like many infants before him, he has traversed the boundary from non-viable to viable. The label non-viable apparently, in this case, meant something like "seriously ill," or "will need lots of high technology treatment." Continuing the pregnancy was clearly not futile, in the sense of "ineffective." Was it inhumane? Did it rob Michael of his humanness? If it did, he seems to have recovered it. When we first meet Michael after transfer to the authors' institution he is an infant with prune belly syndrome, with the most pessimistic prognosis being renal failure "at some point, perhaps in late adolescence"; a more optimistic expert thought he would do even better.

Despite these opinions, the parents were told that "urologic surgery would be futile." The meaning of futility is unclear in this setting. "Ineffective" does not seem to apply, since the worst-case scenario assumed two decades of life, with treatment options for renal failure at that point. "Inhuman" is not a word we usually apply to children who lose renal function in adolescence, or who require dialysis or transplantation thereafter. Presumably the futility label was meant to apply to his other disabilities—his respiratory failure or his severe retardation. Urologic surgery would be futile in correcting either of those. But that is either a tautology or a straw man. Urologic surgery is futile in all cases if we expect it to cure or benefit all bodily dysfunction. It is obvious to the point of triviality to call urologic surgery futile in this sense. I assume, therefore, that the futility applies to the other treatments, or to the idea of keeping him alive by any means. If that is what is meant, then that is what should be said: that Michael's life is not worth living, and no intervention,

*I assume this is what was meant by "non-viable." The authors do not tell us what definition they had in mind. Had they offered one, it would have presumably have been fraught with the same arbitrariness as the futility concept.

including feeding, will change that. Whether or not that conclusion is warranted is, of course, the central issue. My only point is that little light is shed on that central question by labelling the urologic surgery as futile.

In addition to distracting us (and perhaps the parents) from the central issue—is Michael's life worth living, regardless of the intervention—the futility label apparently alienated the parents because of its inaccuracy or ambiguity. They were told once—at 20 weeks' gestation—that he was a non-viable fetus. Then they were told that urologic treatment would be futile, although he might survive 20–40 years. At the least, they were entitled to be confused; at the worst, they had reason to lose trust in the doctors' predictive powers.

"Inhumane," according to the authors, means either painful without compensating benefit, or undignified because it's not a human life. It is not clear whether or how much pain Michael was experiencing. At one point we are told that Michael "had no interaction with his environment except to pain," but later that "Michael was not in constant pain." How do we know how much pain he was experiencing, or whether it was treatable or manageable? As to dignity, it is yet another word requiring definition and instruction on how to apply it. Webster tells us it has to do with "intrinsic worth." Can the authors provide some value-free non-arbitrary guidance as to who or what has intrinsic worth? Is this a restatement of the concept of "personhood," also not defined? Without operational definitions these words will be defined arbitrarily by those who use them as justifications for stopping treatment. Labelling treatment as inhumane or undignified does not constitute an argument for withholding it.

Finally, we are told that treatment was qualitatively futile because the quality of Michael's existence was so poor. Although "not in constant pain he lacked capacities to recognize others or enjoy interacting with them or his environment." Michael's ventilator was discontinued $31\frac{1}{2}$ months after he was born, at 31 weeks' gestation. His adjusted age was 5–6 weeks. His inability to recognize others or enjoy his environment after 6 weeks of ventilator-dependent intensive care would not seem to warrant strong conclusions about his neurologic prognosis.

Perhaps the clinicians had other reasons to believe that Michael would not be able to interact with people and that therefore life had no benefit for him. If this were the case, it doesn't shed light to substitute "undignified" as shorthand for this. It risks letting others use the word to mean anything they think it means, just as "brain dead" is used by some to mean "severely brain damaged," and "vegetative" to mean something similar. We have enough time to say what we mean; to spell out the reasons why we think it is not in Michael's interests to be kept alive.

This, by the way, seems to be a "best interests" argument. If it is, then the treatment would seem to be irrelevant. If he has no interest in living, what difference is it which treatment is keeping him alive? If he does have an interest in living, then the painfulness of treatment doesn't settle the matter. . . .

## Conclusion

"We have clarified the meanings of medical futility and inhumanity," the authors conclude. I wish it were so. Rather, I believe they have done something even more useful; they have clarified the ambiguity of these terms. They conclude that physicians are not required to offer treatments that are futile or inhumane; but the ambiguity of the terms seems to allow physicians to med-icalize a subjective value judgment by labelling treatment as futile or inhumane. If treatment that can prolong life for 12 months is futile, why not 12 years? If physicians disagree how does it clarify the issue for one to label the treatment as "futile" or "inhumane" and the other to insist that it is effective and humane? This kind of debate reminds me of the less-than-persuasive response to "Tastes great"; namely, "Less filling." . . .

With regard to Jecker and Pagon's observation on the need to include families more fully as early as possible, I can only agree. Similarly, their observations on the technophilic tendencies of modern medicine, the hazards of excessive medical optimism, and the often mistaken equation of survival with success are well founded and in need of reiteration. Their courage, candor, and clarity in publicizing their experiences in detail is essential to inform the public and policy-makers of the process, substance, and justifications of decision-making in hospitals. I have little doubt that discussions such as these will "be a springboard for improved understanding and better care."

## Decision Scenario 1

Jecker and Pagon, in a section omitted from the reading, present the case of a newborn girl we'll call Ginny Rutten. Ginny was born with epidermolysis bullosa, a genetic disease involving the blistering and sloughing off of the skin and mucous membranes—the whole thickness, down to the fat and muscle. Ginny cannot drink, because the lining of her mouth is blistered and swollen, and so can take no nourishment by mouth. Areas of her skin have eroded, producing patches of raw flesh resembling third-degree burns. Because of the breakdown of her skin, she suffers constant pain; also, the dehydration it permits produces electrolyte imbalances that put her at risk of heart arrhythmia and death.

Ginny has a disease for which there is no cure and not even a treatment to prevent the blistering and peeling of her skin. In addition to pain from the skin loss, those with the disease lose their fingers and suffer from a drawing up—contracture—of their arms and legs from scarring. They need total care their entire lives. Moreover, there is no case of a spontaneous cure or even a lengthy remission on record.

Ginny has a severe form of the disease and screams in pain when she is awake. She is sedated by a morphine drip and sleeps in brief cycles. Her physicians and the hospital ethics committee debate the question of whether to feed Ginny artificially, either by an IV drip or through a surgical opening into her stomach, and so keep her alive. Her parents ask that no effort to prolong her life be made.

1. According to Jecker and Pagon, what is the relationship between the parents' request and the concepts of medical futility and inhumanity?

2. What would Fost regard as the central issue in this case? Why would he consider the concepts of futility and inhumanity unhelpful or even dangerous?

3. Can Ginny's case be regarded as one involving what Engelhardt calls "the injury of continued existence"?

4. Ginny is apparently neurologically normal, so does Weir's position imply that she ought to be treated?

5. How might the protocols described by Gross be used in this case?

**Decision Scenario 2**

Brookhaven, as we will call it, is a long-term health-care institution in the Washington metropolitan area. Most of Brookhaven's patients are in residence there for only a few months; either they succumb to their ailments and die, or they recover sufficiently to return to their homes.

But for some patients death has no immediate likelihood, nor is recovery a possibility. They linger on at Brookhaven, day after day and year after year. Juli Meyers is such a patient, although that is not really her name.

Juli is seventeen and has been in Brookhaven for six years. But before Brookhaven there were other institutions. In fact, Juli has spent most of her life in hospitals and special-care facilities. But Juli does not seem to be aware of any of this.

At Brookhaven she spends her days lying in a bed surrounded with barred metal panels. The bars have been padded with foam rubber. Although most of the time Juli is curled tightly in a fetal position, she sometimes flails around wildly and makes guttural sounds. The padding keeps her from injuring herself.

Juli's body is thin and underdeveloped, with sticklike arms and legs. She is blind and deaf and has no control over her bowels and bladder. She is totally dependent on others to clean her and care for her. She can swallow the food put into her mouth, but she cannot feed herself. She makes no response to the people or events around her.

There is no hope that Juli will walk or talk, laugh or cry, or even show the slightest sign of intelligence or awareness. She is the victim of one of the forms of Schilder's disease. The nerve fibers that make up her central nervous system have mostly degenerated. The cause of the degeneration is not fully known, nor is it known how to halt the process. The condition is irreversible, and Juli will never be better than she is.

At birth Juli seemed perfectly normal and healthy, but at three months she began to lose her sight and hearing. She made the gurgling noises typical of babies less and less frequently. By the end of her first year, she made no sounds at all and was completely blind and deaf. Also, she was losing control of her muscles, and her head lolled on her shoulders, like a doll with a broken neck.

She became highly subject to infections, and more than once she had pneumonia. Once when she was on the critical list, a specialist suggested to her mother that it would be pointless to continue treating her. Even if she recovered from the pneumonia, she would remain hopelessly impaired. Mrs. Meyers angrily rejected the suggestion and insisted that everything possible be done to save Juli's life.

Although not wealthy, the family bore the high cost of hospitalization and treatments. Mrs. Meyers devoted herself almost totally to caring for Juli at home, and the other four children in the family received little of her attention. Eventually, Mrs. Meyers began to suffer from severe depression, and when Juli was eight and a half her parents decided she would have to be placed in an institution. Since then, Juli has changed little. No one expects her to change. Her mother visits her three times a month and brings Juli freshly laundered and ironed clothes.

1. Would Robertson's arguments support Mrs. Meyers's decision not to allow Juli to die? How might a utilitarian criticize the decision?

2. Would treatment for pneumonia in Juli's case be considered "normal medical measures" in the Roman Catholic view?

3. Are there any grounds for supposing that Juli is being made to suffer what Engelhardt calls "the injury of continued existence"?

4. Would your decision have been the same as Mrs. Meyers's?

5. Is it possible to justify using society's limited medical resources to keep Juli alive?

6. Evaluate the following argument: Opponents of abortion oppose spending public funds for abortion on the grounds that they (the opponents) are being forced to support murder, which is a serious moral evil. Keeping Juli alive is a serious moral evil. Therefore, no public funds should be used for this purpose.

## Decision Scenario 3

Susan Roth was looking forward to being a mother. She had quit her secretarial job three months before her baby was due so she could spend the time getting everything ready. Her husband, David, was equally enthusiastic, and they spent many hours happily speculating about the way things would be when their baby came. It was their first child.

"I hope they don't mix her up with some other baby," Mrs. Roth said to her husband after delivery.

She didn't know yet that there was little chance of confusion. The Roth infant was seriously deformed. Her arms and legs had failed to develop, her skull was misshapen, and her face deformed. Her large intestine emptied through her vagina, and she had no muscular control over her bladder.

When she was told, Mrs. Roth said "We cannot let it live, for her sake and ours." On the day she left the hospital with the child, Mrs. Roth mixed a lethal dose of a tranquilizing drug with the baby's formula and fed it to her. The child died that evening.

Mrs. Roth and her husband were charged with infanticide. During the court proceedings, Mrs. Roth admitted to the killing but said she was satisfied she had done the right thing. "I know I could not let my baby live like that," she said. "If only she had been mentally abnormal, she would not have known her fate. But she had a normal brain. She would have known. Placing her in an institution might have helped me, but it wouldn't have helped her."

The jury, after deliberating for two hours, found Mrs. Roth and her husband guilty of the charge.

1. Are laws against infanticide unjust?

2. Does the fact that the intelligence of the child is normal support the mother's claim that killing was justifiable? Might normal intelligence make the "injury of continued existence" even greater than subnormal intelligence?

3. Why might Robertson consider the mother's action morally wrong?

4. Would the "best-interest"-of-the-infant standard, as presented by Weir, offer any support for the mother's action?

## Decision Scenario 4

Irene Towers had been a nurse for almost twelve years; for the last three of those years she had worked in the Neonatal Unit of Halifax County Hospital. It was a job she loved. Even when the infants were ill or required special medical or surgical treatment, she found the job of caring for them immensely rewarding. She knew that without her efforts many of the babies would simply die.

Irene Towers was on duty the night that conjoined twins were born to Corrine Couchers and brought at once to the Neonatal Unit. Even Irene, with all her experience, was distressed to see them. The twin boys were joined at their midsections in a way that made it impossible to separate them surgically. Because of the position of the single liver and the kidneys, not even one twin could be saved at the expense of the life of the other. Moreover, both children were severely deformed, with incompletely developed arms and legs and misshapen heads. As best as the neurologist could determine, both suffered severe brain damage.

The father of the children was Dr. Harold Couchers. Dr. Couchers, a slightly built man in his early thirties, was a specialist in internal medicine with a private practice.

Irene felt sorry for him the night the children were born. When he went into the room with the obstetrician to examine his sons, he had already been told what to expect. He showed no signs of grief as he stood over the slat-sided crib, but the corners of his mouth were drawn tight, and his face was almost unnaturally empty of expression. Most strange for a physician, Irene thought, he merely looked at the children and did not touch them. She was sure that in some obscure way he must be blaming himself for what had happened to them.

Later that evening, Irene saw Dr. Couchers sitting in the small conference room at the end of the hall with Dr. Cara Rosen, Corrine Couchers's obstetrician. They were talking earnestly and quietly when Irene passed the open door. Then, while she was looking over the assignment sheet at the nursing station, the two of them walked up. Dr. Rosen took a chart from the rack behind the desk and made a notation. After returning the chart, she shook hands with Dr. Couchers, and he left.

It was not until the end of her shift that Irene read the chart; Dr. Rosen's note said that the twin boys were to be given neither food nor water. At first Irene couldn't believe the order. But when she asked her supervisor, she was told that the supervisor had telephoned Dr. Rosen and that the obstetrician had confirmed the order.

Irene said nothing to the supervisor or to anyone else, but she made her own decision. She believed it was wrong to let the children die, particularly in such a horrible way. They deserved every chance to fight for their lives, and she was going to help them the way she had helped hundreds of other babies in the unit.

For the next week and a half, Irene saw to it that the children were given water and fed the standard infant formula. She did it all herself, on her own initiative. Although some of the other nurses on the floor saw what she was doing, none of them said anything to her. One even smiled and nodded to her when she saw Irene feeding the children.

Apparently someone else also disapproved of the order to let the twins die. Thirteen days after their birth, an investigator from the state Family Welfare Agency appeared in the neonatal ward. The rumor was that his visit had been prompted by an anonymous telephone call.

Late in the afternoon of the day of that visit, the deformed twins were made temporary wards of the Agency, and the orders on the chart were changed—the twins were now to be given food and water. On the next day, the county prosecutor's office announced publicly that it would conduct an investigation of the situation and decide whether criminal charges should be brought against Dr. Couchers or members of the hospital staff.

Irene was sure that she had done the right thing. Nevertheless, she was glad to be relieved of the responsibility.

1. Might a utilitarian argument be offered in defense of Dr. Couchers's decision to allow the twins to die?

2. What criticism of such an argument might Robertson offer?

3. Is there a morally relevant distinction between not treating (and allowing to die) and not providing such minimal needs as food and water (and allowing to die)?

4. Does Engelhardt's line of reasoning support the action taken by Irene Towers?

5. Did Irene Towers exceed the limits of her responsibility, or did she act in a morally heroic way?

6. Federal regulations require that impaired infants be given food and water, even if medical treatment can justifiably be withheld. Are there any moral grounds for making the distinction between treatment and nutritional support?

---

## Decision Scenario 5

Dr. Daniel McKay and his wife, Carol, had only a few moments of joy at the birth of their son. They learned almost immediately that the child was severely impaired. Half an hour later, the infant was dead—Dr. McKay, a veterinarian, had slammed him onto the floor of the delivery room.

Mrs. McKay had had problems during pregnancy. An ultrasound test indicated excessive fluid in the uterus, a sign that something might be wrong. Dr. Joaquin Ramos assured the McKays that everything was all right and that the pregnancy should continue. On June 27, 1983, he ordered Mrs. McKay admitted to the Markham, Illinois, hospital so that labor could be induced.

"Don't do any heroic measures," Dr. McKay told Dr. Ramos when Dr. McKay learned that the infant was impaired. Dr. Ramos explained that that was not his choice, for hospital policy required that everything possible be done for babies, even ones like the McKay baby that might not live more than a few months. The child had webbed fingers, heart and lung malfunctions, and missing testicles. It was suspected that the child also had a genetic disorder that might mean kidney malfunctions, mental retardation, and death within months.

Dr. McKay smashed the infant's head against the floor several times, splattering the wall and floor with brain tissue and blood. "Dan, what have you done?" a nurse shouted. Dr. McKay later said that while holding the child he asked himself "Can I accept and love this child, or would it be better off dead?" He had just talked to his wife. "I said to Dan, 'Is it a boy or a girl?' He said it was a little boy. I said, 'Oh, Dan, we got our boy!' Dan really wasn't saying anything. He had tears in his eyes." She then realized that the baby was not crying and asked her husband to go see what was wrong.

Dr. McKay was charged with murder. Two defense psychiatrists testified that he had been temporarily insane. Two others said that he had succumbed to stress. A prosecution psychiatrist said that he was legally sane but that "he made a decision

that he had a moral imperative to do what he did." The jury could not agree whether Dr. McKay was guilty, not guilty, guilty but not mentally ill, or not guilty by reason of insanity. A mistrial was declared, but another trial was scheduled.

1. How might the hospital policy of "doing everything possible" for all impaired infants be criticized in terms of the "best-interest" standard presented by Weir?

2. Would any of the authors here endorse such a policy? If so, on what grounds?

3. Would the McKay infant count as a potential person according to Weir? How does the potential personhood of the infant affect the decision whether or not to withhold treatment?

4. Might one argue that Dr. McKay's action was morally right, whether or not it was legally justifiable?

5. Under what conditions, if any, ought the parents of an impaired infant be allowed to decide how the child is to be treated?

## Decision Scenario 6

On February 8, 1984, Traci Messenger had an emergency caesarean section at the E. W. Sparrow Hospital in East Lansing, Michigan, and her son, Michael, was delivered after only a twenty-five-week gestation period—fifteen weeks prematurely. Michael weighed one pound, eleven ounces; was very likely to have serious brain damage; and was given a 30 to 50 percent chance of survival.

Before Traci Messenger's surgery, Michael's father, Dr. Gregory Messenger, a dermatologist on the staff of the hospital, had spoken with his wife's physicians and requested that no extraordinary measure be taken to prolong the child's life. However, after the child was born, the neonatologist, Dr. Padmoni Karna, insisted that the baby be given respiratory support and diagnostic tests.

About an hour after Michael was delivered, Dr. Messenger went into the child's room and asked the nurses to leave. He then disconnected the life-support

system, setting off an alarm. The child died, and the hospital called the police. A short time later, the county prosecutor, Donald E. Martin, charged Dr. Messenger with manslaughter.

Although most states, including Michigan, allow parents to decide to withdraw life support from their ailing child, Mr. Martin said he had decided to prosecute because Dr. Messenger had not waited for the results of medical tests. "The father appeared to make a unilateral decision to end life for his infant son," Mr. Martin said.

Dr. Messenger's attorney replied that Dr. Messenger had several warnings of severe medical problems during delivery and immediately after birth. Monitoring of the baby suggested that he was not receiving sufficient oxygen and would be severely brain damaged. Blood tests at birth indicated that the baby had a 14 percent level of oxygen, and as a physician testified at a preliminary hearing, five minutes at a less than 50 percent level is enough to damage the brain. "The parents made a decision when the outcome was so grim and the prognosis was so bad they indicated 'we do not want this intervention.' I think it was incumbent on hospital personnel to honor their directive, and they didn't do that."

Dr. Karna said that she would have agreed to removing the life support, given the blood-test results, but that Dr. Messenger had acted without consulting her.

1. Might Michael Messenger be considered likely to suffer "the injury of continued existence"?

2. Robertson would claim that the infant should be treated. On what grounds might he support this claim?

3. Would the infant be a potential person according to Weir's standards?

4. Suppose that after the test results the parents and Dr. Karna disagreed as to whether the infant should be treated. Whose opinion should be decisive?

5. Would Weir's criteria for determining the "best interest" of the infant be of help in resolving a conflict between the Messengers and Dr. Karna?

**Chapter 11**

# Euthanasia and Physician-Assisted Suicide

## Chapter Contents

## Classic Case Presentation

### *Karen Quinlan: The Debate Begins*

At two in the morning on Tuesday, April 14, 1975, Mrs. Julie Quinlan was awakened by a telephone call. When she hung up she was crying. "Karen is very sick," Mrs. Quinlan said to her husband, Joseph. "She's unconscious, and we have to go to Newton Hospital right away."

The Quinlans thought their twenty-one-year-old adopted daughter might have been in an automobile accident. But the doctor in the intensive-care unit told them that wasn't so. Karen was in a critical comatose state of unknown cause and was being given oxygen through a mask taped over her nose and mouth. She had been brought to the hospital by two friends who had been with her at a birthday party. After a few drinks, she had started to pass out, and her friends decided she must be drunk and put her to bed. Then someone checked on her later in the evening and found that Karen wasn't breathing. Her friends gave her mouth-to-mouth resuscitation and rushed her to the nearest hospital.

Blood and urine tests showed that Karen had not consumed a dangerous amount of alcohol. They also showed the presence of .6 milligram of aspirin and the tranquilizer Valium. Two milligrams would have been toxic, and five lethal. Why Karen stopped breathing was mysterious. But it was during that time that part of her brain died from oxygen depletion.

After Karen had been unconscious for about a week, she was moved to St. Clare's Hospital in nearby Denville, where testing and life-support facilities were better. Dr. Robert J. Morse, a neurologist, and Dr. Arshad Javed, a pulmonary internist, became her physicians. Additional tests were made. Extensive brain damage was confirmed, and several possible causes of the coma were ruled out.

### No Longer the Same

During the early days, the Quinlans were hopeful. Karen's eyes opened and closed, and her mother and her nineteen-year-old sister, Mary Ellen, thought that they detected signs Karen recognized them. But Karen's condition began to deteriorate. Her weight gradually dropped from 120 pounds to 70 pounds. Her body began to contract into a rigid fetal position, until her five-foot-two-inch frame was bent into a shape hardly longer than three feet. She was now breathing mechanically, by means of an MA-1 respirator that pumped air through a tube in her throat. By early July, Karen's physicians and her mother, sister, and brother had come to believe it was hopeless to expect her ever to regain consciousness.

Only her father continued to believe it might be possible. But when he told Dr. Morse about some encouraging sign he had noticed, Dr. Morse said to him "Even if God did perform a miracle so that Karen would live, her damage is so extensive she would spend the rest of her life in an institution." Mr. Quinlan then realized that Karen would never again be as he remembered her. He now agreed with Karen's sister: "Karen would never want to be kept alive on machines like this. She would hate this."

### Need to Go to Court

The Quinlans' parish priest, Father Thomas Trapasso, had also assured them that the moral doctrines of the Roman Catholic Church did not require the continuation of extraordinary measures to support a hopeless life. Before making his decision, Mr. Quinlan asked the priest, "Am I playing God?" Father Thomas said "God has made the decision that Karen is going to die. You're just agreeing with God's decision, that's all."

On July 31, after Karen had been unconscious for three and a half months, the Quinlans gave Drs. Morse and Jared their permission to take Karen off the respirator. The Quinlans signed a letter authorizing the discontinuance of extraordinary procedures and absolving the hospital from all legal liability. "I think you have come to the right decision," Dr. Morse said to Mr. Quinlan.

But the next morning Dr. Morse called Mr. Quinlan. "I have a moral problem about what we agreed on last night," he said. "I feel I have to consult somebody else and see how he feels about it." The next day, Dr. Morse called again. "I find I will not do it," he said. "And I've informed the administrator at the hospital that I will not do it."

The Quinlans were upset and bewildered by the change in Dr. Morse. Later they talked with the hospital attorney and were told by him that, because Karen was over twenty-one, they were no longer her legal guardians. The Quinlans would have to go to court and be appointed to guardianship. After that, the hospital might or might not remove Karen from the respirator.

Mr. Quinlan consulted attorney Paul Armstrong. Because Karen was an adult without income, Mr.

Quinlan explained, Medicare was paying the $450 a day it cost to keep her alive. The Quinlans thus had no financial motive in asking that the respirator be taken away. Mr. Quinlan said that his belief that Karen should be allowed to die rested on his conviction that it was God's will, and it was for this reason that he wanted to be appointed Karen's guardian.

## Legal Arguments

Mr. Armstrong filed a plea with Judge Robert Muir of the New Jersey Superior Court on September 12, 1975. He explicitly requested that Mr. Quinlan be appointed Karen's guardian so that he would have "the express power of authorizing the discontinuance of all extraordinary means of sustaining her life."

Later, on October 20, Mr. Armstrong argued the case on three constitutional grounds. First, he claimed that there is an implicit right to privacy guaranteed by the Constitution and that this right permits individuals or others acting for them to terminate the use of extraordinary medical measures, even when death may result. This right holds, Armstrong said, unless there are compelling state interests that set it aside.

Second, Armstrong argued that the First Amendment guarantee of religious freedom extended to the Quinlan case. If the court did not allow them to act in accordance with the doctrines of their church, their religious liberty would be infringed. Finally, Armstrong appealed to the "cruel and unusual punishment" clause of the Eighth Amendment. He claimed that "for the state to require that Karen Quinlan be kept alive, against her will and the will of her family, after the dignity, beauty, promise, and meaning of earthly life have vanished, is cruel and unusual punishment."

Karen's mother, sister, and a friend testified that Karen had often talked about not wanting to be kept alive by machines. An expert witness, a neurologist, testified that Karen was in a "chronic vegetative state" and that it was unlikely that she would ever regain consciousness. Doctors testifying for St. Clare's Hospital and Karen's physicians agreed with this. But, they argued, her brain still showed patterns of electrical activity, and she still had a discernible pulse. Thus, she could not be considered dead by legal or medical criteria.

On November 10, Judge Muir ruled against Joseph Quinlan. He praised Mr. Quinlan's character and concern, but he decided that Mr. Quinlan's anguish over his daughter might cloud his judgment about her welfare so he should not be made her guardian. Furthermore, Judge Muir said, because Karen is still medically and legally alive, "the Court should not authorize termination of the respirator. To do so would be homicide and an act of euthanasia."

## Appeal

Mr. Armstrong appealed the decision to the New Jersey Supreme Court. On January 26, 1976, the court convened to hear arguments, and Mr. Armstrong argued substantially as before. But this time the court's ruling was favorable. The court agreed that Mr. Quinlan could assert a right of privacy on Karen's behalf and that whatever he decided for her should be accepted by society. It also set aside any criminal liability for removing the respirator, claiming that if death resulted it would not be homicide and that, even if it were homicide, it would not be unlawful. Finally, the court stated that, if Karen's physicians believed that she would never emerge from her coma, they should consult an ethics committee to be established by St. Clare's Hospital. If the committee accepted their prognosis, then the respirator could be removed. If Karen's present physicians were then unwilling to take her off the respirator, Mr. Quinlan was free to find a physician who would.

Six weeks after the court decision, the respirator still had not been turned off. In fact, another machine, one for controlling body temperature, had been added. Mr. Quinlan met with Morse and Jared and demanded that they remove the respirator. They agreed to "wean" Karen from the machine, and soon she was breathing without mechanical assistance. Dr. Morse and St. Clare's Hospital were determined that Karen would not die while under their care. Although she was moved to a private room, it was next door to the intensive-care unit. They intended to put her back on the respirator at the first sign of breathing difficulty.

Because Karen was still alive, the Quinlans began a long search for a chronic-care hospital. Twenty or more institutions turned them away, and physicians expressed great reluctance to become involved in the case. Finally, Dr. Joseph Fennelly volunteered to treat Karen, and on June 9 she was moved from St. Clare's to the Morris View Nursing Home.

## The End—After Ten Years

Karen Quinlan continued to breathe. She received high-nutrient feedings and regular doses of antibiotics to ward off infections. During some periods she was more active than at others, making reflexive responses to touch and sound.

On June 11, 1985, at 7:01 in the evening, ten years after she lapsed into a coma, Karen Quinlan finally died. She was thirty-one years old.

Her father died of cancer on December 10, 1996, at the Karen Quinlan Center of Hope, a hospice Joseph and Julia Quinlan had founded in 1980 with money they received from the film and book rights to their daughter's story. Joseph Quinlan continued to support the right of patients and their families to discontinue the use of life-sustaining technologies, but he opposed all forms of physician-assisted suicide.

# BRIEFING SESSION

Death comes to us all. We hope that when it comes it will be swift and allow us to depart without prolonged suffering, our dignity intact. We also hope that it will not force burdens on our family and friends, making them pay both financially and emotionally by our lingering and hopeless condition.

Such considerations give euthanasia a strong appeal. Should we not be able to snip the thread of life when the weight of suffering and hopelessness grows too heavy to bear? The answer to this question is not as easy as it may seem, for hidden within it are a number of complicated moral issues.

Just what is euthanasia? The word comes from the Greek for "good death," and in English it has come to have the meaning "easy death." But this does little to help us understand the concept. For consider this: If we give ourselves an easy death, are we committing suicide? If we assist someone else to an easy death (with or without that person's permission), are we committing murder? Anyone who opposed killing (either of oneself or of others) on moral grounds might also consider it necessary to object to euthanasia.

It may be, however, that the answer to both of these questions is no. But if it is, then it is nec-essary to specify the conditions that distinguish euthanasia from both suicide and murder. Only then would it be possible to argue, without contradiction, that euthanasia is morally acceptable but the other two forms of killing are not.

Someone believing that suicide is morally legitimate would not object to euthanasia carried out by the person herself, but he would still have to deal with the problem posed by the euthanasia/murder issue.

## Active and Passive Euthanasia

We have talked of euthanasia as though it involved directly taking the life of a person, either one's own life or the life of another. However, some philosophers distinguish between "active euthanasia" and "passive euthanasia," which in turn rests on a distinction between killing and letting die.

To kill someone (including oneself) is to take a definite action to end his or her life (administering a lethal injection, for example). To allow someone to die, by contrast, is to take no steps to prolong a person's life when those steps seem called for—failing to give a needed injection of antibiotics, for example. Active euthanasia, then, is direct killing and is an act of commission. Passive euthanasia is an act of omission.

This distinction is used in most contemporary codes of medical ethics (for example, the American Medical Association's Code of Ethics) and is also recognized in the Anglo-American tradition of law. Except in special circumstances, it is illegal to deliberately cause the death of another person. It is not, however, illegal (except in special circumstances) to allow a person to die. Clearly, one might consider active euthanasia morally wrong, while recognizing passive euthanasia as morally legitimate.

Some philosophers, however, have argued that the active–passive distinction is morally irrelevant with respect to euthanasia. Both are cases of causing death, and it is the circumstances in which death is caused, not the manner of causing it, that is of moral importance.

Furthermore, the active–passive distinction is not always clear-cut. If a person dies after special life-sustaining equipment has been withdrawn, is this a case of active or passive euthanasia? Or is it a case of euthanasia at all?

## Voluntary, Involuntary, and Nonvoluntary Euthanasia

Writers on euthanasia have often thought it important to distinguish between voluntary, involuntary, and nonvoluntary euthanasia. *Voluntary euthanasia* includes cases in which a person takes his or her own life, either directly or by refusing treatment. But it also includes cases in which a person deputizes another to act in accordance with his wishes.

Thus, someone might instruct her family not to permit the use of artificial support systems should she become unconscious, suffer from brain damage, and be unable to speak for herself. Or someone might request that he be given a lethal injection, after suffering third-degree burns over most of his body, suffering uncontrollable pain, and being told he has little hope of recovery.

Finally, assisted suicide, in which the individual requests the direct help of someone else in ending his life, falls into this category. (Some may think that one or more of the earlier examples are also cases of assisted suicide. What counts as assisted suicide is both conceptually and legally unclear.) That the individual explicitly consents to death is a necessary feature of voluntary euthanasia.

*Involuntary euthanasia* consists in ending the life of someone contrary to that person's wish. The person killed not only fails to give consent, but expresses the desire not to be killed. No one arguing in favor of nonvoluntary euthanasia holds that involuntary euthanasia is justifiable. Those who oppose both voluntary and nonvoluntary euthanasia often argue that to permit either runs the risk of opening the way for involuntary euthanasia.

*Nonvoluntary euthanasia* includes those cases in which the decision about death is not made by the person who is to die. Here the person gives no specific consent or instructions, and the decision is made by family, friends, or physicians. The distinction between voluntary and nonvoluntary euthanasia is not always a clear one. Physicians sometimes assume that people are "asking" to die, even when no explicit request has been made. Also, the wishes and attitudes that people express when they are not in extreme life-threatening medical situations may be too vague for us to be certain that they would choose death when they are in such a situation. Is "I never want to be hooked up to one of those machines" an adequate indication that the person who says this does not want to be put on a respirator should she meet with an accident and fall into a comatose state?

If the distinctions made here are accepted as legitimate and relevant, we can distinguish eight cases in which euthanasia becomes a moral decision:

1.  Self-administered euthanasia
    a.   active
    b.   passive
2.  Other-administered euthanasia
    a.   active and voluntary
    b.   active and involuntary
    c.   active and nonvoluntary
    d.   passive and voluntary
    e.   passive and involuntary
    f.   passive and nonvoluntary

Even these possibilities don't exhaust the cases euthanasia presents us with. For example, notice that the voluntary–nonvoluntary distinction doesn't appear in connection with self-administered euthanasia in our scheme. Yet it might be argued that it should, for a person's decision to end his life (actively or passively) may well not be a wholly voluntary or free decision. People who are severely depressed by their illness and decide to end their lives, for example, might be thought of as not having made a voluntary choice.

Hence, one might approve of self-administered voluntary euthanasia, yet think that the nonvoluntary form should not be permitted. It should not be allowed not because it is necessarily morally wrong, but because it would not be a genuine decision by the person. The person might be thought to be suffering from a psychiatric disability. Indeed, the current debate about physician-assisted suicide turns, in part, on just this issue.

## Defining "Death"

The advent of new medical technologies, pharmaceutical agents, and modes of treatment raises the question of when we should consider someone dead. Suppose someone's heartbeat, blood pressure, respiration, and liver and kidney functions can be maintained within the normal range of values by medical intervention. Should we still include this individual among living persons, even though she is in an irreversible coma or a chronic vegetative state?

If we consider the individual to be a living person, we need to decide how she ought to be treated. Should she be allowed to die or be maintained by medical means? This is the kind of question faced by families, physicians, and the courts in the *Quinlan* and *Cruzan* cases (see the Case Presentations in this chapter), and it is one faced every day in dozens of unpublicized, though no less agonizing, cases.

But what if an unconscious individual lacking higher cortical functioning is no longer a living person? Could a physician who disconnected a respirator or failed to give an antibiotic be said to have killed a person? If nutrition and hydration are withheld from a "brain dead" individual or even if the individual is given a lethal injection, is it reasonable to say that this is a case of killing? Perhaps the person died when her brain stopped functioning at a certain level. Or perhaps she died when she lapsed into coma.

A practical question that advances in medicine have made even more pressing is when or whether a comatose individual may be regarded as a source of transplant organs. If the individual remains a living person, it may be morally wrong (at least prima facie) to kill him to obtain organs

for transplant. But what if the comatose individual is not really alive? What if he is dead already and no longer a person? Then there seem to be no reasonable grounds for objecting to removing his organs and using them to save the lives of those who need them. (See Chapter 7 for a discussion of organ donation.)

Questions like the ones raised here have prompted various attempts to define the notion of death. In the view of many commentators, the traditional notion of death is no longer adequate to serve as a guide to resolving issues about the treatment of individuals who, through disease or accident, have fallen into states in which many of their basic physiological functions can be maintained by medical means, although they remain comatose or lacking in higher-brain function.

Until recently, the traditional notion of death has been enshrined in laws defining crimes such as homicide and manslaughter. Given the change in medical technology, actions like removing a respirator, which might once have been regarded as criminal for causing the death of a person, perhaps should now be viewed in a different way. Perhaps a person may be dead already, even though major physiological systems are still functioning.

Four major notions or concepts of death have emerged during the last two decades. We'll list each of them, but it's important to keep in mind that there is a difference between specifying the concept of death (or, as it is sometimes put, defining "death") and the criteria for determining that the concept fits in particular cases. This is analogous to defining "the best team" as the one winning the most games, then providing criteria for determining what counts as winning a game.

The concepts are merely sketched and the criteria for applying them only hinted at.

1. *Traditional.* A person is dead when he is no longer breathing and his heart is not beating. Hence, death may be defined as the permanent cessation of breathing and blood flow. This notion is sometimes known as the "cardiopulmonary" or "heart–lung criterion" for death.

2. *Whole-brain.* Death is regarded as the irreversible cessation of all brain functions. Essentially, this means that there is no electrical activity in the brain, and even the brain stem is not functioning. Application of the concept depends on the use of electroencephalographic or imaging data.

3. *Higher-brain.* Death is considered to involve the permanent loss of consciousness. Hence, someone in an irreversible coma would be considered dead, even though the brain stem continued to regulate breathing and heartbeat. Clinical, electroencephalographic, and imaging data are relevant to applying the concept. So, too, are statistics concerning the likelihood of the individual's regaining consciousness.

4. *Personhood.* Death occurs when an individual ceases to be a person. This may mean the loss of features that are essential to personal identity or (in some statements) the loss of what is essential to being a person. Criteria for personal identity or for being a person are typically taken to include a complex of such activities as reasoning, remembering, feeling emotion, possessing a sense of the future, interacting with others, and so on. The criteria for applying this concept have more to do with the way an individual functions than with data about his brain.

Technology makes it necessary to take a fresh look at the traditional notion of death, but technology also provides data that have allowed for the development of new notions. It would be pointless, for example, to talk about brain death without having some means to determine when the concept might be satisfied.

The whole-brain concept of death was proposed by the 1981 *Report of the President's Commission for the Study of Ethical Problems in Medicine* and included in the Uniform Death Act. As a consequence, state laws employing the traditional concept of death generally have been modified in keeping with the whole-brain concept.

The whole-brain concept has the advantage of being relatively clear-cut in application. However, applying the concept is not without difficulty and controversy. In the view of some, the concept is too restrictive and so fails to resolve some of the difficulties that prompted the need for a new concept. For example, both Karen Quinlan and Nancy Cruzan would have been considered alive by the whole-brain criteria. However, those who favor concepts of death based on the loss of higher-brain function or the loss of personhood might argue that both cases were ones in which the affected individuals were, in the respective technical senses, dead.

Furthermore, critics charge, the whole-brain concept is not really as straightforward in its application as it might seem. Even when there appears to be complete lack of cognitive functioning and even when basic brain-stem functions appear to have disappeared, a brain may remain electrically active to some degree. Isolated cells or groups of cells continue to be alive, and monitoring of the brain yields data that are open to conflicting interpretations.

The higher-brain and personhood concepts face even greater difficulties. Each must formulate criteria that are accepted as nonarbitrary and as sufficient grounds for deciding that an individual is dead. No one has yet solved either of these problems for either of these concepts. The fact that there can be controversy over whole-brain death indicates how much harder it is to get agreement about when higher-brain functions are lost. Also, securing agreement on criteria for determining when an entity either becomes or ceases to be a person is a conceptual difficulty far from being resolved to the satisfaction of most philosophers. (See the discussion of persons in connection with abortion in Chapter 9, "Status of the Fetus," for more on this topic.)

## Advance Directives

Like so many issues in bioethics, euthanasia has traditionally been discussed only in the back rooms of medicine. Often decisions about whether to allow a patient to die are made by physicians acting on their own authority. Such decisions do not represent so much an arrogant claim to godlike wisdom as an acknowledgment of the physician's obligation to do what is best for the patient.

Most physicians admit that allowing or helping a patient to die is sometimes the best assistance that can be given. Decisions made in this fashion depend on the beliefs and judgment of particular physicians. Because these may differ from those of the patient concerned, it is quite possible that the physician's decision may not reflect the wishes of the patient.

But covert decisions made by a physician acting alone are becoming practices of the past as euthanasia is discussed more widely and openly. Court cases, such as *Quinlan* and *Cruzan,* have both widened the scope of legally permissible actions and reinforced the notion that an individual has a right to refuse or discontinue life-sustaining medical treatment. Such cases have also made it clear that there are limits to the benefits that can be derived from medicine—that, under some conditions, individuals may be better off if everything that technologically can be done is not done. Increasingly, people want to be sure that they have some say in what happens to them should they fall victim to hopeless injury or illness.

One indication of this interest is that the number of states permitting individuals to sign "living wills" or advanced directives has now increased to include all states. The first living-will legislation was the "Natural Death Act," passed by the California legislature on August 30, 1977. The act is generally representative of all such legislation. It permits a competent adult to sign a directive that will authorize physicians to withhold or discontinue "mechanical" or "artificial" life-support equipment if the person is judged to be "terminal" and if "death is imminent."

The strength of advance directives is that they allow a person to express in an explicit manner how he or she wishes to be treated before treatment is needed. In this way, the autonomy of the individual is recognized. Even though unconscious or comatose, a person can continue to exert control over his or her life. This, in turn, means that physicians need not and should not

## Whose Life Is It Anyway?

A study published in the March 2002 issue of the *Journal of the American Geriatric Society* found that 60 percent of the 1185 Medicare patients surveyed at five teaching hospitals told their doctors to focus on making them comfortable rather than on extending their lives. Yet evidence indicated that more than one-third of the people expressing this wish had it ignored. They were treated more and lived longer than the two-thirds whose wishes were respected. Either their doctors forgot about their preferences, or they deliberately ignored them.

be the decisive voice in determining the continuation or use of special medical equipment.

Critics of advance-directive legislation have claimed that it does not go far enough in protecting autonomy and making death easier (where this is what is wanted). They point out that the directive specified in the California bill and most others would have made no difference in the case of Karen Quinlan. She had not been diagnosed as having a "terminal condition" at least two weeks prior to being put on a respirator, yet this is one of the requirements of the act. Consequently, the directive would have been irrelevant to her condition.

Nor, for that matter, would those people be allowed to die who wish to, if their disease or injury does not involve treatment by "artificial" or "mechanical" means. Thus, a person suffering from throat cancer would simply have to bear the pain and wait for a "natural" death. Finally, at the moment, some states explicitly exclude nutrition and hydration as medical treatments that can be discontinued. The Supreme Court in the *Cruzan* case accepted the notion that the nutrition received by Nancy Cruzan through a feeding tube implanted in her stomach was a form of medical treatment that could be withdrawn. However, the Court did not rule on the Missouri law that forbids withdrawal. Until this law or some other like it is successfully challenged in court, an advance directive does not necessarily guarantee that such treatment will be discontinued, even when requested.

Limitations of such kinds on living wills have led some writers to recommend that individuals sign a legal instrument known as a durable power of attorney. In such a document, an individual can name someone to act on his behalf should he become legally incompetent to act. Hence, unlike the advance directive, a durable power of attorney allows a surrogate to exercise control over novel and unanticipated situations. For example, the surrogate may order the discontinuation of artificial feeding, something that an advance directive might not permit.

The widespread wish to have some control over the end of one's life is reflected in a federal law that took effect in 1991. The Patient Self-Determination Act is sometimes referred to as a "medical Miranda warning."

It requires that hospitals, nursing homes, and other health-care facilities receiving federal funding provide patients at the time of admission with written information about relevant state laws and the rights of citizens under those laws to refuse or discontinue treatment. Patients must also be told about the practices and policies at that particular institution so they can choose a facility willing to abide by their decisions. The institutions must also record whether a patient has provided a written "advance directive" (e.g., a living will or power of attorney for health care) that will take effect should the patient become incapacitated.

Another sign of change is the recent concern with the medical circumstances in which people die. The medical ideal of a "hospital death," one in which the patient's temperature, pulse rate, and respiration are brought within normal limits by medication and machinery, is being severely challenged. This is reflected in the policy of the AMA that holds that it may be morally appropriate to withhold "all means of life prolonging medical treatment," including artificial feeding, from patients in irreversible comas.

A new ideal of natural death also seems to be emerging. In this view, the kind of support a dying patient needs is psychological counseling and contact with family and friends rather than heroic medical efforts. An acceptance of death as a normal end of life and the development of new means of caring for the dying may ease the problem of euthanasia. If those who face imminent death are offered an alternative to either euthanasia or an all-out medical effort to preserve their lives, they may choose that alternative. "Death with dignity" need not always mean choosing a lethal injection.

## Ethical Theories and Euthanasia

Roman Catholicism explicitly rejects all forms of euthanasia as being against the natural law duty to preserve life. It considers euthanasia as morally identical with either suicide or murder. This position is not so rigid as it may seem, however. The principle of double effect (see Part V: Foundations of Bioethics) makes it morally acceptable to give medication for the relief of pain—even if the indirect result of the medication will be to shorten the life of the recipient. The intended result is not the death of the person but the relief of suffering. The difference in intention is thus considered to be a morally significant one. Those not accepting the principle of double effect would be likely to classify the administration of a substance that would relieve pain but would also cause death as a case of euthanasia.

Furthermore, on the Catholic view there is no moral obligation to continue treatment when a person is medically hopeless. It is legitimate to allow people to die as a result of their illness or injury, even though their lives might be lengthened by the use of extraordinary means. Additionally, we may legitimately make the same decisions about ourselves that we make about others who are in no condition to decide. Thus, without intending to kill ourselves, we may choose measures for the relief of pain that may secondarily hasten our end. Or we may refuse extraordinary treatment and let "nature" take its course, let "God's will" determine the outcome. (See Foundations of Bioethics for a fuller discussion of the Roman Catholic position on euthanasia and extraordinary means of sustaining life.)

## Public Views on Euthanasia

|  | Agree | Disagree | Neither |
|---|---|---|---|
| 1. If a person has a fatal illness, that person should have the right to have all life-sustaining devices removed, including feeding tubes. | 79% | 12% | 9% |
| 2. If a person is in a coma that cannot be reversed, relatives should be allowed to tell doctors to remove all life-sustaining devices, including feeding tubes. | 81% | 11% | 8% |
| 3. In case of fatal illness, doctors should be allowed to help that person end his or her life. | 49% | 35% | 16% |
| 4. If a person has been diagnosed as having a fatal illness, he or she should be allowed to take his or her own life. | 39% | 45% | 16% |

*Source: Parade Magazine* (9 February 1992) mail survey of 3750 people aged twenty-one or older; 2203 respondents. Reprinted with permission from *Parade,* copyright © 1992.

At first sight, utilitarianism would seem to endorse euthanasia in all of its forms. Whenever suffering is great and the condition of the person is one without legitimate medical hope, then the principle of utility might be invoked to approve putting the person to death. After all, in such a case we seem to be acting to end suffering and to bring about a state of affairs in which happiness exceeds unhappiness. Thus, whether the person concerned is ourself or another, euthanasia would seem to be a morally right action.

A utilitarian might argue in this way, but this is not the only way in which the principle of utility could be applied. It could be argued, for example, that since life is a necessary condition for happiness, it is wrong to destroy that condition because by doing so the possibility of all future happiness is lost. Furthermore, a rule utilitarian might well argue that a rule like "The taking of a human life is permissible when suffering is intense and the condition of the person permits no legitimate hope" would be open to abuse. Consequently, in the long run the rule would actually work to increase the amount of unhappiness in the world. Obviously, it is not possible to say

there is such a thing as "the utilitarian view of euthanasia." The principle of utility supplies a guide for an answer, but it is not itself an answer.

Euthanasia presents a considerable difficulty for Kant's ethics. For Kant, an autonomous rational being has a duty to preserve his or her life. Thus, one cannot rightly refuse needed medical care or commit suicide. Yet our status as autonomous rational beings also endows us with an inherent dignity. If that status is destroyed or severely compromised, as it is when people become comatose and unknowing because of illness or injury, then it is not certain that we have a duty to maintain our lives under such conditions. It may be more in keeping with our freedom and dignity for us to instruct others either to put us to death or to take no steps to keep us alive should we ever be in such a state. Voluntary euthanasia may be compatible with (if not required by) Kant's ethics.

By a similar line of reasoning, it may be that nonvoluntary euthanasia might be seen as a duty that we have to others. We might argue that by putting to death a comatose and hopeless person we are recognizing the dignity that person possessed in his or her previous state. It might also be argued that a human being in a vegetative state is not a person in the relevant moral sense. Thus, our ordinary duty to preserve life does not hold.

According to Ross, we have a strong prima facie obligation not to kill a person except in justifiable self-defense—unless we have an even stronger prima facie moral obligation to do something that cannot be done without killing. Since active euthanasia typically requires taking the life of an innocent person, there is a moral presumption against it. However, another of Ross's prima facie obligations is that we keep promises made to others. Accordingly, if someone who is now in an irreversible coma with no hope of recovery has left instructions that in case of such an event she wishes her life to be ended, then we are under a prima facie obligation to follow her instructions. Thus, in such a case we may be justified in overriding the presumption against taking an innocent life.

What if there are no such instructions? It could be argued that our prima facie obligation of acting beneficently toward others requires us to attempt to determine what someone's wishes would be from what we know about him as a person. We would then treat him the way that we believe that he would want us to. In the absence of any relevant information, we might make the decision on the basis of how a rational person would want to be treated in similar circumstances. Of course, if anyone has left instructions that his life is to be maintained, if possible, under any circumstances, then we have a prima facie obligation to respect this preference also.

# SOCIAL CONTEXT: THE PHYSICIAN-ASSISTED SUICIDE LAW IN OREGON

On March 24, 1998, an anonymous woman in her mid-eighties became the first known person to choose physician-assisted suicide under an Oregon law authorizing physicians to prescribe doses of drugs that terminally ill patients can use to end their lives.

The woman, who lived in Portland, died shortly after swallowing a lethal dose of barbiturates, which she washed down with a glass of brandy. She was suffering from terminal breast cancer and had been given less than two months to live. In an audiotape she made two days before her death, she said she "looked forward" to her coming suicide. "I will be relieved of all the stress I have." She said she had grown tired of fighting cancer and had trouble breathing and walking. "I can't see myself living a few more months like this," she said. She died about half an hour after taking the prescribed drugs.

The woman may not have been the first person to commit suicide under the provisions of the law. It allows strict privacy, and the woman's death was made public with her consent by an advocacy group that supports the law.

## The Law

Oregon's 1994 "Written Request for Medication to End One's Life in a Humane and Dignified Manner" or Death with Dignity Act is the first physician-suicide measure passed by any state. The measure does not permit a physician to play an active role in ending a patient's life. The major provision of the measure is that it allows physicians to prescribe lethal drugs for terminally ill patients without risking criminal prosecution.

The law spells out a set of conditions that must be met by patients and physicians:

1. A primary-care physician and a consulting physician must both agree that the patient has six months or less to live.

2. The patient must make two oral requests (at least forty-eight hours apart) for drugs to use to terminate his or her life.

3. The patient must wait at least fifteen days after the initial oral request, then make a written request to the physician.

4. If either physician thinks the patient has a mental disorder or is suffering from impaired judgment from depression, they must recommend the patient for counseling.

5.    The patient can terminate the request at any time during the process.

Under the law, a physician is not permitted to assist a patient to die by any means more active than prescribing a medication that can cause death and indicating the manner in which it can be used. Hence, such practices as lethal injections remain as illegal as before.

## A Long Time Coming

In 1994 the Oregon law was approved by the slight margin of 52 percent to 48 percent of the vote. Immediately after it was clear that the law had passed, it was challenged in court. The legal wrangles took three years, and in 1997 opponents of the law mounted an effort through a voter initiative to have it repealed. The effort failed, and the law was approved by 60 percent of the voters.

Despite voter approval, physicians were still uncertain about what might happen to them if they acted in accordance with the law and assisted a patient in killing himself. Thomas Constantine, the head of the Drug Enforcement Administration, responding to pressure by two politically conservative members of Congress, announced that the agency would impose severe sanctions on any physicians who prescribed lethal doses of drugs. Constantine claimed that prescribing drugs for use in suicide wasn't a legitimate medical use under the federal drug laws. Although the DEA cannot cancel a physician's license to practice, it has the power to withdraw the license to prescribe drugs. The threat to physicians was thus very real.

It was not until June 1998 that Attorney General Janet Reno removed the final legal obstacle to implementing the Oregon law. The DEA is a branch of the Justice Department, and Reno said the policy statement threatening to take action against physicians who acted in accordance with the Oregon law had been issued without her knowledge or consent. Overruling Constantine, Reno said the drug laws were intended to block illicit drug dealing and that there was no evidence that Congress ever meant for the DEA

| Survey of Oncologists | |
| --- | --- |
| Support physician-assisted suicide: | 22.5% |
| Taken part in at least one: | 10.8% |
| Taken part in five or more: | 18% |
| Performed euthanasia at least once: | 3.7% |
| Of the previous group, five or more times: | 12% |
| n = 3299 | |

*Source:* Survey by Ezekiel Emanuel of Society of Clinical Oncology, *Annals of Internal Medicine,* October, 2000.

to have a role in resolving the moral problems presented by the Oregon law.

The law explicitly protects only physicians from prosecution. Hence, it leaves in doubt the legal status of nurses. Many terminally ill patients are paralyzed or too weak to take prescribed medications without assistance. Nurses typically help patients take prescribed medications, but what if they help the patient take a lethal dose of drugs? Does this make them liable for legal prosecution?

Also, from a moral point of view, if a nurse is opposed to euthanasia or suicide, does the general responsibility he has to assist a patient require him to help the patient take lethal drugs? Nurses in Oregon are facing these questions, although apparently very few (if any) have had to deal with them in a practical way.

Some pharmacists in Oregon also have trouble with the physician-assisted suicide law. Because they must fill the prescriptions written by physicians, the law makes them, to an extent, participants in the suicide. Some have argued that drugs prescribed for potential use in a suicide should be labeled as such on the prescription. That way pharmacists who object to assisted suicide can avoid becoming involved in one. The prescription could be filled by some other pharmacist.

Physicians object to this proposal, though. They point out that if prescriptions were labeled as potential suicide agents, then the patient's confidentiality would be violated. Particularly in small towns, if word got out, the families of those who chose assisted suicide might become the targets of public criticism or worse.

In March 1998, Oregon state officials decided to make physician-assisted suicide available to residents who cannot pay for it under the state's Medicaid program. The state will have to bear the full cost, because by law federal funds cannot be used to pay for physician-assisted suicide.

Critics claim that the use of state funds is a tacit endorsement of suicide, while supporters claim it is only an extension of the "comfort care" already covered by Medicaid. Those who believe mental health services are underfunded think that supporting physician-assisted suicide is a serious mistake. It suggests to patients that death is the only help available to them. Some observers believe the Oregon legislature will remove physician-assisted suicide as a procedure covered by the state's Medicaid plan.

### Is the Law Needed?

Proponents of the Oregon law would like to see other states pass similar legislation. They point out that terminally ill people who decide to end their lives are often frustrated in carrying out their wishes, even though the society has endorsed in principle a "right to die."

The federal Patient Self-Determination Act requires hospitals to inform patients that they have the right to refuse or discontinue treatment and that by living wills and powers of attorney for health care, they can put their decisions into practice. The Supreme Court in the *Cruzan* decision implicitly acknowledges a "right to die," in that it permits the withdrawal of life-sustaining treatment when clear and compelling evidence shows that this reflects the wishes of an individual. Yet despite the legal possibility of exercising control over medical care during the last stages of one's life, various barriers stand in the way of actual control:

- Surveys of physicians and health-care workers show that many are not aware of the legal options open to patients or are not willing to respect them. Many in health care are not aware of laws that allow them to withhold or discontinue such care as mechanical ventilation, kidney dialysis, or even feeding tubes. Many believe that once a treatment has been started, it is illegal to discontinue it. Courts have repeatedly upheld the right of individuals to decide that, at a certain point in their treatment, they do not want to be provided with food or water, yet 42 percent of health-care workers rejected this as an option patients could choose.

- Many physicians and hospitals simply ignore the oral instructions patients give them about discontinuing their care. In one study of over 4000 seriously ill patients, researchers found that while a third of the patients asked not to be revived by cardiopulmonary resuscitation, 50 percent of the time, "Do not resuscitate" was never written in their charts.

- The living wills or powers of attorney made out by patients may not be followed in practice. In a 1997 study of 4804 terminally ill patients, only 688 had written directives, and only 22 of these contained instructions explicit enough to guide the care they received. Even these instuctions were ignored about half the time, and physicians knew about the patient's instructions only about a quarter of the time.

  Also, advance directives are sometimes not included among the documents constituting a patient's medical chart. In another study, when seventy-one patients were moved to a nursing home, twenty-five of them had living wills that were not sent with them.

  As a result, despite the efforts patients may make to control what happens to them at the end of their lives, they may be forced to accept decisions about their care made by physicians or nurses in accordance with their own values or institutional policies.

- Families may override the wishes expressed by patients in their living wills.

Even though the views of the patient take legal precedence over those of a relative, in practice a physician or hospital may do as the relative wishes. Families never sue because of the overtreatment of a patient, but they do because of withholding or discontinuing treatment.

Laws like the one in Oregon are viewed by many as the only way patients can be sure that in the final days of their lives they can exercise control. Many fear that if they enter a hospital, they cannot trust nurses and physicians to know their wishes and to respect them.

The extent of the desire people have to exercise control over how their lives end is shown by the popularity of Derek Humphry's best-selling *Final Exit.* The book is a guide to effective methods for committing suicide or, as the subtitle puts it, the book is about "The Practicalities of Self-Deliverance and Assisted Suicide for the Dying."

Journalist Betty Rollins's foreword to the book describes the hundreds of letters she received from people who read her book, *Last Wish,* on her mother's suicide because of a terminal illness. The saddest of the letters, she said, were from those who had tried to die, failed in their attempt, and suffered even more as a result. "Until there is a law which would allow physicians to help these people who want a final exit, there is Derek Humphry's book, fittingly named, to guide them."

Various polls suggest that nearly a majority of the American people favor a policy of voluntary physician-assisted suicide, and in cases less well known than the Kevorkian case, in which physicians have been charged with aiding the death of their patients, they have typically been found not guilty or been given suspended sentences.

## How Many Cases?

The Oregon law is written so that only Oregon residents can ask physicians to assist them in suicide under the stipulated conditions. Thus, sick people have not migrated to the state with the idea of getting a physician's help in killing themselves.

Although the way seems clear for any terminally ill Oregon resident to seek help in dying, so far few people seem to have done so. In February 1999 state officials reported that in the first year under the new law, fifteen people in the state ended their lives with drugs legally prescribed for that purpose. (There were 29,000 deaths in Oregon in 1998.) The average age of the eight men and seven women was 69. Thirteen had cancer, one congestive heart failure, and the other chronic lung disease. Fourteen had lived in the state at least six months, and one had come to be with family members.

Eight other people in 1998 were certified as terminally ill and had received authorization to receive lethal doses of drugs, but six died of their diseases without taking the medications. The other two were still alive at the end of the year. For the fifteen who acted under the law, the cause of death was listed as "Drug overdose, legally prescribed."

In 2000, forty-four people obtained drugs under the Death with Dignity legislation, but only twenty-one used them. This was down from twenty-seven people the previous year, the same figure as for 1998. So far only about 125 people have ended their lives with assistance.

According to a state report, those choosing physician-assisted suicide were "not disproportionately poor, uneducated, uninsured, fearful of the financial consequences of their illnesses" or "lacking end-of-life care." The primary factor mentioned by individuals was "the importance of autonomy and personal control." Neither financial worries nor the pain of a long illness was mentioned by them as a decisive factor.

The average time to unconsciousness after taking the prescribed drugs was five minutes (with a range of three to twenty), and the average time to death was twenty-six minutes (with a range of fifteen minutes to eleven and a half hours).

That relatively few have taken advantage of the Oregon law may support the idea of those favoring it that most people simply want to know that if they are terminally ill and in pain, a way out is available to them. To this extent, then, the Oregon experience may support the movement in other states to allow physician-assisted suicide.

## New Federal Actions

In November 2001, Attorney General Ashcroft sent a letter to the Drug Enforcement Agency authorizing agents to take legal action against physicians prescribing drugs for the purpose of ending the lives of terminally ill patients.

Ashcroft wrote that "prescribing, dispensing or administering federally controlled substances to assist suicide" is "not a legitimate medical purpose" and so would violate the 1970 federal Controlled Substances Act. He thus reinstalled the roadblock to the Oregon law that Janet Reno had lifted in 1997.

Critics of Ashcroft claimed he had wrongly interpreted the Act. It is supposed to prevent the illegal trafficking in drugs, not interfere with a state's right to regulate the practice of medicine.

The State of Oregon filed suit against the Justice Department in the Federal District Court in Portland. Justice Robert E. Jones issued a restraining order keeping Ashcroft's directive from being followed, and in April 2002, Jones ruled Ashcroft lacked the authority to decide "what constitutes the legitimate practice of medicine." Ultimately, however, it may take a Supreme Court ruling to settle the issue.

## Case Presentation

### The Cruzan Case: The Supreme Court Upholds the Right to Die in a Landmark Decision

In the early morning of January 11, 1983, twenty-five-year-old Nancy Cruzan was driving on a deserted county road in Missouri. The road was icy and the car skidded, then flipped over and crashed. Nancy was thrown from the driver's seat and landed face down in a ditch by the side of the road.

An ambulance arrived quickly, but not quickly enough to save her from suffering irreversible brain damage. Nancy never regained consciousness, and her physicians eventually concluded that she had entered into what is known medically as a persistent vegetative state, awake but unaware. The higher brain functions responsible for recognition, memory, comprehension, anticipation, and other cognitive functions had all been lost.

Her arms and legs were drawn into a fetal position, her knees against her chest, and her body stiff and contracted. Only loud sounds and painful stimuli evoked responses, but even those were no more than neurological reflexes.

"We've literally cried over Nancy's body, and we've never seen anything," her father, Joe Cruzan, said. "She has no awareness of herself."

Nancy was incapable of eating, but her body was sustained by a feeding tube surgically implanted in her stomach. She was a patient at the Missouri Rehabilitation Center, but no one expected her to be rehabilitated. She could only be kept alive.

"If only the ambulance had arrived five minutes earlier—or five minutes later," her father lamented.

The cost of Nancy Cruzan's care was $130,000 a year. The bill was paid by the state. Because she was a legal adult when her accident occurred, her family was not responsible for her medical care. Had she been under twenty-one, the Cruzans would have been responsible for her medical bills, as long as they had any financial resources to pay them.

## Eight Years Later

In 1991, eight years after her accident, Nancy was almost thirty-three years old, and her physicians estimated she might live another thirty years. She was like some 10,000 other Americans who are lost in the dark, dimensionless limbo lying between living and dying. Those who love them can think of them only with sadness and despair. Given a choice between lingering in this twilight world and dying, most people find it difficult to imagine anyone would choose not to die.

Hope eventually faded even for Nancy Cruzan's parents. They faced the fact she would never recover her awareness, and the time came when they wanted their daughter to die, rather than be kept alive in her hopeless condition. They asked that the feeding tube used to keep her alive be withdrawn. Officials at the Missouri Rehabilitation Center refused, and Joe and Louise Cruzan were forced to go to court.

## Lower Court Decisions

During the court hearings, the family testified that Nancy would not have wanted to be kept alive in her present condition. Her sister Christy said Nancy had told her that she never wanted to be kept alive "just as a vegetable." A friend testified that Nancy had said that if she were injured or sick she wouldn't want to continue her life, unless she could live "half-way normally." Family and friends spoke in general terms of Nancy's vigor and her sense of independence.

In July 1988, Judge Charles E. Teel of the Jasper County Circuit Court ruled that artificially prolonging the life of Nancy Cruzan violated her constitutional right. As he wrote, "There is a fundamental right expressed in our Constitution as 'the right to liberty,' which permits an individual to refuse or direct the withholding or withdrawal of artificial death-prolonging procedures when the person has no cognitive brain function."

Missouri Attorney General William Webster said Judge Teel's interpretation of the Missouri living-will law was much broader than the legislature intended and appealed the ruling. In November 1988, the Missouri Supreme Court in a 4-to-3 decision overruled the decision of the lower court—Nancy Cruzan's parents would not be allowed to disconnect the feeding tube.

The court focused on the state's living-will statute. The law permits the withdrawing of artificial life-support systems in cases in which individuals are hopelessly ill or injured and there is "clear and convincing evidence" this is what they would want done. The act specifically forbids the withholding of food and water. Judge Teel's reasoning in the lower court decision was that the surgically implanted tube was an invasive medical treatment and that the Missouri law permitted her parents, as guardians, to order it withdrawn.

The Missouri Supreme Court held that the evidence as to what Nancy Cruzan would have wanted did not meet the "clear and convincing" standard required by the law. Also, the evidence did not show that the implanted feeding tube was "heroically invasive" or "burdensome." In the circumstance, then, the state's interest in preserving life should override other considerations.

The court found "no principled legal basis" to permit the Cruzans "to choose the death of their ward." Thus, "in the face of the state's strongly stated policy in favor of life, we choose to err on the side of life, respecting the right of incompetent persons who may wish to live despite a severely diminished quality of life." William Colby, the Cruzans' attorney, appealed the ruling to the United States Supreme Court, and for the first time the Court agreed to hear a case involving "right to die" issues.

## Supreme Court Decision

On June 25, 1990, the Supreme Court issued a landmark ruling. In a 5-to-4 decision, it rejected Colby's argument that the Court should overturn as unconstitutional the State of Missouri's stringent standard requiring "clear and convincing evidence" as to a comatose patient's wishes. The decision came as a cruel disappointment to Nancy Cruzan's parents, because it meant they had lost their case.

Yet for the first time in U.S. judicial history, the Court recognized a strong constitutional basis for living wills and for the designation of another person to act as a surrogate in making medical decisions on behalf of another. Unlike the decisions in *Roe v. Wade* and *Quinlan*, which found a right of privacy in the Constitution, the Court decision in *Cruzan* appealed to a Fourteenth Amendment "liberty interest." The interest involves being free to reject unwanted medical treatment. The Court found grounds for this interest in the common-law tradition, according to which, if one person even touches another without consent or legal justification, then battery is committed.

The Court regarded this as the basis for requiring that a patient give informed consent to medical treatment. The "logical corollary" of informed consent, the Court held, is that the patient also possesses the right to withhold consent. A difficulty arises, though, when a patient is in no condition to give consent. The problem becomes one of knowing what the patient's wishes would be.

Justice Rehnquist, in the majority opinion, held that the Constitution permits states to decide on the standard that must be met in determining the wishes of a comatose patient. Hence, Missouri's rigorous standard that requires "clear and convincing proof" of the wishes of the patient was allowed to stand. The Court held that it was legitimate for the state to err on the side of caution, "because an erroneous decision not to terminate treatment results in the maintenance of the status quo," while an erroneous decision to end treatment "is not susceptible of correction."

Justice William Brennan dissented strongly from this line of reasoning. He pointed out that making a mistake about a comatose patient's wishes and continuing treatment also has a serious consequence. Maintaining the status quo "robs a patient of the very qualities protected by the right to avoid unwanted medical treatment."

Justice Stevens, in another dissent, argued that the Court's focus on how much weight to give previous statements by the patient missed the point. The

Court should have focused on the issue of the best interest of the patient. Otherwise, the only people eligible to exercise their constitutional right to be free of unwanted medical treatment are those "who had the foresight to make an unambiguous statement of their wishes while competent."

One of the more significant aspects of the decision was that the Court made no distinction between providing nutrition and hydration and other forms of medical treatment. One argument on behalf of the state was that providing food and water was not medical treatment. However, briefs filed by medical associations made it clear that determining the formula required by a person in Nancy Cruzan's condition and regulating her feeding are medically complex procedures. The situation is more comparable to determining the contents of an intravenous drip than to giving someone food and water.

The Missouri living-will statute explicitly forbids the withdrawal of food and water. However, the law was not directly at issue in the *Cruzan* case, because Nancy Cruzan's accident occurred before the law was passed. The Court's treatment of nutrition and hydration as just another form of medical treatment has since served as a basis for challenging the constitutionality of the Missouri law, as well as laws in other states containing a similar provision.

The Supreme Court decision placed much emphasis on the wishes of the individual in accepting or rejecting medical treatment. In doing so, it underscored the importance of the living will as a way of indicating our wishes, if something should happen to render us incapable of making them known directly. In some states, though, living wills have a legal force only when the individual has a terminal illness (Nancy Cruzan did not) or when the individual has been quite specific about what treatments are unwanted. Because of such limitations, some legal observers recommend that individuals sign a durable power of attorney designating someone to make medical decisions for them if they become legally incompetent.

The Court decision left undecided the question of the constitutionality of assisted suicide. Some state courts have held that, although individuals have a right to die, they do not have a right to the assistance of others in killing themselves. While more than twenty states have passed laws against assisted suicide, only Oregon has made it legal for physicians to prescribe drugs to help patients end their lives.

## A Final Court Ruling

What of Nancy Cruzan? The State of Missouri withdrew from the case, and both the family's attorney and the state-appointed guardian filed separate briefs with the Jasper County Circuit Court asking that the implanted feeding tube be removed. A hearing was held to consider both her medical condition and evidence from family and friends about what Nancy Cruzan would wish to be done. On December 14, 1990, Judge Charles Teel ruled that there was evidence to show that her intent, "if mentally able, would be to terminate her nutrition and hydration," and he authorized the request to remove the feeding tube.

Even after the tube was removed, controversy did not end. About twenty-five protesters tried to force their way into Nancy Cruzan's hospital room to reconnect the feeding tube. "The best we can do is not cooperate with anyone trying to starve an innocent person to death," one of the protest leaders said.

Twelve days after the tube was removed, on December 26, 1990, Nancy Cruzan died. Her parents, sisters, and grandparents were at her bedside. Almost eight years had passed since the accident that destroyed her brain and made the remainder of her life a matter of debate.

"We all feel good that Nancy is free at last," her father said at her graveside.

The *Cruzan* decision, by acknowledging a "right to die" and by finding a basis for it in the Constitution, provides states with new opportunities to resolve the issues surrounding the thousands of cases as tragic as Nancy Cruzan's.

## Case Presentation

### *Dr. Jack Kevorkian: Physician-Assisted Suicide Activist*

On August 5, 1993, Thomas W. Hyde Jr., a thirty-year-old Michigan construction worker with a wife and a two-year-old daughter, was taken inside a battered white 1968 Volkswagen bus parked behind the apartment building in the Detroit suburb of Royal Oak where sixty-five-year-old retired pathologist Dr. Jack Kevorkian lived.

Dr. Kevorkian fitted a respiratory mask over Hyde's face and connected the plastic tubing leading from the mask to a short cylinder of carbon monoxide gas. Dr. Kevorkian placed a string in Hyde's hand. At the opposite end of the string was a paper clip crimping the plastic tubing and shutting off the flow of gas. Hyde jerked on the string, pulled loose the paper clip, then breathed in the carbon monoxide flowing into the mask. Twenty minutes later, he was dead.

Mr. Hyde suffered from amyotrophic lateral sclerosis (Lou Gehrig's disease), a degenerative and progressive neurological disorder. He was paralyzed, unable even to swallow, and, without suctioning, he would have choked to death on his own saliva. He reported that he was in great pain, and like hundreds before him, he approached Dr. Kevorkian to help him end his life.

In a videotape made on July 1, 1993, Mr. Hyde said to Dr. Kevorkian, "I want to end this. I want to die." Dr. Kevorkian agreed to help, and Mr. Hyde became the twentieth person since 1990 whom Dr. Kevorkian had assisted in committing suicide.

## Trial

After the death of Thomas Hyde, Dr. Kevorkian was arrested and charged with violating the 1992 Michigan law that had been enacted specifically to stop his activities. The law applies to anyone who knows another person intends to commit suicide and either "provides the physical means" or "participates in a physical act" by which the suicide is carried out. However, the law explicitly excludes those administering medications or procedures that may cause death, "if the intent is to relieve pain or discomfort."

On May 2, 1994, a jury found Dr. Kevorkian was innocent of the charge of assisting suicide. As one juror said, "He convinced us he was not a murderer, that he was really trying to help people out." According to another, Dr. Kevorkian had acted to relieve Mr. Hyde's pain, and that is allowed by the law.

Several jurors expressed skepticism and resentment at the attempt to legislate behavior falling within such a private sphere. "I don't feel it's our obligation to choose for someone else how much pain and suffering they can go through," one said. "That's between them and their God."

After the decision, Dr. Kevorkian reiterated his position that people have a right to decide when to end their lives. He acted, he said, to protect that right. "I want that option as I get older, and I want it unencumbered, unintimidated, free with my medical col-

leagues," he said. "So I did it for myself, too, just as any competent adult would want to do."

Kevorkian always insisted he practiced physician-assisted suicide only in accordance with stringent safeguards. "You act only after it is absolutely justifiable," he said. "The patient must be mentally competent, the disease incurable." He maintained that other physicians should determine that a candidate for assisted suicide was incurable and that a psychiatrist assess the patient's mental state and determine that he or she was competent. In practice, Kevorkian did not proceed in this fashion, because other physicians refused to cooperate with him.

## Critics

Critics charged that without the safeguard of a psychiatric evaluation, patients who sought out Kevorkian to help them kill themselves were likely to be suffering from depression. Hence, they couldn't be regarded as having made an informed, rational decision to end their lives.

Other critics worried that, if physicians are allowed to play a role in terminating the lives of patients, that role could expand. Physicians might begin by assisting those who ask their help, but then move on to making their own decisions about who should live. Or they might even be recruited to carry out a government policy identifying those who should be "assisted" in dying. The potential for abuse is so serious physicians should not be associated in any way with procedures intended to end the lives of patients.

Finally, some critics, though disagreeing with Kevorkian, believed he had successfully pointed out a major flaw in the health-care system—the medical profession is so committed to preserving life it has not developed ways of dealing with death in cases in which it is inevitable. Rather than help people kill themselves, critics said, physicians ought to surrender the idea of treatment and concentrate on making those with terminal illnesses pain free so they could spend their remaining time enjoying the comfort of their families and friends.

It was in keeping with such an aim that hospitals and other institutions set up hospices to provide nursing care and support for the dying. Even after decades, however, hospices remain at the margins of the medical establishment, and physicians associated with them are given little respect by their colleagues.

## A Charge of Murder

In 1998 the Michigan Department of Consumer and Industry Services, the state agency responsible for licensing physicians, charged that Jack Kevorkian was practicing medicine without a license by assisting forty-two people in committing suicide. (Kevorkian said he assisted about 120 people.)

Although the agency had issued a cease-and-desist order, Kevorkian continued to help terminally ill people die. The Michigan legislature, that same year, passed a law making assisting in suicide a crime, but Kevorkian announced he would continue his activities, despite the law.

In September 1998, Dr. Kevorkian administered a lethal injection to Thomas Youk, a fifty-two-year-old man in an advanced stage of the motor neuron disease ALS (amyotrophic lateral sclerosis). For the first time, Kevorkian by his own direct action caused the death of a person, thus moving from physician-assisted suicide to active euthanasia.

Kevorkian videotaped the event and offered the tape to the CBS program *Sixty Minutes,* which broadcast excerpts from the tape on national television on November 22. About 15.6 million households watched the program.

Kevorkian said he had given the tape to CBS in the hope that it would lead to his arrest and become a test case for assisted suicide and active euthanasia.

"I want a showdown," Kevorkian told a reporter. "I want to be prosecuted for euthanasia. I am going to prove that this is not a crime, ever, regardless of what words are written on paper."

On November 25, the prosecutor of Oakland County, Michigan, filed first-degree murder charges against Jack Kevorkian. David G. Gorcyca, the prosecutor, said that Dr. Kevorkian's actions clearly fit the definition of premeditated murder and that the consent of the man killed was no legal defense.

On April 13, 1999, Jack Kevorkian was found guilty of second-degree murder and sentenced to a prison term of ten to twenty-five years. "This trial was not an opportunity for a referendum," Judge Jessica Cooper said at the sentencing.

Those sympathetic to Jack Kevorkian believe he did more than anyone else to force society to face an issue it has chosen to ignore. His critics believe he made a circus of what should be a serious and deliberative discussion.

## Case Presentation

### *A Canadian Tragedy*

Robert Latimer admitted that he killed his twelve-year-old daughter Tracy by putting her in the cab of his pickup truck, then rolling up the windows and letting the engine run until the cab filled up with deadly carbon monoxide gas.

But he said he did it because he loved her.

Tracy was born with cerebral palsy, a birth disorder involving physical and sometimes mental impairments of varying degrees of severity. A year before she died, Tracy's father said she had been "a happy little girl," living with her parents and three siblings on a 1280-acre wheat and canola farm in Saskatchewan, Canada. Then she had surgery that was supposed to improve her condition. Instead, it turned her into a child who was in constant agony and who could not walk, talk, or feed herself. She lost so much weight that at the time of her death she weighed only forty pounds.

Yet Tracy's doctors wanted her to have additional surgery. They wanted to do extensive surgery on her hip to stabilize the metal rods they had inserted into her back to help her stay upright. They also wanted to insert a feeding tube into her stomach, because the antiseizure medication she had to take interfered with her appetite and her digestion. That was when Bob Latimer decided Tracy would be better off dead.

Latimer was charged with second-degree murder and found guilty by a jury in 1994. The conviction was overturned on a technicality, and although he was convicted a second time, the jury made it clear they had done so reluctantly and only because they were required to consider only the facts presented in court. They took the unusual step of asking the judge to sentence Latimer to only one year in prison.

The general public was as sympathetic toward Latimer as the jury. "Bob Latimer is not a murderer, and he's no threat to society," said one of his neighbors. "It's a shame to take him away from his family and lock him up."

But advocates for the disabled did not share the jury's and public's forgiving attitude toward Latimer. In their view, he deserved to be given a stiff prison term to make it clear that the lives of severely disabled people are worth just as much as the lives of others.

"If you can make your own choice, that's a different thing," said Ron Bort, the president of the local chapter of Voice of People with Disabilities. "For someone else to decide your life is not worth living—that's the scary part."

The point was echoed by the vice president of another advocacy group, the Canadian Association for Community Living. "Tracy Latimer did not choose to die," Diane Richler said. "She was murdered, and justice should be served."

Latimer told a reporter he had felt he had no choice. "People are saying this is a handicap issue, but they're wrong," he said. "This was a torture issue. It was about mutilation and torture for Tracy. She had bedsores, she was in pain all the time, and she wasn't eating well. With the combination of a feeding tube, rods in her back, her leg cut and flopping around, and bedsores, how can people say she was a happy little girl?"

Latimer said he and his wife were never concerned with any legal problems he might have by causing Tracy's death. "We were just concerned with Tracy," he said.

The Canadian Senate debated in 1995 the question of whether a special category should be introduced into the criminal code to cover cases of "mercy killing" like that carried out by Robert Latimer. While a recommendation for such a change was drafted, the law was never changed.

Consequently, despite the jury's wishes, Robert Latimer's conviction of second-degree murder carried with it a mandatory sentence of twenty-five years in prison, with no possibility of parole until after ten years.

# SOCIAL CONTEXT: PHYSICIAN-ASSISTED SUICIDE: THE DUTCH EXPERIENCE

In 2000 the Dutch Parliament passed a law establishing specific rules to allow physicians to assist in the suicide of a terminally ill patient or to kill the patient at the patient's explicit request without risking criminal prosecution. The new law gives a new legal status to a practice that has been followed in the Netherlands for almost fifteen years.

Under a 1993 act, ending a patient's life or assisting in suicide remained illegal, although the law provided physicians with protection from prosecution, if they followed the provisions of the law. The Dutch criminal code previously provided as much as twelve years in prison for anyone who "takes the life of another at his or her explicit and serious request."

In a 1972 case involving a physician who put her mother to death at the mother's request, however, a court refused to impose a penalty. Since then and with the reenforcement of a major court decision in 1984, the extralegal practice of voluntary, active, physician-administered euthanasia became established in the Netherlands. The new legislation made the Netherlands the first nation to legalize assisted suicide.

## Conditions

The 2000 law, following the provisions of the 1993 legislation, requires that a physician follow an extensive checklist to avoid prosecution. The safeguards built into the law include the following:

1.  Patient-initiated request. The physician must be convinced that the patient's request for euthanasia is "voluntary and well-considered." The request must be made entirely of the patient's own free will and not under pressure from others, including family, friends, or physicians. The patient must make the request personally, and relatives cannot make a request on behalf of a patient.

2.  Patient competence. At the time of the decision, the patient must be in a rational state of mind and able to make informed decisions. Those who suffer from dementia or are in a coma are not candidates for euthanasia.

3.  Patient understanding. The patient must have a correct and clear understanding of his or her situation and prognosis.

4.  Informed as to alternatives. The patient must be informed about alternatives to assisted-suicide or euthanasia. The patient

should then be encouraged to discuss them with physicians, family, and advisors.

5. Enduring decision. Requests to physicians made on impulse or ones that may be the result of depression cannot be regarded as legitimate.

6. Unbearable suffering. "The patient must experience his or her suffering as perpetual, unbearable, and hopeless." The physician must be able to make the reasonable judgment that the suffering the patient is experiencing is unendurable. The patient's condition does not have to be terminal.

7. Professional consultation. The physician must consult with at least one other physician who has had experience in dealing with patients requesting euthanasia or help in dying.

8. Medically appropriate. The physician must end the patient's life in a medically appropriate manner.

9. Government report. The physician must submit a report to the government in which the patient's medical history is presented and the physician declares that all the conditions required for assisting in suicide or performing euthanasia have been observed.

The patient must also sign a witnessed explicit authorization for the act to be carried out. Typically, the physician then injects a barbiturate to induce sleep, combined with curare to produce death.

## Minors Excluded

Part of the initial bill would make it possible, in exceptional cases, for minors between the ages of twelve and sixteen to request euthanasia against the wishes of their parents. This provision of the bill was strongly criticized and was eventually withdrawn.

## Statistics

A study conducted by the Dutch government reported that in 1990 there were 2300 deaths by voluntary euthanasia and about 400 cases of assisted suicide. These represented some 2 percent of the total number of deaths in the Netherlands that year. The report also indicated that physicians had reported a total of 9000 requests for euthanasia. Apparently, a majority of requests were turned down.

Between 1990 and 1995, cases of euthanasia rose from 1.8 percent of total deaths to 2.4 percent, but the proportion of cases involving physician-assisted suicide remained about the same.

A preliminary report indicates that 2216 patients were assisted in ending their lives by physicians in 1999, but the actual number is thought to be closer to 5000. (Evidence indicates that, as a rule, only half the cases of physician-assisted suicide are reported.) Almost nine out of ten of the reported cases involved people in the final stages of cancer.

Despite the new law and the fact that physician-assisted suicide has been de facto legal since 1993, physicians are reluctant to practice it. Surveys show that about two-thirds of the people who ask physicians to end their lives are turned down.

An opinion poll conducted in 1993 in the Netherlands showed that 78 percent of those questioned supported the right of the terminally ill to ask for euthanasia. (A previous poll showed that about 50 percent of Roman Catholics also favor this.) Ten percent were opposed, and 71 percent said that physicians who act in accordance with the rules should not have to justify themselves in a court of law. A 2000 poll revealed that about 10 percent of the Dutch people and 10 percent of their physicians are vigorously opposed to the new law.

## No Right

While the new law decriminalizes euthanasia, it does not recognize a right to euthanasia. Physicians have a right to refuse to cooperate if asked to assist in a suicide, even if the conditions required by the law are satisfied.

One difficulty with the new law, even its proponents admit, is that it is unclear about how to deal with cases in which someone has made a request for assisted suicide while of sound mind, then comes to suffer dementia. Should the request be honored? The Dutch Ministry of Health has explicitly stated that dementia itself cannot be grounds for assisted suicide. The patient would have to be suffering from intolerable pain and a very early stage of dementia for a request to be acted on.

## Model for the United States?

Dutch practice and laws are often mentioned in the United States as an example of what a reasonable euthanasia policy might include. In particular, the practice is offered as a model for providing an option to continuing treatment of individuals suffering from a lingering terminal illness. People with AIDS and those suffering from the intractable pain of terminal cancer, for example, have often expressed a wish for a social and legal policy that would permit active, voluntary euthanasia or assisted suicide. These are just the sort of people the Dutch practice has evolved to deal with.

However, the medical care situation in the United States is different in what may be considered a relevant and important way. Dutch citizens are almost universally participants in health plans that cover their medical costs. Hence, individuals are not under economic pressures to make decisions about ending their lives. They need not worry that they are running out of insurance coverage or may be bankrupting their families by remaining alive.

Furthermore, the Dutch practice does not deal with the type of cases that have caused much concern and controversy in this country. Until recently, the proper treatment of individuals in irreversible comas, as in the *Quinlan* and *Cruzan* cases, has been at the focus of dispute. Since the practice in Holland requires that individuals be conscious and intellectually competent, it embodies no principles that could be appealed to for resolving the troublesome issues involved in dealing with those in persistent vegetative states.

Nevertheless, the Dutch experience may still be valuable in showing whether it is possible to have a social policy permitting assisted suicide and voluntary euthanasia without the abuses or corruption of medical power feared by critics.

## READINGS

# Section 1: The Case Against Euthanasia and Physician-Assisted Suicide

## The Wrongfulness of Euthanasia

### J. Gay-Williams

J. Gay-Williams defines *euthanasia* as intentionally taking the life of a person who is believed to be suffering from some illness or injury from which recovery cannot reasonably be expected. Gay-Williams rejects passive euthanasia as a *name* for actions that are usually designated by the phrase but seems to approve of the actions themselves. He argues that euthanasia as intentional killing goes against natural law because it violates the natural inclination to preserve life. Furthermore, both self-interest and possible practical consequences of euthanasia provide reasons for rejecting it.

My impression is that euthanasia—the idea, if not the practice—is slowly gaining acceptance within our society. Cynics might attribute this to an increasing tendency to devalue human life, but I do not believe this is the major factor. The acceptance is much more likely to be the result of unthinking sympathy and benevolence. Well-publicized, tragic stories like that of Karen Quinlan elicit from us deep feelings of compassion. We think to ourselves, "She and her family would be better off if she were dead." It is an easy step from this very human response to the view that if someone (and others) would be better off dead, then it might be all right to kill that person.[1] Although I respect the compassion that leads to this conclusion, I believe the conclusion is wrong. I want to show that euthanasia is wrong. It is inherently wrong, but it is also wrong judged from the standpoints of self-interest and of practical effects.

Before presenting my arguments to support this claim, it would be well to define "euthanasia." An essential aspect of euthanasia is that it involves taking a human life, either one's own or that of another. Also, the person whose life is taken must be someone who is believed to be suffering from some disease or injury from which recovery cannot reasonably be expected. Finally, the action must be deliberate and intentional. Thus, euthanasia is intentionally taking the life of a presumably hopeless person. Whether the life is one's own or that of another, the taking of it is still euthanasia.

It is important to be clear about the deliberate and intentional aspect of the killing. If a hopeless person is given an injection of the wrong drug by mistake and this causes his death, this is wrongful killing but not euthanasia. The killing cannot be the result of accident. Furthermore, if the person is given an injection of a drug that is believed to be necessary to treat his disease or better his condition and the person dies as a result, then this is neither wrongful killing nor euthanasia. The intention was to make the patient well, not kill him. Similarly, when a patient's condition is such that it is not reasonable to hope that any medical procedures or treatments will save his life, a failure to implement the procedures or treatments is not euthanasia. If the person dies, this will be as a result of

his injuries or disease and not because of his failure to receive treatment.

The failure to continue treatment after it has been realized that the patient has little chance of benefiting from it has been characterized by some as "passive euthanasia." This phrase is misleading and mistaken.[2] In such cases, the person involved is not killed (the first essential aspect of euthanasia), nor is the death of the person intended by the withholding of additional treatment (the third essential aspect of euthanasia). The aim may be to spare the person additional and unjustifiable pain, to save him from the indignities of hopeless manipulations, and to avoid increasing the financial and emotional burden on his family. When I buy a pencil it is so that I can use it to write, not to contribute to an increase in the gross national product. This may be the unintended consequence of my action, but it is not the aim of my action. So it is with failing to continue the treatment of a dying person. I intend his death no more than I intend to reduce the GNP by not using medical supplies. His is an unintended dying, and so-called "passive euthanasia" is not euthanasia at all.

## 1. The Argument from Nature

Every human being has a natural inclination to continue living. Our reflexes and responses fit us to fight attackers, flee wild animals, and dodge out of the way of trucks. In our daily lives we exercise the caution and care necessary to protect ourselves. Our bodies are similarly structured for survival right down to the molecular level. When we are cut, our capillaries seal shut, our blood clots, and fibrogen is produced to start the process of healing the wound. When we are invaded by bacteria, antibodies are produced to fight against the alien organisms, and their remains are swept out of the body by special cells designed for clean-up work.

Euthanasia does violence to this natural goal of survival. It is literally acting against nature because all the processes of nature are bent towards the end of bodily survival. Euthanasia defeats these subtle mechanisms in a way that, in a particular case, disease and injury might not.

It is possible, but not necessary, to make an appeal to revealed religion in this connection.[3] Man as trustee of his body acts against God, its rightful possessor, when he takes his own life. He also violates the commandment to hold life sacred and never to take it without just and compelling cause. But since this appeal will persuade only those who are prepared to accept that religion has access to revealed truths, I shall not employ this line of argument.

It is enough, I believe, to recognize that the organization of the human body and our patterns of behavioral responses make the continuation of life a natural goal. By reason alone, then, we can recognize that euthanasia sets us against our own nature.[4] Furthermore, in doing so, euthanasia does violence to our dignity. Our dignity comes from seeking our ends. When one of our goals is survival, and actions are taken that eliminate that goal, then our natural dignity suffers. Unlike animals, we are conscious through reason of our nature and our ends. Euthanasia involves acting as if this dual nature—inclination towards survival and awareness of this as an end—did not exist. Thus, euthanasia denies our basic human character and requires that we regard ourselves or others as something less than fully human.

## 2. The Argument from Self-Interest

The above arguments are, I believe, sufficient to show that euthanasia is inherently wrong. But there are reasons for considering it wrong when judged by standards other than reason. Because death is final and irreversible, euthanasia contains within it the possibility that we will work against our own interest if we practice it or allow it to be practiced on us.

Contemporary medicine has high standards of excellence and a proven record of accomplishment, but it does not possess perfect and complete knowledge. A mistaken diagnosis is possible, and so is a mistaken prognosis. Consequently, we may believe that we are dying of a disease when, as a matter of fact, we may not be. We may think that we have no hope of recovery when, as a matter of fact, our chances are quite good. In such circumstances, if euthanasia were permitted, we would die needlessly. Death is final and the chance of error too great to approve the practice of euthanasia.

Also, there is always the possibility that an experimental procedure or a hitherto untried technique will pull us through. We should at least keep this option open, but euthanasia closes it off. Furthermore, spontaneous remission does occur in many cases. For no apparent reason, a patient simply recovers when those all around him, including his physicians, expected him

to die. Euthanasia would just guarantee their expectations and leave no room for the "miraculous" recoveries that frequently occur.

Finally, knowing that we can take our life at any time (or ask another to take it) might well incline us to give up too easily. The will to live is strong in all of us, but it can be weakened by pain and suffering and feelings of hopelessness. If during a bad time we allow ourselves to be killed, we never have a chance to reconsider. Recovery from a serious illness requires that we fight for it, and anything that weakens our determination by suggesting that there is an easy way out is ultimately against our own interest. Also, we may be inclined towards euthanasia because of our concern for others. If we see our sickness and suffering as an emotional and financial burden on our family, we may feel that to leave our life is to make their lives easier.[5] The very presence of the possibility of euthanasia may keep us from surviving when we might.

## 3. The Argument from Practical Effects

Doctors and nurses are, for the most part, totally committed to saving lives. A life lost is, for them, almost a personal failure, an insult to their skills and knowledge. Euthanasia as a practice might well alter this. It could have a corrupting influence so that in any case that is severe doctors and nurses might not try hard enough to save the patient. They might decide that the patient would simply be "better off dead" and take the steps necessary to make that come about. This attitude could then carry over to their dealings with patients less seriously ill. The result would be an overall decline in the quality of medical care.

Finally, euthanasia as a policy is a slippery slope. A person apparently hopelessly ill may be allowed to take his own life. Then he may be permitted to deputize others to do it for him should he no longer be able to act. The judgment of others then becomes the ruling factor. Already at this point euthanasia is not personal and voluntary, for others are acting "on behalf of" the patient as they see fit. This may well incline them to act on behalf of other patients who have not authorized them to exercise their judgment. It is only a short step, then, from voluntary euthanasia (self-inflicted or authorized), to directed euthanasia administered to a patient who has given no authorization, to involuntary euthanasia conducted as part of a social policy.[6] Recently many psychiatrists and sociologists have argued that we define as "mental illness" those forms of behavior that we disapprove of.[7] This gives us license then to lock up those who display the behavior. The category of the "hopelessly ill" provides the possibility of even worse abuse. Embedded in a social policy, it would give society or its representatives the authority to eliminate all those who might be considered too "ill" to function normally any longer. The dangers of euthanasia are too great to all to run the risk of approving it in any form. The first slippery step may well lead to a serious and harmful fall.

I hope that I have succeeded in showing why the benevolence that inclines us to give approval of euthanasia is misplaced. Euthanasia is inherently wrong because it violates the nature and dignity of human beings. But even those who are not convinced by this must be persuaded that the potential personal and social dangers inherent in euthanasia are sufficient to forbid our approving it either as a personal practice or as a public policy.

Suffering is surely a terrible thing, and we have a clear duty to comfort those in need and to ease their suffering when we can. But suffering is also a natural part of life with values for the individual and for others that we should not overlook. We may legitimately seek for others and for ourselves an easeful death, as Arthur Dyck has pointed out.[8] Euthanasia, however, is not just an easeful death. It is a wrongful death. Euthanasia is not just dying. It is killing.

### Notes

1. For a sophisticated defense of this position see Philippa Foot, "Euthanasia," *Philosophy and Public Affairs,* vol. 6 (1977), pp. 85–112. Foot does not endorse the radical conclusion that euthanasia, voluntary and involuntary, is always right.

2. James Rachels rejects the distinction between active and passive euthanasia as morally irrelevant in his "Active and Passive Euthanasia," *New England Journal of Medicine,* vol. 292, pp. 78–80. But see the criticism by Foot, pp. 100–103.

3. For a defense of this view see J. V. Sullivan, "The Immorality of Euthanasia," in *Beneficent Euthanasia,* ed. Marvin Kohl (Buffalo, N.Y.: Prometheus Books, 1975), pp. 34–44.

4. This point is made by Ray V. McIntyre in "Voluntary Euthanasia: The Ultimate Perversion," *Medical Counterpoint,* vol. 2, pp. 26–29.

5. See McIntyre, p. 28.

6. See Sullivan, "Immorality of Euthanasia," pp. 34–44, for a fuller argument in support of this view.

7. See, for example, Thomas S. Szasz, *The Myth of Mental Illness,* rev. ed. (New York: Harper & Row, 1974).

8. Arthur Dyck, "Beneficent Euthanasia and Benemortasia," Kohl, op. cit., pp. 117–129.

# When Self-Determination Runs Amok

## Daniel Callahan

Daniel Callahan argues against any social policy allowing voluntary euthanasia and assisted suicide. He maintains that self-determination and mercy (the two values supporting them) may become separated. When this happens, assisted suicide for any reason and nonvoluntary euthanasia for the incompetent will become acceptable.

Callahan rejects Rachels's claim that the difference between killing and letting die is morally irrelevant. He holds that the difference is fundamental and that the decision to terminate a life requires a judgment about meaning and quality that physicians are not competent to make.

In general, Callahan warns us, we must not allow physicians to move beyond the bounds of promoting health and exercise the power of deciding questions about human happiness and well-being. Permitting them to make such decisions will lead to widespread abuse and destroy the integrity of the medical profession.

The euthanasia debate is not just another moral debate, one in a long list of arguments in our pluralistic society. It is profoundly emblematic of three important

Daniel Callahan, "When Self-Determination Runs Amok," *Hastings Center Report* 22 (March/April 1992), pp. 52–55.

turning points in Western thought. The first is that of the legitimate conditions under which one person can kill another. The acceptance of voluntary active euthanasia would morally sanction what can only be called "consenting adult killing." By the term I mean the killing of one person by another in the name of their mutual right to be killer and killed if they freely agree to play those roles. This turn flies in the face of a long-standing effort to limit the circumstances under which one person can take the life of another, from efforts to control the free flow of guns and arms, to abolish capital punishment, and to more tightly control warfare. Euthanasia would add a whole new category of killing to a society that already has too many excuses to indulge itself in that way.

The second turning point lies in the meaning and limits of self-determination. The acceptance of euthanasia would sanction a view of autonomy holding that individuals may, in the name of their own private, idiosyncratic view of the good life, call upon others, including such institutions as medicine, to help them pursue that life, even at the risk of harm to the common good. This works against the idea that the meaning and scope of our own right to lead our own lives must be conditioned by, and be compatible with, the good of the community, which is more than an aggregate of self-directing individuals.

The third turning point is to be found in the claim being made upon medicine: it should be prepared to make its skills available to individuals to help them achieve their private vision of the good life. This puts medicine in the business of promoting the individualistic pursuit of general human happiness and well-being. It would overturn the traditional belief that medicine should limit its domain to promoting and preserving human health, redirecting it instead to the relief of that suffering which stems from life itself, not merely from a sick body.

I believe that, at each of these three turning points, proponents of euthanasia push us in the wrong direction. Arguments in favor of euthanasia fall into four general categories, which I will take up in turn: (1) the moral claim of individual self-determination and well-being; (2) the moral irrelevance of the difference between killing and allowing to die; (3) the supposed paucity of evidence to show likely harmful consequences of legalized euthanasia; and (4) the compatibility of euthanasia and medical practice.

## Self-Determination

Central to most arguments for euthanasia is the principle of self-determination. People are presumed to have an interest in deciding for themselves, according to their own beliefs about what makes life good, how

they will conduct their lives. That is an important value, but the question in the euthanasia context is, What does it mean and how far should it extend? If it were a question of suicide, where a person takes their own life without assistance from another, that principle might be pertinent, at least for debate. But euthanasia is not that limited a matter. The self-determination in that case can only be effected by the moral and physical assistance of another. Euthanasia is thus no longer a matter only of self-determination, but of a mutual, social decision between two people, the one to be killed and the other to do the killing.

How are we to make the moral move from my right of self-determination to some doctor's right to kill me—from *my* right to *his* right? Where does the doctor's moral warrant to kill come from? Ought doctors to be able to kill anyone they want as long as permission is given by competent persons? Is our right to life just like a piece of property, to be given away or alienated if the price (happiness, relief of suffering) is right? And then to be destroyed with our permission once alienated?

In answer to all those questions, I will say this: I have yet to hear a plausible argument why it should be permissible for us to put this kind of power in the hands of another, whether a doctor or anyone else. The idea that we can waive our right to life, and then give to another the power to take that life, requires a justification yet to be provided by anyone.

Slavery was long ago outlawed on the ground that one person should not have the right to own another, even with the other's permission. Why? Because it is a fundamental moral wrong for one person to give over his life and fate to another, whatever the good consequences, and no less a wrong for another person to have that kind of total, final power. Like slavery, dueling was long ago banned on similar grounds: even free, competent individuals should not have the power to kill each other, whatever their motives, whatever the circumstances. Consenting adult killing, like consenting adult slavery or degradation, is a strange route to human dignity.

There is another problem as well. If doctors, once sanctioned to carry out euthanasia, are to be themselves responsible moral agents—not simply hired hands with lethal injections at the ready—then they must have their own *independent* moral grounds to kill those who request such services. What do I mean? As those who favor euthanasia are quick to point out, some people want it because their life has become so burdensome it no longer seems worth living.

The doctor will have a difficulty at this point. The degree and intensity to which people suffer from their diseases and their dying, and whether they find life more of a burden than a benefit, has very little directly to do with the nature or extent of their actual physical condition. Three people can have the same condition, but only one will find the suffering unbearable. People suffer, but suffering is as much a function of the values of individuals as it is of the physical causes of that suffering. Inevitably in that circumstance, the doctor will in effect be treating the patient's values. To be responsible, the doctor would have to share those values. The doctor would have to decide, on her own, whether the patient's life was "no longer worth living."

But how could a doctor possibly know that or make such a judgment? Just because the patient said so? I raise this question because, while in Holland at the euthanasia conference reported by Maurice de Wachter . . ., the doctors present agreed that there is no objective way of measuring or judging the claims of patients that their suffering is unbearable. And if it is difficult to measure suffering, how much more difficult to determine the value of a patient's statement that her life is not worth living?

However one might want to answer such questions, the very need to ask them, to inquire into the physician's responsibility and grounds for medical and moral judgment, points out the social nature of the decision. Euthanasia is not a private matter of self-determination. It is an act that requires two people to make it possible, and a complicit society to make it acceptable.

## Killing and Allowing to Die

Against common opinion, the argument is sometimes made that there is no moral difference between stopping life-sustaining treatment and more active forms of killing, such as lethal injection. Instead I would contend that the notion that there is no morally significant difference between omission and commission is just wrong. Consider in its broad implications what the eradication of the distinction implies: that death from disease has been banished, leaving only the actions of physicians in terminating treatment as the cause of death. Biology, which used to bring about death, has apparently been displaced by human agency. Doctors have finally, I suppose, thus genuinely become gods, now doing what nature and the deities once did.

What is the mistake here? It lies in confusing causality and culpability, and in failing to note the way

in which human societies have overlaid natural causes with moral rules and interpretations. Causality (by which I mean the direct physical causes of death) and culpability (by which I mean our attribution of moral responsibility to human actions) are confused under three circumstances.

They are confused, first, when the action of a physician in stopping treatment of a patient with an underlying lethal disease is construed as *causing* death. On the contrary, the physician's omission can only bring about death on the condition that the patient's disease will kill him in the absence of treatment. We may hold the physician morally responsible for the death, if we have morally judged such actions wrongful omissions. But it confuses reality and moral judgment to see an omitted action as having the same causal status as one that directly kills. A lethal injection will kill both a healthy person and a sick person. A physician's omitted treatment will have no effect on a healthy person. Turn off the machine on me, a healthy person, and nothing will happen. It will only, in contrast, bring the life of a sick person to an end because of an underlying fatal disease.

Causality and culpability are confused, second, when we fail to note that judgments of moral responsibility and culpability are human constructs. By that I mean that we human beings, after moral reflection, have decided to call some actions right or wrong, and to devise moral rules to deal with them. When physicians could do nothing to stop death, they were not held responsible for it. When, with medical progress, they began to have some power over death—but only its timing and circumstances, not its ultimate inevitability—moral rules were devised to set forth their obligations. Natural causes of death were not thereby banished. They were, instead, overlaid with a medical ethics designed to determine moral culpability in deploying medical power.

To confuse the judgments of this ethics with the physical causes of death—which is the connotation of the word *kill*—is to confuse nature and human action. People will, one way or another, die of some disease; death will have dominion over all of us. To say that a doctor "kills" a patient by allowing this to happen should only be understood as a moral judgment about the licitness of his omission, nothing more. We can, as a fashion of speech only, talk about a doctor *killing* a patient by omitting treatment he should have provided. It is a fashion of speech precisely because it is the underlying disease that brings death when treatment is omitted; that is its cause, not the physician's omission. It is a misuse of the word *killing* to use it when a doctor stops a treatment he believes will no longer benefit the patient—when, that is, he steps aside to allow an eventually inevitable death to occur now rather than later. The only deaths that human beings invented are those that come from direct killing—when, with a lethal injection, we both cause death and are morally responsible for it. In the case of omissions, we do not cause death even if we may be judged morally responsible for it.

This difference between causality and culpability also helps us see why a doctor who has omitted a treatment he should have provided has "killed" that patient while another doctor—performing precisely the same act of omission on another patient in different circumstances—does not kill her, but only allows her to die. The difference is that we have come, by moral convention and conviction, to classify unauthorized or illegitimate omissions as acts of "killing." We call them "killing" in the expanded sense of the term: a culpable action that permits the real cause of death, the underlying disease, to proceed to its lethal conclusion. By contrast, the doctor who, at the patient's request, omits or terminates unwanted treatment does not kill at all. Her underlying disease, not his action, is the physical cause of death; and we have agreed to consider actions of that kind to be morally licit. He thus can truly be said to have "allowed" her to die.

If we fail to maintain the distinction between killing and allowing to die, moreover, there are some disturbing possibilities. The first would be to confirm many physicians in their already too-powerful belief that, when patients die or when physicians stop treatment because of the futility of continuing it, they are somehow both morally and physically responsible for the deaths that follow. That notion needs to be abolished, not strengthened. It needlessly and wrongly burdens the physician, to whom should not be attributed the powers of the gods. The second possibility would be that, in every case where a doctor judges medical treatment no longer effective in prolonging life, a quick and direct killing of the patient would be seen as the next, most reasonable step, on grounds of both humaneness and economics. I do not see how that logic could easily be rejected.

## Calculating the Consequences

When concerns about the adverse social consequences of permitting euthanasia are raised, its advocates tend to dismiss them as unfounded and overly speculative. On the contrary, recent data about the Dutch experience suggests that such concerns are right on target. From my own discussions in Holland, and from the articles on that subject in this issue and elsewhere, I believe we can now fully see most of the *likely* consequences of legal euthanasia.

Three consequences seem almost certain, in this or any other country: the inevitability of some abuse of the law; the difficulty of precisely writing, and then enforcing, the law; and the inherent slipperiness of the moral reasons for legalizing euthanasia in the first place.

Why is abuse inevitable? One reason is that almost all laws on delicate, controversial matters are to some extent abused. This happens because not everyone will agree with the law as written and will bend it, or ignore it, if they can get away with it. From explicit admissions to me by Dutch proponents of euthanasia, and from the corroborating information provided by the Remmelink Report and the outside studies of Carlos Gomez and John Keown, I am convinced that in the Netherlands there are a substantial number of cases of nonvoluntary euthanasia, that is, euthanasia undertaken without the explicit permission of the person being killed. The other reason abuse is inevitable is that the law is likely to have a low enforcement priority in the criminal justice system. Like other laws of similar status, unless there is an unrelenting and harsh willingness to pursue abuse, violations will ordinarily be tolerated. The worst thing to me about my experience in Holland was the casual, seemingly indifferent attitude toward abuse. I think that would happen everywhere.

Why would it be hard to precisely write, and then enforce, the law? The Dutch speak about the requirement of "unbearable" suffering, but admit that such a term is just about indefinable, a highly subjective matter admitting of no objective standards. A requirement for outside opinion is nice, but it is easy to find complaisant colleagues. A requirement that a medical condition be "terminal" will run aground on the notorious difficulties of knowing when an illness is actually terminal.

Apart from those technical problems there is a more profound worry. I see no way, even in principle, to write or enforce a meaningful law that can guarantee effective procedural safeguards. The reason is obvious yet almost always overlooked. The euthanasia transaction will ordinarily take place within the boundaries of the private and confidential doctor–patient relationship. No one can possibly know what takes place in that context unless the doctor chooses to reveal it. In Holland, less than 10 percent of the physicians report their acts of euthanasia and do so with almost complete legal impunity. There is no reason why the situation should be any better elsewhere. Doctors will have their own reasons for keeping euthanasia secret, and some patients will have no less a motive for wanting it concealed.

I would mention, finally, that the moral logic of the motives for euthanasia contain within them the ingredients of abuse. The two standard motives for euthanasia and assisted suicide are said to be our right of self-determination, and our claim upon the mercy of others, especially doctors, to relieve our suffering. These two motives are typically spliced together and presented as a single justification. Yet if they are considered independently—and there is no inherent reason why they must be linked—they reveal serious problems. It is said that a competent, adult person should have a right to euthanasia for the relief of suffering. But why must the person be suffering? Does not that stipulation already compromise the principle of self-determination? How can self-determination have any limits? Whatever the person's motives may be, why are they not sufficient?

Consider next the person who is suffering but not competent, who is perhaps demented or mentally retarded. The standard argument would deny euthanasia to that person. But why? If a person is suffering but not competent, then it would seem grossly unfair to deny relief solely on the grounds of incompetence. Are the incompetent less entitled to relief from suffering than the competent? Will it only be affluent, middle-class people, mentally fit and savvy about working the medical system, who can qualify? Do the incompetent suffer less because of their incompetence?

Considered from these angles, there are no good moral reasons to limit euthanasia once the principle of taking life for that purpose has been legitimated. If we really believe in self-determination, then any competent person should have a right to be killed by a doctor for any reason that suits him. If we believe in the relief of suffering, then it seems cruel and capricious to deny it to the incompetent. There is, in short, no reasonable or logical stopping point once the turn has been made down the road to euthanasia, which could soon turn into a convenient and commodious expressway.

## Euthanasia and Medical Practice

A fourth kind of argument one often hears both in the Netherlands and in this country is that euthanasia and assisted suicide are perfectly compatible with the aims of medicine. I would note at the very outset that a physician who participates in another person's suicide already abuses medicine. Apart from depression (the main statistical cause of suicide), people commit suicide because they find life empty, oppressive, or meaningless. Their judgment is a judgment about the value of continued life, not only about health (even if they are sick). Are doctors now to be given the right to make judgments about the kinds of life worth living and to give their blessing to suicide for those they judge wanting? What conceivable competence, technical or moral, could doctors claim to play such a role? Are we to medicalize suicide, turning judgments about its worth and value into one more clinical issue? Yes, those are rhetorical questions.

Yet they bring us to the core of the problem of euthanasia and medicine. The great temptation of modern medicine, not always resisted, is to move beyond the promotion and preservation of health into the boundless realm of general human happiness and well-being. The root problem of illness and mortality is both medical and philosophical or religious. "Why must I die?" can be asked as a technical, biological question or as a question about the meaning of life. When medicine tries to respond to the latter, which it is always under pressure to do, it moves beyond its proper role.

It is not medicine's place to lift from us the burden of that suffering which turns on the meaning we assign to the decay of the body and its eventual death. It is not medicine's place to determine when lives are not worth living or when the burden of life is too great to be borne. Doctors have no conceivable way of evaluating such claims on the part of patients, and they should have no right to act in response to them. Medicine should try to relieve human suffering, but only that suffering which is brought on by illness and dying as biological phenomena, not that suffering which comes from anguish or despair at the human condition.

Doctors ought to relieve those forms of suffering that medically accompany serious illness and the threat of death. They should relieve pain, do what they can to allay anxiety and uncertainty, and be a comforting presence. As sensitive human beings, doctors should be prepared to respond to patients who ask why they must die, or die in pain. But here the doctor and the patient are at the same level. The doctor may have no better an answer to those old questions than anyone else; and certainly no special insight from his training as a physician. It would be terrible for physicians to forget this, and to think that in a swift, lethal injection, medicine has found its own answer to the riddle of life. It would be a false answer, given by the wrong people. It would be no less a false answer for patients. They should neither ask medicine to put its own vocation at risk to serve their private interests, nor think that the answer to suffering is to be killed by another. The problem is precisely that, too often in hu-

man history, killing has seemed the quick, efficient way to put aside that which burdens us. It rarely helps, and too often simply adds to one evil still another. That is what I believe euthanasia would accomplish. It is self-determination run amok.

READINGS

# Section 2: The Case for Euthanasia and Physician-Assisted Suicide

## When Abstract Moralizing Runs Amok

John Lachs

John Lachs claims Callahan (see Section 1) fails to grasp the moral problems leading people to consider euthanasia. They are not interested in it as an escape from the suffering inherent in "the human condition," but as an end to pain and a burdensome life.

Callahan holds that even if we have the right to kill ourselves, it intrinsically cannot be transferred to others. But Lachs argues that the idea of a right that cannot be transferred makes no sense.

Callahan also claims that once the principle of taking life has been "legitimized," there can be no good moral reasons for not killing someone for any reason at all. Lachs argues that Callahan's claim rests on the view that judgments about our suffering and the value of our lives are subjective (and so not necessarily shared by others). Yet physicians are able to review objectively a patient's request to die with respect to the patient's condition and situation.

Contrary to Callahan's implication, no one has ever endorsed the principle of autonomy as absolute. It expresses one value among others. But it recognizes that our lives belong to ourselves and that society must justify infringements, and this is what the debate over euthanasia is about.

Moral reasoning is more objectionable when it is abstract than when it is merely wrong. For abstractness all but guarantees error by missing the human predicament that needs to be addressed, and worse, it is a sign that thought has failed to keep faith with its mission. The function of moral reflection is to shed light on the difficult problems we face; it cannot perform its job without a clear understanding of how and why certain of our practices come to seem no longer satisfactory.

It is just this grasp of the problem that is conspicuously lacking in Daniel Callahan's assault on eu-

thanasia in "Self-Determination Run Amok."[1] The rhetoric Callahan unleashes gives not even a hint of the grave contemporary moral problems that euthanasia and assisted suicide, a growing number of people now think, promise to resolve.

Instead, we are offered a set of abstract principles calculated to discredit euthanasia rather than to contribute to a sound assessment of it. Thus, Callahan informs us that suffering "brought on by illness and dying as biological phenomena"[2] is to be contrasted with suffering that comes from "anguish or despair at the human condition." The former constitutes the proper concern of medicine (so much for psychiatry!), the latter of religion and philosophy. Medication is the answer to physical pain; euthanasia can, therefore, be

From *The Journal of Clinical Ethics* 1994; 5(1): 10–13.

only a misconceived response to worries about the meaning of existence. Those who believe in it offer a "swift lethal injection" as the "answer to the riddle of life."

This way of putting the matter will come as a surprise to those who suffer from terrible diseases and who no longer find life worth living. It is grotesque to suppose that such individuals are looking for the meaning of existence and find it, absurdly, in a lethal injection. Their predicament is not intellectual but existential. They are not interested in the meaning of life but in acting on their belief that their own continued existence is, on balance, of no further benefit to them.

Those who advocate the legalization of euthanasia and the practice of assisted suicide propose them as answers to a serious and growing social problem. We now have the power to sustain the biological existence of large numbers of very sick people, and we use this power freely. Accordingly, individuals suffering from painful terminal diseases, Alzheimer's patients, and those in a persistent vegetative state are routinely kept alive long past the point where they can function as human beings. They must bear the pain of existence without the ability to perform the activities that give life meaning. Some of these people feel intensely that they are a burden to others, as well as to themselves, and that their speedy and relatively dignified departure would be a relief to all concerned. Many observers of no more than average sensitivity agree that the plight of these patients is severe enough to justify such desires.

Some of these sufferers are physically not in a position to end their lives. Others could do so if they had the necessary instruments. In our culture, however, few have a taste for blowing out their brains or jumping from high places. That leaves drugs, which almost everyone is accustomed to taking, and which everyone knows can ease one peacefully to the other side.

The medical profession has, however, acquired monopoly power over drugs. And the danger of legal entanglement has made physicians wary of helping patients hasten their deaths in the discreet, humane way that has been customary for centuries. The result is that people who want to die and for whom death has long ceased to be an evil can find no way out of their misery. Current and growing pressures on the medical profession to help such sufferers are, therefore, due at least partly to medicine itself. People want physicians to aid in their suicides because, without such help, they cannot end their lives. This restriction of human autonomy is due to the social power of medicine; it is neither surprising nor morally wrong,

therefore, to ask those responsible for this limitation to undo some of its most noxious effects. If the medical profession relinquished its hold on drugs, people could make effective choices about their future without the assistance of physicians. Even limited access to deadly drugs, restricted to single doses for those who desire them and who are certified to be of sound mind and near the end of life, would keep physicians away from dealing in death.

Unfortunately, however, there is little sensible public discussion of such policy alternatives. And these policy alternatives may, in any case, not satisfy Callahan, who appears to believe that there is something radically wrong with anyone terminating a human life. Because he plays coy, his actual beliefs are difficult to make out. He says the notion that self-determination extends to suicide "might be pertinent, at least for debate."[3] But his argument against euthanasia sidesteps this issue: he maintains that even if there is a right to kill oneself, it is not one that can be transferred. The reason for this is that doing so would lead to "a fundamental moral wrong"—that of one person giving over "his life and fate to another."

One might wonder how we know that transferring power over oneself is "a fundamental moral wrong." Callahan appears to entertain the idea with intuitive certainty, which gives him the moral and the logical high ground and entitles him to demand a justification from whoever disagrees. But such intuitions are problematic themselves: is fervent embrace of them enough to guarantee their truth? Morality would be very distant from the concerns of life if it depended on such guideposts placed here and there in the desert of facts, unrelated to each other or to anything else. Their message, moreover, makes the guideposts suspect: it comes closer to being an echo of tradition or an expression of current views than a revelation of eternal moral truths.

Most important, the very idea of a right that intrinsically *cannot* be handed on is difficult to grasp. Under normal circumstances, to have a right is to be free or to be entitled to have or to do something. I have a right, for example, to clean my teeth. No one else has the right to do that without my consent. But I can authorize another, say my sweetheart or my dental hygienist, to do it for me. Similarly, I can assign my right to my house, my left kidney, to raising my children, to deciding when I rise, when I go to sleep, and what I do in between (by joining the Army), and by a power of attorney even to pursuing my own interest.

To be sure, the transfer of rights is not without limits. My wife and I can, for example, give over our right to our children, though we cannot do so for money. I can contract to slave away for ten hours a day cooking hamburgers, but I cannot sell myself to be, once and for all, a slave. This does not mean, however, that some rights are intrinsically nontransferable. If my right to my left kidney were nontransferable, I could neither sell it nor give it away. But I can give it away, and the only reason I cannot sell it is because sales of this sort were declared, at some point, to be against public policy. We cannot sell ourselves into slavery for the same reason: human societies set limits to the transfer of rights on account of its unacceptable costs.

The case is no different with respect to authorizing another to end my life. If I have a right to one of my kidneys, I have a right to both. And if I can tell a needy person to take one of them, I can tell two needy people to take one each. There is nothing *intrinsically* immoral about this, even though when the second helps himself I die. Yet, by dying too soon, I may leave opportunities unexplored and obligations unmet. Unscrupulous operators may take advantage of my goodwill or naiveté. The very possibility of such acts invites abuse. For these and similar reasons, we may decide that giving the first kidney is morally acceptable, but giving the second is not. The difference between the two acts, however, is not that the first is generous while the second is "a fundamental moral wrong," but that the second occurs in a context and has consequences and costs that the first does not.

Only in terms of context and cost, therefore, can we sensibly consider the issue of the morality of euthanasia. Moving on the level of abstract maxims, Callahan misses this point altogether. He declares: "There are no good moral reasons to limit euthanasia once the principle of taking life . . . has been legitimated."[4] Serious moral reflection, though it takes principles into account, is little interested in legitimating *them*. Its focus is on determining the moral acceptability of certain sorts of actions performed in complex contexts of life. Consideration of the circumstances is always essential: it is fatuous, therefore, to argue that if euthanasia is ever permissible, then "any competent person should have a right to be killed by a doctor for any reason that suits him."[5]

We can achieve little progress in moral philosophy without the ability and readiness to make relevant distinctions. Why, then, does Callahan refuse to acknowledge that there are important differences between the situation of a terminally ill patient in grave pain who wants to die and that of a young father in the dental chair who wishes, for a moment, that he

were dead? Callahan's reason is that he thinks all judgments about the unbearability of suffering and the worthlessness of one's existence are subjective and, as such, parts of a "private, idiosyncratic view of the good life."[6] The amount of suffering "has very little directly to do" with our physical condition, and so the desire to end life is capricious and unreliable. If medicine honored such desires, it would "put its own vocation at risk" by serving "the private interests" of individuals.

I cannot imagine what the vocation of medicine might be if it is not to serve the private interests of individuals. It is, after all, my vision of the good life that accounts for my wish not to perish in a diabetic coma. And surgeons certainly pursue the private interests of their patients in removing cancerous growths and in providing face-lifts. Medicine does not surrender its vocation in serving the desires of individuals: since health and continued life are among our primary wishes, its career consists in just this service.

Nevertheless, Callahan is right that our judgments about the quality of our lives and about the level of our suffering have a subjective component. But so do the opinions of patients about their health and illness, yet physicians have little difficulty in placing these perceptions in a broader, objective context. Similarly, it is both possible and proper to take into account the objective circumstances that surround desires to terminate life. Physicians have developed considerable skill in relating subjective complaints to objective conditions; only by absurd exaggeration can we say that the doctor must accept either all or none of the patient's claims. The context of the young father in the dental chair makes it clear that only a madman would think of switching from novocaine to cyanide when he moans that he wants to be dead. Even people of ordinary sensitivity understand that the situation of an older person whose friends have all died and who now suffers the excruciating pain of terminal cancer is morally different.

The question of the justifiability of euthanasia, as all difficult moral questions, cannot be asked without specifying the details of context. Dire warnings of slippery slopes and of future large-scale, quietly conducted exterminations trade on overlooking differences of circumstance. They insult our sensitivity by the suggestion that a society of individuals of good will cannot recognize situations in which their fellows want and need help and cannot distinguish such situations from those in which the desire for death is rhetorical, misguided, temporary, or idiotic. It would indeed be tragic if medicine were to leap to the aid of lovelorn teenagers whenever they feel life is too much to bear. But it is just as lamentable to stand idly by and watch unwanted lives fill up with unproductive pain.

Callahan is correct in pointing out that, in euthanasia and in assisted suicide, the physician and the patient must have separate justifications for action. The patient's wish is defensible if it is the outcome of a sound reflective judgment. Such judgments take into account the current condition, pending projects, and long-term prospects of the individual and relate them to his or her permanent interests and established values. As all assessments, these can be in error. For this reason, persons soliciting help in dying must be ready to demonstrate that they are of sound mind and thus capable of making such choices, that their desire is enduring, and that both their subjective and their objective condition makes their wish sensible.

Physicians must first decide whether their personal values permit them to participate in such activities. If they do, they must diligently examine the justifiability of the patient's desire to die. Diagnosis and prognosis are often relatively easy to ascertain. But we are not without resources for a sound determination of the internal condition of individuals either: extensive questioning on multiple occasions, interviews with friends and loved ones, and exploration of life history and values of people contribute mightily to understanding their state of mind. Physicians who are prepared to aid individuals with this last need of their lives are not, therefore, in a position where they have to believe everything they hear and act on every request. They must make independent judgments instead of subordinating themselves as unthinking tools to the passing desires of those they wish to help. This does not attribute to doctors "the powers of the gods." It only requires that they be flexible in how they aid their patients and that they do so with due caution and on the basis of sound evaluation.

Callahan is once again right to be concerned that, if allowed, euthanasia will "take place within the boundaries of the private and confidential doctor–patient relationship."[7] This does, indeed, invite abuse and permit callous physicians to take a casual attitude to a momentous decision. Callahan is wrong, however, in supposing that this constitutes an argument against euthanasia. It is only a reason not to keep euthanasia secret, but to shed on it the wholesome light of publicity. Though the decision to terminate life is intensely private, no moral consideration demands that it be kept the confidential possession of two individuals. To the contrary, the only way we can minimize wrong decisions and abuse is to require scrutiny of the decision, prior to action on it, by a suitable social body. Such ex-

amination, including at least one personal interview with the patient, should go a long distance toward relieving Callahan's concern that any law governing euthanasia would have "a low enforcement priority in the criminal justice system."[8] With formal social controls in place, there should be very little need for the involvement of courts and prosecutors.

To suppose, as Callahan does, that the principle of autonomy calls for us to stand idly by, or even to assist, whenever and for whatever reason people want to end their lives is calculated to discredit both euthanasia and autonomy. No serious moralist has ever argued that self-determination must be absolute. It cannot hold unlimited sway, as Mill and other advocates of the principle readily admit, if humans are to live in a society. And morally, it would cut no ice if murderers and rapists argued for the legitimacy of their actions by claiming that they flow naturally and solely from who they are.

The function of the principle of autonomy is to affirm *a* value and to shift the burden of justifying infringements of individual liberty to established social and governmental powers. The value it affirms is that of individual agency expressed in the belief that, through action and suffering and death, the life of each person enjoys a sort of private integrity. This means that, in the end, our lives belong to no one but ourselves. The limits to such self-determination or self-possession are set by the demands of social life. They can be discovered or decided upon in the process of moral reflection. A sensible approach to euthanasia can disclose how much weight autonomy carries in that context and how it can be balanced against other, equally legitimate but competing values.

In the hands of its friends, the principle of self-determination does not run amok. What runs amok in Callahan's version of autonomy and euthanasia is the sort of abstract moralizing that forgets the problem it sets out to address and shuts its eye to need and suffering.

### Notes

1.   D. Callahan, "Self-Determination Run Amok," *Hastings Center Report* 22 (March–April 1992): 52–55.

2.   *Ibid.,* 55.

3.   *Ibid.,* 52.

4.   *Ibid.,* 54.

5.   *Ibid.*

6.   *Ibid.,* 52.

7.   *Ibid.,* 54.

8.   *Ibid.*

## Active and Passive Euthanasia

### James Rachels

James Rachels challenges both the use and the moral significance of the distinction between active and passive euthanasia. Since both forms of euthanasia result in the death of a person, Rachels argues that active euthanasia ought to be preferred to passive. It is more humane because it allows suffering to be brought to a speedy end. Furthermore, Rachels claims, the distinction itself can be shown to be morally irrelevant. Is there, he asks, any genuine moral difference between drowning a child and merely watching a child drown and doing nothing to save it?

Finally, Rachels attempts to show that the bare fact that there is a difference between killing and letting die doesn't make active euthanasia wrong. Killing of any kind is right and wrong depending on the intentions and circumstances in which it takes place; if the intentions and circumstances are of a certain kind, then active euthanasia can be morally right.

For these reasons, Rachels suggests that the approval given to the active–passive euthanasia distinction in the Code of Ethics of the American Medical Association is unwise. He encourages physicians to rely upon the distinction only to the extent that they are forced to do so by law but not to give it any significant moral weight. In particular, they should not make use of it when writing new policies or guidelines.

The distinction between active and passive euthanasia is thought to be crucial for medical ethics. The idea is that it is permissible, at least in some cases, to withhold treatment and allow a patient to die, but it is never permissible to take any direct action designed to kill the patient. This doctrine seems to be accepted by most doctors, and it is endorsed in a statement adopted by the House of Delegates of the American Medical Association on December 4, 1973:

> The intentional termination of the life of one human being by another—mercy killing—is contrary to that for which the medical profession stands and is contrary to the policy of the American Medical Association.
>
> The cessation of the employment of extraordinary means to prolong the life of the body when there is irrefutable evidence that biological death is imminent is the decision of the patient and/or his immediate family. The advice and judgment of the physician should be freely available to the patient and/or his immediate family.

Reprinted by permission from the *New England Journal of Medicine* 292, no. 2 (January 9, 1975): 78–80.

However, a strong case can be made against this doctrine. In what follows I will set out some of the relevant arguments, and urge doctors to reconsider their views on this matter.

To begin with a familiar type of situation, a patient who is dying of incurable cancer of the throat is in terrible pain, which can no longer be satisfactorily alleviated. He is certain to die within a few days, even if present treatment is continued, but he does not want to go on living for those days since the pain is unbearable. So he asks the doctor for an end to it, and his family joins in the request.

Suppose the doctor agrees to withhold treatment, as the conventional doctrine says he may. The justification for his doing so is that the patient is in terrible agony, and since he is going to die anyway, it would be wrong to prolong his suffering needlessly. But now notice this. If one simply withholds treatment, it may take the patient longer to die, and so he may suffer more than he would if more direct action were taken and a lethal injection given. This fact provides strong reason for thinking that, once the initial decision not to prolong his agony has been made, active euthanasia is actually preferable to passive euthanasia, rather than the reverse. To say otherwise is to endorse the option that leads to more suffering rather than less, and is contrary to the humanitarian impulse that prompts the decision not to prolong his life in the first place.

Part of my point is that the process of being "allowed to die" can be relatively slow and painful, whereas being given a lethal injection is relatively quick and painless. Let me give a different sort of example. In the United States about one in 600 babies is born with Down's syndrome. Most of these babies are otherwise healthy—that is, with only the usual pediatric care, they will proceed to an otherwise normal infancy. Some, however, are born with congenital defects such as intestinal obstructions that require operations if they are to live. Sometimes, the parents and the doctor will decide not to operate, and let the infant die. Anthony Shaw describes what happens then:

> . . . When surgery is denied [the doctor] must try to keep the infant from suffering while natural forces sap the baby's life away. As a surgeon whose natural inclination is to use the scalpel to fight off death, standing by and watching a salvageable baby die is the most emotionally exhausting experience I know. It is easy at a conference, in a theoretical discussion, to decide that such infants should be allowed to die. It is altogether different to stand by in the nursery and watch as dehydration and infection wither a tiny being over hours and days. This is a terrible ordeal for me and the hospital staff—much more so than for the parents who never set foot in the nursery.[1]

I can understand why some people are opposed to all euthanasia, and insist that such infants must be allowed to live. I think I can also understand why other people favor destroying these babies quickly and painlessly. But why should anyone favor letting "dehydration and infection wither a tiny being over hours and days"? The doctrine that says that a baby may be allowed to dehydrate and wither, but may not be given an injection that would end its life without suffering, seems so patently cruel as to require no further refutation. The strong language is not intended to offend, but only to put the point in the clearest possible way.

My second argument is that the conventional doctrine leads to decisions concerning life and death made on irrelevant grounds.

Consider again the case of the infants with Down's syndrome who need operations for congenital defects unrelated to the syndrome to live. Sometimes, there is no operation, and the baby dies, but when there is no such defect, the baby lives on. Now, an operation such as that to remove an intestinal obstruction is not prohibitively difficult. The reason why such operations are not performed in these cases is, clearly, that the child has Down's syndrome and the parents and doctor judge that because of that fact it is better for the child to die.

But notice that this situation is absurd, no matter what view one takes of the lives and potentials of such babies. If the life of such an infant is worth preserving, what does it matter if it needs a simple operation? Or, if one thinks it better that such a baby should not live on, what difference does it make that it happens to have an unobstructed intestinal tract? In either case, the matter of life and death is being decided on irrelevant grounds. It is the Down's syndrome, and not the intestines, that is the issue. The matter should be decided, if at all, on that basis, and not be allowed to depend on the essentially irrelevant question of whether the intestinal tract is blocked.

What makes this situation possible, of course, is the idea that when there is an intestinal blockage, one can "let the baby die," but when there is no such defect there is nothing that can be done, for one must not "kill" it. The fact that this idea leads to such results as deciding life or death on irrelevant grounds is another good reason why the doctrine should be rejected.

One reason why so many people think that there is an important moral difference between active and passive euthanasia is that they think killing someone is morally worse than letting someone die. But is it? Is killing, in itself, worse than letting die? To investigate this issue, two cases may be considered that are exactly alike except that one involves killing whereas the other involves letting someone die. Then, it can be asked whether this difference makes any difference to the moral assessments. It is important that the cases be exactly alike, except for this one difference, since otherwise one cannot be confident that it is this difference and not some other that accounts for any variation in the assessments of the two cases. So, let us consider this pair of cases:

In the first, Smith stands to gain a large inheritance if anything should happen to his six-year-old cousin. One evening while the child is taking his bath, Smith sneaks into the bathroom and drowns the child, and then arranges things so that it will look like an accident.

In the second, Jones also stands to gain if anything should happen to his six-year-old cousin. Like Smith, Jones sneaks in planning to drown the child in his bath. However, just as he enters the bathroom Jones sees the child slip and hit his head, and fall face down in the water. Jones is delighted; he stands by,

ready to push the child's head back under if it is necessary, but it is not necessary. With only a little thrash-
ing about, the child drowns all by himself,
"accidentally," as Jones watches and does nothing.

Now Smith killed the child, whereas Jones
"merely" let the child die. That is the only difference
between them. Did either man behave better, from a
moral point of view? If the difference between killing
and letting die were in itself a morally important matter, one should say that Jones's behavior was less reprehensible than Smith's. But does one really want to say
that? I think not. In the first place, both men acted
from the same motive, personal gain, and both had exactly the same end in view when they acted. It may be
inferred from Smith's conduct that he is a bad man, although that judgment may be withdrawn or modified
if certain further facts are learned about him—for example, that he is mentally deranged. But would not the
very same thing be inferred about Jones from his conduct? And would not the same further considerations
also be relevant to any modification of this judgment?
Moreover, suppose Jones pleaded, in his own defense,
"After all, I didn't do anything except just stand there
and watch the child drown. I didn't kill him; I only let
him die." Again, if letting die were in itself less bad
than killing, this defense should have at least some
weight. But it does not. Such a "defense" can only be
regarded as a grotesque perversion of moral reasoning.
Morally speaking, it is no defense at all.

Now, it may be pointed out, quite properly, that
the cases of euthanasia with which doctors are concerned are not like this at all. They do not involve personal gain or the destruction of normal healthy
children. Doctors are concerned only with cases in
which the patient's life is of no further use to him, or
in which the patient's life has become or will soon become a terrible burden. However, the point is the
same in these cases: the bare difference between
killing and letting die does not, in itself, make a moral
difference. If a doctor lets a patient die, for humane
reasons, he is in the same moral position as if he had
given the patient a lethal injection for humane reasons. If his decision was wrong—if, for example, the
patient's illness was in fact curable—the decision
would be equally regrettable no matter which method
was used to carry it out. And if the doctor's decision
was the right one, the method used is not in itself
important.

The AMA policy statement isolates the crucial issue very well; the crucial issue is "the intentional termination of the life of one human being by another."

But after identifying this issue, and forbidding "mercy
killing," the statement goes on to deny that the cessation of treatment is the intentional termination of a
life. This is where the mistake comes in, for what is the
cessation of treatment, in these circumstances, if it is
not "the intentional termination of the life of one human being by another"? Of course it is exactly that,
and if it were not, there would be no point to it.

Many people will find this judgment hard to accept. One reason, I think, is that it is very easy to con-
flate the question of whether killing is, in itself, worse
than letting die, with the very different question of
whether most actual cases of killing are more reprehensible than most actual cases of letting die. Most
actual cases of killing are clearly terrible (think, for example, of all the murders reported in the newspapers),
and one hears of such cases every day. On the other
hand, one hardly ever hears of a case of letting die, except for the actions of doctors who are motivated by
humanitarian reasons. So one learns to think of killing
in a much worse light than of letting die. But this does
not mean that there is something about killing that
makes it in itself worse than letting die, for it is not the
bare difference between killing and letting die that
makes the difference in the cases. Rather, the other
factors—the murderer's motive of personal gain, for
example, contrasted with the doctor's humanitarian
motivation—account for different reactions to the
different cases.

I have argued that killing is not in itself any worse
than letting die; if my contention is right, it follows that
active euthanasia is not any worse than passive euthanasia. What arguments can be given on the other
side? The most common, I believe, is the following:

"The important difference between active and
passive euthanasia is that, in passive euthanasia, the
doctor does not do anything to bring about the patient's death. The doctor does nothing, and the patient
dies of whatever ills already afflict him. In active euthanasia, however, the doctor does something to bring
about the patient's death: he kills him. The doctor who
gives the patient with cancer a lethal injection has himself caused his patient's death; whereas if he merely
ceases treatment, the cancer is the cause of the death."

A number of points need to be made here. The
first is that it is not exactly correct to say that in passive
euthanasia the doctor does nothing, for he does do
one thing that is very important: he lets the patient
die. "Letting someone die" is certainly different, in
some respects, from other types of action—mainly in
that it is a kind of action that one may perform by way

of not performing certain other actions. For example, one may let a patient die by way of not giving medication, just as one may insult someone by way of not shaking his hand. But for any purpose of moral assessment, it is a type of action nonetheless. The decision to let a patient die is subject to moral appraisal in the same way that a decision to kill him would be subject to moral appraisal: it may be assessed as wise or unwise, compassionate or sadistic, right or wrong. If a doctor deliberately let a patient die who was suffering from a routinely curable illness, the doctor would certainly be to blame for what he had done, just as he would be to blame if he had needlessly killed the patient. Charges against him would then be appropriate. If so, it would be no defense at all for him to insist that he didn't "do anything." He would have done something very serious indeed, for he let his patient die.

Fixing the cause of death may be very important from a legal point of view, for it may determine whether criminal charges are brought against the doctor. But I do not think that this notion can be used to show a moral difference between active and passive euthanasia. The reason why it is considered bad to be the cause of someone's death is that death is regarded as a great evil—and so it is. However, if it has been decided that euthanasia—even passive euthanasia—is desirable in a given case, it has also been decided that in this instance death is no greater an evil than the patient's continued existence. And if this is true, the usual reason for not wanting to be the cause of someone's death simply does not apply.

Finally, doctors may think that all of this is only of academic interest—the sort of thing that philosophers may worry about but that has no practical bearing on their own work. After all, doctors must be concerned about the legal consequences of what they do, and active euthanasia is clearly forbidden by the law. But even so, doctors should also be concerned with the fact that the law is forcing upon them a moral doctrine that may well be indefensible, and has a considerable effect on their practices. Of course, most doctors are not now in the position of being coerced in this matter, for they do not regard themselves as merely going along with what the law requires. Rather, in statements such as the AMA policy statement that I have quoted, they are endorsing this doctrine as a central point of medical ethics. In that statement, active euthanasia is condemned not merely as illegal but as "contrary to that for which the medical profession stands," whereas passive euthanasia is approved. However, the preceding considerations suggest that there is really no moral difference between the two, considered in themselves (there may be important moral differences in some cases in their *consequences*, but, as I pointed out, these differences may make active euthanasia, and not passive euthanasia, the morally preferable option). So, whereas doctors may have to discriminate between active and passive euthanasia to satisfy the law, they should not do any more than that. In particular, they should not give the distinction any added authority and weight by writing it into official statements of medical ethics.

### Note

1.  A. Shaw, "Doctor, Do We Have a Choice?" *The New York Times Magazine,* January 30, 1972, p. 54.

---

# Voluntary Active Euthanasia

## Dan W. Brock

Dan Brock examines the possible results of legalizing voluntary euthanasia and assisted suicide and argues that, with procedural safeguards, the value of promoting self-determination and individual well-being outweighs the likely bad consequences.

Brock denies that physician participation in euthanasia is incompatible with the commitment to healing and that it will undermine the moral center of medicine. He argues that medicine's moral center is found in respecting patients' self-determination and promoting their well-being. He regards voluntary euthanasia as compatible with these values and rejects the notion that euthanasia and assisted suicide would undermine the general respect for life or weaken the prohibition against homicide.

## The Central Ethical Argument for Voluntary Active Euthanasia

The central ethical argument for euthanasia is familiar. It is the very same two fundamental ethical values supporting the consensus on patient's rights to decide about life-sustaining treatment that also support the ethical permissibility of euthanasia. These values are individual self-determination or autonomy and individual well-being. By self-determination as it bears on euthanasia, I mean people's interest in making important decisions about their lives for themselves according to their own values or conceptions of a good life, and in being left free to act on those decisions. Self-determination is valuable because it permits people to form and live in accordance with their own conception of a good life, at least within the bounds of justice and consistent with others doing so as well. In exercising self-determination people take responsibility for their lives and for the kinds of persons they become. A central aspect of human dignity lies in people's capacity to direct their lives in this way. The value of exercising self-determination presupposes some minimum of decision-making capacities or competence, which thus limits the scope of euthanasia supported by self-determination; it cannot justifiably be administered, for example, in cases of serious dementia or treatable clinical depression.

Does the value of individual self-determination extend to the time and manner of one's death? Most people are very concerned about the nature of the last stage of their lives. This reflects not just a fear of experiencing substantial suffering when dying, but also a desire to retain dignity and control during this last period of life. Death is today increasingly preceded by a long period of significant physical and mental decline, due in part to the technological interventions of modern medicine. Many people adjust to these disabilities and find meaning and value in new activities and ways. Others find the impairments and burdens in the last stage of their lives at some point sufficiently great to make life no longer worth living. For many patients near death, maintaining the quality of one's life, avoiding great suffering, maintaining one's dignity, and insuring that others remember us as we wish them to become of paramount importance and outweigh merely extending one's life. But there is no single, objectively correct answer for everyone as to when, if at

all, one's life becomes all things considered a burden and unwanted. If self-determination is a fundamental value, then the great variability among people on this question makes it especially important that individuals control the manner, circumstances, and timing of their dying and death.

The other main value that supports euthanasia is individual well-being. It might seem that individual well-being conflicts with a person's self-determination when the person requests euthanasia. Life itself is commonly taken to be a central good for persons, often valued for its own sake, as well as necessary for pursuit of all other goods within a life. But when a competent patient decides to forgo all further life-sustaining treatment then the patient, either explicitly or implicitly, commonly decides that the best life possible for him or her with treatment is of sufficiently poor quality that it is worse than no further life at all. Life is no longer considered a benefit by the patient, but has now become a burden. The same judgment underlies a request for euthanasia: continued life is seen by the patient as no longer a benefit, but now a burden. Especially in the often severely compromised and debilitated states of many critically ill or dying patients, there is no objective standard, but only the competent patient's judgment of whether continued life is no longer a benefit.

Of course, sometimes there are conditions, such as clinical depression, that call into question whether the patient has made a competent choice, either to forgo life-sustaining treatment or to seek euthanasia, and then the patient's choice need not be evidence that continued life is no longer a benefit for him or her. Just as with decisions about treatment, a determination of incompetence can warrant not honoring the patient's choice; in the case of treatment, we then transfer decisional authority to a surrogate, though in the case of voluntary active euthanasia a determination that the patient is incompetent means that choice is not possible. . . .

Most opponents do not deny that there are some cases in which the values of patient self-determination and well-being support euthanasia. Instead, they commonly offer two kinds of arguments against it that in their view outweigh or override this support. The first kind of argument is that in any individual case where considerations of the patient's self-determination and well-being do support euthanasia, it is nevertheless always ethically wrong or impermissible. The second kind of argument grants that in some individual cases euthanasia may *not* be ethically wrong, but maintains

From Dan W. Brock, "Voluntary Active Euthanasia," *Hastings Center Report* (March/April 1992), pp. 11–12, 14–17, 19–21. Reprinted by permission.

nonetheless that public and legal policy should never permit it. The first kind of argument focuses on features of any individual case of euthanasia, while the second kind focuses on social or legal policy. . . .

## Would the Bad Consequences of Euthanasia Outweigh the Good?

The argument against euthanasia at the policy level is stronger than at the level of individual cases, though even here I believe the case is ultimately unpersuasive, or at best indecisive. The policy level is the place where the main issues lie, however, and where moral considerations that might override arguments in favor of euthanasia will be found, if they are found anywhere. It is important to note two kinds of disagreement about the consequences for public policy of permitting euthanasia. First, there is empirical or factual disagreement about what the consequences would be. This disagreement is greatly exacerbated by the lack of firm data on the issue. Second, since on any reasonable assessment there would be both good and bad consequences, there are moral disagreements about the relative importance of different effects. In addition to these two sources of disagreement, there is also no single, well-specified policy proposal for legalizing euthanasia on which policy assessments can focus. But without such specification, and especially without explicit procedures for protecting against well-intentioned misuse and ill-intentioned abuse, the consequences for policy are largely speculative. Despite these difficulties, a preliminary account of the main likely good and bad consequences is possible. This should help clarify where better data or more moral analysis and argument are needed, as well as where policy safeguards must be developed.

Potential Good Consequences of Permitting Euthanasia.    What are the likely good consequences? First, if euthanasia were permitted it would be possible to respect the self-determination of competent patients who want it, but now cannot get it because of its illegality. We simply do not know how many such patients and people there are. In the Netherlands, with a population of about 14.5 million (in 1987), estimates in a recent study were that about 1900 cases of voluntary active euthanasia or physician-assisted suicide occur annually. No straightforward extrapolation to the United States is possible for many reasons, among them, that we do not know how many people here who want euthanasia now get it, despite its illegality.

Even with better data on the number of persons who want euthanasia but cannot get it, significant moral disagreement would remain about how much weight should be given to any instance of failure to respect a person's self-determination in this way.

One important factor substantially affecting the number of persons who would seek euthanasia is the extent to which an alternative is available. The widespread acceptance in the law, social policy, and medical practice of the right of a competent patient to forgo life-sustaining treatment suggests that the number of competent persons in the United States who would want euthanasia if it were permitted is probably relatively small.

A second good consequence of making euthanasia legally permissible benefits a much larger group. Polls have shown that a majority of the American public believes that people should have a right to obtain euthanasia if they want it.[1] No doubt the vast majority of those who support this right to euthanasia will never in fact come to want euthanasia for themselves. Nevertheless, making it legally permissible would reassure many people that if they ever do want euthanasia they would be able to obtain it. This reassurance would supplement the broader control over the process of dying given by the right to decide about life-sustaining treatment. Having fire insurance on one's house benefits all who have it, not just those whose houses actually burn down, by reassuring them that in the unlikely event of their house burning down, they will receive the money needed to rebuild it. Likewise, the legalization of euthanasia can be thought of as a kind of insurance policy against being forced to endure a protracted dying process that one has come to find burdensome and unwanted, especially when there is no life-sustaining treatment to forgo. The strong concern about losing control of their care expressed by many people who face serious illness likely to end in death suggests that they give substantial importance to the legalization of euthanasia as a means of maintaining this control.

A third good consequence of the legalization of euthanasia concerns patients whose dying is filled with severe and unrelievable pain or suffering. When there is life-sustaining treatment that, if forgone, will lead relatively quickly to death, then doing so can bring an end to these patients' suffering without recourse to euthanasia. For patients receiving no such treatment, however, euthanasia may be the only release from their otherwise prolonged suffering and agony. This argument from mercy has always been the strongest argument for euthanasia in those cases to which it applies.[2]

The importance of relieving pain and suffering is less controversial than is the frequency with which patients are forced to undergo untreatable agony that only euthanasia could relieve. If we focus first on suffering caused by physical pain, it is crucial to distinguish pain that *could* be adequately relieved with modern methods of pain control, though it in fact is not, from pain that is relievable only by death.[3] For a variety of reasons, including some physicians' fear of hastening the patient's death, as well as the lack of a publicly accessible means for assessing the amount of the patient's pain, many patients suffer pain that could be, but is not, relieved.

Specialists in pain control, as for example the pain of terminally ill cancer patients, argue that there are very few patients whose pain could not be adequately controlled, though sometimes at the cost of so sedating them that they are effectively unable to interact with other people or their environment. Thus, the argument from mercy in cases of physical pain can probably be met in a large majority of cases by providing adequate measures of pain relief. This should be a high priority, whatever our legal policy on euthanasia—the relief of pain and suffering has long been, quite properly, one of the central goals of medicine. Those cases in which pain could be effectively relieved, but in fact is not, should only count significantly in favor of legalizing euthanasia if all reasonable efforts to change pain management techniques have been tried and have failed.

Dying patients often undergo substantial psychological suffering that is not fully or even principally the result of physical pain.[4] The knowledge about how to relieve this suffering is much more limited than in the case of relieving pain, and efforts to do so are probably more often unsuccessful. If the argument from mercy is extended to patients experiencing great and unrelievable psychological suffering, the numbers of patients to which it applies are much greater.

One last good consequence of legalizing euthanasia is that once death has been accepted, it is often more humane to end life quickly and peacefully, when that is what the patient wants. Such a death will often be seen as better than a more prolonged one. People who suffer a sudden and unexpected death, for example by dying quickly or in their sleep from a heart attack or stroke, are often considered lucky to have died in this way. We care about how we die in part because we care about how others remember us, and we hope

they will remember us as we were in "good times" with them and not as we might be when disease has robbed us of our dignity as human beings. As with much in the treatment and care of the dying, people's concerns differ in this respect, but for at least some people, euthanasia will be a more humane death than what they might have often experienced with other loved ones and might otherwise expect for themselves.

Some opponents of euthanasia challenge how much importance should be given to any of these good consequences of permitting it, or even whether some would be good consequences at all. But more frequently, opponents cite a number of bad consequences that permitting euthanasia would or could produce, and it is to their assessment that I now turn.

**Potential Bad Consequences of Permitting Euthanasia.** Some of the arguments against permitting euthanasia are aimed specifically against physicians, while others are aimed against anyone being permitted to perform it. I shall first consider one argument of the former sort. Permitting physicians to perform euthanasia, it is said, would be incompatible with their fundamental moral and professional commitment as healers to care for patients and to protect life. Moreover, if euthanasia by physicians became common, patients would come to fear that a medication was intended not to treat or care, but instead to kill, and would thus lose trust in their physicians. This position was forcefully stated in a paper by Willard Gaylin and his colleagues:

> The very soul of medicine is on trial . . . This issue touches medicine at its moral center; if this moral center collapses, if physicians become killers or are even licensed to kill, the profession—and, therewith, each physician—will never again be worthy of trust and respect as healer and comforter and protector of life in all its frailty.

These authors go on to make clear that, while they oppose permitting anyone to perform euthanasia, their special concern is with physicians doing so:

> We call on fellow physicians to say that they will not deliberately kill. We must also say to each of our fellow physicians that we will not tolerate killing of patients and that we shall take disciplinary action against doctors who kill. And we must say to the broader community that if it insists on tolerating or legalizing active euthanasia, it will have to find nonphysicians to do its killing.[5]

If permitting physicians to kill would undermine the very "moral center" of medicine, then almost certainly physicians should not be permitted to perform euthanasia. But how persuasive is this claim? Patients should not fear, as a consequence of permitting *voluntary* active euthanasia, that their physicians will substitute a lethal injection for what patients want and believe is part of their care. If active euthanasia is restricted to cases in which it is truly voluntary, then no patient should fear getting it unless she or he has voluntarily requested it. . . . Patients' trust of their physicians could be increased, not eroded, by knowledge that physicians will provide aid in dying when patients seek it. . . .

. . . In spelling out above what I called the positive argument for voluntary active euthanasia, I suggested that two principal values—respecting patients' self-determination and promoting their well-being—underlie the consensus that competent patients, or the surrogates of incompetent patients, are entitled to refuse any life-sustaining treatment and to choose from among available alternative treatments. It is the commitment to these two values in guiding physicians' actions as healers, comforters, and protectors of their patients' lives that should be at the "moral center" of medicine, and these two values support physicians' administering euthanasia when their patients make competent requests for it.

What should not be at that moral center is a commitment to preserving patients' lives as such, without regard to whether those patients want their lives preserved or judge their preservation a benefit to them. . . .

A second bad consequence that some foresee is that permitting euthanasia would weaken society's commitment to provide optimal care for dying patients. We live at a time in which the control of health-care costs has become, and is likely to continue to be, the dominant focus of health-care policy. If euthanasia is seen as a cheaper alternative to adequate care and treatment, then we might become less scrupulous about providing sometimes costly support and other services to dying patients. Particularly if our society comes to embrace deeper and more explicit rationing of health care, frail, elderly, and dying patients will need to be strong and effective advocates for their own health care and other needs, although they are hardly in a position to do this. We should do nothing to weaken their ability to obtain adequate care and services.

This second worry is difficult to assess because there is little firm evidence about the likelihood of the feared erosion in the care of dying patients. There are at least two reasons, however, for skepticism about this argument. The first is that the same worry could

have been directed at recognizing patients' or surrogates' rights to forgo life-sustaining treatment, yet there is no persuasive evidence that recognizing the right to refuse treatment has caused a serious erosion in the quality of care of dying patients. The second reason for skepticism about this worry is that only a very small proportion of deaths would occur from euthanasia if it were permitted. In the Netherlands, where euthanasia under specified circumstances is permitted by the courts, though not authorized by statute, the best estimate of the proportion of overall deaths that result from it is about 2 percent.[6] Thus, the vast majority of critically ill and dying patients will not request it, and so will still have to be cared for by physicians, families, and others. Permitting euthanasia should not diminish people's commitment and concern to maintain and improve the care of these patients. . . .

The [third] potential bad consequence of permitting euthanasia has been developed by David Velleman and turns on the subtle point that making a new option or choice available to people can sometimes make them worse off, even if once they have the choice they go on to choose what is best for them.[7] Ordinarily, people's continued existence is viewed by them as given, a fixed condition with which they must cope. Making euthanasia available to people as an option denies them the alternative of staying alive by default. If people are offered the option of euthanasia, their continued existence is now a choice for which they can be held responsible and which they can be asked by others to justify. We care, and are right to care, about being able to justify ourselves to others. To the extent that our society is unsympathetic to justifying a severely dependent or impaired existence, a heavy psychological burden of proof may be placed on patients who think their terminal illness or chronic infirmity is not a sufficient reason for dying. Even if they otherwise view their life as worth living, the opinion of others around them that it is not can threaten their reason for living and make euthanasia a rational choice. Thus the existence of the option becomes a subtle pressure to request it.

This argument correctly identifies the reason why offering some patients the option of euthanasia would not benefit them. Velleman takes it not as a reason for opposing all euthanasia, but for restricting it to circumstances where there are "unmistakable and overpowering reasons for persons to want the option of euthanasia," and for denying the option in all other cases. But there are at least three reasons why such restriction may not be warranted. First, polls and other evidence support that most Americans believe euthanasia should be permitted. . . . Thus, many more people seem to want the choice than would be made worse off by getting it. Second, if giving people the option of ending their life really makes them worse off, then we should not only prohibit euthanasia, but also take back from people the right they now have to decide about life-sustaining treatment. The feared harmful effect should already have occurred from securing people's right to refuse life-sustaining treatment, yet there is no evidence of any such widespread harm or any broad public desire to rescind that right. Third, since there is a wide range of conditions in which reasonable people can and do disagree about whether they would want continued life, it is not possible to restrict the permissibility of euthanasia as narrowly as Velleman suggests without thereby denying it to most persons who would want it; to permit it only in cases in which virtually everyone would want it would be to deny it to most who would want it.

A [fourth] potential bad consequence of making euthanasia legally permissible is that it might weaken the general legal prohibition of homicide. This prohibition is so fundamental to civilized society, it is argued, that we should do nothing that erodes it. If most cases of stopping life support are killing, as I already argued, then the court cases permitting such killing have already in effect weakened this prohibition. However, neither the courts nor more people have seen these cases as killing and so as challenging the prohibition of homicide. The courts have usually grounded patients' or their surrogates' rights to refuse life-sustaining treatment in rights to privacy, liberty, self-determination, or bodily integrity, not in exceptions to homicide laws.

Legal permission for physicians or others to perform euthanasia could not be grounded in patients' rights to decide about medical treatment. Permitting euthanasia would require qualifying, at least in effect, the legal prohibition against homicide, a prohibition that in general does not allow the consent of the victim to justify or excuse the act. Nevertheless, the very same fundamental basis of the right to decide about life-sustaining treatment—respecting a person's self-determination—does support euthanasia as well. Individual self-determination has long been a well-entrenched and fundamental value in the law, and so extending it to euthanasia would not require appeal to novel legal values or principles. That suicide or attempted suicide is no longer a criminal offense in virtually all states indicates an acceptance of individual self-determination in the taking of one's own life analogous to that required for voluntary active euthanasia. The legal prohibition (in most states) of assisting in suicide and the refusal in the law to accept the consent of the victim as a possible justification of homicide are both arguably a result of difficulties in the legal process of establishing the consent of the victim after the fact. If procedures can be designed that clearly establish the voluntariness of the person's request for euthanasia, it would under those procedures represent a carefully circumscribed qualification on the legal prohibition of homicide. Nevertheless, some remaining worries about this weakening can be captured in the final potential bad consequence, to which I will now turn.

This final potential bad consequence is the central concern of many opponents of euthanasia and, I believe, is the most serious objection to a legal policy permitting it. According to this "slippery slope" worry, although active euthanasia may be morally permissible in cases in which it is unequivocally voluntary and the patient finds his or her condition unbearable, a legal policy permitting euthanasia would inevitably lead to active euthanasia being performed in many other cases in which it would be morally wrong. To prevent those other wrongful cases of euthanasia we should not permit even morally justified performance of it.

Slippery slope arguments of this form are problematic and difficult to evaluate.[8] From one perspective, they are the last refuge of conservative defenders of the status quo. When all the opponents' objections to the wrongness of euthanasia itself have been met, the opponent then shifts ground and acknowledges both that it is not in itself wrong and that a legal policy which resulted only in its being performed would not be bad. Nevertheless, the opponent maintains, it should still not be permitted because doing so would result in its being performed in other cases in which it is not voluntary and would be wrong. In this argument's most extreme form, permitting euthanasia is the first and fateful step down the slippery slope to Nazism. Once on the slope we will be unable to get off.

Now it cannot be denied that it is *possible* that permitting euthanasia could have these fateful consequences, but that cannot be enough to warrant prohibiting it if it is otherwise justified. A similar *possible* slippery slope worry could have been raised to securing competent patients' rights to decide about life support, but recent history shows such a worry would have been unfounded. It must be relevant how likely it is that we will end with horrendous consequences and an unjustified practice of euthanasia. How *likely* and *widespread* would the abuses and unwarranted extensions of permitting it be? By abuses, I mean the performance of euthanasia that fails to satisfy the conditions required for voluntary active euthanasia, for example, if the patient has been subtly pressured to accept it. By unwarranted extensions of policy, I mean later changes in legal policy to permit not just voluntary euthanasia, but also euthanasia in cases in which, for example, it need not be fully voluntary. Opponents of voluntary euthanasia on slippery slope grounds have not provided the data or evidence necessary to turn their speculative concerns into well-grounded likelihoods.

It is at least clear, however, that both the character and likelihood of abuses of a legal policy permitting euthanasia depend in significant part on the procedures put in place to protect against them. I will not try to detail fully what such procedures might be, but will just give some examples of what they might include:

1. The patient should be provided with all relevant information about his or her medical condition, current prognosis, available alternative treatments, and the prognosis of each.

2. Procedures should ensure that the patient's request for euthanasia is stable or enduring (a brief waiting period could be required) and fully voluntary (an advocate for the patient might be appointed to ensure this).

3. All reasonable alternatives must have been explored for improving the patient's quality of life and relieving any pain or suffering.

4. A psychiatric evaluation should ensure that the patient's request is not the result of a treatable psychological impairment such as depression.[9]

These examples of procedural safeguards are all designed to ensure that the patient's choice is fully informed, voluntary, and competent, and so a true exercise of self-determination. Other proposals for euthanasia would restrict its permissibility further—for example, to the terminally ill—a restriction that cannot be supported by self-determination. Such additional restrictions might, however, be justified by concern for limiting potential harms from abuse. At the same time, it is important not to impose procedural or substantive safeguards so restrictive as to make euthanasia impermissible or practically infeasible in a wide range of justified cases.

These examples of procedural safeguards make clear that it is possible to substantially reduce, though not to eliminate, the potential for abuse of a policy permitting voluntary active euthanasia. Any legalization of the practice should be accompanied by a well-considered set of procedural safeguards together with an ongoing evaluation of its use. Introducing euthanasia into only a few states could be a form of carefully limited and controlled social experiment that would give us evidence about the benefits and harms of the practice. Even then firm and uncontroversial data may remain elusive, as the continuing controversy over what has taken place in the Netherlands in recent years indicates. . . .[10]

## The Role of Physicians

If euthanasia is made legally permissible, should physicians take part in it? Should only physicians be permitted to perform it, as is the case in the Netherlands? In discussing whether euthanasia is incompatible with medicine's commitment to curing, caring for, and comforting patients, I argued that it is not at odds with a proper understanding of the aims of medicine, and so need not undermine patients' trust in their physicians. If that argument is correct, then physicians probably should not be prohibited, either by law or by professional norms, from taking part in a legally permissible practice of euthanasia (nor, of course, should they be compelled to do so if their personal or professional scruples forbid it). Most physicians in the Netherlands appear not to understand euthanasia to be incompatible with their professional commitments.

Sometimes patients who would be able to end their lives on their own nevertheless seek the assistance of physicians. Physician involvement in such cases may have important benefits to patients and others beyond simply assuring the use of effective means. Historically, in the United States suicide has carried a strong negative stigma that many today believe unwarranted. Seeking a physician's assistance, or what can almost seem a physician's blessing, may be a way of trying to remove that stigma and show others that the decision for suicide was made with due seriousness and was justified under the circumstances. The physician's involvement provides a kind of social approval, or more accurately helps counter what would otherwise be unwarranted social disapproval.

There are also at least two reasons for restricting the practice of euthanasia to physicians only. First, physicians would inevitably be involved in some of the important procedural safeguards necessary to a defensible practice, such as seeing to it that the patient is well-informed about his or her condition, prognosis, and possible treatments, and ensuring that all reasonable means have been taken to improve the quality of the patient's life. Second, and probably more important, one necessary protection against abuse of the practice is to limit the persons given authority to perform it, so that they can be held accountable for their exercise of that authority. Physicians, whose training and professional norms give some assurance that they would perform euthanasia responsibly, are an appropriate group of persons to whom the practice may be restricted.

### Notes

1. P. Painton and E. Taylor, "Love or Let Die," *Time,* 19 March 1990, pp. 62–71; *Boston Globe*/Harvard University Poll, *Boston Globe,* 3 November 1991.

2. James Rachels, *The End of Life* (Oxford: University Press, 1986).

3. Marcia Angell, "The Quality of Mercy," *NEJM* 306 (1982): 98–99; M. Donovan, P. Dillon, and L. McGuire, "Incidence and Characteristics of Pain in a Sample of Medical-Surgical Inpatients," *Pain* 30 (1987): 69–78.

4. Eric Cassell, *The Nature of Suffering and the Goals of Medicine* (New York: Oxford University Press, 1991).

5. Willard Gaylin, Leon R. Kass, Edmund D. Pellegrino, and Mark Siegler, "Doctors Must Not Kill," *JAMA* 259 (1988): 2139–40.

6. Paul J. Van der Maas et al., "Euthanasia and Other Medical Decisions Concerning the End of Life," *Lancet* 338 (1991): 669–74.

7. My formulation of this argument derives from David Velleman's statement of it in his commentary on an earlier version of this paper delivered at the American Philosophical Association Central Division meetings; a similar point was made to me by Elisha Milgram in discussion on another occasion. For more general development of the point see Thomas Schelling, *The Strategy of Conflict* (Cambridge, Mass.: Harvard University Press, 1960); and Gerald Dworkin, "Is More Choice Better Than Less?" in *The Theory and Practice of Autonomy* (Cambridge: Cambridge University Press, 1988).

8. Frederick Schauer, "Slippery Slopes," *Harvard Law Review* 99 (1985): 361–83; Wibren van der Burg, "The Slippery Slope Argument," *Ethics* 102 (October 1991): 42–65.

9. There is evidence that physicians commonly fail to diagnose depression. See Robert I. Misbin, "Physicians Aid in Dying," *NEJM* 325 (1991): 1304–7.

10. Richard Fenigsen, "A Case Against Dutch Euthanasia," Special Supplement, *Hastings Center Report* 19, no. 1 (1989): 22–30.

### READINGS

# Section 3: Alternatives

## Physician-Assisted Suicide

### Lonnie R. Bristow for the American Medical Association

The AMA, as represented by Lonnie Bristow, rejects physician-assisted suicide as unethical and incompatible with a physician's commitment "to healing and to life." The AMA views recent proposals to legalize physician-assisted suicide as a sign that the needs of patients are not being met by our health-care system and that our society has not adequately addressed end-of-life issues.

The proper response is to provide patients at the end of life with adequate pain control, emotional support, and comfort care. Physicians must respect patient autonomy and maintain good communication, and yet patients must also be educated in ways that help reduce the pressures that might lead them to request physician-assisted suicide.

For nearly 2500 years, physicians have vowed to "give no deadly drug if asked for it, [nor] make a suggestion to this effect." What has changed, that there should be this attempt to make "assisted suicide" an accepted

Statement by Lonnie R. Bristow, President of the American Medical Association, before the United States House of Representatives Committee on the Judiciary, Subcommittee on the Constitution, *Congressional Record,* April 29, 1996.

practice of medicine? Certainly the experience of physical pain has not changed over time. Yet the blessings of medical research and technology present their own new challenges, as our ability to delay or draw out the dying process alters our perceptions and needs. Our efforts in this new paradigm must recognize the importance of care that relieves pain, supports family and relationships, enhances functioning, and respects spiritual needs. Calls for legalization of physician-assisted suicide point to a public perception that these needs are not being met by the current health-care system. In addition, society has not met its responsibility to plan adequately for end-of-life care. It is this issue—how to provide quality care at the end of life—which the AMA believes should be our legitimate focus.

The AMA believes that physician-assisted suicide is unethical and fundamentally inconsistent with the pledge physicians make to devote themselves to healing and life. Laws that sanction physician-assisted suicide undermine the foundation of the patient–physician relationship that is grounded in the patient's trust that the physician is working wholeheartedly for the patient's health and welfare. The multidisciplinary members of the New York State Task Force on Life and the Law concur in this belief, writing that "physician-assisted suicide and euthanasia violate values that are fundamental to the practice of medicine and the patient–physician relationship."

Yet physicians also have an ethical responsibility to relieve pain and to respect their patient's wishes regarding care, and it is when these duties converge at the bedside of a seriously or terminally ill patient that physicians are torn.

The AMA believes that these additional ethical duties require physicians to respond aggressively to the needs of the patients at the end of life with adequate pain control, emotional support, comfort care, respect for patient autonomy, and good communications. Further efforts are necessary to better educate physicians in the areas of pain management and effective end-of-life care. Patient education is the other essential component of an effective outreach to minimize the circumstances which might lead to a patient's request for physician-assisted suicide: inadequate social support; the perceived burden to family and friends; clinical depression; hopelessness; loss of self-esteem; and the fear of living with chronic, unrelieved pain.

### Ethical Considerations

**Physicians' Fundamental Obligation.** The physician's primary obligation is to advocate for the individual patient. At the end of life, this means the physician must strive to understand the various existential, psychological, and physiological factors that play out over the course of terminal illness and must help the patient cope with each of them. Patients who are understandably apprehensive or afraid of their own

mortality need support and comforting, not a prescription to help them avoid the issues of death. Patients who believe sudden and "controlled" death would protect them from the perceived indignities of prolonged deterioration and terminal illness must receive social support as well as the support of the profession to work through these issues. Providing assisted suicide would breach the ethical means of medicine to safeguard patients' dignity and independence.

**Pain Management and the Doctrine of Double Effect.** Many proponents of assisted suicide cite a fear of prolonged suffering and unmanageable pain as support for their position. For most patients, advancements in palliative care can adequately control pain through oral medications, nerve blocks, or radiotherapy. We all recognize, however, that there are patients whose intractable pain cannot be relieved by treating the area, organ, or system perceived as the source of the pain. For patients for whom pain cannot be controlled by other means, it is ethically permissible for physicians to administer sufficient levels of controlled substances to ease pain, even if the patient's risk of addiction or death is increased.

The failure of most states to expressly permit this practice has generated reluctance among physicians to prescribe adequate pain medication. Additional uncertainty is produced by the potential for legal action against the physician when controlled substances are prescribed in large amounts to treat patients with intractable pain. This uncertainty chills physicians' ability to effectively control their terminally ill patients' pain and suffering through the appropriate prescription and administration of opiates and other controlled substances. In this area, states such as California and Texas have developed clear legislative guidance that resolves these concerns for most physicians. The AMA is developing similarly structured model legislation for state medical societies to pursue with their state legislatures and medical licensing boards.

In some instances, administration of adequate pain medication will have the secondary effect of suppressing the respiration of the patient, thereby hastening death. This is commonly referred to as the "double effect." The distinction between this action and assisted suicide is crucial. The physician has an obligation to provide for the comfort of the patient. If there are no alternatives but to increase the risk of death in order to provide that comfort, the physician is ethically permitted to exercise that option. In this circumstance, the physician's clinical decision is guided by the intent to provide pain relief, rather than an intent to cause death. This distinguishes the ethical use of palliative care medications from the unethical application of medical skills to cause death.

**Distinction Between Withholding or Withdrawing Treatment and Assisted Suicide.** Some participants in the debate about assisted suicide see no meaningful distinction between withholding or withdrawing treatment and providing assistance in suicide. They argue that the results of each action are the same and therefore the acts themselves carry equal moral status. This argument largely ignores the distinction between act and omission in the circumstances of terminal care and does not address many of the principles that underlie the right of patients to refuse the continuation of medical care and the duty of physicians to exercise their best clinical judgment.

Specifically, proponents who voice this line of reasoning fail to recognize the crucial difference between a patient's right to refuse unwanted medical treatment and any proposed right to receive medical intervention which would cause death. Withholding or withdrawing treatment allows death to proceed naturally, with the underlying disease being the cause of death. Assisted suicide, on the other hand, requires action to cause death, independent from the disease process.

**The "Slippery Slope."** Physician-assisted suicide raises troubling and insurmountable "slippery slope" problems. Despite attempts by some, it is difficult to imagine adequate safeguards which could effectively guarantee that patients' decisions to request assisted suicide were unambivalent, informed, and free of coercion.

A policy allowing assisted suicide could also result in the victimization of poor and disenfranchised populations who may have greater financial burdens and social burdens which could be "relieved" by hastening death. As reported two years ago by the New York State Task Force on Life and the Law (composed of bioethicists, lawyers, clergy, and state health officials), "[a]ssisted suicide and euthanasia will be practiced through the prism of social inequality and prejudice that characterizes the delivery of services in all segments of society, including health care."

Recent studies documenting reasons for patient requests for physician-assisted suicide speak to our "slippery slope" concerns. Patients were rarely suffering intractable pain. Rather, they cited fears of losing control, being a burden, being dependent on others for personal care, and loss of dignity often associated with end-stage disease.

**The Case of the Netherlands.** While euthanasia and assisted suicide are not legal in the Netherlands, comprehensive guidelines have been established which allow physicians to avoid prosecution for the practice. Despite this environment, Dutch physicians have become uneasy about their active role in euthanasia, prompting the Royal Dutch Medical Association to revise its recommendations on the practice.

Findings of more than 1000 cases of involuntary euthanasia in the Netherlands should raise hackles in the United States, particularly given the stark societal differences between the two countries. Health coverage is universal in the Netherlands, the prevalence of long-term patient–physician relationships is greater, and social supports are more comprehensive. The inequities in the American health-care system, where the majority of patients who request physician-assisted suicide cite financial burden as a motive, make the practice of physician-assisted suicide all the more unjustifiable. No other country in the world, including the Netherlands, has legalized assisted suicide or euthanasia. This is one movement in which the United States should not be a "leader." . . .

## Conclusion

The movement for legally sanctioning physician-assisted suicide is a sign of society's failure to address the complex issues raised at the end of life. It is not a victory for personal rights. We are equipped with the tools to effectively manage end-of-life pain and to offer terminally ill patients dignity and to add value to their remaining time. As the voice of the medical profession, the AMA offers its capability to coordinate multidisciplinary discourse on end-of-life issues, for it is essential to coordinate medical educators, patients, advocacy organizations, allied health professionals and the counseling and pastoral professions to reach a comprehensive solution to these challenging issues. Our response should be a better informed medical profession and public, working together to preserve fundamental human values at the end of life.

# Terminal, but Not Hopeless

## Sandol Stoddard

Sandol Stoddard points out that the debate over assisted suicide has ignored "the care, comfort and dignity" offered to people approaching death by hospices. The debate rests on two false assumptions: that terminally ill people must expect to suffer in ways that make death a welcome alternative and that those who are old, frail, or ill are somehow failures and should depart from life. Hospices, Stoddard claims, provide the sort of care that keeps people from wanting to kill themselves. He ends by warning us that the steps between assisted suicide, homicide, and genocide are short ones.

It is amazing that in all the recent discussion of assisted suicide there has been hardly a reference to hospices as a way of caring for the terminally ill. The American hospice movement has been one of the outstanding expressions in recent years of inventiveness and compassion in combating suffering. At the same time, in hospitals and medical schools, hospice philosophy and expertise are helping to develop more humanely responsible attitudes in the general practice of medicine.

The modern hospice has arisen over the past 25 years to provide care, comfort and dignity to people approaching death. Most hospices in the U.S. today are small, independent nonprofit organizations, though many work in conjunction with local visiting nurse associations, hospitals and medical centers. The interdisciplinary hospice team consists of physicians, nurses, social workers, members of the clergy, therapists of various kinds, nutritionists and specially trained lay volunteers. Family and friends are also part of the team, and continue to receive support during bereavement.

Much of the current suicide controversy seems to be based on a pair of false assumptions. The first is that seriously ill people must expect agonies and humiliations from which death itself is the only merciful release. This is not so. Hospice patients are treated with respect. They are not attached to machines that prolong dying while destroying whatever quality of life remains.

A great deal more can be done today than was possible in the past to relieve the pain of conditions like terminal cancer. Nearly three decades of clinical

From *The New York Times,* 31 August 1991. Copyright © 1991 by The New York Times Company. Reprinted by permission.

experience in America and England have made it clear that skilled hospice teamwork can keep patients quite comfortable, physically and emotionally—often in their own homes—throughout the final stage of life. Studies have also shown that these patients do not become addicted to painkillers, nor do they come to require dangerously high doses. In fact, quite the opposite is true: In the supportive hospice setting, levels of pain medication are frequently reduced.

The second false assumption is perhaps less obvious, but more dangerous to society. Privately, too many of us believe that human perfection can be achieved—that if only we can find the correct program, with all the directions on the package, we can be thin, beautiful, bright, popular, healthy, rich and powerful forever. Such a shallow, simplistic view of life may seem innocent enough on the surface. But underneath it is the unspoken, often unconscious conviction that those who are very ill, very old or very frail have not done it right and should not be here among us. This attitude not only fouls our own lives, but presses the loaded gun, or the overdose, into the hands of sufferers.

Thousands of hospice workers in this country today are witness to the fact that people who are comfortable, secure and lovingly cared for *do not want* to commit suicide. They can also tell us that it is a great and often inspiring privilege to be with these individuals as they travel the last miles of the road that lies before us all. In the meantime we need to remember a lesson history has taught us; that it's but a short step that leads from assisted suicide to homicide, to genocide and the ultimate moral abyss.

# Section 4: Deciding for the Incompetent

## In the Matter of Karen Quinlan, an Alleged Incompetent

### Supreme Court of New Jersey

The 1976 decision of the New Jersey Supreme Court in the case of Karen Quinlan was significant in establishing that a legally based right of privacy permits a patient to decide to refuse medical treatment. The court also held that this right can be exercised by a parent or guardian when the patient herself is in no position to do so. Thus, in the opinion of the court, removal of life-sustaining equipment would not be a case of homicide (or any other kind of wrongful killing), even if the patient should die as a result.

The ruling in the *Quinlan* case has had an enormous impact on decisions about discontinuing extraordinary medical measures. However, the ruling has generally been construed rather narrowly so as to apply only to mentally incompetent patients who are brain dead, comatose, or in an irreversible coma.

**Background Note.** The decision of the court was issued on March 31, 1976. It was delivered by Chief Justice Hughes. The following abridgment omits references and case citations.

## Constitutional and Legal Issues

### I. The Free Exercise of Religion

Simply stated, the right to religious beliefs is absolute but conduct in pursuance thereof is not wholly immune from governmental restraint. So it is that, for the sake of life, courts sometimes (but not always) order blood transfusions for Jehovah's Witnesses (whose religious beliefs abhor such procedure), forbid exposure to death from handling virulent snakes or ingesting poison (interfering with deeply held religious sentiments in such regard), and protect the public health as in the case of compulsory vaccination (over the strongest of religious objections). . . . The Public interest is thus considered paramount, without essential dissolution of respect for religious beliefs.

We think, without further examples, that, ranged against the State's interest in the preservation of life, the impingement of religious belief, much less religious "neutrality" as here, does not reflect a constitutional question, in the circumstances at least of the case presently before the Court. Moreover, like the trial court,

From *In the Matter of Karen Quinlan, an Alleged Incompetent.* Supreme Court of New Jersey, 70 N.J.10, 355 A. 2d 647.

we do not recognize an independent parental right of religious freedom to support the relief requested.

### II. Cruel and Unusual Punishment

Similarly inapplicable to the case before us is the Constitution's Eighth Amendment protection against cruel and unusual punishment which, as held by the trial court, is not relevant to situations other than the imposition of penal sanctions. Historic in nature, it stemmed from punitive excesses in the infliction of criminal penalties. We find no precedent in law which would justify its extension to the correction of social injustice or hardship, such as, for instance, in the case of poverty. The latter often condemns the poor and deprived to horrendous living conditions which could certainly be described in the abstract as "cruel and unusual punishment." Yet the constitutional base of protection from "cruel and unusual punishment" is plainly irrelevant to such societal ills which must be remedied, if at all, under other concepts of constitutional and civil right.

So it is in the case of the unfortunate Karen Quinlan. Neither the State, nor the law, but the accident of fate and nature, has inflicted upon her conditions which though in essence cruel and most unusual, yet do not amount to "punishment" in any constitutional sense.

Neither the judgment of the court below, nor the medical decision which confronted it, nor the law and equity perceptions which impelled its action, nor the whole factual base upon which it was predicated, inflicted "cruel and unusual punishment" in the constitutional sense.

### III. The Right of Privacy

It is the issue of the constitutional right of privacy that has given us most concern, in the exceptional circumstances of this case. Here a loving parent, *qua* parent and raising the rights of his incompetent and profoundly damaged daughter, probably irreversibly doomed to no more than a biologically vegetative remnant of life, is before the court. He seeks authorization to abandon specialized technological procedures which can only maintain for a time a body having no potential for resumption or continuance of other than a "vegetative" existence.

We have no doubt, in these unhappy circumstances, that if Karen were herself miraculously lucid for an interval (not altering the existing prognosis of the condition to which she would soon return) and perceptive of her irreversible condition, she could effectively decide upon discontinuance of the life-support apparatus, even if it meant the prospect of natural death. To this extent we may distinguish [a case] which concerned a severely injured young woman (Delores Heston), whose life depended on surgery and blood transfusion; and who was in such extreme shock that she was unable to express an informed choice (although the Court apparently considered the case as if the patient's own religious decision to resist transfusion were at stake), but most importantly a patient apparently salvable to long life and vibrant health;—a situation not at all like the present case.

We have no hesitancy in deciding, in the instant diametrically opposite case, that no external compelling interest of the State could compel Karen to endure the unendurable, only to vegetate a few measurable months with no realistic possibility of returning to any semblance of cognitive or sapient life. We perceive no thread of logic distinguishing between such a choice on Karen's part and a similar choice which, under the evidence in this case, could be made by a competent patient terminally ill, riddled by cancer and suffering great pain; such a patient would not be resuscitated or put on a respirator in the example described by Dr. Korein, and *a fortiori* would not be kept *against his will* on a respirator.

Although the Constitution does not explicitly mention a right of privacy, Supreme Court decisions have recognized that a right of personal privacy exists and that certain areas of privacy are guaranteed under the Constitution. The Court has interdicted judicial intrusion into many aspects of personal decision, sometimes basing this restraint upon the conception of a limitation of judicial interest and responsibility, such as with regard to contraception and its relationship to family life and decision.

The Court in *Griswold* found the unwritten constitutional right of privacy to exist in the penumbra of specific guarantees of the Bill of Rights "formed by emanations from those guarantees that help give them life and substance." Presumably this right is broad enough to encompass a patient's decision to decline medical treatment under certain circumstances, in much the same way as it is broad enough to encompass a woman's decision to terminate pregnancy under certain conditions.

The claimed interests of the State in this case are essentially the preservation and sanctity of human life and defense to the right of the physician to administer medical treatment according to his best judgment. In this case the doctors say that removing Karen from the respirator will conflict with their professional judgment. The plaintiff answers that Karen's present treatment serves only a maintenance function; that the respirator cannot cure or improve her condition but at best can only prolong her inevitable slow deterioration and death; and that the interests of the patient, as seen by her surrogate, the guardian, must be evaluated by the court as predominant, even in the face of an option *contra* by the present attending physicians. Plaintiff's distinction is significant. The nature of Karen's care and the realistic chances of her recovery are quite unlike those of the patients discussed in many of the cases where treatments were ordered. In many of those cases the medical procedure required (usually a transfusion) constituted a minimal bodily invasion and the chances of recovery and return to functioning life were very good. We think that the State's interest *contra* weakens and the individual's right to privacy grows as the degree of bodily invasion increases and the prognosis dims. Ultimately there comes a point at which the individual's rights overcome the State interest. It is for that reason that we believe Karen's choice, if she were competent to make it, would be vindicated by the law. Her prognosis is extremely poor,—she will never resume cognitive life. And the bodily invasion is very great,—she requires 24-hour intensive nursing care, antibiotics, and the assistance of a respirator, a catheter and feeding tube.

Our affirmance of Karen's independent right of choice, however, would ordinarily be based upon her competency to assert it. The sad truth, however, is that she is grossly incompetent and we cannot discern her supposed choice based on the testimony of her previous conversation with friends, where such testimony is without sufficient probative weight. Nevertheless we have concluded that Karen's right of privacy may be asserted on her behalf by her guardian under the peculiar circumstances here present.

If a putative decision by Karen to permit this non-cognitive, vegetative existence to terminate by natural forces is regarded as a valuable incident of her right of privacy, as we believe it to be, then it should not be discarded solely on the basis that her condition prevents her conscious exercise of the choice. The only practical way to prevent destruction of the right is to permit the guardian and family of Karen to render their best judgment, subject to the qualifications hereinafter stated, as to whether she would exercise it in these circumstances. If their conclusion is in the affirmative this decision should be accepted by a society the overwhelming majority of whose members would, we think, in similar circumstances, exercise such a choice in the same way for themselves or for those closest to them. It is for this reason that we determine that Karen's right of privacy may be asserted in her behalf, in this respect, by her guardian and family under the particular circumstances presented by this record. [Sections IV (Medical Factors), V (Alleged Criminal Liability), and VI (Guardianship of the Person) omitted.]

### Declaratory Relief

We thus arrive at the formulation of the declaratory relief which we have concluded is appropriate to this

case. Some time has passed since Karen's physical and mental condition was described to the Court. At that time her continuing deterioration was plainly projected. Since the record has not been expanded we assume that she is now even more fragile and nearer to death than she was then. Since her present treating physicians may give reconsideration to her present posture in the light of this opinion, and since we are transferring to the plaintiff as guardian the choice of the attending physician and therefore other physicians may be in charge of the case who may take a different view from that of the present attending physicians, we herewith declare the following affirmative relief on behalf of the plaintiff. Upon the concurrence of the guardian and family of Karen, should the responsible attending physicians conclude that there is no reasonable possibility of Karen's ever emerging from her present comatose condition to a cognitive, sapient state and that the life-support apparatus now being administered to Karen should be discontinued, they shall consult with the hospital "Ethics Committee" or like body of the institution in which Karen is then hospitalized. If that consultative body agrees that there is no reasonable possibility of Karen's ever emerging from her present comatose condition to a cognitive, sapient state, the present life-support system may be withdrawn and said action shall be without any civil or criminal liability therefore on the part of any participant, whether guardian, physician, hospital or others. We herewith specifically so hold.

---

### Decision Scenario 1

Jeffry Box was eighty-one years old when he was brought to Doctor's Hospital. His right side was paralyzed, he spoke in a garbled way, and he had trouble understanding even the simplest matters. His only known relative was a sister four years younger, and she lived half a continent away. When a hospital social worker called to tell her about her brother's condition, she was quite uninterested. "I haven't seen him in fifteen years," she said. "I thought he might already be dead. Just do whatever you think best for him. I'm too old to worry about him."

Neurological tests and X-ray studies showed that Mr. Box was suffering from a brain hemorrhage caused by a ruptured blood vessel.

"Can you fix it?" asked Dr. Hollins. She was the resident responsible for Mr. Box's primary care. The man she addressed was Dr. Carl Oceana, the staff's only neurosurgeon.

"Sure," said Dr. Oceana. "I can repair the vessel and clean out the mess. But it won't do much good, you know."

"You mean he'll still be paralyzed?"

"And he'll still be mentally incoherent. After the operation he'll have to be put in a chronic-care place, because he won't be able to see to his own needs."

"And if you don't operate?" Dr. Hollins asked.

Dr. Oceana shrugged. "He'll be dead by tomorrow. Maybe sooner, depending on how long it takes for the pressure in his skull to build up."

"What would you do?"

"I know what I would want done to me if I were the patient," said Dr. Oceana. "I'd want people to keep their knives out of my head and let me die a nice, peaceful death."

"But we don't know what he would want," Dr. Hollins said. "He's never been our patient before, and the social worker hasn't been able to find any friends who might tell us what he'd want done."

"Let's just put ourselves in his place," said Dr. Oceana. "Let's do unto others what we would want done unto us."

"That means letting Mr. Box die."

"Exactly."

1. On what grounds might Gay-Williams object to Dr. Oceana's view?

2. Would Rachels's principles justify active euthanasia?

3. Would the natural law view make the operation discussed a moral mandate?

4. Does Dr. Oceana's reasoning conflict with the AMA position on physician-assisted suicide?

5. Could Justice Stevens's arguments against the majority opinion in *Cruzan* be used to support Oceana's position? (See Case Presentation: "The *Cruzan* Case.")

---

## Decision Scenario 2

On April 8, 1984, William Bartling was admitted to the Glendale Adventist Medical Center in Los Angeles. He was seventy years old and suffered from five ordinarily fatal diseases: emphysema, diffuse arteriosclerosis, coronary arteriosclerosis, an abdominal aneurysm, and inoperable lung cancer. During the performance of a biopsy to diagnose the lung cancer, Mr. Bartling's left lung collapsed. He was placed in the ICU, and a chest tube and mechanical respirator were used to assist his breathing.

Mr. Bartling complained about the pain the respirator caused him, and he repeatedly asked to have it removed. When his physician refused, he pulled out the chest tube himself. This happened so often that eventually Mr. Bartling's hands were tied to the bed to keep him from doing it. He had signed a living will in an attempt to avoid just such a situation.

Although after discussions with Richard Scott, Mr. Bartling's attorney, Mr. Bartling's physician and the hospital administration agreed to disconnect the respirator, the hospital's attorney refused to permit it. He argued that, since Mr. Bartling was not terminally ill, brain dead, or in a persistent vegetative state, the hospital might be open to legal action.

Mr. Scott took the case to Los Angeles Superior Court. He argued that Mr. Bartling was legally competent to make a decision about his welfare and that, although he did not want to die, he understood that

disconnecting the respirator might lead to his death. The hospital's attorney took the position that Mr. Bartling was ambivalent on the question of his death. His statements "I don't want to die" and "I don't want to live on the respirator" were taken as inconsistent and so as evidence of ambivalence. Removing the respirator, the attorney argued, would be tantamount to aiding suicide or even committing homicide.

The court refused either to allow the respirator to be removed or to order that Mr. Bartling's hands be freed. To do so, the court ruled, would be to take a positive step to end treatment, and the only precedents for doing so were in cases in which the patients were comatose, brain dead, or in a chronic vegetative state.

The case was then taken to the California Court of Appeal, which ruled: "If the right of a patient to self-determination as to his own medical treatment is to have any meaning at all, it must be paramount to the interests of the patient's hospitals and doctors. The right of a competent adult patient to refuse medical treatment is a constitutionally guaranteed right which must not be abridged."

The rule came too late for Mr. Bartling. He died twenty-three hours before the court heard his appeal.

1. Is there any merit to the hospital's position that to remove Mr. Bartling's respirator or to free his hands would be equivalent to assisting suicide? How might Brock's arguments apply to this position?

2. On the AMA view as represented by Bristow, would the request to remove the respirator be in effect a request for assistance in committing suicide?

3. How can the reasoning in the *Quinlan* case be extended to Mr. Bartling's case?

4. Can the arguments offered by Callahan be used to support the view that it would be morally wrong even to untie Mr. Bartling's hands?

5. Why might Lachs view Callahan as misunderstanding what is at issue in the case?

---

## Decision Scenario 3

When two plainclothes detectives arrived at Virginia Crawford's suburban apartment at 6:30 on a Sunday morning to arrest her for murder, she was not surprised to see them.

She cried when they insisted on putting her in handcuffs before transporting her to the jail in the county court building. Yet she had more or less expected to be arrested eventually. For almost a month, a police investigation had been conducted at Mercy Hospital, where Ms. Crawford worked as a nurse in the intensive-care unit (ICU). The entire hospital staff knew about the investigation, and Ms. Crawford herself had been questioned on three occasions by officers conducting the inquiry. At the time, her answers had seemed to be satisfactory to the police, and there was no hint that she was under suspicion. Still, she always believed that eventually they would catch up with her.

The investigation centered on the deaths of four elderly patients during the period from February 1979 to March 1980. All of the patients were in the ICU at the times of their deaths. Each had been diagnosed as suffering from a terminal illness, and the chart notation on each case indicated that they had all suffered irreversible brain damage and were totally without higher-brain functions.

The three women and one man were all unmarried and had no immediate family to take an interest in their welfare. All of them were being kept alive by respirators, and their deaths were caused directly by their respirators being turned off. In each instance of death, Ms. Crawford had been the person in charge of the ICU.

After securing the services of an attorney, Ms. Crawford was released on bail, and a time was set for her appearance in court. Through her attorney, Marvin Washington, she made a statement to the media.

"My client has asked me to announce that she fully and freely admits that she was the one who turned off the respirators of the four patients in question at Mercy Hospital. She acted alone and without the knowledge of any other individual. She is prepared to take full responsibility for her actions."

Mr. Washington went on to say that he would request a jury trial for his client. "I am sure," he said, "that no jury will convict Ms. Crawford of murder merely for turning off the life-support systems of people who were already dead."

When asked what he meant by that, Mr. Washington explained. "These patients were no longer people," he said. "Sometime during the course of the treatment, their brains simply stopped functioning in a way that we associate with human life."

Ms. Crawford was present during the reading of her statement, and after a whispered conversation with her attorney, she spoke once for herself. "I consider what I did an act of compassion and humanity," she said. "I consider it altogether moral, and I feel no guilt about it. I did for four people what they would have wanted done, if they had only been in a condition to know."

1. Does the natural law view offer grounds for removing life-support systems from people who are beyond a reasonable hope of recovery? If so, what are they?

2. Why would Gay-Williams's arguments lead us to condemn the actions of Ms. Crawford?

3. Can Brock's arguments favoring voluntary active euthanasia be extended to justify Ms. Crawford's actions?

4. Might Ms. Crawford be right about the patients being dead according to some concept of death?

5. Could a proponent of care ethics defend the actions taken by Ms. Crawford? Could a virtue ethicist?

## Decision Scenario 4

Consider the following four cases.

1. Harvey Shick of Tyler, Texas, on June 1, 1983, shot his wife in the head twice with a .22-caliber pistol. Marie Shick had suffered from severe arteriosclerosis since the late 1970s and suffered extreme pain in her lower legs. The couple had been happily married for forty-five years. Although Mr. Shick was charged with murder, the charges were dismissed by the state district court judge. "I found nothing would be gained in this case by further punishing this man," Judge Donald Carroll said. "This was an act motivated by love," Mr. Shick's attorney said. "He was distressed at the sickness, and additional treatment would have brought only a precarious and burdensome prolonging of life." Mrs. Shick's family supported the action.

2. On September 14, 1984, Thomas Engel, a registered nurse, removed the respirator from Joseph Dohr, a seventy-eight-year-old stroke patient at St. Michael Hospital in Milwaukee. Mr. Engel said Mr. Dohr's family asked that treatment be stopped. His physician said he had refused the request because he believed Mr. Dohr's death was imminent.

Mr. Engel described the bedside scene with Mr. Dohr's daughter that had led him to act: "She was standing there by her father's bed, stroking his arm and cheek and crying and talking to him. He was in a coma, in a steady decline. The only thing keeping him alive was the ventilator breathing for him. 'This isn't right,' she said. Then she looked across the bed at me, right in my eyes, and she said 'If I could do this thing, I would.' Now, what would you do?"

Mr. Engel was charged with practicing medicine without a license. He pleaded guilty and received a twenty-month suspended sentence. His nursing license was revoked for one year.

3. On August 8, 1985, seventy-nine-year-old Abel Montigny walked into the intensive-care unit of Worcester Memorial Hospital in Worcester, Massachusetts, and shot his wife in the head. He then shot himself. Both died from the injuries. Mrs. Leona Montigny, seventy-six, had been in the hospital for several months. She suffered from serious stomach and blood disorders and was recovering from surgery. Her ill-nesses were considered treatable, and she was in no immediate danger of death from them.

4. Roswell Gilbert, a seventy-five-year-old retired engineer, was convicted in Ft. Lauderdale, Florida, on May 9, 1985, for killing his incurably ill seventy-three-year-old wife. The couple had been married fifty-one years. Emily Gilbert had a debilitating bone disease and Alzheimer's disease; as a consequence, she suffered both severe pain and mental disorientation. According to a witness, on the day of the killing Mrs. Gilbert had said to her husband "I'm in pain. I want to die." Mr. Gilbert said later, "Who's that somebody but me? I guess I got cold as ice. I took the gun off the shelf, put a bullet in it and shot her. Then I felt her pulse. I thought, 'Oh, my God, I loused it up.' I put in another bullet and shot her again." Mr. Gilbert was sentenced to twenty-five years in prison with no chance of parole. As he left the courtroom, his daughter cried out, sobbing, "Daddy, Daddy, I don't want to see my daddy in jail—he'll die in jail."

Gilbert lost a chance for clemency when two of the members of the Florida Cabinet rejected the governor's recommendation that he be freed while the case was appealed. "The law does not give one person the right to kill another because of illness or age," said Gerald Lewis, one who voted against clemency. But in August 1990, in failing health, Gilbert was finally freed on probation. He died on September 4, 1994.

1. Compare the issues raised in these four cases. In what ways are the cases the same? In what ways are they different?

2. In which cases, if any, could the action taken be justified by Brock's arguments in favor of voluntary euthanasia?

3. Is it likely that the arguments presented by Rachels could be used to justify any of the actions taken?

4. Would Callahan condemn the actions in all these cases?

5. Would Stoddard's arguments be relevant in any of these circumstances?

## Decision Scenario 5

In 1993 the Netherlands passed a law permitting physicians to assist in the suicide of terminally ill patients. The law requires that the patient's decision to die be informed and irrevocable, and that there be no other solution acceptable to the patient that would improve the situation. (See "Physician-Assisted Suicide: The Dutch Experience" in the Social Context for details.)

1. Can the arguments offered by Brock be used to support a public policy of this kind?

2. Are the procedural safeguards adopted in the Netherlands adequate to prevent deliberate homicide? Are they adequate to prevent people who are temporarily depressed or irrational from killing themselves?

3. What dangers does such a policy pose, according to Callahan?

4. Does the right of an individual to refuse life-sustaining medical treatment imply that an individual has a right to terminate his life by active means? If so, does this mean society has a duty to provide assistance?

5. On what grounds does the AMA object to the Dutch policy? What does it offer as an alternative?

## Decision Scenario 6

In March 1991, Dr. Timothy Quill published an article in the *New England Journal of Medicine* in which he described how he had prescribed barbiturates for Patricia Diane Trumbull, a forty-five-year-old woman suffering from leukemia. In prescribing the medication, Dr. Quill also informed Ms. Trumbull, who had been his patient for a long time, how much of the drug would constitute a lethal dose.

Ms. Trumbull later killed herself by taking an overdose of the barbiturate, and Dr. Quill was investigated by a Rochester, New York, grand jury. Although it is illegal in New York to assist someone in committing suicide, the grand jury decided not to indict Dr. Quill on the charge.

Dr. Quill's actions were later reviewed by the three-member New York State Board for Professional Medical Conduct to consider whether he should be charged with professional misconduct. The board arrived at the unanimous decision that "no charge of misconduct was warranted."

The board, in its report, distinguished between Dr. Quill's actions and those of Dr. Jack Kevorkian. The board pointed to Dr. Quill's long-term involvement in caring for Ms. Trumbull and contrasted it with Dr. Kevorkian's lack of any prior involvement with those whom he assisted in killing themselves.

Moreoever, the board pointed out that Dr. Quill "did not directly participate in any taking of life" and this too made his actions different from those of Dr. Kevorkian. "One is legal and ethically appropriate, and the other, as reported, is not" the board concluded.

1. How might Stoddard view the situation that Ms. Trumbull was in? Would he consider suicide a legitimate option for her?

2. Would Callahan consider Dr. Quill's action to fall within the scope of a physician's legitimate role?

3. Why might Brock view Dr. Quill's action as justifiable?

4. Would Rachels consider this a case of active euthanasia?

5. Would the AMA view this as a case of assisted suicide?

# Part V

# Foundations of Bioethics: Ethical Theories, Moral Principles, and Medical Decisions

# Foundations of Bioethics: Ethical Theories, Moral Principles, and Medical Decisions

## Chapter Contents

"He's stopped breathing, Doctor," the nurse said. She sounded calm and not at all hysterical. By the time Dr. Sarah Cunningham had reached Mr. Sabatini's bedside, the nurse was already providing mouth-to-mouth resuscitation. But Mr. Sabatini still had the purplish blue color of cyanosis, caused by a lack of oxygen in his blood.

Dr. Cunningham knew that, if he was to survive, Mr. Sabatini would have to be given oxygen fast and placed on a respirator. But should she order this done?

Mr. Sabatini was an old man, almost ninety. So far as anyone knew, he was alone in the world and would hardly be missed when he died. His health was poor. He had congestive heart disease and was dying slowly and painfully from intestinal cancer.

Wouldn't it be a kindness to Mr. Sabatini to allow him this quick and painless death? Why condemn him to lingering on for a few extra hours or weeks?

The decision that Sarah Cunningham faces is a moral one. She has to decide whether she should take the steps that might prolong Mr. Sabatini's life or not take them and accept the consequence that he will almost surely die within minutes. She knows the medical procedures that can be employed, but she has to decide whether she should employ them.

This kind of case rivets our attention because of its immediacy and drama. But there are many other situations that arise in the context of medical practice and research that present problems that require moral decisions. Some are equal in drama to the problem facing Dr. Cunningham, while others are not so dramatic but are of at least equal seriousness. There are far too many to catalog, but consider this sample: Is it right for a woman to have an abortion for any reason? Should children with serious birth defects be put to death? Do people have a right to die? Does everyone have a right to medical care? Should physicians ever lie to their patients? Should people suffering from a genetic disease be allowed to have children? Can parents agree to allow their children to be used as experimental subjects?

Most of us have little tolerance for questions like these. They seem so cold and abstract. Our attitude changes, however, when we find ourselves in a position in which we are the decision makers. It changes, too, when we are in a position in which *we* must advise those who make the decisions. Or when we are on the receiving end of the decisions.

But whether we view the problems abstractly or concretely, we are inclined to ask the same question: Are there any rules, standards, or principles that we can use as guides when we are faced with moral decisions? If there are, then Dr. Cunningham need not be wholly unprepared to decide whether she should order steps taken to save Mr. Sabatini. Nor need we be unprepared to decide issues like those in the questions above.

The branch of philosophy concerned with principles that allow us to make decisions about what is right and wrong is called *ethics* or *moral philosophy. Medical ethics* is specifically concerned with moral principles and decisions in the context of medical practice, policy, and research. Moral difficulties connected with medicine are so complex and important that they require special attention. Medical ethics gives them this attention, but it remains a part of the discipline of ethics. Thus, if we are to answer our question as to whether there are any rules or principles to use when making moral decisions in the medical context, we must turn to general ethical theories and to a consideration of moral principles that have been proposed to hold in all contexts of human action.

In the first section, we will discuss five major ethical theories that have been put forward by philosophers. Each of these theories represents an attempt to supply basic principles we can rely on in making moral decisions. We'll consider these theories and examine how they might be applied to moral issues in the medical context. We will discuss the reasons that have been offered to persuade us to accept each theory, but we will also point out some of the difficulties each theory presents.

In the second section, we will examine and illustrate several moral principles that are of special relevance to medical research and practice. These principles are frequently appealed to in discussions of practical ethical problems and are sufficiently uncontroversial to be endorsed in a general way by any of the ethical theories mentioned in the first section. (Those who defend theories without principles do not, of course, endorse them as principles.)

In the third and last section, we will consider the basic concepts of three ethical theories that are usually offered as theories free of principles—virtue ethics, care ethics, and feminist ethics. We will consider how the theories might be used in making moral decisions, but we will also call attention to some of the criticisms urged against each of them.

The three sections are not dependent on one another, and it is possible to profit from one without reading the others. (The price for this independence is a small amount of repetition.) Nevertheless, reading all three sections is recommended. The Case Presentations and Social Contexts presented in the majority of this book can most easily be followed by someone who has at least some familiarity with basic moral theories.

Also, some points in discussions turn upon questions about the applicability of certain familiar moral principles or whether it is possible to operate without any principles. Being acquainted with those principles makes it easier to understand and evaluate such discussions.

# BASIC ETHICAL THEORIES

Ethical theories attempt to articulate and justify principles that can be employed as guides for making moral decisions and as standards for the evaluation of actions and policies. In effect, such theories define what it means to act morally, and in doing so they stipulate in a general fashion the duties or obligations that fall upon us.

Ethical theories also offer a means to explain and justify actions. If our actions are guided by a particular theory, then we can explain them by

demonstrating that the principles of the theory required us to act as we did. In such cases, the explanation also constitutes a justification. We justify our actions by showing that, according to the theory, we had an obligation to do what we did. (In some cases, we may justify our actions by showing that the theory *permitted* our actions—that is, didn't require them, but didn't rule them out as wrong.)

Advocates of a particular ethical theory present what they consider to be good reasons and relevant evidence in its support. Their general aim is to show that the theory is one that any reasonable individual would find persuasive or would endorse as correct. Accordingly, appeals to religion, faith, or nonnatural factors are not considered to be either necessary or legitimate to justify the theory. Rational persuasion alone is regarded as the basis of justification.

In this section, we will briefly consider four general ethical theories and one theory of justice that has an essential ethical component. In each case, we will begin by examining the basic principles of the theory and the grounds offered for its acceptance. We will then explore some of the possibilities of applying the theory to problems that arise within the medical context. Finally, we will mention some of the practical consequences and conceptual difficulties that raise questions about the theory's adequacy or correctness.

## Utilitarianism

The ethical theory known as utilitarianism was given its most influential formulation in the nineteenth century by the British philosophers Jeremy Bentham (1748–1832) and John Stuart Mill (1806–1873). Bentham and Mill did not produce identical theories, but both their versions have come to be spoken of as "classical utilitarianism." Subsequent elaborations and qualifications of utilitarianism are inevitably based on the formulations of Bentham and Mill, so their theories are worth careful examination.

## The Principle of Utility

The foundation of utilitarianism is a single apparently simple principle. Mill calls it the "principle of utility" and states it this way: *"Actions are right in proportion as they tend to promote happiness, wrong as they tend to produce the reverse of happiness."*

The principle focuses attention on the *consequences* of actions, rather than upon some feature of the actions themselves. The "utility" or "usefulness" of an action is determined by the extent to which it produces happiness. Thus, no action is *in itself* right or wrong. Nor is an action right or wrong by virtue of the actor's hopes, intentions, or past actions. Consequences alone are important. Breaking a promise, lying, causing pain, or even killing a person may, under certain circumstances, be the right action to take. Under other circumstances, the action might be wrong.

We need not think of the principle as applying to just one action that we are considering. It supplies the basis for a kind of cost–benefit analysis to employ in a situation in which several lines of action are possible. Using the principle, we are supposed to consider the possible results of each action. Then we are to choose the one that produces the most benefit (happiness) at the least cost (unhappiness). The action we take may produce some unhappiness, but it is a balance of happiness over unhappiness that the principle tells us to seek.

Suppose, for example, that a woman in a large hospital is near death: she is in a coma, an EEG shows only minimal brain function, and a respirator is required to keep her breathing. Another patient has just been brought to the hospital from the scene of an automobile accident. His kidneys have been severely damaged, and he is in need of an immediate transplant. There is a good tissue match with the woman's kidneys. Is it right to hasten her death by removing a kidney?

The principle of utility would probably consider the removal justified. The woman is virtually dead, while the man has a good chance of surviving. It is true that the woman's life is threatened even more by the surgery. It may in fact kill her. But, on balance, the kidney transplant seems likely to produce more happiness than unhappiness. In fact, it seems better than the alternative of doing nothing. For in that case, both patients are likely to die.

The principle of utility is also called the "greatest happiness principle" by Bentham and Mill. The reason for this name is clear when the principle is stated in this way: *Those actions are right that produce the greatest happiness for the greatest number of people.* This alternative formulation makes it obvious that in deciding how to act it is not just my happiness or the happiness of a particular person or group that must be considered. According to utilitarianism, every person is to count just as much as any other person. That is, when we are considering how we should act, everyone's interest must be considered. The right action, then, will be the one that produces the most happiness for the largest number of people.

Mill is particularly anxious that utilitarianism not be construed as no more than a sophisticated justification for crude self-interest. He stresses that in making a moral decision we must look at the situation in an objective way. We must, he says, be a "benevolent spectator" and then act in a way that will bring about the best results for all concerned. This view is summarized in a famous passage:

> The happiness which forms the utilitarian standard of what is right in conduct, is not the agent's own happiness, but that of all concerned. As between his own happiness and that of others, utilitarianism requires him to be as strictly impartial as a disinterested and benevolent spectator. In the golden rule of Jesus of Nazareth, we read the complete spirit of the ethics of utility. To do as you would be done by, and to love your neighbor as yourself, constitute the ideal perfection of utilitarian morality.

The key concept in both formulations of the principle of utility is "happiness." Bentham simply identifies happiness with pleasure—pleasure of any kind. The aim of ethics, then, is to increase the amount of pleasure in the world to the greatest possible extent. To facilitate this, Bentham recommends the use of a "calculus of pleasure and pain," in which characteristics of pleasure such as intensity, duration, and number of people affected are measured and assigned numerical values. To determine which of several possible actions is the right one, we need only determine which one receives the highest numerical score. Unfortunately, Bentham does not tell us what units to use nor how to make the measurements.

Mill also identifies happiness with pleasure, but he differs from Bentham in a major respect. Unlike Bentham, he insists that some pleasures are "higher" than others. Thus, pleasures of the intellect are superior to, say, purely sensual pleasures. This difference in the concept of pleasure can become significant in a medical context. For example, in the choice of using limited resources to save the life of a lathe operator or of an art historian, Mill's view might assign more value to the life of the art historian. That person, Mill might say, is capable of "higher pleasures" than the lathe operator. (Of course, other factors would be relevant here for Mill.)

Both Mill and Bentham regard happiness as an intrinsic good. That is, it is something good in itself or for its own sake. Actions, by contrast, are good only to the extent to which they tend to promote happiness. Therefore, they are only instrumentally good. Since utilitarianism determines the rightness of actions in terms of their tendency to promote the greatest happiness for the greatest number, it is considered to be a *teleological* ethical theory. (*Teleological* comes from the Greek word *telos*, which means "end" or "goal.") A teleological ethical theory judges the rightness of an action in terms of an external goal or purpose—"general happiness" or utility for utilitarianism. However, utilitarianism is also a *consequentialist* theory, for the outcomes or consequences of actions are the only considerations relevant to determining their moral rightness. Not all teleological theories are consequentialist.

Some more recent formulations of utilitarianism have rejected the notion that happiness, no matter how defined, is the sole intrinsic good that actions or policies must promote. Critics of the classical view have argued that the list of things we recognize as valuable in themselves should be increased to include ones such as knowledge, beauty, love, friendship, liberty, and

health. According to this *pluralistic* view, in applying the principle of utility we must consider the entire range of intrinsic goods that an action is likely to promote. Thus, the right action is the one that can be expected to produce the greatest sum of intrinsic goods. In most of the following discussion, we will speak of the greatest happiness or benefit, but it is easy enough to see how the same points can be made from a pluralistic perspective.

## Act and Rule Utilitarianism

All utilitarians accept the principle of utility as the standard for determining the rightness of actions. But they divide into two groups over the matter of the application of the principle.

*Act utilitarianism* holds that the principle should be applied to particular acts in particular circumstances. *Rule utilitarianism* maintains that the principle should be used to test rules, which can in turn be used to decide the rightness of particular acts. Let's consider each of these views and see how it works in practice.

Act utilitarianism holds that an act is right if, and only if, no other act could have been performed that would produce a higher utility. Suppose a child is born with severe impairments. The child has an open spine, severe brain damage, and dysfunctional kidneys. What should be done? (We will leave open the question of who should decide.)

The act utilitarian holds that we must attempt to determine the consequences of the various actions that are open to us. We should consider, for example, these possibilities: (1) Give the child only the ordinary treatment that would be given to a normal child; (2) give the child special treatment for its problems; (3) give the child no treatment—allow it to die; (4) put the child to death in a painless way.

According to act utilitarianism, we must explore the potential results of each possibility. We must realize, for example, that when such a child is given only ordinary treatment it will be worse off, if it survives, than if it had been given special treatment. Also, a child left alone and allowed to die is likely to suffer more pain than one killed by a lethal injection. Furthermore, a child treated aggressively will have to undergo numerous surgical procedures of limited effectiveness. We must also consider the family of the child and judge the emotional and financial effects that each of the possible actions will have on them. Then, too, we must take into account such matters as the "quality of life" of a child with severe brain damage and multiple defects, the effect on physicians and nurses in killing the child or allowing it to die, and the financial costs to society in providing long-term care.

After these considerations, we should then choose the action that has the greatest utility. We should act in the way that will produce the most benefit for all concerned. Which of the possibilities we select will depend on the precise features of the situation: how impaired the child is, how good its chances are for living an acceptable life, the character and financial status of the family, and so on. The great strength of act utilitarianism is that it invites us to deal with each case as unique. When the circumstances of another case are different, we might, without being inconsistent, choose another of the possible actions.

Act utilitarianism shows a sensitivity to specific cases, but it is not free from difficulties. Some philosophers have pointed out that there is no way that we can be sure that we have made the right choice of actions. We are sure to be ignorant of much relevant information. Besides, we can't know with much certainty what the results of our actions will really be. There is no way to be sure, for example, that even a severely impaired infant will not recover enough to live a better life than we predict.

The act utilitarian can reply that acting morally doesn't mean being omniscient. We need to make a reasonable effort to get relevant information, and we can usually predict the probable consequences of our actions. Acting morally doesn't require any more than this.

Another objection to act utilitarianism is more serious. According to the doctrine, we are obligated to keep a promise only if keeping it will produce more utility than some other action. If

some other action will produce the same utility, then keeping the promise is permissible but not obligatory. Suppose a surgeon promises a patient that only he will perform an operation, then allows a well-qualified resident to perform part of it. Suppose all goes well and the patient never discovers that the promise was not kept. The outcome for the patient is exactly the same as if the surgeon had kept the promise. From the point of view of act utilitarianism, there is nothing wrong with the surgeon's failure to keep it. Yet critics charge that there is something wrong, that in making the promise the surgeon took on an obligation. Act utilitarianism is unable to account for obligations engendered by such actions as promising and pledging, critics say, for such actions involve something other than consequences.

A third objection to act utilitarianism arises in situations in which virtually everyone must follow the same rules in order to achieve a high level of utility, but even greater utility can be achieved if a few people do not follow the rules. Consider the relationship between physicians and the Medicaid program. The program pays physicians for services provided to those poor enough to qualify for the program. The program would collapse if nearly all physicians were not honest in billing Medicaid for their services. Not only would many poor people suffer, but physicians themselves would lose a source of income.

Suppose a particular physician believes that the requirements to qualify for Medicaid are too restrictive and that many who urgently need medical care cannot afford it. As an act utilitarian, she reasons that it is right for her to get money to open a free clinic under the program. She intends to bill for services she does not provide, then use that money to treat those not covered by Medicaid. Her claims will be small compared to the entire Medicaid budget, so it is unlikely that anyone who qualifies for Medicaid will go without treatment. Since she will tell no one what she is doing, others are not likely to be influenced by her example and make false claims for similar or less worthy purposes. The money she is paid will bring substantial benefit to those in need of health care. Thus, she concludes, by violating the rules of the program, her actions will produce greater utility than would be produced by following the rules.

The physician's action would be morally right, according to act utilitarians. Yet, critics say, we expect an action that is morally right to be one that is right for everyone in similar circumstances. If every physician in the Medicaid program acted in this way, however, the program would be destroyed and thus produce no utility at all. Furthermore, according to critics, the physician's action produces unfairness. Although it is true that the patients she treats at her free clinic gain a benefit they would not otherwise have, similar patients must go without treatment. The Medicaid policy, whatever its flaws, is at least prima facie fair in providing benefits to all who meet its requirements. Once again, then, according to critics, more seems to be involved in judging the moral worth of an action than can be accounted for by act utilitarianism.

In connection with such objections, some critics have gone so far as to claim that it is impossible to see how a society in which everyone was an act utilitarian could function. We could not count on promises being kept nor take for granted that people were telling us the truth. Social policies would be no more than general guides to action, and we could never be sure that people would regard themselves as obligated to adhere to their provisions. Decisions made by individuals about each individual action would not obviously lead to the promotion of the highest degree of utility. Indeed, some critics say, such a society might collapse, for communication among individuals would be difficult, if not impossible, social cohesion would be weakened, and general policies and regulations would have very uncertain effects.

The critics are not necessarily right, of course, and defenders of act utilitarianism have made substantial efforts to answer the criticisms we have presented. Some have denied that the theory has those implications and argued that some of our generally accepted moral perceptions should be changed. In connection with this last point, Carl Wellman provides an insight into the sort of conflict between moral feelings and rational judgment that the acceptance of act utilitarianism can produce. Concerning euthanasia, Wellman writes:

> Try as I may, I honestly cannot discover great hidden disutilities in the act of killing an elderly person suffering greatly from an incurable illness, provided that certain safeguards like a written medical opinion by at least two doctors and a request by the patient are preserved. In this case I cannot find any way to reconcile my theory with my moral judgment. What I do in this case is to hold fast to act-utilitarianism and distrust my moral sense. I claim that my condemnation of such acts is an irrational disapproval, a condemnation that will change upon further reasoning about the act. . . . That I feel wrongness is clear, but I cannot state to myself any rational justification for my feeling. Hence, I discount this particular judgment as irrational.

*Rule utilitarianism* maintains that an action is right if it conforms to a rule of conduct that has been validated by the principle of utility as one that will produce at least as much utility as any other rule applicable to the situation. A rule like "Provide only ordinary care for severely brain-damaged newborns with multiple impairments," if it were established, would allow us to decide about the course of action to follow in situations like that of our earlier example.

The rule utilitarian is not concerned with assessing the utility of individual actions but of particular rules. In practice, then, we do not have to go through the calculations involved in determining in each case whether a specific action will increase utility. All that we have to establish is that following a certain rule will in general result in a situation in which utility is maximized. Once rules are established, they can be relied on to determine whether a particular action is right.

The basic idea behind rule utilitarianism is that having a set of rules that are always observed produces the greatest social utility. Having everyone follow the same rule in each case of the same kind yields more utility for everybody in the long run. An act utilitarian can agree that having rules may produce more social utility than not having them. But the act utilitarian insists that the rules be regarded as no more than general guides to action, as "rules of thumb." Thus, for act utilitarianism it is perfectly legitimate to violate a rule if doing so will maximize utility in that instance. By contrast, the rule utilitarian holds that rules must generally be followed, even though following them may produce less net utility (more unhappiness than happiness) in a particular case.

Rule utilitarianism can endorse rules like "Keep your promises." Thus, unlike act utilitarianism, it can account for the general sense that in making promises we are placing ourselves under an obligation that cannot be set aside for the sake of increasing utility. If "Keep your promises" is accepted as a rule, then the surgeon who fails to perform all of an operation himself, when he has promised his patient he would do so, has not done the right thing, even if the patient never learns the truth.

Rule utilitarians recognize that circumstances can arise in which it would be disastrous to follow a general rule, even when it is true that *in general* greater happiness would result from following the rule all the time. Clearly, we should not keep a promise to meet someone for lunch when we have to choose between keeping the promise and rushing a heart-attack victim to the hospital. It is consistent with the theory to formulate rules that include appropriate escape clauses. For example, "Keep your promises, unless breaking them is required to save a life" and "Keep your promises, unless keeping them would lead to a disastrous result unforeseen at the time the promise was made" are rules that a rule utilitarian might regard as more likely to lead to greater utility than "Always keep your promises no matter what the consequences may be." What a rule utilitarian cannot endorse is a rule like "Keep your promises, except when breaking a promise would produce more utility." This would in effect transform the rule utilitarian into an act utilitarian.

Of course, rule utilitarians are not committed to endorsing general rules only. It is compatible with the view to offer quite specific rules, and in fact there is no constraint on just how specific a rule may be. A rule utilitarian might, for exam-

ple, establish a rule like "If an infant is born with an open spine, severe brain damage, and dysfunctional kidneys, then the infant should receive no life-sustaining treatment."

The possibility of formulating a large number of rules and establishing them separately opens this basic version of rule utilitarianism to two objections. First, some rules are likely to conflict when they are applicable to the same case, and basic rule utilitarianism offers no way to resolve such conflicts. What should a physician do when faced both with a rule like that above and with another that directs him to "Provide life-sustaining care to all who require it"? Rules which, when considered individually, pass the test of promoting utility, may when taken together express contradictory demands. A further objection to basic rule utilitarianism is that establishing rules to cover many different circumstances and situations results in such an abundance of rules that employing the rules to make moral decisions becomes virtually impossible in practice.

Partly because of such difficulties, rule utilitarians have taken the approach of establishing the utility of a set of rules or an entire moral code. The set can include rules for resolving possible conflicts, and an effort can be made to keep the rules few and simple to minimize the practical difficulty of employing them. Once again, as with individual actions or rules, the principle of utility is employed to determine which set of rules, out of the various sets considered, ought to be accepted.

In this more sophisticated form, rule utilitarianism can be characterized as the theory that an action is right when it conforms to a set of rules that has been determined to produce at least as much overall utility as any other set. It is possible to accept the present forms of social and economic institutions, such as private property and a market economy, as constraints, then argue for the set of rules that will yield the most utility under those conditions. However, it is also possible to be more radical and argue for a particular set of rules that would lead to the greatest possible utility, quite apart from present social forms.

Indeed, such a set of rules might be proposed and defended in an effort to bring about changes in present society that are needed to increase the overall level of utility. Utilitarianism, whether act or rule, is not restricted to being a theory about individual moral obligation. It is also a social and political theory.

We have already seen that rule utilitarianism, unlike act utilitarianism, makes possible the sort of obligation we associate with making a promise. But how might rule utilitarianism deal with the case of the physician who files false Medicaid claims to raise money to operate a free clinic? An obvious answer, although certainly not the only one possible, is that any set of rules likely to be adopted by a rule utilitarian will contain at least one rule making fraud morally wrong. Without a rule forbidding fraud, no social program that requires the cooperation of its participants is likely to achieve its aim. Such a rule protects the program from miscalculations of utility that individuals may make for self-serving reasons, keeps the program focused on its goal, and prevents it from becoming fragmented. Even if some few individuals commit fraud, the rule against it is crucial in discouraging as many as possible. Otherwise, as we pointed out earlier, such a program would collapse. By requiring that the program operate as it was designed, rule utilitarianism also preserves prima facie fairness, because only those who qualify receive benefits.

The most telling objection to rule utilitarianism, according to some philosophers, is that it is inconsistent. The justification of a set of moral rules is that the rules maximize utility. If rules are to maximize utility, then it seems obvious that they may require that an act produce more utility than any other possible act in a particular situation. Otherwise, the maximum amount of utility would not result. But if the rules satisfy this demand, then they will justify exactly the same actions as act utilitarianism. Thus, the rules will consider it right to break promises, make fraudulent claims, and so on. When rule utilitarianism moves to block these possibilities by requiring that rules produce only the most utility overall, it becomes inconsistent: the set of rules is said to maximize utility, but the rules will require actions that do not maximize utility. Thus, rule utilitarianism seems both to accept and reject the principle of utility as the ultimate moral standard.

## Preference Utilitarianism

Some philosophers have called into question the idea of using happiness or any other intrinsic value (knowledge or health, for example) as a criterion of the rightness of an action. The notion of an intrinsic value, they have argued, is too imprecise to be used as a practical guide. Furthermore, it is not at all clear that people share the same values, and even if they do, they are not committed to them to the same degree. Someone may value knowledge more than health, whereas someone else may value physical pleasure over knowledge or health. As a result, there can be no clear-cut procedure for determining what action is likely to produce the best outcome for an individual or group.

The attempt to develop explicit techniques (such as those of decision theory) to help resolve questions about choosing the best action or policy has led some thinkers to replace considerations of intrinsic value with considerations of actual preferences. What someone wants, desires, or prefers can be determined, in principle, in an objective way by consulting the person directly. In addition, people are often able to do more than merely express a preference. Sometimes they can rank their preferences from that which is "most desired" to that which is "least desired."

Such a ranking is of special importance in situations involving risk, for people can be asked to decide how much risk they are willing to take to attempt to realize a given preference. A young woman with a hip injury who is otherwise in good health may be willing to accept the risk of surgery to increase her chances of being restored to many years of active life. By contrast, an elderly woman in frail health may prefer to avoid surgery and accept the limitations that the injury imposes on her physical activities. For the elderly woman, not only are the risks of surgery greater because of her poor health, but even if the surgery is successful, she also will have fewer years to benefit from it.

By contrast, the older woman may place such a premium on physical activity that she is willing to take the risk of surgery to improve her chances of securing even a few more years of it. Only she can say what is important to her and how willing she is to take the risk required to secure it.

These considerations about personal preferences can also be raised about social preferences. Statistical information about what people desire and what they are willing to forgo to see their desires satisfied becomes relevant to institutional and legislative deliberations about what policies to adopt. For example, a crucial question facing our own society is whether we are willing to provide everyone with at least a basic minimum of health care, even if this requires increasing taxes or reducing our support for other social goods, such as education and defense.

Employing the satisfaction of preferences as the criterion of the rightness of an action or policy makes it possible to measure some of the relevant factors in some situations. The life expectancy of infants with particular impairments at birth can be estimated by statistics; a given surgical procedure has a certain success rate and a certain mortality rate. Similarly, a particular social policy has a certain financial cost, and if implemented, the policy is likely to mean the loss of other possible benefits and opportunities.

Ideally, information of this kind should allow a rational decision maker to calculate the best course of action for an individual or group. The best action will be the one that best combines the satisfaction of preferences with other conditions (financial costs and risks, for example) that are at least minimally acceptable. To use the jargon of the theorists, the best action is the one that maximizes the utilities of the person or group.

A utilitarianism that employs preferences has the advantage of suggesting more explicit methods of analysis and rules for decision making than the classical formulation. It also has the

potential for being more sensitive to the expressed desires of individuals. However, preference utilitarianism is not free from specific difficulties.

Most prominent is the problem posed by preferences that we would generally regard as unacceptable. What are we to say about those who prefer mass murder, child abuse, or torturing animals? Obviously, subjective preferences cannot be treated equally, and we must have a way to distinguish acceptable from unacceptable ones. Whether this can be done by relying on the principle of utility alone is doubtful. In the view of some commentators, some other moral principle (or principles) is needed. (See the discussion of justice immediately following.)

### Difficulties with Utilitarianism

Classical utilitarianism is open to a variety of objections. We will concentrate on only one, however, for it seems to reveal a fatal flaw in the structure of the entire theory. This most serious of all objections is that the principle of utility appears to justify the imposition of great suffering on a few people for the benefit of many people.

Certain kinds of human experimentation forcefully illustrate this possibility. Suppose an investigator is concerned with acquiring a better understanding of brain functions. She could learn a great deal by systematically destroying the brain of one person and carefully noting the results. Such a study would offer many more opportunities for increasing our knowledge of the brain than those studies that use as subjects people who have damage to their brains in accidental ways. We may suppose that the experimenter chooses as her subject a person without education or training, without family or friends, who cannot be regarded as making much of a contribution to society. The subject will die from the experiment, but it is not unreasonable to suppose that the knowledge of the human brain gained from the experiment will improve the lives of countless numbers of people.

The principle of utility seems to make such experiments legitimate because the outcome is a greater amount of good than harm. One or a few have suffered immensely, but the many have profited to an extent that far outweighs that suffering.

Clearly what is missing from utilitarianism is the concept of *justice.* It cannot be right to increase the general happiness at the expense of one person or group. There must be some way of distributing happiness and unhappiness and avoiding exploitation.

Mill was aware that utilitarianism needs a principle of justice, but most contemporary philosophers do not believe that such a principle can be derived from the principle of utility. In their opinion, utilitarianism as an ethical theory suffers severely from this defect. Yet some philosophers, while acknowledging the defect, have still held that utilitarianism is the best substantive moral theory available.

## Kant's Ethics

For utilitarianism, the rightness of an action depends upon its consequences. In stark contrast to this view is the ethical theory formulated by the German philosopher Immanuel Kant (1724–1804) in his book *Fundamental Principles of the Metaphysics of Morals.* For Kant, the consequences of an action are morally irrelevant. Rather, an action is right when it is in accordance with a rule that satisfies a principle he calls the "categorical imperative." Since this is the basic principle of Kant's ethics, we can begin our discussion with it.

### The Categorical Imperative

If you decide to have an abortion and go through with it, it is possible to view your action as involving a rule. You can be thought of as endorsing a rule to the effect "Whenever I am in circumstances like these, then I will have an abortion." Kant calls such a rule a "maxim." In his view, all reasoned and considered actions can be regarded as involving maxims.

The maxims in such cases are personal or subjective, but they can be thought of as being candidates for moral rules. If they pass the test imposed by the categorical imperative, then we can say that such actions are right. Furthermore, in passing the test, the maxims cease to be merely personal and subjective. They gain the status of objective rules of morality that hold for everyone.

Kant formulates the categorical imperative in this way: Act only on that maxim which you can will to be a universal law. Kant calls the principle "categorical" to distinguish it from "hypothetical" imperatives. These tell us what to do if we want to bring about certain consequences—such as happiness. A categorical imperative prescribes what we ought to do without reference to any consequences. The principle is an "imperative" because it is a command.

The test imposed on maxims by the categorical imperative is one of generalization or "universalizability." The central idea of the test is that a moral maxim is one that can be generalized to apply to all cases of the same kind. That is, you must be willing to see your rule adopted as a maxim by everyone who is in a situation similar to yours. You must be willing to see your maxim universalized, even though it may turn out on some other occasion to work to your disadvantage.

For a maxim to satisfy the categorical imperative, it is not necessary that we be agreeable in some psychological sense to seeing it made into a universal law. Rather, the test is one that requires us to avoid inconsistency or conflict in what we will as a universal rule.

Suppose, for example, that I am a physician and I tell a patient that he has a serious illness, although I know that he doesn't. This may be to my immediate advantage, for the treatment and the supposed cure will increase my income and reputation. The maxim of my action might be phrased as, "Whenever I have a healthy patient, I will lie to him and say that he has an illness."

Now suppose that I try to generalize my maxim. In doing so, I will discover that I am willing the existence of a practice that has contradictory properties. If "Whenever any physician has a healthy patient, she will lie to him and say he has an illness" is made a universal law, then every patient will be told that he has an illness. Trust in the diagnostic pronouncements of physicians will be destroyed, while my scheme depends on my patients' trusting me and accepting the truth of my lying diagnosis.

It is as if I were saying, "Let there be a rule of truth telling such that people can assume that others are telling them the truth, but let there also be a rule that physicians may lie to their patients when it is in the interest of the physician to do so." In willing both rules, I am willing something contradictory. Thus, I can will my action in a particular case, but I can't will that my action be universal without generating a logical conflict.

Kant claims that such considerations show that it is always wrong to lie. Lying produces a contradiction in what we will. On one hand, we will that people believe what we say—that they accept our assurances and promises. On the other hand, we will that people be free to give false assurances and make false promises. Lying thus produces a self-defeating situation, for, when the maxim involved is generalized, the very framework required for lying collapses.

Similarly, consider the egoist who seeks only his self-interest and so makes "Never show love or compassion for others" the maxim of his actions. When universalized, this maxim results in the same kind of self-defeating situation that lying does. Since the egoist will sometimes find himself in need of love and compassion, if he wills the maxim of his action to be a universal law, then he will be depriving himself of something that is in his self-interest. Thus, in willing the abolition of love and compassion out of self-interest, he creates a logical contradiction in what he wills.

## Another Formulation

According to Kant, there is only one categorical imperative, but it can be stated in three different ways. Each is intended to reveal a different aspect of the principle. The second formulation, the only other we will consider, can be stated in this way: Always act so as to treat humanity, either yourself or others, always as an end and never as only a means.

This version illustrates Kant's notion that every rational creature has a worth in itself. This worth is not conferred by being born into a society with a certain political structure, nor even by belonging to a certain biological species. The worth is inherent in the sheer possession of rationality. Rational creatures possess what Kant calls an "autonomous, self-legislating will." That is, they are able to consider the consequences of their actions, make rules for themselves, and direct their actions by those self-imposed rules. Thus, rationality confers upon everyone an intrinsic worth and dignity.

This formulation of the categorical imperative perhaps rules out some of the standards that are sometimes used to determine who is selected to receive certain medical resources (such as kidney machines) when the demand is greater than the supply. Standards that make a person's education, accomplishments, or social position relevant seem contrary to this version of the categorical imperative. They violate the basic notion that each person has an inherent worth equal to that of any other person. Unlike dogs or horses, people cannot be judged on "show points."

For Kant, all of morality has its ultimate source in rationality. The categorical imperative, in any formulation, is an expression of rationality, and it is the principle that would be followed in practice by any purely rational being. Moral rules are not mere arbitrary conventions or subjective standards. They are objective truths that have their source in the rational nature of human beings.

## Duty

Utilitarianism identifies the good with happiness or pleasure and makes the production of happiness the supreme principle of morality. But, for Kant, happiness is at best a conditional or qualified good. In his view, there is only one thing that can be said to be good in itself: a good will.

Will is what directs our actions and guides our conduct. But what makes a will a "good will"? Kant's answer is that a will becomes good when it acts purely for the sake of duty.

We act for the sake of duty (or from duty) when we act on maxims that satisfy the categorical imperative. This means, then, that it is the motive force behind our actions—the character of our will—that determines their moral character. Morality does not rest on results—such as the production of happiness—but neither does it rest on our feelings, impulses, or inclinations. An action is right, for Kant, only when it is done for the sake of duty.

Suppose that I decide to donate one of my kidneys for transplanting. If my hope is to gain approval or praise or even if I am moved by pity and a genuine wish to reduce suffering, and this is the only consideration behind my action, then, although I have done the morally right thing, my action has no inner moral worth. By contrast, I may have acted *in accordance with duty* (done the same thing as duty would have required), but I did not act *from duty.*

This view of duty and its connection with morality captures attitudes we frequently express. Consider a nurse who gives special care to a severely ill patient. Suppose you learned that the nurse was providing such extraordinary care only because he hoped that the patient or her family would reward him with a special bonus. Knowing this, you would be unlikely to say that the nurse was acting in a morally outstanding way. We might even think the nurse was being greedy or cynical, and we would say that he was doing the right thing for the wrong reasons.

Kant distinguishes between two types of duties: perfect and imperfect. (The distinction corresponds to the two ways in which maxims can be self-defeating when tested by the categorical imperative.) A *perfect duty* is one we must always observe, but an *imperfect duty* is one that we must observe only on some occasions. I have a perfect duty not to injure another person, but I have only an imperfect duty to show love and compassion. I must sometimes show it, but when I show it and which people I select to receive it are entirely up to me.

My duties determine what others can legitimately claim from me as a right. Some rights can be claimed as perfect rights, while others cannot. Everyone can demand of me that I do him or her no injury. But no one can tell me that I must make him or her the recipient of my love and compassion. In deciding how to discharge my imperfect duties, I am free to follow my emotions and inclinations.

For utilitarianism, an action is right when it produces something that is intrinsically valuable (happiness). Because actions are judged by their contributions to achieving a goal, utilitarianism is a teleological theory. By contrast, Kant's ethics holds that an action has features in itself that make it right or in accordance with duty. These features are distinct from the action's consequences. Such a theory is called *deontological,* a term derived from the Greek word for "duty" or "obligation."

### Kant's Ethics in the Medical Context

Four features of Kant's ethics are of particular importance in dealing with issues in medical treatment and research:

1.  No matter what the consequences may be, it is always wrong to lie.

2.  We must always treat people (including ourselves) as ends and not as means only.

3.  An action is right when it satisfies the categorical imperative.

4.  Perfect and imperfect duties give a basis for claims that certain rights should be recognized.

We can present only two brief examples of how these features can be instrumental in resolving ethical issues, but these are suggestive of other possibilities.

Our first application of Kant's ethics bears on medical research. The task of medical investigators would be easier if they did not have to tell patients that they were going to be made part of a research program. Patients would then become subjects without even knowing it, and more often than not their risk would be negligible. Even though no overt lying would be involved, on Kantian principles this procedure would be wrong. It would require treating people as a means only and not as an end.

Likewise, it would never be right for an experimenter to deceive a potential experimental subject. If an experimenter told a patient, "We would like to use this new drug on you because it might help you" and this were not really so, the experimenter would be performing a wrong action. Lying is always wrong.

Nor could the experimenter justify this deception by telling herself that the research is of such importance that it is legitimate to lie to the patient. On Kant's principles, good results never make an action morally right. Thus, a patient must give voluntary and informed consent to become a subject of medical experimentation. Otherwise, he or she is being deprived of autonomy and treated as a means only.

We may volunteer because we expect the research to bring direct benefits to us. But we may also volunteer even though no direct personal benefits can be expected. We may see participation in the research as an occasion for fulfilling an imperfect duty to improve human welfare.

But, just as Kant's principles place restrictions on the researcher, they place limits on us as potential subjects. We have a duty to treat ourselves as ends and act so as to preserve our dignity and worth as humans. Therefore, it would not be right for us to volunteer for an experiment that threatened our lives or threatened to destroy our ability to function as autonomous rational beings without first satisfying ourselves that the experiment was legitimate and necessary.

Our second application of Kant's ethics in a medical context bears on the relationship between people as patients and those who accept responsibility for caring for them. A physician, for example, has only an imperfect duty to accept me as a patient. He has a duty to make use of his skills and talents to treat the sick, but I cannot legitimately insist on being the beneficiary. How he discharges his duty is his decision.

If, however, I am accepted as a patient, then I can make some legitimate claims. I can demand that nothing be done to cause me pointless harm, because it is never right to injure a person. Furthermore, I can demand that I never be lied to or deceived. Suppose, for example, I am given a placebo (a harmless but inactive substance) and told that it is a powerful and effective medication. Or suppose that a biopsy shows that I have an inoperable form of cancer, but my physician tells me, "There's nothing seriously wrong with you." In both cases, the physician may suppose that he is deceiving me "for my own good": the placebo may be psychologically effective and make me feel better, and the lie about cancer may save me from useless worry. Yet, by being deceived, I am being denied the dignity inherent in my status as a rational being. Lying is wrong in general, and in such cases as these it also deprives me of my autonomy, of my power to make decisions and form my own opinions. As a result, such deception dehumanizes me.

As an autonomous rational being, a person is entitled to control over his or her own body. This means that medical procedures can be performed on me only with my permission. It would be wrong even if the medication were needed for my "own good." I may voluntarily put myself under the care of a physician and submit to all that I am asked to, but the decision belongs to me alone.

In exercising control over my body, however, I also have a duty to myself. Suppose, for example, that I refuse to allow surgery to be performed on me, although I have been told it is necessary to preserve my life. Since I have a duty to preserve my life, as does every person, my refusal is morally unjustifiable. Even here, however, it is not legitimate for others to force me to "do my duty." In fact, in Kantian ethics it is impossible to force another to do his or her duty because it is not the action but the maxim involved that determines whether or not one's duty has been done.

It is obvious even from our sketchy examples that Kantian ethics is a fruitful source of principles and ideas for working out some of the specific moral difficulties of medical experimentation and practice. The absolute requirements imposed by the categorical imperative can be a source of strength and even of comfort. By contrast, utilitarianism requires us to weigh alternative courses of actions by anticipating their consequences and deciding whether what we are considering doing can be justified by those results. Kant's ethics saves us from this kind of doubt and indecision—we know we must never lie, no matter what good may come of it. Furthermore, the lack of a principle of justice that is the most severe defect of utilitarianism is met by Kant's categorical imperative. When every person is to be treated as an end and never as only a means, the possibility of legitimately exploiting some for the benefit of others is wholly eliminated.

### Difficulties with Kantian Ethics

Kant's ethical theory is complex and controversial. It has problems of a theoretical sort that manifest themselves in practice and lead us to doubt whether the absolute rules determined by the categorical imperative can always provide a straightforward solution to our moral difficulties. We will limit ourselves to discussing just three problems.

First, Kant's principles may produce resolutions to cases in which there is a conflict of duties that seems intuitively wrong. I have a duty to keep my promises, and I also have a duty to help those in need. Suppose, then, that I am a physician and I have promised a colleague to attend a staff conference. Right before the conference starts, I am talking with a patient who lapses into an insulin coma. If I get involved in treating the patient, I'll have to break my promise to attend the conference. What should I do?

The answer is obvious: I should treat the patient. Our moral intuition tells us this. But for Kant, keeping promises is a perfect duty, while helping others is an imperfect one. This suggests, then, that according to Kantian principles I should abandon my patient and rush off to keep my appointment. Something is apparently wrong with a view that holds that a promise should never be broken—even when the promise concerns a relatively trivial matter and the consequences of keeping it are disastrous.

Another difficulty with the categorical imperative arises because we are free to choose how we formulate a maxim for testing. In all likelihood none of us would approve a maxim such as "Lie when it is convenient for you." But what about one like "Lie when telling the truth is likely to cause harm to another"? We would be more inclined to make this a universal law. Now consider the maxim "Whenever a physician has good reason to believe that a patient's life will be seriously threatened if she is told the truth about her condition, then the physician should lie." Virtually everyone would be willing to see this made into a universal law.

Yet these three maxims could apply to the same situation. Since Kant does not tell us how to formulate our maxims, it is clear that we can act virtually any way we choose if we are willing to describe the situation in detail. We might be willing to have everyone act just as we are inclined to act whenever they find themselves in exactly this kind of situation. The categorical imperative, then, does not seem to solve our moral problems quite so neatly as it first appears to.

A final problem arises from Kant's notion that we have duties to rational beings or persons. Ordinarily, we have little difficulty with this commitment to persons, yet there are circumstances, particularly in the medical context, in which serious problems arise. Consider, for example, a fetus developing in its mother's womb. Is the fetus to be considered a person? The way this question is answered makes all the difference in deciding about the rightness or wrongness of abortion.

A similar difficulty is present when we consider how we are to deal with an infant with serious birth defects. Is it our duty to care for this infant and do all we can to see that it lives? If the infant is not a person, then perhaps we do not owe him the sort of treatment it would be our duty to provide a similarly afflicted adult. It's clear from these two cases that the notion of a person as an autonomous rational being is both too restrictive and arbitrary. It begs important moral questions.

Another difficulty connected with Kant's concept of a rational person is the notion of an "autonomous self-regulating will." Under what conditions can we assume that an individual possesses such a will? Does a child, a mentally retarded person, or someone in prison? Without such a will, in Kant's view, such an individual cannot legitimately consent to be the subject of an experiment or even give permission for necessary medical treatment. This notion is very much in need of development before Kant's principles can be relied on to resolve ethical questions in medicine.

The difficulties that we have discussed require serious consideration. This does not mean, of course, that they cannot be resolved or that because of them Kant's theory is worthless. As with utilitarianism, there are some philosophers who believe the theory is the best available, despite its shortcomings. That it captures many of our intuitive beliefs about what is right (not to lie, to treat people with dignity, to act benevolently) and supplies us with a test for determining our duties (the categorical imperative) recommends it strongly as an ethical theory.

## Ross's Ethics

The English philosopher W. D. Ross (b. 1877) presented an ethical theory in his book *The Right and the Good* that can be seen as an attempt to incorporate aspects of utilitarianism and aspects of Kantianism. Ross rejected the utilitarian notion that an action is made right by its consequences alone, but he was also troubled by Kant's absolute rules. He saw not only that such rules fail to show sensitivity to the complexities of actual situations, but also that they sometimes conflict with one another. Like Kant, Ross is a deontologist, but with an important difference. Ross believes it is necessary to consider consequences in making a moral choice, even though he believes that it is not the results of an action taken alone that make it right.

### Moral Properties and Rules

For Ross there is an unbridgeable distinction between moral and nonmoral properties. There are only two moral properties—rightness and goodness—and these cannot be replaced by, or explained in terms of, other properties. Thus, to say

that an action is "right" is not at all the same as saying that it "causes pleasure" or "increases happiness," as utilitarianism claims.

At the same time, however, Ross does not deny that there is a connection between moral properties and nonmoral ones. What he denies is the possibility of establishing an identity between them. Thus, it may be right to relieve the suffering of someone, but right is not identical with relieving suffering. (More exactly put, the rightness of the action is not identical with the action's being a case of relieving suffering.)

Ross also makes clear that we must often know many nonmoral facts about a situation before we can legitimately make a moral judgment. If I see a physician injecting someone, I cannot say whether she is acting rightly without determining what she is injecting, why she is doing it, and so on. Thus, rightness is a property that depends partly on the nonmoral properties that characterize a situation. I cannot determine whether the physician is doing the right thing or the wrong thing until I determine what the nonmoral properties are.

Ross believes that there are cases in which we have no genuine doubt about whether the property of rightness or goodness is present. The world abounds with examples of cruelty, lying, and selfishness, and in these cases we are immediately aware of the absence of rightness or goodness. But the world also abounds with examples of compassion, reliability, and generosity in which rightness and goodness are clearly present. Ross claims that our experience with such cases puts us in a position to come to know rightness and goodness with the same degree of certainty as when we grasp the mathematical truth that a triangle has three angles.

Furthermore, according to Ross, our experience of many individual cases puts us in a position to recognize the validity of a general statement like "It is wrong to cause needless pain." We come to see such rules in much the same way that we come to recognize the letter A after having seen it written or printed in a variety of handwritings or typefaces.

Thus, our moral intuitions can supply us with moral rules of a general kind. But Ross refuses to acknowledge these rules as absolute. For him they can serve only as guides to assist us in deciding what we should do. Ultimately, in any particular case we must rely not only on the rules but also on reason and our understanding of the situation.

Thus, even with rules, we may not recognize what the right thing to do is in a given situation. We recognize, he suggests, that there is always some right thing to do, but what it is may be far from obvious. In fact, doubt about what is the right way of acting may arise just because we have rules to guide us. We become aware of the fact that there are several possible courses of action, and all of them seem to be right.

Consider the problem of whether to lie to a terminally ill patient about his condition. Let us suppose that, if we lie to him, we can avoid causing him at least some useless anguish. But then aren't we violating his trust in us to act morally and to speak the truth?

In such cases, we seem to have a conflict in our duties. It is because of such familiar kinds of conflicts that Ross rejects the possibility of discovering absolute, invariant moral rules like "Always tell the truth" and "Always eliminate needless suffering." In cases like the one above, we cannot hold that both rules are absolute without contradicting ourselves. Ross says that we have to recognize that every rule has exceptions and must in some situations be overridden.

## Actual Duties and Prima Facie Duties

If rules like "Always tell the truth" cannot be absolute, then what status can they have? When our rules come into conflict in particular situations, how are we to decide which rule applies? Ross answers this question by making use of a distinction between what is actually right and what is prima facie right. Since we have a duty to do what is right, this distinction can be expressed as one between *actual duty* and *prima facie duty.*

An actual duty is simply what my real duty is in a situation. It is the action that, out of the vari-

ous possibilities, I ought to perform. More often than not, however, I may not know what my actual duty is. In fact, for Ross, the whole problem of ethics might be said to be the problem of knowing what my actual duty is in any given situation.

*Prima facie* literally means "at first sight," but Ross uses the phrase to mean something like "other things being equal." Accordingly, a prima facie duty is one that dictates what I should do when other relevant factors in a situation are not considered. If I promised to meet you for lunch, then I have a prima facie duty to meet you. But suppose I am a physician and, just as I am about to leave for an appointment, the patient I am with suffers cardiac arrest. In such circumstances, according to Ross's view, I should break my promise and render aid to the patient. My prima facie duty to keep my promise doesn't make that fact obligatory. It constitutes a moral reason for meeting you, but there is also a moral reason for not meeting you. I also have a prima facie duty to aid my patient, and this is a reason that outweighs the first one. Thus, aiding the patient is both a prima facie duty and, in this situation, my actual duty.

The notion of a prima facie duty permits Ross to offer a set of moral rules stated in such a way that they are both universal and free from exceptions. For Ross, for example, lying is always wrong, but it is wrong prima facie. It may be that in a particular situation my actual duty requires that I lie. Even though what I have done is prima facie wrong, it is the morally right thing to do if some other prima facie duty that requires lying in the case is more stringent than the prima facie duty to tell the truth. (Perhaps only by lying am I able to prevent a terrorist from blowing up an airplane.) I must be able to explain and justify my failure to tell the truth, and it is of course possible that I may not be able to do so. It may be that I was confused and misunderstood the situation or failed to consider other alternatives. I may have been wrong to believe that my actual duty required me to lie. However, even if I was correct in my belief, that I lied is still prima facie wrong.

It is this fact (and for Ross it is a fact) that requires me to explain and justify my action.

We have considered only a few simple examples of prima facie duties, but Ross is more thorough and systematic than our examples might suggest. He offers a list of duties that he considers binding on all moral agents. Here they are in summary form:

1. *Duties of fidelity:* telling the truth, keeping actual and implicit promises, and not representing fiction as history

2. *Duties of reparation:* righting the wrongs we have done to others

3. *Duties of gratitude:* recognizing the services others have done for us

4. *Duties of justice:* preventing a distribution of pleasure or happiness that is not in keeping with the merit of the people involved

5. *Duties of beneficence:* helping to better the condition of other beings with respect to virtue, intelligence, or pleasure

6. *Duties of self-improvement:* bettering ourselves with respect to virtue or intelligence

7. *Duties of nonmaleficence:* avoiding or preventing an injury to others

Ross doesn't claim that this is a complete list of the prima facie duties that we recognize. However, he does believe that the duties on the list are all ones that we acknowledge and are willing to accept as legitimate and binding without argument. He believes that if we simply reflect on these prima facie duties we will see that they may be truly asserted. As he puts the matter:

> I . . . am claiming that we know them to be true. To me it seems as self-evident as anything could be, that to make a promise, for instance, is to create a moral claim on us in someone else. Many readers will perhaps say that they do not know this to be true. If so I certainly cannot prove it to them. I can only ask them to reflect again, in the hope that they will ultimately agree that they also know it to be true.

Notice that Ross explicitly rejects the possibility of providing us with reasons or arguments to convince us to accept his list of prima facie duties. We are merely invited to reflect on certain kinds of cases, like keeping promises, and Ross is convinced that this reflection will bring us to accept his claim that these are true duties. Ross, like other intuitionists, tries to get us to agree with his moral perceptions in much the same way as we might try to get people to agree with us about our color perceptions. We might, for example, show a paint sample to a friend and say, "Don't you think that looks blue? It does to me. Think about it for a minute."

We introduced the distinction between actual and prima facie duties to deal with those situations in which duties seem to conflict. The problem, as we can now state it, is this: What are we to do in a situation in which we recognize more than one prima facie duty and it is not possible for us to act in a way that will fulfill them? We know, of course, that we should act in a way that satisfies our actual duty. But that is just our problem. What, after all, is our actual duty when our prima facie duties are in conflict?

Ross offers us two principles to deal with cases of conflicting duty. The first principle is designed to handle situations in which just two prima facie duties are in conflict: *That act is one's duty which is in accord with the more stringent prima facie obligation.* The second principle is intended to deal with cases in which several prima facie duties are in conflict: *That act is one's duty which has the greatest balance of prima facie rightness over prima facie wrongness.*

Unfortunately, both these principles present problems in application. Ross does not tell us how we are to determine when an obligation is "more stringent" than another. Nor does he give us a rule for determining the "balance" of prima facie rightness over wrongness. Ultimately, according to Ross, we must simply rely upon our perceptions of the situation. There is no automatic or mechanical procedure that can be followed. If we learn the facts in the case, consider the consequences of our possible actions, and reflect on our prima facie duties, we should be able to arrive at a conclusion as to the best course of action—in Ross's view something that we as moral agents must and can do.

To return to specific cases, perhaps there is no direct way to answer the abstract question, Is the duty not to lie to a patient "more stringent" than the duty not to cause needless suffering? So much depends on the character and condition of the individual patient that an abstract determination of our duty based on "balance" or "stringency" is useless. However, knowing the patient, we should be able to perceive what the right course of action is.

Ross further believes that there are situations in which there are no particular difficulties about resolving the conflict between prima facie duties. For example, most of us would agree that, if we can save someone from serious injury by lying, then we have more of an obligation to save someone from injury than we do to tell the truth.

## Ross's Ethics in the Medical Context

Ross's moral rules are not absolute in the sense that Kant's are; consequently, as with utilitarianism, it is not possible to say what someone's duty would be in an actual concrete situation. We can discuss in general, however, the advantages that Ross's theory brings to medical–moral issues. We will mention only two for illustration.

First and most important is Ross's list of prima facie duties. The list of duties can serve an important function in the moral education of physicians, researchers, and other medical personnel. The list encourages each person responsible for patient care to reflect on the prima facie obligations that he or she has toward those people and to set aside one of those obligations only when morally certain that another obligation takes precedence.

The specific duties imposed in a prima facie way are numerous and can be expressed in terms relevant to the medical context: Do not injure patients; do not distribute scarce resources in a way that fails to recognize individual worth; do not lie to patients; show patients kindness and understanding; educate patients in ways useful to them; do not hold out false hopes to patients; and so on.

Second, like utilitarianism, Ross's ethics encourages us to show sensitivity to the unique features of situations before acting. Like Kant's

ethics, however, Ross's also insists that we look at the world from a particular moral perspective. In arriving at decisions about what is right, we must learn the facts of the case and explore the possible consequences of our actions. Ultimately, however, we must guide our actions by what is right, rather than by what is useful, or by what will produce happiness, or anything of the kind.

Since for Ross actions are not always justified in terms of their results, we cannot say unequivocally, "It's right to trick this person into becoming a research subject because the experiment may benefit thousands." Yet, we cannot say that it is always wrong for a researcher to trick a person into volunteering. An action is right or wrong regardless of what we think about it, but in a particular case circumstances might justify an experimenter in allowing some other duty to take precedence over the duty of fidelity.

Fundamentally, then, Ross's ethics offers us the possibility of gaining the advantages of utilitarianism without ignoring the fact that there seem to be duties with an undeniable moral force behind them that cannot be accounted for by utilitarianism. Ross's ethics accommodates not only our intuition that certain actions should be performed just because they are right but also our inclination to pay attention to the results of actions and not just the motives behind them.

## Difficulties with Ross's Moral Rules

The advantages Ross's ethics offers over both utilitarianism and Kantianism are offset by some serious difficulties. To begin with, it seems false that we all grasp the same principles. We are well aware that people's beliefs about what is right and about what their duties are result from the kind of education and experience that they have had. The ability to perceive what is good or right does not appear to be universally shared. Ross does say that the principles are the convictions of "the moral consciousness of the best people." In any ordinary sense of "best," there is reason to say that such people don't always agree on moral principles. If "best" means "morally best," then Ross is close to being circular: the best people are those who acknowledge the same prima facie obligations, and those who recognize the same prima facie obligations are the best people.

Some have objected that Ross's list of prima facie duties seems incomplete. For example, Ross does not explicitly say that we have a prima facie obligation not to steal, but most people would hold that if we have any prima facie duties at all, the duty not to steal must surely be counted among them. Of course, it is possible to say that stealing is covered by some other obligation— the duty of fidelity, perhaps, since stealing may violate a trust. Nevertheless, from a theory based on intuition, the omission of such duties leaves Ross's list peculiarly incomplete.

Further, some critics have claimed that it is not clear that there is always even a prima facie obligation to do some of the things Ross lists. Suppose that I promise to lie about a friend's physical condition so that she can continue to collect insurance payments. Some would say that I have no obligation at all to keep such an un-wise promise. In such a case, there would be no conflict of duties, because I don't have even a prima facie duty to keep such a promise.

Finally, Ross's theory, some have charged, seems to be false to the facts of moral disagree-ments. When we disagree with someone about an ethical matter, we consider reasons for and against some position. Sometimes the discussion results in agreement. But, according to Ross's view, this should not be possible. Although we may discuss circumstances and consequences and agree about the prima facie duties involved, ultimately I arrive at my judgment about the duty that is most stringent or has the greatest degree of prima facie rightness, and you arrive at yours. At this point, it seems, there can be no further discussion, even though the two judgments are incompatible. Thus, a choice between the two judgments about what act should be performed becomes arbitrary.

Few contemporary philosophers would be willing to endorse Ross's ethical theory without serious qualifications. The need for a special kind of moral perception (or "intuition") marks the theory as unacceptable for most philosophers. Yet many would acknowledge that the theory has great value in illuminating such aspects of our moral experience as reaching decisions when we feel the pull of conflicting obligations. Further-more, at least some would acknowledge Ross's prima facie duties as constituting an adequate set of moral principles.

## Rawls's Theory of Justice

In 1971 the Harvard philosopher John Rawls published a book called *A Theory of Justice*. The work continues to attract a considerable amount of attention and has been described by some as the most important book in moral and social philosophy of the twentieth century.

One commentator, R. P. Wolfe, points out that Rawls attempts to develop a theory that combines the strengths of utilitarianism with those of the deontological position of Kant and Ross, while avoiding the weaknesses of each view. Utilitarianism claims outright that happi-ness is fundamental and suggests a direct proce-dure for answering ethical–social questions. But it is flawed by its lack of a principle of justice. Kant and Ross make rightness a fundamental moral notion and stress the ultimate dignity of human beings. Yet neither provides a workable method for solving problems of social morality. Clearly, Rawls's theory promises much if it can succeed in uniting the two ethical traditions we have discussed.

### The Original Position and the Principles of Justice

For Rawls, the central task of government is to preserve and promote the liberty and welfare of individuals. Thus, principles of justice are needed to serve as standards for designing and evaluat-ing social institutions and practices. They provide a way of resolving conflicts among the compet-ing claims that individuals make and a means of protecting the legitimate interests of individuals. In a sense, the principles of justice constitute a blueprint for the development of a just society.

But how are we to formulate principles of justice? Rawls makes use of a hypothetical device he calls "the original position." Imagine a group of people like those who make up our society. These people display the ordinary range of intelligence, talents, ambitions, convictions, and social and economic advantages. They include both sexes and members of various racial and ethnic groups.

Furthermore, suppose that this group is placed behind what Rawls calls "a veil of ignorance." Assume that each person is made ignorant of his or her sex, race, natural endowments, social position, economic condition, and so on. Furthermore, assume that these people are capable of cooperating with one another, that they follow the principles of rational decision making, and that they are capable of a sense of justice and will adhere to principles they agree to adopt. Finally, assume that they all desire what Rawls calls "primary goods": the rights, opportunities, powers, wealth, and such that are both worth possessing in themselves and are necessary to securing the more specific goods an individual may want.

Rawls argues that the principles of justice chosen by such a group will be just if the conditions under which they are selected and the procedures for agreeing on them are fair. The original position, with its veil of ignorance, characterizes a state in which alternative notions of justice can be discussed freely by all. Since the ignorance of the participants means that individuals cannot gain advantage for themselves by choosing principles that favor their own circumstances, the eventual choices of the participants will be fair. Since the participants are assumed to be rational, they will be persuaded by the same reasons and arguments. These features of the original position lead Rawls to characterize his view as "justice as fairness."

We might imagine at first that some people in the original position would gamble and argue for principles that would introduce gross inequalities in their society. For example, some might argue for slavery. If these people should turn out to be masters after the veil of ignorance

is stripped away, they would gain immensely. But if they turn out to be slaves, then they would lose immensely. However, since the veil of ignorance keeps them from knowing their actual positions in society, it would not be rational for them to endorse a principle that might condemn them to the bottom of the social order.

Given the uncertainties of the original situation, there is a better strategy that these rational people would choose. In the economic discipline known as game theory, this strategy is called "maximin," or maximizing the minimum. When we choose in uncertain situations, this strategy directs us to select from the alternatives the one whose worst possible outcome is better than the worst possible outcome of the other alternatives. (If you don't know whether you're going to be a slave, you shouldn't approve a set of principles that permits slavery when you have other options.)

Acting in accordance with this strategy, Rawls argues that people in the original position would agree on the following two principles of justice:

1. Each person is to have an equal right to the most extensive total system of equal basic liberties compatible with a similar system of liberty for all.
2. Social and economic inequalities are to be arranged so that they are both: (a) to the greatest benefit of the least advantaged. . . , and (b) attached to offices and positions open to all under conditions of fair equality of opportunity.

For Rawls, these two principles are taken to govern the distribution of all social goods: liberty, property, wealth, and social privilege. The first principle has priority. It guarantees a system of equal liberty for all. Furthermore, because of its priority, it explicitly prohibits the bartering away of liberty for social or economic benefits. (For example, a society cannot withhold the right to vote from its members on the grounds that voting rights damage the economy.)

The second principle governs the distribution of social goods other than liberty. Although society could organize itself in a way that would eliminate differences in wealth and abolish the advantages that attach to different social positions, Rawls argues that those in the original position would not choose this form of egalitarianism. Instead, they would opt for the second principle of justice. This means that in a just society differences in wealth and social position can be tolerated only when they can be shown to benefit everyone and to benefit, in particular, those who have the fewest advantages. A just society is not one in which everyone is equal, but one in which inequalities must be demonstrated to be legitimate. Furthermore, there must be a genuine opportunity for acquiring membership in a group that enjoys special benefits. Those not qualified to enter medical schools because of past discrimination in education, for example, can claim a right for special preparation to qualify them. (Of course, in a Rawlsian society, there would be no discrimination to be compensated for.)

Rawls argues that these two principles are required to establish a just society. Furthermore, in distributing liberty and social goods, the principles guarantee the worth and self-respect of the individual. People are free to pursue their own conception of the good and fashion their own lives. Ultimately, the only constraints placed on them as members of society are those expressed in the principles of justice.

Yet Rawls also acknowledges that those in the original position would recognize that we have duties both to ourselves and to others. They would, for example, want to take measures to see that their interests are protected if they should meet with disabling accidents, become seriously mentally disturbed, and so on. Thus, Rawls approves a form of paternalism: others should act for us when we are unable to act for ourselves. When our preferences are known to them, those acting for us should attempt to follow what we would wish. Otherwise, they should act for us as they would act for themselves if they were viewing our situation from the standpoint of the original position. Paternalism is thus a duty to ourselves that would be recognized by those in the original position.

Rawls is also aware of the need for principles that bind and guide individuals as moral decision makers. He claims that those in the original position would reach agreement on principles for such notions as fairness in our dealings with others, fidelity, respect for persons, and beneficence. From these principles we gain some of our obligations to one another.

But, Rawls claims, there are also "natural duties" that would be recognized by those in the original position. Among those Rawls mentions are (1) the duty of justice—supporting and complying with just institutions; (2) the duty of helping others in need or jeopardy; (3) the duty not to harm or injure another; (4) the duty to keep our promises.

For the most part, these are duties that hold between or among people. They are only some of the duties that would be offered by those in the original position as unconditional duties.

Thus, Rawls in effect endorses virtually the same duties as those that Ross presents as prima facie duties. Rawls realizes that the problem of conflicts of duty was left unsolved by Ross and so perceives the need for assigning priorities to duties—ranking them as higher and lower. Rawls believes that a full system of principles worked out from the original position would include rules for ranking duties. Rawls's primary concern, however, is with justice in social institutions, and he does not attempt to establish any rules for ranking.

## Rawls's Theory of Justice in the Medical Context

Rawls's "natural duties" are virtually the same as Ross's prima facie duties. Consequently, most of what we said earlier about prima facie duties and moral decision making applies to Rawls.

Rawls endorses the legitimacy of paternalism, although he does not attempt to specify detailed principles to justify individual cases. He does tell us that we should consider the preferences of others when they are known to us and when we are in a situation in which we must act for them because they are unable to act for themselves. For example, suppose we know that a person approves of electroconvulsive therapy (shock treatments, or ECT) for the treatment of severe depression. If that person should become so depressed as to be unable to reach a decision about his own treatment, then we would be justified in seeing to it that he received ECT.

To take a similar case, suppose you are a surgeon and have a patient who has expressed to you her wish to avoid numerous operations that may prolong her life six months or so but will be unable to restore her to health. If in operating you learned that she has a form of uterine cancer that had spread through her lower extremities and if in your best judgment nothing could be done to restore her to health, then it would be your duty to her to allow her to die as she chooses. Repeated operations would be contrary to her concept of her own good.

The most important question in exploring Rawls's theory is how the two principles of justice might apply to the social institutions and practices of medical care and research. Most obviously, Rawls's principles repair utilitarianism's flaw with respect to human experimentation. It would never be right, in Rawls's view, to exploit one group of people or even one person for the benefit of others. Thus, experiments in which people are forced to be subjects or are tricked into participating are ruled out. They involve a violation of basic liberties of individuals and of the absolute respect for persons that the principles of justice require.

A person has a right to decide what risks she is willing to take with her own life and health. Thus, voluntary consent is required before someone can legitimately become a research subject. However, society might decide to reward research volunteers with money, honors, or social privileges to encourage participation in research. Provided that the overall structure of society already conforms to the two principles of justice, this is a perfectly legitimate practice so long as it brings benefits (ideally) to everyone and the possibility of gaining the rewards of participation is open to all.

Regarding the allocation of social resources in the training of medical personnel (physicians, nurses, therapists, and so on), one may conclude that such investments are justified only if the withdrawal of the support would work to the disadvantage of those already most disadvantaged. Public money may be spent in the form of scholarships and institutional grants to educate personnel, who may then derive great social and economic benefits from their education. But, for Rawls, the inequality that is produced is not necessarily unjust. Society can invest its resources in this way if it brings benefits to those most in need of them.

The implication of this position seems to be that everyone is entitled to health care. First, it could be argued that health is among the "primary goods" that Rawls's principles are designed to protect and promote. After all, without health an individual is hardly in a position to pursue other more specific goods, and those in the original position might be imagined to be aware of this and to endorse only those principles of justice that would require providing at least basic health care to those in the society. Furthermore, it could be argued that the inequalities of the health-care system can be justified only if those in most need can benefit from them. Since this is not obviously the case with the present system, Rawls's principles seem to call for a reform that would provide health care to those who are unable to pay.

However, it is important to point out that it is not at all obvious that a demand to reform our health-care system follows from Rawls's position. For one thing, it is not clear that Rawls's principles are intended to be directly applied to our society as it is. Our society includes among its members people with serious disabilities and ones with both acute and chronic diseases. If Rawls's principles are intended to apply only to people with normal physical and psychological abilities and needs, as he sometimes suggests, then it is not clear that those who are ill can be regarded as appropriate candidates. If they are considered appropriate, then the results may be unacceptable. The principles of justice may require that we devote vast amounts of social resources to making only marginal improvements in the lives of those who are ill.

Furthermore, Rawls does not explicitly mention the promotion of health as one of the primary goods. It may seem reasonable to include it among them, given the significance of health as a condition for additional pursuits, but this is a point that requires support. (Norman Daniels is one who has argued for considering health a primary good.) This seems the most promising position to take if Rawls's principles are to be used as a basis for evaluating our current health policies and practices.

It seems reasonable to hold that Rawls's principles, particularly the second, can be used to restrict access to certain kinds of health care. In general, individuals may spend their money in any way they wish to seek their notions of what is good. Thus, if someone wants cosmetic surgery to change the shape of his chin and has the money to pay a surgeon, then he may have it done. But if medical facilities or personnel should become overburdened and unable to provide needed care for the most seriously afflicted, then the society would be obligated to forbid cosmetic surgery. By doing this it would then increase the net access to needed health care by all members of society. The rich who desired cosmetic surgery would not be permitted to exploit the poor who needed basic health care.

These are just a few of the possible implications that Rawls's theory has for medical research and practice. It seems likely that more and more applications of the theory will be worked out in detail in the future.

## Difficulties with Rawls's Theory

Rawls's theory is currently the subject of much discussion in philosophy. The debate is often highly technical, and a great number of objections have been raised. At present, however, there are no objections that would be acknowledged as legitimate by all critics. Rather than attempt to summarize the debate, we will simply point to two aspects of Rawls's theory that have been acknowledged as difficulties.

One criticism concerns the original position and its veil of ignorance. Rawls does not permit those in the original position to know anything of their own purposes, plans, or interests—of their conception of the good. They do not know whether they prefer tennis to Tennyson, pleasures of mind over pleasures of the body. They are allowed to consider only those goods—self-respect, wealth, social position—that Rawls puts before them. Thus, critics have said, Rawls has excluded morally relevant knowledge. It is impossible to see how people could agree on principles to regulate their lives when they are so ignorant of their desires and purposes. Rawls seems to have biased the original position in his favor, and this calls into question his claim that the original position is a fair and reasonable way of arriving at principles of justice.

A second criticism focuses on whether Rawls's theory is really as different from utilitarianism as it appears to be. Rawls's theory may well permit inequalities of treatment under certain conditions in the same way that the principle of utility permits them. The principles of justice that were stated earlier apply, Rawls says, only when liberty can be effectively established and maintained. Rawls is very unclear about when a situation may be regarded as one of this kind. When it is not, his principles of justice are ones of a "general conception." Under this conception, liberties of individuals can be restricted, provided that the restrictions are for the benefit of all. It is possible to imagine, then, circumstances in which we might force individuals to become experimental subjects both for their own benefit and for that of others. We might, for example, require that all cigarette smokers participate in experiments intended to acquire knowledge about lung and heart damage. Since everyone would benefit, directly or indirectly, from such knowledge, forcing their participation would be legitimate. Thus, under the general conception of justice, the difference between Rawls's principles and the principle of utility may in practice become vanishingly small.

# Natural Law Ethics and Moral Theology

The general view that the rightness of actions is something determined by nature itself, rather than by the laws and customs of societies or the preferences of individuals, is called *natural law theory*. Moral principles are thus regarded as objective truths that can be discovered in the nature of things by reason and reflection. The basic idea of the theory was expressed succinctly by the Roman philosopher Cicero (103–43 B.C.). "Law is the highest reason, implanted in Nature, which commands what ought to be done and forbids the opposite. This reason, when firmly fixed and fully developed in the human mind, is Law." The natural law theory originated in classical Greek and Roman philosophy and has immensely influenced the development of moral and political theories. Indeed, all the ethical theories we have discussed are indebted to the natural law tradition. The reliance upon reason as a means of settling upon or establishing ethical principles and the emphasis on the need to reckon with the natural abilities and inclinations of human nature are just two of the threads that are woven into the theories that we have discussed.

## Purposes, Reason, and the Moral Law as Interpreted by Roman Catholicism

The natural law theory of Roman Catholicism was given its most influential formulation in the thirteenth century by St. Thomas Aquinas (1225–1274). Contemporary versions of the theory are mostly elaborations and interpretations of Aquinas's basic statement. Thus, an understanding of Aquinas's views is important for grasping the philosophical principles that underlie the Roman Catholic position on such issues as abortion.

Aquinas was writing at a time in which a great number of the texts of Aristotle (384–322 B.C.) were becoming available in the West, and Aquinas's philosophical theories incorporated many of Aristotle's principles. A fundamental notion borrowed by Aquinas is the view that the universe is organized in a teleological way. That is, the universe is structured in such a way that each thing in it has a goal or purpose. Thus, when conditions are right, a tadpole will develop into a frog. In its growth and change, the tadpole is following "the law of its nature." It is achieving its goal.

Humans have a material nature, just as a tadpole does, and in their own growth and development they too follow a law of their material nature. But Aquinas also stresses that humans possess a trait that no other creature does—reason. Thus, the full development of human potentialities—the fulfillment of human purpose— requires that we follow the direction of the law of reason, as well as being subjected to the laws of material human nature.

The development of reason is one of our ends as human beings, but we also rely upon reason to determine what our ends are and how we can achieve them. It is this function of reason that leads Aquinas to identify reason as the source of the moral law. Reason is practical in its operation, for it directs our actions so that we can bring about certain results. In giving us directions, reason imposes an obligation on us, the obligation to bring about the results that it specifies. But Aquinas says that reason cannot arbitrarily set goals for us. Reason directs us toward our good as the goal of our action, and what that good is, is discoverable within our nature. Thus, reason recognizes the basic principle "Good is to be done and evil avoided."

But this principle is purely formal, or empty of content. To make it a practical principle we must consider what the human good is. According to Aquinas, the human good is that which is suitable or proper to human nature. It is what is "built into" human nature in the way that, in a sense, a frog is already "built into" a tadpole. Thus, the good is that to which we are directed by our natural inclinations as both physical and rational creatures.

Like other creatures, we have a natural inclination to preserve our lives; consequently, reason imposes on us an obligation to care for our health, not to kill ourselves, and not to put ourselves in positions in which we might be killed. We realize through reason that others have a rational nature like ours, and we see that we are bound to treat them with the same dignity and respect that we accord ourselves. Furthermore, when we see that humans require a society to make their full development possible, we realize that we have an obligation to support laws and practices that make society possible.

Thus, for example, as we have a natural inclination to propagate our species (viewed as a "natural" good), reason places on us an obligation not to thwart or pervert this inclination. As a consequence, to fulfill this obligation within society, reason supports the institution of marriage.

Reason also finds in our nature grounds for procedural principles. For example, because everyone has an inclination to preserve his life and well-being, no one should be forced to testify against himself. Similarly, because all individuals are self-interested, no one should be permitted to be a judge in his own case.

Physical inclinations, under the direction of reason, point us toward our natural good. But, according to Aquinas, reason itself can also be a source of inclinations. For example, Aquinas says that reason is the source of our natural inclination to seek the truth, particularly the truth about the existence and nature of God.

Just from the few examples we have considered, it should be clear how Aquinas believed it was possible to discover in human nature natural goods. Relying upon these as goals or purposes to be achieved, reason would then work out the practical way of achieving them. Thus, through the subtle application of reason, it should be possible to establish a body of moral principles and rules. These are the doctrines of natural law.

Because natural law is founded on human nature, which is regarded as unchangeable, Aquinas regards natural law itself as unchangeable. Moreover, it is seen as the same for all people, at all times, and in all societies. Even those without knowledge of God can, through the operation of reason, recognize their natural obligations.

For Aquinas and for Roman Catholicism, this view of natural law is just one aspect of a broader theological framework. The teleological organization of the universe is attributed to the planning of a creator—goals or purposes are ordained by God. Furthermore, although natural law is discoverable in the universe, its ultimate source is divine wisdom and God's eternal law. Everyone who is rational is capable of grasping natural law. But because passions and irrational inclinations may corrupt human nature and because some people lack the abilities or time to work out the demands of natural law, God also chose to reveal our duties to us in explicit ways. The major source of revelation, of course, is taken to be the biblical scriptures.

Natural law, scriptural revelation, the interpretation of the Scriptures by the Church, Church tradition, and the teachings of the Church are regarded in Roman Catholicism as the sources of moral ideals and principles. By guiding one's life by them, one can develop the rational and moral part of one's nature and move toward the goal of achieving the sort of perfection that is suitable for humans.

This general moral–theological point of view is the source for particular Roman Catholic doctrines that have special relevance to medicine. We will consider just two of the most important principles.

**The Principle of Double Effect.** A particular kind of moral conflict arises when the performance of an action will produce both good and bad effects. On the basis of the good effect, it seems it is our duty to perform the action; but on the basis of the bad effect, it seems our duty not to perform it.

Let's assume that the death of a fetus is in itself a bad effect and consider a case like the following: A woman who is three months pregnant is found to have a cancerous uterus. If the woman's life is to be saved, the uterus must be removed at once. But if the uterus is removed, then the life of the unborn child will be lost. Should the operation be performed?

The principle of double effect is intended to help in the resolution of these kinds of conflicts. The principle holds that such an action should be performed only if the intention is to bring about the good effect and the bad effect will be an unintended or indirect consequence. More specifically, four conditions must be satisfied:

1. The action itself must be morally indifferent or morally good.

2. The bad effect must not be the means by which the good effect is achieved.

3. The motive must be the achievement of the good effect only.

4. The good effect must be at least equivalent in importance to the bad effect.

Are these conditions satisfied in the case that we mentioned? The operation itself, if this is considered to be the action, is at least morally indifferent. That is, in itself it is neither good nor bad. That takes care of the first condition. If the mother's life is to be saved, it will not be *by means of* killing the fetus. It will be by means of removing the cancerous uterus. Thus, the second condition is met. The motive of the surgeon, we may suppose, is not the death of the fetus but saving the life of the woman. If so, then the third condition is satisfied. Finally, since two lives are at stake, the good effect (saving the life of the woman) is at least equal to the bad effect (the death of the fetus). The fourth condition is thus met. Under ordinary conditions, then, these conditions would be considered satisfied, and such an operation would be morally justified.

The principle of double effect is most often mentioned in a medical context in cases of abortion. But, in fact, it has a much wider range of application in medical ethics. It bears on cases of contraception, sterilization, organ transplants, and the use of extraordinary measures to maintain life.

**The Principle of Totality.**  The principle of totality can be expressed in this way: An individual has a right to dispose of his or her organs or to destroy their capacity to function only to the extent that the general well-being of the whole body demands it. Thus, it is clear that we have a natural obligation to preserve our lives, but, by the Roman Catholic view, we also have a duty to preserve the integrity of our bodies. This duty is based on the belief that each of our organs was designed by God to play a role in maintaining the functional integrity of our bodies, that each

has a place in the divine plan. As we are the custodians of our bodies, not their owners, it is our duty to care for them as a trust.

The principle of totality has implications for a great number of medical procedures. Strictly speaking, even cosmetic surgery is morally right only when it is required to maintain or ensure the normal functioning of the rest of the body. More important, procedures that are typically employed for contraceptive purposes—vasectomies and tubal ligations—are ruled out. After all, such procedures involve "mutilation" and the destruction of the capacity of the organs of reproduction to function properly. The principle of totality thus also forbids the sterilization of the mentally retarded.

As an ethical theory, natural law theory is sometimes described as teleological. In endorsing the principle "Good is to be done and evil avoided," the theory identifies a goal with respect to which the rightness of an action is to be judged. As the principle of double effect illustrates, the intention of the individual who acts is crucial to determining whether the goal is sought. In a sense, the intention of the action, what the individual wills, defines the action. Thus, "performing an abortion" and "saving a woman's life" are not necessarily the same action, even in those instances in which their external features are the same. Unlike utilitarianism, which is also a teleological theory, natural law theory is not consequentialist: The outcome of an action is not the sole feature to consider in determining the moral character of the action.

### Applications of Roman Catholic Moral-Theological Viewpoints in the Medical Context

Roman Catholic ethicists and moral theologians have written and developed a body of widely accepted doctrine. We will consider only four topics.

First, the application of the principle of double effect and the principle of totality have definite consequences in the area of medical experimentation. Since we hold our bodies in trust, we are responsible for assessing the degree of risk present in an experiment in which we are asked to be a subject. Thus, we need to be fully informed of the nature of the experiment and the risks that it holds for us. If after obtaining this knowledge we decide to give our consent, it must be given freely and not as the result of deception or coercion.

Because human experimentation carries with it the possibility of injury and death, the principle of double effect and its four strictures apply. If scientific evidence indicates that a sick person may benefit from participating in an experiment, then the experiment is morally justifiable. If, however, the evidence indicates that the chances of helping that person are slight and he or she may die or be gravely injured, then the experiment is not justified. In general, the likelihood of a person's benefiting from the experiment must exceed the danger of that person's suffering greater losses.

A person who is incurably ill may volunteer to be an experimental subject, even though she or he cannot reasonably expect personal gain in the form of improved health. The good that is hoped for is good for others, in the form of increased medical knowledge. Even here, however, there are constraints imposed by the principle of double effect. There must be no likelihood that the experiment will seriously injure, and the probable value of the knowledge expected to result must balance the risk run by the patient. Not even the incurably ill can be made subjects of trivial experiments.

The good sought by healthy volunteers is also the good of others. The same restrictions mentioned in connection with the incurably ill apply to experimenting on healthy people. Additionally, the principle of totality places constraints on what a person may volunteer to do with his or her body. No healthy person may submit to an experiment that involves the probability of serious injury, impaired health, mutilation, or death.

A second medical topic addressed by Roman Catholic theologians is whether "ordinary" or "extraordinary" measures are to be taken in the preservation of human life. While it is believed that natural law and divine law impose on us a moral obligation to preserve our lives, Catholic moralists have interpreted this obligation as requiring that we rely upon only ordinary means. In the medical profession, the phrase "ordinary means" is used to refer to medical procedures that are standard or orthodox, in contrast with those that are untried or experimental. But from the viewpoint of Catholic ethics, "ordinary" used in the medical context applies to "all medicines, treatments, and operations which offer a reasonable hope of benefit for the patient and which can be obtained and used without excessive expense, pain, or other inconvenience." Thus, by contrast, extraordinary means are those that offer the patient no reasonable hope or whose use causes serious hardship for the patient or others.

Medical measures that would save the life of a patient but subject her to years of pain or would produce in her severe physical or mental incapacities are considered extraordinary. A patient or her family are under no obligation to choose them, and physicians are under a positive obligation not to encourage their choice.

The third medical topic for consideration is euthanasia. In the Roman Catholic ethical view, euthanasia in any form is considered immoral. It is presumed to be a direct violation of God's dominion over creation and the human obligation to preserve life. The Ethical Directives for Catholic Hospitals is explicit on the matter of taking a life:

> The direct killing of any innocent person, even at his own request, is always morally wrong. Any procedure whose sole immediate effect is the death of a human being is a direct killing. . . . Euthanasia ("mercy killing") in all its forms is forbidden. . . . The failure to supply the ordinary means of preserving life is equivalent to euthanasia.

According to this view, it is wrong to allow babies suffering from serious birth defects to die. If they can be saved by ordinary means, there is an obligation to do so. It is also wrong to act to terminate the lives of those hopelessly ill, either by taking steps to bring about their deaths or by failing to take steps to maintain their lives by ordinary means.

It is never permissible to hasten the death of a person as a direct intention. It is, however, permissible to administer drugs that alleviate pain. The principle of double effect suggests that giving such drugs is a morally justifiable action even though the drugs may indirectly hasten the death of a person.

Last, we may inquire how Roman Catholicism views abortion. According to the Roman Catholic view, from the moment of conception the conceptus (later, the fetus) is considered to be a person with all the rights of a person. For this reason, direct abortion at any stage of pregnancy is regarded as morally wrong. Abortion is "direct" when it results from a procedure "whose sole immediate effect is the termination of pregnancy." This means that what is generally referred to as therapeutic abortion, in which an abortion is performed to safeguard the life or health of the woman, is considered wrong. For example, a woman with serious heart disease who becomes pregnant cannot morally justify an abortion on the grounds that the pregnancy is a serious threat to her life. Even when the ultimate aim is to save the life of the woman, direct abortion is wrong.

We have already seen, however, that the principle of double effect permits the performance of an action that may result in the death of an unborn child if the action satisfies the four criteria for applying the principle. Thus, *indirect* abortion is considered to be morally permissible. That is, the abortion must be the outcome of some action (for example, removal of a cancerous uterus) that is performed for the direct and total purpose of treating a pathological condition affecting the woman. The end sought in direct abortion is the destruction of life, but the end sought in indirect abortion is the preservation of life.

## Difficulties with Natural Law Ethics and Moral Theology

Our discussion has centered on the natural law theory of ethics as it has been interpreted in Roman Catholic theology. Thus, there are two possible types of difficulties: those associated with natural law ethics in its own right and those associated with its incorporation into theology. The theological difficulties go beyond the scope of our aims and interests. We will restrict ourselves to considering the basic difficulty that faces natural law theory as formulated by Aquinas. Since it is this formulation that has been used in Roman Catholic moral theology, we shall be raising a problem for it in an indirect way.

The fundamental difficulty with Aquinas's argument for natural law is caused by the assumption, borrowed from Aristotle, that the universe is organized in a teleological fashion. (This is the assumption that every kind of thing has a goal or purpose.) This assumption is essential to Aquinas's ethical theory, for he identifies the good of a thing with its natural mode of operation. Without the assumption, we are faced with the great diversity and moral indifference of nature. Inclinations, even when shared by all humans, are no more than inclinations. There are no grounds for considering them "goods," and they have no moral status. The universe is bereft of natural values.

Yet, there are many reasons to consider this assumption false. Physics surrendered the notion of a teleological organization in the world as long ago as the seventeenth century—the rejection of Aristotle's physics also entailed the rejection of Aristotle's teleological view of the world. This left biology as the major source of arguments in favor of teleology. But contemporary evolutionary theory shows that the apparent purposive character of evolutionary change can be accounted for by the operation of natural selection on random mutations. Also, the development and growth of organisms can be explained by the presence of genetic information that controls the processes. The tadpole develops into a frog because evolution has produced a genetic program that directs the sequence of complicated chemical changes. Thus, no adequate grounds seem to exist for asserting that the teleological organization of nature is anything more than apparent.

Science and "reason alone" do not support teleology. It can be endorsed only if one is willing to assume that any apparent teleological organization is the product of a divine plan. Yet, because all apparent teleology can be explained in nonteleological ways, this assumption seems neither necessary nor legitimate.

Without its foundation of teleology, Aquinas's theory of natural law ethics seems to collapse. This is not to say, of course, that some other natural law theory, one not requiring the assumption of teleology, might not be persuasively defended.

## MAJOR MORAL PRINCIPLES

Making moral decisions is always a difficult and stressful task. Abstract discussions of issues never quite capture the feelings of uncertainty and self-doubt we characteristically experience when called upon to decide what ought to be done or to judge whether someone did the right thing. There are no mechanical processes or algorithms we can apply in a situation of moral doubt. There are no computer programs to supply us with the proper decision when given the relevant data.

In a very real sense, we are on our own when it comes to making ethical decisions. This does not mean that we are without resources and must decide blindly or even naively. When we have the luxury of time, when the need to make a decision is not pressing, then we may attempt to work out an answer to a moral question by relying upon a general ethical theory like those discussed earlier. However, in ordinary life we rarely have the opportunity or time to engage in an elaborate process of reasoning and analysis.

A more practical approach is to employ moral principles that have been derived from and justified by a moral theory. A principle such as "Avoid causing needless harm" can serve as a more direct guide to action and decision making than, say, Kant's categorical imperative. With such a principle in mind, we realize that, if we are acting as a physician, then we have a duty to use our knowledge and skills to protect our patients from injury. For example, we should not

expose a patient to the needless risk of a diagnostic test that does not promise to yield useful information.

In this section, we will present and illustrate five moral principles. All are ones of special relevance to dealing with the ethical issues presented by decisions concerning medical care. The principles have their limitations. For one thing, they are in no sense complete. Moral issues arise, even in the context of medicine, for which they can supply no direct guidance. In other situations, the principles themselves may come into conflict and point toward incompatible solutions. (How can we both avoid causing harm and allow a terminally ill patient to die?) The principles themselves indicate no way such conflicts can be resolved, for, even taken together, they do not constitute a coherent moral theory. To resolve conflicts, it may be necessary to employ the more basic principles of such a theory.

It is fair to say that each of the five basic moral theories we have discussed endorses the legitimacy of these principles. Not all would formulate them in the same way, and not all would give them the same moral weight. Nevertheless, each theory would accept them as expressing appropriate guidelines for moral decision making.

Indeed, the best way to think about the principles is as guidelines. They are in no way rules that can be applied automatically. Rather, they express standards to be consulted in attempting to arrive at a justified decision. As such, they provide a basis for evaluating actions or policies as well as for making individual moral decisions.

They help guarantee that our decisions are made in accordance with our principles and not according to our whims or prejudices. By following them we are more likely to reach decisions that are reasoned, consistent, and applicable to similar cases.

### The Principle of Nonmaleficence

"Above all, do no harm" is perhaps the most famous and most quoted of all moral maxims in medicine. It captures in a succinct way what is universally considered to be an overriding duty of anyone who undertakes the care of a patient. We believe that in treating a patient a physician should not by carelessness, malice, inadvertence, or avoidable ignorance do anything that will cause injury to the patient.

The maxim is one expression of what is sometimes called in ethics the principle of non-maleficence. The principle can be formulated in various ways, but here is one relatively noncontroversial way of stating it: *We ought to act in ways that do not cause needless harm or injury to others.* Stated in a positive fashion, the principle tells us that we have a duty to avoid maleficence, that is to avoid harming or injuring other people.

In the most obvious case, we violate the principle of nonmaleficence when we intentionally do something we know will cause someone harm. For example, suppose a surgeon during the course of an operation deliberately severs a muscle, knowing that by doing so he will cripple the patient. The surgeon is guilty of maleficence and is morally (as well as legally) blameworthy for her action.

The principle may also be violated when no malice or intention to do harm is involved. A nurse who carelessly gives a patient the wrong medication and causes the patient to suffer irreversible brain damage may have had no intention of causing the patient any injury. However, the nurse was negligent in his actions and failed to exercise due care in discharging his responsibilities. His actions resulted in an avoidable injury to his patient. Hence, he failed to meet his obligation of nonmaleficence.

The duty imposed by the principle of non-maleficence is not a demand to accomplish the impossible. We realize that we cannot reasonably expect perfection in the practice of medicine. We know that the results of treatments are often uncertain and may cause more harm than good. We know that the knowledge we have of diseases is only partial and that decisions about diagnosis and therapy typically involve the exercise of judgment, with no guarantee of correctness. We know that an uncertainty is built into the very nature of things and that our power to control the outcome of natural processes is limited. Con-

sequently, we realize that we cannot hold physicians and other health professionals accountable for every instance of death and injury involving patients under their care.

Nevertheless, we can demand that physicians and others live up to reasonable standards of performance. In the conduct of their professions, we can expect them to be cautious and diligent, patient and thoughtful. We can expect them to pay attention to what they are doing and to deliberate about whether a particular procedure should be done. In addition, we can expect them to possess the knowledge and skills relevant to the proper discharge of their duties.

These features and others like them make up the standards of performance that define what we have a right to expect from physicians and other health professionals. In the language of the law, these are the standards of "due care," and it is by reference to them that we evaluate the medical care given to patients. Failure to meet the standards opens practitioners (physicians, nurses, dentists, therapists) to the charge of moral or legal maleficence.

In our society, we have attempted to guarantee that at least some of the due-care standards are met by relying upon such measures as degree programs, licensing laws, certifying boards, and hospital credentials committees. Such an approach offers a way of ensuring that physicians and others have acquired at least a minimum level of knowledge, skill, and experience before undertaking the responsibilities attached to their roles. The approach also encourages such values as diligence, prudence, and caution, but there is of course no way of guaranteeing that in a particular case a physician will exhibit those virtues. Haste, carelessness, and inattention are always possible, and the potential that a patient will suffer an injury from them is always present.

The standards of due care are connected in some respects with such factual matters as the current state of medical knowledge and training and the immediate circumstances in which a physician provides care. For example, in the 1920s and 1930s, it was not at all unusual for a general practitioner to perform relatively complicated surgery. This was particularly true of someone practicing in a rural area. In performing surgery, he would be acting in a reasonable and expected fashion and could not be legitimately charged with violating the principle of non-maleficence.

However, the change in medicine from that earlier time to the present has also altered our beliefs about what is reasonable and expected. Today, a general practitioner who has had no special training and is not board certified and yet performs surgery on her patients may be legitimately criticized for maleficence. The standards of due care in surgery are now higher and more exacting than they once were, and the general practitioner who undertakes to perform most forms of surgery causes her patients to undergo an unusual and unnecessary risk literally at her hands. Their interest would be better served if their surgery were performed by a trained and qualified surgeon.

Such a case also illustrates that no actual harm or injury must occur for someone to be acting in violation of the principle of nonmaleficence. The general practitioner performing surgery may not cause any injury to his patients, but he puts them in a position in which the possibility of harm to them is greater than it needs to be. It is in this respect that he is not exercising due care in his treatment and so can be charged with maleficence. He has subjected his patients to *unnecessary risk,* risk greater than they would be subject to in the hands of a trained surgeon.

It is important to stress that the principle of nonmaleficence does not require that a physician subject a patient to no risks at all. Virtually every form of diagnostic testing and medical treatment involves some degree of risk to the patient, and to provide medical care at all, a physician must often act in ways that involve a possible injury to the patient. For example, a physician who takes a thorough medical history and performs a physical examination, then treats a patient with an antibiotic for bacterial infection cannot be held morally responsible if the patient suffers a severe drug reaction. That such a thing might happen is a possibility that cannot be foreseen in an individual case.

Similarly, a serious medical problem may justify subjecting the patient to a serious risk. (Gaining the consent of the patient is an obvious consideration, however.) A life-threatening condition, such as an occluded right coronary artery, may warrant coronary-bypass surgery with all its attendant dangers.

In effect, the principle of nonmaleficence tells us to avoid needless risk and, when risk is an inevitable aspect of an appropriate diagnostic test or treatment, to minimize the risk as much as is reasonably possible. A physician who orders a lumbar puncture for a patient who complains of occasional headaches is acting inappropriately, given the nature of the complaint, and is subjecting his patient to needless risk. By contrast, a physician who orders such a test after examining a patient who has severe and recurring headaches, a fever, pain and stiffness in his neck, and additional key clinical signs is acting appropriately. The risk to the patient from the lumbar puncture is the same in both cases, but the risk is warranted in the second case and not in the first. A failure to act with due care violates the principle of nonmaleficence, even if no harm results, whereas acting with due care does not violate the principle, even if harm does result.

## The Principle of Beneficence

"As to diseases, make a habit of two things—to help or at least to do no harm." This directive from the Hippocratic writings stresses that the physician has two duties. The second of them ("at least to do no harm") we discussed in connection with the principle of nonmaleficence. The first of them ("to help") we will consider here in connection with the principle of beneficence.

Like the previous principle, the principle of beneficence can be stated in various and different ways. Here is one formulation: *We should act in ways that promote the welfare of other people.* That is, we should help other people when we are able to do so.

Some philosophers have expressed doubt that we have an actual duty to help others. We certainly have a duty not to harm other people, but it has seemed to some that there are no grounds for saying that we have a duty to promote their welfare. We would deserve praise if we did, but we would not deserve blame if we did not. From this point of view, being beneficent is beyond the scope of duty.

We need not consider whether this view is correct in general. For our purposes, it is enough to realize that the nature of the relationship between a physician and a patient does impose the duty of acting in the patient's welfare. That is, the duty of beneficence is inherent in the role of physician. A physician who was not acting for the sake of the patient's good would, in a very real sense, not be acting as a physician.

That we recognize this as a duty appropriate to the physician's role is seen most clearly in cases in which the physician is also a researcher and her patient is also an experimental subject. In such instances, there is a possibility of a role conflict, for the researcher's aim of acquiring knowledge is not always compatible with the physician's aim of helping the patient. (See Chapter 1 for a discussion of this problem.)

The duty required by the principle of beneficence is inherent in the role not only of physicians but also of all health professionals. Nurses, therapists, clinical psychologists, social workers, and others accept the duty of promoting the welfare of their patients or clients as an appropriate part of their responsibilities. We expect nurses and others to do good for us, and it is this expectation that leads us to designate them as belonging to what are often called "the helping professions."

The extent to which beneficence is required as a duty for physicians and others is not a matter easily resolved. In practice, we recognize that limits exist to what can be expected from even those who have chosen to make a career of helping others. We do not expect physicians to sacrifice completely their self-interest and welfare on behalf of their patients. We do not think their duty demands that they be totally selfless. If some do, we may praise them as secular saints or moral heroes, but that is because they go beyond the demands of duty. At the same time, we would have little good to say of a physician who always put his interest above that of his patients,

who never made a personal sacrifice to service their interests.

Just as there are standards of due care that explicitly and implicitly define what we consider to be right conduct in protecting patients from harm, so there seem to be implicit standards of beneficence. We obviously expect physicians to help patients by providing them with appropriate treatment. More than this, we expect physicians to be prepared to make *reasonable* sacrifices for the sake of their patients. Even in the age of "health-care teams," a single physician assumes responsibility for a particular patient when the patient is hospitalized or treated for a serious illness. It is this physician who is expected to make the crucial medical decisions, and we expect her to realize that discharging that responsibility may involve an interruption of private plans and activities. A surgeon who is informed that her post-operative patient has started to bleed can be expected to cancel her plan to attend a concert. Doing so is a reasonable duty imposed by the principle of beneficence. If she failed to discharge the duty, in the absence of mitigating circumstances, she would become the object of disapproval by her patient and by her medical colleagues.

It would be very difficult to spell out exactly what duties are required by the principle of beneficence. Even if we limited ourselves to the medical context, there are so many ways of promoting someone's welfare and so many different circumstances to consider that it would be virtually impossible to provide anything like a catalog of appropriate actions. However, such a catalog is hardly necessary. Most people most often have a sense of what is reasonable and what is not, and it is this sense that we rely on in making judgments about whether physicians and others are fulfilling the duty of beneficence in their actions.

The principles of nonmaleficence and beneficence impose social duties also. In the most general terms, we look to society to take measures to promote the health and safety of its citizens. The great advances made in public health during the nineteenth century were made because the society recognized a responsibility to attempt to prevent the spread of disease. Water treatment plants, immunization programs, and quarantine restrictions were all in recognition of society's duty of nonmaleficence.

These and similar programs have been continued and augmented, and our society has also recognized a duty of beneficence in connection with health care. The Medicaid program for the poor and Medicare for the elderly are major efforts to see to at least some of the health needs of a large segment of the population. Prenatal programs for expectant mothers and public clinics are among the other social responses we have made to promote the health of citizens.

Less obvious than programs that provide direct medical care are ones that support medical research and basic science. Directly or indirectly, such programs contribute to meeting the health needs of our society. Much basic research is relevant to acquiring an understanding of the processes involved in both health and disease, and much medical research is specifically aimed at the development of effective diagnostic and therapeutic measures.

In principle, social beneficence has no limits, but in practice it must. Social resources like tax revenues are in restricted supply, and the society must decide how they are to be spent. Housing and food for the poor, education, defense, the arts, and the humanities are just some of the areas demanding support in the name of social beneficence. Medical care is just one among many claimants, and we must decide as a society what proportion of our social resources we want to commit to it. Are we prepared to guarantee to all whatever medical care they need? Are we willing to endorse only a basic level of care? Do we want to say that what is available to some (the rich or well-insured) must be available to all (the poor and uninsured)? Just how beneficent we wish to be—and can afford to be—is a matter still under discussion (see Chapter 8).

## The Principle of Utility

The principle of utility can be formulated in this way: *We should act in such a way as to bring about the greatest benefit and the least harm.* As we dis-

cussed earlier, the principle is the very foundation of the moral theory of utilitarianism. However, the principle need not be regarded as unique to utilitarianism. It can be thought of as one moral principle among others that present us with a prima facie duty, and as such it need not be regarded as always taking precedence over others. In particular, we would never think it was justified to deprive someone of a right, even if by doing so we could bring benefit to many others.

We need not repeat the discussion of the principle of utility presented earlier, but it may be useful to consider here how the principle relates to the principles of nonmaleficence and beneficence. When we consider the problem of distributing social resources, it becomes clear that acting in accordance with the principles of nonmaleficence and beneficence usually involves trade-offs. To use our earlier example, as a society we are concerned with providing for the health-care needs of our citizens. To accomplish this end, we support various programs—Medicare, Medicaid, hospital-building programs, medical research, and so on.

However, there are limits to what we can do. Medical care is not the only concern of our society. We are interested in protecting people from harm and in promoting their interests, but there are many forms of harm and many kinds of interest to be promoted. With finite resources at our disposal, the more money we spend on health care, the less we can spend on education, the arts, the humanities, and so on.

Even if we decided to spend more money on health care than we are currently spending, there would come a point at which we would receive only a marginal return for our money. General health would eventually reach such a level that it would be difficult to raise it still higher. To save even one additional life, we would have to spend a vast sum of money. By contrast, at the start of a health-care program, relatively little money can make a relatively big difference. Furthermore, money spent for marginal improvements would be directed away from other needs that had become even more crucial because of underfunding.

Thus, we could not spend all our resources on health care without ignoring other social needs.

The aim of social planning is to balance the competing needs of the society. Taken alone, the principles of nonmaleficence and beneficence are of no help in resolving the conflicts among social needs. The principle of utility must come into play to establish and rank needs and to serve as a guide for determining to what extent it is possible to satisfy one social need in comparison with others. In effect, the principle imposes a social duty on us all to use our resources to do as much good as possible. That is, we must do the most good *overall,* even when this means we are not able to meet all needs in a particular area.

The application of the principle of utility is not limited to large-scale social issues, such as how to divide our resources among medical care, defense, education, and so on. We may also rely on the principle when we are deliberating about the choice of alternative means of accomplishing an aim. For example, we might decide to institute a mandatory screening program to detect infants with PKU but decide against a program to detect those with Tay–Sachs. PKU can often be treated successfully if discovered early enough, whereas early detection of Tay–Sachs makes little or no difference in the outcome of the disease. Furthermore, PKU is distributed in the general population, whereas Tay–Sachs occurs mostly in a special segment of the population. In general, then, the additional money spent on screening for Tay–Sachs would not be justified by the results. The money could do more good, produce more benefits, were it spent some other way.

The principle of utility is also relevant to making decisions about the diagnosis and treatment of individuals. For example, as we mentioned earlier, no diagnostic test can be justified if it causes the patient more risk than the information likely to be gained is worth. Invasive procedures are associated with a certain rate of injury and death (morbidity and mortality). It would make no sense to subject a patient to a kidney biopsy if the findings were not likely to affect the course of treatment or if the risk from the biopsy were greater than the risk of the sus-

pected disease itself. Attempts are well under way in medicine to employ the formal theories of decision analysis to assist physicians in determining whether a particular mode of diagnosis, therapy, or surgery can be justified in individual cases. Underlying the details of formal analysis is the principle of utility, which directs us to act in a way that will bring about the greatest benefit and the least harm.

## Principles of Distributive Justice

We expect (and can demand) to be treated justly in our dealings with other people and with institutions. If our insurance policy covers up to thirty days of hospitalization, then we expect a claim against the policy for that amount of time to be honored. If we arrive in an emergency room with a broken arm before the arrival of someone else with a broken arm, we expect to be attended to before that person.

We do not always expect that being treated justly will work to our direct advantage. Although we would prefer to keep all the money we earn, we realize that we must pay our share of taxes. If a profusely bleeding person arrives in the emergency room after we do, we recognize that he is in need of immediate treatment and should be attended to before we are.

Justice has at least two major aspects. Seeing to it that people receive that to which they are entitled, that their rights are recognized and protected, falls under the general heading of *noncomparative justice.* By contrast, *comparative justice* is concerned with the application of laws and rules and with the distribution of burdens and benefits.

The concern of comparative justice that is most significant to the medical context is *distributive justice.* As the name suggests, distributive justice concerns the distribution of such social benefits and burdens as medical services, welfare payments, public offices, taxes, and military service. In general, the distribution of income has been the focus of recent discussions of distributive justice. In medical ethics, the focus has been the distribution of health care. Is everyone in the society entitled to receive health-care benefits, whether or not she or he can pay for them? If so, then is everyone entitled to the same amount of health care? (See Chapter 8 for a discussion of this issue.)

Philosophical theories of justice attempt to resolve questions of distributive justice by providing a detailed account of the features of individuals and society that will justify our making distinctions in the ways we distribute benefits and burdens. If some people are to be rich and others poor, if some are to rule and others serve, then there must be some rational and moral basis for such distinctions. We look to theories of justice to provide us with such a basis. (See the earlier discussion of John Rawls's theory for an outstanding recent example.)

Theories of justice differ significantly, but at the core of all theories is the basic principle that "Similar cases ought to be treated in similar ways." The principle expresses the notion that justice involves fairness of treatment. For example, it is manifestly unfair to award two different grades to two people who score the same on a multiple-choice exam. If two cases are the same, then it is arbitrary or irrational to treat them differently. To justify different treatment, we would have to show that in some relevant respect the cases are also dissimilar.

This fairness principle is known as the *formal* principle of justice. It is called "formal" because, like a sentence with blanks, it must be filled in with information. Specifically, we must be told what factors or features are to be considered *relevant* in deciding whether two cases are similar. If two cases differ in relevant respects, we may be justified in treating them differently. We may do so without being either irrational or arbitrary.

Theories of distributive justice present us with *substantive* (or *material*) principles of justice. The theories present us with arguments to show why certain features or factors should be considered relevant in deciding whether cases are similar. The substantive principles can then be referred to in determining whether particular laws, practices, or public policies can be considered just. Further, the substantive principles can be employed as guidelines for framing laws and policies and for developing a just society.

Arguments in favor of particular theories of justice are too lengthy to present here. However, it is useful to consider briefly four substantive principles that have been offered by various theorists as ones worthy of acceptance. To a considerable extent, differences among these principles help explain present disagreements in our society about the ways in which such social "goods" as income, education, and health care should be distributed. Although the principles themselves direct the distribution of burdens (taxation, public service, and so on) as well as benefits, we will focus on benefits. The basic question answered by each principle is "Who is entitled to what proportion of society's goods?"

### The Principle of Equality

According to the principle of equality, all benefits and burdens are to be distributed equally. Everyone is entitled to the same size slice of the pie, and everyone must bear an equal part of the social load. The principle, strictly interpreted, requires a radical egalitarianism—everyone is to be treated the same in all respects.

The principle is most plausible for a society above the margin of production. When there is enough to go around but not much more, then it is manifestly unfair for some to have more than they need and for others to have less than they need. When a society is more affluent, the principle may lose some of its persuasiveness. When greater efforts by a few produce more goods than the efforts of the ordinary person, it may be unfair not to recognize the accomplishments of a few by greater rewards. Rawls's theory remains an egalitarian one, while providing a way to resolve this apparent conflict. According to Rawls, any departure from equality is arbitrary, unless it can be shown that the inequality will work out to *everyone's* advantage.

### The Principle of Need

The principle of need is an extension of the egalitarian principle of equal distribution. If goods are parceled out according to individual need, those who have greater needs will receive a greater share. However, the outcome will be one of equality. Since the basic needs of everyone will be met, everyone will end up at the same level. The treatment of individuals will be equal, in this respect, even though the proportion of goods they receive will not be.

What is to count as a need is a significant question that cannot be answered by a principle of distribution alone. Obviously, basic biological needs (food, clothing, shelter) must be included, but what about psychological or intellectual needs? The difficulty of resolving the question of needs is seen in the fact that—even in our affluent society, the richest in the history of the world—we are still debating the question of whether health care should be available to all.

### The Principle of Contribution

According to the principle of contribution, everyone should get back that proportion of social goods that is the result of his or her productive labor. If two people work to grow potatoes and the first works twice as long or twice as hard as the second, then the first should be entitled to twice as large a share of the harvest.

The difficulty with this principle in an industrialized, capitalistic society is that contributions to production can take forms other than time and labor. Some people risk their money in investments needed to make production possible, and others contribute crucial ideas or inventions. How are comparisons to be made? Furthermore, in highly industrialized societies it is the functioning of the entire system, rather than the work of any particular individual, that creates the goods to be distributed. A single individual's claim on the outcome of the whole system may be very small.

Nonetheless, it is individuals who make the system work, so it does seem just that individuals should benefit from their contributions. If it is true that it is the system of social organization itself that is most responsible for creating the goods, then this is an argument for supporting the system through taxation and other means. If individual contributions count for relatively little (although for something), there may be no real

grounds for attempting to distinguish among them in distributing social benefits.

### The Principle of Effort

According to the principle of effort, the degree of effort made by the individual should determine the proportion of goods received by the individual. Thus, the file clerk who works just as hard as the president of a company should receive the same proportion of social goods as the president. Those who are lazy and refuse to exert themselves will receive proportionally less than those who work hard.

The advantage of the principle is that it captures our sense of what is fair—that those who do their best should be similarly rewarded, while those who do less than their best should be less well rewarded. The principle assumes that people have equal opportunities to do their best and that if they do not it is their own fault. One difficulty with this assumption is that, even if the society presents equal opportunities, nature does not. Some people are born with disabilities or meet with accidents, and their misfortunes may make it difficult for them to want to do their best, even when they are given the opportunity.

Each principle has its shortcomings, but this does not mean that adjustments cannot be made to correct their weaknesses. A complete theory of justice need not be limited in the number of principles that it accepts, and it is doubtful that any theory can be shown to be both fair and plausible if it restricts itself to only one principle. Although all theories require adjustment, theories fall into types in accordance with the principles they emphasize. For example, Marxist theories select need as basic, whereas libertarian theories stress personal contribution as the grounds for distribution. Utilitarian theories employ that combination of principles that promises to maximize both private and public interests.

Joel Feinberg, to whom the preceding discussion is indebted, may be mentioned as an example of a careful theorist who recommends the adoption of a combination of principles. Feinberg sees the principle of equality based on needs as the basic determination of distributive justice. After basic needs have been satisfied, the principles of contribution and effort should be given the most weight.

According to Feinberg, when there is an economic abundance, then the claim to "minimally decent conditions" can reasonably be made for every person in the society. To have one's basic needs satisfied under such conditions amounts to a fundamental right. However, when everyone's basic needs are taken care of and society produces a surplus of goods, then considerations of contribution and effort become relevant. Those who contribute most to the increase of goods or those who work the hardest to produce it (or some combination) can legitimately lay claim to a greater share.

The principles of justice we have discussed may seem at first to be intolerably abstract and so irrelevant to the practical business of society. However, it is important to keep in mind that it is by referring to such principles that we criticize our society and its laws and practices. The claim that society is failing to meet some basic need of all of its citizens and that this is unfair or unjust is a powerful charge. It can be a call to action in the service of justice. If the claim can be demonstrated, it has more than rhetorical power. It imposes upon us all an obligation to eliminate the source of the injustice.

Similarly, in framing laws and formulating policies, we expect those who occupy the offices of power and influence to make their decisions in accordance with principles. Prominent among these must be principles of justice. It may be impossible in the conduct of daily business to apply any principle directly or exclusively, for we can hardly remake our society overnight. Yet if we are committed to a just society, then the principles of justice can at least serve as guidelines when policy decisions are made. They remind us that it is not always fair for the race to go to the swift.

## The Principle of Autonomy

The principle of autonomy can be stated this way: *Rational individuals should be permitted to be*

*self-determining.* According to this formulation, we act autonomously when our actions are the result of our own choices and decisions. Thus, autonomy and self-determination are equivalent.

Autonomy is associated with the status we ascribe to rational beings as persons in the morally relevant sense. We are committed to the notion that persons are by their very nature uniquely qualified to decide what is in their own best interest. This is because, to use Kant's terms, they are ends in themselves, not means to some other ends. As such, they have an inherent worth, and it is the duty of others to respect that worth and avoid treating them as though they were just ordinary parts of the world to be manipulated according to the will of someone else. A recognition of autonomy is a recognition of that inherent worth, and a violation of autonomy is a violation of our concept of what it is to be a person. To deny someone autonomy is to treat her or him as something less than a person.

This view of the nature of autonomy and its connection with our recognition of what is involved in being a person is shared by several significant moral theories. At the core of each theory is the concept of the rational individual as a moral agent who, along with other moral agents, possesses an unconditional worth. Moral responsibility itself is based on the assumption that such agents are free to determine their own actions and pursue their own aims.

Autonomy is significant not only because it is a condition for moral responsibility, but because it is through the exercise of autonomy that individuals shape their lives. We might not approve of what people do with their lives. It is sad to see talent wasted and opportunities for personal development rejected. Nevertheless, as we sometimes say, "It's his life." We recognize that people are entitled to attempt to make their lives what they want them to be and that it would be wrong for us to take control of their lives and dictate their actions, even if we could. We recognize that a person must walk to heaven or hell by her own freely chosen path.

Simply put, to act autonomously is to decide for oneself what to do. Of course, decisions are never made outside of a context, and the world and the people in it exert influence, impose constraints, and restrict opportunities. It is useful to call attention to three interrelated aspects of autonomy in order to get a better understanding of the ways in which autonomy can be exercised, denied, and restricted. We will look at autonomy in the contexts of actions, options, and decision making.

## Autonomy and Actions

Consider the following situations: A police officer shoves a demonstrator off the sidewalk during an abortion protest. An attendant in a psychiatric ward warns a patient to stay in bed or be strapped down. A corrections officer warns a prison inmate that if he does not donate blood he will not be allowed out of his cell to eat dinner. A state law requires that anyone admitted to a hospital be screened for the HIV antibody.

In each of these situations, either actual force, the threat of force, or potential penalties are employed to direct the actions of an individual toward some end. All involve some form of coercion, and the coercion is used to restrict the freedom of individuals to act as they might choose. Under such circumstances, the individual ceases to be the agent who initiates the action as a result of his or her choice. The individual's initiative is set aside, wholly or partially, in favor of someone else's.

Autonomy is violated in such cases even if the individual intends to act in the way that is imposed or demanded. Perhaps the prison inmate would have donated blood anyway, and surely some people would have wanted to be screened for HIV. However, the use of coercion makes the wishes or intentions of the individual partly or totally irrelevant to whether the act is performed.

Autonomy as the initiation of action through one's own intervention and choice can clearly be restricted to a greater or lesser degree. Someone who is physically forced to become a subject in a medical experiment, as in a Nazi concentration camp, is totally deprived of autonomy. The same is true of someone tricked into becoming a subject without knowing it. In the infamous Tuskegee syphilis studies, some participants were led to believe they were receiving appropriate medical treatment, when in fact they were part of a control group in the experiment. The situation is somewhat different for someone who agrees to become a subject in order to receive needed medical care. Such a person is acting under strong coercion, but the loss of autonomy is not complete. It is at least possible to refuse to participate, even if the cost of doing so may be extremely high.

In situations more typical than those above, autonomy may be compromised, rather than denied. For example, someone who is by nature nonassertive or someone who is poor and uneducated may find it very difficult to preserve his power of self-determination when he becomes a patient in a hospital. Medical authority, represented by physicians and the hospital staff, may be so intimidating to such a person that she does not feel free to exercise her autonomy. In such a case, although no one may be deliberately attempting to infringe on the patient's autonomy, social and psychological factors may constitute a force so coercive that the patient feels she has no choice but to do what she is told.

## Autonomy and Options

Autonomy involves more than freedom from duress in making decisions. There must be genuine possibilities to decide among. A forced option is no option at all, and anyone who is in the position of having to take what he can get can hardly be regarded as self-determining or as exercising free choice.

In our society, economic and social conditions frequently limit the options available in medical care. As a rule, the poor simply do not have the same choices available to them as the rich. Someone properly insured or financially well off who might be helped by a heart transplant can decide whether or not to undergo the risk of having one. That is an option not generally available to someone who is uninsured and poor.

Similarly, a woman who depends on Medicaid and lives in a state in which Medicaid funds cannot be used to pay for abortions may not have the option of having an abortion. Her choice is not a genuine one, for she lacks the means to implement it. The situation is quite different for a middle-class woman faced with the same question. She may decide against having an abortion, but whatever she decides, the choice is real. She is autonomous in a way that the poor woman is not.

Those who believe that one of the goals of our society is to promote and protect the autonomy of individuals have frequently argued that we must do more to offer all individuals the same range of health-care options. If we do not, they have suggested, then our society cannot be one in which everyone has an equal degree of autonomy. In a very real sense, those who are rich will have greater freedom of action than those who are poor.

## Autonomy and Decision Making

More is involved in decision making than merely saying yes or no. In particular, relevant information is an essential condition for genuine decision making. We are exercising our autonomy in the fullest sense only when we are making *informed* decisions.

It is pointless to have options if we are not aware of them; we can hardly be said to be directing the course of our lives if our decisions must be made in ignorance of information that is available and relevant to our choices. These are the reasons that lying and other forms of deception are so destructive of autonomy. If someone with a progressive and ordinarily fatal disease is not told about it by her physician, then she is in no position to decide how to shape what remains of her life. The lack of a crucial piece of information—that she is dying—is likely to lead her to make decisions different from the ones she would make were she in possession of the information.

Information is the key to protecting and preserving autonomy in most medical situations. A patient who is not informed of alternative forms of treatment and their associated risks is denied the opportunity to make his own wishes and val-

ues count for something in his own life. For example, someone with coronary artery disease who is not told of the relative merits of medical treatment with drugs but is told only that he is a candidate for coronary artery-bypass surgery, is in no position to decide what risks he wishes to take and what ordeals he is prepared to undergo. A physician who does not supply the patient with the information the patient needs is restricting the patient's autonomy. The principle of autonomy requires *informed* consent, for consent alone does not involve genuine self-determination.

Making decisions for "the good" of others (paternalism), without consulting their wishes, deprives them of their status as autonomous agents. For example, some people at the final stages of a terminal illness might prefer to be allowed to die without heroic intervention, while others might prefer to prolong their lives as long as medical skills and technological powers make possible. If a physician or family undertakes to make a decision in this matter on behalf of the patient, then no matter what their motive, they are denying to the patient the power of self-determination.

Because autonomy is so bound up with informed consent and decision making, special problems arise in the case of those unable to give consent and make decisions. Patients who are comatose, severely brain damaged, psychotic, or seriously mentally impaired are not capable of making decisions on their own behalf. The nature of their condition has already deprived them of their autonomy. Of course, this does not mean that they have no status as moral persons or that they have no interests. It falls to others to see that their interests are served.

The situation is similar for those, such as infants and young children, who are incapable of understanding. Any consent that is given must be given by others. But what are the limits of consent that can be legitimately given for some other person? Consenting to needed medical care seems legitimate, but what about rejecting needed medical care? What about consenting to becoming a subject in a research program? These questions are as crucial as they are difficult to resolve.

## Restrictions on Autonomy

Autonomy is not an absolute or unconditional value. We would regard it as absurd for someone to claim that she was justified in committing a murder because she was only exercising her power of self-determination. Such a defense would be morally ludicrous.

However, we do value autonomy and recognize a general duty to respect it and even to promote its exercise. We demand compelling reasons to justify restricting the power of individuals to make their own choices and direct their own lives.

We will briefly examine four principles that are frequently appealed to in justifying restrictions on autonomy. The principles have been discussed most in the context of social and legal theory, for it is through laws and penalties that a society most directly regulates the conduct of its citizens. However, the principles can also be appealed to in justifying policies and practices of institutions (such as hospitals) and the actions of individuals that affect other people.

Appealing to a principle can provide, at best, only a prima facie justification. Even if a principle can be shown to apply to a particular case in which freedom of action is restricted, we may value the lost freedom more than what is gained by restricting it. Reasons suggested by the principle may not be adequately persuasive. Furthermore, the principles themselves are frequently the subjects of controversy, and, with the exception of the harm principle, it is doubtful that any of the principles would be universally endorsed by philosophers and legal theorists.

**The Harm Principle.**  According to the harm principle, we may restrict the freedom of people to act if the restriction is necessary to prevent harm to others. In the most obvious case, we may take action to prevent violence like rape, robbery, killing, or assault. We may act to protect someone who is in apparent risk of harm from the action of someone else. The risk of harm need not be the result of the intention to harm. Thus, we might take steps to see that a surgeon whose skills and judgment have been impaired through drug use is not permitted to operate.

The risk that he poses to his patients warrants the effort to keep him from acting as he wishes. The harm principle may also be used to justify laws that exert coercive force and so restrict freedom of action. Laws against homicide and assault are clear examples, but the principle extends also to the regulation of institutions and practices. People may be robbed at the point of a pen, as well as at the point of a knife, and the harm produced by fraud may be as great as that produced by outright theft. Careless or deceptive medical practitioners may cause direct harm to their patients, and laws that regulate the standards of medical practice restrict the freedom of practitioners for the protection of patients.

**The Principle of Paternalism.**  In its weak version, the principle of paternalism is no more than the harm principle applied to the individual himself. According to the principle, we are justified in restricting someone's freedom to act if doing so is necessary to prevent him from harming himself. Thus, we might force an alcoholic into a treatment program and justify our action by claiming that we did so to prevent him from continuing to harm himself by his drinking.

In its strong version, the principle of paternalism justifies restricting someone's autonomy if by doing so we can benefit her. In such a case, our concern is not only with preventing the person from harming herself, but also with promoting her good in a positive way. The principle might be appealed to even in cases in which our actions go against the other's known wishes. For example, a physician might decide to treat a patient with a placebo (an inactive drug), even if she has asked to be told the truth about her medical condition and her therapy. He might attempt to justify his action by claiming that if the patient knew she was receiving a placebo, then the placebo would be less likely to be effective. Since taking the placebo while believing that it is an active drug makes her feel better, the physician may claim that by deceiving her he is doing something to help her.

Paternalism may be expressed in laws and public policies, as well as in private actions. Some have suggested the drug laws as a prime example of governmental paternalism. By making certain drugs illegal and inaccessible and by placing other drugs under the control of physicians, the laws aim to protect people from themselves. Self-medication is virtually eliminated, and the so-called recreational use of drugs is prohibited. The price for such laws is a restriction on individual autonomy. Some have argued that the price is too high and that the most the government should do is warn and educate the individual about the consequences of using certain drugs.

**The Principle of Legal Moralism.** The principle of legal moralism holds that a legitimate function of the law is to enforce morality by turning the immoral into the illegal. Hence, the restrictions placed on actions by the law are justified by the presumed fact that the actions are immoral and so ought not to be performed.

To a considerable extent, laws express the values of a society and the society's judgments about what is morally right. In our society, homicide and theft are recognized as crimes, and those who commit them are guilty of legal, as well as moral, wrongdoing. Society attempts to prevent such crimes and to punish offenders.

The degree to which the law should embody moral judgments is a hard question. It is particularly difficult to answer in a pluralistic society like ours, in which there may be sharp differences of opinion about the moral legitimacy of some actions. Until quite recently, for example, materials considered obscene could not be freely purchased, birth-control literature could not be freely distributed nor contraceptives legally prescribed in some states, and the conditions of divorce were generally stringent and punitive. Even now many states outlaw homosexual solicitation and acts, and prostitution is generally illegal. The foundation for such laws is the belief by many that the practices proscribed are morally wrong.

The current heated debate over abortion reflects, in some of its aspects, the conflict between those who favor strong legal moralism and those who oppose it. Many who consider abortion morally wrong would also like to see it made illegal once more. Others, even though they may oppose abortion, believe that it is a private moral matter and that the attempt to regulate it by law is an unwarranted intrusion of state power.

**The Welfare Principle.** The welfare principle holds that it is justifiable to restrict individual autonomy if doing so will result in providing benefits to others. Those who endorse this principle are not inclined to think that it demands a serious self-sacrifice for the welfare of others. Rather, in their view, an ideal application of the principle would be the case in which we give up just a little autonomy to bring about a great deal of benefit to others.

For example, transplant organs are in short supply at the moment because their availability depends mostly on their being freely donated. The situation could be dramatically changed by a law requiring that organs from the recently dead be salvaged and made available for use as transplants.

Such a law would end the present system of voluntary donation, and by doing so it would restrict our freedom to decide what is to be done with our bodies after death. However, it would be easy to argue that the tremendous value that others might gain from such a law easily outweighs the slight restriction on autonomy that it would involve.

These four principles are not the only ones that offer grounds for abridging the autonomy of individuals, but they are the most relevant to decision making and policy planning in medicine. It is important to keep in mind that merely appealing to a principle is not enough to warrant a limit on autonomy. A principle points in the direction of an argument, but it is no substitute for one. The high value we place on autonomy gives its preservation a high priority, and compelling considerations are required to justify compromising it. In the view of some philosophers, who endorse the position taken by Mill, only the harm principle can serve as grounds for legitimately restricting autonomy. Other theorists find persuasive reasons to do so in other principles.

# THEORIES WITHOUT PRINCIPLES

Most of traditional Western ethics is based on the assumption that ethical beliefs are best represented by a set of rules or abstract principles. Thus, Kant's categorical imperative, Mill's principle of utility, and Ross's list of prima facie duties attempt to supply guides for moral action and decision making that apply in all circumstances.

Moral decisions thus typically involve bringing a case under a rule, in much the same way that law courts apply statutory laws to cases brought before them. Much ethical dispute, like much legal dispute, is over whether an abstract rule does or does not apply in a concrete case.

In recent decades, some ethical theorists have turned away from the principle-governed, legalistic approach to ethics in favor of another approach from the Western tradition. Some of the new theorists have emphasized the importance of character as the source of moral action, whereas others have stressed the central role of shared concerns and the crucial importance of social practices and institutions in shaping our moral lives.

We will present brief sketches of ethical theories that (according to their proponents) cannot be reduced to sets of abstract principles. Although moral theorists debate such questions as whether the virtue of being a truthful person (a character trait) isn't ultimately derived from the duty to tell the truth (a principle), we will steer clear of these issues. Rather, as with theories based on principles, we will restrict ourselves to a general statement of each theory, indicate how it might be applied in a medical context, and then discuss some of the difficulties it faces as a moral theory.

The three theories discussed here have been presented by their proponents in a variety of versions, some of them quite elaborate and philosophically sophisticated. Keep in mind that we are presenting only sketches.

## Virtue Ethics

J. D. Salinger's character Holden Caulfield dislikes "phonies" and dreams of standing in a field and keeping little kids from running off the edge of the cliff beyond. He wants to be a "catcher in the rye."

Millions of us who have read *The Catcher in the Rye* have admired Holden and wanted to be like him in some ways. We too would like to avoid phoniness, particularly in ourselves, and we would like to do something to make the world a better place, particularly for children. Holden isn't a perfect person, but even so, he's a moral hero, a sort of icon or example of what we wish we could be in some respects.

Every culture is populated by real and fictional characters representing the sort of people we should try to become. Some characters are seen as perfect, while others are people who, despite their flaws, show what they were capable of in confronting life's problems and struggles. To name only a few historically important people, consider Socrates, Jesus, Gautama Buddha, Moses, Florence Nightingale, Confucius, Martin Luther King, Susan B. Anthony, Anne Frank, Gandhi, and Mother Teresa. It would be easy to make an even longer list of fictional characters who evoke our admiration and make us feel we would be better people if we could be more like them.

*Virtue ethics* is ethics based on character. Its fundamental idea is that a person who has acquired the proper set of dispositions will do what is right when faced with a situation involving a moral choice. Thus, virtue ethics doesn't involve invoking principles or rules to guide actions.

The virtuous person is both the basic concept and the goal of virtue ethics. The virtuous person is one who acts right, because she or he is just that sort of person. Right actions flow out of character, and the virtuous person has a disposition to do the right thing. Rules need not be consulted, calculations need not be performed, abstract duties need not be considered.

People become virtuous in the way they become good swimmers. Upbringing, education, the example of others, reflection, personal effort, and experience all play a role. As with swimming, some people may be more naturally inclined to become virtuous than others. Those who are naturally patient, reflective, and slow to anger may find it easier than those who are impatient, impulsive, and possessed of a fiery temper.

Families and social institutions—like schools, clubs, and athletic teams, as well as religious institutions—play a role in shaping our moral character. They tell us how we should behave when we lose a school election or win a softball game. They teach us what we should do when we have a chance to take money without anyone's finding out, when we witness a case of discrimination, when we ourselves are treated unfairly.

Quite apart from explicit teachings or doctrines, the lives of historical figures like Jesus, Mohammed, and Buddha have served as examples of what it is possible for a person to become. Perhaps no one believes she or he can achieve the level of moral perfection that such people represent, but they offer us models for fashioning ourselves. In the way a swimmer may study the backstroke, we can study the way moral heroes have dealt with the moral questions that face us.

When a Christian asks, "What would Jesus do?" it is not typically an attempt to call on divine guidance. Rather, it is an occasion for reflection, of attempting to imagine what someone trying to live a life like Jesus's would do. We try to improve our character by becoming more like those who are admirable. Hence, in addition to education and social influences, we must engage in self-criticism and make deliberate efforts to improve.

## The Virtues

The virtuous person is disposed to demonstrate virtues through behavior. *Virtue* is a translation of the Greek word *arete,* which also has much the same meaning as *excellence.* (Virtue ethics is also called *aretaic ethics.*) The excellent tennis player demonstrates in playing tennis that he possesses characteristics needed to play the game well. Similarly, the virtuous person demonstrates through living that she possesses the appropriate range of excellences.

Virtues have traditionally been divided into moral and practical, or nonmoral, virtues:

*Moral virtues:* benevolence, compassion, honesty, charity, sincerity, sympathy, respect, consideration, kindness, thoughtfulness, loyalty, fairness, and so on

*Nonmoral virtues:* rationality (or intelligence), tenacity, capability, patience, prudence, skillfulness, staunchness, shrewdness, proficiency, and so on

The distinction between moral and nonmoral virtues is far from clear, but the rough idea is that those in one set are associated with living a good (moral) life, whereas those in the other are associated with the practical aspects of living. A thief can be patient (a nonmoral virtue), but not honest (a moral one). By contrast, an honest (moral virtue) person may lack patience. (How to classify *courage* has always been a problem. A courageous thief may be more successful than a cowardly one, but a benevolent person lacking the courage to put his views into practice will be ineffective.)

## Virtue Ethics in the Medical Context

Consider Dr. Charles Holmes, an emergency room trauma surgeon who chose his specialty because the money is good and the hours reasonable. He treats the patients, then he goes home. Holmes is technically expert, but he lacks compassion for his patients and is not interested in their worries or fears. He shows no tact in dealing with patients and barely acknowledges they are people.

Dr. Holmes is far removed from our notion of what a physician as a compassionate healer should be. In treating his patients as broken machines, he may help them in important ways, but his skills as a physician are deficient. Holmes, we might say, lacks the dispositions necessary to be a good physician.

From at least the time of the ancient Greeks, the Western tradition has expected physicians to be virtuous, and more recently, we have broadened that expectation to include nurses, medical technicians, and all who care for patients. The tradition is resplendent with stories of those who behaved in ways that make them moral examples for all who commit themselves to providing patient care. Scores of European physicians at the time of the Black Death (the bubonic plague) in the fourteenth century tended to their patients, even though they knew they risked infection themselves. The eighteenth century American physician Benjamin Rush did his best to help cholera sufferers, although he knew he was likely to get the disease. Florence Nightingale, braving harsh conditions and the risk of sickness, helped care for British troops during the Crimean War and fought to establish nursing as a profession.

Virtue ethics calls attention to the strength of medicine at its moral (and practical) best. Courage, loyalty, integrity, compassion, and benevolence, along with determination and intelligence, are virtues associated with physicians and others who provide what we consider the right sort of care for their patients. We expect everyone involved in patient care to display in their behavior a similar constellation of virtues. Virtue ethics, with its emphasis on character and behavioral dispositions, comes closer to capturing our concept of the ideal health professional than does a rule-based view of moral decision making like Kant's ethics or utilitarianism.

### Difficulties with Virtue Ethics

A fundamental difficulty with virtue ethics is that it provides us with no explicit guidance in deciding how to act in particular circumstances. Suppose someone is terminally ill, in great pain, and asks assistance in dying. Should we agree to help? We may ask, "What would Jesus do?" and the answer may be, "I don't know." If we have been brought up to be virtuous, perhaps we should have no need to ask such questions. But how are we to know who among us has been properly brought up, and for those of us who aren't sure, what should we do?

Medicine is repeatedly faced with the problem of deciding about what actions ought to be taken, but virtue ethics is about character and dispositions. However, even a benevolent person

(one disposed to act benevolently) may not know how to distribute organs that are in scarce supply. Further, virtue ethics does not supply any clear way to resolve moral conflicts. What if Assiz thinks it would be wrong to abort a fetus twenty-four weeks after conception, but Puzo does not. How can they go about resolving their dispute? The answer is not clear.

Also, virtues, like duties, can be incompatible when they are translated into action. If I am a transplant coordinator and try to express my gratitude to my physics teacher by allowing her to jump to the head of the waiting list for a new liver, this will conflict with my commitment to fairness. But if virtues are not ranked, how do I decide what to do in such a case? Surely we don't think it would be right for me to put my teacher at the head of the list, but on what grounds can virtue ethics say that it would be wrong?

## Care Ethics

Care ethics is an outgrowth of feminist ethics or, perhaps more accurately, is a particular strand of feminist ethics. Care ethics is not a unified doctrine that can be captured in a set of abstract statements. Indeed, care ethics, like feminist ethics in general, rejects abstract principles as the basis for ethics. It is perhaps best characterized as a family of beliefs about the way values should be manifested in character and in behavior. It is unified by a set of shared concerns and commitments, as well as by the rejection of the traditional philosophical view that ethics can be adequately represented by rules and principles.

Much of the philosophical work in care ethics has been developed on the basis of psychologist Carol Gilligan's research on moral development. Lawrence Kohlberg's earlier studies suggest that women are "less developed" in their moral reasoning skills than men because they are not as adept at applying moral principles to particular cases. Gilligan does not conclude that Kohlberg is wrong but, rather, that women have a *style* of moral reasoning that is entirely different from the style employed by men. The title Gilligan gave to her book, *In a Different Voice,* is an allusion to the impression she formed in listening to women discuss how they would resolve moral difficulties that she was hearing a voice different from the strident and judgmental male voice of traditional ethical theory.

Gilligan claims that when women are presented with cases of moral conflict, they focus on the details of the people involved in the situation and their personal relationships. They then try to find a way to resolve the conflict that will avoid causing harm to anyone and satisfy, to the extent possible, the interests of everyone concerned. To accomplish such a resolution, women are prepared to look for compromises and points of agreement, to be flexible in their demands, and to take novel approaches to find resolutions that all parties to the dispute will accept.

Unlike the approach taken by women, Gilligan claims, when men are presented with a case of moral conflict, they focus on analyzing the situation with the aim of deciding what abstract rule it would be appropriate to follow to resolve the case. They take little interest in the people as individuals who have their own concerns and needs. Once men have identified a rule they believe fits the case at hand, they act (and try to make others act) in a way that most closely conforms to it. Men are prepared to follow rules in the interest of justice, even if securing justice involves sacrificing the interests of some of the people involved in the conflict.

Gilligan characterizes the way women respond to situations of moral conflict as expressing an *ethic of care* and the way in which men respond as expressing an *ethic of justice.* She emphasizes, however, that there isn't a perfect correlation between these types of response and gender. Ideally, according to Gilligan, moral agents should employ both approaches in moral decision making. Not only is there room for both, but there is also a need for both.

Some philosophers have refined Gilligan's original distinction and divided "feminist ethics" from "care ethics." *Feminist ethics,* they emphasize, involves acknowledging the validity of women's experience in dealing with people and society, expressing a commitment to social equality, and exploring ways to empower women (see the discussion of feminist ethics later in this chapter). *Care ethics* need not have such explicit feminist concerns, although it shares the same general aims and point of view.

Even so, most feminists see the question of whether care ethics should be distinguished from feminist ethics as less important than the need to make sure women's perspectives and concerns are represented within ethics. According to them, the tradition of philosophical ethics has concentrated on the development of comprehensive abstract theories that fail to acknowledge the importance of values prized by women and thus assign those values no role in moral decision making or the moral life. Care ethics is a means of bringing women's concerns with the lives of individual women, children, families, and the society into ethics.

## Values, Not Principles

Ethical theories as diverse as utilitarianism and Kantian ethics have in common a reliance upon abstract principles both as an expression of the theory and as a means of resolving moral conflicts. Thus, to decide whether an action is morally legitimate, we can appeal to the principle of utility or to the categorical imperative. Moral theories can be viewed as providing a decision procedure for arriving at morally justified conclusions in particular cases—to justify an action, bring it under a rule.

Care ethics holds that it is not even appropriate to think in terms of rules or principles where certain kinds of relationships are concerned. Do we need to perform a utilitarian calculation before giving a friend a ride to the hospital? Should parents consult the categorical imperative before deciding whether to immunize their children against polio? Of course not. These relationships require that we give of ourselves and provide assistance and care of an appropriate sort. Such a requirement is bound up with the nature of being a friend or a parent. Other relationships—being a nurse, physician, teacher, manager, therapist, trainer—have similar requirements bound up with them. In general, rules and principles seem both inappropriate and unnecessary where certain human relationships are concerned.

Care ethics rejects outright the idea that abstract principles can capture everything relevant to making moral decisions. Hence, feminist/care ethics explicitly denies there can be a decision procedure consisting only in bringing a case "under a rule" or showing it to be an "instance" of a general principle. What is crucial for care ethics, rather, is an understanding of the complexities of the particular situation in which a moral problem has occurred. It requires a deep and detailed understanding of the people and their interests and feelings. Only then is it possible to resolve the problem in a way that is sensitive to the needs of everyone.

In understanding a complex situation, we must use intelligence to grasp relationships and details about the people, the circumstances, and the problem. But equally important, we must use *empathy* to understand the concerns and feelings of the people involved. We must identify with those in need or conflict, see what is at stake from their point of view, and ascertain their worries and concerns. We must also bring to the situation of moral conflict or doubt such traditional "women's values" as caring, consideration, kindness, concern for others, compassion, understanding, generosity, sympathy, helpfulness, and a willingness to assume responsibility.

These are the very values we must rely on to resolve moral conflicts and see to the needs of the people involved. The point is not to show who is in the wrong or being treated unfairly. Rather, the point is to find a way out of the conflict that takes into account the concerns and feelings of those involved.

According to care ethics, the traditional ethical model of a disinterested, detached, and dispassionate judge reviewing the objective facts in a case and then issuing an impartial decision about the moral acceptability of an action is inappropriate and mistaken. It excludes the very values that are most relevant to moral situations and most important to the people who are in-

volved. Moral decisions should not be impartial, in an abstract and bloodless way, rather, they should show partiality to *everyone* involved.

Like virtue ethics, care ethics emphasizes the development of an appropriate character. As a society we should make an effort, by teaching and example, to develop individuals, male and female, who respond appropriately to moral situations. They should be people who recognize the importance of personal relationships, respect individuals, and accept responsibility. In their dealings with others, if they have acquired the proper character, they will bring to bear the values (see above) we associate with caring for and about people.

## Care Ethics in the Medical Context

Suppose the parents of a severely impaired newborn boy are told by the child's physicians that his treatment ought to be discontinued and he should be given only "comfort care" and allowed to die. The parents' initial response is to reject the recommendation and insist that everything possible be done to continue the life of their child. How might such a conflict be resolved by the approach advocated by care ethics?

The parties in the conflict must discuss freely and openly each of their positions. (We need not assume only two positions are involved.) The physicians must explain in detail the baby's medical condition, discuss the therapy they may be able to offer, and be forthcoming about its limitations. If they believe the baby will die in a few hours or days, no matter what they do, they must be frank about their expectation. They might point out that the only therapy possible involves extensive and painful surgery, that it is almost certain to be unsuccessful, that it will be expensive, and that it will demand the resources of the hospital, the society, and the parents themselves.

For their part, the parents might talk about their hopes for the child and their willingness to love and nurture even a child with severe physical and mental problems. They might discuss the guilt they would feel about giving up the struggle and allowing the child to die. They might discuss their experiences with other children or talk about the difficulties they had conceiving the one who is now not expected to live.

No particular outcome can be predicted from such a discussion. We might imagine education taking place and compromises developing among all the participants. We might imagine the physicians coming to a greater appreciation of what the child means to the parents and why they are so reluctant to allow the child to die. The parents, for their part, might come to understand that the physicians are concerned with their child and are also frustrated and saddened by their inability to help the child get better.

The outcome might involve adjustments on the part of all participants. The parents might come to realize that their child is almost sure to die no matter what is done. The physicians might realize that they might make the child's death easier for the parents to bear by allowing the parents to hold the child and spend time with him.

Other moral conflicts or questions might be approached in a similar fashion. Should Ladzewell's request that he be assisted in dying be followed? Should Terema's request for an abortion in the second trimester of pregnancy be honored? Dozens of similar questions arise in the area of health care, and care ethics suggests that the proper approach is not to invoke principles, but instead to deal with the people involved as individuals and behave in accordance with the values of care.

Medicine, nursing, and allied areas have traditionally been associated with the values of caring. We have expected practitioners to manifest in their character and conduct concern, compassion, sympathy, kindness, and willingness to take responsibility and to help patients in their charge. In this respect, care ethics is asking us to recognize a traditional approach to patients. However, care ethics also reassures us that this approach is legitimate, even though no abstract principles are involved. More than this, though, it tells us to rely on those same values and dispositions when we are faced with moral conflicts in medicine. Again, care ethics reassures us that we can put our trust in the values of care and need not reach for principles to resolve the conflict.

## Difficulties with Care Ethics

A frequent criticism of care ethics is that Gilligan's empirical claims about the differences between the moral reasoning of women and men do not stand up to the challenge of more recent data. Without taking a stand on this question, it is enough to observe that Gilligan's empirical claims are not crucial to care ethics. It is enough for the care ethics theorist to demonstrate the importance of the values that belong to the ethic of care by showing how they can play a role in the moral life of individuals and society and how they can be employed as guides in resolving cases of moral doubt and conflict.

Also, not all care advocates have accepted a radical division between two "ethics." Some critics have pointed out, for example, that the principle of beneficence ("Act so as to promote the good of others") can be construed as implying the need for caring. Hence, according to this line of criticism, care ethics can be seen as a part of the traditional enterprise of philosophical ethics. Care ethics usefully emphasizes values and approaches relatively ignored or unappreciated in traditional ethical theory, but it does not stand as an alternative to a moral theory like utilitarianism or even Ross's intuitionism.

A more important criticism may be that, like virtue ethics, which also rejects principles as necessary to ethics, care ethics provides us with no obvious way to resolve moral conflicts. We may bring to a conflict the ethics of care, but we may still not know how to make a decision. When a number of people are in need of the same kidney for transplant, how should we decide who gets the kidney? Should we, in the manner suggested by care ethics, have a discussion with them all, assess their needs and feelings, then make a decision? It seems unlikely such a group could reach a consensus, particularly in the short time allowed under such circumstances. If we make the decision affecting them, then most would probably claim they had been treated unfairly.

Such cases suggest that the abstract principle of justice may yield more satisfactory results than the values of care ethics alone.

Finally, values, like virtues and duties, can be incompatible when they have to be translated into action. While I may be moved by sympathy and want the mother with two young children to receive the bone marrow that may save her life, I may also be moved by my compassion for the sufferings of a six-year-old boy who might have a long life ahead of him and want him to receive it. If I am forced to choose who gets the bone marrow, even if I learn much more about the people involved, my choice ultimately seems arbitrary.

These objections might be answered satisfactorily by a care ethics theorist. Even so, they are prima facie shortcomings that require serious responses.

## Feminist Ethics

Feminist ethics in general, like care ethics in particular, rejects the traditional notion that ethics can be represented by a set of abstract rules or principles and that the morality of actions and policies can be assessed by reference to them.

From the feminist perspective, the "principlism" of traditional ethics is compromised by the facts of the social world. The unequal distribution of political and social power and the inequalities attached to the accidents of birth, race, and gender mean that even such an apparently basic principle as the autonomy (self-directedness) of the individual is restricted in its application. In some states, for example, a woman who cannot pay for an abortion is not free to get one. Thus, her autonomy as an abstract right is meaningless in practical terms. The focus of ethics, according to feminist philosophers, must be on social arrangements, practices, and institutions, not abstract principles. Further, the overall aim of ethics must be to eliminate (or at least reduce) the oppression of women, races, and other subordinate groups in societies throughout the world.

Although care ethics originated in feminism, some feminists regard associating it with feminism as a threat to feminism. They fear that caring will be seen as a uniquely female trait and that feminist ethics will be undercut. First, it may be dismissed as based on an inferior form of reasoning (Gilligan's "ethic of care") more appropriate to the largely female "helping" professions of nursing and social work than to the predominantly male profession of medicine. Second, the view that caring is a woman's way of thinking may reinforce the stereotypes that confine women to the lower ranks of the health-care hierarchy. Caring has a legitimate place in feminist ethics, but it must be seen as a disposition desirable for all people to have across all divisions of gender, race, and class.

For many feminist philosophers, *equality* lies at the core of ethics. Their primary concern is with gender equality, and their aim is to critique the institutions and practices of society to expose the ways they keep women subjected to men. More broadly, though, most feminists support an effort to expose and eradicate the domination of any one group by another. They recognize that women may suffer compound injustices because they belong to races and classes that have been subordinated. A woman who is Asian, sick, and old needs to have all the ways she is subordinated addressed by ethics and redressed by society.

For feminists, ethics is part of the ongoing effort to uncover and eliminate the sources of social inequality. As Susan Sherwin puts the point, feminist ethics cannot be satisfied just by calculating increases in happiness and invoking moral principles. Rather, it must also ask *whose* happiness is increased and how the principles affect the oppressed as well as the oppressor. In the final analysis, she writes, "Positive moral value attaches to actions or principles that help relieve oppression, and negative value attaches to those that fail to reduce oppression or actually help to strengthen it."

Traditional ethics is among the practices scrutinized by feminist philosophers. As discussed earlier, the concept of individuals as self-directing, or autonomous, is compromised by social realities. Equality is necessary for the

exercise of autonomy, and under present conditions, most people are not autonomous. Thus,
appealing to the principle of autonomy is more a
way of saying that those who are socially privileged and economically and politically powerful
may do as they wish than a way of putting power
into the hands of people who are oppressed.
People limited by social disadvantages, dependence on others, or responsibility for the care of
others are not equal to those free of such burdens, and thus lack their autonomy.

Because of the importance feminists attach
to social equality, they are concerned with the
ways medicine as a social institution tends to
subordinate women to men. They point to the
fact that most nurses are still female, while most
physicians are male. Also, some feminists tend to
see the "medicalization" of women's reproductive lives—through assisted-reproduction
procedures like in vitro fertilization, hospitalized
deliveries by obstetricians, or hormone-replace-
ment therapy at menopause—as ways for men to
exercise control over women. Further, some feminists view the techniques of assisted reproduction as a means for powerful males to produce
genetically connected offspring at the expense of
subordinated females.

Various feminists also question some of society's fundamental assumptions about the value of
medicine. For example, some have argued that
providing expensive health care for the very sick
is not the best way to pursue health. It could be
more effectively pursued by the equal distribution
of resources like food, shelter, security, and education that help keep people healthy. We could
get (as it were) more health by distributing our
resources than we could by treating sick people
with expensive drugs, equipment, and expertise.

## Feminist Ethics in the Medical Context

Because feminist ethics can't be represented by a
set of principles and isn't a unified set of beliefs,
it's not likely that particular examples of how
feminist doctrines might be put into practice
would be accepted as accurate by most feminists.

Nevertheless, we can at least suggest in a general
way how a few cases might be approached from
the perspective of feminist ethics.

Feminist ethics, because of its views about
how reproduction and child rearing have been
employed to keep women subordinate to men,
supports the idea that women must have unfet-
tered access to abortion. Without such access,
women cannot control their own lives and are
forced to submit to regulation by others. They are
therefore in a state of subjection. On the question of when abortions are permissible—whether
late-term abortions are acceptable or whether
abortions are permitted when contraception has
not been used, when it has been used, or only
when a rape has occurred—feminist theorists
differ. Even on the topic of abortion, not all feminists agree; some argue that the ready availability
of abortion deprives women of the strongest
support for saying no to male sexual aggression.

Assisted reproduction is another area in
which feminists disagree among themselves.
Some hold that the new technologies that allow
women who would otherwise be infertile (even
postmenopausal women) to have a child empower women. Others hold, however, that reproductive technology is dangerous to women
and an instrument of male dominance, a way of
forcing women to have children. Women who
seem to seek out such technology on their own
may simply have been misled by our male-dominated society to believe that their choice is free.

A feminist ethics approach to a particular
case might involve asking questions about the
power relations among those involved. For example, suppose a seventy-two-year-old woman
with leukemia is considering whether she should
refuse a second course of chemotherapy and wait
for death with only home care and no further
medical intervention. Feminist ethics would want
us to ask: (1) whether the attitude of the mostly
male hospital staff that an old woman has no
useful life is influencing her decision; (2) whether
her experience of caring for others is making her
reluctant to impose a burden on her daughter or
daughter-in-law, whereas an old man might
simply feel entitled to care; (3) whether society's

view that an old woman has no function might not result in her thinking of herself in the same way—thus ignoring herself as a repository of wisdom and a link with the past or (assuming she regains her health) as someone able to exercise her skills in whatever way she sees fit. In sum, from the perspective of feminist ethics, instead of regarding the decision to discontinue treatment as a straightforward matter of exercising autonomy, we are enjoined to look at the hidden factors that may be influencing the woman's decision and making it less than free.

## Difficulties with Feminist Ethics

Proponents of traditional ethical theories question whether feminist ethics can be of much use in actual cases in which decisions must be made. What does it mean to promote gender equality when deciding whether life support should be terminated or late-term abortion allowed? How do we go about practical decision making? Even asking a feminist doesn't seem to be of much use, because they differ among themselves on how such questions should be answered.

The multiplicity of feminist views has led some critics to charge that feminist ethics is not a unified and coherent ethical theory in the way that, say, utilitarianism is. Feminists respond that they reject the notion of moral knowledge as essentially theoretical and deny that the role of ethics is to tell us what to do. (Those in power may believe or wish this were so, but that is only because traditional ethics allows them to employ principles to subjugate women.) Rather, ethics is about people, and it has the aim of facilitating their mutual understanding and adjusting the differences among them. Working together, they resolve conflicts and find a solution to their problems.

One problem with this view of ethics is that, like care and virtue ethics, it appears to provide us with no way to resolve moral conflicts. Suppose someone who is HIV positive claims he has no responsibility to warn sexual partners of his HIV status or to practice safe sex. "It's their lookout," he says. What, from the point of view of

feminist ethics, might he be told to persuade him he has an obligation not to put others at risk of a deadly disease by his behavior? Or what grounds could be offered to support his position? The answer is not clear. And if the approach assumed in these questions (asking for "grounds") is wrong, what is the right approach to resolve the problem of someone's acting in ways that will endanger others needlessly?

A second difficulty of this view of ethics is that it seems to open feminist ethics to the charge of relativism. If ethics is (in Margaret Urban Walker's phrase) "socially embodied" and can only facilitate agreement among those who accept the values of a particular culture, how can feminist ethics criticize the culture? More to the point, even if the culture is one that subjugates women, feminist ethics seems to be committed to going along with its practices and values.

In fact, some cultural practices, such as so-called female circumcision (genital mutilation) in some countries, have divided feminists. Many want to condemn it, but the feminist view of ethics doesn't seem to provide a means for doing so. As with virtue ethics and care ethics, the commitment to doing without principles or rules doesn't seem to offer a way of assessing actions, policies, and practices from the outside.

---

# RETROSPECT

The two major tasks of this chapter have been to provide information about several important ethical theories and to formulate and illustrate several generally accepted moral principles. One aim in performing these tasks was to make it easier to follow the arguments and discussions in this book.

Another and ultimately more serious aim has been to call attention to ethical theories and principles you may wish to consider adopting. From this standpoint, the problems and issues raised in the Case Presentations and Social Contexts can be considered tests for the theories and principles.

You may find that some of the theories that we have discussed are inadequate to deal with certain moral issues in the medical context, although they may seem satisfactory in more common or simpler cases. Or you may discover that certain commonly accepted moral principles lead to contradictory results or to conclusions that you find difficult to accept. Other theories or principles may appear to give definite and persuasive answers to medical–moral problems, but you may find that they rest on assumptions that it does not appear reasonable to accept. Such a dialectical process of claims and criticism is slow and frustrating. Yet it offers the best hope of settling on theories and principles that we can accept with confidence and employ without misgivings.

During the last quarter century, a great amount of effort has been expended addressing the moral problems of medical practice and research. Without question, progress has been made in developing a better understanding of a number of issues and securing agreement about how they are to be dealt with. Nevertheless, a large number of moral issues in medicine remain unsettled or even unexplored. Even in the absence of moral consensus on these issues, the demands of practical decision making generate a force that presses us for immediate solutions.

In such a situation, we cannot afford to try to settle all doubts about moral principles in an abstract way and only then apply them to problems in medicine. The dialectical process must be made practical. Formulating and testing theories and principles must go on at the same time as we are actually making moral decisions. We must do our best to discover the principles of aerodynamics while staying aloft.

To a considerable extent, that is what this book is about. Biomedical ethics is still an area in which there are more legitimate questions than there are satisfactory answers, but the answers that we do have are better supported and better reasoned than those available even twenty years ago.

# Notes and References

## Chapter 1: Research Ethics and Informed Consent

The Jesse Gelsinger Case Presentation draws heavily from Paul Gelsinger's statement to the National Human Research Protections Advisory Committee Meeting at Bethesda, Md. on 29 January 2002. Additional information is from Sheryl Gay Stolberg, "The Biotech Death of Jesse Gelsinger," *New York Times Magazine* (28 November 1999).

The Baby Fae Case Presentation is based on the following *New York Times* stories: L. K. Altman, "Learning from Baby Fae" (18 November 1984); Philip M. Boffey, "Medicine Under Scrutiny" (20 November 1984); Sandra Blakeslee, "Baboon Implant in Baby Fae Assailed" (20 December 1985). For a detailed discussion, see Ronald Munson, *Raising the Dead: Organ Transplants, Ethics, and Society* (New York: Oxford University Press, 2002), Chapter 7.

Materials on clinical trials, HIV, and pregnancy were drawn from the *New York Times* articles S. G. Stolberg, "Research on AIDS in Poor Nations Raises an Outcry" (17 September 1997) and "Defense for Third-World HIV Experiments" (1 October 1997); Howard W. French, "AIDS Research in Africa: Juggling Risks and Hopes" (8 October 1997); on discontinuing placebos, see Sheryl Gay Stolberg, "Placebo Use Is Suspended in Overseas AIDS Trials" (19 February 1998); for more recent

results, see Lawrence K. Altman, "Report Dims Hope for AIDS Therapy to Protect Babies" (7 July 2000) and "AIDS Studies on Infants Appear to Conflict" (13 July 2000).

The Social Context on radiation research is based on *New York Times* articles: Keith Schneider, "Nuclear Scientists Irradiated People in Secret Research" (17 December 1993); "1950 Memo Shows Worry over Radiation Tests" (28 December 1993); "Signatures in Experiment Called Forgery" (12 April 1994); and John H. Cushman Jr., "Study Sought on All Testing on Humans" (10 January 1994). More recent developments are reported in the *New York Times:* Philip J. Hilts, "Secret Radioactive Experiments to Bring Compensation by the U.S." (20 November 1996) and Matthew L. Wald, "Rule Adopted to Prohibit Secret Tests on Humans" (29 March 1997). See also the Associated Press story "Settlement Is Reached in Suit over Radioactive Oatmeal" (31 December 1997).

Details of the experiments in the Willowbrook case are taken from Saul Krugman and Joan P. Giles, "Viral Hepatitis: New Light on an Old Disease," *JAMA,* 212 (1970): 1019–1021. "Echoes of Willowbrook or Tuskegee?" is based on Philip J. Hilts, "Ethics Officials to Investigate Drug Experiments on Children," *New York Times* (15 April 1998).

The account of Nazi experiments is from the indictment in *United States vs. Karl Brandt*, excerpted in *Hastings Center Report,* "Special Supplement: Biomedical Ethics and the Shadow of Nazism" (6 August 1976): 5. On drug testing, see Ross J. Baldessarini, *Chemotherapy in Psychiatry* (Cambridge, Mass.: Harvard University Press, 1977), pp. 4–11.

The paternalistic view of consent is expressed in Eugene G. Laforet, "The Fiction of Informed Consent," *JAMA* 235 (12 April 1976): 1579–1585. Placebos are discussed in Sissela Bok, "The Ethics of Giving Placebos," *Scientific American* 231 (November 1974): 17–23. The discussion of research and children is indebted to Jean D. Lockhart, "Pediatric Drug Testing," *Hastings Center Report* 7 (June 1977): 8–10. Prisoners and research is discussed in Jessica Mitford, *Kind and Usual Punishment* (New York: Knopf, 1973). The historical cases of research on the poor are from M. H. Pappworth, *Human Guinea Pigs* (Boston: Beacon Press, 1961), pp. 61–62. The Tuskegee case details are from the "Final Report of the Tuskegee Syphilis Study Ad Hoc Advisory Panel," U.S. Public Health Service (Washington, D.C., 1973), excerpted in S. J. Reiser et al., *Ethics in Medicine* (Cambridge, Mass.: MIT Press, 1977), pp. 316–321. On fetal experimentation, I am indebted to "Individual Risks vs. Societal Benefits: The Fetus," in *Experiments and Research with Humans: Values in Conflict* (Washington, D.C.: National Academy of Sciences, 1975), pp. 59–90. HSS regulations on children as research subjects were published in the *Federal Register* (8 March 1983). They are summarized in "Finally, Final Rules on Children Who Become Research Subjects," *Hastings Center Report* 13 (August 1983): 2–3. See also Robert Pear, "Proposal to Test Drugs in Children Meets Resistance," *New York Times* (30 November 1997).

Statistics about researchers and financial conflicts are from E. A. Boyd and L. A. Bero, "Assessing Faculty Financial Relationships with Industry," *JAMA*, 284 (1 November 2000): 2209–2214.

On the tamoxifen trial, see "Scientists Cancel Tamoxifen Test," Associated Press (7 April 1998). On foreign drug testing, see Elisabeth Rosenthal, "For More Drugs, First Test Is Abroad," *New York Times* (7 August 1990) and

Warren E. Leary, "U.S. Ethics Are Questioned by Critics of Vaccine Test in Italy and Sweden," *New York Times* (13 March 1994).

The account of the controversy over the use of the Pernkopf anatomy is based on Nicholas Wade, "Doctors Question Use of Nazi's Medical Atlas," *New York Times* (26 November 1996).

## Chapter 2: Physicians, Patients, and Others

The Classic Case Presentation is based on the documentary film *Dax's Case,* by Unicorn Medical (Dallas, Texas) for the Council for Dying (New York, N.Y.); produced by Donald Pasquella and Keith Burton; directed by Donald Pasquella.

On development of licensing procedures for physicians, see John Duffy, *The Healers: The Rise of the Medical Establishment* (New York: McGraw-Hill, 1977). An influential account of the doctor–patient relationship as a social role is Talcott Parsons, "Illness and the Role of the Physician: A Sociological Perspective," in Clyde Kluckhohn and H. A. Murray, eds., *Personality in Nature, Society, and Culture* (New York: Knopf, 1961). The multiple sclerosis study is reported in *Hastings Center Report* 13 (June 1983): 2–3. On recent developments about privacy, see Robert Pear, "Bush Rolls Back Rules on Privacy of Medical Data," *New York Times* (9 August 2002).

On the medical ID question, see Sheryl Gay Stolberg in the *New York Times:* "Health Identifier for All Americans Runs into Hurdles" (19 July 1998) and "Medical I.D.'s and Privacy" (26 July 1998). The Social Context on pregnancy and prosecution is based on Martha Field, "Controlling the Woman to Protect the Fetus," *Law Medicine and Health Care* 2 (1989): 114–129 for the Monson and similar cases; *New York Times* (15 January 1986; 30 August 1988) for effects of alcohol and other drugs; (4 May 1989; 9 May 1989) for the Illinois cases; (2 February 1990) for a Wyoming case; (30 May 1990) for the New York court ruling; (18 August 1992) for the Connecticut Supreme Court ruling; (19 July 1990) for racial bias; (28 October 1992) for the Gillespie case; (24 July 1992) for the Florida Supreme

Court decision; *Time* (19 September 1988) for statistics about crack babies and hospital experiences in California and South Carolina. See also the following *New York Times* articles: Tamar Lewin, "Detention of Pregnant Woman for Drug Use Is Struck Down" (28 April 1997); "Florida Court Says Hurting One's Fetus Isn't Crime" (31 October 1997); "Abuse Laws Cover Fetus a High Court Rules" (30 October 1997); Rick Bragg, "Defender of God, South and Unborn Addict" (13 January 1998). See also Associated Press, "Woman Who Used Crack Is Guilty in Death of Fetus" (3 December 1997) and "More Women Report Alcohol Use in Pregnancy" (25 April 1997). The Supreme Court decision is reported in Linda Greenhouse, "Drug Tests Curbed During Pregnancy," *New York Times* (21 March 2001).

The Twitchell Case Presentation draws substantially from David Margolic, "Death and Faith, Law and Christian Science," *New York Times* (6 August 1990). Other sources were *New York Times* (3, 6 July 1990) and "Convicted of Relying on Prayer," *Time* (16 July 1990). The overturn of the conviction was reported on CNN in November 1994.

## Chapter 3: HIV/AIDS

The Thompson case is based on accounts by a number of people with AIDS. On AIDs and suicide, see Seth Mydans, "AIDS Patients' Silent Companion Is Often Suicide," *New York Times* (25 February 1990). On combination therapy, see Michael Waldhoz, "AIDS Drug Cocktails in Use Since 1996 Cause Steep Drop in Deaths Study Finds," *Wall Street Journal* (26 March 1998); A.P., "AIDS Related Deaths Fall by 26 Percent in 1996" (10 January 1998); L. K. Altman, "AIDS Deaths Drop 48% in New York," *New York Times* (2 February 1998); A.P., "HIV Infection Rate Steady, but Rate of AIDS Has Slowed" (24 April 1998); S. G. Stolbert, "Despite New AIDS Drugs, Many Still Lose the Battle" (21 August 1997); Sheryl Gay Stolberg, "In AIDS War, New Weapons and New Victims," *New York Times* (2 June 2001); on drug resistance, see Lawrence K. Altman, "Study Re-

ports Drug Resistant Strains Have Increased to 14 Percent Among New HIV Cases," *New York Times* (7 February 2001).

On HIV drug advertising, see Stuart Elliott, "A Campaign for AIDS Drug Adds Warning," *New York Times* (10 May 2001). On the history of the disease, see L. K. Altman, "Study of HIV Family Tree Places Origins a Decade Earlier," *New York Times* (3 February 1998); on infection estimates, see the following *New York Times* articles: Robert Pear, "New Estimate Doubles Rate of HIV Spread" (25 December 1997); Elizabeth Olson, "AIDS Infections Rise Globally," (25 November 2000); Ian Fisher, "Stigma Lingers as AIDS Spreads Across Ukraine" (26 January 2002); L. K. Altman, "Many Gay Men in U.S. Unaware They Have HIV" (7 July 2002); on prevention, see S. G. Stolbert, "President Decides Against Financing Needle Programs," *New York Times* (20 April 1998). On the Bergalis case, see Lawrence K. Altman's articles in *New York Times*: "AIDS Mystery That Won't Go Away" (5 July 1994) and "AIDS and a Dentist's Secrets" (6 June 1993). Also, see Gina Kolata, "The Fact That Haunts," *New York Times* (10 July 1994).

On vaccine, see *New York Times* articles: L. K. Altman, "Vaccine Protects Two Chimps from AIDS" (30 April 1997) and "U.S. to Begin Study of Vaccine's Ability to Suppress HIV Levels" (11 May 2000); Nicholas Wade, "DNA Innovation Lets Team Undermine the AIDS Virus" (31 July 2000); Gina Kolata "New Kind of Vaccine, Made of DNA, Controls Virus in Early Tests on Monkeys" (2 October 2000); also see Geoffrey Cowley, "Can He Find a Cure?" *Newsweek* (11 June 2001); J. S. Fischer, "Searching for That Ounce of Prevention," *U.S. News and World Report* (17 July 2000) and Carol Ezzel, "Hope in a Vial: Will There Be an AIDS Vaccine Anytime Soon?" *Scientific American* (June 2002): 28–35.

On AIDS in Africa, see *New York Times*: Rachel L. Swarns, "AIDS Is Chief Cause of Death in South Africa, Study Says" (16 October 2001) and "Newest Statistics Show AIDS Still Spreading in Africa" (1 March 2001); David A. Sanger, "South African Links AIDS to Broader Issue of Poverty" (27 June 2001); on financing, see editorial, "Toward a Global AIDS Fund" (2 May 2001); Barbara Crossette, "Annan in Washington to Seek AIDS Funds" (10 May 2001); David E. Sanger, "Bush Says U.S. Will Give $200 Million to World AIDS Fund" (11 May 2001); Jane Perlez, "U.N. Chief Calls on U.S. Companies to Donate to AIDS Fund" (1 June 2001). On drugs and treatments, see from the same source Rachel L. Swarns, "AIDS Drug Battle Deepens in Africa" (8 March 2001) and "Despite Legal Victory, South Africa Hesitates on AIDS Drugs" (21 April 2001); Sheryl Gay Stolberg, "Africa's AIDS War: Pressure for Affordable Medicine" (9 March 2001); Rachel L. Swarns, "Drug Makers Drop South African Suit over AIDS Medicine" (20 April 2001); Barbara Crossette, "A Wider War on AIDS in Africa and Asia: Experts Say That Cheaper Drug Treatments Alone Are Not Enough" (27 April 2001); Stephanie Flanders, "In the Shadow of AIDS, a World of Other Problems" (24 June 2001) on infectious diseases; Jennifer Steinhauer, "U.N. United in AIDS Fight but Split over What to Do" (27 June 2001). Also see Scott Hensley, "Pharmacia Nears Generics Deal on AIDS Drugs for Poor Nations," *Wall Street Journal* (24 January 2003). For the impact cheap generics can have and for the Bush administration's commitment to spend funds needed to treat two million additional people, see Rachel L. Swarns, "Free AIDS Drugs in Africa Offer Dose of Life," *New York Times* (4 February 2003). Sections of the U.N.'s Declaration are reprinted in *New York Times,* "From the U.N. Statement on AIDS" (29 June 2001). For a picture of worldwide health issues, see C. Everett Koop, Clarence E. Pearson, and M. R. Schwarz, eds., *Critical Issues in Global Health* (San Francisco: Jossey-Bass, 2002).

# Chapter 4: Race, Gender, and Medicine

The Tuskegee Case Presentation is based on the classic study, James H. Jones, *Bad Blood: The Tuskegee Syphilis Experiment, New and Expanded Edition* (New York: Free Press, 1993) and Alison Mitchell, "Survivors of Tuskegee Study Get Apology from Clinton," *New York Times* (17 May 1997).

The best guide to statistics in this area, one I have drawn from heavily, is *Health, United States, 2002* (Washington, D.C.: Department of Health and Human Services, Centers for Disease Control and National Center for Health Statistics, 2002). The publication is available at www.cdc.gov/nchs/hus.htm. For a survey of the range of ethnic health issues, see Thomas A. LaViest, ed., *Race, Ethnicity, and Health: A Public Health Reader* (San Francisco: Jossey-Bass, 2002).

The section on African American health issues draws from the *New York Times* articles: W. E. Leary, "Discrimination May Impair Black's Health" (24 October 1996) and "Even When Covered by Insurance  Black and Poor People Receive Less Health Care" (12 September 1996); Lynda Richardson, "An Old Experiment's Legacy: Distrust of AIDS Treatment" (21 April 1997); C. K. Yoon, "Families Emerge as Silent Victims of Tuskegee Syphilis Experiments" (10 March 1997); P. T. Kilborn, "Black Americans Trailing Whites in Health, Studies Say" (26 January 1998); S. G. Stolberg, "Cultural Issues Pose Obstacles in Cancer Fight" (14 March 1998); Richard Rothstein, "Linking Infant Mortality to Schooling and Stress" (6 January 2002); editorial, "Subtle Racism in Medicine" (22 March 2002); James Sterngold, "Los Angeles Inner City Beset by Chronic Health Problems" (2 May 2002); S. G. Stolberg, "Racial Disparity Is Found in AIDS Clinical Studies" (1 May 2002); Nicholas Wade, "Race Is Seen as Real Guide to Track Roots of Disease" (30 July 2002).

See also Christine Gorman, "Why Do Blacks Die Young?" *Time* (16 September 1991); "Collaboration Urged to Ease Prostate Cancer Burden, Especially Among African Americans," *Nation's Health* (February 1998); Office of Minority Health Affairs, "Progress Report for: Black Americans," n.d. (issued in 1998) and "Trends in the Health of African American Children," n.d. (issued in 1998); D. S. Pinkney, "Barriers to Health Care Remain, Especially for Blacks," *American Medical News* (28 November 1994), p. 20ff. For an analysis of the roots of long-standing distrust of medicine by Blacks, see V. N. Gamble, "Under the Shadow of Tuskegee," *American Journal of Public*

*Health* (November 1997): 1773–1779. See also H. E. Flack and E. D. Pellegrino, eds., *African-American Perspectives on Biomedical Ethics* (Washington, D.C.: Georgetown University Press, 1992). For recent studies on Blacks and cardiac catheterization and differential treatment, see Sheryl Gay Stolbert, "Blacks Found on Short End of Heart Attack Procedure," *New York Times* (10 May 2001) and Reuters, "Racial Gap in Cancer Survival Is Not Biological, Study Finds." The CDC review of "health indicators" is reported by Associated Press (24 January 2002). See too the following studies: Arnold M. Epstein et al., "Racial Disparities in Access to Renal Transplantation," *New England Journal of Medicine,* 343 (23 November 2000): 1537–1544; Peter B. Bach et al., "Survival of Blacks and Whites After a Cancer Diagnosis," *JAMA* 287 (24 April 2002): 2106–2113. For an outstanding historical perspective, see Linda A. Clayton and W. Michael Byrd, *An American Health Dilemma: A Medical History of African Americans and the Problems of Race: Beginnings to 1900* (New York: Routledge, 2002).

The discussion of the health problems of American Indians and Alaska Natives is based on Office of Minority Health Affairs, "Progress Report for American Indians and Alaska Natives," n.d. (issued in 1998); Jo Ann Kauffman and Yvette K. Joseph-Fox, "American Indian and Alaska Native Women," in Marcia Bayne-Smith, ed., *Race, Gender, and Health* (Thousand Oaks, Calif.: Sage Publications, 1996), pp. 121–171, and Indian Health Service, "Comprehensive Health Care Program for American Indians and Alaska Natives" (Indian Health Service, website, posted 16 February 1999). On the problems of Asian Americans and Pacific Islanders, see R. H. True and Tessi Guillerno, "Asian/Pacific Islander American Women," in Bayne-Smith, pp. 94–120, and Department of Health and Human Services, "Progressive Review: Asian Americans and Pacific Islanders" (13 September 1997). On the problems of Hispanics/Latinos, see A. L. Gichaello, "Latino Women," in Bayne-Smith, pp. 21–171, and Department of Health and Human Services, "Progressive Review: Hispanic Americans" (29 April 1997).

On bridging cultural gaps, see the following *New York Times* articles: Gina Maranto, "Nurses Bridge Cultures to Give Better Care" (1 October 2002); and Lynette Clemetson, "A Neighborhood Clinic Helps Fill the Gaps for Latinos Without Health Care" (6 October 2002). The definitive book illustrating medical cultures in conflict is Anne Fadiman, *The Spirit Catches You and You Fall Down: A Hmong Child, Her American Doctors, and the Collision of Two Cultures* (New York: Farrar, Straus, and Giroux, 1997).

Comparative figures for disease incidence and mortality for all ethnic groups are from *Health, United States, 2002* as cited above. I have also used information supplied by the Office of Minority Health Resources Center of the Department of Health and Human Services. Of general relevance is Office of Minority Health, *Standards for Culturally and Linguistically Appropriate Services in Health Care: Executive Summary* (Washington, D.C.: March 2001).

The National Institutes of Health's Office of Research on Women's Health (www.od.nih.gov/orwh) serves as a focal point for women's health research conducted under the auspices of NIH. Its website contains information about the Women's Health Initiative, research involving women, recruiting women as investigators, and the "Strategic Plan to Address Health Disparities Among Diverse Populations of Women."

The discussion of the lack of women as research participants is based on Office of Minority Health, "Including Women and Minorities in Clinical Trials," *Closing the Gap* (December/January 1998), p. 11; Michael Wines, "In Research, the Sincerest Form of Concern Is Money," *New York Times* (22 June 1997); the American Medical Association Council on Ethical and Judicial Affairs' report and the Public Health Service's report of the Task Force on Women's Health Issues are quoted in John M. Smith, *Women and Doctors* (New York: Delta Books, 1992); on treatment, see references in Lawrence K. Altman, "Mastectomy Alternative Often Ignored, Study Says," *New York Times* (19 May 1998). The GAO report charging recent failures of researchers to enroll a sufficient number of women in studies is reported in Robert Pear, "Studies Find Research on Women Lacking," *New York Times* (29 April 2000). See Nancy Wartik, "Hurting More, Helped Less," *New York Times* (23 June 2002) on whether women's complaints are taken seriously and dealt with appropriately.

For the Hmong Case Presentation, see "Girl Flees After Clash of Cultures on Illness," *New York Times* (12 November 1994); for follow-ups on the case of Lor Lee, see *Fresno Bee* (2 November 1996) and (2 February 1995).

The Social Context on the mammography debate draws from *New York Times* articles: Gina Kolata, "Mammograms for Women in 40s Debated by Experts" (22 January 1997); "Mammogram Talks Prove Indefinite" (25 January 1997); "Stand on Mammograms Greeted by Outrage" (25 January 1997); "Women Benefit from Breast Screening in 40s" [Letters], (28 January 1997); Kathy Conway, "Luckily, I Had a Mammogram" (24 February 1997); "Let Mammography Be Guided by Facts" [Letters], (4 February 1997); Marjorie Connelly, "On Breast Cancer, the Vote Favors Aggressive Screening" (22 June 1997); Sandeep Jauhar, "Dense Breasts May Need Sonograms to Detect Cancer" (19 September 2002); Michael Moss, "Spotting Breast Cancer: Doctors Are the Weakest Link" (27 June 2002); and "Mammogram Team Learns from Its Errors" (28 June 2002); other material was drawn from Sharon Begley, "The Mammogram War," *Newsweek* (24 February 1997); Jeffry Kluger, "Mammogram Two-Step," *Time* (7 April 1997); and Associated Press, "Risk of False Alarm from Mammogram Is 50% over Decade" (15 April 1998). For continuation of the debate, see these *New York Times* articles by Gina Kolata: "Expert Panel Cites Doubts on Mammogram's Worth" (23 January 2002); "Dispute Builds over Value of Mammography" (1 February 2002). On "genetic signatures" as predictors, see Gina Kolata, "Breast Cancer Genes Are Tied to Death Rates," *New York Times* (19 December 2002). The Susan Arcadan case is based on an interview with a breast cancer patient at Johns Hopkins Hospital

conducted in March 1998; the name and details have been changed.

An excellent history of the debate over mastectomy versus lumpectomy (and associated issues) is Barron H. Lerner, *The Breast Cancer Wars: Hope, Fear, and the Pursuit of a Cure in Twentieth-Century America* (New York: Oxford University Press, 2001).

The prostate cancer section draws from Jaroff, "The Man's Cancer," *Time* (1 April 1996); Patrick Walsh and Janet Worthington, *The Prostate: A Guide for Men and the Women Who Love Them* (Baltimore: Johns Hopkins University Press, 1996); Robert Lipsyte, "Hot Gland," *American Health* (March 1994); W. E. Leary, "Men Are Told to Reconsider How to Treat the Prostate Gland," *New York Times* (9 February 1994); "Collaboration Urged to Ease Prostate Cancer Burden, Especially Among African Americans," *Nation's Health* (February 1998). See also the following *New York Times* articles: A. E. Pollack, "Routine Screening for Prostate Cancer Is Said to Cut Deaths" (19 May 1998); David Kirby, "More Options for Men with Prostate Cancer" (3 October 2000); Kenneth Chang, "Findings Fuel Debate on Prostate Test" (2 May 2000); Gina Kolata, "Dilemma on Prostate Cancer" (17 September 2002); anonymous, "Mixed Reviews for Prostate Exams (3 December 2002); and Susan Brink, "Prostate Dilemmas," *U.S. News & World Report* (22 May 2000).

## Chapter 5: Genetic Control

The Classic Case Presentation discussion of obtaining stem cells is indebted to National Institutes of Health, "Stem Cells: A Primer" (May 2000), www.nih.gov/news/stemcell/primer/htm. For a discussion of the therapeutic possibilities of stem cells and extensive references, see Ronald Munson, *Raising the Dead: Organ Transplants, Ethics, and Society* (New York: Oxford University Press, 2002), Chapter 11, "Grow Your Own Organs: Stem-Cell Engineering and Regenerative Medicine." The official Roman Catholic view of stem cells is found in Pontifical Academy of Life,

"Declaration on the Production and the Scientific and Therapeutic Use of Human Embryonic Stem Cells," issued at Vatican City (25 August 2000). For accounts of the recent research and criticisms, I am indebted to the magisterial series of articles by Nicholas Wade in the *New York Times:* "Embryo Cell Research: A Clash of Values" (2 July 1999); "Stem Cells Yield Promising Results" (31 March 2001); "Findings Deepen Debate on Using Embryonic Stem Cells" (3 April 2001); "Experiment Offers Hope for Tissue Repair" (22 January 1999). On the continuing debate, see Sheryl Gay Stolberg, *New York Times:* "Bush's Bioethics Panel Recommends a Moratorium, Not a Ban, on Cloning Research" (11 July 2002); "U.S. Rule on Stem Cell Studies Let Researchers Use New Lines" (6 August 2002); and Debra Rosenberg, "Stem Cells Slow Progress," *Newsweek* (12 August 2002). The President's Council on Bioethics report, *Human Cloning and Human Dignity: An Ethical Inquiry* (July 2002), is available at www.bioethics.gov.

The account of PKU screening draws from National Academy of Sciences, *Genetic Screening: Programs, Principles, and Research* (Washington, D.C.: National Academy of Sciences, 1975). For an account of alpha-fetoprotein screening, see Barbara Gastel et al., eds., *Maternal Serum Alpha Fetoprotein: Issues in the Prenatal Screening and Diagnosis of Neural Tube Defects* (U.S. Department of Health and Human Services Publication HE 20.2: M41, 1981). For social problems caused by PKU laws and sickle-cell screening, see Philip Reilly, "There's Another Side to Genetic Screening," *Prism* (January 1976): 55–57.

Genetic screening and the problems it poses for rights is considered by Susan West, "Genetic Testing on the Job," *Science* 82 (September 1982): 16. See also Morton Hunt, "The Total Gene Screen," *New York Times Magazine* (19 January 1986). Specific uses of genetic engineering are reported in *New York Times* (25 June 1995) on flu vaccine; (30 May 1997) on mouse-human hybrids; (1 May 1997) on increasing muscle growth; (30 October 1997) on sickle-cell model.

The Human Genome Project account draws from the following *New York Times* articles by Nicholas Wade: "Genetic Code of Human Life Is Cracked by Scientists" (27 June 2000), "Big Stride for Researchers in Human Gene Mapping" (15 March 1997), "Genome's Riddle" (13 February 2001), "Now the Hard Part: Putting the Genome to Work" (27 June 2000). For a patient-centered discussion, see Lois Wingerson, *Mapping Our Genes: The Genome Project and the Future of Medicine* (New York: Dutton, 1990); for the genome from the point of view of the chromosomes, see Matt Ridley, *Genome: The Autobiography of a Species in 23 Chapters* (New York: Harper-Collins, 1999); for the story of the scientific "race," see Kevin Davies, *Cracking the Genome: Inside the Race to Unlock Human DNA* (New York: Free Press, 2001).

The Huntington's disease Case Presentation relies heavily on Gina Kolata, "Closing in on a Killer Gene, *Discover* (March 1984): 83–87. See also Lawerence K. Altman, "Researchers Report Genetic Test Detects Huntington's Disease," *New York Times* (9 November 1983) and Albert Rosenfield, "At Risk for Huntington's Disease," *Hastings Center Report* 14 (June 1984): 5–8. Nancy Wexler's views on genetic testing are quoted from Mary Murray, "Nancy Wexler," *New York Times Magazine* (13 February 1993), pp. 28–31. For a profile of Wexler, see *Time* (10 February 1992). On more recent developments, see the following *New York Times* articles: Sandra Blakeslee, "Unusual Clues Help in Long Fight to Solve Huntington's Disease" (27 October 1992); and Natalie Angier, "Action of Gene in Huntington's Is Proving a Tough Puzzle" (2 November 1993).

On genetic testing, see Sandra Blakeslee, "Cause of Brain Cells' Death in 7 Diseases Is Discovered," *New York Times* (8 August 1997); Nicholas Wade, "Two Gene Discoveries Help Explain Misfires of Epilepsy in the Brain," *New York Times* (30 December 1997), "Newly Discovered Gene Offers Clues on Deafness" (14 November 1997), "Gene Mutation Tied to Colon Cancers in Askenazi Jews" (26 August 1997), "Gene from a Mideast Ancestor May Link 4 Disparate Peoples" (22 August 1997) on familial Mediterranean fever disease; and "Genetic Cause Found for Some

Cases of Human Obesity" (27 June 1997); Denise Grady, "Gene Link to Incurable Eye Disease Is Found," *New York Times* (19 September 1997); Associated Press, "Blood Test Uncovers Inherited Diseases in Fetuses" (4 November 1996), and "Two Genes Found to Be Causing Some Diabetes" (5 December 1996); Natalie Angier, "Scientists Zero in on Gene Tied to Prostate Cancer," *New York Times* (22 November 1996). For an account of how getting good news about Huntington's disease can be stressful and disorienting, see Patrick Cooke, "A Genetic Test for Huntington's Let Colin MacAllister See His Future, and That's When His Free Fall Began," *Health* (July–August 1993): 81–86. On recent breast cancer conclusions, see Jeffry Kluger, *Time* (26 May 1997). Poll results are from a 1994 *Time*/CNNA survey cited in *Time* (17 January 1994), p. 50.

On genetic disorders that worsen over generations, see Anastasia Toufexis, "The Generational Saga of the Vicious Gene," *Time* (17 February 1992): 72; and Gina Kolata, "Discovery Upsets Geneticists' Ideas on Inherited Ills," *New York Times* (6 February 1992). As background on genes affecting breast cancer, see Rachel Nowa, "Breast Cancer Gene Offers Surprises," *Science,* (23 September 1994): 1796–1799; Gregory Cowley, "Family Matters: Hunt for a Breast Cancer Gene," *Newsweek* (6 December 1993): 46–52; and Kenneth Offit, "Hostage to Our Genes?" *New York Times* (22 September 1994). On cystic fibrosis, see Andrew Purvis, "Laying Siege to a Deadly Gene," *Time* (24 February 1992), and Natalie Angier, "Researchers Trace Primary Cause of Cystic Fibrosis to the Stone Age," *New York Times* (1 June 1994). The account of the discovery of the cystic fibrosis gene is based on Sandra Blakeslee, "Discovery May Help Cystic Fibrosis Victims," *New York Times* (24 August 1989). See the Associated Press stories "Gene Defect for a Type of Dwarfism Is Found" (31 July 1994) on Canavan disease; "Researchers Find Key to Rare Brain Disorder" (4 October 1993); "Gene Linked for First Time to High Blood Pressure" (7 October 1992); "Gene Linked to Diabetes Found" (12 January 1993); and "Genetic Defect Linked to Alzheimer's" (23 October 1992). See E. Pennisi, "Free-Radical

Scavenger Gene Tied to ALS," *Science News* (6 March 1993). See the following *New York Times* stories: Tim Hilchey, "Researchers Find Genetic Defect That Causes Rare Immune Disease" [namely, severe-combined-immunodeficiency disease] (9 April 1993); and Natalie Angier, "Gene Is Found That Causes Rare Type of Hypertension" (16 January 1992). For a discussion of issues of genetic discrimination, see *Science News* (21 January 1989): 40–42; Gina Kolata, "Nightmare or the Dream of a New Era in Genetics," *New York Times* (7 December 1993); Sharon Begley, "When DNA Isn't Destiny," *Newsweek* (6 December 1993): 53–55; and George J. Annas, "Who's Afraid of the Human Genome?" *Hastings Center Report* (July/August 1989): 19–21. Guidelines on sickle-cell testing are in Warren E. Leary, "Sickle-Cell Screen Urged for All Newborns," *New York Times* (28 April 1993); on treatments, see Leary's "Intractable Pain of Sickle Cell Begins to Yield," *New York Times* (7 June 1994). The discussion of ethical issues about testing and children is based in Gina Kolata, "Should Children Be Told If Genes Predict Illness?" *New York Times* (26 September 1994). For general review and references, see Philip Kitcher, *The Lives to Come: The Genetic Revolution and Human Possibilities* (New York: Simon and Schuster, 1996).

The gene therapy Case Presentation draws from Eve K. Nicholas, *Human Gene Therapy* (Cambridge: Mass.: Harvard University Press, 1988). The plan to initiate ADA gene therapy is described in Natalie Angier, "Gene Implant Therapy," *New York Times* (8 March 1990), and her account of the first case is in "Girl, 4, Becomes First Human to Receive Engineered Genes" (15 September 1990). Biographical details of Ashanthi Desilva and additional treatments are reported in Larry Thompson, "The First Kids with New Genes," *Time* (7 June 1993): 50–53. The first case, as well as plans for future ones, is discussed in W. French Anderson, "Human Gene Therapy," *Science* (8 May 1992): 808–813. An excellent review of the ethical issues is Leroy Walters and Julie Gage Palmer, *Ethics of Human Gene Therapy* (New York: Oxford University Press, 1996). For the adverse events in France, see "Gene Tampering,"

*Time* (14 October 2002); and Sheryl Gay Stolberg, "Panel Advises Resuming Gene Studies," *New York Times* (10 October 2002). In the Gelsinger case (see Chapter 1, Classic Case Presentation), a gene-therapy trial went badly wrong, thus calling into question the wisdom of additional trials.

## Chapter 6: Reproductive Control

Statistics about assisted reproduction are from Centers for Disease Control, "1998 Assisted Reproduction Success Rates," Reproductive Health Information Source (cdc.gov/art98). In 2003 these remain the most recent statistics.

Statistics on fertility treatments are cited in S. G. Stolberg, "U.S. Publishes First Guide to Infertility," *New York Times* (18 December 1997). For report on personal experiences, see Stolberg, "For the Infertile, A High-Tech Treadmill," *New York Times* (14 December 1997). For information about techniques, see Lawrence J. Kaplan and Rosemarie Tong, *Controlling Our Reproductive Destiny* (Cambridge: MIT Press, 1996). On fertility clinics see *New York Times:* Gina Kolata, "Reproductive Revolution Is Jostling Old Views" (11 January 1993); and Glenn Kramon, "Infertility Chain: The Good and Bad in Medicine" (19 June 1992). The account of the debate about the selling of ova is based on Gina Kolata, "Young Women Offer to Sell Their Eggs to Infertile Couples," *New York Times* (10 November 1991). On transplanting ovaries from aborted fetuses, see Gina Kolata, *New York Times,* "Fetal Ovary Transplant Is Envisioned" (6 January 1994). For problems over embryos, see Gina Kolata, "Frozen Embryos: Few Rules in a Rapidly Growing Field," *New York Times* (5 June 1992). The historical background on artificial insemination is presented in R. Snowden and G. D. Mitchell, *The Artificial Family* (London: Allen and Unwin, 1981).

The influential New York law regulating surrogacy is summarized in Lisa Belkin, "Childless Couples Hang on to Last Hope, Despite Laws," *New York Times* (28 July 1992). The Kim Cotton case is reported in the A.P. story, "Surrogate Mother's Child in English Court Custody" (9 January 1985).

The cloning Case Presentation ("Hello, Dolly") is indebted to Michael Specter with Gina Kolata, "After Decades and Many Missteps, Cloning Success," *New York Times* (3 March 1997); Gina Kolata, "Panel Recommends a Ban on Human Cloning Efforts," *New York Times* (8 June 1997); "Clinton Seeks to Ban Human Cloning," Associated Press (9 June 1997); Sharon Begley, "Little Lamb Who Made Thee," *Newsweek* (10 March 1997): 53–59; Wray Herbert et al., "The World After Cloning," *U.S. News & World Report* (10 March 1997): 59–63; Madeline Nash, "The Age of Cloning" (10 March 1997): 64–65; Gina Kolata, "For Some Fertility Experts, Human Cloning Is a Dream," *New York Times* (7 June 1997). For recent developments, see Gina Kolata, "In Big Advance in Cloning, Biologists Create 50 Mice," *New York Times* (27 July 1998). The Hall and Stillman "twinning" experiments are discussed in Geoffrey Cowley, "Clone Hype," *Newsweek* (8 November 1993): 60–64; and David Gelman, "How Will the Clone Feel," same issue, (65–66). The cloning story is told in Gina Kolata, *Clone* (New York: William Morrow, 1998), and in Ian Wilmut, Keith Campbell, and Colin Tudge, *The Second Creation: Dolly and the Age of Biological Control* (Cambridge, Mass.: Harvard University Press, 2000).

The Louise Brown Case Presentation is based in *Newsweek* (7 August 1978); *Time* (7 August 1978); and *U.S. News & World Report* (7 August 1978). On Louise Brown, see "Where Are They Now," *Time* (15 August 1996). "Motherhood after Menopause" draws on "World's Oldest Mother Just Wanted Baby," A.P. (27 April 1997); Gina Kolata, "A Record and Big Questions as a Woman Gives Birth at 63," *New York Times* (24 April 1997); Claudia Kalb, "How Old Is Too Old?" *Newsweek* (5 May 1997); Margaret Carlson, "Old Enough to Be Your Mother," *Time* (10 January 1994): 41; A.P., "California Woman, 53, Gives Birth to Twins" (11 November 1992); Gina Kolata, "When Grandmother Is the Mother, Until Birth," *New York Times* (5 August 1991). Also see Gina Kolata, "Clinics Enter a New World of Embryo 'Adoption,'" *New York Times* (23 November 1997), and "Scientists Face New Ethical Quandaries in Baby-Making" (19 August 1997); M. D. Lemonick, "Sorry Your Time Is Up," *Time* (12 August 1996).

The septuplets Case Presentation is based on Pam Belluck, "Iowan Makes U.S. History, Giving Birth to 7 Live Babies," *New York Times* (20 November 1997), and "Heartache Frequently Visits Parents with Multiple Births," *New York Times* (3 January 1997); Gina Kolata, "Many Specialists Are Left in No Mood for Celebration," *New York Times* (21 November 1997). For personal details of the family, see also M. D. Lemonick, "'It's a Miracle,'" *Time* (1 December 1997): 35–39; on technology, see Lemonick's "The New Revolution in Making Babies," pp. 41–46.

Information on the Davis case is from a UPI story (21 September 1989); *New York Times* (22 April 1989; 8 August 1989); Ronald Smothers, "Court Gives Ex-Husband Rights on Use of Embryos" (2 June 1992); and "Doctor's Act on Embryos Sends Case Back to Court" (4 June 1992); and AP stories (26 May 1990; 13 September 1990). Information about the Baby M case is drawn from *New York Times* articles (4, 5, 6, 10, 26, 27 January 1987; 2, 3, 9, 10, 11, 17 February 1987; 5, 9, 10, 31 March 1987; 2 April 1987). Additional information about the Rios case is from James Lieber, "The Case of the Frozen Embryos," *Saturday Evening Post* (October 1989), pp. 50–53. The Calvert case is based on Carol Lawson, "Couple's Own Embryos Used in Birth Surrogacy," *New York Times* (12 August 1990); Seth Mydans, "Surrogate Loses Custody Bid in Case Defining Motherhood," *New York Times* (22 October 1990); and *Time* (22 August 1990).

## Chapter 7: Scarce Resources

The Brattle County, Texas, Case Presentation is fictional, but it represents the problem faced by dialysis centers when programs were starting. For the classic account of a committee (at Swedish Hospital, Seattle, Washington, in 1961),

see Shana Alexander, "They Decide Who Lives, Who Dies," *Life* (1962).

For a discussion (with extensive references) of major issues in organ transplants, see Ronald Munson, *Raising the Dead: Organ Transplants, Ethics, and Society* (New York: Oxford University Press, 2002). For current survival rates, see the United Network for Organ Sharing website. On special topics see R. W. Evans et al., "The Potential Supply of Organ Donors," *JAMA* 259 (1992): 1546–1547; P. A. Singer et al., "Ethics of Liver Transplantation with Living Donors," *New England Journal of Medicine* 321 (1989): 620–622; S. J. Younger and R. M. Arnold, "Ethical, Psychosocial, and Public Policy Implications of Procuring Organs from Non-Heart-Beating Cadaver Donors," *JAMA* 269 (1993): 2769–2774. On selling organs, see the following *New York Times* articles: Peter S. Young, "Moving to Compensate Families in Human Organ Market" (8 July 1994); Sanjoy Hazarka, "India Debates Ethics of Buying Transplant Kidneys" (17 August 1992); Chris Hedges, "Egypt's Doctors Impose Kidney Transplant Curbs" (23 January 1992); and "Egypt's Desperate Trade" (22 September 1991). See also, "Trading Flesh Around the Globe," *Time* (17 June 1991): 61. The classic sociological study on dialysis and transplants is Renee C. Fox, "A Sociological Perspective on Organ Transplantation and Hemodialysis," *Annals of the New York Academy of Sciences* 169 (1970): 406–428. On recent controversies about defining death, see Stuart J. Youngner, Robert M. Arnold, and Rene Scapiro, *The Definition of Death: Contemporary Controversies* (Baltimore: Johns Hopkins University Press, 2001).

The facts and opinions in the Ayala case are presented in Lance Morrow, "When One Body Can Save Another," *Time* (7 June 1991): 54–58; the Associated Press story, "Mom, 43, Having Baby to Save Daughter's Life" (17 February 1990); Irene Chang, "Bone Marrow Baby Is Born to the Ayalas," *Los Angeles Times* (6 April 1990); the marriage of Anissa is reported in Rebecca Norris, "Made in Heaven," *American Health* (October 1994): 100.

The account of the public debate on fetal-cell transplants is based on J. Eric Ahlskog, "Cerebral Transplantation for Parkinson's Disease: Current Progress and Future Prospects," *Mayo Clinic Proceedings* 68 (1993): 578–591; Associated Press, "Fetal Tissue Study Approved, the First Since the Ban Was Lifted" (4 January 1994); "Fetal Tissue Grafts Reverse Parkinson's," *Science News* (28 November 1992): 372; and the following *New York Times* articles: Warren Leary, "Call to Regulate Transplant Tissue" (15 August 1993); Gwen Ifill, "House Approves Fetal Tissues in Federally Funded Research" (26 June 1991); and Gina Kolata, "Fetal Tissue Implant Said to Be Aiding a Parkinson Patient" (2 February 1990).

On the shortage of Betaseron, see Associated Press, "Computer Lottery Will Distribute a New M.S. Drug" (2 September 1993); Tamar Lewis, "Prize in Unusual Lottery: A Scarce Experimental Drug," *New York Times* (7 January 1994); and Laura Johanes, "New Drug Aims to Win over Sufferers," *Wall Street Journal* (20 April 1996).

For the Sepulveda case, see Bruce Lambert, "Jesse Sepulveda Is Dead at Seven," *New York Times* (18 July 1993). For the Bosze case, see Isabel Wilkerson, "Search for Marrow Donor Questions Nature of Altruism and Child Rights," *New York Times* (30 July 1990), and "Setback for Boy Needing Marrow," Associated Press (28 September 1990). For the Benton case, see Terry Trucco, "Sales of Kidneys Prompt New Laws and Debate," *New York Times* (1 August 1990).

## Chapter 8: Paying for Health Care

The Case Presentation is a composite, one representing the situation of the 44 million Americans lacking health insurance. These are most often people with jobs or small businesses.

The discussion of rights in the Briefing Session is indebted to Joel Feinberg, "The Nature and Value of Rights," *Journal of Value Inquiry* 4 (1970): 243–257. See also Charles J. Dougherty, *American Health Care: Realities, Rights, and Reforms* (New York: Oxford University Press, 1988).

An excellent source for information about health spending is *Health, United States, 2002* (Washington, D.C.: Department of Health and Human Services, Centers for Disease Control and National Center for Health Statistics, 2002). The publication is available at www.cdc.gov/nchs/hus.htm. I have drawn a variety of statistics from this source.

The materials on health-care costs and controversies are also drawn from the following *New York Times* articles: Robert Pear, "In a First, Medicare Coverage Is Authorized for Alzheimer's" (30 March 2002); "Propelled by Drugs and Hospital Costs, Health Spending Surged in 2000" (7 January 2002); Sam Howe Verhovek, "Frustration Grows with Cost of Health Insurance" (16 September 2000); Robin Toner, "Harry and Louise Were Right, Sort Of" (24 November 1996); Stuart Elliott, "Harry and Louise II: The Same but Somehow Different" (5 May 2002); Robin Toner, "Rising Drug Costs a Powerful Issue for National and State Politicians" (1 April 2002); Peter Kilborn, "Looking Back at Jackson Hole" (22 March 1998); Paul Krugman, "Bad Medicine" (19 March 2002); John M. Broder et al., "Problem of Health Benefits Is Reaching into Middle Class" (25 November 2002); Robert Pear, "Decade After Health Care Crisis, Soaring Costs Bring New Strains" (10 August 2002); "After Decline, the Number of Uninsured Rose in 2001" (29 September 2002). On HMOs and proposals for change, see David Sibley, "Nasty, Costly Battle Shapes Up over Changing Managed Care" (3 June 1998), "What the Texas Experiment Shows About HMO Liability" (7 August 1998); Lasette Alvarez, "A Conservative Battles Corporate Health Care" (12 February 1998); Milton Freudenheim, "Health Insurers Seek Big Increases in Their Premiums" (24 April 1998); Robert Pear, "Study Tells U.S. to Pay More for the Best Medical Care" (22 October 2002); Gina Kolata, "More May Not Mean Better in Health Care, Studies Find" (2 July 2002). On attempts to extend care to particular groups, see Milton Freudenheim, "Some Tentative First Steps Toward Universal Health Care" (7 December 2002); Robert Pear, "Expert Panel Wants States to

Test Ideas in a Health Crisis" (19 November 2002); "Policy Changes Fail to Fill Gaps in Health Coverage" (8 August 1998); "Senators Reject Bill to Regulate Care by HMOs" (9 October 1998); "Health Care Bills Don't Meet Goals, Budget Aides Say" (2 July 1997); "Clinton Ordering Effort to Sign Up Medicaid Children" (28 December 1997); "Clinton to Expand Medicaid for Some of the Working Poor" (3 August 1998); "New Health Plans Due for Elderly" (9 June 1998); Peter T. Kilborn, "States to Provide Health Insurance to More Children" (21 September 1997); Adam Clymer, "With Health Overhaul Dead, a Search for Minor Repairs" (28 August 1994); Robin Toner, "Maine at Front Line in Fight over the High Cost of Drugs" (11 May 2002); Robert Pear, "U.S. in Court Filing Backs Maine's Drug Discount Plan" (31 March 2002). On costs and consumer complaints, see Ian Fisher, "HMO Premiums Rising Sharply, Stoking Debate on Managed Care" (11 January 1998); Peter T. Kilborn, "Complaints About HMOs Rise as Awareness Grows" (10 October 1998). For more on costs, see Milton Freudenheim, "Health Care Costs Edging Up and a Bigger Surge Is Feared" (2 January 1997); Peter T. Kilborn, "HMO Fiscal Incentives Linked to Doctor's Discontent" (19 November 1998), "Doctor's Pay Regains Ground Despite the Effects of HMOs" (22 April 1998). On the uninsured or underinsured, see Peter T. Kilborn, "Illness Is Turning into Financial Catastrophe for More of the Uninsured" (1 August 1997), "The Uninsured Find Fewer Doctors in the House" (30 August 1998). For a general review, see Karen Tumulty, "Health Care Has a Relapse," *Time* (11 March 2002). For an examination of problems associated with HMOs, see George Anders, *Health Against Wealth: HMOs and the Breakdown of Medical Trust* (Boston: Houghton-Mifflin, 1996).

Statistics in the Canadian Case Presentation are mostly drawn from Karen Dnelan et al., "All Payer, Single Payer, Managed Care, No Payer: Patients' Perspectives in Three Nations [U.S., Canada, Germany]," *Health Affairs* 15 (1996): 256–265. The case is also based on the following *New York Times* articles: James Brooke, "Full Hospitals Make Canadians Wait and Look South" (16 January 2000); Anthony De Palma, "Doctor, What's the Prognosis for Canada" (15 December 1996); also used were Anthony Schmitz, "Health Assurance," *Health* (January/February 1991): 39–47; and *Consumer Reports* (September 1992): 579–592. For a detailed comparison of the U.S. system with those in Canada and Germany, see Donald Drake, Susan Fitzgerald, and Mark Jaffe, *Hard Choices: Health Care at What Cost?* (Kansas City: Andrews and McMeel, 1993). For U.S. waiting problems, see Gale Scott, "Waits Are Common for Colonoscopies," *New York Times* (9 July 2002).

# Chapter 9: Abortion

The Finkbine Case Presentation is based on Allen F. Guttmacher, *The Case for Legalized Abortion* (Berkeley, Calif.: Diablo Press, 1977), pp. 15–17.

On birth defects, see the following *New York Times* articles: Kurt Eichenwald, "Push for Royalties Threatens the Use of Down Syndrome Test" (25 May 1997); Denise Grady, "Research Finds Risk in Early Test of Fetus" (27 January 1998); and the Associated Press, "Small Amount of Folic Acid Bars Defects" (4 December 1997). For specific developmental or genetic anomalies, see Charles B. Clayman, ed., *American Medical Association Encyclopedia of Medicine* (New York: Random House, 1989).

The Social Context Gallup statistics are cited in Robin Toner, "The Abortion Debate, Stuck in Time," *New York Times* (21 January 2000). The statistics from the *New York Times*/CBS poll cited in the Social Context appear in the newspaper for 16 January 1998; I have also drawn from Carey Goldberg and Janet Elder, "Public Still Backs Abortion but Wants Limits, Poll Says" on the same date and the following *New York Times* articles: Tamar Lewis, "Debate Distant for Many Having Abortions" (17 June 1998); Carey Goldberg, "Shifting Certainties in the Abortion War" (11 January 1998); Kate Zernike, "Thirty Years After the Abortion Ruling, New Trends but the Old Debate" (20 January 2003).

On the "partial-birth" abortion debate, see *New York Times:* Linda Greenhouse, "Overturning of Late-Term Abortion Ban Is Let Stand" (24 March 1998); Deborah Sontage, "'Partial Birth' Just One Way, Physicians Say" (21 March 1997); Neil A. Lewis, "Ban on Method of Late Abortion Passes House Despite Veto Threat" (9 October 1997); Katharine Q. Seelye, "Senate Votes Ban on Late Abortion: Bill Faces a Veto" (21 May 1997); "Medical Group Supports Ban on a Type of Late Abortion" (19 May 1997); "As Federal Bans Face a Veto, States Outlaw Late Abortions" (3 May 1997); "Group Defends Late-Term Abortion Procedure" (27 February 1997); Frank Burni, "The Partial Truth Abortion Fight" (9 March 1997); Sheryl Gay Stolberg, "Definition of Fetal Viability Is Focus of Debate in Senate" (15 May 1997); Linda Greenhouse, "Justices to Rule on Law That Bans Abortion Method" (14 January 2000); and on the Nebraska and Colorado decisions, "Court Rules That Government Can't Outlaw Type of Abortion" (28 June 2000).

On legal and policy decisions, information about the Pennsylvania case (Casey) and the U.S. Supreme Court decision from *New York Times* (22 January 1992; 23 April 1992; 30 June 1992; 13 May 1993; 30 January 1994). Information about the *Webster* case is from *Newsweek* (1 May 1989; 17 July 1989) and *Time* (1 May 1989). Response to the *Webster* decision is based on Linda Greenhouse, "Supreme Court Upholds Sharp State Limits on Abortion," *New York Times* (4 July 1990); and E. Dionne, "On Both Sides, Advocates Predict a 50-State Battle" in the same issue. Difficulty in getting access to abortion is covered in *New York Times* (5 January 1992; 15 March 1992). The Court ruling on access to clinics and its background is reported in *New York Times* (25 January 1994; 1 July 1994). See too Linda Greenhouse, "High Court Upholds Buffer Zone of 15 Feet at Abortion Clinics," *New York Times* (20 February 1997); and on the Colorado law, "Court Rules That Governments Can't Outlaw Types of Abortion" (28 June 2000); Peter T. Kilborn, "Definition of Abortion Is Found to Vary Abroad" (23 November 1999); Frank Bruni and Marc Lacey, "Bush Acts to Deny Money Over-

seas Tied to Abortion" (22 January 2001); Daniel E. Pellegrom, "A Deadly Global Gag Rule" (27 January 2001). On recent federal policies, see Todd S. Purdum, "U.S. Blocks Money for Family Clinics Promoted by the U.N.," *New York Times* (22 July 2002); and Robert Pear, "Bush Rule Makes Fetuses Eligible for Health Benefits, *New York Times* (27 September 2002).

The Social Context on RU-486 is based on *New York Times* stories: (28 October 1994; 28 March 1994; 18 February 1994; 2, 20 April 1993; 27 July 1990; 22 June 1990; 18 November 1993; 23 February 1992; 13 October 1993; 23 September 1989; 26, 27, 29, 30 October 1988; 22 February 1988). It also draws from *Newsweek* (22 November 1993); *Time* (14 July 1993; 4 June 1994; 4 October 1992; 7 November 1988); and Steven Greenhouse, "A Fierce Battle," *New York Times Magazine* (12 February 1989). For an account of the seizure of RU-486 by U.S. Customs, see *New York Times* (2, 17 July 1992). More recent material on RU-486 is drawn from Gina Kolata, "Abortion Pill Tests Well in the United States, Drug's Sponsor Says" (30 April 1998); and "Doctors Looking at Abortion Pill Are Often Unaware of Obstacles" (30 September 2000); Nancy Gibbs, "The Pill Arrives," *Time* (8 October 2000); Associated Press, "Pills Used in Six Percent of Abortions, Study Says" (16 January 2003). On emergency contraception involving "preconceptive" drugs, see the *New York Times* articles: Tamar Lewin, "A New Procedure Makes Abortions Possible Earlier" (21 December 1997) and Jane Brody, "Personal Health" (2 September 1997), and Gina Kolata, "Morning After Pill Becomes Available Without a Doctor" (8 October 2000).

The facts in the Visna case are from Suzanne Siegel and Bill Roy, "Youth, Incest, and Abortion," *Newsweek* (10 August 1998).

## Chapter 10: Impaired Infants and Medical Futility

Information in the Social Context on premature infants is drawn from the following series of articles from *New York Times:* Elisabeth Rosenthal, "As More Tiny Infants Live, Choices and Burdens Grow" (29 September 1991); Gina Kolata, "Parents of Tiny Infants Find Care Choices Are Not Theirs" (30 September 1991); Jane E. Brody, "A Quality of Life Determined by a Baby's Size" (30 September 1991); Sheryl Gay Stolberg, "As Premature Babies Grow, So Do Their Problems" (8 May 2000); Tamar Lewin, "Learning Problems of Premature Infants Are Broader Than Once Thought, Study Finds" (5 July 2000). For a discussion of the Saigal study, see Associated Press, "Tiniest Babies Face Hurdles to Learning" (7 February 2000). See also David Harvey, R. W. I. Cooke, and G. A. Levitt, *The Baby Under 1000g* (London: Wright, 1989), and Jane E. Brody, "Steroid Therapy Is Saving Lives of Premature Babies," *New York Times* (9 March 1994). For the functioning of a hospital ethics committee and the struggle of parents to make a decision about life-sustaining treatment for their child, see Lisa Belkin, *First, Do No Harm* (New York: Simon and Schuster, 1993).

The statistics on when abortions are performed are calculated from the data in Barbara A. Kantrowitz, "A Bitter New Battle over Partial Birth Abortions," *Time* (17 March 1997).

Details of the Baby K case are from Linda Greenhouse, "Court Order to Treat Baby Prompts a Debate on Ethics," *New York Times* (19 February 1994). The Gregory Messenger Scenario is based on Suzan Chira, "Medical and Legal Quandary in Father's Letting Baby Die," *New York Times* (3 August 1994). "The Baby Doe Cases" is based on George J. Annas, "Disconnecting the Baby Doe Hotline," *Hastings Center Report* 13 (June 1983): 14–16, and "Baby Doe Redux," *Hastings Center Report* 13 (October 1983): 26–27; Bonnie Steinbock, "Baby Jane Doe in the Courts," *Hastings Center Report* 14 (February 1984): 13–19; Thomas H. Murray, "The Final Anticlimactic Rule on Baby Doe," *Hastings Center Report* 15 (June 1985): 5–9; and *Time* (14 November 1983): 107. Also, see the following articles from *New York Times:* Marcia Chambers, "U.S. Suing for L.I. Records of Baby in Surgery Dispute" (3 November 1983); and "Letting Panels

Decide the Fate of Defective Infants" (15 January 1984); Harold M. Schmeck Jr., "Life, Death and the Rights of Handicapped Babies" (18 June 1985); Stuart Taylor Jr., "High Court Upsets U.S. Intervention on Infants' Lives" (10 June 1986); and Andrew H . Malcolm, "Ruling on Baby Doe: Impact Limited" (11 June 1986).

The Baby Owens case is based on an actual case presented in James M. Gustafson, "Mongolism, Parental Desires, and the Right to Life," *Perspectives in Biology and Medicine* 16 (1973): 529–557; and in Milton D. Heifetz and Charles Mangel, *The Right to Die* (New York: G. P. Putnam's, 1975), pp. 59–60. The R. S. Duff and A. G. M. Campbell article referred to is "Moral and Ethical Dilemmas in the Special-Care Nursery," *New England Journal of Medicine* 289 (1973): 75–78.

The Juli Decision Scenario is based on a case reported in B. D. Colen, *Karen Ann Quinlan: Dying in the Age of Eternal Life* (New York: Nash, 1976), pp. 130–137. The Susan Roth Scenario is based on a case reported in Richard Trubo, *An Act of Mercy* (Los Angeles: Nash, 1973), pp. 149–150. The Irene Towers Scenario is based on a Chicago case reported by the Associated Press (18 May 1981). The Dr. Daniel McKay Scenario is based on E. R. Shipp, "Mistrial in Killing of Malformed Baby Leaves Town Uncertain About Law," *New York Times* (18 February 1985). The AMA policy decision is reported in Andrew H. Malcom, "Reassessing Care of the Dying," *New York Times* (16 March 1986). The Bartling case is based on *New York Times* (28 December 1984) and George J. Annas, "Prisoner in the ICU: The Tragedy of William Bartling," *Hastings Center Report* 14 (December 1984): 28–29. The Virginia Crawford Scenario is based on a Baltimore case reported by United Press International (25 February 1979). The facts in the Shick case are from a United Press International story (8 February 1983); the Dohr-Engel case was reported in *New York Times* (20 March 1985); the Montigny case was reported by the Associated Press (8 August 1985). The original policy endorsed by the Netherlands Supreme Court was outlined in a *New York Times* story (27 November 1984).

# Chapter 11: Euthanasia and Physician-Assisted Suicide

The Quinlan Case Presentation is based on Phyllis Battelle, "The Story of Karen Quinlan," *Ladies' Home Journal* 93 (September 1976): 69–76, 172–180. Direct quotations are from Battelle. I have also drawn from B. D. Colen, *Karen Ann Quinlan: Dying in the Age of Eternal Life* (New York: Nash, 1976) and *In the Matter of Karen Quinlan: The Complete Legal Briefs, Court Proceedings, and Decisions* (Arlington, Va.: University Publications of America, 1975). On the death of Joseph Quinlan, see Robert Hanley's obituary in *New York Times* (11 December 1996).

On the Oregon measure, see Associated Press, "Voters in Oregon Allow Doctors to Help the Terminally Ill" (10 November 1994); and "Suicide Plan Would Permit Prescription for Lethal Drugs" (15 October 1994). For more background, see the following *New York Times* stories: Timothy Egan, "Suicide Law Placing Oregon on Several Uncharted Paths" (20 November 1994); for criticisms, Robert A. Burt, "Death Made Too Easy" (16 November 1994); the first statistics are from Sam W. Verhovek, "Legal Suicide Has Killed 8, Oregon Says" (18 August 1998); on Ashcroft's letter and more recent statistics, see Sam W. Verhovek, "U.S. Acts to Stop Assisted Suicides" (7 November 2001); for the suit see "Stay Extended Against U.S. on Oregon's Suicide Law" (20 November 2001); "As Suicide Approvals Rise in Oregon, Half Go Unused" (7 February 2002); "Government and Oregon Vie over Doctor-Assisted Suicide" (22 March 2002); Adam Liptak, "Judge Blocks Bid to Ban Suicide Law" (18 April 2002).

The Social Context on the Cruzen case draws from *Time* (11 December 1989; 19 March 1990; 9 July 1990); *Newsweek,* Marcia Angell, "The Right to Die in Dignity" (23 July 1990); *New York Times* (17 November 1988; 29 July 1988; 25 July 1989; 19 January 1990; 26, 27 June 1990; 23 July 1990).

The discussion of Kevorkian and assisted suicide draws material from *Time* (31 May 1993); *New York Times,* David Margolick, "Jurors Acquit Dr. Kevorkian in Suicide Case" (3 May 1994); "Michigan Panel Narrowly Backs Suicide" (5 March 1994); Lawrence K. Altman, "A How-to Book on Suicide Surges to the Top of the Best-Seller List" (August 1991); and Jane Gross, "Voters Turn Down Legal Euthanasia" (7 November 1991).

The discussion on euthanasia in the Netherlands is based on articles from the *New York Times:* Tom Kuntz, "Helping a Man Kill Himself as Shown on Dutch TV" (includes partial transcript of dialogue during the process) (14 November 1994); Marliese Simons, "Dutch Move to Enact Law Making Euthanasia Easier" and "Dutch Parliament Approves Law Permitting Euthanasia" (9, 10 February 1993); and F. X. Klines, "Dutch Quietly in Lead in Euthanasia Requests" (31 October 1986). See also Reuters, "Dutch Legalize Euthanasia, the First Such National Law" (1 April 2002); Maurice A. M. de Wachter, "Euthanasia in the Netherlands," *Hastings Center Report* (April 1992): 23–33 and Robert I. Misbin, ed., *Euthanasia,* "Part II: Euthanasia in the Netherlands" (Frederick, Md.: University Publishing Group, 1992), pp. 55–107. On the California Natural Death Act, see Karen Lebacqz, "On 'Natural Death,'" *Hastings Center Report* 7 (1977): 14. The Timothy Quill Scenario is based on "State Won't Press Case on Doctor in Suicide," *New York Times* (17 August 1991).

# Foundations of Bioethics: Ethical Theories, Moral Principles, and Medical Decisions

My discussion of ethical theories is generally indebted to Richard B. Brandt, *Ethical Theory* (Englewood Cliffs, N.J.: Prentice Hall, 1959) and William K. Frankena, *Ethics,* 2nd ed. (Englewood Cliffs, N.J.: Prentice-Hall 1973).

My treatment of utilitarianism owes much to the excellent introductory essay by Paul Taylor in his *Problems of Moral Philosophy* (Belmont, Calif.: Dickenson, 1971), pp. 137–151. Mill's statement of the principle of utility is from *Utilitarianism* (Indianapolis: Bobbs-Merrill, 1971), p. 18; the second quotation is from p. 24. In the discussion of act and rule utilitarianism and their attendant difficulties, I am indebted to Michael D. Bayles and Kenneth Henley's introduction in their *Right Conduct* (New York: Random House, 1983), pp. 86–94; and to Carl Wellman, *Morals and Ethics* (New York: Scott, Foresman, 1975), pp. 39–42, 47–50. The quotation is from p. 49.

The statements of Kant's categorical imperative are more paraphrase than literal translations. They are from his *Groundwork of the Metaphysics of Morals,* translated by H. J. Paton (New York: Harper & Row, 1964). Other translations and editions are easily available. Some of the criticisms of Kant are based on those of Brandt (*Ethical Theory,* pp. 27–35) and Frankena (*Ethics,* pp. 30–33).

The quotation from Ross is from his *The Right and the Good* (New York: Oxford University Press, 1930), p. 24. The prima facie duties are found on pp. 21–22 and the "rules" for resolving conflict on pp. 41–42. My exposition is indebted, in part, to G. J. Warnock, *Contemporary Moral Philosophy* (New York: St. Martin's Press, 1967) and to Fred Feldman, *Introductory Ethics* (Englewood Cliffs, N.J.: Prentice-Hall, 1978), pp. 149–160.

Rawls's theory is presented in *A Theory of Justice* (Cambridge, Mass.: Harvard University Press, 1971). The principles are quoted from p. 203; "natural duties" are discussed on pp. 340–350. My statement of the theory is indebted to Norman Daniels's introduction to *Reading Rawls* (New York: Basic Books, 1976). The first criticism is one made by Thomas Nagel, "Rawls on Justice" (Daniels, pp. 1–16) and Ronald Dworkin, "The Original Position" (Daniels, pp. 16–53). The second criticism is urged by R. M. Hare, "Rawls's Theory of Justice" (Daniels, pp. 81–108) and David Lyons, "Nature and Soundness of the Contract and Coherence Arguments" (Daniels, pp. 141–169).

For Aquinas's view on "man," see his *Summa Theologica,* Part II (First Part), vol. 6, translated by Fathers of the English Dominican Province (London: Burns Oates and Washbourne, 1914). For his views on natural law and law in general, see vol. 8, "Treatise on Law." For an interpretation of Aquinas, see Frederick Copleston, *A History of*

*Philosophy,* vol. 2, part 2 (New York: Doubleday, 1962), pp. 126–131, to which my account is indebted. For the presentation of the current Catholic natural law view I am indebted to Charles J. McFadden, *Medical Ethics,* 6th ed. (Philadelphia: F. A. Davis, 1967). The doctrine of double effect is treated on pp. 121–155; euthanasia, extraordinary means, and medical experimentation, pp. 239–270. The quotations from the Directives are from the appendix in McFadden: abortion, p. 441, euthanasia, p. 442.

My discussion of moral principles is indebted to Tom L. Beauchamp and James F. Childress, *Principles of Biomedical Ethics* (New York: Oxford University Press, 1979), pp. 56–201, and to Beauchamp and LeRoy Walters's introduction in *Contemporary Issues in Bioethics,* 2d ed. (Belmont, Calif." Wadsworth, 1982), pp. 26–32. The discussion of liberty-limiting principles is based on Joel Feinberg, *Social Philosophy* (Englewood Cliffs, N.J.: Prentice-Hall, 1973), pp. 20–33, as is the discussion of principles of justice, pp. 98–119.

The account of virtue ethics is indebted to Louis P. Pojman, *Ethics: Discovering Right and Wrong,* 2nd ed. (Belmont, Calif.: Wadsworth Publishing Company, 1995), pp. 166–181. See also Alasdair McIntyre, *After Virtue* (University of Notre Dame Press, 1981), the book that revived current discussions of virtue ethics, and Philippa Foot, *Virtues and Vices* (Oxford: Blackwell, 1978), a collection of essays by a virtue ethicist who addresses problems in medical ethics.

For the beginnings of feminist-care ethics, see Carol Gilligan, *In a Different Voice* (Cambridge, Mass.: Harvard University Press, 1982); for its philosophical development, see Annette Bair, *Postures of the Mind* (Minneapolis: University of Minnesota Press, 1985). Care ethics and feminist ethics are points of view still developing, and my sketch of them represents the ideas of no one theorist. Nell Noddings in *Caring: A Feminine Approach to Ethics and Moral Education* (Berkeley: University of California Press: 1988) argues that everyone ought to follow the ethic of caring and abandon abstract principles. Some feminist writers are concerned not to have the emphasis on care overwhelm feminism and its concerns. See Susan Sherwin, *No Longer Patient: Feminist Ethics and Health Care* (Philadelphia: Temple University Press, 1992) and Helen B. Holmes and Laura M. Purdy, eds., *Feminist Perspectives in Medical Ethics* (Bloomington: Indiana University Press, 1992). See the *Resources for Chapters and Topics,* found at the book's website, for more references.